Do-It-Yourself
HOUSEBUILDING
THE COMPLETE HANDBOOK

George Nash

Illustrations by Roland Dahlquist

STERLING PUBLISHING CO., INC.
NEW YORK

Acknowledgments

For almost two decades, I made my living building and renovating houses. For the last five years, I've made my living writing about building and renovating houses. Over a quarter of a century you can learn and forget so much. This book was written by osmosis from all the things I've learned about housebuilding. It's my attempt to shore up the levee of memory and a desire to share something useful before I forget it.

There are so many individuals to whom I am grateful for what they've taught me. From some, I've learned hands-on, side by side, and from others, I've learned from what they've written. Some have been mentors, others employees or clients or competitors. To all of you, thanks.

Thanks are also due to good friend Steve Topping for the connection that got this project started; to Charlie Nurnberg at STERLING PUBLISHING, for taking Steve at his word; to "Denver prognosticator" Kim Long, for the encouragement to write my own "Great American How-to Book"; to John Larowe, Phoenix designer/builder and fellow martial arts enthusiast, for his architectural and grammatical critique of Chapter One; to Vermont designer and Renaissance man Howard Romero, for his critical editing of the material on solar and structural engineering; to my New Hampshire brother-in-law, Lenny "the Furnace Man," for his input to the sections on heating and cooling; and to Vermont designer/builder Ted Zilius, for sharing his elegantly simple techniques for making kitchen cabinets and clever built-in furniture and his pruning of some of the more rank excesses of the first draft.

Thanks very much to Patti Gilmartin, for loaning me the photographic record of her housebuilding, and to my wife, Jane, whose fine photographs add so much to this book. And thanks to Rudy and Misty Henninger of AZ Photo Lab, for their work in turning my collection of old negatives, prints, and snapshots into usable photos.

Thanks also to my illustrator, Roland Dahlquist, of Phoenix, whose labors had to be of love since he certainly wasn't paid what they were worth. Without his clear drawings to explain the text, this would have been an impenetrable book.

And finally, thanks to John Woodside, editorial director, and my editor, Rodman Neumann, for fitting the manuscript into the "box" allotted for it while managing to preserve its style and content.

Library of Congress Cataloging-in-Publication Data

Nash, George, 1949-
  Do-it-yourself housebuilding : the complete handbook / George Nash;
  illustrations by Roland Dahlquist.
      p. cm.
  Includes bibliographical references and index.
  ISBN 0-8069-0424-0
  1. House construction—Amateurs' manuals. I. Title.
TH4815.N37 1995
690′.837—dc20   94-2371
  Edited and designed by Rodman Neumann   CIP

10 9 8 7 6 5 4

Published by Sterling Publishing Company, Inc.
387 Park Avenue South, New York, N.Y. 10016
© 1995 by George Nash
Distributed in Canada by Sterling Publishing
% Canadian Manda Group, One Atlantic Avenue, Suite 105
Toronto, Ontario, Canada M6K 3E7
Distributed in Great Britain and Europe by Cassell PLC
Wellington House, 125 Strand, London WC2R 0BB, England
Distributed in Australia by Capricorn Link (Australia) Pty Ltd.
P.O. Box 6651, Baulkham Hills, Business Centre, NSW 2153,
Australia
Manufactured in the United States of America
All rights reserved

Sterling ISBN 0-8069-0424-0

Disclaimer

There's always more than one way to do a job. Although the author has made every attempt to present safe and sound building practices, he makes no claim that the information in this book is by any means complete or that it complies with every local building code. The author recommends that the reader refer to the titles listed in the Bibliography for further information and seek professional advice or have all plans professionally reviewed before undertaking any project. As the author and publisher have no control over how the reader chooses to utilize the information presented in this book or any capability of determining the reader's level of proficiency or physical condition, they are not responsible for mishaps or other consequences that result from the reader's use of the information in this book.

For Dad

This is the answer to your question,
if I wanted to be a carpenter,
why did I spend four years in college?

The miracle that is a brick will be forever lost
to the man who never lays one. Build with your
own hands as much as you can; you'll never
regret it.

Malcolm B. Wells
"An Ecologically Sound
Architecture Is Possible"

Photo Credits

Contents

Preface   8

PART I   Ground Work   11

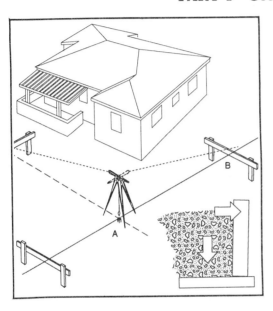

1   Getting Organized
    From Idea to Reality:
    An Overview of the Design Process   11

2   Getting Started
    Site Work   27

3   Foundations   37

4   Physical Matters
    Structural Engineering for Homebuilders   85

PART II   Frame Work   101

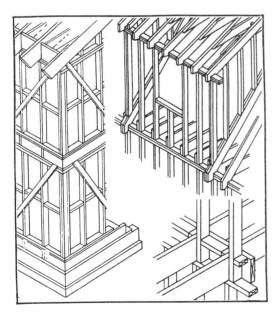

5   An Overview of Framing Systems   101

6   Framing the Floor
    Checking the Foundation   115

7   Wall and Ceiling Framing   139

8   Roof Framing   171

9   Roofing   233

PART III   Outside Work   271

10   Access
     Stagings, Scaffolds, and Safety   271

11   Exterior Trim and Siding   280

12   Windows and Exterior Doors   307

13   Decks, Garages, and Other Attachments   327

14   Painting and Staining   347

PART IV   Mechanical Work   355

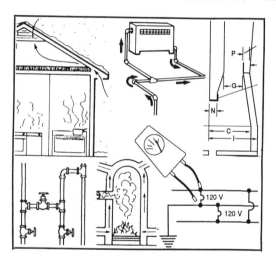

15   Plumbing Rough-In   355

16   HVAC Systems   385

17   Chimneys, Fireplaces, and Woodstoves   425

18   Electrical Rough-In   445

19   Insulation   483

PART V   Inside Work   515

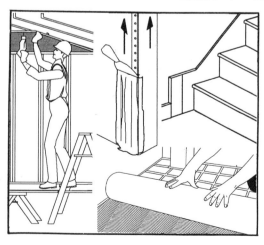

20   Stair-Building   515

21   Interior Finish
     Walls and Ceilings   537

22   Flooring   569

PART VI Finish Work 587

23 Tile Work 587

24 Interior Trim 608

25 Kitchen Cabinets and Other Built-Ins 629

26 Finish Details 659

27 Landscape Construction 666

Appendices 684

Common Woods and Their Uses 684

Western Dimension Lumber Base Values 686

Adjustment Factors for Base Values 687

Conversion Diagram for Rafters 689

Western Lumber Span Tables 690

Floor Joists 690

Ceiling Joists 691

Roof Rafters 692

Bibliography 693

Metric Conversion 696

Index 697

Preface

The question that anyone contemplating building his or her own house needs to ask is not, can I save money, but rather, will I save enough to make it worthwhile? And if not, are there other rewards that would justify the time, energy, and stress that owner-building requires?

Building on a foundation of solid "book learning," with common sense, a bit of luck, and minimal hands-on construction experience, by doing your own contracting you're likely to save some or even most of the 15 percent fee professional contractors normally charge. If you can substitute your own labor for that of carpenters and subcontractors, you could save even more. Since materials and other "hard" costs account for roughly 60 percent of the total cost of the modern home, it's *theoretically* possible to save up to 40 percent by doing it all yourself.

Most owner-builders, however, keep poor records of actual costs. Many of those who've managed to tabulate

While you certainly can save money doing it, ultimately the best reason to build your own house is for the pleasure of it.

every invoice and receipt will frankly admit that the final savings weren't all that impressive. If it were possible to assign a cash value to the endless hours of worry and emotional dislocations that they endured throughout their undertaking, the final costs are likely to be much higher than the original estimate.

Unlike contractors (who do it for a living), few of us have the luxury of putting aside three or four months to concentrate exclusively on the work of building a house. There are livings to earn and families to tend to in the meantime. Necessarily sandwiched between these competing demands and conditions, owner-housebuilding can drag on for months, or even years.

Yet, certainly, the risks seem worth taking. Short of having a baby (in which case, a man's level of involvement is a moot point), there's little else most of us can do in our lives that involves a greater commitment, requires more energy and expense, or is potentially more rewarding than building one's own house. This is one reason why even people who can afford to do otherwise still choose to build (or supervise the building of) their homes.

The compulsive attraction of housebuilding springs from a deeper source than the simple desire to save money. I'd argue that, ultimately, the best reason to build your own house is for the pleasure of it. Homebuilding represents a convergence of cultural values and self-expression. By giving public shape to private dreams, it's a creative, challenging, and socially valued form of applied art.

But, when it comes to houses, at least, the catchphrase "They really don't build 'em like they used to" is quite true. For instance, whether for a luxury mansion or a humble cottage, gypsum wallboard is the material of choice; no one uses plaster lath anymore. You probably couldn't afford it if you did. Whether you buy or build yourself a house, it costs just about as much as you can afford. The desire for quality control—that is, getting your money's worth—is one of the best reasons to consider building or contracting your own house. As an owner-builder, you'll be free (to some extent) from the pressures of a contract and tight scheduling. You can make changes, scrounge used materials, and shop around for bargains. You can spend the time it takes to "do it right" that speculative homebuilders dismiss as unaffordable and unnecessary. Proceeding with the caution of inexperience, you'll tend to overbuild, rather than cut corners.

Modern commercial homebuilding is an intensely competitive industry largely driven by unpredictable fluctuations in the costs of money and materials. An "efficient" professional homebuilder makes a profit by assembling the smallest possible amounts of the least costly materials into a minimally adequate structure as fast as possible.

Building codes only mandate the *minimum* acceptable standards, not the highest; code approval of a given material or practice isn't the same thing as a guarantee of quality. And mistakes that are hidden aren't the same as mistakes that are fixed. The selling of a house may confuse the appearance of quality with the presence of substantiality. In this way, house-buying isn't too much different from buying a new car. It's just harder to find "test results" and "product reviews."

Eighteen years as a professional building and renovation contractor, consultant, and teacher of owner-building and home design courses have confirmed for me the notion that a great many homebuyers don't have the slightest idea of what goes into the truly "well-built" house. To be fair, except to experienced and conscientious professionals, a lot of the important stuff isn't obvious. That's one good reason to read this book, whether you're thinking of buying, contracting, or building your house. Even more than skill and experience, knowledge, together with perseverance, is the main ingredient in any recipe for successful do-it-yourself homebuilding.

The blossoming of my housebuilding career coincided with the mortgage crunch of the late 1970s, just when double-digit interest rates squeezed the middle out of the new-home market and made it a great time to be in the remodelling business. While those who had the cash were still commissioning luxury homes, that limited market was super-saturated with established contractors. At the other end of the spectrum, subsidized housing through the FmHA program was "the only game in town." Neither I, nor the underpaid and overeducated young rural professionals who comprised my clientele, would consider building the "plywood boxes" that were the prototypical FmHA house. My challenge was to design and build energy-efficient, solid houses that were elegant enough to satisfy the brand-name tastes of clients on a generic budget—and somehow make a profit doing it. Fortunately, this turned out not to be as impossible as it sounded. The techniques I utilized are featured in this book.

A lot of the materials and methods of modern carpentry were developed to meet the demands of large-scale production builders and aren't suited to the owner-builder. Also, some of the several standard ways to solve any particular problem call for a level of skill or investment in equipment that can't be justified for a nonprofessional or novice builder. Therefore, my discussion is limited to methods that are simple, practical, and specifically adapted to the owner-builder or the beginning, rather than experienced, professional. Of course, I'd like to think that there's always something professionals can learn from any book, even one aimed at do-it-yourselfers. I've certainly found that to be true in my own reading and work experience.

Since profitable commercial homebuilding depends on economies of scale, quality construction is necessarily secondary to productivity. Every structural component of this "luxury" house has been carefully engineered to meet minimum standards at the least possible cost and fastest possible assembly so that the developer can maximize square footage as well as the cosmetic features that upscale homebuyers associate with "quality" building. A desire for integral rather than just surface quality is one reason to build your own home.

One particular quality—and strength—of this book as distinct from many other how-to books is that real-life carpentry is an inexact art. Real walls aren't always perfectly square, and real studs sometimes get nailed on the wrong side of the line. A difference between the professional builder and an amateur is that the pro practises preventative carpentry. The pro has a whole arsenal of techniques designed to keep things in line. Another difference is that a pro knows how to fix his or her own mistakes or the mistakes of others with a minimum of fuss and expense. With that in mind, I've included some of my favorite "recipes" for *fudge*—one of the most important ingredients in any successful building project.

Another thing you'll notice as you read this book is a distinct bias towards the use of "natural" minimally processed materials and an emphasis on what, for lack of a better term, is still called "appropriate technology."

Housebuilding at the end of the 20th century and beginning of the 21st is largely a problem of choice. New building products are constantly being introduced and promoted, many of which aren't necessarily better than the materials they're intended to replace. Building uses up resources. As builders, when we choose the materials for our houses, I think we have a responsibility to ask, Is this the best material for the job or is there something else which will accomplish the same purpose, as far as we can ascertain, with less long-term environmental damage? One thing for certain, "natural" materials, unlike their synthetic analogs, age gracefully. Wood, for example, "weathers,"

9

whereas plastics "degrade." Of course, some modern manufactured building products are a vast improvement over their more natural antecedents. Fibreglass and foam plastic insulations and synthetic weatherstripping reduce overall energy consumption and make life comfortable. Plywood sheathing is not only much stronger than old-fashioned board sheathing, but it reduces the volume of lumber, and hence the number of trees that must be cut, to frame a house as well.

Although houses have historically taken many forms and have been built from many different materials, my experience convinces me that the standard wood-framed house, with a simple roofline, is the easiest to build—at least for beginners. Certainly, logs, brick, stone, adobe, ferrocement, and other more exotic materials can be, and have been, successfully utilized by owner-builders. And underground houses, double-envelope "geothermal" construction, geodesic, octagonal, and other geometrically irregular shapes all have their advocates. Whatever their merits or drawbacks, most of these kinds of houses don't meet all my criteria for real-world owner-building; that is, an easily understood method of rapid and inexpensive assembly that provides comfortable and aesthetically pleasing shelter while requiring only a minimum of skill, specialized equipment, and backbreaking or tedious labor—and using readily available and time-tested materials that give pre-

The facade of this Southwestern house was built with machine-made adobe blocks, which gives it a much more traditional appearance than the stucco-over-wood-frame "Santa Barbara–style" houses that are the hallmark of contemporary Sunbelt housing. Nevertheless, for most owner-builders, wood-frame construction is still the easiest and most practical way to build.

dictable and dependable performance and that maximize energy efficiency and minimize environmental degradation. Many so-called "alternative" construction systems are undeniably extremely energy-efficient. But, often, this advantage is gained at the expense of simplicity or economy, or even worse, comfort.

With the few exceptions of plywood, fibreglass insulation, plastic plumbing, and amateur-friendly electrical wiring, most of the components of the modern house were invented or already in use in the decades immediately preceding and following the turn of the 20th century. By then, stick framing had already proven itself through almost three-quarters of a century of service. Except, perhaps, for what may seem to be stilted language and the poor quality of photographs, today's carpenter would find his or her great-grandfather's carpentry manual remarkably and reassuringly familiar. The inherent conservativism of the building trade and its often slow and suspicious embrace of new techniques are its hidden strengths. Traditional materials and traditional practices have withstood the test of time. Continuity is important; a house, whether well or poorly built, is likely to last a long time. It's too big and too expensive to throw away if you botch the job. By conscientiously adapting what is still valid and true of the past to the needs of the present, you can build a house that is a blessing rather than a blight upon the landscape.

Building your own house does presuppose some basic skill with carpentry tools. Building a garden shed or another small project first is a good way to get used to working with tools before you undertake such a huge project. Another way to gain valuable hands-on construction experience and design skills is by attending a course or series of weekend seminars offered by one of the many owner-builder schools throughout the country.

One thing housebuilding *doesn't* require is brute strength. But, as with any physical activity involving a lot of lifting, tugging, climbing, and stretching, you'll perform better and risk less injury if you're in reasonably good physical condition. Accommodate and work within your limits.

No one book, no matter how thorough, can completely or adequately convey all the accumulated knowledge an average tradesperson draws upon during his or her routine activities. And the art of housebuilding encompasses the activities of at least a dozen skilled subtrades. To distill the experience of so many lifeworks into print would require a work of truly encyclopedic proportions. Even if such a volume were to be compiled, it would be obsolete almost before it was finished. This helps to explain the perennial appearance of new homebuilding and do-it-yourself skill books. It's also the reason that I include a list of suggested readings in the bibliography of this one.

George Nash

1 Getting Organized

From Idea to Reality: An Overview of the Design Process

Much of what passes for "correct" house design is a product of cultural convention, the fashion of the moment, rather than the application of any truly universal underlying principles. While it's hardly a requirement for developing your own design, learning something about the principles, and even the jargon, of architectural discourse can be both interesting and useful. Reading a good "idea" book helps you integrate housebuilding into its larger social context. Some of my favorite titles are listed in the Bibliography.

Most houses are already built in the imagination long before their builders pick up paper and pencil or boards and nails. We all carry an image of our ideal home in our heads (see 1-1). A "good" house design must distill these dream images into a practical plan for a house that meets the requirements of the site and budget as well as the personal needs of its future occupants—while at the same time being aesthetically pleasing not only to the owners but also to the community in which it will be built. Houses are unique in that they exist in both public and private realms; they should fit into the neighborhood.

At the beginning of a course for owner-builders that I used to teach, I'd ask my students to sketch and describe the house they'd like to build. At the end of the course, I asked them to reevaluate their original designs. Besides showing me what my students had learned, the exercise illustrated the relationship between dream and reality.

A good way to begin designing your house is by collecting your dream images in a "design notebook." When you go for a drive, make a point of noticing the kinds of houses that seem more appealing to you than others. Draw quick sketches or take photos of window arrangements, rooflines, trimwork details, siding patterns, porch treatments, landscaping, or anything else that catches your eye and stirs your spirit. Clip or photocopy pictures and advertisements from building, architectural, or interior design magazines and books and paste them into your notebook. The "field guides" to historical and regional house styles, which you'll find at your local bookstore or library, are especially helpful. As you browse through the architectural epochs, note which kinds of house styles and details speak most pleasingly to you, and add them to your notebook. Gradually, the *gestalt* of your ideal house should

begin to emerge from your collection of resonant details. By observation and reflection, you'll make the connection between the general form of your house and your inner sense and image of domestic comfort. This sort of preliminary design work is especially valuable when, as is most likely the case, more than one person is involved in defining the outlines of their home. Since 80 percent of

1-1 *Dream houses are built in the imagination long before anyone picks up paper and pencil or boards and nails.*

1-2 *A good building site is more than a piece of land with a view. Soil and climate conditions, vegetation, and the general community are just some of the components of a good site. (Notice the tile of a dug well in the upper right corner of the field.)*

homes are built by couples, taking two different, deeply held ideal images and finding a harmonious convergence is likely to be a difficult but necessary prerequisite to the successful outcome of the building project (as well as, perhaps, the survival of the marriage).

The next step is to fill in this somewhat fuzzy outline of the general shape of your house with what architects call "the building program." This is a list of such things as the number and type of rooms, their general layout, the kind of living arrangements needed to fit your lifestyle, and, of course, the budget that will contain all these wants and needs. The more specific you can be with developing your program list, the easier it will be to translate its requirements into a tentative floor plan.

Ultimately, house design is a product of aesthetics, social patterns, and physics. Since the answer to the question of which positions, patterns, shapes, materials, and textures "look" best arises from a dialogue between personal and public values, aesthetics is always a slippery issue. If it were something simple, there wouldn't be libraries of design books, or any ugly houses.

Social *patterns*—as opposed to social *conventions* (e.g., in our society the front door is supposed to face the road)—are concerned with the realities of daily use. Social patterns reflect practicalities, such as if your arms are full of groceries, you can't grab a handrail to help yourself up a steep set of stairs. Nor do you want to carry those groceries across an icy deck. Heating your house with wood implies a place to store it and to dispose of the ashes. The design consequences might be different when household garbage is collected weekly at the curbside rather than stored for a monthly trip to the local landfill. A long, sloping driveway may be quite desirable until you consider the cost and

inconvenience of snow removal. The same goes for maintaining a large lawn area. And these are just a few examples of the practical considerations of social patterns.

The use and arrangement of interior spaces is largely determined by social patterns as well. Surveys have shown that most people (in this culture anyway) agree that backyards are private and front yards more formal. Thus, rooms reserved for family activities tend to face the backyard, while more formal activities take place in rooms that face the front. Likewise, it's a design convention that rooms intended for quiet or private activities are situated at some distance from noisier, more public spaces. Presently, our culture also places a premium on informal cooking and dining, so that large eat-in kitchens are the norm, while formal dining rooms are often eliminated altogether. And changing attitudes towards the bathroom have transformed this once utilitarian cubicle into a sybaritic retreat.

Since housebuilding is a social as well as an individual act, it has consequences that could affect the health and safety of the entire community, which is the rationale behind building codes and zoning ordinances. Codes are a lot like mandatory helmet and seat-belt laws; they're intended to protect society from the burdens imposed upon it by the foolhardiness of its individual members. While you might feel that you have a perfect right to build a house that falls down on your head or is a firetrap, society has a legitimate interest in protecting the heads of anyone who might buy it from you or those who have to answer your emergency call. Although some owner-builders might consider code requirements to be an unwarranted intrusion upon their creative expression, it's a lot smarter to work with the code rather than around it. If your conception of adequate shelter does not happen to be shared by the local building inspector, you'll still have to fix whatever isn't up to standard, even if that means tearing it all down and starting over. By specifying the approved types, dimensions, and spacings of materials and their fasteners as well as minimum room dimensions and window openings, building codes guarantee that whatever you build is at least minimally safe and sound.

Although critical, the answers to the types of design questions that arise out of social patterns aren't necessarily "right" or "wrong." This is certainly not the case with the design challenge posed by physical variables. As will become clear in following chapters, the location of a house, its general shape and roofline, its foundation design, the arrangement of framing members, selection of exterior finish, and choice of energy systems are all to some degree a response to sun, wind, water, snow, temperature, soil type, and site conditions.

Ultimately, the importance of these physical constraints argues for the primacy of site selection in the design process. It's easier to design a house to fit a particular real-world site than it is to find or adapt a site to fit a particular plan. It's certainly okay to have a general idea of the kind of house you want to build—and even a very specific program—but you shouldn't try to refine these preliminary concepts into working drawings before you select the building site. While this could be construed as an argument against buying a set of prefabricated plans from one or another house-plan service, I don't mean it to be taken as an absolute prohibition. Plan books have a long and honorable tradition, going back at least to the "pattern books" imported from England by 18th-century carpenters. Many people have found that a particular pattern-book design was exactly the house they were looking for. A predrawn plan can catalyze your own original design. Likewise, with so many plans available, you're likely to find at least one that will only require a few modifications to fit your particular program. In any case, generic plans will fit generic sites. But whether you draw your plans yourself or hire an architect to do them for you, a truly inspired integration of house and site is always pleasing to look at, comfortable to live in, and easier to maintain.

WHAT MAKES A GOOD BUILDING SITE?

A building site is more than a piece of land with a nice view. "Real" estates are located within the matrix of the larger community. So the first rule of site selection might be summed up as "Build your house where you want to live" (see **1-2**).

Unless you're an "empty nester," the quality of the school system is one of the most important factors to consider; so is the distance between your house and the nearest schoolbus stop. In most communities the quality of schools is also proportional to property tax rates. Can you afford the taxes on the house you'll build? Does the community

offer the level of municipal services and kinds of amenities you find necessary or desirable? How convenient are hospitals, libraries, parks, recreational programs, and retail outlets? Which are you willing to forego in exchange for other benefits? If you build on the edge of a growing community, you could find yourself someday forced to pay the cost of hooking up to a municipal sewer extension even though you already have an on-site sewage-disposal system. The same might be true for a municipal water connection. And, if you choose to live out back of beyond, can you survive without cable TV or cellular phones?

Choosing a compatible community affects your ultimate comfort; whereas choosing the right real estate affects your everyday comfort—that is, how "liveable" your house will be. Zoning is where these two realms of site interface.

Local health regulations specify zones of isolation between existing wells and leach fields so your neighbors won't wonder if the effluent from your septic system is leaching into their drinking water. And, like a good fence, minimum setback requirements between your house and the property lines help to ensure privacy. If a future addition is part of your house plan, be sure that it will fit within the prescribed setbacks.

In rural areas, the capability of your soil to accommodate a septic system is perhaps the single most important determinant of its value as a potential building site. In fact, in many states, you won't be able to get a building permit unless the site has already passed a percolation test. Ask the seller to furnish documented proof of satisfactory "perc" test results before you sign the contract. Otherwise, make the contract conditional thereupon.

Local and state regulatory agencies have established standards and detailed specifications to prevent the contamination of drinking water by on-site sewage disposal systems. Unfortunately, there is one potentially even more hazardous contaminant which may already exist on your site that is virtually ignored by present codes, builders, and most trade publications. Under the right conditions, radon—an invisible radioactive gas that occurs naturally in many soils and in groundwater—can become concentrated to carcinogenic levels in poorly ventilated basements, crawl spaces, and even the living areas of a home. Radon build-up is usually worse in tight, well-insulated energy-efficient homes, especially if they are earth-bermed or built over a full basement in wet soils. Like water, radon gas will leak into a basement through cracks and penetrations in the foundation, especially through floor drains.

Most states and the regional offices of the EPA have established advisory boards of one kind or another to help homebuilders and buyers (often the worst radon problems are in existing houses) deal with radon pollution. Relatively inexpensive do-it-yourself radon detection kits are now available. Fortunately, its a lot easier and cheaper to keep radon out of a new home than it is to retrofit an existing home with a mitigation system. Thorough waterproofing of foundation walls, minimizing joints in concrete floor slabs, sealing openings in the basement slab and walls, and installing a waterproof PVC membrane over an under-slab gravel bed fitted with drainpipes for exhausting the gas have proven effective. The NAHB (National Associ-ation of Homebuilders) is currently developing radon-proofing standards for inclusion in the national building codes. Contact your State radon control office to find out if you should be concerned about radon pollution on your site (see **1-3**).

A good building site for a tract house developer isn't the same thing as a good building site for an owner-builder. Developers prefer level, open sites that permit easy move-ment of machinery and materials and minimize clearing, grading, and infrastructure improvement costs. While a level site is certainly easier to build on—especially if you plan to use a slab-on-grade foundation—sloping sites have a lot to recommend them.

Depending on how saturated the soil is—and where the natural water table lies—it could be hard to build a dry basement on a flat site, especially when the site lies in a floodplain or valley bottom where subsurface water tends to pond up. Such sites also collect cold air. Hilltop "view" sites must balance the advantages of a commanding vista with the heightened exposure to heat-robbing winds and with the usually higher taxes that are assessed. On sloping sites gravity works in your favor to divert surface runoff. Temperature extremes and winds are also somewhat mit-igated on slopes. Cutting into the bank of the hillside and piling the fill up against the sides of your house is an economical way both to excavate a cellar and to utilize the energy-saving properties of earth berming at the same time (assuming, of course, a south-facing slope).

In general, houses should face into the sun and turn away from the wind in cold regions—and turn away from

1-3 *This map, released by the EPA, actually shows deposits of granite, uranium, shale, and phosphate—all potential sources of radon gas.*

the sun and face into the breezes in hot regions. But, in many cases, the social convention which dictates that houses should face the street overrules solar orientation. This is unfortunate because, even if you do nothing else, orienting your house towards the south will significantly reduce its heating load (see **1-4**). It's not necessary for the house to face true south to take advantage of solar gain. Facades oriented up to 25 degrees east or west of south still receive 85 percent to 95 percent of the available solar energy.

The prospects for solar orientation should always be an important factor in evaluating a potential building site (see **1-5**). Is access to the sun blocked by neighboring buildings, a hillside, or tall trees? Does optimal solar orientation con-flict with the best view? Wide overhangs won't shade west

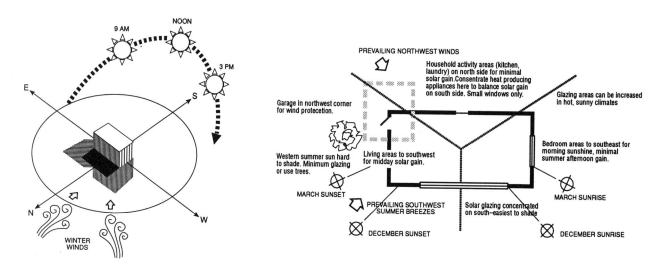

1-4 *Besides the compass orientation of the building facade, the intensity of the sunlight falling on each building surface is also affected by the diurnal and seasonal variations of the sun's position.*

1-5 *Strive to integrate your house with its site: Here the deciduous trees shade the south-facing wall in the summer while allowing solar gain and providing a pleasant scene in the winter.*

or east walls from the summer sun; shade trees, on the other hand, can provide an effective sunscreen. Tree plantings are not only useful for windbreaks, but in the proper combination of shape, size, and density, they can also channel cooling air flows into the house.

UNDERSTANDING PLANS

When people hear the word "plan," the image that springs to mind is usually that of the *floor plan*. This is quite understandable since this particular drawing represents the plane of the house on which its inhabitants live. It shows the relationship between the rooms, walls, windows, doors, stairwells, and large appliances of the home from the designer's and homeowner's point of view. The floor plan is also the most important plan to the builder, since it gives the dimensions he or she will need to draw up materials and labor estimates, and lay out the actual construction. But the floor plan is only one of a set of drawings that together make up a complete house plan.

A *site plan* (also known as a *plot plan*) is almost always required as part of the application for a building permit (see 1-6). At the very least it must show the property lines, the location of the house and its setbacks from the property lines, the driveway, and town highway. If there is no hookup to municipal water or sewers, the location of the well and on-site sewage disposal system and the distances between them and any existing septic systems and wells on adjoining properties must be marked. Most health codes mandate at least a one-hundred-foot isolation zone between a water source and a sewage disposal field, and they usually require that the latter be downgrade of the former.

Although you may be able to satisfy the permit requirements with a simple dimensioned plan that isn't drawn to scale, for anything but a simple house on a treeless level lot a scaled drawing will be a great deal more useful, at least to the excavator. A complete site plan includes such things as the layout of utility lines (either overhead or buried), water and sewer hookups, trees and boulders to be left standing or removed, any surface drainage swales and subsurface curtain drains, the outlet pipe for the foundation drain system, and the existing and finished contours of the property, particularly the elevation of the top of the foundation wall relative to grade of the site. This tells the excavation contractor how deep a hole to dig. One small detail which, if overlooked, can cause you a great deal of trouble is the existence of any utility rights-of-way that cross your land. If you happen to put part of your house in a right-of-way, the utility company would probably make you move it.

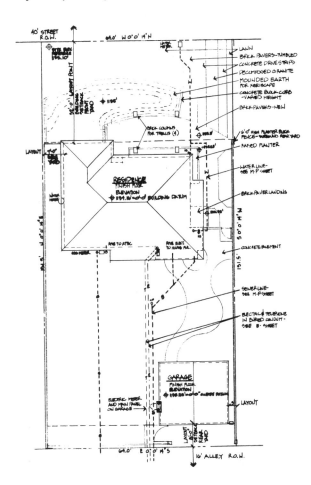

1-6 *In addition to property lines, minimum setbacks, and other legal aspects of the building lot, a site plan also gives the benchmark elevation from which all other site contours are measured.*

Depending on the size of your drawing paper and the level of detailing, site plans are typically scaled at one inch equal to 10 feet or to 25 feet; these are architecturally notated as 1":10' or 1":25'.

Foundation plans typically include a horizontal and (sometimes) a vertical *section* (see 1-7). (A section is a view, or "slice," through the plane of the building. Horizontal and vertical sections are simply other names for a plan view and a cross section, respectively.) The foundation plan shows the layout and dimensions of all footings, walls, piers, and other components, and the location of any *Rebar* (reinforcing steel) *rods* (horizontal), *dowels* (vertical), or wire mesh. If not otherwise shown on the site plan, the foundation plan also establishes the elevation of the first floor from a fixed point of reference (called a *benchmark*, or *control point*—usually a stake at the high-point of the excavation or the elevation above sea level as

determined by a survey). The normal convention is to designate the finished floor (or the top of the foundation wall (T.O.W.) as 0'-0" and measure all construction height from there with plus (+) or minus (−) elevations (e.g., (−)3'-6" or (+) 1'-2"). The height of any penetrations in the foundation wall for such things as water, sewer, and other utility lines are usually dimensioned relative to the T.O.W. For example, the location for the center of the sewer line might read *Sewer: (−)4'-6" T.O.W.*, which indicates that the pipe is supposed to be four feet six inches below the top of the wall.

When extra detail would be helpful, as, for example, to show footing drains, perimeter insulation details, Rebar rod and dowel locations, and backfill placement, these items are shown in footing-to-rafter-plate *typical section* view described below. Clarifications of complicated foundations that involve changes of level are usually shown as

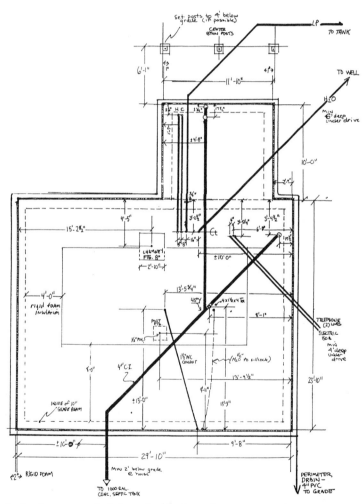

1-7 *A separate plan isn't always needed for a basic foundation since there's usually room enough for all the necessary information on the "typical section" and "elevation" drawings. But, with slab foundations, a plan is necessary to accurately position utility pipes because they cannot be moved after the concrete is poured.*

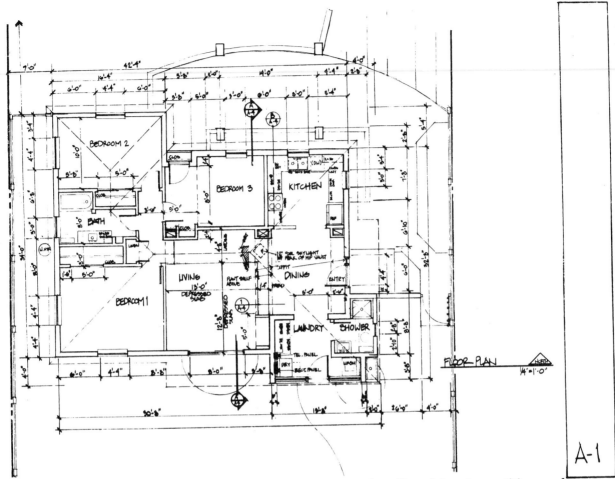

1-8 *Since it shows the layout and dimensions of all the outside walls and interior partitions and the location of window and door openings, the floor plan is the most important drawing for both the builder and the homeowner. In fact, many houses have been built using nothing more than a floor plan and a few notes about details and finishes.*

dashed below-grade lines on one or more of the regular *building elevation* drawings. (An elevation is a straight-on vertical view, i.e., perpendicular to a cross section.)

For matters of convenience, there's often a difference between "compass north" and "plan north." (It's a lot easier to think of the "top" of the plan as "north" even though it might be 15 degrees NNE of north.) Both compass north and plan north are always shown on the site plan. Subsequent drawings only show plan north.

Except for detailed drawings, which are always shown close up, a ¼ inch to the foot scale is large enough to show enough detail and still fit on 18″ × 24″ sheets of drafting paper (which is what you'll use unless you have a professional drawing table that can accommodate 24″ × 36″ sheets). Except for the site plan and the building elevations, the same scale is used for all the subsequent plans that make up a full set of working drawings.

In floor plans, at least, outside sheathing and siding, and inside wallboard "don't exist," or rather, have no dimensioned thickness (see 1-8). Unless otherwise indicated, floor plan dimensions always represent *rough*, as opposed to *finished*, measurements. Thus, if a plan shows 6′-11″ between interior partitions, the measurement is the distance between the actual framing studs and not the room size after sheetrock is added. But don't forget to account for the difference between *nominal* and *actual* dimensions of the framing lumber when you translate your plan dimensions into your actual framing layout. Since, for example, a so-called 2×4 is 3½″ wide, this and not four inches is assumed to be the thickness of a partition wall. Fractions of inches add up. When finished size is critical, as, for example, with the framing for a bathtub or shower stall enclosure, the desired finish or rough dimensions should always be so labelled on the plan.

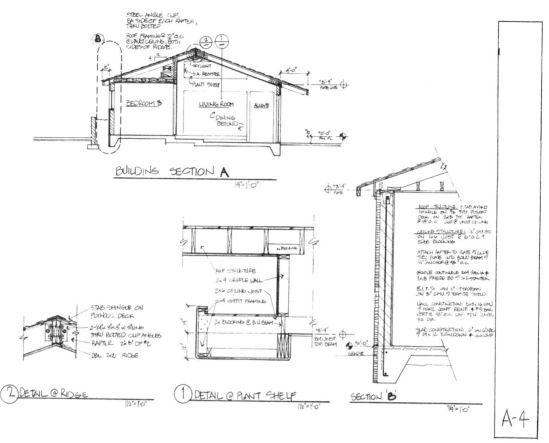

1-9 *When the design includes changes in level, roofline, or other special "conditions," a keyed symbol refers the builder from the floor plan to a separate drawing that clarifies the situation. Likewise, keyed symbols on the main drawings are used as necessary to refer to special large-scale close-up drawings when greater detail is needed to show the construction of a particular situation.*

Besides the floor plan, you'll need a typical *wall section* and sometimes one or more *building sections* to make a comprehensible set of plans (see **1-9**). This typical wall section shows the heights of rough and finished floors, ceilings, and window headers, and it gives a profile of the framing, insulation, inside and outside finish, roofing, and rafter tail cut. The typical section assumes that the composition and relative shape of the house is constant throughout the plane of the drawing (hence the designation "typical"). Special *building sections* are used as required to show the vertical relationship of floor levels, changes of width, and roofline or any other deviations from the assumed normal section. These are shown by letter- or number-keyed arrows on the main floor plan that refer to the appropriate supplemental drawings.

In addition to special sections, one or more *framing plans* for walls, floors, or a roof might be needed to clarify the structure of particularly complicated designs. It's a lot easier and cheaper to experiment with unusual connec-

tions or solve problems on paper than to discover it can't be done with real wood in real time. One sign of a competent architect is the number of details that the plans don't leave to a builder's discretion. Otherwise, for normal residential construction, framing lumber sizes and spacings are briefly noted on the floor plan or typical section, and standard framing practice is simply assumed.

Special sections and other details (called *conditions*, in architect lingo) are appended to the floor plans. Depending on the level of magnification necessary, these are drawn with ½":1', 1":1', or 1½":1' scales.

Each floor level of living space requires its own floor plan. Unless they're very basic, separate *mechanical plans* (see **1-10**) that show heating ventilating and air-conditioning (*HVAC*) ductwork, plumbing systems, and the electrical or other electronic systems superimposed over a simplified floor plan are less confusing than a single all-purpose floor plan, especially when you're putting each system out for bid to subcontractors.

18

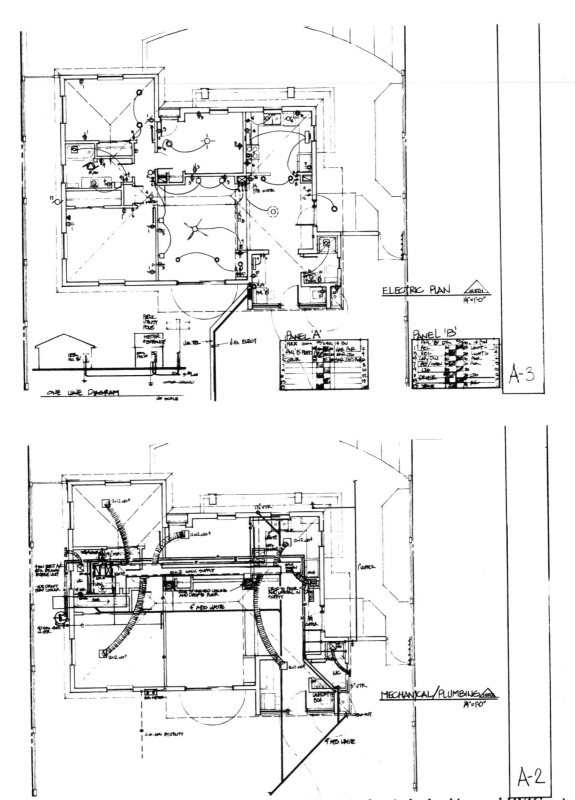

1-10 Simple houses seldom require separate drawings for their electrical, plumbing, and HVAC systems. As long as it can be shown without confusion, all the necessary information is usually combined into a single "mechanical" drawing.

Artist's Rendering

(Elevation labels visible: NORTH ELEVATION 1/4"=1'-0", EAST ELEVATION 1/4"=1'-0", WEST ELEVATION 1/4"=1'-0", SOUTH ELEVATION 1/4"=1'-0")

1-11 *Elevations show exterior finish details and the relationship between various levels of the building, such as floor and ceiling and window and door heights and steps in the foundation and/or roofline. Isometric projections give the illusion of three dimensions but remain true to scale. An artist's rendering usually displays a perspective view in which the scale does not stay true. But both isometric projections and artist's renderings can be more useful than elevations for visualizing the shape of a complicated structure.*

Building or *exterior elevations* show the finished exterior of the house (see **1-11**). In addition to specifying finish siding and general trim and window placement, elevations are useful for finding window and door heights, floor levels, ceiling heights, and understanding other level changes. Combining all four elevations on a single sheet makes it easier to compare the visual composition of the house design. For simple plans that don't require any great amount of detail, typically a ⅛":1' scale is used to fit them all on a single sheet.

The very same lack of visual perspective which makes it possible to scale off dimensions from elevations makes it hard to visualize the overall shape of the house, especially where complex shapes and rooflines intersect each other. *Artist's renderings* do this much better, but are hard to draw well and can't be used for scaling. *Isometric projections* create the illusion of depth without the complications of perspective drawing. Superimposing diagonal axes over the 90-degree grid of ordinary two-dimensional drawing allows the horizontal lines of the plan to remain true to scale, even though they appear to be at 45-degree angles to the vertical lines of the drawings. Of course, the same perceptual trick that lets you see two sides of the building

at once means that rooflines or other angled planes aren't in scale. But, when you want to impress a bank officer with the beauty of your custom design, these are the drawings you should have.

The dream home that is summed up by your architectural elevation or perspective drawing can be comprehended and easily "read" by not only the builder, but also bankers and bureaucrats. But, it is in your own interest that you also be fluent in the language of plans. To speak and understand that language, you've got to master the architectural symbols that comprise the alphabet of residential construction (see **1-12**).

THE LOGIC OF BUILDING: AN OVERVIEW OF THE BUILDING PROCESS

Okay, you've got a set of plans, a site, and your construction loan approved: How do you go about turning all this into a well-built house without injuring your health or running out of time and money?

Except for differences of scale, you and a commercial construction manager must both meet the challenge of scheduling materials and labor to arrive in the right quantities so that they can be installed before they're stolen or

Architectural Symbols in Building Plans

MATERIAL	PLAN	ELEVATION	SECTION
WOOD	FLOOR AREAS LEFT BLANK	SIDING / PANEL	FRAMING / FINISH
BRICK	FACE / COMMON	FACE OR COMMON	SAME AS PLAN VIEW
STONE	CUT / RUBBLE	CUT / RUBBLE	CUT / RUBBLE
CONCRETE			SAME AS PLAN VIEW
CONCRETE BLOCK			SAME AS PLAN VIEW
EARTH	NONE	NONE	
GLASS			
INSULATION	SAME AS SECTION	INSULATION	
PLASTER	SAME AS SECTION	PLASTER	STUD / LATH AND PLASTER
STRUCTURAL STEEL		INDICATE BY NOTE	
SHEET METAL FLASHING	INDICATE BY NOTE		SHOW CONTOUR
TILE	FLOOR	WALL	

Mechanical Symbols for Plumbing and Heating

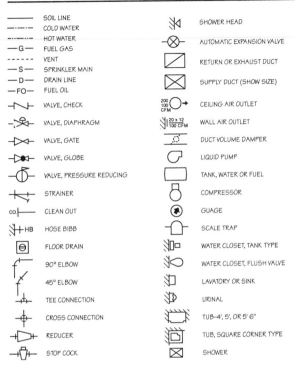

SOIL LINE
COLD WATER
HOT WATER
G — FUEL GAS
VENT
S — SPRINKLER MAIN
D — DRAIN LINE
FO — FUEL OIL
VALVE, CHECK
VALVE, DIAPHRAGM
VALVE, GATE
VALVE, GLOBE
VALVE, PRESSURE REDUCING
STRAINER
CO — CLEAN OUT
HB — HOSE BIBB
FLOOR DRAIN
90° ELBOW
45° ELBOW
TEE CONNECTION
CROSS CONNECTION
REDUCER
STOP COCK

SHOWER HEAD
AUTOMATIC EXPANSION VALVE
RETURN OR EXHAUST DUCT
SUPPLY DUCT (SHOW SIZE)
CEILING AIR OUTLET
WALL AIR OUTLET
DUCT VOLUME DAMPER
LIQUID PUMP
TANK, WATER OR FUEL
COMPRESSOR
GUAGE
SCALE TRAP
WATER CLOSET, TANK TYPE
WATER CLOSET, FLUSH VALVE
LAVATORY OR SINK
URINAL
TUB–4′, 5′, OR 5′ 6″
TUB, SQUARE CORNER TYPE
SHOWER

Architectural Symbols in Building Plans

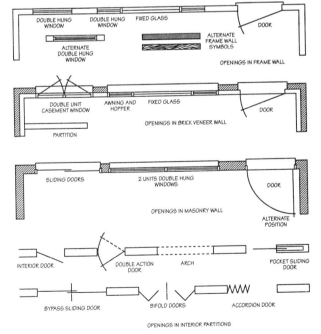

DOUBLE HUNG WINDOW
DOUBLE HUNG WINDOW
FIXED GLASS
DOOR
ALTERNATE FRAME WALL SYMBOLS
ALTERNATE DOUBLE HUNG WINDOW
OPENINGS IN FRAME WALL

DOUBLE UNIT CASEMENT WINDOW
AWNING AND HOPPER
FIXED GLASS
DOOR
PARTITION
OPENINGS IN BRICK VENEER WALL

SLIDING DOORS
2 UNITS DOUBLE HUNG WINDOWS
DOOR
OPENINGS IN MASONRY WALL
ALTERNATE POSITION

INTERIOR DOOR
DOUBLE ACTION DOOR
ARCH
POCKET SLIDING DOOR

BYPASS SLIDING DOOR
BIFOLD DOORS
ACCORDION DOOR

OPENINGS IN INTERIOR PARTITIONS

Electrical Symbols

WIRING IN WALL OR CEILINGS
WIRING IN FLOOR
WIRING EXPOSED
CONDUIT W/ NUMBER OF WIRES
SERVICE WEATHER HEAD
GROUND FAULT PROTECTED OUTLET
PANELBOARD OR MAIN SWITCH
DUPLEX RECEPTACLE
TRIPLEX RECEPTACLE
DUPLEX SPLIT–WIRED
SPECIAL–PURPOSE OUTLET
RANGE OUTLET
CEILING LIGHT FIXTURE
WALL BRACKET LIGHT FIXTURE
FLUORESCENT LIGHT FIXTURE
PULL CHAIN LIGHT FIXTURE

BLANKED OUTLET
JUNCTION BOX
SINGLE POLE SWITCH
THREE–POLE SWITCH
LOCK OR KEY SWITCH
SWITCH AND PILOT LIGHT
SWITCH AND DUPLEX RECEPTACLE
CEILING FAN
CLOCK RECEPTACLE
TELEPHONE
SIGNAL PUSH BUTTON
BUZZER
BELL
TELEVISION
INTERCOM STATION
SOUND SYSTEM

1-12 *(Continued next page)*

Symbols for Plumbing, Appliances, and Mechanical Equipment

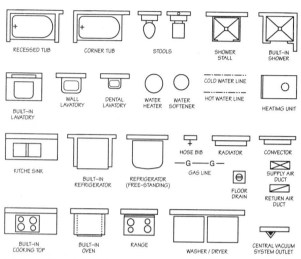

1-12 *(Continued)*

damaged by weather—or your workers are hampered by confusion and delay. Everything must proceed as quickly as possible, yet not so fast that production outstrips your ability to pay for it. While keeping in touch with the day-to-day progress (if not actually doing the work itself), you've got to prepare for the next phase. Whether it's resolving labor–management tensions, dealing with the demands of intractable bureaucrats, or mollifying a neglected spouse or reconnecting to a forgotten family, there are myriad conflicting demands.

Viewed as a seamless whole, building a house can seem like a very large and, perhaps, even incomprehensibly daunting undertaking. Fortunately, like any grand enterprise, the whole of housebuilding is easily reduced to the orchestration of many small, discreet, and readily accomplished tasks that proceed, one after another, in a logical and orderly process. The outline which follows gives a general overview of the housebuilding process and illustrates that careful organization is almost as important in successful housebuilding as careful craftsmanship. Depending on whether you're "vertically" or "horizontally" oriented, you can use the outline as a guide to drawing up a simple "TTD" (Things-To-Do) checklist or as the basis for a more graphic time-and-task flow chart similar to the ones used by professional construction managers. One thing that constructing a chart should make painfully obvious is that contracting is not much more than glorified "gofering." If you can handle making lists and checking and rechecking them to the edge of paranoia, and if you can make phone calls like a telemarketer, you'll probably avoid any truly costly scheduling conflicts. As an owner-contractor, it also helps to be skilled in juggling parallel lives.

The entire process begins long before any dirt is disturbed—just as soon as you've crystallized your design into a set of working drawings. The "preparational" phase, which consists mostly of a few meetings, a lot of telephone calls, and reams of paperwork, precedes the actual construction by at least several months. Groundbreaking initiates the transition from planning to actual building. Faced with the substantial outlay for excavation and foundation subcontracts, cash-poor homebuilders often opt for labor-intensive alternatives that require minimal site work. The outline assumes a standard full-basement poured concrete foundation. In the best of circumstances, this phase of construction should be completed within two to three weeks. Advance notice and frequent phone calls notwithstanding, some subcontractors may have an annoying habit of taking on other commitments in the interim, which will throw your coordinated schedule off track. Even when everyone is ready on time, uncooperative weather, such as late snow cover or heavy rains and soggy soil conditions, can cause extensive delays.

Except in frost-free regions where year-round building is possible, housebuilding is a decidedly seasonal activity. Planning is winter work. The bidding and permit process begins in early spring. Site work follows in late spring, after the ground has thawed and dried out enough to permit efficient excavation. For best results, concrete should be poured after the weather is above freezing. The long, dry days of summer provide a window of opportunity for framing and closing in the house. The outside "shell" is finished in early fall, before cold weather makes painting problematic. If scheduling and weather permit, the grounds are finish-graded and seeded. At the same time, mechanical systems and insulation are installed so that the house can be kept warm while interior work continues. The interior finish work continues throughout that winter and into the next spring. If necessary, finish-grading and seeding can be left until late into this second spring.

The construction phase theoretically divides into exterior shell, mechanical installation, and interior finish phases, although, in real-life building, work on at least two of the three phases usually occurs simultaneously.

Working with subcontractors, a professional four-person crew can typically build a small (1500 square feet) no-frills "Cape"-style house in about six weeks from start to finish. This represents a labor input of about 1000 hours for carpentry alone. Assuming about 100 hours each for the plumbing/heating, wiring, drywall/painting subcontractors, who normally work concurrently with the carpenters, that adds another 300 hours. Not counting the excavation and foundation work, it takes at least 1300 hours—or 32½ forty-hour person-weeks—to build a simple house "all by yourself." As a relatively unskilled amateur you won't have the tools or the experience to work as fast as a professional, so it might take you at least half again as many hours. Realistically, if you did nothing else but work on your house forty hours a week, it would take almost a year to build your own place. Few of us have the luxury to indulge in such a single-minded pursuit; the typical do-it-yourself builder will need to figure on a two- or three-year project, with some time to recuperate in between major phases. A realistic goal for the first year might be to build a minimally habitable shell. The second and third years would be devoted to interior finish and fine cabinetry. Of course if you're building with the bank's money, you'll be forced to complete the house on the bank's timetable, which means that you'll have to speed up the pace by subbing out a lot more work than you might otherwise be inclined to. Time limits are just one of the more compelling reasons why owner-contracting is more common than strictly owner-building.

OUTLINE OF THE HOUSEBUILDING PROCESS

1. Obtain a second opinion. Homemade plans should be reviewed by a knowledgeable professional before you consider them final. Revise them as needed.
2. Do a "takeoff" from plans and specifications lists. Submit materials lists to suppliers for bids and/or price estimates. (Note: Some lumber yards offer this service to their customers gratis.)
3. Interview potential subcontractors and submit plans to mechanical and other subcontractors for bid.
4. Redesign plans to eliminate budget overruns after initial price estimates and bids. Bargain for best prices with subs when appropriate. Confirm bid choices. Have your lawyer review any contract documents.
5. Check with accountant/insurance agent about providing workmen's comp, premises liability, and other insurance if you are acting as either general contractor or employer.
6. Set up construction escrow account.
7. Set up tentative materials delivery schedule with suppliers and advance-order windows and other custom components with long delivery times. Arrange tentative scheduling with subcontractors so that they'll be available to do your job when you're ready.
8. Obtain a **Building Permit**. This assumes a favorable "perc test" before land was purchased. Submit plans for approved on-site sewage disposal system designed by a registered civil engineer with application. Besides the obvious, such as electrical, plumbing, and fire safety, check your plans for conformance with all other applicable codes (e.g., sewer and water, environmental, hazardous waste disposal, etc.). The difficulty of administrative hurdles varies considerably between municipalities, so leave a margin of safety between initiating the application process and the commencement of construction.

1-13 *Scheduling is an important part of the construction process. For example, well drilling, which is very noisy, is best done before construction begins. Also, having water on site for the masons is a lot more convenient than hauling it in.*

9. Contact the road commissioner or highway department for driveway or "curb cut" permit.
10. Contact the power company to provide a temporary "service drop." Have your electrician install a meter and temporary power panel so that you'll have something to plug your extension cords into. If using underground power, permanent service is installed after the foundation is finished.
11. Call the phone company to have an on-site phone line connected as soon as possible. Typically, for a nominal fee, your present home phone number can ring at both locations.
12. Schedule your well-drilling ahead of construction—especially so that you won't have to listen to the possibly annoying drilling noise while you're working on site (see 1-13). Stake the well location before the driller arrives.
13. Check with suppliers to be sure prices haven't changed since your first materials quote.
14. Meet with the excavator to mark off building lines, and rough-in the driveway and parking area.
15. Notify concrete subcontractor to be ready.

16. Supervise digging of the cellar hole. Set up batter boards and strings for foundation layout. Check that the driveway is solid enough to support a fully loaded concrete truck and that excavation gives sufficient access to the foundation walls. Provide a drainage trench to grade so that the foundation will not become a lake if it rains.
17. Set up forms for footings, and pour them.
18. Strip footing forms, set up wall forms, and pour walls. Let walls "cure" for two or three days before stripping forms.
19. Waterproof the foundation wall.
20. Arrange foundation/footing inspection as required by building permit. Call floor slab subcontractor to be ready.
21. Arrange for excavator to dump gravel into cellar hole for slab base. Spread and compact gravel; install vapor barrier, basement floor drain and/or underfloor radon drains, and wire mesh in preparation for floor slab.
22. Excavate leach field, and set septic tank. Arrange for inspection of same before covering.
23. Pour and finish concrete basement floor slab.
24. Have the excavator dig trenches for underground utilities. Unless you do the work yourself, arrange for the well driller or plumber to install the water line and well pressure tank and pump. Connect the sewer drain line to the septic tank or arrange for municipal water and sewage connection. Install underground fuel tank for oil-fired heating system or LP (liquid propane) gas at this time. If needed, have an electrician run underground power (if any) and telephone wire into a service panel. Call for any required inspections of same. Seal and waterproof penetrations through foundation walls.
25. Apply perimeter insulation to foundation walls; install perimeter footing drains and outlet to grade.
27. Notify lumber supplier to ready framing lumber delivery.
26. Backfill all trenches and the leach field. Place crushed stone over drain tiles and partially backfill foundation trenches with gravel.
27. Store and organize materials on site.
28. Check foundation walls for squareness and level. Set sills.
29. Frame cellar girders, lay floor joists, and sheath floor deck.
30. Frame first-floor walls. For single-storey buildings, walls are often sheathed before tilting up. For multi-storey buildings, interior partitions must be framed before ceiling joists and second-floor deck. Coordinate delivery of one-piece bath/shower stall before framing bathroom partitions or else leave unframed.
31. Take out fire insurance policy on value of materials "in place." Arrange for delivery of dumpster for disposal of construction debris.
32. Arrange for mason to begin building chimney (and/or fireplace) so that it will go through roof sometime before shingling, if possible.
33. Rent scaffolding as needed. Frame rafters or install roof trusses.
34. Sheath roof deck.
35. Install fascia-board trim at eaves and cover rakes of roof and waterproof deck with tarpaper. Gable-end and rough stair framing can then be saved for "rainy day work," if necessary.
36. Confirm window and door delivery date. Alert mechanical subcontractors that they will soon be needed. Order exterior trim lumber so that boards can be prepainted or prestained.
37. Sheath exterior walls, if not previously done. Store windows inside until after shingling is finished.
38. Lay roofing shingles, and flash chimney.
39. Order exterior siding. Begin prepainting or prestaining. Complete rough stairs, if not done earlier. Coordinate delivery of furnace and basement fuel oil tank with plumber before building cellar stairs since installation may be impossible after stairs are built.
40. Install windows and doors.
41. Update fire insurance, and add theft coverage now that house can be locked up.
42. Arrange for framing inspection as required.
43. Have the plumber and electrician (either together or sequentially) "rough-in" plumbing, heating, and wiring.
44. Meanwhile, make sure corner trim boards, cornice work, and soffit trim are installed on exterior.
45. Arrange for inspection of roughed-in mechanical work.
46. Depending on weather or scheduling concerns, either install insulation yourself or hire a subcontractor, and apply exterior finish siding after finish-coating outside trim.
47. Build (any) porches and decks.
48. Apply finish coat of paint or stain to siding. Return rented scaffolding.
49. (Meanwhile) you or drywall contractor hangs, tapes, primes, and first-coats inside walls. If local codes require, arrange drywall inspection before taping. Or install plaster lath for real plaster—or install wood panelling.
50. Order finish lumber and cabinet materials.
51. Test well water as a precondition to obtaining certificate of occupancy from the health board.
52. In cool weather provide heat to dry out plaster or cure drywall compound. Store finish lumber in a warm, dry place before prestaining or varnishing. Arrange for furnace hookup. If furnace cannot be installed at this point, rent portable LP heaters, salamanders, or install temporary wood stove.

53. If weather permits, finish-grade the site, and complete landscape plantings or lawn seeding.
54. Install finish ceilings, if other than drywall.
55. Begin framing kitchen cabinets and other built-ins.
56. Hang interior doors, and trim windows.
57. Set sinks in countertops. Lay finish floors in bathrooms. Do tile work as needed.
58. Have the plumber complete the finish installation of all fixtures. Electrician does same for outlets and fixtures.
59. Final inspection for electrical, plumbing, and other mechanicals—also fire inspection, if needed, for smoke detectors, wood stove installation, etc.
60. Touch up trim paint or varnish. Apply final coat on walls.
61. Finish kitchen cabinets.
62. Finish stairs and balusters.
63. Install finish-wood flooring, sand, and varnish. Lay tile floors; grout and seal. Install vinyl sheet flooring.
64. Install baseboard trim.
65. Install kitchen appliances.
66. Install carpeting.
67. Final "punch list" for touch-up, mistakes, and oversights. Complete interior cleanup.
68. Final cleanup of site. Finish landscaping if not previously done or arrange to complete later when weather permits.
69. Final inspection; obtain occupancy permit. Readjust insurance policy to full homeowner's coverage. Arrange bank inspection for conversion of construction loan to conventional mortgage. Pay all bills, release liens—or sue subcontractors for failure to carry out contract provisions.
70. Move in with the furniture, etc., and celebrate with a housewarming party.

TOOLS TO DO THE JOB

One obvious difference between amateur and professional builders is the quality and quantity of their tools. When you're earning your living with your tools, it's only prudent to invest in heavy-duty commercial-grade tools. And specialized tools are justified by increased efficiency and productivity. But, tools are seductive; their acquisition can easily become an end in itself. While there's no such thing as really having too many tools, it's easy to have a lot of tools that you won't use enough to be worth owning—or to spend too much for a level of quality that you don't really need. In general, nonprofessionals will find that mid-grade tools offer the most reasonable compromise between cost and performance. Avoid the bargain bins, and, with the possible exception of tools you'll use constantly, forego the top-of-the-line brands. Even professionals find it more sensible to *rent* specialized tools, for jobs like drilling through concrete, sawing brick, or laying hardwood flooring, than to own them.

Specific tools are discussed in the appropriate chapter. You'll need a good selection of hand and power tools and probably you'll want to have more than you absolutely need. Hopefully, you'll already own quite a few of them. Otherwise, a realistic tool allowance will add at least (US) $2500 to your homebuilding budget.

TOOLS FOR THE DO-IT-YOURSELF SUBCONTRACTOR

If you're planning on doing your own electrical and plumbing work, you'll find that a heavy-duty ½-inch right-angle drill is pretty much a necessity. Although it is expensive, this tool is still a lot cheaper than paying for an electrician or plumber. Ordinary drills don't have enough torque to drive an *18-inch-long electrician's auger* or a *four-inch plumber's hole saw* through layers of built-up framing lumber, beams, and flooring. Other required electrical tools include a pair of *insulated electrician's pliers*, *needlenose pliers*, a *wire stripper*, an *insulated screwdriver*, a *test meter* or *neon-bulb tester*, and a *cable jacket stripper*.

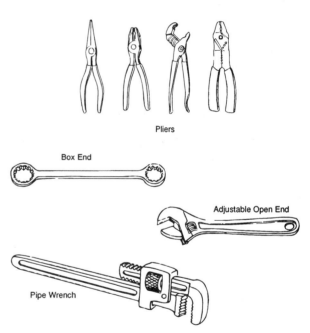

Pliers

Box End

Adjustable Open End

Pipe Wrench

Modern plastic and copper pipe has made do-it-yourself plumbing much easier. In addition to a set of *adjustable and box end wrenches*, the basic home plumber's tool kit should include *slip-joint pliers* (also called "water pump" pliers) for working with drain tubing, a pair of *pipe wrenches*, a *tubing cutter* and *tubing benders* for flexible copper tubing, a *propane or Mapp gas soldering torch* (Mapp gas produces the extra heat needed to sweat-solder the one-inch and larger diameter copper tubing used in some hydronic and solar heating installations), a *flaring tool* for making LP gas and fuel oil tubing connections, and a *basin wrench* for reaching the otherwise inaccessible

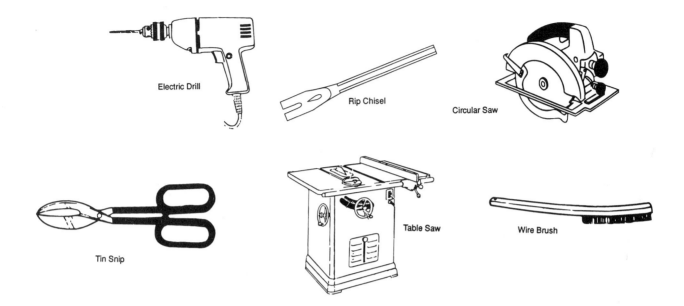

Electric Drill

Rip Chisel

Circular Saw

Tin Snip

Table Saw

Wire Brush

faucet lock nuts. Tools for cutting cast iron or threading black-iron pipe (used for natural and LP gas lines) can be rented. You'll also need *right- and left-handed and circle-cutting "aviation" snips, straight shears*, and a *stovepipe crimping tool* and *sheetmetal-bending pliers* for installing your own heating and air-conditioning ductwork. The latter tool is also handy for roofing and flashing work.

Drywall finishing tools include an *aluminum palette* for the joint compound, a *taping knife* for applying the base coat of compound, and a *10-inch and 14-inch taping paddle* for feathering out the finish coats. A sanding screen that mounts on a *telescoping fibreglass extension pole* lets you reach the ceiling without stepladders. The same pole will hold a paint roller.

Brickwork, concrete blockwork, and stonework all fit under the rubric of masonry. You'll need one or more high-quality *mortar trowels* (the cheap ones are too flimsy), a *brick chisel*, a *mason's hammer*, a *joint striker* for shaping mortar joints, and a *wire brush* for cleanup of the finished work. *Masonry-cutting blades* for your circular saw give more precise cuts with less breakage than a hammer and chisel, but don't last very long. Other than a rented professional tile saw, they're the best tool for cutting slate and quarry tile.

2 Getting Started

Site Work

While many would-be homebuilders own at least a few tools of the trade, few own a bulldozer or backhoe or have the skill to run rented heavy equipment (see **2-1**). So, unless you have an inordinate fondness for hand shovels, site work is almost always subcontracted to an excavator. Nevertheless, you'll need to work closely with your excavator to make sure everything is carried out according to plan.

Clearing your own building site and roadway may be a good way to begin saving money. The work is well suited to weekends and occasional afternoons, and, if started far enough in advance of construction, it can proceed at an unhurried and even enjoyable pace. If the site is well wooded rather than brushy, it could also yield saw logs or firewood to sell or use yourself. But beware: The potential payback of marketable timber must be weighed against the potential danger of chain saw work.

FELLING TREES

The key to safe tree felling is controlling the direction and speed of the tree's fall (see **2-2**). Select a landing zone that is clear of any trees that could hang up the falling tree or be injured by its momentum. The tree's center of balance should lean slightly towards the direction of fall. Look for heavy branches which would pull the tree off

course. On slopes there's less chance of the butt end bouncing back at you if the tree is felled downhill. Pay particular attention to the direction of wind; never try to fell a tree against the wind. Better still, don't cut trees on a windy day. Finally, always have an escape route in mind in case the tree falls the wrong way. And if you absolutely must work by yourself—I don't recommend it—a transportable cellular telephone or two-way radio could save your life in case of an accident.

2-2 *Siting a house to take advantage of a wooded lot calls for careful tree felling.*

2-1 *Few owner-builders have either the skill or inclination to do their own excavating work. For those who do, renting heavy equipment is always an option to hiring a subcontractor.*

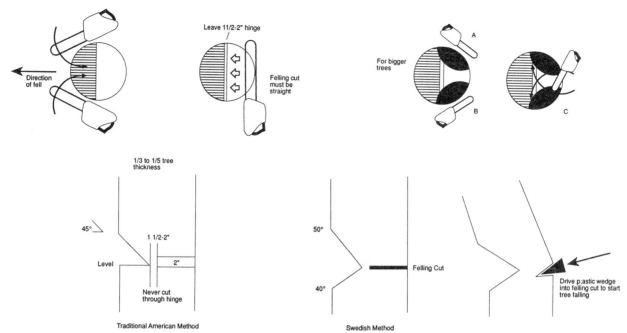

2-3 *The initial level base cut of the felling notch is made by pivoting the sawblade from both sides of the trunk. With the traditional "American" method, the notch is cut at about a 45-degree angle to the base. The felling cut itself is made about two inches above the base cut. With the "Swedish" method, there's less chance of a dangerous kickback since the butt won't tend to get hung up on the sloped base cut of the notch (the "barberchair"). When felling a large tree, make the initial felling cut from both sides of the trunk, and then finish it off cutting evenly and carefully from opposite sides, a bit at a time, towards the hinge until the tree can be wedged to start the fall.*

Once you've chosen the path of fall, clear a safe work zone by trimming any low branches and brush. The felling cut is a three-step process (see **2-3**). Rest the head of the saw motor against the trunk and let the bar pivot into the trunk as it makes a level cut (some chain saws are outfitted with a flat metal felling spike to steady the saw). For softwood, cut no more than about a fifth of the way through the trunk—for hardwood, a third. The line of the finished cut should be perpendicular to the intended direction of fall. For large trees or small saws, make two overlapping pivot cuts from opposite sides of the trunk. Next, holding the saw on a diagonal to the back of the base cut, saw downward from the face of the cut to remove a wedge-shaped section. The felling cut is made from the back of the tree, level, and about two inches higher than the base cut. Cut carefully, waiting for the first sign that the tree is beginning to lean. Shut off the saw, nudge the tree to help it along, and step back and towards the side. As you do, keep your eyes on the butt of the falling tree, in case it suddenly twists the wrong way or kicks back.

DRIVEWAY LAYOUT

A rural or suburban building site at some remove from a paved highway isn't much good if you can't get to it. Yet many owner-builders don't think about the requirements for a proper driveway until the moment the ready-mix truck buries itself up to its axles in their muddy track. Building a finished driveway as soon as the site is cleared prevents stuck delivery trucks and provides a dry and level place to store your building materials (see **2-4**).

Begin by stripping the sod and topsoil and laying a base of at least 12 inches of coarse gravel, compacted by repeated passes of a bulldozer. Top the base with 4 to 6 inches of finer silt-bearing gravel for good compaction, and crown it for drainage (see **2-5**). Wherever possible, divert existing water courses away from the roadbed with ditches or surface swales instead of expensive culverts.

In rural areas, you'll have to install a culvert where the driveway enters the public highway as a condition of your building permit. In more thickly settled areas, you may have to lay a paved apron instead. You or your excavator should already have obtained the necessary *curb cut* specifications from the local road commissioner or zoning board during the preliminary planning phases of the project. Be sure that your estimates include the cost of a paved driveway and/or any required walkways.

For ease of travel and snow removal, unpaved rural or suburban drives should be at least 12 to 14 feet wide and end in a vehicle turnaround. When planning turnarounds, consider not only the turning radius of your vehicle, but those of any vehicles which will make vital deliveries to your house, such as an LP gas tank truck. Faced with backing up a steep icy drive because of no turnaround, the driver may decide to wait until spring.

Lay out the drive so that it doesn't interfere with or detract from lines of view. On densely wooded lots, a well-planned driveway can increase privacy while a poorly planned drive will diminish it. A drive with broad or numerous curves costs more to build and maintain, and it offers no more screening from the road than one with a gentle curve. Check to see if the power company will let its lines follow your drive or insist on cutting across it—and what the company specifies for the minimum width of any such right-of-way.

Driveway design is one example of how site development costs must be analyzed in terms of one-time outlays that build long-term equity versus ongoing expenses that only yield increased carrying costs. In other words, while it may cost less to run in power overhead, underground power won't interfere with the view and will increase your property value. A steeper driveway may cost less than one that requires several switchbacks to reach a dramatic site, but you'll need an expensive four-wheel drive vehicle to negotiate it. A drainage swale that diverts surface water away from your foundation or a curtain drain to intercept groundwater may increase your excavation costs, but these are both cheaper than repairing a wet basement. Likewise, the seeming advantages to locating the garage under the house may be offset by the added cost and maintenance of retaining walls or the problem of maneuvering your car up or down an icy sloped driveway.

2-4   *In rural areas a well-built driveway not only adds to the beauty and value of the property but it can save time and expense getting materials onto the building site.*

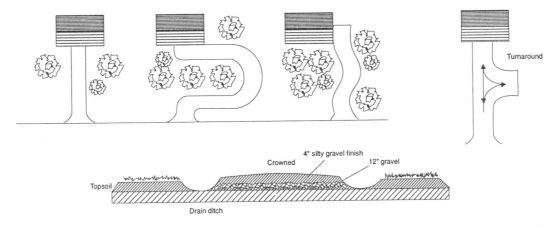

2-5   *The optimal driveway layout shouldn't detract from the view, complicate maintenance, or require too much finesse to negotiate under adverse conditions. A gentle curve is preferable to a straight run or a broad curve, both visually and functionally. A base of compacted coarse gravel and contours sloped for good drainage will preserve its stability. Where the house is situated at some distance from the street, provide a turnaround area large enough to accommodate delivery vehicles (such as the lumberyard truck) as well as guest parking.*

29

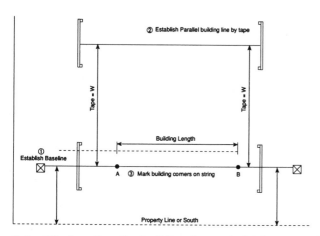
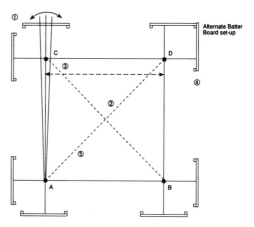

2-6 *The baseline for building layout is laid out parallel with a convenient property line. Where minimum setback requirements aren't critical or solar orientation is not a consideration, the baseline is laid out arbitrarily or along an east–west axis as determined by a compass reading (1). After the line is marked by a string, the opposite building line (CD) is established by parallel measurement (2). The building corners are located on the baseline (3) and a right angle is set up by moving the string AC (4) until it matches the 3-4-5 at A. Set strings BD by parallel measurement from AC (5). Check accuracy of corners by the equal diagonals method (6).*

LAYOUT OF BUILDING LINES

The accurate layout of the building lines will not only satisfy zoning setback requirements, but it will also simplify excavation and foundation construction. It's the critical step towards a square and level house. Although your excavator will do the digging, it's usually up to you to tell him where to dig and how deep.

Assuming that the property lines are already marked by surveyor's stakes, use the setback dimensions given on the site plan to locate the building lines (see **2-6**). Begin by taping off whichever building line is easiest to lay out using the property lines as a reference point (the one that parallels a property line or a public road, or is the longest line, for example). A string stretched between two 2×2 wood stakes driven in the ground at your initial measurement points establishes this *baseline* from which all the other building lines will be laid out. The baseline should be 10 to 20 feet longer than the actual building line itself. If the plan calls for the baseline to be oriented towards the south rather than any specific property line, hold a compass over the string with its needle pointing south. Then adjust the string so that it lines up with the east and west points of the compass rose.*

Straddle the baseline with a pair of sharpened 2×4 stakes spaced four to five feet apart and driven securely into the ground four to 10 feet beyond the approximate location of your first building corner (point A, in **2-6**), and then set a second pair of stakes a like distance beyond the approximate location of the opposite building corner (point B). Nail a level 1×6 board between each pair of stakes just beneath the string, and mark the boards where they're crossed by the string. These are your first two *batter boards.*

Tape off the width of the building from baseline AB and set up a second guide string on another pair of batter boards to lay out the second building line parallel to the first. Check that the strings are parallel once more, and then drive a nail or make a saw kerf in the 1×6 so that the strings can be taken down and set up again as you find it necessary.

Measuring in from the property line or other benchmark, mark the precise location of the first building corner (point A) on the baseline string with an indelible marker. Have a helper hold the end of your tape against the string over this point, and measure the exact length of the building; mark point B on the string.

---

*Since the North Pole isn't the same as magnetic north, there's also a corresponding difference between solar south and compass south. The amount of this *isogonic variation* changes throughout the country and can be found on US Geodetic Survey topographic maps or in charts such as those published in the *ASHRAE* [American Society of Heating, Refrigeration, and Air-Conditioning Engineers] *Handbook of Fundamentals* or in any good passive solar design manual. Hence, the orientation of your baseline string should be adjusted to the requisite compass heading rather than an east–west heading. Some compasses allow the dial to be adjusted with a thumbscrew so that the magnetic deviation is allowed for and readings become true. The compass layout should also reflect any intentional deviation from solar south that you may wish your building to have, e.g., 15 degrees east of south.

To position the other two building corners so that the remaining building lines form true right angles, center a third pair of batter boards four to 10 feet back from points A and B. Set up a fourth pair of batter boards behind the opposite building line to straddle the corner points that your eye tells you are directly across from the already established building corners (refer to **2-6**). Stretch a string between the first pair of these batter boards so that it crosses the mark for point A on baseline AB and appears to form a right angle to it.

It takes only seconds to find the true length of the diagonal generated by the actual building sides. With this number in hand, tie the string to the batter board behind the first building corner, and stretch it tight while your helper holds your tape over point B on the baseline string and you hold the other end at the correct length on the adjacent guide line. Then simply move the string back and forth until it coincides with this intersection. Before marking point C on this guide string, check to be sure that the other end of your movable string still runs through point A. If it does, then you can secure the loose end to the other batter board. If it has shifted, then you'll have to adjust its attachment to the batter board, and remeasure the diagonal. Once line AC is established, its opposing building line is easily found by measuring down the length of the guide string from point C, marking point D, and then stretching a string between the batter boards across points B and D (refer, again, to **2-6**). As a final check for square, measure both diagonals. They should be equal.

Even though this method is more accurate than projecting from a 3-4-5 triangle, it's still slow and fairly cumbersome—especially since it's unlikely to get an exact right angle on the first try. Squaring the corners with a transit level is faster and more accurate (see **2-7**).

Transit levels are inexpensively rented, so there's no reason for a nonprofessional to own one. But since the delicacy of the tool almost guarantees its abuse, be certain that the one you rent has been checked for accuracy. Otherwise, you won't be able to level the base—no matter how many times you adjust the mounting screws.

Transit levels are often confused with *builder's levels* (also termed *dumpy levels*). The difference is that the transit level pivots vertically as well as horizontally, making it possible to read along angled lines of sight. A builder's level is fixed and can only read horizontal sight lines. It costs less to buy, but it is not actually as useful for building layout.

To lay out right angles for your building lines with a transit, attach a plumb bob to the clip under the tripod head, and center it directly over your building corner (point A in **2-8**). Level the scope. Unlock the vertical pivot screw so that the scope is free to swing up and down, and sight along the baseline string (in the direction of point B in **2-8**) until it lines up with the cross hairs. Set the horizontal graduated circle scale to the zero-degree mark. Then rotate the scope until the scale reads exactly 90

2-7 *A transit level makes layout work so much easier that it's almost a necessity.*

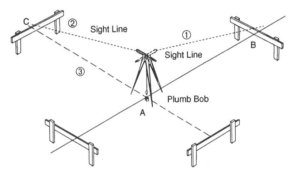

2-8 *Right angles are easy to make with a transit level. A plumb bob hung from a clip on the underside of the tripod head is centered over the building corner point A, and the scope is sighted along the baseline AB (1). The index vernier is set to zero degrees on the horizontal graduated circle. The scope is then rotated until the scale reads 90 degrees (2). The point of sight that falls on the batterboard or other benchmark at C then demarcates line AC, which is a perfect right angle with the baseline (3). This method also makes the layout of angles other than right angles especially easy.*

degrees. Sight the batter board for point C, and mark where the cross hairs line up on it. The resulting line AC will be at an exact right angle to baseline AB. Rather than moving the transit to repeat this procedure at each building corner, tape off the remaining building lines from the first two.

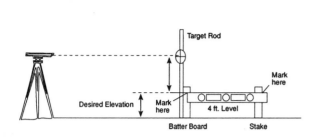

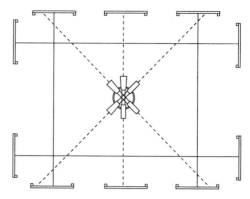

2-9 *To mark level points with a transit, set the levelling rod so that its bottom rests on the desired benchmark. Note the resultant reading. Use the rod to transfer this reading to as many other points on batterboards or grade stakes as needed.*

Setting all the batter boards to the same height will simplify foundation layout (refer to Chapter 3). To use the transit for levelling, mark a batter board stake at the desired elevation (see **2-9**). While your helper holds the target rod upright with its bottom resting on the mark, sight the rod in the cross hairs of the scope. Note the reading, and transfer it to each set of batter boards, moving the target rod up and down until the desired number lines up with the cross hairs. Mark a single stake for each set of batter boards, and then level the boards across the stakes using a four-foot level.

EXCAVATION

Some builders prefer to dig first and check later. They roughly locate the building corners to allow for a margin of error in the excavation, and set up their batter boards for the exact building line layout after the excavator finishes digging. Excavators usually use a hand-held sight level set against a benchmark stake—rather than a transit—to check the hole for proper depth. This shortcut is effective for a simple rectangular cellar hole when building line setback and solar orientation aren't critical. Otherwise, it's safer and wiser to lay out precise building lines, and remove the strings for the excavator.

To leave enough room to set the foundation form work and drain tiles, the excavation is typically about two feet wider than the actual building lines (see **2-10**). A wider trench increases backfilling costs considerably, since gravel is usually trucked in for fill. The angle of the backslope of the excavation depends on the stability of the soil: The

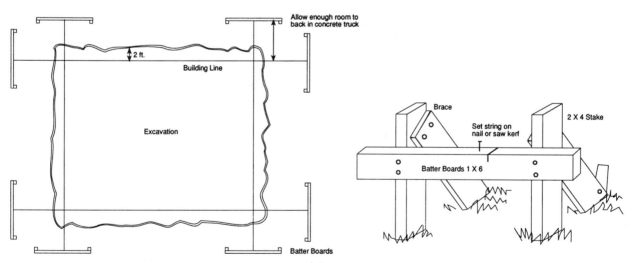

2-10 *Batterboards should always be set back far enough from the actual excavation so that they won't be disturbed by the machinery or the spoils. The batterboard stakes should be driven firmly into undisturbed soil and be staked and braced to prevent shifting, that would throw off the measurements.*

looser the soil, the flatter the cut and the wider the trench. A nearly vertical trench would be stable in heavy clay. In loose, sandy soil, a safe backslope would approximate a 45-degree angle.

The batter board stakes should be set well beyond the perimeter of the building line where they'll be out of the way of the machinery. Even strong and stable stakes should be braced with diagonals to reduce the chances of accidental misalignment (refer to **2-10**). The excavator should also take care not to pile the spoils where they'll interfere with the strings. Otherwise, you'll be faced with some remedial hand shovel work.

Although a skilled excavator can operate a bulldozer or backhoe with amazing finesse when he has to, his natural inclination won't be towards excessive sensitivity. Be sure to mark any trees that are to be left on the site before digging begins. When shaping the final grade, keep in mind that trees will die, if more than a foot of new soil is piled up against their trunk. Likewise, decide on a strategy for the removal of stumps. Is it possible to bury them on site without leaving an unsightly moraine? Or will they have to be hauled to a landfill or chipped on site at considerable expense? Even where burning is permitted, stumps are troublesome to dispose of. Chipping, at least, yields a useful mulch and is also an ecological way to dispose of the piles of limbs and brush left from land clearing.

Your contract should also specify what happens to the topsoil that must be stripped from the excavation (see **2-11**). Standard practice calls for it to be piled up and saved for finish grading. Unscrupulous excavators have been known to haul it off and sell it to someone else.

Every time a piece of heavy equipment is moved to a site, you pay a moving charge. Excavators are usually under a lot of pressure to keep all their machines working. So if you can furnish gainful employment for the equipment that's already on your site, your excavator may not be tempted to remove the machines to other jobs, and you won't have to pay the extra moving charges when it's brought back to yours. Usually, the cellar hole is dug with a bulldozer or bucket-type excavator, and then the machinery is withdrawn to a different job while you wait for the foundation contractor to arrive. After the foundation is finished, the excavator returns for backfilling. If you can coordinate the digging of utility trenches and the installation of the septic system with this phase of the excavation work, you'll eliminate a future round of heavy equipment "musical chairs" as well as lower the level of stressful jobsite noise and confusion during construction.

As should be clear from the outline of the construction process in Chapter One, the timely installation of utilities prior to construction is an important preliminary to housebuilding (see **2-12**). Having working electricity, telephone, and water on site is a necessity, not a convenience.

The type of power and the cost of its installation depend on the distance of your site from existing power lines and

2-11 *Topsoil stripped from the excavation area should be stored on site for reuse during finish grading.*

2-12 *In many housing developments, the developer runs the primary electric service underground and power to each building lot is taken from a ground-level transformer enclosed in a fibreglass or steel case. Only a licensed electrician can make the transformer connections. Note the enclosure for the underground telephone cable visible behind the transformer box and the building materials stacked close to the foundation.*

your aesthetic preference. The main advantage of overhead wire is that it costs less than underground wire. Because it can dissipate heat into open air, overhead conductors can be thinner than the wire needed to carry the same amount of power underground. Also the neutral conductor for underground cable must be insulated to protect it from moisture-induced corrosion. Because the thickness of a conductor must increase with its length to prevent a loss of voltage, overhead wiring is the least expensive way to bring power to a house at some distance from the main line—especially since most utility companies will run wire overhead to one additional pole at no extra cost. (Spans of up to 400 feet between poles are not uncommon.) But overhead wires can interfere with your view, and, on wooded sites, require a substantial clear cut for maintenance and safety. Underground power is also free from the threat of interruption by ice storms and falling trees. Some builders strike a compromise between the economy of overhead service and the aesthetic benefits of underground installation by splitting the difference: They run power overhead to a utility-furnished pole and then proceed underground from there to the house.

Whichever you choose, unless you need to extend the high-voltage main line, power companies supply only the *service drop*, which is the overhead cable that runs from

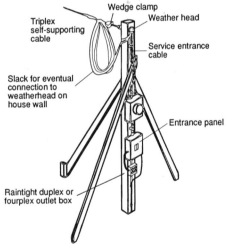

2-13 *Temporary support for an overhead power connection is provided by a braced 4×4 pole (your local utility may specify minimum pole size). The service drop line from the transformer on the primary pole runs to the temporary pole and is spliced to a cable that drops down to the meter and disconnect switch. This switch is sometimes combined with the meter box or else is part of a main-disconnect and outdoor-type panel which feed several smaller branch circuit breakers that, in turn, feed weatherproof outlets. Power is then supplied to the house through one or more heavy-duty (10- or 12-gauge) extension cords.*

the transformer at the main-line pole to the anchor on the wall of your house, or to an extra pole somewhere on your site. For underground service, the utility just connects their transformer to your wire at their pole. When you buy a lot in a development that has underground power on site, the transformer will be located under a fibreglass shell sitting on a concrete pad at curbside. The installation of the meter socket and the rest of the service hardware is your (or your electrician's) responsibility. Check to see if your local code allows you to make outside service connections yourself or whether they must be installed by a licensed electrician.

The main disadvantage of overhead connection is that you can't do it until the shell of the house is finished, since the service drop cable is anchored to the wall of the house or a steel mast that rises up through the roof overhang. The power company will provide you with a temporary service drop instead (see 2-13). This may be nothing more than a conduit or cable that runs down the utility pole into a steel box, which holds the meter and a main circuit breaker or disconnect switch. Since this will be rated at 100 amps or more, you'll need to add another box with two or more standard 20-amp breakers to deliver the proper current to the outlets mounted in a weatherproof box. If the utility pole is much more than 100 feet from the house, even an extra-heavy-duty No. 10 extension cord won't be enough to offset the resultant voltage drop. The solution is a temporary power pole made from two 2×4's spiked together and braced with tripod like legs (refer to 2-14). The service drop cable (which is left long enough to reach the future house) remains coiled up at the top of the temporary pole and is run into the meter/disconnect box.

Underground power avoids the disadvantage of temporary service drops; the connection at the pole is permanent. From the meter/disconnect box, the service cable runs through PVC plastic electrical conduit under or through the foundation wall and into the service entrance panel screwed to a piece of plywood attached to the basement wall. Outlets can be mounted on the plywood next to the service panel and wired into circuit breakers as needed. Ordinary extension cords will then deliver power throughout the house without excessive voltage drop.

Local codes specify the minimum depth for underground power trenches, typically 32 or 36 inches. However, even if your code permits otherwise, it's always a good idea to bury the power and any underground utility below the depth of maximum frost penetration for your area. In the coldest parts of the country, this will be four feet or more. Where the line runs under a driveway or other plowed area, frost penetration will be deeper, and the lines should likewise be buried deeper (six feet is the minimum in a four-foot frost zone). Otherwise, soil movement caused by frost can break the joints of the conduit, allowing moisture to enter—or even pinch the wires together until they short out. To protect against the possibility of damage from stones, the conduit is first covered with six inches of clean sand or carefully hand-shovelled stone-free native soil before backfilling by machine (see **2-14**).

Professional electricians will usually pull cable through the conduit after it's buried or laid in the trench. As each section of conduit is glued together, they pull a nylon cord through it. Later, the end of the rope is attached to the cable (which has been greased with a special wire-pulling compound or talcum powder) so that it pulls the cable through the conduit as it's withdrawn. Since underground service cable is quite stiff and heavy, this method is limited to relatively short runs. For longer runs, it's easier to lay the cable in the trench, and, starting at the foundation wall, slip sections of conduit over it—sliding them towards the opposite end and gluing them in place as you go. Since the cable can't negotiate sharp bends, broadly curved *sweep elbows* are used to facilitate changes of direction.

Underground telephone cables are usually run in the same trench as the electric service. Telephone wire is designed for *direct burial*, i.e., it doesn't have to be run through conduit (except where it passes through the foundation wall). Although the cable is almost indestructible, it's standard practice to run two lines. Then, if one should fail, or you decide to add another phone number at a later date, the spare line can be activated. Even if you need multiline service to begin with, it's still a good idea to run an extra line. Underground cable is usually furnished free of charge by your local telephone company.

The biggest problem with phone service is getting the line activated soon enough to be useful. Since it inevitably seems to take several weeks for the telephone company just to determine the shortest distance between a telephone pole and the system interface on the wall of your house, you can expect that it may take months before your service is actually working. If you contact the phone company

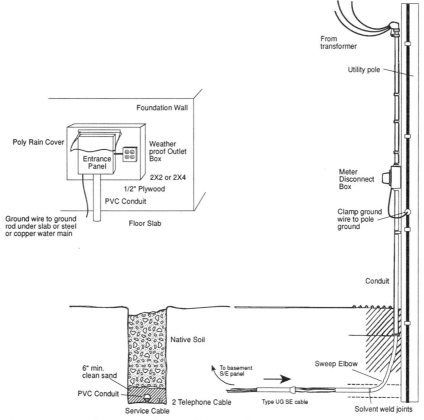

2-14 *Permanence is one major advantage of an underground power connection. A cable or conduit is typically run down the pole from the transformer to a meter-disconnect box and from there through buried conduit (some codes allow direct burial of the cable and require conduit only between the meter and the end of the sweep elbow) into the basement of the house, where it enters the actual service entrance attached to a plywood panel on the foundation wall. To protect the buried cable from damage by stones, always lay it in six inches of clean sand before backfilling the trench with native soil.*

about the same time as your begin reviewing your house plans, you may have a working phone a week or so after you install the underground line. Build a waterproof plywood box to protect the phone on site until the house is built around it, and take the phone home with you at night.

If a fuel oil storage tank or an LP gas tank is to be buried underground, the best time to do it is while the excavator is digging trenches for the other utilities. This is a more efficient use of the machinery than a return trip at a later date to dig up a previously backfilled grade. Otherwise, since the line from a surface LP gas storage tank is buried only a foot deep, it is installed at a later date in a hand-dug trench.

The connection to a municipal water line or sewer system will probably be done by your local utilities (see **2-15**). Advance planning is necessary. But the majority of homes still rely on drilled wells for water supply. Your

2-15 *In frost-free climates the connection to the municipal water supply is close enough to the surface that the water meter and main shutoff can be installed in a concrete caisson at curbside rather than inside the cellar. The meter-reader lifts the steel cover plate with a special forked wrench.*

excavator should include a trench from the well casing to the foundation in the contract price. If the well is drilled in advance of excavation or foundation, it will be easier to coordinate the installation of the water line and pump with the return of the excavator. Some codes allow water and electrical lines to use the same trench; others don't.

The well-driller usually includes the installation of the submersible pump, water line, and pressure tank and its electrical connections as an option with the drilling contract. Although this installation isn't beyond the abilities of an experienced owner-builder, it is not necessarily a smart way to save money. Most well-drillers warrant their installation against failure for at least five years. Since this includes the expensive submersible pump motor, professional installation may be cheaper in the long run. In any case, the quality of the installation is likely to be better than any that you could do yourself.

Be sure that the well-driller disinfects the well by pouring a quart of chlorine bleach down the casing before capping the well. When the pump is connected, flush the system to remove drilling grit and other impurities by letting the water run until several hundred gallons have flowed through it. Then collect a sample to send to the appropriate agency for testing. Sometimes the disinfection process must be repeated before the test shows no bacterial contamination. Your water *must* pass this health test before you can be issued a certificate of occupancy. You may also discover that your well water contains an unacceptably high level of minerals or particulates, in which case you'll have to add a water softener and/or filtration system to your plumbing installation. Depending on their configuration, these systems can also remove malodorous sulfur and fixture-staining iron. In areas where groundwater has been identified as a source of radon, it's important to test your well water for this contaminant too. Contact your State radon control office for the proper procedure you need to follow.

It's a good idea to have your excavator install the leach field and septic tank too, before backfilling the foundation. The tank is placed about eight feet from the foundation, just far enough so a standard 10-foot length of cast-iron sewer pipe can fit into the tank and penetrate an eight-inch concrete wall while leaving a stub sufficient to attach a coupler fitting on the basement side (about four inches). Since every on-site sewage system must be inspected before it can be covered over, installing it while all the other trenches are open avoids the danger of cutting across previously installed utility lines, and makes for the most efficient use of the excavation machinery. Open trenches are always hazardous, so it's a good idea to fill them in before the carpentry begins.

3 Foundations

The foundation serves three purposes: It distributes the weight of the building over the soil; it anchors the building to the ground, preventing movement; and it protects the house from decay and insect attack by preventing direct contact between earth and wood. Although there are many different types of foundation, all of them consist of three parts that together accomplish these purposes. These are: the bed—usually, but not always, the earth upon which the foundation rests; a footing, which spreads the weight of the building over the bed while anchoring the foundation in the earth; and a wall or pier that supports the building on the footing and holds it above grade.

SOIL MECHANICS AND FOUNDATION DESIGN

Although the load-bearing capacity of soils varies considerably according to composition, most are capable of supporting the loads typical of wood-frame residential construction *so long as the soil bed is dry*. Soils lose strength in proportion to water content. The ability of a soil to hold water is explained by the physical structure of its particles. The film of water that sticks tenaciously to the plate-like particles of a clayey soil acts like a lubricant under

pressure (see **3-1**). Thus, clayey soils drain poorly and can loose more than half their strength when wet.

Muck, a spongy soil derived from rotted plant material, and organic fill (dirt filled with stumps and brush that cause it to settle as they rot) are too unstable to build on.

The excellent drainage of sandy and gravelly soils is explained by the rough irregular shape of their particles. Even when tightly packed, the particles still have voids—pore space—through which water moves rapidly. Fine sand, with its more uniformly sized particles, can hold more water than gravel—defined as an amalgam of particles ranging from coarse sand to small boulders. The variety of particle sizes in gravel prevents close packing and ensures high porosity.

Silts are extremely fine particles of sand or clay. When present in sand or gravel, they fill up the interstices between the coarser particles—reducing pore space and, thus, dramatically reducing soil porosity.

It might seem that bearing capacity should be a consideration when the construction plans call for a massive stone fireplace or masonry thermal mass wall (see **3-2**). But, distributed over an 8' × 10' (80 sf) footing, 60 tons of stone impose a load of only 1500 psf (pounds per square foot) on the foundation bed.

Even if it didn't adversely affect the strength of soils, soilborne water can still threaten the stability of a foundation in two ways: *hydrostatic pressure* and *frost heave*.

Water weighs 62.5 pcf (pounds per cubic foot). A column of water five feet high and one foot square would exert slightly more than 312 psf of hydrostatic pressure at its base. If that column were a pool of water five feet deep and 100 feet square, the pressure at the foot of the pool

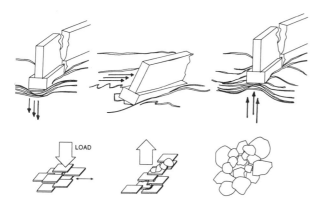

3-1 *Clayey soils are inherently unstable under load because the film of water that adheres to their plate-like particles acts as a lubricant, causing them to slip sideways past each other under pressure. When water trapped between the soil particles freezes, it pushes them upwards, causing the soil to "heave." The coarse irregular structure of gravelly soils lets water drain rapidly. Foundations can fail when saturated clay soils settle under loading, when hydrostatic pressure has the effect of pushing them inward, or when frost penetrates beneath a footing and lifts it upwards.*

3-2 *Load-bearing capacity of soils (sf = square feet; psf = pounds per square foot).*

	tons/sf	psf
Bedrock	80	160,000
Ledge rock	20	40,000
Hardpan or hard shale	10	20,000
Compacted sand and gravel	8	16,000
Loose gravel	6	12,000
Coarse dry sand or hard dry clay	4	8,000
Fine dry sand	3	6,000
Silty sand and clay mixed, wet sand or firm clay	2	4,000
Soft clay	1	2,000
Alluvial muck, organic fill	0.5	1,000

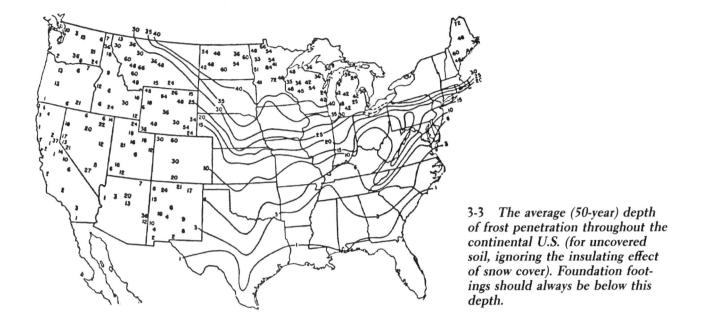

3-3 *The average (50-year) depth of frost penetration throughout the continental U.S. (for uncovered soil, ignoring the insulating effect of snow cover). Foundation footings should always be below this depth.*

wall would be 312,500 psf or 2,170 psi (pounds per square inch). If you think of poorly drained soil saturated with groundwater as a lake, then your concrete foundation wall is a rather thin dam. Concrete has very little tensile strength, i.e., it will break before it bends very far (refer to **3-1**). Hydrostatic pressure acts equally in all directions so that its effect is to subject the walls to a lateral (sideways) bending force.

A critical property of water is that it expands when it freezes. When the water trapped in the pores between soil particles freezes, it pushes them upwards since there's no room for them to move sideways or down. This upward movement of frozen soil is called *frost heave*. When frost penetrates below the depth of the footings, they'll be carried upwards with the expanding soil. This might not be such a problem if the soil expanded uniformly at all points; like a boat on the rising tide, the foundation would lift and fall a few inches. In reality, frost penetration is uneven. Subjected to uneven forces, an inelastic concrete foundation simply breaks apart. Furthermore, since a cellar hole is, in effect, a void in the soil, the pressures generated by frost heave can push laterally against its foundation walls like a monstrous hydraulic jack. The caved-in ruins of abandoned old cellars attest to these powerful forces. Despite the addition of reinforcing steel, an overstressed foundation will still crack, but the pieces will stay together after the wall cracks.

A stable foundation depends on two things: proper footing depth and proper drainage. At the very least, the bottom of a footing should always be at least a foot below the depth of average frost penetration (see **3-3**). Since this varies greatly throughout the country, local building codes generally specify the minimum allowable footing depth.

The frost penetration depths shown in **3-3** are for bare, undisturbed earth. The thickness and duration of local snow cover significantly limits frost penetration. Protected by an undisturbed insulating blanket of snow, the ground may not freeze at all, whereas frost could reach much deeper than the expected average in the compacted soil under a plowed driveway. To be safe, footings or water lines in such areas should be buried half again as deep and/or covered with rigid insulation board.

IMPORTANCE OF GOOD DRAINAGE

Good drainage is perhaps even more important than footing depth. Soils that don't hold water can't freeze or heave.

Surface runoff is water from rain or melted snow. Depending on the porosity of the soil and its vegetative cover, some portion of this water will run off to join the local watershed and some will percolate down through the soil to join with the reservoir of water held in the porous soil or strata immediately overlying an impermeable layer. The *water table* is the seasonally fluctuating surface level of this *aquifer*.

Thus, an adequate drainage system must divert both surface runoff water and groundwater away from the foundation (see **3-4**). *Gutters* (also called *eavestroughs*) at the lower edge of the roof catch the runoff from the roof and channel it away from the foundation through *leaders* (also called *downspouts*). The leaders should discharge two to three feet away from the house onto a stone slab or into a shallow pit filled with crushed stone. The leaders can also drain into a system of underground pipes that empty at a convenient point on the site or into the municipal storm drain system (if permitted). To prevent clogging with debris washed from the roof, install a ½-inch wire

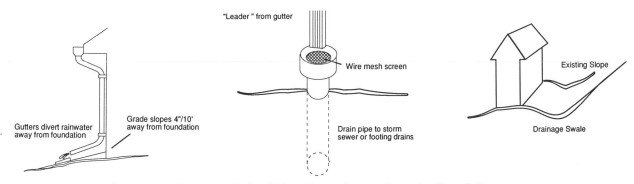

"Leader" from gutter

Wire mesh screen

Gutters divert rainwater away from foundation

Grade slopes 4"/10' away from foundation

Drain pipe to storm sewer or footing drains

Existing Slope

Drainage Swale

3-4 *To prevent damage, surface runoff should be diverted away from the foundation.*

mesh screen at the junction of the leader and the drainpipe. For the same reasons, it's recommended that the roof drainage system be separate from any cellar drain or foundation drainage system.

To ensure what architects call *positive drainage*, the finish grade should slope away from the foundation wall at a minimum of four inches per ten feet. If the natural contour of the site is such that water would tend to flow towards the foundation, a *swale*—a broad, shallow trough—is used to divert the runoff. Swales are preferable to narrow drainage ditches, which are hard to mow and maintain and can become an impediment, if not outright hazard, to enjoyment of the property.

THE PROS AND CONS OF CELLARS

Ninety percent of the foundations in northern regions of the United States are of the full-basement type. The fact that at least 40 percent of these cellars leak or suffer from chronic dampness is more likely the result of their builder's inattention to the details of proper waterproofing and drainage than to the inherent difficulty of achieving a dry and stable basement in the saturated and frost-heave-prone clay soils endemic to these regions.

In the days before mechanical refrigeration, the cellar provided a cool, freeze-proof place to store root vegetables and winter foods. The cellar also kept cold winter winds from sweeping under the floorboards. Later, it was the logical place to put the furnaces and coal bins of early central-heating systems. Automatic washing machines and water pumps were also put in the cellar because they tended to be noisy and to leak. But as the huge boilers and dirty coal bins of primitive heating systems were supplanted by modern heating plants, the cellar evolved into the "rec room" of the 1950s and 1960s. Meanwhile, due to the increasing popularity of the low-pitched ranch-house-style roofline, and the rising cost of building, the attic—the traditional repository of domestic surplus—became extinct or was converted into living space. The cellar assumed the attic's storage function, and became the domain of the weekend handyman as well.

Whatever your feelings are about having a cellar, a house needs some kind of foundation. It seems only sensible to choose a foundation that can offer usable space as well as support—especially since, compared with other options, a cellar is the cheapest heated space you can build. Excavation and concrete work for a standard cellar typically comprise eight percent or less of the total cost of a new home. In cold climates, an insulated cellar could eventually pay for itself by significantly reducing the overall heat loss from the house.

Full basements are best suited to deep soils (see **3-5**). If ledge or shallow bedrock is encountered, the foundation is either raised and backfilled or else the rock is blasted or jackhammered out. Since the first strategy usually results in an aesthetic affront and the second is very expensive, it makes more sense to use an alternative foundation design rather than do violence to the site while trying to accommodate a full basement.

3-5 *On an open site in deep soil, a day's work or less with a bucket loader or bulldozer is usually all it takes to get a cellar hole ready for foundation form work.*

39

3-6 *Level batter boards and strings make it easy to set footing forms for the foundation. Here, a concrete slab will be poured on top of the crushed-stone base.*

COST-EFFECTIVENESS OF BUILDING YOUR OWN FOUNDATION WALL FORMS

The only real drawback to a full-basement foundation is that building one is a bigger job than the average do-it-yourself homebuilder will want to tackle. Although professional concrete work isn't cheap, forming and pouring your own concrete foundation won't necessarily save you enough money to be worth the effort either. Materials (ready-mix concrete, reinforcing steel, wire mesh, anchor bolts, and two cellar windows) make up roughly half the cost of the typical concrete foundation subcontract. The rest is labor, overhead, and profit. The plywood and lumber needed for site-built form work is no small expense. Although some of the materials can be recycled into the framing, much of it will be damaged or unusable. Besides, you've still got to buy metal "snap" ties to hold the wall forms together and rent clamps to secure them to their 2×4 stiffeners (called *walers*). When you can find commercial form panels to rent, the cost won't be low.

Unless you've had prior experience, forming and pouring an eight-foot concrete wall is one of the few jobs that really is better left to professionals. They'll testify from their own experience that there's nothing that rivals the helpless feeling of seeing a truckload of wet concrete blow apart a jerry-rigged form.

However, since the possibility of form failure increases with height, a foundation form four feet or under won't need as much stiffness and bracing as a taller wall. Here, building your own forms and pouring the concrete could easily be cost-effective.

Concrete-block foundations are also touted as a low-cost owner-builder alternative to poured concrete foundations. Unfortunately, block walls have much less resistance to lateral forces than poured concrete walls. In heavy, wet clay soils, the mortar joints soon crack apart and the wall buckles inward and/or leaks. In light, dry soils, where frost heave is not a significant concern, a block foundation offers some significant advantages. Other than a footing, there's no form work to set up or build. Unlike concrete, which must be poured all at once, block walls can be built a little at a time as your schedule permits. Blocks and mortar are relatively cheap, and the techniques of block-laying are fairly easy to master (although you won't begin to approach the speed of a professional mason).

FOOTING LAYOUT, FORM WORK, AND POURING

Whether you choose to pour your own foundation walls or subcontract them to professionals, you should consider forming and pouring your own footings, both as a cost-saving measure and to guarantee that the foundation at least starts off square and level.

The batter boards that were used to lay out the building lines for excavation of the cellar hole are also used to guide the layout of the foundation (see **3-6**).

Unless otherwise specified by your local building code, the footings for your foundation will be twice as wide as the wall, and as deep as the wall is thick (see **3-7**). The distance between the edge of the footing and the wall should be half the width of the wall. For a standard eight-inch-thick concrete wall, footings are thus 16 inches wide and eight inches deep, with a four-inch projection, or "toe," beyond the wall. Although some local codes may require it, reinforcing rod (Rebar) isn't ordinarily used for footings on stable soils.

To lay out the footings, "drop" a plumb line from the strings that mark the building corners. In many how-to books, this operation is performed with a plumb bob. In real life, where breezes swing the bob in perpetual motion and you can't hold the plumb bob string over the layout strings and mark the ground with the same pair of hands, it's a lot easier to transfer the corner point with a four-foot level and a straight-edged board (see **3-8**, drawing 1). After the corner points are located, drive 10-inch log-cabin spikes into the ground to mark them.

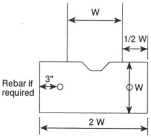

3-7 *The width (W) of a standard footing is twice the width of the wall it supports. Its depth is the same as the wall width. If required, Rebar should be centered in the footing and set at least three inches in from its outside edge.*

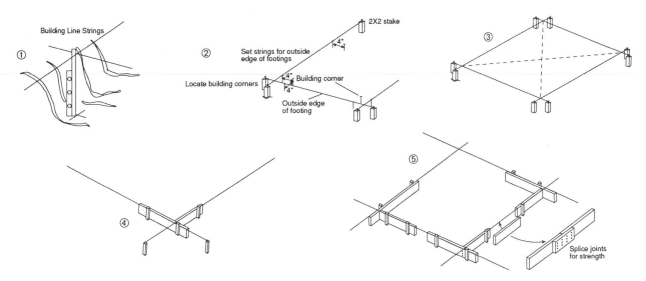

3-8 *Layout and construction of footing forms. Drawing numbers are cited in text. (Continued on next page.)*

Since the outside edge of the footing lies four inches beyond the building line, mark a second set of points that distance beyond the corner points (see **3-8,** drawing 2). Run strings through these points and tie them to nails in the tops of stakes driven into the ground. Check the layout for square once more by measuring the diagonals (see **3-8,** drawing 3). The inside edge of the outside footing form board will line up with these strings (see **3-9**).

Carpentry manuals typically advise that, in firm undisturbed soils, you can dispense with footing form boards and pour the concrete directly into trenches, using grade stakes to establish a more-or-less level surface. This results in a footing even with, or slightly below, the grade of the cellar floor. Since floor slabs should always be poured over a compacted gravel base, this method can only be used with crawl-space foundations that will have a bare earth floor. Another complication is that the perimeter drainpipes are then laid on top of the footing rather than along its bottom edge, which could allow water to seep under the footings and into the basement. In my opinion, a trenched footing is the kind of shortcut that can lead to long-term problems.

Although some concrete contractors construct their footing forms with 1× boards, 2×10 planks are easier to set and level. The extra depth of the plank (9¼ inches) allows a margin of error in the footing base. Beginning at a corner, nail two planks together (see **3-8,** drawing 4). Drive a sharpened 2×4 stake against the outside face of the corner, taking care that the stake is plumb and doesn't push the form plank off the line. Drive another set of stakes at the opposite ends of each plank. Repeat this procedure at the remaining building corners. Next, add or cut pieces as needed to fill in between the planks for the long walls (see **3-8,** drawing 5). Splice the joints together by nailing a short piece of plank (a *scab*) over them. Drive more stakes about six feet apart along the length of the forms.

3-9 *Two-by-ten planks make strong and accurate form boards for footings. Since they can be reused for staging, this system is well suited to the owner-builder. Note the batter board strings used for layout.*

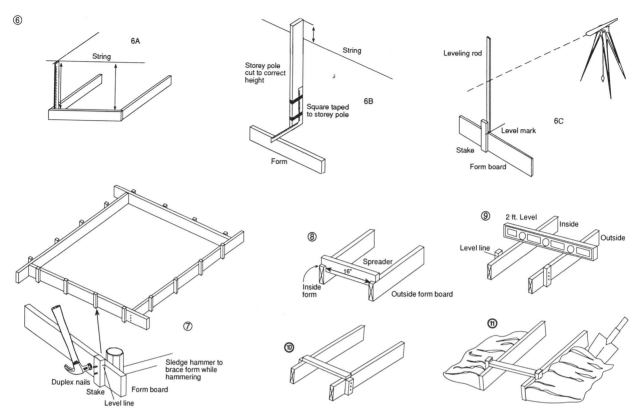

3-8 *(Continued.) Layout and construction of footing forms. Drawing numbers are cited in text.*

If the building line strings were set on level batter boards, the footing form can be levelled by measuring down from the strings (see **3-8,** drawing 6, A through C). First, check the distance between the string and the foundation bed at the corners and several points along the footing to find the high and low points of the excavation. If there is an overall difference of more than an inch or two, lower the high spots by hand-digging. To prevent possible settlement and cracking, footings must always be laid on a solid bed of undisturbed soil, so never yield to the temptation to fill in the low spots instead. Always remove any loose dirt or debris from the footing bed. Minor bumps can be levelled off with the claw of your hammer or a mattock. Shallow depressions will simply result in a slightly deeper footing.

Cut a straight piece of 1×3 or 1×4 board to the same length as the distance between the top of the footing at the control corner and the building line string. Since the footings themselves lie outside of the building line, tape your framing square to the bottom edge of this *storey pole* (see **3-8,** drawing 6B). Holding the top of the pole plumb under the building line string, mark the stakes where the blade of the square crosses them. These are the level lines for the top of the footing form. If you have a transit available, set it up in the center of the cellar hole and

shoot the level marks directly onto the stakes instead (see **3-8,** drawing 6C). Then, holding the top of the plank to the mark, drive *duplex* (double-headed) form nails *through the stakes and into the planks* (see **3-8,** drawing 7). The forms will be a lot easier to pull apart than if nails had been driven flush with the stakes instead. Take care not to knock the stakes off the line while nailing them to the planks. A sledgehammer held against the back of the form makes a solid brace for nailing. Check the forms for alignment with the string, adjusting them as necessary, and once more for level with your story pole. If you need to raise a board slightly, lever it up with your hammer claw or pry bar and shim the form under its bottom edge with a flat stone. Tamp the soil against the stake. If the forms need to be lowered instead, scrape out the dirt under their bottom edge and tap the stakes gently downward as needed.

Once the outside form is secured and levelled, setting the inside forms is easy. Use a *spreader*—a notched piece of board cut to the width of the footing (see **3-8,** drawing 8)—to align the inside form planks parallel to the outside form and drive stakes alongside them as before. Measuring across from the outside form with a two-foot level, mark the inside form stakes for height and nail the planks to them (see **3-8,** drawing 9). Saw the tops of the stakes off flush with the form board, and nail 1×3 *spacers*—cut to the outside width of the form, i.e., 19 inches (see **3-8,** drawing 10)—to the top of the planks at each stake to keep the forms from spreading when they're filled with concrete (see **3-10**). Shovel loose dirt against the outside faces of the form planks to anchor them and fill in the gaps under any low spots (see **3-8,** drawing 11). Check the completed forms for level once more.

FOOTINGS AND FOUNDATIONS FOR SPECIAL CONDITIONS

On sloping lots, footings are stepped to accommodate the change in grade (see **3-11**). Each step should be at least two feet long horizontally and at least one foot high. In any case, the steps should be designed to accommodate standard form panel sizes or, for a block foundation, standard block modules, both vertically and horizontally. To prevent the upper level from slumping, the lower level is poured first and allowed to stiffen somewhat.

In wet and unstable soils, building codes require a wider footing (typically three times the width of the wall) to distribute the building load over a wider area of the bed. Rebar is also used to disperse the tensional stress—that would otherwise cause cracking—evenly throughout the footing and to help it bridge any settled areas. If a test excavation indicates possible soil problems, your footing design should be done by a structural or civil engineer. In earthquake zones, footings and their reinforcement almost always require certified professional design to gain code approval.

3-10 *Professional concrete crews can set and pour footing forms in a few hours.*

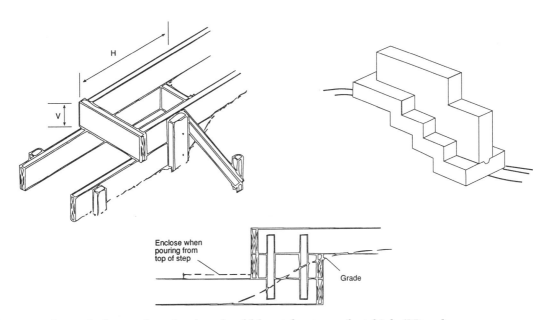

Enclose when pouring from top of step

Grade

3-11 *For strength, vertical steps in a footing should be at least one foot high (V) and run at least two feet horizontally (H). The top of the lower footing form should be covered to keep wet concrete from bulging upwards before it can set.*

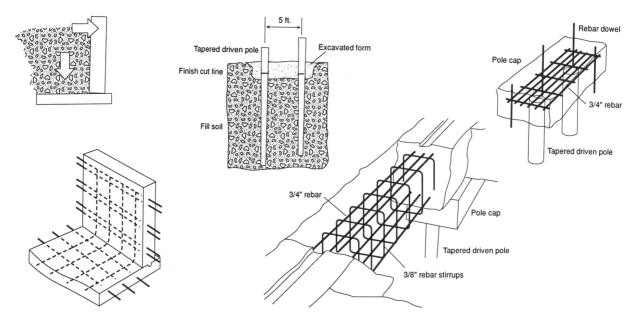

3-12 *A cantilevered retaining wall is used when a foundation must be designed to withstand greater than normal lateral stress. A reinforced grade-beam footing resting on pairs of tapered poles driven deep into the ground will support a foundation on unconsolidated fill or wet muck soils otherwise unsuited for load-bearing. The first pole compacts the surrounding soil, inhibiting the second pole from being driven as deep. The poles are capped with a thick reinforced concrete slab that in turn carries the grade-beam footing proper. Nonstandard foundations should always be designed by a professional engineer.*

The weight of the earth piled over the toe of the footing acts to anchor the foundation wall in the ground. But, as has been mentioned, this same earth exerts a lateral force against the wall. Normally, opposing walls and the rigidity of the floor deck act to cancel out or balance this stress. But in long walls taller than eight feet—particularly where the distribution of forces is unequal as in an earth-bermed foundation or a retaining wall—the lateral stress may be too great. *Pilasters*—concrete columns cast into the wall at equal intervals along its length—add stiffness. But the best resistance to the stresses that might lead to structural failure is provided by a *cantilevered retaining wall* (see **3-12**). Here, the toe of an extra-wide heavily reinforced footing projects four feet or more outside the equally heavily reinforced foundation wall to which it is tied by a lattice of continuous rebar. The weight of the earth on the toe of the footing resists the lateral forces against the wall. Design specifications for these kinds of walls can be found in professional concrete construction handbooks.

In unstable soils, where a deep layer of unconsolidated fill or muck overlies firmer strata, pilings are used to support a *grade-beam footing*. Treated-wood poles, typically 25 feet or more long, tapering from 12 inches to 9 inches in diameter, are hammered into the ground by a power pile-driver until they reach "refusal depth" (they won't go any deeper, despite repeated hammering) (refer to **3-12**). These are capped with a reinforced concrete pole cap which is then tied to a horizontal continuous grade beam that serves as a footing for the walls. Each pile is capable of supporting an enormous load (50 tons or more). Most of the load is transferred to the surrounding soil through the mechanism of simple friction against the piles. The grade beam is reinforced with a cage of rebar so that it resists bending stresses in all directions, allowing it to act like a bridge over the soft soil between poles. The design of this and any other foundation system where soil load-bearing capacity is questionable should always be left to professional engineers.

Bearing capacity is not a consideration for foundations on bedrock or solid ledge; neither is frost-heave. In order to ensure a dry cellar or crawl space and a stable foundation, the footings must be firmly anchored to the underlying rock. With a backhoe, scrape as much of the overlying soil from the rock as possible. Remove any remaining soil by hand. Use a pressure washer to scrub the rock clean (see **3-13**, drawing 1). Even a trace of dirt will cause a poor bond with the concrete. While there isn't any structural reason to use footings on a solid rock bed, it's a lot easier to scribe short sections of stepped footing forms to the irregular contour of the rock than to fit cumbersome wall forms (see **3-13**, drawing 3). A site-built contour gauge can be made from 1×3 strapping clamped between 1×2 horizontal pieces. Maintain a minimum footing thickness of three inches over high spots.

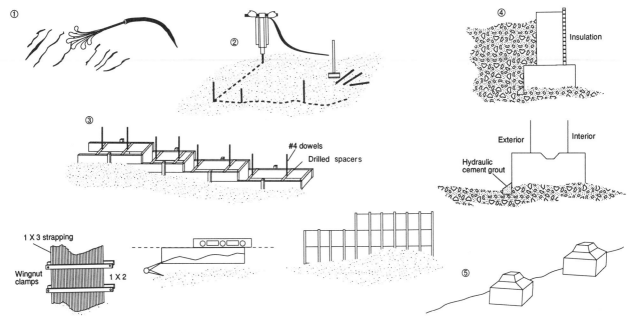

3-13 *A foundation on bedrock. (Drawing numbers are cited in text.)*

With a rented heavy-duty electric impact hammerdrill, bore six-inch-deep ½-inch-diameter holes into the rock (see **3-13**, drawing 2). There should be a hole within a foot of each side of a building corner, at least every six feet along the length of the walls, and two holes in each footing step longer than two feet. Two- to three-foot-long No. 4 rebar dowels (reinforcing rod is sized in ⅛-inch increments; No. 4 rod = ½ inch, No. 3 = ⅜ inch, etc.) driven into the holes will anchor the footings to the rock. To prevent the forms from shifting while placing concrete, drill the spacers to fit over the rebar dowels.

Because some of the water seeping across the uneven surface of impermeable ledge won't be diverted into the perimeter drain, the joint between the rock and the footing should be grouted with waterproof hydraulic cement to keep water from seeping under the footings (see **3-13**, drawing 4). This joint should be sealed whether the foundation is to be backfilled or left exposed. In milder climates where an insulated and fully enclosed foundation is not necessary for comfort, concrete or masonry piers cast or built directly on top of the exposed rock offer an alternative to a continuous footing (see **3-13**, drawing 5).

After the footing forms have been filled with concrete they're "screeded" off by pushing a board back and forth across the top of the form boards while it is also pulled forward. Screeding levels the concrete and brings water and fine particles to the surface. It also leaves a rough surface that improves the bond with the foundation wall.

When the concrete has begun to set, but is still soft, press a bevelled 2×3 strip of wood into the middle of the footings (see **3-14**). The resulting *keyway* provides a me-

chanical connection between the wall and footing, enabling it to resist the lateral overturning force of the backfill soil. The keyway also makes it harder for water to seep between the wall and its footing.

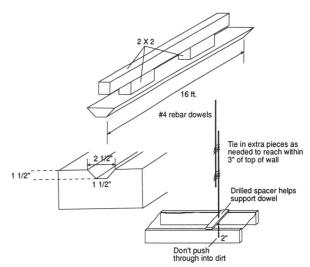

3-14 *Rather than rip a bevelled strip for the entire footing, you can make the keyway by repeatedly pressing a 16-foot (or shorter) form into footing concrete just before it sets up. Since this may interfere with the screeded surface, many foundation contractors simply insert rebar dowels into the stiffened concrete through holes predrilled in the form spacers.*

45

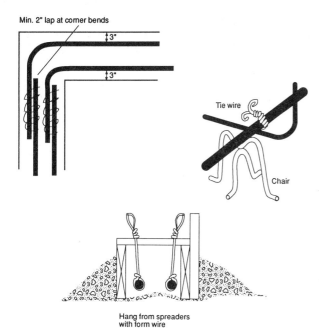

Min. 2" lap at corner bends

Tie wire

Chair

Hang from spreaders
with form wire

3-15 *Except in earthquake-prone regions or in wet, unstable clay soils, rebar is not normally used in footings for single-storey houses. Still, it doesn't hurt to hang two No. 4 bars from the spacers. Use No. 9 form tying wire and position the bars so that they are centered and about three inches in from the edges of the footings. Use metal or plastic Rebar "chairs" to support bars or wire-mesh reinforcement for slabs.*

3-16 *Concrete contractors use prefabricated form panel systems. The panels for the outside of the wall are set first, working from corner to corner. The inside wall panels will be joined to the snap ties seen projecting from the outside walls.*

A simple alternative to the keyway that works just as well in dry soils is to force vertical rebar dowels five to six inches into the center of the footing concrete just as it's beginning to set up. Don't drive them into the ground because this will cause them to rust. These dowels needn't be much more than three or four feet long since longer pieces can be tied to them later when forming the walls. Use one dowel within a foot of each corner and space the rest at six-foot intervals along the length of the footing.

If your design specifications require Rebar in the footings, the pieces should be bent around corners, overlap each other by at least two feet, and be tied together with wire (see **3-15**). Never rest rebar on *brickbats* (scraps of broken brick) or stone shims; these will weaken the concrete. Use steel or plastic rebar "chairs" that can be purchased from masonry suppliers.

WALL FORMS FOR A FULL-BASEMENT FOUNDATION

"Green" concrete (fresh concrete actually does have a greenish tint) is quite soft for the first day or two after the pour. Leave the form boards in place to protect the edges of the footings when laying out the wall forms.

Restring the batter boards and transfer the building corner marks onto the footings. Check them for square once more, and then snap chalk lines on the footings. The inside edge of the wall forms will follow these lines.

Each of the many different kinds of manufactured form panel systems has its own unique hardware and setup procedure (see **3-16**). Your dealer should furnish specific instructions for whichever system you rent. The Symons wedge-bolt system is one of the most widely used, easiest to set up, and strongest, prefabricated form panel systems. Steel "snap" form ties are inserted into slots between abutting edges of standard modular 2×8 steel-framed plywood panels, and each section is locked together with wedge-shaped pins that can be tightened or loosened by a light hammer blow.

As with the footing forms, assembly of wallforms begins at the corner of the outside wall. The bottom of the panels are tacked to the footings with hardened masonry nails. A special fractional-sized panel (e.g., one foot, 8 inches, 4 inches, etc.) or custom-cut piece of plywood is used to fill in the gap between the last full-sized panel and the ending wall corner. A special steel corner piece (presized to account for the difference between inside and outside form lengths) starts the inside wall form layout. Once the forms for both walls are tied together, the entire unit is straightened and stiffened by a continuous 2×4 *waler* clamped to the top course of the wall ties (see **3-17**). The form is now so stable that only an occasional diagonal brace is needed to hold it to the layout line once the corners have been checked for plumb.

The plywood face of some prefabricated form panels is coated with plastic to create a smooth finish and prevent it from sticking to the concrete. Others are sprayed with form-release coatings before each use. Your form rental contract usually requires the forms to be returned clean and sprayed with release coating.

Site-built forms must be strong enough to withstand the forces generated during concrete placement. Forms for walls up to eight feet high can be assembled from four-by-eight sheets of ¾-inch exterior sheathing-grade plywood ("CDX") stiffened with 2×4s horizontally at their top and bottom edges and vertically every 16 inches (see **3-18**). Manufactured form ties are inserted through holes spaced one foot down from the top and one foot up from the bottom—and at the three-foot and five-foot points along the second and third vertical stiffeners of each panel. These intermediate ties can be omitted for walls only four feet high or less. As the panels are set to the chalk line, they're nailed into the footing through their bottom edge.

3-17 *The completed form setup is straightened by a single course of 2×4 walers clamped to the top of the wall. Since it's essentially self-supporting, the form needs only a few diagonal braces to hold it plumb and square.*

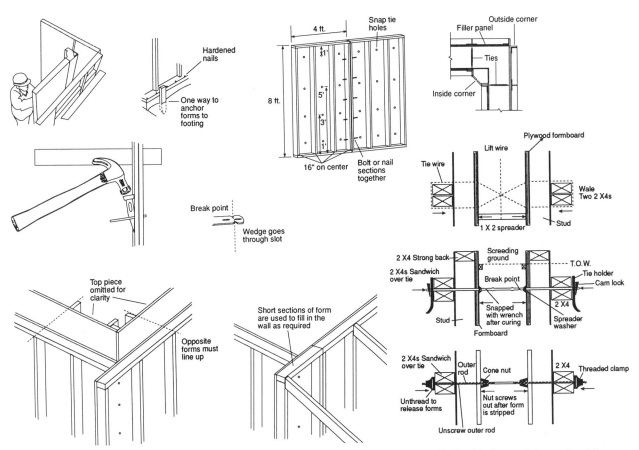

3-18 *Site-built wall forms can be assembled from plywood and 2×4s. Inch-thick plywood is preferable for wall forms over four feet high; otherwise, use ¾-inch plywood, which can be recycled for subfloor sheathing. There are several different systems available for setting up homemade forms: Form wire is twisted to pull the form panels tight against wood spacers that are removed as the concrete is poured; commercial systems typically use snap ties: in one, snap ties are locked against the walers with a cam; in another, the clamp threads on the end of the tie. Some systems use a special wedge clamp that is driven into a slot in the tie.*

Two-by-four walers are clamped to each course of ties. For maximum stiffness, use sixteen-foot lengths of 2×4 and stagger the joints so that they don't "break" over each other. For a strong corner, overlap the walers, and spike them together. Nail or bolt each form panel to the next one as well. Since the snap ties also serve as spacers, their overall length must accord with the particular setup of your forms and walers (refer to **3-18**).

Even with four courses of walers, site-built forms aren't quite as strong or stable as manufactured forms. They have a pronounced tendency to float upwards on the rising tide of concrete or to bulge outward along their bottom edge. Diagonal bracing should be firmly attached to both sides

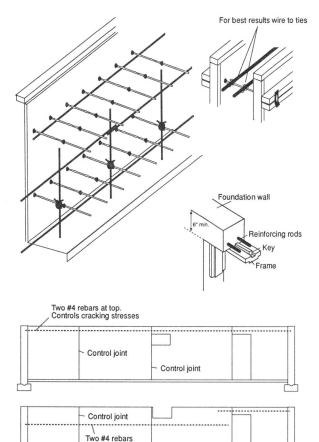

of the form every four to six feet. Concrete form work is one place where overbuilding is always preferable to minimal adequacy.

Unlike footings in normal soil where Rebar isn't usually required, it should always be used in walls, not so much for strength, as to relieve the thermal stresses that could otherwise cause it to crack around openings or along its length (see **3-19**). In residential construction Rebar eliminates the need for *expansion control joints* in all but the longest walls. At the very least, two pieces of horizontal Rebar are wired to the top course of metal snap ties and over and under any window openings. More often, the Rebar is laid across each course of snap ties. Rebar can also be wired to the vertical Rebar dowels projecting from the footings. Since it isn't possible to slide 20-foot lengths of Rebar between the snap ties after the forms are tied together, the Rebar is laid across each layer of snap ties before attaching the inside form panels. To gain the full benefit of its strength and prevent long-term corrosion, Rebar must be surrounded by at least three inches of concrete. Don't lay it any closer than this to the sides or the top and bottom of the walls or footings. Rebar can be cut with an ordinary hacksaw, albeit slowly; rent a Rebar cutter instead. Likewise, to bend Rebar, you can use a length of pipe slipped over the bar or else rent a Rebar bender.

FORMS FOR WALL OPENINGS

Core boxes inserted between the wall panels are used to form the openings for windows, doors, and other penetrations, indentations, or changes of level in the foundation wall (see **3-20**). Leaving the forms for doors and windows in place furnishes a convenient base for nailing trim or attaching jambs. Use pressure-treated lumber for any wood left in contact with concrete or masonry. Nail a key to the back of the core box to help anchor it to the concrete. A removable core box is called a *buck*. To facilitate removal from hardened concrete, bucks are normally sawn almost all the way through and temporarily braced by tacking a piece of plywood over the saw kerf. After the forms are stripped, the buck is snapped along the cuts and quickly removed.

Core boxes or bucks can be eliminated entirely by installing prefabricated cellar vent window units directly between the form panels. Depending on the above-grade elevation of the foundation wall, these windows are usually installed level with the top of the foundation wall. Otherwise, set the window unit at least six inches below the top of the wall to allow sufficient thickness for the concrete to form a strong lintel. As shown in **3-19**, two pieces of Rebar are then laid in the form over the window.

To form the opening for the household sewer line, nail an empty one-gallon paint can between the wall forms, or cut a piece of six-inch-diameter PVC pipe (see **3-21**). Use sleeves cut from PVC conduit for the penetrations of water, power, telephone, and gas lines. Since the forms

3-19 *Rebar adds strength and prevents cracking caused by thermal stress. When window or door openings are set at least six inches below the top of the wall, the rebar should run above them. Otherwise, run the bars beneath the window opening. Expansion control joints—interlocking but structurally discontinuous caulked seams—are not needed in normal residential foundations unless a wall is 60 feet or more long.*

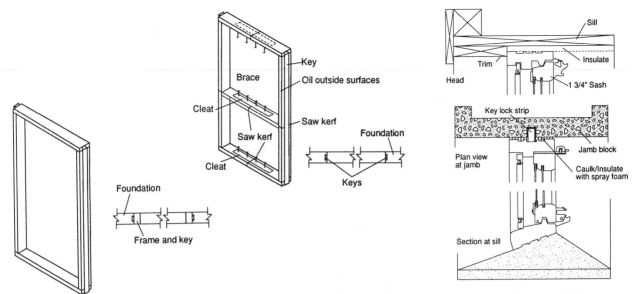

3-20 *The corebox form for an opening can be left in place to provide a nailing base for the window or door unit. Use pressure-treated wood and a dovetail-shaped keyway to lock the form into the concrete. The key for removable forms—bucks—should be rectangular to facilitate removal. Prefabricated cellar windows do not require corebox forms and are usually set flush with the top of the wall. In concrete block construction, special keyed jamb blocks lock the window unit in place, and the sill is packed with sloped mortar.*

will spread slightly when filled, don't rely on friction to hold the sleeves in place. Instead, shape a scrap of board to fit inside the conduit and nail it through the sides of the pipe; then anchor it to the wall forms with drywall screws.

In order for a cellar floor drain to empty into the perimeter footing drain, it must pass through the bottom of the footing. Notch the footing forms to slip over a short length of drainpipe, installed so that its bell end is facing the inside of the footing.

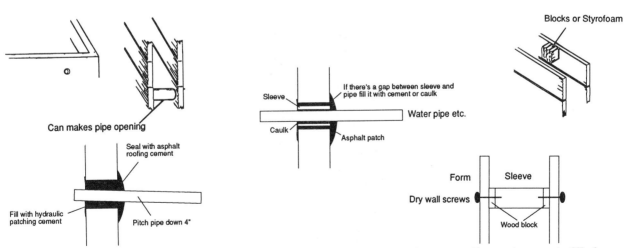

3-21 *The gap between cast-iron sewer pipe and the hole prepared with a one-gallon paint can is filled with hydraulic patching cement and sealed on the outside with asphalt flashing cement. The gaps between conduit or pipes and PVC sleeves are caulked and sealed with asphalt on the outside wall. A wood block cut to fit inside the sleeve provides support for screwing it to the form panels. Wood or Styrofoam blocking is used to form beam pockets.*

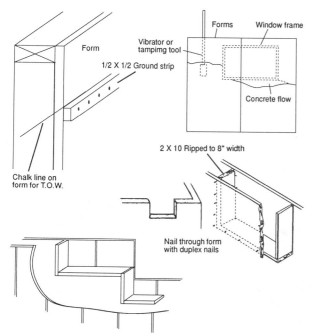

3-22 *Steps, indentations, and levelling grounds using 2×10 planks ripped to eight inches and ½-inch-square ground strips.*

To form steps in the top of the wall for changes in level, or indentations for beam pockets, use 2×10 boards ripped to an eight-inch width and nailed between the wall forms (see **3-22**). Be sure to work the concrete thoroughly to eliminate any voids beneath the forms.

Full-sized wall form panels are eight feet tall; but foundation walls are often only 7'-6" or 7'-8" high. Snap a level chalk line to mark the T.O.W. and tack a ½-inch-square wood strip under the line. This *ground strip* makes a handy rest for your trowel when you float the finished wall pour (refer to **3-22**).

ESTIMATING, ORDERING, AND PLACING CONCRETE

Concrete is ordered by the cubic yard (CY). To estimate the amount of concrete to order, multiply the width by the depth (or height) by the length—all measured in feet—and divide by 27. Use decimal feet equivalents for inches. Thus, a 24' × 32' footing is 16" wide and 8" deep and runs for 112 (24+32+24+32) linear feet (LF). So this footing would require 1.33' (16") × 0.66' (8") × 112'/27 = 3.64 CY. You would phone in an order for 3⅔ CY. An eight-foot-high, eight-inch-thick wall poured on the same footing would need an additional 21.9 CY of concrete. Since it's always better to have a little bit of ready-mix left over than to run a little short, if you divide by 26 instead of 27, you'll build in a four-percent allowance for waste and odd inches (since the perimeter mea-

surement doesn't take into account the eight-inch thickness of the walls where they meet at each corner, the original calculation already includes a small cushion, too). By this rule of thumb, you would order 3¾ CY and 22¾ CY, respectively.

Unless they're very busy, most concrete suppliers need little advance notice to arrange a delivery. Usually, if you call first thing in the morning, you can have your concrete within a matter of hours. Just be sure that you've realistically left yourself enough time to finish setting up the forms and make any final adjustments before the ready-mix truck arrives. There's a steep penalty charged for waiting time.

When you phone in your order, the dispatcher will most likely ask how many *bags* you want your mix to be. This refers to the number of 94-pound sacks (one cubic foot) of Portland cement in each cubic yard of concrete. Concrete is a mixture of coarse and fine aggregate (crushed stone up to 1½ inch and washed sand), water, and Portland cement powder (made from ground limestone heated in kilns with shale or clay). The proportion of cement powder in the mix determines the strength of the concrete. A five-bag mix is the minimum for standard residential foundations. A six-bag mix is used in floor slabs and reinforced footings and/or walls. Alternatively, you can order concrete by its compression strength. A 2500-psi rating is equivalent to the standard five-bag mix; a 3000-psi rating is a six-bag mix. The dispatcher may also ask you how much *slump* (a measure of its stiffness or consistency—basically, how high wet concrete can be piled before it collapses) you want it to have. A five- to seven-inch slump is standard for footings.

The most difficult part of concrete placement may well be in figuring out how to get the truck to do most of the work for you. A conscientious excavator can help by leaving a clear route for the truck to the back corner of the foundation. Since you're responsible for the truck once it leaves curbside, the question of access to the foundation should be decided well in advance of the truck's arrival. Concrete trucks are very heavy; getting one unstuck is a challenge. It's better to wait until the ground has dried out enough to support the truck than risk a pour too early in the season or too soon after heavy rains.

The chute on a concrete truck has a reach of about 16 feet straight back from the hopper (see **3-23**). If you specifically ask for one when you order your concrete, the driver will bring an extension chute, as well. Chained to the hydraulic chute, this adds another 12 feet or so to its reach. If even this extra length won't reach all the way to the farthest part of your foundation, use a makeshift chute fashioned from a couple of 2×4s nailed on edge to a one-foot-wide strip of plywood. This is a lot easier than ferrying the concrete to the forms with a wheelbarrow. As more length is added to the chute, its angle decreases, which means the concrete has to be dragged along with a shovel or hoe, especially since it won't slide on the rough plywood of a homemade chute in the first place (I've solved this problem by nailing a strip of aluminum flashing metal to the plywood first).

As much as possible, avoid dragging the concrete over long distances through the forms (more than three feet) or dropping it from heights greater than five feet. This tends to *segregate* the coarse aggregate from the fines and cement paste, weakening the finished product. Concrete with a five-inch slump is too stiff to "seek its own level." It has to be laboriously pushed, poked, and pulled to settle it around Rebar and into the forms. But don't yield to the temptation to save time and sweat by adding water to the concrete to make it "runny." Each extra gallon added to a yard of concrete reduces its ultimate strength by five percent. To gain some leeway for adding water, order the concrete stronger than specified.

Wall forms must be strong and well braced to withstand the lateral pressure of fresh concrete. Since concrete weighs about 150 pounds per cubic foot, the pressure against the forms at the bottom of an eight-foot wall would theoretically be 1200 psf. Fortunately, concrete is to some extent self-supporting. The actual pressure depends on the rate at which the concrete is placed, its water content, the air temperature, and the amount of mechanical vibration during placement.

To reduce lateral pressure, concrete is generally placed continuously in separate layers, or *lifts*, of 12 to 18 inches at a time, rather than pouring the full height of the wall all at once. A rate of four to five vertical feet per hour is recommended. The warmer the air temperature, the faster concrete will harden and the lower the lateral pressure it exerts on the forms will be. At 40 degrees F (4.4 degrees C), for example, the pressure is almost twice as much as it would be at 90 degrees F (32.2 degrees C).

When placing concrete in below-freezing weather, it's important to prevent the concrete from freezing before it can set up. Heated water is standard. Per your request, an accelerant (usually two percent calcium chloride) will be added at extra cost. Increasing the volume of accelerant will speed up setting, but it will also reduce ultimate strength. To retain the heat generated as the concrete cures, the finished pour is insulated with a plastic membrane covered with straw or rigid foam insulation.

In hot weather, concrete can cure faster than you can place it. Retarders are then added to the mix. Once the pour is finished, curing is controlled by wetting down the surface and covering it with plastic sheeting to keep it moist. A commercial curing compound can also be sprayed on the walls to retard water loss and yield a stronger end result. Overly rapid curing causes hairline shrinkage cracks (known as *crazing*) on the surface.

The higher the water content of freshly placed concrete, the more closely it assumes the hydraulic characteristics of a true liquid. This is another good reason to avoid adding water to speed up placement. In order to assure a smooth surface free of *honeycombs*, and a strong,

3-23 *Proper placement of concrete in wall forms requires judgment and experience to maintain strength and prevent blow-outs. The worker in the background is pounding on the forms with a hammer to settle the concrete.*

uniform mix, concrete is *consolidated* by working a stick or shovel up and down in the mix as it's placed, to bring fines and water to the surface (see **3-24**). Commercial contractors often use mechanical vibrators, especially on large pours. But excessive vibration (more than 10 seconds in one location with a power vibrator), whether by hand or power tools, causes the mix to become more liquid—increasing the pressure on the form walls towards the theoretical maximum. This is one of the most common causes of form failure, or *blowout*. Hammering on the filled forms with a rubber mallet gives smooth walls with less chance of a blowout.

3-24 *"Honeycombing" occurs when concrete is poured too stiff or not tamped enough to force the fines to the surface.*

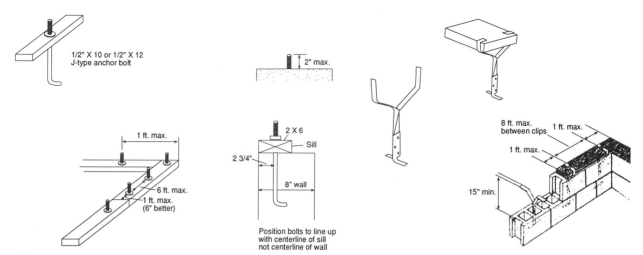

3-25 *For sills narrower than a 2×8, center the anchor bolt with respect to the sill, not the wall itself. Galvanized-steel strap anchors that fold over and are nailed to the top of the sill can be used instead of anchor bolts. These anchor straps are most often inserted in mortar-filled cores of block foundations.*

Although the average ready-mix truck driver can maneuver a loaded truck into some amazing places, on steeply sloped or otherwise difficult sites it may prove impossible to reach a point where the delivery chute is higher than the footing or the wall forms. The only way to get concrete to flow uphill is to pump it. A hose attached to an articulated boom mounted on the bed of the pumper truck delivers concrete to otherwise inaccessible forms within its 100-foot reach. Since it just about doubles the cost of the concrete, pumping should be a remedy of last resort. An alternative foundation design or some degree of site recontouring may be more cost-effective.

3-26 *After two or three days the forms are stripped and then about another week is allowed before breaking the snap ties. Note how the wood window frames are cased, in place, at the top of the walls.*

FINISHING THE FULL-BASEMENT FOUNDATION

J-shaped ½-inch by 10-inch anchor bolts should be installed in the top of the foundation wall immediately after it's screeded off (see **3-25**). Rest a drilled spacer block across the forms or ground strips to support the bolts until the concrete hardens. Inserting the bolts after the concrete has partially set up makes a weaker bond. The bolts must be carefully positioned with respect to the sills; use the foundation plan to determine the lengths of your sill stock and its placement on the wall. Space the anchor bolts so that there's one within six inches of the ends of each sill piece and intermediate bolts every four to six feet apart. The threaded end of the bolt should project 1½ to 2 inches above the T.O.W.

To ensure adequate curing, leave the forms in place on the wall for at least two days. In cold weather, you may have to wait an extra day or two before you begin stripping the forms. Since it can take a considerable amount of force to pry the forms from the wall, you could crack a wall that hasn't hardened up.

Concrete is actually porous, and soil-borne water, especially when under pressure, will migrate through it. The first line of defense against a wet basement is to waterproof the outside face of the foundation wall below grade.

Once the forms are stripped and after about a week of further hardening, the ends of the snap ties that protrude from the face of the wall are "snapped" or twisted off (see **3-26** and **3-27**). In lieu of a tie-breaking tool, use a straight claw hammer or a length of pipe slipped over the tie to break it (see **3-28**). Seal the crater with asphalt flashing cement to keep water from seeping in along the entrapped metal.

3-27 *The protruding ends of the snap ties will be broken off with a length of pipe or a special tool. The footing is swept clean; note the small footing which will support cast piers for a shed addition.*

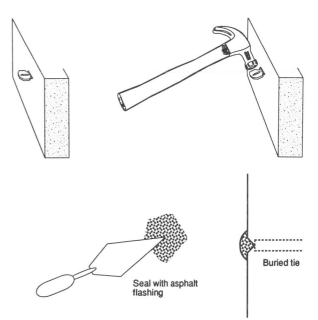

3-28 *The projecting ends of flat-type snap ties can be broken off with a hammer or a special notched lever-like tool. Use a short length of pipe to twist off round snap ties.*

3-29 *Asphalt foundation coating is mopped onto the below-grade portion of the foundation wall to waterproof it. Note the opening for the sewer line in the wall and the perforated perimeter drainpipe at the base of the footing.*

Clean any loose concrete and dirt from the toe of the footing and apply asphalt foundation coating to the wall and footing toe with a long-handled tar brush (see **3-29**). Work the coating thoroughly into the joint between the wall and the toe and into any honeycombs or other rough spots on the walls. Asphalt spreads with difficulty at temperatures below 60 degrees F (15.5 degrees C). Leave the buckets in a warm place overnight or heat them over an open fire or a portable LP gas stove.

In wet soils, a single coat of hand-mopped foundation waterproofing provides minimally adequate protection at best. One or more coats of heated asphalt sprayed under high pressure by a foundation waterproofing contractor provides a much more reliable seal for a nominal extra cost. Another method is to press a sheet of 10-mil black polyethylene into the freshly applied asphalt, draping it down the wall, over the footings, and under any drainpipe.

With underground and earth-bermed houses, reliable waterproofing is even more important. Architects typically specify either bituthane, a self-sealing butyl rubber or 45-mil EPPM (ethylene propylene polymer membrane), like the kind used to seal flat roof decks, or bentonite (a special clay, packed in kraft paper bags that expands when wet) to make an impervious barrier.

FOUNDATION INSULATION

Since the recommended thickness of attic and wall insulation has increased, heat lost through the foundation wall has accounted for a correspondingly greater percentage of the overall building envelope heat loss. Over the past decade or so, building codes and energy-conscious builders have taken steps to reduce this heat loss by insulating the foundation (see **3-30**). Presently, the most common method is to apply tongue-and-groove panels of extruded polystyrene rigid foam insulation (Styrofoam, also called blueboard) to the outside of the wall. The question as to whether this insulation isn't better applied to the inside of the wall has not been definitively settled; there are arguments in favor of both approaches. Placing the insulation on the outside requires special construction techniques to accommodate the increased size of the foundation. There are also questions concerning its long-term performance. But, because foam insulations give off toxic gases when they burn, building codes typically require them to be covered with ⅝-inch fire-rated drywall when used on interior building surfaces. While not difficult, fastening foam and drywall to concrete adds labor and expense, while subtracting possibly useful space from the cellar. Some experts argue that placing insulation on the inside of the foundation is *too efficient*; they feel that a certain amount of heat transfer to the outside keeps the soil immediately adjacent to the foundation wall from freezing, thus preventing frost-heave problems. There's also some evidence that interior insulation can cause the outside face of the concrete to *spall* (flake off).

Extruded polystyrene, which is waterproof, relatively noncompressible, and has a high R-value per inch, shouldn't be confused with the less expensive and less efficient *expanded polystyrene* "beadboard" (Korolite), which soaks up water and decomposes rapidly in exterior applications.

Since the greatest heat loss occurs in the exposed above-grade portion of the foundation and tapers off rapidly below grade, except in the coldest climates it isn't necessary or cost-effective to extend the Styrofoam panels more than four feet below grade or past the frost line. To keep the foam stuck to the wall until it can be backfilled, drive a hardened masonry nail through a roofer's "tin" (a thin half-dollar-sized metal disc that keeps tarpaper from blowing off the roof deck). Two or three nails per 2×8 panel are usually sufficient. If the nails are in the below-grade portion of the foam, they won't have to be removed after backfilling (refer to **3-30**).

Polystyrene, like most petrochemical-based building materials, degrades upon prolonged exposure to ultraviolet light. Above-grade insulation panels must be protected from UV and physical damage. There are several com-

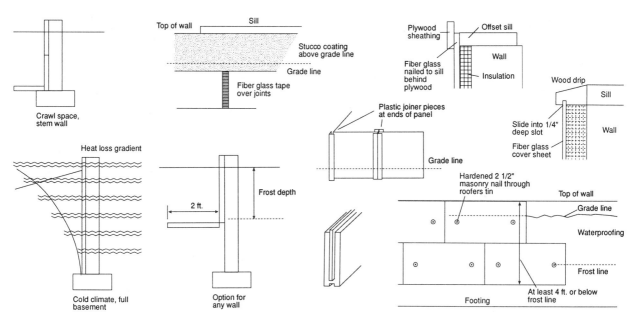

3-30 *Because most of the heat loss through a cellar wall occurs above and within the first few feet below grade, it's not considered cost-effective to insulate to the bottom of a full basement foundation. The insulation should extend to at least the maximum frost penetration depth; laying foam horizontally at the frost line is sometimes done for additional protection against frost heave. The foam panels are held in place by hardened masonry nails driven through roofer's tins. The above-grade portion is protected by a stucco coating or fibreglass sheet. The method of finishing depends on whether the sill extends over the foam or ends flush with the concrete wall (see also 3–31).*

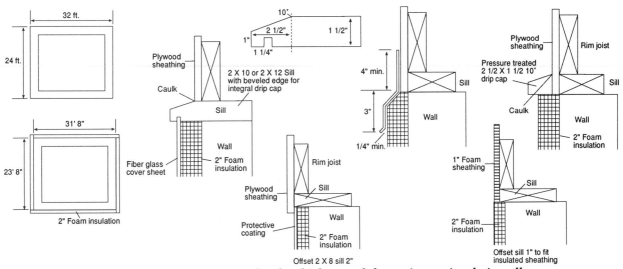

3-31 *Adjusting the foundation to account for the thickness of the perimeter insulation allows the framing to line up flush with the face of the insulation. Otherwise, the requisite drip-cap detail could complicate exterior trimwork or clash with the lines of the design. Custom-formed metal flashing is also an option.*

mercially available latex-augmented and fibreglass-reinforced stucco coatings available for this purpose. In general, the foam is prepared for a good bond by roughening with a wire brush, fibreglass tape is applied over seams, and one or two coats of the stucco mix is trowelled on. Refer to the manufacturer's product literature for specific application methods. For speed and neatness, apply the stucco before backfilling or finish-grading.

A more costly but less labor-intensive alternative, which offers better protection against physical damage than stucco, is to cover the foam with thin fibreglass panels (Insulgard). The top edge of the 1×8 or 2×8 panel is nailed to the wall sheathing or slipped into a slot cut into a wooden drip cap and glued to the wall with foam panel adhesive (refer to **3-30**). Special plastic moulding strips cover the vertical joints between panels.

Currently, the recommended R-value for exterior foundation insulation is R-10 in the coldest regions and R-5 everywhere else but the warmest regions, where it's not needed (for a discussion of R-value see Chapter 19). Extruded polystyrene has an R-value of five per inch. Thus, unless otherwise compensated for, providing adequate exterior foundation insulation can add up to four inches (two inches to each wall) to the overall dimensions of the building lines. The details of integrating the insulation with the framing should be worked on in advance in your framing or foundation drawings to avoid unpleasant surprises during construction.

The design problems presented by foundation insulation are mostly aesthetic and only somewhat structural (see **3-31**). If it's important that the insulation and the vertical line of the building appear to lie in a single plane, the overall dimensions of the foundation must be reduced to make up for the thickness of the insulation. For example, if the floor plan measures 24 feet by 32 feet, the foundation would be 23'-8" by 31'-8". Foundation subcontractors really dislike these kinds of less-than-full-width modules, and they may try to charge extra for the fill-in form work required. But the alternative—adding the extra width to the frame—would be very wasteful and costly indeed; full sheets of plywood sheathing would fall short of the last wall stud, and floor joists would have to be two feet longer to gain a few inches. Some builders shrink the foundation and let the framing overhang the insulation. The problem with this approach and two-inch-thick insulation is that, with 2×4 framing, more than half of the building load carried on the end walls (i.e., those parallel to the floor joists) won't be supported by the foundation. Fortunately, end walls rarely carry more than their own weight, and the critical loads carried by the walls perpendicular to the floor joists are transferred to the foundation through the joists themselves (see Chapter Four).

If, instead of plywood, the exterior frame is sheathed with inch-thick insulating foam, then the sills need only overhang the foundation wall one inch, and the wall insulation will neatly line up with the foundation insulation.

Rather than shrink the foundation or overhang the sills, you can use a wood drip cap or preformed metal flashing to emphasize the junction as a design element (refer to **3-31**). For a one-piece installation, cut a 10-degree bevel on the projecting edge of a 2×10 or 2×12 sill to shed water. To reduce the profile of the drip cap while suggesting traditional elegance, install a decorative band of trim.

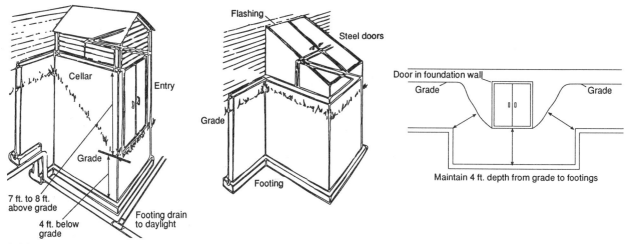

3-32 *Entrance to the cellar can be accomplished with variations on a bulkhead or a simple cellar door depending on grade conditions: A bumped-out bulkhead with foundation at same level as foundation wall on a level site; a bumped-out bulkhead on sloping grade requires a stepped-down foundation and perimeter drain below frost, as well as a simple cellar door in foundation wall with foundation stepping down below door.*

BULKHEADS AND CELLAR DOORS

Either as a convenience or a necessity, a separate outside entrance into the cellar is well worth the added cost (see **3-32**). On level sites, the foundation wall is simply "bumped out" to accommodate a prefabricated sloped steel bulkhead, according to dimensions supplied by the distributor. The bulkhead should always be thermally isolated from the cellar to prevent excessive heat loss. Insert a pair of keyed pressure-treated 2×4s or 2×6s into the wall forms to provide a nailing base for attaching the insulated steel door unit. The carriage for the bulkhead stairs can be nailed directly to the bulkhead sidewalls.

On sites where a steep grade slopes away from the house, the foundation for the bump-out is stepped down at the main wall so that the foundation wall immediately beneath the bulkhead entry doors is below frost line (refer to **3-32**). For example, assuming four feet to frost line and an eight-foot foundation wall, the bump-out wall is twelve feet high. The bulkhead is closed in with a custom-built gable-roofed cover. Since these walls are also retaining walls, they should be heavily reinforced with Rebar. The perimeter drain system will also drop down to the level of the bulkhead footings and drain to grade at that point. To reduce hydraulic pressure on the walls, backfill is typically done with coarse crushed stone instead of gravel.

If the grade slopes parallel to the foundation, no bump-out is needed. Instead, the foundation wall is stepped down so that its footings are below frost line at all points of the finished grade, particularly under the opening of the door, which is formed in the foundation wall itself.

INSTALLING FOUNDATION DRAINS

Perforated four-inch plastic pipe has almost entirely superseded the cement and clay tiles and asphalt-fibre Orangeburg pipe which were formerly used for foundation drains. Unlike its predecessors, plastic pipe is easily cut with a handsaw, and its bell and hub design and wide range of fittings make connections easy. ADS corrugated black polyethylene pipe, which is available in 250-foot-long coils, and widely used for shallow agricultural subsoil drainage, isn't strong enough for full-foundation drains.

Following the path of least resistance, groundwater from a rising water table and surface water percolating down along the foundation wall flow into the porous layer of crushed stone surrounding a continuous loop of pipe laid level with the *bottom of the footings*, perforations perpendicular to the ground (see **3-33**).

3-33 *Perforated plastic drainpipe has been laid along the base of this foundation, which was waterproofed with a special rubber-based coating. Since the native soil of this desert site is basically pure rock, gravel backfill is not needed.*

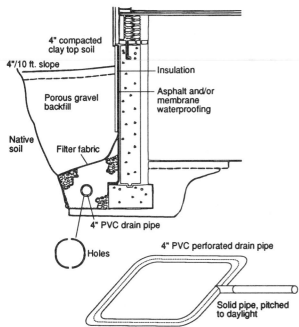

Labels in figure:
- 4" compacted clay top soil
- 4"/10 ft. slope
- Porous gravel backfill
- Native soil
- Filter fabric
- Insulation
- Asphalt and/or membrane waterproofing
- 4" PVC drain pipe
- Holes
- 4" PVC perforated drain pipe
- Solid pipe, pitched to daylight

3-34 *A standard foundation drain system utilizes asphalt waterproofing and perforated PVC pipe set in a bed of crushed stone along the base of the footings, draining into a drywell, sewer, or grade-level discharge point downhill of the footings. Filter fabric between the stone and the porous gravel backfill prevents soil fines from infiltrating the pipe and clogging it. To divert surface runoff away from the foundation, the backfill is typically topped with a layer of relatively nonpermeable clay soil.*

The perforated, four-inch foundation drainpipe should theoretically pitch continuously at one inch to 20 feet to keep it from getting clogged with mud. In reality, as long as measures are taken to keep soil fines from washing into it, a level pipe won't clog—and is a lot easier to install. However, if the pipe were laid *on top* of the footing, it wouldn't intercept water rising from below before it seeped under the footing and into the cellar. The water collected by the perforated drainpipe flows through a solid pipe (which *is* pitched) to an outlet at grade. This opening is covered with a wire-mesh screen to keep out rodents and other vermin. This trench should always be dug at the same time as the cellar hole to help prevent the excavation from flooding after a rain.

Because of its size (one to two inches) *chestnut stone* won't fall through the openings in the drainpipes or plug them up as pea stone (¼ to ½ inch) often will; it's also more porous. The stone is covered with a layer of filter fabric to keep soil particles from washing through the gravel (see **3-34**). This is a more costly, but more dependable, alternative to rosin-coated building paper, burlap, and straw mats used by some builders.

The foundation trench is backfilled with washed gravel. By effectively dropping the level of the water table below the drain tile, the gravel facilitates the rapid movement of water, preventing the buildup of hydrostatic pressure and frost heave against the foundation wall. Backfilling with native soil (unless it is broken rock, gravel, or pure sand) can compromise the effectiveness of the drain system. Clay and silty sand and gravel drain slowly and can hold water like a sponge, increasing the pressure on the wall.

On sites where trucked-in gravel is too expensive, special drainage mats applied directly against the foundation, just like rigid insulation, are an alternative. A rigid fibreglass-based panel that combines the functions of foundation insulation and drainage in a single product has recently become available. In very wet soils, special membranes are sometimes used to provide additional waterproofing.

On a level site—particularly on an small urban or suburban building lot—it may not be possible to "daylight" the drain line anywhere on the property. If local codes don't allow connection with storm sewers (assuming any are available), the foundation is often drained into a *dry well*. Basically an underground pit lined with perforated concrete tiles or dry-stacked concrete blocks and filled with crushed stone, a dry well holds water for gradual absorption into the adjacent soil. But, if the seasonal water table rises higher than the dry well—or if the surrounding soil isn't permeable enough—the flow can reverse with the foundation drains becoming waterlogged. Under such conditions, a dry basement is a virtual impossibility. This is a strong argument against building on level sites, particularly in flood plains or heavy wet soils. Incidentally, it's also the reason why some codes don't allow cellar floor drains to connect with the footing drains. Some do allow the foundation drain to empty into a sump pit in the cellar floor, where the water is then pumped onto the lawn or an open drainage ditch at some distance from the house.

PREPARING FOR THE FLOOR SLAB

Many builders prefer to pour the cellar floor slab later in the construction sequence—after the floor deck has been laid—especially if the plumber must install sewer and water lines first. In cold weather, when both the ground and the concrete must be protected against freezing, and the decked-over cellar can be warmed with a portable kerosene salamander or LP gas heater, it makes sense to postpone pouring a floor slab. Otherwise, the buildup of exhaust fumes from the gasoline-powered power trowel typically used to finish the slab is so noxious that it seems a lot more healthful, and more sensible, to pour the floor slab before the floor deck is built—either just before or after installing the perimeter drains.

Pouring the slab after the floor deck requires that the posts or steel lally columns which carry the floor girders rest on cast-concrete piers whose tops are just above the finished slab, rather than on the floor itself.

BUILT-IN RADON PROTECTION

When it comes to radon, **prevention** is always the best remedy. Fortunately, the same measures used to waterproof the foundation also keep out radon (see **3-35**). These include sealing any and all penetrations through the foundation wall proper with silicone caulk, and using a keyed footing to increase the difficulty of water penetration. Large gaps can be packed with oakum before caulking or filled with hydraulic cement mortar. Where radon is definitely known to occur, a soil–gas barrier of PVC plastic (Trocal) laid over roofing felt on top of crushed stone is often substituted for the standard 6-mil polyethylene vapor barrier.

Proper sealing of the joint between the floor slab and the foundation is especially important. Although many slab contractors neglect this step, a slab should never be poured directly against the wall for two reasons. First, different rates of thermal expansion between the two surfaces could cause the slab to crack or push the wall off its footing, and all foundations settle slightly; a slab bonded to the walls could crack as they moved downwards. Second, although the joint appears tight, it isn't completely waterproof. A ½-inch- or ¾-inch-thick gasket of moulded asphalt or a saturated polyurethane foam gasket inserted along the perimeter before the floor is poured solves the problem. Several types are available from masonry suppliers. The gasket should be flexible enough to maintain a watertight (and gas-proof) seal despite the temperature-related fluctuations in gap width, and yet it should be rigid enough to withstand impact. As a bonus, it doubles as a screed guide for levelling the slab pour.

Subgrade depressurization is another recommended precaution against radon gas. A short length of drainpipe is inserted through the slab into the crushed stone base. One pipe is sufficient for every 500 SF of floor area. Should a radon test kit eventually show a buildup of the gas in the cellar, the pipe is simply extended through the building to the attic, where it is fitted into a fan that exhausts to the outside air. Running the fan depressurizes the subslab and exhausts the gas to the outside without the heat-loss problems associated with the very effective but not terribly energy-efficient strategy of leaving the cellar vent windows wide open throughout the winter. If no radon shows up, the pipe is simply left capped.

3-35 *Where tests have shown a potential radon problem, a heavy membrane is laid over compacted gravel or crushed stone. All joints between the soil and the foundation are sealed. In block construction, the top course is filled with concrete or capped with solid block. All penetrations through the foundation wall must be tightly sealed. A perforated pipe with a vertical connection should be laid in the aggregate. Then, if the soil–gas barrier and the caulking don't prove effective, the pipe can be extended to the attic or outside the building and exhausted by natural or fan-powered convection. Earth-floored crawl space foundations are protected similarly by a gas/vapor barrier and vent, if needed.*

When planning to pour a slab, never set treated wood or steel posts on footings under the slab, since this can provide a path for radon, water, or termite infiltration. Instead, for solid anchoring, rest them on a footing pier whose top is not more than an inch below the slab surface (refer to Chapter Five).

Even more than pouring a foundation wall, the proper finishing of a concrete floor is a skilled art—so much so that many foundation contractors subcontract slab work out to specialists themselves. But it's still the responsibility of the general contractor or you, as owner-builder, to prepare for the slab pour.

Concrete slabs shouldn't be poured directly onto the subgrade (the earth under the slab, i.e., the *bed*). A four-inch (minimum) layer of pea stone or gravel lowers the likelihood of future dampness by reducing the capillary action of the soil, which otherwise tends to draw moisture into the floor. Since wet soil also conducts heat faster than dry soil, the air spaces in the gravel bed have an insulating effect. Because of its greater porosity, pea stone—or even coarser stone—is better than gravel as a slab underlayment where radon gas or water levels are a problem.

The subgrade is raked clean of loose debris, and any obvious high spots are lowered. Determine the level of the finished floor, and set a grade stake at the floor drain location. While floor drains are useful for draining a water heater or plumbing system, unless you've done something wrong, there is no justification for installing them to remove any water that might seep through the foundation. At best floor drains are optional; at worst, in areas where radon is a problem, they are a major point of entry for the gas. Your local building code may still require drains—having not yet been amended to address this problem.

In any case, if a floor drain is included in your foundation, set the grate fitting an inch below the level of the finished floor, and connect the pipe to the stub previously installed through or under the footing.

With a backhoe or bucket loader, dump the gravel or pea stone into the cellar at convenient points along the foundation wall. (Since the foundation isn't backfilled yet, this is another good reason not to dig a wide foundation trench.) Rake the underlayment evenly over the subgrade. Thoroughly compact the gravel with a rented gasoline-powered tamper (known as a *jumping jack*). The tamper is heavy and awkward; to lower or raise it safely over the cellar wall, chain it to the backhoe bucket. Add underlayment material as needed until the tamped grade is flush with the top of the footing (if more ceiling height is desirable, the finish grade can be two inches lower than this). Check the grade by stretching strings on spacer blocks between the footings. When fully compacted, it should be within ½ inch or so of level.

Install a moisture barrier membrane of 6-mil UV-stabilized polyethylene over gravel, using the widest sheets available to minimize seams (which are overlapped about one foot). The edge of the membrane should rest on the footings, extending slightly up the wall—but not so far as to show above the finished floor. If, instead of gravel, the membrane is installed over pea stone, protect it from puncture by spreading an inch of sand over the stone first.

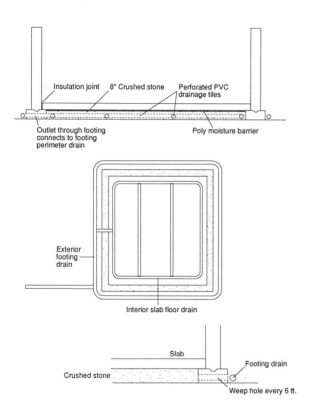

Insulation joint   8" Crushed stone   Perforated PVC drainage tiles

Outlet through footing connects to footing perimeter drain   Poly moisture barrier

Exterior footing drain

Interior slab floor drain

Slab

Footing drain

Crushed stone

Weep hole every 6 ft.

3-36 *Perforated drain pipes laid in eight inches of crushed stone can collect water under a slab, and drain it into the exterior footing drain. An alternative that doesn't require internal drainpipes is to provide two-inch-diameter "weep holes" through the footings every six feet to allow the under-slab water to drain into an external footing drain system.*

DRAINING WATER UNDER SLABS

Sometimes, despite the installation of footing drains, in very wet soils groundwater will seep up into the cellar from a spring under the slab itself. Two-inch-diameter "weepholes" that are run through the footings at six-foot intervals will let water move through the subslab gravel and out to the footing drain (see **3-36**). An even more effective solution is to lay one or more lines of perforated drainpipe on the inside of the foundation under a crushed-stone subgrade. This interior drain connects with the outside perimeter drain through the footing. The only other alternative is to build a sump pit in the cellar floor to collect water moving under the slab, and then pump it outside the cellar.

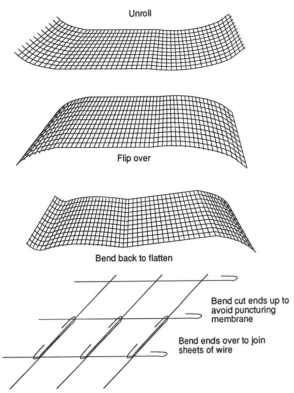

Unroll

Flip over

Bend back to flatten

Bend cut ends up to avoid puncturing membrane

Bend ends over to join sheets of wire

3-37 *Laying wire-mesh reinforcement can be tricky.*

Walls

Level chalk line on wall or slab edge gasket

Fill in and trowel after removal

Screed board

Screeded concrete

Unscreeded concrete

Reposition for screeding next section of slab

Sub grade

Rebar pins

Temporary screed guide

3-38 *Unlike a slab foundation, you can't use the form boards as a guide when screeding a cellar floor. Instead, temporary screed guides consisting of a length of 2×4 (pros use special magnesium bars) and Rebar stakes are set flush with finish floor level.*

CONTROLLING CRACKS IN FLOOR SLABS

Besides the gasket at the wall, several other measures are used to help floor slabs withstand internal stresses without cracking. These include a stronger (3000 psi) mix, control joints, and welded wire reinforcing mesh (see **3-37**). Except for outdoor concrete work such as sidewalks, patios, and driveways, which are subject to greater thermal stress than a foundation slab, control joints are seldom used in residential work. This is mainly because the joint, which is anywhere from one-fifth to full depth of the slab, would leave an unsightly caulked line in the floor. But even if not required by code, welded six-inch by six-inch 10-gauge wire mesh reinforcement is a good idea. The mesh is unrolled over the polyethylene membrane and cut to length with pliers or bolt cutters. To straighten the up-curved sheet of wire so that it will lay flat, flip the piece over, lift an end, and walk it backwards on itself. Bend the cut ends back on themselves so that they won't puncture the plastic membrane. Use form wire to tie sheets together along their edges.

To be effective, the mesh must be placed in the middle of the slab—and not at its bottom or top. Rebar chairs can be used to position it at the proper height, although most contractors simply pull the mesh up into the freshly poured concrete with a hooked tool or bent piece of Rebar.

FINISHING A CONCRETE SLAB

The concrete is placed and raked to grade. With a large-enough crew, screeding can start while the rest of the slab is still being poured (see **3-38**). When a slab is poured on grade, the ends of the screed board, which is simply a long length of straight 2×4, can rest on the footing forms. Since the basement walls are in the way, you can't do this with a cellar floor slab. A temporary screed guide is used instead; this is a long 2×4, staked into the subgrade with Rebar so that its top edge is level with the finish grade. As a section of slab is poured and screeded off, the guide is pulled up and reset for the next section. One end of the screed rests on the freshly screeded section of slab (which should be starting to stiffen) while the other end rests on the screed guide. The screed rests on top of the gasket at the walls, or else is held against a chalk line that has been snapped to show grade.

As soon as the screeding is complete, move a rented *bull float*—a wide, flat, lightweight magnesium trowel, attached to a very long handle—over the surface of the slab in broad arcs to level any high spots, fill in depressions, and smooth off the ridges left by screeding.

When the water sheen has disappeared and the slab appears frosted or "sugared," it's ready for final finishing. The concrete should have set hard enough so that foot-square plywood kneeling boards won't sink any deeper than ¼ inch under your weight. A steel trowel is used to polish the slab to a hard smooth finish; but hand trowelling is tiresome and time-consuming work. A rented gasoline-powered finishing trowel does a faster and much better job. Timing is absolutely critical for a proper trowel finish. If the concrete is too soft, the trowel will tear it apart; if it's too hard, it can't be worked. For power-trowelling, the slab should be hard enough to walk on without leaving an imprint, but not yet so fully set that it can't be softened, as necessary, with a little water.

BACKFILLING

Although concrete continues to harden for years, it is, for all practical purposes, fully cured within a month. But even a cured wall, if otherwise unsupported, can crack when subjected to the sudden load of backfilled soil. Foundation trenches should not be completely backfilled until after the floor deck is built. The floor deck transmits the loads from opposing walls onto each other, thereby cancelling

them out (see **3-39**). The trenches can be filled to grade at the building corners since they're already self-supporting, while the midspans of the walls are filled only enough to cover the drainage stone. If a long wall has been stiffened by the addition of one or more pilasters, it can probably be filled. Since an unfilled foundation trench is hazardous to the framing carpenters, some builders prefer to brace the foundation walls with opposing diagonal planks as shown in **3-39**, and then backfill the trench before the framers arrive.

When placing backfill gravel, make sure that no boulders are within a foot of the foundation wall. Frost could eventually work them against the wall, crushing the insulation, if not actually cracking the concrete.

The trench is filled with gravel to rough grade and allowed to settle—a good hard rain is helpful here—before being capped with about four to six inches of clay soil during the finish grading, just prior to seeding and landscaping. To divert surface runoff away from the foundation, this relatively impermeable layer is sloped at a minimum of four inches over ten feet.

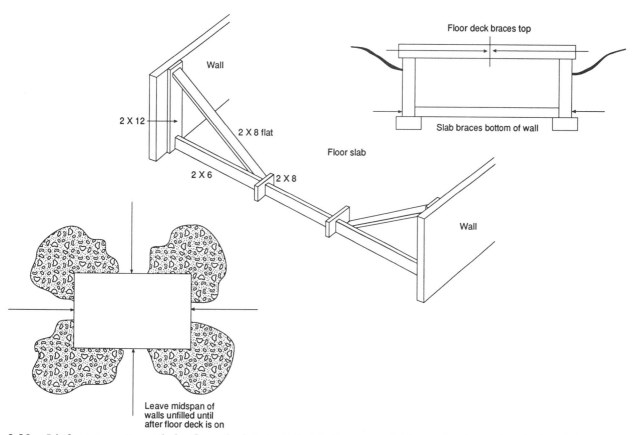

3-39 *It's best to wait until the floor deck is installed before completely backfilling a foundation. Since this can make framing awkward, if not hazardous, many builders prefer to wedge temporary bracing between the walls as shown so that they can backfill before framing. For walls more than about 36 feet long, corners and shorter end walls are filled and the rest left unfilled until the floor deck is framed.*

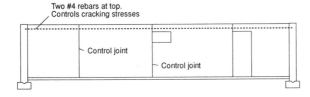

Two #4 rebars at top.
Controls cracking stresses

Control joint

Control joint

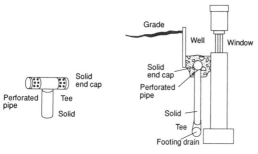

Grade

Well

Window

Solid
end cap

Perforated
pipe

Tee

Solid

Solid
end cap

Perforated
pipe

Solid

Tee

Footing drain

3-40 *To prevent leakage into the cellar and ice damage, fill the bottom of the window well with crushed stone and install a short perforated drainpipe that tees into the footing drain.*

Cellar windows that are below grade are protected by pressed steel or concrete tile window wells (see **3-40**). The steel wells must be bolted into the foundation wall before backfilling. Concrete tiles are set during the fill. A pleasing low-cost alternative is to simply lay up a small retaining wall for the window well using old brick, stones, or treated timbers. In any case, the bottom of the well area should be filled with six to twelve inches of coarse crushed stone laid over a short piece of perforated drainpipe, teed into the footing drain system. An undrained window well can trap water and ice against the wall.

TERMITE PROTECTION

Some builders consider a partially filled foundation trench an ideal repository for construction debris. Unfortunately, scraps of framing lumber, piles of sawdust, and buried stumps and roots also attract termites (see **3-41**).

Many species of termites occur naturally in woodlands, where they play an important role in the breakdown of dead plant material. Unfortunately, to a termite, wood in a house tastes just as good as wood in a tree. Subterranean

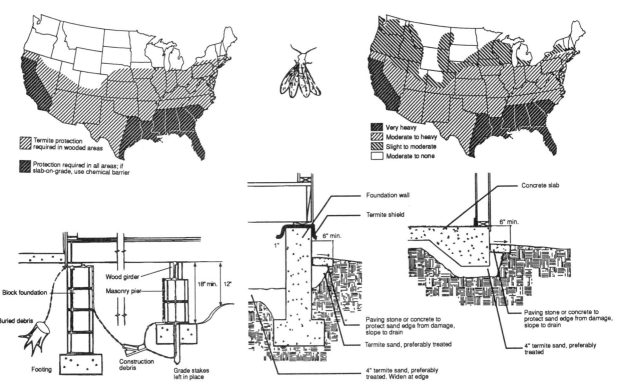

Termite protection required in wooded areas

Protection required in all areas; if slab-on-grade, use chemical barrier

Very heavy
Moderate to heavy
Slight to moderate
Moderate to none

Wood girder

Masonry pier

Block foundation

Buried debris

Footing

Construction debris

Grade stakes left in place

18" min.   12"

Foundation wall

Termite shield

6" min.

1"

Concrete slab

6" min.

Paving stone or concrete to protect sand edge from damage, slope to drain

Termite sand, preferably treated

4" termite sand, preferably treated. Widen at edge

Paving stone or concrete to protect sand edge from damage, slope to drain

4" termite sand, preferably treated

3-41 *As the maps show, termite infestation is endemic in many areas of the country. Preventative measures include blocking routes of infiltration and avoiding burying wood construction debris near the foundation. Provide at least 18 inches of clearance between joists and the base of any masonry foundation piers. Provide a metal termite shield between masonry and wood sills. Termite sand and diatomaceous earth have been shown to be effective deterrents as well.*

termites, which are the most destructive, are found throughout the U.S. wherever the average annual air temperature is above 50 degrees F (10 degrees C) and the ground contains sufficient moisture (refer to **3-41**). Termites have been known to eat their way through bad flashing to get to wood.

Termite infestation has historically been prevented by chemically poisoning the soil under slabs and around footings. Chlordane, formerly the most widely used termiticide, has been shown to be a potent and long-lasting carcinogen, and its use has now been restricted. While there are other chemicals approved for this purpose, the question of long-term hazards from their use has not been satisfactorily resolved. Even if chemicals are used, termite control still depends heavily on blocking easy routes of entry from the soil into the wooden parts of the house structure.

Besides buried debris, any footing form work or grade stakes left in place also provides termites with a base camp for their forays into the foundation. Floor joists over an open crawl space should be at least 12 inches off the ground (18 inches where supported on masonry piers). Any penetrations through the foundation wall and joints between slabs and walls should be thoroughly waterproofed. Since termites have been known to tunnel behind foundation insulation to reach the framing, use pressure-treated lumber for sills and drip caps—and anywhere else where wood is in direct contact with masonry. Metal termite shields should also be installed between the sill and the top of the foundation wall and between any supporting masonry piers and wood girders. Because this angled flashing sticks out past the masonry, termites cannot build their protective mud-walled entry tubes over its sharp edge. Recent tests have shown that special *termite sand* is an effective barrier with or without chemical treatment. Compacted in a four-inch layer beneath slabs, along foundation walls, and over crawl space areas, the 1.7 to 2.4 millimeter grains are too large for the termites to move with their jaws—and yet small enough so that they can be packed too tightly for the termites to tunnel through.

Most of the various species of wood borers, powderpost beetles, annobids, carpenter ants, and other insects that cause structural damage unfortunately are typically built into the house in the form of infested framing lumber. This is a special hazard of building with logs or cordwood, as some alternative housebuilders advocate. Many species have very specific habitats. Some can live only in sapwood; others only in a certain kind of wood; others need dry wood or the right temperature range. Visually inspect timbers and boards for evidence of infestation before using them. Don't pile firewood inside the house or in the cellar. And since carpenter ants need moisture to survive, use tight flashings to keep water out of the building. Insect attack is seldom a problem in new construction. But all "new" houses eventually become old houses. Generally, the measures taken to prevent moisture and wind infiltration also keep out wood-destroying insects.

3-42 *The roof of this earth-bermed house slopes to within a few feet of ground level at the north wall while the two-storey-high facade captures solar energy on the south side. The foundation steps down the slope from back to front and the backfill is held in place by railroad-tie retaining walls that form terraced plant beds.*

Other Foundation Types

For all their advantages, full-basement foundations are expensive, difficult to build, and not always suitable for every site, climate type, or soil condition. Following is a description of several alternative foundation types.

PARTIALLY ENCLOSED OR EARTH-BERMED FOUNDATION

Replacing part or all of the front wall of a full basement foundation with wood framing is a good way to fit a house into a sloped site and turn ordinary cellar space into living area while benefitting from the heat conserving effects of *earth-buffering* (see **3-42**). The earth itself is a poor insulator; but when it is piled against a structure, the temperature difference between inner and outer surfaces that drives the rate of heat transfer is smaller.

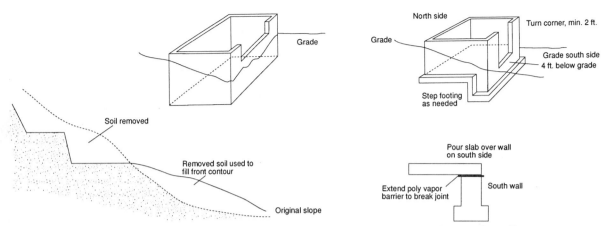

3-43 *A bermed foundation is economical and ideally suited for sloped sites. The south wall can be framed with wood at grade or else be bermed halfway up.*

The arrangement of "steps" in the foundation walls depends on whether the south wall is fully or only partially wood framed (see **3-43**). The slope of the final grade must be such that the footings are always below frost line. For strength, turn the side walls at least two feet into the south wall corners before stepping them down. If, as a design element, the finish siding follows the line of the grade rather than the steps in the foundation wall, it can be nailed to a sheet of pressure-treated plywood glued to the perimeter insulation.

Although it uses slightly less concrete than a conventional full-basement foundation, the steps in the form work offset any cost-savings; but excavation is generally more economical. The soil removed from the bank cut can be piled against the foundation on the downhill side of the slope or used to shape the contours of the site (refer to **3-43**).

PERIMETER OR CRAWL-SPACE FOUNDATION

A perimeter, or crawl space, foundation is a short wall that is set on a footing in a shallow excavation just below frost line (see **3-44**). Crawl-space foundations are less expensive and easier to build than full-basement foundations, with which they are often used in conjunction. Because any number of treated support posts or masonry piers can be set on footing pads laid on the crawl-space floor, then the span and the depth of the floor joists can be reduced. The earth floor of the crawl space is covered with a polyethylene moisture barrier extending up to the top of the inside wall. Four inches of fine sand is laid over the barrier to protect it from puncture.

Depth to frost line or code requirements notwithstanding, the perimeter wall itself should be high enough to allow sufficient room between the ground and the underside of the floor joists for comfortable installation of plumbing, wiring, and heating ducts. Furthermore, for termite control, no wood framing should be closer to the ground than 12 inches.

In unvented crawl spaces, radon control is accomplished by a ventilation standpipe inserted under the moisture barrier membrane. In vented crawl spaces, constant air circulation prevents radon buildup. The pipe penetrations and other pathways into the living areas should be caulked in either case.

To protect the plumbing from freezing and keep the floors warm in severe climates, the crawl space is usually heated. Rigid foam insulation is equally effective applied to either the exterior or the interior of the walls. Two or more screened vents will promote a cooling cross-ventilation air flow in summer and discourage the growth of wood-rotting fungi. These vents are shut and insulated during the winter (refer to **3-44**). In milder climates, they can be left open year round. Where there is no need to heat the crawl space, the floor joists are insulated instead—both to warm the floors in winter and aid in summer cooling. Whether the crawl space is heated or not, the foundation walls should always be waterproofed and their perimeter drained the same as a full basement.

SLAB-ON-GRADE FOUNDATIONS

Throughout much of the South and Southwest of the United States, where the temperature seldom falls below 25 degrees F (−4 degrees C), cooling is more important than heating, and termite protection is crucial. In these regions, on level sites, the *monolithic slab-on-grade* foundation is much preferred over full-basement and crawl space types. It's also just about the least expensive and quickest foundation you can build yourself.

Since it is, in effect, one footing (hence "monolithic") this kind of slab foundation distributes the building weight over its entire surface area, and thus imposes the lowest psf soil loading. The thickness of a standard slab is four inches, thickened an extra eight inches under any con-

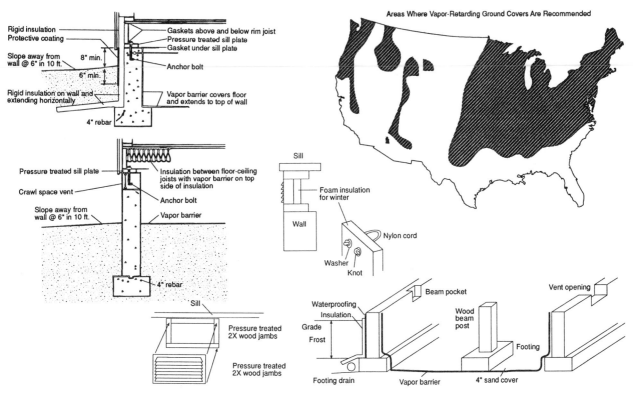

Areas Where Vapor-Retarding Ground Covers Are Recommended

Rigid insulation
Protective coating
Slope away from wall @ 6" in 10 ft.
8" min.
6" min.
Rigid insulation on wall and extending horizontally
4" rebar

Gaskets above and below rim joist
Pressure treated sill plate
Gasket under sill plate
Anchor bolt
Vapor barrier covers floor and extends to top of wall

Pressure treated sill plate
Crawl space vent
Slope away from wall @ 6" in 10 ft.
Insulation between floor-ceiling joists with vapor barrier on top side of insulation
Anchor bolt
Vapor barrier
4" rebar

Sill
Pressure treated 2X wood jambs
Pressure treated 2X wood jambs

Sill
Wall
Foam insulation for winter
Nylon cord
Washer
Knot

Beam pocket
Waterproofing
Insulation
Grade
Frost
Footing drain
Vapor barrier
Wood beam post
Footing
4" sand cover
Vent opening

3-44 *The outside of the wall to the crawl space should be well insulated with rigid foam as shown. To prevent buildup of moisture and condensation problems, lay a vapor barrier over the grade and extend it up over the walls, gasketing it to the framing. Cover the barrier with four inches of sand to prevent puncture during construction and routine maintenance. The shaded areas of the map indicate regions where crawl space vapor barriers are recommended. A good rule of thumb is to install a ground cover in cool climates wherever the annual precipitation is greater than twenty inches.*

centrated loads, such as a bearing post, partition, or a chimney. For extra strength and adequate clearance to the framing at grade, the outer edge of the slab is "turned down" eight to twelve inches (see **3-45**).

Excavation and form work for a monolithic slab is simple. After the site is scraped free of topsoil and levelled, the outer edge of the slab is formed just like a footing. The form boards for the sloping inside edge of the turn-

down are temporarily held at the desired angle as gravel for the subslab is spread and compacted behind it (refer to **3-45**). Then they are removed. A poly vapor barrier is laid on the gravel, extending to the edge; Rebar is laid on chairs at the bottom of the edge form, as required; and then the wire mesh is installed. Since it won't be tied to another opposing form board, the outside edge form should be well braced and staked.

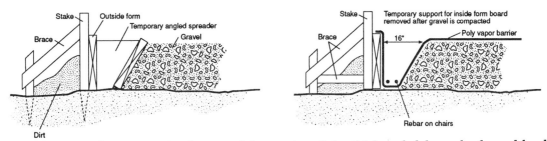

Stake
Brace
Outside form
Temporary angled spreader
Gravel
Dirt

Stake
Brace
Temporary support for inside form board removed after gravel is compacted
16"
Poly vapor barrier
Rebar on chairs

3-45 *Where soil conditions permit, the turned-down edge of the thickened slab can be formed by digging a trench in the undisturbed grade. An angled spreader supports the temporary form board for the four-inch gravel slab base. Bracing is required in soils too loose to support a trench.*

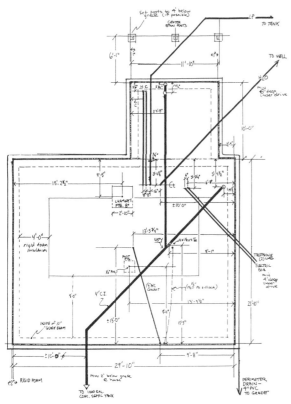

3-46 *With a slab foundation, all under-slab mechanicals are set out in a separate foundation plan so that all the utility conduits can be positioned accurately before the concrete is poured—since they cannot be moved afterwards.*

3-47 *Precise placement of sub-slab drain and utility lines is critical with a slab-on-grade foundation. For all practical purposes, mistakes aren't fixable. The PVC sleeves will house electrical runs, LP gas lines, and telephone and water lines.*

The layout of all under-slab mechanicals must be carefully planned and installed before pouring the concrete (see **3-46**). Any heating ducts should be insulated. Water lines and electrical wires should be run through plastic conduit so that they can be replaced if necessary at a later date. Cast-iron pipe is used for all drain lines that will be buried under the concrete or in the ground.

One big disadvantage of a slab floor is the permanence of any under-slab mechanicals. Mistakes are costly to correct, and future changes and extensions difficult (see **3-47**). One way to overcome this drawback is to construct a 16-inch- or 24-inch-high crawl space on top of the slab.

3-48 *In the hot and arid Southwest, the runoff from infrequent rains doesn't penetrate into the rocky subsoil, so that perimeter drainage isn't normally needed. Here, footings are poured directly into shallow trenches, on which a 12- to 18-inch-high six-inch-wide poured concrete foundation wall will be set.*

This not only simplifies mechanical installation, but also allows some underfloor storage area. The floor could also be kept comfortably warm by installing a downdraft furnace that utilized the crawl space as a warm-air plenum.

Since most of the heat loss through a slab occurs at its edges, rigid foam insulation should always be glued to the perimeter of the slab. For protection in areas subject to occasional light frosts, a two-foot-wide strip of rigid insulation is also extended horizontally out from the wall just below grade. Where ground- or surface water may be a concern, a perforated perimeter drain and crushed stone can also be laid against the bottom of the slab (see **3-48**, **3-49**, **3-50**, and **3-51**).

3-49 *Anchor bolts are set that will tie the wall sole plates to the foundation.*

3-50 *The area inside the perimeter wall has been filled with compacted gravel to within four inches of its top. Note the mechanicals. Although soil moisture isn't a problem in an arid climate, an under-slab membrane is still a good idea since it protects against radon, which is endemic to much of the intermountain West and Southwestern deserts of the United States. Since standards for radon protection have not yet been incorporated into most building codes, this developer didn't install a barrier.*

3-51 *The slab is poured level with the top of the foundation perimeter wall. The slightly rough floated surface will make a better base for tile flooring than a smooth machine-trowelled finish. The markings are for partition layout and ceiling heights. The drain stubs have been sealed with duct tape, and the water supply risers have been capped off or looped.*

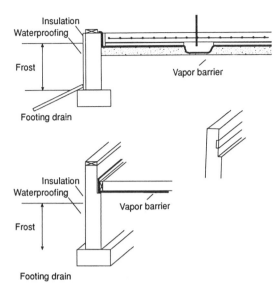

3-52 *A frost-wall slab foundation is similar to a crawl-space foundation. The slab is separated from the wall by a compressible nonrotting material to allow for thermal expansion. Some builders rest the slab on a shelf in the wall; the wall can then be extended so that the framing is higher above grade.*

A FROST-WALL SLAB FOR COLD CLIMATES

Floor slabs are an ideal low-cost way to build in the extra thermal mass it takes to store heat collected by south-facing windows in passive solar homes. In cold regions, building codes typically require the slab to be protected against frost heave by a *frost wall* (see **3-52**). This is nothing more than the familiar perimeter wall of the crawl-space foundation, with a ledge at the top on which the slab rests—otherwise, the isolation joint would be exposed to the living area. If the frost wall is formed so that it is higher than the floor slab, the wall framing can be raised above the finish grade without having to raise the floor too. Key a 2×2 strip of pressure-treated wood into the bottom face of the extension to serve as a nail base for the wall finish.

Either gravel or crushed stone can be used for the base. In dry soils, waterproofing of the frost wall isn't necessary, as long as a moisture barrier is installed under the slab itself. Since they're backfilled on both sides, there's no unequal lateral pressure against the perimeter walls.

Insulation is especially important with thermal slabs. In addition to both faces of the frost wall, the area under the slab itself is also insulated. Since very little heat transfer occurs in the middle of a passive-solar heat-storage slab, it isn't cost-effective to extend the insulation more than four feet in from the edge on all but the south wall "target area," where it should extend to eight feet. However, the entire sub-slab area should be insulated when it contains radiant heating coils.

3-53 *Double 2×12 forms are used for the modified grade beam that will form the turn-downed edge of this cold-climate slab-on-grade foundation. Note the chestnut stone base that ensures good drainage and the snap ties clamped to vertical strongbacks with rented form hardware.*

A MONOLITHIC SLAB-ON-GRADE FOUNDATION FOR COLD CLIMATES

The cost and soil-loading benefits of the monolithic slab foundation are pretty much nullified by the frost-wall requirement. Superior drainage and good insulation are the key to building a frostproof monolithic slab in cold climates.

Since most codes call for a minimum of eight inches between grade and wood siding, the bottom of an ordinary turned-down-edge slab is barely below grade. Unfortunately, building the form work for a deeper turndown strong enough to withstand the outward pressure of wet concrete is impractical. A modified grade beam, however, requires only a narrow, deeper-than-normal footing form.

After the topsoil is removed and the subgrade levelled, spread and compact six inches of chestnut stone (pea stone isn't coarse enough), extending about two feet beyond the building lines. Using 2×12 planks, build a form for a ten-inch-wide footing (see **3-53**). Predrill holes in the outer form planks four inches up from their bottom edges spaced three feet apart, and transfer the center markings to the inside form planks. Insert round snap ties designed for a ten-inch wall and 2×4 *strongbacks* (vertical walers) into the holes to tie the forms together.

3-54 *Rebar is overlapped at corners and wired to snap tie bars for strength.*

A double course of No. 5 rebar is wired to the snap ties (see **3-54**). Set a second 2×12 form—drilled for snap ties four inches down from its top edge—on top of the first form. Insert the snap ties through the forms, and clamp them to the strongbacks, which should be about six inches higher than the finished forms.

With a crowbar, level and line the form up with the building line strings and drive an occasional corner stake or brace to hold it for the pour. Bend four-foot lengths of No. 4 rebar at right angles, and tie them to the snap ties and outer course of horizontal rebar so that they project about two or three inches above the top of the forms (see **3-55**). Check all measurements once again before pouring the concrete.

After the concrete has set, strip off only the inside form boards, and install foam insulation to within two inches of the top of the grade beam. Install any further underslab mechanicals, as needed, and fill the subgrade with compacted gravel to within two inches of the top of the beam. Lay a 6-mil polyethylene vapor barrier over the gravel. Then set a 2×4 or 2×6 (for a 3½-inch- or 5½-inch-thick floor) on top of the outside form board, nailing it into the strongbacks to form the outside edge of the floor slab. Install rigid foam insulation over the vapor barrier, butting it tight to the top of the grade beam. Tie 6×6 wire reinforcing mesh to the ends of the bent-over Rebar, and support it on Rebar chairs (refer to **3-55**). Pour the slab. Before it sets, push bent anchor bolts into the edge of the slab. Since the depth of the grade beam and the elevation of the slab above grade depend on the height of the form boards, extra form work for the slab is not needed when the beam is made shallower, allowing the second tier of forms to be used for the slab pour as well.

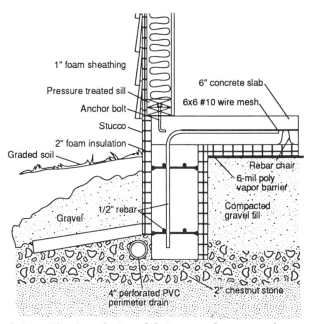

3-55 *The foundation slab is poured on top of a deep, reinforced concrete beam footing resting on an under-slab drainage bed of coarse stone and gravel backfill, providing excellent perimeter drainage and insulation.*

Strip the outside forms, and glue rigid foam insulation against them. Lay perimeter drainpipe at the base of the beam, covering it with more chestnut stone and then with a horizontal sheet of foam insulation, before backfilling with gravel.

69

The porous subgrade, the depth of the perimeter insulation, and the structural connection between the beam and floor slab all work together to make this a stable foundation. Nevertheless, since it may be unfamiliar to your building inspector, you may have to hire a structural engineer to convince the inspector of its soundness.

CONCRETE AND MASONRY PIER FOUNDATIONS

Pier and post foundations are used when minimal site disturbance is desirable or the costs of a full-basement or crawl-space foundation is unaffordable but the site isn't level enough for a slab. Since the quantity of concrete they require is small enough to mix by hand, pier and post foundations are an obvious choice for hand-dug foundations on sites too steep and/or heavily wooded to reach

with ready-mix trucks or excavation machinery. Because piers place concentrated loads on relatively small footings, soil load-bearing capacity is a factor in the design of a stable pier foundation. The load on each pier is basically equal to the total load of the building divided by the number of piers. Soil settling is one factor that causes many pier foundations eventually to tilt. Increasing the area of the footings to spread the load requires very specific reinforcement. Plans for any such pier footings should be reviewed by a structural engineer.

Round pressed-fibreboard *Sonotubes* have all but replaced site-built square plywood forms. Depending on soil conditions and excavation methods, there are several different ways to set up Sonotube forms (see **3-56**).

Set batter board strings to mark the center of each pier. Then dig holes down to the required depth below frost. In loose and stone-free soils, a hand shovel or post-hole

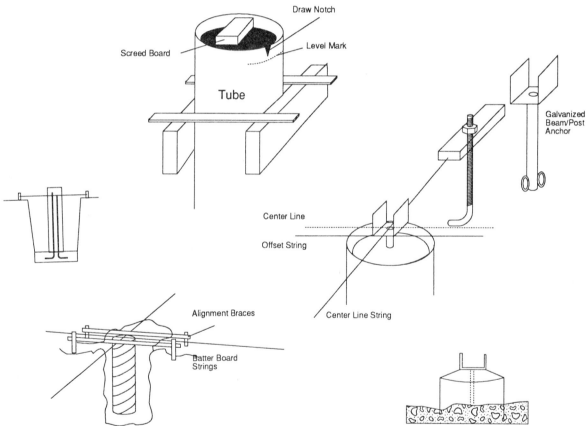

3-56 *Pouring concrete pier foundations in stable soil involves using batterboard strings to center the cylindrical cardboard forms in their excavations and drywall screws to suspend them from staked boards. Threaded steel rods, standard anchor bolts, special steel post/beam anchors, or even lengths of Rebar are pushed into the concrete to provide a solid connection to the sill beams or other support girders. When the cross-sectional area of the beam is smaller than that of the tube, set the anchor at least an inch above the concrete so that you can make a sloped mortar cap that will drain water away from the bottom of the beam. Check local codes; in earthquake zones, for instance, the individual piers may have to be connected by a continuous footing.*

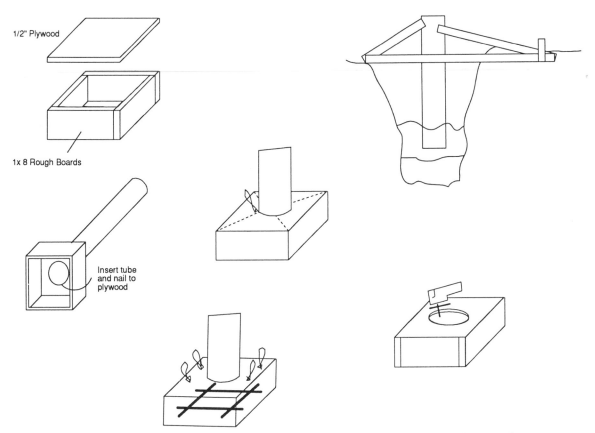

3-57 *Site-built forms allow piers and their footings to be poured at the same time in loose soils or in the outsized holes left by backhoe excavation. Use braces at the top or partial dirt at the bottom to hold the forms in position while pouring. The wood forms should be removed after the concrete has set.*

digger may suffice. Gas-driven post-hole augers are hard to handle and potentially dangerous, particularly in rocky soil; the resulting hole is usually too small anyway. Consider renting or hiring a tractor-mounted auger, or have a utility pole contractor drill them instead.

To leave room for a footing, the hole should be at least twice as wide as the diameter of the pier. Cut the Sonotube to the desired length with a handsaw, and set it six to eight inches above the bottom of its hole to leave room for the footing. The tube is held plumb by screwing it either to staked support boards or to diagonal braces.

To figure the amount of concrete needed to fill a Sonotube form, use the formula for finding the volume of a cylinder ($pi \times 2r \times h$, where $pi = 3.14$). Pour a stiff mix to keep the concrete from pushing out at the bottom as it fills the tube. The top of the form should extend to the height of the beam that will carry the floor framing. Use level batter-board strings to calculate the overall length of each tube—or shoot a level mark on the tubes with a transit level—and saw them off about an inch above the mark. Cut a notch in the side of the tube down to the mark (refer to **3-56**). This will allow water to escape and

also provide a screeding guide. Use a small block of wood for a screed. The concrete tends to settle after a while and will need topping off. As it begins to stiffen up, push two pieces of L-shaped Rebar long enough to reach the footing into each pier. Finally, use the batter-board strings to precisely center galvanized metal beam anchors or threaded anchor rods for tieing the foundation to the house frame.

Since any holes dug in unconsolidated, sandy, or rocky soils must be oversized to prevent cave-ins, pouring a pier and footing simultaneously in the pit left by a backhoe calls for extra form work (see **3-57**).

First, build a footing form by nailing 1×6 or 1×8 boards together into a two-foot square. Tack a piece of ½-inch plywood to the top of this form. Center the Sonotube on the square, and scribe its outline onto the wood. Cut out the circle, and insert the Sonotube into the hole; nail it into the edge of the plywood. Any required Rebar for the footing is hung from wires tacked to the plywood cap. Position the form in its hole and shovel about a foot of dirt over it to hold the bottom steady. Plumb and brace the tube at the top as described above.

The finished piers must line up perfectly level and straight, if the floor beams are to bear solidly upon their anchors. With Sonotubes, the required degree of precision can be difficult to achieve. Concrete is unforgiving of errors; you can't shave an inch or two off a pier that's too high or too far off-center. For wood decks, where the loads are relatively light, the problem of height is solved by pouring the piers just slightly above grade, and then cutting treated-wood posts to fit between the anchors and the floor framing (see 3-58). But even if this type of connection weren't already dangerously unstable under the loads imposed by an entire house, the problem of horizontal alignment would still be a significant problem. Normally, strap-type and threaded-bolt anchors allow some margin of lateral error. The metal strap can be bent to fit the beam or the bolt-hole offset without harm as long as the pier is not so far out of line that the beam does not bear solidly upon it. Hence, it's always a good idea to oversize the piers to provide extra bearing area. Since a cast-in-place rigid steel anchor can't be realigned, it will have to be sawn off. A new anchor can be attached with expansion bolts set into holes drilled in the concrete. Since this isn't as strong as a cast-in-place anchor, it may not be permitted by local codes.

Differences in height between piers are corrected by inserting shims between the pier and the beam to increase the pier height or by notching the beam over the pier that is too high, as needed (refer to 3-58). Unless done carefully, both adjustments can weaken the structural integrity of the connection. It is always a good idea, for any of these solutions, to consult a structural engineer and check local codes.

Because they are built piece by piece rather than cast in place, it's easier to control the height and anchor placement in masonry piers (concrete block, stone, or brick) than in poured concrete piers. The bulk of their individual units ensures a broad bearing surface.

The tops of all perimeter foundation piers should be sloped to prevent water from getting trapped under the wood framing—piers under the midspan of floor beams are already protected. The anchors are set an inch or two above the top of the poured concrete and the pier is finished with a sloping mortar cap after the concrete has set.

TREATED-WOOD-POST FOUNDATIONS

The fact that it's a lot easier to attach wood to wood than wood to concrete is just one reason why treated-wood posts have become an increasingly popular alternative to concrete Sonotubes, not only for deck and light shed foundations, but for entire houses as well. Since the only concrete needed is for the footing pads (this can be mixed

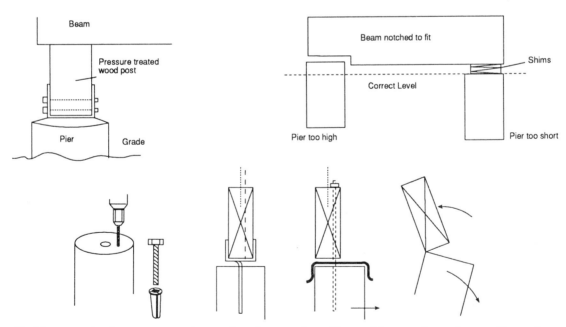

3-58 *Problems anchoring concrete piers to framing can be addressed in a variety of ways. Treated-wood posts are often used with heavy-duty steel post anchors to support sill beams and girders. Saw off misaligned anchors, and use a carbide-tipped masonry bit to drill a hole for a lead expansion-shield bolt anchor. Sometimes, a light-gauge strap-type anchor can be bent to shift it when the pier is only slightly off-center. Sill beams that bear on the outer edge of a pier will tend to twist outward and push the pier inward under load, unless the floor joists are set flush with the beams rather than on top of them. When a pier is too high, the beam can be notched to fit.*

and cast off site), a wood-post foundation is an obvious choice for hard-to-reach sites and low-budget owner-builder installation.

Footing pads for wood-post foundations should be pre-cast so that they can cure for at least a week before loading (see **3-59**). This can be done at a convenient location, and then brought on site when needed. Pour 3000-pound concrete into $16'' \times 16'' \times 8''$ or $24'' \times 24'' \times 8''$ rough-board frames set on top of a sheet of scrap plywood. Hang rebar from wires on temporary wood supports. Wire a bent length of No. 5 or No. 6 rebar to the horizontals so that it projects vertically eight to twelve inches from the middle of the footing pad (refer to **3-59**).

Compact the bottom of the post hole with a hand tamper and set the footing pad level, tamping any added soil. Line up the rebar pin with the post center point dropped plumb from the batter-board strings.

Drill a hole into the center of an 8×8 treated-wood post, and apply a thick coat of asphalt roofing cement to the bottom of the post to prevent it from soaking up water. Set the post on the footing pin, using a sledgehammer and protective wood block (or a fence post maul, which won't split the wood) to seat it firmly and check for plumb. Square it up with the centerline string (if the post won't turn on the pin, use a peavy or forked wood lever to rotate the entire footing) and stake it with temporary diagonal braces (refer to **3-59**). The posts are cut to approximate height only, and trimmed to exact level after backfilling.

To strengthen the connection between post and footing, drive galvanized spikes into the base of the post, and tangle chicken wire or scraps of reinforcing mesh between them and the ends of the wires used to hang the rebar from the wood cleats. Backfill the hole to the edges of the form *by hand*, and cover the reinforcement with concrete.

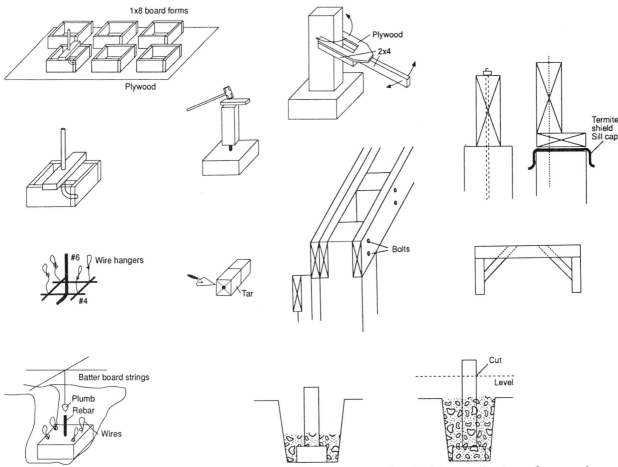

3-59 *Setting up a wood-post foundation involves casting footings ahead of time and using rebar as reinforcement and as an anchor pin. Posts are trimmed to exact level after backfilling and tamping. Sill beams can be pinned to the top of their posts or spiked to a continuous sill plate that is lag-screwed or bolted to the posts. Diagonal braces needed for lateral stability are easily installed with wood-post foundations.*

3-60 *The floor girders for this house rest on recycled creosote-treated telephone poles buried below frost line. The square pads between the posts and girders assure solid bearing.*

Depending on construction details, the floor beams will rest either on top of the finished posts or on notches cut into their sides. A variety of strong anchors can be easily applied after the beam is precisely positioned. Unlike concrete, wood posts are readily braced to resist lateral forces by adding angle braces between them and the floor beams.

One possible objection to a treated-wood foundation is its relatively short service life. Unlike concrete, treated wood will eventually rot. Southern yellow pine CCA-treated (chromated-copper-arsenate-treated) wood intended for direct contact with the ground absorbs more preservative than other grades and is warranted by the manufacturer for 40 years. This is probably a conservative estimate; it could last much longer. In termite-infested zones, CCZA-treated (chromated-copper-zinc-arsenate-treated) wood is even more resistant to termite attack. Termite shielding and soil treatment are critical components of a successful wood foundation in these areas.

Creosote-treated utility poles are considerably more expensive than squared CCA timbers, but can have a useful service life of 75 years or more—and are almost completely immune to termite attack (see **3-60**). In either case, removing and replacing foundation piers one at a time from under an existing house is actually fairly easy, if and when it becomes necessary to do so.

PROBLEMS WITH PIER AND POST FOUNDATIONS

Concrete pier and wood-post foundations suffer from two climate-related drawbacks which make them less than ideal in cold regions. In wet soils subject to frost action, foundation piers eventually begin to tilt and must often be replaced or straightened (see **3-61**). As mentioned above, pier movement is sometimes attributable to excessive loading of the soil bed, particularly since clayey soil becomes plastic when wet.

Even though its footing is below the frost line, a pier can still be uplifted by *frost-jacking* at the surface—the uplift that results when frozen soil grips the column like a lever. Over the years, this seasonal uplift and subsequent settling leads to instability. Furthermore, since the soil on the south side of a pier thaws out just a tiny bit faster than the north side, the slight but steady lateral push of frost begins to tilt the pier. A critical situation is reached when the building load distribution and the tilting force cause the piers to topple over or break. The relatively weak mortar bonds between the courses of concrete block or stone piers make them particularly susceptible to the lateral forces generated by frost-jacking and soil settling.

Frost-jacking can be ameliorated by wrapping the pier with polyethylene plastic sheeting to break the bond between the soil and the concrete. Square wood posts are protected with a two-foot vertical collar of rigid foam insulation laid just below grade.

Since a strong mechanical bond between the pier and its footing also resists the pull of frost-jacking, concrete piers are probably a better choice in wet soils subject to freezing than wood posts. The weight of the overlaying earth holds the footing down. The wider the footing, the more difficult it will be to push over the column it carries. This is why on a hillside, unstable, or earthquake-prone sites, piers are often joined to a continuous reinforced grade beam footing.

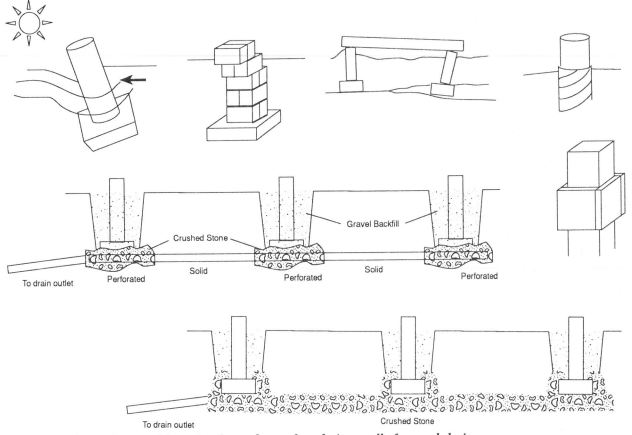

3-61 *Preventing frost problems in pier and post foundations calls for good drainage.*

The only way to guarantee the stability of a pier or post foundation in wet soil is to provide drainage (refer to **3-61**).Crushed stone under the footings by itself is useless, since there's no outlet for the water that collects there. Instead, lay a short length of perforated pipe in a foot of crushed stone under each footing, and connect them all with solid pipe to a pipe pitched to an outlet. Backfill each pier with fast-draining gravel rather than native soil. As an alternative to pipe, crushed stone can be laid in a continuous trench and the footings set on top of it. Of course, this makes it impossible to adhere to a building philosophy of minimal site disturbance.

However, another disadvantage of pier or post foundations in cold climates is in fact their greatest asset in hot, humid climates: heat loss. Since the rate of heat loss is increased by air movement, some kind of skirting is needed to keep cold winter winds from sucking heat out through the exposed underbelly of the floor platform. The problem with skirting is twofold: in termite zones, it provides a direct link from the soil to the framing (see **3-62**). And, in frost-prone soils a skirting laid tight to the ground would be shoved up against the sill beams, either lifting the house off its piers or crushing itself.

3-62 *An owner-builder faux pas: The framing for this wood foundation should be pressure-treated to prevent rot and insect infestation. It's also much too close to grade and will be heaved up by frost.*

75

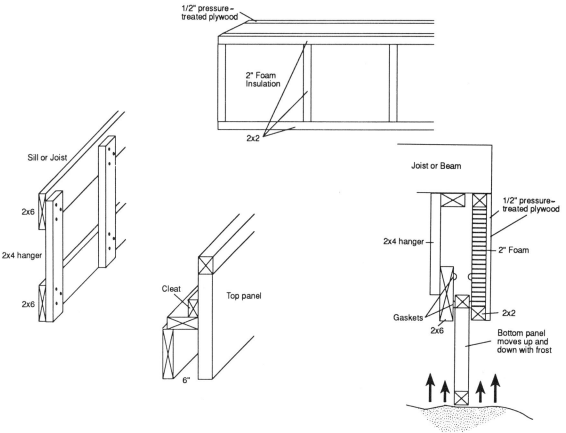

3-63 *Unless allowance is made for movement, frost action will buckle wind-skirting under a pier foundation. Slip-jointed skirting allows a lower panel to move freely up or down.*

A continuous metal termite shield installed between the skirting panels and the floor beams solves the first problem. A two-piece slip-joint skirting panel consisting of a pressure-treated 2×2 frame and a ½-inch pressure-treated plywood skin alleviates the second concern (see **3-63**). Like the sashes of a double-hung window, the upper panel is fastened to the underside of the sill beams, while the bottom panel rests on the ground—free to move up or down against the upper panel in gasketed tracks fastened to the side of the wood foundation post and attached to a cleat on the upper panel. Both panels should be filled with two-inch-thick rigid foam insulation (this requires a two-inch by 1½-inch framework or else 1½-inch-thick foam). A tight fit between the panels and a round concrete pier is somewhat more difficult. Angle iron screwed into masonry anchors drilled into the face of the concrete will require wedge-shaped shims to bring it in line with the plane of the panels.

Even with skirting, the earth under the floor platform of a pier foundation will eventually freeze solid. Thus, water lines entering the house and drain lines leaving it must be protected from freezing (see **3-64**). The usual cheap fix is to spiral an electric heat tape around the exposed water pipe and wrap it with insulation; but heat tapes have an annoying habit of burning out. Since they're also a potential fire hazard if improperly installed, their use may be prohibited by local codes. And should the power fail during a cold snap, they won't be working when they're needed most.

More reliable and less costly to operate freeze protection can be had by building an insulated "hot box" around the water pipes, similar to the slip-jointed skirt board in **3-63**. Depending on its size, the enclosure could be heated by the regular house heating system, or by a separate thermostatically controlled electric heater. For a small, well-insulated enclosure, a single 60- or 100-watt light bulb will generally provide all the heat needed to keep a water pipe from freezing (refer to **3-64**). In regions with relatively mild winters, a thick blanket of insulation alone may be all that is needed to keep the pipes from freezing. In any case, the bottom of the hot box should be below frost line. For additional protection, to allow for any ground movement, add a flexible section to the incoming water line.

If the house sewer drainpipe is hung too close to the ground, it can be pushed upwards by frost heave just enough so that water trapped in the resulting low point will freeze (refer to **3-64**). As the drain is used, water will continue to freeze as it moves over the existing ice, until the drain is eventually plugged up. The sewer pipe should be a minimum of four inches above grade where it enters the ground. At this point it should turn into a 90-degree elbow to drop vertically below grade. It is best if the drain-

pipe is also protected against frost-jacking by a collar of rigid foam insulation.

Water lines running under the floors in an exposed unheated crawl space or skirted pier foundation can freeze, even if they are covered with insulation or run between insulated floor joists. Furthermore, the traps that must be installed in every fixture drain should always be confined to the heated side of the floor since they contain water at all times.

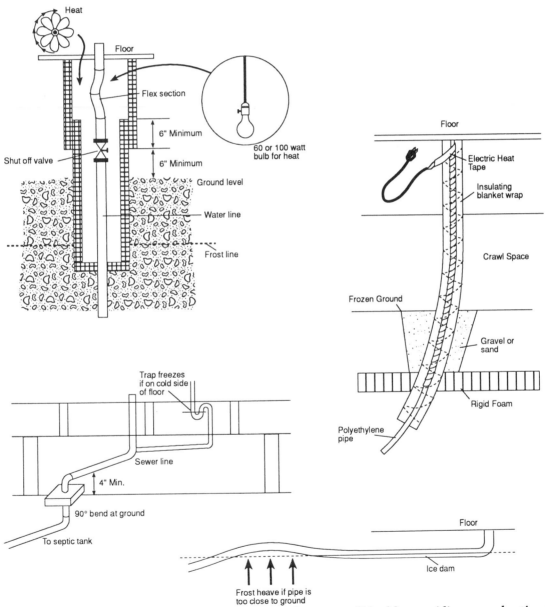

3-64 *Protection for pipes in unheated crawl spaces can be accomplished by providing some heating to the vulnerable pipes. When running sewer lines or other drains under the floor of a pier or post founda-tion, hang the pipe from the joists so that it can't be lifted by the frost.*

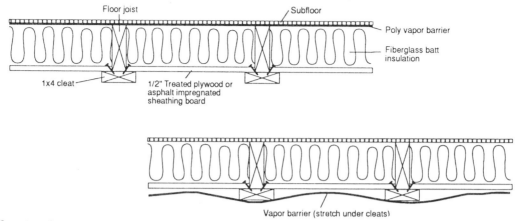

Floor joist
Subfloor
Poly vapor barrier
Fiberglass batt insulation
1x4 cleat
1/2" Treated plywood or asphalt impregnated sheathing board

Vapor barrier (stretch under cleats)

3-65 *When insulating crawl spaces, the vapor barrier must be against the warm side in colder regions. In humid warmer regions, it's placed on the outside wall.*

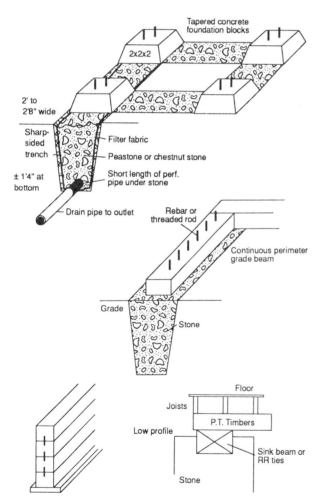

Tapered concrete foundation blocks
2x2x2
2' to 2'8" wide
Sharp-sided trench
Filter fabric
Peastone or chestnut stone
± 1'4" at bottom
Short length of perf. pipe under stone
Drain pipe to outlet
Rebar or threaded rod
Continuous perimeter grade beam
Grade
Stone
Floor
Joists
Low profile
P.T. Timbers
Sink beam or RR ties
Stone

3-66 *Ballast trench foundations are a good choice for very wet soils. Individual piers or a continuous cast beam or treated timber can be used to support the sills.*

The awkward and extremely unpleasant task of lying on your back in the dirt of a cramped and dark crawl space to install insulation between the floor joists can be avoided by installing the insulation from above, after the floor platform is framed (see **3-65**). Assuming standard two-by dimension lumber floor joists, nail a 1×4 cleat to the underside of each joist, before installing them. The resultant "shelf" carries strips of ½-inch pressure-treated plywood or asphalt-impregnated sheathing board laid between each joist to support the underside of the insulation—and to protect it from colonization by rodents and other vermin (rigid foam insulation is self-supporting, but it also seems especially attractive to mice). Sealing the underside of the floor joists is especially important when the floor platform is left open to encourage circulation of cooling breezes. The traditional chicken-wire support netting is not only vulnerable to infestation, but won't prevent a strong wind from blowing away the insulation.

Fill the bays between the floor joists with fibreglass blanket insulation, and staple a sheet of 6-mil polyethylene over the tops of the floor joists before laying the subfloor decking. This will not only serve as the required vapor retarder on the warm side of the insulation, but also protect it from getting wet if it should rain before the rest of the house is framed and closed in. In hot, humid regions, where it's recommended that vapor retarders be installed on the outside of the building envelope, the plastic sheeting must be stapled to the underside of the joists instead.

BALLAST TRENCH FOUNDATIONS

There is one foundation system—the ballast trench—which is well suited to heavy clay soils that requires little or no form work and only minimal excavation (see **3-66**). With a backhoe, dig a level or slightly sloping trench along the entire house perimeter to a depth at least a foot below frost line. For best results, the sides of the excavation should be clean cut and nearly vertical, which requires a stiff clay soil. Line the trench with filter fabric and fill it to grade with chestnut or pea stone, compacting it in six-inch lifts. Bury a single length of perforated pipe under the stone and connect it to a solid drain line pitched and run out to daylight. Cast two-foot-square by 1½- to two-foot-high concrete foundation blocks at the building corners—and at any other intermediate points as required to carry the sill beams. The block forms can be levelled to each other by working them down into the stone. Carefully align and support beam anchors from the form work before pouring the concrete.

A ballast trench foundation is similar to a railroad ballast bed. The crushed stone provides excellent drainage, and its depth protects it against frost heave. The weight of the house is distributed over the entire trench.

As an alternative to cast-in-place concrete blocks, a continuous footing, prestressed concrete beams, pressure-treated timbers, or railroad ties can be laid on top of the stone to provide even better weight distribution and block out the wind without a skirt board. The floor joists should be at least 12 inches above grade and an access port and cross-ventilation openings provided—in case it's ever necessary to crawl under the floor deck for future repairs or changes.

CONCRETE BLOCK FOUNDATIONS

Pouring a concrete foundation wall is a one-shot proposition, requiring a significant commitment of money and time. Because a concrete-block foundation can be built piecemeal, it's well suited to the erratic schedule and finances of owner-building (see **3-67**). As was mentioned at the beginning of this chapter, because of their low lateral strength—and added vulnerability to moisture—block foundations should only be used in sandy, light, and well-drained soils.

Standard concrete blocks have a nominal size of eight-by-eight-by-sixteen inches; their actual size is ⅜ of an inch smaller across all dimensions to allow for normal ⅜-inch mortar joints. The nominal size is used to estimate the number of block needed for the job. It takes 112.5 eight-inch-high by sixteen-inch-long blocks or 225 four-inch-high blocks to build 100 square feet of wall surface—and about 8.5 or 13.5 cubic yards of mortar, respectively, to bond them together. Multiply the perimeter by the height to find the total wall area (in square feet)—then divide by 100 and multiply by 112.5 (or 225) to find the total number of wall blocks. An 80-pound sack of premixed mortar makes about one cubic foot. Although convenient, this is hardly an economical way to supply the several cubic yards of mortar needed for the average foundation. Instead, buy masonry cement in 94-pound sacks and mix it with clean, fine sand. Use one part cement to 2¼ to three parts damp sand and enough water to make a mortar that is plastic but not squishy. For extra strength mortar, add one-part Portland cement mix (used for making concrete) to each part mortar cement, and use four to six parts sand. Mortar can be mixed in small batches in a contractor's wheel-

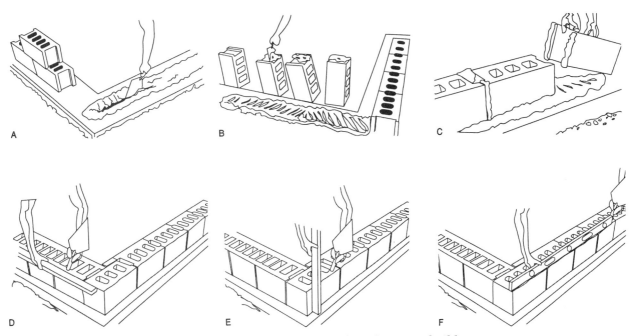

3-67 *Laying up a concrete-block foundation is well suited to the owner-builder.*
(Continued on the following pages.)

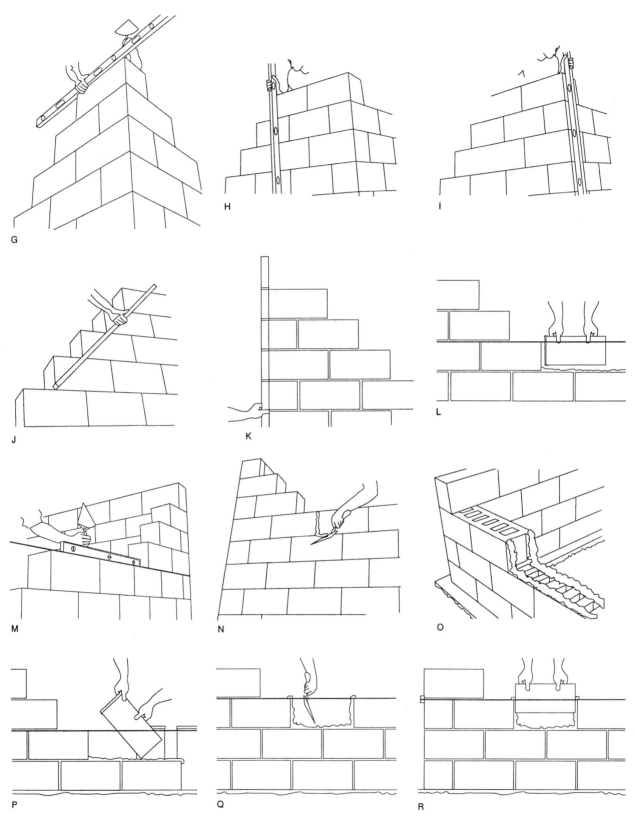

3-67 *(Continued) Laying up a concrete-block foundation.*

barrow or mortar tub, but an electric mixer makes for a lot less work and better-quality mortar. Buying your own light-duty one-cubic-foot mixer is a justifiable, relatively small additional expense.

Begin laying block by snapping a chalk line along the footing to mark the outside edge of the wall (refer to **3-67**). Then starting at a corner, lay a bed of mortar down the centerline of the wall, and spread it out into two beads with the point of the trowel; masons call this step *furrowing*. Next, stand a few blocks on end and "butter"—with mortar—their edges where they will butt against each other. Grasp a block by its webs, and set it onto the mortar bed. As each succeeding block is set, tap it into position firmly with the butt of the trowel to align it with the chalk line and the preceding blocks. It's important to check the alignment of these first-course blocks for vertical and horizontal plumb with a four-foot level since the accuracy of the following courses will depend on it. Carefully build up each corner four or five courses high before filling in the rest of the wall. This way, they become vertical and horizontal guides for it. The blocks for each course are interlocked so that the eight-inch face of one course is covered by the sixteen-inch face of the next (refer to **3-**

67). Regular blocks have one end face smooth and the other with ears. *Stretcher blocks* have ears at both ends and are used to fill in the runs between regular corner blocks. In reality, most suppliers deliver—and most masons use—both kinds of block together indiscriminately.

Attaching plastic mason's line blocks to each corner, stretch a guide string along the length of the wall to keep the outside top edge of each course running straight and level. A storey pole is also helpful to keep incremental differences in the thickness of each mortar bead from throwing the height of the wall off line.

Since it's unlikely that the last closure block in each course will be full or half-length, you'll have to cut it to fit. Make a deep scoring cut on both faces of the block with a *brick set* (a wide, hardened chisel) and a hammer; then break it cleanly along the line with a few sharp blows on the chisel. Or use a masonry-cutting blade in an old circular saw (the dust from repeated cutting can ruin a good saw) to make a deeper scoring cut that is less apt to break haphazardly.

Strike the excess mortar from the joints with the edge of the trowel after it has partially set. Tooling the joints into a concave shape compacts the mortar and helps them

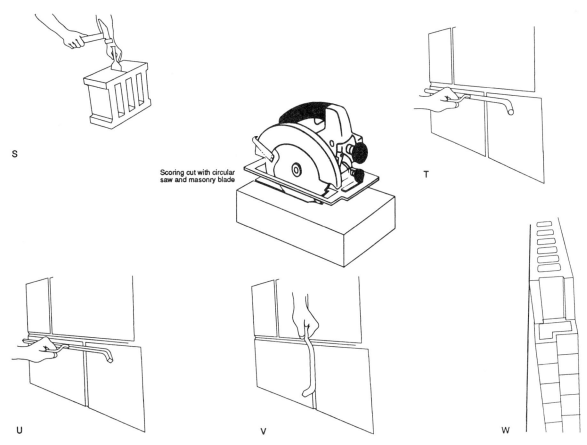

Scoring cut with circular saw and masonry blade

S

T

U

V

W

3-67 *(Continued) Laying up a concrete-block foundation.*

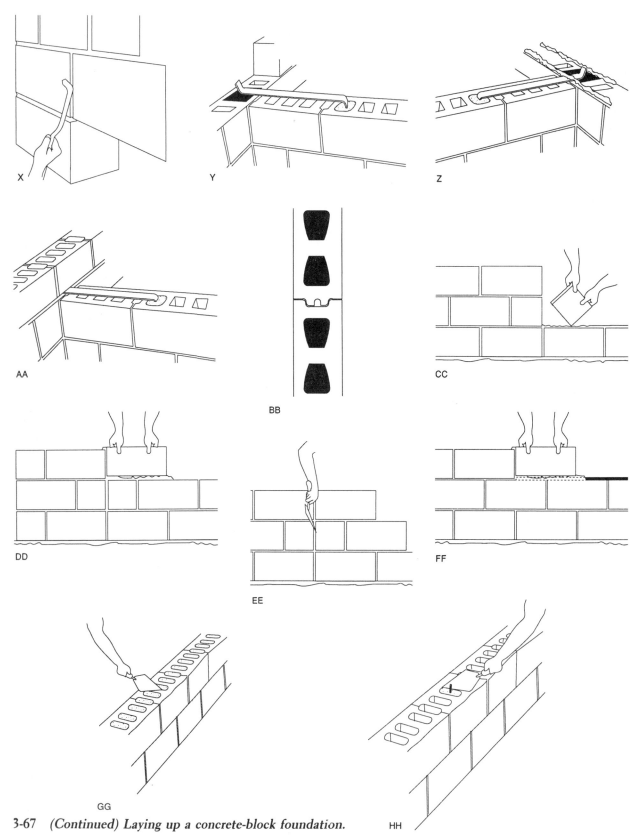

3-67 *(Continued) Laying up a concrete-block foundation.*

to shed water better. A joint tool is essentially a two-foot length of ⅝-inch-diameter pipe bent up on one end so it won't dig in with a handle welded to it. An S-shaped brick jointer is used to tool the vertical joints. Mortar smears can be cleaned from the block face with a wire brush.

Openings for windows or doors must be supported by lintels (refer to **3-67**). These are either precast concrete, steel angle irons, or special U-shaped lintel blocks temporarily supported on wood forms and filled with Rebar and concrete. In most foundations, vent windows are usually placed in the top course of block, where they are covered by the wood sill. Splines on the window jambs slip into channels in the ends of special jamb blocks.

Special metal tie bars are embedded in every four or five courses at intersections of bearing walls. Control joints are not often required in block foundations unless they happen to be unusually long—or contain abrupt changes in height, door openings, or foundation thickness. In unreinforced walls, control joints are placed every 40 feet. (A control joint is a continuous full-height vertical joint, designed to relieve cracking stresses.) The mortar in the joint is raked out to a depth of ¾ of an inch and filled with caulk. Special tongue-and-groove blocks filled with caulk instead of mortar are also used.

It's a good idea to reinforce concrete block walls by casting full-length Rebar dowels in the footing at three- to five-foot intervals. Fill the voids in the block cores surrounding the Rebar with concrete. Since concrete block is a good conductor of heat, the remaining cores should be filled with vermiculite insulation to increase the energy efficiency of the wall—but since vermiculite can contain *asbestos*, wear a respirator when handling it. Finally, the last course of block should be filled solid with concrete. The vermiculite will support the concrete. Otherwise, stuff the cores with fibreglass insulation first. Concrete is preferable to mortar; its greater strength provides better holding power for the sill anchor bolts. The continuous filling also closes off a common entry route for radon into the cellar.

The finished block walls are waterproofed by *parging* them with two ¼-inch coats of Portland cement mortar stucco. The mortar is coped at the bottom of the wall to shed water, and a coat of asphalt waterproofing is applied over the entire wall.

SURFACE-BONDED CONCRETE BLOCK

The problem with conventional concrete block foundations is that block-laying is time-consuming, takes a fair amount of skill to do well, and the wall itself is ultimately not very strong. Surface-bonded block is a lot faster, easier, and stronger than conventional block-laying (see **3-68**). Once the first course of block has been laid in a furrowed mortar bed, the remaining courses are simply dry-stacked on top of it (the ends of the first course are butted, not battered). Guide strings are still used to keep the courses aligned; also, because there's no mortar bead to compensate for small irregularities in the size of the blocks, corrugated galvanized metal brick ties inserted between the courses as necessary are used as shims to keep the blocks running level.

Because the actual size of the blocks is less than the nominal size, estimating the number of blocks to order involves a lot of fractions. In lieu of a calculator, use the table given in **3-69**. Since concrete blocks are not quite uniform, add ¼ inch to every 10 feet of wall length, and measure a trial stack to find the actual vertical height.

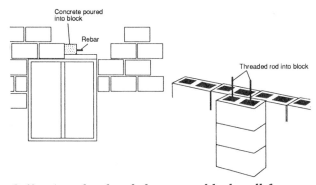

3-68 A surface-bonded concrete-block wall foundation is fast and strong: The first course is bedded in mortar on the footings, and blocks are simply dry-stacked, using metal shims, as needed, to keep them level (mortar fulfills this purpose in standard block walls). Then Rebar is inserted and voids filled with concrete to reinforce walls at pilasters, in corners, near openings, and at four-foot intervals along the walls; pour concrete into special lintel blocks to form headers over openings.

3-69 Height and length dimensions for surface-bonded block.

Number of courses	Height of wall	Number of blocks	Length of wall
1	0'-7⅝"	1	1'-3⅝"
2	1'-3¼"	2	2'-7¼"
3	1'-10⅞"	3	3'-10⅞"
4	2'-6½"	4	5'-2½"
5	3'-2⅛"	5	6'-6⅛"
6	3'-9¾"	6	7'-9¾"
7	4'-5⅜"	7	9'-1⅜"
8	5'-1"	8	10'-5"
9	5'-8⅝"	9	11'-8⅝"
10	6'-4¼"	10	13'-0¼"
11	6'-11⅞"	11	14'-3⅞"
12	7'-7½"	12	15'-7½"
13	8'-3⅛"	13	16'-11⅛"
14	8'-10¾"	14	18'-2¾"
15	9'-6⅜"	15	19'-6⅜"

A coating of Portland cement laced with chopped fibreglass is trowelled over the stacked blocks. A 50-pound bag of commercially prepared block-bonding mix covers about 50 square feet of wall surface. Since it isn't cheap, you can save about 35 percent by mixing your own. To make 25 pounds of stucco, it takes 19½ pounds of Type 1 Portland cement, 3¾ pounds of hydrated lime, one pound of alkali-resistant Type K glass fibre filament chopped into ½-inch lengths (available from plastic and chemical supply dealers, boatyards, and some masonry materials suppliers), ½ pound of calcium chloride flakes or crystals (from concrete or masonry suppliers), and ¼ pound of calcium stearate, wettable technical grade (from chemical distributors). Mix the powdered ingredients together with the exception of the calcium chloride. Since the chemicals are corrosive, wear a respirator. Add the glass fibres, avoiding overmixing, which can break them up into filaments that hamper application. Finally, mix the calcium chloride with a gallon of water, and then add the solution to the powder. Add another ½ gallon of water, and mix thoroughly. The finished mix should be creamy yet thick enough for trowelling. Since the stucco begins to set as soon as the calcium chloride is added, don't mix more than 25 pounds at a time.

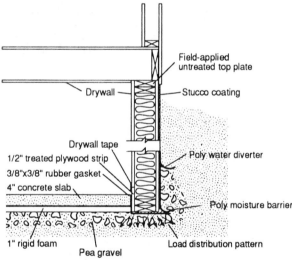

3-70 *Every detail of the all-weather wood foundations (AWWF) must be carefully engineered to resist moisture penetration and withstand soil and hydraulic pressures. The cast floor slab is needed to keep the bottom of a full-basement wood wall from shifting. In crawl spaces, without a slab, the wall must extend several feet beneath the gravel backfill.*

The tensile strength of a surface-bonded wall is almost equal to that of unreinforced concrete and almost six times greater than that of mortar-bonded block. It's also considerably more watertight, although an application of asphalt waterproofing is still required below grade.

The stucco mix is applied from the top down, with flat sweeps of the trowel over a two- to three-foot-high, five-foot-wide area. The surface is evened out by trowelling again, with the blade slightly angled. Moving downwards, the process is repeated. Cover as much area as you can in 15 or 20 minutes; then clean the trowel in water, and go over the surface once more with long, firm, arced strokes of the trowel for a smooth finish.

Anchor bolts and reinforcement steel can be embedded in concrete-filled voids of block just as for a mortar-bonded block wall. For added strength, build interlocked pilasters at eight-foot intervals along the inside of the wall (refer to **3-68**). These should be filled with Rebar and concrete as well.

ALL-WEATHER WOOD FOUNDATIONS

In the past decade, the all-weather wood foundation (AWWF) has become increasingly popular among professional builders (see **3-70**). The main advantages of a wood foundation are lower costs and speedy construction. In addition, rather than wait for a concrete subcontractor, the builder can use his or her own carpenters to build the foundation. And, because there are no problems with freezing and curing, AWWF foundations can be erected in winter.

The typical AWWF foundation begins with a carefully leveled 20-inch-wide crushed-stone-filled trench below frost line. A 2×10 or 2×12 footing plate is laid on the gravel and a 2×6 or 2×8 16-inch on-center stud-framed wall faced with ½-inch plywood is set on top of it. The exterior of the wall is covered with a polyethylene or EPDM plastic waterproofing membrane. The interior of the wall is filled with fibreglass insulation. If the concrete floor slab is poured before the wall forms are built, backfilling will be easier, since the bottom of the wood wall will be braced against the edge of the slab; forms for the slab can be tacked directly to the footing plate. The floor platform must also be built before backfilling the foundation trench.

Wood foundations require careful design to withstand lateral soil pressures. Unlike conventional concrete foundations, it's critically important that a considerable part of the building load be transferred to the floor deck. Since soil conditions are also important design criteria, the plans for any AWWF foundation should be reviewed by a qualified structural engineer.

4 Physical Matters

Structural Engineering for Homebuilders

Ideally, a house shouldn't move—at least, not very much by itself (sometimes a house is moved to a new site, but that's a different kind of movement). What little movement does occur shouldn't affect the structural stability of the frame and the weathertightness of its covering (see **4-1**). How well your house fulfills this ideal is a measure of both your skill as a builder and your understanding of the physical laws that govern structural design.

If a structure such as a house is to remain standing for any length of time, it must be heavy enough or well-enough anchored to its foundation so that it can't shift. The materials used in its frame and their connections must be strong enough to withstand the forces created by their own weight as well as the weights they carry. Its walls and roof must resist the wind pushing against them; it must bear the weight of snow piling up on the roof and of people and furniture piling up or moving about inside it.

The abstractions of classical mechanics have very important consequences for real-life buildings. If you can remember anything at all of high school physics, it's probably Newton's law which says that for every force there is an equal and opposite *reaction*. A *force* is something that, if unopposed, acts on an object to produce motion. To a structural engineer, a force applied to the frame of a building is called a *load*. How a building reacts to a load determines whether or not it will stand straight and strong for generations or sag, pull apart, and collapse. Stability depends on equilibrium: When a load and its reaction are equal but opposite, they cancel each other out—balance—and nothing moves. But when either the force or its reaction are unequal, an imbalance, or *moment*, arises. Basically, all anyone but an engineer needs to know about moments is summed up by the colloquial expression "Something's got to give." Unequal moments are resolved by motion in the direction of the smaller side of the equation, either by a circular movement called *rotation* or a straight-line movement perpendicular to the direction of the force, called *translation*—or some combination of both. There are, of course, extenuating circumstances: In a building, loads and their reactions do not always occur at the same place. The effects of forces acting over a distance are experienced as *leverage*.

There are two kinds of loads that a building must withstand and a builder must understand. These are: *dead load* and *live load*. The minimum design values for these loads that building codes require a structure to withstand are somewhat arbitrary—being based on such things as the averages of local climate conditions, the physical properties of building materials and how they are used, and empirical experience.

4-1 *The individual members of a house frame must be assembled so that they minimize movement and resist stresses or conduct them in the proper direction.*

4-2 Typical assumed dead loads for residential wood-frame construction in pounds per square foot (psf).

Roof (asphalt or wood shingles, felt paper, ½-inch plywood)	10 psf
Attic floor (unfloored)	10
Attic floor, floored for storage use	20
Floors (plastered ceilings or drywall)	20
Floors (no ceiling)	10
Bearing partition (8-foot wall)	20
Nonbearing partition	5

A dead load is the weight of the building materials themselves. Designers and building codes normally use assumed values for a given structural component expressed as pounds per square foot (psf), rather than the sum total of the additive weights of individual components, to calculate dead loads. Thus, rather than add together the psf weights of asphalt roofing, plywood, framing lumber, etc., the dead load of a normal roof is simply assigned a design value of 10 psf (see **4-2, 4-3,** and **4-4**). Careful calculation of dead load components is only necessary under unusual design conditions. The fact that the assumed dead load is almost always greater than the total loads of its parts adds a built-in margin of safety to ordinary design.

The *live load* is the weight added to the dead load of the floors by the occupants or the use of the building (see **4-5**). It includes such things as the weight of furniture, furnishings, and people. For example, a 600-pound piano or a half-ton waterbed will increase the load on a 100-sf floor by 6 and 10 psf, respectively. Thirty adults at an average weight of 150 pounds each would increase the live load on that floor by 45 psf. Since such a concentration of mass would seriously hamper most forms of ordinary social interaction, scattering that same group across the floor of a 12-foot by 18-foot living room would increase the load distribution to 23 psf. If this same group happened to be dancing a polka, the collective impact of their stamping feet could conceivably double the force. Since the actual live load is impossible to predict at any given moment, building codes specify minimum safe values for different types of activities. The sizes and spacing of floor and ceiling joists are chosen to safely carry these prescribed design loads.

4-4 Weight of common materials in pounds per cubic foot (pcf).

Soil, depending on moisture content and type	60–120 pcf
Brick	120
Stone	132–168
Water	64
Ice	56
Fresh snow	8

4-3 Dead loads of common building materials in psf.

Asphalt composition roll or shingles	3 psf
Five-ply buildup flat roof with gravel	6
Wood shingles	2
¼-inch slate	10
Cement and clay tiles	12–19
Sheet-metal standing seam	2
Skylight (glass)	5
Galvanized-steel sheets	1–3
Softwood, per inch thickness	3
¾-inch softwood boards	2.5
½-inch plywood	1.4
¾-inch plywood	2.1
½-inch fibreboard sheathing	0.8
25/32-inch standard hardwood flooring	4
Wood lath and ¾-inch plaster	5
Metal lath and ¾-inch plaster	6
½-inch drywall	2.5
Softwood joists, per ft. span per in. depth	0.33
Cement, per inch thickness	12
Ceramic or slate floor tiles per in.	12
Concrete slab, 4-inch thick	48
Carpet	0.5
Foam insulation, per inch	0.2
Glass, single pane, double strength	1.5
Glass, ¼-inch plate	3.5

Snow load is considered as a separate live load that acts on the roof independently of the live load on the floors and is the primary design consideration for sizing rafters. The minimum allowable snow load design values are based on a 90% average of annual snow pack, which means that they will be exceeded once every 10 years (see **4-6**).

Snow load values assume that all the snow which falls on the ground also sticks to the roof. This is unlikely, since most roofs are sloped to a greater or lesser degree. Thus some local building codes allow a reduction in snow load capacity for every degree of roof pitch over 20 degrees—a 20-degree roof rises 4.5 inches vertically for every foot of horizontal run, i.e., it's slightly steeper than the typical ranch-house-style roof (see **4-7**).

4-5 Minimum allowable live loads in psf.

Dwelling floors used for social purposes (typically ground floors)	40 psf
Attic floors (used for light storage only)	20
Dwelling floors used for private purposes (typically bedrooms, second floors)	30
Garages (passenger cars)	80
Banquet halls, assembly rooms	100
Fire escapes and balconies	100
General commercial storage purposes (machinery, warehouses, hay lofts, etc)	250

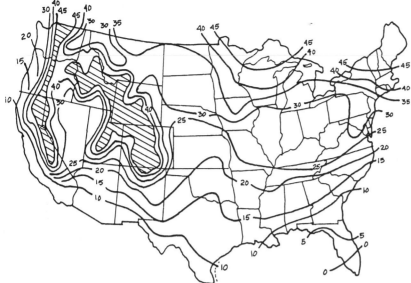

4-6 *Minimum design values for snow loads on roof in psf is shown. The snow weight in the shaded areas varies greatly and should be determined from local weather records or code requirements.*

Since a cubic foot of freshly fallen snow weighs about eight pounds, it would seem that a roof built to withstand a 40-psf load would be more than strong enough in most parts of the country. Suppose, however, that a roof is already covered with a foot of old compacted snow (which weighs about twice as much as new snow) when a blizzard dumps three feet of fresh snow on it right before it warms up and rains heavily. Before it melts, the live load of this wet blanket can easily exceed 50 psf. This, and the fact that the design load is already estimated to be exceeded at least once every ten years, is a good reason not to economize on rafter size and spacing—even if local codes allow it. In some exceptionally snowy areas, codes call for an extra 10 psf as a safety margin.

In the same way that it pushes against your hand held out the window of a car while cruising down a highway, wind also is a live load on the building. Wind pressure is not only a function of velocity, that is, the speed of the vehicle, but also of angle; changing the pitch of the roof modulates the force of the wind just as feathering the angle of your palm does.

For purposes of calculation, wind loads are considered to act at both right angles to the roof and horizontally against the walls of the house (see **4-8**). But since a house is more than a plane surface, the actual effects of wind force are more complicated. As wind moves over the roof and around the corners, the pressure on the leeward side of the house drops. Since the air inside the house is now at a higher pressure than the air moving around its outside, an uplifting force on the underside of the roof is created. Wide overhanging eaves tend to amplify these uplifting forces; so does the crawl space of an unskirted pier foundation.

4-7 *Formula for calculating allowable reduction in snow load design value on pitched roofs.*

$$R = P \times (L/40)/2$$

Where: R = allowable reduction in psf
P = degrees of pitch over 20 degrees
L = snow load design value as per Code

(Example: For a 45-degree roof pitch and a 40-psf load, R = 25 × (⁴⁰⁄₄₀)/2 or 12.5 psf.)

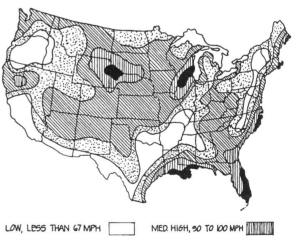

LOW, LESS THAN 67 MPH ☐   MED. HIGH, 90 TO 100 MPH ▥

MED. LOW, 67 TO 80 MPH ░   HIGH, OVER 100 MPH ■

MEDIUM, 80 TO 90 MPH ▨

4-8 *Average wind pressure data is used to determine live load on house walls and roofs.*

4-9 *Metal foundation anchors such as this strap embedded in the corner of the foundation wall and nailed to the wall studs through the sheathing are often required by building codes in earthquake-prone or high-wind areas.*

4-10 *Steel straps also tie upper and lower wall frames together particularly when floor trusses rather than solid trimmer joists are used. Otherwise, a horizontal band of plywood sheathing should span this zone of potential weakness.*

The net effect of all the various forces generated by the action of wind against the surfaces of a house is a tendency towards a moment of simultaneous rotation and translation, more commonly known as *overturning*. This is why a house must be anchored to its foundation (see **4-9**), its exterior walls rigidly braced (see **4-10**), and its roof frame tied down to them. Fortunately, standard framing methods are more than capable of withstanding all but the worst hurricane-force winds. As **4-11** shows, even a 90-mph wind exerts only about 20 psf of force on the walls. Thus, except in regions where extremely high winds are common, wind loads usually don't require any particularly elaborate design details.

Wind and snow loads are often combined into a single live roof load. Building codes prescribe a combined wind/snow load value based on local weather conditions, usually 40 to 60 psf.

The reaction of building materials, especially framing lumber, to the forces generated by live and dead loads is of critical concern to architects and structural engineers and is important to the homebuilder insofar as these prin-

4-11 *Relationship between wind speed and wind pressure.*

Wind speed (mph)	Wind Pressure (psf)
5	0.06
10	0.25
20	1.0
25	1.6
40	4.1
60	9.2
80	16.4
90	20.7
100	25.6
120	36.8

ciples are embodied in such things as code specifications for minimum allowable sizes and spacing of girder spans, floor and ceiling joists, rafters, and the number and types of fasteners used to join them.

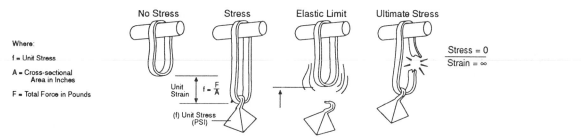

No Stress   Stress   Elastic Limit   Ultimate Stress

$$\frac{Stress = 0}{Strain = \infty}$$

Unit Strain $f = \frac{F}{A}$

(f) Unit Stress (PSI)

4-12 *A weighted rubber band is the classic demonstration of the relationship between stress and strain.*

When an external force is applied to a material, the internal force exerted by one part of the body on an adjoining part that tends to resist the applied force is called *stress*. Stress is measured in terms of force per unit area. Materials under stress tend to change shape—*deform*—in proportion to that stress. This deformation is called *strain*. There are different kinds of stress; the two for which forces are *perpendicular* to the area under consideration are *tensile stress*—when a body is subject to a pull—and *compressive stress*—when a body is being pushed, i.e., supporting a load.

Imagine a rubber band looped around a dowel: If a weight is attached to its free end, the band stretches; the greater the weight, the more the band stretches (see **4-12**). The total change in shape divided by the band's original shape is defined as *unit strain*. When the term "strain" is used alone, it invariably means unit strain. With a particular material—in this case the rubber band—up to a certain point the stress experienced remains proportional to the strain produced. This means that when weight is removed, the band returns to its original shape. The band attains its *elastic limit* when it will no longer quite return to its original shape when the weights are removed. A permanent elongation has been produced. At some point as more weight is applied, the band will exhibit a behavior that does not conform to the earlier stress–strain proportionality; this point is called the *yield strength*. If increasing weight is continuously applied, a maximum stress that the band is able to withstand is reached—called the *ultimate strength*. Beyond this point, elongation continues until the *breaking point*—here the rubber band snaps (for materials, in general, this is termed the *fracture point*).

When dealing with building materials rather than rubber bands, a material's elastic limit and its ultimate strength are not quite as important as the broad region that lies beneath them, which is its working, or *allowable stress*. The ratio of ultimate stress to allowable stress which defines the boundaries of this zone for any given material is its *safety margin*.

There are three different kinds of stress that arise when a building or its members and their connections are subjected to the force of a load. These are tensile stress or *tension*, compressive stress or *compression*, and shearing stress or *shear*. Shear differs from tension and compression in that the external and internal forces are *parallel* (rather than perpendicular) to the stressed cross-sectional area (the shear plane) under consideration. Other stresses are similar to these basic stresses or a combination of them. For instance, *bending*—or transverse—stress is important in a building, but a bending stress in a beam actually is a combination of tensile, compressive, and shearing stress (see **4-13**).

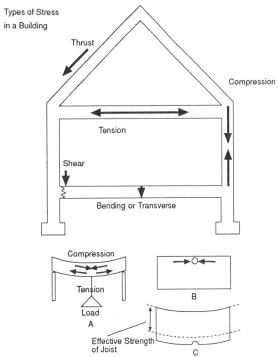

Types of Stress in a Building

Thrust

Compression

Tension

Shear

Bending or Transverse

Compression

Tension

Load

A

B

Effective Strength of Joist

C

4-13 *A load of a roof causes an outward thrust against the walls, placing the ceiling joists in tension. As the load is transmitted down to the foundation, the wall frame is in compression. Even without a load, beams supported at their ends tend to sag in the middle under their own weight. The interaction between tension, compression, and shear stress is described as a bending (transverse) stress.*

When a load is applied at right angles to a wood structural beam, it creates tension stresses that act to stretch and tear the fibres on the outside of the bend apart. Thus, in extreme cases, an overloaded beam will snap just like the rubber band in the example when it was under too much tension. The resistance of wood to tension stresses is one of the two main criteria used to size joists and other structural beams.

In houses, the load of a pitched roof exerts an outward force or *thrust* on the walls which also subjects the floor joists that tie them together to significant tensile stress. In most cases, the effects of this tension within the wood itself are of less concern than the possibility that the connectors between pieces of wood under tension will fail.

Except in foundation design for unstable soils, compression, which in housebuilding typically is the stress that results from the downward force on a supporting wood column, is only of marginal concern. Wood has such an extremely high compressive strength parallel to its grain that it is almost impossible in normal housebuilding to load a wood column to its breaking point. Failure occurs not from the actual crushing of wood fibres in compression but rather from sideways bending and diagonal shearing along planes of internal weakness. This presupposes that the supporting post is cut exactly square so that the load bears evenly across its entire cross-sectional area. The load is transferred only to the portion of the post in actual contact with it. An uneven post under a heavy load creates a moment that causes it to kick out sideways. Compression can also occur perpendicular to the grain, as, for example, when the fibres along the edge of a joist supporting a heavily loaded post are crushed.

Shear is the stress which tends to cause different materials or layers of the same material to slide past each other. It can be either external, as, for example, the *horizontal shear stress* caused by wind pressure against a wall, or internal, such as the splitting or checking of a fresh-sawn timber as it dries out. Shear is also what cause nailed joints to slide past each other, the unsupported ends of loaded joists to split open, and an overloaded beam to snap right next to its supporting column. Wood has virtually unlimited shear resistance across its grain and relatively low resistance parallel to its grain. Cross-grained lumber is especially vulnerable to shear stresses and should not be used for structural purposes.

When a horizontal beam supported at both ends is loaded over its span, it reacts to the resulting stress by tending to bend, i.e., it sags. This characteristic response to transverse stress—more properly called *deflection*—is of immediate concern to every housebuilder. Resistance to deflection is commonly experienced as *bounciness*, a quality not highly desirable in floors. Hence, building codes don't permit floor joists to deflect vertically more than 1/360th of their horizontal spans (about 1/2 inch over 15 feet). The span lengths given in tables used for sizing floor joists and rafters are normally listed as "limited by deflec-

tion" (1). Because of the above-mentioned reduction in load with increased roof pitch, deflection limits for roof rafters are calculated at 1/240th and 1/180th of span. The 1/240l rating is also used for attic ceiling joists not used for storage.

Besides choosing properly sized joists and rafters, builders compensate for deflection by installing them "crown" up. (As a plank dries, it tends to shrink parallel to the grain. The characteristic signature of this stress is a "crown," or bow, in the plane of its widest dimension.) Orienting joists and rafters with crowns up prestresses the frame to resist deflection as it is loaded. It also ensures a level floor and a flat roof deck.

As a beam deflects under load, the bending or transverse stress includes components of compression and tension at the same time. The practical consequences for carpenters and plumbers is that holes for pipes bored through the lower edges of a floor joist will significantly reduce the strength of that joist; whereas the same hole bored through the upper regions of the joist won't have any serious consequences. Knots have high resistance to compression (try hammering a nail through one) but almost none to tension (their grain is at right angles to the grain of the beam, which is why they fall out so easily). A knot under tension is the structural equivalent of a hole. Any floor joist or rafter with large knots in its lower third shouldn't be used.

To an engineer, a "beam" is any horizontal load-bearing structure supported at both ends subject to transverse stress. To a builder, a beam is either a solid-wood timber, a built-up *girder*, or a steel I-beam. Although the terms are often used interchangeably, joists are narrow two-by horizontal supports and beams are horizontal supports more than four inches wide. For example, 4×8s, 6×6s, 8×8s, and 8×10s are often referred to as either beams or joists, but a single 2×10 or 2×12 is always called a joist and never a beam. For engineers and builders alike, the important question is what size beam is needed to safely carry a given design load?

With wood, *strength* and *stiffness* aren't exactly the same thing. Strength is measured in psi by a quality called *extreme fibre strength* (Fb), which is basically the internal resistance of wood cells to the compression and shear forces that arise when wood bends under load. Stiffness is its resistance to deflection under load; it is the ratio of stress to strain expressed as a number called the *modulus of elasticity* (E). Both the extreme fibre stress and the modulus of elasticity for common species of wood used in construction have been determined through laboratory testing; tables listing their values are used by structural engineers and architects to calculate the allowable spans for rafters and joists of a given size subjected to a chosen combined live and dead design load.

Other things being equal, the usefulness of a wood beam depends on its *section modulus*, which is a technical term for the ratio of depth to width. Strength is propor-

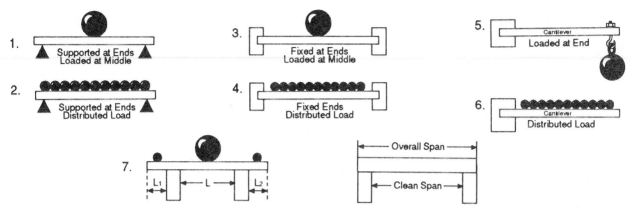

4-14 *These simplified diagrams show the basic categories of structural beams and their load distribution.*

tional to the *square* of depth, but stiffness is proportional to its *cube*. Thus, a 4×8 beam on edge is four times stronger and eight times stiffer than a 4×4 beam (4×4 = 16 and 8×8 = 64; while 4×4×4 = 64 and 8×8×8 = 512). For beams of equal depth, both strength and stiffness are directly proportional to width. Thus, a 2×12 flatwise is twice as strong and twice as stiff as a 2×6 flatwise.

Finally, when both width and depth of a beam are equal, its strength is inversely proportional to the length of its span while its stiffness is inversely proportional to the cube of its span. Thus, a 2×8 spanning six feet is twice as strong as a 2×8 that spans twelve feet. And it will deflect under load only one-eighth as much as the longer beam.

The physics of beams is further complicated by the fact that they behave differently when loads are concentrated at one or more points or uniformly distributed along their entire span (see **4-14**). Distributed loads are typical of stud-frame construction while concentrated loads are the norm with traditional post-and-beam timber framing. Furthermore, the manner in which a beam is supported also influences its resistance to stress. A beam supported at both ends is a *simple beam*. A beam supported at just one end is a *cantilevered beam*. And a beam supported by some combination of the other two is an *overhanging beam*. Different engineering formulas must be used to calculate safe loads for each design case (refer to **4-14**). And, to make things even more interesting, a beam that merely rests on its supporting posts can deflect in any direction, whereas a beam whose ends are fixed before the stress is applied can only deflect in a compound curve, which almost doubles its relative stiffness. Carpenters apply this principle when they install rigid blocking between floor joists at the ends and midpoints of their spans.

In order to determine the suitability of a given type of wood to a particular load or span, an architect or structural engineer begins by looking up the *base values* for its extreme fibre stress, modulus of elasticity, and any other applicable stress-related factors. (Consult the tables for base values for Western dimension lumber in the Appendices, provided courtesy *Western Wood Products Association*.) These values vary not only according to species groups, but with grade within a particular group as well. This is only logical since the highest grades of wood are most free from knots, splits, and other defects that would compromise strength. The base values are then adjusted by other multipliers to account for such things as the moisture content of the wood, the size of the framing member, whether it will be used in vertical or horizontal compression, its intended use, and its duration.

Base values for fibre stress and modulus of elasticity assume "dry" (i.e., having a moisture content not greater than 19 percent) and "clear" (i.e., knot-free) wood. Depending upon species, "green" wood has 20 to 50 percent less resistance to shear than dry wood, which may be why it's so much easier to drive nails into and pull them out of fresh-sawn wood than seasoned wood.

Like people, wood under stress eventually gets "tired"; its strength decreases with time. Working loads account for this by incorporating a margin of safety based on the ratio of ultimate strength to a more or less arbitrary 10-year allowable working stress. A safe working load is defined as one where that ratio is at least a factor of eight. For example, Eastern white spruce has an extreme fibre stress of 9800 psi and a 10-year average stress of about 1200 psi. This gives a safety margin of 8.2, which makes it a good choice for framing lumber.

Wood can carry substantially greater maximum loads for short periods than for long durations. Typical short-term loading adjustment factors of the normal 10-year working stress (by which *Fb* is multiplied) are 1.15 for a "two month" (i.e., snow) load, 1.25 for a "seven-day" load, such as piling up construction materials on a floor and roof deck, 1.60 for "10 minute" (severe wind and earthquake) loads, and 2.00 for impact resistance, such as the momentary concentrated stress of dancing or dropping a heavy object on a floor.

After the base values are multiplied by the requisite adjustment factors, the calculated design values can be used in several ways. You can find out which grade and species of wood your local lumberyard carries, look up its F_b and E values, and use these to check the suitability of the dimensions and/or spacing of the joists or timbers you'll need to bridge the spans and carry the loads of your design. You may find that span lengths or framing dimensions must be modified to fit affordable and readily available lengths of lumber, a steel beam substituted for wood, or spans for intermediate posts and carrying beams added. Fibre stress and modulus of elasticity values are a prerequisite when using beam formulas to calculate timber frame members.

All these different forces, stresses, and design criteria are awfully complicated. Fortunately, in the course of ordinary framing, there's seldom any reason to do any structural calculations. Instead, the lengths and sizes of rafters and joists can be found by referring to standard span tables such as those found in the Appendices (*courtesy Western Wood Products Association*). Since the stresses that a particular joist or rafter is subjected to depend on the use to which it's put, there's no single span table that works for all cases of rafter and joist selection. Instead, span tables are arranged according to grades of lumber and types of combined dead and live loads. Among other things, the tables distinguish between floor joists in living areas, ceiling joists for attics and whether or not they will be used for storage, ceilings with plaster or drywall, and flat, low-sloped, and steeply pitched roof rafters with either light or heavy roofing materials, as well as other various dead and live load conditions. Also, since the tables for rafter spans are calculated horizontally, the lengths must be corrected for the actual length of the rafter for a given roof pitch. An appropriate conversion matrix accompanies the rafter span tables in the Appendices.

Even though most houses aren't so structurally complicated or unusual that they must be designed by an engineer or that an experienced and conscientious builder wouldn't almost intuitively know which size framing lumber is best for a particular purpose, span tables are indispensable to the novice builder and useful to the professional alike.

The basic problem of frame design has always been: What is a reasonable margin of safety? How much can be trimmed before a structure is unsafe? The recommendations of span tables are based on mathematics and laboratory testing tempered by experience. As we have seen, every species and every grade of lumber varies in strength. The strength of each individual piece is affected by knots, grain patterns, and other defects. One reason that old houses seem so much better built than modern houses is that lumber cut from the old-growth forests was much stronger than that cut from today's second-, third-, and fourth-growth forests. The loosely packed cell structure of young fast-growing wood has less resistance to rot and weathering, warps and twists easier, shrinks more, and is weaker than dense old wood.

Although the extreme fibre stress of a modern web frame is about 15 percent greater than that of its individual units, much of its strength also depends on the skill and integrity of its assembly. The right size and the best lumber won't amount to much if it is improperly nailed or carelessly erected. In any case, even with all the adjustments for moisture content, grades, defects, and anticipated loads, engineering formulas still describe generalized cases rather than the specific house with its peculiar idiosyncrasies of misalignment and cumulative small errors. Since it's ultimately impossible to predict with absolute certainty the kinds of stress a house will endure over several generations, it is prudent to size framing members conservatively.

And because the minimal use of wood has both ecological and economic benefits, common sense dictates that a frame should be stronger than absolutely necessary but not more than is sensible. The safety margin of a real-life frame should be large enough to accommodate unseen or knowingly ignored defects, honest miscalculations of framing sizes, and some degree of substandard workmanship. Ultimately, it should be strong enough, not just to withstand "average" loads, but a once-in-a-century load.

THE IMPORTANCE OF LEVEL, PLUMB, AND SQUARE

The physics of building loads dictates, as was just discussed extensively, that a safe working load be designed into the house frame to accommodate inevitable stresses. Physics also dictates that maintenance of equilibrium is fundamental to the stability of a frame. Even the most rigid or overbuilt frame won't last if a moment is built into it from the start. This is exactly what happens when a builder does not respect and insist on the carpenter's trinity of *level*, *plumb*, and *square*.

For example, suppose one corner of a wall is built out of plumb (true vertical). If the top and bottom lengths of that wall are equal, then the opposite end of that wall must also be out of plumb (see **4-15**). Instead of a stable rectangle, the wall is now a rather unstable parallelogram; a moment waiting to be resolved. Although a frame is in reality braced by its sheathing, over the life span of the house this added stress could exacerbate any future structural problems.

If the floor deck on which this hypothetical wall is raised happens to be off level, the wall studs themselves may be plumb, but the top plate that joins them together won't be horizontal (see **4-16**). Not only will the floor deck that the wall carries tilt, but also the edges of the plywood exterior sheathing panels won't fall on the center of studs or line up with the top and bottom of the wall. Out-of-plumb or off-level walls also create difficulties for fitting windows, doors, and kitchen cabinets, and skew the sightlines of exterior and interior trim.

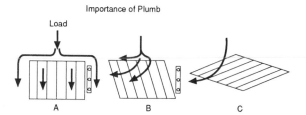

Importance of Plumb

A   B   C

4-15 *A load on a plumb wall is transmitted safely to the foundation. If the wall is out of plumb, the load tends to act as a sideways thrust, which can collapse the wall.*

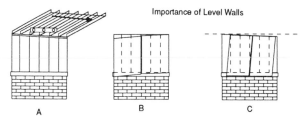

Importance of Level Walls

A   B   C

4-16 *A floor deck or foundation out of level will cause the rest of the house to be off level too. It also causes the plywood sheathing to run off the studs or the top and bottom plates (exaggerated).*

An out-of-square wall can't be both plumb and level at the same time. But a level platform such as a floor deck or foundation can be out of square, yet level. Insofar as mechanical equilibrium is concerned, this poses no problem. Once again, the difficulty comes in fitting rectangular subfloor panels to skewed floor joists.

A foundation or floor platform can also be out of square because a wall is longer or shorter than the others, making the building wider or longer on one side or another. Since the roof rafters are (supposed to be) all the same length

and pitch, the ridge to which they join won't be level and the rafters won't seat evenly on the top of the wall (see **4-17**). The only way to connect two unparallel lines (e.g., the ridge beam and the wall) is to change the lengths of the connectors (the rafters). But shortening or lengthening rafters to fit a skewed wall also increases or decreases the depth of the seat cut where the rafters rest on the wall, which throws off the line where the interior wall meets the ceiling. Uncorrected errors don't disappear, they compound.

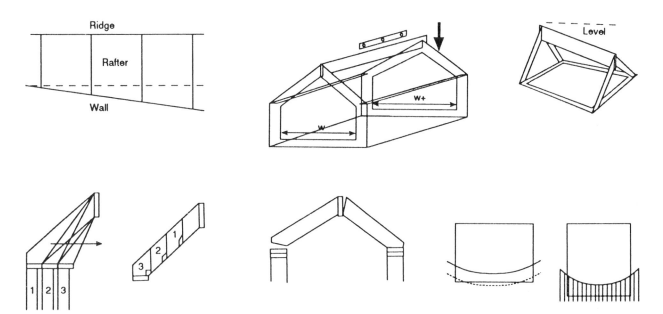

4-17 *Small errors add up to big problems in roof framing. When a wall is off-level, the rafters must change length for the ridge to be level. If the ridge is set level and the building width isn't the same, the rafter will drop down the ridge as width increases. If the rafter lengths stay the same, the ridge will drop off-level. If the ridge is dropped, the rafters either won't bear tight against it or won't seat flat on the wall. Successively lengthening the rafters to follow an increase in wall width also changes their pitch and the angles of each bearing surface. If the rafter pitch is held constant, the depth of the seat cut must change with wall width. A bow in the wall will show up in the cornice if the rafter ends are kept the same length. If the rafter ends are cut to a straight line, the bow still shows up on the underside of the cornice.*

4-18 *Despite its appearance of massive strength, a traditional timber frame owes its rigidity to the small triangles formed by the knee braces at the corner and intermediate posts.*

Unless counteracted or avoided, small errors at each stage of wall and floor framing eventually add up to major problems in roof rafter framing and cornice trim (refer to **4-17**). While framing can't and shouldn't be as precise as finish carpentry, there's no reason why a frame should be more than a quarter to half-inch off of dead square and level by the time it reaches the ridge. Anything more than this will show, and anything less is usually a pleasant surprise. There are numerous opportunities to correct misalignments at each step of the framing process. A conscientious builder takes advantage of them; a sloppy builder ignores them. The traditional building trade aphorisms "close enough for government work" and "can't see it from my place" express the natural tension between the desire for quality workmanship and the limitations of budget, time, materials, and tools.

RACKING

Racking is the distortion of a frame due to horizontal shear stress generated by wind pressure or some other horizontal force on the walls. A house frame must be rigid enough to resist racking.

If a frame were a solid seamless cube, stresses would be distributed evenly throughout it and racking could not occur. But since a frame is made up of many individual pieces, each of which acts and is acted upon by an adjoining member, every joint and discontinuity in the frame is a potential fulcrum upon which a moment can be resolved. The junction between the foundation and sill, the wall frame with the ceiling and floor platforms, walls with

adjacent walls, and walls with roofs are all, structurally speaking, hinges which must not be allowed to swing open. By themselves mechanical fasteners or complex joints won't prevent racking. The rectangle of an unbraced timber frame or a stud wall alike can be transformed into a rapidly collapsing parallelogram by a strong push. Adding a diagonal brace turns a rectangle into a stable and strong triangle. There are no hinges in the plane of a triangle. So long as the joints at the apexes hold, no pivoting movement can take place unless the sides actually break.

The rigidity of a traditional timber frame was almost entirely a result of the relatively small diagonal knee braces between the upright posts and the horizontal beams rather than the massive size of the timbers themselves (see **4-18**). Before the adoption of plywood sheathing, the corner studs of stick-framed construction were notched to receive *let-in* 1×4 or 2×4 diagonal braces. Because nails are less resistant to shear forces than wood, *cut-in* bracing (angled pieces are cut to fit between the studs on a diagonal line) is not as strong as let-in bracing.

The greater the number of braced triangles, the stronger a frame will be. Besides the actual bracing, the sandwich of finish siding, sheathing, framing, interior sheathing and plaster lath all tend to increase rigidity, especially if the individual layers are perpendicular to each other (see **4-19**). The cumulative effect of all the individual fasteners and overlapping joints in a complete wall section is to more or less distribute stress along diagonal lines. But because this resistance arises from purely mechanical connections rather than integral triangles, horizontal and vertical overlapping by itself isn't strong enough to resist strong racking forces.

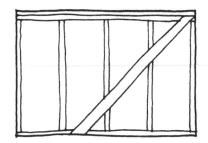

LET-IN 2×4
RESISTANCE = 2.6

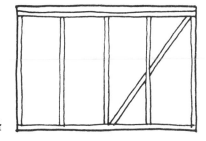

CUT-IN 2×4
RESISTANCE = 1.6

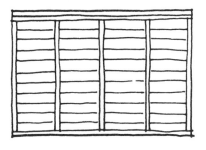

HORIZONTAL 3/4" T&G
BOARDS, NAILED TO STUDS
RESISTANCE = 1

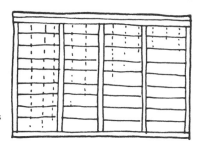

3/4" VERTICAL BOARDS
NAILED OVER
3/4" HORIZONTAL BOARDS
RESISTANCE = 2.0

DIAGONAL 3/4" T&G BOARDS
NAILED TO STUDS
RESISTANCE = 4.3

3/4" DIAGONAL T&G BOARDS
W/OPENINGS
RESISTANCE = 1.0

OPENINGS GREATLY REDUCE RESISTANCE TO
RACKING OF ANY WALL CONSTRUCTION.

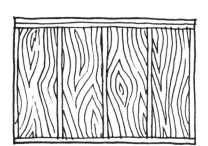

1/4" PLYWOOD
  NAILED: 4.2
  GLUED: 24.0
1/2" PLYWOOD
  NAILED: 6.0
  GLUED: 34.0

1/2" PLYWOOD W/OPENINGS
  NAILED: 2.8
  GLUED: 5.1

4-19 *Comparative resistance to racking of various sheathing techniques. The numbers given represent an arbitrary comparative racking resistance factor based on 2×4 wall framing at 16-inch on-center, with horizontal T & G sheathing assigned a base value of 1.0.*

95

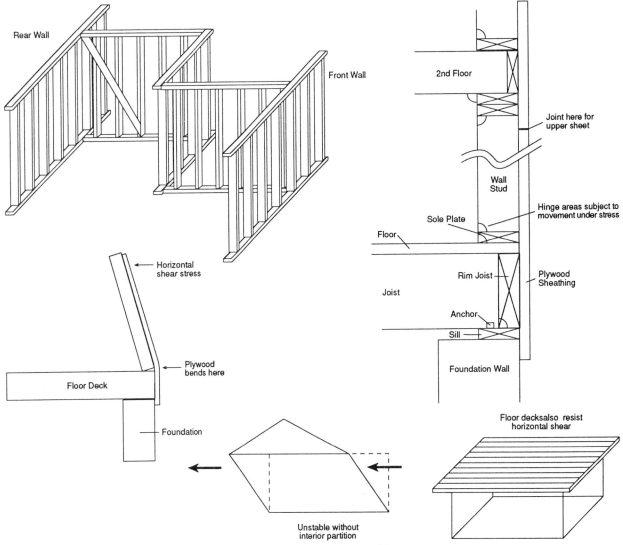

4-20 *Plywood sheathing and interior partitions help prevent racking.*

Structurally speaking, plywood sheathing, with its perpendicularly alternating glue-bonded plies, contains an infinite series of triangles, which is why it offers the greatest racking resistance of any common building material (see **4-20**). Likewise, when properly applied, it bridges the structural "hinges" between the sills and floor frame and between floor and wall framing. Racking forces can still have an effect perpendicular to the plane of the wall. Normally, the interior partitions and the web of floor platform satisfactorily resist forces from this direction (refer to **4-20**). With open space designs, however, special measures are needed to ensure the stability of the frame in this plane.

The rigidity of a wall is greatly reduced by openings. Thus, as much as possible, openings should be cut from whole sheets of plywood rather than filled in with odd scraps. Plywood sheets should also bridge the joint between the walls studs and the second-floor framing. When a wall contains more openings than solid sheathing, as for example, with a south-facing "window wall," the plywood should be glued and screwed to the studs, not nailed, for maximum shear resistance. Window walls facing into strong prevailing winds also benefit from an additional layer of ¼-inch plywood glued to the interior wall.

THE NATURE OF WOOD

Wood is an ideal building material. It's widely available, relatively inexpensive, and can be obtained with a minimum of environmental degradation. It can be recycled as fuel. It's adaptable to an infinity of uses. It's easily worked by hand or machine tools, durable, sound- and heat-

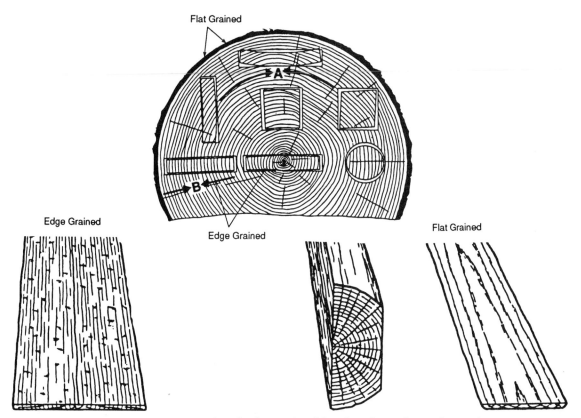

4-21 *The difference between flat-grained and edge-grained lumber depends on the angle of the saw blade to the growth rings.*

absorbent, and has a high strength-to-weight ratio. It's also beautiful, and finally, it grows on trees.

Wood species are somewhat arbitrarily classed as hardwoods and softwoods. Although this has more to do with whether they are broad-leaved or coniferous species, as a rule most hardwoods are considerably denser, heavier, and stronger than softwoods. These same properties that make hardwoods prized for flooring, furniture, cabinetry, and fine ornamental woodwork also make them unsuitable for most frame construction. Softwood lumber is more workable, much lighter, and less prone to warp than hardwood. The species commonly used for lumber are also more plentiful and rapid-growing, and hence, less expensive than hardwoods. (Refer to the table listing the characteristics of common woods and their uses provided in the Appendices.)

LUMBER NOMENCLATURE

When a log is sawn into lumber, the angle of its annular rings to the surface of the board will yield two different kinds of lumber, depending on how it is sawn (see **4-21**). If the angle of the saw blade is more or less tangential to the annular rings, *flat-grained* (for softwood) or *plain-sawed* (for hardwood) lumber is the result. If the angle is

more or less perpendicular to the rings, the lumber is *edge-grained* or *quarter-sawed*, respectively. Since plain-sawing produces more lumber with less waste, it is the more common. Because edge-grained lumber shrinks and warps less than flat-grained lumber and holds paint better, it is specified for high-quality exterior trim and interior cabinetry, flooring, and especially for locations subject to extreme conditions such as saunas. It is considerably more expensive than ordinary lumber and so often must be specially-ordered.

Wood shrinks because of the arrangement of its cellular structure. As it dries out, the water held inside the cells is lost first. Then, at around 30-percent MC (moisture content), as the water held within the cell walls themselves is in turn lost and the walls shrink, the bundles of wood fibres grow smaller.

General construction lumber is considered dry—whether produced in temperature- and moisture-controlled kilns or left in stickered stacks to air-dry—when it reaches 19-percent MC. The only difference between the two methods is that there is less waste in the kiln-drying process since humidity can be carefully controlled to prevent the lumber from drying too fast and warping. Once out in the lumberyard or on the job site, wood will con-

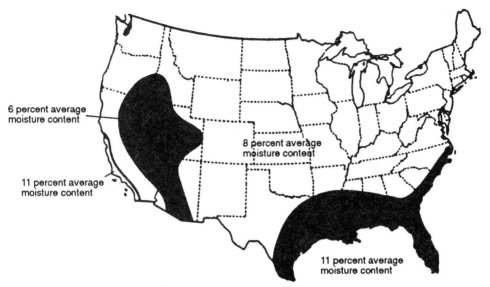

4-22 *Moisture content of interior woodwork varies throughout the country.*

6 percent average moisture content

8 percent average moisture content

11 percent average moisture content

11 percent average moisture content

tinue to dry (and shrink) until its MC is the same as the air surrounding it—unless it is stacked so that air can't circulate around it. In a heated building, wood continues drying until it reaches an average MC of eight percent. In the arid Southwest, the MC is typically six percent, while in the hot and humid South it's as high as 11 percent (see **4-22**).

In any case, this gradual drying out as the house is heated will make the house frame settle slightly and the joints between tightly laid floor and trim boards open up. Most of this shrinkage occurs during the first heating season, although there is always some inevitable swelling and shrinkage due to seasonal changes in ambient moisture levels. This is why, in quality construction, "dry" finish lumber is stacked inside in a heated space with plenty of air circulation several weeks before installation.

A board dries from its outermost layers inward; as the outside edges shrink, one side of the board becomes smaller than the other (see **4-23**). In response to these drying stresses, the wood will either split apart into *checks* or *shakes*, or it will curl upward, *cupping* across the grain. This is why stair treads and flooring boards are always laid *heart side up*; a convex cup is less objectionable than a concave trough. Extreme cupping is likely whenever the ratio of width to thickness of a board exceeds eight. This is why siding boards are seldom more than eight inches wide. When wood warps along the grain instead of across it, the resulting curve is either a *bow* or *crook*, depending on the plane of its direction. A *twist* is a compound curve. Other common defects that affect the strength of wood are large—*loose knots*, *splits*, *pitch pockets*, *waney edges*, and *red rot* (decay caused by fungus). The discoloration caused by *blue stain* fungus may render a board unsuitable for finish work, but it has no effect on its strength.

Except for ungraded lumber that is produced by small neighborhood sawmills, commercial lumber is either visually graded by defects or mechanically graded by fibre stress.

While there are many different grading systems in use, all lumber is classified into one of three broad categories, according to its cross-sectional modulus. These are *boards*, *dimension lumber*, and *timbers*. Boards are defined as one to 1½ inches thick and at least two inches wide. Dimension lumber is by definition two to five inches thick and at least two inches wide. Timbers are five inches or more in both thickness and width. Lumber is further differentiated according to its intended use. *Yard lumber* is for general construction. *Structural lumber* is reserved for specialized and high-stress applications. *Factory and shop lumber* (F&S) is used for furniture-making and other high-grade millwork.

In general, softwood boards are graded for appearance as well as intended use. Some grades apply only to a particular species such as redwood or Western red cedar. The highest grade board is usually *clear* (*clear heart*, for redwood and Western red cedar), which indicates free of any defects other than an occasional tiny knot. *Select* grades (often further distinguished by A and B select) have a few small tight knots. Depending on whether they are "No. 2" or "No. 3," *common* boards have a few more to "more than a few" defects.

To further confuse the issue, hardwood lumber is graded with a system different from softwood lumber. Since the names of the grades and their specifications varies between regions and among lumber products associations, check with your local supplier. It's not unusual for a lower-grade batch of lumber purchased from one distributor to be of better quality than a supposedly higher-

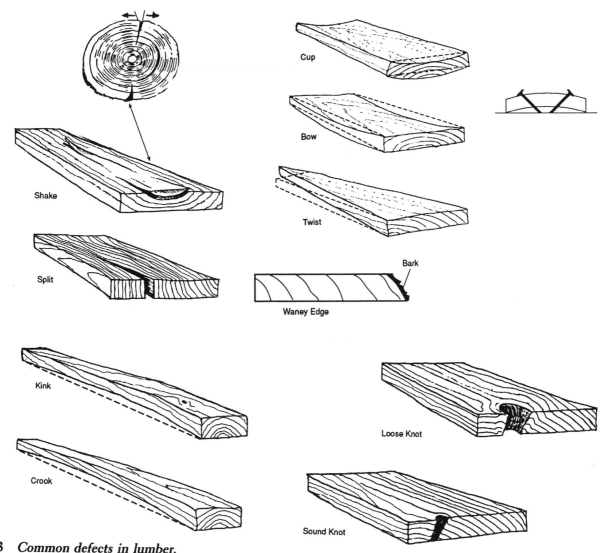

4-23 *Common defects in lumber.*

grade batch from another mill. For economy, choose the lowest grade that will meet the job specifications.

Dimension lumber up to 4×4 is divided into into *light framing* and *structural light framing* categories, according to its strength. Planks six inches and wider are classed as *structural joists and planks*. Each of these broad categories is broken down into several grades. Light framing is rated in order of decreasing quality as *construction, standard, utility,* and *economy*—with standard and utility grades most often used for general-purpose framing. *Stud* and *economy stud* grade are special categories, limited to studs 10 feet and under only. Economy-grade lumber can be so full of knots, red rot, or waney edges that it's hardly a worthwhile bargain. Grading for structural lumber runs from *select structural* down through No. 1, No. 2, No. 3, and economy grades. It is used for engineered applications such as truss construction and form work, as well as general rafter and framing purposes.

When pricing lumber, always look for the grade stamp. The price differential between a lumberyard and a discount do-it-yourself warehouse may reflect a higher-grade product.

Suppliers who cater to the weekend carpenter typically price lumber by the piece or *lineal* (also called *running*) foot. This makes it hard to compare the true cost of different sizes of lumber to each other. Professional builders price lumber by the *board foot*. One board foot is a volumetric measurement equal to a piece one inch thick and 12 inches square, or 144 cubic inches. Converting individual pieces to board-foot measure simplifies cost estimates. For example, your supplier quotes a price for 2×4s of "485 M," i.e., 485.00 US dollars per 1000 board feet.

4-24 *Nominal (rough-sawn) and actual (dressed) sizes of lumber and board foot per lineal foot.*

1×1	¾″ × ¾″	0.08 BF	2×3	1½″ × 2½″	0.5 BF
1×2	¾″ × 1½″	0.16	2×4	1½″ × 3½″	0.66
1×3	¾″ × 2½″	0.25	2×6	1½″ × 5½″	1.00
1×4	¾″ × 3½″	0.33	2×8	1½″ × 7¼″	1.33
1×5	¾″ × 4½″	0.41	2×10	1½″ × 9¼″	1.66
1×6	¾″ × 5½″	0.50	2×12	1½″ × 11¼″	2.00
1×8	¾″ × 7¼″	0.66	4×4	3½″ × 3½″	1.25
1×10	¾″ × 9¼″	0.83	4×6	3½″ × 5½″	2.00
1×12	¾″ × 11¼″	1.00	4×8	3½″ × 7¼″	2.66
			4×10	3½″ × 9¼″	3.33
⁴⁄₄*	²⁵⁄₃₂″		4×12	3½″ × 11¼″	4.00
⁵⁄₄	1⁵⁄₃₂″		6×6	5½″ × 5½″	3.00
⁶⁄₄	1¹³⁄₃₂″		6×8	5½″ × 7¼″	4.00
⁷⁄₄	1¹⁹⁄₃₂″		8×8	7¼″ × 7¼″	5.33
⁸⁄₄	1¹³⁄₁₆″		8×10	7¼″ × 9¼″	6.66
			8×12	7¼″ × 11¼″	8.00

*The nominal sizes for hardwood and select-grade finish board lumber of thicknesses greater than 1″ are often listed in "quarters." E.g., "⁴⁄₄" or "four quarters." Because of milling and drying shrinkage, the actual size of quarter-sized stock is ⁵⁄₃₂″ smaller than its nominal size.

Your takeoff from the plans totals 260 2×4×8s, 56 2×4×10s, 75 2×4×14s, and 20 2×4×16s. How much will this cost? Most builders refer to a table that shows board footage for given sizes and lengths. You can use a pocket calculator and the following formula just as easily.

$$\text{Bd ft} = \frac{\text{No. of pieces} \times \text{Thickness} \times \text{Width} \times \text{Length}}{12}$$

So then,

$$260 \times 2 \times 4 \times 8 / 12 = 1386.6 \text{ BF } +$$
$$56 \times 2 \times 4 \times 10/ 12 = 373.3 \text{ BF } +$$
$$75 \times 2 \times 4 \times 14/ 12 = 700 \text{ BF } +$$
$$20 \times 2 \times 4 \times 16/ 12 = 213.3 \text{ BF}$$

$$2673.2 \text{ BF} \times .485$$
$$= \$1296.50$$

Novice builders are often confused by the difference between the *nominal* and *dressed* sizes of boards and dimension lumber (see **4-24**). When it first comes from the log, a *rough-sawn* 2×4 has a nominal size of approximately two inches by four inches. Before modern laser-guided sawmills, the actual size of the lumber would vary somewhat according to the accuracy of both the machinery and its operator. *Dressing*, or planing, and shrinkage during drying yield a finished size which convention has established at 1½ inches by 3½ inches. Of course, lumber producers could just as easily oversize the rough-sawn dimensions to yield "full-size" dressed lumber, but this would just have resulted in a different set of rough-sawn and dressed dimensions and probably have cost more and slowed production. Unless otherwise noted, the values cited in span tables are for dressed lumber, not rough lumber.

The actual dimensions listed in **4-24** are for *dry* planed lumber. If planed when green, an extra ¹⁄₁₆ inch is added to the actual dimensions as an allowance for shrinkage. Occasionally, particularly with 2×8s through 2×12s, the actual finished width of the planks may be a quarter-inch different either way. Check your joist and rafter stock for true width, and adjust layout calculations, as needed. Width variations are likely if your supplier delivers mixed-lot lumber that was purchased from several different distributors.

5 An Overview of Framing Systems

Since tools for cutting timbers or rigid poles did not yet exist, early structures that served as living spaces were made by lashing bent saplings together and thatching them with twigs and bark. Modern carpentry began around 700 B.C., when iron tools became generally available. It was then possible to cut and shape timbers and poles and to assemble them into rigid skeletal frames of beams and braced posts that supported the roof and floors, an approach that is still the basis for framing systems today (see 5-1). The rigid frame allowed the builder to choose among a wide range of sheathing materials. Like the human frame, the strength of the traditional house was in its "bones," or, more precisely, in the joints which held them together. Thus, as buildings became larger and more complex over the next two and a half millennia, timber joinery logically evolved into an elaborate art.

In the colonial North America of two hundred and fifty years ago, wood was abundant and really more of a nuisance to be cleared away than a resource to be husbanded and renewed. The over-building represented by a log cabin or the heavy timber frame was in its time actually an economy of sorts, dictated by practical necessity. While early water-powered sawmills were a great improvement over the ancient hand-powered pit saws, the production of board lumber was a luxury well into the middle of the 19th century. It was easier and faster to hew logs into beams and planks than to saw them into studs and boards.

The modern "stick," or web-frame, style of building, in which loads are distributed across a matrix of relatively light framing members covered with a rigid structural skin, arose as a logical consequence of the introduction of steam-powered sawmills. These sawmills could turn out great quantities of boards and dimensioned lumber. At the same time, the invention of machinery for the mass production of nails and the advent of dependable long-distance rail transportation virtually assured the growth of the nascent building industry.

The framing systems that we take for granted today must have seemed both miraculous and threatening to the carpenters of the mid-19th century. Miraculous, because amazingly strong frames could be rapidly assembled from thin, "flimsy" sticks by relatively unskilled laborers using nails instead of complicated joints; and threatening because carpentry became an accessible, democratic art—no longer the jealously guarded preserve of a guild. A single family of homesteaders working by themselves could easily build their own house anywhere within wagon range of a railroad. The rapidity and ease of stick framing underwrote the incredible growth of cities and villages as the territories and states of the expanding United States were settled to the west.

5-1   *Modern "stick" framing allows structures of great strength to be quickly and easily assembled from light modular framing units.*

101

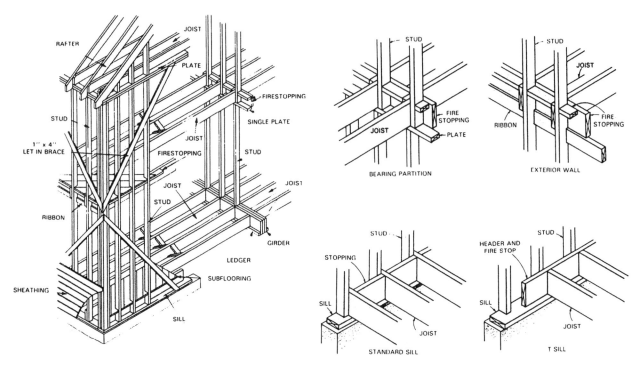

5-2 *The main difference between balloon and modern framing is that the wall studs run continuously from sill to plate while the floor joists for the second floor rest on a let-in ribbon. Installing the numerous pieces of firestop blocking is laborious.*

STICK FRAMING

Although not quite extinct, the balloon frame which is the predecessor of the modern platform, or "western," frame, is seldom used today. In balloon framing, the exterior wall studs run continuously from the sill to the rafter plate (see **5-2**). The ends of the second-floor joists rest on a let-in *ledger* (also called a *ribbon* or *ribband*) and are also nailed to the side of each stud. Solid blocking must be installed in each *stud cavity* (also called a *bay*) as a *firestop* to prevent a continuous chimney-like air channel. Balloon framing was well suited to the traditional plaster interior finishes of early times, before the widespread use of gypsum wallboard. Because it has so little cross-sectional lumber, the shrinkage which would crack plaster walls is practically eliminated, even with somewhat green framing. This also makes balloon framing a good choice when a stuccoed exterior finish is called for. Because it also contains fewer *hinges*, a two-storey balloon frame is more rigid and earthquake-resistant than a platform frame. Despite these particular advantages, balloon framing is more awkward and labor-intensive than platform framing. Furthermore, both two-storey houses and 18-foot- to 20-foot-long studs are less common and more costly nowadays.

In platform or western framing, the first-floor deck is built on top of the foundation before the walls are framed (see **5-3**). This provides an ideal open and level work platform, upon which the wall frames are easily and rapidly laid out and assembled. The second-floor deck bears directly on top of the walls and interior partitions. Platform framing is adequate for structures up to four stories tall. Since the settlement caused by shrinkage is even and uniform throughout the structure, it has no significant effects as long as dry wood is used for framing. Firestops are also built into the floor platforms. As long as it bridges the joints between floor decks and wall studs, plywood sheathing confers more than sufficient rigidity upon even a multi-storey platform frame.

All things considered, platform framing is probably the best system to use for building your own house within a reasonable amount of time for a reasonable amount of money. No other system is quite as easy to master or more forgiving of inevitable small mistakes. The genius of platform framing is that it breaks the complex whole of a house frame into several discrete, easy-to-understand, easy-to-build parts. Since errors can be corrected or compensated for at each stage, presupposing just ordinary competence, the chance of making a really serious mistake is quite small.

The main elements of a platform frame are the floor deck, walls, interior partitions, second-floor deck, roof frame, and exterior sheathing (see **5-4**).

102

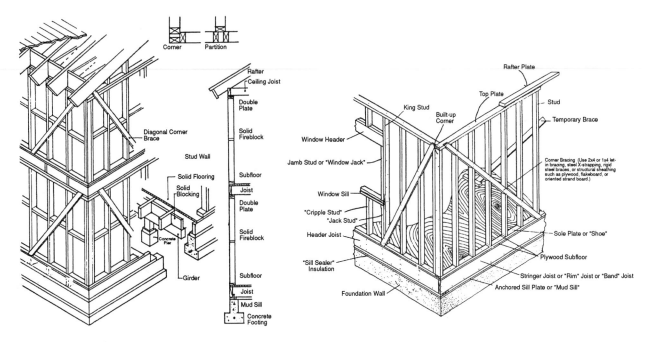

5-3 *Note how the floor platforms resting on top of the wall frames and the joist headers provide the firestop between floors. The relative absence of blocking and the shorter walls make this a very fast way to frame.*

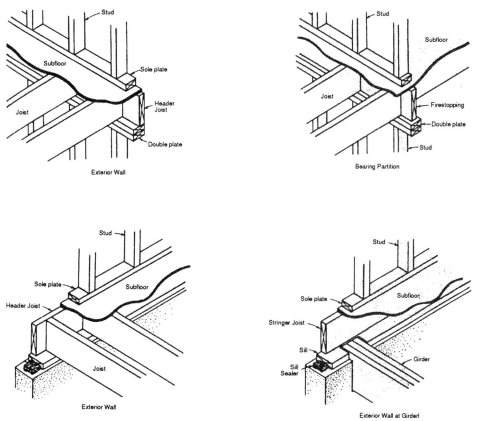

5-4 *Elements of a platform frame.*

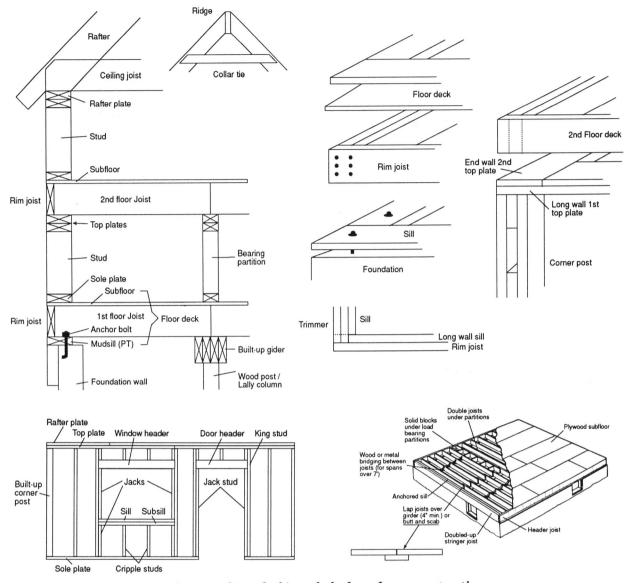

5-5 *Vertical alignment and horizontal interlocking of platform frame construction.*

The *mudsill* (or just plain *sill*) is the flatwise 2×6 (sometimes 2×8 or 2×10) that is bolted down to or otherwise attached to the top of the foundation wall (see **5-5**). Because wood in contact with masonry will absorb water by capillary action, which can cause it to rot or invite termite infestation, most building codes today require the sill to be pressure-treated wood. With pier-and-wood-post foundations, the sill is a beam, either of solid timber or of planks nailed together.

Depending on the area of the floor plan and the spans of the floor joists, one or more *girders*, or *carrying beams*, supported on wood posts or concrete-filled steel *lally columns*, span the foundation and carry one end of the floor joists. The other end of the joists is nailed to the sill. The ends of the joists butt perpendicularly against a *rim* (also called a *band* or *header*) *joist*. The first and last floor joists (*stringer* joists), which run parallel to the sill, are doubled up to provide a bearing surface for the end walls of the house. Solid *blocking* or open wood or metal *bridging* is nailed between the joist spans to stiffen them. A *subfloor* of plywood (formerly diagonally applied tongue-and-groove board) is nailed and/or glued across the joists to complete the floor deck (refer to **5-5**).

A typical wall frame consists of vertical *studs* nailed between two horizontal *plates*. The bottom plate is the *sole plate*, or *shoe*. Since it transmits the brunt of the building load to the studs, the *top plate* is always doubled up (the uppermost plate, to which the rafters are attached, is the *rafter plate*).

Stick framing is always vertically aligned (see **5-6**)—i.e., each rafter is nailed to the rafter plate directly over a wall stud, which in turn is nailed to a sole plate directly over a floor joist. This not only simplifies the framing process, but takes full advantage of the great strength of wood in compression by transmitting loads downwards to the foundation through solid wood.

In addition to vertical alignment, stick frames are horizontally interlocking. Just as the mortar joints in a block wall are staggered, the joints between the horizontal layers of a frame are offset for shear resistance. This requires some forethought, not only for sizing various framing members, but as to the order of their assembly. For example, the end wall sills are normally cut to fit between the long wall sills which run the full length of the house, i.e., perpendicular to the run of the floor joists. The rim (or header) joist follows the run of the long wall sill, overlapping the face of the doubled or tripled-up stringer joist and conveniently tying the sills together at their corner joint (refer to **5-5**). The rafter plate is set back at the corner post so that the end wall rafter plate ties the corners together. The second-floor deck strengthens this connection by overlapping it just as with the sill.

House frames are also directional. The layout for the spacing of each element of the frame—i.e., the joists, the studs, and the rafters—always starts from the same end of the house and proceeds in the same direction to maintain vertical alignment. By keeping everything "on the right side of the line," mistakes are avoided, especially with overlapping sets of floor joists. This symmetry also aids in locating studs behind finished walls.

When studs must be cut to make room for a window or door opening, the portion of the building load that the amputated studs would have carried must be shifted horizontally to intact studs by a *header* (refer to **5-5**). Since they carry the loads of more than one stud like a beam in tension, headers must be thicker than doubled-up plates. Like any beam, the depth of a header depends on its span and on the load it must carry. Whatever the size of a header, it must always bear solidly on a shorter *jack* (or *trimmer*) stud, nailed into a full-length *king* (or *backer*) stud. Doubling up studs adds the stiffness it takes to resist the heavier compression load of the header. Jack studs for doors extend from the header to the sole plate. For windows, the jack stud usually rests on a sill, which is in turn carried on a shorter stud. The rest of the short *cripple* studs between the windowsill and the sole plate aren't actually load-bearing, but are used to maintain the spacing module for nailing the sheathing and wall finish.

Openings in a floor deck for a stairwell or in the roof for a dormer or skylight are structurally analogous to wall openings (see **5-7**). The extra loads are carried on doubled- or tripled-up *trimmer* joists or rafters. In floor decks, the

5-6 *Vertical alignment allows each member of a stick frame to transmit a small part of the building load continuously from the rafters to the foundation.*

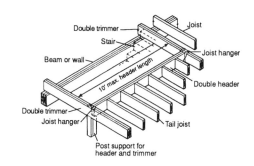

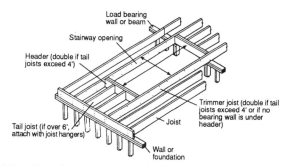

5-7 *Detail of stair-opening framing.*

layout of the framing depends on whether the opening is parallel with or perpendicular to the run of the joists and the length of the short (*tail*) joists.

When the plans call for a second storey, the second-floor deck is framed exactly the same as the first, except that the outer ends of the joists rest on the top plate while their interior ends are supported by a *bearing partition*. These walls are always centered over a girder or otherwise continuously and solidly supported.

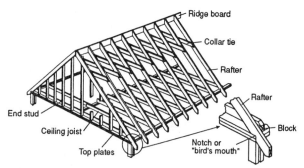

5-8 *Typical rafter-framing for a pitched roof.*

As the span tables make clear (refer to the Appendices), an attic floor joist can also be a ceiling joist, but a ceiling joist isn't necessarily a floor joist. The term ceiling joist generally refers to lighter joists whose structural purpose is to tie the walls together to resist the outward thrust of the roof load. The fact that they support a finished ceiling is almost incidental. Attic joists are load-bearing ceiling joists.

A rafter is a sloped ceiling joist. In conventional framing, one end of the rafter is notched to rest on top of the rafter plate and the other end is cut on an angle to fit against the *ridge* board (see **5-8**).

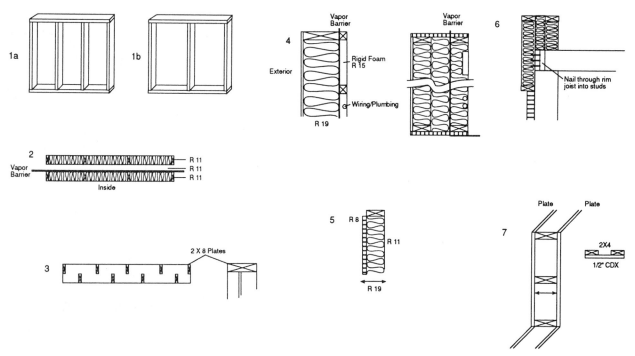

5-9 *Alternative framing systems for increased energy efficiency: (1a) With a standard 2×4 16-inch on-center wall, the stud cavities can hold 3½ inches (R-11) of fibreglass insulation; (1b) 2×6 on 24-inch on-center framing accommodates 5½ inches (R-19) of fibreglass; (2) with "double-wall" framing, two separate 2×4 wall frames joined by a 10½-inch-wide plywood plate are filled with three layers of 3½-inch fibreglass (total of R-33); if the vapor barrier is installed behind the innermost layer of fibreglass instead of over it, pipes and wires can be run through the wall without puncturing the barrier; (3) since they require only 2×8 plates, "staggered stud" walls use up less interior space; but, unless filled with blown cellulose insulation (which can be packed to greater density than fibreglass batts), this method offers only R-22 with the same lumber cost as a double-wall; (4) the horizontal bays formed by nailing 2×2s (16 inches on-center) across 2×6 wall studs filled with fibreglass batts and covered with a continuous vapor barrier are a convenient raceway for wiring and plumbing; when these bays are filled with 1½ inches of "Hi-R" polyisocyanurate rigid foam (approx. R-10), the wall has a very respectable R-value of 29; (5) Hi-R foam panels can also be applied to either the interior or exterior side of a standard 2×4 frame to make an R-19 wall; (6) by hanging the non-load-bearing third of this double-wall frame outside the foundation wall, not quite as much interior space need be sacrificed to energy efficiency; (7) some builders have used simple plywood and 2×4 vertical trusses to frame 16- to 24-inch-deep walls for the R-50 to R-60 values of blown-in insulation called for by superinsulated construction in arctic climates; the channels between the soles and plates makes a convenient raceway for wiring.*

Besides exerting an outward thrust against the walls, roof rafters also tend to sag in mid-span. *Collar ties* nailed horizontally across each pair of rafters are necessary to resist both these tendencies. In single-storey and storey-and-a-half Cape designs, collar ties also serve as ceiling joists. Inexperienced builders can create structural problems by omitting collar ties or failing to provide a structural equivalent in cathedral and other vaulted-ceiling designs.

Today, more homes are probably framed with prefabricated *roof trusses* than with conventional rafters. Labor savings make roof trusses attractive to amateur and commercial builders alike. Since the bottom chord of the roof truss also functions as a ceiling joist, bearing partitions aren't necessary, and the interior partitions can be framed after the roof is on. Roof trusses could make a big difference if getting the house closed-in as fast as possible is critical.

In stick framing, (vertical) sheathing and (horizontal) decking not only cover the frame, but act structurally to distribute loads to the framing members and to resist racking forces. They fulfill the same role as the knee braces of a timber frame.

ADAPTATIONS OF STICK FRAMING FOR INCREASED ENERGY EFFICIENCY

In response to the sudden rise in the cost of fossil fuels during the "energy crisis" of the 1970s, the homebuilding industry developed framing techniques that permitted thicker insulation to be installed in the *building envelope*—the architectural term for the surfaces of the house that enclose its heated portions. The most widely adopted was the switch from 2×4 framing on 16-inch centers to 2×6s on 24-inch centers. Super-insulated houses using a repertoire of entirely new framing and finishing methods were devised to increase insulation to an even greater level and to create a virtually air-tight building envelope. Some of these techniques, shown in **5-9,** are still experimental or of questionable cost-effectiveness. But the importance of maintaining the integrity of the interior vapor barrier has been established beyond doubt.

The widespread adoption of rigid foam insulation panels applied either to the outside of the frame as non-structural sheathing, or to the inside under the drywall, was also another way to increase energy efficiency while utilizing inexpensive 2×4 framing.

TRADITIONAL MORTISE-AND-TENON FRAMING

Post-and-beam heavy timber framing with traditional mortise-and-tenon pegged-wood joints is enjoying something of a renaissance among owner-builders and high-end custom homebuilders alike (see **5-10**).

The basic framing module of the traditional one-and-a-half- to two-storey post-and-beam frame is the *bent*, which usually consists of two full-height corner posts, a center post, and a connecting beam called a *girt* (see **5-11**). Bents run parallel with the end walls. The bottoms of the posts are joined to a continuous heavy sill beam, which is bolted to the foundation wall.

5-10 *Traditional mortise-and-tenon timber framing is attractive to many owner-builders. The infill framing between the posts allows a great deal of freedom with window placement.*

5-11 *An owner-builder and friends raise an 8×8 bent. Note the post tenons about to slip into the sill mortise and the half-lapped sill joints. Also note how the next bent has already been assembled on the floor deck.*

5-12　Raising the end girt. Floor joist beams will drop into the mortises notched in the girts.

5-13　Even with a lot of helping hands, lifting a heavy plate beam into position is a big job. Note the come-along and chain used to pull the connecting girts together and the shouldered joints that they rest on in the post.

5-14　The plate beam is set over the post tenons to lock the front wall and connecting girts together.

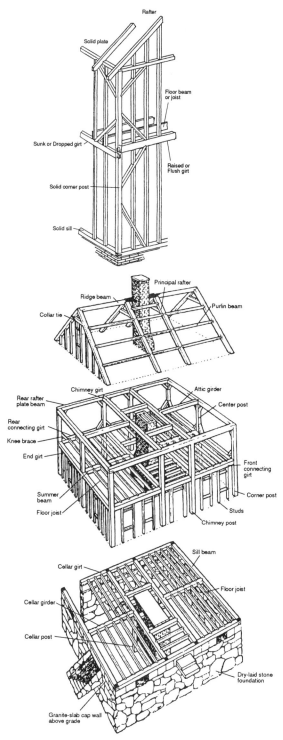

5-15　There are an almost infinite number of variations on the timber frame. Shown are a typical frame corner for a one-and-a-half storey traditional New England Cape and the two-storey "braced frame" design, which immediately preceded the evolution of the stick frame.

108

A typical small traditional Cape-style frame contains two *end girts*—one for each end wall of the house (see **5-12**)—and two intermediate *chimney girts*, whether or not there is a central chimney. Girts junction like oversized ceiling joists to tie the long walls of the house together and resist the outward thrust of the roof. The bents are joined to each other at the tops of the end posts by a continuous *rafter plate beam* (see **5-13** and **5-14**). The floor joists for the second floor or attic floor are carried by front and rear *connecting girts* mortised between each set of bents (see **5-15**). At midspan, these joists are mortised into a heavy *summer beam*, which is supported by the end girt and chimney girt center posts. As an alternative to the summer beam, the floor joists can be run perpendicular to the girts instead. Roof framing is similar.

Principal rafters carry lighter horizontal *purlin beams* or else heavy timber rafters run from the rafter plate beam to the ridge beam as in a conventional frame.

Contrary to popular image, except for complicated roof designs, most timber frame joints aren't especially intricate or difficult to make. But since the strength and squareness of the frame as well as its appearance depend on a tight fit, every joint must be very carefully and accurately cut. Thus, traditional timber framing is not for the impatient or unskilled.

Although it may take several hundred joints to connect the timbers in an average house frame, all but a few of them will be variations or combinations of three basic joints: the mortise-and-tenon, the lap joint, and the dovetail (see **5-16**).

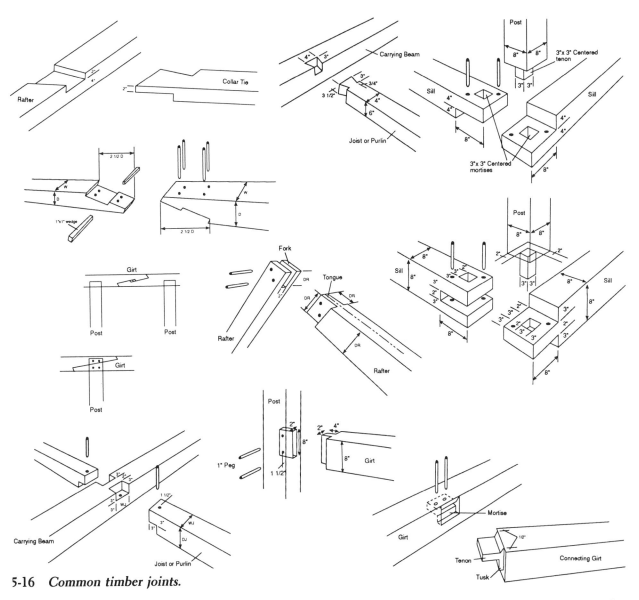

5-16 *Common timber joints.*

DIFFERENCE BETWEEN TIMBER FRAMING AND STICK FRAMING

In timber frames, the building loads are concentrated by heavy horizontal beams onto a relatively few upright posts. The traditional wall sheathing of horizontal boarding nailed to haphazard studs contributed very little to the stiffness of the frame. This arrangement puts a great deal of stress on the joints between framing members. A joint must be designed not to pull apart and be of sufficient stiffness to withstand the internal shear and compression forces that would cause the wood to break.

Although it might seem that a traditional timber frame is massively overbuilt, there is a structural necessity for the outsized dimensions of its timbers. There must be enough "meat" on the timbers to cut a suitably strong joint. While smaller timbers could certainly carry the loads, the section modulus of their joints would be too small to hold together.

In a stick frame, building loads are dispersed across many more framing members so that no one joint is subjected to any significant shear stress. Besides resisting racking, the wall sheathing stiffens the frame, which helps it to carry the loads by making it act like a composite beam. The forces are so dispersed that thin wire nails make sufficiently strong connections in most situations.

CLOSING IN THE POST-AND-BEAM FRAME

Since the building loads are carried by posts spaced at wide intervals in the walls, large openings can be framed without headers. While this does allow a great deal of flexibility in the sizing and patterning of windows, it doesn't actually save as much framing lumber as it would seem. Two LF (linear feet) of 8×8 beam contain 10.6 BF (board feet) of lumber. Two LF of 2×6-framed stud wall contains 14 BF. But the building envelope must still be attached to something. Until recently, this was usually a 2×4 or 2×6 nonstructural framework, built between the timber bays—the *in-fill* method—or hung from the outside of frame—the *curtain-wall* method (see **5-17**). Al-

though no window headers are required, and studs can be installed horizontally between posts for siding nailers, post-and-beam framing actually uses more, not less, framing lumber and labor than conventional framing.

The advantage of the in-fill method is that the timber frame and filler frame are tied together by the exterior plywood sheathing. This provides racking resistance and also eliminates or reduces the need for mortised-in knee braces. Not only does this allow more leeway in window layout and a less cluttered finished appearance in a small house, it also saves a lot of time-consuming and precise notching.

The disadvantage of in-fill framing is that a wall thick enough to be energy-efficient leaves most of the timber frame hidden behind it. Furthermore, attaching windows and door jambs directly to large, usually green, timbers can cause infiltration problems, cracking of drywall joints, and sticking of doors and windows as the timbers shrink.

The *curtain wall* approach addresses these drawbacks by hanging the shell of the house on the outside of the timber frame. A lip must be built into the foundation wall or the timber frame must be set back on the floor deck in order to provide support for the bottom of the curtain wall. Adding a layer of rigid foam insulation to the inside of the curtain wall between each timber bay will increase energy efficiency without drastically reducing the exposure of the timbers.

Beginning in the 1980s, many timber framers began to close in their frames with prefabricated *stress-skin* panels instead of conventional stick framing (see **5-18**). The term stress-skin panel technically refers to the plywood-skinned wood framework that functions like a torsion beam under load, and which had been used for many years in commercial construction. As adapted to post-and-beam framing, nonstructural panels consist of a 5½-inch layer of extruded polystyrene (EPS) foam insulation laminated to a sandwich of plywood or waferboard facing and drywall. The waferboard provides a nailing base for the exterior siding while the drywall is the interior finish. To protect the drywall facing against rain, the panels aren't installed until after the frame is roofed over. (An entire house can be closed in a single day.) Some builders prefer structural

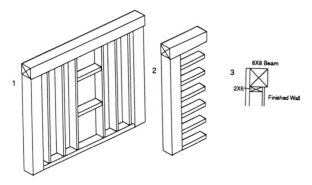

5-17 *Post-and-beam framed walls can be finished by in-filling between the timbers or by setting an external curtain wall on a ledge built into the foundation.*

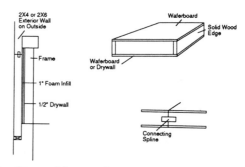

5-18 *Stress-skin panels.*

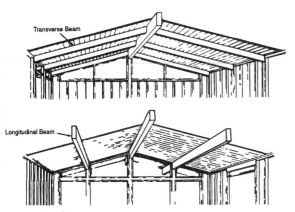

5-19 *In the* transverse beam *system of plank-and-beam framing, rafters rest directly over wall posts which are braced against lateral movement by filler panel frames. The tops of the rafters are attached to the side or supported on top of a heavy ridge beam. In a* longitudinal beam *frame one or more pairs of beams running parallel to the ridge beam carry the roof planking instead.*

5-20 *This post-and-beam framing utilizes built-up header beams lapped and bolted to built-up posts in a system developed by architect and owner-builder advocate Alex Wade.*

panels, consisting of waferboard on both faces. There is no need to protect them from the weather, and when spiked to the frame, they make it structurally rigid. Timber knee braces are likewise unnecessary. Unfaced nonstructural panels can also be installed between timber bays. Structural panels containing urethane insulation are considerably more expensive than polystyrene, but offer more R-value per inch. These are often used for roof decks. Structural panels can also be used entirely on their own, without any timber frame at all.

Stress-skin panels suffer from several of their own drawbacks. There are currently about a dozen different types of panels produced by more than 75 different manufacturers. Not all of them have been approved for use by local building codes.

The application of asphalt shingles directly over stress-skin panels (or rigid foam insulation) will void some manufacturer's warranties. Heat buildup causes shingles to wear out prematurely. Compliance with fire codes may also be a problem. Some panel manufacturers offer vented roofing panels. An effective, but expensive, solution is to apply the shingles to a deck nailed to vertical strapping laid over the panels.

Carpenter ants seem to have an inordinate fondness for tunnelling through the foam. Termite shields, pressure-treated wood at sills, and treating the foundation, surface grade, and lower portions of the panel with persistent insecticides are all recommended prevention strategies.

Running wires and plumbing through panels can often be problematic. Many builders prefer to sidestep these difficulties by concealing mechanicals behind surface-mounted raceways. Although the panels themselves are

light enough to be assembled by hand, they can be awkward to handle and cut. For safety's sake, roofing panels are best lifted into place with a boom truck or light crane.

Finally, the energy efficiency of stress-skin panels isn't cheap. While professional builders find that the high cost of the panels compared to the materials for conventional stick framing is usually offset by savings in labor, the same economy doesn't necessarily work for an owner-builder—particularly when the added cost of a timber frame is factored in.

Another purported advantage of post-and-beam framing is that the underside of the floor decking or roof planks can also serve as a finished ceiling, thereby saving on materials and labor. But, once again, the absence of concealed spaces in outside walls and ceilings requires careful planning for the successful integration of wiring, plumbing, and HVAC systems.

A timber frame isn't inherently stronger, longer-lived, or more energy-efficient than a well-built stick-framed house. Ultimately, the decision to build a timber frame rests not on considerations of economy, but on aesthetics. People are willing to pay a premium for a timber-frame house because it is undeniably beautiful to look at and comfortable to live with.

ALTERNATIVES TO TRADITIONAL TIMBER FRAMING

There are several contemporary alternatives to traditional timber framing that are much less labor-intensive (see **5-19** and **5-20**).

Because interior supporting posts are almost entirely eliminated, plank-and-beam construction allows the maximum use of open space design. The bays between posts are filled in with conventional wall framing. The only joints required for plank-and-beam framing are simple butt and lap joints. These are usually reinforced with heavy-duty factory-made metal connectors or steel dowels. Unless somehow concealed, the appearance of standard heavy-framing anchors and connectors will detract from the design. On the other hand, intentionally exposed custom-forged or architectural-grade-steel connectors and heavy carriage bolts or lag screws can be an attractive design feature.

Modern *glu-lam* (glue-laminated) timbers, which can be manufactured to virtually any load specification, permit greater architectural freedom than traditional timber framing. Other than the need for a crane to place the beams, this kind of timber framing is no more complicated than ordinary stud-wall construction.

STICK-FRAMED WALLS AND A TIMBERED CEILING

Much of the appeal of a timber-frame house is in its massive exposed ceiling beams. The hybrid system shown in **5-21** combines the aesthetic beauty of timber ceiling joists with the speed and flexibility of platform framing.

Except for the omission of window and door headers, the exterior walls are conventionally framed with 2×4s at 16 inches on-center. The walls carry 6×8 *rim beams* instead of rim or header joists. This leaves two inches of beam showing on the finished interior wall. For 2×6 framing, an 8×8 rim beam will give the same reveal. The outside of the frame is then covered with one-inch foam sheathing.

5-21 *This hybrid timber-and-stick framing system uses mortised beams set on top of conventional 2×4 wall frames. The timber floor joists create an exposed-beam ceiling.*

Notches for 4×8 floor joists on 32-inch centers are cut 3½ inches deep across the interior face of the rim beam. This depth allows the joist to bear a full 1½ inches on the stud wall rather than being carried by the mortise. Because they run across the entire depth of the rim beam, the notches are easily made by chiselling out repeated scoring cuts of a circular saw.

The other end of the joist rests in a 1½-inch-deep, full cross-section notch cut into an 8×10 or 8×12 summer beam. Use a two-inch-wide Forstner bit (which cuts a clean-sided flat-bottomed hole) to remove the stock between the outlines of the notch and square up the corners with a two-inch timber-framer's chisel. The finished notch should be tight enough so that the joist has to be pounded into it, but not so tight that its edges are crushed. "Easing," or *chamfering*, the edges of the notch with a block plane helps. A fence post maul (a flat-faced, heavy cast-iron hammer that should never be used to strike anything but wood) is a useful "persuader."

The corners of the rim beams are joined by simple vertical half-lap joints, and secured with pins made from 12-inch lengths of ½-inch Rebar. These are pounded into predrilled holes with a two-pound sledge. The rim beams themselves are toenailed to the doubled wall plate with 20d spikes every two feet along their outside face. Toenailing will usually pull a bowed timber back into line. If the timber bows up from the wall instead, use a pipe clamp or heavy bar clamp to pull it down before driving six-inch ring-shank *pole-barn* nails up through the wall plates and into the beam at roughly six-foot intervals along the walls and within three feet of each corner.

Drive two 12-inch-long "log-cabin" spikes through the face of the rim beam into the ends of each joist. Toenail two 20d spikes through the top of each joist at the summer beam.

Unless it ends at a central stairwell or chimney, the summer beam normally runs the full length of the house. It's easier to splice two beams over a center post than to use a single-span beam. If exposed, this joint should be given ornamental treatment.

The end of the summer beam that will be buried in the wall frame is supported on a built-up 2×4 post and locked into place with full-length studs at each side (see **5-22**).

Use a template to check the accuracy of the summer-beam joint faces. A boatbuilder's slick, which looks like an oversized chisel with an extra-long handle, is used to finish the faces of the joints mirror smooth. The flat of the blade is held against the work and the handle is pushed like a plane, not struck like a chisel. Check the joint for fit before lifting it into place. If the top of the joint is tight while the bottom is open or if only one face closes, cut carefully down along the line of the joint with a sharp handsaw to relieve the excess stock and tighten the fit.

Sawhorses stout enough for timber framing should be built from 2×8 or 2×10 stock (see **5-23**). Always treat

5-22 *The intersection of the summer beam and the end wall girts clearly shows the reveal that will remain exposed after the interior walls are installed. A 2×8 false post milled from the same lumber as the timbers will be set under the 8×12 summer beam before nailing up the wall boards.*

5-24 *Two-by-fours on edge on 16-inch centers are laid across 4×8 beams with 32-inch centers.*

framing timbers like finish lumber, not framing lumber; wash your hands before handling them, and don't walk on them or rest them on a dirty deck or on the ground. Use a protective block when pounding joints together. A short length of 1½-inch or 3-inch PVC pipe makes a handy roller for moving timbers about on the floor deck. To raise or carry even very heavy green timbers from the floor deck to the sawhorses, slide a 2×3 or 2×4 hardwood cradle under each end, and lift from both sides. Using planed, rather than rough-sawn, timbers makes it much easier to cut and fit accurate joints. If the finished dimensions of the timbers also match dimension lumber standards, they can be combined with ordinary framing lumber, as needed.

Instead of nailing tongue-and-groove decking over the timber floor joists, nail 2×4s on edge at 16 inches on-center across them (see **5-24**). When covered with ¾-inch tongue-and-groove underlayment plywood, glued and nailed, this subfloor system makes it a lot easier to conceal wiring and plumbing (see **5-25**).

5-23 *Beams are supported for notching on extra-strong sawhorses. A 12-inch circular saw can accurately make cuts through an 8×8 beam in two passes. Note the steel diagonal brace in the partition wall; you can't have too much bracing in an open-plan house.*

5-25 *A subfloor deck of ¾-inch tongue-and-groove plywood is nailed and glued to the stringers. Note the dovetailed notch in the summer beam over the center post.*

113

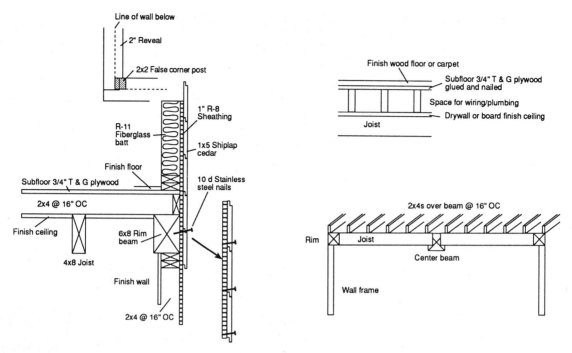

5-26 *The finish ceiling is hung from the undersides of 2×4 stringers on which a tongue-and-groove plywood subfloor deck is glued and nailed—making a convenient chase for plumbing, wiring, and heating runs.*

Unlike solid decking, no special measures are needed to protect the floor from water or construction damage. The finished ceiling is hung from the underside of the 2×4s between the exposed joists.

Finally, 2×8 stock—cut from the same wood as the timbers—is screwed to the built-up posts under the sum-mer beam (and any other carrying beam) and 2×2 stock under each corner to imitate structural center and beam posts. When the finished interior wall is butted to them, these false posts are indistinguishable from the reveal of a true post. For best appearance, the screws are countersunk and plugged with wood dowels.

6 Framing the Floor

Checking the Foundation

A square and level house begins with the foundation (see **6-1**). It's a moment of truth, cast in solid concrete. Sight down the edge of the wall. Except for an inevitable slight dip over a window opening, the top of the wall should appear almost perfectly straight and level (see **6-2**). Since an "eyeball level" can pick up deviations as small as $1/32$ of an inch, some small humps and bows will always show up.

Just because the top of a wall "reads" *straight*, doesn't mean that the plane of the foundation is *level*. This initial check should be confirmed with a transit level. Pencil the transit readings onto the concrete for future reference. The first reading is the *benchmark*. Readings above this show how much the wall is below the benchmark; numbers below it, how much higher the wall is than it should be (refer to **6-2**). Since it will "disappear" into the general "slop" of the frame, an overall difference of a quarter-inch or less between transit readings taken at all four corners and midway points along the top of each wall indicates that the wall is, for all practical purposes, level.

Since a level floor requires a level wall, differences greater than this must be corrected by shimming up low spots or hewing down high ones. Dips can be levelled out by filling them in with grout made of patching concrete (unlike regular concrete, patching concrete can be feathered to a fine edge). For humps, the underside of the sill is hewn to fit with a chisel or power plane. Unless prohibited by local codes—except for a small dip or hump—it's much easier to let the mudsill follow the foundation wall and make the adjustments in the rim and stringer joists instead.

6-1 *Before you start framing, check the top of the foundation wall for level with a transit level.*

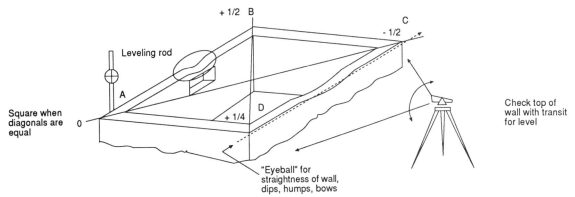

6-2 *If the length of the diagonals AC and BD are equal, the foundation is square. In this example, if the initial reading at point (A) is the control point and point (B) reads $1/2$ inch high, (C) is $1/2$ inch low, and (D) is $1/4$ inch high, the overall difference between (B) and (C) of one inch and between (D) and (C) of $3/4$ inch are both unacceptable. The floor deck must be lowered $1/2$ inch from (A) towards (B), raised $1/2$ inch from (B) towards (C), and raised $1/2$ inch from (D) to (C). The simplest way to do this is to assign the control point to the lowest reading and lower the floor deck at the other points to make it level (refer to 6-9).*

115

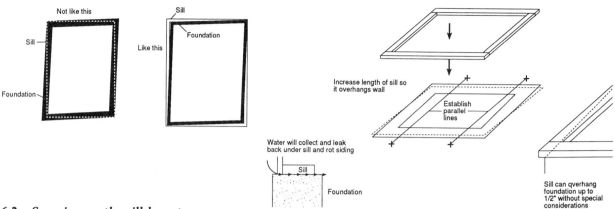

6-3 *Squaring up the sill layout.*

After checking the foundation wall for level, check it for square by measuring the diagonals (see **6-3**). Given the nature of concrete form work, it's unlikely that they'll measure exactly the same. Anything under an inch is *de facto* perfect. The foundation is squared up by overhanging or setting back the mudsills slightly at opposite corners, as necessary. The guide lines to which the mudsills will be set are moved in or out on the foundation wall to make true right angles. Adjustments of up to a half-inch won't be easily detectable or cause any structural problems.

However, if the foundation is several inches out of square, squaring up the sills will increase the width or length of the floor deck, which could require extra sheathing and longer floor joists—and more framing lumber. Since this will be costly in both materials and labor, it's a good idea to withhold the concrete subcontractor's final payment until after the foundation is checked for square and level.

SETTING THE SILLS

Sweep the top of the wall clean. Assuming the foundation wall is square, measure in from the face of the wall (or the "adjusted" face of the wall if the foundation is not square) and make *tick* marks on the concrete at each corner at a point equal to the width of the mudsill less the amount it overhangs the foundation insulation—e.g., for a 2×8 sill with a one-inch overhang, the mark is at 6¼

inches. Snap a chalk line from mark to mark along the length of each wall; the inside edge of the mudsill will follow this line. (Experienced carpenters carry two chalk reels, one for red chalk, the other for blue. Red shows up better on concrete and doesn't rub or wash off as easily as blue chalk, which is better for roofing and siding, where it won't stain finished work.)

Just because their location was shown on the foundation plan doesn't mean all the anchor bolts will actually be in the right places. If there isn't a bolt within six to 12 inches of each end and at least every six feet of each piece of sill stock, one must be retrofited (see **6-4**). To prevent damage, allow the concrete to harden before drilling and setting any expansion anchors. Also, rather than depend on the concrete subcontractor to leave nuts and washers on every bolt, keep an extra supply on hand.

There are two ways to mark the location of the anchor bolts on the sill (see **6-5**). First, set a length of sill stock on edge against the bolts, and mark their centers on the wood. Then, measure in from the chalk line to the bolts, and locate the second center line on the first. The second method is much faster but won't give accurate results if the sill stock is bowed. With a helper, or else by resting it on blocks, lay the sill on top of the bolts, and line it up to the chalk line on the wall with a square or wood block. Hit the board with your hammer over each bolt so that the board will be marked by the bolts.

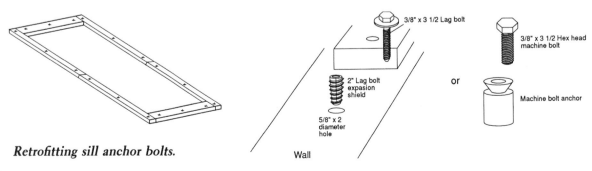

6-4 *Retrofitting sill anchor bolts.*

116

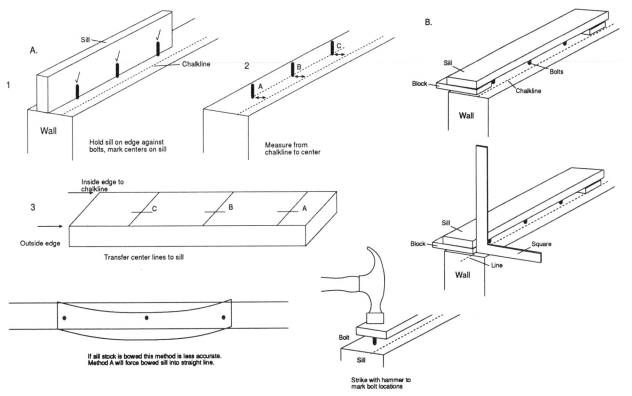

6-5 *Since the sill stock will be turned over, make sure to transpose the marks to the correct edge of the board when measuring back from the chalk line to the centerpoints of the anchor bolts. Unlike the second method, the first will straighten bowed sill stock.*

Drill a ⅝-inch hole through the sill at each bolt mark. The extra play makes it easier to fit the sill over the ½-inch anchor bolts. The drilled sills can be used as a template to mark the holes in the sheet-metal termite shield (if required). If preformed shield stock is not available in your area, it can be fabricated at a sheet-metal shop from 12-inch-wide 26-gauge galvanized steel or aluminum (see 6-6). Whether or not a termite shield is used, install the *sill sealer*—a thin batt of insulation that compresses to block infiltration through the crack between the masonry and the sill—just before setting the sills. It doesn't take much of a breeze to blow it off the bolts.

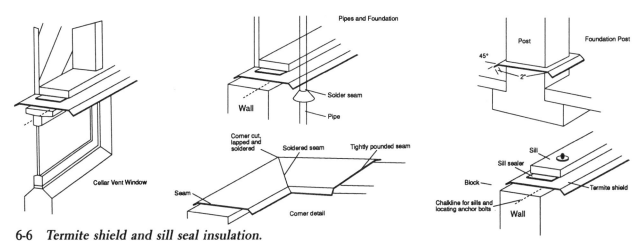

6-6 *Termite shield and sill seal insulation.*

Building codes have been amended to specify that pressure-treated lumber must be used for sill stock as a defense against decay and insect damage. Pressure-treated lumber can vary noticeably in width and quality, especially if batches from different shipments are mixed to fill your order. Personally select straight, square-edged, and fairly knot-free pieces for sill stock, rather than count on the luck of your supplier's draw.

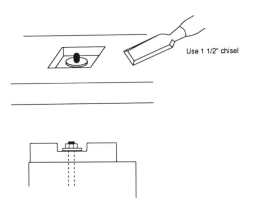

Use 1 1/2" chisel

6-7   *Notching sills for short anchor bolts.*

If the anchor bolts were properly set, they should project about two inches above the concrete, which allows just enough purchase to start the nut on the bolt. Otherwise, cut a recess in the face of the sill with a 1½-inch-wide chisel, and countersink the washer and nut (see **6-7**). Tighten down the bolts with a socket wrench, and toenail the sills together at the corners to bring their faces flush.

SETTING THE RIM AND STRINGER JOISTS

Select straight stock for rim joists. A crowned rim joist won't rest flat on a level sill. The toenails that attach the rim joist to the sill will split its bottom edge before pulling it very far down. If there isn't enough straight stock in your joist pile or you forgot to check, use a bar clamp to pull the joist down tight against the sill (see **6-8**). Another fix for a bowed rim joist is to set it with the crown facing downwards. Nail the tangential area to the sill first, and then pull down the ends of the joist by standing on them as you nail them to the sill. It usually helps to work out the bow gradually by nailing at intervals along the length of the joist rather than trying to close the entire gap with a single toenail. In any case, the rim joist will almost always flatten out once the floor joists are nailed into it and the floor deck is laid. To help close the gap, don't toenail the floor joists to the mudsill.

Since the stringer joist is ordinarily doubled up, any bow is easily straightened by toenailing the crown of the high joist downwards onto the other joist.

If the foundation happens to be seriously uneven or out of level, the depth of the rim joist and/or stringer joists must be adjusted to level the floor platform (see **6-9**). With a transit level, find the lowest point of the rim joist, and snap a level chalk line from there around the perimeter. Cut off the high portions above the line with a circular saw. On foundations with level corners and humped midsections, the string will also show where to hew down the rim. Gaps between the rim and the sill caused by dips in the wall rather than bows in the joist can be shimmed with pressure-treated wedges driven into the gap at one-foot intervals. If the depth of the rim joist is shrunk, the floor joists must be notched where they cross the mudsill so that their top edges will be flush with the top edge of the rim.

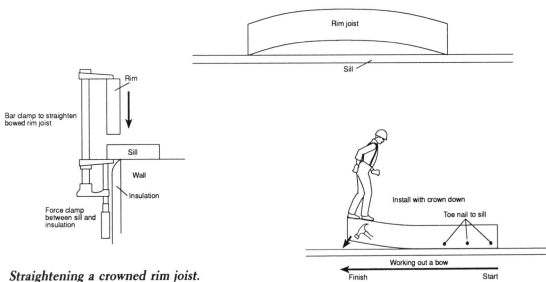

6-8   *Straightening a crowned rim joist.*

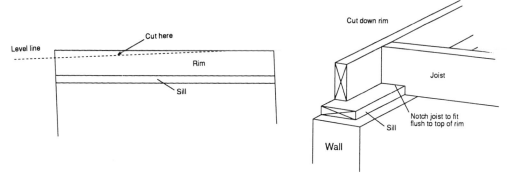

6-9   *Adjusting the rim joist to correct for an off-level foundation.*

GIRDER SELECTION AND CONSTRUCTION

Girder pockets are usually formed into the top of the foundation somewhere near the middle of its end walls. Both pockets should be the same distance from the corner; otherwise, the girder won't be parallel with the walls. If the girder pocket is too far off the line, you'll have to chisel out the side.

Cut out the part of the mudsill that overlays the pocket. Then stretch a string across the sills from one wall to the other to keep the top edge of the girder running straight and level. Measure down from the string to the floor and subtract the thickness of the girder stock to find the height of the girder support post. If a post anchor pin hasn't already been cast in the floor slab, drill a hole at least three inches deep and drive a six-inch length of Rebar into it.

The girder size and the location of its support posts should be indicated on the framing plans. If not, the girder size must match the girder load. The girder load can be calculated by multiplying the girder span times its *load area* times the total floor load (see **6-10**). The span is the width between supports. Since half of the load on the floor joists is carried by the walls, the load area is half the span of the joists carried by the girder times the girder span. The total floor load is the pfs sum of all the dead and live loads for the building except for the roof load (which is carried by the outer walls, unless the rafters are braced to the attic ceiling joists). The product of these three factors is the total load on the girder in pounds. Dividing the total girder load by the girder span gives the load per linear foot, which can be used to size girders by their E and Fb values.

The size of the girder needed to carry the total load can be derived from beam formulas, appropriate single-use lumber span tables, or local code specifications. Typical safe loads for some common girders are given in **6-11**.

Because timbers would be hard to lift and also tend to check more than planks, solid girders are rarely used in modern frame construction. Instead, girders are "built-up" in place by nailing overlapping two-by planks together on top of their supporting posts. The slight reduction in strength is seldom a problem since the typical girder (usually three or four 2×12s on a 10-foot to 12-foot span) has a large built-in margin of safety.

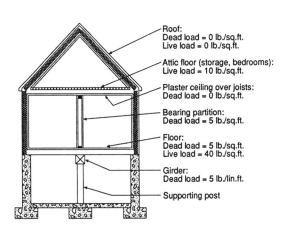

6-10   *Example of girder load determination.*

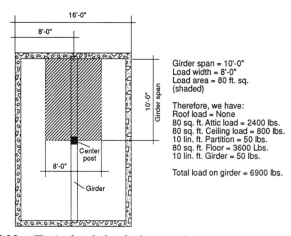

6-11   *Typical safe loads for wood girders.*

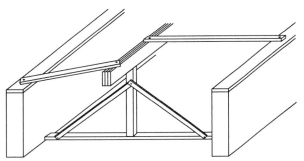

6-12 *Temporary bracing supports the posts and girders.*

Posts for girders are also built up from straight-grained defect-free 2×6 lumber. A good rule of thumb is to spike together as many 2×6s as there are layers in the girder. Some builders prefer to use steel posts with an adjustable threaded top section which can be turned up later to correct for shrinkage. When using such posts, it's important that the bearing cap be large enough so that it can support the entire width of the girder. With cheap threaded posts, the connection between the bearing cap and the screw thread can fail, rolling the girder or kicking the post out sideways. Concrete-filled Lally columns are much stronger. Since they must be ordered cut to exact height, temporary wood posts are used to support the girder until you can accurately measure the post length. If, despite everything, the lolly column is just a bit too short, drive steel shims between its bearing cap and the girder.

Use temporary diagonal 2×4 braces to hold the girder posts upright and plumb. Since you can't nail the bottom ends of these braces into the concrete slab, spike them to 2×6's (2×4's are too "wiggly") wedged between the foundation walls and the posts as shown in **6-12**. Coat the bottom of the post with asphalt roofing cement so that it won't absorb moisture from the concrete.

Once the first layer of the girder sandwich is tacked to the posts, the others are added; they are spiked together with three or four 16d nails in rows spaced about 16 to 24 inches apart (see **6-13**). Joints between planks should be staggered and located over a post. To gain extra stiffness without increasing girder depth or shortening the span, glue ½-inch plywood "flitch plates" between each plank.

Crown each piece of girder stock by sighting along its edge and draw an arrow pointing upwards in the direction of the bow, across the face. Use toenails to pull each piece of stock downwards so that their top edges will be flush with each other, before face-nailing them together. A crowned girder will tend to level itself out as it settles under load—and have greater resistance to deflection.

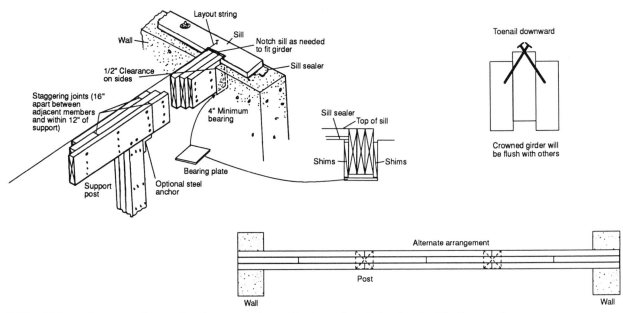

6-13 *Using a layout string makes it easy to keep the top of a girder level with the mud-sill and to find the correct support-post length.*

Hold the completed girder to the string with temporary 2×4 braces so that it won't shift sideways when the floor joists are installed. Since the beam pocket will be somewhat oversized, drive cedar shim shingles between the girder and the concrete to anchor it sideways in its pocket and to bring it flush to the top of the sill.* Even when not required by local code, it's still a good idea to slip a steel bearing plate between the masonry and the bottom of the girder to protect it from rot and to give good bearing. The girder should have no less than four inches of bearing in the pocket.

STEEL BEAMS

Steel beams are often used in residential construction where longer spans than wood girders can safely support or where extra headroom is called for. The size and span lengths of steel beams are calculated in the same way as for wood girders. Of the two common types of steel beams, the "S" (standard) and the "W" (wide-flange), the W beam is most often used in residential construction (see 6-14). It has a wide flat flange, which provides a better bearing surface for attaching wood framing members than the narrow curved profile of the S beam.

The designation for a steel beam gives its height in inches, a letter for its type, and its weight in pounds per linear foot, e.g., 8W15.0 (refer to 6-14).

There are several ways to attach wood framing to steel beams (see 6-15). Normally, the beam is set level with the top of the foundation wall (about 1/8 inch higher if sill sealer is used), and the beam pocket is filled with grout under the beam. Steel beams should never bear on wood posts; always use concrete-filled Lally columns. Bearing caps should be welded to the top and bottom of the columns. The top cap is either drilled and bolted to the beam flange or welded in place. Holes drilled through the flange at the bottom of the column allow it to be lag-bolted into the concrete floor.

Use bolts, or a Ramset gun—a tool that uses blank cartridges to shoot special hardened fasteners—to secure a 2×6 to the top flange of the beam as a bearing pad for the floor joists (see 6-16).

If the joists must be flush with the bottom of a steel beam, they are notched on their bottom edge to fit over the beam flange (see 6-17). A second, deeper, notch at the top edge accommodates the top flange of the beam. The ends of the joists are toenailed into a two-by ledger ripped to fit and bolted to the beam web.

---

*Some experts recommend setting wood girders 1/4 to 3/8 inch higher than the sill to account for the difference in shrinkage between a 12-inch-wide plank and a two-inch-deep sill. While this may make sense with unseasoned lumber, it would also make a hump in the subfloor over the trimmer joist. Since the pressure-treated wood now required for mudsills tends to shrink more than untreated wood, the whole issue is probably moot.

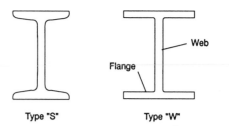

6-14 *The wide flange of a Type "W" beam permits easy attachment of wood framing.*

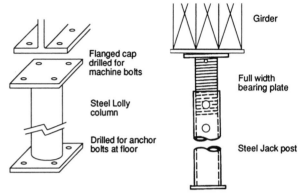

6-15 *Attaching steel beam supporting columns.*

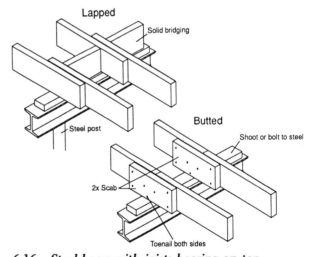

6-16 *Steel beam with joists bearing on top.*

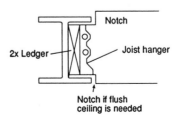

6-17 *Steel beam with joists flush to bottom.*

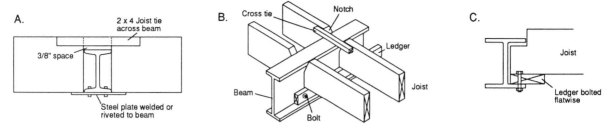

6-18 *Joists supported by ledger on a steel beam.*

LAYOUT AND INSTALLATION OF FLOOR JOISTS

In most cases, the floor joists will be deeper than the steel beam. A two-by ledger bolted to the web and bearing edgewise on the flange—or else bolted flatwise to the flange itself—is used to position the joists at the desired height (see **6-18**). The top edges of the joists are notched to fit around the top flange of the beam, in any case. Nail a two-by joist tie across the beam. Since the joists will eventually shrink and the steel won't, leave a ⅜-inch space between the beam and the tie.

LAYOUT AND INSTALLATION OF FLOOR JOISTS

The position of the floor joists is laid out on the rim joist and the girder. To prevent small measuring errors, use a 100-foot steel (or fibreglass) tape instead of a pocket tape to mark all the joists along the entire length of the wall. Unlike a pocket tape, the hook of a long tape also stays put as the tape is extended.

Back along the length of the rim joist (or slide backwards while straddling the girder) with one hand stretching the tape tightly, and, with the other hand, draw a V pointing to each spacing interval (see **6-19**). Then, with a combination square, draw a straight line through the point of each V across the top of the girder and down the inside

face of the rim joist. Place an X at the side of these lines to show the position of the floor joist. An X always marks where a joist, rafter, stud, or any other framing unit will be nailed. Framing is normally spaced 16 or 24 inches *on center* (o.c.) so that 4×8 sheets of plywood and wallboard, or any standard modular building material, will "break" over the middle of a joist or stud, with a minimum of trimming or waste. Since the layout lines actually correspond to edges and not centers, they must be offset half the width of the stud or joist. For example, for two-by's at 16 inches o.c., the first mark is at 15¼ inches, the next at 31¼ inches, 47¼ inches, and so on. Each mark is "three-quarters under," because planed two-by dimension lumber is 1½ inches thick. Full-dimension, rough-sawn lumber would be marked an "inch under."

A single floor joist seldom spans the width of the building. Most framing plans require multiple sets of joists carried on one or more girders or bearing partitions. While the ends of joists can be cut to butt each other over a girder, this is an unnecessarily time-consuming method—especially since the butted joints must be stiffened against deflection with overlapping "scabs" of short joist stock. It's a lot easier to let the joists "run by" (overlap) each other at the girder (see **6-20**).

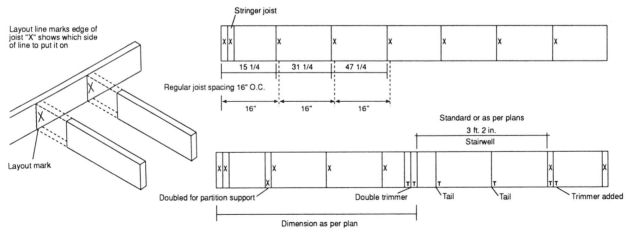

6-19 *The accuracy of the entire layout depends on how accurately you draw the "V" mark that transfers the joist spacing from the tape measure to the rim joists and girders. Remember that small errors add up to noticeable mistakes.*

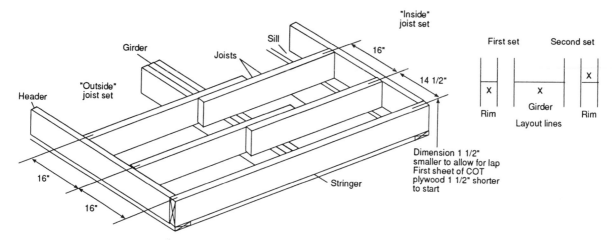

Labels in figure: Girder, Joists, Sill, "Inside" joist set, 16", 14 1/2", "Outside" joist set, Header, 16", 16", Stringer, First set, Second set, X, X, X, Rim, Girder, Rim, Layout lines, Dimension 1 1/2" smaller to allow for lap / First sheet of COT plywood 1 1/2" shorter to start

6-20 *Running joists by each other over a girder is not only faster, but makes for a stronger splice.*

Before nailing any joists, always double-check the layout to make sure that all the Xs are on the right side of their layout lines. On frames with two or three girders and lots of overlapping joists, a layout mistake won't show up until the plywood starts running off the joists.

Floor joists aren't always nailed over the top of a girder, especially if the girder must be raised for extra headroom or the underside of the girder must be flush with the joists for an uninterrupted ceiling surface. One way to accomplish this is to nail a 2×4 ledger to the bottom edge of the girder, which bears on a shallow beam pocket. The ends of the joists are butted and toenailed to the face of the girder—and connected by two-by cross ties scabbed to their top edges (see **6-21**). If the joist stock is long enough, tails can be cut into the ends of the joist, instead, and run by each other over the top of the girder. Using metal joist hangers eliminates the need for the ledger and allows the bottoms of the joists to be flush with the bottom of the girder as well (see **6-22**).

Labels in figure 6-21: Scab or cross tie, Subfloor, Joist, Toe nails, Ledger, Ledger, Girder, Ledger, Girder

6-21 *When girders are deeper in cross section than the floor joists, set the joists slightly above the top of the girder. The resulting gap between the subfloor and the girder allows for differential shrinkage.*

6-22 *Strong steel joist hangers are used when the joist must be flush with the girder.*

123

LINING THE RIM AND STRINGER JOISTS

Just because the bottom edges of the rim and stringer joists have been toenailed to a straight sill doesn't mean that their top edges are also straight. After a day or two of exposure to the weather, the rim beam tends to cup—or twist out of vertical alignment. Before nailing the floor joists, stretch a string over spacer blocks (scraps of 1×2 or 2×4) nailed to each corner of the floor frame at the top edge of the joists. A gauge block (cut from the same scrap as the spacer blocks) held between the string and the rim shows how far in or out it must be moved to keep a straight line (see **6-23**). *Lining* is used repeatedly at different points in the framing process to keep the frame running straight and true.

Nail one end of the floor joist into the rim joist. Before nailing its other end to the girder, check the alignment of the rim joist with the string. To move the rim in or out, push or pull on the girder end of the joist. The girder should also be braced to the mudsill so that it can't be pushed off its line either. Then, toenail the joist to the girder.

Sometimes a floor joist will be cupped or twisted so that it doesn't line up with the layout line on the rim (see **6-24**). Usually, once the first nail is driven home, you can work the joist back onto the line simply by pulling on it. If the joist is a real "pretzel," have your helper "nail it home" while you push it over to the line with your feet. A 2×4 levered against the preceding joist will also bring a twisted joist into line. But any joist that takes this much force to hold will probably split out along the nails. Use such a twisted joist only as a last resort when you don't have any joists to spare. Otherwise, warped stock is best cut up for blocking.

NAILING PATTERNS

It's just as easy to use *too many* nails in framing as *too few*. Since nails tend to act like wedges that split the grain, too many or too big a nail can actually weaken the joint. Building codes specify in general terms the types of nails and other fasteners and the required spacings. For example, the UBC—Uniform Building Code, upon which many local codes are modelled—states that nails used for

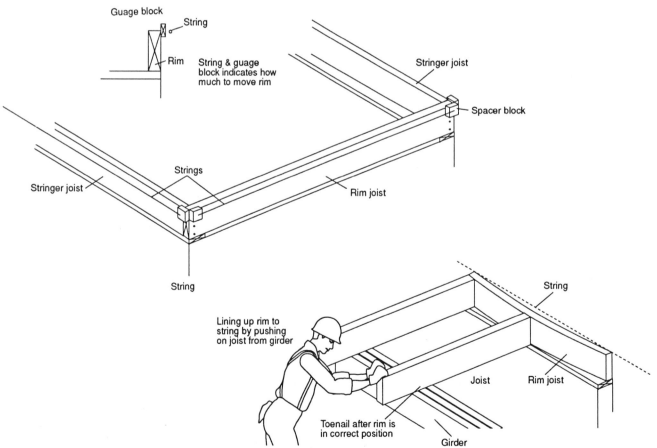

6-23 *Rim joists are particularly susceptible to bowing at their midpoints. Doubled or tripled stringer joists are much less likely to twist off line.*

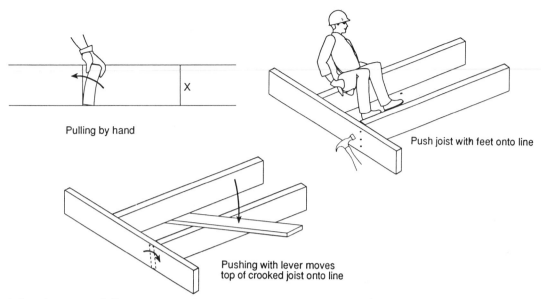

6-24 *Straightening warped floor joists at the rim.*

standard framing should not be spaced closer than half their length nor closer to the edge of a framing member than a quarter of their length. Using 3½-inch-long 16d nails and a 2×10 joist, the nails shouldn't be any closer than ⅞ inch to the edge of the joist and spaced about 1¾ inches apart. Since a nail much closer than an inch to the edge of a plank would risk splitting it, most carpenters naturally tend to drive four nails spaced about two inches apart into a 2×10. A good rule of thumb is: Use two nails with 2×4s; three with 2×6s and 2×8s; four with 2×10s; and four or five with 2×12s.

The lateral strength, resistance to withdrawal, and the risk of splitting of a nail are more or less determined by its length and diameter (see **6-25**), which is why different kinds of nails are recommended for different framing applications. Three-and-one-half-inch-long 16d nails are used for general framing. Two-and-one-half-inch-long 8d nails are used for toenailing 2×4s and for face-nailing sheathing and decking. Three-inch-long 10d nails are used

to face-nail two-by dimension lumber together without penetrating through to the other side. Since it's easy to forget to clinch over a 16d nail, using shorter nails for doubled-up studs and trimmers can prevent nasty accidents.

While *common* nails (also called bright nails, because of their shiny bare steel finish) are widely used, many carpenters find other kinds of general framing nails more versatile. Cement-coated *sinkers* have a lubricating resin that makes them easier to drive into the wood but harder to pull out. Sinkers are also slightly smaller in diameter than common nails of similar size. Because *box* nails are considerably thinner than common nails, some carpenters use them for toenailing rafters and joists, where a longer nail with more holding power is desirable. *Galvanized box* nails resist rusting and seem to have more withdrawal resistance than other nails. Some carpenters use them for all their framing as well as for exterior finish work, siding work, and deck building.

6-25 *Common and box nail information.*

Penny	Length (in)	Diameter		Approx. No./lb	
		Common	Box	Common	Box
4d	1½	.102	.083	316	473
6d	2	.115	.102	181	236
8d	2½	.131	.115	106	145
10d	3	.148	.127	67	94
16d	3½	.165	.134	48	71
20d	4	.203	.148	31	52
40d	5	.238	.165	18	35

6-26 *Because the architect designed a stairwell opening that falls in the middle of the house, instead of the usual single center girder this floor frame has two stairwell girders.*

FRAMING OPENINGS IN THE FLOOR

When laying out the joist spacings on the rim, all the regular joist locations are marked first. The trimmer joists that will frame openings are located from the plan dimensions and marked next. Try to design the floor plan so that an ordinary joist can also serve as the first trimmer wherever there is an opening (see **6-26**). The length of the headers at either end of a stairwell opening is found by measuring between the layout marks for the trimmer joists. Standard stairwells are framed 3'-2" wide (see **6-27**). Transfer the marks for the tail joists from the rim onto the headers.

For maximum strength as well as convenience, the order in which the stairwell headers and trimmers are assembled is important (see **6-28**). The inside trimmer is installed first. The first of the doubled headers are nailed between the trimmers. The tail joists are nailed through the headers. The second header is installed next. Then

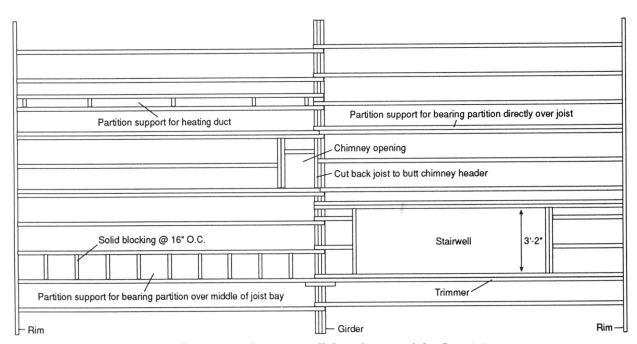

6-27 *The headers of stairwell openings that are parallel to the run of the floor joists are carried by doubled trimmer joists.*

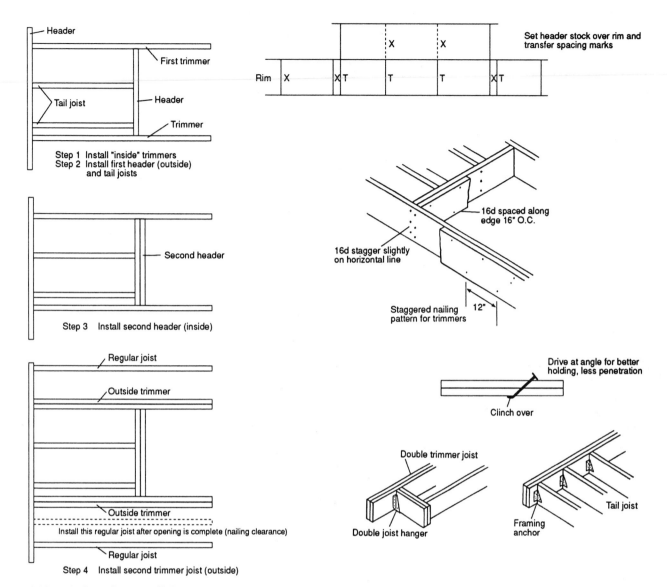

Step 1 Install "inside" trimmers
Step 2 Install first header (outside) and tail joists

Header
First trimmer
Tail joist
Header
Trimmer

Step 3 Install second header (inside)

Second header

Step 4 Install second trimmer joist (outside)

Regular joist
Outside trimmer
Outside trimmer
Install this regular joist after opening is complete (nailing clearance)
Regular joist

Set header stock over rim and transfer spacing marks
Rim

16d spaced along edge 16" O.C.
16d stagger slightly on horizontal line
Staggered nailing pattern for trimmers   12"

Drive at angle for better holding, less penetration
Clinch over

Double trimmer joist
Double joist hanger
Tail joist
Framing anchor

6-28 Order of stairwell framing.

the second trimmers are nailed to the face of the first trimmers. When a regular floor joist is close enough to a trimmer to interfere with nailing, it should not be installed until after the opening is framed. Tail joists under four feet long only require a single header. Those over six feet long should be attached to the header with joist hangers rather than face-nailed. As long as the length of the opening is parallel to the floor joists, this technique is capable of supporting a uniform load of 50 psf without additional supports.

Openings that run perpendicular to the floor joists will require more support (see **6-29**). Tripling the trimmer joists is usually sufficient for an ordinary stairwell opening up to about 11 feet.

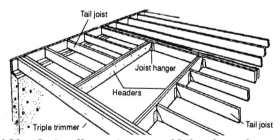

Tail joist
Joist hanger
Headers
Tail joist
Triple trimmer

6-29 Stairwell openings over 11 feet long that run perpendicular to the floor joists will require posts for extra support. Posts are also needed under the inside corner of an L-shaped stairwell of any length.

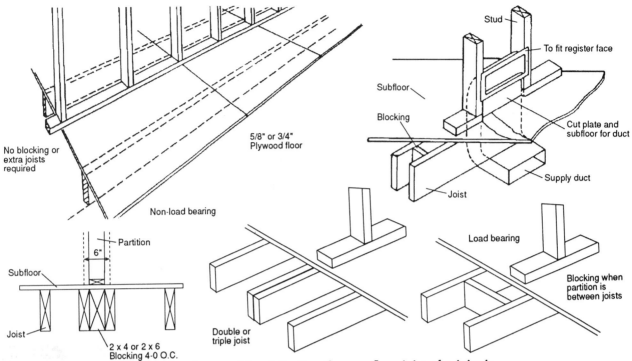

6-30 *When a parallel load-bearing partition falls directly on a floor joist, the joist is stiffened by doubling or tripling. When the partition falls between joists, full-width solid blocking nailed between the joists adds the required stiffness. Lay out the framing so that it will accommodate heating ducts wherever possible without having to cut any floor joists (girders are never, under any circumstances, cut).*

FRAMING FOR SPECIAL CONDITIONS

Extra support is also required under load-bearing partitions that run parallel with the joists (see **6-30**). A joist directly under the partition can be doubled or tripled. Otherwise, nail solid blocking 16 inches o.c. between a pair of floor joists. Nonload-bearing partitions require no additional blocking or added support as long as ⅝-inch or ¾-inch plywood is used for the subfloor.

The dead load of bathroom fixtures adds about 10 to 20 psf to the ordinary floor load. A tile floor set in mortar can add another 30 psf to the dead load. Since the joists that are supposed to support this 50-psf dead load are often cut to accommodate drain lines, bathroom floor framing requires special attention (see **6-31**). The lip of a heavy cast-iron tub should rest on a ledger nailed to the enclosure partition. Both the joist under this partition and

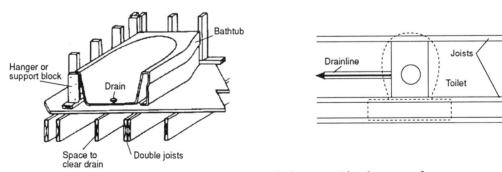

6-31 *Joists under bathroom fixtures can be offset as needed to provide clearance for running the drain lines. Since bathtub enclosure walls are effectively bearing partitions, always double the joists beneath them as well as under the unsupported lip of the tub.*

128

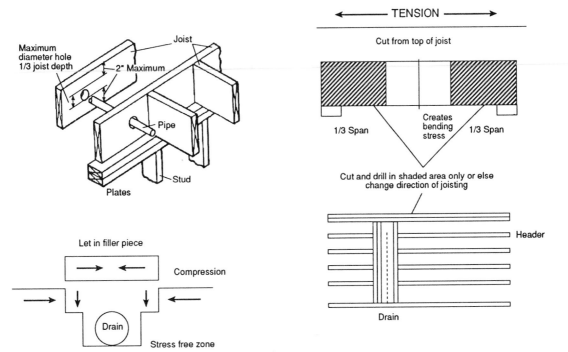

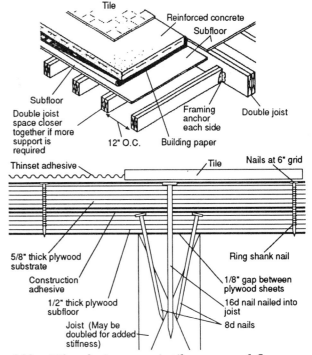

6-32 *Always try to confine cuts or holes to the regions of a joist that are under the least stress (i.e., along the neutral axis or close to the ends of the span).*

the joist under the opposite side of the tub should be doubled. Study the plumbing plans, and offset joists, as necessary, so that they don't coincide with the run of the drain lines. Extra blocking between joists under a toilet will help stiffen the subfloor so that the toilet flange doesn't tend to settle and leak.

A joist under load is in compression along its top and in tension at its bottom—as you will remember from Chapter Four. At changeover point, roughly near the middle—from top to bottom—of the joist, the stress is zero. Since the bending forces are also greater at midspan of a joist than near its ends, the best place to drill a hole for a drain line would be through the middle somewhere close to the bearing (see **6-32**). Limiting the depth of a cut to a quarter of the total depth of the joist will not cause any significant reduction in its strength. When a joist has to be cut rather than drilled, saw from the top down, and tack a piece of blocking in the hole afterwards to reduce the tension forces on the lower portion.

Where quarry tile or slate is used in combination with other types of flooring, the joists and decking must be set so that the finished floors are flush with each other (see **6-33**). The recommended substrate for a tile floor is a layer of ⅝-inch plywood glued and screwed over the subfloor plywood. Since the joists under the tiled area are usually smaller than the regular floor joists, they are doubled and spaced 12 inches o.c. for the extra stiffness needed to keep the tiles joints from cracking.

6-33 *When laying ceramic tile over wood floor, special precautions are needed to increase stiffness so that the grout joints don't crack. The installation of fasteners is critical.*

129

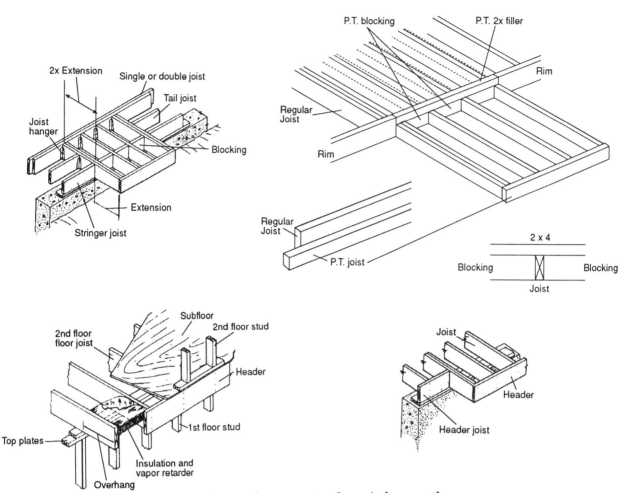

6-34 *Cantilevered floor joists are often used to support a bay window or other "bump-out" in lieu of a foundation.*

Overhangs and projections also require special support similar to that used with stairwell openings (see 6-34). As a rule of thumb, cantilevered joists for projections perpendicular to the run of the regular floor joists should extend back to a trimmer joist a distance equal to twice the width of the overhang. Projections or overhangs parallel with the regular joists require only an extension of the joist length—except at the sides of the projection, where they are doubled to carry the walls the same as a stringer joist. Nail solid blocking between the joists over the foundation wall to close in the space and add rigidity.

If the cantilevered joists are intended to support an open deck or porch rather than a walled-in extension of the house proper, use pressure-treated lumber instead of regular dimension lumber. Since, to keep water out, any such outdoor deck should be at least two inches lower than the interior floor level, scab shallower pressure-treated joists to full-depth floor joists that end just behind the pressure-treated blocking at the rim or stringer.

6-35 *Working from planks laid across the joists, metal "speed" bridging is nailed to the tops of the floor joists before laying down the subfloor.*

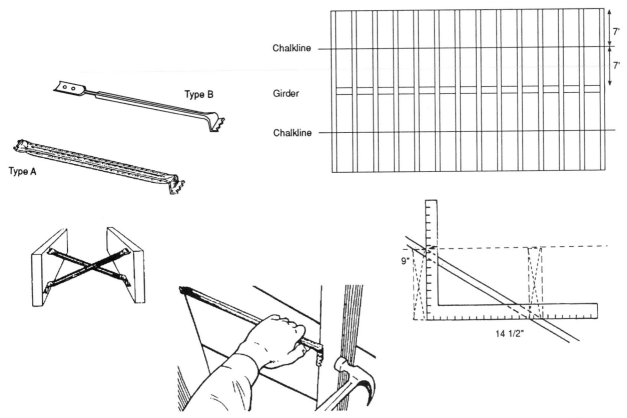

6-36 *When installing wood bridging, use solid blocking to fill in odd-width joist bays and over girders and bearing walls. To lay out the cuts for wood bridging on a radial-arm saw, line up the joist depth with the tongue of the square and the joist bay width with the blade.*

BRIDGING AND BLOCKING

Cross-bridging or solid blocking is nailed between floor joists to help distribute the loads and to keep the bottoms of the joists from twisting sideways. Although studies have shown that this bracing is superfluous with a strong subfloor and properly secured joists, many codes still require it anyway. Considering the marginal cost, the extra stiffness bridging imparts to the floor is a justifiable excess. Because it takes more time to install, traditional "herring-bone" cross-bridging of 1×3s set diagonally between the floor joists in an X pattern has been almost entirely supplanted by steel "speed bridging" (see 6-35). However, wood bridging can be quickly cut with a radial-arm or chop saw. Use a framing square as shown in 6-36 to lay out the angle cuts. The pieces are nailed to the top edges of the floor joists before the subfloor is laid. The bottom ends are nailed after the floor deck is finished. Metal bridging requires no nails and can be quickly installed any time after the floor deck. Leaving the bottom ends of the bridging unsecured lets you straighten out bowed floor joists as the subfloor plywood is laid and makes it easier to run wiring and plumbing along the joist bays (see 6-37).

6-37 *The bottom ends of the bridging aren't nailed into place until after the wiring and plumbing are finished. This also allows the joists to be shifted as needed to line up with the spacing marks on the subfloor plywood.*

Because it relies on the compressive strength of the wood itself rather than the shear strength of nails, solid blocking cut from badly crowned or otherwise unusable joist stock (there's always some in every lumber delivery) provides more resistance to joist deflection than open bridging (see **6-38**). It's generally required by code—under bearing partitions that run parallel to a girder and with regular cross-bridging—to fill in the odd-width bays between offset joists and trimmers. Solid blocking is more trouble to install than steel bridging and must be drilled for pipes and wires. But the added stiffness is worth the effort.

Blocking or bridging is installed on alternate sides of chalk lines snapped across the joist spans at intervals of no more than seven feet. (Usually this results in a single course down the centerline of each set of joists and a course over the girder.)

If this were a perfect world—with perfect carpenters—the space between each joist would be exactly the difference between 16 inches o.c. and one-half the thickness of each joist, i.e., 14½ inches; then, you could simply cut a pile of blocking or pieces of cross-bridging all to the same length and nail them in place. In the real world, the spacings, when measured between the joists at the rims, always vary slightly. Some are ¹⁄₁₆ inch or even ⅛ inch

over or under the line. Measure each joist bay (at the rim or girder—not at midspan—since unblocked joists bend and twist); write the measurements down in order on a scrap of wood; and then cut the blocking to size, numbering each one for the corresponding bay. This keeps the joists from "crowding" each other off parallel alignment, which always seems to happen when using same-sized blocking. Wood bridging that sticks out past the bottom of the joists will tend to push the joists sideways unless it is trimmed. Since they bend to fit, the anchor flanges of steel bridging are more tolerant of imperfect spacings.

With a glued and nailed plywood subfloor over an unfinished cellar ceiling, blocking and bridging can be replaced by 1×3 strapping nailed to the bottoms of the joists. If the ceiling must be strapped for installation of drywall or other finish, anyway, no other bracing is needed.

INSULATING STRINGER JOISTS
With 2×6 wall framing, the width of the stringer joist must be increased to provide adequate bearing for the wall above. Tripling a stringer joist is expensive and unnecessary. Instead, nail blocking between two joists. The cavities between these pieces must be filled with insulation before the floor deck is nailed down (see **6-39**). (In cold

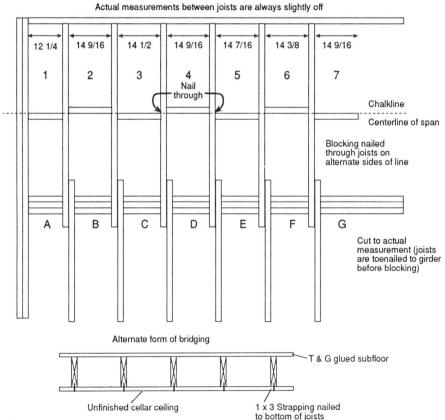

6-38 *Installing solid wood blocking.*

climates, frost will form on the inside face of the joist.) Include a sheet of 1½-inch-thick rigid foam insulation with the framing lumber order. Foam is easily cut to fit the pockets and won't get soggy like fibreglass if it rains before the frame is closed in. Use rigid foam insulation to fill in the cavities between the blocking in built-up corner post studs and partition backers as well (see **6-40**).

FLOOR TRUSSES

Prefabricated computer-engineered floor trusses permit long, clear spans uninterrupted by girders and posts (see **6-41**). The open web of 2×4s simplifies plumbing, HVAC, and wiring installation. Designed for installation either directly on top of a wall plate or hung from the mudsill, the individual trusses are light enough to be set quickly and easily by hand (see **6-42**).

6-39 *Blocking has been installed to double up a header joist for the second-floor frame. The cavities should be filled with rigid foam insulation before laying the floor deck. The cavity in the built-up corner post should also be insulated before sheathing.*

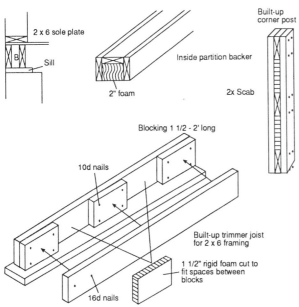

6-40 *Insulating stringer joists and other built-up framing members.*

6-41 *The higher cost of computer-designed floor trusses over standard floor joists is offset by the elimination of girders and support posts under long spans and the rapidity with which they can be installed.*

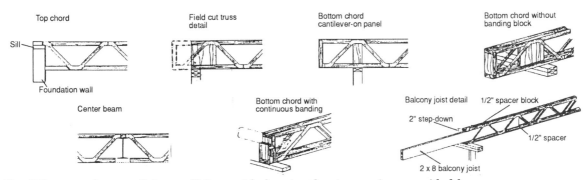

6-42 *When weather conditions call for rapid close-in, the time savings provided by prefabricated floor trusses may be worth their extra cost.*

6-43 *Although they increase the overall height of a building when used for a second storey, the extra depth of floor trusses is useful for concealing HVAC ducts. Note how the trusses extend over the wall at the right to conveniently frame the cantilever for the second story. Note, also, the steel framing anchors tying the upper and lower wall frames across the trusses.*

6-45 *A subfloor deck makes an excellent level platform for assembling the wall frames. Note the sheets of plywood laid over the stairwell opening for safety. Note, also, the T-square used to cut plywood and to mark the sheets for nail spacing and the built-up corner post under construction.*

Truss spacing, depth, and splicing details and installation requirements vary according to manufacturer and application (see **6-43**). Get the exact specifications from your supplier before finalizing your working drawings. Rapid installation and versatility are some of the advantages that have led to widespread use of floor trusses in commercial construction. In most situations, however, floor trusses are too expensive for the homebuilder on a tight budget.

INSTALLING THE SUBFLOOR
A sheet of plywood is about as perfectly square as anything made of wood can be. So, if the edge of a plywood sheet starts "running off" the joists, either the joists are skewed because something was nailed on the wrong side of the line, or the initial sheets weren't laid square to the framing or the frame itself isn't square. To keep the plywood sheets running straight and square to each other and the floor joists, even if the rim is slightly bowed, snap a chalk line across the joists four feet in from the rim (see **6-44**).

Codes allow ½-inch CDX plywood to be used for a subfloor with joists at 16 inches o.c., as long as horizontal 2×4 blocking is nailed between them to support the edges of the plywood. Although this makes a minimally adequate subfloor for a wood finish floor, most conscientious builders prefer to use ⅝-inch or ¾-inch plywood instead (see **6-45**).

Although not required by code, the strong and squeak-free floor that results with ¾-inch tongue-and-groove exterior-grade underlayment plywood glued and nailed to the joists is well worth the extra cost compared to a standard CDX subfloor.

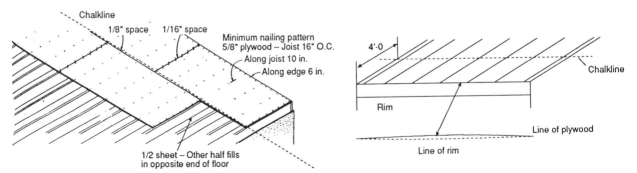

6-44 *Setting the floor deck plywood back about ¼ inch from the edge of the rim allows for slight bows without having to trim off any overhanging edges that would otherwise make bumps in the wall sheathing.*

Before plywood came into use, subfloors and walls were sheathed with 1×6 tongue-and-groove boards nailed diagonally across the joists and studs for racking resistance. The time it would take to lay such a subfloor is reason enough to explain the popularity of plywood even without considering its other advantages. Plywood uses about half the board footage compared to tongue-and-groove boards of board sheathing while making a house frame that's at least twice as strong.

There are many grades and types of plywood and related structural wood product panels used in residential construction. In general, plywood is classified as either *exterior* or *interior*, according to the type of the glue used to bond the plies together. Exterior glue is waterproof while interior glue is merely water-resistant. Exterior plywood can be used for all applications. Interior plywood is rated *Exposure 1* and *Exposure 2*, according to its degree of water-resistance, and it should only be used in protected locations or where exposure to moisture will be of limited duration, such as a subfloor underlayment.

A grade lettering system is used to indicate the quality of the face veneers. *Type A* is smooth and paintable. *Type B* has a solid, slightly rougher surface with some small knots and minor defects. *AB* plywood is often used for cabinet carcasses, doors, and shelving, where the A face is exposed to view and the B side is more or less hidden. *C grade* plywood has more knotholes, splits, and defects. Less expensive than AB plywood, AC is a good choice for a cabinet base, where only the smooth face will show. *D grade* has the most allowable defects. Inexpensive *CD* (also called, *CDX*, i.e., exterior) plywood is widely used for sheathing and subfloor decking where it will be covered by something else. For best results, the somewhat smoother and more weather-resistant C veneer should always face up. If the face veneer is to be left natural or varnished, *premium type N* plywood, which has no obvious defects, is used instead.

Underlayment (or *PTS*, i.e., "touch-sanded," also called Sturd-I-Floor) plywood isn't exactly the same as subfloor plywood. It has one smooth-sanded face veneer, which makes it suitable as a structural substrate for direct application of resilient flooring, ceramic tile, or carpet. Underlayment plywood usually has a tongue-and-groove long edge. Standard CDX plywood is used as a subfloor for wood-finish floors. Hardboard or other underlayment panels must be installed over it as a base for other types of flooring.

Plywoods used for decorative cabinetry are manufactured in a wide range of hardwood veneers, with either plywood or solid lumber cores. Plastic-laminate-coated plywoods are also available for specialized interior and exterior applications. In fact, there are so many varieties of plywood for so many different applications that most builders and lumber dealers have never even heard of or seen many of them.

Because they cost up to 30 percent less than plywood, structural panels manufactured from various wood wastes have become widely used in modern construction. Waferboard—also known as Aspenite, flakeboard, or chipboard—and oriented-fibre strand board (OSB) are composites of variously sized wood chips, flakes, sawdust, and glue, heated and compressed into 4×8 panels for use as sheathing and decking. These products have a lesser degree of resistance to bending and shear stresses than plywood of similar thickness. Some also swell up when their edges are exposed to moisture for any length of time. None of them hold nails as well as plywood; but all of them do meet minimum code requirements and represent a recycling of what would otherwise be sawmill waste.

Economical one-quart tubes of construction adhesive are applied with an oversized caulking gun. Run a ¼-inch bead of subfloor adhesive along the tops of the joists (use two ⅛-inch beads at the end joints) and a ⅛-inch bead along the groove of the underlayment sheet. Installing tongue-and-groove plywood is a two-person job (see **6-46**). One worker stands, legs akimbo, on the back edge of the sheet and distributes his or her weight so as to force the tongue to line up with the groove of the preceding sheet. The other worker, standing on the front edge, closes the gap by driving a cushion block (a scrap of 2×4 long enough to bridge at least three joists) against it with a sledgehammer. The sheet is then tacked into place with a few strategic nails. Manufacturer's recommendations call for a ⅛-inch gap between the ends of sheets. The tongues and grooves are milled so that they don't quite close tight. Slip a couple of nails between the sheets to space them at their sides.

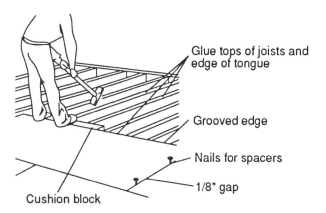

Glue tops of joists and edge of tongue

Grooved edge

Nails for spacers

1/8" gap

Cushion block

6-46 *When glued to the joists with construction adhesive and solidly nailed, tongue-and-groove plywood makes an extremely strong and stable floor deck.*

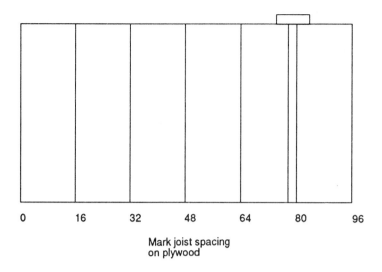

| 0 | 16 | 32 | 48 | 64 | 80 | 96 |

Mark joist spacing
on plywood

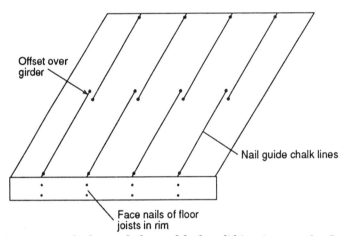

Offset over
girder

Nail guide chalk lines

Face nails of floor
joists in rim

6-47 *Marking the nailing lines on each sheet of plywood before lifting it onto the floor deck speeds up nailing and makes it easy to space the centers of the floor joists to the lines by eye.*

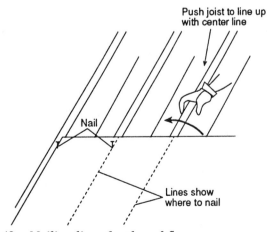

Push joist to line up
with center line

Nail

Lines show
where to nail

6-48 *Nailing lines for the subfloor.*

If steel bridging is used in lieu of solid blocking, the joists must be spaced to run straight and to line up square to the plywood (see **6-47**). With a drywall T-square, draw lines at 16-inch centers across the length of each sheet, before sliding them up onto the deck. Push each joist back and forth until its center coincides with the lines on the plywood, and then tack the sheet down to the joist. These same lines will also serve as nailing guides (see **6-48**).

Solid blocking effectively prespaces the joists. With less than seven feet between fixed points, they won't move enough to make a difference anyway. When the last sheet of underlayment is tacked down, snap nailing lines across the entire floor along the centerlines of the floor joists. Use 8d common or box nails or 6d ring-shank underlayment nails spaced 12 inches apart (six inches apart on the edges).

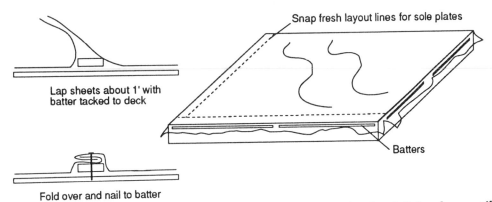

Snap fresh layout lines for sole plates

Lap sheets about 1' with batter tacked to deck

Batters

Fold over and nail to batter

6-49   *In climates with changeable weather, protective plastic sheeting is often left in place until after the roof is tar-papered. Once the sole plates are nailed down, the battens can be removed.*

PROTECTING THE SUBFLOOR AGAINST WEATHER

Exterior plywood should withstand repeated exposure to rain. But after a week or more of heavy soaking, especially if puddles of standing water collect on the deck, the face plies can absorb so much moisture that they swell, buckle, and come apart, particularly along their edges. While this is more likely to happen with the (sometimes) inferior brands carried by discount chains, even good-quality plywood is not immune to the effects of prolonged exposure to moisture. The only cure for serious delamination is replacement. Covering the deck with a sheet of polyethylene plastic is cheap insurance (see **6-49**). The rest of the roll can be used to cover lumber piles or for the insulation vapor barrier (see **6-50**).

Poly film is available in widths up to 24 feet. If the entire deck could be covered with a single sheet, there wouldn't be any seams to leak. But since the covering must overlap the edge of the deck by a few inches to protect from wind and be watertight—and most floors are at least 24 feet wide—at least one seam is inevitable. Tack a piece of 1×2 or 2×4 to the deck along what will be the seamline. Overlap the sheets about a foot; then fold the seam over on itself, and staple it to the underlying batten. The resulting raised *pan* is temporarily waterproof. The rest of the sheet is stapled to the edges of the floor deck and anchored with 1×3 battens.

Chalk won't stick to unscuffed plastic. Snap the chalk lines for the sole plates of the wall frames on the floor deck before covering it.

6-50   *Materials on the job site should rest on skids and be covered to protect them from the elements. Note that the floor deck has also been covered with a poly sheet to protect it against rain.*

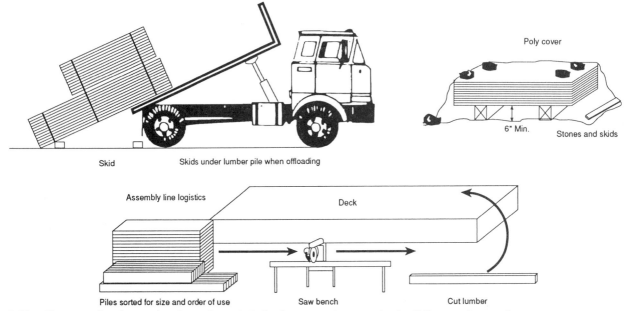

Poly cover

6" Min.

Stones and skids

Skid

Skids under lumber pile when offloading

Assembly line logistics

Deck

Piles sorted for size and order of use

Saw bench

Cut lumber

6-51 *Try to unload your lumber where it is both convenient to the building and out of the way of traffic and work patterns. As soon as possible, sort the load into piles according to their order of use as well as size.*

JOB-SITE LOGISTICS

For professional builders, profit depends in large part upon efficient logistical organization and labor orchestration. While not all of the practices of production carpentry are suited to the owner-builder, saving time and steps certainly is, especially if you're paying for hired help.

Lumber stored on site must be properly stacked and protected against weather; at the same time it must be located as close as possible to where it will be used but not so close that it will be in the way (see **6-51**). It should be convenient, but out of the way.

Your framing lumber order will usually arrive banded with steel straps so that the delivery truck can use its tilt bed to dump it in a pile. As soon as the leading edge of the pile contacts the ground, push a scrap lumber "skid" under it. Position a second skid near the tailgate of the truck so that the pile will come to rest on the skids once it slides free of the truck.

As soon as you can, hire a couple of neighborhood kids or a helper to pull the load apart, sort, and restack it according to length and order of use. Your lumberyard may be willing to deliver some extra skids or old pallets with the load or you might be able to get some free for the hauling from the cull pile at a local sawmill. Separate the joists from the studs (if they're both included in the

first shipment) and the plywood. Set the skids so that the piles will be more or less in the same plane, if not actually level; this will help keep the lumber from warping. The bottom of the stacks should be at least six inches above the ground. Cover the piles with poly or canvas tarps to keep out rain and snow, using stones and skids to batten down the sides. Moisture trapped between the layers of lumber will cause it to swell and also promote the growth of wood-destroying fungi and mildew discoloration. Water-soaked wood will also warp excessively as it dries out. Wood exposed to strong sunlight will also warp.

If possible, locate the piles over gravelled areas rather than in the grass or mud. Try to visualize the shortest path for the lumber from pile to point of use. Before the floor deck is built, the chop saw or radial-arm saw bench is usually set up parallel with the house and close to it. Ideally, you should be able to pull a joist or stud off the pile, slide it onto one end of the saw bench, cut it, and slide it onto the floor deck or into a pile within lifting distance of the foundation at the other end. This assembly-line efficiency may have to be postponed until after the floor deck is built and the foundation completely back-filled. Once the first-floor walls are framed, the saw bench is generally relocated onto the floor deck for the remainder of the framing process.

7 Wall and Ceiling Framing

The motions and tasks of a skilled framing crew are as carefully choreographed as those of a dance troupe (see **7-1**). As two of the crew are nailing the studs to the plates, another is cutting the window *jack studs*, sills, and header pieces they'll soon need, while the foreman is laying out the next section of wall so that the work can stay ahead of the workers.

Whether you are building with a crew or by yourself, a "cut list" is a useful organizational tool (see **7-2**). The window and door schedule, which is normally part of every framing plan, identifies each opening with a key letter that refers to the dimensions of its *rough opening*. Rough openings always give the width first, followed by height. Instead of rough opening (r.o.) dimensions, doors are sometimes designated by their size only, e.g., $3'-0'' \times 6'-8''$. Unless otherwise specified, adding 2½ inches to the door dimensions will give an adequate r.o. for an exterior door. For interior doors, which normally use thinner jamb stock, add two inches instead.

The length of headers and sills always equals rough opening width plus the jack studs (r.o. + 3"). The jack studs for the sides of the window rough opening (also called *jamb studs*) are the same as the r.o. height. Some carpenters prefer to run their jack studs full-length from header to sole plate rather than interrupt them with a sill.

7-1 *Carpenters steady a wall section until it can be nailed and braced to the floor deck. Safely lifting long sections of frame calls for at least two pairs of helping hands, and more when the frames include one or more heavy built-up headers.*

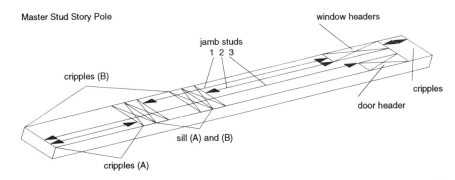

R.O. KEY #	HEADER	SILLS	JAMB STUD	HEADER CRIPPLES	SILL CRIPPERS
A	(2) 2X8 X 3'-2"	"	2@ 3-0	none	
B	(2) 2X8 X 5'-8"	"			
C (door)	(2) 2X6 X 3'-5' 1/2"	none	2@ 6' - 10' 1/2"	none	none
D	(2) 2X10 X 9'-3"	"	2@5'-3"		

7-2 *A "cut list" lets you precut all the parts for framing window and door openings so that you won't lose time or make mistakes when knocking together the wall frame. A master storey pole is a full-scale typical wall section that is used to find the lengths of common, jack, and cripple studs.*

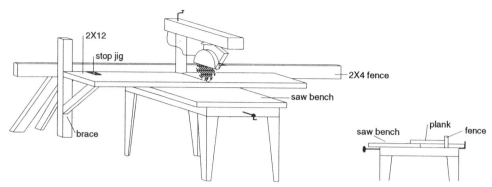

7-3 *Even without a 16- to 20-foot cutting bench, a radial-arm saw is likely to stay exactly where it's been set up on the job site until you're done with it; so choose the saw's location carefully.*

The lengths of the *cripple studs* under the sills and over the header (if any) can only be determined approximately from the plans. The actual length is "determined in the field" (as an architect would say). This is done by making a storey pole or *master stud*. Mark the header, sill, and plate heights on a floor-to-ceiling-length stud, and then measure the intervals in between these components to find the length of cripples. Mark and measure carefully with a sharp pencil. Lumber-marking pencils are too clumsy for close and accurate layout work; use a sharpened No. 2 pencil instead. With a storey pole as a reference, all the parts for all the openings can be cut ahead of the actual frame assembly. Likewise, headers, corner posts, and partition backers are all preassembled so that they will be ready when needed.

Whether you use a circular saw, a radial-arm saw, or a chop saw, repetitive cuts for framing members are much

faster and more accurate if you use a jig that can be set to length on a work surface. For a radial-arm saw, screw a 16-foot 2×12 plank to its work table with a 1×4 fence dropped between table sections—with three-fourths of its overall length offset to one side (see **7-3**). Nail 2×4s to the back edge of the plank to serve as extensions for cutting long stock. Make sure that the saw cuts perpendicular to the fence. The long end of the bench and any extensions are solidly braced to keep the cuts running square.

Building a cutting table for a chop saw is a little more complicated (see **7-4**). The saw is secured to a plank with machine bolts (use wing nuts for quick attachment). Spacers cut from two-by stock support a second plank so that its surface is flush with the cutting table of the chop saw. For added length, extend the upper plank and its fence beyond the lower plank. An overall length of 18 to 20 feet makes a very versatile cutting bench that isn't any

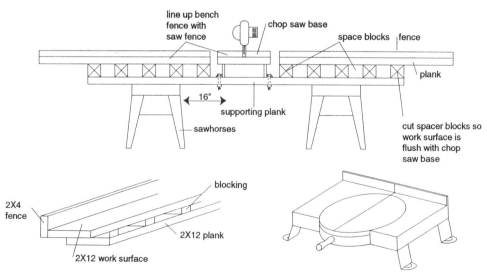

7-4 *What a chop saw lacks in capacity it more than makes up for in portability. A chop saw and cutting bench is ideal for cutting wood siding and trim.*

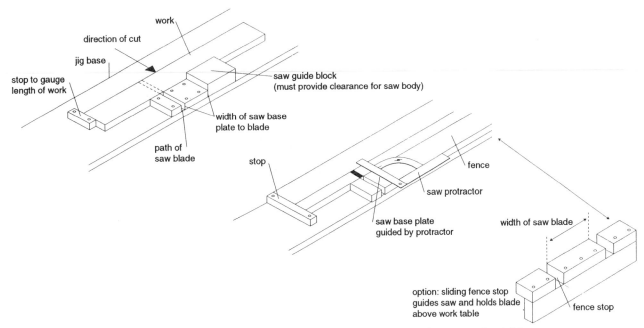

work
direction of cut
jig base
stop to gauge length of work
saw guide block (must provide clearance for saw body)
width of saw base plate to blade
path of saw blade
stop
fence
saw protractor
saw base plate guided by protractor
width of saw blade
option: sliding fence stop guides saw and holds blade above work table
fence stop

7-5 *This jig allows you to make repetitive cuts for length quickly and accurately. Adding a stop to the fence piece that holds the saw base above the work allows you to slide it along the edge of the work table.*

more cumbersome to transport than an extension ladder. The table is supported on sawhorses.

If you only own a circular saw, the jig bench requires only a block to guide the saw base and another to raise it flush with the face of the piece to be cut (see **7-5**). Use drywall screws or clamps to secure the stop blocks instead of nails. If you own a saw protractor/cut-off guide, then the cutting bench needs only a stop for the length and a fence to rest the protractor against.

DOUBLE-SOLE-PLATE FRAMING SYSTEM
Standard ceiling height, measured from the subfloor to the bottom of the ceiling joists, is 7'-8". Trimming eight-foot studs to 7'-3½" (7'-8" less the 4½-inch thickness of the sole plate and doubled top plate) wastes both wood and time. For professional framers, time is profit, which is why it's cheaper for them to use more expensive *precuts* (studs factory-cut to 8'-7½") instead. Since do-it-yourself labor is usually cheaper than materials—and the trimmings make great kindling—using precuts isn't as economical.

Doubling up the sole plate is a cost-saving technique that also offers some other benefits (see **7-6**). Codes usually require a minimum ceiling height of 7'-6". A double sole and double top plate (total thickness equals six inches) permits the use of seven-foot studs made by cutting 14-footers in half. Since 14-foot studs use 12½ percent less material than two eight-footers, the cost of the extra sole

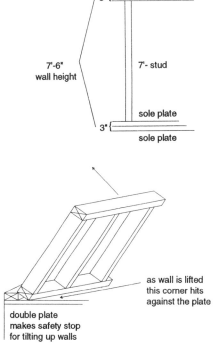

rafter plate
top plate
3"
7'-6" wall height
7'- stud
sole plate
3"
sole plate

as wall is lifted this corner hits against the plate
double plate makes safety stop for tilting up walls

7-6 *Doubling up the sole plate lets you cut 14-foot studs in half to make a 7'-6" ceiling with no scrap.*

141

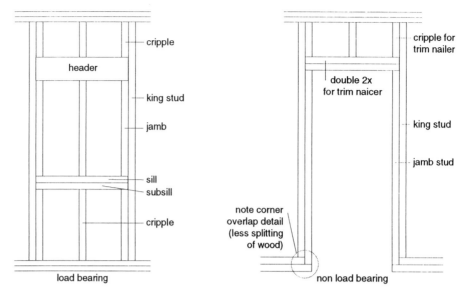

cripple

header

king stud

jamb

sill
subsill

cripple

load bearing

cripple for trim nailer

double 2x for trim naicer

king stud

jamb stud

note corner overlap detail (less splitting of wood)

non load bearing

7-7 *Even though they aren't required above a header, cripple jamb studs are often installed next to the king studs to provide solid nail-backing for the door or window finish trim in both bearing walls and nonbearing partitions.*

plate is still cheaper than precuts. The double sole plate method also offers several advantages for wall framing; it's a very effective batten where plastic sheets are used to protect the subfloor deck. When used with interior partitions, it makes a life-sized layout template. It also provides a safety stop to keep wall sections from sliding off the deck as they are tilted up into place. Finally, nailing baseboard trim is easier since you don't have to worry about missing the studs hidden behind the wall finish.

There are several other places where it makes sense to use more wood than is required by code or structural necessity. For example, I always double the sill under window openings and fill in a cripple stud above the header next to the king stud (see 7-7). This gives solid support where it's needed most for nailing the window casing trim. For the same reason, I also double the flatwise header studs over door openings in nonload-bearing partitions.

LAYOUT FOR A WALL FRAME

Whether you're using a single or double sole plate, the layout for a wall frame begins with a chalk line. Measure $3\frac{1}{2}$ inches in at the corners for 2×4 framing ($5\frac{1}{2}$ inches in for 2×6 framing), and snap lines between the marks. Like the line for the sill on top of the foundation, these lines keep the wall frame running straight.

Nail the first sole plate to the chalk line with two 16d nails driven through the subfloor into the rim and into each floor joist. Cut out the door openings so that water will drain and dirt can be swept off the deck.

Reserve the straightest 2×4s for plate stock. Plate sections are usually the longest pieces that can divide more or less evenly into the wall—e.g., two 16-footers for a 32-foot wall, or, since 14 feet doesn't break evenly on 16-inch centers, two 14-footers for a 26-foot 2×4 wall, or a 12-footer and a 14-footer for a 2×6 wall at 24 inches o.c.

Snapping lines longer than 16 feet is best done with two sets of hands (see 7-8). The line is hooked over a nail driven into the mark (or over a convenient edge), and held by one person at the other mark. The other person pins the line down at its midspan, and then snaps each side separately. When snapping a long line from one end, there's a good chance that it will run off in the middle or snag on a splinter or hump somewhere along its length. For clear and accurate lines, stretch the string as tight as you can and pluck it crisply.

7-8 *Snapping a chalk line.*

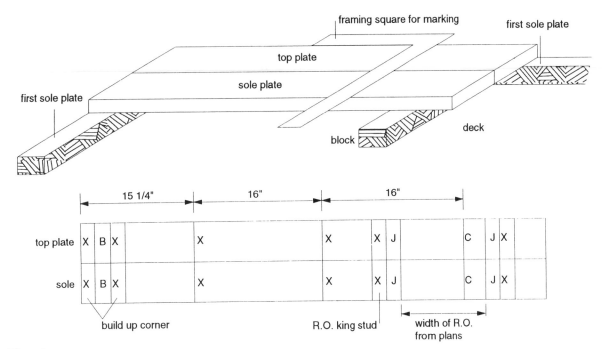

	15 1/4"				16"			16"						
top plate	X	B	X		X			X	X	J		C	J	X
sole	X	B	X		X			X	X	J		C	J	X

build up corner   R.O. king stud   width of R.O. from plans

7-9 *Plate layout.*

Plate layout begins with the longest wall (see **7-9**). Trim a pair of 2×4s to exact length. High-quality milled lumber is usually clipped ¼ inch to ½ inch longer than its nominal length (otherwise you couldn't cut it into two equal pieces since the saw kerf is at least ⅛ inch wide). Set a short block alongside the first sole plate and lay the two pieces of plate stock side by side, over the first plate and the blocking. Check to see that their ends are exactly flush with the end of the wall. Trim and butt the next pair of plates against the ends of the first. Before trimming the final pair, check to see if it overhangs the end of the wall or falls short of it. The actual length of the wall may be a fraction of an inch longer or shorter than the plan length; always go by the actual length. That little bit extra on the untrimmed plate might be just enough to close up the gap.

Stretch your long tape down the entire length of the plates, and mark the position of the common studs, using an X as with floor joist layout. Then, locate the centerlines of the rough openings for the doors and windows as shown in the framing plans or elevations, and measure to the sides of the openings. Indicate each king (also called a backer) stud with an X and the jack studs with a J. Cripple studs are marked with a C. Corner posts are designated by XBX (B for blocking—any short piece sandwiched between framing members). After all the locations for the regular and extra studs are marked, draw the location lines across both plates at the same time with a framing square. Use the 1½-inch-wide tongue of the square to draw the layout marks for king and jack studs.

Since the exterior walls are laid out so that the sheathing breaks over the studs, the spacing of the first stud on the end wall plates (i.e., the wall over the trimmer joist) must be offset to account for the thickness of the wall it abuts (see **7-10**). Hold the end of the tape 3½ inches past the end of the plate (for 2×6 framing, overhang the tape 5½ inches). If you hook the tape over a scrap of 2×4, there's less chance of small spacing errors from repositioning the tape.

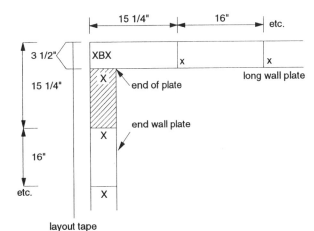

7-10 *The spacing marks for an end wall must be offset by the width of the adjacent long wall plate. It's not uncommon for novices to mistakenly begin the layout at the end of the plate instead.*

143

CORNER POSTS AND PARTITION BACKERS

Built-up corner posts provide a strong structural connection between wall sections at the building corners, a structural connection for overlapping the top plates, and support for nailing the interior and exterior wall finish (see 7-11).

Although some argue that the traditional built-up corner post, consisting of three or four 12-inch pieces of blocking nailed between two studs, is overbuilt, in my opinion it provides much more solid support than the approved alternatives—metal "backup" clips or an "open" corner post—especially for nailing exterior corner trim boards. The cost of one additional stud per corner is worth the security of knowing that your drywall corner joints won't crack if someone bumps into them.

Dropping the blocking of a built-up corner post slightly below the ends of the full-length studs makes it easier to square the ends of the post (see 7-12). Nail the blocking to the stud with 10d nails, and nail the second stud to it with 16d nails. Some carpenters stagger the nailing pattern along the length of the studs. In my opinion, two nails driven in a line helps keep built-up posts from twisting. Use toenails to drive the edges of any bowed studs flush with each other.

Corners for 2×6 wall framing require another layer of blocking to gain the added thickness. They are indicated on the plate by an "XBBX."

If you opt not to use double sole plate framing, nail blocking to the bottom of the corner posts to provide a nailing surface for the baseboards.

Partition backer posts are used wherever an interior wall abuts the perimeter wall or interior walls intersect (see 7-13). The essential principle is to provide a solid connection to tie the walls together and backing for nailing the wall finishes to the corners. Solid partition backers are most often used where a regular stud can be used as one of the backers. A 2×6 (or 2×8 for 2×6 framing), nailed flatwise, also makes a solid backer when the intersection falls between stud spacings. This is easier than the alternative favored by some carpenters of nailing a 1×8 board to a ladder of horizontal 2×4s.

Depending on whether it faces towards the interior or the exterior of the wall, the location of partition backer layout lines will be different at the top and sole plates. To make it easier to tilt up finished sections, the exterior side of the wall frame faces upwards. The sole plate will be next to the edge of the floor platform and the top plate will be farthest from it. If a header is inadvertently nailed to the sole plate instead of the top plate, you could frame the entire opening upside down before noticing the mistake (see 7-14). To avoid confusion label the plates as "top" and "bottom." Draw directional arrows on them to keep the frame sections properly aligned from left to right.

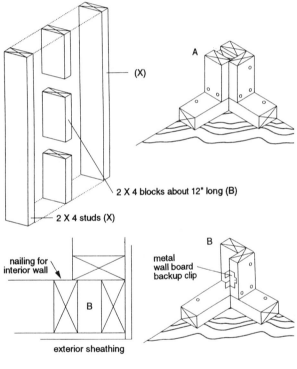

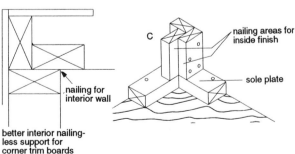

7-11 *Although they require more lumber, a built-up corner post is structurally stronger than other kinds of corner post frames.*

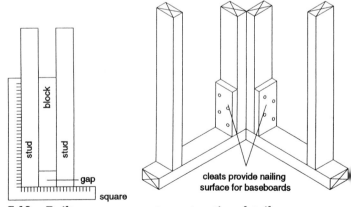

7-12 *Built-up corner post construction details.*

144

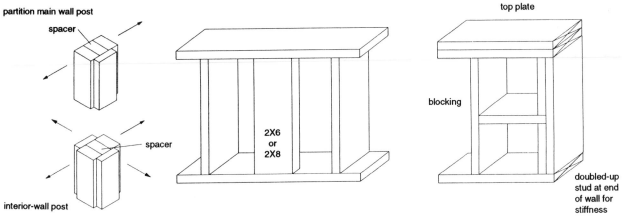

7-13 *A two-by laid flatwise or a built-up post provides a solid attachment for an intersecting partition and good backing for nailing the finish walls into the corners.*

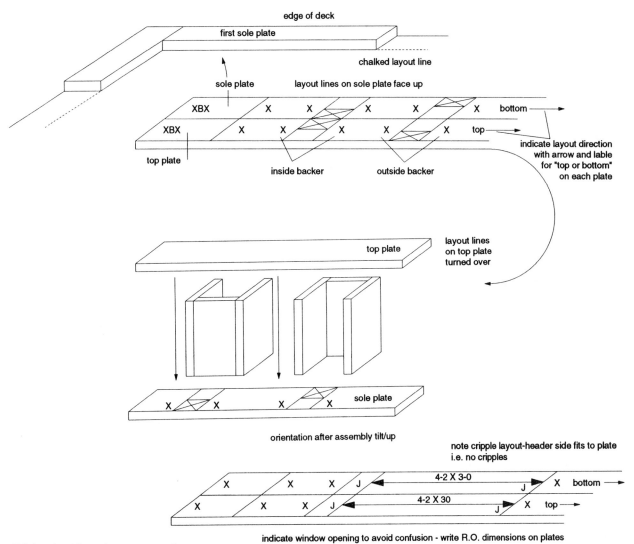

7-14 *Avoiding layout mistakes.*

The lines on the sole plate face the way the wall will be built. The lines on the top plate face upside down. When the top plate is properly positioned, a layout line for a partition backer marked on its outside edge will rotate to the inside edge. Overlook this twist and you'll nail the partition backer in backwards.

HEADERS

Typical header spans for the two most common loading conditions are given in **7-15**. Theoretically, the size of a header depends on the width of the opening and the type of load it carries. In reality, header sizing is often stipulated by local codes.

Furthermore, the real limiting factor for the depth of a header (and hence its span) is the height of the wall frame. It's an established principle of good design that windows look best if their tops are all at the same level. According to custom and studies of comfortable fields of view, this is 6'-8". Thus, maximum header depth is ultimately the difference between 6'-8" and stud length plus the sole plate. In standard framing, this isn't all that much. For example, at 7'-3" (the height of a double sole plate and seven-foot studs) the headers are limited to 2×8s (since a 2×8 is 7¼ inches deep, the header height is actually 6'-7¾"—close enough to 6'-8" to ignore). A 7'-8" ceiling height (precut studs and a single sole plate) allows a 2×10 header. A 2×12 header requires a minimum ceiling height of 7'-10".

So the widths of the windows are limited by the header spans and/or ceiling height. The design principle of vertical symmetry says that window patterns look more balanced when same-sized windows are placed directly above each other or when the upper storey windows are smaller than the first storey windows. The net result is, structural considerations notwithstanding, that the upper storey header shouldn't be any longer than the lower storey header. All of these considerations should have been resolved during the initial design phase, long before you're actually assembling headers.

Headers for a standard 6'-8" door opening are placed at 6'-10½". Despite the difference in heights, the finish trim of the door will match the line of the finish trim of the windows. Make door headers for 7'-6" ceilings by ripping down 2×6 stock to 4½ inches.

7-15 *Typical recommended header spans.*

Header dimensions doubled, on edge	2nd storey load (ceiling and roof)	1st storey load (ceiling, roof, floor)
2×4	3'-6"	3'-0"
2×6	6'-0"	5'-0"
2×8	8'-0"	7'-0"
2×10	10'-0"	8'-0"
2×12	12'-0"	9'-0"

When you're framing with rough-sawn lumber, any differences in width between the studs will be on the outside of the wall, where they more or less "disappear" under the sheathing and siding. The inside face will be in the same plane, simplifying finish work and allowing a flat wall.

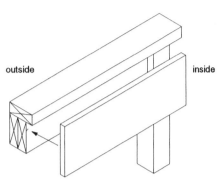

outside / inside

option add 1/2" plywood to header after wall framing

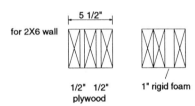

for 2X6 wall

5 1/2"

1/2" 1/2" plywood

1" rigid foam

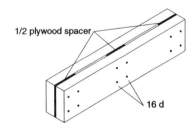

1/2 plywood spacer

16 d

header construction - plywood spacers are placed 16 to 24 in. apart on centers also use rigid foam

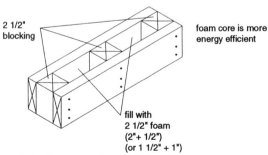

2 1/2" blocking

foam core is more energy efficient

fill with 2 1/2" foam (2"+ 1/2") (or 1 1/2" + 1")

7-16 *Header assembly details.*

Since a header doubled up for 2×4 wall framing will be only three inches thick, a filler of ½-inch CDX plywood is usually sandwiched between the planks (see **7-16**). Two filler pieces are needed for the tripled headers used with 2×6 wall framing. If ½-inch CDX wasn't included in your initial framing lumber order, the filler strips can be nailed to the interior face of the header instead, after the frame is closed in. To reduce heat loss through a solid wood header, use ½-inch or one-inch rigid foam insulation instead of plywood. With 2×6 wall framing, a tripled header permits longer spans relative to header depth. However, in most situations a doubled header is all that is structurally necessary. The energy efficiency of the header can be increased even further by nailing the stock to 2½-inch-thick blocking instead of a third plank and filling the cavities with 2½ inches of rigid foam insulation.

Because they can eliminate the need for short cripples between the top of the header and the underside of the plate, many framers use full-depth headers even when they aren't called for structurally (see **7-17**). This forces electricians to route wiring under the windows even when it would be more convenient to run a cable above the header. Because a wide, solid header will shrink more than a narrower one, it's more likely to cause cracks in the drywall.

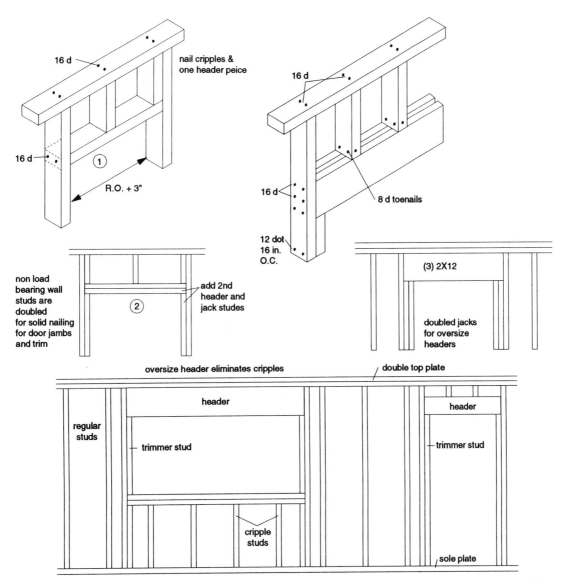

7-17 *Sequence is important in framing openings in nonbearing partitions. Nail the cripples to the flatwise header first. Then nail the assembly to the king studs and top plate. Add a second flat piece to provide nail-backing for finish trim, and then add the jack studs.*

147

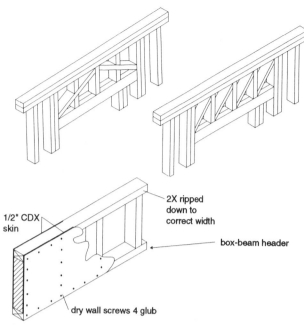

1/2" CDX skin

2X ripped down to correct width

box-beam header

dry wall screws 4 glub

7-18 *Trussed headers can be used in place of solid, built-up headers where spans and loads are excessive. Where there is adequate headroom, plywood-skinned box beams are even stronger.*

When cripples can't be avoided, they should be nailed through the top plate with 16d nails and toenailed into the header with 8d nails. Headers aren't needed for non-load-bearing interior partitions. Nail the cripples to a single flatwise header, and then face-nail a second header stud under it to provide solid nailing for the door trim.

Trussed headers are used for unusually long spans or extra-heavy loads, such as a garage door opening in a split-level house (see **7-18**). While the building inspector may require a design for an unusual condition to be certified by a structural engineer, in most cases, trussed headers are nothing more complicated than cripples reinforced by diagonal braces. *Box beams*, which are similar to a floor truss skinned with plywood, are used where solid timbers are impractical or insufficient for the load or span and where depth clearance isn't limited. Since oversized headers need more bearing surface to counteract increased shear forces, double their jack studs.

ASSEMBLING THE WALL FRAME

The length of the individual sections of wall frame is limited by the help available to tilt it up. Lifting more than 12 feet of wall by yourself is hard on your back, if not downright dangerous. A four-person crew can easily tilt up walls as long as 32 feet, if they don't contain too many large, heavy headers.

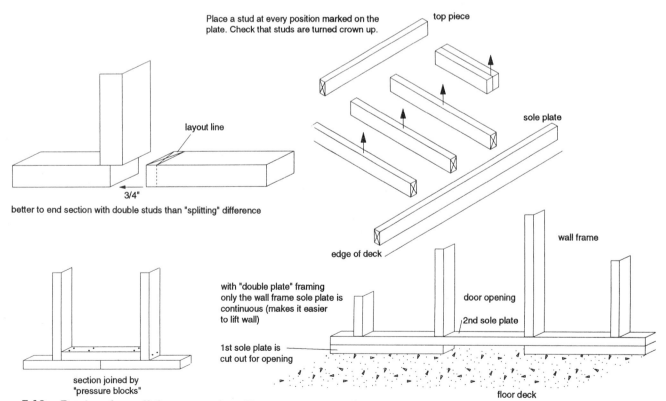

Place a stud at every position marked on the plate. Check that studs are turned crown up.

top piece

sole plate

layout line

3/4"

better to end section with double studs than "splitting" difference

edge of deck

wall frame

section joined by "pressure blocks"

with "double plate" framing only the wall frame sole plate is continuous (makes it easier to lift wall)

door opening

2nd sole plate

1st sole plate is cut out for opening

floor deck

7-19 *Putting the wall frame together. Frame openings only after nailing all the regular studs first.*

To assemble the wall frame, lay the sole plate on edge about a foot away from the end of the floor deck; pay attention to the sequence that assembly requires (see 7-19). Distribute the regular studs next to their layout lines. Lay the top plate next to them. To make it easier to lift the walls, don't cut out the sole plates for any door openings at this time. Wait until after the frame is tilted up; then use a handsaw (or reciprocating saw) to make the cuts.

Check each stud for crown before nailing it in place. Any bows should face upwards, towards the exterior of the wall. Rather than build humps into the finished wall, cut up any badly warped studs for blocking or short cripples. Start two 16d nails in the sole plate, and then, holding the stud to the line with one hand and pushing the top edge of the sole plate flush to the stud with your foot or knee, drive the nails home. Nail the corner studs and all the regular studs, first to the sole plate and then to the top plate. Then assemble the opening frame members and other special backer posts. End each section of plate with a full stud. This allows the wall sections to be solidly nailed to each other with a doubled stud. "Splitting" the last stud between the plates is a lumber-saving alternative. Sections of wall frames can also be joined by nailing a piece of blocking to the plates between the last studs as shown in 7-19.

As with a stairwell opening in the floor deck, the order in which the framing members for a window opening are assembled is important (see 7-20). The opening is built from the header on down. First, nail the king studs in place. Then nail the header to the top plate and through the king studs. (Leave out any regular stud that will interfere with nailing room alongside the header and sill until after the window opening is finished.) Cripples, if required above the header, will position it at the proper height. Next, nail the jamb studs under the header. Transfer the cripple stud spacings to the *subsill*—the bottommost of the doubled-up sill pieces—from the sole plate, and lay the two pieces in place under the jack studs; but don't nail them yet. Check the cripples for proper fit, and trim them, if necessary. Nail the cripples to the sole plate and subsill. Then drive the sill proper into place, and nail it to the king studs and the subsill. Using only straight stock for king studs will make it easier to plumb doors, windows, and trim boards in their rough openings. To prevent nasty accidents, be sure that any nails sticking through the doubled studs are clinched over before you even prepare to lift the wall.

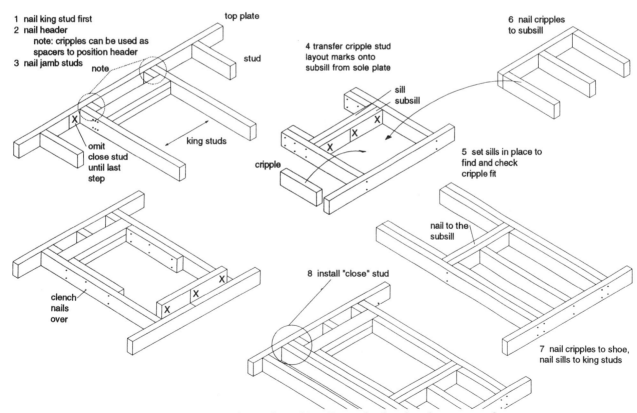

7-20 *Window and door openings are framed working from the header down towards the sole plate with a nailing pattern that maximizes the strength of the connections while minimizing wasted time and motion.*

149

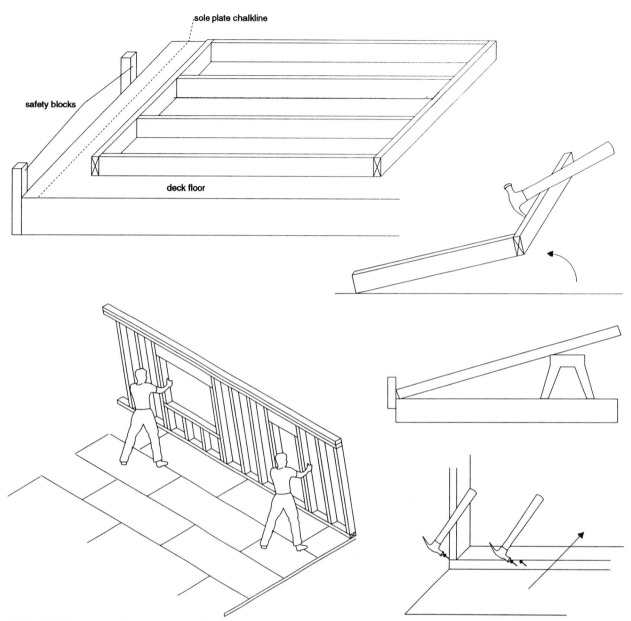

sole plate chalkline

safety blocks

deck floor

7-21 *Tilting up wall sections and nailing down the sole plate.*

Tilting up wall sections is one job where it makes sense to hire some extra help (see **7-21**). One of the advantages of a straight-claw framing hammer is that you can sink the claw into the top plate and save your back by lifting the frame off the floor with the hammer. Lifting a wall frame is a lot like pressing weights; the tricky place is where you switch from pulling to pushing. If the frame is too heavy, prop it up on a sawhorse while you reposition yourself for the push. Nail blocking to the outside of the rim joist for a safety stop. This will keep the bottom of the frame from sliding off the deck if you lose control of it while lifting. Set the frame on the chalk line or on top of the first sole plate, and, while your helper holds it upright, check to see that it's lined up with the end of the wall. If it isn't, nudge it into place by toenailing through the end of the sole plate or adjust it with a few gentle taps of a sledgehammer. Then nail the sole plate down with two 16d nails in each stud bay. Some framers use a special lever-like tool to pull the sole plate in or push it out to the chalk line (or first sole plate), but you can use your hammer claw for the former and a flat bar or pinch bar for the latter.

150

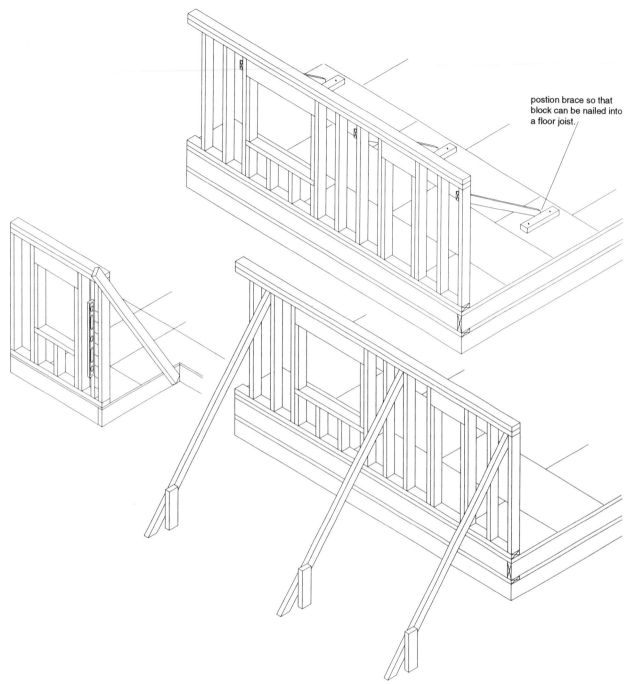

position brace so that block can be nailed into a floor joist.

7-22 *Temporary bracing; the braces can be secured to the top or sides of the floor deck or attached to stakes driven into the ground on the outside of the building.*

Don't let go of the wall until it's nailed off at the sole plate. On a windy day, your helper shouldn't let go of it until it's secured with temporary braces (see **7-22**). Tack a 2×4 to the end of the top plate on the outside of the wall, and plumb it with your four-foot level, while your helper tacks the other end of the brace to the stringer joist. As each section of wall is tilted up and nailed to the end stud of the preceding section, tack more temporary 2×4 braces to the face of the studs just below the top plate and to blocking nailed to the subfloor over a joist.

7-23 *This frame mixes conventional platform construction with a balloon-framed high wall section. Note the notches in the studs for the floor ledger. Notice that because its top plate has not yet been installed, the long wall is bowed where its sections are joined together. No temporary diagonal braces are needed prior to lining, since numerous corners tend to make wall frames self-supporting.*

Don't be too concerned about making everything perfectly plumb yet, and don't nail the braces too solidly. At this point, their main job is simply to keep the walls standing upright while you tilt up all the sections and double the top plates (see **7-23**).

Before you nail the walls together at a corner, check to see that the studs are tight both to the sole plate and to the top plate. They tend to pull apart when the walls are tilted up. The corner post might also be out of square. Snug up the joints by whacking the top plate over each stud with a sledgehammer. Toenail the outside edges of the corner post studs flush with each other before spiking them solidly together.

Plumb the wall in the plane of its length by tacking a brace from the top inside corner down across the studs to the sole plate. Once all the walls sections are tilted up and braced, the top plate is doubled (see **7-24**). As before, choose long, straight lumber for plate stock. If possible, center the upper plate over the end joints in the lower plate—or, at the very least, overlap them by a minimum of four feet. Toenail the plates to bring them together flush before driving two 16d nails over the middle of each stud bay. If you begin at one end of the plate and work along its length, the uppermost plate acts like a lever to pull the lower wall sections into a straight line.

The plates should also overlap each other at the corners as was mentioned in Chapter Five. Hold back the topmost plate where it intersects a partition wall, and overlap the partition top plate onto the lower top plate of the wall to make a strong connection.

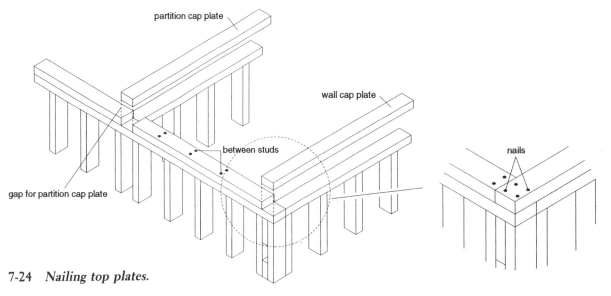

7-24 *Nailing top plates.*

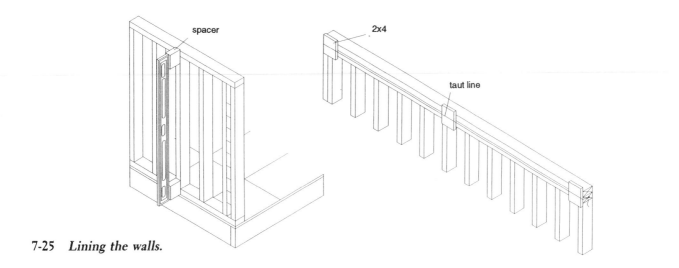

7-25 *Lining the walls.*

LINING THE WALLS

In lieu of more substantial bracing, the frame is likely to be shoved out of whack by the time you get all the wall sections up and nailed together. The plates also tend to bow somewhat, and the sections flex at inherently weak joints such as those at the edges of door openings and long window headers. Lining the walls trues up the frame (see **7-25**). Reinforced bracing holds it in place so that the sheathing and rafters, partitions, or second-floor deck can be added.

As with the rim joists, nail spacer blocks to each corner of the building flush with the top plate, and stretch a string between them. Check the corners for plumb in both directions (i.e., parallel and perpendicular to the plane of the wall), adjust the braces as needed, and nail them solidly to the deck and wall. Drive a nail wherever the brace crosses a stud. Check the spacing at intervals along the string, and bring the wall into alignment by pushing out or pulling in on the braces and adding more braces, as needed.

Lining assumes that if the corners are plumb and the sole plate is straight, then the top plate must be straight if it is plumb to the sole plate. Nevertheless, a plumb wall isn't always a straight wall; sometimes, the sole plate isn't perfectly straight, or the top plates aren't exactly flush. Within reason, a perfectly straight wall is a higher priority than a perfectly plumb wall. The rafters or the floor deck will fit better. If the wall is within ⅛ inch of the string, it's straight enough. You might have to "split the difference" between plumb and straight to bring the wall into line.

Pushing or pulling on a brace might not be enough to move a wall in or out or hold it to the line once you've moved it (see **7-26**). You can gain extra leverage by inserting a 2×4 or pinch bar under the end of the brace and prying upwards. If more force is needed, wedge a 2×8 or 2×10 plank flatwise between a block nailed to

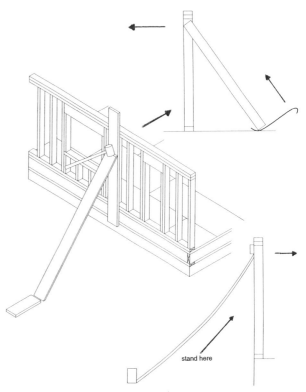

7-26 *Nail braces to the insides of the wall studs so that they won't have to be moved or trimmed off to sheath the walls.*

the subfloor and another plank leaning against the wall, and pound its top edge down with a sledgehammer. Nail the planks together when the wall is on the line. You can also use this technique to push a wall inward from outside the building by wedging the plank against a stake driven into the ground.

153

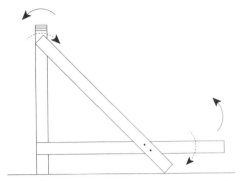

7-27 *This powerful lever can move even the most stubborn walls in or out.*

Another technique which works equally well for pushing outward or pulling inward is to spike a 2×4 diagonally to the wall stud just beneath the top plate, nail a second 2×4 horizontally to the bottom of the stud, and then nail the two braces together at their apex (see 7-27). Lifting upwards on this lever pushes the top of the wall outward. Pushing downwards pulls it inward.

Once you've pulled a wall section into satisfactory alignment, brace it well. The blocking to which the ends of the braces are nailed should be solidly nailed to the joists, not just to the subfloor. Braces in the plane of the wall are left in place until the walls are sheathed (see 7-28). Braces perpendicular to it shouldn't be removed until after the interior partitions are built and the roof is framed and shingled. Until then, these braces are the only thing that keeps the walls straight and prevents them from moving back and forth. Try to place the braces so that they won't have to be moved in order to make room for a partition.

The most important thing to remember about lining and bracing is: Don't assume that something is plumb just because it has been plumbed and braced once before. Until the framing and sheathing is finished, things tend to sneak out of line, especially when braces are moved and removed. The weight of piled-up building materials, the weakness of temporary bracing, and the stresses and strains of the construction process all conspire to twist and tug at the frame. Check and recheck walls and corners before the next step makes them more rigid and harder to fix.

SHEATHING THE WALLS

Although permitted by some codes, ⅜-inch sheathing doesn't provide a very solid nail base for any kind of finish siding unless the siding is nailed directly to the studs. Nominal inch-thick board sidings should always be nailed to the studs, no matter how thick the plywood. But other finish sidings such as wood shingles, clapboard, and hardboard siding can be nailed into ½-inch CDX with 16-inch o.c. stud spacing or ⅝-inch CDX with 24-inch o.c. spacing. If used with 16-inch o.c. spacing, the thicker sheathing makes a much stronger frame that offers significantly more long-term resistance to siding nail withdrawal. This could be a design/budget consideration for high-wind areas.

Plywood sheathing is generally applied vertically since this orientation provides the most effective racking resistance (see 7-29). With 10-foot to 12-foot high walls, the top course of sheathing can be horizontal. Space 8d nails five to six inches apart along the edges of the sheets and 10 to 12 inches apart elsewhere. Leave a ⅛-inch expansion gap between long edges and a 1/16-inch between the short ends of the sheets. Double this spacing in humid or wet weather.

For maximum shear resistance, the bottom edge of the sheathing should overlap the rim joist and mudsill. Instead of fussing with a precise fit between the bottom of the sheathing and the top of the foundation wall, set the mudsills so that the sheathing runs down over the wall about ½ inch. This helps seal out infiltrating drafts and hides

7-28 *The temporary braces that hold the wall corners plumb and prevent lateral movement in the plane of the wall are left in place until after the wall is sheathed.*

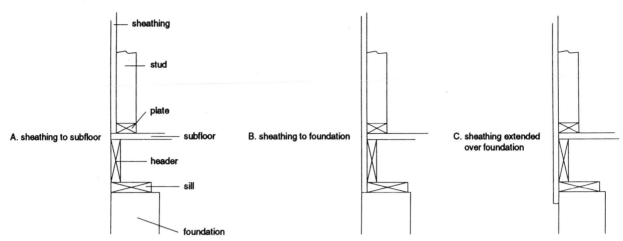

7-29 *Application of plywood sheathing.*

A. sheathing to subfloor

sheathing
stud
plate
subfloor
header
sill
foundation

B. sheathing to foundation

C. sheathing extended over foundation

any flaws in the foundation. With a single-storey building, most framers prefer to run the sheathing flush with the top plate downwards. This is fine, as long as its bottom edge overlaps at least half the depth of the rim joist. If it doesn't, the studs must be anchored to the rim with metal ties. In any case, these tie-down anchors are a good idea—if not a code requirement—in high-wind or earthquake regions. With two-storey buildings, the top edge of the sheathing should end a few inches below the bottom of the top plate or on the second-floor rim joist so that it ties together the frame components.

Normally, owner-builders will find it easier to sheath the walls after they're framed. Mark the centerlines of the studs on each sheet before nailing them. If you're working alone, snap a level chalk line across the top of the frame and tack a jig to it as shown in **7-30** to hold the top edge of the sheet for nailing. The jig is reversed to anchor the bottoms of second-storey sheets.

If job site security is a concern, don't cut out the window openings until just before the windows and doors are installed. Tack sections of 2×4 around the inside of the door opening to make a stop against which you can nail the door cut-out when you leave for the day (see **7-31**). If you own an electric chain saw or a reciprocating saw with a long blade, you can saw out the openings from the inside. Countersink any jamb or sill nails so that you won't hit them with your saw blade. Since it doesn't require any marking of lines or working from ladders, this method is fast. But, it also splinters the face of the sheathing. It's messy. Some builders prefer to drive a nail through the sheathing to mark the corners of the openings and then snap lines on the outside face of the sheathing and saw out the openings with a circular saw set for depth.

If security isn't an overriding issue, it's even easier to cut the openings before nailing the sheathing to the studs. Hold the sheet in place and scribe the cut marks against its back side (refer to **7-31**).

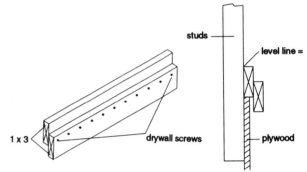

studs
level line =
1 x 3
drywall screws
plywood

7-30 *"Extra hand" wall sheathing jig.*

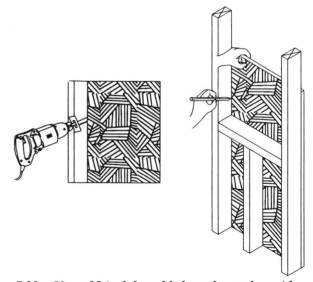

7-31 *Use a 12-inch-long blade and rest the guide shoe of the saw against the inside edge of the wall studs when cutting an opening with a reciprocating saw.*

155

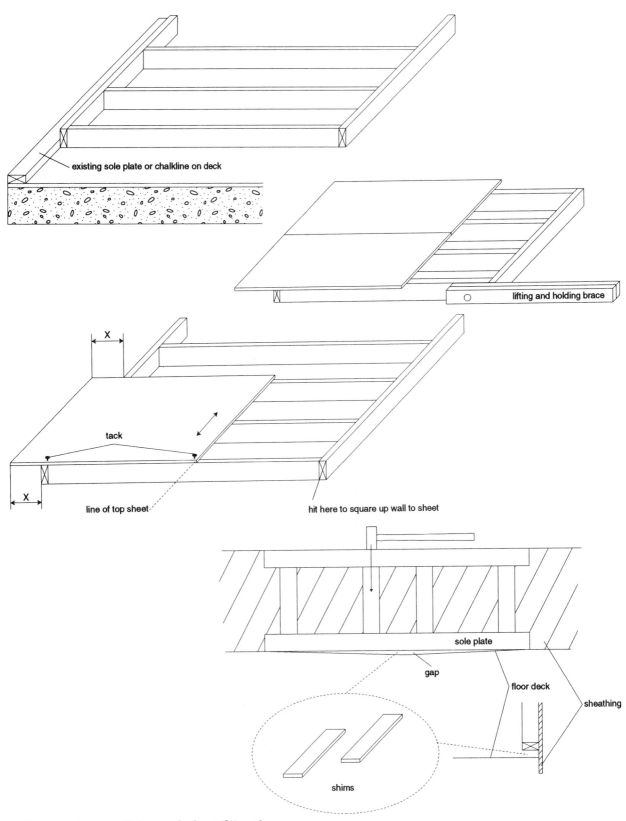

7-32 *Sheathing wall frames before tilting them up.*

156

When extra hands are available, there are some advantages to sheathing the walls before tilting them up (see 7-32 and 7-33). It's easier to nail plywood to a horizontal surface than a vertical one. And, temporary bracing in the plane of the walls can be eliminated.

The frame must be squared up before the sheathing is nailed to it (refer to 7-32). Establish a baseline by pushing the sole plate of the wall section tight to the first sole plate already nailed to the deck. If you're using only a single sole plate, toenail it to a chalk line snapped across the floor deck. Although some builders lay the sheathing flush with the top of the wall, it's structurally sounder to overhang the sole plate enough to completely cover, or at least fasten onto, the rim joist. Align the first sheet of plywood to the edge of the corner post at the proper height. Tack it with a nail at its top and bottom edge. Measure the overhang at the other end of the sheet. If it's the same, the frame is square. If it's not, use a sledgehammer to coax the top plate in or out until the measurements are equal. Snap chalk lines for nailing guides, and nail the sheathing to the studs. So long as the spacing of the overhang is even on subsequent sheets, the wall will stay square. For maximum strength, the sheathing should overlap joints between wall sections rather than break on them.

Since it's hard to get a firm grip on the studs in a sheathed wall, tack two or three temporary braces to the studs; use a single nail so that they can pivot outward as the wall is tilted up. Lift carefully; the added weight of the sheathing makes the wall sections heavier and more awkward to maneuver, especially since there's no safety stop-block nailed to the rim joist. Any dips in the floor platform will show up as a gap under the sole plate. Check to make sure the studs are nailed tight to their plates, and "adjust" them with a sledgehammer, if necessary. Otherwise, wedge wood-shingle shims into the gap to prevent the wall from settling.

NONSTRUCTURAL SHEATHING
Unless you happened to have your own sawmill or other source of cheap boarding, it's unlikely that you'd choose to sheath your house with traditional diagonal 1×6 tongue-and-groove boarding. It's not so much the expense as that it's just too time-consuming. But there are two alternatives to conventional plywood sheathing that are worthy of consideration.

Asphalt-impregnated sheathing (IB) board has a long history as a cheap alternative to plywood sheathing (see 7-34). The panels—made from vegetable-fibre waste materials, such as ground corn stalks and bagasse (sugar cane residuum), coated with asphalt for water resistance—have twice the insulating value of plywood (R2 per inch). IB board can be cut with a utility knife or a saw and is fastened to the studs with large-headed galvanized roofing nails. Exposed factory edges are waterproof, but cut edges aren't. Install blocking behind any unsupported edge joints.

7-33 *In this house, the first-floor wall frames were covered—before tilting them up—with ⁷/₁₆-inch Aspenite waferboard structural sheathing panels, a popular low-cost alternative to CDX plywood. Note the full-storey front wall and the rear knee-wall configuration characteristic of a traditional saltbox-style roofline.*

Since their introduction in the 1980s, aluminum-foil-faced polyisocyanurate and phenol-formaldehyde plastic foam sheathing panels have become widely used. The considerable expense of this insulating foam is offset by the elimination of plywood sheathing and the lower cost of 2×4 framing without sacrificing the energy efficiency of a 2×6 wall. (Depending on the manufacturer, foam sheathing panels have an R value of between 7 and 8 per inch. Coupled with the R-11 of 3½-inch fibreglass, a 2×4 framed wall is more or less equivalent to an R-19 2×6 wall.)

7-34 *Nonstructural asphalt-impregnated sheathing (IB) board is another very inexpensive alternative to plywood, particularly when the walls will be sided with vertical or horizontal inch boards. Plywood is used at the corners and between the window panels in lieu of, or in addition to, diagonal bracing to provide extra racking resistance.*

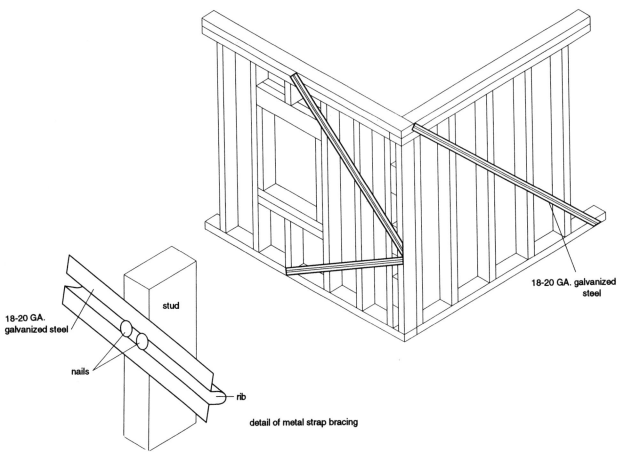

18-20 GA. galvanized steel

stud

18-20 GA. galvanized steel

nails

rib

detail of metal strap bracing

7-35 *Metal let-in wall braces; use two 8d nails at each stud.*

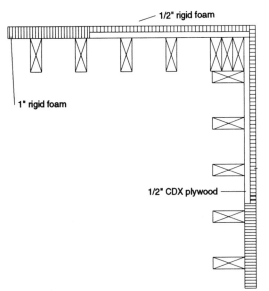

1/2" rigid foam

1" rigid foam

1/2" CDX plywood

7-36 *Run vertical full-width sheets of plywood at each building corner when using rigid foam or IB nonstructural sheathings.*

Since both IB board and plastic foam panels are nonstructural, however, they offer no racking resistance. Let-in wood bracing is labor-intensive and not as strong as plywood, especially when the wall is perforated by window and door openings. T-shaped steel braces aren't quite as strong as wood braces, but they are inexpensive and so easy to install that what they lack in strength individually can be overcome by strength of numbers (see **7-35**). Snap a chalk line diagonally across the outside of the frame, and make a cut along the line with a circular saw set to depth. The brace fits into the saw kerf and is face-nailed through its flange into the studs with 8d nails.

Just the same, I wouldn't trust metal bracing on its own merits. Since the racking resistance of the wall is concentrated at its corners, I recommend sheathing them from sill to top plate with a full-width sheet of ½-inch plywood (see **7-36**). If you use one-inch foam instead of IB board, overlap the plywood corners with ½-inch foam to increase the R-value, and bring them flush to the rest of the sheathing. Since diagonal bracing is virtually ineffective in walls with large areas of glass, those walls should be sheathed with plywood over their entirety.

Nonstructural sidings cannot be used as a nailbase either. Unless it is end-matched, the finish siding must be nailed directly to the studs or strapping.

INTERIOR PARTITIONS

Interior partitions are built after the outside walls are erected, lined, and braced (see 7-37). The layout of interior partitions is done directly on the subfloor with a chalk line and pencil (see 7-38). The exterior walls provide the baselines and reference points for establishing parallel layout lines and measuring plan dimensions. You can use your four-foot level and framing square to draw and extend perpendicular layout lines. Use X's to mark the side of the line where the partition will be nailed. Check all dimensions for accuracy and squareness before cutting and nailing down the first sole plates.

With the exception of headers, which aren't required in nonload-bearing partitions, interior walls are framed exactly the same as exterior walls. Any interior walls which are load bearing should have solid blocking beneath them. Provide backer studs and nailers wherever walls abut. Interior partitions are plumbed to each other and to the outside walls, and temporarily braced, as needed. Once they are tied together by the floor deck, interior partitions provide most of the racking resistance across the span of the house. Keep this fact in mind when considering open-space designs. In any case, it's a good idea to include diagonal metal braces in any major partitions that intersect the outside walls at right angles whenever possible.

7-37 *Nonload-bearing interior partitions don't need built-up headers. But the doubled flat header provides solid nailing for the door trim. Notice the opening in the floor for the chimney.*

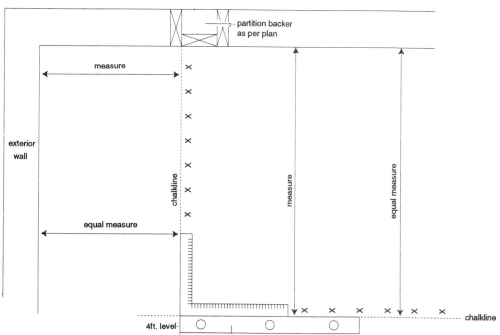

7-38 *Since interior partition lines are established by parallel measurement from them, the squareness of the exterior walls determines the accuracy of the interior layout.*

159

SPECIAL CONDITIONS

As with the floor joists, plumbing fixtures and drain lines typically require special framing techniques to accommodate them. The most common adaptation is the *wet wall* (see 7-39). The main soil stack vent of a household plumbing system is either four inches inside diameter (I.D.) cast iron or three inches I.D. ABS plastic pipe—neither of which will fit into a 2×4 partition. The wet wall is a partition framed with 2×6s which provides room for the vent stack and which may also contain all the plumbing supply and drain lines for a bathroom on one side and the kitchen or utility room on the other. The extra width of the studs also permits boring for horizontal 1½-inch and 2-inch diameter drain lines without compromising structural strength.

Since a vent stack that penetrates the top plate of a bearing partition can significantly compromise the plate's strength, the plate is reinforced by nailing 2×4 scabs against both sides of the pipe on top of the plate. Likewise, if the studs must be notched for drainpipes, they are similarly reinforced with let-in pieces of 1×2. It's also common practice to protect the pipes from nails by covering the face of the notch with a steel plate. Where a stud and part of the sole plate must be cut to accommodate a hot-air register, two 2×4s are nailed flatwise to the adjoining studs.

Some carpenters prefer to frame a double row of flatwise studs on a 2×6 or 2×8 plate instead. This way, horizontal drain lines can be run between the studs without any notching at all. Staggered 2×4 studs on a 2×6 plate

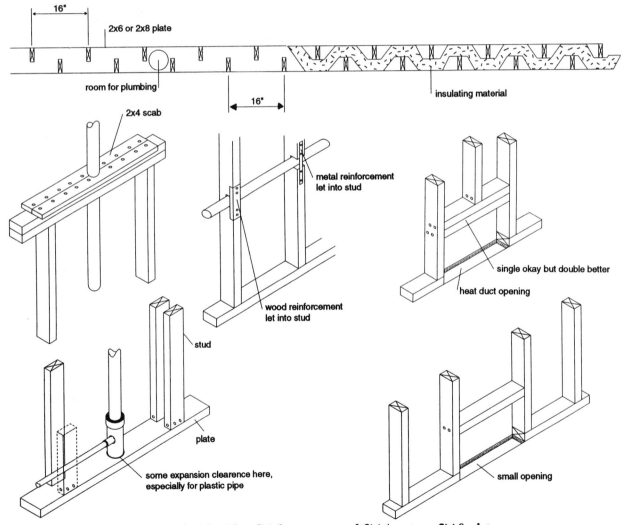

7-39 *Wet walls can be framed with either 2×6s or staggered 2×4s set on 2×8 plates. In bearing walls, always provide proper reinforcement for any notches or holes. Leftover side panels of gang-type electrical boxes can be used for covering the notches when drainpipes run close to the face of wall studs.*

160

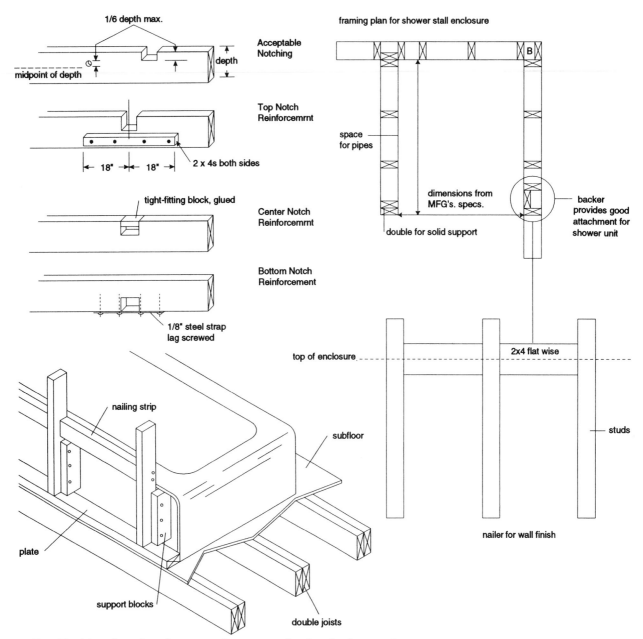

7-40 *Blocking for tubs, shower enclosures, and other bathroom fixtures. (Continued on next page.)*

maintain 16-inch spacing for the wall finishes and allow blankets of insulation to be woven between them for soundproofing (refer to **7-39**). This is desirable when a private room and a bathroom, kitchen, or utility room share a common wall.

Bathroom framing has the lowest tolerance for error of just about any room in the house, including the kitchen (see **7-40**). Standard tubs fit between walls framed at exactly 5'-0". The framing for one-piece moulded fibreglass shower units and one-piece bath-and-shower enclosures must be precisely dimensioned, plumb, and square. You can get a booklet which gives the framing measurements for your plumbing fixtures and fittings from the manufacturer or distributor; this is an essential part of your planning library. It's not a good idea to have a one-piece tub enclosure on site until after the frame is closed in. Since one-piece enclosures won't fit through a standard bathroom door opening, leave two or three studs out of the bathroom wall partition so that you can slide the enclosure through the opening after it is delivered.

161

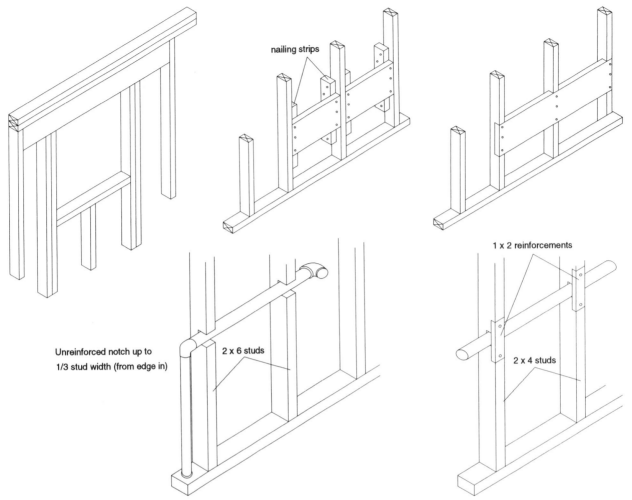

nailing strips

1 x 2 reinforcements

Unreinforced notch up to
1/3 stud width (from edge in)

2 x 6 studs

2 x 4 studs

7-40 *(Continued.) Blocking for tubs, shower enclosures, and other bathroom fixtures.*

Flatwise 2×4 blocking should be nailed between the studs to support the top edge of tub-and-shower enclosures and to provide solid backing for the wall finish. Standard bathtubs also require solid blocking along the bottom edge of the wall finish. Because of their weight, cast-iron tubs need additional support, either from a horizontal ledger nailed to the wall backing or from vertical 2×6 blocking nailed to each wall stud under the lip of the tub.

Backings for mounting wall-hung lavatories, wall cabinets, and other fixtures are nailed between the studs as shown in **7-40**. Check with the manufacturer or your plumber for mounting recommendations.

Blocking is also used in the sidewalls of closets to provide support for the closet shelf and clothes-pole mounting brackets (see **7-41**). Nail a 2×8 or 2×10 between the studs at about five and a half to six feet from the floor.

To gain space, the short wall that subdivides a closet between two rooms is sometimes framed with 2×2 stock or 2×4s toenailed flatwise to 2×2 plates. Unless they are shorter than two feet and anchored on both ends to standard walls, such thin walls will be too shaky, even for a closet.

Switches that control room lights are often mounted close to the edge of doors (see **7-42**). Nail one or two six- to eight-inch pieces of 2×4 blocking to the back of the jamb studs centered at 48 inches off the floor for mounting the switch box. Multiple ganged switch boxes need solid mounting support on both sides.

Fin walls are partitions that aren't attached to another wall at one end (see **7-43**). The last stud of a fin wall should be doubled up to increase its stiffness. It's also a good idea to nail two or three pieces of horizontal blocking between the doubled end stud and the last regular wall stud. One of these can also serve as a mounting support for ganged switches.

The more you can anticipate and provide for what will come later, the more solidly built and problem-free your house will be. You'll also avoid cutting into freshly finished

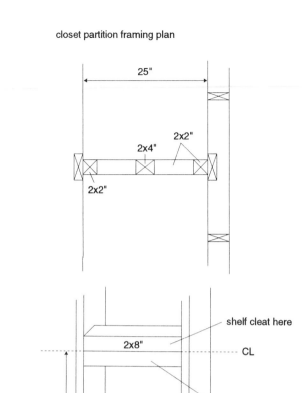

closet partition framing plan

25"

2x2"

2x4"

2x2"

shelf cleat here

2x8"

CL

5'-6" to 6-0"

closet pole bracket here

7-41 *Closet framing details; use 2×2 party wall framing to gain extra space in adjoining closets.*

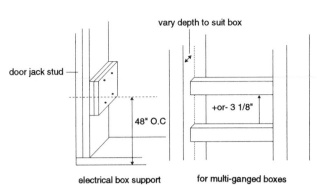

vary depth to suit box

door jack stud

48" O.C

+or- 3 1/8"

electrical box support

for multi-ganged boxes

7-42 *Blocking an electrical box next to a door opening provides clearance between the finish casing and the switch or outlet cover plate.*

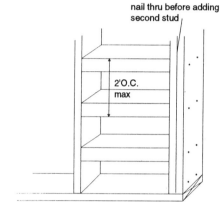

nail thru before adding second stud

2'O.C. max

7-43 *Without the extra stiffness provided by doubling and blocking, the drywall joints of a fin wall tend to crack.*

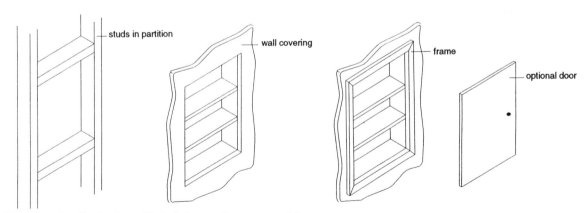

studs in partition

wall covering

frame

optional door

7-44 *Framing details for in-wall shelving and storage cabinets.*

walls to retrofit framing details and mounting supports that you've overlooked. Framing for in-wall medicine cabinets, ventilators, kitchen spice racks, and other in-between-studs storage shelves and cabinets are typical of the kinds of details that should be included in your partition framing (see **7-44**). Unless a stud must be cut, these types of details require only a 2×4 flatwise header at the top and bottom of the opening.

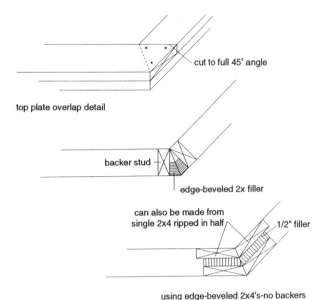

cut to full 45° angle

top plate overlap detail

backer stud

edge-beveled 2x filler

can also be made from
single 2x4 ripped in half

1/2" filler

using edge-beveled 2x4's-no backers

7-45 *Since they don't require ripping any oblique angles, 45-degree wall corners are easy to frame.*

Besides adding an element of drama to interior design, an angled wall can also be a practical way to provide access to rooms where hallway circulation space is limited. As long as the partition is confined to 45-degree angles, layout and framing won't confound the novice framer. Bisecting the angle is the key to framing a 45-degree corner post (see **7-45**). Draw layout lines for both sides of the sole plate. A line connecting the inside and outside corner points divides the angle into two 22½-degree angles. This

step is necessary because the face of a 45-degree bevel cut is longer than the face of a 90-degree cut; bisecting the angle yields two identical 22½-degree filler pieces that can be accurately joined to make a solid corner post. It's also considerably easier to rip a 2×4 on a 22½-degree bevel than on a 45-degree bevel. The bevelled pieces can be nailed to the face of the backer studs at the corner— or else nailed flatwise to each other and a spacer strip of ½-inch plywood in lieu of the backer stud. The end cuts of the sole plate and the first top plate should follow the angle of the studs. The second top plates should be cut at 45 degrees so that they'll overlap the first plate.

CEILING FRAMING

Since the first-floor ceiling joists of a two-storey house are the floor joists for the second floor, they are framed exactly like the first-floor deck except that instead of, or in addition to, girders, the joists typically overlap on bearing partitions (see **7-46**).

With single-storey houses and with the attic of a two-storey house, the ceiling joists differ from floor joists in that they're sometimes smaller, and that header or stringer joists aren't needed at the plates. Your building code will generally specify the minimum size of ceiling joists, depending on whether the attic will be used for storage or not and on what type of ceiling will be attached to them. If there's enough headroom under the rafters, it's foolish to suppose that the attic will never be converted into living space sometime in the future. It makes much more sense to plan for this by using stronger ceiling joists than absolutely necessary rather than undersizing them to save on materials.

7-46 *The first-floor ceiling joists of a two-storey house are the floor joists for the second floor. Note that these joists are fastened flush to a built-up center girder with joist hangers.*

164

If you do intend to use your attic for more than storage, I recommend that you frame a conventional floor platform complete with rim joist instead, and attach the rafters to a single plate nailed to the top of the floor deck to gain a little bit of extra headroom (see **7-47**).

Traditional Cape-style houses can also be framed with a storey-and-a-half wall. This attic *knee wall*, which typically varies in height from two to four feet, adds extra usable space below the roofline (see **7-48**). Since a platform-framed knee wall would be too weak to resist the outward thrust of the roof, the floor joists are supported semi-balloon fashion, on a ledger let into the wall studs, which are platform-framed to full height. If your code permits it, make the ledger from the same (or deeper) stock as the floor joists, and nail it directly over the studs instead of letting it into them. In either case, the joists can be attached to the ledger with joist hangers—instead of resting on it and being nailed to the sides of the studs. Face-nailing the ledger doesn't interfere with the thickness of the insulation in the wall. Otherwise, use rigid foam behind a let-in ledger.

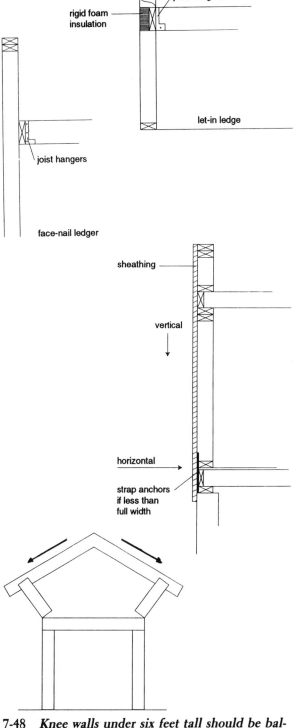

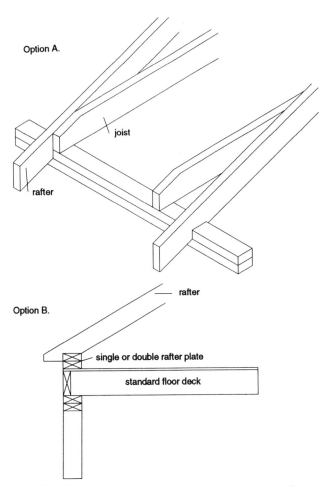

7-47 *Two ways to frame a load-bearing attic floor.*

7-48 *Knee walls under six feet tall should be balloon-framed whenever possible.*

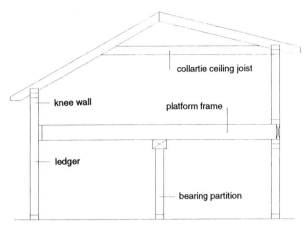

7-49 Raising the rear wall of a saltbox-style frame adds to the usable living space of the upper storey.

The traditional salt-box style house is framed with a combination of both methods (see **7-49**). The floor platform is hung from a ledger at the rear wall and rests on a single-storey plate at the front and side walls.

Although joists normally run across the narrow dimensions of the building, their direction can be turned at right angles to reduce the length of their spans where the layout of interior partitions permits a bearing wall (see **7-50**).

In large rooms, the ceiling joists may need to be supported at their mid-span by a beam. Such carrying beams are usually set flush with the bottoms of the joists. Where a beam might interfere with HVAC ducts, it is sometimes placed on top of the joists, which are then hung from it with metal hangers.

Although they can be attached anywhere on a double top plate, ceiling joists usually follow the same spacing module as the wall studs. An exception might be for an unfloored attic and a roof with rafters spaced on two-foot centers. Even if the walls were framed at 16 inches o.c., the ceiling joists would follow the rafter layout since the rafters are always nailed to the sides of the joists.

Toenail the joists to the rafter plate first. Although 10d common nails are recommended for toenailing joists and rafters, 16d box nails hold much better with little risk of splitting, especially if you blunt the tip of the nail first. Use one nail in each side of the joist.

When a toenail is driven through horizontal, as opposed to vertical, grain, as is the case with a joist versus a stud, the likelihood of splitting is much greater. Make it a habit to always blunt the tip of any toenails, especially when nailing the bottom ends of joists and rafters to the plates. To further reduce the chances of splitting, drive *only one* toenail on each side to position the piece, and then use framing anchors for the actual structural connection. Toenails are less troublesome when used to anchor the bottoms

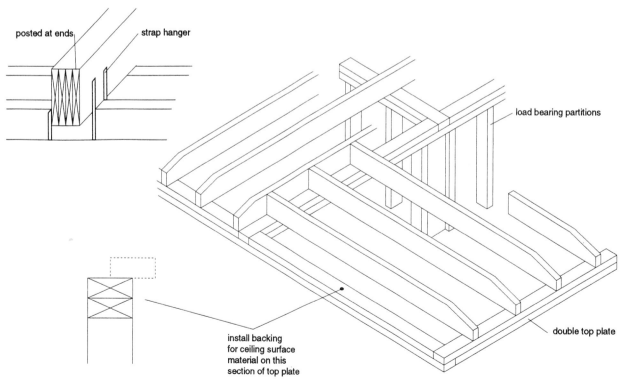

7-50 Built-up girders can be used instead of bearing partitions to carry the ceiling joists.

of studs, jacks, and cripples that are installed after the sole plate is already nailed down. Here, the difficulty is that driving the nail pushes the stud off the line. Experienced framers automatically adjust by starting the stud ahead of the line. The nail on the opposite face also pushes the stud back, as necessary. A beginner might consider using a toenailing jig—basically a piece of blocking cut to the stud interval—to keep the stud from moving as it is nailed.

This tendency to push a framing member away is exploited when using toenails to pull bowed pieces flush. To coax a particularly stubborn piece into line, drive two blunted box nails simultaneously. The doubled head area increases the holding (or pushing) power without increasing the chance of splitting an edge.

Although four 8d toenails (two on each wide face) will suffice to attach a stud to a sole plate, six nails (one each in the edge faces as well) will do a better job. Each toenail should be driven at about a 60-degree angle. If the angle is steeper, it'll split the wood, and if it's too shallow, it won't hold.

Use five 10d nails to join the rafters to the floor joists. Rather than depend on toenails for strength, secure the rafter and the joist to the plate with steel framing anchors (see **7-52**). In high-wind areas, special anchors are used to tie the joists to the wall studs as well.

A blunt nail will crush the wood fibres rather than split them apart like a wedge as it's hammered into them. Hold the head of the nail against something solid like another nail head, a metal framing anchor, or concrete, and strike its tip with your hammer (see **7-51**).

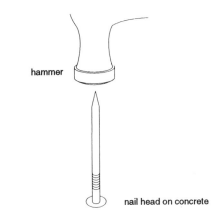

hammer

nail head on concrete

7-51 *To avoid splitting the bottom edges when toenailing joists and rafters, use box nails instead of the thicker common nails and always blunt the tip.*

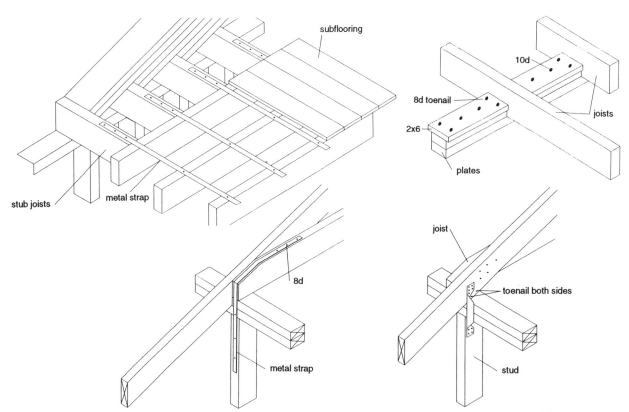

7-52 *Steel framing anchors make for quality construction even where high winds aren't a problem.*

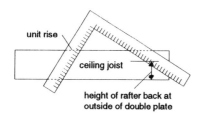

7-53 *Once you've determined how much to clip off, use one joist for a pattern to mark the others.*

With most roof pitches, the top edge of the ceiling joist will stick up past the top edge of the rafter. Usually, the required cut is small enough so that it can be done—after the rafters are installed—with a handsaw, a chainsaw, or even a hatchet (see **7-53**).

An exception is where the joists intersect a low-pitched hip roof. Here the cut might be long enough so that the joists are best cut before installing them. Use your framing square to lay out the cut line on the joist.

With hip roofs and other low-pitched roofs where the ceiling joists run parallel to the edge of the roof, the outermost ceiling joist will interfere with the slope of the roof in the same way that the top edge of the joists sticks up past the backs of the rafters. The problem is solved by framing the ceiling with *stub joists* running perpendicular to the regular joists (see **7-54**). Stub joists are generally short enough so that the regular joist need not be doubled to carry them. However, installing *pressure blocks* between each stub joist guarantees stiffness. Another option, which works just as well and uses considerably less lumber, is to lay an offset 2×6 across the top plate as a backer for the finish ceiling and to install the first joist flatwise. The flat joist is stiffened with 2×4 *strongbacks* nailed to the blocking at the plate and at the first vertical joist.

Unfloored ceiling joists are spaced where they cross a bearing partition or girder. In addition to this, they should be stiffened and properly spaced at their mid-spans before toenailing them to the tops of the interior partitions. This is usually accomplished by nailing a continuous course of

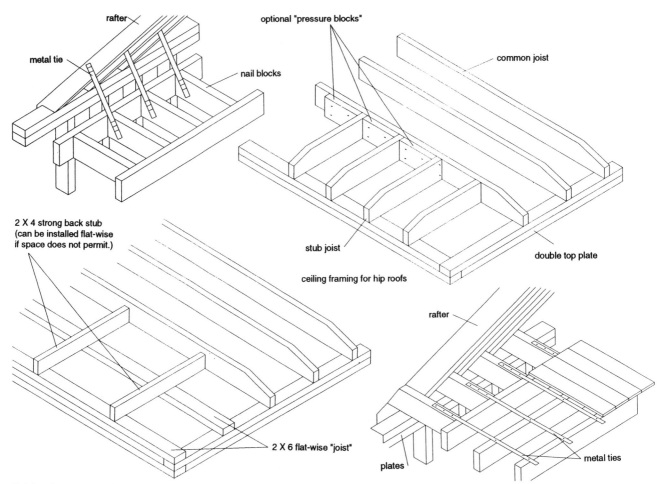

7-54 *Strapping the ceiling-joist nailing blocks to the rafters provides excellent resistance to wind uplift, which is important if the roof has a wide overhang.*

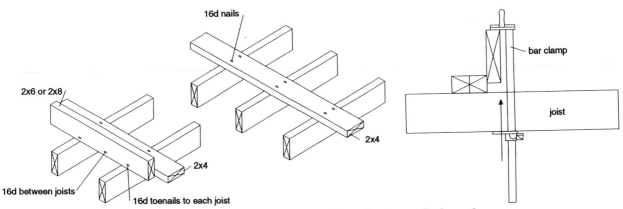

7-55 *You can also use a bar clamp to draw a stubbornly bowed joist up flush to the bottom of the strongback.*

2×4s—with the joist spacing intervals taped off on them—flatwise to the tops of the joists down the center of each joist span, similar to the way bridging or blocking was installed in the floor frame. However, with long uninterrupted spans, strongbacks are often used not only to space the joists and stiffen the ceiling, but also to level out crowns and dips in the joists so that the finish ceiling appears flat (see 7-55). Lay out the joist spacings on the 2×4 strongback as you would for wall plates, and nail it to a chalk line that has been snapped across the top of the ceiling joists at mid-span. Then nail one end of a straight 2×6 or 2×8 on edge to the strongback. Working down the length of this stiffener, step on the strongback or the stiffener to bring the edges flush to each other as you toenail

the stiffener to the joists, and face-nail it to the strongback with 16d nails.

Ceiling joists that run perpendicular to interior partitions are simply toenailed to them. Check for plumb first. To avoid splitting the bottom of joists, use a bar clamp to close any gap between the joist and the partition plate instead of trying to draw it down with toenails.

Partitions that run parallel to the joists are attached with *ladders*, which also carry a backer for nailing the finish ceiling (see 7-56). With the blade of your framing square, mark layout lines at two-foot intervals along the inside faces of the joist bay, 1½ inches up from the joist bottoms. Next, center and nail a 2×6 nailer flatwise over the top of the partition on the double plate.

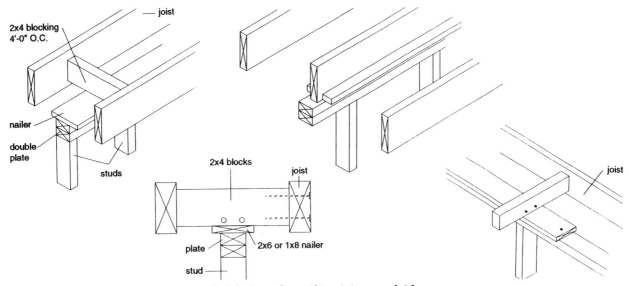

7-56 *If the partitions will be installed before the ceiling joists are laid, you can save time by nailing the ceiling backers to their top plates before installing the ladder pieces. Otherwise, install the ladders, then the backer; then nail the partition plate to it.*

169

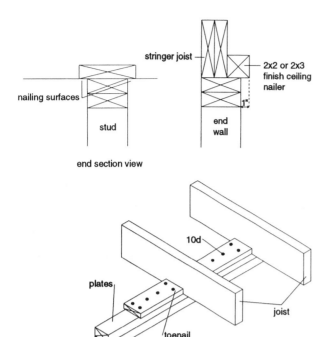

nailing surfaces

stringer joist

2x2 or 2x3 finish ceiling nailer

stud

end wall

end section view

10d

plates

joist

toenail

7-57 *Backing for nailing finish ceilings.*

Then nail 2×4 *rungs* flatwise between the joists over the top of the 2×6 backer. Check the partition for plumb, and then nail the ladder rungs into the backer. The same procedure in slightly different order is used when partitions are framed after the ceiling joists—as would be the case with a truss roof. Here, the ladders are nailed first; then the partition layout line is plumbed up to them and offset one inch for the backer. The backer is nailed into the ladders, and then the partition is framed and attached to it.

When partitions fall directly under—or slightly to the side of—a ceiling joist, nail a flatwise 2×4 or 2×2 to one or both sides of the joist as needed.

Many builders don't bother with backing over partitions that run perpendicular to the joists, since the ceiling finish is considered stiff enough to span the gap. But it is just this sort of cost-cutting detail that distinguishes true quality construction from ordinary work. If you want to save a little, substitute pieces of 1×6 or 1×8 boards for two-by blocking; but don't scrimp on nailer backing (see **7-57**).

Backing should also be nailed to the trimmer joists along the end walls; use 2×4 or 2×2 stock. Where the trimmer joist is omitted, nail a 2×4 across the edges of the end wall studs instead.

8 Roof Framing

ROOF TYPES AND TERMS

Among novice builders, there is a definite feeling that since it requires the layout and cutting of angles instead of simple butt joints, roof framing is a tricky business (see **8-1**). The complexity of roof construction is directly related to the design of the roof (see **8-2**). For example, building a *flat roof* is no more difficult than building a floor deck. The modernistic *shed roof* and the traditional *gable roof* require only the parallel layout of a single angle using nothing more mysterious than a bit of simple geometry and arithmetic and a framing square. The barn-like *gambrel roof* can be thought of as a combination of two separate gable roofs, while the traditional *salt-box-style roof* is really a shed-like extension of the basic gable roof. Because all four sides of a *hip roof* slope towards a central point, the angles of a hip roof are more complicated. The framing for a *mansard roof* is akin to a combination of a hip and gambrel roof. Any of these basic roof types can be combined with each other and with changes in direction, slope, and level, to create roof designs and layout problems of truly daunting perplexity and complexity. Simple roof framing, however, is well within the compass of the amateur homebuilder.

8-1 *Laying out the angled cuts of a rafter is considered a daunting challenge by many novice builders.*

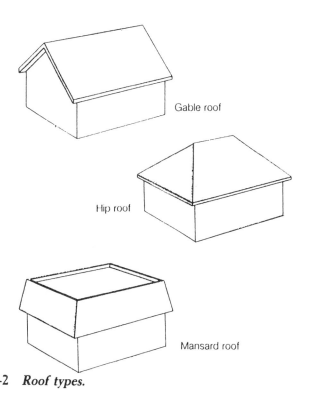

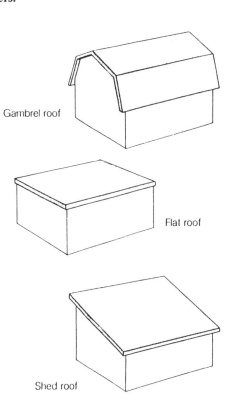

Gable roof

Gambrel roof

Hip roof

Flat roof

Mansard roof

Shed roof

8-2 *Roof types.*

Although it's unlikely that you'd ever build such a thing, the hypothetical frames shown in **8-3** depict the relationship of the various components of the roof frame to each other.

In general, roof framing pieces are broadly called *rafters*; they are further identified by their location and their function. *Common* rafters run at a right angle from the rafter plate to the ridge board. *Hip* rafters run from the rafter plate (usually at the building corners) to the ridge at a 45-degree angle. They can be thought of as a sloping ridge that supports two intersecting roof planes. *Valley* rafters are similar to hip rafters in that they also run diagonally from the ridge to the plate, but they lie in the hollow (hence, "valley") formed by the intersection of two

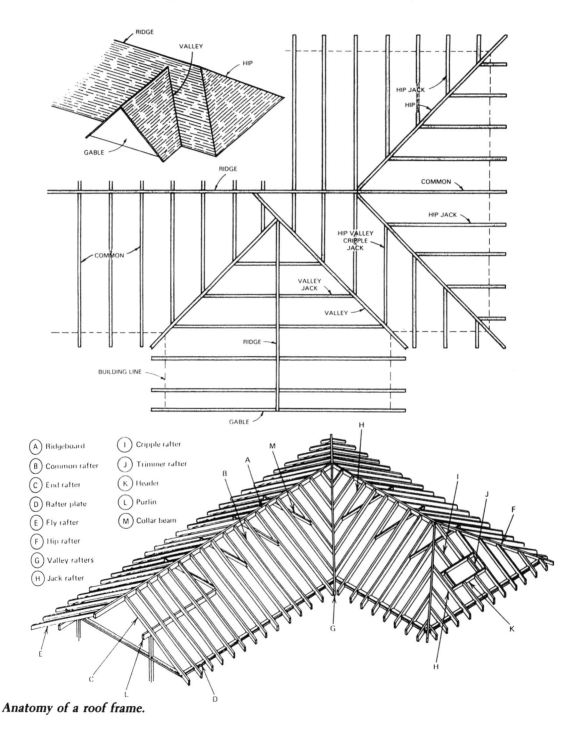

A Ridgeboard
B Common rafter
C End rafter
D Rafter plate
E Fly rafter
F Hip rafter
G Valley rafters
H Jack rafter
I Cripple rafter
J Trimmer rafter
K Header
L Purlin
M Collar beam

8-3   Anatomy of a roof frame.

172

roof planes at right angles to each other. There are three kinds of less-than-full-length *jack* rafters. A *valley jack* has the same upper end as a common rafter, but its lower end is cut on a *compound mitre*—an angle cut across the *face* of the rafter that adds a bevel perpendicular to it—to fit against the face of a valley rafter. A *hip jack* has the same lower end as a common rafter and a compound mitre at its upper end to fit against a hip rafter. A *cripple jack* has cuts at both ends to fit between a valley and a hip; it doesn't connect to either the plate or the ridge. The compound mitre cuts of jack rafters are called *cheek cuts*.

Besides the rafters, roof frames often include some form of *collar tie* to help stiffen the rafters and counteract the outward thrust on the walls. Depending on the roof design, collar ties can also function as ceiling joists. Although they can end flush with the outside of the wall plate, most rafters have *rafter tails*, which extend past the wall to form an overhang that diverts rainwater away from the walls and shades them from the sun. The overhang perpendicular to the slope of the roof is the *eaves*. The *rake* is the overhang parallel to it. On a gable roof, the end wall rafter is called the *gable* rafter. The rafter which frames the rake is hung from the underside of the projecting roof decking or from blocking attached to the main rafters. Since it isn't attached to the plate or the ridge board, it's called a *fly*, or *false*, rafter. Just as they are joined at their top ends by the ridge board, the ends of the rafter tails are often nailed to a *subfacsia* to provide a solid attachment for the eaves trim work.

Understanding the meaning and relationship between certain terms is essential to rafter layout (see **8-4**). The length of a rafter is the hypotenuse of a right triangle whose base is the *run* of the roof and whose altitude is its *rise*. The run of a rafter is the horizontal distance from the outside edge of the rafter plate to the ridge centerline. This is different from the *span* of the roof, which is the horizontal distance between the outside edges of the rafter plates. Unless the ridge is off center, the run will be half the span.

Most novice builders quite logically assume that the rise is the vertical distance between the rafter plate and the top edge of the rafter, where it runs into the ridge; it isn't. The *measuring line*, upon which rafter length calculations are based, is an imaginary line running from the outside of the rafter plate, parallel to the edge of the rafter, to the centerline of the ridge (refer to **8-4**). The rise is the vertical distance between the top of the plate and the point where the measuring line intersects the ridge centerline, which is somewhere below the top of the ridge.

Roof *slope* is the ratio of the roof rise to run, expressed as a function of 12—i.e., inches of rise per foot of run—which is how the framing square is calibrated for rafter layout (see **8-5**). This is distinguished from roof *pitch*, which is the ratio of rise to span, expressed as a fraction—e.g., a six-foot rise with a 24-foot span has a *6 to 12 slope*, but a *¼ pitch*. Since saws are calibrated in degrees, roof pitches and slopes are also sometimes converted into degrees of angle so that a protractor or special framing square can be used to set up compound mitre cuts and angled gable studs.

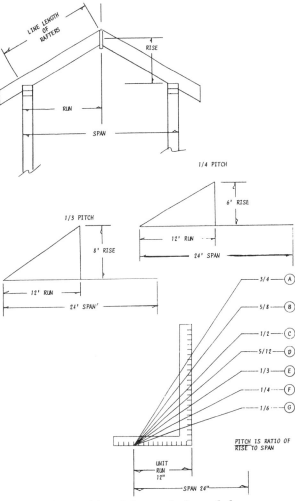

8-5 *Relationship of slope, pitch, and degrees.*

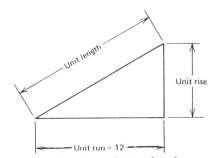

8-4 *Understanding the relationship between the measuring line and the actual line length is the key to rafter layout.*

173

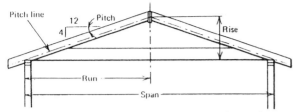

8-6 *Simple rafter layout consists of making three basic cuts.*

All common rafters have at least two angled cuts, a *plumb* cut across the face at the ridge and plate, and a *seat* cut at the plate (see **8-6**). If the rafter extends past the plate, the seat cut and the plumb cut are combined into a notch called the *bird's-mouth*. The *line length* is the distance between the apex of the plumb cut extended to the centerline of the ridge and the plumb line extended to the top edge of the rafter from the outside of the rafter plate. It's actually the measuring line transposed to the top edge of the rafter. The line length reflects the upward shift of the measuring line to compensate for the depth of the plumb cut at the rafter plate (its *raising line*). The line length is the theoretical length of the rafter. The true length of the rafter is the line length less half the thickness of the ridge plus the length of the rafter tail (if any).

While these cuts are not difficult to make, it's important that all rafter cuts be made accurately so that the rafter fits snugly against the plate and ridge—both for neat appearance and for solid bearing.

HOW TO LAY OUT A COMMON RAFTER

Laying out a common rafter is a two-step process. First, you find its line length; then you locate and mark the plumb and seat cuts. You can do this either empirically, by scribing, or computationally, with a framing square (see **8-7**).

The simplest way to determine the length of a common rafter is to look it up in tables like those packaged with a newly purchased framing square or Speedsquare. But the tables won't take the place of your framing square for laying out the rafter cuts. It's a good idea to know how to use the square to find rafter length anyway, just in case you lose that booklet.

Find the whole number on the inch scale of the long blade of the square that corresponds to the roof pitch as given in the plans. Below this, on the first line of the rafter tables marked *"length common rafters per foot of run,"* is the number representing the *unit line length* of the *unit run*, which is the line length (hypotenuse) for each foot of run (base) for "x" inches of rise (altitude). The unit line length is thus the square root of the sums of the squares of 12 (one "unit" in inches) and the number representing the roof slope. (E.g., under a rise of "9" on the square, you'll find "15"; $12^2 + 9^2 = 225$, whose

square root is 15.) Multiplying the unit line length by the feet of actual run gives the overall line length of the rafter.

Of course, you don't need a framing square to find the line length; by applying the Pythagorean theorem, you can calculate the total rise (in inches) by multiplying the unit rise by the total run, and then add the square of that number to the square of the total run (in inches) and then take the square root of the sum of the squares of both sides. The point is, it's already figured out for you on the framing square.

Because calculations involving feet, inches, and fractions are cumbersome, it helps to convert mixed fractions to decimals. A pocket calculator is handy for this and other rafter computations. (If you plan to stay in the building business, buy a builder's calculator that crunches fractions and decimals and that does rafter calculations automatically.)

Suppose, for example, that the plans show an 8-in-12 roof slope and the building span measures 26 feet. The number under "8" on the rafter table of the framing square is 14.42. The rafter run is 13 feet, so the line length of the rafter is 14.42 multiplied times 13, or 187.46 inches. If you own a high-quality framing square it will have a decimal-to-sixteenths conversion scale stamped into the corner of the side opposite the rafter table. Otherwise, multiply 46 by 16 and divide by 100. Either way, 0.46 works out to just about ⁷⁄₁₆ of an inch, and, expressed so that you can read it on your tape measure, the rafter line length is 15'-7⁷⁄₁₆".

In the above example, the run was a whole number. If it weren't, you'd use your calculator to convert the odd

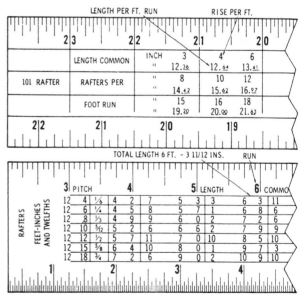

8-7 *The tables on a framing square contain all the information you need to lay out even complicated rafters.*

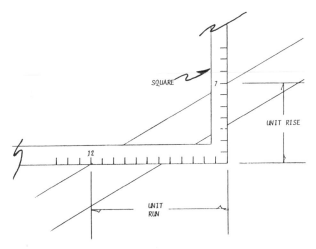

8-8 *Rafter layout always begins with marking the plumb cut at the ridge end.*

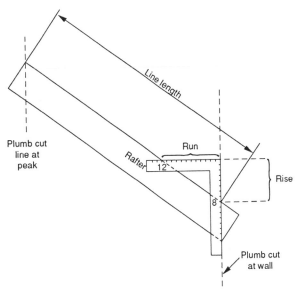

8-9 *The plumb cut at the plate can be laid out after measuring off the rafter's line length.*

inches into a decimal by dividing by 12. (E.g., if the run were 13'-3¼", you'd divide 3.25 by 12 to get 0.27, and then add it to the unit run. Continuing with the example, you'd then multiply 14.42 by 13.27 to get a line length of 191.35 inches—or 15'-11⁵⁄₁₆".)

Select and crown a straight piece of stock to use for the pattern rafter. Hold your framing square so that its short blade (the "tongue") is horizontal and its long blade is on your right, pointing downwards. You'll be looking at the "back" side (the one on which the 100ths to ¹⁄₁₆ths scale is stamped). Find the mark on the *outside* edge of the blade that corresponds to the unit rise (8 in our example), and line it up with the top edge of the rafter at the peak end. Locate the unit run (this is always 12 for common rafters) on the outside edge of the tongue, and line it up with the top edge of the rafter, as well. Then draw a line along the outside edge of the long blade. This is the plumb cut for the peak of the rafter (see **8-8**).

Now measure the line along the top edge of the rafter from the plumb cut line towards the tail. Turn the square so that its tongue is on the right, and the blade is pointing downwards. Position the unit rise line on the outside edge of the blade at the mark for the line length at the top edge of the rafter. Then line up the unit run mark on the outside edge of the tongue with the top edge of the rafter as well. Drawing a line along the outside of the blade will mark the plumb cut at the outside of the wall (see **8-9**).

The next step is to lay out the seat cut (see **8-10**). Seat cuts are normally equal in length to the width of the rafter plate. This provides both solid bearing and a simple transition between the ceiling and wall finishes (where the rafters also carry the ceilings). Turn the square so that the tongue is on the right, pointing upwards. Lay the outside edge of the tongue on the plumb line, and move it up and down until the marking for the width of the wall on the bottom edge of the blade coincides with the bottom

edge of the rafter. (E.g., 3½" for a 2×4 wall. The sheathing isn't included unless the rafters must be notched to fit over it.)

If the rafter ends at the wall, the extra stock along the plumb cut line and beneath the seat cut is sawed off. It's more likely that the rafter will extend past the wall to frame the roof overhang. The area between the inside of the plumb line and below the seat cut is removed to make the bird's-mouth notch after the tail layout is finished (refer to **8-10**).

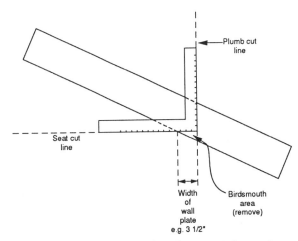

8-10 *The seat cut is simply a line at right angles to the plumb cut, whose location is determined by the width of the wall plate. The two cuts together comprise the bird's-mouth notch.*

175

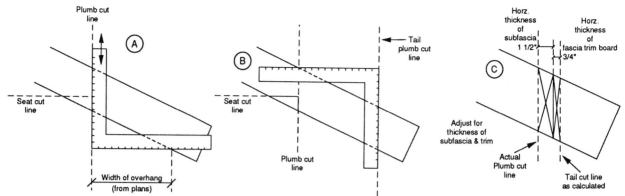

8-11 *Layout of the rafter tail.*

The length of the rafter tail is determined by the width of the roof overhang as measured horizontally from the wall sheathing to the outside face of the fascia trim board (see **8-11**). Flip the framing square over so that it's "face" side is up and the tongue is on the left, pointing upwards. Line up the back edge of the tongue with the plumb cut line, and slide the square up and down until the measurement for the bottom of the blade intersects the bottom of the rafter tail at the point coinciding with the width of the eaves overhang. Reposition your square, as above, and draw another plumb line through this point. Deduct the thickness of the trim board and subfascia (if any) to locate the actual tail cut for the rafter. (When you're figuring tail length, it is also important that you do not forget to allow as well for the thickness of both the siding and the sheathing so that the *finished* width of the soffit will be correct.)

Although there is no one particular layout which is inherently better than any other, you can save a lot of expensive trim material and thin down the profile of the finished eaves and rake by ripping down the tails of rafters wider than 2×6s to that width or even to a 2×4. (A 2×6 subfascia is trimmed with a 1×8 fascia board; a 2×4 subfascia supports a 1×6 fascia.) Draw a line parallel with the top of the rafter to mark the desired width of the tail. A good way to save on the cost of stock is to cut the rafter off at the plumb cut and scab a length of 2×4 along its edge for a tail extension. This is especially the case with the wide rafters required for shed-type and flat roofs.

As will be explained later in this chapter and in further detail in Chapter Ten, the installation of eaves and cornice trimwork is greatly simplified when the rafter tail ends in a *square cut*—i.e., perpendicular to the edge of the rafter—rather than a plumb cut (see **8-12**).

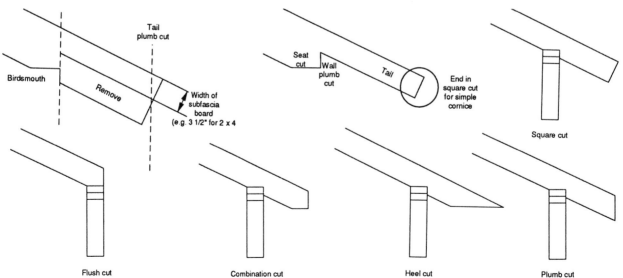

8-12 *Whichever of the various treatments you choose, the rafter tail length should be shortened by the thickness of the subfascia and finish trim boards.*

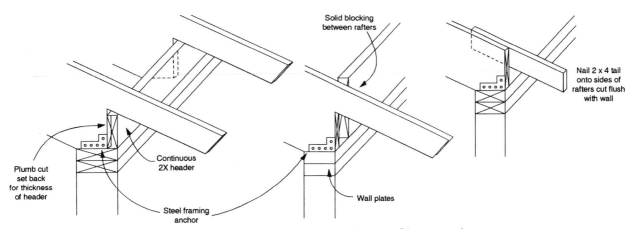

Solid blocking
between rafters

Nail 2 x 4 tail
onto sides of
rafters cut flush
with wall

Plumb cut
set back
for thickness
of header

Continuous
2X header

Steel framing
anchor

Wall plates

8-13 *When the bird's-mouth notch is eliminated, steel anchors and/or a continuous header are needed to secure the rafters to the plate. In high-wind areas, special long steel tie-down strap anchors are also used.*

Trimming the rafter tail to less than full width eliminates the bird's-mouth notch and leaves only toenails in the seat cut to resist the outward thrust of the roof load. Steel framing anchors are then needed on both sides of the rafter to join it to the plate (see **8-13**). Solid blocking can be nailed between each rafter. A better solution is to set the rafter plumb cut back 1½ inches and toenail a continuous header to the top plate below the tail.

Before you cut the pattern rafter, measure the span at both end walls and at the middle of the building. Even with bracing and lining, there's still enough slop in the framing for the measurements to vary by a half inch or

more. Use the *widest* span measurement to calculate the rafter line length (see **8-14**). The difference will show up as a relatively small gap where the seat cut overhangs the wall—especially if it is split between both sides of the building. If, for some reason, one end of the building is considerably wider than the other, you can divide the difference evenly between the rafter pairs to maintain the width of the overhang. For example, if the difference amounted to one inch, distributed over 16 rafter pairs, the line length of the rafters would increase by 1/32 of an inch with each succeeding rafter pair. Adding 1/16th of an inch to every other pair would be close enough.

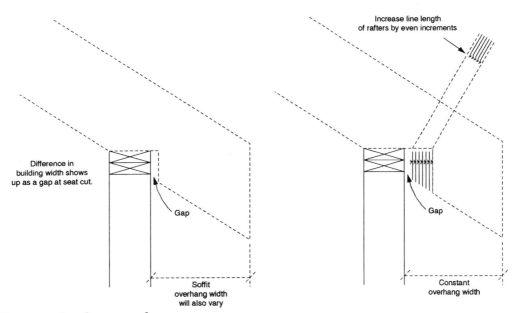

Increase line length
of rafters by even increments

Difference in
building width shows
up as a gap at seat cut.

Gap

Soffit
overhang width
will also vary

Gap

Constant
overhang width

8-14 *Compensating for unequal spans.*

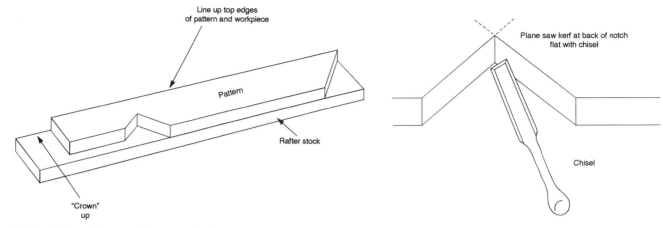

Line up top edges
of pattern and workpiece

Pattern

Rafter stock

"Crown"
up

Plane saw kerf at back of notch
flat with chisel

Chisel

8-15 *Select the straightest stock for pattern rafter and gable end rafter layout.*

Since the first rafter will be used as a pattern to cut all the subsequent rafters, it must be very carefully laid out and precisely cut (see **8-15**). Use a sharp pencil, and double check all measurements for accuracy and squareness. When cutting the bird's-mouth, finish the cut with a handsaw, and plane off any ridges between saw kerfs at the back of the notch with a sharp chisel. Write "pattern" on both sides of the pattern rafter so it won't get mixed up with the others.

As you select and cut your rafter stock, orient each piece crown up. Align the pattern with the top edge of the stock so that any variation in width won't change the relative position of the bird's-mouth. This is especially important if you use rough-sawn lumber for rafter stock; don't use any stock that is badly twisted or that has large knots or splits. Save the straightest rafters for the gable ends.

Rented pipe scaffolding makes roof framing easy. Set up a platform so that the ridge will fall somewhere between chest and shoulder level. There should be enough room to slide the staging platforms back and forth along the ridge without getting hung up on the bottoms of the rafters. Two sections of staging spanned by a couple of planks will allow you to frame at least a 24-foot section of ridge and rafters at a time.

Using your pattern rafter, select and cut another straight rafter to make up a test pair, and try them out for fit before cutting any more rafters (see **8-16**). The easiest way to test the rafters for fit is with three pairs of hands. Tack a block of 2×4 to the end of one rafter to represent the

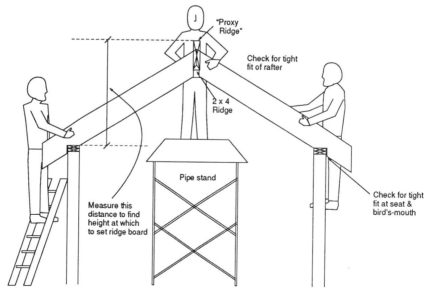

"Proxy
Ridge"

Check for tight
fit of rafter

2 x 4
Ridge

Pipe stand

Measure this
distance to find
height at which
to set ridge board

Check for tight
fit at seat &
bird's-mouth

8-16 *Fitting the first rafter pair also determines the correct height of the ridge board.*

8-17 *With a saltbox-style roof, the ridge board is set and levelled at the height taken from the plans. (See the next section, "An Alternative method of Rafter Layout.") The temporary posts which support it will be removed once the rafters are installed and the roof has been sheathed.*

ridge board; while your helpers hold the bird's-mouths (or outside plumb cuts) against the wall plates at the building corners, bring the two rafters together at the peak. If the layout was correct and the cuts accurate, the test rafters will butt tightly against the proxy ridge, rest level on their seat cuts, and sit flush against the wall at the bird's-mouth. A level held vertically against the face of the plumb cuts should read plumb; if the cuts run off at a noticeable angle, something isn't right. Check your calculations and measurements, and adjust the pattern accordingly—or make a new one. (If the mistake isn't too big, you can probably recycle the pattern rafter as a common rafter with the aid of some shingle shims.)

If the test fitting is satisfactory, measure from the end wall plate to the top of the temporary ridge to find the height at which to set the permanent ridge board.

SETTING THE RIDGE
Although the rafters bear against it, the ridge board in a conventional roof (cathedral roofs are an exception) isn't really load-bearing. Its function is to maintain spacing and alignment and provide a strong nailing backer to tie the rafters together. Thus, it needs only temporary support until the rafters can carry it (see **8-17**).

If the rafters aren't going to be nailed to ceiling joists already installed, mark their spacings on the plates. Since the rafters can bear anywhere on a double plate, increasing

the rafter depth and switching to 24-inch o.c. spacing may offer some cost-saving advantages. Nevertheless, rafters usually follow the stud spacing.

Select straight stock for the ridge board. Since the length of the plumb cut increases with slope, the depth of the ridge stock will increase correspondingly (see **8-18**). The next dimensional increment is usually sufficient—e.g., a 2×8 ridge for 2×6 rafters, 2×10 for 2×8s, and so on. To support 2×12 rafters, slip a 2×4 in the gap between the plumb cuts under a 2×12 ridge.

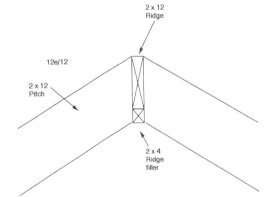

8-18 *Matching depth of ridge to length of plumb cut.*

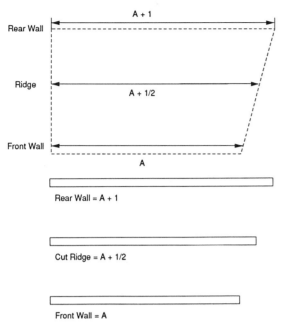

Rear Wall = A + 1

Cut Ridge = A + 1/2

Front Wall = A

8-19 *Any difference in the length of the long walls can be split at the ridge board.*

Check the ridge for crown, and mark off the rafter spacings on both sides of the ridge to match those on the plates. If there's a difference in the lengths of the rafter walls, split it between the spacing for the gable rafter and the last regular rafter on the ridge (see **8-19**). For example, if the south wall is an inch longer than the north wall, you'd lengthen the ridge one-half inch to bring the peak of the gable rafters into line with the end wall. The slip-up is less obvious when both gable rafters run slightly off square than it would be if only one rafter were skewed.

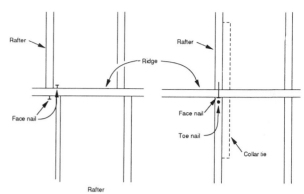

8-20 *Spacing for rafters on ridge.*

Some carpenters prefer to alternate rafter spacing from one side of the line to the other across the ridge so that they can nail all the rafters through the ridge (see **8-20**). If the rafters are spaced across from each other, one set must be toenailed instead. This may seem like too much trouble, but it's a lot easier to nail the collar ties to the rafters if each pair is in the same plane.

Cut a 2×4 post to fit under the ridge, and tack and brace it plumb to the center of the end wall top plate. Tack and brace another post to the floor deck under the far end of the ridge, and check the ridge for level.

The end of the ridge should be plumb with the outside face of the end wall frame. You can check it with a plumb bob, but a straight 2×4 and a level is a lot faster, especially on a windy day (see **8-21**).

Like the wall plates, the ridge is usually built in segments—each as long as can be comfortably handled from the staging platform. The sections should break *between* a rafter pair rather than *over* one. Splice them together with a plywood gusset or scrap of blocking (see **8-22**).

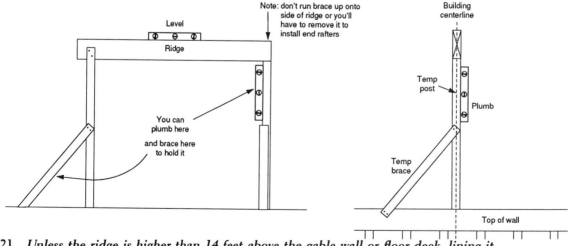

8-21 *Unless the ridge is higher than 14 feet above the gable wall or floor deck, lining it up with a straightedge is easier than a plumb bob.*

AN ALTERNATE METHOD
OF RAFTER LAYOUT

The foregoing description of rafter layout can be thought of as proceeding from the plate up. The rafter pattern was developed first and used to establish the height at which the ridge board was set.

It's also possible to lay out the rafters from the ridge on down (see **8-23**). At first glance, this would seem like a much easier way to lay out rafters than using a framing square. All you have to do to calculate the height at which to set the ridge is to multiply the unit rise by total run. Then, you'd set up the ridge and hold a piece of rafter stock against it and the plate at the corner of the wall and scribe the cut lines on the back of the piece. You can use a sliding T-bevel or a saw protractor to transfer the angle of the plumb cut from the peak to the tail end of the rafter—or else mark it on the face of the rafter with a level.

The only hitch is that the height calculation is based on the measuring line and not the top edge of the rafter.

8-22 *A rafter that rests on the blocking used to splice sections of ridge together must be shortened correspondingly.*

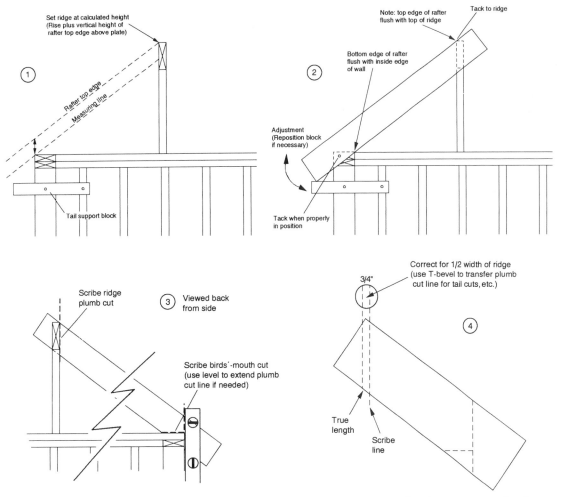

8-23 *When the ridge beam is already in place, it's a simple matter to scribe the pattern rafter layout.*

You'll have to correct for this by adding the *estimated* length of the plumb cut at the rafter plate (measured between the top of the plate and the top of the rafter) to the calculated height of the ridge above the plate. Because of the odd fractions and decimals, there'll still be some slight disagreement between the calculated and actual height of the ridge—that's one of the reasons why rafters are *always* tried out for fit *before* setting up the ridge in the other method. But even though the slope might not

be perfectly accurate, it will probably be close enough not to make much difference.

The advantage of this method is that you can use it *working by yourself*. Tack a block to the wall near the plate; rest the tail end of the rafter stock on this, and align the peak with the ridge. Tack the stock to the ridge, and readjust the tail end so that the bottom of the rafter lines up with the inside edge of the rafter plate. Recheck the ridge, and tack the rafter against the plate.

RAFTER INSTALLATION

Rafters are always installed in pairs to balance the pressure on the ridge and keep it on the line (see **8-24**). As soon as you've nailed down a half-dozen or so rafter pairs, check to see if the gable rafters and ridge are still plumb with the end wall. Nail a 2×4 diagonal brace at least 16 feet long to the underside of the rafters, from the peak on down to the wall plate, to hold the gable plumb (see **8-25**). Measure the spacing intervals between the rafters and tack the brace to each rafter it crosses. Nail a second brace to the undersides of the rafters on the opposite side of the ridge. Another pair is added at the opposite end wall when all the rafters are in place. These braces are left in place until the roof is completely sheathed. Without them, there's a very real danger that the rafters could topple over in a strong wind or even from their own weight. The braces must be left in place permanently when board sheathing is used—except in the case of hip roofs, where the diagonal hip rafters act as braces.

As you nail the rafters in place, sight along the ridge to make sure it's still running more or less straight. You could also line the top edge of the ridge with a string and spacer blocks. A curved ridge means that the rafters are either pushing or pulling it to one side or the other. Check to make sure the walls are still lined with their strings. Sometimes braces shift and the walls bow outward.

8-24 *Common rafters are always installed in opposing pairs to balance the push against the ridge, which might otherwise make it run off line. In some parts of the country, nailing a tree to the first pair of rafters is an ancient ritual harking back to the Druids, intended to appease the spirits of the trees that gave up their wood for lumber. It's customary for the owner to provide the appropriate libations for the "wetting the bush" party that is traditionally held at the close of rafter-framing day.*

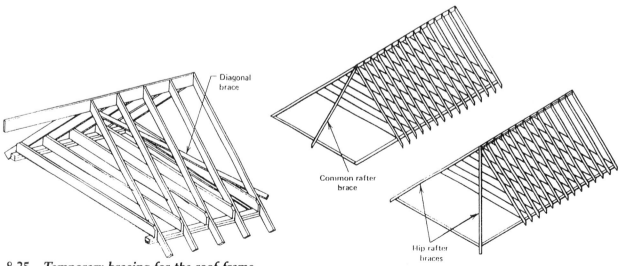

8-25 *Temporary bracing for the roof frame.*

182

COLLAR TIES

The longer the rafter span, the more a roof frame tends to bend under its own weight and pull the ridge down. Collar ties stiffen the rafters against this tendency. But until you can install them, put temporary support posts under the middle of each ridge section to keep it from sagging (see 8-26). If you rest the bottom of the post on a small hydraulic jack (or an automobile scissors jack) you can lift a sagging ridge or crown it slightly (about ¼″) before installing the ties.

Collar ties also help neutralize the outward thrust of the roof against the walls. In effect, the rafters become part of a self-supporting rigid arch. Collar ties frequently double as ceiling joists (see 8-27). But they impart the most strength when placed at a point two-thirds of the way between the plate and the peak. Depending on the slope of the roof and the presence or absence of a knee wall, this may be too high for a ceiling. Rather than add a set of ceiling joists, most builders prefer to lower the collar ties. So long as the rafters are of more than minimal depth, this won't have any significant effect on the strength of the frame.

Mark a level line for the bottom of the collar tie stock across the gable end rafters at both ends of the building (see 8-28). Snap a chalk line across the undersides of the rafters between them. Hold a piece of 2×6 tie across the rafters on the lines, and scribe where it intersects their top edges. Use this pattern to cut the collar ties. Nail the ties to the rafter with five 16d nails in each end.

Unless you use a load-bearing ridge, transverse beams, or special trusses, some form of collar tie or its structural equivalent is always needed to keep the roof from pushing the walls out. Exposed collar ties are often a feature of cathedral ceilings with either conventional rafters or exposed timbers. Solid timbers—such as 3×8s or 4×10s—or built-up and cased-in beams are commonly installed on every third or fourth rafter pair. This provides adequate stiffness without a cluttered appearance.

8-26 *Temporary braces keep the front walls of this saltbox plumb until the gable walls are framed in. The vertical post which keeps the ridge from sagging is also left in place until after the roof is sheathed.*

8-27 *Collar ties add stiffness and double as ceiling joists. Note that the center tie is left out until after the chimney opening is framed in.*

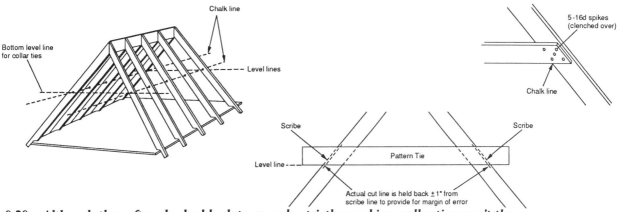

8-28 *Although they often do double duty as such, strictly speaking, collar ties aren't the same thing as ceiling joists.*

183

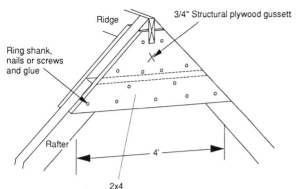

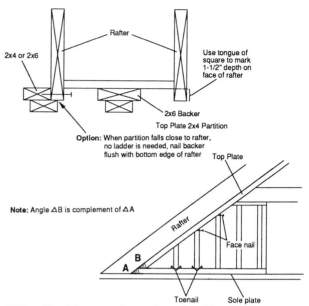

8-29 *To create a more open cathedral ceiling, plywood gussets can be substituted for collar ties. Always have such a design and any other deviation from standard practice approved by a structural engineer.*

A rigid plywood gusset at the apex of the roof is an alternative to collar ties where an even more open ceiling is desired (see 8-29). Nail and glue ¾-inch structural-grade plywood to both sides of the rafter pairs. Insert a piece of 2×4 between the gussets at their bottom edge for added stiffness and to serve as a ceiling nailer. The gussets should be at least four feet long at their base. Always have this kind of framing design checked by a structural engineer.

Purlins are often used for long rafter spans that need more support than collar ties alone can provide or where ties aren't used (see 8-30). The purlin itself is a 2×4 nailed flatwise across the undersides of the rafters at their midspans. The purlins are braced with short 2×4s that rest, ideally, on a bearing partition below. They can also be nailed to a strongback attached to the top of the ceiling joists. Although the exact angle isn't critical, the purlin

8-31 *Partitions under a sloped ceiling.*

brace will be stronger if it's installed perpendicular to the rafter slope.

Just as the interior partitions of the first floor add racking resistance to the side walls of the building, attic partitions also tend to stiffen and support the roof. Except for the fact that their top plates are at an angle, partitions that run parallel to the rafters are attached with the same ladder-and-backer system used for floor joists (see 8-31). The partition frames are assembled in place rather than tilted up. The studs are toenailed to the sole plate and face-nailed through the tip of their angle cut at the top plate.

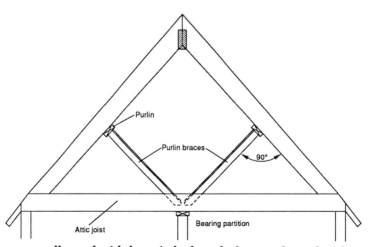

8-30 *Purlin braces are generally used with low-pitched roofs that are framed with conventional rafters. The use of prefabricated roof trusses has made them rare in modern carpentry.*

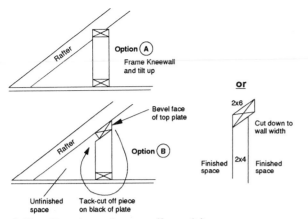

8-32　*Framing a knee-wall partition.*

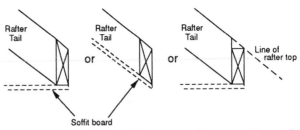

8-34　*Use a full-scale drawing to lay out rafter tail length and subfascia bevel cuts so that the fascia trim board will line up correctly with both the top of the rafter and the soffit trim board.*

While not necessarily intended to be load-bearing, the framing for a knee wall—which is often used to separate usable living space from "dead" storage space under a sloping ceiling—is similar to purlin framing (see **8-32**). Some carpenters prefer to cut bird's-mouths into the rafters and tilt the knee wall frame into place against a top plate nailed to the seat cut of the notch. It's a lot easier and just as effective to bevel the edge of the top plate and use angled studs instead. Since the angled edge of a 2×4 knee wall stud is longer than the face of the 2×4 top plate, rip the plates out of 2×6 stock instead. If you're doubling up the top plates, you can nail the leftover bevelled strip to the back edge of a bevelled 2×4 to save a little material. But unless the knee wall is also intended to bear part of the roof load, there's no need to double up the top plates. Likewise, if the backside of the knee wall won't be finished, there's no reason to bevel the back edge of the top plate either.

SUBFASCIAS AND LOOKOUTS

The line of the rafter tails should be checked for straightness and, if need be, trimmed (see **8-33**). In fact, many carpenters won't bother to cut the rafter tails at all until this point. Snap a chalk line from end to end across the top edge of the rafter tails. With a T-bevel or torpedo level, drop a plumb line across the face of any rafter tails that stick out past the chalk line—one advantage of square-cut rafter tails is that it's easier to mark a square-cut than a plumb-cut. If more than one or two rafter tails fall short of the line, it's better to shift the line inward than to shim the tails out to the subfascia.

For some reason, although every framer I've known uses it, the vast majority of carpentry textbooks and how-to manuals fail to mention the *subfascia*, a continuous band of two-by nailed across the ends of the rafter tails (see **8-34**). Instead, most sources recommend nailing the fascia trim board directly to the ends of the rafter tails. In addition to the difficulty of doing this neatly—and that it needlessly complicates the rest of the cornice construction—it also makes it harder to sheath the roof. Even more

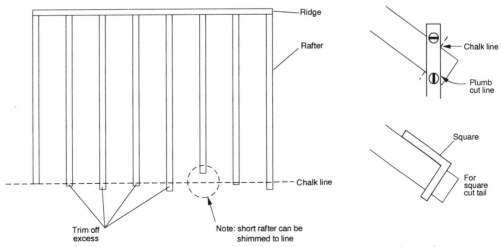

8-33　*Mark both sides of the rafter tails for trimming so that they can be cut from the least awkward (and safest) direction with a circular saw.*

of the rafter tails rather than to a horizontal cornice. The extra labor involved in cutting and fitting bevels and plumb cuts is a good argument in favor of square-cut rafter tails (see **8-35**). In any case, the width of the subfascia should match that of the rafter tail. Rather than bevel its top edge, some carpenters prefer to drop the subfascia so that its outermost corner doesn't stick up past the line of roof decking. Although this does allow the use of narrower stock, it doesn't provide as much nail-backing for the bottom edge of the plywood.

When ordering subfascia stock, keep in mind that it will carry the false rafter at the bottom of the rake overhang. Since a standard rake typically projects about a foot past the gable wall, the subfascia stock must be two feet longer than the building wall. The other end should break over the center of the rafter tail.

Mark the spacing between the rake false rafter and the gable rafter, and then mark off the regular rafter spacings on the inside face of the subfascia (see **8-36**). While your helper holds the far end, nail it to the gable rafter tail. Move the far end up and down like a lever to bring the subfascia flush with the top (or bottom) edge of each rafter tail in succession. As you approach the end, you may have to toenail a stubborn bow downwards or pry a rafter tail upwards to make a good match. "Working down" the subfascia straightens out the inevitable small dips and humps in the rafter tails and ensures that the plane of the eaves is flat. Also, move the rafter tails sideways, as needed, to line them up with the spacing lines. After even only a brief exposure to the sun and rain, the unfixed ends of a rafter begin twisting. The subfascia keeps them straight until they're secured by the roof decking and soffit trim.

8-35 *Sixteen-foot-long rafters were just long enough to bear on the plate; the tail pieces were scabbed onto the sides of the rafters. Note the square-edged subfascia; a bevelled piece would provide better support for the bottom edge of the roof sheathing.*

than a double sole plate or the subsill under a window opening, nailing a subfascia across the rafter tails is an inexpensive extra framing detail that greatly improves the ease and quality of the finish work.

Depending on whether the rafters are square-cut or plumb-cut, the subfascia can be either square-edged or bevelled on its top edge. The bottom edge is left square-cut unless the soffit board will be attached to the underside

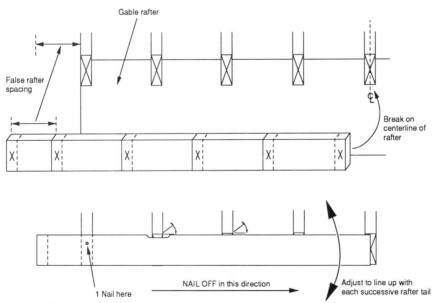

8-36 *Subfascia installation.*

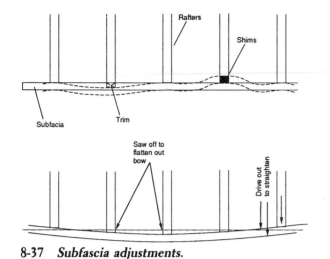

Subfacia / Trim / Rafters / Shims

Saw off to flatten out bow / Drive out to straighten

8-37 Subfascia adjustments.

Sight down the finished subfascia (see **8-37**). It should appear to run in a straight line; if you botched trimming the rafter tails, it won't. Where there's a noticeable outward bow, pull the nails, and trim the tail back with a handsaw. If the bow is inward, drive the subfascia away from the rafter tail, and shim behind it. If things managed to really get away from you during rafter framing, and the subfascia humps upwards or downwards with the plane of the rafters, there isn't anything you can do to adjust the subfascia. Instead, you can create the illusion of a straight line when you install the fascia and rake trim (refer to Chapter Ten).

For roofs with a relatively lightweight 2×4-framed rake overhang not more than a foot wide, it's much easier to hang the false rafter which carries the rake fascia from the roof sheathing than to support it with special *lookout* framing (see **8-38**).

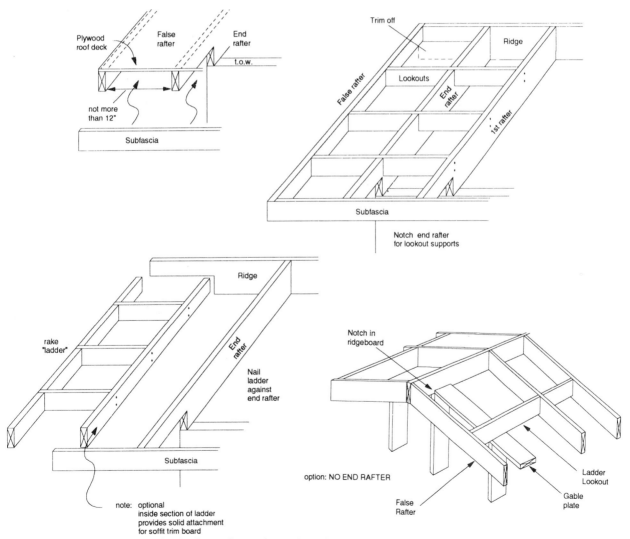

8-38 The framing for a rake lookout depends on how far out from the end wall it projects.

8-39 *The false—or fly—rafter for this roof frame has been nailed to the subfascia and an extension of the ridge beam cut down to the width of the false rafter. Blocking stiffens the false rafter and keeps it running straight.*

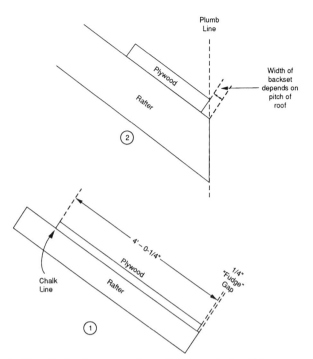

8-40 *If the bottom edge of the roof sheathing sticks out past the rafter tail, it will throw the fascia board off plumb.*

Where the roof design calls for a wider and/or deeper rake profile, the false rafter is carried by framing analogous to the stub joists used to support the header joist of a floor deck projection (see **8-39**). The ridge board should extend out past the gable rafter the full width of the rake. In most cases, you'll have to trim its bottom edge so that it matches the depth of the false rafter stock.

In order of increasing complexity and overhang projection, lookout framing can vary from simple blocking set between the false rafter and the gable rafter to flatwise 2×4s let into notches at the top of one or more rafters. (As with floor projections, two-thirds of the length of the rake projection supports should be on the inside of the gable rafters.) As long as the rafter stock is deeper than the lookout stock (e.g., 2×12 rafters and 2×6 lookouts), the lookouts can also run edgewise through notches cut into the gable rafter and a trimmer-backed common rafter. For very wide rake overhangs and profiles, eliminate the gable rafter and one or more common rafters, and let the lookouts bear on the top plate of the sloping gable stud wall frame, tying them back to a trimmer (i.e., doubled) rafter.

ROOF SHEATHING

Plywood roof sheathing is laid with its face grain perpendicular to the rafters (i.e., the "long way"). If the rafter tails are square-cut, measure up 4'-0¼" from the edge of the subfascia at the gable ends, and snap a line across the rafters to mark the top edge of the first course of plywood. Holding the plywood back slightly from the edge of the subfascia prevents it pushing the back of the fascia trim board outward (see **8-40**). If the rafter tails are plumb-cut, this backset should be increased according to the steepness of the roof and/or the thickness of the sheathing. For example, a ⅝-inch backset works for ½-inch plywood and a 12/12 slope.

Line the gable rafters with a string and spacer block, and brace them temporarily back to the other rafters. Draw rafter centerlines across each sheet of plywood with your T-square. Position the first sheet of sheathing with its top edge on the chalk line—and so that its end overhangs the gable rafter by about two feet. The first nailing centerline will coincide with the outside edge of the gable rafters, and the other lines will fall over the center of the succeeding rafters. Each course of sheathing is offset from the one below it so that the ends don't break consecutively on the same rafter. If the rafters are spaced two feet o.c., building the rake overhang so that the outside of the false rafter is no more than eleven inches from the gable rafter will almost eliminate wasted plywood. Instead of alternating full-width and half-width sheets, use "starter" sheets cut into three-foot and five-foot pieces.

Tack only the upper corners of the sheets for the entire first course of sheathing. This way you can adjust them if they don't run square to each other and the rafters, and

188

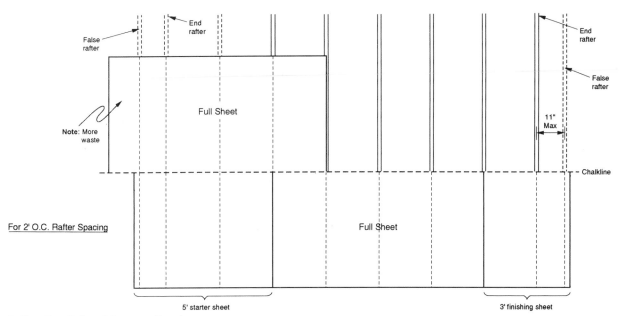

8-41 *Roof sheathing application.*

Labels in figure 8-41: False rafter, End rafter, Full Sheet, Note: More waste, For 2' O.C. Rafter Spacing, Full Sheet, End rafter, False rafter, 11" Max, Chalkline, 5' starter sheet, 3' finishing sheet

stay on the chalk line. The subfascia makes a handy scaffold for positioning the sheets (see **8-41**). Push the rafters sideways, as needed, to line them up with the spacing marks on the sheathing as you nail it down. On small houses, builders often wait until they're ready to start shingling before setting up staging along the eaves. When the slope is too steep to stand on, they hook their legs under a pair of rafters and hang themselves down over the sheet to nail off its bottom edge. Although not for the faint-hearted, the technique is probably not anywhere near as dangerous as it looks; but a scaffold is a lot safer.

Nail a 2×4 to the deck about a foot below the top edge of the first course of sheathing (see **8-42**). This is what will keep you from falling off the roof as you lay the rest of the deck, so make sure the nails are driven into the rafters and not just through the plywood. Add another *rung* to this *ladder* with each course of plywood. Hold the ends back from the rake overhang so that they don't get in the way of the saw when you trim the edges of the sheathing.

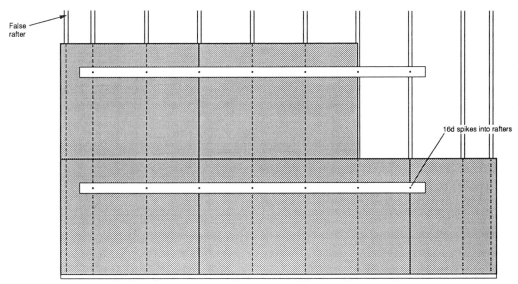

Labels in figure 8-42: False rafter, 16d spikes into rafters

8-42 *Always sweep the roof deck clean of any sawdust. This is especially important when using wafer-board sheathing, where even a slight dusting will make its naturally waxy surface dangerously slippery.*

"H" Clip

8-43 *H clips also provide the spacing between horizontal edges recommended by the manufacturer to prevent buckling when the sheets are exposed to moist conditions: A plywood lift is a necessity if you're sheathing the roof without extra help.*

8-44 *Carpenters prepare to snap a chalk line for trimming the rake. Note the 2×4 "chicken ladder" staging nailed to the roof deck. The pieces are set back so that they won't be in the way of the saw. Note that the far rake has already been trimmed. The long 2×4s will be removed as the deck is tar-papered from the top on down.*

At 24 inches o.c., rafters are too far apart to adequately support ½-inch plywood, unless the long edges of the panels are stiffened by slipping special metal H clips between them (see **8-43**). You could also use ⅝-inch plywood instead. Even though codes permit ⅜-inch sheathing, it tends to sag noticeably between the rafters—especially in snow country.

As you work your way higher up the rafters, getting the plywood up onto the deck is an increasing challenge. Collar ties make an excellent temporary staging. Pile enough sheets on the roof to finish the last course before you close over the only available access. And have a ladder handy to climb down off the finished deck unless you want to cut the chimney opening "ahead of schedule."

There's a lot less lifting involved in sheathing the roof of a single-storey house, especially if you build a plywood lifter (refer to **8-43**). Tack a pair of braced 2×4s against the subfascia. Another set of two-by's is nailed across them somewhere near waist height and back to the wall studs. The projecting ends of these bottom pieces will support a dozen or more sheets of plywood so that you can pull them up onto the roof from their top edges.

HANGING THE FALSE RAFTERS

The end of the subfascia should already have been trimmed to the width of the rake. Measure the same amount out from the ridge and snap a chalk line down along the edge of the sheathing (see **8-44**). If the gable end is farther out at the peak than it is at the ends of the long walls, you can square up the roof deck by narrowing the width of the overhang. A tapering rake soffit board is less noticeable than a skewed line in the roofing shingles. Carefully cut the sheathing along this line.

Make a special effort to pick out the straightest possible stock you can find for false rafters. Whenever possible, use pieces long enough to span the length of the rake without splices. Make an appropriate plumb cut at the top (and bottom, if not square cut) of the false rafter, and position it carefully at the peak (see **8-45**). Since there is no ridge to butt against, tack a short board along the centerline of the ridge out along the overhang to help locate the meeting point of the opposing false rafters. Rather than rely on measurements, scribe the lower end against the edge of the subfascia for an exact fit. Then, holding the false rafter even with the edge of the overhang, drive 8d nails, spaced four inches apart, through the plywood to pull the rafter up tight.

If it doesn't clash with the style of your house, the *clipped* rake characteristic of early New England homes

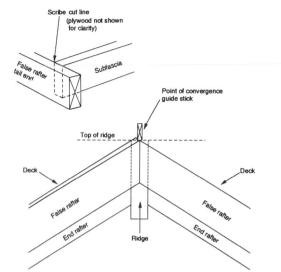

8-45 *Hanging a false rafter.*

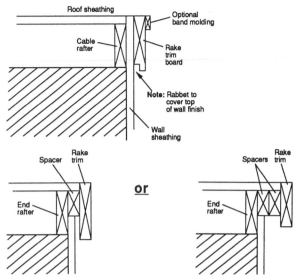

8-46 *Clipped rakes do away with the need for rake faming but leave the upper wall siding more vulnerable to the weather. Use a strip of trim to hide doubled spacers from view.*

is noted for its severe simplicity and economy of materials and labor (see **8-46**). The roof sheathing is trimmed flush with the face of the gable rafter, which is then covered by the wall sheathing. The fascia board is applied either directly over the wall, or else, for a little more relief, to a spacer rafter nailed to it.

DORMERS AND OTHER ROOF OPENINGS

Gable dormers are used to bring light and ventilation into attics and living areas under sloping roofs. Gable dormers are usually fairly narrow—often barely wider than the single window they contain. Since they can have a dramatic effect on the overall appearance of the house, the proportions and placement of gable dormers should be carefully considered. Shed dormers aren't subject to the same limitations of size as gable dormers. They can run the full length of the roof, in which case the roof line begins to resemble a saltbox. Although they don't appear as elegant as gable dormers, shed dormers create large amounts of more usable interior living space and are much easier to frame than gable dormers.

Either type of dormer can be built as an extension of the house wall or else set back at some point in the plane of the roof (see **8-47**). In any case, the framing for a dormer opening is similar to framing an opening for a stairwell in the floor deck or a window in a bearing wall. An opening for the dormer is left between the common rafters; the trimmer rafters that frame the sides of the dormer opening are installed. With 2×4 framing, insert a ½-inch plywood spacer between the two trimmers so that the rafter equals the width of the wall studs it will carry. Add a nailer for the roof sheathing to its top outside edge. The trimmer rafter for a really wide dormer gable should be tripled.

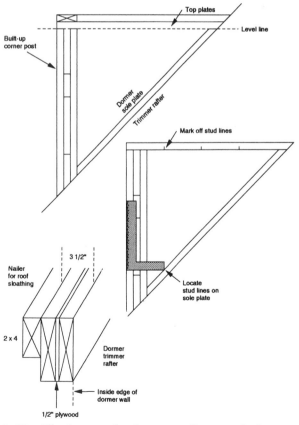

8-47 *The layout of a dormer wall proceeds from a plumbed and braced built-up corner post set on a firred-out trimmer rafter.*

191

Construct a built-up corner post, and nail it plumb to the trimmer where the front wall of the dormer will start. Level a line from the top of the corner post back to the trimmer rafter to mark the location of the top plate. Although you can nail the dormer side wall studs directly to the trimmer rafter, I prefer nailing a sole plate to it first. The bottom end of the plate is cut on the same angle as the rafter plumb cut and butts against the back of the corner post. Its top end is cut to the same angle as the rafter seat cut so that the top plate will rest on it. Nail the top plate to the post and to the trimmer. Mark the stud layout on the underside of the top plate. To speed the layout on the sloped sole plate, set the long blade of the framing square flush with the outside edge of the post, and slide it up or down until the end of the tongue falls across the edge of the sole plate. As long as you proceed from longer to shorter studs, this layout method works for any angled wall. Nail flatwise blocking between the studs at the sole plate for backing the sidewall flashing and finish siding. Instead of measuring and marking pieces of blocking one at a time, hold a length of 2×4 against the studs, and scribe where they cross it (see 8-48). You'll find this method is a lot quicker, with less chance of error, especially where the blocking is angled.

When the front of the dormer falls directly over the building side wall, nail a header joist over the ends of the floor joists instead of clipping them back to match the rafter slope (see 8-49). Then you can frame the front wall on the deck just like a conventional wall, and tilt it up to fit in between the side walls. With most building facades, however, it's unusual for the front wall of the dormer to extend without interruption into the front wall of the

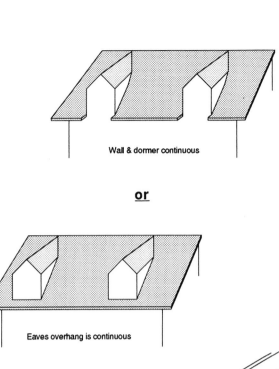

Wall & dormer continuous

or

Eaves overhang is continuous

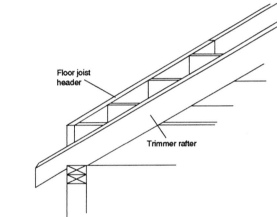

Floor joist header

Trimmer rafter

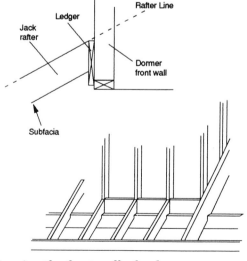

Jack rafter

Ledger

Rafter Line

Dormer front wall

Subfacia

8-49 *Framing the front wall of a dormer.*

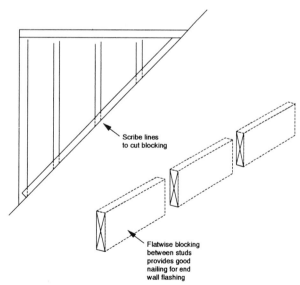

Scribe lines to cut blocking

Flatwise blocking between studs provides good nailing for end wall flashing

8-48 *Flatwise blocking nailed between the studs provides much more solid backing for nailing end-wall flashings than sheathing plywood alone.*

building. Traditionally, the bottom edge of the dormer is skirted by the eaves overhang. Snap a chalk line across the front wall frame and nail short jack rafters between the subfascia and to the wall studs.

If the dormer is set back in the roof frame so that its front wall doesn't bear on the floor deck, nail a doubled, spaced header plumb between the trimmers to support the sole plate of the dormer front wall and to carry the upper ends of the lower jack rafters.

The intersection of a gable dormer roof with the main roof creates a valley between the rafters. One way to solve this framing problem is to run the dormer ridge board and the valley rafters into a double header nailed at right angles to the trimmer rafters (see **8-50**). The ends of the upper jack rafters are also attached to this header. To locate the header, first establish the height of the ridge (use the dormer end wall rafters and a temporary ridge block as you did with the main roof). Tack a storey pole to the corner post of the dormer, and level the ridge height back across the face of the trimmer rafter. The point where the ridge line meets the top edge of the trimmer is where the header goes. Transfer this mark to the other trimmer.

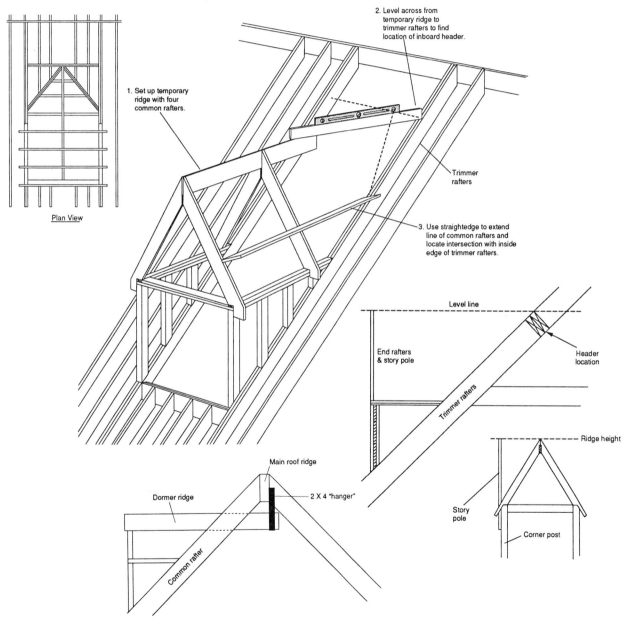

8-50 *Locating the dormer header.*

If the peak of the dormer roof is close to the main ridge, you can dispense with the header, and, instead, extend one of the valley rafters up into the main ridge board (see **8-51**). The other valley rafter butts against the first one, and the dormer ridge fits into the junction. Another approach is to extend the dormer ridge through the plane of the main roof and hang it from the main ridge. The valley rafters then butt against the sides of the dormer ridge.

Although it varies with the framing technique, in general the line length of the dormer valley rafter is the diagonal distance from the intersection of the centerlines of the dormer ridge and header to the centerline of the intersection of the dormer top plate and the trimmer rafter (see **8-52**). (The actual length is adjusted as explained in the discussion of valley rafter layout on pages 202–209.) The common rafters and jack rafters are installed after the valley rafters.

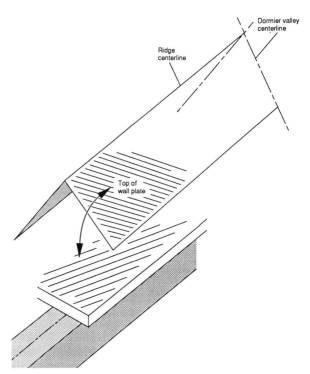

8-52 *Visualizing the length of a dormer valley rafter.*

Since they usually have only a short span, dormer ceiling joists are framed with 2×4s (see **8-53**). The last joist, which is nailed between the trimmer rafters, is beefed up to carry the ends of the main roof ceiling joists. Always install a temporary support beam and post under the attic ceiling joists before cutting them to install the dormer ceiling header.

Shed dormer framing is considerably less complicated. Although you can use the same method of side wall framing for both kinds of dormers, it's a lot faster to nail the

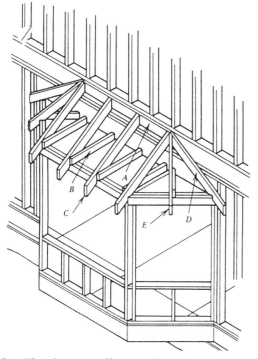

8-51 *The dormer valley can be carried on a valley board set on the rafters rather than on valley rafters or on the main roof sheathing, with the dormer header set at ceiling height. Another variation of the dormer is a bay window roof; to frame it, cut ridgeboard (A) the same length as the wall header; attach ceiling joists (B) and common rafters (C). Then drop a line for cutting hip rafter (D), which will have a single 45-degree cheek cut. Use a string to establish length of rafter (E) or else use 8.5 (one-half of 17, i.e., 22½ degrees) as the unit run on the square and the same rise as the common rafters.*

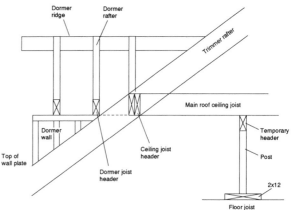

8-53 *Dormer ceiling joist framing detail.*

194

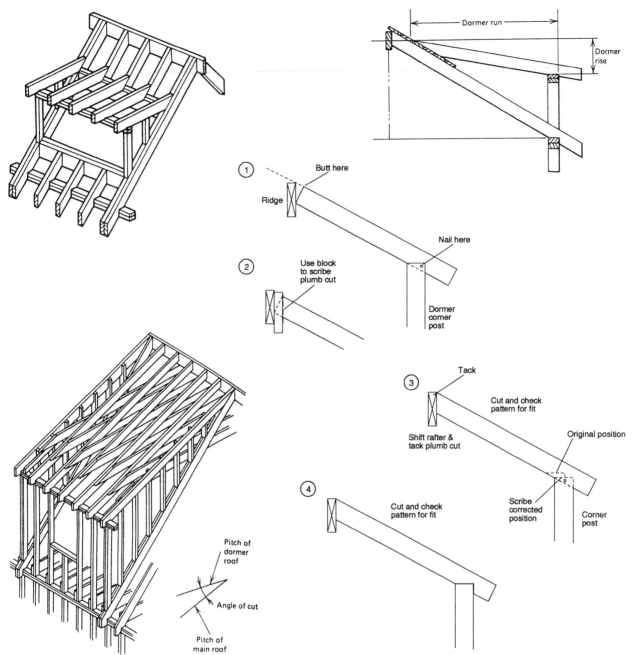

8-54 *With shed dormers you have the option of notching the side wall studs into the end rafters or running the side wall plate into the trimmer like a gable dormer and filling in with short studs later.*

side wall studs to the dormer rafters instead. With shed dormers, the ceiling joists are nailed to the sides of the rafters, or against them over the front wall plate, as with standard ceiling joists or collar ties.

Most of the time, shed dormer rafters run into the ridge of the main roof. Since the height of the dormer front wall is usually fixed by the plans and the ridge is fixed by the rafters of the main roof, the exact slope of the dormer roof and the plumb cut of its rafters is determined after the fact by scribing, rather than a priori, by calculation (see **8-54**). Butt the upper end of the shed dormer against the ridge, and tack its lower end to the corner post. Use a level or framing square to scribe the plumb cut against the ridge (or the seat cut against the trimmer rafter). Make the plumb cut, and reposition the rafter to scribe the bird's-mouth cut.

195

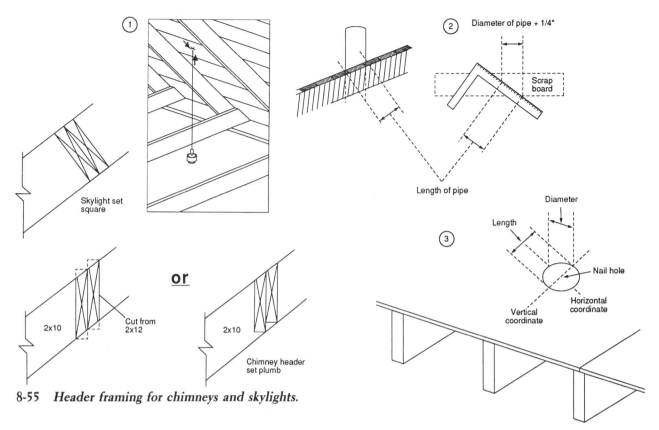

8-55 *Header framing for chimneys and skylights.*

OTHER ROOF OPENINGS

The framing for skylight and chimney openings in the roof is similar to the framing for openings in the floor deck (see **8-55**). The rafters at the sides of the opening are doubled, and doubled headers are used at its top and bottom.

Since the headers for chimney openings are set plumb between the rafters, with their top edges bevelled to the angle of the roof slope, they must be cut from deeper stock. If a ceiling will be attached to the bottom of the rafters, the underside of the headers is also bevelled. Skylight openings are framed square with the rafters.

8-56 *The cuts for all the rafters for this complex shed roof, including those for the gable dormer, were laid out by the empirical method. Note how the framing for the lookouts for the wide overhang at the shed rake are notched into the end rafter. The false rafter will eventually line up with the rake of the main roof. Note also the let-in steel diagonal braces.*

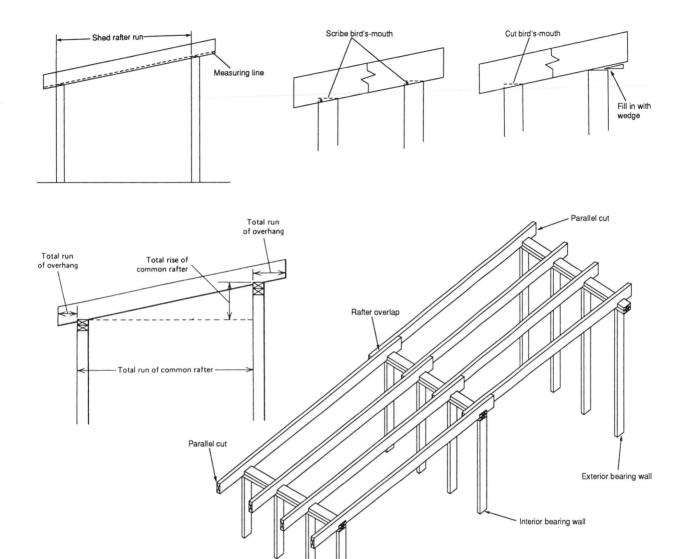

8-57 *Shed roof rafters are almost always laid out by scribing rather than calculation.*

SHED ROOF RAFTER LAYOUT

Although you could use a framing square, the empirical method described earlier is the most practical way to lay out shed roof rafters or any other rafters supported on bearing walls or beams, such as salt box and extended low-pitch gable roofs (see **8-56**).

Since the rafters of a shed roof can have bird's-mouth cut-outs at both ends, the difference in height between the front and rear top plates is the total rise (see **8-57**). The run is the distance between the outside of the lower rafter plate and the inside of the upper rafter plate (i.e., the distance between the bird's-mouth notches). With a little calculation, you could convert total rise and run to unit rise and run for laying out plumb cuts and calculating lengths (e.g., a six-foot rise over a 24-foot run equals a 3-in-12 slope). But one of the main advantages of a shed roof is that a perfectly accurate pitch isn't a requirement. Shed roof layout is almost foolproof because the roof pitch and the rafter fit can be arbitrarily determined by the height of the building walls.

Like floor joists, the spans of most shed roofs are usually too long to bridge with a single rafter. Multiple sets of rafters are run by each other over carrying beams or bearing partitions. Even single-span roofs are often extended past the main building walls to enclose an ell or open shed.

8-58 *This shed roof was framed by stretching strings between the upper and lower walls to locate the height of the middle beam on which both sets of rafters would bear.*

When the heights of two bearing walls are already established, the easiest way to determine the height of the roof extension bearing wall is by strings (see 8-58). Lay out and install the first set of rafters using the empirical method described above. Then plumb and brace a 2×4 storey pole at the next bearing point. Attach a string to the upper end of the rafter, and extend it along its top edge (see 8-59). Mark where it crosses the storey pole.

Tack your pattern rafter stock to the storey pole and to the first end wall rafter. Scribe the cut where the first and second sets of rafters intersect. Remember that the succeeding rafters will run by each other rather than butt together. Draw a plumb line across the tail end of the pattern rafter to represent the line of the wall, and level or square another line across it to lay out the seat cut so that it will coincide with the inside edge of the bearing

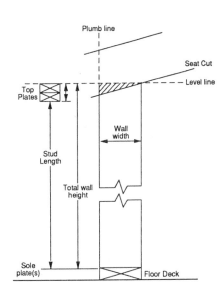

8-59 *Rafter layout for extended shed roof.*

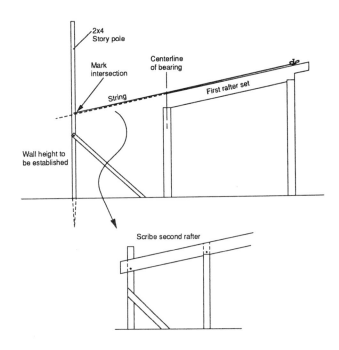

198

wall rafter plate. Measure down to the floor and deduct the thickness of the sole plate and of the top plates to find the stud length for the bearing wall or the height at which to set the top of the carrying beam. Build the bearing wall, cut and try the pattern rafter for fit, and use the string to check that the rafters run in a straight line without dips or humps at their bearing points.

Where the outside bearing walls are already established and you need to find the height of an intermediate bearing partition or carrying beam, stretch a string along the full length of the rafter run so that it marks either the bottom or the top edge of the rafters (see 8-60). You'll probably need to nail a stick to the wall to hold the string in the right position. Set up a storey pole at the intermediate bearing point, and lay out the bird's-mouth notch on a pattern rafter held to the string; then determine stud height as above.

Because it begins at the bird's-mouth, the run of the tail portion of a shed rafter will be longer by the width of the seat cut at the upper wall, even though the actual overhang beyond the building will be the same at both walls. Rather than cut a notch which will reduce the effective depth of the rafter at the upper wall, some builders eliminate one or both bird's-mouths, and cut wedges to fit under the rafters at the plate (see 8-61). Steel framing anchors and solid blocking should be used with shed rafters in any case, even with full bird's-mouths.

Sometimes the design calls for a roof extension to change slope where it intersects the main roof (see 8-62). The empirical method is used here as well; the only difference is that where the end wall rafters meet on the plate, a simple plumb cut can't be used for the butt joint. The cut must be scribed at an angle if the top edges of each rafter are to meet evenly. The bottom ends of the other rafters will also have to be trimmed off where they run by each other.

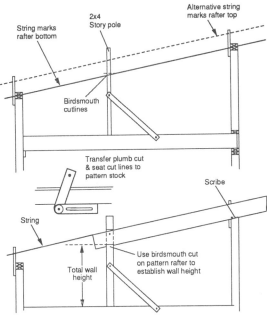

8-60   When cutting studs for an intermediate bearing wall to length, don't forget to deduct the thickness of the plates.

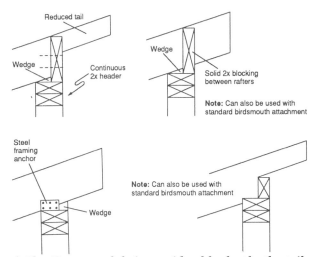

8-61   Because of their considerable depth, the tails of shed rafters are almost always reduced, making a continuous header a logical choice for closing in the space between the rafters.

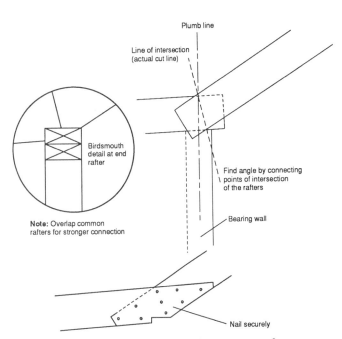

8-62   The meeting angles of a change in roof pitch can also be found by making a full-scale layout on the floor deck.

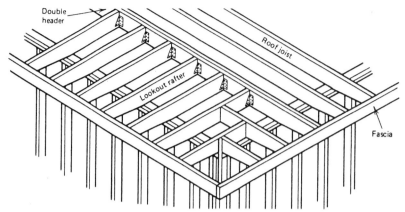

8-63 *Flat roofs can also be framed with prefabricated trusses similar to floor trusses.*

FLAT ROOFS

Although flat roofs are actually pitched slightly (usually 1-in-12 or less) for drainage, their rafters (which are called *roof joists*, since they support both the roof and the finished ceiling) are not ordinarily laid out with plumb and seat cuts. Instead of bearing against a ridge board, the ends of the roof joists typically run by each other over a girder or bearing partition (see **8-63**). The angle of a 1:12 slope is so negligible that it's easier to fill the gap between the roof joist and the wall plate with shingle shims than to take the time to make a seat cut. Leaving the tails square-cut tilts the fascia slightly inward at the bottom, which helps direct roof runoff away.

Because of the heavier loads they must carry, roof joists are framed with 2×10s or 2×12s and, depending on code and structural considerations, spacings may be reduced to 12 inches o.c. Since this would require a very wide fascia, the rafter tails are often tapered (which preserves their stiffness) rather than cut down.

Lookout rafters supported by doubled roof joists frame the overhang perpendicular to the run of the cantilevered roof joists. With overhang projections of two feet or less, the lookout framing for the corner requires only a short piece of diagonal blocking, which serves as a nailer for the soffit boarding. For wider overhangs, a diagonal, doubled *king rafter* provides the required stiffness to prevent the corners from sagging. Support the subfascia corner (and add a slight crown) with a temporary post until the king rafter and all the jack roof joists are installed.

GAMBREL ROOFS

Despite its well-known association with barns, the gambrel roof is frequently used in residential building to obtain the most usable headroom under a sloping roof.

Rafters of a true gambrel roof are equal chords inscribed in a semicircle whose radius is the run of the roof (see **8-64**). But not all gambrel-style roofs are necessarily true gambrels. Because it's easy to work with 30-60-90-degree complementary angles, many gambrel-type roofs are laid out with upper and lower roof slope angles of 30 degrees and 60 degrees, respectively.

In any case, the simplest way to find the lengths and cuts for gambrel rafters is to draw a full-size layout on the

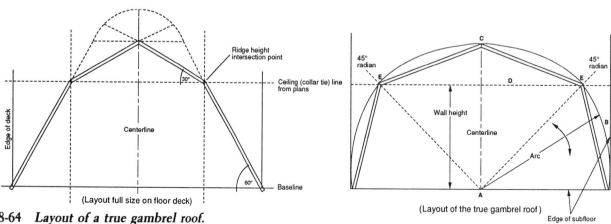

8-64 *Layout of a true gambrel roof.*

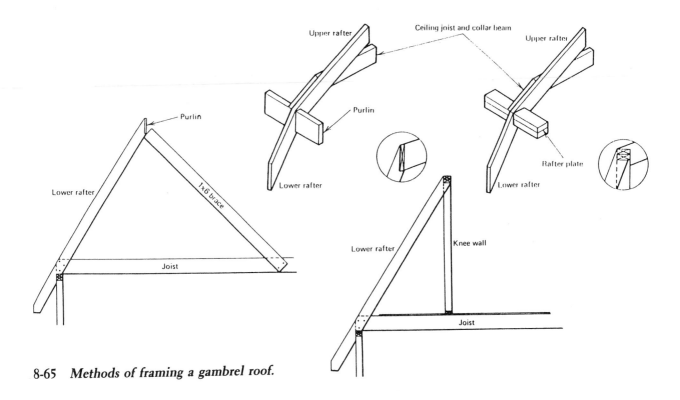

8-65 *Methods of framing a gambrel roof.*

floor deck. Begin by snapping a baseline and perpendicular centerline. For a true gambrel, swing an arc and mark the points where it is intersected by the 45-degree radians and the centerline (refer to **8-64**). The top of the arc is the top of the ridge. The intermediate points mark the transition between the upper and lower roofs at the top, outside edge of the purlin. A line connecting them represents the bottom of the collar tie.

For other than a true gambrel, simply measure off the heights and spans as given in the framing plans. Use the layout lines to find the angle of the rafter cuts and their lengths. If you bisect the angle where the two roofs meet, the end cuts for both rafters will be identical.

Once the rafter layouts have been determined, there are (at least) three ways to assemble the roof frame (see **8-65**). You can temporarily support a continuous purlin, analogous to a ridge board, while attaching the lower set of rafters. The upper rafters are installed next, and supported under their ridge beam until everything is tied together by the collar ties (ceiling joists). Or, you can replace the purlin with a bearing partition or an exposed beam resting on posts or cross-partitions, lay the collar ties across it like floor joists, and then erect the rafters. An advantage of this bearing-wall/carrying-beam approach is that prefabricated roof trusses can be substituted for the collar ties and upper roof rafters. Finally, you could do away with the purlin and the collar ties by building the entire arch assembly as a truss. The connections between the rafter members are either overlapped or else gusseted

with plywood and glue stiffeners, as shown in **8-65**.

Because of the concentrated outward thrust on the rafter plates, framing anchors are required. The rafter tails themselves can be notched over the plate and joined back to the wall studs by lookouts. The traditional "Dutch bonnet" eaves are formed by ending the rafters flush against the plate and nailing a short 2×4 square-cut lookout against its face (see **8-66**).

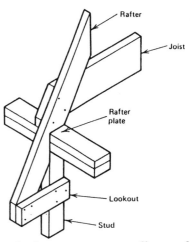

8-66 *Since gambrel trusses are normally attached to plates laid on top of the floor deck, the rafter tails are tacked on afterwards.*

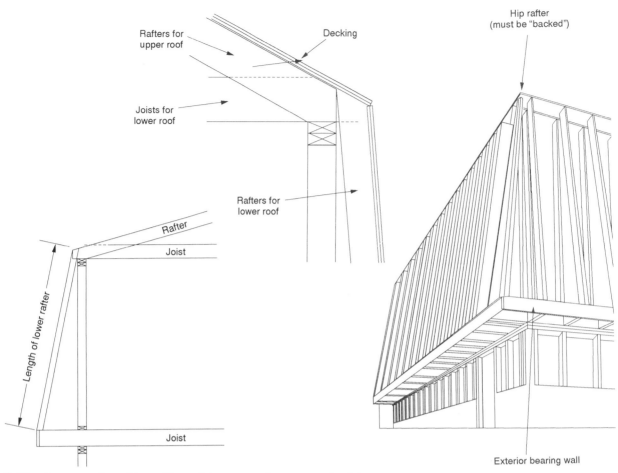

8-67 *A mansard roof is really nothing more than a standard hip roof with a very long rafter-tail extension.*

MANSARD ROOFS

In most parts of the country, the mansard roof, named after its 17th-century originator, French architect François Mansart, is today more likely to be found in association with a strip mall than in a housing development. Yet, the mansard design offers even more usable living space than a gambrel roof—in fact, it owes its origin to property taxes being assessed by how many floors a house had; the design permitted a usable floor where the tax assessor was forced to define the level as "roof." The framing for a mansard roof consists of a low-pitched hip roof set on top of a conventional full second-floor frame (see **8-67**). The rafter tails project far enough past the top plate to attach the lower roof rafters. These, in turn, bear on a 2×4 nailed to the tops of the extended floor joists and cantilevered lookout joists of the floor deck that form the roof overhang. The lower-level rafters are nonstructural, and only serve to carry the roofing material. Dormers or window wells set in the vertical wall are normally used to provide light and ventilation.

To frame a mansard roof, the upper roof is built first. The lower rafters are scribed to the floor joists and upper rafter tails. The only tricky part in framing the lower section is to find the *backing cuts* (refer to following section) of the hip rafter at the corner. Since this rafter slopes in two planes, its top edges will have a double bevel.

UNCOMMON RAFTERS

Hip roofs offer several worthwhile advantages over a conventional two-pitch gable roof. Depending on your level of aversion to heights, the experience of siding, trimming, and painting a high gable wall can range from mildly challenging to outright terrifying. A hip roof has no gable walls; its eaves are all at the same level. It takes less material to finish the walls. The streamlined profile of a hip roof and its continuous eaves make it ideally suited to regions with high winds and heavy rains. The payback for these benefits is that a hip roof is considerably harder to frame than a common rafter roof.

Hip-and-valley roof framing is where most novices draw the line. If you found yourself initially confused by the layout of common rafters, trying to follow the descriptions of hip-and-valley rafter layout presented in most building books may leave you—as it leaves most beginners and not a few experienced carpenters—totally lost. This alone might be good enough reason to stick to simple roof framing—at least until after you've gotten good at it.

One of the problems with hip-and-valley framing is that its hard to visualize the various ways in which different planes cut through a three-dimensional object—like a piece of rectangular rafter stock that's descending in two directions at once. If you study the drawing of a roof frame in 8-68, you'll see that hip-and-valley rafters are the diagonals of squares whose sides are common rafters and the outside wall plates or ridge boards, respectively.

If you think of the wall plate (or ridge) as the base of a triangle (with a unit run of 12) and the common rafter as its altitude (with a unit rise of 12), then the unit run of the hip or valley rafter, which is its hypotenuse, is 17 (the square root of the sum of the squares of 12 and 12, which is 16.97, rounded off for purposes of calculation).

This rounded off number replaces the 12 in hip-and-valley calculations.

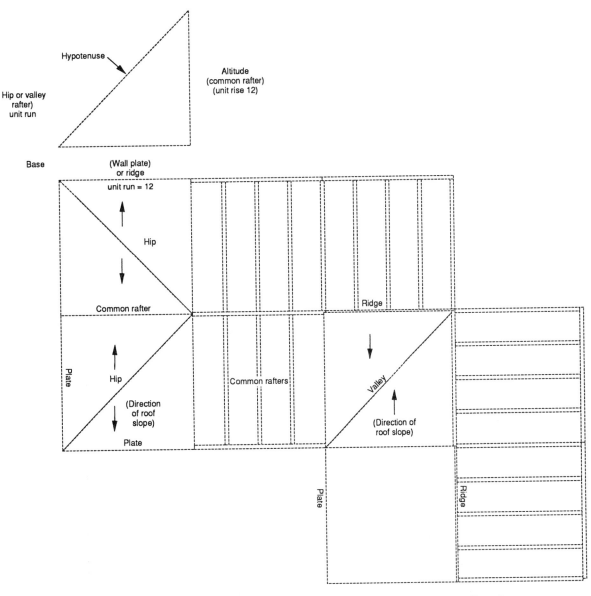

8-68 *Because most people have trouble projecting a two-dimensional situation onto a flat plane, even some experienced carpenters resort to laying out hip-and-valley rafters by the trial-and-error method.*

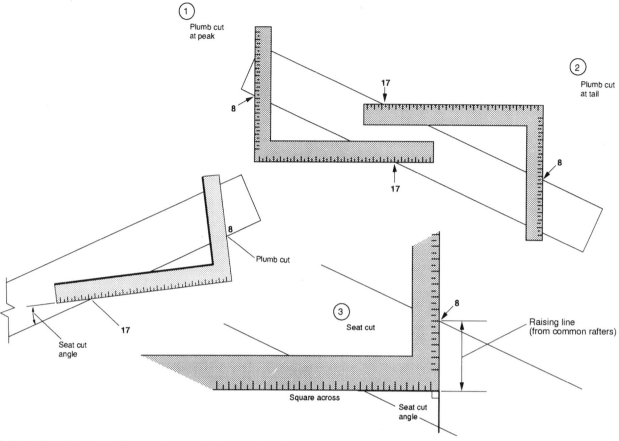

8-69 *The hip-and-valley unit run tables on the rafter square are based on 17, not 12.
The tables won't work for roofs that intersect in unequal pitches.*

So, to find the line length of a hip or valley rafter you'd look up the appropriate number on the second line of the rafter table "Length hip or valley per foot of run"—under the number for roof slope—and multiply it by the common rafter run (see **8-69**). For example, with an 8-12 slope, and a run of 14 feet, the line length of the hip or valley rafter would be 18.76 times 14, which equals 262.64 inches, or 21'-10⅝". And when you laid out your plumb and seat cuts, you'd line up the blade of the square on 17 instead of 12. Although the top edge of the rafter will be in the same plane as the common rafters, its seat cut will be longer—since it crosses the plate at a 45-degree angle. With your square, measure off the *raising line* down from the top of the rafter along the plumb cut. Square the seat cut across the rafter from the bottom of the raising line.

Because the line length of a hip or valley rafter is measured to the centerlines of its intersection with the ridge board, it must be shortened at the ridge and mitred to fit snugly against it (see **8-70**). At first glance, this *cheek* (also called *side*) cut, which represents half the thickness of the hip or valley rafter, appears to be simply half the length

of a 45-degree diagonal squared across the top edge of the ridge, which, whether you measure it or calculate it by square roots, for planned standard two-by lumber (*and* intersecting roofs of equal pitch), works out to 1 1/16 inch.

But, when a 45-degree line drawn across the top edge of a hip or valley rafter is projected downwards as the rafter rotates away from that flat plane—i.e., its pitch increases—the angle of intersection with the ridge grows increasingly less than 45 degrees. Think of a how the hole where a pipe penetrates the roof is an ellipse whose length increases with the slope. As the pitch of a hip or valley rafter changes, two plumb and parallel lines (the equivalent of the pipe) drawn across its face will generate different angles when extended diagonally across the rafter's top edge.

To find the angle of the cheek cut, draw a plumb line parallel to the shortening line, at a distance equal to half the thickness of the rafter stock measured horizontally. Square the two lines across the top of the rafter. Locate the center point of the shortening line on the top edge of the rafter. Connect the corners of the second line to the center point of the shortening line, and measure the resulting angle with your protractor to set your saw blade.

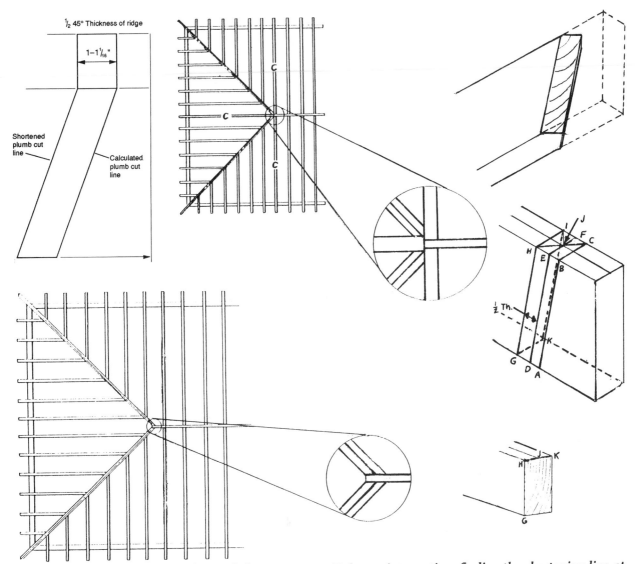

8-70 *Because it represents a diagonal drawn across a 45-degree intersection, finding the shortening line at the ridge is one of the trickiest parts of hip-and-valley rafter layout.* To make a single cheek cut for the meeting of hip rafters at the ridge:

1. *Draw the centerline along the top of the rafter;*
2. *Mark plumb cut AB;*
3. *Square the plumb cut line across the top of the rafter (BC);*
4. *Beginning at point (B), mark off line EB, which is equal to half the 45-degree thickness of the ridge (or common rafter);*
5. *Draw the shortening line (DE) parallel with AB;*

6. *Mark off, from point (E), line EH, which is equal to half the thickness of the hip (or valley) rafter stock;*
7. *Draw cut line GH at this point;*
8. *Square line (HI) across the top of the rafter;*
9. *To mark the cheek cut bevel line, draw a line from point (H) through (J) to (K); line HK is the bevel angle of cheek cut GH;*
10. *To make the opposing cheek cut, draw a line from point (I) through (J) to (L); line IL is the bevel angle of cheek cut LM.*

To make a double cheek cut at the ridge (also used for the tail cut of a hip rafter at the subfascia), mark off lines AB, ED, GH, BC, and HI as above. Then draw lines from points (H) and (I) to (J). The first cheek cut is along line GH with the bevel angle following line HJ. The second cheek cut is along line IK (on the opposite side of the rafter) with the bevel angle following line IJ.

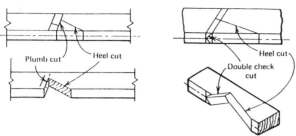

8-71 *One method for bird's-mouth cuts for hip-and-valley rafters.*

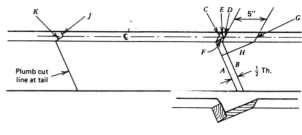

8-72 *Another method for bird's-mouth cuts for hip-and-valley rafters.*

You can also use line six, "Side cut hip or valley use," of the rafter table on your framing square to lay out the side cut in one step. The numbers in this table are based on 12. Line up the bottom edge of the blade with the rafter and the 12 mark set back so that the blade intersects the shortening line at the center of the rafter edge. Line up the tongue of the blade with the rafter on the number from the table (e.g., 10⅞ for an 8-12 pitch), and scribe the angle across the top edge of the rafter. Square across both lines, and draw another diagonal to bisect the first one. Extend plumb lines down the face of the rafter on both sides to mark the cut lines; the same technique is used to mark the tail side cuts as well.

There are two ways to deal with the bird's-mouth cut of a hip rafter, one elegant and time-consuming, and the other "quick and dirty," but effective (see **8-71** and **8-72**). Mark the centerline on the bottom edge of the rafter tail. Lay out the angle for the double cheek cut with your square or T-bevel. You'll find that the rest of the tail gets in the way of a circular saw blade, and you'll have to finish all but part of one face of the cut with a handsaw and chisel. The alternative is to lay out the angles for the cheek cuts, and cut square across their base. Marking the length of the cheek cuts on the corners of the rafter plate, draw a diagonal between them. "Dub" off the corner of the top plate to accept the bird's-mouth. Since the direction of the cheek cuts are reversed on a valley rafter, most of the cut can be made with a circular saw and the rafter plate doesn't need to be dubbed off.

The centerline of a hip or valley rafter is where the opposing roof surfaces actually meet. The edges of a hip rafter or the center of a valley rafter will stick up past the plane of the jack rafters so that you can't lay the roof sheathing flat. Carpenters in a hurry solve this problem by "dropping" both kinds of rafters, deepening the seat and plumb cuts, and lowering the peak at the ridge so that their edges are at the right height (see **8-73**). The slight gap where the sheathing meets a dropped rafter makes it hard to get solid nailing and increases the chances of mistakes when attaching the jack rafters.

Because they don't know how to find the angle of the bevel necessary to properly *back* a hip or valley rafter to make its top edge co-planar with the roof, inexperienced carpenters will often attempt, with varying degrees of success, to hew the rafter down by trial and error with a power plane, a circular saw, or even a hatchet. There are two simple methods to find the proper backing angle: using a square (see **8-74**), and the "test block" method (see **8-75**). The test block is made by cutting the rafter seat on one end of a short block and a square cut on the other end. The stock need only be as thick as the rafter stock; its width doesn't matter.

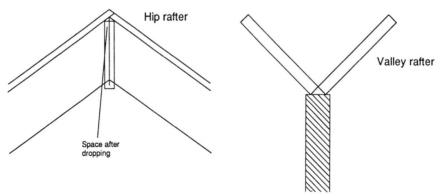

8-73 *Although it saves time, dropping the rafter doesn't provide a very good bearing surface for nailing down the valley or hip sheathing.*

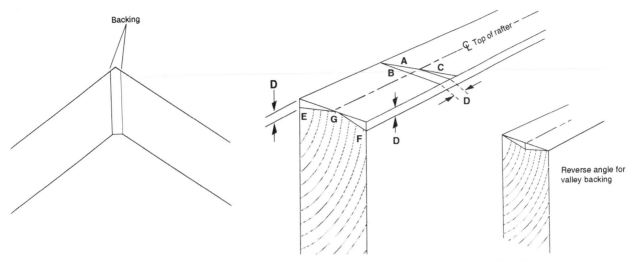

8-74 *Using a square to find the backing angle:*

1. *Draw the centerline down the top edge of the rafter;*
2. *Draw plumb line A across the top of the rafter (at any convenient point);*
3. *Square one side of this line across the top edge (B);*
4. *At the intersection of the plumb line and the*

centerline draw square line C;
5. *Measure the distance (D) between line B and line C;*
6. *Mark off this distance down both sides of the rafter;*
7. *The resulting lines EG and FG are the cutting lines for the backing angles; use a bevel square and a protractor to convert the angle to degrees for setting your table-saw blade.*

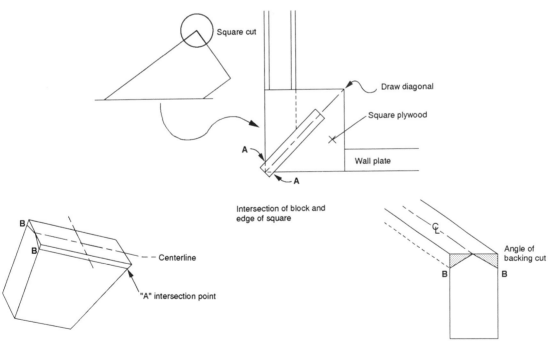

8-75 *Test block method for finding backing cut:*

1. *Set test block on corner and mark point A on both sides of block;*
2. *Scribe line A along both sides of the top edge*

of the test block to the square cut end (point B);
3. *Connect point(s) B to the centerline; this is the angle of the backing cut; measure it with a protractor to find the saw-blade angle.*

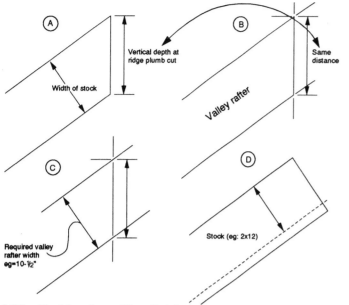
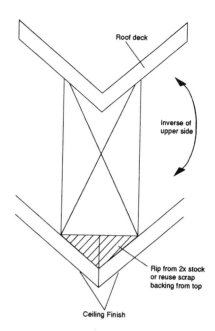

8-76 *Backing for ceiling finish.*

If the hip or valley rafter carries a cathedral ceiling, its bottom edge should also be backed to provide solid nailing for the ceiling finish (see **8-76**). The backing on this edge will be the opposite of the backing on the top. This bottom backing should line up flush with the bottoms of the jack rafters. It might be possible to tack the leftover from the top backing cut to the bottom. Otherwise, rip a two-by strip to fit.

The length of the tail of a hip or valley rafter is the diagonal of a square whose sides are the length of the jack rafter or common rafter overhang (see **8-77**). You could measure that diagonal by constructing a full-scale drawing, but the easiest way to deal with hip or valley rafter tails is to leave them overlong and cut them to fit when you install the subfascia.

If the valley or hip rafter tail intersects a corner formed by the two common rafters (a cross-gabled roof is one example of this condition), it's often less trouble to leave off the tail entirely (see **8-78**). The common rafters are mitred at 45 degrees along their plumb cuts to meet in a 90-degree corner against which the hip rafter terminates. Blocking installed between the corner and the subfascia supports the sheathing and soffit as required.

Valleys and hips are really nothing more than descending ridge boards. As such, they should also be cut from stock at least two inches wider than the rafters to provide full bearing for the cheek cuts of the jack rafters. Although, in most cases—except for excessively long runs—there's no strictly structural necessity for so doing, I prefer to double the valley-and-hip rafters anyway, since they are subjected

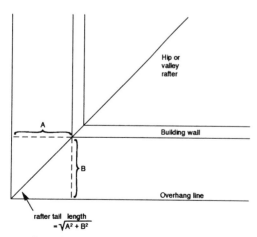

8-77 *Finding hip or valley rafter tail length.*

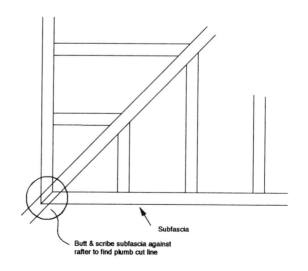

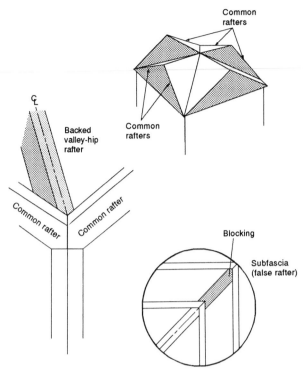

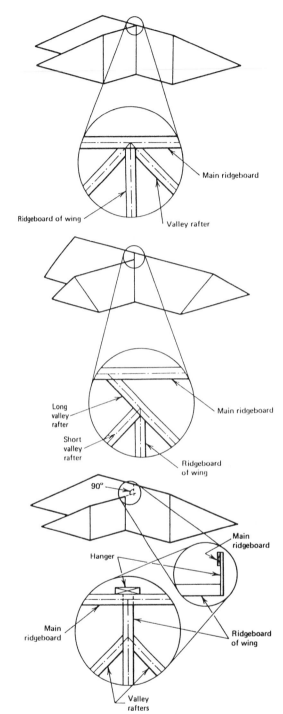

8-78 *Since the tail of a hip rafter is normally reduced, some carpenters end the valley rafter at the plate and cut a 2×4 tail to fit.*

to slightly more downward stress than an ordinary ridge. (The added stiffness seems only prudent in light of the 100-year stress theory of framing.) In any case, the added width makes for better sheathing attachment and easier execution of the backing cut, especially for a valley rafter, where the cuts slope inward. Single cheek cuts are also easier to cut than double ones.

BLIND VALLEY RAFTERS

Framing for the intersection of two gable roofs of equal pitch but different spans is similar to the framing for a large gable dormer (see **8-79**). Since the ridge of the minor-span roof will be lower than the ridge of the major-span, one of the valleys, the *blind valley*, is extended from the plate to the major ridge. It rests against the ridge with a single side cut instead of a double one; the opposing valley is supported against it. To locate the intersection of the two valleys, measure in along the major ridge the distance from the last common rafter to the center of the building (or to the centerline of the minor ridge if the minor roof isn't centered on the major one). Transfer that distance to the center of the blind valley rafter. The intersection of the valleys is where the minor roof ridge begins. The side cut of the short valley is a square cut where it runs into the blind valley—and so it is shortened by half the 90-degree thickness of the valley rafter.

8-79 *When ridges are at equal heights but the rafter spans are different, the pitches of the major and minor roofs are different. If the pitches of the roof are the same, the minor-roof ridge must be lower than the major-roof ridge. Hanging the minor ridge from the major one is an alternative to framing a blind valley for fairly small (i.e., lightweight) projecting roofs.*

209

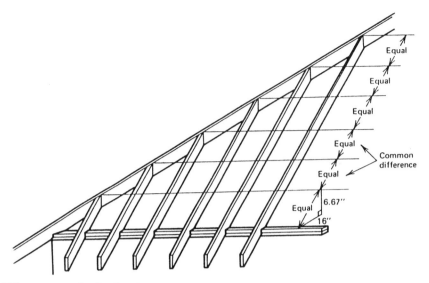

8-80 *The common difference method of jack rafter sizing works only when everything else is perfectly cut and framed.*

JACK RAFTERS

A valley jack rafter has the same plumb cut as the common rafters at its top end and a cheek cut at its lower end. A hip jack rafter has the same bird's-mouth as the common rafters with the cheek cut at its upper end. Other than that, the layout principles for the two kinds of rafters is the same; the only tricky part is to find the angle of the cheek cut.

The easiest way to find the line length of a jack rafter is by the *common difference* method (see 8-80). When evenly spaced, each successive hip or valley rafter will be predictably and identically longer or shorter than the one before it.

Instead of trial and error, the easiest way to find the common difference between jack rafters for roofs of known whole-number pitches is to look it up on line three, "Diff

in length of jacks 16 inches centers," or line four, "Diff in length of jacks 2 feet centers," on your framing square. To lay out the first jack pattern rafter, subtract the amount given by the table from the line length of the common rafter (measured from the plumb line at the plate to the center of the ridge) (see 8-81). Shorten the line length of the jack rafter by half the 45-degree thickness (horizontal) of the hip (or valley). Then subtract half the horizontal thickness of the jack rafter. A diagonal extended through the centerline of the rafter between the shortening line and the second plumb cut mark gives the mitre angle for the cut. You can also use the numbers from line five of the rafter table, "Side cut of jacks use" as before when laying out the side cuts for hip and valley rafters. The bottom edge of the blade is lined up on 12 so that it crosses the rafter at the intersection of the shortening line

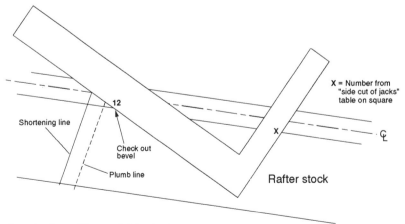

8-81 *Layout of cheek cuts for valley and hip jacks.*

210

8-82 *Making the cheek cuts for hip-and-valley jack rafters with a handsaw is tedious and difficult work. A circular saw set to the complement of the bevel angle and held against the end of the plumb cut will save a good deal of that hand work. The rafter board is clamped on edge to the sawhorse by blocks nailed against it.*

and the centerline. As before, the plumb cut of the cheek cut is laid out with 17 and the common roof rise.

If the first jack rafter fits, the others are laid out in order by deducting the common difference from the actual length of the pattern and each succeeding rafter. Don't cut all the jack rafters before trying them for fit. If your hip or valley isn't running perfectly true, or the spacing layout is off square, they may need adjustments in length. Cut the jack rafters in pairs of equal length with the cheek cuts in opposite directions. To avoid getting confused as to the orientation of the angles and sides, mark the *long point* and *short point* of the angle layouts on the rafter stock.

The angles of jack rafter cheek cuts are normally greater than 45 degrees, which means they can't be cut in the usual manner with a circular saw. A chain saw is possibly dangerous and definitely inaccurate. It takes too much skill and elbow grease to cut them with a handsaw (see **8-82**). This is one situation where it pays to have a radial-arm saw on the job. If you don't, you can use the following method to make most of the cut with your circular saw (see **8-83**). Saw the plumb cut square with the face of the rafter. Tack the rafter on edge to a sawhorse. Then set the saw blade to the complementary angle of the desired face cut angle. Hold the base of the saw against the edge face of the plumb cut (at right angles to its face), and cut along the edge. A standard 7¼-inch saw blade won't cut all the way through, but what's left is a lot easier to finish with a handsaw. Smooth off any differences between the two saw kerfs with a block plane or a sharp timber-framing chisel.

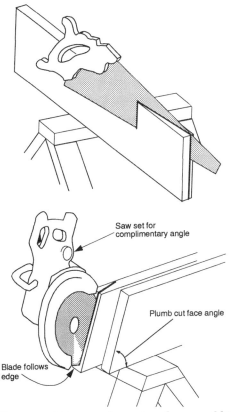

Saw set for complimentary angle

Plumb cut face angle

Blade follows edge

8-83 *Because of the much greater danger of kickback, only experienced carpenters should attempt to cut along the edge of a board with a power saw.*

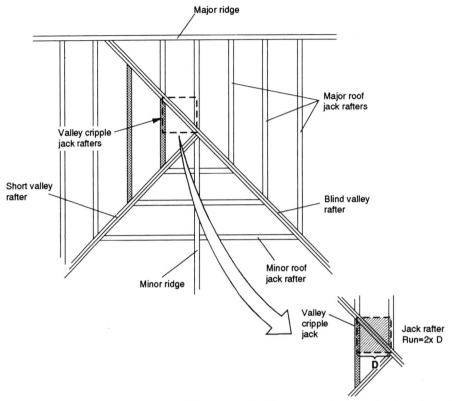

8-84 *The only difference between cripple rafters and other jack rafters is in finding the line length.*

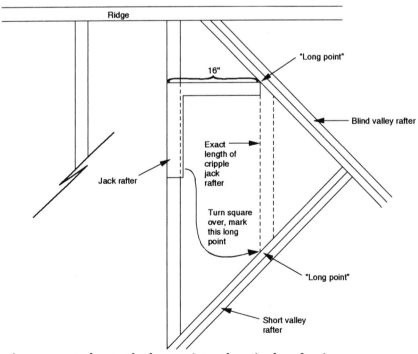

8-85 *Using the framing square to locate the long points of a cripple rafter is more accurate than finding the length by calculation.*

CRIPPLE RAFTERS

In the case of the blind valley rafter discussed above, depending on the difference in height between the major and minor ridge, one or more rafters must be framed between the two valleys. The angle of the cheek cut at the top of this *valley cripple jack* rafter is the reverse of the cheek cut at its lower end. The run of a valley cripple is twice the distance from the centerline of the rafter to the intersection of the centerlines of the two valley rafters (see **8-84**), which is the side of an imaginary square formed by the jack and cripple rafters. Its rise is the same as the main roof. The line length of a valley cripple is shortened at each end by half the 45-degree thickness of the rafter stock. The side cuts are the same as jack rafters.

Since the "long point"-to-"long point" length of a valley cripple is also the hypotenuse of the triangle formed by the intersection of the outside edges of the blind and short valley rafters, you could also measure the spacing interval from the last jack rafter with the blade of the square, and mark where it falls on the valley rafters (see **8-85**). You simply measure between the two points to find the length of the cripple jack without having to make any shortening adjustments.

In roofs that feature a hip sloping down into a valley, *hip-valley cripple jacks* are needed. The only difference in layout approach is that since they are the side of a square parallel to the wall plate, the run of these rafters is the distance between the centers of the hip-and-valley rafters as measured along the plate (see **8-86**). Also, if the taping-off method is used, the measurement will be from long point to short point, instead, since the cheek cuts are at parallel angles.

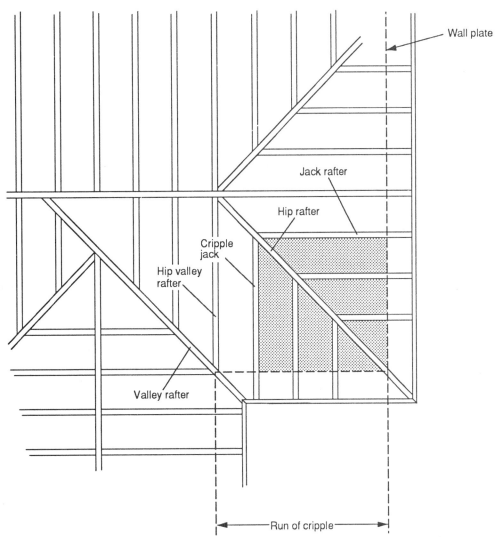

8-86 *Hip-valley cripple jack rafters have both a long point and short point measurement to locate.*

213

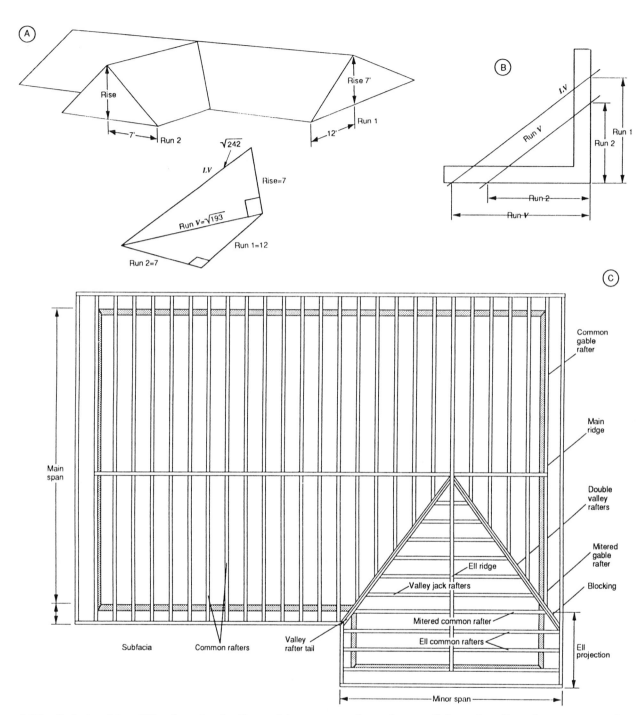

8-87 *Relationship of line length of valley or hip rafter to rise and run for roofs of unequal pitch:*

A: *The line length of the valley or hip rafter for an unequal-pitch roof is the hypotenuse of a triangle formed by the rise and the hypotenuse of the triangle formed by the runs of the major and minor roofs.*

B: *You can also use a framing square to find*

the unit run of the rafter: Lay the square on the floor deck. Mark the run of the major roof on the blade (R1) and the run of the minor roof (R2) on its tongue. Connect the two points. Mark the rise of the roof on the tongue. Measure the length between these two points (use the 1/12th scale) to find the unit run of line LV.

C: *The framing plan for a typical unequal-pitched roof.*

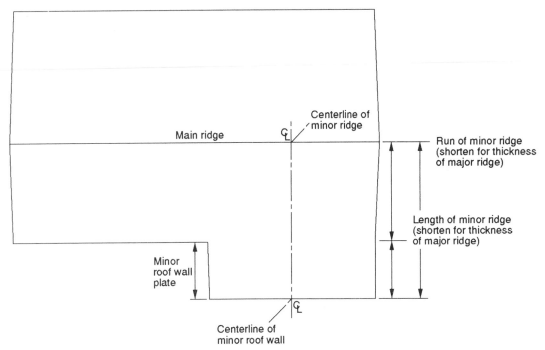

Main ridge

Centerline of minor ridge

Run of minor ridge (shorten for thickness of major ridge)

Length of minor ridge (shorten for thickness of major ridge)

Minor roof wall plate

Centerline of minor roof wall

8-88 *The first step in valley rafter layout is setting the minor ridge.*

FRAMING FOR ROOFS OF UNEQUAL PITCH

The intersection of two roofs of unequal pitch involves complicated geometrical relationships that are difficult to visualize, let alone lay out. The constants given in the framing square rafter tables apply only to roofs of *equal pitch*. Trigonometric manipulations and complicated graphic projections are two of the alternatives to the trial-and-error approach to finding line lengths and laying out cheek and plumb cut angles. Although a first-time builder should probably avoid such roofs, there's an empirical strings-and-level method that works and has much to recommend it, even to experienced roof framers.

The roof shown in **8-87** is a fairly common example of intersecting unequal-pitch roofs. Because the spans are different and the ridges are at the same level, the slopes of the roofs are different, even though their rise is the same. The measuring-line length of the hip or valley rafter for such a roof is the hypotenuse of a triangle laid out on the hypotenuse of another triangle. The sides of the first triangle are the runs of the two roofs; the base of the second triangle is the hypotenuse of the first (i.e., the run of the valley rafter). Its side is the common rise of both roofs and its hypotenuse is the length of the hip or valley rafter.

For example, referring to **8-87**, the major roof has a run of 12 feet at a 7-12 pitch, and the minor roof has a run of seven feet at some as yet undetermined pitch; the rise of both roofs is 7. Add the squares of Run 1 and Run 2 (144 plus 49) to find Run V (193). Add this sum to

the square of the rise (49) to get 242, and take its square root to find LV, the measuring-line length of the valley rafter, or 15'-6⅝". The square root of Run V is 13.892 or 13⅞. Set the blade of the square on this number and the tongue to the pitch to lay out the plumb cuts.

This part of the operation is relatively straightforward, but it isn't much help in laying out the side cuts and backing cuts, which will be different for each side of the rafter. The faces of the side cuts won't meet at the centerline of the rafters and the opposing jack rafter pairs won't be the same length or line up directly across from each other. The rafter tails will be different lengths, too. These can all be found by graphing them out on paper. But it's a lot easier to do the layout in place instead (see **8-88**).

In the roof frame of the example, the common rafters of the major roof are framed first. Next, locate the centerline of the minor roof gable wall plate and nail a ridge support post over it. Transfer this centerline location to the major ridge. The length of the minor ridge equals the run of the main roof (less half the thickness of the major ridge) plus the length of the minor roof wall plate. Mark the rafter spacing on the minor ridge from the gable end inward, and set it on top of its support post. Nail it to the major ridge; check it for level. Make a pattern for the minor-roof common rafters using the empirical method described earlier, leaving the tail unmarked for the moment, and tack it in place.

215

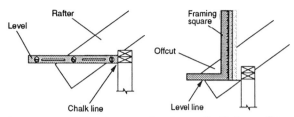

8-89 *Layout of minor-roof rafter tail; if the soffits of an unequal-pitched roof are at the same level, the more steeply pitched roof will have a narrower-width soffit.*

For the subfascia to run across the rafter tails of both roofs at the same level, the overhang of the minor roof must be shorter than the major-roof overhang. To determine where to cut them you'll have to project the major-roof common rafter tail onto the minor-roof common rafter pattern (see **8-89**). First, level across the bottom of the major-roof common rafter to the wall itself. Measure the distance between this mark and the top of the wall plate, and transfer the measurement to the minor-roof wall plate. Extend this line across the bottom of the minor-roof rafter pattern. Measure the length of the tail plumb cut (or

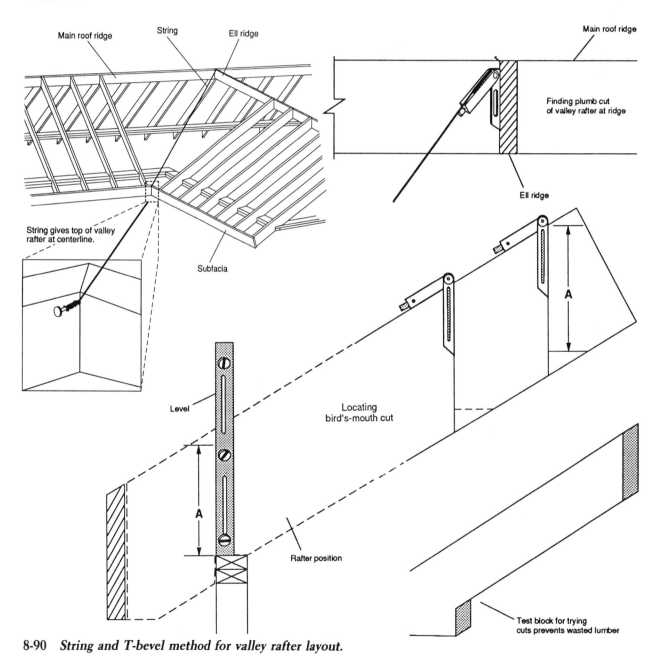

8-90 *String and T-bevel method for valley rafter layout.*

square cut) on the major-roof rafter, and slide your framing square horizontally across the level line on the pattern rafter until it measures off a vertical line equal in length to the plumb cut of the major-roof rafters. Take down the pattern, cut the tail, and lay out and install the remaining common rafters.

To find the length and pitch of the valley rafter, nail the subfascias to the common rafter tails, extending them to meet in a 45-degree mitre at the inside corner at the end of the valley rafter tail. Since the bevels on the top edges of the subfascias will match their respective roof slopes, you'll have to trim the steeper one off with a small plane or chisel to make a smooth match.

Stretch a string from the outside corner of the subfascia to the centerline of the ridge intersection (see **8-90**). Measuring the length of the string between the inside of these two points gives the actual length of the valley rafter (along its centerline) without any need to adjust for ridge thickness. Align a T-bevel vertically with the string to find the angle of the plumb cut at the intersection of the valley rafter and ridge. This angle is also used for the heel cut of the bird's-mouth and for the tail cut. Align the T-bevel horizontally with the string to find the angle of the side cut. Instead of a T-bevel, you can also find the angles by holding a scrap block on the string and scribing the cut with another block or the blade of your square.

To locate the bird's-mouth, use a level to plumb up to the string from the outside corner of the plate, and measure the rising distance. Measure the distance between the tail and the level along the string. Locate this point on the top edge of the rafter, and draw a plumb line downwards. Its length should match the measured rising distance.

Before laying out the cuts on the valley rafter proper, transfer these angles onto a short piece of stock, and make a test block to try them out for fit; it costs less to fix a mistake on scrap than on a full-size rafter.

Since the string marks the centerline of the valley rafter, layout is a lot less trouble if the rafter is doubled, especially since the angles of side cuts and backing cuts will be different on each side of the centerline. You can use the layout method described earlier to find the backing cut angles or draw the angle across the face of the rafter peak test block (see **8-91**). Since this piece will be plumb cut, you can't transfer the angle to a square-cut piece for conversion into degrees of saw-blade angle. Just keep making trial cuts and adjusting the blade until its kerf lines up with the scribe line of the test block.

To make sure that the valley rafter runs straight, leave the centerline string in place until all the jack rafters are installed. Use temporary braces to hold it to the line, as needed.

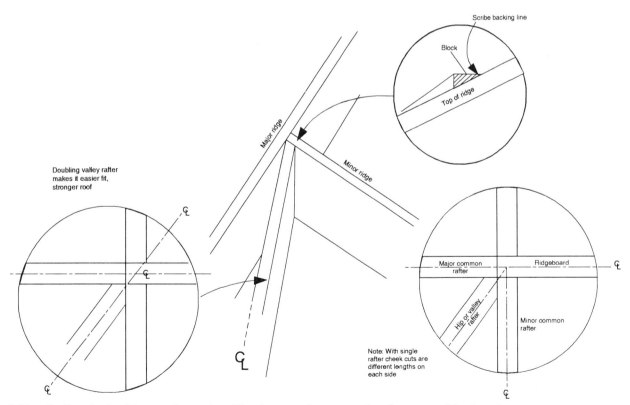

8-91 *Scribe the backing angle at the ridge intersection on a plumb-cut test block and find the correct saw-blade angle by trial-and-error cuts on the table saw.*

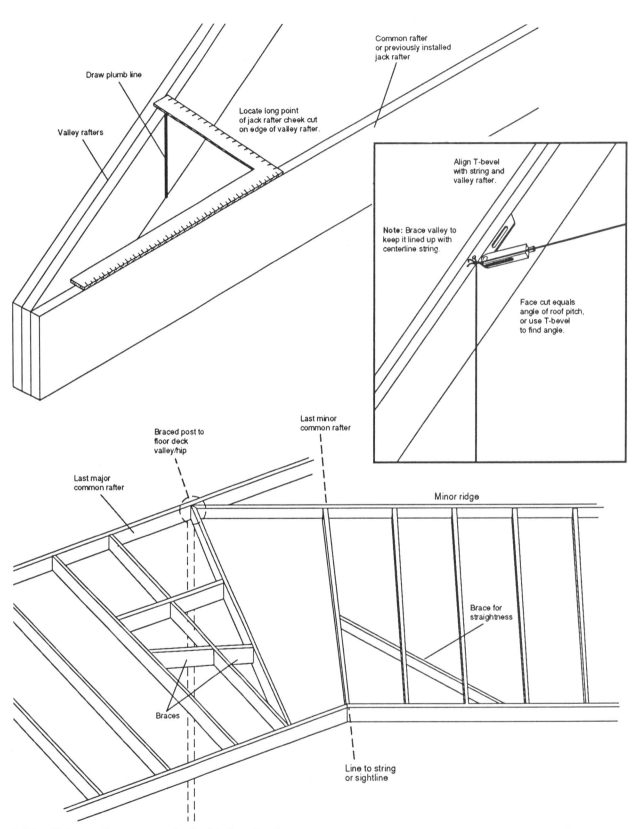

8-92 *String-and-square method of jack rafter layout.*

The layout lines for the jack rafters should have been marked on both ridges prior to their installation. The center of the first jack rafter will be 16 inches or 24 inches from the center of the last common rafter. Eyeball the common rafter for straightness, and take out any bow with a temporary brace back to the plate. For 16-inch centers, align the blade of your framing square with the outside top edge of the common rafter (use the tongue for 24-inch centers), and slide it up or down until the tip of the tongue intersects the outside edge of the valley rafter (see 8-92). Plumb a line down the face of the valley rafter at this point. Stretch a string between this point and the spacing mark at the top of the ridge board. Measuring along the string gives the exact length of the top edge of the jack rafter. Set your T-bevel along the string, and line it up with the edge of the valley rafter to find the jack rafter cheek-cut angle. The blade and the center of the T-bevel handle must be in the same plane when lined up with the string. Since even a small twist will give an incorrect angle, make a test block for this end of the jack rafter first, and try it for fit before marking the actual jacks. You can use it as a pattern to lay out the rest of the cuts.

Make the compound cheek cuts before measuring off the rafter length and making the plumb cut at the ridge end, to ensure a good fit. After the first jack rafter is installed, you can find the common difference by measuring it. The lengths of the succeeding jacks are shortened by this amount. Even if you bothered to calculate it, it's unlikely that the pitch of the minor roof will be a whole number; so you couldn't use the rafter tables to find the common difference even if you wanted to.

Mark the intersection with the valley for each following jack rafter by setting the framing square along the edge of the preceding one. By setting the square on the outside edge, you can mark the long point of the jack rafter cheek cut.

Whenever possible, angles should be laid out from the *long point* since that's the safest, easiest, and most accurate way to orient a circular-saw blade to the stock. If you need to determine a *short point* measurement, set the square to the inside of the rafter instead. The distinction between long point and short point when laying out and measuring angle and bevel cuts is one which carpenters have many occasions to make. When making a cut list for a number of pieces, the measurements are often followed by an "LP" or "SP" to show their direction and prevent miscuts (e.g., 56″ LP-SP; 56″ SP-SP; 56″ LP-LP—or 56″ LP, indicating one end is square-cut).

The valley-to-ridge measurements should agree with the length as derived from the subtraction of common difference. If it doesn't, something is out of square. In this case, it's more important for the sake of the sheathing that the spacing intervals remain constant and the jacks stay parallel to the common rafters than that the actual length of the jack rafters equal the predicted length of the common difference method. Sixteenths and smidgeons always seem to conspire against the congruence of theory and actuality.

With same-pitch valley-and-hip roofs, the jack rafters of the opposing roofs line up in pairs perpendicularly across from each other; in an unequal-pitch roof, the cheek cuts aren't mirror images so that the jack rafter pairs won't line up across from each other (see 8-93). Since the cuts are different, it's only sensible to work up one side of the valley or hip at a time rather than installing opposing pairs. The ridge intersection should be temporarily supported by a post, and the valley rafter braced both vertically and horizontally, to keep the jack rafters from running off.

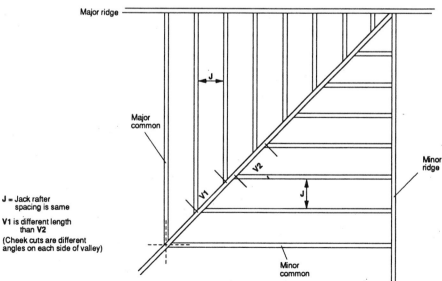

8-93 *Spacing difference of jack rafters on opposite sides of the valley.*

8-94 *Calculating rafter cuts can require a working knowledge of trigonometry or the art of geometric projections. But it is easier to establish a level subfascia parallel to the run of the top plate and stretch strings to the ridge or (in this case) the common center point of the radial rafters.*

THE NO-VALLEY ROOF FRAMING TECHNIQUE

Beginners and any carpenter afflicted with "fear of ciphering" will find that the empirical method described above works even better for framing equal-pitch hip-and-valley roofs and octagonal roofs (see **8-94** and **8-95**). Unless they happen to be architects, most beginners wouldn't think of trying to frame a wall that runs at 30 degrees or 45 degrees to the line of its eaves—or a wall that slices vertically through the plane of the roof. Although calculations are possible to enable doing it, the string-and-level method is the most accessible and practical way to lay out uncommon rafters for creative roof forms.

The so-called "California roof" is a quick-and-dirty shortcut to framing intersecting roofs that requires no valley rafter at all (see **8-96**). This method, which basically boils down to framing the minor roof on top of the deck of the major roof, is often used by remodellers to join the roof of an addition or ell onto the main roof. It will work for any roof with flat ceiling joists at plate level and where the main roof has a cathedral ceiling that shares no connection with the minor roof. It's also a simple and effective way to install a small gable dormer. Once the dormer roof is completed, the underlying rafters are cut and headed off between the trimmers.

8-95 *Seen from below: If the top edges of the rafters are to coincide with the top edge of the previously established level subfascia, the bottom edges—the seat cuts— will vary according to their location along the wall. In effect, the depth of the rafters changes, which is why shims must be installed between the rafters and the plate. Later, tapered strips will be added to the bottom edges of the rafters so that the finish ceiling ends even with the top of the wall plate.*

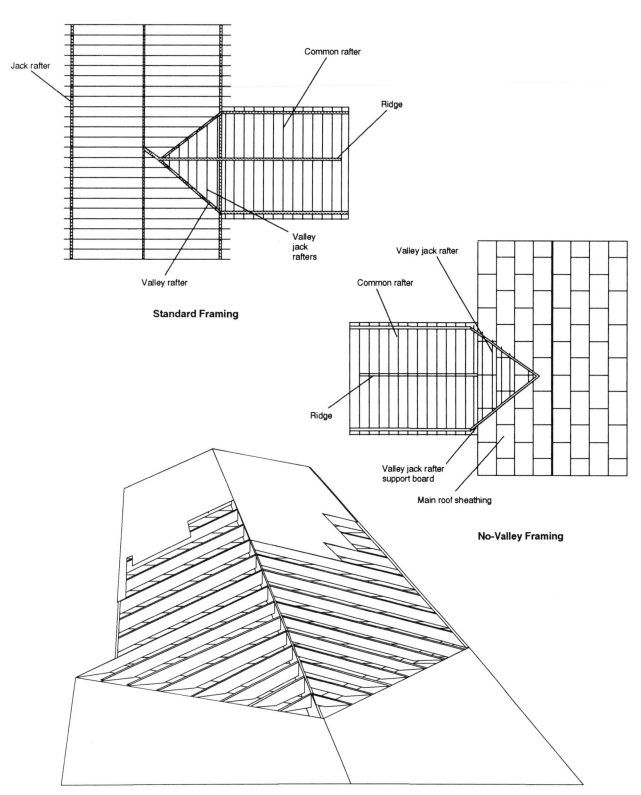

Jack rafter

Common rafter

Ridge

Valley
jack
rafters

Valley rafter

Standard Framing

Valley jack rafter

Common rafter

Ridge

Valley jack rafter
support board

Main roof sheathing

No-Valley Framing

8-96   *The California roof: After the minor roof is framed, cut through and remove some of the major roof sheathing under the jack rafter area so that the attic spaces of both roofs are contiguous—both for access and ventilation purposes.*

221

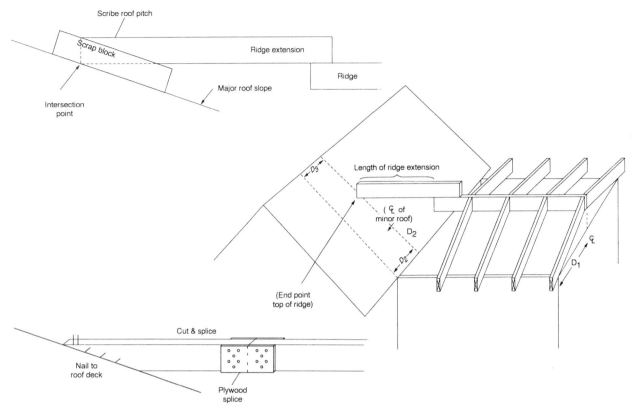

8-97 *Locating the ridge for a California roof.*

After the major roof is framed and sheathed, but before the finish trim is applied to the subfascia, lay out the gable pattern rafters for the minor roof and determine its ridge height. To locate the intersection of this ridge with the major roof deck, first locate its centerline, which is the run of the ell roof plus the length of the major roof eaves beyond it (see **8-97**). Transfer that measurement to the main roof at two points in from its rake so that you can snap a vertical line between them. Plumb a ridge support post/storey pole over the center of the minor roof gable wall, and extend a level line from it to the centerline marked on the major roof. If the run of the minor ridge is longer than the ridge stock, support its far end with a temporary post. You can mark the angle of the cut where the ridge meets the main roof with your framing square (it's the same as the major common rafter seat cut). Otherwise, slide the ridge extension stock over the first ridge until its bottom touches the locating mark on the major roof. Check it for level; then scribe the angle against it with a scrap of 2×4. The point where the extension piece overlaps the first piece of ridge stock is also the length of the extension. If the ridge is short enough to reach the major roof in a single piece, rest the far end on top of its support post, hold it level to the major roof, and scribe the angle.

To locate the valley line, first extend the plane of the minor roof onto the major roof by resting a two-by across the tops of a few common rafters, and marking where it hits the main roof (see **8-98**). Snap a chalk line from the upper edge of the ridge intersection down across the major roof through this point—and beyond to the edge of the major roof. Repeat the procedure on the other side of the ridge.

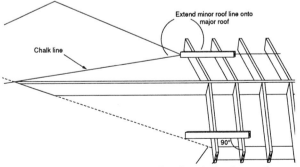

8-98 *To ensure accuracy, the 2×4 that's used to extend the line of the minor-roof rafter to locate the lower end of the valley centerline must be at right angles to the common rafter.*

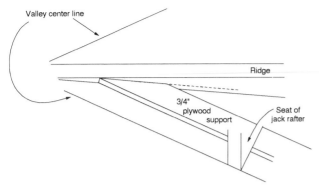

8-99 *Once you've determined the proper back-off distance, snap a second chalk line for installing the support strips.*

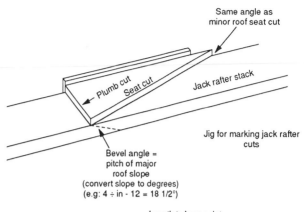

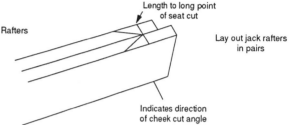

8-100 *Jack rafter seat cut layout.*

Provide extra support under the tail ends of the jack rafters by nailing a strip of ¾-inch plywood to the roof deck down the length of—but not on—the valley guide lines. Hold the plywood back from the line so that the top edge of the jack rafters will line up in the same plane as the valley lines even though they won't actually intersect it (see **8-99**). Stretch a string from the valley line to the ridge and set the plywood where its top edge touches the string. The point of the jack rafter tail cut will then line up with the edge of the plywood.

The plumb cut of the jack rafters at the ridge and the seat cut, which extends across the entire tail end of the jack, are the same angle as the corresponding cuts on the minor-roof common rafters, except that the seat cut is also bevelled at the angle of the major-roof slope (see **8-100**). Measure it with a protractor, and set your saw blade to the correct angle. You can make a simple jig to lay out the cuts: lay out and cut the rise and run of the minor roof onto a board of the same width as the rafter stock. Nail a one-by alignment fence to the top edge of this jig. Line it up with the length marks on the jack rafter stock to mark the seat cut.

If you coordinate the length of the ell with the rafter spacing so that the last common rafter of the minor roof falls exactly in the corner, then the first jack rafter will be shorter by the common difference for the slope and spacing of the minor roof. If the last common rafter doesn't fall over the corner, square across from it to the valley line, and measure the distance between that point and the jack rafter spacing mark at the ridge (see **8-101**). Since the actual rafter ends on the support board and not the valley line, shorten the measurement by the horizontal distance between the valley line and the bottom edge of the support board.

Try out the first jack rafter for fit. It should run parallel with the common rafter and the extension of its point should end on the valley line. If the bevel cut is correct, its face will also be plumb.

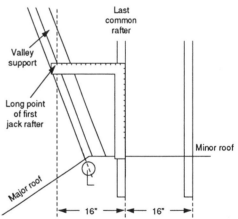

8-101 *Laying out the first jack rafter; unless specifically designed that way, it's unlikely that the last common rafter will coincide with the corner of the valley.*

Once the first jack is installed, the lengths of the other jacks are calculated by deducting the common difference as determined from the rafter tables or else by direct measurement. In either case, use your framing square as described earlier to maintain parallel spacing intervals. Lay out the jack rafters in pairs of equal length with opposite bevels at their long points. Mark the direction of the bevel cut across the correct side of the seat cut. Install the jacks in pairs working up the roof.

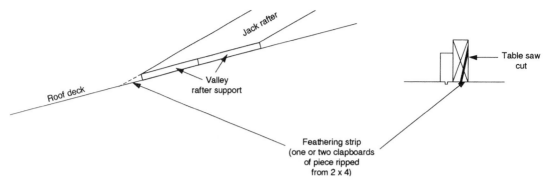

8-102 *Backing roof sheathing.*

The only drawback to this method of valley framing is that it's difficult to bevel the underside of the minor roof sheathing so that it feathers into the major roof slope, since the angle of the cut will typically exceed the capabilities of your saw. Although many carpenters do it, butting a square edge can cause a slight hump in the valley lining—and even an eventual leak. Scribe the bevel of the cut across the end of a 2×4 and rip it on a table saw set to its complement (see 8-102). Tack this feathering strip along the edge of the sheathing. Applying the sheathing noticeably shifts the finished valley line an inch or two past the layout line; this is of consequence only when the valley is to be centered over the inside corner of the subfascia trim, which should be finished after the minor-roof sheathing. Finally, cut out a section of sheathing in the major roof to provide access to the minor roof attic area.

8-103 *With this house, the roof trusses were set at an angle; the truss bottom chord was joined to the end wall below by nailing a plate to its underside and filling in the gap between the two walls with short lengths of blocking. The garage was framed with ordinary extension rafters. Note the mix of IB and CDX wall sheathing.*

ROOF TRUSSES

A truss is a rigid frame engineered to carry a load between two points (see 8-103). The braced triangles of a typical roof truss distribute the compression and tension forces of the roof load so effectively that only very light framing members are required to carry relatively large spans. Two-by-fours are typical for residential roofs with spans of up to 24 feet. Two-by-six top members are used for longer spans and/or heavier design loads. The important thing to remember about roof trusses is that their design isn't arbitrary. The dead and live load conditions, the span, the type and direction of stresses, the grade and species of the truss members, their dimensions, and the kinds of connectors used to join them are just some of the factors that must be considered. This is the main reason why most trusses are delivered to the job site preassembled and pre-engineered according to your specifications or a standard form.

Truss roofs are generally less expensive than conventionally framed roofs when the total costs of materials and labor are compared. Because a roof truss combines rafters and ceiling joists into one frame that bears only on the outside walls, the arrangement of the floor plan isn't restricted by bearing partitions or supporting girders. In fact, the interior partitions aren't even built until after the trusses are erected and the roof and walls are sheathed over. Also, since the entire roof frame can be erected in a few hours or less, trusses are ideal if there's a premium on getting the house closed in as quickly as possible. One of the advantages of roof trusses is also their disadvantage: that they are most economical for low-pitched roofs (slopes of 5-12 or less) where the attic space won't be used.

Of the many types of roof trusses, the "W," or *Fink*, truss (named after its inventor) is the most widely used in residential construction (see 8-104). The *Double W* truss allows lighter members to carry longer spans and/or heavier loads. A *scissors truss* is used when the design calls for sloping ceilings (see 8-105). A variant of the Double-W truss (which might be called the "W-and-a-half" truss) is used for low-pitched salt-box style rooflines. When set on walls of unequal height, it provides a sloped ceiling and

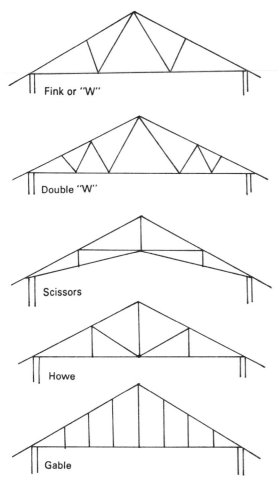

Fink or "W"

Double "W"

Scissors

Howe

Gable

8-104 *Roof trusses commonly used in residential construction.*

8-105 *Scissors trusses are used to frame a vaulted ceiling in lieu of cathedral or transverse beam framing. The scissors truss provides space for better ceiling insulation and for a roof pitched more steeply without excessively high ceiling heights.*

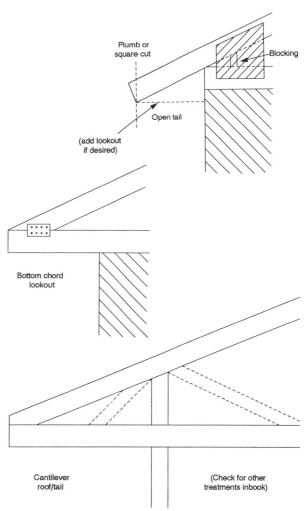

Plumb or square cut

Blocking

Open tail

(add lookout if desired)

Bottom chord lookout

Cantilever roof/tail

(Check for other treatments in book)

8-106 *An open tail is limited to overhangs shorter than two feet. Otherwise, add a horizontal lookout to keep the eaves from sagging.*

a streamlined roof slope with an ideal orientation for installing solar collectors. A modified *Howe* truss is often used to provide space for the extra-thick insulation required for energy-conserving designs. Scissors and W trusses can also be adapted for this purpose.

Whatever type of truss you use, order a pair of special *gable trusses* with vertical studs at normal spacing intervals to frame the end walls.

Where the eaves overhang isn't much more than a foot wide, the truss span is normally lengthened so that its bottom chord serves as a soffit lookout. Wider overhangs require the addition of a vertical web between the top and bottom chords at the plate bearing point. Otherwise, the truss terminates at the plate, and its top chord is extended into a rafter tail that can either frame a pitched soffit or support a lookout for a horizontal one (see **8-106**). Depending on design requirements, the tail overhangs can be cantilevered in various ways to support a porch roof or other wide overhang.

8-107 *Heavy timber site-built trusses are laid out with the aid of jig blocks nailed to a convenient concrete slab. The multiple laminations are power-nailed and glued together.*

SITE-BUILT TRUSSES

If you do decide to build your own roof trusses, most lumberyards can provide you with a truss design engineered to meet local code requirements for your roof span and load conditions—free of charge. In most cases, this is likely to be a W truss framed with structural-grade 2×4 lumber and fastened together with glued-and-nailed ½-inch plywood gussets or steel gang-nail truss plates (see 8-107).

To build a truss, make a full-size layout on a flat surface like a floor deck with your chalk line, framing square, and straightedges. Align the stock with the layout to mark its length and cuts. Starting with the top and bottom chords, cut each member precisely, and tack it to the deck. A chord under load tends to sag. To compensate, the bottom chord is raised slightly at its midspan. For a standard, 24-foot truss, the amount of this built-in *camber* is normally about one-half inch. Check all the pieces for accuracy of

8-108 *The gable-end truss is hoisted into place and tacked to plumbed braces nailed to the end wall. Note how the trusses are being unloaded onto the walls from a lift-bed delivery truck.*

length and fit. Then nail blocks firmly to the deck along the sides of each truss member to make an alignment jig. Remove the truss members, and label them for use as patterns. A radial-arm saw is ideal for making the many required repetitive cuts accurately and quickly.

Set the pieces in the truss jig, and apply the plywood gussets with waterproof truss glue and ring-shank nails spaced about three inches apart in double rows. Carefully flip the assembled truss frame over, and apply the gussets to the back. To prevent the joints from pulling apart (especially when gang-nail plates are used instead of plywood), always carry trusses in a vertical position.

ERECTING ROOF TRUSSES

Large roof trusses are too awkward and heavy to maneuver safely by hand and are generally lifted onto the wall plates with the aid of a small crane or a "cherry-picker" (truck-mounted hydraulic boom). Smaller 2×4-framed trusses up to 30 feet wide can be easily set by hand with a three- or four-person crew.

Ask for your trusses to be delivered on roof-raising day by a truck equipped with a lift bed. Also remember to specify that the first and last truss in the stack be a gable truss. Back the truck up parallel with the end wall, and raise the bed of the truck until the top of the pile is even with the wall plates. Slide the trusses off flatwise across the plate, carefully dropping the peak end down towards the floor as soon as it clears the end wall, so that the truss hangs upside down on the wall plates. Slide it along the wall in this position to the opposite end of the building. Be especially careful when handling gable trusses. They're flimsier than regular trusses. As you continue to slide the trusses down along the walls, leave enough room to clear the peaks when you tilt them up. If a lift truck is unavailable, unload the trusses onto the floor deck, and lift them up onto the plates one side at a time.

Somewhere near the one-third and two-thirds point of the end wall span, toenail two 2×6s on edge to the gable wall so that they will project above the slope of the truss. Check them for plumb; then lift the gable truss up into place, and tack it to these temporary braces (see **8-108**).

A crew member perched on top of the wall plate at each end of the truss keeps it from sliding, and pulls upwards as another crew member pushes its peak up with a notched 2×4 "push stick" (see **8-109**). If you have the extra help, balance the truss with a safety rope from the opposite direction.

Toenail the truss through the bottom chord into the plate. "Brace and space" it to the preceding truss by tacking a piece of strapping or 2×4 across it (see **8-110** and **8-111**). When only four or five trusses are left to erect, tilt them all up against the previously installed truss. Tack a gable brace to the wall and work from the end backwards to finish the installation.

8-109 *Even with a 2×6 top chord, these trusses are light enough to tilt up into position with three workers. Note the pipe scaffolding on the floor deck and the horizontal blocking between the studs that will provide nailing for vertical board exterior siding and interior paneling.*

8-110 *The trusses are braced and spaced to each other with short lengths of 2×4 nailed across the top chords.*

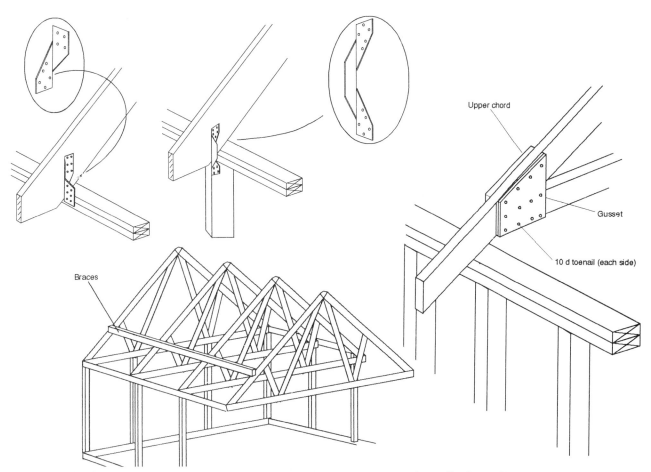

8-111 *Check with local code requirements for anchoring trusses to the wall plates. Keep the trusses plumbed and properly centered by tacking premarked strips of 1×3 or 2×4 across their top chords at the centers and just below the peaks.*

Although you can clamber across the chords at this point, a truss roof before it's closed in isn't very strong. Lateral bracing must be installed at right angles to the plane of the trusses (see **8-112**). Depending on the size and type of the truss, code requirements and design specifications, these can range from one or more courses of strong backs along the midspans of the bottom chord with a diagonal brace from the peak of the gable truss down to the strongback, to continuous horizontal braces nailed to one side of the compression webs and zigzag diagonal braces to the other.

CLOSING IN

If you're building in a climate where the possibility of rain can throw a damper on your schedule, it makes sense to hold off on the wall sheathing and gable wall framing so that you can get the roof sheathing on as quickly as possible and waterproof it with tarpaper or plastic sheeting. Framing-in the gable, as well as building interior partitions and rough stairs, are ideal rainy-day jobs.

Covering the deck with an underlayment of 15-lb asphalt saturated felt paper ("tarpaper") is still a good idea even if waterproofing isn't an immediate concern. Besides

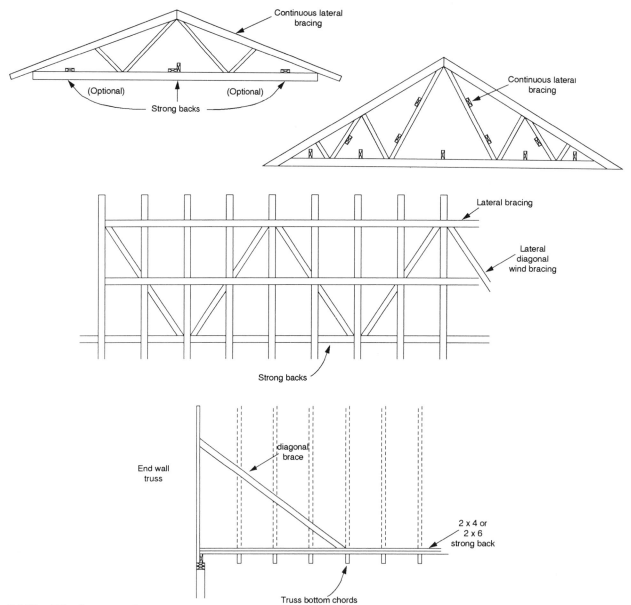

8-112 *The larger and steeper the truss, the more lateral wind-bracing is needed; a structural engineer should always be consulted.*

228

8-113 *A roof frame ready for tar paper and shingles. Although it's technically part of the exterior finish, the fascia trim is installed before the tar paper and is thus a prerequisite for roofing.*

protecting the sheathing from water damage until the shingles can be laid, the paper is a secondary line of defense against the infiltration of wind-driven rain and snow under the shingles. It also extends the life of asphalt shingles by preventing the resins in the sheathing from slowly dissolving their undersides.

Even with a roof pitch as low as 4-12, there's a good chance that you'll tear the tarpaper if you walk on it. On a steeper roof, this is not only annoying but dangerous. To avoid unnecessary traffic on the tarpaper, don't lay it down until after you've installed the fascia trim boards over the subfascia (see **8-113**)—refer to Chapter Ten for installation details.

Tarpaper is traditionally secured with 1×3 battens tacked to the roof deck or roofing nails driven through *roofer's tins* (half-dollar-size, thin steel discs) that prevent the paper from tearing off the nail (see **8-114**). But battens interfere with the shingle layout chalk lines, and it takes forever to nail tins. Instead, I use a staple hammer to fasten the tins. In order to take advantage of this time-saving shortcut, of course, the tins must be thin enough so that the staples can penetrate them. Not all tins fill the bill.

Unless it has a pitch low enough to walk on, the roof deck will already have 2×4 ladder stagings nailed to it. If you apply the tarpaper across the length of the roof starting at the ridge, and remove the ladder staging as you work your way down the roof, you'll always have something to stand on—and you will end up with a clear and uninterrupted deck when you're done. The first sheet should overlap the ridge by about a foot. Staple a single line of tins spaced about two feet apart across the middle of the sheet. Slide the top edge of the second sheet two inches up under the bottom edge of the first, using the factory-applied guide line to keep it running straight. Staple only a single tin in the middle of the edge to hold the sheet

as you roll it out and move it up or down to the line. Then staple tins along the overlapping edge, and stagger a second line of tins along the middle of the sheet. Repeat this procedure with each succeeding sheet. Lap sheets at their ends by at least six inches, and run them onto the opposing roof at valleys.

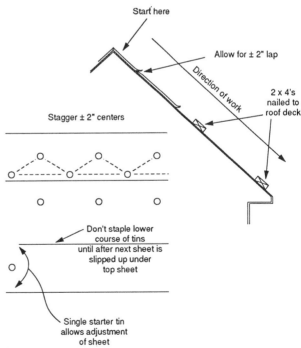

8-114 *Laying tar paper from the ridge on down saves time and virtually eliminates the chances of accidental tearing prior to shingling.*

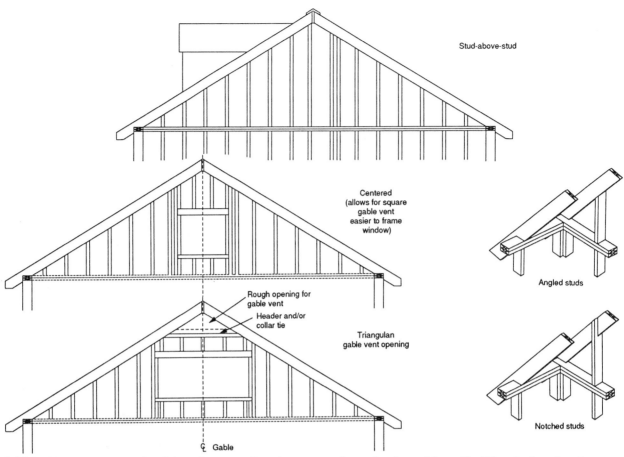

Stud-above-stud

Centered
(allows for square
gable vent
easier to frame
window)

Rough opening for
gable vent

Header and/or
collar tie

Triangular
gable vent opening

Gable

Angled studs

Notched studs

8-115 *Every carpenter has his or her own favorite way to frame in the gable walls. The choice also depends on whether or not a pitched attic louvre will be installed in the wall.*

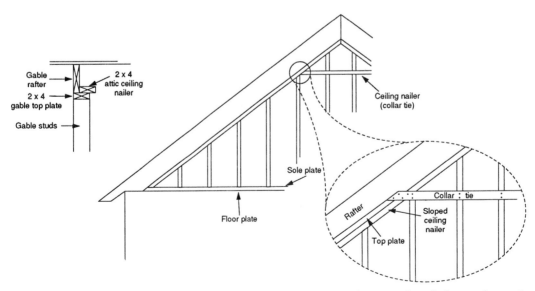

Gable
rafter

2 x 4
attic ceiling
nailer

2 x 4
gable top plate

Gable studs

Ceiling nailer
(collar tie)

Sole plate

Floor plate

Collar tie

Rafter

Sloped
ceiling
nailer

Top plate

8-116 *In unfinished attics, the ceiling nailer and top plate can be eliminated and the studs can be notched or bevelled to fit against the rafters.*

230

GABLE WALL FRAMING

Besides providing rainy-day work, framing the gable wall after the roof deck is on also offers one other advantage: it's easier to fill in a wall under an existing rafter than to lay out the top plate angle before the rafter is in place (see **8-117**).

Many carpenters save lumber by eliminating the top plate entirely, and simply notch the tops of the studs to fit against the gable rafter or bevel them to fit under it (see **8-115**). This method is minimally adequate for an unfinished attic. But when the area under the roof will be used for living space, nail backing must be provided for the finished walls and ceilings.

Gable framing in this case is similar to the technique used to provide ceiling backers for a partition running parallel with a joist (see **8-116**). Nail a 2×4 flatwise to the bottom of the gable rafters so that its edge is flush with the outside face of the rafter. This is the gable-wall top plate. Transfer the stud spacing from the end wall onto a sole plate nailed to the floor deck. Plumb the tallest gable stud, and scribe it for angle and length against the top plate. Once the first stud is installed, you can use your framing square to locate the long point of the next stud on the top plate—just as for jack rafter layout. After all the studs are framed, level across to the wall from the collar ties, and nail an angled 2×4 flat against the studs for a ceiling nailer. Nail a 2×4 flatwise against the inside edge of the gable rafter on top of the wall plate to make a nailer for the sloped part of the ceiling.

Depending on the height of your roof, locating and nailing long gable-wall studs can be awkward. Furthermore, unless you use a ridge-line ventilator, quite a few of them will have to be cut when you install the gable louvre. An alternative framing technique is to nail a collar tie between (not over) the gable rafters (see **8-118**). Then nail a 2×4 flatwise to the inside edge of the collar tie for the ceiling nailer. Cut two more flatwise 2×4s, and nail them flush with the inside bottom edge of the gable rafters below the collar tie.

8-117   *The 2×6 nailed flatwise to the back of the gable end rafter will become the backer for the gable wall top plate. This piece ends against a 2×6 nailed to the back of a gable end collar tie. Note the false rafter hung from the underside of the roof deck and how the fascia board reveal allows for the thickness of the soffit board.*

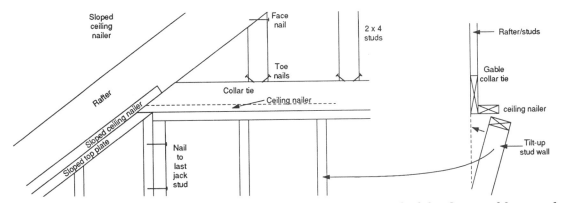

8-118   *Two-step method for gable wall framing; this is the preferred method for Cape-, saltbox-, and gambrel-style roofs, which enclose substantial volumes of living space.*

8-119 *This gable wall was framed in two steps—a tilt-up standard end wall was installed under the collar tie, and then notched and angled filler studs were toenailed into the underside of the gable rafters. Note the thin band added over the top edge of the fascia board for decorative effect.*

Build a tilt-up wall frame to fit under the collar tie area (see **8-119**). Nail top plates to the sloping ceiling nailers and fill in the angled jack studs. To fill in the area above the collar tie, cut studs so that they can be installed flatwise between the tie and the underside of the gable rafter. You can frame in the opening for a prefabricated wood gable louvre at this time or you can wait until later to cut through the studs and sheathing to install an adjustable-pitch aluminum louvre—and then block between the sawn-off studs, as necessary.

9 Roofing

Chances are, for most people the word *roofing* is associated with asphalt shingles (see **9-1**). While it's true that the majority of roofs today are covered with this inexpensive, easy-to-apply, and versatile material, there are many reasons to consider roofing your house with traditional wood shingles or shakes, clay or concrete tiles, and galvanized or enamelled steel sheets. The choice of roofing material depends on its suitability to the climate and roof slope, its initial cost and long-term durability, and its aesthetic qualities. The texture, color, and line of roofing materials have a visual impact that can add to or detract from the overall appearance of the house.

The fire rating of a roofing material can also determine whether of not it is permitted by local codes. Organic felt-based asphalt shingles have a Class C rating, which is the lowest most building codes will permit. Fibreglass-based asphalt shingles have a Class B rating, which makes them a good choice in zones where brush and forest fires are a frequent threat. Since wood shingles have a Class C rating only when they are treated with fire-retardant chemicals, they may not be allowed in regions of fire hazard. Noncombustible cement and clay roofing, with its Class A rating, may make more sense. In general, heavier types of roofing are a good choice where high winds are prevalent. Some kinds of roofing, such as corrugated aluminum, are vulnerable to corrosion caused by saltwater spray. Local tradition and regional variation is also an important influence on the selection of roofing materials.

Despite differences in materials, all roofing shares a common vocabulary. Roofing is estimated and sold by the *square*, which is the amount it takes to cover 100 square feet of finished roof surface, whatever the actual surface area of the given pieces.

Since roofing must overlap to shed water, all roofing material has a specified *head-* and *side-lap*, which is the amount that the lower unit is covered by the upper one.

The portion of the roofing which is uncovered is its *weather exposure*. The durability of a roofing material depends on the ability of the exposed portion to resist wind, rain, temperature cycles, and rot. Most types of roofing require single or double *coverage*—one or two overlapping thicknesses for protection. Increasing the coverage by decreasing the exposure improves the weather-tightness of the roof and enables the material to be used on shallower slopes than would be otherwise permitted.

Wherever a pipe penetration, a valley, or sidewall interrupts the regular placement of the roofing, *flashing* is used to prevent leaks. Usually metal, flashing can also be formed from the roofing material itself or from special rubber or plastic fittings.

9-1 *Guide lines chalked across the tar paper at intervals equal to the exposure of courses of shingles (20 inches) help ensure straight shingling.*

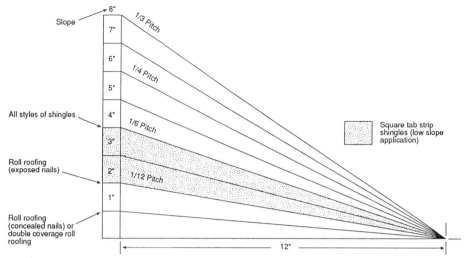

9-2 *The water-tightness of a given roofing material is largely dependent on the roof slope.*

In general, the steeper the pitch of the roof, the less watertight each individual roofing unit must be (see **9-2**). Depending on their coverage and composition, shingles—whether of wood, asphalt, metal, clay, or concrete—should generally not be used for roof slopes less than 4-in-12. Roll roofing can be used for roofs with slopes as low as 1-in-12. Below this, any one of several built-up membrane systems must be used to ensure watertightness.

ASPHALT ROOFING

Although some of the older styles of asphalt shingles are once again becoming available, the strip shingle is the only kind of asphalt shingle most building suppliers carry (see **9-3**). Strip shingles come in two different styles: the traditional three-tab and the tabless random-embossed self-aligning shingle. Besides being somewhat easier to apply than three-tab shingles (hence their common appellation,

		Per square	
		Approximate shipping weight	Bundles
Multi-thickness "Architect"	Self-sealing random-tab strip shingle	285# to 390#	4 or 5
Single-thickness	Self-sealing random-tab strip shingle	250# to 300#	3 or 4
Three-tab	Self-sealing square-tab strip shingle	215# to 300#	3 or 4
No-cutout "Jet shingle"	Self-sealing square-tab strip shingle	215# to 290#	3 or 4
Basic design	Individual "lock" shingle	180# to 250#	3 or 4

	Approximate shipping weight	
	Per roll	Per square
Mineral surface roll	75# to 90#	75# to 90#
Mineral surface roll double coverage "Selvage"	55# to 70#	110# to 140#
Smooth surface roll	40# to 65#	40# to 65#
Saturated felt (non-perforated) "Tarpaper"	60#	15# to 30#

9-3 *Asphalt roofing is available in several styles of shingles and rolls of various thickness.*

jet shingle), the finished appearance of tabless shingles has a strong horizontal emphasis. The *shadow line* formed by the brick-like interwoven coursing of the cut-outs of traditional three-tab shingles shifts the visual impression towards the vertical. Except as noted, application procedures for both types of strip shingles are basically the same.

The service life of an asphalt shingle depends on its weight per square, which in turn is determined by the depth and size of the granules that coat its *butt*—the portion exposed to the weather. Standard shingles, with a weight of 235 pounds per square, are typically warranted for 20 years. If properly applied, you can expect them to last about 25 years in most regions of the United States, except the Sunbelt (the Southwest), where their average life expectancy can be as short as seven years.

Premium-grade (260 or 305 pounds per square) shingles, which cost about 35 percent more than standard-weight shingles, can be expected to last about five years longer. Heavier shingles are more likely to be chosen for their highly textured appearance than because of the anticipated 20 percent gain in service life. At 320 pounds or more per square, multithickness "architect" shingles cost almost as much as wood shingles, whose texture and random pattern they are designed to invoke. Of course, it is a lot less work to install the multithickness shingles than wood ones.

Besides individual shingles, asphalt roofing also is manufactured in mineral-surfaced rolls. Cheap and easily applied, roll roofing is most often used on roofs with slopes less than 4-in-12. Because of its relatively short life and an appearance that many find objectionable, it's seldom used where it can be seen from the ground.

INSTALLATION

When applying the last course of tarpaper to the deck at the eaves, hold the nails back at least six inches from its bottom edge so that you can slip a metal drip edge under it (see 9-4). Preformed galvanized-steel drip edges are sold in 10-foot lengths with a five-inch or eight-inch width (before folding). Although primarily used for reroofing, the wider drip edge is used at the eaves in new work where a square-cut fascia and subfascia would preclude solid nailing for the narrower width. Drip edge is also available in several colors of enamel-finished aluminum to blend unobtrusively with the color of the shingles and/or the fascia trim or gutters.

Lay the drip edge at the eaves first, overlapping each piece by about an inch. The ends of the drip edge should be flush with the face of the rake fascia trim. Cut the tar paper back just above the edge of the metal. To block wind-driven water, install the rake drip edge on top of the tar paper, folding the corner over at the eaves as shown in 9-4. Install the drip edge up the rake, so that each piece overlaps the one beneath it. For maximum weather protection at the peak of the roof, cut the last piece to fold over onto the opposite rake.

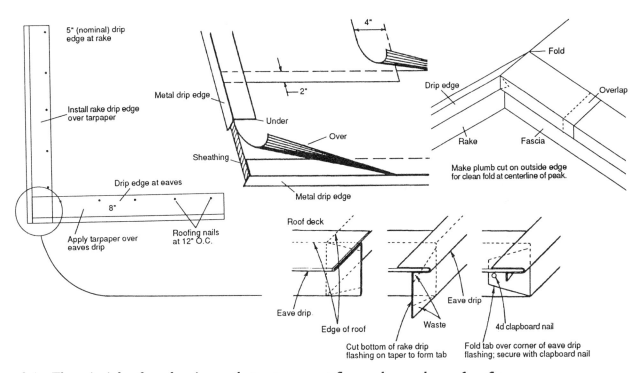

9-4 *The principle of overlapping so that water cannot flow under any layer of roofing also extends to the installation of drip edge.*

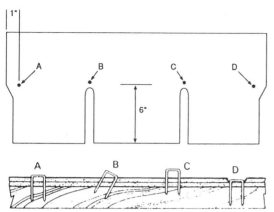

9-5 *Roofing nails have oversize heads so that they won't pull through the face of the shingles. Hot-dipped galvanized nails resist rust longer than electroplated nails. Roofing staplers are designed so that the crown of the staple will seat just above the surface of the shingle.*

Asphalt shingles are fastened with special galvanized large-headed roofing nails (see **9-5**). The length used should be sufficient to just barely penetrate the sheathing (e.g., one-inch nails with new roofing over plywood, 1¼ inch with rough board sheathing, 1½ inch for reroofing over existing shingles). Performance of the roofing depends on where and how the nails are driven. With standard three-tab shingles, the nails are driven about an inch above the cut-outs, just below the self-sealing cement line. Since they lack cut-outs, the two inside nails of a jet-type shingle are spaced approximately evenly apart by eye. To

9-6 *Many professional roofers use air-powered staplers to lay asphalt shingles. Building codes and manufacturer's warranties are very adamant about staple installation specification. Improper application voids the warranty and, more important, seriously compromises the wind resistance of the shingles.*

keep the shingle from buckling, nail it at one end first, and then continue nailing across towards its opposite end. Drive the nail perpendicular to the roof so that the edge of the nail head doesn't cut into the asphalt. To prevent leaks, don't overdrive the nail—so that it breaks through the surface of the asphalt—or under-drive it—so that the head sticks up and cuts into the back of the overlying shingle.

Modern shingles are manufactured with a bead of thermoplastic cement which glues the courses of the shingles to each other after a few hours of exposure to the sun and makes them highly wind-resistant. In the days before such self-sealing shingles, two nails were called for over each cut-out.

Although they save a tremendous amount of labor, air-driven roofing staples are somewhat controversial (see **9-6**). Manufacturer's warranties and building codes both specify that the crowns of the staples must be aligned horizontally to the run of the shingle and driven to the proper depth. Even so, stapled shingles are much more likely to blow off the roof in high winds than nailed-down shingles.

Unless the roof terminates in a valley or against an end wall, shingling from the center of the roof out towards the rakes rather than across the roof from one rake to the other generally requires fewer steps and makes more efficient use of roof staging (see **9-7**). It also "splits the difference" when, as it sometimes happens, the measurements between the rakes are slightly different at the ridge than at the eaves. A shadow line that runs off evenly at both rakes tends to be less noticeable than one where the taper is confined to just one side of the roof.

To start the layout from the center, measure across the roof at the ridge and the eaves to see where the centerline will fall; then determine how much to offset it (refer to **9-7**). A 36-inch-long three-tab shingle is divided by its cut-outs into three one-foot-wide sections, or "tabs." The tabs are staggered six inches between courses so that the cut-outs of any given course always break over the middle of the adjoining course. The goal is to arrange the layout of the roof so that whatever filler piece you end up with at the rake is at least two, and preferably three or more, inches wide. Even if you could nail an inch-wide filler without breaking it, it would still look awful and could eventually cause a leak. Offsetting the centerline avoids this problem. For example, assuming the roof measures 36'-2" across, if you ran the shingles out from a centerline at 18'-1", you'd end up with one-inch fillers at both ends of the first course and seven-inch and eleven-inch fillers in the second. Shifting the starting line two inches to either side of dead center lets you finish up at one side with alternating courses of three-inch and nine-inch pieces and with 11-inch and five-inch pieces at the other. Once you've determined where the adjusted centerline should be, measure over six inches to one side of it, and snap parallel chalk lines between both pairs of marks.

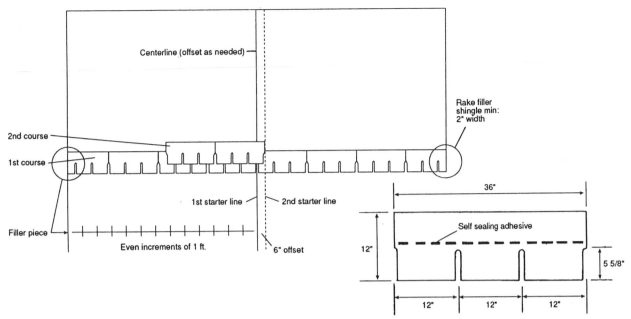

9-7 *Keep a calculator in your tool kit to help determine whether and how much to off-set the center starting lines—especially if you happen to be using metric-based shingles with an English-based tape measure.*

Jet shingles are normally offset half the width of a full shingle, so the starting lines should be adjusted accordingly and spaced 18 inches apart.

You probably won't find parallel starting lines mentioned in any descriptions of shingling application. That's because the standard recommendation is to continue off-setting each successive course six inches past the one preceding it. Following this recommendation, the tabs of each course step up the roof like the courses of blocks in a wall (see **9-8**). Once you lay the last piece in a vertical series, you have to run the shingles out horizontally across the roof before you can resume shingling upwards. If the roof is too steep to work on without staging, the staging must also run out across the roof before you can shingle up towards the peak. With parallel layout lines, the shingles are offset only half a tab. If you leave the ends of the overlapping courses unnailed until you can slip a shingle under them, you can run the shingles vertically up the entire length of the roof before shifting the staging sideways. You'll cover more roof area with less back-and-forth motion. Also, since you'll only need to cut two different-size filler pieces for each rake, they can be cut ahead of time. Although there's normally a slit in the top edge of most strip shingles six inches in from its ends to mark the offset, it takes less time, and your shadow lines will run straighter with parallel guide lines. The only objection to this method of starting is that the line where the ends of the shingles butt together tends to be less noticeable when the pattern is broken up across several courses.

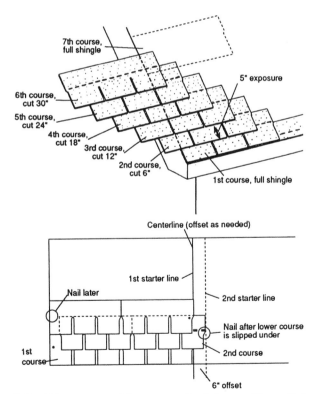

9-8 *The staggered layout method is equally useful when starting from the center of the roof or from the rake.*

237

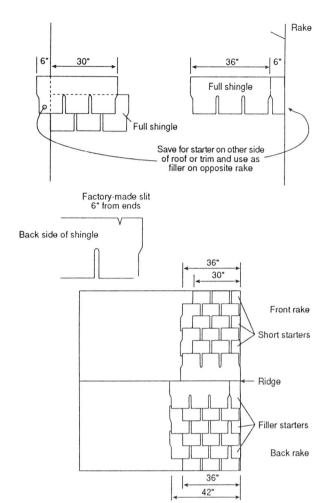

9-9　As long as the rake runs square to the eaves, starting at the rake is the easiest way to shingle an addition that ends at a side wall.

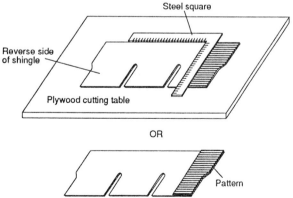

9-10　Once shingles have softened on a warm day, a utility knife is the only tool that can cut them neatly.

The same method can be used if you start shingling at the rake instead of the center (see 9-9). Prepare rake "starter" shingles on the ground by cutting six inches (half a tab) off a full-width shingle. Make sure the cut edge will face the drip edge. Alternate a dozen or so cut shingles with full-width shingles and carry this "starter bundle" onto the roof. Save the cut-off pieces for filling in at the far end of the roof or alternate them with full shingles for rake starters on the other side of the roof.

The granules will soon dull your knife when you cut a shingle through its face side. Turn it over and make a scoring cut on the back instead with your utility knife (see 9-10). Use a scrap of plywood as a cutting table. I use a rusty old steel square for a cut-off guide. If your knife is sharp and your hand steady, you can also use a pattern shingle to make the cuts. Although it is useful for cutting roll roofing and tar paper from the face side, the traditional hooked roofer's knife is no match for the speed and accuracy of a utility knife when it comes to cutting shingles.

A starter strip is used at the eaves to provide the requisite double coverage under the cut-outs of the first course (see 9-11). This can be mineral-surfaced roll roofing of a matching color or else an ordinary strip shingle nailed butt-end up. Lay another course of shingles on top of this strip—offset half a tab and with the butts facing downwards. The starter course should overhang the drip edge by about one quarter of an inch to keep it from rusting at the outermost edge.

Measure 17 inches up from the bottom of the starter course and snap a line across the roof to guide the installation of the second course (see 9-12). (Strip shingles are 12 inches wide with a five-inch exposure; so the top edge of the second course will be 17 inches above the bottom edge of the starter course.) This way, if the line of the drip edge is less than perfectly straight, the chalk line straightens out the following course of shingles.

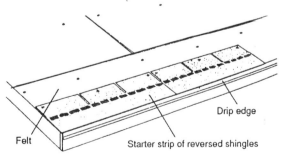

9-11　Some roofers feel that cutting the eaves starter shingle in half lengthwise gives better results than laying a full-width shingle upside down. Some roofers also run half shingles along the rakes. The resulting slight cambre helps divert runoff water away from the edge, where it could work under the shingles.

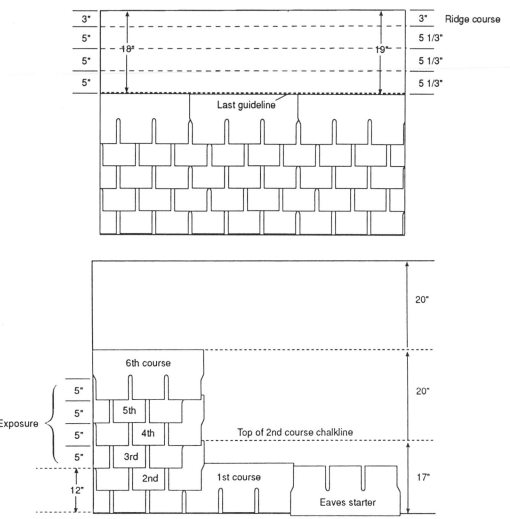

9-12 *Horizontal shingling guide lines.*

Theoretically, the courses of strip shingles are spaced by lining up the bottom edge of the uppermost course with the top of the cut-outs of the underlying course. In practice, individually imperceptible deviations soon add up to a noticeable drift. This is why even professional roofers snap guide lines every 20 inches (i.e., four courses) apart up the entire vertical run of the roof (starting with the 17-inch baseline). The course alignment is constantly corrected before it has a chance to get too far out of line.

Similarly, since the cut-outs at the ends of a jet shingle automatically align it with the top edge of the underlying shingle, horizontal layout lines shouldn't be necessary. While experienced shinglers probably can run jet shingles without guide lines, for the amateur it's a good idea to use them anyway.

There's one thing to watch for when using guide lines; sometimes, the shingles will vary in width by as much as a quarter-inch from bundle to bundle. Some brands are worse in this regard than others. Since the top edges are lined up to the guide lines, if differences in width go undetected the exposure line can become noticeably uneven. If you do notice a variation in width between shingles, raise or lower their top edges relative to the guide line to finish out the course.

Although it shouldn't be a problem if you framed the roof properly, on roofs longer than 24 feet or so, it's a good idea to snap chalk lines from the middle of the roof outward towards the eaves rather than across the entire roof at once. Measure the 20-inch spacing at both rakes and at the center. Likewise, make sure that the line isn't thrown off by wrinkles in the tar paper.

Measure the interval between the last guide line and the peak of the roof. If it varies from one end of the roof to the other, split the difference between the last four courses so that the shingles will line up evenly with the ridge.

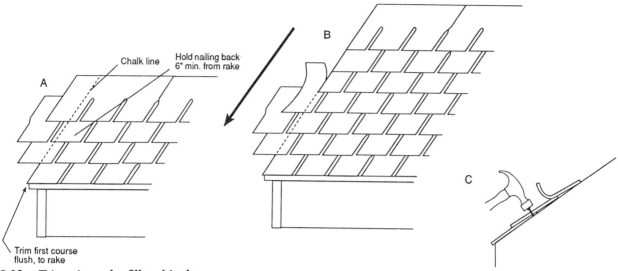

9-13 *Trimming rake filler shingles.*

While you could cut each rake filler shingle to fit as you install it with your knife and square, it's neater and much faster to trim them off all at once (see **9-13**). Let the last full tab or rough-cut filler pieces overhang the rake. Use only one nail driven as far as possible back—at least two inches—from the edge to hold each filler piece. Make sure no nail heads are exposed between cut-outs of the overlying shingle. Early in the morning, before the shingles have had time to soften in the sun, snap a chalk line even with the edge of the rake, and trim off the overhanging shingles with a pair of roofing shears—ordinary tin snips turn into roofing shears when their edge is dulled by the mineral granules of the shingles. Cut from the ridge downwards, and then nail off the fillers, working from the eaves back upwards. If the nails are too close to the edge of the rake, you won't be able to lift the shingle far enough up to slip the shears under it. Work quickly; roofing shears gum up and won't cut cleanly once the shingles soften.

The joint between shingles at the peak of the roof—and along any other hip roof intersection—is covered by special *ridge caps* or *hips* (see **9-14**). The last course of regular shingles on both sides of the roof overlaps the ridge and is nailed to the opposite side of the roof along its top edges. If there isn't enough shingle left to fold over the ridge, trim the shingles flush instead.

Ridge caps for both three-tab and jet shingles are cut from ordinary three-tab shingles. You'll need to include a bundle or two of matching tab shingles for this purpose if you use jet shingles. The ridge shingles for multiple-ply architect-style shingles are special-ordered.

Turn the shingle over, and score it on an angle back from each cut-out. The angle keeps the unsurfaced part of the shingle from showing when the cap shingle is folded over the ridge.

Center the ridge cap over the ridge so that its bottom edges will cover the cut-outs of the last course of shingles. Snap a chalk line along the most noticeable side of the ridge to keep the shingles running evenly. Lay the caps in whatever direction is opposite to the prevailing wind direction. Nail the caps with one nail on each side, penetrating the caps below them and leaving about five inches exposed to the weather. To prevent cracking, nail all the ridge caps on one side only, and allow them to soften before bending them over the peak to nail off the opposite side. In cold weather, store ridge caps in a warm place, and bring them up onto the roof in small batches; bend and nail off both sides as you install them. The last piece of ridge shingle is cut to width and surface-nailed. Cover the exposed nail heads with a daub of roofing cement. To figure how many ridge-cap shingles you'll need, multiply the length of the ridge and/or hips by 12 and divide by five; divide the result by three to get the number of shingles you'll need. There are 27 shingles in a full (one-third square) bundle of standard strip shingles.

VALLEY TREATMENTS

Valleys are a potential trouble spot that require waterproof *flashing* to ensure that water drains off freely and that snow and ice buildup doesn't cause leaks.

Valley flashings must be installed before laying the shingles. Mineral-surfaced roll roofing (90-lb roll) is widely used as valley flashing for asphalt singles (see **9-15**). First, lay an 18-inch-wide strip of smooth-surfaced (60-pound) roll roofing down the center of the valley. (If your supplier doesn't stock 60-pound roll, you can use 90-pound mineral-surfaced roll, laid facedown.) Lap any joints at least 12 inches. If you unroll the roofing and let it soften in the sun for an hour or so, it will conform to the bend of

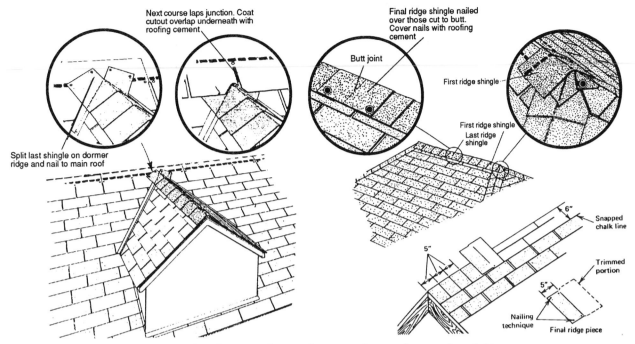

9-14 *Ridge cap shingles; hip shingles must be neatly cut and must be weather-tight at their intersection with the ridge.*

the valley without cracking. Nail off one side first, and use your knee to form the roofing into the valley before nailing off the other edge. Center a second sheet of 36-inch-wide mineral-surfaced roll roofing over the first, and form and nail it as before. Seal any laps with asphalt flashing cement. The underlying roofing cushions the valley so that it lasts longer, and provides a second line of defense against leaks should the top layer wear through.

As you run out the shingles into the valley, trim them roughly to its centerline. Hold the nailing back just as was described above for rake filler shingles. After all the shingles along the run of the valley are laid, snap trimming guide lines down each side of the valley. Measure three inches to both sides of center at the top, and increase the valley width about one-eighth of an inch for every foot of run (e.g., a 20-foot valley would be six inches wide at its top and 8½ inches wide at its bottom outlet). Trim the shingles along the line with your roofing shears, working downwards as with the rake fillers. Working up the valley, nail off the ends of the shingles. Hold the nails back at least three inches from the edge of the trimming line. The corner of the last shingle at the top of the valley is cut at about a 45-degree angle to the valley to prevent water from flowing under it, and then it is sealed with flashing cement.

You could also snap the trimming lines first, and then cut the shingles to it as you install them. It's harder to make a neat line this way, but you might not have any choice if you're shingling in hot weather.

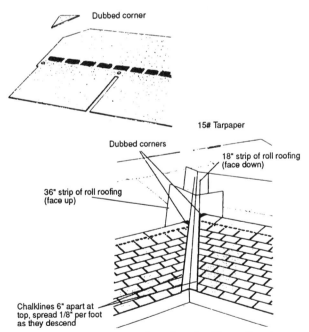

9-15 *Use care; mineral-surfaced roll roofing is easily punctured and torn in warm weather, and it is brittle in cold. If the valley is damaged, a patch isn't likely to hold. Instead, cut the valley at the injury, and overlap the sheets, sealing the joint with flashing cement.*

241

The valley treatment just described is known as the *open valley*; some roofers use a *woven* or *closed-cut valley*, instead (see **9-16**). These are best suited to climates where little or no snow or ice buildup is likely. First, run a 36-inch-wide strip of 60-pound smooth-surfaced roll roofing down the center of the valley. Lay the shingles so that they straddle the center of the valley by at least a foot on each side. To provide this coverage, shift full-length shingles towards the valley as needed and fill in behind them with pieces trimmed to single- or double-tab length. Alternate the overlap between succeeding courses of shingles from one side of the valley to the other. Hold the nails back at least six inches from the valley centerline. A closed-cut valley differs from a woven valley in that the shingles are extended across the valley from one side only. The minor-roof shingles are trimmed along a line held two inches back from the valley centerline. Both of these techniques can only be used with strip shingles.

Because of the high volume of water they carry, mineral-surfaced open valleys tend to wear out sooner than the rest of the roofing. Also, in cold climates their rough surface encourages the buildup of ice and snow. For these reasons, many roofers prefer to use sheet metal for valley flashings (see **9-17**). It's a requirement for long-lasting roofing materials such as wood shingles.

Sheet-metal valley construction is similar to roll roofing. Begin by weaving the horizontal courses of tar paper across the valley, and then run a full-width strip of ordinary tar paper down the center of the valley. Center a strip of 24-inch or 36-inch-wide flashing metal in the valley, tacking it at the top with a single nail. The wider flashing should always be used with roof slopes under 8-in-12. The flash-

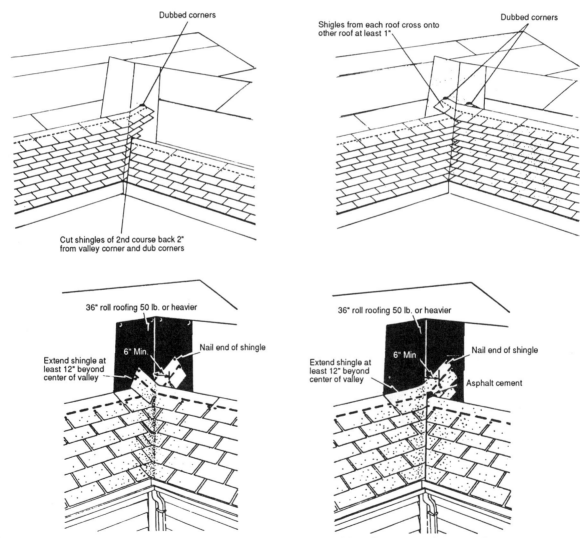

9-16 *Woven or closed-cut valleys provide extra protection and last longer in regions of heavy rainfall but little or no snow.*

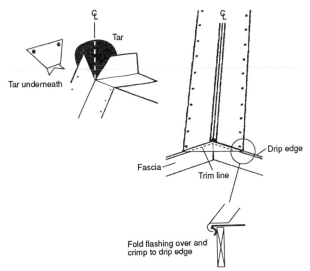

9-17 *Galvanized sheet metal must be kept painted once it begins to rust. Flashing coated with a factory-applied, baked-epoxy enamel finish never needs repainting.*

ing should run about two feet past the top of the valley and far enough beyond its bottom to overhang the drip edge by at least an inch along its full width at the eaves. As with roll roofing, nail off one side from top to bottom, and press the metal into the valley with your knee; work carefully to avoid wrinkling the metal. Take care that it lies flat against the roof at the ridge intersection.

Cut the flashing on a line that represents the vertical extension of the minor ridge up onto the plane of the major roof, and fold it flat over the ridge. Trim off the points parallel to the line of the main roof. Install and trim the flashing for the opposing valley. Before nailing down the overlapping seam, coat the area between the cut edges, and the metal that will be overlapped, with flashing cement. Cut a triangular cover piece to fit over the gap of the second valley flashing, and embed it in flashing cement as well.

Trim the flashing to a three-quarter-inch overhang at the eaves, and crimp it over the drip edge with a sheet-metal-bending plier (rented or bought). Where one side of the valley terminates on the major roof rather than at its eaves, trim the flashing so that it ends evenly above the exposed shingles and so that its edge is completely covered by the next course.

With roofs of unequal pitch, there's a tendency for the water to rush across the valley and up under the shingles of the shallower roof. To break the force of the water, the centerline of the valley is crimped by bending it over the edge of a 2×4 with a block and hammer (For better results, run the 2×4 through your table saw to remove its factory-milled rounded edge first. Even better, have the *splash rib* fabricated at a sheet-metal shop.)

Copper, galvanized steel, aluminum, and lead are the most commonly used flashing metals. Because of a property called *galvanic action*, different metals react with one another in the presence of water. Following is the galvanic ranking of metals commonly used in residential construction from most active to least. The more electrochemically active metal will corrode when in contact with a less active metal. The farther apart the two metals are in the series, the sooner and more extensively the corrosion will occur.

| 1. Aluminum |
| 2. Zinc |
| 3. Steel |
| 4. Tin |
| 5. Lead |
| 6. Brass |
| 7. Copper |
| 8. Bronze |

To prevent corrosion, always use fasteners of the same metal as the flashing. If this isn't practical, use noncorroding stainless-steel nails or factory-applied, enamel-coated steel flashing instead.

OTHER FLASHING CONDITIONS

Various kinds of flashing are also required wherever a roof is penetrated by a vent pipe or a chimney, at skylights, and at the intersection of a dormer or other vertical wall (see 9-18). It's a lot harder to describe flashing work than it actually is to do it. Shingle-type roofing materials shed water because they overlap each other. The primary rule for watertight flashing is: Never allow water to flow under a shingle. The corollary is: Use caulking cement for backup, not primary, waterproofing.

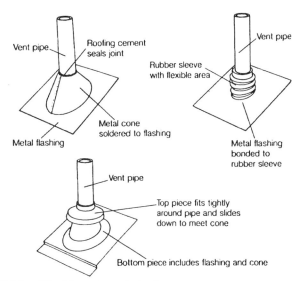

9-18 *Flashing at vent stacks.*

243

A ready-made, vent-stack flashing makes waterproofing a pipe penetration foolproof. Cut the top shingle to fit snugly around the vent pipe. Install the flashing boot so that its bottom edge will lay over the lower shingle course and its top will be under the next course. For best results seal under the base flange with flashing cement, and set the top course of shingles in cement as well. Seal the joint between the neoprene flashing gasket and the pipe with flexible butyl or silicone caulk.

Because the wood framing of the house naturally contracts and expands and the foundation under a chimney can settle, the flashing around a chimney must allow movement without breaking its watertight seal. *Counterflashing*, which consists of two overlapping layers—a *base flashing* joined to the roofing and a *cap flashing* embedded between the mortar joints of the chimney, having no bond between them—is the solution (see **9-19**).

Fold the tar paper underlayment up three to four inches against the shingles. The metal front-base flashing is installed once the roofing reaches the bottom of the chim-ney. It should be long enough to extend five to six inches beyond the front of the chimney and wide enough to run at least eight inches over the shingles and up against the chimney (refer to **9-19**). Use either standard-width 14-inch or 20-inch metal. The front-base piece is nailed over the top of the shingles just like a vent-pipe flashing. Cut and fold a *step flashing* fashioned from eight-inch-by-eight-inch or eight-inch-by-ten-inch pieces of metal bent at right angles, over each corner, as shown in **9-19**. Continue installing step flashing up the sides of the chimney between each course of shingles. Set the bottom edge of each step flashing just above the shingle cut-out and so that it overlaps both the shingle and the chimney four to five inches. Nail them only at the top edge. A similar piece of base flashing is installed at the back of the chimney so that it overlaps the last piece of step flashing, which is bent around the corners. Cement the flange of the back flashing to the shingles with a generous bed of flashing cement. When the chimney penetrates the roof through the ridge instead of below it, a double-length piece of step

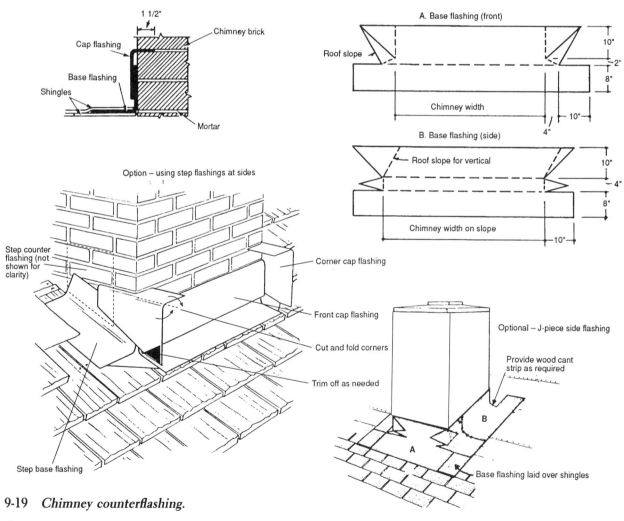

9-19 *Chimney counterflashing.*

flashing is cut and folded over the ridge in a manner similar to a valley flashing.

The cap flashing is fitted about 1½ inches into the mortar joints of the chimney masonry while it is being built—and then it is notched and bent to fit over the base flashing when the roof is shingled. This is a lot easier than raking out finished mortar joints to install cap flashing after the chimney is finished. Running the chimney through the roof deck before the roof is shingled also avoids staining the shingles with spilled mortar. Cap flashing should be long enough to overlap the base flashing by at least four inches; it should be trimmed to follow the pitch of the roof. Inexperienced roofers sometimes make the cap flashing too long, folding and nailing it to the shingles.

Galvanized-steel or aluminum chimney flashing is the sign of an inferior job. Aluminum tends to break along fold lines and is hard to seal tightly. Unless it's kept painted, galvanized steel soon rusts and stains the roof. Replacing or maintaining a not readily accessible chimney flashing is a lot of trouble. In contrast, both copper and lead are very malleable and long-lasting. Lead, in particular, can be hammered to lie flat and conform to irregular contours in the masonry, making it ideal for flashing a stone chimney. It's also less expensive than copper.

Unless you live in an arid climate, if your chimney is wider than normal or goes through the roof more than a few feet below the ridge, you'll have to build a *cricket* on the back side of the chimney to divert water around it and to prevent trapped ice and meltwater from backing up under the shingles (see 9-20). This dormer-like rooflet, constructed on top of the roof sheathing, consists of a ridge board supported by two rafters set against the back of the chimney, covered by two pieces of plywood. Unless they are exceptionally large, chimney crickets aren't shingled. Instead, a single width of flashing metal is cut to form both the valleys and base flashing against the chimney. Unless you're an experienced metal worker, don't attempt to cut and fold this flashing in place. Make a pattern from sheets of cardboard or kraft paper instead.

The upper edges of the cricket are sealed to the roof deck with flashing cement, and the main-roof shingles are trimmed to within about two inches of the mini-valley centerlines. The corner step flashings at the back of the chimney should run under the cricket. It's a good idea to seal the underside of all corner flashing folds with flexible, high-grade caulking. Use an elastomeric acrylic copolymer like Geocel, which can stretch many times its original size without breaking the bond.

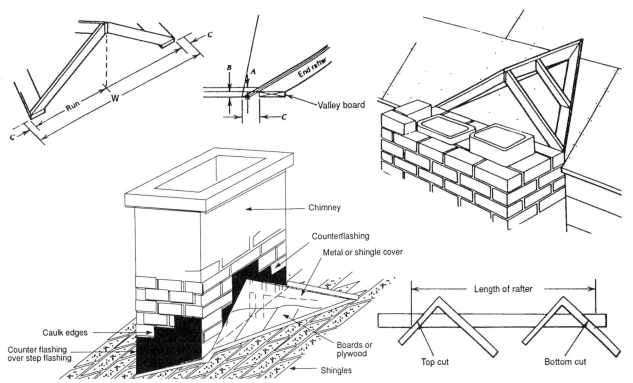

9-20 *A very small cricket can be framed with only a single pair of end rafters set against the chimney and two triangular sheets of plywood. Building a larger cricket is like framing a small California roof. Slope the end rafters at the same pitch as the main roof. The run of the rafters is half the overall width of the chimney where it passes through the roof (W) minus the combined vertical thickness (C) of the valley board (B) and the cricket sheathing (A).*

245

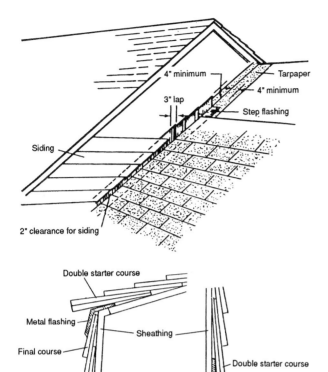

9-21 *Step flashings are used wherever shingle courses butt against a vertical wall.*

Metal flashing is also used wherever shingles abut a dormer or the side or end wall of the house (see **9-21**). Since the sidewall flashing is counterflashed by the finished siding, the roof flashing is always installed before the wall siding. As with the step flashing for a chimney, right-angle pieces of flashing are nailed over the top of each course of shingles. It is not necessary to nail the flashing to the wall sheathing since it will be held in place by the finish siding. To prevent rot, the finish siding shouldn't contact the roof surface. Maintain a two-inch flashing exposure.

Flashing at the face of a dormer or a wall parallel to the run of the shingles is made from continuous pieces of metal—similar to a base flashing—installed over the shingles and folded around the corners of the dormer. Where a window opening is less than four inches higher than the roof, the flashing should also fold up over the subsill. The underlayment must also extend up against this and any other vertical wall.

To cut and fit shingles against an end wall, butt the full-width shingle against the wall smooth-side up (i.e., reversed), and mark where its end overlaps the edge of the last full shingle (see **9-22**). Trim it off on this mark.

ASPHALT ROOFING FOR LOW-PITCHED ROOFS

Asphalt shingles applied to a roof with a slope of less than 4-in-12 won't be watertight. Mineral-surface roll roofing, which can be used with slopes as low as 1-in-12, would normally be used for low-pitched roofs. However, when the roof is visible from the ground the appearance of roll roofing may be objectionable. Strip shingles can be used with roof slopes as low as 2-in-12 if special measures are taken to provide a waterproof underlayment (see **9-23**). In this case the shingles are mostly ornamental.

Formerly, the recommended procedure was to overlap each course of felt underlayment 19 inches, beginning with a 19-inch starter strip. In regions where the average January daily temperature is less than 25 degrees Fahrenheit (minus four degrees Celsius), the plies should also be cemented together along the eaves and up the rake to two feet inside of the building walls.

Much better protection against water penetration can be obtained by covering the deck with an adhesive rubberized asphalt membrane (e.g., Ice and Water Shield) instead of tar paper. Remove the backing paper as you unroll the material across the roof; proceed carefully. The membrane is very sticky and once it contacts the roof you won't be able to lift it to straighten it out. Lap each sheet about four inches. No nails are needed. Unlike tar paper, the membrane is flexible and tends to seal itself around the punctures caused by the shingle nails. As long as you use self-sealing shingles, they can be installed over the membrane without any other precautions. Avoid penetra-

9-22 *Save all trimmings for possible rake fillers until the installation is complete.*

9-23 *Laying strip shingles on low-pitched roofs.*

tions in low-pitched roofs wherever possible; otherwise, exercise extreme care to make sure that any flashing is watertight. Use flashing cement under all flashings and the shingles that overlay them.

Exposed-nail roll roofing is used with slopes between 2-in-12 and 4-in-12 (see **9-24**). *Double coverage* (also called *selvage* or *half-lap*) roll roofing is used for roofs between 1-in-12 and 2-in-12 (see **9-25**). Since it lasts about 50 percent longer than exposed-nail roofing—and looks better, too—it's usually used for all low-pitch roofing applications.

Ninety-pound mineral-surfaced roll is used for exposed-nail roofing. The first sheet is nailed full width to the deck, overhanging the drip edge by about one-quarter inch. Nail within an inch of the top edge first, spacing the nails three inches apart; then fold the sheet back over on itself, and apply a bead of flashing cement along the eaves and rake drip edge. Flip the sheet back over, and press it into the cement. Drive nails along the edges and ends of the sheets spaced as above. End-lap sheets by six inches, cement between them with *cold cement*—asphalt compound similar to foundation coating made especially for roll-roofing application—and secure them with a double row of nails spaced four inches apart. The subsequent courses are also nailed along their top edges first so that they overlap the previous sheets two to four inches (the roofing comes with a factory-applied chalk line to mark the overlap). Flip the sheets back up and apply cold cement to the lap; nail off the edges as for the first sheet.

Half-lap roll roofing is *blind-nailed* (refer to **9-25**). Cut the roll down the middle and cement the smooth-surfaced "selvage" portion to the roof deck along the eaves with

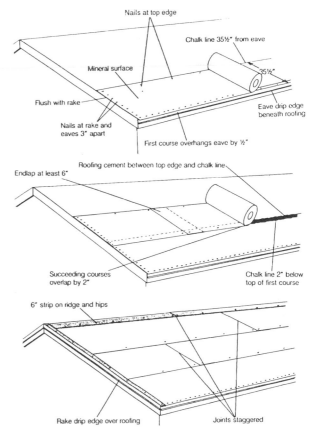

9-24   *Exposed nail roll roofing; note how the rake drip edge is applied over the roofing to keep wind from lifting up the edges.*

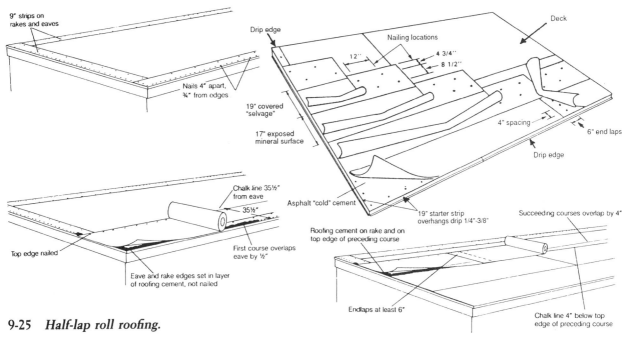

9-25   *Half-lap roll roofing.*

247

cold cement, applied with a mop. Nail the first course of full-width selvage roll over this starter course. Use two staggered lines of nails, spaced about a foot apart at about five inches and thirteen inches from the top edge; don't nail any ends or lap joints yet. Install the next course so that it overlaps the first course by 19 inches, leaving a 17-inch exposure. Continue applying the courses until you reach the ridge. Then, beginning at the top of the roof, carefully lift up and roll back the mineral-surfaced portion of each course on itself; you'll need at least one helper to do this without tearing the sheets. Working from the eaves up, mop cold cement across the smooth selvage portion, and flip the sheets down into the cement. Smooth out any wrinkles in the sheet by shuffling your feet from the center outward to the rakes. Nail the selvage portion of any lap joints and ends of sheets before spreading cement on the next course. Save the mineral-surfaced portion of the starter sheet for use at the ridge or as a filler sheet. End and lap joints can be face-nailed for greater wind resistance.

Whenever roll roofing is used to flash against an end wall or as a base flashing against a chimney or skylight, a 45-degree wood *cant strip* is used to ease the bend so that the roofing doesn't crack (see **9-26**). Since roll roofing wears out relatively quickly, don't nail the finish siding over it. Seal the joint with long-lasting, metal counterflashing instead. The pattern for cutting chimney base flashing is shown in **9-26**. Roll roofing should be unrolled across a driveway swept clean of stones that might puncture it and left to soften in the sun before it is installed.

BUILT-UP ROOFING

There are a lot of reasons why an amateur roofer should shy away from built-up roofing (see **9-27**). Although it's not especially difficult, it's potentially hazardous work; you've got to hoist pails of liquid coal tar (*bitumin*) or asphalt heated to 450 to 525 degrees Fahrenheit (232 to 273 degrees Celsius) onto the roof and spread them over its surface with a mop. Spilling the tar on yourself causes nasty burns; its fumes can make you ill. However, if you remain determined to do it yourself, you can certainly rent the propane-fired "kettle" used to melt the 60-pound blocks of solid tar. You'll also need to build a simple tripod hoist with a single pulley to lift the five-gallon pails of hot tar onto the roof. Since some spills are unavoidable, install built-up roofing before the finish siding or windows to avoid ruining them.

A built-up roof begins with a base layer of 30-pound felt applied to the sheathing with galvanized nails and roofer's tins spaced six inches apart along the ends and edges and 18-inches o.c. across the sheets. Lap the sheets four inches; this layer keeps the tar from seeping through the joints in the sheathing and also makes it a lot easier to rip off the old roofing when the time eventually comes to replace it. For added protection against rot caused by an undiscovered leak, some builders substitute pressure-treated plywood for ordinary roof sheathing. Each of the three or four succeeding layers of 15-pound asphalt-saturated felt are mopped in place with hot tar (fibreglass-based felts are stronger, and, unlike organic-fibre-based felts, they won't rot). For three-ply coverage, start with a

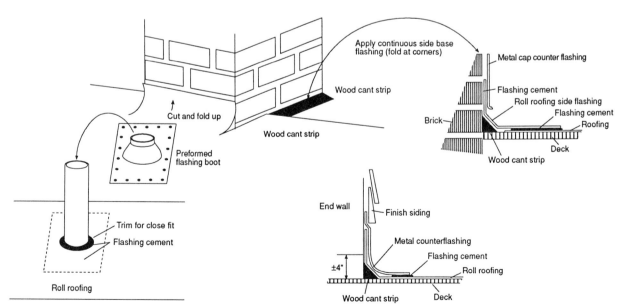

9-26 *Roll roofing is cut and folded against the sides of the chimney to make the base. The side pieces should be long enough to fold around the corners. Always cut the roofing to fit snugly against vent pipes—seal all joints and coat the entire area under the flashing boot with cement before nailing it in place.*

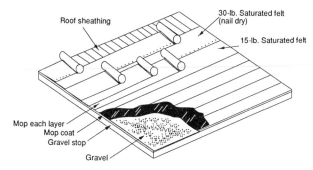

9-27 *Although mostly used for flat roofs, built-up roofing can be used on slopes up to 3-in-12. Use ¼-inch to ⅝-inch gravel.*

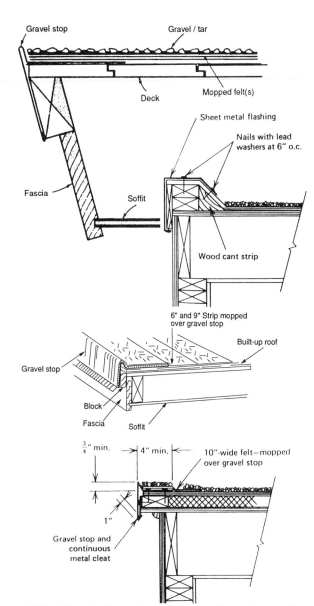

9-28 *The design of a gravel stop depends on the profile of the finished cornice.*

12-inch-wide sheet butted to the roof edge; cover it with a 24-inch-wide piece, and then a 36-inch piece. The rest of the sheets are laid full-width, with a 12-inch exposure. Use a nine-inch exposure for four-ply coverage. After all the felts are in place, the entire surface is given a thick hot tar *flood coat* and covered with light-colored crushed stone, gravel, or mineral slag. The stone protects the asphalt from the abrasion and the weather, prolongs the life of the underlayment, and reflects sunlight, keeping the roof cooler. It also acts as ballast to keep the membrane from blowing off the roof.

The tars used for cementing built-up roofing are classified according to their melting point. It's important to select the grade that's appropriate for your particular application. For flat roofs, where standing water is likely, use *dead-flat* asphalt, which actually flows very slowly at ordinary temperatures, enabling it to seal itself. For sloping roofs or in hot climates, *steep* asphalt, which has a higher melting point, is used.

A galvanized-steel *gravel stop*, which is like an oversized drip edge with a vertical rather than horizontal projection, is nailed to the edge of the roof deck over the plies (see **9-28**). The joint is sealed with a special base flashing of self-sticking fibreglass-reinforced asphalt membrane (since it is sold in 36-inch-wide rolls, you'll have to cut a strip to width) and then covered with the flood coat. The stop keeps the loose gravel on the roof, and makes a clean edge with the fascia board. Depending on the profile of the stop, it may require wood backing or it may attach to a retaining clip on the fascia or overlap a gutter.

Flat roofs also often terminate against a parapet wall of wood or masonry, particularly with adobe-style houses of the American Southwest (see **9-29**). Although this short wall is usually framed on top of the roof deck, a stronger connection results if the studs are nailed to the sides of the roof joists instead. Use pressure-treated plywood for the sheathing on the side of the wall facing the roof. Nail a 3½-inch-wide 45-degree *cant strip* to the base of the parapet wall to support the roofing where it bends up

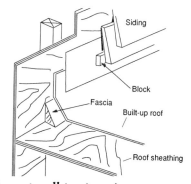

9-29 *Parapet wall treatment.*

against the wall. The felts are run up a few inches onto the walls and overlaid with a strip of fibreglass-reinforced base flashing that extends at least eight inches and preferably 12 inches up over the wall sheathing. Metal counterflashing seals the joint between the base flashing and the finish siding. Because it is soft enough to fold up out of the way for reroofing and will last indefinitely, copper is the metal of choice for counterflashing.

Even ostensibly flat roofs are pitched slightly so that water doesn't pond up on them. Normally, the area adjacent to the cant strip or gravel stop serves as a gutter. A hole drilled through the deck and lined with a metal collar drains into a downspout. In parapet walls, a *scupper*—an opening lined with metal—directs the water through the wall and out away from the house.

Despite the difficulties associated with its installation, built-up roofing performance is tried-and-true. Yet in the last decade or so, synthetic elastomeric copolymers such as silicone, neoprene, acrylic and polyurethane rubber, EPDM (Ethylene Propylene Diene Monomer), and Hypalon have become increasingly popular with commercial roofers. Although expensive, they are extremely flexible and resistant to UV (ultraviolet radiation), fire, chemicals, weather, and abrasion. They also come in a variety of colors. Most of these *membrane systems* are applied in liquid form with a trowel or roller. Special attention must be paid to mixing, curing, solvents, and application details; some products give off toxic fumes during application.

Some elastomers are available in sheets. Of these, EPDM, which has the feel of a rubber inner tube, is the most accessible to the do-it-yourself roofer. A single ply of EPDM glued to the roof deck or over insulation makes a watertight roof. It must be protected from the weather with a layer of loose gravel.

One of the problems characteristic of built-up roofs is that there is no simple or effective way to ventilate the insulation between the roof deck and the waterproof membrane. Vapor migrating through the roof sheathing can be trapped under the membrane, causing it to blister and the deck to rot. In climates where the average January temperature is 40 degrees Fahrenheit (4½ degrees Celsius) or less (or the relative humidity is more than 50 percent)—i.e., most of the United States—a tight vapor barrier must be installed between the insulation and the finish ceiling. A ventilation channel should also be provided between the top of the insulation and the underside of the roof deck. This complicates fascia and soffit construction, especially if mechanical ventilation is required. An entirely different approach is to lay the vapor barrier on top of the deck and cover it with rigid foam insulation (see **9-30**). The foam itself is covered with a protective sheathing of ½-inch fibreboard and then an EPDM membrane is glued over it to waterproof the assembly, which is covered with a protective layer of gravel ballast.

PROTECTION AGAINST ICE DAMS

In cold climates, heat escaping through the attic tends to melt the snow cover on a shingle roof from underneath. Solar radiation, especially on the south side, also contributes to snow melt. In contrast to the roof over heated areas, the eaves overhang is exposed to the cold. Water that has trickled down the roof tends to freeze when it reaches the eaves, eventually forming a reverse "glacier." The water trapped behind this *ice dam* seeps underneath the shingles and into the building, where it can cause severe damage to the walls and ceilings. That's why the sight of a homeowner perched on top of a ladder hacking away at the edge of the roof is such a common sight in

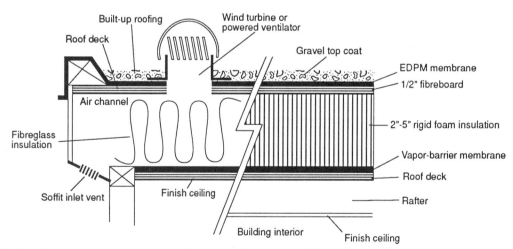

9-30 *Placing the insulation on top of the roof solves the problem of providing ventilation under the roof deck and permits unobstructed mechanical runs between the roof-joist bays. Wind turbines or mechanically powered ventilators are usually needed to draw air through the ventilation channel between insulation and roof deck.*

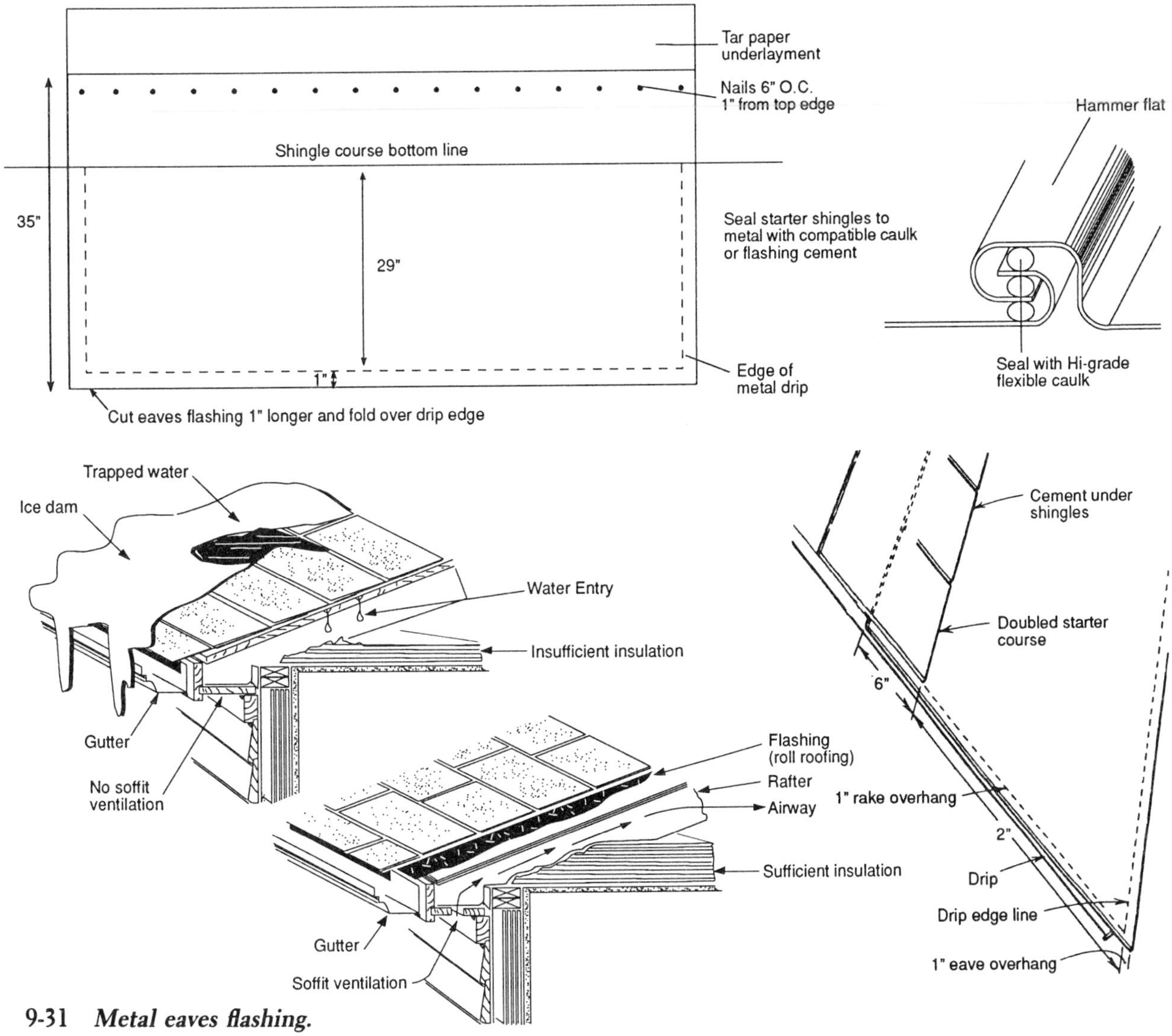
Tar paper underlayment
Nails 6" O.C. 1" from top edge
Shingle course bottom line
35"
29"
1"
Seal starter shingles to metal with compatible caulk or flashing cement
Edge of metal drip
Cut eaves flashing 1" longer and fold over drip edge
Hammer flat
Seal with Hi-grade flexible caulk
Trapped water
Ice dam
Water Entry
Insufficient insulation
Gutter
No soffit ventilation
Flashing (roll roofing)
Rafter
Airway
Sufficient insulation
Gutter
Soffit ventilation
Cement under shingles
Doubled starter course
6"
1" rake overhang
2"
Drip
Drip edge line
1" eave overhang

9-31 ***Metal eaves flashing.***

snow country. This is not only a bothersome and potentially dangerous chore, but one that's hard on the roofing, too.

A better solution to ice dams would be preventative, not reactive. Cold-cement smooth-surfaced roll roofing or 30-pound felt to the deck from the eaves drip edge to a point at least two feet inside of the building walls over all heated areas. Two courses, i.e., six feet, of coverage are better, especially for roof slopes of 6-in-12 or less. A self-adhesive membrane like Ice-and-Water Shield is more costly, but less messy and much faster to install.

While this will generally keep any water or ice that backs up under the shingles from seeping through to the sheathing, it doesn't affect the growth of the ice dam. A slippery, wide metal eaves flashing makes it a lot harder for the ice to build up in the first place (see **9-31**).

Galvanized-steel 28-gauge flashing metal is relatively inexpensive, but must be kept painted or else it will rust. Since paint won't adhere to fresh galvanized steel, many builders prefer to let it "ripen" for a year or two first. Otherwise, you've got to strip the oily coating off the new metal with paint thinner, paint it with a special galvanized metal primer, and then recoat it with two coats of high-quality metal enamel. Even so, the flashing will need periodic repainting. Since painting from a ladder is a lot of work, it makes more sense to use steel with a factory-applied baked-on epoxy enamel finish that's good for at least 20 years. The metal color can match or complement the roofing.

For a premium installation, cement the underlayment or the membrane to the deck as described above. Measure up from the drip edge to a point equal to the width of the flashing metal less one inch. (I recommend 36-inch-wide metal, hence, 35 inches.) Snap a chalk line across the roof. Cut the metal to the length of the roof plus two inches. Tack the top corner of the metal to the line and unroll it as you would when tar papering. Wear leather gloves, and don't work in windy weather. Nail off the edge at six-inch intervals, working from the center towards the rakes to minimize buckling. Crimp the overhanging edge of the flashing over the drip edge at the eaves and up the rake with a sheet-metal tool or a wood block and hammer.

A sheet of steel 30 feet long will expand about one-quarter of an inch over a 100 degrees F (55½ degrees C) change in temperature. A single sheet of flashing metal running the full length of the eaves will tend to ripple visibly on hot days. This occasional visual imperfection is less of a problem than the possibility of leaks between overlapping joints. If joints are unavoidable, overlap each piece 1½ inch, and form an interlocking seam joint that can be sealed with flexible caulk to allow some room for movement.

Snap a chalk line six inches below the top edge of the flashing, and lay butts of the starter course shingles to it. This will leave 29 inches of flashing exposed. Since you'll want to avoid scratching or climbing over the metal to shingle the roof—on steep roofs at least—it's a good idea to leave the starter course out and begin shingling with the second course. Snap a chalk line 46 inches up from the drip edge to mark the top of the second course of shingles and nail them through their *top edges only*. Continue shingling the roof in the normal manner. The flashing is installed only after the shingling is completed and all staging is removed. Slip both layers of the starter course up under the tabs of the second-course shingles and seal them to the flashing with a bead of butyl rubber caulking.

THE "COLD ROOF" SYSTEM

Besides the problem of ice dams in winter, the surface of a roof gets very hot in summer. A significant portion of that heat is absorbed by the attic insulation and radiated from the ceilings into the living areas, making them uncomfortably hot in the late afternoon, when they are most often occupied, and driving up cooling costs.

For better than two decades, the *cold roof* (also called the *double roof*) has been used throughout the United States to reduce both summer overheating and winter ice dam problems (see 9-32). Two layers of sheathing are separated by a course of vertical strapping with continuous intake and outlet vents at both the soffit and ridge that form a ventilating cavity. The air movement in this space carries off attic heat that would otherwise melt the snow cover in winter—and it reduces attic heat buildup in the summer. By improving attic ventilation in general, the continuous ridge vent of the cold roof also helps prevent condensation on the attic side of the sheathing and in the insulation. A vertical distance of at least five feet between the intake and exhaust vents is necessary to create the *thermal head* to start the air circulation flowing.

Since the first layer of sheathing in a cold roof doesn't carry any roofing, it only needs to be strong enough to support your weight while you apply it. Inexpensive material such as waferboard or ⅜-inch plywood will suffice. Leave a two-inch-wide horizontal gap in the sheathing directly over the soffit vent and at the peak of the ridge. Nail 1×4 or 1×3 strapping vertically over each rafter; these should butt against a nailer laid over the subfascia at the eaves. The second layer of sheathing is nailed to the strapping and shingled as with a standard roof deck.

Until the past few years, none of the prefabricated ridge vents looked good or performed as intended. Custom-built

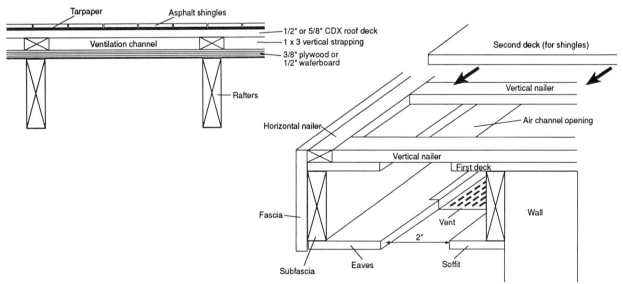

9-32 *Cold roof construction for asphalt shingles.*

Typical cold roof air intake at eaves

9-33 *This steel roofing is capped with a custom-built continuous ridge ventilator; factory-made ventilators that fit metal roofing aren't available. Note the skylight flashing, which utilizes a malleable, lead base flashing originally designed for European tile roofing that can be formed on site to conform with the profile of the roofing.*

9-35 *Modern steel roofing has a prominent ribbed profile that goes equally well with contemporary and traditional house styles. The roofing sheets are also available with a baked-on enamel finish in a wide range of colors.*

ventilators were the only durable and effective alternatives (see **9-33**). Several new, improved types of ridge ventilators designed for installation with asphalt roofing—and that are unobtrusive, easy to install and fitted with integral baffles to make them water- and windproof, and work well—are now widely available (see **9-34**). Cor-A-Vent, one of the better ones, nails to the roof with long nails and is covered with ordinary ridge-cap shingles. A special piece is also available for venting the intersection of a roof with a vertical wall.

GALVANIZED STEEL-SHEET ROOFING

Traditional *standing seam* metal roofing makes a handsome, durable, and virtually leakproof roof (see **9-35**). Unfortunately, the tools and the knowledge needed to install it aren't available to most professional roofers, let alone the do-it-yourself homebuilder. Installing a standing seam roof is an expensive subcontract.

In contrast, steel-sheet roofing (e.g., Paneldrain and Channeldrain, manufactured by Wheeling Corrugated, Inc.), which is available with either a plain galvanized finish or a baked-on enamel finish in a range of colors—if properly applied—makes a long-lasting, relatively inexpensive, watertight roof that can be quite handsome and is easily applied by the do-it-yourselfer.

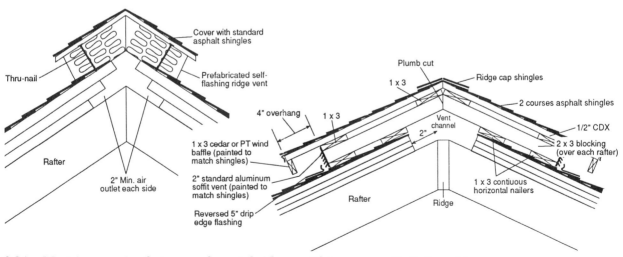

9-34 *Most inexpensive factory-made metal ridge ventilators are easily flattened by snow cover. Others lack a baffle for keeping out wind-driven rain or snow. Corrugated plastic ventilators don't compress, are long-lasting, and are easily installed.*

9-36 *Steel roofing is often applied over spaced purlins nailed across the rafters, such as the rough-sawn 1½×4s used on this barn roof.*

Steel roofing does entail some unique installation problems. It takes considerably more skill to make accurate cuts and to ensure watertight flashings for valleys, dormers, end walls, and penetrations with steel roofing panels than with shingle-type roofing. Cut edges are very sharp, and the sheets can be a challenge to handle on a windy day. They should not be used on slopes of less than 4-in-12, since water and ice can work up under the long edge seams at low pitches.

One of the most attractive features of steel roofing, at least to low-budget builders, is that it doesn't require a solid roof deck (see **9-36**). Instead, it's nailed to horizontal *purlins* (also called *nailers*, *strapping*, or *lathing*) spanning the rafters on 16-inch centers. While such a roof is ideal

for a barn or unheated garage, it causes problems in cold climates where the insulation is installed between the rafters. Water vapor condenses readily on the chilled metal, saturates the insulation, and drips from the ceiling and walls. A cold-roof system should always be used with metal roofing (see **9-37**).

Light decking is installed over the rafters and covered with 15-pound felt underlayment. Strapping (you can use inexpensive rough-sawn 1×4) is nailed parallel over each rafter to form the ventilating air channel. A second course of strapping is nailed perpendicular to the first, at 16-inches o.c., to furnish the purlins to which the roofing sheets are nailed.

Commercially available ridge vents don't interface with the raised ribs of steel roofing. Building a custom ridge ventilator is labor-intensive (see **9-38**). You can't safely stand on metal roofing with a pitch in excess of 4-in-12. There's no convenient way to attach a staging to steel roofing once it's installed. Instead of straddling the ridge, spike a 2×4 kneeling board to a purlin at a convenient working height near the ridge. Fill the nail holes with caulk and roofing nails after removing the staging.

The most salient feature of steel roofing is its absolute regularity. Unlike a shingle roof, metal sheets have no tolerance for out-of-square framing or the occasional odd dimension. The rake overhang must be sized to fit the steel coverage (which, because of the overlap at the long edges, isn't quite the same as the width of the sheets—and varies according to the brand of roofing). Because it's unlikely that the roof will end up perfectly square, the far rake is left unfinished until the last sheet of steel is ready to install.

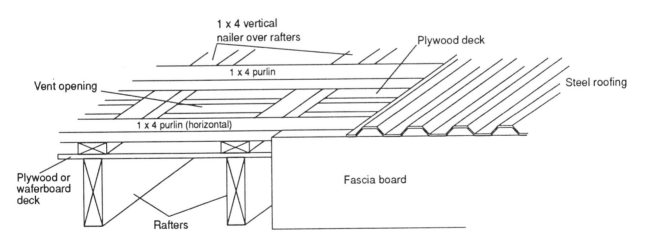

Soffit and intake vent
not shown

9-37 *Cold roof system for steel roofing.*

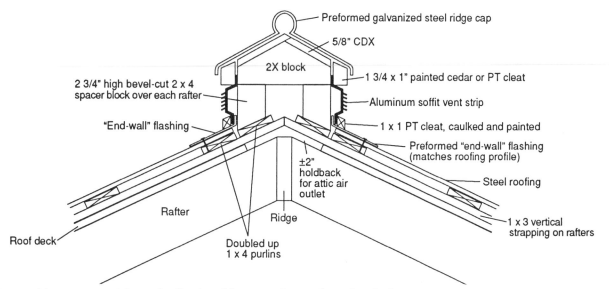

9-38 *Building a watertight and effective ridge vent for steel roofing isn't easy.*

Align the starting sheet so that its edge overhangs the rake fascia board by one-half inch (see **9-39**). The bottom edge overhangs the eaves fascia board by three-quarters of an inch to one inch. Use a gauge block to line it up with the fascia board. No drip edges are required. As with ridge-cap shingles, lay the sheets so that their vertical seams overlap away from the direction of the prevailing wind (start on the downwind rake). If the overhang at the eaves varies from one side of the sheet to the other, something is out of square. If it happens to be the roof, then you can usually split the difference between the rake and eaves or run the sheet out slightly more at the rake. One-

eighth of an inch variation isn't critical or noticeable; the following sheets will drop a like amount to keep the eaves overhang dimension more or less constant.

Measure the length of the roof from eaves to ridge before ordering your steel. Standard lengths are available in two-foot increments from eight feet up to 20 feet. With six weeks advance notice, most manufacturers can supply sheet precut to the exact length you need or supply extra-long sheets. The overall length, including an allowance for a one-inch eaves overhang, should be two inches shorter than the distance to the peak to permit air circulation from the cold roof and attic into the ridge vent.

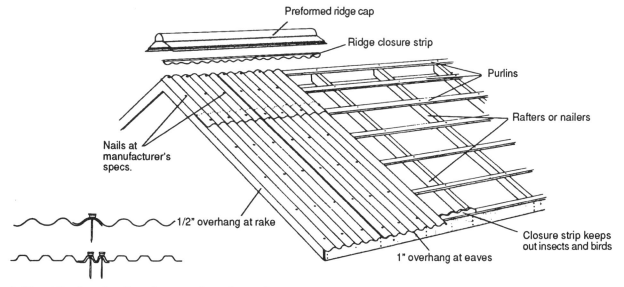

9-39 *Aligning the first sheet to the rake and eaves.*

255

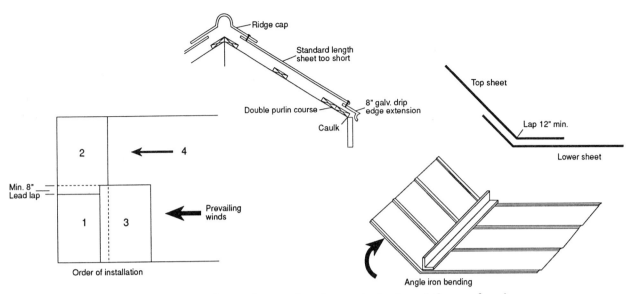

9-40 *To prevent leaks, always lay the roofing so that the vertical edge of the overlapping sheet is opposite the prevailing wind.*

If a standard sheet is only an inch or two short of the required length, install eight-inch-wide galvanized-steel drip edge at the eaves instead of a small unsightly extension piece or a special order. If standard sheets are a bit too long, trim them at the top edge, which will be hidden under the ridge flashing. (Most sheets are directional; the bottom edge is marked by an embossed trademark or the rib overlap pattern is such that it can only go one way.)

Extra-long sheets are subject to greater thermal stress, which tends to loosen their nails over time. Overlapping sheets don't look quite as handsome and can leak under the wrong conditions. I'd stick with full-length sheets up to about 24 feet—especially if you use neoprene washer nails—which will maintain a watertight seal even with some movement of the sheets.

Sheets should overlap vertically at least eight inches (see **9-40**). Plan the overlap so that the bottom edge of the top sheet falls over a nailer—or add an extra course of strapping in the vicinity of the overlap. If an overlap occurs at a point where the roof changes pitch, the sheets must be folded. Set the edge of a piece of two-inch-angle iron over the ribs, and bend the sheet by pulling it against the iron. Don't crease the sheet so sharply that you split the ribs instead of just deforming them.

If you do use overlapping sheets, run each course vertically up the entire length of the roof before laying the next course. Otherwise, the splice between the sheets is likely to leak. Drive a single nail through the top of each rib into the purlin. Don't nail the last rib until it's overlapped by the next sheet. Likewise, leave off the nails along the top edge of the sheets at the ridge (or between overlaps) since they will be secured when the ridge flashing (or top sheet) is nailed down.

There are three types of fasteners used to install steel roofing (see **9-41**). The best (and most expensive) is a hex-head self-tapping screw with a steel washer and rubber gasket. Use a hex-head nut driver attachment for your electric drill or power screwdriver. These screws can be ordered with a baked-enamel finish that matches the color of the roofing. Nails are cheaper, easier to drive, and give fairly good service although they don't hold as well as screws. "Lead heads" have a soft lead washer under a wide galvanized-steel head and a spiral thread to increase holding power; the washers can and do break off or split apart. Neoprene-gasket nails have an annular shank and a rubber gasket that maintains a better seal. They cost more than lead heads, but you get more per pound as well. Whatever type of fastener you use, it should be long enough to penetrate through the rib and at least three-quarters of an inch into the purlins. Drive the fastener

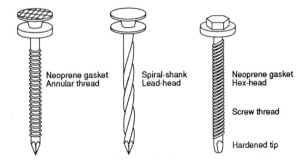

9-41 *Self-drilling hex-head fasteners are mainly used for installing the wall panels of steel buildings.*

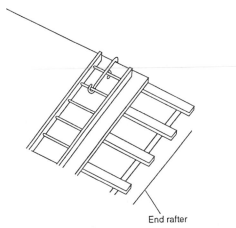

9-42 *When you're using ladder hooks, it's always a good idea to tie a safety rope to the wall framing or the purlins on the opposite side of the roof.*

just enough to seat the washer. Overdriving will break it or buckle the rib; an under-driven nail will leak.

The nailing purlins provide a comfortable ladder staging for installing the roofing. Reach across each sheet and nail the overlap first, working back towards yourself. There is a little bit of sideways play in the vertical seams. You could gain almost an inch across the run of a long enough roof if you're trying to straighten out a skewed one.

Don't nail the last two or three ribs of the second-to-last sheet. Depending on the rib pattern and the width of the sheets, you may need to overlap the last sheet on an inner rib to avoid trimming off the edge at the rake. The strapping at the unfinished rake should extend at least 14 inches beyond the gable rafter.

Since it's hardly possible to sit on the strapping and install the last sheet over it at the same time, work from a ladder resting on the roofing and held to the ridge with

a *ladder hook* (see **9-42**). If you can't find one to rent or buy, the ladder guides of a wooden extension ladder make good substitutes.

Mark the top and bottom edges of the last sheet where it falls over the strapping (see **9-43**). Set the sheet aside. Measure back from these marks a distance equal to the width of the fascia board plus the one-half-inch rake overhang. Snap a chalk line down the strapping, and saw it off. Nail the false rafter beneath the strapping and the rake fascia board flush with its top face. If you've planned the layout of the roof well, this rake overhang won't be appreciably wider than the other one. If the roof is out-of-square, it will show up now as a difference in the width of the rake soffit from peak to eaves. Since the eye tends to skew parallel lines in perspective anyway, anything but the most flagrant discrepancy won't be noticeable, or at least, not as obvious as a tapered cut along the edge of the steel.

If, as was mentioned above, overlapping the last sheet at its full width will result in an excessively wide rake overhang, it can overlap an inner rib (refer to **9-43**). Since the pattern is often double-crimped on the last rib, you may need to cut it off for a neat fit. If necessary, ignore the stipulation about the weather and run the end piece under the second-to-last piece. Sometimes, you can cut a sheet in two, and use each piece to finish off the opposite ends of the roof.

Steel roofing can be cut with tin shears, although it's a lot of work. Since the cut edges can be razor-sharp, wear leather work gloves to protect yourself. Electric metal-cutting shears are the safest and easiest tool to use, but they tend to wander easily off the cutting line. Abrasive metal-cutting circular saw blades don't last very long. You'll achieve better results with an old sawblade set backwards in the circular saw. Wear a safety shield to protect your face from flying red-hot shrapnel. The noise produced by this method is fearsome; hearing protectors are also a good idea. However you make it, a cut edge shouldn't show (except at a valley, where it's unavoidable).

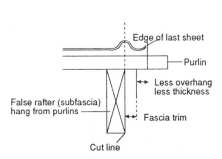

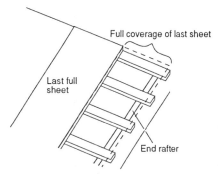

9-43 *A cut edge at the rake always looks sloppy. Try to frame the rake overhangs so that they will be as close to equal width as possible and still end on a full sheet. When offsetting the ending sheet, trim off its doubled "prime" rib so that it lies flat under the last full sheet.*

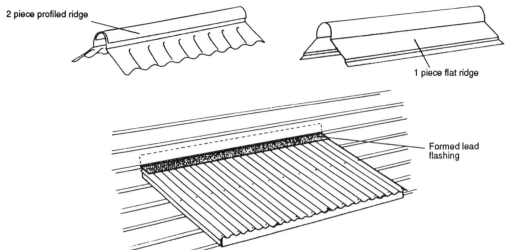

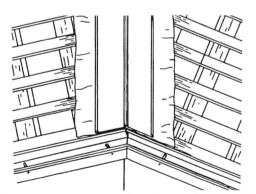

Formed lead flashing

9-44 *Flashing details for steel roofing; for best results, provide extra blocking around all penetrations for attaching the roofing sheets and flashing.*

FLASHING STEEL ROOFING

Flashing with metal roofing is similar to flashing with roll roofing (see **9-44**). Step flashing isn't required since there are no overlapping courses to protect against water penetration. Base flashing for chimneys and dormers is the same as the special factory-made *end-wall flashing* with a bottom section that matches the profile of the roofing sheets and a top section that lays flat against the wall or chimney. End-wall flashing is used wherever the roofing intersects a vertical obstruction across its width. When the intersection is parallel to the length of the sheet, allow four to six inches extra and cut it to fold upwards against the wall. Trim the rib off the edge so that the sheet will lay flat beneath the finish siding or will fold easily; counterflash as needed. Where flashing must join to the roof instead, as with a flange, it is always caulked under the seam.

For vent pipes, you can cut a hole in the sheet, slip a metal or plastic flashing boot over the pipe, and seal it to

the roof. A more watertight job is guaranteed if two overlapping sheets are used instead. The lower sheet, which contains the hole, ends about a foot above the penetration. The flashing flange is installed next. The second sheet is cut to fit around the pipe and laid over the flange just as is done with a shingle.

Always seal any flashings with caulk, such as Geocel, and secure them to the roofing with self-tapping sheet-metal screws. Otherwise, you can anticipate where flashings will go and add extra nailing purlins beneath them.

You can usually order ridge-cap flashing in eight-foot or 10-foot lengths that more-or-less match the profile of the roofing. Some ribs of some kinds of roofing won't line up across opposite sides of the ridge. Interlocking two-piece flashing solves the problem.

Valleys and hips are best avoided with steel roofing, since it's hard to cut a neat valley line across the sheets (see **9-45**). Hips have to be covered with flat sheet metal since the ribs will be at an angle to the run of standard

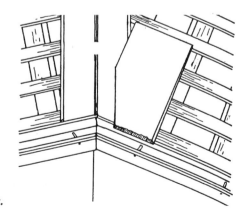

9-45 *Valley trimming for steel roofing and wood shingles.*

ridge flashing. This makes for a fairly shoddy job. Install a 12-inch- to 16-inch-wide course of boards or plywood over the vertical strapping to provide solid nailing support down the run of the valley. Snap a chalk line down the edge of the valley, and make a template from a scrap piece of roofing to guide the cuts of the sheets. Cut them longer than necessary, and check for their alignment with the guide line. If the fit is good, trim the top edge of the sheet off where it will be hidden, rather than shorten the valley cut.

Lead is the best material to form custom flashings. However, because it will corrode steel, the metals should be isolated from each other with a coating of paint or flashing cement.

WOOD SHINGLES AND SHAKES
Until the introduction of asphalt roofing, *wood shingles* and *shakes* were the most widely used roofing material in America (see **9-46**). Made from durable, naturally rot-resistant woods like Western red and Eastern white cedar, redwood, cypress, and pine, wood roofing is highly prized for its color and texture. It also stays much cooler in the summer and warmer in the winter than asphalt or metal roofing. Although some people confuse the two, shingles and shakes aren't different words for the same kind of wood roofing. The main difference between a shake and a shingle is in the method of manufacture; a shake is split from a bolt of wood along its grain whereas a shingle is sawn. Since the face of a shake follows the natural cleavage planes of the wood, the cells on its face will be closed. As the saw blade rips through a shingle it tears the face cells apart, making them more likely to absorb water and to rot sooner than a shake. The durability of shakes is also enhanced by their thickness, which is two to three times that of a shingle. The premium cost of shakes (about twice that of wood shingles and three to four times more than asphalt roofing) is offset by their longevity. Depending on the severity of local conditions, wood shingles typically last about twice as long as asphalt roofing (25–50 years). Shakes can easily last a lifetime or more. Both types of roofing are labor-intensive; but, unlike asphalt roofing, wood roofing is light and clean. Working with it can be quite enjoyable.

Because of its extremely rugged texture, shake roofing is best suited to steep-pitched roofs, where it can be shown to advantage. Shingles will work with any roof pitch suitable for standard asphalt shingles. The only real drawback to wood roofing is its flammability. Unless the wood is specially treated with fire-retardant chemicals, many building codes won't permit its use. You may find that your fire insurance premium is higher with a wood roof even when such a roof is permitted by code. Recently, a special asbestos-fibreglass underlayment has been proved to reduce the flame spread rate of wood roofing to within acceptable code limits. However, using asbestos carries its own set of problems which many don't want to consider.

9-46 *Many homeowners find the rugged texture of genuine wood shake roofing exceptionally beautiful. Note that the ridge boards have been applied over a continuous ventilator. Also, note the cables for the lightning protection system.*

Traditionally, wood shakes and shingles have been nailed to spaced lathing, which allowed them to dry out between soakings and ensured their longevity (see **9-47**). Neither tar paper nor solid sheathing was used under wood shingles. Unfortunately, providing ventilation conflicts with the need to control infiltration and heat loss, at least in snow country. Here, ice can build up on the roof as snow melts and work its way between the shingles, causing a great deal of havoc.

The solution to the problem is to use a system analogous to the cold roof used with steel roofing, described above. Lay 15-pound felt over a waferboard or plywood deck, and run 1×3 strapping up the rafters. Space the horizontal laths to accommodate the shingle nailing line (usually five inches o.c. for five-inch exposure and 16-inch shingles). The air channel keeps the undersides of the shingles dry and provides the other benefits of a cold roof.

Open lathing is the preferred method where the climate is mild and humid, if not downright wet, most of the time. This is one reason why shakes and shingles are associated with coastal regions.

Shingles and shakes are available in at least three grades. Use only No. 1 grade, 100-percent clear heart edge-grain shingles for roofing. The other grades have too many defects, sapwood, and flat grain to last as long or remain leak-free; they're fine for undercoursing and sidewall shingling. Shingles also are manufactured in three standard

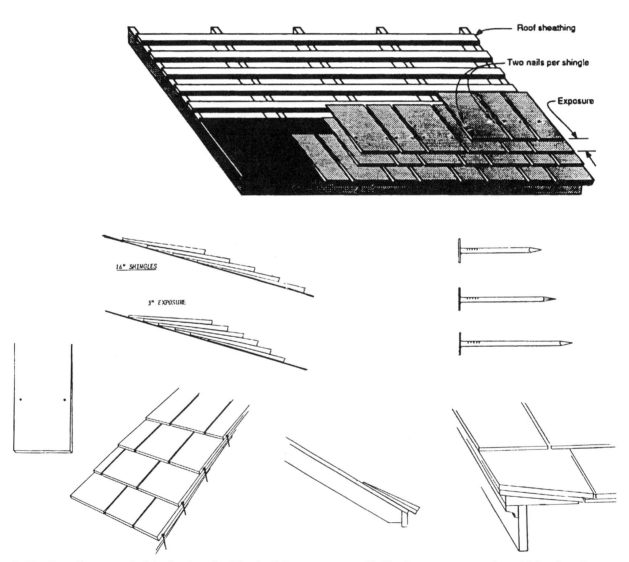

9-47 *Installing wood shingles is a lot like building a stone wall. You've got to vary the width of each shingle for pleasing effect and the most efficient use of your material while maintaining the correct side-lap. This requires constant attention to selecting and saving out the right widths as you work.*

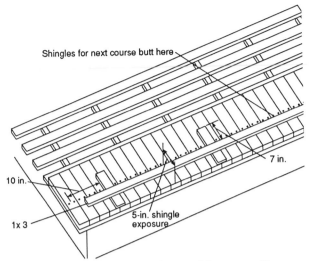

Shingles for next course butt here

10 in.

1x3

5-in. shingle exposure

7 in.

9-48 *Using a roofing stick to guide course lines.*

lengths: 16-inch, 18-inch, and 24-inch for exposures of 5 inches, 5½ inches, and 7½ inches, respectively, on roofs with slopes of 5-in-12 and greater, allowing triple coverage at these exposures. On lower slopes, the exposures are reduced to 3¾ inches, 4¼ inches, and 5¾ inches, respectively, for quadruple coverage. Either way, four bundles of shingles make up a square.

Metal drip edge is not normally required with wood roofing. Instead the shingles are allowed to overhang one inch at the eaves and three-eighths of an inch at the rake. To direct water away from the rakes, a clapboard is often run along its length (the fascia trim is raised to hide the edge). The starter course at the eaves is doubled.

Use only two 3d or 4d *hot-dipped* galvanized shingle nails for each shingle. (The zinc coating on electroplated nails soon wears off and they rust.) Space the nails within three-quarters of an inch of the edges and about one to 1½ inches above the butt line of the next course. The joints of alternate courses should never line up (refer to **9-47**). Keep a minimum offset of 1½ inches. Since the shingles will swell up when they absorb water, leave an eyeball space of about an eighth to a quarter of an inch between them so that they don't buckle. (This spacing rule applies only for Western red cedar shingles, which are usually fairly dry. Eastern white cedar shingles are generally "green," and will shrink upon application. You can let them touch each other.) Shingles wider than 10 inches should be scored down the middle, and treated as two shingles; otherwise they'll split at some future time.

A *roofing stick* is a straightedge used to keep the courses of shingles running straight (see **9-48**). Nail three 3-inch-by-12-inch strips of flashing metal to a 12- to 16-foot length of straight 1×3. This straightedge is lined up with a chalk line that marks the butt of the course you're about

to lay. Tack the straps to the shingles where the nail holes will be covered by the overlying shingle, which is left out until the roofing stick is removed. Experienced roofers add a butt gauge to the roofing stick, as shown in **9-48**, so that they don't have to bother with snapping any chalk lines. But until you develop the habit of automatically checking your shingle courses for straightness, it's a good idea to rely on chalk lines anyway.

As with asphalt shingles, check to make sure the courses are running parallel to the ridge before you get too close to the top. Adjust the guide lines accordingly. If the exposure between the last course and the ridge works out to three inches or less, it's a good idea to juggle the exposure of the preceding courses so that the last course comes closer to full width for a better appearance.

To lay ridge boards on an unventilated roof, run a strip of 15-pound felt down the length of the ridge (see **9-49**). (If the boards will be painted, run the tar paper an inch or so wider than the finished ridge to protect the shingles from drips when you apply the touch-up coat, and trim it off afterwards.) Use clear edge-grain Western red cedar or redwood 1×6 for the ridge stock. The joint between the ridge boards should be bevelled to match the angle of the roof. To find the angle of the cut, lay a scrap board against one side of the ridge, and scribe the line where the blade of your square crosses it from the opposite side of the ridge. Since the boards will butt rather than meet in a mitre, one must be wider than the other so that the overall width of the ridge is even.

Snap a chalk line along the most visible side of the ridge. Nail the bottom edge of the narrow ridge board to it (its top edge is flush with the peak) with 8d stainless-steel ring-shank nails driven into the rafters. Run a bead of clear caulking along the upper edge and nail the wider ridge board to it. Stand on the ridge to flatten the lower edge of the wide ridge board against the roof, and nail it. Caulk between end butt joints, and cover them with a strip of copper flashing metal.

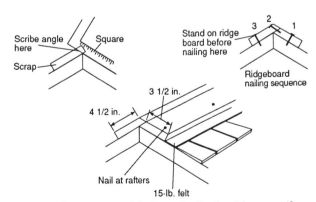

Scribe angle here

Square

Scrap

Stand on ridge board before nailing here

3 2 1

Ridgeboard nailing sequence

3 1/2 in.

4 1/2 in.

Nail at rafters

15-lb. felt

9-49 *The same prefabricated plastic ridge ventilator that is used for asphalt roofing works equally well with wooden ridge boards.*

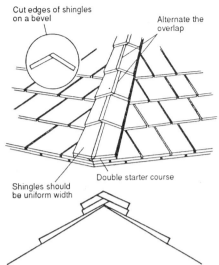

Cut edges of shingles on a bevel

Alternate the overlap

Shingles should be uniform width

Double starter course

9-50 *The fitted opposing bevels of a traditional "Boston" hip or ridge are both handsome in appearance and time-consuming to make.*

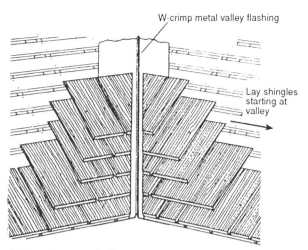

W-crimp metal valley flashing

Lay shingles starting at valley

9-51 *Snap a chalk line on the valley metal, and lay the precut angled valley shingles for each course first, working from the valley outward and filling in with straight shingles selected for minimal trimming with a block plane.*

For a cold roof, end the ridge course of shingles two inches below the peak. Glue a Cor-A-Vent to the shingles, and nail the ridge boards over it, using stainless-steel nails long enough to penetrate into the rafter strapping.

You can also cover the ridge with shingles instead of a ridge board (see **9-50**). Set the fence of your table saw to the width of the exposure, and set the blade for the angle of the ridge bevel. Saw the shingles in stacks of two with alternating tapers (i.e., the butt of one shingle and the tip of the other face you). Reverse the order of the next alternating pair. This way, the lap at the ridge will alternate from side to side with each pair of ridge caps. Lay a strip of 30-pound felt over the peak, and nail the cap shingles over it to a chalk line snapped on both sides. Maintain the same exposure as the roof shingles and use two 5d nails on each ridge shingle. This same technique can be used to cover a prefabricated ridge ventilator and to shingle a hip.

Since it can be fiendishly difficult to remove and replace wood shingles when mending a corroded valley (or any other) flashing, copper is the only sensible flashing metal to use with wood roofing, despite its cost. Crimp a standing seam into the middle of the valley sheet and lay it over 36-inch-wide 30-pound felt. Use boards or ¾-inch plywood to provide at least 12 inches of solid backing under each side of the valley, and butt regular horizontal laths to it.

The width of the valley is narrower with wood shingles than with asphalt; start at four inches (see **9-51**). Snap guide lines down both sides of the valley. Save the widest shingles in the bundle for filling in the valley. Make a template shingle, and use it to precut a supply of mitred valley shingles on your table saw. You can also scribe shingles to fit, and trim them with a sharp utility knife and a square. Any small adjustments are easily made with a block or trim plane. Instead of filling in between the last regular course and the valley, start laying the shingles from the valley outwards.

WOOD SHAKES

Wood shakes also come in three standard lengths: 18 inches, 24 inches, and 32 inches, with recommended maximum exposures of 8½ inches, 10 inches, and 13 inches, respectively. Like wood shingles, shakes are normally nailed to open lath, with or without a cold roof system. Because their roughly grooved surface permits more air circulation than shingles, shakes can also be applied to lath nailed across solid sheathing or IB board in cold climates.

A system of prefabricated panels is also available (see **9-52**, bottom).

Installation techniques for shakes are similar to wood shingles with one major exception (see **9-52**, top). Start the application by laying a 36-inch-wide strip of 30-pound felt along the eaves. Lay the doubled starter course. Then lay 18-inch-wide strips of 30-pound felt between each regular course. The bottom of the felt should be twice the regular exposure from the butts of the shingles it overlaps. Since shakes are thicker than shingles, use 6d or 7d nails to secure them. Don't overdrive the nails to the point that they crush the surface grain of the shake. Space the shingles one-quarter to three-eighths of an inch apart. Base flashings at chimneys and side walls should extend at least six inches under the shakes. Cut the ridge shakes in alternating pairs as described above for wood shingles.

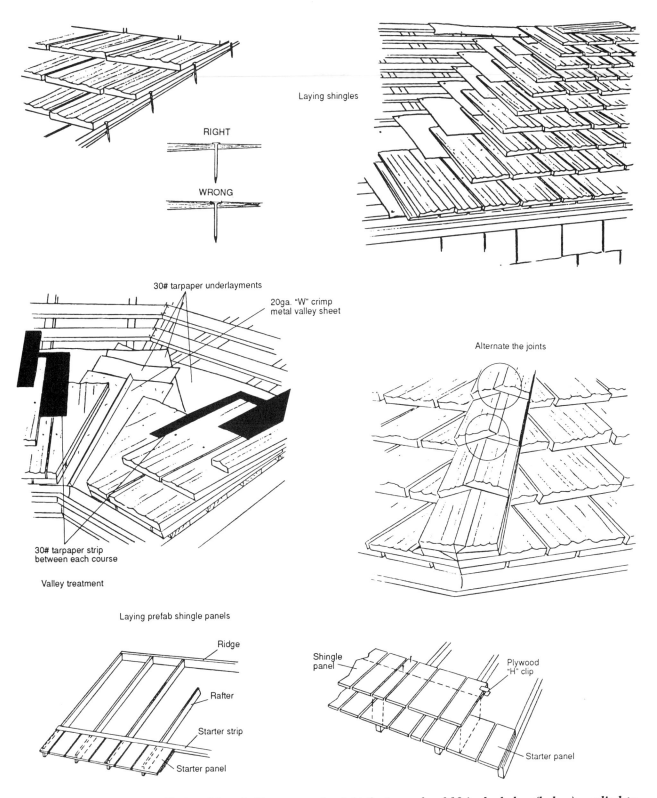

Laying shingles

RIGHT

WRONG

30# tarpaper underlayments

20ga. "W" crimp metal valley sheet

Alternate the joints

30# tarpaper strip between each course

Valley treatment

Laying prefab shingle panels

Ridge

Rafter

Starter strip

Starter panel

Shingle panel

Plywood "H" clip

Starter panel

9-52 *Wood shake installation (above). Factory-made eight-foot panels of 18-inch shakes (below) applied to plywood strips that are nailed directly to the rafters allow sheathing and roofing to be applied at the same time. Special starter panels are aligned with a starter strip or a chalk line across the rafters.*

9-53 *Tile roofing is equally at home in humid hot and cold climates and with a variety of a house styles. It's one of the most common roofing materials throughout northern Europe.*

CONCRETE AND CLAY TILE ROOFING

Although popularly associated with the Spanish Mission style of the Southwest and southern California in the United States, clay tiles have been used for roofing throughout all of North America since the earliest settlements (see **9-53**). Due to a shift in the canons of style, they fell out of fashion during the late 19th century everywhere but in the Spanish Southwest of the United States. Discarded fashions have a way of recycling themselves, and once again, traditional tile roofing is becoming popular. Concrete shingles in both traditional and modern profiles that mimic wood shakes are also gaining acceptance. Clay and concrete roofing is durable in all climates. It won't rot, moss can't grow on it, nothing can eat it. It withstands freeze–thaw cycles, blistering heat, and the corrosive effects of salt spray and industrial pollution. Completely inflammable, it has a Class A fire rating. Its weight also makes it very resistant to high winds.

Although that same weight is an objection often raised against tile roofing, ordinary roofs are designed to withstand a dead load of at least three asphalt roofings, which is about the weight of a typical clay tile roof. In most cases, increasing the depth of the rafters from 2×8s to 2×10s and/or decreasing the spacing from 24 inches to 16 inches o.c. is the only modification needed to support a tile roof. High cost, of course, is the other objection to tile roofing; but, just as with wood shakes, standing seam, or slate roofing, the life-cycle cost of any premium roofing that can last a century or more is actually less than that of asphalt shingles.

The specific installation techniques vary with the style of the roofing and are supplied in detail by the manufacturer (see **9-54**). The most popular tile roofing today is the Mission style, which comes in either the traditional two-piece barrel tile consisting of a concave trough (*tegula*) and convex cap (*imbrex*) or the more recent one-piece S tile, in which the cap and trough are joined in a single piece.

Accurate layout is important because of the strong vertical line of tile roofing (see **9-55**). Courses are indicated by chalk lines snapped on a felted solid roof deck. (Cold roofs and open lathing can also be used.)

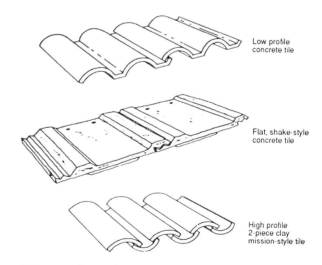

Low profile concrete tile

Flat, shake-style concrete tile

High profile 2-piece clay mission-style tile

9-54 *Modern tile roofing is available in traditional two-piece Mission-barrel and S-shaped "Spanish" clay style or low-profile and flat-shake pattern concrete and ceramic tiles, with a glazed or natural finish.*

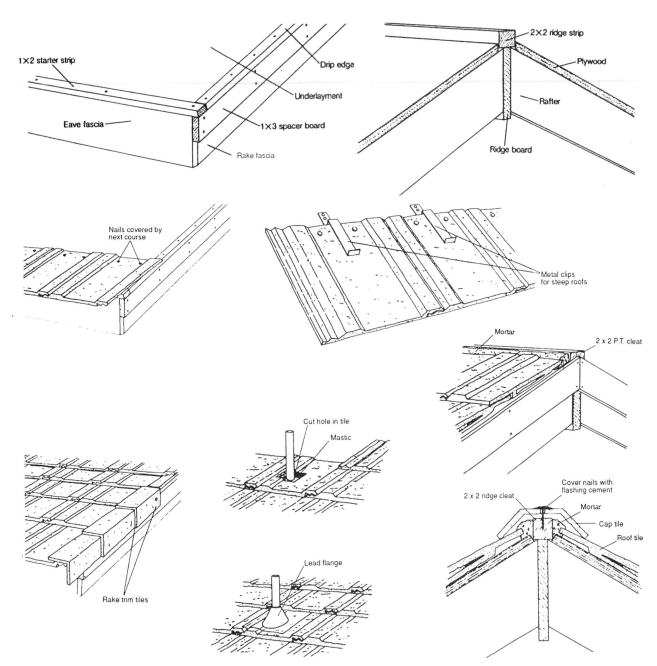

9-55 *The location of the nail holes in two-piece Mission-barrel tiles depends on whether they are cap (imbrex) or trough (tegula) tiles. Tiles are stacked six high, with the piles spaced one tile-width apart. Tile roofing is not doubled at the eaves. Instead, the eaves fascia board is raised or a 1×2 starter strip is tacked to the roof deck to raise the butt of the starter course tiles into the same plane as the rest of the tiles. A special drip edge or a strip of flashing metal crimped over a standard drip edge keeps water from "ponding" up under the starter tiles. Depending on the style of tile, nailers may also be needed along the rakes. Lugged tiles hook over the battens and require no nails. Other kinds of tiles are nailed to them through predrilled holes. Special dealer-supplied clips that match the particular tile style are used to anchor tile butts to steep roofs or to hold their sides down in very windy areas. At the ridges and hips, the final course of tiles is trimmed back about 1½ inches from a wood ridge strip. The gap and the edges of the tiles are covered with a bed of mortar, and the hip or ridge-cap tiles are nailed down before the mortar hardens.*

9-56 *To keep from walking on them, roofing tiles are stacked on the roof before their installation.*

Some tiles are designed to be mounted on vertical or horizontal battens (see **9-56** and **9-57**). Others have integral interlocking ridges.

With Mission tiles, the installation begins with the gable rake tiles. These can be special profile pieces nailed to the deck or else standard barrels supported on a vertical batten. Several courses of field tegulas are run vertically and horizontally before capping them with the imbrexes. Since the top of the cap tiles are well above the roof deck, they are either nailed to vertical battens or else secured to the deck by extra-long tile nails. All fasteners used for tile work should be corrosion-resistant. Copper nails are the best.

Clay plugs are used at the eaves to prevent birds and other creatures from nesting under the tiles. At the ridge or hip, the field tiles are butted to a vertical board and the cap tiles are mortared over them (see **9-58** and **9-59**). Some manufacturers also make special rounded-off ridge closure tiles. Lead flashing is used to seal the ridge with some low-profile cement or clay tiles. Tiles are generally closed with mortar at valleys. Production cutting of tiles is done with a diamond-blade wet saw. Although you can rent one, it's probably a better idea to avoid complex roof shapes that call for a lot of cuts. Masonry cutting blades for circular saws don't last all that long, but they're cheap.

As with asphalt shingles, clay tiles used on slopes of less than 4-in-12 are basically decorative; the underlying membrane roof provides the waterproofing.

If you have to walk on a tile roof, you should do so carefully. Step on the reinforced lugs or over the battens or in the troughs to avoid breaking unsupported tiles. If you do break a tile, all the tiles in the row above it will have to be removed in order to replace it. Some roofers walk or kneel on cushions made from sawdust-filled burlap sacks. Tile installation on steep-pitched roofs is done from ladders hooked over the ridge.

GUTTERS AND LEADERS

Rainwater falling freely from the eaves can contribute to wet cellars or exacerbate the effects of frost heave and hydraulic pressure on the foundation wall. Dirt splashed up against the bottom of the siding can nourish decay, attract termites, and detract from the appearance of the house. A cascade of water is also detrimental to the health of nascent foundation plantings.

At one time, *eavestroughs* (or *gutters*, as they are more commonly known) were built on top of the roof, formed into the eaves, or attached to the cornice. When clear-

9-57 *These glazed concrete tiles have a lug at their upper edge that hooks over the wood battens nailed to the roof. Note the V-crimp in the center of the metal valley flashing and how the tar paper overlaps it.*

9-58 *These concrete tiles have a lower profile than Mission-style clay tiles. Note the closed valley construction and the intersection of the ridge and rake caps.*

9-59 *The method of rake closure depends on the type of tile. With some systems, the rake tiles are laid first and overlapped by the field tile. Here, the rake tiles overlap the field tiles.*

heart Douglas fir, cedar, and redwood were less expensive than they are today, a wood gutter incorporated into the fascia was considered a hallmark of quality construction. Properly maintained, a wood gutter was supposed to last as long as the house. Since gutter maintenance is a low priority for most homeowners, very few wood gutters lived out their normal lifespan. You can still buy wood gutter stock or build a gutter into the eaves, but it's hard to justify the trouble and expense of installing and maintaining one (see **9-60**).

Metal gutters used to be made from copper or galvanized steel. Today, a copper gutter system would make wood gutters look cheap. Galvanized steel had to be soldered, and, unless kept painted, would soon begin to rust. Since the 1960s, aluminum and vinyl plastic have rendered any other gutter system virtually obsolete. I consider aluminum gutters to be one of the few sensible uses of that metal as a building material; with a factory-applied enamel finish, they are virtually immune to corrosion. They're stronger and hold up a lot better than vinyl plastic, which tends to become brittle with age.

Gutters are sized by the area of their watershed, i.e., the square footage of the slope that directly drains into them, not the area of the whole roof. The rule of thumb is: Use four-inch gutters for areas up to 750 sf; five-inch gutters for areas between 750 and 1400 sf; and six-inch gutters for larger areas. The diameter of the *downspouts* (also called *leaders*) also depends on roof area: use three-inch pipe for areas up to 1000 sf and four-inch pipe for larger roofs.

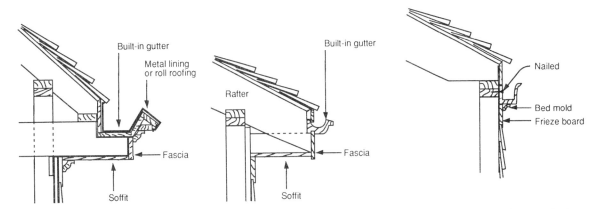

9-60 *Wood gutters are milled from costly clear redwood or Douglas fir stock. They must be regularly cleaned and patched to prevent leaks that could seriously damage the cornice or wall construction. Although less involved than the other installation methods, mounting a wood gutter directly against the wall makes it impossible to ventilate the soffit.*

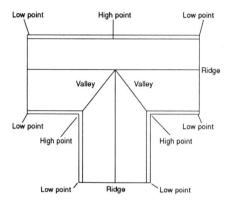

9-61 *The gutters should have just enough pitch so that a pail of water dumped into the high end will drain off reasonably fast.*

Although a level gutter will drain eventually, it should be sloped so that the water will drain fast enough to clean it out (see **9-61**). Ideally, this would be a pitch of about one inch in 20 feet. Since such a noticeably skewed line tends to be aesthetically disturbing, gutters are often installed at about half that pitch. The general practice is to pitch the gutters from a high spot at the middle of a long eaves—or the outlet of a valley—downward towards the low spot at the rakes. Thus the leaders are located at the ends of the building and away from doorways. Since most roofs have overhangs, elbows are used to carry the leader back against the house wall, where it will be less conspicuous and less vulnerable to damage.

There are three basic systems for mounting gutters (see **9-62**). With one of them, the gutter is hung from a strap that is nailed to the roof deck. The other two allow the gutter to mount directly against the fascia trim board, either by means of a special bracket nailed to the fascia at 30-inch intervals or by a spike that passes through both sides of the gutter and through a sleeve (the *ferrule*) that keeps the gutter from buckling, and then into the ends of every other rafter tail or the subfascia board. With the strap hanger, the gutter must be installed before the roofing; this is a good reason to avoid strap hangers entirely. Otherwise, with asphalt roofing, you can fill in the starter course after the shingling is complete and the gutters are

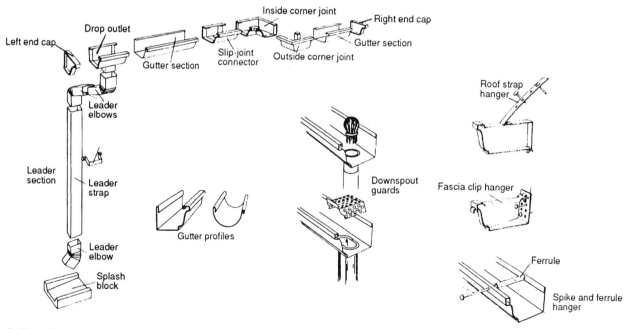

9-62 *To prevent the gutter from buckling, use a helper or two to lift a long section onto its mounting brackets.*

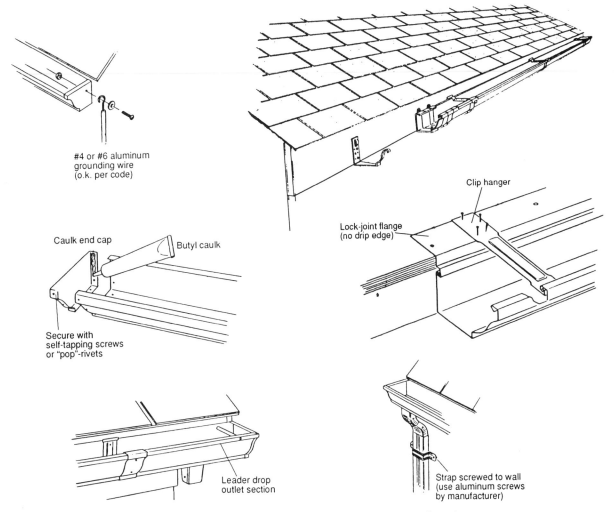

9-63 *Modern gutter systems are made from anodized aluminum that never needs painting or from UV-resistant plastics—in both round and rectangular profiles.*

installed or, for straight runs, with no inside or outside corners, hang the gutter and then dismount it while you install the roofing—and remount it when everything is done and you're ready to take down the staging.

With the other two systems, you can attach the gutter directly to the fascia trim after the roofing is complete.

Depending on whether the top edge of the gutter will slip beneath the bottom lip of the drip edge (special extra-wide drip edge flashing is included with some gutter systems for this purpose) or lie against the fascia, snap a chalk line (or stretch a string) at the desired pitch across the fascia to align the top (or bottom) edge of the gutter.

Assemble the entire length of the gutter run on the ground, and then position it on the previously installed fascia brackets (see **9-63**). For spike-and-ferrule mounting, tack the gutter to the pitch line with nails until you can install the ferrules. Although the spike will penetrate the front lip of the gutter if you hold the ferrule behind it, it's better to drill the hole first to avoid any chance of buckling the metal.

Most gutter stock is assembled by slipping connectors over the ends of the pieces to be joined (refer to **9-63**). The joint is waterproofed with special caulking compounds supplied by the dealer. Although the connectors will hold by friction alone, it's a good idea to secure them with "pop" rivets or self-tapping screws (if you do use screws, they must be aluminum, not plated steel, to avoid corrosion). Inside and outside corner pieces, end caps, and downspout flanges are all joined the same way.

The crimped end of leader pipe and elbows should always run downwards into the smooth flange of the next piece. Use crimping pliers to add corrugations to the cut ends, as needed. Rivet the leader mounting straps to the pipe once it is secured to the wall.

269

Gutter and leader stock is easily cut with tin snips and a hacksaw or with a chop saw equipped with a fine-toothed carbide blade.

A roof drainage system is an integral part of the well-built house wherever rainfall is heavy and winters are mild. In snow country, they're usually more trouble than benefit. Ice-jammed gutters split apart or are torn from the fascia. They generate ice dams that invade the soffit and back up under the shingles. The downspouts burst apart at their seams. By springtime, when they are most needed, they're not in any shape to work. I'd put the money into a good foundation drain system instead. Or else I'd consider a system recently introduced as an alternative to gutters in snow country. Basically a grille that attaches to the fascia, it doesn't collect roof runoff water, but, rather, breaks it up into tiny droplets that drizzle gently and harmlessly to the ground. Since ice can't build up on the open grille, there are no ice dams or ruined gutters.

10 Access

Stagings, Scaffolds, and Safety

One important aspect of framing and roofing which has only been mentioned in passing in previous chapters is how to reach and work safely on heights (see **10-1**). Many would-be owner–builders discover that it's a lot easier to draw a high wall or a steep roof than it is to build one. If you're afraid of heights, don't build a high house. Build a house with eaves you can reach from a stepladder or from planks resting on sawhorses and with a roof that has a slope that you can walk on. Or else hire someone to scale the heights for you.

The type of staging (also called scaffolding) to use and whether it can be built on-site or should be rented depends on how high it will be and how many workers and how much building materials it will carry. Convenience, that is, how long it takes to set up and dismantle relative to how long it will be used, and whether it can be used for more than one type of operation without major reconfiguration should also not be overlooked.

RENTED SCAFFOLDING

In most parts of the country, pipe scaffolding is so readily available and inexpensive to rent that it doesn't pay to build your own scaffolding (see **10-2**). The pairs of panel-like sections joined with X-braces can be assembled into strong and stable scaffolding up to 30 feet high. They can be interlocked horizontally to span the entire length of the building or set up as units that can be picked up and carried around the perimeter or floor deck to follow the work.

10-1 *The peak of a gable wall can be 30 or more feet above grade, which is beyond the reach of most extension ladders. Arranging safe access to high places is one of the skills that comes with experience.*

The panel frames range in width from two feet to five feet and in height from three feet to 10 feet. Depending on the corresponding length of the cross braces, they can be set up to form units five feet to 10 feet long. Ladder frames, which provide both intermediate staging settings and built-in ladders, are more versatile than shallow-truss frames. Rubber-tired casters can be rented to make rolling scaffolds for working on high ceilings. Since rolling scaffolds are more easily tipped over than stationary ones, the height of the platform should not be more than four times the smallest base dimension.

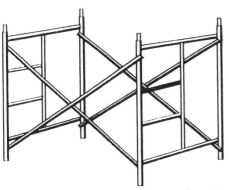

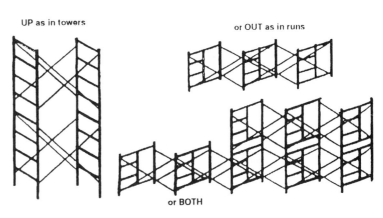

UP as in towers

or OUT as in runs

or BOTH

10-2 *Pipe scaffolding setup and options.*

10-3 *With only minor repositioning, this setup can be used for shingling, soffit construction, installing the upper-storey windows, and sheathing and siding the walls. Note the diagonal braces which stiffen the jack posts.*

Never set the bottom of the panels directly on the ground. Instead, place a scrap of 2×10 planking under each leg. The panels should be eyeball level in both directions. Cross braces that won't attach easily are a symptom of skewed panels. If anything, the staging should lean slightly towards the building and never away from it. On uneven ground, use additional blocking to level up the panels. If possible, rent adjustable jack-screw type extension legs to level out big differences. As an added safety precaution, tie tall scaffolding back to the building with form wire or rope. Use guard rail supports and toeboard clamps (rented separately) as required by code or common sense.

Although single planks are more easily maneuvered, two 2×10 or 2×12 planks laid across the uprights and tacked together at their midspan with a plywood scrap will provide a stronger and more stable working platform. Experienced carpenters know that their lives can depend on a single piece of wood. They're especially careful about using only good planks for staging.

The ends of the planks should overlap the staging panels by about six inches and each other by at least one foot. Nail cleats to the underside of the planks or bend nails around the pipe frame to keep them from sliding sideways, especially where frost can make the metal dangerously slippery. Tack overlapped ends together. When using pipe scaffolding for masonry or roofing, a wider and stronger platform made from ½-inch or ¾-inch CDX plywood tacked to three or four 2×12 staging planks can hold heavy materials and provide a more convenient work area.

Although it is much easier to set up and disassemble than site-built staging, anything more than a couple of sections of pipe scaffolding takes so long to erect that you won't want to move it anytime soon. This is why most builders only rent or own a few sections for roof framing, chimney building, and other relatively limited operations.

Pump jack scaffolding is a lot more versatile (see **10-3**). Pump jacks resemble an automobile bumper jack. They are designed with a cam-action foot pedal that forces them against the jack post and raises them when "pumped" up. A pump jack in good working order will support more than a ton without slipping. The jacks slide up and down on posts made of straight-grained knot-free 2×4s lapped at least four feet and spiked together into poles anywhere from 16 feet up to 30 feet long (see **10-4**). To set up a pump jack scaffolding, slip the anchor brace over the top of the pole and tilt it up against the building. Hold it eyeball plumb and drive a 16d or two 8d nails through the anchor brace flanges into the adjacent building structure and bend them over. Space the pump jacks about eight to ten feet apart and lay doubled 2×12 stagings over them.

Raise the staging by lifting up on the foot pedal and alternating from jack to jack, or have assistants operate each jack to raise the staging evenly. Brace the bottoms of the poles to the building with perpendicular and diagonal two-bys. When the staging rises higher than 10 feet, nail 2×4 cross bracing between the poles.

Tilting up or taking down a 24-foot-long pump jack pole requires balance and strength (see **10-4**). When raising or lowering poles, remember that the anchor brace can swing freely and cause damage if you get careless or loose control.

Since pump jacks can be raised or lowered to any position along their poles, they are ideal for sites too uneven

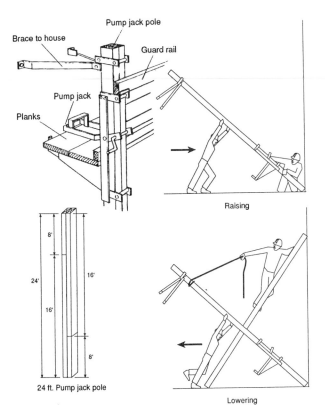

10-4 *Pump jack scaffolding.*

10-5 *A pump jack staging is used to lift a heavy window unit up to its third-floor opening.*

for regular scaffolding. Another advantage of pump jacks is that they can be used for several different tasks throughout the course of the job. A window too heavy or awkward to safely carry up a ladder or slide out a rough opening unassisted can simply ride the pump jack staging up from ground level (see 10-5). Finally, the stagings are raised or lowered according to the needs of trim board and finish siding installation and painting.

Although pump jacks can be rented, their long-term rental is much higher than that of pipe scaffolding. Unless you only need them for a day or two, it's cheaper to buy two pairs than to rent them. As an alternative, and since they can be quickly repositioned and also moved from one site to another, steel brackets that nail to the walls are used by carpenters to support stagings. So long as they're secured with four 16d or 20d nails driven directly into the studs, these are probably safe enough for light low-level work. A more secure bracket, which should always be used on high walls, bolts through a hole drilled in the sheathing and anchors against a piece of blocking over two studs (see 10-6). Both of these can be rented.

These wall-mounted brackets shouldn't be confused with *ladder jacks*, which are used to support simple single-plank scaffolds for quick repair jobs and painting (see 10-7). The brackets have braces that hook over the top rung to support a plank between two ladders at the same height.

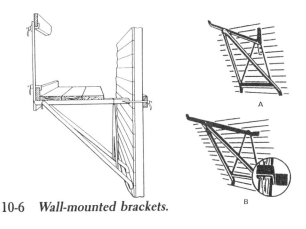

10-6 *Wall-mounted brackets.*

10-7 *Ladder jack stagings.*

273

10-8 *Such substandard staging is more often the rule than the exception with light-duty noncommercial work or owner-building, where staging safety is often a trade-off between common sense and expediency.*

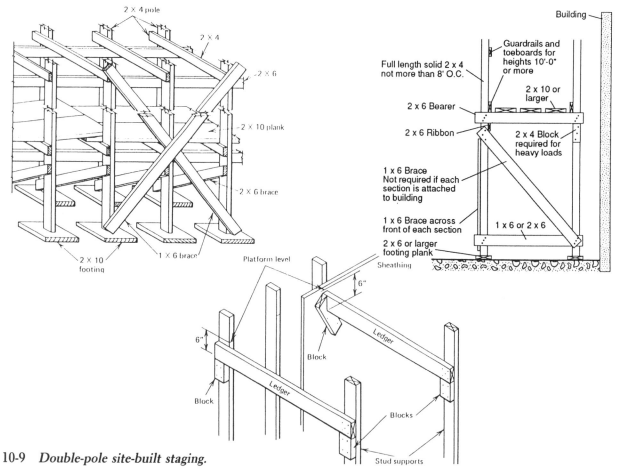

2 × 4 pole

2 × 4

2 × 6

2 × 10 plank

2 × 6 brace

2 × 10 footing

1 × 6 brace

Building

Guardrails and toeboards for heights 10'-0" or more

Full length solid 2 x 4 not more than 8' O.C.

2 x 6 Bearer

2 x 10 or larger

2 x 6 Ribbon

2 x 4 Block required for heavy loads

1 x 6 Brace Not required if each section is attached to building

1 x 6 Brace across front of each section

2 x 6 or larger footing plank

1 x 6 or 2 x 6

Platform level

Sheathing

6"

6"

Ledger

Block

Ledger

Block

Blocks

Stud supports

10-9 *Double-pole site-built staging.*

274

10-10 *This solidly built single-post scaffold can easily shoulder the fairly heavy loads typical of roof shingling.*

SITE-BUILT STAGING

If, for some reason, you must build your own scaffolding, there are three basic options. These are oversized sawhorses, single- and double-pole scaffolds, and outrigger stagings (see **10-8**).

Planks spanning 30-inch-high sawhorses may be all you need to work on a low wall. Custom-built sawhorses up to six feet high with supports at regular intervals make a stable stepladder-like support for staging planks.

The double-pole scaffold will hold the most weight, but it's also the most trouble to build, since it must be rigidly braced to keep from toppling sideways (see **10-9**).

Because single-post scaffolding is attached to the building, it doesn't require much diagonal bracing (see **10-10**). Since it is easier to set up on uneven ground than pipe staging, this system would be a good choice with clay tile or other roofing materials that might be too heavy for pump jacks (see **10-11**).

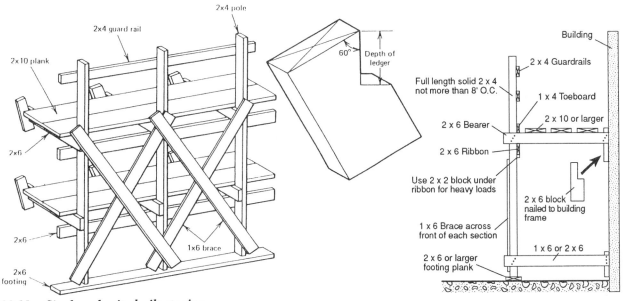

10-11 *Single-pole site-built staging.*

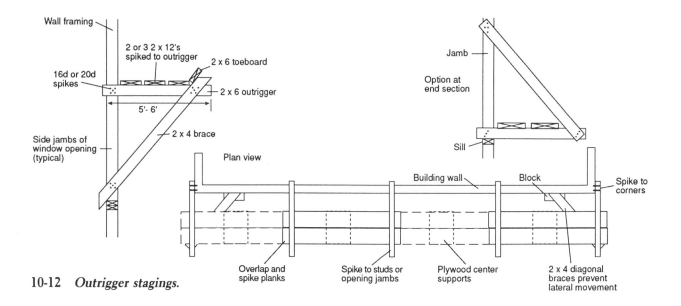

10-12 *Outrigger stagings.*

Labels (figure 10-12): Wall framing; 2 or 3 2 x 12's spiked to outrigger; 2 x 6 toeboard; 16d or 20d spikes; 2 x 6 outrigger; 5'-6'; Side jambs of window opening (typical); 2 x 4 brace; Jamb; Option at end section; Sill; Plan view; Building wall; Block; Spike to corners; Overlap and spike planks; Spike to studs or opening jambs; Plywood center supports; 2 x 4 diagonal braces prevent lateral movement

Outrigger stagings are strong and easily built (see **10-12**). But because there's no simple way to build a safety railing into them, many builders prudently choose not to use them even where there may not be proscribed. And yet, because an outrigger staging can be four or more feet wide, there's plenty of room between you and the back edge. The inside end of the horizontal 2×6 outriggers, or "bearers," to which the staging planks are (always) nailed, are themselves spiked to the sides of the wall studs with four 16d or 20d nails. The 2×4 or 2×6 diagonal braces which support them are also nailed equally firmly to each other. Extending the end of the brace allows a toeboard to be tacked to it for safety. Each outrigger should also be diagonally braced back to the wall in the plane of the staging planks to keep the assembly from twisting sideways.

Outrigger stagings are most often used with unsheathed walls where the exposed studs offer a multitude of convenient attachment points. They can also be used with sheathed walls by nailing them to the jamb studs of window rough openings and to the sides walls at the building corners (see **10-13** and **10-14**). The outriggers can also be hung from diagonal braces nailed above, instead of beneath, the staging, particularly when working over existing sheathing.

10-13 *Note the diagonal brace that ties the left end of the staging to the window rough opening. This is needed to prevent lateral movement of the staging, which could otherwise pry the outrigger nails from the wall.*

10-14 *The view from inside the outrigger staging shows the double-headed spikes used to fasten the outriggers to the window jack studs.*

276

10-15 *It's actually quite easy and not at all unsafe to ride a jack up or down the pole without a staging plank if you ever have to; but exercise caution in any unconventional maneuver.*

As an owner-builder and not an employer, you won't be subject to OSHA safety inspections. But, for your own safety, you should still follow design specifications for staging as listed in your local or state building codes. Nevertheless, it's more often the more experienced worker who gets hurt due to overconfidence and a lapse in attention rather than the cautious beginner (see **10-15**).

LADDER LORE
A high-quality extension ladder is an indispensable tool for building any house more than one storey high. Like pump jacks, the most difficult part of working with ladders is setting them up and taking them down (see **10-16**). If you are working by yourself, set the bottom of the ladder against the building (or something equally immovable) and push the ladder upwards with your hands over your head as you walk forward. As with raising a pump jack pole, it's a lot easier if you have a helper "foot" the ladder for you. Once you've got the ladder standing straight up, braced against your chest and shoulder, it will balance quite easily. As long as you keep it upright, you can move it about, even if fully extended. Ladders should also be footed when they are lowered.

There are at least six basic rules for ladder safety:

- First, the base of the ladder should be set at a distance from the wall equal to a one-quarter of its height, which works out to about a 60-degree angle, and when used to reach the edge of a roof, the ladder should extend above it about three feet.

- Second, don't extend the ladder more than 80 percent of its total length; at least three rungs should always overlap.

- Third, when working from a ladder, don't reach out too far to the side. This is especially true of aluminum ladders, which will slide quite easily against a metal drip edge. If you need to reach sideways, either at the edge

of a roof or against a wall, or to straddle a narrow window, use a ladder stabilizer bracket to keep it from sliding sideways and/or to hold it away from the gutter.

- Fourth, always keep one hand on the ladder rail as you climb the ladder.

- Fifth, if you're using the ladder on smooth surfaces such as trowel-finished concrete, make sure it has rubber safety shoes to keep it from sliding.

- Sixth, don't use metal ladders where they could contact a power line or when working with electricity; use nonconductive wood or fibreglass. You don't have to make actual contact to get electrocuted. If you can't avoid working near a power line, maintain a six-foot-minimum clearance at all times.

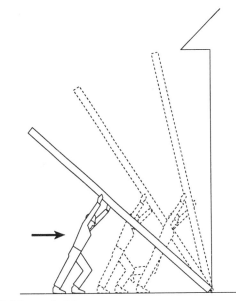

10-16 *Raising a ladder.*

277

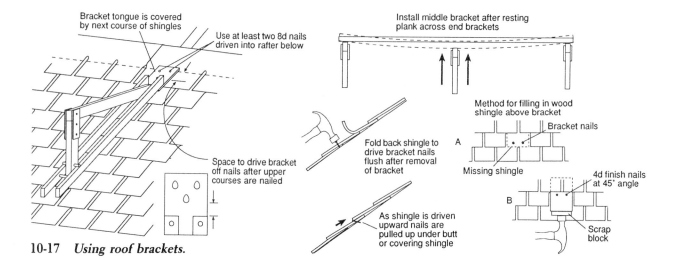

10-17 *Using roof brackets.*

Labels in figure:
Bracket tongue is covered by next course of shingles
Use at least two 8d nails driven into rafter below
Space to drive bracket off nails after upper courses are nailed
Install middle bracket after resting plank across end brackets
Method for filling in wood shingle above bracket
Bracket nails
A
Missing shingle
4d finish nails at 45° angle
B
Scrap block
Fold back shingle to drive bracket nails flush after removal of bracket
As shingle is driven upward nails are pulled up under butt or covering shingle

For stepladders, the basic rules are:

- First, don't set foot on the ladder without checking to make sure that the braces between the legs are fully extended.

- Second, never use the top two rungs of the ladder as steps.

- Third, make sure the ladder is firmly and levelly footed.

- And finally, don't use the top step for a tool rest; use the foldout shelf instead.

ROOF STAGING

With asphalt roofing, the uppermost limit of a roof slope that can safely be negotiated without some means of staging is somewhere between 5-in-12 and 6-in-12. This helps to explain some of the appeal of the 4-in-12 roof pitch to commercial builders and roofers.

Laying the starter course and the first few courses at the eaves is always the slowest and most difficult part of shingling. If you're working alone, shingling the eaves from a ladder may take less time than setting up a pipe scaffold or pump jacks by yourself.

Once the shingle courses are run up as high as you can comfortably reach, you're ready to install the roofing

10-18 *Some of the brackets that were used for shingling are left in place for building the chimney above the roof. Note the pump jacks used for applying the clapboards.*

278

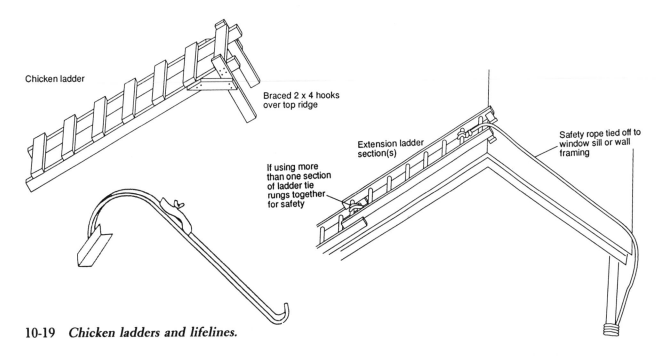

Chicken ladder

Braced 2 x 4 hooks over top ridge

Extension ladder section(s)

If using more than one section of ladder tie rungs together for safety

Safety rope tied off to window sill or wall framing

10-19 *Chicken ladders and lifelines.*

brackets (or *roof jacks*) that will support 2×10 staging planks (see **10-17**). Roof brackets are made from steel or hardwood and are adjustable to make a level staging at standard roof pitches (see **10-18**). They are nailed directly above the cutouts so that the nail holes will be covered by the shingles of the next course.

Set the first course of brackets so that you can safely and comfortably step from the ladder onto the staging plank. Although some roofers use two brackets spaced about 10 feet apart to carry a 12-foot plank, the center of the plank tends to sag enough under load that it can damage the mineral coating on the shingles it rubs against. Use three brackets, spaced one foot in from the ends and one in the middle of 14-foot or 16-foot planks. Don't install the middle bracket until after the plank is resting across the end brackets. Bridge the spans between stagings with shorter planks tacked to the others. Secure the nails to the deck with 8d common nails (not skinny box nails), one in each of its three mounting holes. Make sure that

at least one nail of each bracket catches solidly into a rafter and not just the sheathing. Properly nailed brackets will easily support your weight and the weight of at least a square of shingles distributed across the length of the staging plank. Ideally, you'd have enough brackets on hand to set up enough staging to shingle the entire roof deck without having to reposition any. At six brackets per staging course and three or four courses, this can mean 18 to 24 brackets. A dozen is the bare minimum needed for shingling half the roof at a time. The same staging brackets are also used for wood shingle and wood shake installation.

As mentioned, brackets can't be used with steel or tile roofing. Fortunately, you can walk safely on the battens at slopes up to 12-in-12. Site-built "chicken ladders" that hook over the ridge are also handy and more trustworthy than a ladder hook (see **10-19**). On steep roofs or any metal roof that's wet, it's always a good idea to tie a lifeline rope around your waist, and secure it to something solid on the other side of the building.

11 Exterior Trim and Siding

The cornice, which is the proper architectural term for the projection of the roof at the eaves and rake, has been given elaborate ornamental treatment since classical antiquity (see **11-1**). Even when stripped of its traditional grandeur, the modern cornice is still the most prominent decorative element of the facade. The cornice overhang also diverts runoff water away from the house walls and foundation. The shading afforded by the cornice is also one of the main ways to control excessive solar heat gain; its sizing is an important part of solar design.

CORNICE CONSTRUCTION DETAILS

Cornice construction is considered here as part of the exterior trim work. In the actual order of building, the structural underpinnings for the cornice are an element of the roof frame, and one of its finished components, the fascia trim, is best installed before the roofing itself, well in advance of any other exterior trim.

Cornices are either open, closed, or boxed (see **11-2** and **11-3**). Open cornices are commonly associated with rustic, log cabin, Swiss-chalet, craftsman-style, or Japanese-influenced designs, especially when heavy timber rafters are featured.

An open cornice is a no-frills roof overhang (see **11-4**). Although it has no soffit or other trim, a fascia board is recommended to protect the exposed end grain of the rafter tails. Since the underside of the roof sheathing is visible, use finish-grade boards (such as 1×6 V-groove decking) instead of plywood to sheathe the eaves and rakes.

The solid blocking that would normally be nailed plumb between each rafter over the wall plate to keep out wind and animals makes it hard to install an intake for venting the attic. One solution is to drill two-inch holes through the blocking, before you install it, and fit them with pop-in louvres. Another solution is to divide the blocking into two pieces and staple a strip of screen or soffit vent between them.

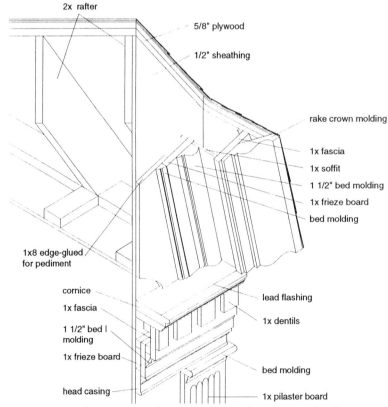

11-1 *In spite of its apparent complexity, even the most detailed cornice is built up from simple layers of boards and mouldings.*

11-2 *Since it requires no angled cuts, the square-cut, boxed cornice is the easiest to build.*

11-3 *This boxed cornice is combined with a clipped-rake fascia for a simple traditional profile.*

The treatment of the transition between the wall siding and the blocking is also a matter of some concern. Even when neatly cut, notching the siding to fit around the rafter tails looks ungainly. Covering the transition with a horizontal band of trim makes a clean break.

Besides the problems with ventilation and closure, the open cornice roof overhang provides a sheltered homesite for birds, wasps, spiders, etc. Closing in the cornice with a soffit board discourages colonization by any of these potential pests to a large extent.

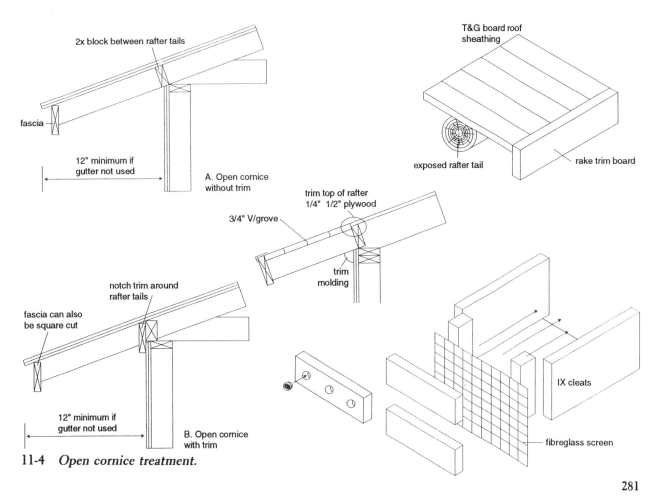

2x block between rafter tails

fascia

12" minimum if gutter not used

A. Open cornice without trim

T&G board roof sheathing

exposed rafter tail

rake trim board

trim top of rafter 1/4" 1/2" plywood

3/4" V/grove

trim molding

notch trim around rafter tails

fascia can also be square cut

12" minimum if gutter not used

B. Open cornice with trim

IX cleats

fibreglass screen

11-4 *Open cornice treatment.*

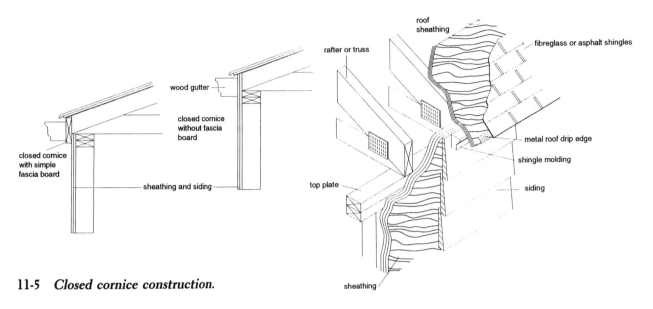

11-5 *Closed cornice construction.*

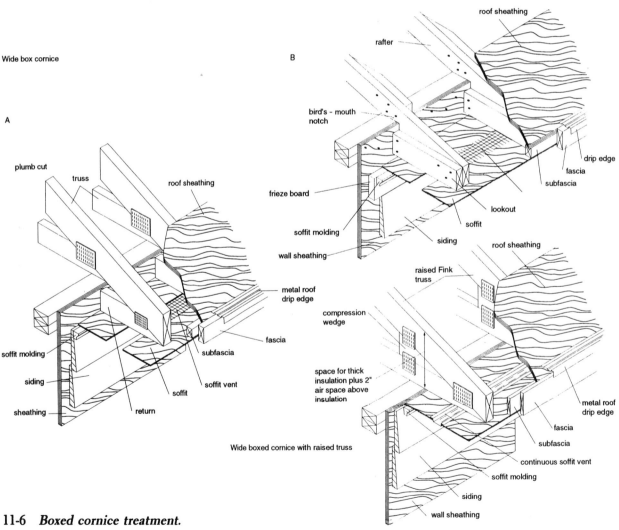

11-6 *Boxed cornice treatment.*

Because it doesn't protect the walls against roof runoff, the closed cornice is (or was) most often used with built-in wood gutters (see **11-5**). In its most severe form, the traditional closed cornice consisted of flat trim board (called the *frieze* or *plancher* board) nailed directly over the ends of the rafters, which were cut flush with the wall. It was sometimes given a slight projection by extending the bottom of the roof sheathing and covering the edge with an ornamental moulding or a flat board bevelled on both edges. Since they make no provision for the installation of soffit venting, these forms of the closed cornice aren't recommended for modern construction except where rigid foam insulation has been applied on top of the roof deck over a cathedral ceiling.

To provide better protection for the walls without a great deal of extra framing and to allow for soffit venting, the closed cornice can be extended into a narrow boxed cornice by cutting the rafter tails level and attaching the soffit to them (see **11-6**). Modern soffits are built in two pieces to accommodate a continuous two-inch-wide soffit vent louvre (see **11-7**).

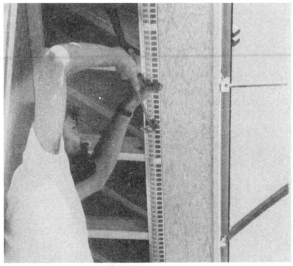

11-7 *Preformed aluminum soffit vents can be spray-painted or are available with a plain, white, or brown enamelled finish.*

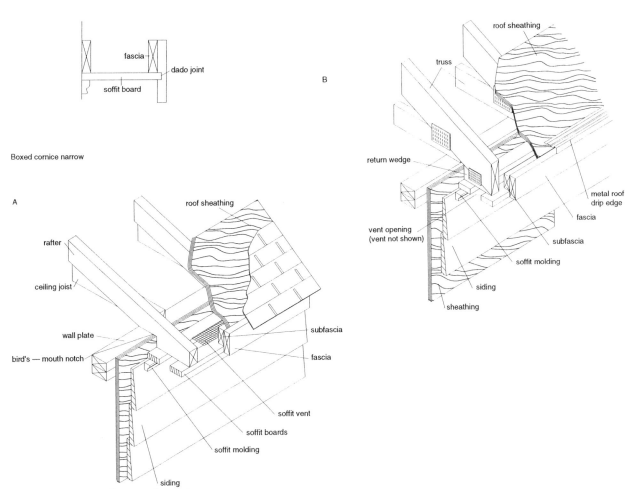

11-6 *(Continued) Boxed cornice treatment.*

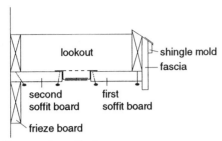

11-8 *Soffit vent installation.*

Install the first soffit board against the back of the fascia board (see **11-8**). Some consider it a sign of good construction to cut a *dado* (shallow groove) in the back of the fascia board to receive the edge of the soffit; but the extra support isn't needed when a subfascia is used. Don't nail the inside edge of the board until after you've slipped the flange of the soffit vent up under it. Then fit the second soffit board into place between the louvre and the wall. Check to see that each soffit vent strip is facing the same way. Overlap the ends of each section about ¼″ over a rafter tail or other solid support.

Because it provides more flexibility in width and architectural detailing, the wide, boxed cornice is the most widely used type of cornice construction (see **11-9**). Two-by-four lookouts are nailed between the subfascia and a ledger attached to the building wall. Level across from the bottom of the rafter tails and snap a line along the sheathing. Nail the 2×4 ledger into each stud. Toenail the lookouts into the ledger. The bottom chord of a truss rafter can also double as a cornice lookout.

Since the amount of protection offered by the rake is minimal, the clipped rake, which was a prominent detail of early colonial style, can be used with any type of cornice

construction (see **11-10**). Here, instead of a false rafter, a subfascia is nailed over the sheathing following the gable rafter. This is covered with a slightly wider fascia to hide and weatherproof the top edge of the siding. The subfascia can also be *rabbeted* (notched along an edge, as opposed to dadoed) to overlap the siding or frieze board.

Soffit installation usually begins at the rake (see **11-11**). Where the false rafter is hung from the sheathing, snap a chalk line equal to the width of the false rafter along the top edge of the gable wall. Nail a 2×4 or 2×2 cleat to the line to make a nailer for the inside edge of the rake soffit board. The outside edge is nailed to the false rafter. If the rake is constructed with lookouts instead, no wall cleat is needed.

Many builders use ⅜-inch exterior AC plywood for soffit stock. This is an economical material when the trim work will be painted (not stained), especially for wide soffits. In my opinion, however, the utilitarian look of a plywood soffit is at odds with the concept of the cornice as a piece of decorative finish work. In any case, use only good-quality kiln- (or air-) dried wood for cornice construction.

Start the installation at the peak. Mitre the ends of the soffit boards to match the angle of the roof. To make a tight joint that won't open up even after it shrinks, use 45-degree mitre cuts instead of butt joints between sections of soffit (and fascia) boards (see **11-12**). In a boxed cornice, the bottom end of the rake soffit is left over-long, since it will be covered by the trim at the cornice *return* (see **11-13**). Insert a prybar between the inside edge of the soffit board and the wall to close up any gaps between the outside edge of the soffit board and the back of the fascia board.

Depending on the design of the cornice, the junction of the rake and the eaves overhang can be the most difficult

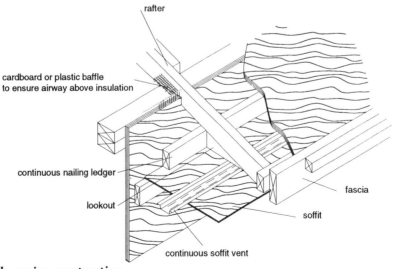

11-9 *Wide, boxed cornice construction.*

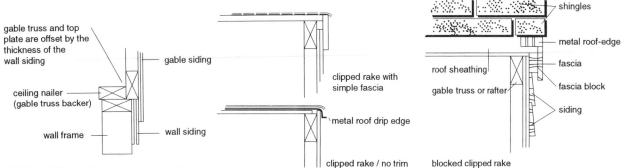

11-10   *Clipped rake construction.*

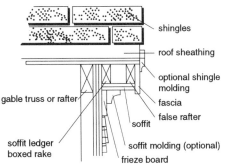

11-11   *Rake soffit nailing support.*

part to build. This cornice return, or *rebate*, has traditionally been the locus of the most lavish elaboration. The simplest way to form a cornice return is to use a clipped rake with a plumb-cut eaves fascia. The eaves fascia turns a simple mitre corner and follows the lookout back onto the house wall. The rake fascia runs into the return. The triangular space in between both trim boards is filled in by extending the subfascia.

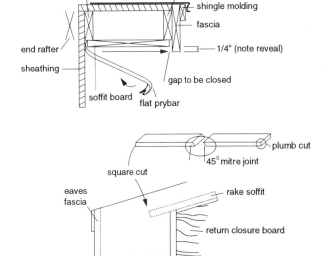

11-12   *Soffit board installation.*

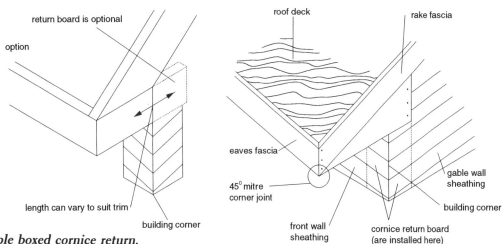

11-13   *Simple boxed cornice return.*

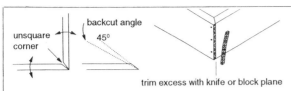

11-14 *Backcutting a mitre joint.*

When making mitre joints between the rake and eaves fascia board, backcut the heel of the 45-degree cut slightly with a sharp utility knife or block plane to make a tight fit (see **11-14**). If the joint doesn't meet perfectly, use the same tools to trim off the projecting edge. The end grain will be invisible from the ground. Protect it from exposure by rubbing paintable caulking into it.

When the rake projects beyond the gable walls, the return is a bit more complicated (see **11-15**). First, frame in the bottom of the return with 2×4 by adding a lookout to the false rafter and extending the lookout ledger out beyond the wall. Next, run the rake soffit down past the end of the wall. Then add a vertical corner support between the return corner and the underside of the rake soffit. Cut a closure board, and nail it to the back of the return. Then fill in the triangular area under the rake fascia with a piece of trim stock scribed to match the roof pitch. Since the grain of this board should be oriented level and not parallel to the run of the rake, rest a template against the bottom edge of the rake fascia when scribing the eaves soffit and closure lines. Add ¼ inch to the scribe marks to make a *reveal*—a slight overhang, usually ¼ inch to ½ inch—between the end of the fascia board and the face of the soffit board.

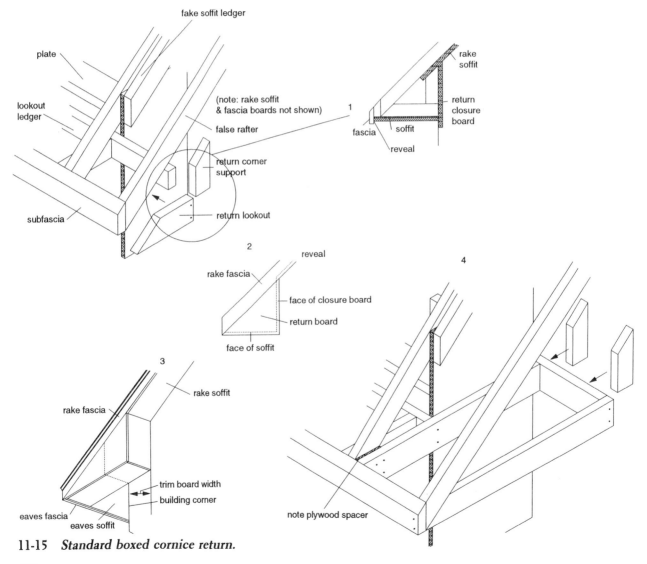

11-15 *Standard boxed cornice return.*

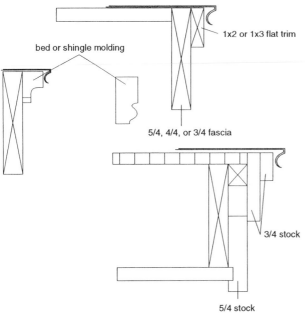

bed or shingle molding

1x2 or 1x3 flat trim

5/4, 4/4, or 3/4 fascia

3/4 stock

5/4 stock

11-16 *Some cornice detail options.*

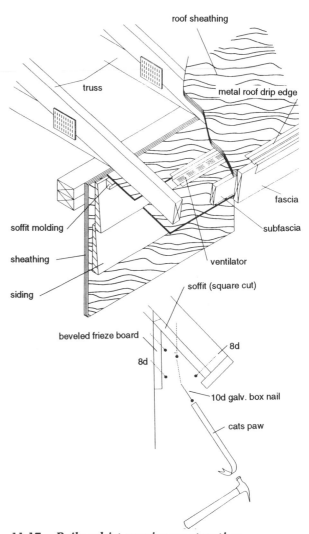

roof sheathing

truss

metal roof drip edge

fascia

subfascia

soffit molding

sheathing

ventilator

siding

soffit (square cut)

beveled frieze board

8d

8d

10d galv. box nail

cats paw

11-17 *Railroad jet cornice construction.*

Cornice returns can be as complicated and decorative as your fancy and budget permit. They can faithfully duplicate the layered mouldings of traditional pedimented neoclassical and colonial cornices or simply echo them with pared-down flat band mouldings which are a lot easier to cut and fit (see **11-16**). A simple way to add proportion and depth to a cornice is to run a strip of 1×2 or 1×3 over the top edge of the fascia board; this is done before the drip edge is installed. The frieze board is another traditional trim element nailed to the wall beneath the soffit.

Most of the difficulties with cornice return treatment arise from the meeting of the pitched rake soffit with the horizontal eaves soffit. The so-called *railroad jet* ("jet" is a regional term for overhang), which can be thought of as a closed-in open cornice, solves the problem by eliminating it (see **11-17**). The eaves soffit is fastened directly to the underside of the rafter tails so that it can simply turn the corner and run up the rake without changing planes.

Because the soffit board of the railroad jet follows the rafter tails, the installation becomes more awkward as the pitch of the roof increases and the space between the soffit and the wall narrows. To avoid marking the finish wood, drive the nails at a steep angle with a nail set (see **11-18**). Bevel the lower edge of the soffit board to fit snugly against the back of a plumb-cut fascia.

Cornice trim is often painted or stained, even when the siding on the house itself isn't. To save labor and make a neat job, all cornice trim stock, including the fascia boards, should be stained or painted entirely, prior to installation. Apply a touch-up coat afterwards.

11-18 *This closeup of a railroad jet soffit shows how tight the nailing can be.*

11-19 *The exterior walls reveal the character of the home owners.*

FINISH SIDING AND EXTERIOR TRIM WORK

The exterior walls of a house are at once both structural and decorative. The lattice of frame and sheathing, of course, hold the house together; but, more than this, the walls are the face the house shows to the world (see **11-19**). Which of the many possible siding materials you choose for your house, like roofing, depends on more than such simple considerations as cost and convenience.

Siding materials can be grouped into five general categories: board sidings, plywood panels, wood shingles, mineral sidings (such as stucco and fibre-cement siding), and manufactured sidings (such as hardboard, aluminum,

and vinyl). Of these, board, wood shingle, and stucco sidings have been in continuous use since the earliest settlements.

Back when houses were sheathed with boards rather than plywood, building paper was stapled over the sheathing to keep out the wind. This was either the pink rosin-coated paper or 15-pound asphalt-saturated tar paper. (Heavier coated felts and waterproof papers were not used since they would create an unwanted vapor barrier on the outside wall.) Plywood, rigid foam, and fibreboard sheathing make such a tight building membrane that no underlayment paper is needed (see **11-20**). A spun plastic membrane such as Tyvek that is permeable to water vapor but

11-20 *Underlayment paper is not really needed for siding over panel-type sheathings. Taping the joints between the sheets blocks air infiltration. The windows have been sealed with caulking so that tar paper flashing strips aren't needed either. Nevertheless, you must follow your building code, even if it doesn't reflect these changes in materials and practices.*

impervious to moisture and wind is recommended for energy-conscious construction. I might use it instead of tar or rosin paper when underlayment is required by code, but I'm not convinced that it is needed over panel sheathing. An exception is with vertical board siding, where the joints between boards are only incidentally watertight. Underlayment is also required behind stucco finishes since cement plaster will wick moisture out of the air.

The kind of siding you choose determines whether or not the exterior trim must be completed prior to or after siding installation. The edges of wood shingles and clapboards, for example, butt against trim boards at the corners of the building and at windows and doors. With other forms of board siding and plywood siding, the window and door trim and corner boards are applied over the siding. With some variations, the siding itself forms a corner or joints are covered with special manufactured flashings or joining pieces. In many styles of building, the corner trim and a frieze board are also elements or extensions of the cornice treatment.

BOARD SIDINGS

Although the spectrum of choice has diminished somewhat over the past half-century, there are still many different types of board siding in use today, for both horizontal and vertical application. These can be classed according to their general profile as either bevel, rabbet, tongue-and-groove, or board-and-batten. Within each type, there are at least several varieties of pattern, some of which may be regional, or even local, products, unknown elsewhere.

CLAPBOARDS AND BEVEL SIDING

The original clapboard was simply a flat board nailed to the studs so that its bottom edge overlapped the top of the lower board (see 11-21). Later, they were riven, like shingles, from long bolts of straight-grained wood, which gave them their traditional wedge-shaped profile. With the introduction of power saws, it was possible to mass-produce them by sawing flat boards in half on an angle. The main difference between clapboards and bevel siding is thickness and width. Clapboards vary in width from four to six inches and are generally about 7/16 inch wide at the butt and, depending on regional variations, taper to an edge anywhere between nothing and 3/16 inch. Bevel siding ranges from eight to 12 inches in width and from 1/2" to 1/4" at the butt with a uniform taper to 3/16."

Depending on where you live, clapboards and bevel siding may be locally manufactured from naturally rot-resistant, stable, premium woods like cedar, redwood, or cypress, or common species like pine or spruce. As with all finish materials, grades and costs vary according to visible defects, edge- or face-grain sawing, and heartwood or sapwood exposure. *Extra clears* are free from any visible defects or knots on the exposed portion. *Second clears* contain occasional small tight knots. *Cottage grade* have

11-21 *Clapboard siding makes a durable, weathertight wall that's equally at home with contemporary and traditional lines.*

defects and unsound knots that must be sawed out, but are less costly. *Mechanics grade* are an economy grade, with lots of knots and often unsquare end cuts, with heartwood and sapwood mixed indiscriminately.

In general, the costly clear grades are used for painted finishes or where a sleek natural appearance is desired, while the less expensive, knottier grades are adequate for stained finishes or where a rustic appearance is not objectionable. Additionally, all bevel sidings and some clapboards are reversible, with the smooth-planed face intended for painting, and the rough-sawn side for a stained or natural finish (see 11-22).

11-22 *Second-clear grade unstained redwood siding is used on this contemporary interpretation of a classical French provincial farmhouse.*

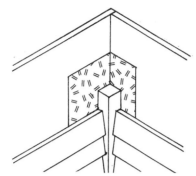

11-23 *Inside corner trim.*

The weather exposure of a clapboard depends on its width. A good rule of thumb is that the exposure should equal half the width plus ¼ inch. Because of its thicker profile, bevel siding only requires a minimal overlap (one inch for six-inch siding, one and a half inch for eight- to twelve-inch siding). To estimate the quantity of clapboards or bevel siding required for a given coverage, multiply the area by the width of the clapboard and divide by its exposure to find the lineal footage to order. Deduct the area of window and door openings, and add ten percent for waste.

INSTALLING CLAPBOARDS

The corner trim boards must be installed before the clapboards. There are any number of ways to treat the outside corners, depending on the appearance you want and the time you're willing to put into the job. The simplest approach is to butt the two boards together. Don't use the same-width boards for each side of the corner; instead, nail the next smaller-sized board to whatever width board you've chosen so that the assembled corner appears to be the same width on each side (e.g., use a 1×5 with 1×6 corners or a 1×3 with 1×4s). Corner boards can also be joined with a 45-degree mitre. This may be nearly invisible when first installed, but the joint eventually opens, looking more like a flaw than the simple butt joint. An elegant corner detail is achieved by butting corner boards against a quarter-round moulding.

The bottom end of the corner boards should extend about ½ inch below the bottom edge of the wall sheathing. Depending on the design of the cornice, butt the top of the corner board against the cornice return, the frieze board, or the soffit. In most cases, the rake-side corner board will be longer than the eaves-side corner board and will also have an angled cut. Cut this board first and tack it in place; then butt the other board to it, and drive a nail through their common edges. Remove the boards and nail the entire edge before installing it against the wall as a unit. Also before installing the corner board, fold a strip of tar paper around the corner for long-term waterproofing, since any caulking will ultimately fail.

The easiest way to trim an inside corner is to nail a 1×1 (or other appropriate size) into the corner and butt the siding to it (see **11-23**). Once again, fold underlayment into the corner first.

If a frieze board is part of your cornice design, it's usually nailed to the wall under the soffit between the corner boards at the eaves and against the cornice return closure board at the rakes. The bottom edge of the frieze can be rabbeted to cover the top of the last course of clapboards or wood shingles (you can also use a piece of shiplap siding with one edge cut off in lieu of cutting the rabbet).

It's important to use the right kind of nails for exterior trim work. At the very least, these should be hot-dipped, galvanized 8d box nails. Even galvanized nails will eventually stain unpainted wood; therefore, I recommend ring-shank, stainless-steel siding nails for all unpainted exterior trim and siding, even though they are more expensive. Don't use finish nails for outside trim; they have too little holding power to resist the movement caused by weather and temperature changes.

Windows and doors, of course, must be installed before the clapboards (see Chapter Twelve).

Both clapboards and bevel siding are installed with the aid of a storey pole (see **11-24**). Mark off an eight-foot piece of 1×2 in increments that equal the exposure of the siding courses. If your foundation and wall sheathing are level, you can assume that the bottom edges of the corner boards are level all the way around the house. If the floor frame had to be adjusted, shoot a transit line to establish level corners before running the corner boards. This should be done in any case where the house walls step up or down several changes of level.

Set the storey pole on the wall next to the corner trim board. Its bottom should be flush with the bottom of the trim board. Transfer the clapboard spacing marks onto the

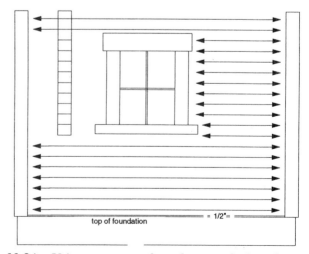

11-24 *Using a storey pole to lay out clapboard spacings.*

wall sheathing. Repeat at the far corner. Snap chalk lines across the wall from corner to corner. Where windows and doors interfere with the run of the lines, set the storey pole on the last continuous line next to the obstruction and mark spacings on both sides of the window or door.

Nail a cant strip cut from the top half of a dirty or damaged clapboard to the bottom edge of the wall so that the first clapboard will have the correct slant (see 11-25). Cut a 1×4 spacer block equal to the exposure of two courses. Hold the top edge of the spacer block on the chalk line, marking the butt of the third course. The bottom of the spacer block lines up with the butt of the first course. Unlike bevel siding, the feather-thin top edges of clapboards are too uneven to use for layout purposes, which is why the exposure is gauged from the butt instead.

An alternative method is to install the first two courses to a level line and then space the following courses with a jig as shown in 11-26. The cleat hooks under the butt of the previously nailed course, and the next course rests on top of it. The length of the jig can also mark the nailing spacing. Since this method trades off the accuracy of chalk lines for speed, check the courses for level at frequent intervals.

Both clapboard and bevel siding can also be installed from the top of the wall down. This works especially well for high walls where the staging can be removed from the wall as the sections above it are finished. In this case, the exposure lines for the bevel siding would mark the butts instead of the top edge, just like clapboards. No jigs are needed to lay the siding to the chalk lines. Nail the topmost course through its upper portion only so that you can slip the next course up under its butt. Tack the succeeding

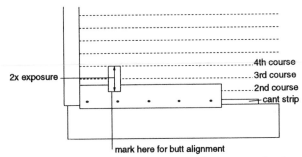

11-25 *A two-course spacer jig and a cant strip for clapboards.*

courses lightly along their butt edges. If you drive the nails home, you'll have trouble sliding the clapboards under the butts.

Clapboards are nailed about 12 inches apart, ¼ inch to ½ inch above the butt edge with 4d galvanized nails. Unlike bevel siding, whose end joints must be cut to break on a stud, the end joints of clapboards can be butted together wherever they happen to fall, so long as they are staggered at least three inches between courses. The ends of the clapboards as they come from the bundle may or may not be cut perfectly square or may be a bit rough. Since all butt joints are visible, saw them carefully.

Make a pattern piece to mark the long, angled cuts for fitting against the rake soffit or frieze board. Since a clapboard doesn't lie flat against the wall, add about ⅛ inch to the thick end of the cut and adjust it for fit with a sharp hand plane.

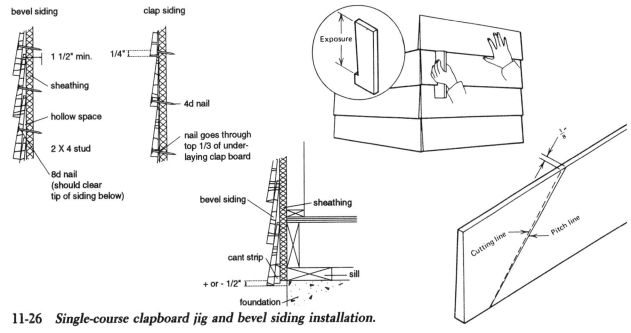

11-26 *Single-course clapboard jig and bevel siding installation.*

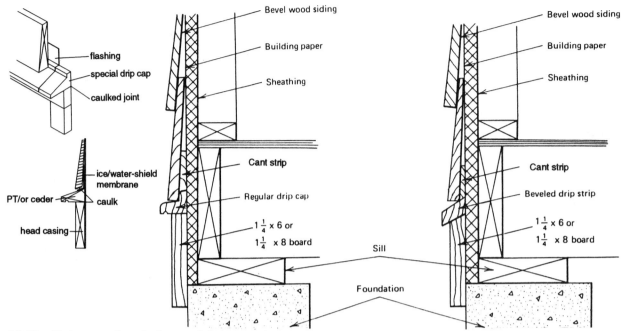

11-27 *Drip caps for window and door openings.*

The tops of window and door openings should always be protected by a wood drip cap moulding (see **11-27**). You can cut these from pressure-treated or naturally rot-resistant wood such as cedar or redwood. Use only high-grade "lifetime" caulk in the joint between the drip cap and the sheathing. Most experts recommend covering the drip cap with metal flashing. Since preformed metal flashing that matches the profile of the wood doesn't always lie flat over the edge of the drip cap, consider using a strip of adhesive water- and ice-shield membrane stuck to the drip cap just beyond the butt of the clapboard. Drip caps should be used above any window and door header that is more than a foot below the soffit board.

BOXBOARD SIDING

If there is a custom sawmill in your neighborhood, you might consider ordering "boxboard" siding. Although the finished appearance of these inexpensive rough-sawn ½-inch-thick boards, edged on only one side like waney-edged bevel siding, may be too "rustic" for a house, boxboard is a good choice for sheds, barns, or other outbuildings.

The boards will vary considerably in actual width. Sort them according to usable exposure. Snap chalk lines eight or 10 inches apart across the studs or insulating sheathing and lay the sawn, top edge of each board to the line (see **11-28**). Nail directly into the studs with 8d galvanized box

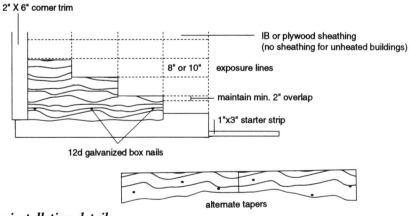

11-28 *Boxboard siding installation details.*

292

nails. Break joints over studs. Try to alternate tapers between courses to keep the exposure lines balanced, and select boards so that they are about the same width at their butt joints.

Because boxboarding is thicker than bevel siding, its bottom edge will stick out beyond the face of ordinary one-inch trim. Use 1¼-inch or 1½-inch-thick stock for corner boards and casings.

RABBETED AND TONGUE-AND-GROOVED SIDING

Rabbeted, wide-bevel siding is thicker than ordinary bevel siding. Its rabbeted edge lets the board lay flat against the sheathing, which not only reduces its apparent thickness by ¼ inch, but allows the use of an extra face nail without danger of splitting the board. The biggest advantage of rabbeted siding, whether bevelled or flat-faced, is that it is self-aligning, once you've installed the first course level. Minimum rabbet depth is usually ⅜ inch. Some custom patterns feature ½-inch rabbets. Tongue-and-groove siding (also called *planned-and-matched*) usually has a ¼-inch overlap. The other difference between the two patterns is that rabbeted siding is face-nailed with 8d galvanized box or stainless-steel siding nails, and tongue-and-groove (T&G) siding is blind-nailed, usually with 8d galvanized finish nails. Both types of boards are available in nominal widths from 1×4 up to 1×8.

One big "plus" of flat siding is that the corner boards and window/door casings can be installed afterwards, on top of the siding (see **11-29**). A drawback to this method is that you have to cut out the siding above the windows and doors to install the drip cap flashing beneath its bottom edge. You can't rely on caulk to seal a drip cap against the siding. One way around this would be to plumb and

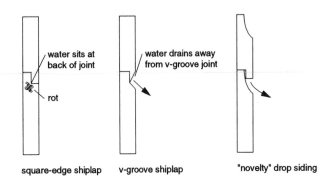

square-edge shiplap   v-groove shiplap   "novelty" drop siding

water sits at back of joint — rot

water drains away from v-groove joint

11-30 *The profile of horizontal board siding must shed water.*

level the window unit in its opening, tack it to the sheathing, scribe where the top edge of its head casing falls, remove the window, and install the drip cap and flashing above this line. Otherwise, set the drip edge over the top of the installed window, scribe a line about ¼ inch above its top edge, and saw through the siding with a circular saw set to depth. Finish the corner cuts with a sharp chisel and/or handsaw. You could also avoid the entire problem by butting and/or notching the siding to fit against the window trim as with bevelled sidings.

It's important that the profile of any board siding intended for horizontal application be shaped in so that it directs water away from the joint (see **11-30**). Standard square-edged rabbets tend to trap water against the back of their shelf-like edge. A V-groove profile or the scooped-out curve of "novelty" drop siding prevents this.

Regular clapboard and bevel siding not only takes a long time to install, but the wood itself is quite expensive. One way to emulate the look of a traditional clapboard siding while benefitting from the low cost and quick installation of rabbeted siding, is to lay standard rabbeted boards "clapboard-style" by dropping the lip of the upper board down past the edge of the lower board (see **11-31**). Like all rabbeted siding, this technique is self-aligning, but the corner board stock must be thicker. Custom-planed stock with a finished thickness of 1¼ inches looks better than the nominal two-inch (i.e., 1½-inch-thick) stock.

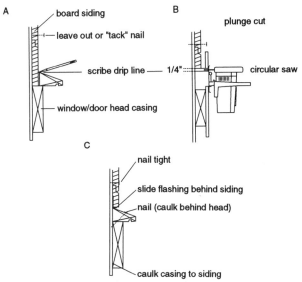

A — board siding — leave out or "tack" nail — scribe drip line — window/door head casing

B — plunge cut — 1/4" — circular saw

C — nail tight — slide flashing behind siding — nail (caulk behind head) — caulk casing to siding

11-29 *Fitting drip caps to siding boards.*

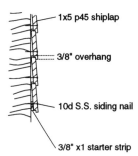

1x5 p45 shiplap — 3/8" overhang — 10d S.S. siding nail — 3/8" x1 starter strip

11-31 *Clapboard-style shiplap siding.*

11-32 *Vertical shiplapped board siding has a clean, contemporary look that can still go well with traditional lines.*

Both shiplap and T&G patterns can be installed vertically (see **11-32**). *Channel rustic* (also called board-and-gap) siding uses a ½-inch lap over a 1¼-inch channel to make a prominent ¾-inch-wide shadow line; it is one of the most common patterns. Like bevel siding, one face is rough-sawn and the other smooth-planed. Tongue-and-groove board can also be installed diagonally. Diagonal joints shed water well, while the boards also provide racking support, eliminating the need for let-in bracing.

Corner boards are optional with vertical siding. Many builders prefer to butt the rabbets together or trim them off and butt the full-thickness boards. It's also a fairly simple matter to notch and butt vertical siding against the sides of windows and doors. With rabbeted siding, it's easy to trim a tapered piece and recut a rabbet in the edge to fit an odd-width space if necessary.

Since plywood sheathing alone won't provide enough long-term nail-withdrawal resistance to keep the boards from eventually twisting off the wall with seasonal and daily temperature cycles, all vertically applied siding needs a solid nailing base beneath it (see **11-33**). The traditional approach was to nail horizontal 2×4 blocking flatwise between the studs, but nailing 1×3 strapping on two-inch centers over the sheathing on the outside of the wall is a much more efficient alternative, particularly with foil-faced, rigid-foam sheathing.

When rigid-foam insulating sheathing was first introduced, there was some concern that the aluminum-foil facing on the panels would cause condensation problems and paint failure or warping of the siding since it would act as an exterior vapor barrier, trapping moisture behind the finish siding. Some experts suggested ways to ensure sufficient ventilation. The current wisdom is that no particular ventilation strategy is necessary in most climates as long as the siding doesn't exceed an eight-inch width and is fastened with stainless-steel ring-shank nails that penetrate at least one inch into the studs (for clapboard-style shiplap, this requires 10d nails). Also, when the siding is to be painted, it must be primed on the back side to prevent unequal moisture absorption and related stresses. The vapor-barrier effect of the foil face appears to be nullified when it's punctured by the siding nails; but, for board sidings that lie flat against the sheathing, it's best to provide a ventilation channel by nailing vertical strapping over the studs. Because clapboard-style shiplap and standard bevel sidings already have built-in air channels behind them, strapping is unnecessary (see **11-34**). If you use plywood instead of nonstructural sheathing, the blocking or strapping for vertical boarding can be eliminated by fastening the siding with screws instead of nails. The screws should be long enough to penetrate at least ¼ inch beyond the inside face of the sheathing.

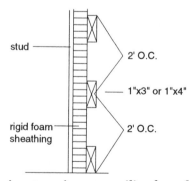

stud

2' O.C.

1"x3" or 1"x4"

rigid foam sheathing

2' O.C.

11-33 *Exterior strapping as a nailing base for vertical siding.*

BOARD-AND-BATTEN SIDING

Because you can use relatively inexpensive rough-sawn green boards, board-and-batten siding has long been used to cover sheds, barns, rustic houses, and cabins. When properly and carefully applied, board-and-batten siding is not only watertight and durable, but can also be quite elegant (see 11-35).

Basically, board-and-batten siding consists of square-edged boards applied vertically to the wall and the joints between them covered with another layer of boards (see 11-36). In the most common variant, wide boards are installed first and covered with narrow battens. Or, with the *reverse batten* system, the battens are installed first and overlaid with the boards to expose a narrow channel (this is also the effect mimicked by the previously mentioned channel rustic shiplapped boarding). In the *board-on-board* pattern, battens are replaced with boards of the same or varying widths. The finished appearance of the siding depends mainly on the quality of the material you use.

The main problem with board-and-batten siding is the tendency of the boards to split and check as they contract and expand in response to seasonal changes in humidity. If you place your order far enough in advance of construction, and store them under cover after delivery, your boards will be reasonably dry by the time you use them. Proper nailing techniques are more critical in preventing splitting and checking than moisture content, in any case. Furthermore, since the weather-tightness of board-and-batten siding depends mainly on the underlayment membrane and flashings, a few splits or knotholes won't seriously compromise the effectiveness of the siding. In addition to proper nailing, the best way to prevent cupping is to back-prime the boards with whatever finish you will use for the face side. If no finish is planned, then coat them with a water-repellent preservative instead.

11-35 *Short and long sections of rough-sawn board-and-batten siding and horizontal drip mouldings create an interesting effect on this house.*

11-34 *With this house, rigid-foam sheathing was nailed to the studs and sealed with two-inch-wide polyethylene tape. Shiplap is being applied clapboard style with 10d siding nails driven through the insulation and into the wall studs.*

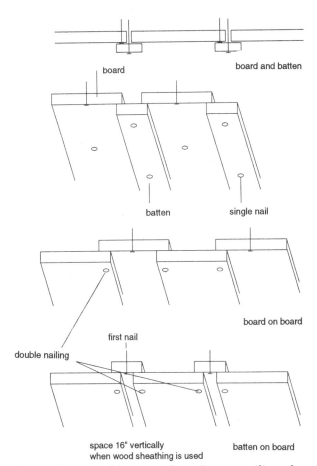

11-36 *Board-and-batten siding. Proper nailing allows the boards to shrink as they dry without splitting.*

The California Redwood Association recommends nailing boards less than eight inches wide with one nail in the center. For wider boards, use two nails, spaced equidistantly to divide the board in thirds. The battens, which should overlap the edges of the boards by at least ½ inch, are secured by a single nail driven through their centerline.

An alternative nailing pattern, which leaves only the batten nails exposed, is to nail only one edge of the board as shown in **11-36.** Nailing both edges would increase the chances of the board splitting down the middle when it shrinks. With the board-on-board and reverse batten patterns, the nailing doesn't divide the boards into thirds. Instead, the top boards overlap the lower boards by about 1½ inch and are nailed within ¼ inch of the edges of the underlying board. The portion of the nail that isn't embedded in the wood allows enough flex to prevent it from splitting.

If the boards aren't being applied to strapping, snap chalk lines over the underlayment to mark the centers of the nailing lines. The easiest way to nail long boards to the wall is with a helper who works from a ladder or pipe-scaffold staging while you work from the ground. This is one case where pump jacks won't work as well. Since redwood and cedar can be brittle, you may have to drill pilot holes to nail their ends without splitting them.

Where boards aren't long enough to cover the wall in one piece, join them together over a nailer with a 45-degree scarf joint. The bevelled edge of the upper board should overlap the lower board to shed water. Angle the nails to catch both boards. For extra protection, coat the end grain of the scarf with clear wood preservative before installing the boards.

Nail the battens on as soon as the boards are applied. If you wait too long, the boards will already be cupped and they won't flatten out without cracking when the battens are nailed down. This can happen within hours on a sunny south wall.

Installing the siding around windows and doors can be a little tricky. Before you begin nailing the boards, use a scrap piece to mark where the boards will go on the wall so that you can see how they'll end up against the window or door jamb. Ideally, the battens should be balanced to fall equally over the ends of the header. Varying the spacing (up to 1½ inches) to shift the layout won't be noticeable.

Depending on the type of units you use, there are (at least) three ways to fit board-and-batten siding to windows and doors (see **11-37**). With self-flashing aluminum or vinyl-clad windows that mount to the wall by a flange, the underlayment paper is sealed to the flange with asphalt caulking and the boards are carefully cut to fit around the window. If the combined thickness of the board and batten is greater than the projection of the window, you'll have to add a drip cap above the window header and a bevelled apron trim below the sill to butt the battens against. To make this fix look intentional, run a narrow band of similar-thickness boards along each side jamb of the unit.

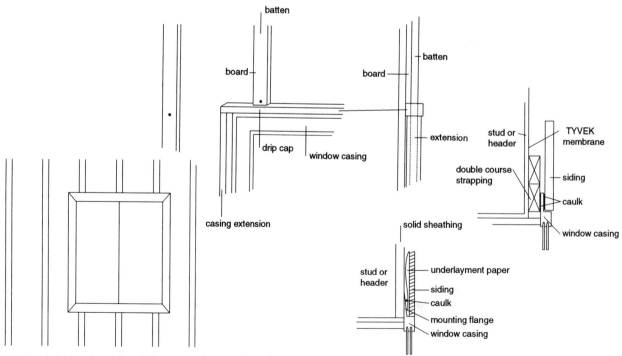

11-37 *Fitting board-and-batten siding to self-flashing windows.*

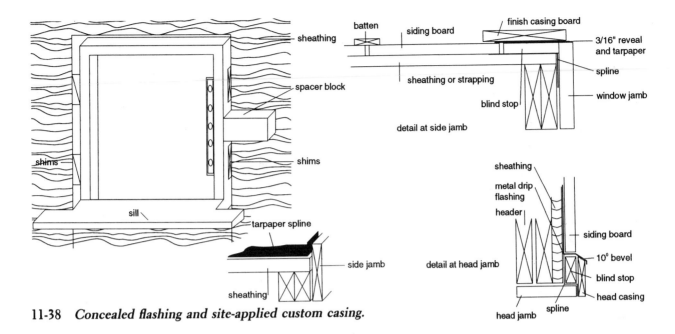

11-38 *Concealed flashing and site-applied custom casing.*

Labels for figure 11-38: sheathing; spacer block; shims; shims; sill; tarpaper spline; side jamb; sheathing; batten; siding board; finish casing board; 3/16" reveal and tarpaper; spline; window jamb; blind stop; sheathing or strapping; detail at side jamb; sheathing; metal drip flashing; header; detail at head jamb; head jamb; spline; head casing; blind stop; 10° bevel; siding board

Windows and doors fitted with factory-applied brick-mould or flat casings can be installed over the sheathing and fitted with a wood drip edge or metal flashing. The boards and battens are cut to fit, as with self-flashing units. Since factory-applied casings aren't made from the same wood as the siding, many builders prefer to order their windows and doors without a casing (see **11-38**). In this case, the units are shimmed plumb and square in their openings with wood shingle wedges before the boards are installed. Use a scrap of siding held against the jamb as a gauge so that the outside of the jamb will be flush with the face of the boards. Staple crisply folded tar paper splines up against the bottom and side jambs of the window. Although you can butt the boards directly against the splines, a much tighter seal is formed if you batten the tar paper against the window jambs with "blind stops" made from 1½-inch-wide strips of siding. Nail metal drip cap flashing above the head jamb before installing the tar paper spline and blind stop. This method eliminates the need for a separate wood drip cap. Once the boards are installed, trim out the window with flat casings cut from siding boards. For best appearance, these should be at least one inch wider than the batten strips. Butt the battens against the head and apron casings. Set the casings far enough back from the edges of the jamb to leave a visually pleasing reveal but still hide the bottom of the head flashing flange.

One trim detail which is especially effective with vertical boarding of all types is horizontal decorative bands that divide the wall into visually distinct sections (see **11-39**). They can be used at the bottom of the wall to ease the transition into the foundation insulation. On multistorey facades, a drip cap, with or without an underlying horizontal trim board, also enables you to cover the wall with convenient lengths of boards rather than harder-to-handle long boards or visually disruptive splices. A common treatment for the transition to the rake at gable walls is to run vertical boards over horizontally applied sidings. These can butt on a drip edge or else be nailed to strapping so that they project over the lower siding. Any board which butts against a drip edge should be bevelled at least 10 degrees to shed water.

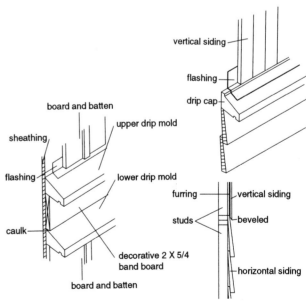

Labels for figure 11-39: board and batten; sheathing; flashing; caulk; upper drip mold; lower drip mold; decorative 2 X 5/4 band board; board and batten; vertical siding; flashing; drip cap; furring; studs; beveled; vertical siding; horizontal siding

11-39 *Horizontal band mouldings used with board-and-batten and other sidings.*

11-40 *Wood shingles are a handsome traditional siding material. Note the temporary plastic film that will do until the owner can install the windows.*

WOOD SHINGLES

The main difference between applying wood shingle siding and wood shingle roofing is the allowable exposure and grade of shingle. Since wall shingles won't leak as easily as roof shingles, the maximum exposure is half the length of the shingles less ½ inch (see **11-40**). No. 2 grade shingles are suitable for sidewall applications that will be left natural or stained. No. 1 shingles are used for painted walls.

A special rebutted, rejointed shingle, available in both #1 and #2 grades, is used where tight-fitting joints and even-sized shingles are desired. Also called wall shakes, these shingles have parallel sides and are available with a smooth-sanded or grooved face. They are most often painted. With the renaissance of Victorian and Queen Anne styles, a wide selection of "fancy butt" shingles sized to (more or less) even widths and cut in traditional decorative shapes has become readily available (see **11-41**). Many sidewall shingles are also available prestained or prepainted.

Wood shingle siding is nailed and spaced as for roofing shingles. The shingles may be applied over solid sheathing or nailed to 1×3 strapping (o.c. spacing equal to exposure) over nonstructural sheathing or open studs. Like clapboards, the shingles are usually butted against corner trim boards and casings (see **11-42**). Unlike clapboards, they can also be mitred at outside corners, or woven—or laced—at the inside or outside like the "Boston" ridge used to cover the peak or hips.

As with clapboards, level a starting line and mark off the butts of the courses with a storey pole. But don't snap chalk lines on the sheathing. After installing the starter course, snap the lines across each course of previously applied shingles, instead. Instead of laying the shingles to the chalk line, tack a strip of shiplapped board to it so that the lip of the rabbet holds the butt of the shingle against the wall. As with roof shingling, this straight edge is held to the wall by strips of metal tacked to the shingles where the nail holes can be covered by the next course. Adjust exposures as needed to bring courses parallel with windows and to end up with a reasonably proportioned filler piece at the eaves frieze board.

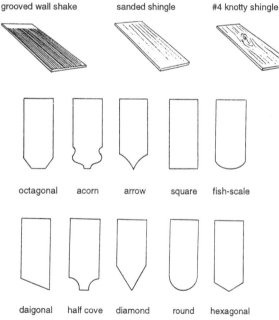

grooved wall shake   sanded shingle   #4 knotty shingle

octagonal   acorn   arrow   square   fish-scale

daigonal   half cove   diamond   round   hexagonal

11-41 *Decorative "fancy-butt" shingles.*

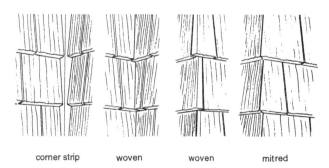

corner strip   woven   woven   mitred

11-42 *Corner treatment for shingle siding.*

Double-coursing, where two layers of shingles are placed directly over each other, is used to provide increased weather protection while permitting greater exposure (see **11-43**). As long as you use No. 1 grade shingles for the top course, you can use a 12-inch exposure with 16-inch shingles. An inexpensive No. 4 grade *undercoursing* shingle is used for the covered course. The shingles are laid so that the butts of the covering course overhang the butts of the undercourse by about ½ inch.

Be careful when fitting the top course of shingles. Since the nails will be exposed, many builders prefer to use galvanized finish nails in place of headed shingle nails. Predrill the holes to avoid splitting. Finally, if you're using No. 2 face-grain shingles, turning them pith- (i.e., heart-) side up will tend to reduce cupping—or at least result in convex cups that shed water better.

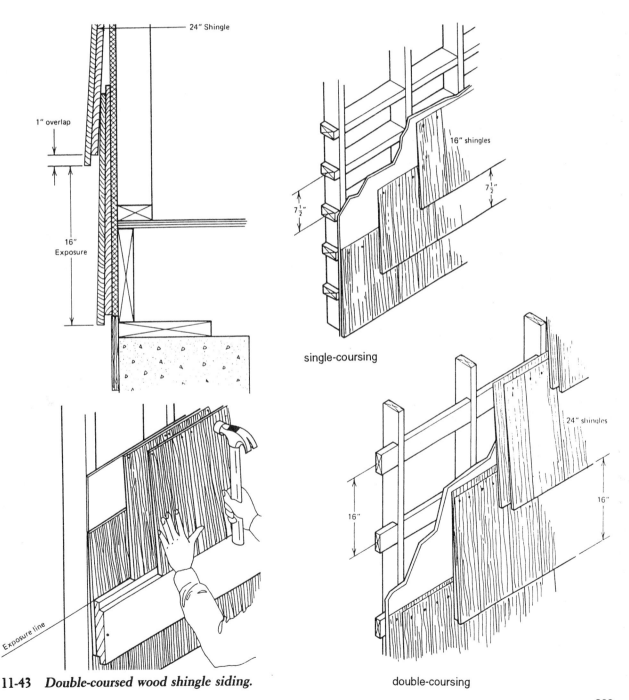

11-43 *Double-coursed wood shingle siding.*

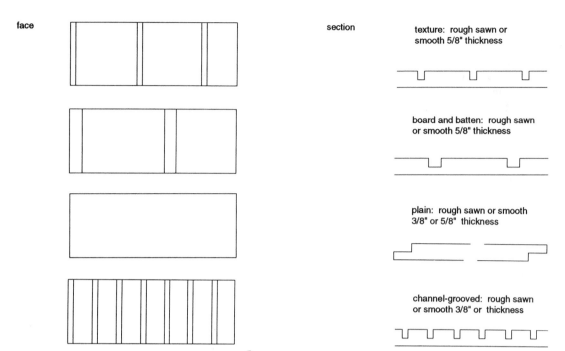

11-44 *Typical patterns for APA 303 plywood siding.*

PLYWOOD AND HARDBOARD SIDING

There are two classes of plywood panels used for exterior siding: *Medium-density overlay* (MDO) and the American Plywood Association's so-called *APA 303* series of plywood panels.

MDO has a uniformly smooth, waterproof resin-impregnated surface veneer that provides an excellent base for paint. The colored surface can also be used as it comes from the factory. Vertical battens are frequently applied to MDO panels for decorative effects. Horizontal battens should be bevelled along their top edge to shed water. MDO panels are also used as a decorative element to provide visual emphasis with board and other sidings. Typical applications include fill-in panels above and below windows, and continuous horizontal bands at various levels of the wall.

A wide variety of surface textures and patterns are available in fir, redwood, cedar, and yellow pine veneers in the APA 303 series of plywood panels, most of which are designed for a stained finish (see **11-44**). Depending on their thickness (which varies from 5/16 inch to 5/8 inch), the panels can be applied to studs spaced either 16 inches or 24 inches o.c., with or without underlying sheathing. Besides the standard 4×8 panel, most APA 303 sidings are available in 4×9 and 4×10 sizes as well, so that you can span the wall from sill to plate with a single, vertical sheet.

A 5/8-inch rough-sawn APA 303 panel milled with shiplapped edges and grooved channels intended to look like channel rustic board siding—known as *Texture*, or *T 1-11*—is the most well known APA 303 siding. Because T 1-11 provides both structural sheathing and finish siding in one operation, you can save money and time using it. Viewed from a distance, it tries to mimic rough-sawn boarding; however, up close, its machined regularity belies its true nature. Further, T 1-11 does not age gracefully. It works well as an interim siding with the assumption that you'll eventually cover it over with real siding. Since lenders consider T 1-11 to be a finished siding, you can satisfy completion requirements which would be impossible if you left the house otherwise sheathed and unsided.

Plywood siding panels are installed vertically. With T 1-11 siding, the grooved channels are designed to fall over stud spacings, which helps to make the nails less obvious. Joints should always break on a stud (see **11-45**). Insert solid blocking between studs to back up any horizontal joints. Whether shiplapped or butt-jointed, the panels should be spaced about 1/16 inch apart at vertical joints.

It's a good idea to seal the joints with caulking even when they are covered with battens or the rabbet of the shiplap. Horizontal joints between panels can be sealed by overlapping them at a gable wall or else with special metal "Z" flashing or wood drip caps (called *watertable moulding*).

Like sheathing, plywood siding panels are often nailed to the studs before the wall frame is tilted up; don't nail the edges above headers. You'll need to trim them back to slide drip flashing up under them before installing window and door units.

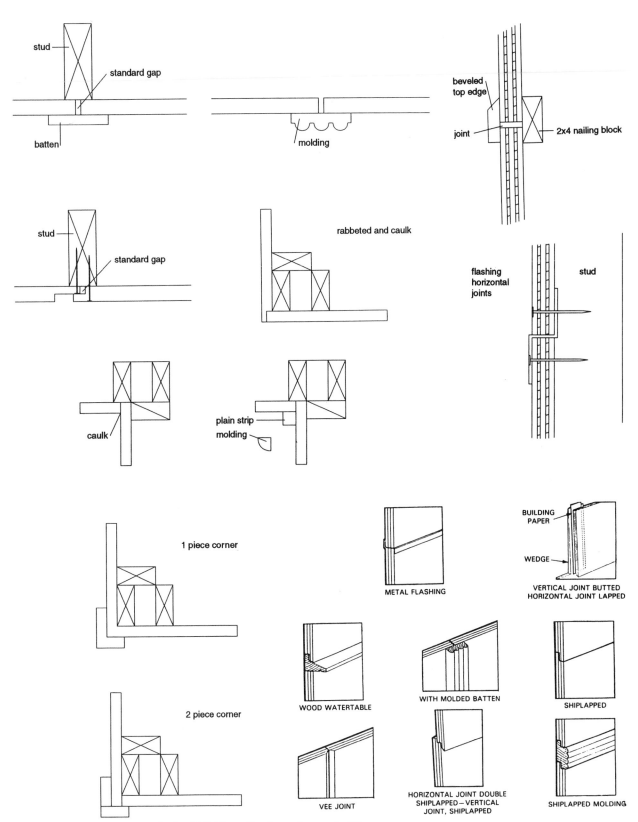

11-45 *Installation details for T 1-11 and other plywood sidings.*

301

Both MDO-finished and textured plywoods are also available with lap siding. These panels, which install like oversized bevel siding, are 12 inches to 24 inches wide and up to 16 feet long. As with other plywood sidings, they can be installed directly to the studs over underlayment paper or nonstructural sheathing or else nailed to plywood sheathing. A minimum head lap of 1½ inch is required. With lap siding wider than 12 inches, a wood shingle wedge is nailed to each stud to provide support against buckling. The wedge is also used behind all vertical end joints, which must also be sealed with caulk. Corners are mitred or butted against corner boards or covered with special metal corner-trim flashing.

Hardboard siding, which is a composite of sawdust and glue, is now a durable product that is easy to apply. It also comes with variously textured surface treatments and factory-applied painted finishes. Earlier problems with moisture, buckling, and appearance have been overcome. Hardboard sidings are applied like wide bevel sidings or plywood lap siding (see 11-46). Since the hardboard expands more than plywood, a ⅛-inch gap is recommended between panels and against trim boards. Fill in the gaps with caulking. Unless you use special metal butt-joint connectors, butt joints should always occur over a stud, even when the wall is sheathed. As with plywood lap siding, special metal pieces are available for use with inside and outside corners.

My reservations about the appearance and long-term performance (average life is 20 years for plywood and 30 years for hardboard, with proper maintenance) of these materials are mild compared to my opinions about aluminum and vinyl siding. At least plywood and hardboard are wood products from renewable and recycled resources as opposed to energy-intensive aluminum and nonrenewable petroleum. Whenever you choose a building materials, ask yourself whether there's a better alternative given the use intended, the life of the product and its appearance, as well as how its manufacturing process and eventual disposal impacts on the environment.

The selling point of aluminum and vinyl siding is freedom from maintenance, specifically painting and repainting. Increased energy efficiency is raised as a secondary benefit. But neither product looks all that well at the end of its 30-year life cycle, which is considerably shorter than the 50-plus-year useful life of properly applied wood shingle, bevel, or board siding. The finish eventually fades, and you're faced with the same need to paint. And, unlike wood, you can't stain aluminum or vinyl. The energy-conservation benefits are actually due to foam insulation backers rather than the thermal properties of the siding material itself. My litany of objections continues: insulation backers can cause condensation problems and structural rot; aluminum siding can rattle in the wind; vinyl siding offers less fire resistance even than wood shingles; repairing dents or punctures in aluminum or splits and cracks in vinyl is difficult and more noticeable compared to wood siding.

CEMENT SIDINGS

Fibre-cement lap siding (such as Hardieplank and FibreCem) is a relatively new product that combines the advantages of manufactured sidings such as aluminum, vinyl, hardboard, and plywood with many of the benefits of wood siding. As such it satisfies a need for a durable, ecologically benign, and attractive product. It is composite of Portland cement, ground sand, and cellulose fibre, but it contains no asbestos—unlike the old-fashioned cement–asbestos siding that it slightly resembles. It's warranted for 50 years by the manufacturer, equalling or exceeding the best wood siding. It's noncombustible, immune to rot and salt spray, inedible to vermin, and (because of its cellulose fibre content) won't dent or crack easily. Fibre-cement lap siding is available in several different surface textures, including wood grain, and a small range of preprimed colors beyond its basic cement grey. Because it won't absorb moisture, swell, or shrink, if you do paint it, you can expect the finish to last at least twice as long as it would on boards.

The siding comes in 12-foot-long, 7½-inch or 9½-inch-wide panels or eight-inch shiplap. It's applied like any lap siding, with stainless-steel nails driven through the edges into the studs.

STUCCO

Contrary to popular perception, cement stucco can be used for an attractive, durable, inexpensive, low-maintenance wall finish in regions of the United States outside the Southwest (see 11-47). Although commercial stucco subcontractors use pressure sprayers to apply the coating, applying your own stucco with a trowel is not hard to do, so long as you observe the manufacturer's directions (see 11-48).

Stucco is a lime-based mortar applied to a wall. The most common formula is one part Portland cement combined with four parts sand and about two-thirds part builder's lime and 1½ parts water. This translates into five-

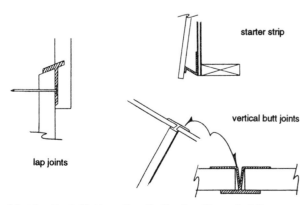

starter strip

vertical butt joints

lap joints

11-46 *Installation details for hardboard siding.*

11-47 *Cement stucco can be used in any climate. This uniform finish is a spray-gun application.*

11-49 **Rigid-foam insulation is fastened to the studs with roofing nails and woven wire mesh is stapled over the foam. Since the stucco does not contact the framing, no tar paper underlayment is needed. The stucco will be trowelled directly onto the moistened concrete blocks.**

11-50 *Closeup shows expanded-diamond, reinforcement mesh stapled to an outside corner.*

gallon pails as six pails sand, 1½ pails cement, 1 pail lime, and 1¼ pails water. The key to a successful stucco application is achieving a workable mix; it must be plastic enough to form a smooth and level coat, but not so runny that it sags after application.

Stucco can be applied over any rigid substrate. Concrete block is ideal (see **11-49**). Wood-frame walls must have solid sheathing or else be very well braced. "Self-furring" expanded-metal lath reinforcement can be applied over solid sheathing or open studs. Woven wire and welded wire mesh (resembling chicken wire fencing) should only be used over solid sheathing (see **11-50**). If you don't use self-furring lath, use special furring nails or metal furring strips to hold the reinforcement ¼ inch above its base. Nails should penetrate at least ¾ inch into the sheathing. Lap the edges of expanded lath at least one inch and make joints over solid nailing. Apply No. 15 tar paper underlayment over the sheathing before installing the lath.

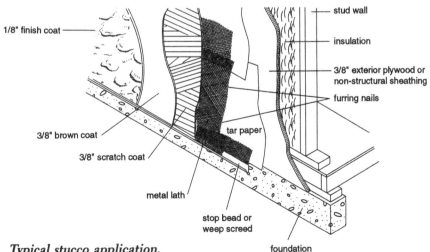

1/8" finish coat

3/8" brown coat

3/8" scratch coat

metal lath

stop bead or weep screed

tar paper

stud wall

insulation

3/8" exterior plywood or non-structural sheathing

furring nails

foundation

11-48 *Typical stucco application.*

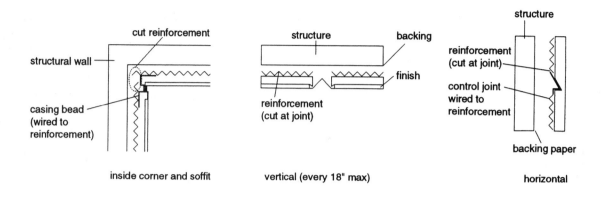

inside corner and soffit

vertical (every 18" max)

horizontal

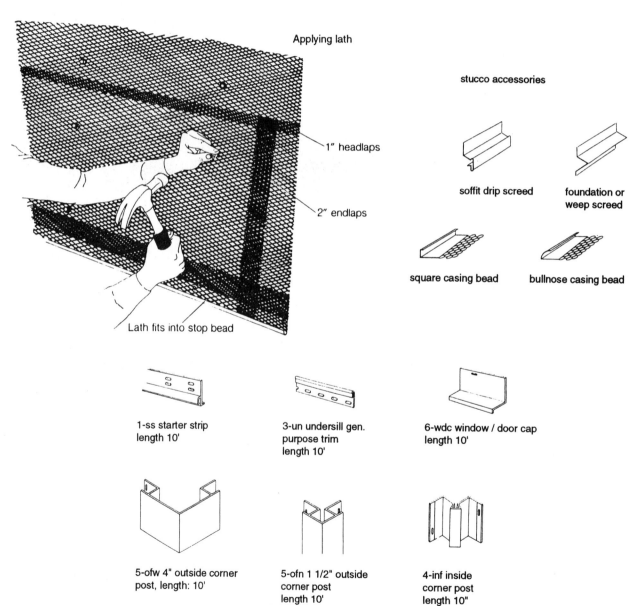

Applying lath

1" headlaps

2" endlaps

Lath fits into stop bead

stucco accessories

soffit drip screed

foundation or weep screed

square casing bead

bullnose casing bead

1-ss starter strip length 10'

3-un undersill gen. purpose trim length 10'

6-wdc window / door cap length 10'

5-ofw 4" outside corner post, length: 10'

5-ofn 1 1/2" outside corner post length 10'

4-inf inside corner post length 10"

11-51 *Preparation strips for stucco application.*

Special metal mouldings are applied at the edges and next to windows and door openings to "key" the stucco to the wall (see **11-51**). Metal *casing beads* are also used to reinforce outside and inside corners. A *weep screed* moulding installed at the lower edge of the finish wall allows moisture that collects between the underlayment and the stucco or plywood to drain. Screeds are also used where the wall meets a drip edge or soffit. The corners of all openings are also reinforced with wire mesh (see **11-52**).

Proper stucco application is a two- or three-coat process (see **11-53**). The base coat, the *scratch coat*, should completely fill the metal lath and cover it about ⅛ inch deep. The surface is scored (hence, "scratch" coat) for good bonding with the next coat. It should be kept moist for at least 12 hours to prevent shrinkage cracks caused by too-rapid curing. The optional middle coat, called the *brown coat*, because more sand is added to the mix, should not be applied sooner than 48 hours. It is trowelled to a fairly smooth ⅜-inch-thick finish rather than scored, and left to cure for seven days after being kept moist for 12 hours. For best results with the finish coat, apply a factory mix instead of a homemade mix, and follow the manufacturer's instructions carefully. The finish coat only needs to cure for two days. It should be ⅛- to ¼-inch thick and trowelled to a smooth finish.

11-52 *To prevent stress cracks, the corners of all openings are strengthened with reinforcing mesh.*

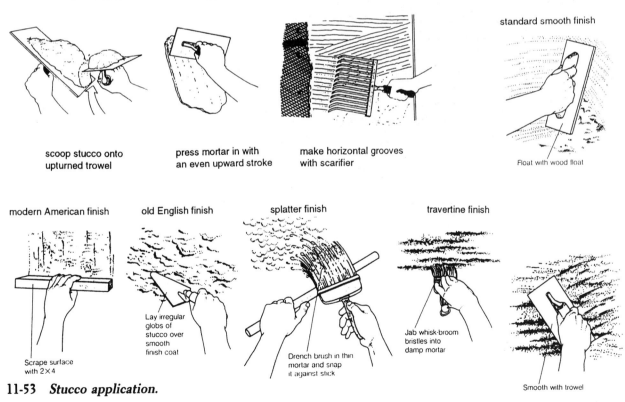

loading the trowel

scoop stucco onto
upturned trowel

mortar application

press mortar in with
an even upward stroke

scarifying the scratch coat

make horizontal grooves
with scarifier

Applying the finish coat

standard smooth finish

Float with wood float

modern American finish

Scrape surface
with 2 × 4

old English finish

Lay irregular
globs of
stucco over
smooth
finish coat

splatter finish

Drench brush in thin
mortar and snap
it against stick

travertine finish

Jab whisk-broom
bristles into
damp mortar

Smooth with trowel

11-53 *Stucco application.*

11-54 *Simple plywood forms are all that is needed to create the curved arches of this stuccoed entryway. The columns are precast concrete.*

The finished building walls can be quite handsome (see 11-54). Although it's often done, painting a stucco finish is a usually bad idea. If you ever wish to apply a new coat of stucco at some later date, all the paint must be removed first. Furthermore, even the best paints, specifically formulated for the application, have a short service life since moisture absorbed into the plaster will inexorably break the bond between the paint film and the stucco. The best results come from using a color-tinted finish coat mix instead.

When applying stucco over wood walls, provide vertical expansion joints at minimum horizontal intervals of 18 feet. Horizontal control joints are also added so that no unrelieved sections of wall area exceed 150 square feet. The joints allow the underlying structure to move slightly and the stucco to contract and expand with temperature and moisture changes without cracking. Cut the reinforcement lath beneath the expansion joint, and wire a metal expansion bead to it. For horizontal expansion joints, conceal the metal bead under the finish coat instead of leaving it exposed.

12 Windows and Exterior Doors

Modern windows are mass-produced to high standards of quality and performance that far exceed the capabilities of the average woodworker or custom shop. Even so, windows and doors account for 10 to 15 percent of the total construction budget. Yet the expense is justified, since well-made wood-framed windows can give trouble-free service for as long as the house lasts, and besides light and ventilation, they provide a psychological extension of the living space into the outside world (see **12-1**).

WINDOW TYPES

Despite advances in materials technology, wood is still the best window material because of its natural insulating qualities and the ease with which it can be machined. Wood windows can also be painted or stained to match any color scheme or siding. Windows made of steel or aluminum require complex engineering to avoid conducting heat (or cold) through their frames. Solid metal frames are seldom used; instead, wood or rigid foam frames are clad with an anodized aluminum or steel skin that requires no painting or other maintenance. Wood windows are also available with a vinyl plastic cladding (see **12-2** and **12-3**). Like vinyl siding, clad windows are intended to be maintenance-free. Since they mount to the wall by a flange concealed under the siding, replacing them 30 years or so later when the vinyl eventually breaks down may be a major undertaking.

12-1 *Windows can have a profound effect on the comfort of the house's occupants. This "greenhouse" bay window links the natural landscape outside to the house plants inside.*

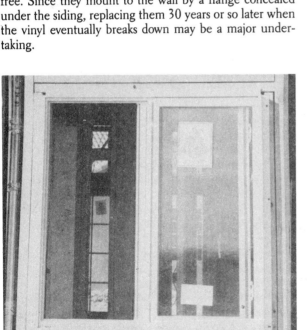

12-2 *Developers favor vinyl-clad window units since they require no trim or painting.*

12-3 *The narrow reveal of a vinyl-clad window echoes the profile of the steel window frames that were widely used with masonry and stuccoed construction from the beginning of the 20th century until the early 1960s.*

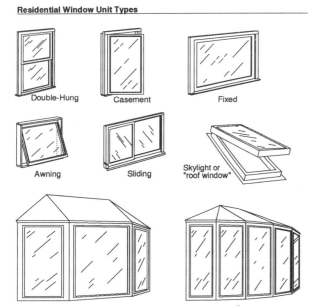

12-4 *Window types.*

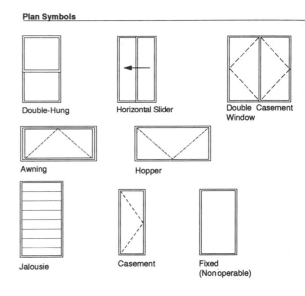

Unlike plastic or metal cladding, the long-term performance of standard wood-framed windows is well established. Since they are installed by nailing through the casings into the sheathing, wood windows can be removed or repaired relatively easily, if necessary. The units are supplied either preprimed or with bare wood. They should always be painted or sealed with a wood-preserving stain or clear finish before installation. Failure to keep window trim, particularly the exposed sills, painted is the most common cause of window problems and premature failure.

12-5 *Installing this window in the frame before the siding is applied complicates exterior trimwork and risks breakage.*

Depending on their mode of operation, windows are classed as either sliding, swinging, or fixed. There are several types of windows within each of these general categories (see **12-4**).

The *double-hung* window, consisting of two bypassing sashes that move vertically in their frame (the top sash of a *single-hung* window is immovable), is the most familiar of the sliding windows. Instead of the troublesome concealed cords and sash weights that formerly held the movable sash in position, contemporary double-hungs operate by friction- or spring-type hardware. Double-hung windows are popular because they are less expensive than most other window types, easy to operate, don't interfere with furniture or activities, and are available in many versions to suit a wide range of architectural styles (see **12-5**).

Horizontal sliding windows—also called sliders or gliders—are the least expensive of the operable windows. They contain two or more sashes, at least one of which can slide in horizontal tracks, and are often used for high windows in bedrooms, baths, and kitchens. Improvements in locking hardware and built-in stops have eliminated the traditional "stick" laid between the sash and jamb for security. Like the related double-hung windows, sliders don't interfere with curtains and furniture.

The *casement* window is the oldest type of swinging window—in use since the Middle Ages, but remarkably suited to contemporary styles.

The casement sash is hinged at the top and bottom to one side of the frame so that it can swing outward or lock tight when closed. The opening hardware is a simple crank or push bar. This style is practical where having to

12-6 *Roof windows, as distinguished from fixed glazing units, i.e., skylights, can bring light deep into the interior as well as provide ventilation or solar gain.*

12-7 *A bay window can increase the sense of interior space, providing a cozy nook, window seat, or plant bench, and add visual interest to the house outside.*

lean over a countertop or furniture to open a double-hung or sliding window would be awkward. Casement windows can provide good ventilation depending on the prevailing breeze, but their outward swing can interfere with outside activities.

Awning windows are hinged at the top edge to open outward and upwards. These windows are most often used for ventilation in tandem with fixed windows. Mounted low in the wall, they act as intake vents, but may cause outside interference. High in the wall, they exhaust hot air and admit light while maintaining privacy. Awning windows are placed side by side for clerestory lighting.

Hopper windows are essentially awning windows hinged at the bottom to open inward, especially for easy washing. Hopper windows are most often used in basements.

The *roof window* is the current term that goes beyond the more commonly used *skylight* to connote a fully operable window designed to be watertight and energy-efficient rather than just an immovable pane of glass or plastic bubble (see **12-6**). Equipped with venetian blinds,

it can be used to control both ventilation and light. It can convert attic space into living space at a fraction of the cost of a dormer, provide light and privacy in bathrooms, and bring natural light into stairwells and hallways.

Because *fixed windows* don't have a moveable sash or hardware, they are fairly simple and inexpensive to build yourself, on-site. Standard patio-door replacement glass is often used for this purpose. However, even if more expensive, factory-made fixed windows have the advantage that their sizes and trim details will match the modules and style of operable units.

Ever since it was first popularized by the 19th-century landscape-architect-turned-design-guru Andrew Jackson Downing, the *bay window* has been favored as a means of "bringing the outdoors inside" (see **12-7**). Bay windows typically consist of a fixed, picture window with a double-hung or casement window on each side, usually at a 45-degree angle to the plane of the central unit. *Bow windows* are a more elegant and substantial form of the bay window. Typically, five or more fixed and operable units of the same size are combined into a flattened curve.

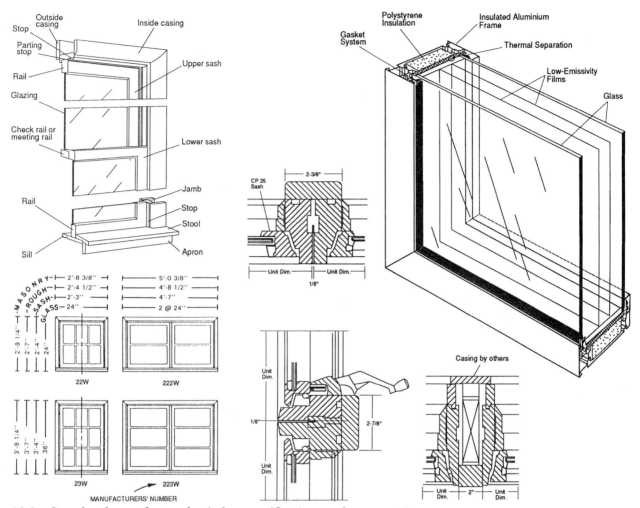

12-8 *Sample of manufacturer's window specifications and cross sections.*

Manufacturer's catalogs contain complete listings, detailed cross-sectional drawings, installation specifications, and dimensions for their product line (see **12-8**). This is your source for determining window rough opening sizes. Catalogs also list the overall unit dimensions, which architects find useful for drawing elevations, as well as the sash size and glass size, which you'll need to replace a broken unit and an engineer might use for detailed heat-load calculations.

GLAZING CHARACTERISTICS AND THERMAL PERFORMANCE

For the past quarter-century, the industry standard has been to use at least *double-glazed* windows for new construction. Except for outbuildings and summer houses, single-glazed windows are not used. "Double-glazing" is a loose term, whose use does not always distinguish the precise technical meaning. Welded insulating glass, or

Thermopane, indicates two panes joined together at their edges into a single piece with the space between them filled with dry air. Mechanical double-glazing means two panes joined with a sealant to a metal frame where a desiccant is added to absorb moisture from the air between them. And yet, in practice, double-glazing can also refer to standard single-pane windows which have been covered with a storm window panel. Most builders, and homeowners, have found that any method of double-glazing still lets in too much heat in the summer and too much cold in the winter.

To increase the poor insulating value of glass, window manufacturers introduced triple-glazed windows in the 1970s. But it wasn't until the 1980s, with the introduction of high-performance low-emissivity ("low-e") coatings, that a fundamental and significant technological advance was incorporated into window design. Applied to the outer surface of the inner pane of the double-glazing, this invisible metallic coating admits light but blocks heat re-

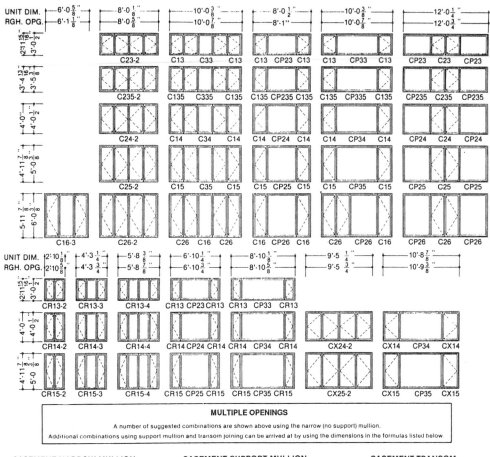

12-8 *(Continued) Sample of manufacturer's window specifications and cross sections.*

radiation, thus increasing the insulating value of the glass 50 to 75 percent over conventional glass. When applied to the inside of the outer pane, the coating will keep heat out.

Insulated glass works because the "dead" air trapped in the space between the glazing is a relatively poor conductor of heat. However, adding more glazing increases both window weight and sash bulk while reducing light transmission. Manufacturers found that low-e coatings applied to one or two layers of plastic film suspended between the glass could boost insulating values up to 300 percent above conventional low-e double-glazing without significantly increasing weight or reducing transmission. Further improvements substituted low-conductivity inert gases such as argon or krypton for the air between the layers.

As the thermal performance of glazing is improved, proportionately more heat is lost through the edges of the glazing and the window frames. This is an argument against *divided lights* (an individual pane is called a "light"); multiple panes have more edges and lose more heat than a single large pane. The latest generation of high-tech modifications is concentrated on improving the thermal performance of the window frames.

Moderately high-efficiency windows with low-e coatings and argon-gas filling cost about 10 to 15 percent more than standard air-filled insulating glass. The super-efficient windows with triple-glazing or two suspended plastic films, low-e coatings, and inert gas filling cost 40 to 50 percent more than insulated glass windows. The cost-effectiveness of windows depends on the severity of your heating and cooling season, fuel costs, the percentage of possible sunshine, and your investment recovery period, i.e., the length of time you expect to live in your house. It's not necessary, or even desirable, that all facades of the house receive the same level of window treatment. Western windows are amenable to heat blocking in almost all climates, while northern windows are more vulnerable to heat loss in the northern hemisphere.

311

INSTALLING FACTORY-BUILT WINDOWS

To allow time for painting and staining the casings, order your windows and doors to arrive a few days ahead of installation. Store the units upright leaning against a wall inside the building. Tack a sheet of plywood to a couple of 2×4s nailed to a partition or wall studs to protect the window stack from accidental collisions and to keep it from falling over.

Measure the window and check it against the rough opening for adequate clearance. Leave any temporary braces or spacer blocks in place until after the window is shimmed and plumbed in its opening. Remove the shipping blocks that are usually stapled to the underside of the sill and corners of the jambs.

Even if you don't use underlayment paper, cut 8-inch to 10-inch-wide tar paper splines and fold them over the edges of the rough opening, tacking them to the sheathing (see 12-9). Cut and overlap the corners as carefully as if you were flashing a chimney. It's a good idea to run a bead of caulk around the opening before installation. Place the window unit into its opening from the outside. Rest the window on the rough sill, and center it between the jambs. Set wedge blocks under the window sill to raise it to the correct height as shown on the plans. Check the window for plumb by holding a level against its side casing. Drive a nail partway through the casing at one of the corners and adjust the window up or down in the opening

to plumb it. Check the corners with a framing square. Open the window to make sure it operates smoothly. Multiple units should be supported by wedge blocks. When you're satisfied that the frame is level and plumb, nail the window to the framing behind the sheathing with 16d or 20d galvanized finish nails. Space the nails about 12 to 16 inches apart, angling them, if needed, to catch into solid wood.

"Brickmould," a profiled casing about 1⅜ inches thick and two inches wide, is standard with factory-built wood-frame windows and doors. You can order flat casings or no casings to fit your design scheme. For casement windows, be sure to specify which way you want them to swing.

BUILDING FIXED WINDOWS

Factory-made double-glazing panels are available at wholesale prices in stock sizes (typical sizes are 28″ × 76″, 34″ × 76″, and 46″ × 76″) intended for sliding patio doors replacement units. Custom panels can also be fabricated by your local glass shop in virtually any size or shape you specify. Building codes require tempered safety glass for any glazing within 10 inches of a door and 18 inches of the floor and for sloping or overhead glazing.

Frames for site-built fixed windows should be cut from high-grade, warp-free, clear pine, cedar, or redwood. The

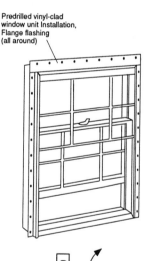

Wood Casement Unit

Predrilled vinyl-clad window unit Installation, Flange flashing (all around)

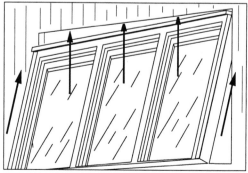
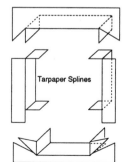
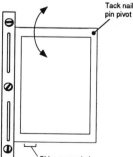

Tarpaper Splines

Tack nail pin pivot

Shim as needed

12-9 *Installing ready-made windows.*

frame can be assembled as a unit and installed in the rough opening, or else, if the openings themselves are framed carefully (as for example, with a greenhouse "window wall," where the posts between each individual sash are usually structural and the sill is laid in one continuous piece), the side and head jambs are nailed directly to the framing with a minimal amount of shimming (see 12-10). Although it is often done, I don't recommend sealing the glazing directly to the framing itself without an intervening jamb.

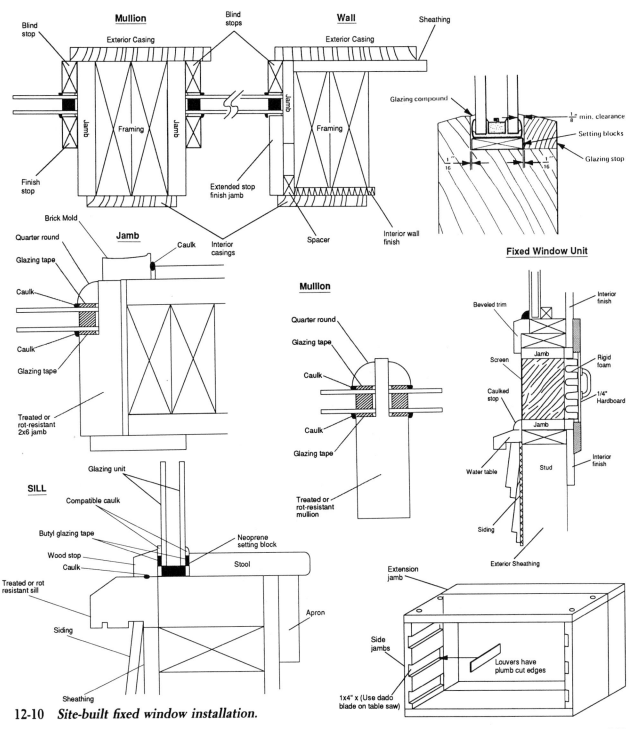

12-10 *Site-built fixed window installation.*

Since the panels weigh about seven pounds per square foot, use 1½-inch-thick jamb stock for preassembled frame units or where the frame will be rabbeted to form an integral glazing stop. Use one-inch stock if the glazing will rest against an overlaid stop instead. Rabbeted stops offer better protection against infiltration and leakage. The glazing actually floats in the frame, resting on two four-inch-long neoprene rubber *setting blocks* placed on the sill a quarter of the way in from each corner. (Allow for the thickness of the blocks when sizing the frame opening.) You can't remove the window (at least not easily) once the glass contacts applied ½-inch double-faced glazing tape, so be sure that it will fit and that the opening and the glazing unit itself are both square. Apply a second layer of tape over the outside edges of the glazing. Fill, but don't overstuff, the space between the setting blocks with sealant and then install the outside stops. Both the outside sill and the stop must be bevelled to drain water away from the bottom of the window; use a 10-degree or 15-degree bevel. Cut a ¼-inch-deep kerf into the under-side of the sill about ½ inch in from its outside edge. This drip-groove stops water from being sucked behind the fin-ish siding by capillary action. Carefully seal the glazing to the stop with a bead of compatible caulking. Just in case any moisture should manage to penetrate the seal at the sill, drill ⅛-inch-diameter upward-angled "weep holes" through the stop at both sides of each setting block.

Using fixed windows in combination with site-built ven-tilating louvres is one way to avoid the costs of operable windows without sacrificing their comfort-control func-tions. Standard wood louvres designed for installation in attic gables won't normally match the size of your window modules. But it doesn't require a great deal of skill to build your own from bevel-edged 1×4 or 1×6 stock set in grooved jambs. Staple screening across the back of the unit, and apply a set of larger extension jambs to provide a stop for a board-faced, rigid-foam insulating shutter on the interior side of the unit.

The use of fixed glass in conjunction with ventilation louvres should be weighed against the important consid-eration that operable windows also provide emergency fire exits. Indeed, building codes state that at least one window in each bedroom must be an "egress" window (the area of the opened sash must be large enough so that an adult can crawl out).

PREHUNG DOOR INSTALLATION

Like windows, doors are usually factory-assembled units that arrive on-site *prehung*, that is, hinged and hung in the frame, ready for installation in the rough opening, or else, in the case of large sliding units, in kit form. These *knocked-down* (or *K.D.*) frames have precisely machined joints and carefully packaged parts that, together with the detailed instructions supplied by the manufacturer, make them easy to assemble on-site.

Exterior doors are available in many variations of three basic types: flush, panelled, or panelled with lights (inset panes of glass—see **12-11**). The door *blanks* may be man-ufactured from solid or composition wood, or urethane foam clad with smooth steel or a wood-grain plastic finish.

Wood doors feature a mortise-and-tenon *rail* (horizon-tal) and *stile* (vertical) framework in which thin wood panels float freely (see **12-12**). This allows the door to respond to changes in atmospheric moisture without warp-ing or splitting. To seal out moisture and keep the door from swelling and shrinking, all the surfaces of the door, especially the edges, should be sealed—varnished or painted—before installation. Because of the high-grade wood and joinery, a rail-and-stile door may be expensive. In addition, since the ¼-inch-thick panels offer little in-sulation, wood-frame doors are normally installed in tan-dem with a wood storm door.

Wood-composite exterior doors are made by gluing face veneers over a particleboard core rimmed with solid wood edging. These *solid-core* doors can be flush, or have applied mouldings that suggest panels and/or inset lights (see **12-13**). As long as they are kept sealed, relatively inexpensive solid-core doors are actually more dimen-sionally stable than wood-frame doors, and offer better insulation than thin panels.

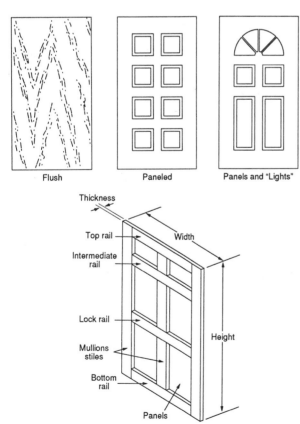

12-11 *Types of exterior doors.*

Because of their superior insulating qualities, complete dimensional stability, and economical cost, steel-clad, urethane-foam core doors are widely used in standard residential construction (see **12-14**). These units are also available in a wide range of flush, raised-panel, and lighted styles, preprimed for painting. Because little adjustment is possible, steel doors are always prehung. Storm doors are not installed with insulated steel doors, since heat buildup between them could cause the steel cladding to buckle.

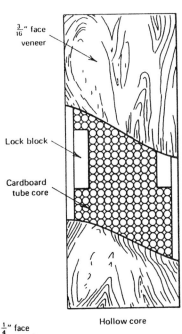

$\frac{3}{16}$" face veneer

Lock block

Cardboard tube core

Hollow core

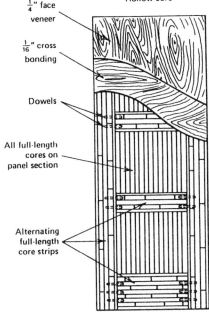

$\frac{1}{4}$" face veneer

$\frac{1}{16}$" cross bonding

Dowels

All full-length cores on panel section

Alternating full-length core strips

Solid core

12-13 *Structure of solid and hollow core doors.*

12-12 *Hardwood doors that feature raised panels and stained- or bevelled-glass inserts are an important visual feature of the house's exterior, perhaps justifying the expense.*

12-14 *The low cost and utilitarian look of prehung, insulated-steel doors makes them well suited for basement, garage, and other secondary entrances.*

315

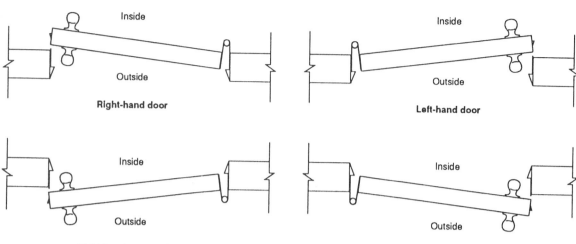

Inside

Outside

Right-hand door

Inside

Outside

Left-hand door

Inside

Outside

Right-hand reverse door

Inside

Outside

Left-hand reverse door

12-15 *Determining "handedness" of doors.*

12-16 *Prehung steel-clad foam core doors are easy to install.*

Urethane-core doors with a prepainted faux wood finish have been making inroads into the steel door market. The best of these are hard to distinguish from real wood and offer unmatched thermal performance. But the superior performance of these units comes at the cost of authenticity; they lack the hefty feel of a real wood door. Some home owners opt for real wood at the main entrance and insulating doors elsewhere.

When ordering doors (interior or exterior), it's important to specify the "handedness," or direction of swing—the side the hinges are attached to, as viewed from the "outside" of the door—the street side for exterior doors or the corridor side for interior doors (see **12-15**). In residential construction, exterior doors swing inward. In public buildings, fire codes require outside doors to swing outward. An "outswing" door is also called a *reverse* door, and would be specified as either "LHR" or "RHR."

To install a prehung door, check the rough opening dimensions (see **12-16**). Although not always required, it's a good idea to flash the area under the sill (see **12-17**). Tar paper will work, but an adhesive butyl-rubber, ice-and-water shield membrane is more reliable. Run a double bead of caulking over the sill area, particularly in the corners next to the studs, and set the unit in the opening. Plumb the side and head jambs and nail the unit through the outside casing as for a window. Insert wood-shingle wedges between the jambs and framing. Use five wedges on each side: one behind each hinge point, and two in between—top and bottom and lock strike and in between on the other side. Don't remove the wood spacer shims that are factory-inserted between the edges of the door and the jambs until after the door unit is nailed and wedged in the opening. The threshold on most prehung door units can be moved up or down by its adjustment screws to close evenly against the door bottom weatherstripping, even when the sill itself is slightly off-level.

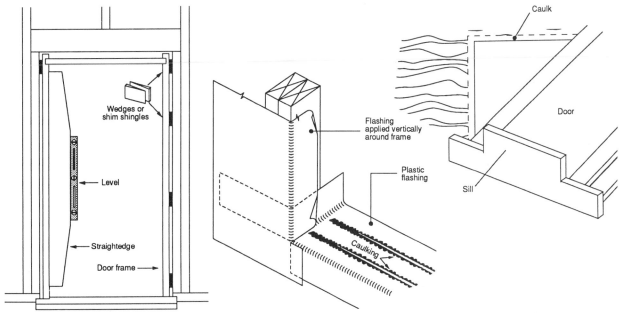

12-17 *Flashing, caulking, wedging, and adjusting prehung doors.*

Whatever type of sill your door has—usually oak or aluminum—its top should always be level with or overlap the finish floor (see **12-18**). Some types of sills are designed with a bevelled lip that overlaps the flooring; others butt against it and rely on a threshold to cover the gap between the flooring and the sill; others are formed into a concrete or block wall. Depending on the thickness of the finish floor, it may be necessary to cut away part of the subfloor or even part of the rim joist to drop the sill low enough. Some carpenters simply set the sill on the subfloor and increase the slope and depth of the inside bevel so that the sill won't be a tripping hazard.

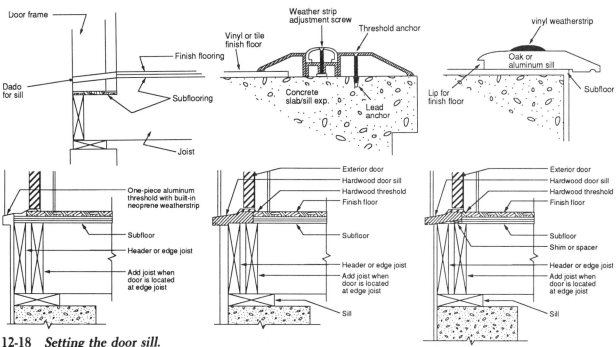

12-18 *Setting the door sill.*

12-19　*Building your own entry door can be visually and psychologically rewarding.*

12-20　*With this door, custom-forged hardware augments a wood slab applied over copper-clad plywood trimmed with a hardwood board frame.*

HANGING AND BUILDING YOUR OWN DOORS

Many builders prefer to use recycled or antique doors, or to customize factory-made doors, rather than install pre-hung units (see **12-19**). Building a door frame isn't much harder than framing a fixed window (see **12-20**).

You can buy specially kerfed jamb stock (the kerfs prevent it from cupping) or else cut your own. Because of the weight and thickness of exterior doors, their jambs are generally thicker than the typical ¾-inch interior door frames. The extra thickness not only provides more support, but also allows a ½-inch rabbeted stop. The integral stop is more weather-tight and sturdier than a nailed-on stop. The jamb can be made in two interlocking pieces as shown in **12-21** so that its width can be adjusted to fit walls of irregular thickness. The jambs can also be double-rabbeted to accommodate a storm door, although these are more typically hung from the edge of the outside casing. The width of the rabbet(s) equals the thickness of the door(s). For strength, the head jamb is notched into

a dado cut about one inch below the ends of the side jambs. Glue the head jamb, and nail it through the side jambs with three 8d box nails. The sill is also nailed through the jambs. Predrill holes in the oak to keep the nails from bending. The "ears," or "horns," of the sill are cut long enough to project past the edges of the outside casing boards which will butt to them. Some carpenters prefer to install the sill after the frame is nailed to the jambs. If the sill has horns on both sides, it must be installed after the frame, since it can't slip into the rough opening. Interior doors have no sill; the bottom of the jambs are held in place with a temporary spacer board.

When cutting the jambs to length and width, allow for the thickness of the sill and also provide ⅟₁₆-inch clearance at the top and hinge sides of the door, ⅛-inch at the strike side, and ¼-inch to ⅜-inch at the sill, depending on the design of the threshold weatherstripping. For interior doors, provide enough clearance at the bottom to clear the finish floor—usually one inch for carpet and wood, and ⅝ inch for sheet floorings.

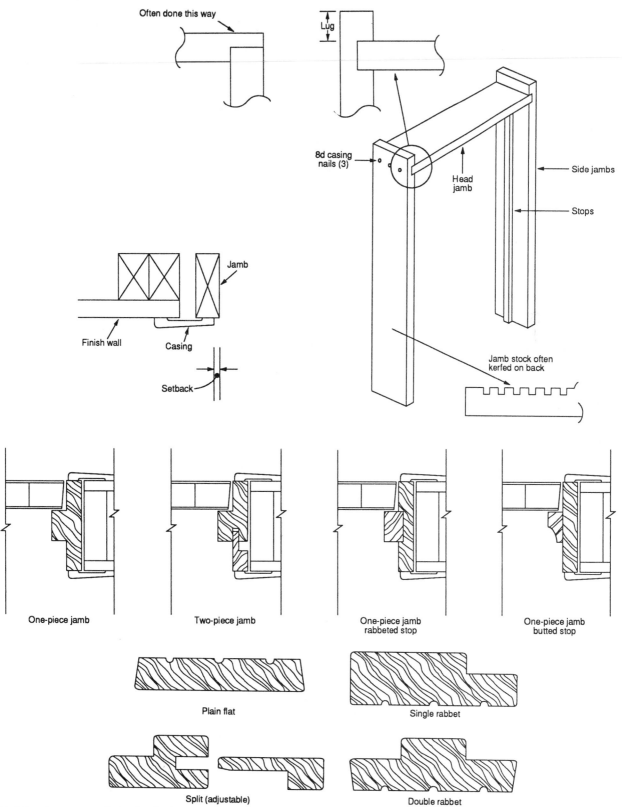

Often done this way

Lug

8d casing nails (3)

Head jamb

Side jambs

Stops

Jamb

Finish wall

Casing

Setback

Jamb stock often kerfed on back

One-piece jamb

Two-piece jamb

One-piece jamb rabbeted stop

One-piece jamb butted stop

Plain flat

Single rabbet

Split (adjustable)

Double rabbet

12-21 *Anatomy of site-built door frame.*

Standard exterior doors are 1¾ inches thick and 36 inches wide. Some may be two inches thick and 42 inches wide. The size of the hinges depends on the size and weight of the door (see **12-22**). In general, three hinges should be used for exterior doors. Although only two hinges are necessary for interior doors, three hinges will help keep any door from warping. Use four-inch by four-inch or 4½-inch by 4½-inch hinges for standard exterior doors. Five-inch by five-inch hinges will support two-inch-thick doors up to 48 inches wide. To prevent the barrel of the hinge from pinching against the edge of the inside casing board, the hinge is backset ¼ inch from the outside face of the door. The smaller hinges used with thinner doors can sometimes fit into the reveal between the jamb and the casing board without a backset. The top hinge carries most of the weight of the door and is therefore set five to seven inches down from the top of the door. The bottom hinge is set nine to eleven inches up from the bottom. The middle hinge is centered between the two.

Lay the assembled frame on a flat surface. Set the door in the frame, resting on the stops, and check it for clearance and squareness. Mark the position of the hinges on

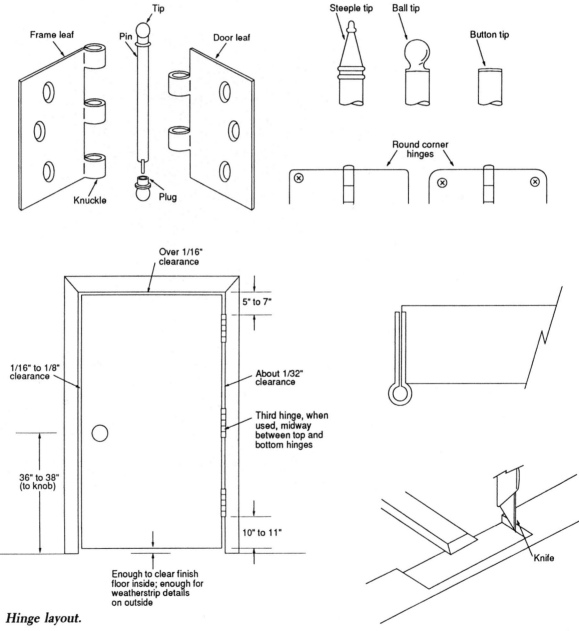

12-22 *Hinge layout.*

the edges of the door and jambs. Remove the door. Use one leaf of the hinge as a pattern to mark its outline on the door edge at the correct backset. Use hinge mortise butt gauges or a utility knife to incise the scribe marks. If you're using round-corner hinges (designed for installation with a router bit) instead of square-cornered hinges, use the edge of the hinge as a template to guide the knife and make careful repeated scoring cuts. Cut the hinge *gain*, or mortise, with a *sharp* chisel; a dull chisel is dangerous, clumsy, and can't cut a clean mortise. Professional finish carpenters cut perfectly flat-bottomed hinge gains with a router and a special hinge-mortising template. A professional template, however, won't pay for itself and a home-made model is a lot of trouble for a one-shot deal.

The gain should be only as deep as the thickness of the hinge. To avoid cutting too deeply, hold the chisel with its bevelled edge against the wood, and push it (rather than striking it) with the grain. To smooth the gain, lay the blade of the chisel flat against the wood and work it back and forth like a plane. Check the hinge for fit and screw it to the door. Repeat the procedure for the hinge gains on the door jambs. Some carpenters prefer to install the hinges on the door first and then use a storey pole to transfer their location to the jambs of the frame, which has already been installed in the rough opening. Others simply prop and shim the hinged door in the opening and scribe where the hinges contact the jamb.

Although you can leave the hinges screwed to the door and then set them in the jamb gains, it's easier to separate them, and screw the hinge leaves to the door jamb by themselves. Use only one screw in each jamb leaf (repeated unscrewing and screwing will loosen the grip of the screws). Set the door in the frame and pin the leaves together. If they don't fit perfectly, adjust them. You may need to strike the hinge barrel with your hammer to "pop"

the leaves together. Install the rest of the screws, and then drive a 4d finish nail through the jamb into the edge of the door to keep it from swinging open as you lift it (afterwards, push on the door to free it and pull the nail through the jamb with a pair of pliers). You can also tack a spacer board across the jambs. Set the unit into the rough opening. Plumb and level the jambs to the studs and shim with opposing shingle wedges. You can either attach the exterior casings to the unit before installing it or afterwards. Preinstalled casings make it easier to attach the frame to the opening and avoid having to fill in the nail heads that are otherwise driven through the jambs. Shim behind the jambs as described above in either case.

The leading edge of the door should be bevelled about three to five degrees (plus/minus 1/8 inch) so that it won't bind against the jamb as it closes. If the door pinches at its hinge edge, it can be shifted slightly toward the lock side by "springing" the hinge (see **12-23**). Place the head of a nailset between the leaves of the hinge, and gently close the door on it. If the door needs to shift towards the hinge side instead, spring the hinge inward with an adjustable wrench placed over the barrel. Protect the finish by inserting a strip of heavy cloth between the wrench and the hinge.

Sometimes the problem isn't in the door hanging but rather in the wall in which the unit is installed. Sight diagonally across the door from the inside to the outside jambs. They should appear parallel. If they aren't, one of the walls is skewed, and the door will swing open or shut on its own. Use a sledgehammer to "adjust" the wall sole plate and drive a wedge under it to keep it from shifting back (see **12-24**).

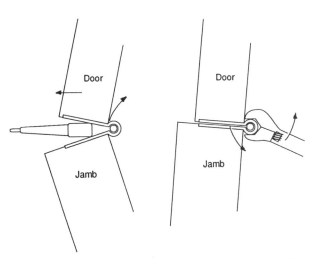

12-23 *Barrel hinges can be twisted slightly to adjust the door to close perfectly against its stops.*

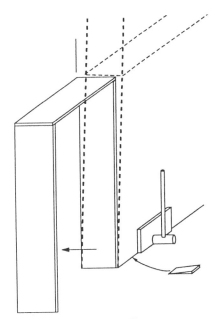

12-24 *Adjusting a skewed wall.*

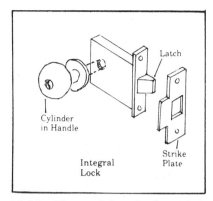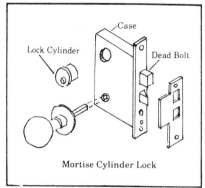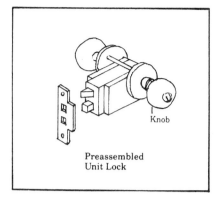

12-25 *Types of door locks and deadbolts.*

Once the door is installed and checked for proper closure, replace two of the top hinge screws with 2½-inch-long screws. These will anchor the hinge directly to the underlying framing and help keep the weight of the swinging door from loosening the hinges over time.

The lockset is installed next (see **12-25**). Mortise locks provide high security and are often used in apartment buildings. But they require cutting a large rectangular opening in a solid core or rail-and-stile door to accommodate the lock body. Cylindrical locks are sturdy enough

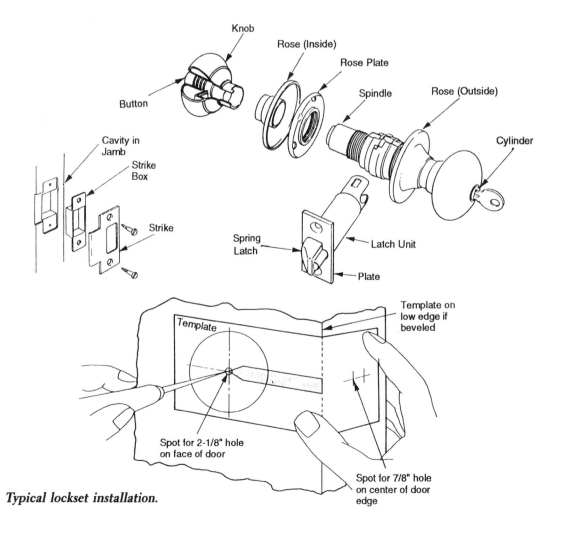

12-26 *Typical lockset installation.*

to provide adequate security for exterior doors. A large hole is bored in the door face to fit the lock body, and a smaller hole is required in the edge for the bolt. The installation of tubular locks is basically the same, except that they require boring a smaller hole in the door face. Because of their thinner cross section and generally lighter-duty construction, tubular locks are better suited to interior doors. Unit lock sets are installed in a cutout in the edge of the door and, since the lockset need not be disassembled to install or remove it, are most often used in apartments where locksets are changed with each new tenant.

Deadbolts provide extra security. The rim cylinder type attaches to the inside face of the door so that the bolt engages a strike notched into the edge of the casing. Tubular deadbolts engage a strike that resembles a deeper version of an ordinary door latch. A single-acting cylinder is keyed from the outside only. A double-acting cylinder, which is keyed from both sides, offers more security but less convenience and possible hazard in case of fire.

Professional door hangers use boring jigs and other specialized tools to install locksets accurately and quickly. The paper templates supplied with the lockset work well enough for the occasional door hanger (see **12-26**). The latch hole (typically, $7/8$ inch) can be done with a spade bit or a bit-and-brace. The lock hole (typically, $2\frac{1}{8}$ inch) is best cut with a hole saw.

Install weatherstripping after the lockset. The performance and difficulty of installation varies greatly with the type of weatherstripping (see **12-27**). One of the easiest to install that gives good service is Portaseal weatherstripping, which consists of a compressible vinyl gasket embedded in the edge of a $1\frac{3}{8}$-inch-wide stop moulding which is nailed to the jambs so that it lightly contacts the closed door. The smaller $3/4$-inch size is used for storm doors.

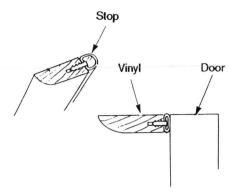

12-27   *Door weatherstrip moulding.*

There are also many different types of threshold weatherstrippings, ranging from simple sweeps to extruded aluminum thresholds fitted with a compressible vinyl bulb. (These are discussed in more detail in Chapter Nineteen.)

BUILDING YOUR OWN DOORS

When boards subject to seasonal shrinkage and swelling are fixed to a rigid frame they're likely to split if the frame doesn't deform first. Unless a homemade door duplicates the rail-and-stile floating panel construction of a high-quality factory-made door, the door may not stay tight for very long. The tendency towards distortion can be reduced by using inherently stable woods such as cedar, redwood, or cherry, appropriate angle braces, and thorough sealing, especially of end grain (see **12-28**). Homemade board-and-frame doors are better suited to interior use and for barns and sheds where a weather-tight seal is not critical.

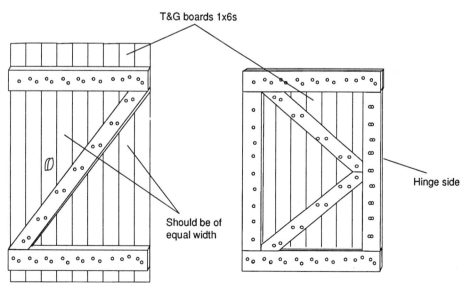

12-28   *Z-brace board-and-frame door.*

Sandwiching ¾ inch to 1½ inches of rigid-foam insulation between two sheets of ⅜-inch plywood and/or opposing board facings gives greater dimensional stability and excellent thermal performance. Seal the edges thoroughly and band them with solid wood (see **12-29**). With board overlays, greater racking resistance is obtained by orienting the boards on one face perpendicular or diagonal to those on the other. A sandwich door is apt to be too heavy and thick to be supported by ordinary square butt hinges, but most heavy-duty tee-strap hinges are too utilitarian for a fancy entrance door. You'll probably need to order custom-forged ornamental hinges. The leading edge of a door much thicker than two inches will strike against the jamb of an ordinary frame; the edge of the door must be bevelled accordingly. For a tight fit, add a bevelled stop to the jamb. Extend the board facing an inch beyond its edge-frame to make a self-sealing lip. Another approach to custom door construction is to glue decorative moulding or ⅜-inch-thick board panelling to solid-core flush doors. You can also cut an opening for a stained-glass insert or sheath the door with copper sheets according to your own ideas.

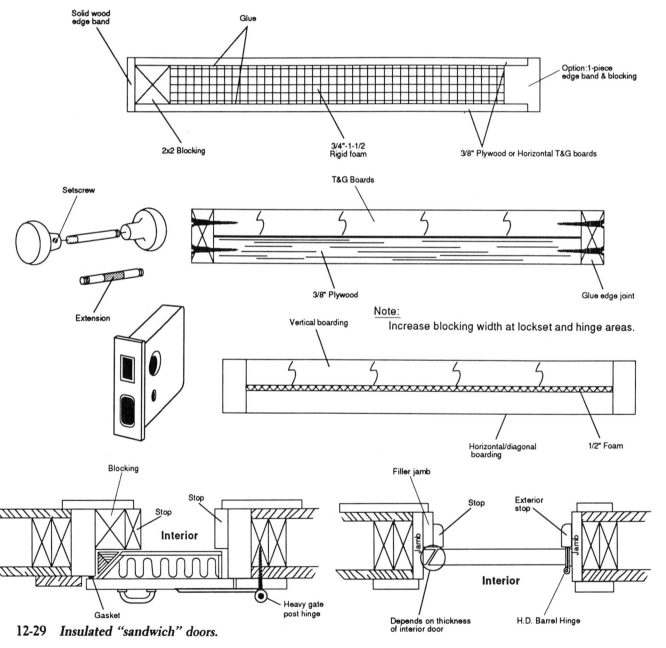

12-29 *Insulated "sandwich" doors.*

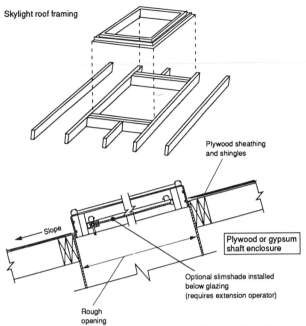

Skylight roof framing

Plywood sheathing and shingles

Slope

Plywood or gypsum shaft enclosure

Optional slimshade installed below glazing (requires extension operator)

Rough opening

12-30 *Typical roof window installation details.*

ROOF WINDOW INSTALLATION

Modern roof windows are installed in rough openings framed between the rafters (see **12-30**). Complete installation instructions are supplied with the unit. In general, metal angle brackets screwed to the unit frame and the roof deck support the roof window at the proper height above the roof. Be sure to order the flashing kit appropriate for the type of roofing material. Roof windows cannot be installed in roofs with slopes of less than 3-in-12 without leaking. If you still want to install an operable roof window rather than a fixed-glass skylight in a low-pitched roof, the roof window can be adapted to fit a projecting curb of the correct slope.

Prefabricated plastic-bubble or site-built fixed-glass skylights that seal to a wood-framed curb are normally used for flat roofs and as a low-cost alternative to roof windows (see **12-31**). Prefabricated units are generally dependable, but building your own leak-proof fixed-glass skylight can be problematic. Some builders screw tempered insulated-glass sashes to a curb flashing. The face of the sash is cut flush with the glazing at its bottom edge to shed water. But even with regular maintenance, the caulked seal between the glazing and the sash tends to leak.

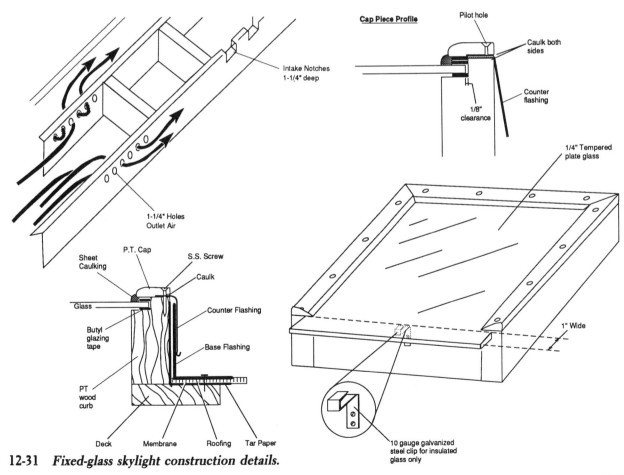

Intake Notches 1-1/4" deep

1-1/4" Holes Outlet Air

Cap Piece Profile

Pilot hole

Caulk both sides

Counter flashing

1/8" clearance

1/4" Tempered plate glass

P.T. Cap

S.S. Screw

Sheet Caulking

Caulk

Glass

Counter Flashing

Butyl glazing tape

Base Flashing

PT wood curb

1" Wide

Deck   Membrane   Roofing   Tar Paper

10 gauge galvanized steel clip for insulated glass only

12-31 *Fixed-glass skylight construction details.*

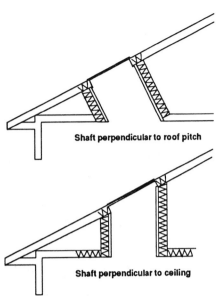
Shaft perpendicular to roof pitch

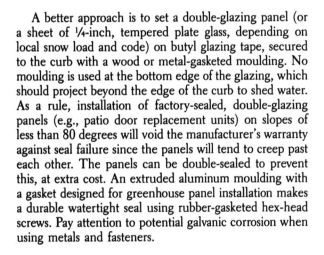
Shaft perpendicular to ceiling

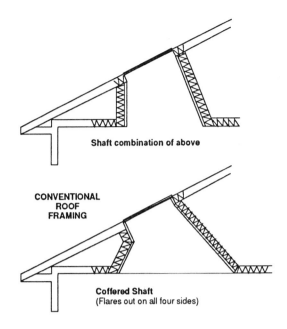
Shaft combination of above

**CONVENTIONAL
ROOF
FRAMING**

Coffered Shaft
(Flares out on all four sides)

12-32 *Skylight shaft configurations.*

A better approach is to set a double-glazing panel (or a sheet of ¼-inch, tempered plate glass, depending on local snow load and code) on butyl glazing tape, secured to the curb with a wood or metal-gasketed moulding. No moulding is used at the bottom edge of the glazing, which should project beyond the edge of the curb to shed water. As a rule, installation of factory-sealed, double-glazing panels (e.g., patio door replacement units) on slopes of less than 80 degrees will void the manufacturer's warranty against seal failure since the panels will tend to creep past each other. The panels can be double-sealed to prevent this, at extra cost. An extruded aluminum moulding with a gasket designed for greenhouse panel installation makes a durable watertight seal using rubber-gasketed hex-head screws. Pay attention to potential galvanic corrosion when using metals and fasteners.

Unless they are installed in a cathedral ceiling, both skylights and roof windows require a shaft—or light well (see **12-32**). The lower edges of some roof window jambs are rabbeted so that finish trim or wall surface can slip neatly behind them. The orientation of the shaft walls to the skylight determines how much light it will admit and the field of view through the window. The coffered type lets in the most light. A side perpendicular to the roof pitch lets light farther into the house than one perpendicular to the ceiling. Shaft angle can be utilized to block unwanted afternoon solar gain.

The space around the skylight shaft should be well insulated. With cathedral ceilings, notch or bore the top edges of the trimmer rafters so that the insulation vent cavity below the roof window can connect with the unobstructed vent cavities to either side.

13 Decks, Garages, and Other Attachments

From about 1840 until 1940, the front porch was where the private life of the home intersected with the public life of the street. As the parade of street life was given over to the automobile, and extended families shrank to nuclear dimensions, the front porch disappeared from the facade of the home, and the focus of sociability shifted to backyard patios and decks of an emerging suburbia.

BUILDING DECKS

There are several good reasons why, over the past decade or so, the outdoor deck has become the most popular home improvement in America (see **13-1**). Adding a deck is the simplest and least expensive way to increase the effective living area of a house. It requires no complicated foundations or roofing. The framing techniques, which are similar to floor framing, are accessible to the casual do-it-yourselfer. Unlike interior remodelling, deck building doesn't disrupt the normal use of the house. And, unlike the more formal porch, decks are more suited to the current casual style of outdoor living.

Many of the basic principles of deck construction were touched upon in the discussion of foundation systems in Chapter Three. The main difference between a pier foundation and a deck foundation is the scale of the support posts and their footings (see **13-2**). In most cases, pressure-treated 4×4s or, at most, 6×6s are adequate for the relatively light loads involved. Soil conditions permitting, holes for the deck support posts can be dug by hand or drilled with a post-hole auger.

13-1 *A well-proportioned porch can moderate the apparent height of the facade, and the porch roof can be used as a deck, as in this case—once the railings are finished.*

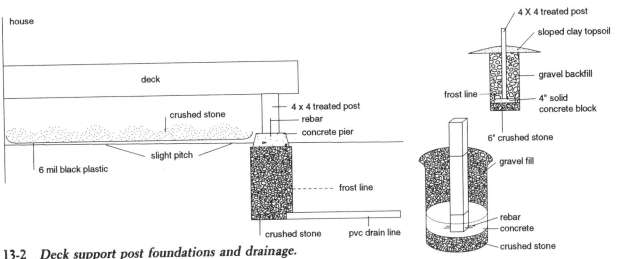

13-2 *Deck support post foundations and drainage.*

Although most designers recommend attaching the support posts to, or embedding them in, poured concrete piers that extend from frost line to just above grade, unless local codes require it, concrete foundation piers aren't really necessary. Treated posts can be set directly on a six-inch bed of tamped, crushed stone laid in the bottom of the hole, and they are easy to adjust.

Steel post anchors are actually a weak structural link, especially when used with tall, relatively thin posts. Side-ways bending stresses on the post base can split it apart at the through-bolts or make the deck wobble back and forth when you walk on it. A post that is continuous down to its footing will be stiffened by the backfill and much more resistant to sideways stresses, especially if its cross section is increased to counteract bending. If additional anchorage is needed (e.g., a steep sloping site, posts higher than six feet above grade, or in earthquake zones), drill two perpendicular holes through the post base, drive $1/2$-inch or $3/4$-inch rebar anchors through them, and pour a concrete collar around the post before backfilling it with well-tamped gravel to grade.

As was discussed in the foundation chapter, the key to long-term stability of any pier foundation is good drainage. A gravel or crushed-stone footing in a heavy, poorly drained chronically wet soil won't provide effective protection against frost heave or settlement since there is no outlet for the water that seeps into it. Under such conditions, the post footings should be drained by a continuous crushed-stone bed or perforated pipe to an outlet at grade (refer to 13-2). An alternative (for low decks only) is to fill a drainage trench from frost line to grade with crushed stone and support the deck framing on cast-concrete anchor blocks set directly on top of the stone.

The ground under most decks (and porches) won't be protected by a blanket of snow, so frost penetration can be deeper than normal. It's a good idea to set the footings for any intermediate support posts a foot or so deeper than standard frost depth.

Finally, since it's difficult or impossible to get to any weeds that might grow under the deck, strip the sod off and lay down a black plastic membrane covered with crushed stone under the deck area. The subgrade should pitch slightly to drain surface water away from the house foundation.

Freestanding decks are relatively rare; most decks are attached to at least one wall of the house. Assuming the house itself is square, this makes it relatively simple to lay out the deck support posts (see 13-3). Tack a string to the far corner of the end wall of the house and extend it along the wall to a batterboard or stake beyond the edge of the deck. The string will be a continuation of the house line. Do the same at the opposite wall if the deck runs the full length of the house wall; otherwise, measure in from the string along the wall, tack a nail to the sill at the correct point, and extend a string outward from it. Measure over from the first string to correctly position the second string, distance A. The string for the outside face of the deck supports is located by measuring off a line parallel to the house wall, distance B. If the walls aren't square, hide the difference in the least obtrusive side. It's more important for the sightline along the end of the deck to be straight than that the deck be perfectly square. Any difference in the width of the deck from one end to the other, distances C and D, can be "disappeared" by varying the spacing between the deck boards.

Pressure-Treated Lumber Pressure-treated wood is classified according to the type of preservative it contains. Creosote, an oily, smelly derivative of coal tar, is widely used in marine, farm, and heavy construction applications, and for treating railroad ties and utility poles. "Penta" (pentachlorophenol) is a petroleum-based preservative used for fencing and other outdoor applications. Both of these long-lived preservatives are carcinogenic and have a high residual toxicity; they have no place in residential construction. The familiar green-ish-hued wood that is widely used in outdoor construction is treated with one or more of several combinations of water-borne metallic salts. Some of the most common are ACA (ammoniacal copper arsenate), CCA (chromated copper arsenate), ACC (acid copper chromate), CZC (chromated zinc chloride), and FCAP (fluoro chrome arsenate phenol). Copper is a fungicide, arsenic is an insecticide, and chromium is the bonding agent that fixes the salts to the wood.

Pressure-treated wood is rated for either "Ground Contact" or "Above Ground" use. Ground contact lumber generally has more preservative and will last longer than above-ground wood. Tests have shown that the average expected service life of treated yellow pine in contact with the ground is about 42 years; untreated yellow pine would last about three years. The life expectancy of naturally rot-resistant woods like red or white cedar or redwood varies greatly with its resin content, climate conditions, application, and many other factors; in general, it ranges from eight to 25 years.

Many people are concerned about the toxicity of pressure-treated wood with normal use. The advantage of water-soluble preservatives is that once they dry, they become permanently fused to the wood cells; there is no oily exudate or leaching out of toxic compounds. After it reaches this state, the wood is basically nontoxic. Of course, when working with the stuff, you should always wash your hands before eating, smoking, or touching other parts of your body. As much as possible, wear gloves when handling the lumber. Wear a dust mask when cutting or machining it and do so outdoors. Never burn the scraps in an open fire. Don't use it in horse barns or where farm animals and pets could chew on it.

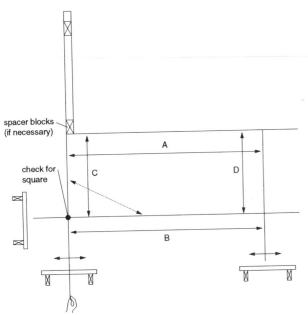

13-3 *Laying out a square deck. (Letters cited in text.)*

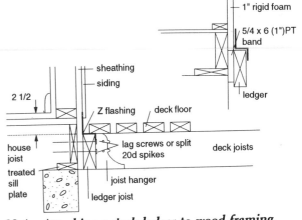

13-4 *Attaching a deck ledger to wood framing.*

Ideally, the finished surface of an unprotected deck should be about a standard stair step (7½ inches) below the sill of any doors that open onto it. In practice, this can vary from four inches to eight inches. The deck is usually not made flush with door openings since it's almost impossible to keep water and ice from seeping under the sill, even with proper flashing.

It is best if all or part of the ledger that carries the deck floor joists can be spiked (use 20d spikes) or lag-screwed directly to the wall sheathing at the rim joist and sill (see **13-4**). Nonstructural sheathing such as IB board and rigid foam should be cut back the width of the ledger (or at least six inches) and filled in flush with pressure-treated

plywood, 1×6 or ⁵⁄₄×6, treated boards to provide solid backing for the ledger. Otherwise it will eventually slip downwards against the compressible sheathing under load.

Special anchors are used to attach the ledger to poured concrete or concrete block or brick masonry (see **13-5**). Snap a level chalk line for the top of the ledger and temporarily support it against the masonry with boards tacked to the blocks of equal thickness nailed to the sills. Drill holes for the lag-screw or machine bolt fasteners through the ledger at the required locations—about two inches in from the top and bottom edges of the ledger, spaced no more than 24 inches apart, but offset to fall between joist spacings. Make the holes 1/16 inch larger than the diameter of the lag screws. Allow the drill to just barely mark the masonry. Then remove the ledger and bore the holes for the anchors with a carbide-tipped masonry drill. Lead expansion shield anchors are used in concrete and brick. Toggle-bolt anchors work better in hollow concrete block—avoid drilling into the solid parts of the block when locating fasteners.

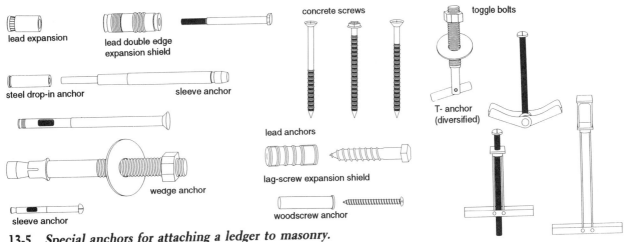

13-5 *Special anchors for attaching a ledger to masonry.*

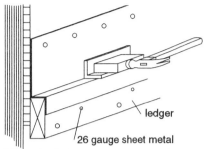

13-6 *Flashing the ledger.*

ledger

26 gauge sheet metal

In new construction, the deck ledger is always fastened to the wall sheathing and flashed before the finish siding is applied. The bottom of the siding itself is kept two inches above the finished decking. If the deck is being added to an existing structure, you'll need to remove the lower courses of siding first. Make the flashings from 14-inch copper or corrosion-proof enamelled aluminum or steel coil stock. They should extend at least four inches up the wall beneath the finish siding and bend over the top and down onto the face of the ledger (see **13-6**). Nail the top edge of the flashing to a level line across the sheathing

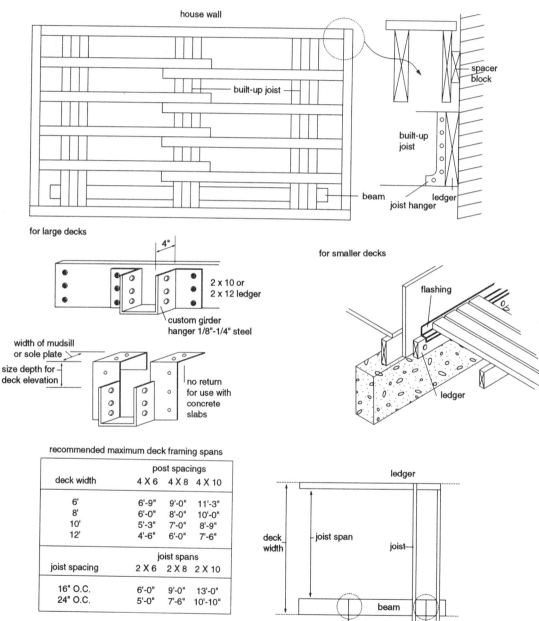

13-7 *Supporting girders and layout of joists.*

recommended maximum deck framing spans

	post spacings		
deck width	4 X 6	4 X 8	4 X 10
6'	6'-9"	9'-0"	11'-3"
8'	6'-0"	8'-0"	10'-0"
10'	5'-3"	7'-0"	8'-9"
12'	4'-6"	6'-0"	7'-6"
	joist spans		
joist spacing	2 X 6	2 X 8	2 X 10
16" O.C.	6'-0"	9'-0"	13'-0"
24" O.C.	5'-0"	7'-6"	10'-10"

and use an angle-iron bar or a square-edged board to fold the metal into the corner and bend it over the ledger. Flashing the ledger before installing the deck joists avoids notching it to fit over the tops of the joists and the attendant risk of leakage.

For light-duty decks, the joists are attached directly to the face of the ledger with galvanized-steel joist hangers or else notched or rested on an attached cleat at the bottom of the ledger and toenailed to it (see **13-7**). With large and/or complex decks that must carry significant loads (such as a hot tub or spa) the ledger may support the ends of large beams that carry the floor joist system instead.

As with any floor system, the size and run of the deck joists and the need for intermediate girders is determined by their span and the live load requirements. I recommend a working load of 50 pfs, since you can never tell how many people or how much snow will pile up on your deck. Decking usually runs parallel to the house wall, requiring the joists to be perpendicular to the ledger but effectively limiting their overall span to about ten feet unless intermediate support girders are added for multiple sets of joists. For a different configuration, doubled or tripled joists can be used to carry joists parallel with the ledger and the decking be run at right angles or diagonals to the house wall.

If you're working alone, tack a short piece of furring to the top edge of the joist so that it sticks out past each end (see **13-8**). These "hangers" hold the joist in position so that you can nail it to the ledger and header beam with metal joist hangers; many carpenters will nail joist hangers to the joist first. Brush wood preservative on all exposed end grain; pressure-treating may not have penetrated completely to the core.

"Boxed" girders or header joists offer as much, if not more, stiffness than built-up girders with a much stronger structural connection to their support posts (see **13-9**). A pair of planks are fastened to each side of a support post

and bridging blocks on 16-inch centers are nailed between them. If greater stiffness is required, one of the members is inset and a trimmer joist is nailed to it after the bridgers are installed.

One advantage of this method is that 4×4 posts can extend upwards through the decking to furnish a very solid support for the deck railing. In light-duty decks, the girders or header joists are normally through-bolted to the support posts or set on top of them. Notching the faces of the posts ¾ inch deep to receive the full width of the joist or girder beams is much stronger. The remaining post is still two inches; strong enough to carry the railing. Using 6×6 support posts provides greater resistance against sideways bending and also allows full-width support of the girders. The 6×6 posts are typically cut off flush with the top of the joists, and more proportional railing designs are used.

Treated 2×6 is the most widely used decking material. Wider planks tend to cup objectionably. Some builders prefer to use higher-grade ⁵⁄₄×6 boards milled especially for decking; its pronounced rounded edge is less likely to cause splinters and the surface is planed smoother than all but the highest-grade 2×6 lumber. These boards require 16-inch o.c. joist spacing, whereas 2×6s can be used with 24-inch spacing. Use two 16d (or 8d, with ⁵⁄₄ stock) hot-dipped, galvanized- or stainless-steel nails or 2½-inch deck screws over each joist. Lay the decking bark-side up (heart down) so that the boards will shed water if they do cup.

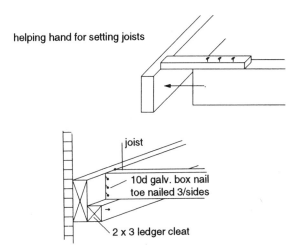

13-8 *Attaching joists to the ledger.*

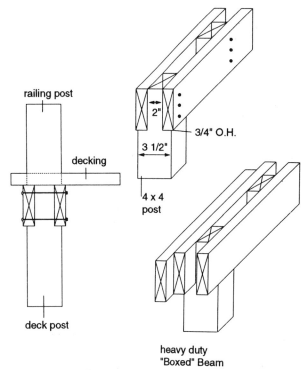

13-9 *Boxed beam construction.*

331

For a clean line and even reveal, begin laying the decking at the outer edge of the deck and work back towards the house. The first piece should overhang the deck support (or its fascia trim board) by about one inch (see **13-10**). Notch the pieces to fit neatly around railing posts. Except for the first board or two, which should be trimmed to exact length, leave the ends of overhanging boards long and trim them off all at once with a circular saw following a chalk line. An option which duplicates the "clean" edge of the starting board overhang is to cut the ends of the decking back about ¼ inch to ½ inch over the stringer joist and screw a narrow strip of wood across the exposed ends.

Space the decking ¼ inch or ⅜ inch apart for adequate drainage, using spacers cut from scrap. Toenail obviously bowed boards tight against the spacers to straighten them out. Sight along the run of the decking from time to time to make sure it isn't starting to curve, and measure the distance to the house wall to make sure it is running parallel. If necessary, vary the spacing in increments so that you don't end up with a tapered piece at the wall. Also, divide the distance to be covered by the width of the decking plus the spacing, and adjust it as needed so that the last piece isn't a narrow strip either; if need be, you can also rip a slightly wider ending piece from a 2×8.

When a deck turns a corner, standard practice calls for the decking to intersect at a 45-degree mitre. This angle must be precise if the edges of the cuts are to meet evenly; otherwise, if one face angle is longer than the other, the decking will soon run off its spacing. Check the decking to make sure each opposing piece is of equal width; pressure-treated boards often vary in width. The underlying angled joist is doubled up and mitred into the header joists.

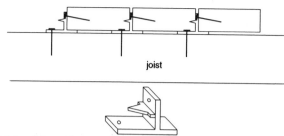

13-11 *Manufactured Dec-Klips fasteners allow a nail-free deck surface.*

Dec-Klips fasteners are an alternative to face-nailing that automatically space the boards for drainage while eliminating unsightly nail heads and the problems associated with nail popping (see **13-11**). The base of the clip slides under the free edge of the decking and is nailed into its edge with a 16d nail. The other side of the base is nailed into the joist. The edge of the following board is held down by tapping it against a point that sticks out of the clip.

Marine-grade plywood is an alternative to lumber or board decking where a spaced deck might be objectionable (e.g., where the space below the deck is also intended to double as a storage area but a porch roof is not desired). Another special plywood, designed for use on docks and outdoor commercial walkways, has a laminated waterproof phenolic plastic face that's roughened for safe traction. It comes with tongue-and-grooved edges which should be caulked before installation.

The fact that one side of a deck is attached to a relatively immovable house won't stop the deck from shaking or

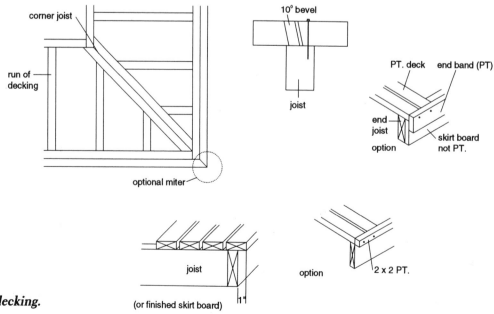

13-10 *Laying decking.*

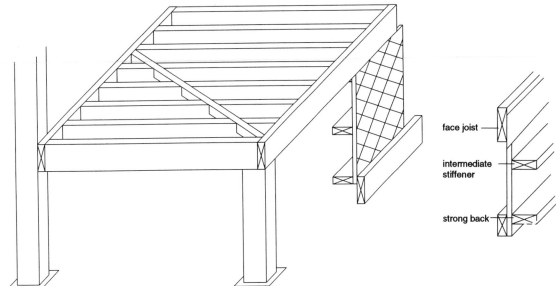

13-12 *As the height of the deck increases, lateral racking resistance becomes more critical.*

shifting back and forth when people walk on it. The support posts along the outer rim are still free to shift sideways, especially if they are tall and relatively narrow. Nailing let-in 2×4, flatwise diagonal braces to the tops of the deck joists can substantially dampen this sideways motion, at least for a low deck (see **13-12**). Tall decks need knee-bracing or X-bracing between the support posts to completely eliminate the wobble.

Other than code requirements which specify the heights of the top and middle rails (any deck more than 16 inches above the ground is required to have a 42-inch-high railing) and the spacing requirements for vertical rails (a six-inch sphere, e.g., a child's head, should not be able to pass between them), the design of deck railings, benches, planters, and other built-in furniture is limited only by one's imagination and budget (see **13-13**).

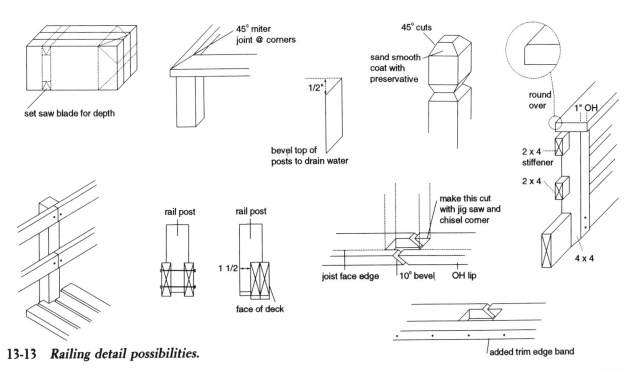

13-13 *Railing detail possibilities.*

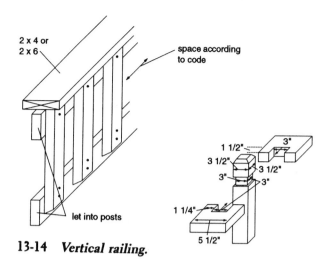

13-14 *Vertical railing.*

Another popular railing design utilizes vertical 2×2 balusters screwed six inches o.c. to a horizontal top and bottom rail (see **13-14**). The top end of the balusters butts against a flat top rail, and the bottom end is usually cut on a decorative 45-degree bevel. Construct a simple jig to predrill holes for the screws in each baluster. Round over and sand the edges of hand rails of any design to prevent splinters.

Although it's often done, a plumb railing doesn't provide a comfortable backrest for a bench. The backs of most seating are at least 10 to 15 degrees off-vertical. You can set your railing uprights at this angle or else add backrest supports to vertical uprights (see **13-15**).

If you feel that outward-leaning railings or extra backrest supports detract from the aesthetics of the deck, but you want comfortable seating, a compromise is to taper the backrest portion of a 2×6 upright up to about two inches (see **13-16**). Although the resulting angle is only about half of the standard backrest tilt, it's a lot more comfortable than vertical—and it allows the design to neatly integrate the benches with ordinary vertical railings.

Laid flat, a 2×4 or 2×6 bench requires supports at frequent intervals. This can make for a cluttered appearance. Building benches by laying 2×4s (or 2×3s) on edge allows supports to be spaced up to six feet apart. The two-bys can be spaced with squares of ½-inch pressure-treated plywood or ⅜-inch shims ripped from boards, which look and weather better than the exposed end grain of plywood. Glue the shims to the bench stock with construction ad-

Railing uprights that are not extensions of the deck support posts should be bolted to the header joist. Always use two bolts to prevent sideways movement. The uprights can be set either on the inside or on the outside of the joist and be either full-width or lap-notched to reduce the profile and length of the bolts. Horizontal railings are either lagged or screwed to the face of the uprights or, for better support, let into them. A flatwise top rail both stiffens the railing and protects the end grain of the uprights from exposure.

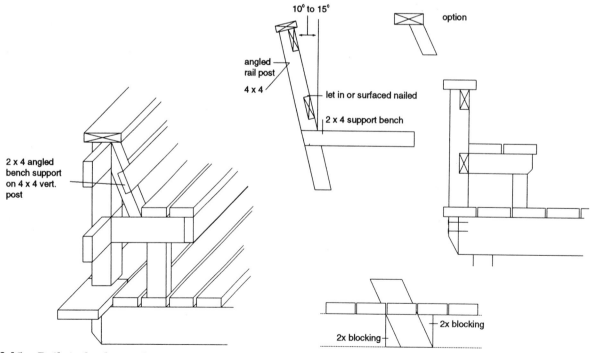

13-15 *Built-in backrests for deck benches.*

334

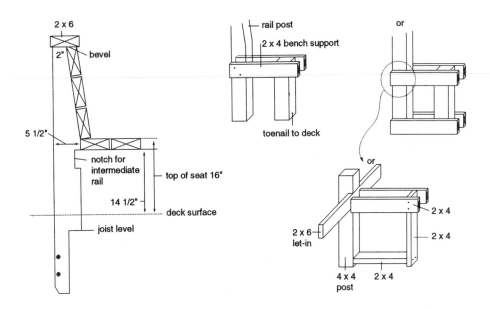

13-16 *This design is a reasonable compromise between comfort and simplicity.*

hesive rated for use with pressure-treated wood and drive 16d galvanized nails alongside each shim to join each piece to the next (see **13-17**). The ends of the bench pieces can be left as they are or else banded with a trim piece mitre-jointed to the long edges of the bench. Sand the spacer shims smooth and flush to the top of the bench. You can also bore each piece using a jig or an extension bit and bolt the bench together with recessed threaded ½-inch rods.

Instead of ordinary framed two-by bench supports, consider laminating 2×4s together with glue and nails to make a complementary pedestal for your laminated benches (see **13-18**). The supports can be secured by lag screws driven into their bottoms from below or by bolts inset in the base piece of the pedestal prior to lamination. To increase durability, reduce the contact area between supports and decking. The benches can be lagged down to the pedestals or secured by cleats with screws and adhesive.

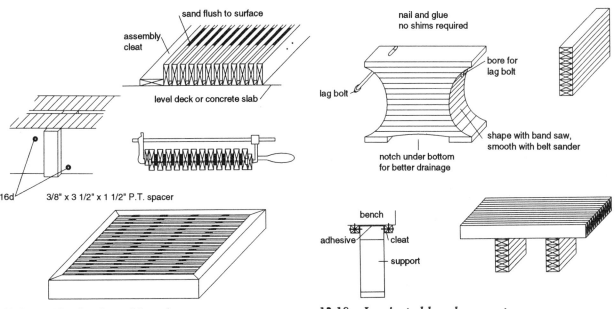

13-17 *Edge-laminated benches.*

13-18 *Laminated bench supports.*

13-19 *Gable-end porches weren't common on 1860s farmhouses, but there were enough so that this modern version seems quite at home.*

PORCHES

The addition of a roof turns a deck into a porch (also called a veranda). In small towns and rural villages, where people can still stroll along the sidewalks at twilight, the classic front porch is, once again, making a comeback, especially with the revival of neo-Victorian, Gothic, and Craftsman-style house plans (see **13-19**).

Unlike patios and decks, even long rambling porches are normally relatively narrow—eight feet being the most common and practical width. A wider porch creates problems integrating its roof into the main house wall or main roofline; a narrower porch doesn't allow enough space for furniture and circulation.

Porches can be either open, semi-enclosed, or fully enclosed according to both their intended use and architectural style (see **13-20**). Since an open porch lacks a railing between its cylindrical columns or turned or squared wood posts, its deck can't be more than two steps above grade, by code. The semi-enclosed porch features either an ornamental balustrade between the posts or else a half-wall, with a wide sill. Many semi-enclosed porches are designed so that removable screen and/or storm window panels can be installed between their posts as the season dictates. Fully enclosed porches have permanently installed regular operable windows or *jalousie* windows for privacy and ventilation. Instead of the post-and-infill framing of the true porch, the enclosed porch is typically stud-framed; it's more often an extension of the house proper than a transition zone.

In general, porch floor framing is very similar to deck construction. Both use a flashed ledger attached to the house wall to carry the floor frame. The girder and/or joist header beam are both supported on wood posts or concrete piers. The main difference is that porch floor joists always run parallel to the house wall so that the floor boards themselves will run at right angles to the house. The floor boards are typically pitched away from the house wall at about one inch over eight feet to drain away wind-blown rain or other water. Because of their greater degree of protection, unlike decking, porch floor boards are laid tight.

Tongue-and-groove Douglas fir is the traditional porch flooring material in edge-grained clear $5/4 \times 4$ boards. To prolong the longevity of this expensive wood, soak the boards in a trough of clear wood preservative for at least three minutes and let them dry for two days before painting them with primer and two coats of high-quality oil-based porch and deck enamel on *all* faces and edges. Run a thin bead of caulk between each joint as you nail down the floor.

Using pressure-treated decking instead assures longevity without the trouble of painting. Since treated $5/4 \times 6$

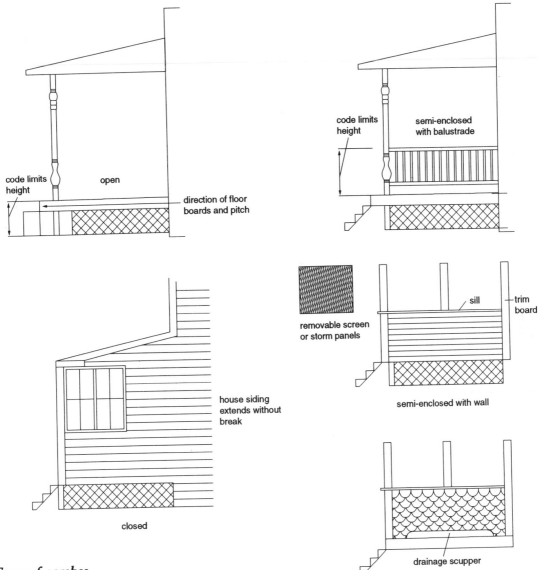

13-20 *Types of porches.*

decking is only milled with square edges, you'll have to run the boards through a shaper (or router) to custom-cut the tongue-and-groove joints. For best appearance and minimal warpage, stain the decking on all sides. Since porch floor joists are close to the ground and some moisture will eventually become trapped between the underside of the decking and the tops of the framing, use pressure-treated lumber for the floor framing, no matter what kind of wood you use for the floor boards.

The exposed end grain of porch decking should be protected also. Cut a one-inch-wide strip off the edge of a piece of decking and round over its corners into a bull nose shape (see **13-21**). Coat the ends of the flooring with preservative, run a bead of caulking, and nail the edge bead to them.

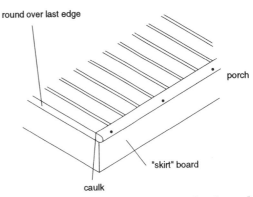

13-21 *Bull-nose moulding for the ends of porch floorboards.*

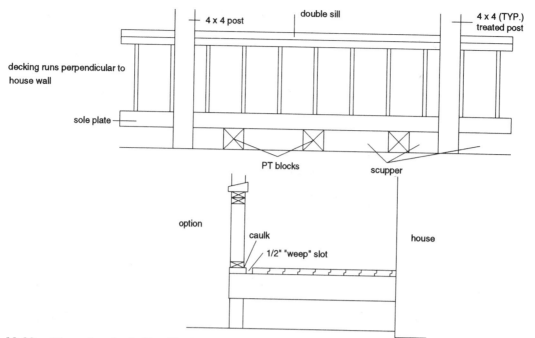

13-22 *The sole of a half-wall of a semi-enclosed porch is always raised above the floor boards for drainage unless the porch will be protected by permanent screen and/or storm panels.*

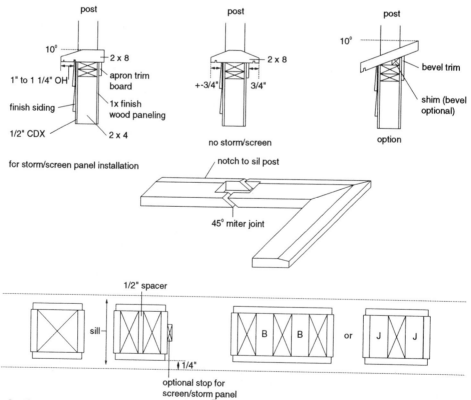

13-23 *Frame built-up posts into the half-wall and notch the sill to fit against them. Bed the finish post trim in caulking where it butts against the sill to make a watertight joint.*

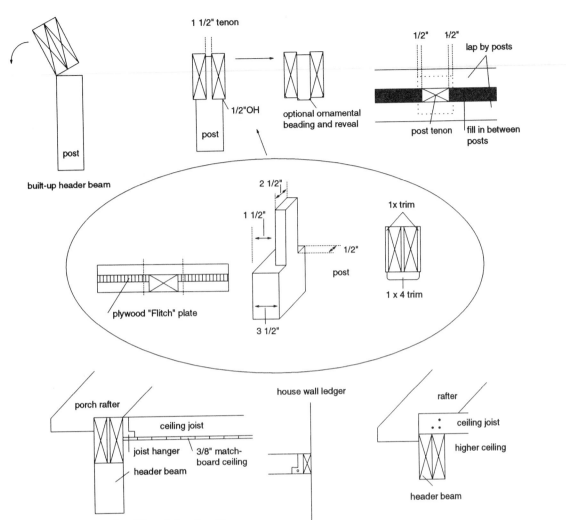

13-24 *Header beam and ceiling joist details.*

Porches are more likely to rot than the rest of the house because of the great number of exposed joints and faces in the trim and railing details which are capable of trapping water. The most important part of porch construction is still careful attention to configuring joints to shed rather than collect water and to avoid exposed end grain, which sucks up water.

With a semi-enclosed half-wall porch, the infill panels are framed like a regular wall, using pressure-treated lumber for the sole plate, which is set on spacer blocks above the decking to form drainage scuppers (see 13-22). If the porch is always protected by screens and/or glazing panels, the wall can be caulked tight to the deck since the small amount of water that normally blows through a screen panel can be mopped up before it has a chance to do much damage. The floor boards could also run parallel with the house and the drainage scuppers in the porch wall could be eliminated.

With or without screen panels, the sill of any semi-enclosed porch should be cut from a single piece of two-by stock (heart-side up) whenever possible and notched to fit against the porch posts (see 13-23). Any splices should be bevelled. Use mitre joints at outside corners. The sill itself is bevelled 10 degrees on one or both sides (depending on whether or not it will be fitted with screens and storms), or bevelled on its leading edge and installed at an angle (refer to 13-22).

If the header beam which carries the porch rafters is set on top of the porch posts, it will tend to roll outwards under load. It's a better idea to set the beam on notches cut into each side of the uprights (just like the deck box-beam described earlier), or to piece the header in between the posts and tie everything together with a rafter plate (see 13-24).

Stiffening the connection between the post and the header beam, however, only transfers the outward thrust

339

of the roof load onto the support posts. Running horizontal ceiling joist ties from the header to a ledger on the building wall substantially increases the structural stability of the porch roof assembly. Two-by-fours are normally adequate for ceiling joist stock. Beaded ⅜-inch-thick "matchboard" is the traditional porch ceiling finish, but any less expensive board finish is preferable to plywood.

Unless your house has a storey-and-a-half sidewall, if the porch roof is to have a pitch steep enough to permit shingle or corrugated sheet roofing, it will have to extend onto the deck of the main roof (see **13-25**). The framing and end wall siding and flashing techniques are basically the same as those used for shed dormers. Since both the porch roof and the main roof must have full-width starter shingles at their eaves, the exposure of the last few courses of porch roof shingles will probably have to be adjusted to blend more or less unnoticeably with the main roof shingles. If the porch roof is attached to a sidewall, pay close attention to the flashing details, especially if window sills are located close to the roof.

ROOFTOP DECKS
A flat roof, with or without a parapet wall, would seem to offer an ideal outdoor living area. Unfortunately, walking on the gravel surface of built-up roofing can cause the stones to puncture the underlying membrane. Half-lap roofing is also damaged by excessive traffic and is too steeply pitched for comfortable use, in any case.

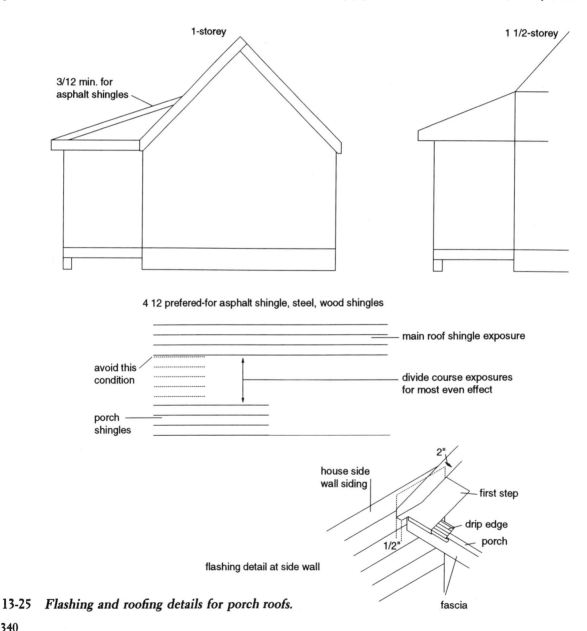

13-25 *Flashing and roofing details for porch roofs.*

Fortunately, it's easy to build a level deck over any flat or low-pitched roof by using tapered pressure-treated *sleepers* to hold the deck level above the underlying roof (see **13-26**). Don't spread any gravel under the deck area when applying the flood coat for built-up roofing or ballast cover for EPDM membrane roofing. Since the membrane will be shielded by the deck, there's no need to protect it with gravel. Setting the sleepers on gravel would have the same effects as walking on it. Bed the sleepers in cold cement spread over 12-inch-wide strips of 90-pound mineral surface roll roofing which have also been cold-cemented to the flood coat. This way, if it ever becomes necessary to replace the sleepers, the mineral strips can be torn up without damaging the underlying built-up membrane. The sleepers themselves are laid parallel with the run of the rafters so that they don't interfere with roof drainage. For 24-inch o.c. rafter spacing, lay a sleeper over each rafter; with 16-inch o.c. spacing, lay the sleepers over every other rafter if you use 2×6 decking, or on each rafter for 2×4 or 5/4×6 decking.

Since a slope of 1/4-in-12 (1 inch over 12 feet) is steep enough to prevent ponding, but close enough to level not to interfere with the use of the deck, it's probably not worth the trouble to taper the sleepers. To provide both better nailing and more stable bearing, use 4×4s instead of flat- or edge-laid 2×4s. On slightly steeper pitches, the sleepers should be at least one inch deep at their thinnest dimension so that the deck nails won't penetrate into the underlying roof surface. Such an oversight could lead to real leakage problems.

To keep windblown debris and birds from accumulating under the deck, extend the sleepers slightly beyond the edge of the roof drip edge (if the deck does not butt a parapet wall) and cover the exposed ends with a fascia board that overhangs the drip edge. Leave at least a 1/2-inch-wide gap behind the fascia to allow water to drain freely. Where heavy ice buildup is likely, the extension will have to be greater to prevent an ice jam. Plywood decking can also be used instead of spaced decking to eliminate the runoff problem.

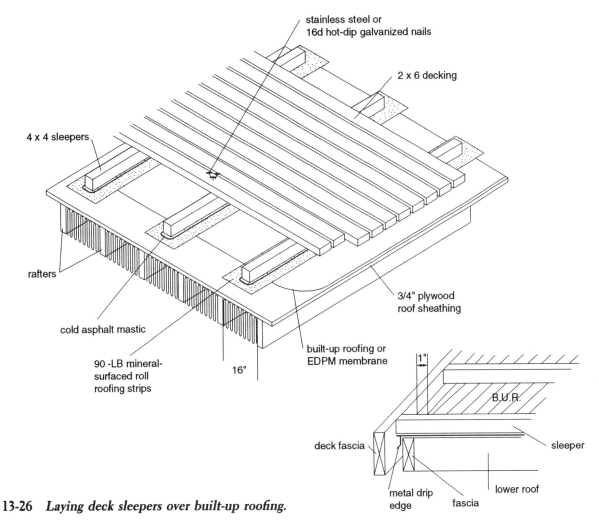

13-26 *Laying deck sleepers over built-up roofing.*

Unlike a flat, pitched roof, where the weight of the deck and the tenacity of the cold cement will keep the sleepers in place without any need for nails, sleepers must be firmly attached to the deck of a low-slope roof so they won't creep down along its slope (see **13-27**). Furthermore, the taper needed to level out a steeper slope will exceed the depth of a 4×4 for any deck wider than a narrow catwalk. While you could toenail tapered floor joists bedded in mastic to half-lap roofing, long-term watertightness would be hard to guarantee. Toenail the tapered joists directly to the roof sheathing and nail cant strips along their edges, folding an ice-and-water-shield membrane over them and onto the membrane covering the rest of the roof. The area under the deck needs no further protective roofing surface. Although the membrane is self-sealing, coat the top of the joists with asphalt or butyl caulking when you nail down the decking. The joists can also be doubled up for greater sideways stability or else nailed through their bottom edges to a flat-laid 2×4 sleeper.

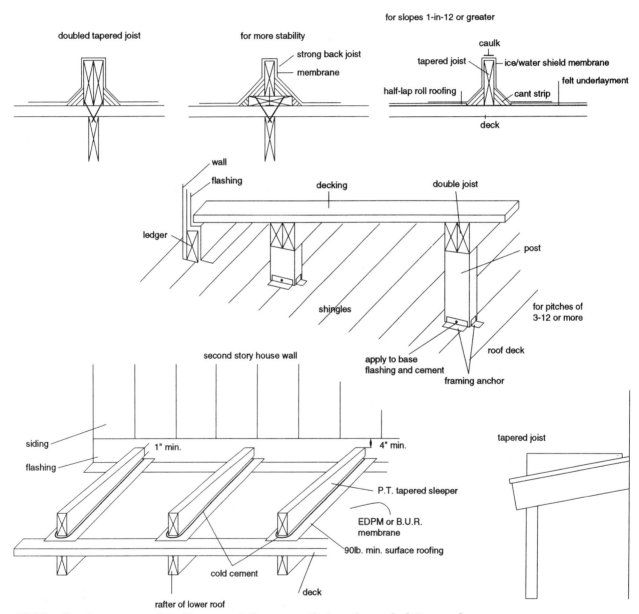

13-27 *On slopes up to 3-in-12, tapered sleepers nailed to the underlying roofing are flashed with a membrane for watertightness. On steeper pitches, deck joists are supported on posts flashed to the roofing like any standard penetration.*

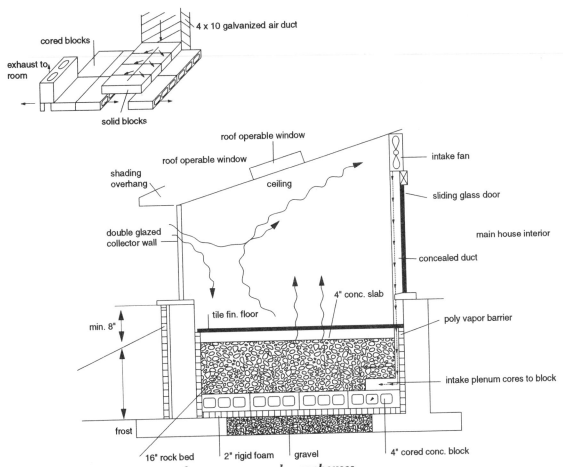

13-28 *Hybrid heat-storage floor system for sunspaces and greenhouses.*

On steeper pitches, secure bevelled posts to the roof deck with galvanized framing anchors and flash them with membrane and mastic as for any roof penetration (refer to **13-27**). The posts carry girders to support the deck floor joists. Provide diagonal cross bracing between the posts to keep the deck from shifting sideways.

GREENHOUSES AND SUNSPACES

In areas with long, cold winters, the amount of outdoor living afforded by a deck is limited. Although the glass-enclosed sunspace and attached greenhouse were initially promoted as a way to utilize passive solar energy to reduce heating costs, their ensuing popularity had more to do with an expansion and rediscovery of the traditional sunporch. Even if their construction details are similar, the functions of a greenhouse and sunspace are entirely different. Factors which increase the efficiency of a sunspace as a solar collector can make it unsuitable as a greenhouse.

A sunspace is basically a fancy version of a glassed-in porch that can be opened to the house during the day and isolated at night or on cloudy days; it is thus subjected to wide temperature swings, which are totally unacceptable for growing plants. Even with sufficient thermal mass, a properly functioning greenhouse won't add very much supplemental heat to the rest of the house, since as much as 30 percent of the incoming solar radiation is absorbed by the metabolic processes of the plants themselves. And those same processes can increase the indoor humidity to unacceptable levels or require venting. A greenhouse will also almost always need supplemental heat from the house at night to keep the plants at the right temperature.

Nevertheless, heat storage mass is the key element of both a successful solar greenhouse and a sunspace (see **13-28**). It extends the comfort range of the space by damping extreme temperature swings. One drawback to 100 percent passive solar heat storage is the relatively low efficiency of heat transfer into the storage slab. Heat storage systems which use small blower fans must overcome complex mechanical inefficiencies to achieve any significant increase in the rate of heat storage. A large and turbulent surface area in good mechanical contact with the radiant mass has been shown to be the key to efficient thermal charging by forced convection.

343

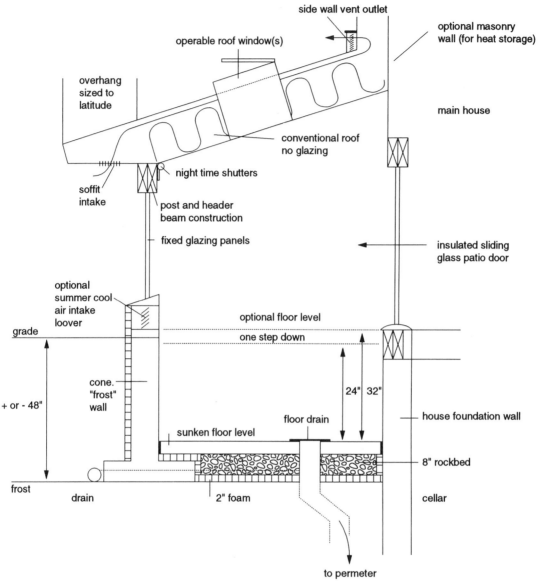

13-29 *Schematic of typical greenhouse/sunspace construction.*

One way of achieving this is to align the cores of four-inch concrete blocks into a system of parallel ducts over rigid insulation. Solar-heated air is drawn from the upper levels of the space by a thermostatically controlled small blower into a duct to a plenum that connects with the concrete block cores where the rough surface of the blocks increases the efficiency of heat extraction and transfers to a four-inch radiant slab poured over the blocks. The ends of each duct are joined to another plenum where the cooled but still warm air heats the space or can be drawn into the main house. Adding a 16-inch-deep rock bed between the block ductwork and the radiant floor slab provides long-term, deep-storage capacity.

Greenhouse and sunspace additions are available in kit form in a wide variety of styles, materials, sizes, and price ranges, for dealer/contractor or skilled do-it-yourself installation. I strongly recommend that, before you buy any kit, you be sure the manufacturer is willing to back up the performance specifications of the unit with stamped engineering calculations by a registered professional engineer. Ask the dealer for references from satisfied customers and arrange to inspect a completed installation. Examine the installation manual; you should be confident of your ability to follow it before you buy. Ask if the manufacturer has a detailed professional installation video, which could save many hours of confusion. Check the

344

details of the glazing system; not only must it comply with local codes and support the expected ice and snow loads for your region—and be leakproof—but it should contain weep channels and interior gutters on all four sides of the glass to drain condensation that would otherwise damage the interior of the structure and any furnishings it contains. Finally, consider the range of options and accessories such as ventilation systems and nighttime insulation and summer-shading mechanisms that are either offered with the kit or are compatible to it. The National Greenhouse Manufacturers Association (P.O. Box 567, Pana, IL 62557) offers a brochure that describes types of sunspaces and offers suggestions for siting and code requirements.

In general, sloping glazing greatly complicates the construction of a weather-tight sunspace/greenhouse and the installation of effective shutters and shades. Formerly, the rule of thumb held that the optimum glazing angle was equal to latitude plus 15 degrees. However, at latitudes of 45 degrees North and more, a vertical wall performs almost as well as the idealized 60-degree slope, especially where reflection off the winter snow cover can make up for the loss of overhead insolation. Although substituting a conventional roof for overhead glazing does sacrifice a dramatic view of the sky, it makes it much easier to control heat loss, summer overheating, and condensation problems. More than sufficient overhead light and ventilation can be provided by operable roof windows at a fraction of the cost of glazing (see **13-29**).

"Wrapping" the house walls around the sunspace or greenhouse is a more efficient configuration than "bumping" the addition out beyond the main wall of the house. If this is unavoidable, the end walls should be solid and opaque, rather than glazed, to prevent excessive winter heat loss and summer overheating. The sunspace/greenhouse can face up to 20 degrees off of solar South without any meaningful loss of insolation.

SOME THOUGHTS ABOUT GARAGES
In frost country, garages are built on frost-wall foundations. In less severe climates, they can be built on a concrete slab-on-grade poured over a compacted gravel base. In either case, it's important that the sole plate of the garage wall be at least eight inches above the garage floor, since it's frequently wet. Some builders set a course of cement-filled concrete blocks around the perimeter of a slab-on-grade foundation, but even with anchor bolts the connection to the slab is relatively weak. Forming and pouring an extension wall directly on top of the slab makes a stronger connection. Some builders also prefer to pour the slab against a shelf formed in the frost wall.

The garage door opening must be laid out precisely since the jambs of the garage door will rest against it (see **13-30**). The dimensions of the finished frame opening for a garage door are usually the same size as the door itself; so the rough openings are thus three inches wider and 1½ inches higher than the finished size.

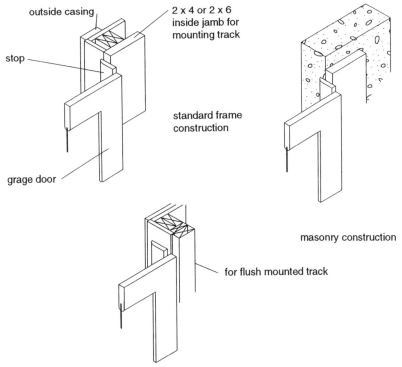

outside casing

2 x 4 or 2 x 6 inside jamb for mounting track

stop

standard frame construction

grage door

masonry construction

for flush mounted track

13-30 *Details and options for garage door construction.*

Most contractors prefer to purchase their overhead garage doors from specialized dealers who also install them in a matter of minutes. But the actual assembly and installation of a sectional garage door isn't difficult, although it does take quite a bit longer to do it yourself. Any door you buy will come with detailed and easy-to-understand assembly and installation instructions.

Garages attached to or built underneath the house require special construction to prevent poisonous automobile exhaust fumes from seeping into the living areas and to protect the rest of the house against fire. Building codes call for one-hour fire-rated (fire code) ⅝-inch drywall on walls and ceilings. All joints and seams must be taped with joint compound to provide a good seal. Tight-fitting steel doors and caulked trim should also be used to seal out the fumes. Install a smoke detector on the garage ceiling.

Although it is considered standard, I don't recommend that you put a drain in the garage floor. The fluids that drip from your car are toxic and should not be introduced to the sewer system or ground water table by means of the house drainage system. Soak up any spills with kitty litter instead, and dispose of it properly in a hazardous-waste landfill.

Finally, whether your garage is attached or detached, try to keep from building it *too small*. The minimum dimensions for a two-car garage should be 24 feet by 24 feet. A 20 foot by 20 foot structure will admit two cars, but there won't be room for anything else.

14 Painting and Staining

The first-known oil-based paint, a mixture of red ochre earth and animal fat that decorated the walls of caves in the south of France, was invented about 30,000 years ago. The ancient Greeks (about 3000 years ago) bound their colors with honey and egg whites. The first modern house paint appeared in the late 1700s, when white lead was mixed with linseed oil to create a bright and durable finish. That basic formula remained essentially unchanged until the invention of water-based "latex" paints as an outgrowth of the post–World War II development of polymer chemistry. Likewise, faster-drying, petroleum-based alkyd polyester resins replaced natural linseed oil as the vehicle in modern oil paints. Professionals and amateurs alike have argued about whether an oil or a water base makes the best paint ever since.

Oil paints form a hard, nonporous film, and have a reputation for durability and a smooth, rich finish among professional painters. Although the lead that formerly gave oil paint much of its "body" has been eliminated since 1978, the volatile organic compounds (VOCs) that are the solvents for the film-forming resins are nonetheless hazardous to health in confined areas.

Latex paints, which were routinely dismissed by professionals as inferior products suited only to the weekend painter, have been improved to the point where their performance and durability equals—or surpasses—that of the best oil paints in most cases. The linked molecular structure of acrylic latex polymer is more "breathable" than the hard film of oil paints. This is why you can paint damp wood with latex. When dry, a latex film is also more flexible, enabling it to withstand the contraction and expansion of the wood better than a brittle oil film. Latex paint has less odor, lower toxicity, better resistance to mildew and UV degradation, dries faster, and is easier to clean up than oil paint.

Despite being "water-based," latex paints are formulated with small amounts of petrochemical solvents and emulsifiers to improve workability and drying time as well as pigment dispersion. Many of these compounds are still present in potentially harmful amounts. A new generation of so-called green or low-toxic paints, originally developed in Europe, is now finding a place in the North American market. These paints are based on natural emulsifiers such as linseed oil, beeswax, turpentine, and citrus terpene and contain extremely low levels of petroleum distillates and little or no fungicides or other biocides. Because of their low VOC levels, they are "kinder" to the environment, although some chemically sensitive individuals may still be irritated by their aromatic fumes, especially when they are used indoors.

GUIDELINES FOR SUCCESSFUL PAINTING

Moisture is the main cause of premature paint failure. Water vapor migrating through the house walls from the interior will break the bond between the paint film and the wood siding, causing the paint surface to blister. Moisture, in the form of actual water or ice, can leak through uncaulked or improperly flashed joints between siding and trim. Proper interior ventilation, the installation of a continuous vapor retarder, and avoidance of living habits that produce excessive amounts of water vapor all are necessary to control the generation of internal moisture. Meticulous caulking of joints and seals and the use of gutters and drip edges help prevent external moisture problems. Keeping a clearance of at least eight inches between wood siding and the ground also helps.

Proper surface preparation is also important. Although not as much of a problem with new wood as with repainting, the bare wood should be free of dirt, sawdust, oily grime, fingerprints, and bird droppings.

Before priming, coat the wood with a *paintable* water repellent/wood preservative or, at the very least, with a clear wood preservative. Water repellents prolong the life of the paint film by reducing the normal swelling and shrinkage of the wood in response to soaking/drying cycles. It's also important to use this preservative/repellent treatment prior to staining and when the wood will be left "natural" with no other finish. Allow the preservative to dry for three days before *brushing* on a single coat of *oil-based* primer. The brush works the coating into the wood fibres better than a sprayer or roller. As mentioned earlier, wood siding that will be painted or stained should always be "back-primed" on all hidden faces and edges before installation so that it won't absorb moisture that would otherwise blister the face coat.

Despite their widespread use, experts recommend against shellac-base primer/sealers outdoors. These products are very effective for sealing resinous knots so that they don't "bleed" through the top coat. But they also tend to fail before the rest of the finish.

Follow the manufacturer's recommendations as to how long to wait before applying the finish coat and then brush on two coats of exterior acrylic latex housepaint. Even though the paint may have enough body to give single-coat coverage, doubling the number of coats is worth the effort since it doubles the life of the paint and, more important, the interval between repainting.

Finally, dispose of the leftover paint properly. Let the cans sit uncovered in a safe place outdoors where animals, pets, and children can't reach them, until the solvent evaporates; then dispose of the solidified pigment in an approved landfill. In some cities, you can bring your unused paint to a recycling center. Don't rinse out petrochemical solvents in the sink or dump them on the ground where they can wreak havoc on your septic tank, percolate into the ground water, or contaminate your municipal sewer system.

Whether you use oil or latex paint, always buy only the very best. Ask professional painters which brands they prefer. If the same name comes up repeatedly, it's probably the one you should use. But do make sure that the product you buy is suited to the intended use. If it's latex, make sure it's 100 percent acrylic, not vinyl, which is not as resistant to UV degradation. It's important that the paint also have high levels of mildewicide in humid regions. Paint also has a limited shelf life. Make sure yours is fresh.

The satisfactory appearance of the finished job is a direct result of how the paint is applied. Contrary to popular impression, applying paint with a sprayer isn't all that much faster than brushing it on ordinary siding when the time-consuming masking of windows and trimwork and protection against overspray is taken into account. Indoors, sprayers are effective only when everything is the same color. Rollers are a lot more useful. Sprayers are great on railings, fence boards, and ornamental trim. One big advantage of a sprayer is that, when properly used, drips are avoided.

Good paint needs a good brush (see **14-1**). Use natural hog bristle for oil paints and polyester or nylon bristles for latex paints (natural bristles get soft and soggy in water). A good brush is shaped to an axe-like taper. The ends of its bristles are "blown" or "flagged" (i.e., split) to spread the paint evenly. To test for quality, push the brush against a flat surface; there shouldn't be any gaps between the bristles which will leave streaks in the paint.

Three different-sized brushes will carry you through most paint jobs: a four-inch-wide brush is used for rapid coverage of siding and other large areas. The two-inch size is used for trim work. A one-inch-wide "sash" brush, with either a square or angled edge, is used for *muntins* (window dividers) and cutting in against the edges of trim boards.

Always follow the manufacturer's recommendations for coverage. Don't thin the paint to extend it; and don't spread it too thick either. Excessive thickness is a common cause of wrinkling and "alligatoring."

The **when** of outdoor painting is at least as important as the **how**. Don't paint unless no rain is expected for at least 24 hours before *and* after you begin—and the temperature isn't expected to dip below 50 degrees Fahrenheit (10 degrees Celsius) during that time. Apply latex paint only when the temperature is between 50 and 70 degrees Fahrenheit (10 to 21 degrees Celsius). Experienced painters learn to follow the sun; in hot weather, they try to stay painting in the shade. Excessively fast drying causes paint to crack. In cooler weather, they'll try to stay working in the sunshine to keep the paint warm. And they won't paint into the early evening on the cool side of the house where nighttime dew can water down latex paint, causing streaking and color fading. On the other hand, since latex can be applied over slightly damp wood, they can get an earlier start on a shaded wall than with oil paint, where they'll have to wait until all of the wood has completely dried.

Finally, latex paint is ruined by freezing. Lumberyards and farm stores sometimes forget to put their latex paint into heated storage before a hard frost comes. If you find a large amount of clear liquid sitting on top of a mass of doughy pigment when you open the can, suspect previously frozen paint.

The temperature sensitivity of latex paint is one reason why painters in northern regions of the United States like the state of Vermont, where July is the only month of the year that temperatures are likely to stay above 50 degrees F (10 degrees C) during most nights, have traditionally used oil paints, which can be safely applied down to 40 degrees F (about 4½ degrees C).

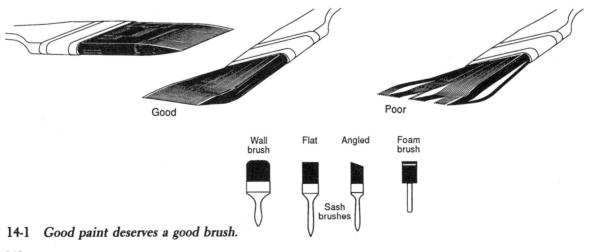

Good   Poor

Wall   Flat   Angled   Foam
brush   brush

Sash
brushes

14-1   *Good paint deserves a good brush.*

TO PAINT OR STAIN?

Painting means repainting. Even the very best paints have a useful life of only 10 years under normal conditions (see 14-2). The problem with any film-forming finish is that a loose and flaking film provides a poor base for repainting. Hence, all loose and flaking paint must be scrapped down and the bare wood spot-primed before the new paint can be applied. Ideally, if you manage to recoat the paint before it starts failing, you'll prolong the interval between repaintings. Eventually though, the accumulated paint film will become too thick to repaint and every bit of it will have to be scraped off. No matter how you do it, once you've opted for paint, you're stuck with having to remove it sooner or later.

Paint works best and lasts longest when applied to smooth, stable, edge-grain woods like cedar and redwood clapboards and products whose surfaces are especially designed for paint, like MDO panels and factory-primed hardboard or cement siding. The flat-grained boards typical of wood siding won't hold paint anywhere near as well. Plywood, with its minute surface checks, is even worse.

14-2 *Performance estimates of various exterior wood finishes expressed as suitability and expected life (years). NR indicates "not recommended."*

		Water-repellent preservatives	Semi-transparent stains	Paints
Cedar, redwood siding	Smooth (vertical grain)	Good (1-2)	Moderate (2-4)	Good (4-6)
	Rough-sawn or weathered	Good (2-3)	Excellent (5-8)	Moderate (3-5)
Pine, fir, spruce siding	Smooth (flat grain)	Good (1-2)	Low (2-3)	Moderate (3-5)
	Rough (flat grain)	Good (2-3)	Good (4-7)	Moderate (3-5)
Shingles	Sawn	Good (2-3)	Excellent (4-8)	Moderate (3-5)
	Split	Good (1-2)	Excellent (4-8)	NR
Plywood siding (Douglas fir, southern pine)	Sanded	Low (1-2)	Moderate (2-4)	Moderate (3-5)
	Textured (smooth)	Low (1-3)	Moderate (2-4)	Moderate (3-5)
	Textured (rough-sawn)	Low (2-3)	Good (4-8)	Moderate (3-5)
	Medium-density overlay	NR	NR	Excellent (6-8)
Plywood siding (cedar, redwood)	Sanded	Low (1-2)	Moderate (2-4)	Moderate (3-5)
	Textured (smooth)	Low (1-2)	Moderate (2-4)	Moderate (3-5)
	Textured (rough-sawn)	Low (2-3)	Excellent (5-8)	Moderate (3-5)
Millwork (pine)	Windows, shutters, doors, exterior trim	Good	Moderate (2-3)	Good (3-6)
Decking (not pressure-treated)	New (smooth)	Good (1-2)	Moderate (2-3)	Low (2-3)
	Weathered (rough)	Good (2-3)	Good (3-6)	Low (2-3)

14-3 *The light-colored, semi-transparent stain (and the front deck) gives this house a more modern feel than the darker stain used on the house in 14-4.*

Because they don't form any film to crack and peel, penetrating oil stains are ideal for rough-sawn woods, wood shingles, and textured plywood. They can be applied by dipping or brushing. Semi-transparent stains are distinguished from solid-color stains by the amount of pigment they contain. With a semi-transparent stain, the grain and other features of the wood show through the finish (see 14-3 and 14-4). Solid-color stains contain enough pigment to mask the wood almost as well as paint. In addition to better UV protection, this extra body also means that solid-color stains form a film. Fortunately, it's considerably thinner than a paint film, so many more layers can be applied before it becomes necessary to remove the flaking surface. In most cases, the film is weak enough so that scouring with a stiff brush, rather than scraping, is all that is needed to recondition the surface.

Latex stains are basically watered-down paint. They are more flexible and thinner than oil-based paint (but not oil-based stains). Because the film doesn't penetrate into the wood grain, they don't last very long compared to either oil-based, solid-color stain or latex paint applied over a primer. But, once again, they're usually easier to remove.

A good strategy to wean yourself from the tyranny of repainting is to scrape down the failed areas every few years and recoat them with a solid-color stain formulated to match the paint color. Eventually, you'll have replaced all the original paint piecemeal and then can recoat the entire house with a solid-color or semi-transparent stain. I particularly believe that this makes a lot more sense than covering everything over with vinyl or aluminum siding.

According to conventional wisdom, pressure-treated lumber is difficult to paint or stain. Many builders would recommend that the home owner wait six months or so for the preservative-saturated wood to dry out before attempting to do so. Recent studies have shown that CCA-treated wood will accept most penetrating wood finishes if it has a chance to air-dry for just two to three weeks. For paint, the wood should be dead-dry (a moisture content, M.C., of eight to 14 percent).

Solid-color stains and paints work best when applied to vertical surfaces. Light-colored semi-transparent stains are best for decks. The wood will be less noticeable as the stain wears away and the old stain will blend in better with the new when it is recoated.

Left untreated in any way, properly applied wood bevel and shingle siding can last a century or more, so long as it has a chance to dry out between rains and is modestly protected by an eaves or rake soffit. However, the constant swelling and shrinkage causes cracks and splits to develop along the grain of the siding. Nails act as conduits for moisture, encouraging rot, and the structure of the surface cells breaks down after prolonged exposure to UV. As the surface comes apart, it is more rapidly eroded by wind and rain. Cracks and splits in the surface allow both water and cold air to infiltrate into the walls.

Clear water-repellent finishes prevent moisture absorption and thereby limit the contraction/expansion stresses that cause the siding to split. Preservatives protect against dry-rot and mildew. These finishes must be reapplied every two or three years for maximum effectiveness. Although

14-4 *Another version of the same basic house, but in darker, semi-transparent stain.*

it's easy enough to do with a garden-type sprayer, few home owners are so compulsive, since there is no readily discernible loss of color or visually repugnant reminder of the fading protection.

Although most of these repellent/preservative finishes do darken the wood slightly, they don't arrest the natural color changes that are the hallmark of weathering. Not everyone finds this random and uncontrollable process beautiful; naturally weathering wood may be considered an eyesore in your area, proscribed by zoning laws. Fortunately, there are special finishes that contain antoxidants to preserve the natural hue of the wood as it weathers. To maintain this protection, the coating must be periodically reapplied. A companion coating is available to bring previously weathered wood back to a shade that approximates new wood.

Don't be tempted to coat outdoor wood with any kind of clear varnish, urethane, or shellac. Despite any manufacturer's claims to the contrary, all these finishes will crack and peel within a few years. Extensive sanding or complete removal down to bare wood will be necessary for recoating. The only exception might be a doorway sheltered from direct exposure to sunlight or weather.

Ideally, the time for siding and painting will coincide with the height of the summer building season; both tasks require warm dry weather. In any case, prestain or prepaint your trim stock and siding material at your earliest opportunity. Besides saving a lot of time, another benefit of prefinishing the siding is that no bare wood will show when the joints between boards shrink and open up. Other time-saving techniques include applying the touch-up coat to cover exposed nail heads and smudge marks on the rake trim and other hard-to-reach places as each piece is installed or before removing the scaffolding. Do this touch-up work before applying the siding so that you won't have to worry about dripping paint on the finish or cutting-in against edges. It's also a good idea to prestain and/or varnish your interior trim boards ahead of time too, while the weather is still warm and you can work out doors.

SOME THOUGHTS ABOUT INTERIOR PAINTING

Since the primary purpose of interior paint is decorative, it's important to understand how color can affect our perceptions of space, light, and mood.

Reflectance is one of the most important properties of color. A bright, white paint reflects up to 98 percent of the received light. Dark green paint, in contrast, reflects only about nine percent of the available light. Thus a dark hallway can be brightened by painting it with light colors and deep cupboards won't appear dark when their backs are painted white. One important point is that white paint is cheaper than lamps or windows.

The quality of a color also affects our perception of space. Light colors appear to "recede" to the eye. Painting walls flat white or in light, "neutral" shades increases the apparent size of a room. Painting a ceiling white makes it appear higher. Conversely, painting it dark "drops" it, and painting walls in warm dark hues makes a large room feel more snug and cozy. Color can also draw attention to woodwork details or ease transitions by minimizing differences. Too many colors can intensify a cluttered feeling, while the unrelieved overuse of a monochromatic scheme can be inhospitable. It's important to keep in mind rugs, window treatments, countertops, fabric patterns, and other large areas of texture and color—as well as personal taste—when choosing the color scheme for wall and ceiling surfaces.

Besides affecting our perception of space, colors also influence moods. We speak of a color as "cool" or "warm," which may reflect the degree of blue or black versus red in its makeup (a black color can be warm when it contains red). Bright primary colors are perceived as stimulating or detracting. Darker colors can foster relaxation—or deepen a mood of depression. Pastel hues can be cheerful or soothing—and, in some instances of too much, oppressive.

When light is reflected off a surface directly into your eyes, the result is uncomfortable glare. When the light is bounced at odd angles by a (perhaps microscopically) rough-textured surface, the reflected light strikes your eyes at oblique angles. This diffuse light is much more useful and less fatiguing.

High-gloss paints, which have a large ratio of binder to pigment, form a highly reflective film that is abrasion-resistant and easy to clean, but very conducive to glare. It also shows surface imperfections very clearly. High-gloss paints are generally reserved for floors and marine applications where durability is at a premium.

Flat paints have more pigment relative to binder, which tends to diffuse reflected light internally, making them easy on the eyes. The lack of a hard film makes them less wear-resistant and harder to keep clean. Satin or "eggshell" paints contain a bit more binder than pure flat paints, giving them better wearing qualities without greatly increasing their glare. They are most often used on walls. True flat finishes are usually reserved for ceilings, where imperfections in the surface finish would be otherwise highly visible. A flat, highly textured ceiling paint is excellent for diffusing both natural and artificial light, and (to a lesser extent) softening sounds. As a general rule, ceilings should never be glossier than the walls.

Semi-gloss enamels strike a balance between the desirable qualities of hard enamels and flat paints. They combine excellent cleanability with low glare, making them an ideal choice for woodwork, kitchen wall and cabinet surfaces, and bathroom and children's rooms.

When selecting colors, bear in mind that all paints darken slightly when they dry. You can't always trust the color chips that you get from the paint store when trying to match up or coordinate hues. If you're unsure of the color, buy the smallest possible can (generally a pint) and apply it to a test scrap of wood or wallboard before mixing up the whole batch. Some interior designers recommend applying the test color in a large swath directly to one of the intended surfaces and viewing it dry under several lighting conditions (natural and artificial) before you are satisfied to go ahead with a paint scheme.

APPLICATION TIPS AND TECHNIQUES FOR INTERIOR PAINT

Although interior painting comes much later in the scheme of construction—after the installation of the ceiling and wall finishes, and just before the finish flooring—much of what has been said about exterior painting also applies to painting inside.

As you might expect, a good interior paint job begins with proper surface preparation; the walls must be dust-free. Vacuum every surface thoroughly with a powerful, rented commercial vacuum cleaner especially designed to pick up drywall dust, which will quickly clog an ordinary vacuum cleaner. Sand unfinished woodwork lightly to improve adhesion with the primer. Knots and other stains can be sealed with a shellac-based primer. Fill any nail holes or blemishes with wood putty or spackle. Use spackle or joint compound on wallboard.

Oil-based primers should not be used directly on previously unfinished drywall. The oil will raise the fibres on the paper face, making a rough finish. Use a latex primer specifically formulated for drywall instead. Since a flat white primer can show through even two strongly colored top coats—especially on woodwork—you can reduce the need for a third topcoat by tinting the primer the same hue as the top coat.

Alkyd (synthetic) oil-based paints dry faster and retain a higher gloss than paints based on natural fish, soy, tung, or linseed oils. But alkyd oil paints are harder to brush on than latex paints; they tend to be runny, and leave streaks. They also produce stronger fumes, which take longer to disperse. Latex paints dry much faster, often within less than an hour before recoating, and are easier to brush on, although they do tend to spatter more when applied with a roller. They also will not adhere to a gloss finish, which can make repainting over old oil paint difficult.

As with brushes, don't be tempted to buy a cheap roller for applying interior wall paint. A cheap roller doesn't hold paint as well and quickly falls apart, seeding the paint with bits of fuzz as it does so. Match the length and type of nap with the paint. Different types of rollers are required for oil and latex paints and for smooth or textured surfaces, and flat, semi-gloss, or enamel finishes. Cheap disposable sponge applicators or rollers work best with oil-urethane stains and varnishes, although the solvents in some products will cause their foam to disintegrate. Except for cutting-in against trim and other edges, brushes aren't used for walls, but are reserved for woodwork and floors. Rollers should not be used to apply clear floor finishes since they can produce bubbles which can remain trapped in the finish as it dries.

Most painters prefer to paint the edges of trim first and cut-in the finish wall against it. Begin by cutting-in the close areas between wall corners, ceilings, and against trim

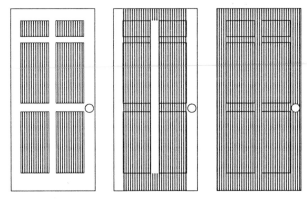

14-5 *Brushing a rail-and-stile door.*

with a brush. While this makes it easier to avoid hitting the woodwork with your roller, unless you're careful (and skilled) the edge of the roller can leave a lap mark on the brushed area. This is why some painters prefer to roll first and brush later.

Even on normal-height ceilings, using an adjustable fibreglass extension pole to roll paint saves moving a ladder and increases both your speed and control over the paint application. Paint ceilings in long, narrow strips. Don't let the edges of one strip dry before you lap it over with the next.

The extension handle is also handy for rolling walls. Cover walls from ceiling to floor in two-foot-wide vertical sections. Begin by rolling the excess paint off the roller with a short vertical stroke in the middle of each section, and then roll horizontally across the top and bottom of the wall section over your cut-in brush work. Finish the section with continuous top-to-bottom vertical strokes. To avoid leaving lap marks, don't lift the roller until the stroke is completed. As with ceiling painting, move steadily across the wall, overlapping each section before it has a chance to dry. You may have to go over the laps once or twice with a dry roller to smooth out the lap.

Most people find it difficult to paint a door or window without leaving brush marks. The secret is the order and direction in which you paint each part (see **14-5**). For panel doors, begin by painting each panel first, working top to bottom and brushing with the grain. Keep working top-to-bottom as you paint the horizontal rails next and finish with the vertical stiles.

On flush doors, work in small sections, applying the paint first vertically, then smoothing it out with horizontal strokes, followed by a vertical sweep and a final horizontal sweep across the section. Repeat for each overlapping section as you work down the door.

When it comes to painting window muntins and sashes, or baseboard and ceiling crown moulding, masking tape is usually more trouble than it's worth. The paint should lap over onto the glass to seal the glazing compound to it. Scrape off the excess with a single-edged razor blade.

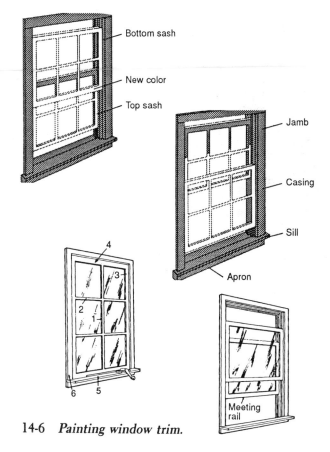

14-6 *Painting window trim.*

(With oil-based paint, do this as soon as it dries; it's a lot harder to do after a day or so.) To protect the joint from the razor blade, hold a drywall-taping knife or wide paint scraper against the glazing compound and scrape against it with the blade.

There are often small gaps between the wall and the baseboard or crown moulding that runs along it. These should be filled with paintable caulking tooled smooth with a moistened fingertip before painting. A careful painter with a steady hand can usually cut-in against these mouldings freehand. A 14-inch drywall-taping paddle makes a good edger.

As with doors, windows are also painted in a precise order (see **14-6**). Begin with the vertical muntins, then do the horizontal muntins, followed by the vertical sash, horizontal sash, the sill, the header casing, and then the side casings. With double-hung windows, it's often easiest to remove the sashes from the frames and paint them separately. Otherwise, slide the top sash down and the bottom sash up to expose the meeting rail. The slide tracks of wood windows work better if they are left unpainted and instead rubbed with wax for lubrication and to seal out moisture. Modern double-hungs use metal or plastic slides that should *never* be painted. Weatherstripping should never be painted either.

353

14-7 *Even with all windows open, the high VOC content of urethane varnish can be hazardous to your health. The painter should be wearing a respirator.*

SAFETY

Unlike exterior-grade plywood, exterior paint can't be used indoors with equanimity. It may well contain levels of toxic additives that are unsafe to use inside a house. Since an interior paint doesn't need to be fortified against UV radiation, mildew, and moisture, they're generally cheaper and certainly contain fewer hazardous substances than exterior paint. But that doesn't mean that you shouldn't take safety precautions during and immediately after application. Although formulated with lower levels of VOCs, applying interior paints can be even more dangerous to your health than exterior paints, since the fumes become concentrated in enclosed spaces rather than diffused into the outside air.

The instructions on the label say to provide "adequate" ventilation. This means, open all windows and doors, and set up a fan to blow the fumes out the window. If you're painting in the winter, you'll have to trade heat loss for your health. Always wear an activated-charcoal cartridge respirator approved for organic vapors (see **14-7**). (If you're working with shellac, the standard cartridge won't protect you against the methanol which is contained in the vehicle.) Wear inexpensive rubber gloves when working with penetrating finishes or any paint that carries a warning label against prolonged skin contact.

SAFETY NOTES ON REMOVING OLD PAINT

Although lead has not been allowed in paints since 1978, some old paints contain up to 40 percent of this very dangerous compound. The best cure for old lead paint is to leave it right where it is; paint over it. If it can't get into the environment, it can't hurt you.

However, when the paint must be removed, you should take extreme care to avoid contamination, both of the human and surrounding environment. Children are particularly susceptible to lead poisoning; once trapped in their body cells, lead stays there forever. The effects of lead poisoning are insidious, debilitating, and not always easy to diagnose.

Never strip paint with a blowtorch. Not only will this expose you to highly toxic fumes containing lead vapors, but the flames can get sucked up under loose siding and start hidden fires within the house walls. Scraping, sanding, and wire brushing all create hazardous dust and leave chips that can contaminate the soil and water next to the house.

Remove all interior drapes and fabrics which can collect dust when working inside. Outside, use plastic ground clothes taped to the building sill to collect the chips. Better yet, use a chemical stripper or a low-temperature heat gun to loosen the film. One safe new process uses a fabric mask embedded into the paint which has been loosened with a stripper to remove it in large sections without dust or flakes. The effect is similar to laying a piece of masking tape on semi-dry paint.

Dispose of lead paint scrapings and dust carefully in an approved landfill or hazardous waste disposal site.

15 Plumbing Rough-In

Professional builders usually dread "rough-in" time—that hiatus in the carpentry when the exterior shell is just about complete but the interior finish work cannot yet begin (see 15-1). It's then that the plumbers, electricians, HVAC installers, and insulation, drywall, and painting subcontractors preempt the house and the contractor must find other work for the carpenters on the crew. For the owner-builder, the completion of the shell is as significant a rite of passage as the long-ago first bite of the bulldozer blade into the undisturbed sod. You now have a shelter—rough shelter, but a lot more substantial than a tent out under the stars. You could live in it if you had to.

It's also a time when the work leaves the accessible realm of carpentry and enters into the arcana of pipes and wires. Most everyone who dreams about or actually starts building their own house somehow feels more comfortable with the thought of nailing wood than soldering pipe or running cable. I have a theory that this is because the logic of building seems so obvious and directly sensible that compliance with the building code which governs its every aspect is almost intuitive. With plumbing and electrical work, the presence of the code is far more onerous. It seems a Byzantine labyrinth of often arbitrary and minute regulations, more a product of unbridled bureaucratic excess than common sense.

But when you really stop and think about it, plumbing and wiring are a lot less complicated than carpentry. The sizes and types of fittings, conductors, connections, everything is spelled out in minute detail. Mechanical work lives up to its name: unlike carpentry, it is never for a moment "creative." Never for a moment will a plumber or an electrician have to stand back from the drawings and wonder, "How am I supposed to do that?" The complexity of these crafts is an illusion.

15-1 *In the Southwest of the United States, where rain seldom occurs during the building season, it's not unusual to rough-in the mechanicals before the walls are sheathed. The exhaust vent stack for the clothes dryer is visible in this photo.*

15-2 *Even pros sometimes forget to set a one-piece fibreglass tub/shower enclosure in place before framing the bathroom partitions. Another method for accommodating these units—which won't fit through any opening less than 34 inches wide—is to leave out two studs in the partition wall until after the tub is installed.*

15-3 *The capped stub of the black-iron gas line is visible behind the water main. The electrical cable provides temporary power. The insulated lines are sealed, freon-filled tubes that will connect to the air conditioner.*

This isn't to say that there isn't a lot that you need to know in order to plumb or wire a house or install a heating or air-conditioning system. It's just that, unlike carpentry, you can usually follow the directions (see **15-2**). And, with the acceptance of user-friendly materials into the codes, home-plumbers and home-electricians are fully capable of installing their own systems without recourse to highly paid specialists or expensive tools, and intractable materials.

AN OUTLINE OF A DOMESTIC PLUMBING SYSTEM

A household plumbing system is really two separate sub-systems (a third subsystem is added with hot-water heating or solar-heating), the distribution system and the DWV (drain/waste/and vent) system. Fresh water enters the house under pressure from either a private on-site source

or a municipal water main (see **15-3**). This single one-inch or ¾-inch diameter pipe divides at the water heater into hot and cold distribution lines that run, usually parallel to each other, throughout the house, delivering water to each fixture or appliance. High-quality installations use ¾-inch main lines and ½-inch branch lines. This configuration prevents that familiar and unwelcome sudden change in water temperature when more than one fixture is used simultaneously. Less expensive systems use ½-inch pipe throughout.

Besides valves at each point of use (faucets) a good system also features stopcocks, boiler-drain valves, or other shut-off valves before each fixture and at other critical locations so that the fixtures can be isolated or various parts of the system can be shut down and/or drained as necessary for repairs or seasonal operation. Horizontal runs should slope slightly downward so that they'll drain when the highest tap is opened.

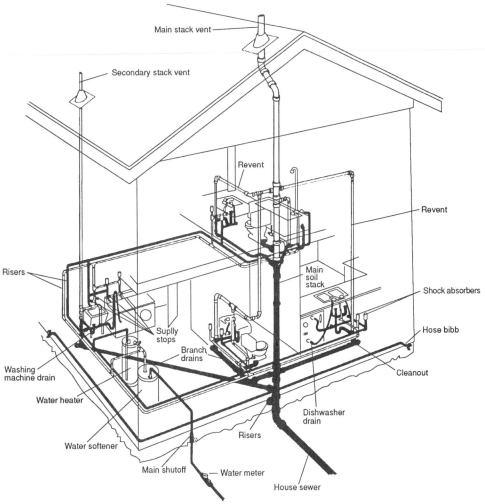

15-4 *Schematic of typical plumbing system—for illustration only. Check code requirements for specific DWV requirements.*

The drawing shown in **15-4** assumes some basic techniques that will help reduce the cost of your plumbing system and improve its operation:

1. Pipe and fittings are expensive: ergo, keep pipe runs as short as possible. Use "wet wall" layouts to group fixtures on opposite sides of a common wall or else use a plumbing column layout to stack bathrooms directly over each other and over basement utility rooms (see **15-5**).
2. Put the water heater as close to the main point of use as possible. Long pipe runs also lose expensive heat.
3. Insulate supply pipes. This is an obvious corollary of point number two for hot water runs, but in hot and/or humid climates, it's just as important to insulate cold water pipes to prevent structural damage caused by condensation.

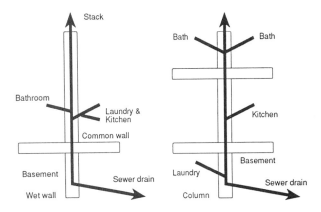

15-5 *Wet wall and plumbing column layout. It's inherently more difficult to design a concentrated plumbing layout for a spread-out single-storey house than a two-storey structure.*

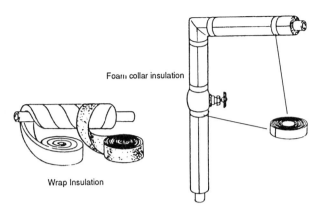

Foam collar insulation

Wrap Insulation

15-6 *Pipe insulation helps keep cold water pipes from "sweating" in humid weather.*

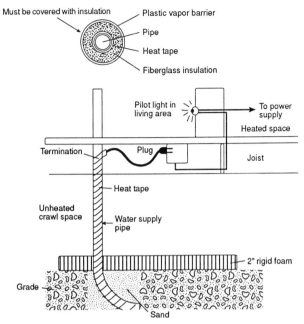

Must be covered with insulation

Plastic vapor barrier
Pipe
Heat tape
Fiberglass insulation

Pilot light in living area

To power supply

Heated space

Termination

Plug

Joist

Unheated crawl space

Heat tape

Water supply pipe

2" rigid foam

Grade

Sand

15-7 *Heat tape installation. Since heat tapes run on household current, a winter power outage can render them useless during the very time when they're needed most.*

Flexible neoprene rubber foam insulation that slips snugly over the pipe is the best material to use for this purpose (see **15-6**). Fibreglass will get soggy, and polyurethane is too brittle. Seal the joints with duct tape, and cut corner pieces on a 45-degree mitre to fit tightly.

4. Never run supply pipes in exterior walls (except in frost-free climates) or through unheated crawl-spaces and attics. Heat tapes are not a guaranteed protection against frozen pipes. If you do use a heat tape, make sure to follow installation directions carefully (see **15-7**). To prevent heat build-up that could melt the cable and cause a fire and/or short circuit, the heating cables should not cross over each other. Heating cables are only used with metal pipe, never plastic. Install a pilot light or switch at some convenient point so that you can tell when the cable is turned on.

Outdoor hose bibcocks should be protected against freezing by an inside shutoff valve or a frost-proof self-draining faucet (see **15-8**). A frost-proof hydrant is also a handy way to obtain water outdoors in winter. The faucet handle is connected by a long rod to a self-draining valve buried at the foot of the hydrant, well below the frost line. Fill the area around the base of the hydrant with some gravel to aid in drainage.

5. Design a system that can be shut down and drained off if you need to leave your house unoccupied for any length of time. Leaving mineral-laden water in pipes for a long time will corrode them. Pitch lines downward, eliminate high-spots, and provide drain valves at low points and at each appliance and a sump or other connection to the foundation drain system or (code permitting) house sewer.

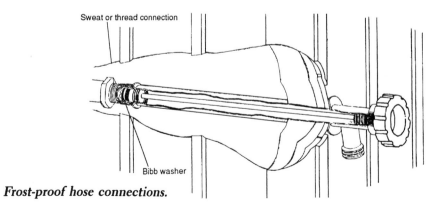

Sweat or thread connection

Bibb washer

15-8 *Frost-proof hose connections.*

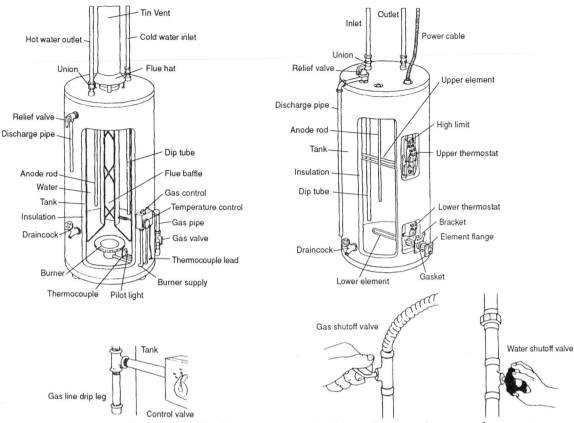

15-9 *Shut-off valves, union fittings, and flexible connectors (in that order) permit easy replacement or repair of appliances such as water pumps, heaters, boilers, and softeners.*

6. No appliances last forever. Provide union-type couplers for all appliances (e.g., water heaters, furnace boilers, pumps) to facilitate repair and/or replacement (see **15-9**).

7. Install shutoff valves on every fixture riser. A corollary of point number six, it would seem obvious that you shouldn't have to turn off the entire water system to fix a leaky faucet or runny toilet or repair a broken fitting. Since fittings absorb the brunt of the shock when a slug of water slams into them, they tend to loosen over time, no matter which type of plumbing system you use. In any case, the sound of water slamming to a sudden stop can be annoying. This is especially true for appliances such as washing machines and dishwashers that use quick-acting, solenoid-operated valves to control water flow. Air chambers consisting of an 18-inch to 24-inch vertical extension beyond the valve feed line act as shock absorbers to prevent water hammering (see **15-10**). In a quality system, air chambers are installed at every fixture riser. For added safety, the chamber is made from a larger pipe.

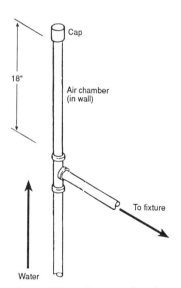

15-10 *Air chambers. Water hammering is more than an annoyance. The shock waves of surging water can cause leaks and damage valves and controls.*

359

8. Provide access panels for hidden connections. You don't want to tear a wall apart to replace a shower control valve.

9. Protect the pipes and preserve the framing. Know where the pipes are when you nail finish siding and drywall to the studs. Protect them with steel plates if they are too close the surface. Avoid drilling or sawing joists for drain lines in places that will weaken them. Drilling is always preferable to sawing. Plan the framing to accommodate plumbing runs in advance (refer to **6-31** and **6-32** in Chapter 6 and **7-39** in Chapter 7). Be familiar with the required rough-in dimensions for your fixtures and design the framing around them. Although most rough-in dimensions are standard, some will vary according to specific fixtures (see **15-11**). This is often a problem with European imports.

10. Finally, learn to love the code. If you're building where plumbing codes are in force, you have no choice but to follow their guidance. Everything you need to know about system design, installation requirements, and materials to use are either described or can be extrapolated from code specifications. Plumbing guidebooks that utilize an edited, annotated, or expurgated version of the code as a template are the most accessible.

DRAINAGE

The used water is carried off to a municipal sewer system or an on-site sewage disposal system by a separate system of drain pipes (see **15-12**). Sanitation engineers and codes distinguish between *drain* lines that carry *grey* water from the sinks and laundry, and larger *waste* or *soil* pipes that carry *black* water from the toilet. U-shaped, water-filled traps are installed in the drain lines at each fixture (toilets have built-in traps) to keep sewer gases and odors from seeping into the house. The drain system must be vented to allow the gases blocked by the traps to escape through the roof and to prevent water from being siphoned out of the traps when the drains are filled with water. Horizontal drain lines always have a slight downward pitch, from ¼ inch to ½ inch per foot. Vent lines, on the other hand, must have an upward pitch. A vent line that also serves as a drain line is called a *wet vent*. Some codes don't allow wet venting or else limit the conditions under which it can be used.

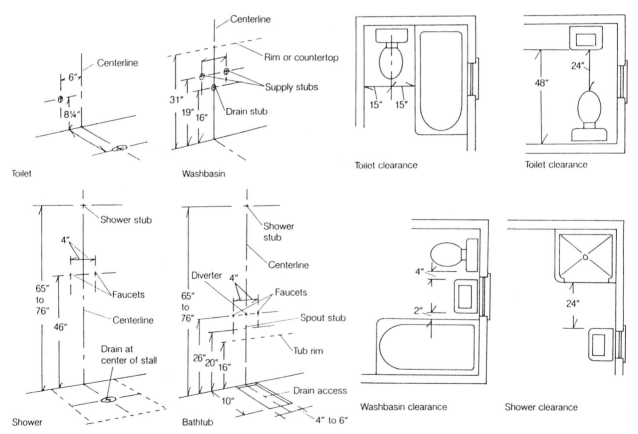

15-11 *Typical fixture rough-in dimensions.*

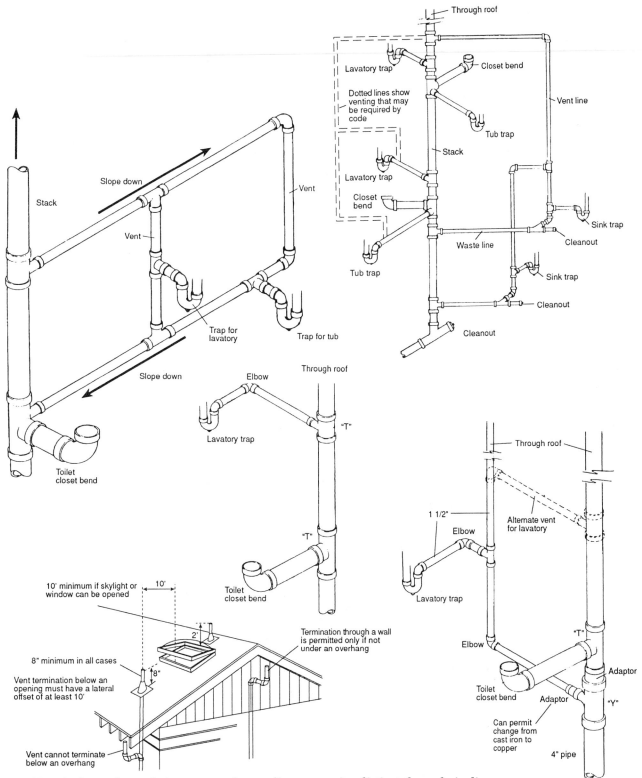

15-12 *As far as the code is concerned, vent lines are quite distinct from drain lines. The general installations shown are based on the Uniform Plumbing Code, for illustration only. Always consult your local code for specific requirements.*

The toilet is connected to the main vent or "stack" pipe, which is 3 inches or 4 inches in diameter (unless otherwise specified, pipe sizes are measured by their inside diameter, "I.D.," and not their "O.D.," or outside diameter). Smaller (1½-inch) *secondary vents* serve each fixture (see **15-13**). In order to avoid excessive penetrations through the roof, these are usually *revented* into the main stack at a specified height above the fixture drain or else in the attic ceiling.

In cold regions, when a secondary vent goes through the roof, it's usually increased in diameter so that it can't be plugged solid by frozen moisture. As a general rule of thumb, the horizontal distance (in feet) between the fixture *trap weir* (its outlet) and the vent shouldn't exceed roughly twice the diameter of the trap arm pipe size in inches. (E.g., the code says that a fixture with a 1½-inch drain line can't be more than 3'-6" from its vent and limits a two-inch drain to 5'-0". Using the rule guarantees code

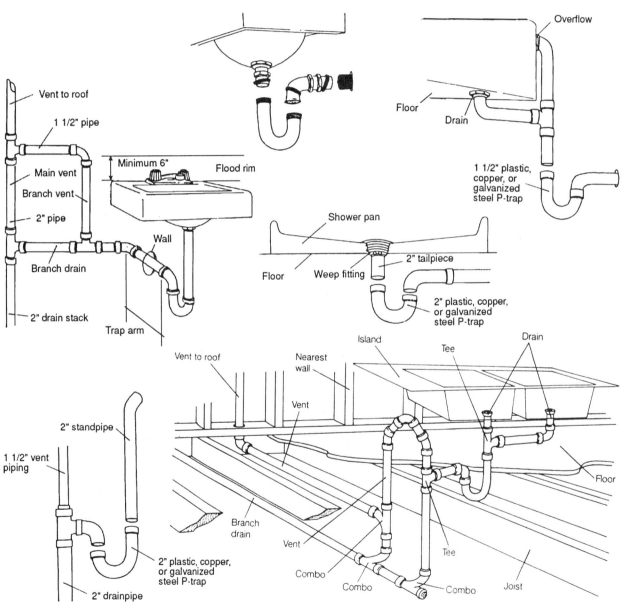

15-13 *Trap and vent relationships. Vertical vent lines cannot change to horizontal within six inches of the "flood rim" (overflow) level of a fixture. A vent line that connects to a horizontal drain from the side must do so above the center of the drain. The vent line for a vertical drain must connect to it at a 45-degree angle, and not a 90-degree angle.*

compliance). Remember that just because a certain kind of trap is sold at your local hardware store doesn't mean that it is allowed by the code.

The DWV system also includes cleanouts at each horizontal run. These wye fittings have a removable plug that provides access for a drain auger if the pipe ever becomes plugged with congealed grease, soil, or lost household objects.

Like a river and its tributaries, the drainage system more-or-less increases in diameter from top to bottom, i.e., with the volume of flow. Since drain lines work by gravity, not pressure, they must be larger to reduce internal friction, and be sloped to hasten the flow. Drain fittings are designed and installed so as not to create barriers or turbulence in the flow which could lead to obstruction (see **15-14**).

In general, drain pipe size is a function of the amount of water the fixture uses along with the number of fixtures draining into the line. Toilets need three-inch lines (the same size as the stack vent). Washing machines and shower stalls use two-inch lines. Bathtubs, sinks, washbasins, and other fixtures generally require 1½-inch lines, unless they share a common drain, in which case a two-inch line is called for. The sewer line should be at least four-inch pipe to be adequate.

A large section of the plumbing code is devoted to specifying distances between traps and fixtures and vents, the length and diameters of drain lines, and the manner in which fixtures are to be vented. Since these can and do vary in each jurisdiction, check with your local plumbing inspector before you make your plans and/or buy any materials. Codes can be educational in other ways, particularly in specifying permitted materials. For example, you may learn that plastic water pipe isn't allowed in your town even though the local hardware store carries it and plumbers in the neighboring towns use it regularly. This is one reason why plumbing how-to books describe only general techniques and materials and not specific installation procedures. Refer to the drawing in 15-6: it shows how a generic DWV system might be put together. The particulars of your layout will be determined by your local code requirements.

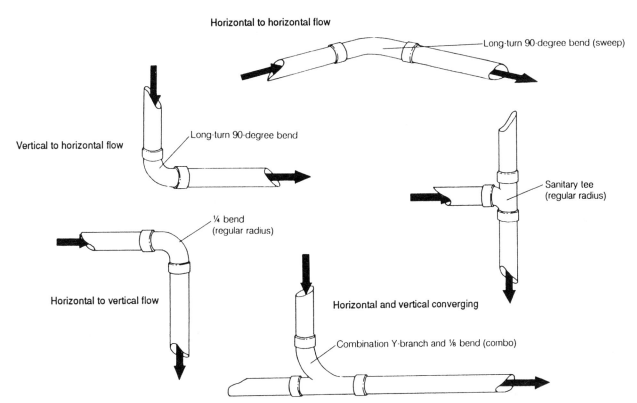

15-14 *Fittings and flow in the DWV system. The code measures waste water flow in "fixture units" which are used to size the diameter of drain and vent pipes. It also distinguishes between direction of flow and whether a line is wet or dry when determining what kinds of drainage fittings are allowed. For example, sanitary tees and standard ¼ bend (90 degree) fittings can only be used where the direction of flow changes from horizontal to vertical. Most codes also require cleanouts upstream of any combination of horizontal and vertical changes of direction that exceed 135 degrees.*

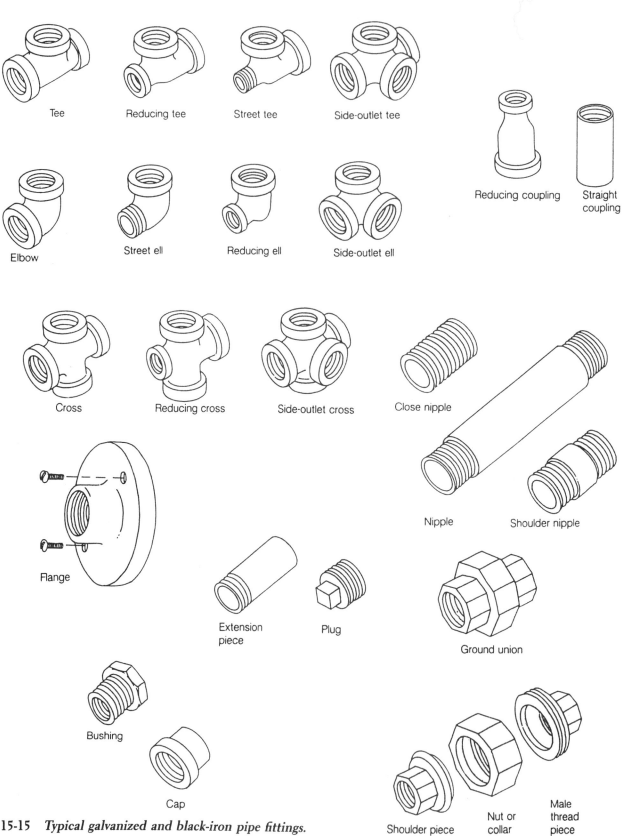

15-15 *Typical galvanized and black-iron pipe fittings.*

Plumbing Materials and Tools and Their Use and Installation

The wide-spread acceptance of plastic pipe, both for DWV and (to a lesser extent) for supply lines, has threatened the formerly unassailable hegemony of the professional plumber. Do-it-yourself plumbing is a lot easier than it used to be when galvanized steel, cast iron, and copper were the only standard pipe materials.

STEEL PIPE

Although galvanized steel pipe is seldom used in modern residential plumbing or heating systems, there are still some conditions where no other material can offer the same strength and durability (see **15-15**). Pipe for supply lines from deep-water wells and buried outdoor plumbing or exposed greenhouse or irrigation lines are some typical cases. Although it will eventually burst, steel pipe can usually withstand some moderate amount of freezing without damage. The biggest drawback of galvanized steel pipe is that its rough surface increases flow friction and also attracts mineral deposits and sediment that eventually clog it. It's also prone to leaks caused by corrosion.

Ungalvanized *black-iron* pipe is still widely used for steam and hydronic heating systems, and it is generally required by code for natural gas lines. The techniques for working it are the same.

Galvanized pipe, in diameters from ⅜ inch to 3 inches is available already threaded in stock lengths up to 21 feet along with a complete selection of fittings. The tools for custom cutting and threading are easy to rent and use (see **15-16**). A basic used commercial or new noncommercial setup is also fairly inexpensive, should you desire to add one to your collection.

To make a clean and square cut, you'll need a *pipe-cutter* (which resembles a heavy-duty tubing cutter). A hacksaw just won't do the job as well. A cone-shaped *reamer* is used to clean out the burr that the cutter will leave on the inside edge of the pipe. The pipe is inserted into a *pipe vise* which keeps it from rotating while it is threaded; a bench vise that is equipped with pipe jaws will also do the job. The actual thread is cut with a *die* held in a *die stock* which is a ratcheted handle that applies the leverage necessary to turn the die. Turn the stock clockwise (to the right) about a half turn and then turn it back to the left (counterclockwise) a quarter turn to remove the waste and to keep the die from clogging. Lubricate the die with pipe-cutting oil as your repeat the cutting operation.

When cutting pipe to length, always be sure to measure between the face of the fittings and add the length of the pipe that enters into the fittings at both ends. Coat the threads with pipe-joint compound or wrap them with Teflon tape (in the direction of rotation) to assure a waterproof joint and to make it easy to disassemble the joint at a later date. To prevent any corrosion caused by galvanic action, always use Teflon tape when joining fittings made of dissimilar metals.

You'll need a pair of pipe wrenches to work with steel pipe. One wrench is used to grip the pipe or the fitting while the other turns it. Since the serrated jaws of the pipe wrench scar the surface, pipe wrenches shouldn't be used on soft or polished materials.

Threaded pipe is directional—that is, you can only assemble it in one direction. The last piece in a run can't turn into fittings and fixtures on both of its ends. You will need to use an adaptor or a union fitting to finish the connection.

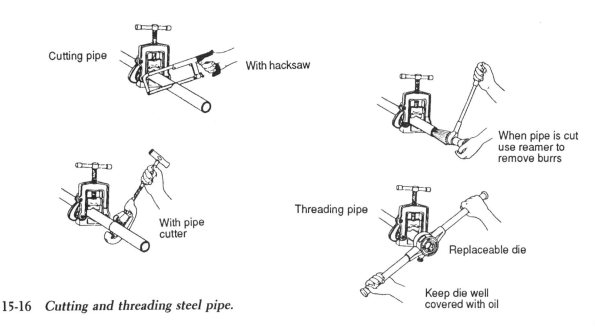

Cutting pipe

With hacksaw

With pipe cutter

When pipe is cut use reamer to remove burrs

Threading pipe

Replaceable die

Keep die well covered with oil

15-16 *Cutting and threading steel pipe.*

**WROT COPPER
90° ELLS
SOLDER TO SOLDER**

**WROT COPPER
90° FITTING ELLS
FITTING TO SOLDER**

**WROT COPPER
90° FITTING ELLS
FITTING TO FITTING**

**WROT COPPER
FEMALE ADAPTERS
SOLDER TO FPT**

**WROT COPPER
FEMALE FITTING ADAPTERS
FITTING TO FPT**

**WROT COPPER
45° ELLS
SOLDER TO SOLDER**

**WROT COPPER
45° FITTING ELLS
FITTING TO SOLDER**

**WROT COPPER
45° FITTING ELLS
FITTING TO FITTING**

**WROT COPPER
MALE ADAPTERS
SOLDER TO MPT**

**WROT COPPER
MALE FITTING ADAPTERS
FITTING TO MPT**

**WROT COPPER
TEES
SOLDER TO SOLDER TO SOLDER**

**WROT COPPER
REDUCING TEES
SOLDER TO SOLDER TO SOLDER**

**WROT COPPER
90° ELLS
SOLDER TO FPT (Forged Brass)**

**WROT COPPER
90° ELLS
SOLDER TO MPT (Forged Brass)**

**WROT COPPER
FITTING REDUCERS EXTENDED
FITTING TO SOLDER**

**WROT COPPER TEES
SOLDER TO SOLDER TO FPT
(Forged Brass)**

**WROT COPPER
UNIONS
SOLDER TO SOLDER**

**WROT COPPER
FLUSH BUSHINGS
FITTING TO SOLDER**

**WROT COPPER
FLUSH BUSHINGS
FITTING TO FPT**

**WROT COPPER CROSSES
SOLDER TO SOLDER TO SOLDER TO SOLDER
(Forged Brass)**

**TUBE STRAP
PERFORATED COPPER**

**WROT COPPER
COUPLINGS ROLLED STOP
SOLDER TO SOLDER**

**WROT COPPER
COUPLINGS STAKED STOP
SOLDER TO SOLDER**

**WROT COPPER
COUPLINGS WITHOUT STOP
SOLDER TO SOLDER**

**WROT COPPER
CAPS**

**WROT COPPER
FITTING PLUGS
(Brass Rod)**

**WROT COPPER
REDUCING COUPLINGS
SOLDER TO SOLDER**

**WROT COPPER
ECCENTRIC COUPLINGS
SOLDER TO SOLDER**

**WROT COPPER
RETURN BENDS
SOLDER TO SOLDER**

**WROT COPPER
SUCTION LINE P-TRAPS
SOLDER TO SOLDER**

15-17 *Typical copper and bronze "sweat" fittings.*

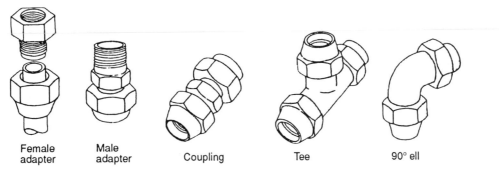

Female adapter   Male adapter   Coupling   Tee   90° ell

15-18 *Flare fittings.*

COPPER TUBING

Copper tubing is considered to be the hallmark of a quality plumbing system. Although it's considerably more expensive and softer than steel pipe, it's also more durable and easier to install. It's less prone to the build-up of scale and virtually corrosion-proof under normal conditions, but it will split more readily if allowed to freeze.

Copper tubing is sold as either "hard" rigid pipe in 10-foot and 20-foot lengths or else in 30-, 60-, or 100-foot coils of "soft" flexible tubing. The pipe is further rated according to the thickness of its wall as either type M, L, or K (thin, medium, and thick, respectively). Type M pipe is more than adequate for most residential plumbing applications. Your local code may require type K for pipe that will be buried or in heating systems. Both types L and K are generally specified for commercial or industrial installations.

Fittings used for copper pipe are almost always soldered ("sweated") together. The variety of sweat fittings and related adaptors that mate copper pipe to other systems is extensive (see **15-17**). Brass sweat fittings are also available for heavy-duty applications.

Sweat fittings can also be used with flexible tubing. In some cases, brass *flare* fittings are used in lieu of soldered fittings to provide self-sealing joints that can be quickly taken apart with a pair of open-ended wrenches. Since they cost more than sweat fittings, flare fittings are seldom used in water lines except for prefabricated installations.

They're mainly used for fuel oil and LP gas lines, where sweated fittings aren't allowed (see **15-18**). Flare fittings for water lines are thinner than those used for oil and gas and *are not* interchangeable.

Copper pipe and tubing can be cut with a hacksaw, but it leaves a rough edge that interferes with a good solder joint. Use a tubing cutter instead. To avoid distorting the pipe, tighten the handle gradually as you turn the cutter wheel around the pipe. Use the attached triangular reamer to smooth any burrs off the completed cut. Use a "mini" cutter when there isn't enough room to turn a full-sized cutter around the pipe.

Even though it costs more than rigid pipe, flexible tubing saves time and money by eliminating elbows throughout the run. Short lengths are often used as risers between rigid pipe and faucets. It also can withstand a few freezings. Flexible tubing can be bent into gentle curves by hand. To make a tighter bend without kinking it, slide a coil-spring bender of matching diameter over the tubing and apply gentle pressure as you form the curve.

To make a flare joint, first make a smooth, square cut in the tubing. Slip the flare nut over the tubing and grip the end of the tubing in a flaring vise (see **15-19**). Slide the flaring tool ram onto the vise so that the cone-shaped tip of the ram is against the tubing and tighten it down to flare the tubing. The finished flare must be smooth and even or it will leak.

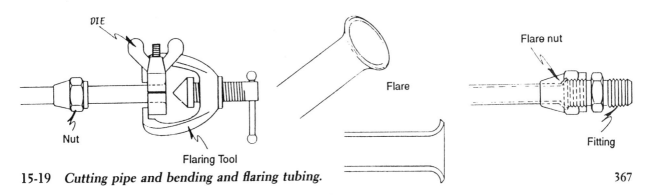

DIE

Nut

Flaring Tool

Flare

Flare nut

Fitting

15-19 *Cutting pipe and bending and flaring tubing.*

Making a watertight soldered joint is simple in theory but does take a bit of practice to do well. Begin by checking to make sure that the fitting and the pipe end are both free of dents and aren't out-of-round (see **15-20**). Polish the contact surfaces (the outside of the pipe and the inside of the fitting) with steel wool or fine emery cloth. A special conical wire brush makes polishing the inside of fittings a lot easier. Don't touch the polished surfaces with your fingers or otherwise allow them to get dirty.

Apply a liberal coating of soldering flux to the contact surfaces with a small flux brush; the solder won't bond without it.

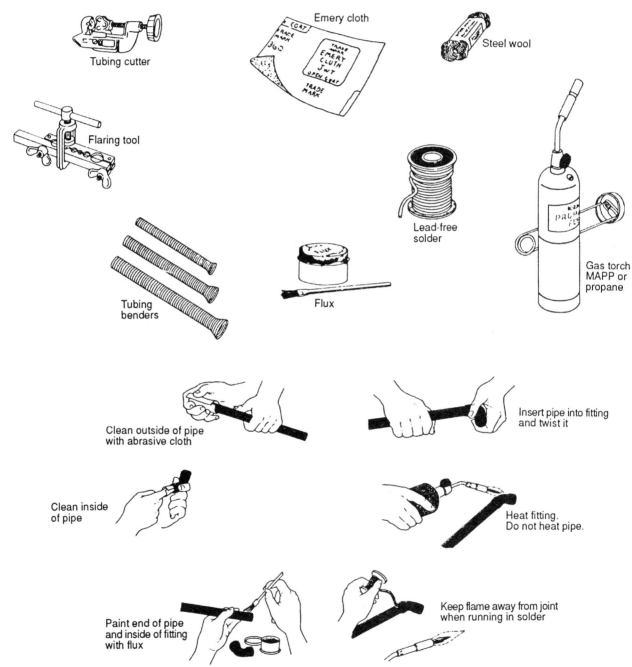

Tubing cutter

Emery cloth

Steel wool

Flaring tool

Tubing benders

Flux

Lead-free solder

Gas torch MAPP or propane

Clean outside of pipe with abrasive cloth

Insert pipe into fitting and twist it

Clean inside of pipe

Heat fitting. Do not heat pipe.

Paint end of pipe and inside of fitting with flux

Keep flame away from joint when running in solder

15-20 *Sweat soldering copper pipe. Note that because of its lead content, 50-50 solder (i.e., the percent of tin and lead) is no longer allowed in many locales. Its replacement, silver/tin solder, is much more expensive and has a higher melting point.*

Slip the fitting onto the pipe and apply heat to the fitting until it is hot enough to melt the solder. The key to a good joint is to let the heated metal melt the solder, not the torch flame. Touch the tip of the solder to the joint. If the pipe is hot enough, the solder will melt instantly and flow into the joint, filling it by capillary action. Keep applying the solder until it forms a full ring around the joint. Remove the flame so that you don't overheat the joint and make the solder flow out. You can wipe excess solder from the joint with a quick swipe of the emery cloth or a rag. But don't move the joint or cool it with water until at least 30 seconds after it has lost its shine.

If you are soldering tubing to a shutoff valve, remove the valve body first to avoid burning its rubber or nylon washers. Note that the valve body will be stamped with an arrow that should point in the direction of the flow in order to make a leak-proof seal.

An ordinary propane torch is adequate for sweat soldering 1/2-inch and 3/4-inch copper fittings. One-inch and larger diameter pipe and heavy cast brass fittings take more heat than a propane torch can quickly produce. Use a special torch and a cylinder of hotter-burning *MAPP gas*.

When soldering fittings close to walls or wood framing, protect the combustible surfaces with a heat shield such as a piece of thin sheet metal.

After all the connections have been soldered together and cooled down, open the shutoff valve and check for leaks, the presence and location of which, in most cases, will be immediately obvious. But you should also be aware

that there's a possibility that some joints many not leak for several minutes or several hours, or that the leaks will be so slow that they won't show up for some time. Don't leave the water on overnight when you go home until the system has remained leak-free for the entire day.

In the likely event that you'll have at least one or two joints to resolder, make sure to completely drain the pipe before attempting the repair. Even a few drops of water will keep the solder from melting or bonding. If you cannot drain the fitting well enough to melt the solder and pull it apart, you'll have to cut it out with your mini-cutter and splice in a union fitting or coupler. Otherwise, pull the defective joint apart, wipe the hot solder clean with a rag, apply flux, and resolder. Sometimes, a shutoff valve won't seat properly, and a trickle of water will continue to drip through the pipe. Plug the pipe with a ball of compressed white bread. If you work quickly, you'll have enough time to resolder the joint before the bread soaks through.

Ring-type compression fittings are normally used to connect 3/8-inch diameter chrome-plated toilet supply tubing to a shutoff valve installed at the terminus of the riser (see **15-21**). The same type of connection is also frequently used for faucet supply connections. Slide the compression nut over the tubing first, and then slip the brass compression ring onto its end. Insert the ring in the fitting and then tighten the nut down to expand it against the seat. Be careful not to overtighten the nut. Instead, turn on the water and tighten it down just enough to keep it from leaking.

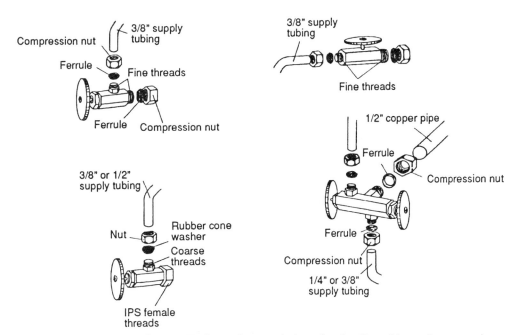

15-21 *Installing a compression fitting. To keep from twisting the fragile tubing, always use two wrenches, one to hold the threaded fitting and the other to tighten the nut down onto it.*

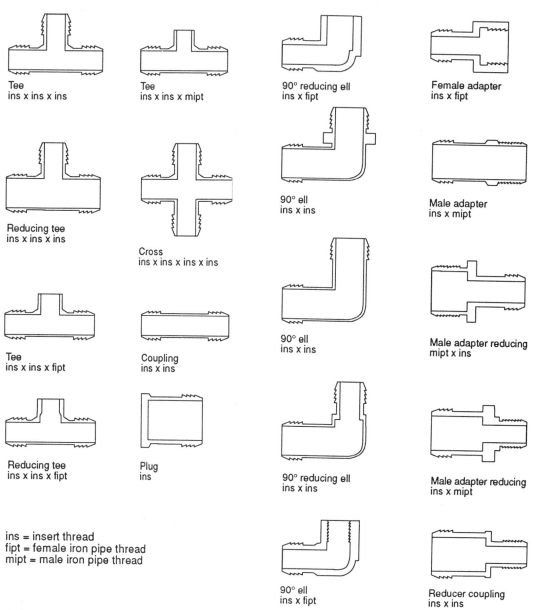

15-22 *Polyethylene pipe fittings. Polyethylene pipe is almost exclusively used for direct burial when running the supply line directly from a well or spring to the pump or pressure tank inside the house.*

PLASTIC SUPPLY PIPE

There are four types of plastic pipe presently approved for use in water supply systems by the plumbing codes—although not all of them are allowed for hot water and one of them, polybutylene, is not allowed by all codes for any purpose. Even where permitted, codes require special installation precautions. For example, the plastic must be isolated from the wall of a water heater by a long brass nipple. Check with your local plumbing inspector for conditions governing plastic pipe installation.

Polyethyelene "black plastic" pipe is permitted for cold water use only. Its low cost and long-length coils, and its immunity from scale build-up make it ideal for piping water from the well into the house without any buried couplers that could spring a leak. It should not be used for distribution lines inside the house however. Its low structural strength will cause it to sag between supports. It's also particularly vulnerable to stress failures at couplers and other fittings. These tend to leak simply as a function of the time they're in use. PE pipe also begins to melt at

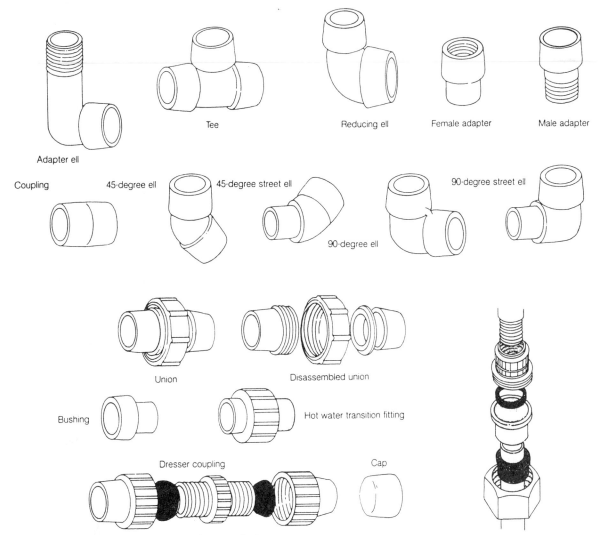

15-22 *(Continued) PVC and CPVC pipe fittings.*

120°F (49°C), and should be isolated from heat sources. Coils of pipe for water supply use are rated for 100, 120, and 160 psi (pounds per square inch). Use higher pressure ratings for deep wells or long runs.

PE pipe is used with barbed, insert-type nylon fittings, secured by stainless-steel screw clamps (see **15-22**). To install a fitting, cut the pipe squarely with a sharp utility knife (you can also use a fine-toothed hacksaw, as long as you clean off the burrs with a knife). Slip the clamp over the pipe, and push the fitting into it all the way onto its shoulder. If the pipe is cold, soak it in hot water until it softens a bit. Never heat it with a torch, which could permanently warp the plastic. Slide the clamp to about ¼ inch back from the shoulder, and tighten the screw down. But don't tighten it so far that the plastic squeezes through the clamp slots which can cause the pipe to split. If the connection will be inaccessible, use two clamps on each

side of the fitting. Nylon fittings buried underground can sometimes shear off; use brass fittings instead.

Rigid PVC (polyvinyl chloride) and CPVC (chlorinated PVC) pipe is strong enough for use in pressurized water systems. PVC is approved only for cold water, while CPVC is approved for both hot and cold water use, since it will withstand temperatures up to 150°F (65°C). On the other hand, CPVC and PVC plastic become very brittle when cold, and the pipe and fittings will shatter if water freezes in them. Both kinds of pipe are available in 10 foot and 20 foot lengths and with a full line of threaded or cement-type (also called solvent welded) fittings. The relatively low cost along with fast and easy assembly are the main advantages of rigid plastic plumbing systems. However, the long-term durability of the system is open to question. It won't do anything for the resale value of your house either.

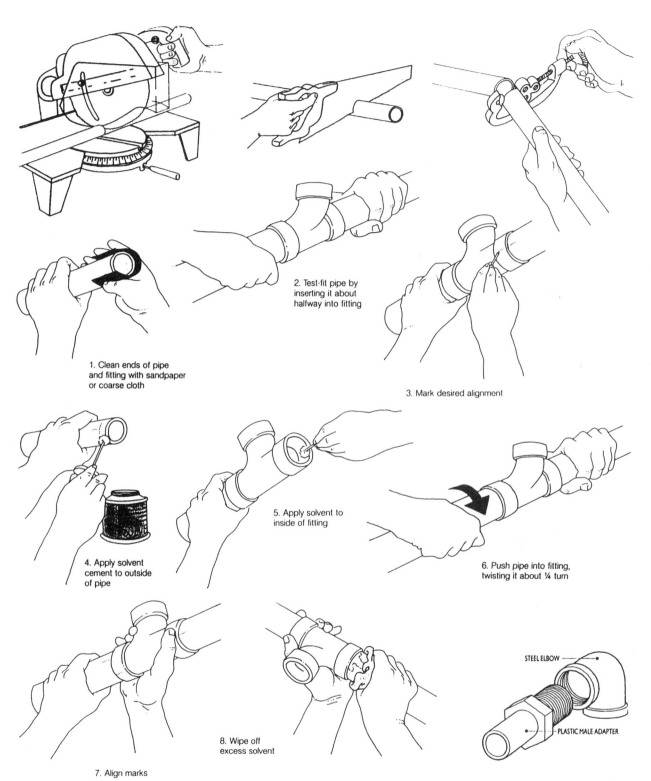

1. Clean ends of pipe and fitting with sandpaper or coarse cloth

2. Test-fit pipe by inserting it about halfway into fitting

3. Mark desired alignment

4. Apply solvent cement to outside of pipe

5. Apply solvent to inside of fitting

6. Push pipe into fitting, twisting it about ¼ turn

7. Align marks

8. Wipe off excess solvent

STEEL ELBOW

PLASTIC MALE ADAPTER

15-23 *Solvent-welding plastic pipe fittings. When joining plastic pipe to steel or copper always wrap the male threads with Teflon pipe tape. Don't use pipe thread "dope" which can weaken the plastic. Female plastic adapters can expand and leak when threaded onto metal male threads. Whenever possible, use male plastic adapters with female metal threads.*

To solvent-weld PVC or CPVC pipe, first make a smooth cut with a fine-toothed saw, a tubing cutter, or special plastic-pipe cutting shears (see **15-23**). Preassemble as many of the joints as possible. Mark the orientation of the fittings with a pencil or marking pen. CPVC requires a special cleaner/primer before cementing. Other types of pipe do not. Check to make sure that the cement is the right kind for the pipe you're using. In any case the surfaces to be joined should be dry and free of grease and dirt. Don't sand the edges of the pipe.

Brush a thick coat of solvent cement on the pipe and a slightly thinner coat on the fitting and then *immediately* push the pieces together with a slight twisting motion (about one o'clock past 12) until the pencil lines match up. You should see a bead of excess solvent around the edge of the fitting. If it isn't there, quickly pull the joint apart and reapply more cement. If it is, hold the joint for about 30 seconds or so until it sets to make sure the pipe doesn't back out under pressure of the solvent. Once the cement has set, you won't be able to pull the joint apart. If you make a mistake you'll have to cut out the fitting and insert a new one. Fortunately, both fittings and couplers are cheap. Wait at least an hour before turning on the water in a supply line and at least 15 minutes before testing an unpressurized drain line.

Polybutylene (PB) plastic pipe is very flexible, can withstand temperatures as low as $-50°F$ ($-45°C$) without damage, will handle water up to $180°F$ ($82°C$), and is available in either continuous coils up to 1000 feet long or short semi-rigid five foot lengths. The relatively high cost of the fittings (slip-on, crimp-over, or compression-type) is offset by the low cost of the pipe and the ease with which the system can be assembled. The pipe can be snaked through walls and around corners like electrical cable. Since bends as sharp as ten times the radius of the pipe can be made without danger of kinking, very few elbows are needed.

Despite these many advantages and HUD and FHA approval, PB plumbing has not yet been accepted by all plumbing codes. In fact, most plumbers become quite agitated at the very mention of it, and in some areas of the country, it's still hard to find. To be perfectly fair, there have been problems reported with PB plumbing systems which had nothing to do with installer malfeasance. Flaws in the design of the early fittings caused them to fail. The manufacturers claim to have corrected the problems.

Compression-type PB fittings have proven both durable and easy to install (see **15-24**). Begin by slipping a compression nut over the end of the pipe (use a utility knife to cut it). Slide the stainless steel retaining ring over the end of the pipe, and then push the compression ring against it so that about $1/8$ inch of the pipe is exposed. Seat the fittings together and tighten down the compression nut about a full turn past the point that it squeaks. Overtightening can strip the soft plastic threads. Use threaded copper or brass bushings (not galvanized steel) wrapped with Teflon tape to mate PB fittings to dissimilar materials. Special tools are required to make crimp-joint connections. Slip-on fittings have proved less durable. Support the tubing every 32 inches of horizontal run (running it through wall studs provides adequate support) and every 48 inches vertically, with plastic clips loose enough to allow movement. Provide six inches of slack for thermal expansion in every 50 feet of tubing. Never sweat solder any fittings connected to PB adapters.

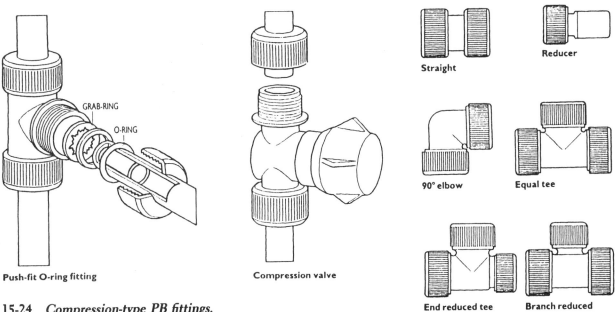

Straight

Reducer

90° elbow

Equal tee

End reduced tee

Branch reduced

Push-fit O-ring fitting

GRAB-RING

O-RING

Compression valve

15-24 *Compression-type PB fittings.*

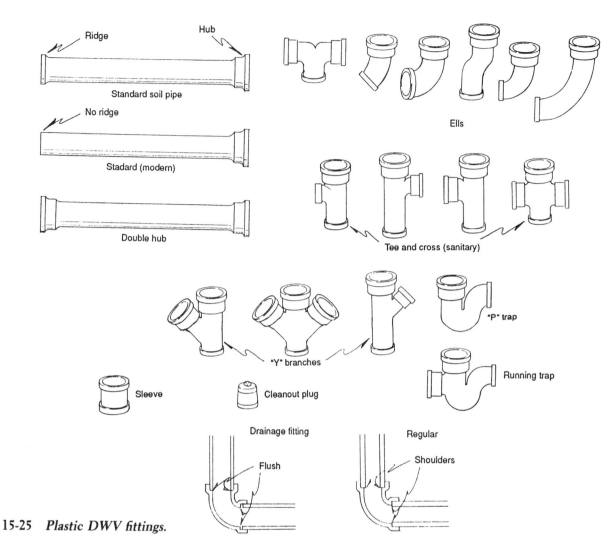

15-25 *Plastic DWV fittings.*

PLASTIC DWV PIPE

Copper and cast iron DWV pipe have been almost entirely replaced by plastic pipe in residential work. Thin-walled copper is too costly to be used today and cast iron is too cumbersome and difficult to work with. Although widely used in the home plumbing market, cream-colored or white PVC DWV pipe is not generally approved by the code. Black ABS (acrylonitrile-butadiene-styrene) plastic pipe is considerably stronger and has both greater impact and thermal resistance than PVC pipe. Vent fittings are slightly different from drain fittings, which have eased curves and no internal shoulders to interfere with waste flow (see **15-25**). Keep runs as direct as possible, slope horizontal pipes, and make sure bends are not too sharp or convoluted. Plastic has an affinity for sticky fat molecules, so be sure to provide clean-out Tees or Wyes.

Plastic DWV pipe is assembled by solvent welding. Except for long horizontal runs, which should be supported with plastic hangers, it is rigid enough to be self-supporting. Special adapters enable the pipe to join with the cast-iron sewer pipe.

The pipe can be cut with a tubing-type cutter or any fine-toothed saw. But it's hard to follow a straight line with a handsaw or hacksaw. A chop saw makes a much quicker and more accurate cut. As with all cuts, remove the burr along the edges with a utility knife or reamer.

CAST-IRON DWV

Although seldom used in residential plumbing installations except where codes still don't permit ABS plastic, cast-iron pipe is always used to connect from the house drain to the septic tank or municipal sewer line and for any situations where extra strength and durability are called for, such as when lines must be buried under a concrete slab. Standard pipe lengths are 5 feet and 10 feet. As with other pipe systems, a fairly extensive line of fittings are available. And as with ABS pipe, regular vent fittings aren't interchangeable with shoulderless drainage fittings.

374

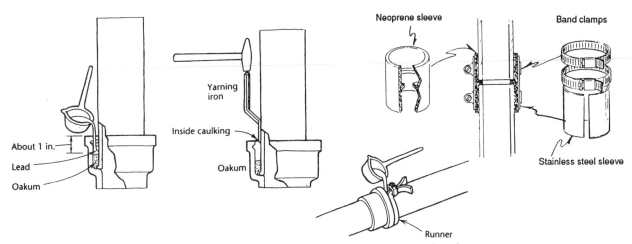

15-26 *Making caulked lead joints in cast-iron pipe. Caution: molten lead is dangerous. Work in a well-ventilated area and avoid breathing fumes.*

The caulked and leaded joints of the old-fashioned *hub-and-spigot* pipe system are time-consuming and occasionally dangerous, but not actually all that difficult to make (see **15-26**). The actual seal is made by packing the joint space with *oakum* (tarred rope fibres) caulking using an offset chisel called a *yarning iron* to compress it solidly until the hub is half full. Molten lead is poured into the space and tamped tight (when cool) to anchor the oakum and keep the joints from moving. An *inside iron* is used to bevel the lead ring against the spigot, followed by an *outside iron* (with a reverse bevel) against the hub. The propane-heated lead pot and long-handled ladle can be rented along with the yarning and leading irons. Use a special asbestos gasket called a *joint runner* clamped around the pipe to lead a horizontal joint. The lead is poured into it through a hole at the top of the runner and the gasket is left in place until the lead solidifies.

Molten lead can splatter explosively when moisture in a damp joint turns to steam. Always wear protective gloves, eye protection, and an apron when making a joint with

hot lead. Keep the ladle well away from you when pouring the lead.

Fortunately, most codes now permit the use of hubless cast iron, which is a lot easier and safer to work with. A neoprene rubber sleeve is slipped over one side of the joint and folded back on itself (see **15-27**). The gasket is then rolled over the other half of the fitting. A stainless steel sleeve slips over the neoprene, and the entire assembly is secured by tightening down two band clamps (which may or may not be integral with the stainless steel sleeve). When exposed, rather than buried, hubless pipe can be easily disassembled for repairs or remodelling.

Although it's possible to cut cast iron pipe by scoring it with a hacksaw about $\frac{1}{16}$-inch deep, supporting one side on a block, and then repeatedly and carefully tapping the score line with a cold chisel or hammer, the possibility of shattering the brittle pipe is still fairly high (see **15-28**). The best solution is to rent a ratchet-powered, chain-type, cast-iron pipe cracker instead; it does the job quickly and accurately.

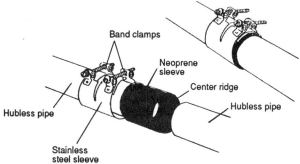

15-27 *Joining "no-hub" cast-iron pipe. The nuts on the band clamps must be turned down to 60 pounds with a torque wrench.*

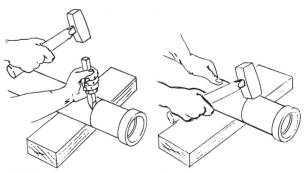

15-28 *Cutting cast-iron pipe. You can also cut cast iron with a circular saw fitted with a metal-cutting blade.*

375

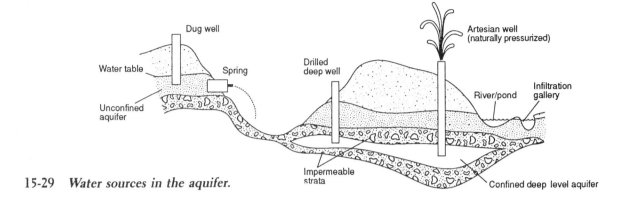

15-29 *Water sources in the aquifer.*

DEVELOPING ON-SITE WATER SUPPLY

Rainwater falling on the ground percolates into the soil and collects in porous layers called *aquifers*. The level of ground water in the aquifer will rise and fall according to seasonal changes in rainfall and snowmelt (see **15-29**). The top of this saturated layer is called the *water table*. A spring or seep marks the coincidence of the water table with the surface.

15-30 *The steel casing for a drilled well extends downward until the well bore reaches solid rock at which point the walls of the bore hole are stable and self-sealed with the ground-rock grout produced by the drilling.*

In rural areas, a natural source of potable water close to the surface has always been one of the criteria of a good building site. You may actually find an old stone or wooden "spring box" on your property. Or you may find a wet spot where the spring trickles to the surface. This shouldn't be confused with a bog or "sink" which is the ponding of surface water in a low spot over impermeable underlying soil.

Forty percent of American homes still get their water from individual wells drilled on the property (see **12-30**). The only difference between a spring, a shallow dug well, and a deep-drilled well is how far down the water is and the horsepower it will take to pump it up. A naturally pressurized artesian well is created by tapping a vein of water confined between impermeable strata in a deep aquifer and a recharging level that is higher than the top of the well. The column of water in an artesian well pipe will continue to rise until its weight equals the pressure of the water in the aquifer at which point it is said to have reached its *static* level. With a true artesian well, that pressure will be high enough that the water will erupt from the ground like a geyser. Such wells typically require a pressure-reducing valve to make them safe for home delivery.

Since the water in a spring or shallow-dug well lies at or close to the surface, it costs a lot less to develop than a drilled well (see **15-31**). Once you've located a likely area, the overlying soil is excavated until you reach the actual source, which is typically a layer of saturated gravel or a crack in the bedrock. A pencil-thin trickle is more than enough to supply a household. Clear the bottom of the excavation of loose mud and debris. Take care not to dig through or disturb the underlying impermeable layer. Excavate an area about six feet to eight feet in circumference and spread a six-inch layer of clean *washed* chestnut stone over the bare earth. Set a perforated, precast concrete spring tile onto the stone. As you set the succeeding solid tiles, seal their joints with mortar to keep silt from seeping into the spring bottom. It's a good idea to line the bottom and sides of the excavation with filter fabric as well.

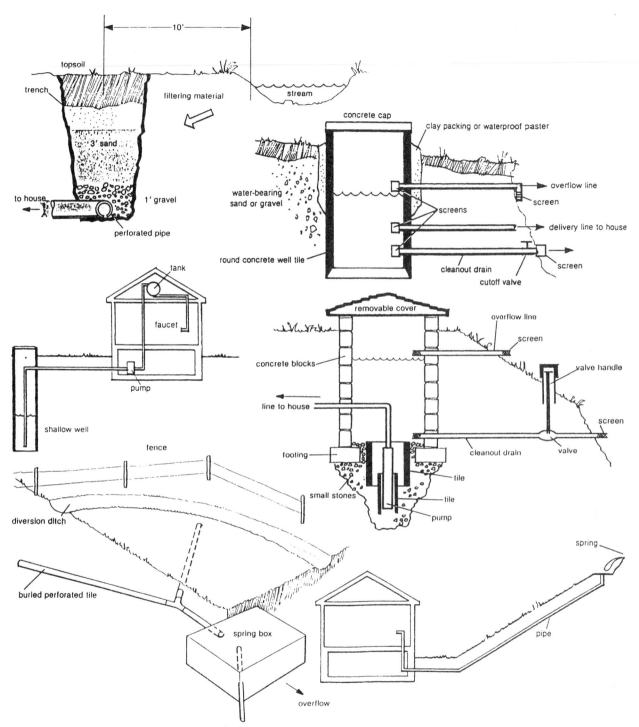

15-31 *Developing a spring for household water supply. Spring boxes are generally bottomless unless they collect water only from above; springs can also be built from mortared and parged concrete block; protect the spring area from surface contamination by fencing and surface diversion ditches; when gravity cannot supply sufficient pressure alone a pump can be used to boost the water up to an attic storage tank to create a hybrid system; infiltration galleries can be used to filter water collected from a nearby stream or lake for household use. However, the filtration effect is limited and the safety of the water cannot be assured.*

377

If the bottom of the spring is high enough above the house to allow gravity flow, the intake pipe must be installed through a hole in the first spring tile (chisel through the flanges where the tiles join if there is no precast hole). If the water must be pumped to the house, it doesn't make any difference at which point the pipe enters the spring box as long as it is at least a foot below frost and it extends to within two inches of the bottom of the spring. The end of the pipe is fitted with a combination strainer and *footvalve*. This one-way valve keeps the pipe full of water when the pump shuts off. Otherwise, the pump would "lose its prime" (the water drains back and the pump sucks air until it burns out). Since flow is always downhill with a gravity-feed line, no footvalve is needed.

Backfill the hole with crushed stone to the level of the first tile or the source outlet, and then continue filling with clean, washed gravel to within a foot or so of grade. This permeable layer filters ground water as it seeps into the spring and acts as a reservoir to increase the capacity of the spring tiles. Cover the top of this layer with tar paper and pack it firmly with heavy clay to grade. Install an overflow pipe, if necessary, and set the spring tile cover. Grade around the spring box so that surface water drains away from the tiles, and fence out grazing animals (if you have them) within a 50-foot radius. Pour about one-half gallon of bleach into the water, and let it sit for a day or so; then draw off the water through your household tap until you can't taste the bleach. Fill a sample bottle for the water test kit obtained from your local health officer according to the instructions provided. The water must test free of coliform bacteria to obtain your certificate of occupancy.

A spring of this kind must be surrounded by relatively impermeable clay soil. If your property is near a river, stream, or lake, an *infiltration gallery* will allow you to safely utilize this surface water for household supply. An infiltration gallery is basically a horizontal spring box made from a large-diameter perforated pipe, culvert, or spring tiles set in a gravel-filled excavation in permeable soil at least 50 feet away from the surface water source. This allows the water to be filtered as it seeps through the soil from the adjoining river or lake and eventually collects in the gallery. Tapping a river or lake for water can be risky, given the kinds of pollutants that they can collect. Testing for a broad spectrum of contaminants is expensive and not necessarily cost-effective.

A water purification system installed in the house is the only sure way to guarantee safe drinking water (see **15-32**). While a deep, drilled well is unlikely to be contaminated with bacteria from surface runoff, any aquifer is vulnerable to pollution from toxic chemicals that have seeped into the ground water. Naturally occurring minerals or dissolved radon can also make well water unusable without additional treatment. If you do install a treatment

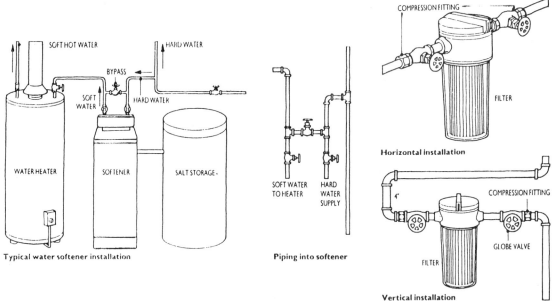

15-32 *Water softeners remove the calcium, magnesium, and iron salts that clog pipes. Since softened water has a high salt content it shouldn't be used for lawn and garden watering or drinking (where dietary sodium levels are a concern). Thus, the softener is typically only connected to treat the hot water used for clotheswashing, dishwashing, and bathing. In-line filters with or without disposable cartridges can be used to remove undesirable minerals salts, sediment, or chemicals from the drinking water at the point of use or else a whole-house filter can be installed in the supply main.*

system, remember that a water softener isn't the same thing as a water filter. Softeners remove minerals that cause "hard" water, corrosion, and stains. A reverse osmosis filtration system (either whole-house or point-of-use, under-sink unit) and activated charcoal filters are required to remove pollutants, particulates, and bacterial contaminants. Water purification systems can cost hundreds to thousands of dollars and vary widely in performance. Don't trust the claims of the person trying to sell you the system; consult a reliable, unbiased source in selecting the right purification system.

If your house is sufficiently downhill of your water source, you'll have a *gravity-feed supply* (see **15-33**). The rule of thumb is that the pressure at the tap is half the difference between the source and its outlet. For example, if your source is 40 feet above the kitchen sink tap, you'll have about 20 psi at that point, which is enough to run a modern washing machine or dishwasher.

Several conditions affect the performance of gravity-feed water supply. First, the delivery pipe must be sufficiently large to minimize flow friction. Use at least one-inch polyethylene pipe for runs under 500 feet long. For runs over 500 feet, use 1¼-inch pipe. Second, pressure is a function of *hydraulic head*. If your second floor shower head is only two feet below the actual level of the inlet at the bottom of the spring, you'll only have about one psi of pressure at that point. The usual cure is to pressurize the system once the water is brought into the house.

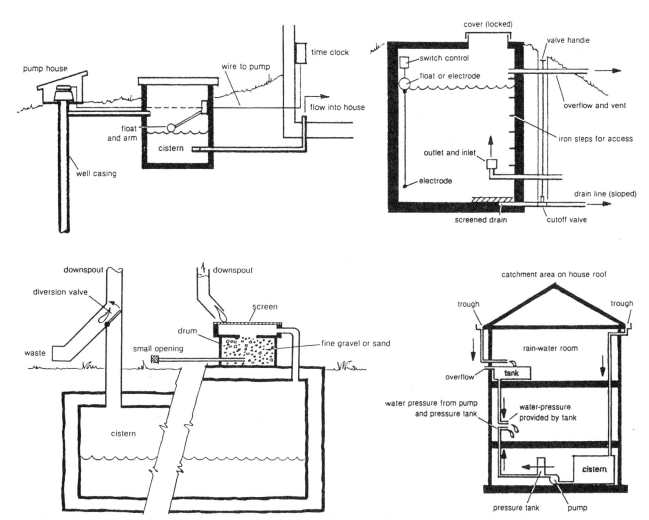

15-33 *Cistern for roof collection or gravity-feed supply. A catchment system once used in Victorian homes featured a cistern on the upper story to deliver gravity-pressurized water. This might be an option for remote sites where power is unavailable. Since its capacity is limited only by the available space, a concrete cistern in the basement fitted with a pump for constant pressure is preferable. Cisterns may also be used as reservoirs for low-yield wells. The system can be set up with a timer to run the pump at regular intervals and a float switch to shut it off so that the level in the system remains fairly constant.*

In regions where rain is frequent and of intense but brief duration and ground water is not available or is contaminated by salt water, rainwater is often collected from the roof and stored in underground *cisterns* for household use. A diverter valve and strainer is installed in the downspout so that the first few minutes of runoff can wash the roof clean. Metal, tile, or asphalt roofing are all suitable for roof-collection systems. A pump installed on the cistern cover pressurizes the water lines. A hand-operated pump provides backup for power failures.

It's unlikely that most sites will provide you with a gravity-feed or artesian water supply. In most cases, water will have to be *pumped* from its source. The type of pump depends on the depth of the source.

A *piston pump* uses suction to lift water. Raising the piston creates an area of low pressure in the chamber behind it, and atmospheric pressure pushes a column of water up the pipe. Since the weight of the water column will eventually be more than the lift provided by atmospheric pressure (15 psi at sea level), piston pumps are limited to a vertical lift of about 25 feet. The horizontal pull, however, is virtually unlimited, except by internal friction against the sides of the delivery pipe. Large diameter pipes reduce friction.

Centrifugal pumps use a rapidly rotating paddle (the impeller) to create a powerful suction that can draw water faster and more efficiently than piston pumps. The deepwell *jet pump* uses a second pipe to force a high-velocity stream of water across the intake, lowering its pressure and providing more lift. This enables the same centrifugal pump to pull water up from depths as great as 140 feet. Jet-type centrifugal pumps are relatively inexpensive and, since they are surface-mounted, they can be installed in a basement or separate pump-house where they are accessible for repairs.

Because it is located at the bottom of the well, a deepwell *submersible pump* can push, rather than pull, the water column up the pipe. This takes a lot less energy, enabling a relatively small motor to deliver water from wells up to 500 feet deep. Being mounted in the bottom of the well, they take up no indoor space and can't be heard in the house when running.

The only drawback of a submersible pump is its vulnerability to damage by lightning strikes. The long cable which connects it to the household wiring is an attractive ground for lightning. Modern pumps are somewhat protected by being bathed in an insulating oil bath. Lightning arresters installed across the pump control relay also block lightning surges from travelling up the motor wires and into the household wiring.

Do-it-yourself submersible pump installations are possible (see 15-34). The motor is lowered into the well by its attached power cable, and high-pressure 160-psi-rated polyetheylene delivery pipe (steel pipe is required for wells deeper than 400 feet). Foam plastic spacers keep the pipe centered in the bore hole. The power cable exits out the

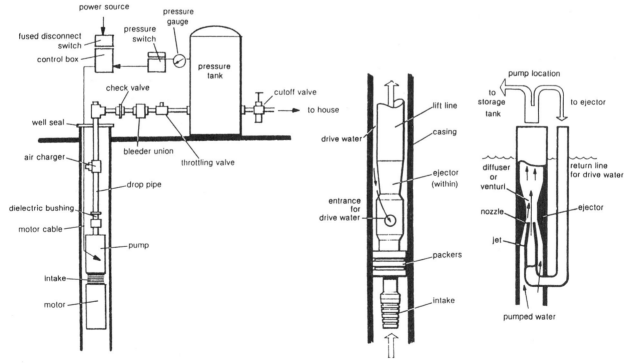

15-34 *Schematic of submersible pump installation with pressure tank and typical controls.*

well head and is run through a galvanized pipe to the house. It is connected through a motor-control relay switch to a 240-volt circuit. The delivery pipe is joined to a brass *pitless adaptor* installed in the wall of the steel well casing below the frost line. An oxy-acetylene torch is needed to cut the hole for the adaptor fitting. The line should run from the well into the house in one continuous length, without any other fittings. If this isn't possible, or you need to add a branch line to an outbuilding, use brass fittings and double stainless hose clamps for all of the buried connections.

Since a do-it-yourself installation by its very nature can't have a five-year warranty against lightning damage or other failures offered by professional installers, most homeowners prefer to let the well-driller also install at least the pump if not the rest of the system up to and including the *pressure tank*.

Except for submersible pumps, which are self-priming, since they push the water up the pipe, suction pumps must be primed before they will operate. The pipe must be purged of air by filling it with water. With a short run, this can be done by pouring water into the priming hole on top of the pump body with a funnel (look for a square threaded plug on top of the impeller chamber). Keep filling until water squirts out of the priming hole instead of air when the pump is turned on. Leave the plug screwed in loosely so that the water doesn't spray all over the cellar. With long runs, slugs of trapped air will make it almost impossible to fill the pipe with water by hand, especially if there's a high spot in the line. Rent a *force pump* (an aqueous version of a bicycle pump) to pump water from a bucket into the pipe under pressure. The foot valve at the well end of the line keeps the water from draining out of the pipe as the air is forced towards the pump end. Even with a force pump, it can take an hour or more and repeated cycling and filling of the pump impeller to work all the air out of the line. You'll hear a distinct change in the sound of the pump when it starts pulling water instead of air.

If the system depended on only the pump to maintain its pressure, the pump would cycle every time a tap was opened or water was otherwise drawn off. These sudden surges of pressure are not only hard on the pump and the plumbing fittings, but they waste energy as well. A pressure tank installed between the pump and the rest of the system uses a cushion of compressed air to maintain the system water pressure within predetermined limits after the pump shuts off (see **15-35**). A pressure-sensitive control switch turns the pump off and on at those points. The set points are adjusted by tightening or loosening screws inside the pressure switch control box mounted on top of the pump or pressure tank line. A modern pressure tank fitted with a rubber diaphragm is shown in **15-35**. Old-fashioned tanks which lacked the diaphragm would eventually become "waterlogged" as their internal air was replaced by water. With a submersible pump, a one-way check valve is usually installed in the line to the pressure tank to keep water from siphoning back down the well.

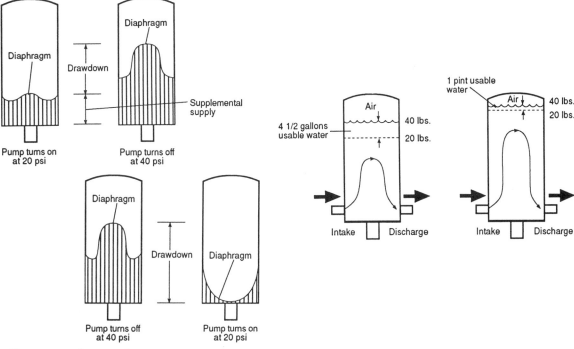

15-35 *Pressure-tank operation.*

ON-SITE SEWAGE DISPOSAL

Roughly one in three homes treats its household waste water on site with a septic system (see **15-36**). When correctly sized and properly installed in suitable soils and regularly maintained, such systems are a safe and effective way to purify waste water and return it to the ground water supply (see **15-37**).

Household sewage (black water) and drainage water (grey water) are carried by a four-inch diameter, cast-iron pipe set about two feet below the ground into a large, sealed concrete *septic tank* whose top is about a foot or so beneath the surface. The tank is generally within eight feet of the house wall so that only a single standard ten-foot length of pipe is required. Tank sizes are correlated to the number of bedrooms in the house, on the assumption that more people will be using the facilities. Although the minimum size for a two-bedroom house is 500 gallons, a 1000-gallon tank is not that much more expensive and provides a safety margin of excess capacity. It's pretty much considered to be the standard for houses up to five bedrooms (here, the capacity should be increased to at least 1250 gallons). Adding an in-sink garbage disposal doubles the required tank capacity.

The inlet into the septic tank is about one inch higher than the outlet. Internal baffles prevent mixing of inflow and outflow. Complex anaerobic (without oxygen) bacterial action breaks down solid wastes into a liquid effluent, sewer gas (which is what you smell issuing from the vent stack), and an undigestible sludge which sinks to the bottom of the tank. Eventually the sludge builds up to a point where it interferes with the action of the tank and must be pumped out. Rather than discover this when your toilet backs up or when the smell of sewage oozing from your lawn is evident, pump the tank out regularly—at least once every two years. Plant a perennial flower patch or some other sort of marker over the clean-out hole to make it

15-36 *The 1000-gallon, precast concrete septic tank is installed close enough to the house so that it is connected to the cellar by a single length of 10-foot cast-iron sewer pipe. Tanks are set about one to two feet below the finish grade. Mark the access cover with a stake or other landmark and/or record it's location on a map (e.g., the site plan) so that you can find it again when it's time to pump it out.*

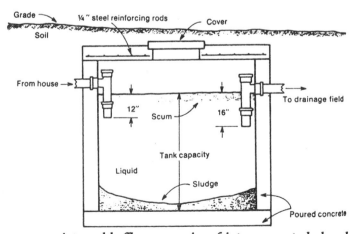

15-37 *Instead of one or more internal baffles or a series of interconnected chambers, this septic system tank design uses the difference in inlet and outlet pipes to separate incoming sewage from effluent. Any system must be designed by a licensed professional.*

easy to locate when the time comes to dig it up. The actual pumping is done by professionals with special trucks.

The effluent portion of the digested sewage flows from the tank through a solid PVC four-inch plastic pipe into the *distribution box*, which is a small concrete plenum that distributes the outflow to the requisite number of perforated drain pipes laid in gravel- and/or crushed stone-filled *absorption trenches*. The pipes slope away from the box at one inch in 25 feet. Aerobic bacteria in the trenches and the surrounding soil that together comprise the *leach field* further digest the partially treated sewage until it is rendered harmless.

The right kind of soil is one key to how well the septic system will function and the total linear footage of the absorption trenches is another. The soil must not absorb water so quickly that the effluent doesn't get a chance to be digested by the bacteria. On the other hand, an excessively slow-draining soil will become waterlogged and go anaerobic. Both overly sandy and heavy clay soils are difficult to work with. The best would be sandy-gravelly loam.

You can estimate the absorption capacity of your proposed leach field by digging a one-foot-square hole to the depth of the absorption trench (about three feet) and filling it with six inches of water. Time how many minutes it takes for the water level to drop an inch (see **15-38**). You can also time how long it takes for all six inches to disappear and average the results. The area of the absorption field is sized in units of square feet per bedroom according to the percolation rate of the water, with a minimum area of 150 square feet.

The figures in **15-38** are subject to modification by a number of other factors. For example, the seasonal high water table must always be at least four feet below the bottom of the leach field. This is the reason why soil testing is usually done during the wettest part of the year. On questionable sites, you may be required to install vertical perforated pipes to monitor changes in ground water levels throughout the year before gaining approval of your system design. The depth to bedrock also affects system design. At least five feet is required between the bottom of the trench and the underlying rock. The presence of a stream or another disposal field or a well will also affect system design. In some cases, especially with shallow dug wells, a *curtain drain* may be required to isolate the ground water from the leach field. This is a line of subterranean perforated drain pipe, laid at the bottom of a gravel-filled and fabric-filter-lined four to six foot deep trench uphill of the leach field that corrects for a high water table or wet soils in a manner similar to the foundation drain system. Other site modifications may be required when the slope is so steep that there is a danger of the effluent flowing out onto the surface instead of down into the ground. Furthermore, you may be required to have enough acceptable land area to provide a replacement field if your primary field fails.

Many local ordinances require that soil percolation testing be done by a registered civil engineer or approved by a state environmental technician. This is especially important when designing an alternative system for marginal conditions. Usually, any systems must also be certified as meeting state or local standards, and the installation must be inspected and approved by local health officers before it can be covered. The actual installation is usually included in the excavation subcontract.

Since partially digested effluent that gets into the ground water table can wind up miles away in someone else's drinking water, proper septic system design is a community health issue. Because of the complexity of system design and regulation, and the effect it could have on your housebuilding plans, you should never buy a building lot without making the sale contingent upon passing a perc test and/or being furnished with a copy of an approved on-site design for the plot.

15-38 *Estimating the absorption capacity of your proposed leach field.*

Minutes for water to fall one inch	Absorption Area (sqft/bdrm)
<2	85*
3	100
4	115
5	125
10	165
15	190
30	250
60	330
>60	Special design case

*Percolation rates <5 may require special design systems in some states.

ALTERNATIVES

Despite the claims of their advocates, waterless toilets are unlikely to make much of an impact upon the mainstream of sanitary engineering. Even putting aside the question as to the level of involvement most people are willing to commit to the disposal of their bodily wastes, the argument that the high cost of factory-built, composting waterless toilets could be offset by the elimination of the septic system is, unfortunately, not true. The grey water still needs treatment before it can be released into the water table. And so far, the only approved method for treating grey water is still a conventional septic system and leach field. Some municipalities permit a reduction in the size of the absorption area. But others insist that it remain the same in case the present or future owners choose to replace the waterless toilet with a flush toilet. The larger composting-type waterless toilets also require a large area of

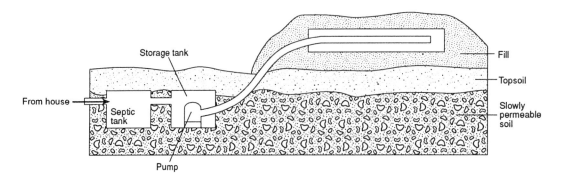

15-39 *For a mound system on a sloped site, the mound is located downhill of the storage tank so that it can be charged by a maintenance-free, automatic dosing siphon instead of a mechanical pump.*

warm basement space. Smaller composting toilets take up less space but use electricity to run a ventilation fan and/or small heater. They also are pretty much limited to vacation-cottage or occasional use, rather than continuous use by a large family.

But, on the positive side, your septic system will last longer if it handles only grey water, and you may be able to install it in soils with otherwise marginal absorption capacity.

Of the many designs for owner-built waterless toilets, the only one that is sure to gain approval by local health officers without an uphill battle, is the venerable pit privy. Properly built and screened against flies and rodents, it is safe on almost any rural site. The drawbacks, however, are obvious enough that most privies are a temporary expedient until a conventional system can be installed.

Alternative on-site, water-borne sewage disposal systems that are approved for marginal or wet sites are generally a variation of the *mound system* (see **15-39**). A mound system is basically a disposal field built on top of the ground. Permeable soil or sand is placed on the surface, and the leach pipes are laid in this fill. Sewage flows from the tank to a storage tank where it is pumped or siphoned to the mound in large doses that keep the pipes from clogging. In order to work well, the mound fill must overlay marginally permeable soil or else such soil must be added to the site first. Because of the great deal of fill, mound systems tend to be very expensive. The pump also imposes maintenance problems. The dosing siphon works automatically, but adds extra costs. Yet mound systems may be the only practical alternative for some sites unsuited for standard systems.

16 HVAC Systems

For many reasons that are both conscious and unconscious, the United States is almost entirely dependent on fossil fuels to heat and cool our homes. Nevertheless, there are proven alternatives which have been available in one form or another for almost a half century. Fortunately, as the costs of electricity and heating fuels have continued to creep upwards, many conservation techniques that only a few decades ago would not have been considered have been adopted by the mainstream building industry. For example, the average "tight" tract home built since 1980 exchanges its warm inside air with cold outside air about 75 percent more slowly than houses built 20 or 30 years earlier, and about 150 percent slower than a house 50 or more years older. Meanwhile, the modern super-insulated home has an air-change rate half that of the standard "energy-efficient" home.

ENERGY CONSERVATION CONSIDERATIONS

Most of these energy savings have been achieved through conservation—that is, more and better insulation, tighter and better-built windows and doors, careful sealing of air leaks with caulking, weatherstripping, and other anti-infiltration measures, and an improvement in the overall efficiency of heating and cooling equipment. However, an unintended consequence has been the emergence of an awareness or concern for the quality of indoor air.

The widespread use of solar energy for supplemental space heating and full-time water heating could make an even bigger difference in energy efficiency. Depending on the investment in equipment and design, and the suitability of the site, in many parts of the United States, solar energy can carry most of the residential heat load. There's almost no region where it couldn't provide at least an economically significant portion.

Any prospective home builder would be remiss not to include measures for reducing heat loss or gain into their house design. At the very least, except in the hottest, sunniest parts of your country or region, orient the house to face south. It doesn't cost any more to do this, and it will reduce heat loss to some degree, no matter what. In the Southwest of the United States, summer shading or heat reflective windows will counteract summer heat and still allow you to utilize solar gain in the winter in lieu of conventional heating.

A corollary of this orientation principle is: minimize undesirable exposures. In the northern hemisphere consider building into a slope and/or a low north wall profile, earth berming, and concentrating the glazing on the south wall. Eliminate or reduce north-wall glazing in cold cli-mates. Likewise, attach garages and sheds on the north side to buffer against wind and reduce heat loss. In hot climates, build garages and carports on hard-to-shade east or west walls and use white roofing to reflect summer sun. (In the southern hemisphere, read north for south and vice versa.)

Insulate well; use at least six inches of fibreglass or its equivalent in walls and 12 inches in the attic ceiling (for more on insulation, see Chapter Nineteen). Control infiltration, which causes even more heat loss, with tight construction, caulking, good windows, and insulated attic access panels. Prevent conduction heat losses by using plastic instead of steel electrical boxes. Insulate pipes. Install gaskets at penetrations.

At the very least, utilize the "solar tempering" effect of south-facing glazing to supplement conventional heating. For most areas of the country, the total gain of solar radiation through south-facing windows on a sunny day more than balances the heat loss through them during the night. To reflect the contribution of south-facing windows to the seasonal heat load, don't include them in the sum total of glazing areas when figuring heat loss.

Use insulating shutters or thermal curtains to lower nighttime heat loss through windows. Use double glazing on south walls and triple glazing on all others.

To aid in lowering heat gain, ventilate the attic well. Use trees to shade walls in summer. Promote passive natural cooling by operable low and high vent windows oriented to prevailing summer breezes. Thermal mass also improves summer comfort in climates with hot days and cool nights.

Do a heat/cooling load calculation so that you won't oversize your system. Short cycling entails higher operating costs, lower seasonal efficiency, and shorter service life. When installing heating and cooling ducts, avoid running them through the attic, if possible. Insulate them, and tape all joints with duct tape (up to 25 percent of the heat or cool is lost through loose duct joints).

Buy only the most energy-efficient appliances. For example, side-by-side refrigerator–freezers use up to 40 percent more energy than over/under appliances. Use microwaves for cooking in summer. Setting the water heater temperature down to 120 to 125°F (49 to 52°C) saves 50 percent on fuel. Using low-flow shower heads not only conserves water, but also saves on fuel to heat it.

Utilize efficient natural and artificial lighting. Emphasize task lighting over general lighting. Use energy-efficient, low-heat fluorescent instead of incandescent bulbs; some of the newest fluorescent bulbs screw into

16-1 *The shadow lines on the walls of these houses clearly show how south-facing facades receive more sunlight than other walls do. Note also the shading effect of the overhangs on the upper walls.*

ordinary fixtures and give a more natural, less harsh light. When using incandescent lighting, use one large bulb instead of several small bulbs in multiple fixtures. Reflective surfaces increase the effectiveness of both natural and artificial light. Finally, avoid recessed fixtures that penetrate into the attic. They cannot be insulated.

SOLAR HEATING STRATEGIES

In general, some level of passive solar space heating will be cost-effective no matter where you live. This can range from simply using south-facing glass to supplement your fossil-fuel system to a nearly 100 percent solar installation. The trick is to find the most efficient mix of solar and conventional heating systems for the region in which you live (see **16-1**).

There's a commonly held notion that passive solar heating is nothing more than a lot of south-facing glass. While south-facing fenestration is the most prominent feature of solar architecture, it doesn't necessarily follow that more is better. The relationship between the glazing area and the living area is critical. Building codes and standard practice assume an overall window area equal to 10 to 20 percent of the floor area, more-or-less uniformly distributed on the exterior walls. Experience has shown that a house lacking any provision for heat storage other than the mass of the house itself will overheat on a sunny day if the area of the south-facing glazing exceeds roughly seven percent of total floor area. Temperature swings of up to 30 degrees Fahrenheit (17 degrees Celsius) are not uncommon. Adding extra thermal mass to absorb and store the heat captured by this *direct gain* strategy allows an increase in south-facing glazing area without the concomitant overheating. This can be achieved by several different methods. Partition cavities can be filled with scraps of drywall. You can cover walls opposite of or adjacent to the south windows with two layers of ⅝-inch drywall. (Make sure the joists and partitions are sturdy enough to carry the increased load.) Integral thermal mass such as an insulated concrete slab floor or a vertical structural masonry wall are also cost-effective, since they fulfill other vital functions at the same time (see **16-2** and **16-3**).

16-3 *Advantages and disadvantages of passive solar heating.*

Pro	Con
Cheapest, makes use of integral structures	Overheats easily, wide temperature swings
Compatible with standard building techniques	Needs frequent backup heat
Easy to install thermal shades on vertical windows	Window sizing a problem unless extra mass added
Oriented for view and natural lighting	Southern orientation can cause siting problems, glare, undesirable view, fabric fading
Pleasing appearance	

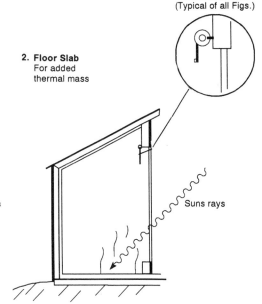

16-2 *Direct gain (one zone) passive solar heating.*

1. **Solar-tempered**
Heat storage only in house-mass

South

Suns rays

North

2. **Floor Slab**
For added thermal mass

Thermal shutter
(Typical of all Figs.)

Suns rays

The most familiar and successful example of the mass wall approach is the *Trombe wall* (after the designer Felix Trombe). Here, a vertical, dark-colored masonry wall is placed directly behind the glazing (see **16-4**). An alternative, which permits more architectural freedom at the cost of decreased efficiency, is to place the mass wall at some point within the living space of the house, but still in direct sunshine. Water-filled containers can be substituted for masonry. Usually, 10 inches of concrete, 16 inches of filled-core concrete block, 12 inches of brick, or six inches of water will furnish enough mass to prevent wide temperature swings.

Although mass wall systems entail added cost, they can be justified because of their relatively high thermal efficiency. Temperatures on the dark side of a Trombe wall can exceed 150°F (66°C). Up to 80 percent of the incoming solar radiation will be stored as heat in the wall.

This efficiency is considerably reduced as the mass wall is moved further back into the room. Since there is no access to the space between the Trombe wall and its glazing, insulating nighttime shutters and reflective summer heat shades must be installed on the outside of the glazing. Another drawback of the Trombe wall is that because the glazing will be quite cold at night, a good part of the heat stored in the wall will tend to radiate outward to the glazing rather than inward to the house (see **16-5**).

Many builders, long on enthusiasm, but short on physics, mistakenly assume that incorporating a fireplace, chimney, or wood stove into an interior mass wall will supplement its solar heat storage capabilities. Heat absorption is driven by temperature difference. As a thermal mass is warmed, its capacity to absorb further heat decreases. A wood stove will warm a thermal mass so quickly that it will be incapable of absorbing any solar heat. A mass wall

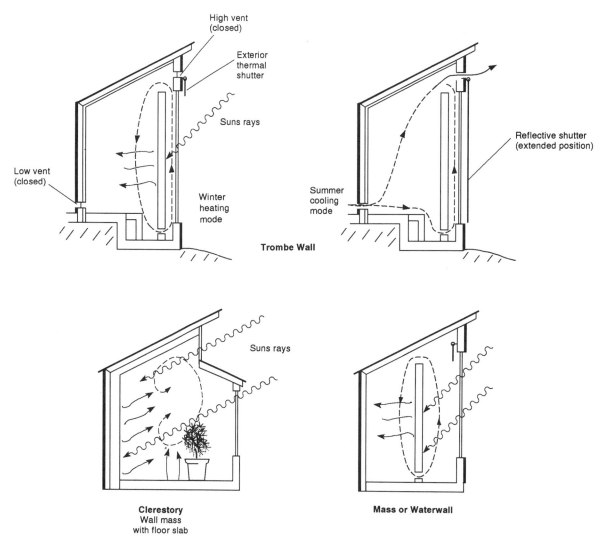

Trombe Wall

Clerestory
Wall mass
with floor slab

Mass or Waterwall

16-4 *Mass wall (two-zone system).*

16-5 Advantages and disadvantages of mass wall systems.

Pro	Con
More even temperature swings	Exterior shutters, access problems
High efficiency, does not overheat living spaces	Can block view, exterior appearance may be ungainly
Will block bad view	Interior mass wall takes up living area
Uses relatively inexpensive materials	Not structural, can need extra support, foundation
More efficient than floor slab, well suited as back wall for greenhouse and sunspace	

designed to absorb furnace heat will be quite efficient. But it should never be combined with a mass wall intended to absorb solar heat.

The thermosiphon system utilizes a passively induced natural convection loop to circulate solar-warmed air or water into a storage bin (see **16-6**). The storage must always be at least six feet higher than the collector surface and (typically) below the living areas. The stored heat is transferred to them by direct radiation from a floor slab poured over the storage bin (see **16-7**). Depending on system configuration and dynamics, a blower or a circulating pump may be needed to overcome internal resistance and deliver a usable quantity of heat. Dampers or some other control are also required to prevent reverse thermosiphoning (heat flows from storage back to a cold collector at night or on cloudy days). Thermosiphons are well-suited to steeply sloping sites where the collector can be placed at some distance from the house.

16-7 Advantages and disadvantages of thermosiphons.

Pro	Con
Natural power	Requires specific site
	Extra construction costs
Collector isolated from house	
Does not require insulation	Low efficiency, slow to heat, easily overcome, reverse siphoning
Does not interfere with facade or use of living area	
No overheating, no overhang or shading	Engineering problems, need for mechanical assistance

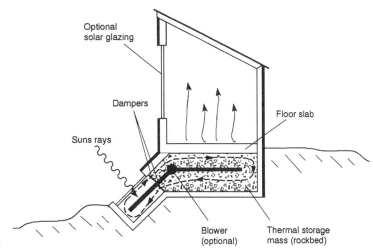

Optional solar glazing
Dampers
Suns rays
Blower (optional)
Thermal storage mass (rockbed)
Floor slab

16-6 Thermosiphon.

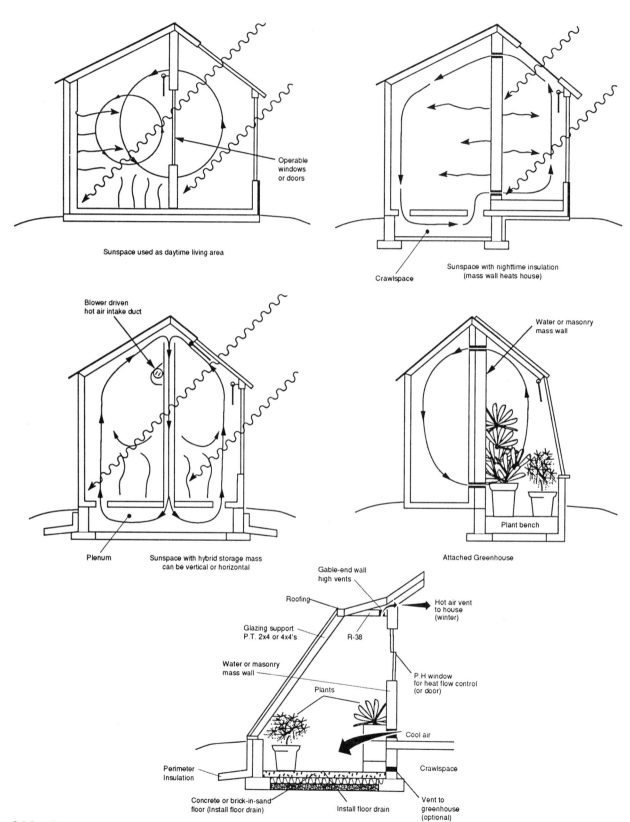

Sunspace used as daytime living area

Crawlspace

Sunspace with nighttime insulation
(mass wall heats house)

Operable
windows
or doors

Blower driven
hot air intake duct

Plenum

Sunspace with hybrid storage mass
can be vertical or horizontal

Water or masonry
mass wall

Plant bench

Attached Greenhouse

Gable-end wall
high vents

Roofing

Hot air vent
to house
(winter)

Glazing support
P.T. 2x4 or 4x4's

R-38

Water or masonry
mass wall

P.H window
for heat flow control
(or door)

Plants

Cool air

Perimeter
Insulation

Crawlspace

Concrete or brick-in-sand
floor (Install floor drain)

Install floor drain

Vent to
greenhouse
(optional)

16-8 *Sunspace and attached greenhouse (two-zone systems).*

390

16-9 *Advantages and disadvantages of sunspaces and greenhouses.*

Pro	Con
Pleasant interior environment (psychological benefits)	Efficiency problems
Natural light, dramatic design	Greenhouse use conflicts with living area use
Extra daytime living space	Expensive to build or buy large glazing area
Used to grow food, extend season	Can block direct access to view, south
Controls temperature swings	Nighttime heat losses can need supplemental heat for greenhouses, need shutters
Hybrid systems can store large amounts of heat, low-backup heating	
No shutters for isolated sunspaces	Humidity, ventilation problems, summer heat gain
Available as add-on kit or subcontract	

The difference between a sunspace and an attached greenhouse and the details of its construction have already been discussed in Chapter Thirteen. Both are popular additions to living space in regions of the country where they can act as an antidote to winter cabin fever (see **16-8** & **16-9**).

The distinguishing concept of the double-envelope "geothermal" house design is a novel construction technique that thermally isolates the inner living space from the outer walls on the north and south sides of the house (see **16-10**). A continuous convective loop runs between an inner and outer wall, under the roof, and down to a crawl space. According to its proponents, solar-heated air, warmed by an integral attached sunspace rises through the wall duct to the peak of the roof, where, as it cools, it flows down the north wall duct space into the sealed crawl space. The natural drive of the system pulls this cool air up through the open decking of the sunspace floor to continue the cycle. During the night, the cycle is said to reverse as "lukewarm" air from the earth-floored crawl space would rise up the north wall and down into the sunspace. In summer, hot air could be cooled by being drawn down into the crawl space area. The temperature of the living space was not supposed to fall below the base temperature of the crawl space, even without supplemental heat.

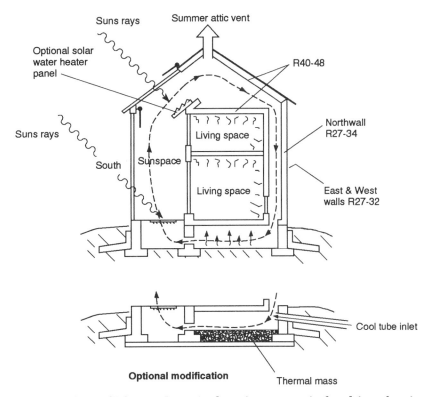

16-10 *Double-envelope "geothermal" house. In revised versions, an attic fan drives the circulation loop and forces warm air into a rock-bed or sand-bed thermal storage bin in the crawl space.*

The many envelope houses which were built do, without exception, maintain remarkably even internal temperatures. But the contribution of the heat-duct loop and the earth-floored storage space proved difficult to establish. Tests by independent researchers established that although the passive-solar aspects of the sunspace and the high levels of insulation worked very well, there was little actual air circulation through the supposed convective loop. The base temperature of the crawl space (about 45°F or 7°C) actually acted as a thermal sink, absorbing, not radiating, heat.

Subsequent revamping of the design focused on insulating the crawl space and filling it with sand or rock to convert it into a heat storage bin and adding fan-forced circulation to the convective envelope. Others reduced the width of the loop to only the middle third of the south wall. Ultimately, the most cost-effective and energy-efficient solution was to eliminate the loop entirely and utilize a blower-driven duct to charge thermal storage mass. The crawl space can be effective for summer cooling.

The double-walled envelope proved difficult and expensive to build. The inaccessibility of the duct would be a problem if an animal nested or died in it. The duct also makes an excellent chimney for spreading a fire while the earth-floored crawl space could contribute to the buildup of excessive humidity. These are just some of the reasons why envelope houses have fallen from grace. In any case, these drawbacks had nothing to do with the real attractions of the design, which were its dramatic sunspace and the living area it contained. Despite the lackluster performance of the air loop, the concept was so exciting that envelope houses enjoyed a brief vogue among the ecologically chic and well-heeled.

In general, passive techniques are almost always cost effective, or at least aesthetically satisfying. All solar systems employ a *collector* to harvest the sunlight, and a *storage system* to concentrate it and release it to the living areas. The difference between passive and active systems is in the efficiency of the collector and the addition of a powered fluid *distribution system* to increase the rate of heat transfer from the collector into storage and from storage into the living area. In passive systems, the collector is simply a window. The storage system is the thermal mass directly in front of the window (*target mass*) and/or scattered about in the house structure and its furnishings (*distributed mass*). Heat transfer is always by direct radiation from the heated mass to cooler room areas.

In active systems, a heat-transferring fluid (typically water, propylene glycol antifreeze, or air) circulates through pipes or ducts between the collector and the storage medium. The typical flat-plate collector consists of tubing bonded to a black heat-absorbing material set in a glass- or plastic-covered box. If water or glycol is the heat transfer medium, it circulates through a heat exchanger immersed in a large water-filled storage tank. Hot water from the tank can be drawn off for household use and/or

circulated through a second exchanger where air blown across the fins is warmed for space-heating use. The water from storage won't be hot enough on its own to heat conventional, baseboard hot-water radiators efficiently. If air is the heat-transfer fluid, it circulates through an insulated, rock-filled storage bin. The stored heat is drawn off through ducts to heat the house.

The problem with active systems is that they require a lot of expensive hardware. Except in the sunniest regions, active systems are not a cost-effective way to heat your house. Some may feel that the emotional satisfaction of energy-independence or the social status of ecological awareness is worth the cost no matter what. And there's always the possibility that new technologies will emerge over the next few years that will shift the economics of domestic energy use in favor of active solar systems.

As was mentioned earlier, the biggest drawback of passive solar space heating is the relatively low efficiency of heat transfer. Hybrid systems utilize small thermostatically driven fans to increase heat transfer rates by forcing large volumes of solar-warmed room air through rock storage bins that heat the living areas by radiation from an overlying concrete slab. A well-designed hybrid system can eliminate the overheating and wide temperature swings typical of direct-gain passive systems. Unlike active systems, the ductwork and controls are simple and inexpensive.

On the other hand, active systems are very cost-effective for heating hot water for domestic use in every region of the United States right now. You can choose from a wide range of high-quality, off-the-shelf components or else purchase entire kits ready for installation. If you live in the Southwest or South, there's no real excuse for not installing solar water heating instead of a conventional fossil-fuel or electric water heater. Even in areas as cloudy and cold as northern Vermont, it's still possible to provide 50 percent of your domestic hot water by solar panels.

The real question is not whether passive or active solar heating is best, but what is the most efficient way to build houses that conserve energy. Given a fixed budget, is it better spent on thermal mass and south-facing windows, Trombe wall, or on double-wall construction, super-insulation and triple-glazed windows? Which combination of insolation and insulation, sunlight and Styrofoam is best?

The *super-insulated* house is not exactly a passive solar house but it's certainly energy efficient (see **16-11**). The basic conservation techniques of reducing outside air infiltration and cutting interior heat loss are applied with a vengeance. A virtually leak-proof vapor barrier and careful attention to plugging every conceivable source of air leakage results in houses with an air exchange rate of only 0.1 to 0.3 per hour. Double-wall and staggered stud construction techniques permit the use of inexpensive fibreglass or blown cellulose insulation with R-values of R 35 to R 44 in walls and R 50 to R 60 in ceilings, and R 28 in foundations. Triple-glazed window areas are kept small to avoid overheating and are fitted with thermal shutters against nighttime heat loss. Because the south-facing glazing doesn't exceed six percent of floor area, there is no need for added thermal mass. Overall heat loss is so low that the entire heating load is often met with the waste heat generated by household appliances and limited direct solar gain. Except on the coldest and cloudiest days, even a small wood stove or space heater will overheat a super-insulated house. This is the one case where electric resistance heat is practical and economical; no chimney is required.

Because the building envelope is so tight, special measures must be taken to supply fresh air without losing heat. Otherwise, there's a definite and serious threat of indoor air pollution from cooking and other household activities, outgassing of formaldehyde from building components, and radon accumulation. Excess humidity, odors, mold spores, and lingering smoke can also cause discomfort, respiratory difficulties, and structural problems.

Super-insulated houses utilize an air-to-air heat exchanger to exhaust stale indoor air and bring in fresh air while transferring about 80 percent of the heat contained in the exhaust air to the incoming cold fresh air. These units, which typically mount above the bathroom or kitchen ceiling or in the basement, are now widely available from HVAC suppliers. In this application, electric appliances are recommended over gas. Fluorescent lighting, and careful attention to limiting the production of moisture

(e.g., keeping lids on pots when cooking or using microwaves) are all part of adapting to the super-insulated lifestyle. The incremental cost of super-insulation is said to amount to only two to five percent of the overall cost, which would be rapidly repaid by the virtual elimination of heating costs.

CONVENTIONAL HEATING SYSTEMS

Fuel Cost Comparisons. In most cases, solar heating will supplement, rather than replace a conventional heating system. Even with a 100 percent solar house, you'd still need some kind of back-up heating system to deal with prolonged stretches of cloudy, cold weather.

Before you choose the type of heating system to install, you should decide which kind of fuel to burn (see **16-12**). Availability, cost per Btu, and combustion efficiency are factors which influence the selection of one fuel over another. Each fuel has its own heat equivalent, that is, the number of Btu's it contains per gallon, pound, cubic foot, etc. Each particular type of heating appliance converts those theoretically available Btu's to heat with more or less greater efficiency. Not all fuels are equally available in all areas. The use of LPG bottled gas, for example, is prohibited or severely restricted by fire codes in most urban areas. Natural gas lines are even scarcer in rural areas than cable TV. Fuel wood varies greatly in cost, availability, and quality. The table in **16-12** compares the heat content of various fuels in terms of a gallon of oil.

16-11 *Advantages and disadvantages of the super-insulated house.*

Pro	Con
Very even temperatures	Claustrophobic, small window areas
Very quiet, draft-free	
Energy-savings of 60 to 80 percent with little extra cost	Construction techniques to master, attention to detail extremely important
Easy to cool, little back-up heat needed	Humidity, odor, pollution problems, needs air-to-air exchanger
No chimney needed	
Long thermal carry-over period, solar orientation not needed	Limited aesthetics, lack of space because of thick walls
Adaptable to conventional housing (doesn't look like a "solar" house)	
Will work anywhere (including hot climates)	

16-12 *Heating equivalents for various fuels.*

Fuel type	Btu/unit	Equivalent to one gallon oil
Oil (No. 2)	139,000/gal	——
Natural gas	1025/cu ft or 100,000/"therm"	136 cu ft 1.39 therms
LPG gas	91,500/gal (2500/cu ft)	1.5 gal (36.6 cu ft/gal)
Electricity	3413/kwh	40kwh
Coal, soft hard	25,000,000/ton 28,000,000/ton	0.005 ton (10lbs)
Dry hardwood	25,500,000/cord (128 cu ft)*	0.007 cord (0.6 cu ft), or one 6-8" × 2' log

*While all values in this table are approximate, the Btu content of wood is highly variable. A dry hardwood like oak burned at 100 percent efficiency would theoretically yield about 32,500,000 Btu's. But the average firewood pile is a mix of types and moisture contents. The figure above is an average of 12 common firewood species, both hard and soft, and "dry" (12 percent MC) and "green"(>20 percent MC).

16-13　*The decision to use wood as either a primary or backup heating fuel entails solving the problem of convenient, ample sheltered storage to keep the wood dry. Because of the high moisture content of unseasoned logs and the possibility of insect infestation, basements should not be used for extensive wood storage. Attached woodsheds are a hidden cost of wood heat.*

Natural gas, where available, is the cheapest fuel. But the cost of running gas pipe from the main to your house could be considerable. Liquified petroleum gas (LPG), or bottled gas, costs about the same as fuel oil, which is about twice the cost of natural gas. Fuel oil deliveries are generally quite dependable in urban and suburban areas, and less so in rural locations, where LPG may be the only reasonable option. Both kinds of fuel require large storage tanks, either underground or above ground (oil and LP) or in the basement (oil only). At least a 1000 gallon tank is needed for LP gas in cold climates. Codes permit two 220 gallon fuel oil tanks in the basement, as long as they are fitted with a switching valve so that only one tank can drain (or leak) at a time. If regular fuel oil delivery service is available, a single 220 or 275 gallon tank is usually adequate for most heating seasons. An underground or basement storage tank location is better in cold climates. Water tends to condense in half-filled or very cold tanks. Even if it doesn't freeze and block the fuel flow, water will still shut down the fire in the heating unit.

Where locally available, bulky fuels like wood and coal are almost always cheaper than fuel oil, but far less convenient, since there are no dependable automatic feed systems (see **16-13**). At a U.S. national average in 1994 of 7.9 cents per kwh (kilowatt-hour, i.e., 1000 watts used for one hour) electricity is about three times as expensive as fuel oil (figured at about 1.05 U.S. dollars per gallon). In some areas of the United States, electricity costs as much as 16 cents/kwh. In most cases, the high cost of electricity *as a heating fuel* makes it unaffordable, except where cheap hydroelectric or subsidized power production keep the cost well below market rates.

The actual cost of a fuel is modified by the efficiency with which it is converted to heat. For example, electricity is 100 percent efficient (of course, the generation process itself is only about 40 percent efficient, which is one significant reason that it costs so much). Electric resistance heating is also the cheapest and easiest system to install (although, not so to run). In a super-insulated house, where backup heat will seldom be needed, the life-cycle cost of electric heating may even be lower than other alternatives when you consider its high efficiency and the low cost of equipment and maintenance.

While modern oil- and gas-burning systems can both achieve relatively high efficiencies, oil burners have more parts that require more maintenance than gas burners. Where natural gas is available, it will be cheaper than oil, especially since you can burn it in an ultra-high-efficiency, condensing "pulse" furnace or boiler that can attain efficiencies of 97 percent, unequalled by any other fuel except electricity. The flue gases produced by these burners have a temperature of only about 130°F (55°C), which means they can be exhausted through the roof or sidewall with a two-inch ABS plastic pipe. Because they are ignited by a spark plug, no pilot flame is needed. They produce a noncorrosive liquid condensate that can be drained into the house sewer. The substantially higher cost of a high-efficiency burner can be offset by the elimination of a chimney.

The only meaningful way to compare heating costs is to convert everything to cost per Btu of delivered heat. To do this, divide the price per unit of fuel in U.S. dollars (lbs, cu ft, gals etc.) by the Btu content per unit times the AFUE (see **16-14**). Since a single Btu is a very small quantity of heat, multiply the result by 10^6 (1,000,000) to convert it to a useful number for comparison.

For example, suppose you wanted to compare the cost of oil at $1.05 per gallon burned in a boiler rated for 80 percent efficiency with firewood at $95 per cord burned at 60 percent efficiency to LP gas at $1.10 per gallon and 95% AFUE, and natural gas at $0.59 per therm at 75 percent efficiency:

$$1.05 / (139,000 \times .80) \times 10^6 = \$9.44$$

$$95.00 / (25,500,000 \times .60) \times 10^6 = \$6.20$$

$$1.10 / (91,500 \times .95) \times 10^6 = \$12.65$$

$$0.59 / (100,000 \times .75) \times 10^6 = \$7.86$$

The above comparisons show that even when operating at a lower efficiency, natural gas is still cheaper than burning LP gas in a high-efficiency condensing furnace.

To compare the seasonal cost of various fuels and heating systems, you need to extrapolate the annual heat load from the hourly heat loss figure for your house. Since the hourly heat loss figure is the number that is used to size your heating system, it's a prerequisite to any installation. Assuming you have that figure, the annual heat load in Btu's is equal to the sum of 24 times the hourly heat load (there are 24 hours in a day) divided by the indoor design temperature base—this is generally 65°F (18°C). It's assumed that the internal heat produced by house appliances, etc., accounts for five degrees of the desired indoor temperature of 70°F, multiplied by the heating degree days for your climate zone (see **16-15**). Degree days, (DD) are supplied by the weather bureau or utility company. Because it represents the difference between the low temperature recorded for a given day and the design temperature base of 65°F and it's assumed that

16-14 The average AFUE (annual fuel utilization efficiency) of various types of burners. Ask your supplier for the efficiency specs of your particular burner or boiler.

Electric resistance:	100 percent
Standard gas or oil burner:	70–80 percent
High-efficiency gas burner or condensing boiler	85–97 percent
Coal burner:	60–75 percent
Modern, air-tight wood stove (radiant type with catalytic combustor) or furnace	60–70 percent
Modern, air-tight wood stove (circulating type)	50–60 percent
Franklin-type, old-fashioned wood stove	40 percent
Standard masonry fireplace	(−)10 to 10 percent
Rumford fireplace with outside combustion air and glass doors	15–25 percent
Heat recirculating fireplace with same	30 percent

heat must be provided to make up the difference, degree days provide a convenient way to estimate heating needs. Cooling degree days are used with a 70°F base to estimate air-conditioning costs. Statistics are based on 30-year seasonal averages.

For example, suppose your heat loss figures show an hourly heat load of 30,000 Btu's and you live in an area with 6000 DD:

$$24 (30,000) / 65 \times 6000 = 66,461,538 \text{ Btu's.}$$

Using the figures provided by the fuel cost comparisons above, it would cost you 627 dollars to heat your house with oil, 412 dollars with wood, 840 dollars with bottled gas, and 522 dollars with natural gas.

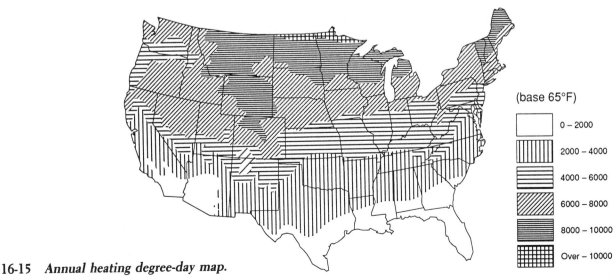

16-15 Annual heating degree-day map.

(base 65°F)

	0 – 2000
	2000 – 4000
	4000 – 6000
	6000 – 8000
	8000 – 10000
	Over – 10000

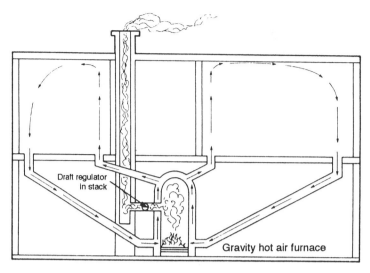

Draft regulator
in stack

Gravity hot air furnace

16-16 *Gravity systems are simple but slow and inefficient.*

Overview of Conventional Domestic Heating Systems

Like active solar systems, conventional domestic heating systems rely on warmed air or hot water as a heat transfer medium. Radiant-heating systems that utilize either water or electricity are also becoming popular once again. Despite some obvious drawbacks, electric "heat pumps" are also widely promoted as an efficient heating and cooling system. In some parts of the United States wood burners provide the bulk of the heat load, supplemented by a fossil-fuel-burning backup heater. In smaller houses, individual space heaters may make more sense than central heating systems.

WARM-AIR HEAT

In a warm-air heating system, air heated by a furnace* is circulated through the house either by gravity or a motor-driven blower.

The gravity-flow, warm-air system is one of the oldest forms of central heating (see **16-16**). Because it is less dense, warm air will move upwards through ducts and enter the rooms through registers. As it cools, it becomes heavier and falls down into return air ducts and flows back to the furnace. Air circulation in a gravity system depends on a suitable temperature difference between rising warm air and falling cool air. However, the physics of convective heat flow places strong limitations on the effectiveness of

gravity heating. The furnace must be centrally located at the lowest point of the structure. Because the amount of heat that air can carry is fairly small and the volume and speed of the air delivered by gravity flow is also not very large, it takes a long time to warm a room after the thermostat calls for heat. The small amount of heat delivered relative to the large amount of fuel consumed is very inefficient. The slight pressure of a gravity system requires very large and short ducts to reduce friction. Each register, both hot and cold, is supplied by a duct that runs directly from and to the furnace. This requires both a lot of ducting and takes up a lot of cellar space. The hot-air registers will be located close to the furnace on the inside walls of the rooms. The return air registers are located on the outside walls. The outer edges of the rooms can become quite chilly on a cold night. Even with short ducts and large pipes, the flow pressure isn't strong enough to overcome the resistance of an air filter, so gravity heat is "dirty" heat.

The main advantage of gravity heat is its low cost. Since there are no moving parts, it's also silent. Gravity heat will work with any relatively compact and open space, one- or two-storey house design where the furnace can be centrally located. On the other hand, the rambling layout of the modern single-storey ranch house leaves no option but forced circulation.

According to present day standards of comfort, gravity heating has so many disadvantages that there's hardly any

---

*****Furnaces** heat air, **boilers** heat water. A furnace is basically a box that contains the fire surrounded by another larger box. The flue for the exhaust gases passes through the outer box to the chimney, but there is no connection between the two that would allow smoke to contaminate the heated air. As the fire heats the air in the space between the inner and outer boxes (or a convoluted system of cast metal flues called the heat exchanger) it rises into a chamber called the plenum. Basically, a boiler is a box that contains the fire so that it can warm the water-filled heat exchanger.

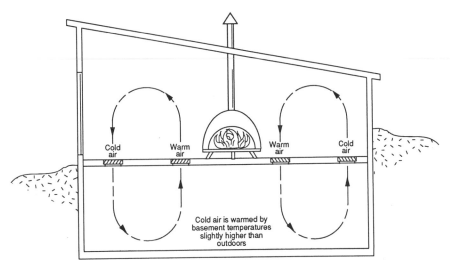

16-17 *An efficient gravity heating system.*

good reason to use it. One exception might be a small, open-space house designed intentionally for ductless gravity heating in the form of a centrally located wood stove. The prototype is a house built by a man named Wendell Thomas in the mountains of North Carolina (see **16-17**). The house utilized south-facing windows with earth-berming on the north and west walls to reduce heat loss. An earth-floored crawl space acted as a cold-air return plenum for the centrally located wood stove. Air heated by the stove would rise to the ceiling and flow down the walls as it cooled and through a continuous perimeter register into the crawl space where it was drawn up through a floor grate under the stove.

Adding an electrically powered blower to drive the air circulation turns a gravity system into a forced, warm-air system (see **16-18**). Forced, warm-air heating is the most popular residential heating method in use today for many reasons, foremost of which are low cost and ease of installation. Another advantage of forced warm-air is that the furnace can be located anywhere in the house. Since the blower can pull or push air in any direction, the ducts don't have to be located directly above the furnace either, as they do with a gravity furnace. Standard *upflow highboy* furnaces are installed in a full basement. The shorter *upflow lowboy* is designed for low-headroom installation. A horizontal furnace that can be mounted in the attic or a low crawl space is available for houses that lack a full basement. Upright *counterflow* or *downflow* furnaces on the main floor force warm air downward into the subfloor ducts of mobile homes and into crawl spaces.

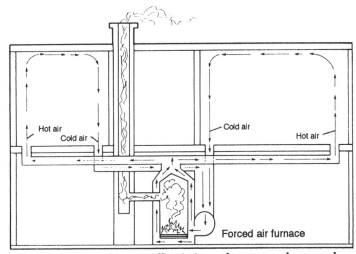

16-18 *In a forced, warm-air system the blower pulls air into the return ducts and pushes it through a heat exchanger in the furnace and out to the supply ducts.*

Because the air moves rapidly, the furnace can be much smaller than a gravity-feed system, which makes it more efficient. It has a quick response time when the thermostat calls for heat. The biggest advantage of warm-air heating is the ease with which the humidity of the air can be controlled for comfort. Moist air carries more heat than dry air does. An automatic humidifier is generally installed in the supply duct to maintain the relative humidity of the house between 20 percent to 40 percent throughout the heating season. The solenoid-actuated valve that feeds water to the humidifier is controlled by a *humidistat* mounted just ahead of the humidifier.

In the typical humidifier, a rotating foam pad powered by a 24-volt motor, controlled by the humidistat, absorbs water from a pan. The level of the water is maintained by a float valve. In summer, a bypass duct circumvents the humidifier. This system is more satisfactory than humidifiers that operate by spraying heated water vapor into the return air duct, which was found to leave mineral deposits on the draperies. Freestanding portable humidifiers are needed for hot-water heating systems.

Without humidification, forced warm-air heat tends to shrink woodwork and furniture and cause respiratory problems in the winter. In super-insulated houses, removal of excess humidity is much more of a concern and humidifiers are not needed. The map in **16-19** shows the average number of hours a year when the indoor relative humidity falls below 30 percent at 70°F (21°C).

Another major advantage of warm-air heating is that the same ductwork and blower can be used to cool the house with central air-conditioning. Since conditioned air is drier, the problem of excessive summer humidity is generally solved by air-conditioning. Where humidity levels are quite high, a separate room-size dehumidifier can be used to remove the moisture. A dehumidifier can also be installed in the furnace ductwork, although this is usually only done with systems that don't include central air-conditioning.

Because the strong convection currents create turbulence, untreated warm air tends to be dusty. However, electrostatic air filters are capable of removing particles and pollutants down to microscopic size. (Electrostatic air filters should not be confused with electronic air cleaners which have been found to create ozone.)

There are some disadvantages to forced warm-air heat as well. The blower can be noisy. Usually, increasing the size of the fan and slowing its speed will lower the noise level. Connecting the ductwork to the supply plenum with a flexible fire-resistant fabric coupler will also help reduce sound transmission into the ducts. Since the heat is delivered in intermittent blasts of warmed air, the room temperatures can fluctuate somewhat uncomfortably. Also, the need to locate warm-air registers under windows and along the outside walls can interfere with the placement of drapery and furniture. The only substantial objection to warm-air heating is the need for a separate water heating appliance and the extra installation and operating costs that entails.

HOT WATER HEATING

Using water instead of air as a heat transfer medium takes full advantage of the inherent efficiency of water's much greater heat capacity. As with warm-air systems, old-fashioned hot-water heating systems relied on gravity to drive the circulation. Water, like air, becomes less dense as it's heated. As you might expect, gravity hot-water heating is

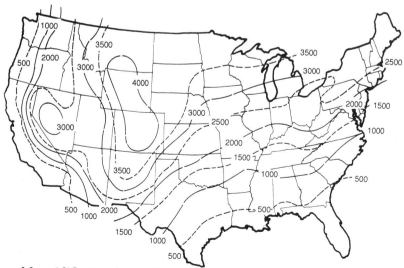

16-19 *Average annual humidification hours. Since the decreasing numbers represent increasing indoor humidity levels and vice versa, the map shows where excess humidity or dryness could cause problems.*

neither fast nor efficient, which is why it's not used today. The addition of a small circulating pump in the boiler return line and the substitution of a closed expansion tank for the open tank of the gravity flow system creates a modern forced, hot-water or *hydronic* system that produces faster and more even heat and permits the use of small-diameter copper piping. The hot water gives up its heat as it circulates through relatively unobtrusive, finned baseboard *convectors* or the traditional bulky cast-iron radiators. Although most of the heating from hot-water radiators occurs by convection rather than direct radiation (the radiators mostly warm air that passes over them) the relatively low temperature of the water and the radiator results in gentle air flows so that hydronic heat doesn't tend to dry out the household air or raise as much dust as a warm-air system does. And since the water in the radiators remains warm for quite a while after the boiler shuts off, the room temperature is more even. Hydronic heating systems are silent and extremely compact. Some modern, high-efficiency hydronic boilers are no larger than a suitcase. The system is also easier to control. Heat can be delivered to individual rooms or zones as desired by separate thermostatically or manually controlled valves.

One of the biggest advantages of hydronic heat is that the same boiler also heats the water for household use, which is much more efficient than heating it with a separate appliance, at least during the heating season (see **16-20**). No separate flues or appliances are needed.

The main disadvantage of hydronic heat is its high installation cost. Even with layouts designed to minimize the length of pipe runs, copper plumbing is expensive. Boilers and their controls also cost more than warm-air furnaces. Since there is no blower or ductwork in a hot-water system, these must be installed at extra expense if central air-conditioning is desired. This is probably why most hydronic systems are installed in parts of the United States where heating is much more important than air-conditioning. A separate room-size humidifier may also be needed if indoor relative humidity falls too low during the winter.

Another drawback of hot-water heat is it's vulnerability to damage caused by frozen pipes should a prolonged power outtage occur in very cold weather. To provide protection against this possibility, nontoxic propylene glycol antifreeze (as opposed to the very toxic ethylene glycol used in your car's cooling system) is sometimes circulated through the system instead of water. The problem with glycol is that it eventually breaks down and becomes corrosive. Also, each time the system purges fluid, the glycol is diluted as fresh water is drawn in. The fluid should be tested every year and replaced as necessary.

When hydronic heat is used for a vacation home, the boiler should be wired into the security system so that it will sound an alarm at the local fuel supplier or service contractor, should it run out of fuel or otherwise fail. The best insurance against freeze damage is to make the system

16-20 *Modern hydronic gas-fired boilers can be extremely compact and efficient.*

fully drainable or to provide a backup source of power for the circulator pump.

There are several different possible piping arrangements for hydronic heat. The *series loop* is the most economical and simplest (see **16-21**). Hot water from the boiler goes into a single supply main that feeds each radiator in succession before returning to the boiler to be reheated.

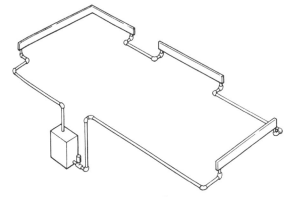

16-21 *Series loop hydronic heating.*

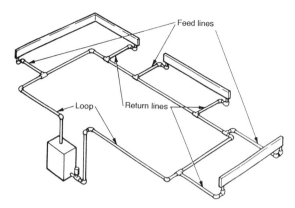

16-22 *Schematic of one-pipe hydronic heating.*

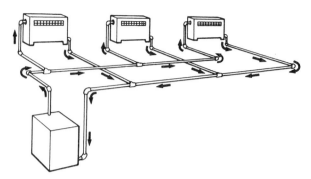

16-23 *Schematic of two-pipe hydronic heating. Using separate supply and return lines increases the efficiency of heat delivery.*

The system isn't very flexible, since no one radiator can be shut off without shutting down the entire loop. Also, since all the radiators are either heating up or cooling down at the same time, and the water temperature is dropping as it moves farther down the line, a series loop system is best suited to small homes where separate temperature zones aren't needed, and where the overall run of the system is short enough to prevent excessive temperature drops.

The main difference between a series loop and a *one-pipe* set-up is that a branch pipe from a continuous hot-water main supplies each radiator while another pipe returns the spent water (see **16-22**). The same pipe serves as both supply and return main. A shutoff valve installed in the supply riser to each radiator can be open or closed to control the amount of hot water entering the radiator, which makes it much easier to "balance" the heat flow to each room. Thus the flow to radiators closest to the boiler might be restricted somewhat so that more heat is available for radiators at the end of the loop. If no heat is needed, the valve is shut down, and the radiator is simply bypassed. Although it requires more tubing, a one-pipe system offers greater flexibility.

The two-pipe system is often used with large houses (see **16-23**). Because there is a separate supply and return line for each radiator, hot and cool water never mix, and, except for some heat loss incidental to the length of the pipes, there's very little temperature difference between the first and last radiators. This makes the two-pipe arrangement ideal for large houses. It also makes it more costly.

Both warm-air and hydronic heating systems can be *zoned* to control the amount of heat delivered to different regions of the house. In split-level and two-storey homes, warm air tends to rise to the upper level through the stairways. If the same amount of heat were provided to both levels, the upper storey would become too warm. Dividing the house into two or more heating zones, each controlled by its own thermostat, enables different amounts

of heat to be supplied to each as comfort and patterns of use require.

With warm-air systems, the degree of control is not very precise. Thermostatically controlled, motorized dampers that close off individual supply ducts are expensive and breakdown prone. Hand-operated dampers are inconvenient.

Although it is theoretically possible to install separate automatic zone valves in the risers to each radiator of one-pipe or two-pipe hydronic systems or to split the main into two or more valve-controlled separate subsystems, until recently, automatic zone valves for hydronic heat tended to be both expensive and unreliable. Zone control was achieved instead by running individual series loops to each radiator or a series of radiators that together comprised a single zone, each supplied by its own thermostatically controlled circulator pump (see **16-24**). One-way check valves were used to prevent hot water from circulating through each loop by gravity when the circulators weren't running.

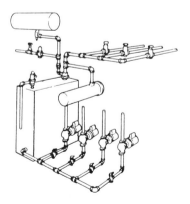

16-24 *Hydronic zoned heating arrangement. In this system, the supply line for each separate zone has its own circulating pump. Automatic zone valves can also be used in place of individual circulators.*

Eventually, circulators became more costly and the reliability of zone valves improved. Today, the zoned series loop arrangement is probably the best compromise between comfort, flexibility, cost and maintenance for most medium to large houses. Thermostatically operated zone valves, mounted in line on a supply manifold, automatically regulate the flow of hot water to the radiator(s) piped in a series loop for each zone. Since only a single, powerful circulating pump drives the entire system, there are fewer parts to install or to fail than there are with the previous set-up.

ELECTRIC RESISTANCE HEATING

If you pass a lot of electricity through a special ceramic conductor, its resistance (the electrical equivalent to friction) will make it heat up. The glowing red hot coils heat the air that circulates over them. That's the principle of electric resistance heating in a nutshell.

As mentioned earlier, lightweight electric baseboard heaters are the least-expensive heating system to install and the most expensive to operate. In a typical installation, a separate 20-amp, 240-volt circuit is provided for each heating circuit. (As long as the total current draw of the individual heating units doesn't exceed the maximum allowed, anywhere from one to several baseboard units of different lengths and output ratings can be connected in series on the same circuit.) The two-conductor wire runs from the circuit box to a line-voltage thermostat, and then to the heater. In lieu of a thermostat, some baseboard heaters have a built-in control for manually setting the heat output.

In an electric central furnace, air is heated by being blown across resistance coils in the ductwork. To protect against coil burnout and fire if the fan should fail, a sail switch installed in the airstream energizes the heater circuit only when the blower is running. There are also electric boilers for hydronic systems. They work exactly like the heating elements of a household water heater, except that the multiple elements are timed to turn on in sequence about 60 seconds apart to avoid excessive current drain.

Even with above-average levels of insulation, electric heating is still too expensive except as a backup system intended to occasionally supplement solar or wood heat. The only real advantage that electric heating offers over fossil-fuel burners is that its heating output can be easily downsized to meet the low-calorie heat load of super-insulated construction. It's hard to find a fossil-fuel-burning furnace or boiler with a heat output small enough to match the backup heating needs of truly energy-efficient construction. Since there's no combustion, electric heat doesn't require an outside air supply, and so it doesn't give off gases that need to be vented through a heat-robbing chimney. Electric heat is also very clean and even. Although it's expensive, electric heat can be right under certain conditions.

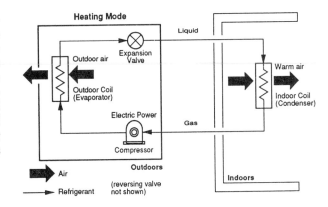

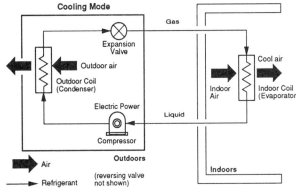

16-25 *Heat pump heating/cooling cycle. It's ability to reverse the direction of heat flow allows a heat pump to both cool or warm the house air as needed.*

HEAT PUMPS

Many experts claim that heat pumps are the wave of the future. Others claim that they are an expensive white elephant. In any case, they certainly aren't a panacea.

A heat pump can be thought of as a two-way air-conditioner (see **16-25**). In its cooling mode, warm refrigerant gas from inside the house is compressed to a liquid at about 210 psi in an outdoor condenser coil. As the gas condenses, it gives up its heat to air blown over the coil. The liquid is then pumped through a filter–dryer to an indoor evaporator where a special and very complicated TEV (thermostatic expansion valve) drops its pressure to 69 psi, allowing it to turn back into a gas and thereby absorbing heat from the household air that's passing over the evaporator coil. In heating mode, automatic or manual reversing valves reverse the refrigerant flow, and the indoor evaporator functions as a condensing coil and the outdoor condensing coil as an evaporator. The chilled refrigerant will absorb heat from the cold, outdoor air so long as the temperature of the refrigerant is lower than that of the air. Inside the house, the fluid gives up its heat as it suddenly expands into a gas.

The problem with a heat pump is that as the outside temperature approaches and drops below 40°F (4°C), there's not enough usable heat in the cold air, and the pump becomes inefficient. Auxiliary electric heat is supplied to the coil instead, or a gas- or oil-fired furnace takes over. If a gas- or oil-fired furnace must be installed as a backup, why bother with the very large expense of a heat pump in the first place?

One way to overcome the inherent inefficiency of air-to-air heat pumps is to use a water-to-air heat transfer system. Water is circulated through several hundred feet of pipe buried six feet underground, where it absorbs heat from the ground, which is more or less a constant (and ideal) 50°F (10°C). The cost of the excavation and the piping and its controls and pump can easily double the cost of the installation. Some systems extract ground heat from deep well water instead. Once used, the water is considered polluted and must be disposed of in a dry well. This is not only expensive, but environmentally insensitive.

Heat pumps can be efficient in climates with relatively mild winter temperatures and hot summers. One way to increase the useful temperature range of the system is to use solar panels to preheat water circulating in a closed loop to the 60 to 90°F (15 to 32°C) range in which a water-to-air heat pump operates most efficiently.

Another drawback of the heat pump is its service life of only 8 to 10 years. This compares to the 20-plus year life of an oil or gas furnace or boiler. Over the course of its brief life, a heat pump will require regular servicing by a professional technician. Finally, even in its very efficient cooling mode, it still costs more to operate on an annual basis than a gas hot-air system with central air-conditioning. Newer, more efficient, and less complicated designs are being developed at this writing. Once they are brought to market, the economics of heat-pump heating may change dramatically.

RADIANT HEATING

Forced warm-air and hot-water or electric baseboard heat are convective systems since they use air as their primary heat transfer medium (the main function of a radiator is to warm the air that passes over it). Stratification (the layering of air according to its temperature) and heat loss to the ceiling are characteristic drawbacks of any convective heating system.

Radiant heating is the direct flow of heat from any warmer body to a cooler one by waves of infrared energy. If the temperature of the walls, floor, or ceiling is higher than the temperature of your body, heat will flow from them to you by radiation. This is why you feel the warmth when you sit in front of a fireplace.

There are a lot of advantages to radiant heating. Heating engineers have shown that with radiant heat, people will be comfortable at temperatures six to eight degrees Fahrenheit (three to four-and-a-half degrees Celsius)

lower than convective systems. Thus heat-loss calculations for radiant systems are based on an indoor design temperature of 60°F (15°C) instead of the standard 65°F (18°C) for convective heating. Since the temperature difference between the ceiling and the floor averages only three degrees Fahrenheit (two degrees Celsius), with the floor typically being warmer than the ceiling, stratification is nonexistent. And, because there's no relatively hot air flowing across relatively cold outside walls or ceilings, the heat loss caused by outside air infiltration which is driven by the temperature difference between the inside and outside, will be significantly less. It's estimated that radiant heating can reduce the heat load in a well-insulated house by 25 percent to 35 percent over convective heating.

Another advantage of radiant heat is that it has no effect on the moisture content of the air. Humidification is unnecessary. There's no air or dust blown around the house or registers and baseboards to complicate furniture placement.

Radiant heating systems installed in the 1950s and 1960s, which circulated hot water through flexible copper tubing buried in a concrete floor slab or run between ceiling joists, proved to be unreliable. Oxygen dissolved in the boiler water corroded the pipes. Finding and repairing a leaking pipe buried in concrete was difficult and expensive. Although more immediately obvious, a leak in the ceiling was equally disastrous. Electric radiant heating installations, either in the form of factory-made ceiling-mounted panels or heating cables buried in the slab, were less troublesome, but expensive to operate if used as a primary heat source (see **16-26**).

When all the system life-cycle costs are taken into account, however, electric radiant heating could be cost effective in a modern well-insulated house, even though the price of electricity is about three times that of natural gas and twice that of oil. Unlike combustion heating systems, there's no boiler to replace, repair, and maintain in an electric radiant system. There are no filters or flues to clean, no chimney, and no parts to wear or burn out or valves to corrode and pipes to freeze up or drain. Armored by a PVC jacket over lead sheathing that protects a copper core against moisture, modern high-quality radiant heating cable is virtually indestructible.

Electric radiant heating cable must be precisely sized for each specific room and its heating load. The cable is cut to length at the factory and nonheating leads are prespliced to both ends. You can't make any on-site modifications. If you provide the distributor with accurate floor plans, insulation R values, and details of building cross sections for heat loss calculations, he/she will provide you with a computer-generated schedule for the length of the cables and their required loop spacing to provide the correct heating wattage for each room. Since there's no need to heat the slab under closets, cabinets, bathtubs, and major appliances, the floor area they take up is subtracted from the total living area.

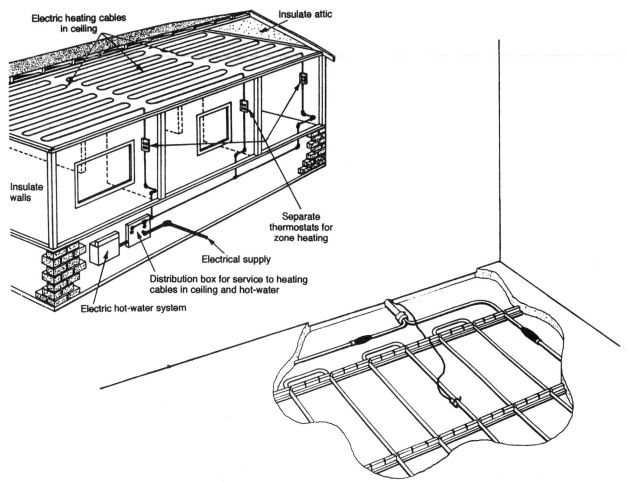

16-26 *Electric radiant systems can utilize heating cables in ceiling panels or buried in lightweight concrete poured over the subfloor. Codes require leads to be protected where they exit the slab. A ¼-inch PVC conduit sweep elbow is adequate.*

The cables themselves are stapled to the underside of the subfloor between ceiling joists or supported on strapping for ceiling installations or stapled to the plywood subfloor and covered with a thin layer of special lightweight, fibre-reinforced concrete for floor installation.

When the cables are installed in an ordinary four-inch concrete slab, they are tied to the wire mesh reinforcement with plastic cable ties. Some systems use special plastic mounting strips to hold and space the tubing or cables instead.

Depending on the wattage of the heating circuit, a 120-volt or 240-volt line (12-2 wire) is run from the service panel to each thermostat. The heating cable lead runs from the other side of the thermostat down the wall cavity and through a code-mandated rigid conduit sweep elbow into the floor slab (refer to **16-26**).

The spacing between each loop of the cable is critical in preventing hot and cold spots in the floor and delivering the correct amount of wattage per square foot to the room heat load. The first and last cable runs at each side of the room should be spaced half the standard loop spacing from the wall. At the end of each run, where it loops back, the cables should also be spaced half the loop width from the walls. A staple gun outfitted with a special notched attachment that straddles the cable anchors the loop to chalk-lines snapped across the felt underlayment which protects the subfloor from any moisture absorbed by the concrete. The location of partitions, appliances, closets, and other nonheated areas should also be marked on the underlayment.

Test the cables for continuity after installing them and also, once again, before burying them in the concrete. Touch the leads from a continuity tester or an ohmmeter to each end of the cable leads. If the tester indicates that there is a break in the cable you'll have to tear it up and replace it.

16-27 *An ultra-high efficiency gas-fired water heater supplies warm water to polyethylene radiant heating tubing embedded in a concrete floor slab.*

HOT-WATER RADIANT HEATING SYSTEMS

New types of plastic pipe (e.g., crosslinked, polyethylene thermoplastic tubing), developed over the last decade, can withstand high temperatures and freezing and to eliminate corrosion caused by oxygen diffusion, have led to a comeback of hot-water radiant heating. A hot-water radiant system offers all the advantages of an electric system at a lower installation and operating cost. Any small standard boiler or a special high-efficiency, gas-fired water heater can be used to heat the water (see **16-27**). Since the system operates at much lower water temperatures (90°F to 130°F instead of 190°F to 200°F; i.e., 32°C to 54°C instead of 88°C to 93°C) than a hydronic system, considerably less energy is required to achieve a much greater level of comfort. Zone control is simple: each loop of tubing, which can be cut to size on the job, is connected to a manually or thermostat-controlled valve on a central

flow and return manifold (see **16-28**). As with electric systems, the length and spacing of the tubing runs are determined by the distributor.

With both electric and hot-water radiant systems, it's important that any slab on grade be well insulated. Since the winter ground temperature is somewhere between 40°F and 60°F (4°C and 15°C), a good deal of the heat imparted to the slab from the cables or coils can otherwise radiate downwards into the cold ground instead of upwards into the room. Two inches of rigid foam insulation over a vapor barrier are sufficient to eliminate this potential "heat sink." It's especially important to insulate the outside edges of the slab and/or any frostwall, since the greatest heat loss occurs at the perimeter.

If your in-slab radiant heating system is used as the primary heat source, you won't be able to use the same slab as thermal mass for passive solar heating (at least, not at the same time). Heat storage capacity is a function of temperature difference. As the slab warms up, its storage capacity diminishes. If it's warmer than the room, it can't store any incoming solar radiation. Radiant heating can be used as a backup system to carry a house heated by a solar slab and woodstove through stretches of cloudy weather or periods when the house is unoccupied.

SOME THOUGHTS ABOUT DO-IT-YOURSELF HEATING AND AIR-CONDITIONING

It's not hard to understand why plumbers have traditionally been responsible for the installation of home heating systems. In the late 19th century, when both central heating and indoor plumbing were becoming widespread, gravity-flow steam and hot-water heating were a major improvement over the gravity warm-air furnaces of the time. The plumber was the only tradesperson with the skills and tools to work with the heavy piping these systems required. This natural hegemony was consolidated soon after the turn of the century, with the invention of small electric motors that made forced-circulation hot-water and warm-air heating and home water pumps practical. The introduction of central air-conditioning just after World War II initiated a split in the traditional role of the plumbing/heating contractor that has culminated in the present day HVAC (Heating, Ventilation, Air-Conditioning) specialist. While this specialization is almost universally true of commercial work, it varies geographically with residential work in the United States. In the North, where heating is more important than cooling, the plumber still wears the traditional double hat of domestic heating contractor. In the South and Southwest, where heating and air-conditioning needs can be met by a single forced-air system, AC-heating contractors are listed separately from plumbing contractors in the telephone Yellow Pages. Technologies such as radiant heating and heat pumps have also spawned their own subspecialists. As solar water and space heating become more widely used, the trend towards increased specialization will continue.

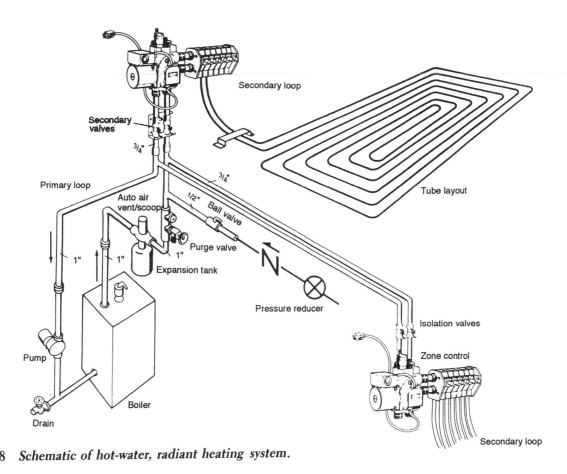

Secondary loop

Secondary valves

3/4"

Primary loop

3/4"

Auto air vent/scoop

1/2" Ball valve

Purge valve

Tube layout

Expansion tank

1" 1" 1"

N

Pressure reducer

Isolation valves

Zone control

Pump

Drain

Boiler

Secondary loop

16-28 *Schematic of hot-water, radiant heating system.*

Just about every municipality has regulations preventing an unlicensed individual from engaging in the *business* of electrical, heating, plumbing, and cooling system installation. But there are absolutely no laws that prevent you from doing your own work on your own home. The regulations only require that whatever work you do has to pass the same inspection and meet the same code requirements as work done by licensed professionals. Granted, the inspectors will scrutinize your work more closely than that of a contractor with whom they are familiar.

This is probably one reason why most do-it-yourself home building guides describe the options available for different types of heating systems, and then more or less assume that the installation will be done by a professional contractor. While it's true that furnaces and air-conditioners must be properly matched to the calculated heating and cooling needs of your particular house, and that those calculations are quite involved, they're still only an approximation based on assumed design values and climactic averages. Within broad limits, there's a wide margin of safety. While you could certainly do your own heat load calculations, most heating/cooling-equipment dealers can be persuaded to do them for you to clinch a sale. And

while it's also true that a modern heating system has many controls and valves which must be calibrated and synchronized for proper and safe performance, most heating plants are sold with their controls preassembled and/or with the same complete installation, wiring, and plumbing instructions that the professionals use to install them.

The design of an efficient heating and cooling system requires a great deal of expertise. As with the heat loss calculations, in most cases, the equipment dealer or the fuel supplier will provide you with all the relevant information concerning pipe or duct sizes, system layout, control installation and safety requirements. A secret of the trade is that most heating contractors don't do their own calculations or system design either. Although they have to know how to do it in order to get their license, there are so many factors, pages of charts, and other data that enter into system design, that the average contractor is just as happy to rely on the engineering services furnished by his or her supplier as you would be. Some suppliers, like Sears Roebuck, that specifically target the do-it-yourself market, offer complete design and installation support. Failing this, you could hire a professional engineer or heating contractor to design a system for you or simply to review your plans.

Once you understand how heating/cooling systems and their controls work in general, the actual assembly is no more difficult than any other kind of plumbing or wiring. Of course, there are some operations which do require experienced technicians or specialized test equipment. Air-conditioning compressors and heat-pump components, for example, can be easily damaged or destroyed when an unknowing amateur tries to repair them. Few do-it-yourselfers have either the equipment or expertise for the start-up calibrations of an oil-burning furnace. Proper installation techniques are extremely important to guarantee the safety of gas or fuel-oil lines. But if you're capable of doing your own plumbing and wiring, you can certainly install your own heating and central air-conditioning system.

Since the specific hookup of individual systems varies according to the manufacturer's instructions, the descriptions which follow are only intended as a *rough guide*. You should get all the advice you can from your dealer and local code officials and other competent professionals before attempting to install any system yourself. If you still have doubts about your capabilities, then be sure to hire a professional.

INSTALLING A WARM-AIR SYSTEM

The location of the furnace and the size of the house, and its structural layout, are the main factors in determining how the ductwork will be laid out. To keep the length of the furnace flue pipe short, the furnace is located as close to the chimney as possible. The location of the chimney usually follows aesthetic and structural impera-

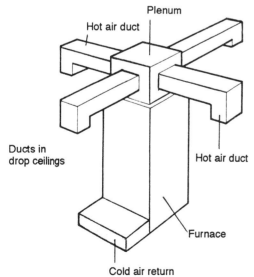

Plenum
Hot air duct
Ducts in drop ceilings
Hot air duct
Furnace
Cold air return

16-29 *Ceiling duct warm air system. Since the ductwork for this system runs through dropped ceilings no special insulation is needed.*

tives, and so it is not necessarily designed with a particular duct layout in mind. It's simply another limit within which the heating-system designer must work. The heating demand for each room, the static pressure of the system, the velocity of the air in the system, the desired noise level, blower capacity, the length of the ducts, heat loss, and space limitations all are factors which professional heating engineers consider to properly size the ductwork itself. Duct runs should be as short and have as few changes in direction as possible. The *registers* (*diffusers* or *outlets*) must be located for proper air distribution. The cross-sectional area of the ducts must permit airflow at suitable but moderate velocities to avoid waste of energy and noise. An adequate duct system is the best compromise between all the variables. There are so many pages of tables and charts to pour over that it may well be worth paying for having a professional develop a detailed design based on your scale drawing.

The *ceiling duct* system makes sense for a small house, especially if it's built on a slab (see 16-29). The furnace is installed in a closet on the first floor and hot air is routed through a supply duct installed in a section of dropped ceiling (usually the hallways). Short supply ducts to individual rooms branch off the main duct as needed. A single cold-air inlet is located at the bottom of the furnace itself. Any furnace in a closet should always have a louver door or other means of insuring and adequate supply of *outside* combustion air.

The *radial perimeter duct system* which was originally developed for gravity warm-air heating and later modified for under-slab installations is widely used in full basements where space is not a problem (see **16-30**). Under a slab, warm air feeds through more-or-less diagonal ducts to the corners of a continuous loop at the perimeter of the house where registers deliver it into the rooms. Insulated metal ducts are laid in the gravel subbase before pouring the concrete. In full basement and crawl space installations, the supply ducts just radiate outward from the plenum to the perimeter walls like the tentacles of an octopus, without the continuous loop. Each room can also have its own cold air return duct that runs back to the plenum. Because dampers can be installed in each supply line, this system provides a good deal of control and wastes less heat than other systems, although it does require considerably more ductwork. Radial ducts are usually used when the furnace can be placed in the middle of the cellar.

Another variation on the radial duct system is to run the ducts across the tops of the attic joists and, as with the ceiling duct system, put the cold-air return at the base of the furnace (see **16-31**). In general, however, running heating or cooling ducts through unheated spaces and attics should be avoided, since even with four inches of insulation around them, there's still more heat loss than with basement ducting, particularly in very cold climates. Floors may also tend to be draftier when there's only a single cold air return.

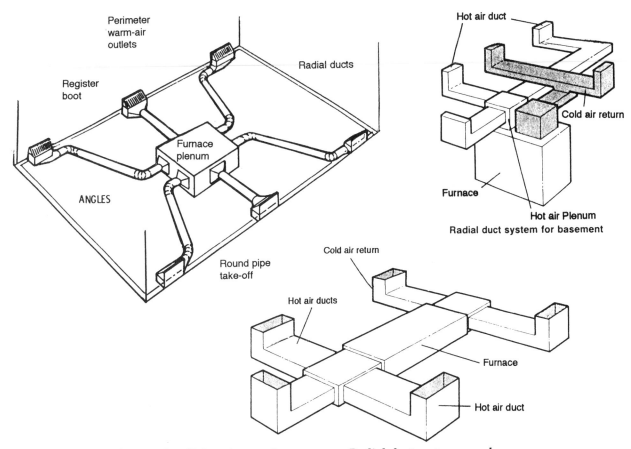

Perimeter
warm-air
outlets

Register
boot

Radial ducts

Furnace
plenum

ANGLES

Round pipe
take-off

Hot air duct

Cold air return

Furnace

Hot air Plenum

Radial duct system for basement

Cold air return

Hot air ducts

Furnace

Hot air duct

16-30 *Perimeter loop and radial perimeter duct systems. Radial duct systems can be buried in slab floors, connected to a horizontal flow furnace for a crawl space, or with a basement furnace in one- or two-storey houses.*

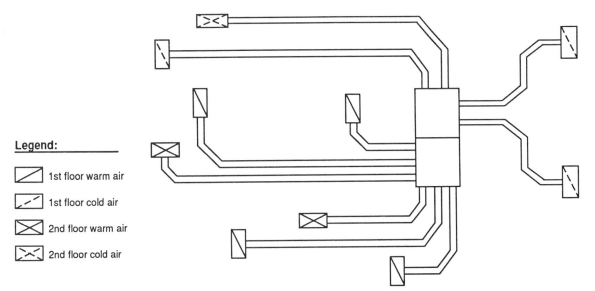

Legend:

◻ 1st floor warm air

◻ 1st floor cold air

◻ 2nd floor warm air

◻ 2nd floor cold air

16-31 *Radial ducts for attic installation. Houses built on slabs will use this system when ceiling ducts would interfere with design considerations.*

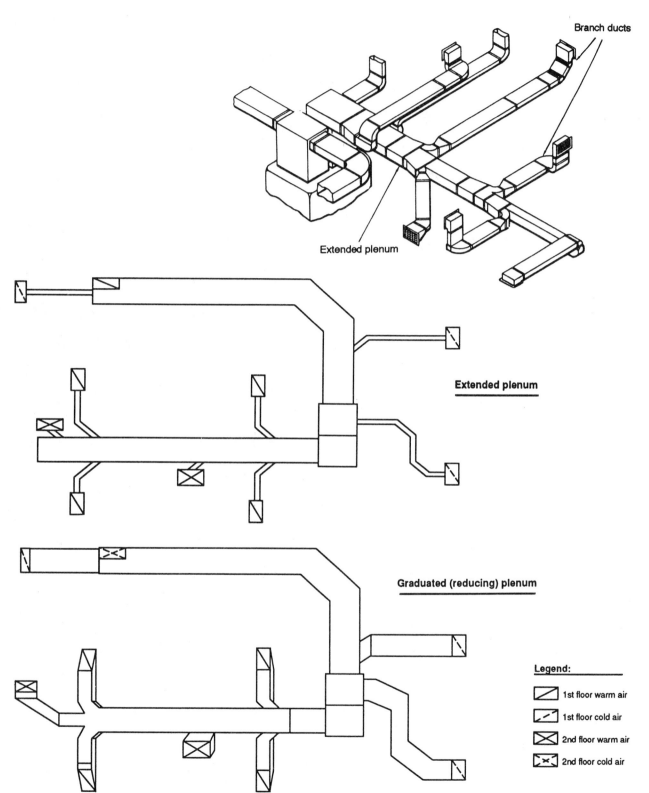

16-32 *Extended reducing plenum duct systems. The extended plenum uses round take-off ducts to deliver heat to each room. The reducing plenum system utilizes rectangular ducts of decreasing cross-sectional area throughout.*

The *extended reducing plenum system* consists of a large rectangular duct that runs straight out from the plenum down the center of the basement (or ceiling, etc.). As round feeder ducts are taken off to supply each room, the cross-sectional area of the plenum duct is decreased (see **16-32**). As a rule, the overall length of extended plenum ducts should be limited to 35 feet. Depending on the location of the furnace, the duct can run in both directions or just one; this is handy if the furnace is located at the far end of the house.

Space permitting, round ducts are preferred for warm-air feeder lines since they have the least surface area relative to the greatest cross-sectional area—which means they have less resistance to air flow than rectangular ducts. Although it eliminates elbows and is useful for making otherwise difficult bends, flexible round duct (*"flexduct"*) is not widely used because of its greater cost. One exception is attic installations, where its integral insulation is better than ordinary duct pipe.

Wide, flat, rectangular ducts are generally used where the warm-air lines run below the joists and are almost always used for plenum extensions since it's easier to fit the round feeder ducts into a rectangular main duct than into a round one.

Cold-air returns for extended plenums don't have to be entirely made of metal. Usually a piece of sheet metal is simply nailed (and caulked) to the bottom of the floor or ceiling joists. These feeder returns are joined by an adaptor to an extended cold-air return duct. Local codes determine whether vertical, cold-air return ducts in the wall must be metal or not.

Six-inch diameter round duct (sold in five-foot sections that slip together like stovepipe) is normally used for most feeder lines. The sections, one end of which is crimped to fit into the plain end of the other section, are sold "open," and must be assembled by snapping their length-wise tongue-and-slot seam together. There is no need to hammer the joint. Cut the sections before they're snapped together with a pair of straight tin snips. It's a lot harder to do it afterwards with a hacksaw. If the assembled pipe needs trimming, a pair of right- or left-hand-cutting aviation shears will do a neat job.

When cutting sections to length, cut off and discard the uncrimped end. Otherwise, you'll need a pair of hand crimping pliers to form a new end. The crimped ends of the ducts should always point away from the furnace. This helps to keep pressurized warm air from otherwise being forced out the joint.

Square duct also comes in preformed two- to five-foot-long sections. Special cleats are used to join the sections (see **16-33**). Cut a one-inch deep slit in the corners of the sections to be joined, and bend the sides back flat to form a flange. Slide a factory-made S cleat over the ends of the top and bottom edges of the ducts. Slip a preformed *drive clip* over the side flanges, and drive it downwards to lock the joint together. No screws are needed.

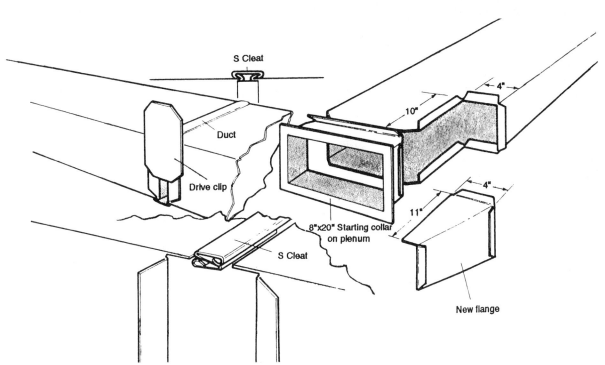

16-33 *Joining sections of rectangular duct. Use the S cleat to bend the flange. Note how a custom-made triangular flange can be used to match a large duct to a smaller plenum.*

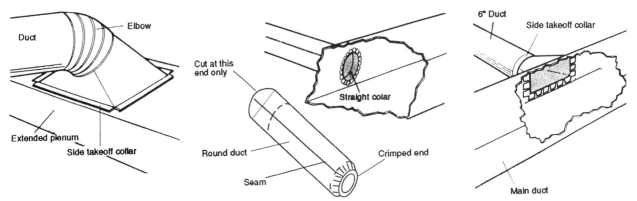

16-34 *Take-off collars for joining round to rectangular duct. Tabs can be cut into any standard section of round duct in lieu of a straight collar.*

Round duct is fitted to the main duct with one of two kinds of take-off collars (see **16-34**). A straight collar is a short section of round duct with tabs cut into the end where the crimp would be. The collar slips into a circular hole cut in the side of the duct, and the tabs are bent over to secure it. The other kind of take-off collar is screwed through flanges to a rectangular cut-out. The other end of the collar is formed into a flexible elbow for connection to the round duct.

The easiest way to cut a hole in the duct is to scribe the outline of the duct on the metal (or use a compass), and then punch a starter hole with a screwdriver. Insert a pair of circle-cutting snips into the hole and cut outwards towards the line. Wear leather gloves. The curled edges of the scrap are razor sharp. Use straight cutters for rectangular openings, and cut diagonally towards the corners until you can turn a straight line.

Register boots are used to mate a round duct to a rectangular floor register. A *stack boot* adapts it to a standard 3¼-inch by 12-inch rectangular duct that fits in between wall studs. Various elbows will enable you to make 45 degree and 90 degree turns in or perpendicular to the plane of the duct.

All these fittings are sold by heating suppliers and they are designed to slip together like stovepipe. All joints should be secured with self-tapping, pan-head or hex-head sheet metal screws and sealed with duct tape (untaped ducts can loose up to 25 percent of their heat). Warm-air ducts and air-conditioning ducts should always be insulated and wrapped with an outside plastic vapor barrier as well. If it's impossible to avoid running ductwork through the stud cavities in external walls, then simply slip a piece of rigid foam insulation behind it.

Although it's logical to assume that cold-air returns would be located at floor level, in modern installations the return register is actually fairly high on the wall, especially if the system is also used for air-conditioning. Raising the return encourages warm air released at floor level to circulate completely as it's pulled into the duct by the furnace blower. And, if it was located at floor level in air-conditioning mode, the cooled air would just flow across the floor and return to the plenum without cooling the warm air in the upper part of the room. Return registers should be placed on interior walls. To avoid dispersing moisture and odors throughout the house, don't locate any in the kitchen or bathroom.

The size of the cold-air return duct isn't quite as critical as that of warm-air supply ducts, so long as the area of its return register is equal to the total area of the individual supply registers that it serves. A good rule of thumb for sizing rectangular return ducts (which are always eight inches high by "x" inches wide) when using six-inch supply ducts is that the width of the return duct is equal to two times the number of six-inch registers plus two inches. For example, if the main duct supplied eleven registers, then $11 \times 2 = 22$ and this $+ 2 = 24$; so that the return duct would have to be eight inches by twenty-four inches (or some other combination that would yield the same cross-sectional area).

Whatever arrangement you utilize for your duct runs, they'll all eventually tie into the sheet metal plenum which fits on top of the furnace outlet and against the side of the blower cabinet. Few amateur tinsmiths possess the tools—or the skill—necessary to bend flat sheet metal stock into a tight-fitting plenum. The job is best done by a local sheet metal shop to whom you've given the particular dimensions needed.

The controls on a forced warm-air furnace are simple (see **16-35**). Codes no longer require the familiar red, oil-burner shutoff switch to be installed at the top of the stairs. Instead, a shutoff switch is mounted on the furnace body, and fire protection is afforded by a *fusible link*. This is a device similar to an automatic fire sprinkler, which will melt at a preset temperature, and shut the burner off. Fusible links are generally installed on the ceiling above the boiler or furnace. They aren't always required for gas burners, but they are a good idea anyway. Check local code requirements, as always.

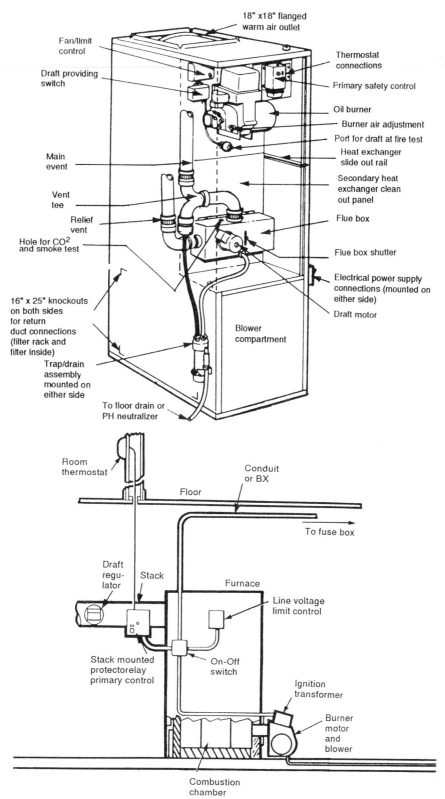

18" x18" flanged warm air outlet

Fan/limit control

Draft providing switch

Thermostat connections

Primary safety control

Oil burner

Burner air adjustment

Port for draft at fire test

Main event

Heat exchanger slide out rail

Secondary heat exchanger clean out panel

Vent tee

Relief vent

Flue box

Hole for CO^2 and smoke test

Flue box shutter

16" x 25" knockouts on both sides for return duct connections (filter rack and filter inside)

Electrical power supply connections (mounted on either side)

Draft motor

Blower compartment

Trap/drain assembly mounted on either side

To floor drain or PH neutralizer

Room thermostat

Conduit or BX

Floor

To fuse box

Draft regulator

Stack

Furnace

Line voltage limit control

Stack mounted protectorelay primary control

On-Off switch

Ignition transformer

Burner motor and blower

Combustion chamber

16-35 *Typical oil furnace automatic controls. By code, furnace control wiring must be run with flexible, armored cable or metal conduit.*

411

With an oil burner, when the room thermostat senses a temperature drop and calls for heat, it sends a signal to the *primary control*, which energizes the burner motor and ignition transformer that provides the spark to ignite the oil sprayed into the combustion chamber by the burner oil pump. If the flame does not become established after a predetermined time delay, the primary control will shut the burner down. Formerly, the *primary safety relay* was mounted in the stack and would infer a rise in temperature as evidence of successful ignition. New burners rely on a cadmium sulfide "electric eye" integral with the primary control to "see" the flame instead.

When the burner raises the furnace air temperature to 130°F (54°C) the *fan control* starts the fan motor. The control will allow the fan to keep running until the furnace temperature drops to about 90°F (32°C). The fan control is usually combined in a single case with the *limit control* (in which case it is often called a *high–low limit control*). This is another safety control that will shut off the burner if the furnace temperature exceeds 200°F (93°C), as it would do if the fan stopped running for any number of reasons. The limit control will restart the burner after the furnace cools down to 160°F (71°C).

There are also some differences between oil-fired and gas-fired furnaces (and boilers) in the way the flue pipe is connected. In both cases, the pipe should pitch upwards towards the chimney at least ¼ inch per foot with a maximum horizontal run that should not exceed 75 percent of the vertical run. But, in most cases a *barometric damper* is installed in the flue pipe of an oil burner to regulate the chimney draft for efficient operation while the burner is running—whereas dampers are *never* installed in a gas-fired flue, since they would interfere with the *draft hood* (or *draft diverter*) which these appliances require for safe operation. A barometric damper shouldn't be confused with an *automatic flue damper*. Installed in the flues of either type burner, this electrically operated control stops warm air from leaking out the chimney when the burner is turned off.

Internal safety controls for gas-burning furnaces are built into the automatic gas valve and its pilot light assembly. Other than this, the high–low limit control that drives the fan and controls burner ignition is similar. Wiring diagrams furnished with the furnace show the connections for all controls which aren't already prewired.

The output of a newly installed, warm-air heating system must be *balanced* so that the heat is evenly distributed to all areas. This requires patience and a bit of experience. Open all of the dampers in the feeder ducts branching off the main warm-air duct, and open all of the registers in each room. Buy enough identical thermometers to put in the middle of each room (it helps if you keep them all in one place for a few hours first to equilibrate their readings), and record the temperatures. Push the thermostat five degrees Fahrenheit (three degrees Celsius) or so above the room temperature to start the furnace blower (to bal-

ance the air-conditioning, set the thermostat five degrees Fahrenheit [three degrees Celsius] below the room temperature in summer). If you do this when the outside temperature is around 40°F (4½°C) or less, the house won't become insufferably hot. Run the furnace long enough to record a definite temperature change in each room (anywhere from one to three hours), and write them down, noting which rooms increased the fastest from their initial temperatures. Close down the feeder duct dampers in those rooms by about one quarter. Let the furnace run for about a half hour more, and check the temperatures in all the rooms once again. Keep adjusting the dampers until all of the rooms are at basically equal temperatures, allowing about a half hour for the rooms to stabilize between each adjustment.

INSTALLING A HOT-WATER SYSTEM

Sizing baseboard radiation is at least as complicated a piece of engineering as sizing warm-air ductwork. The manufacturer's spec sheets for radiator heat output (typically in terms of Btuh per lineal foot per gallon of flow per minute [typically one to three gals] at 190°F to 200°F [88°C to 93°C]) are plugged into the heat load calculations for each room or zone to figure the lineal footage of baseboard radiation it will take to heat the room to the design temperature.

Even though they are small, modern boilers are still heavy. Some are shipped in several pieces, which are assembled on site; others arrive whole. Determine in advance how you'll manage to maneuver your boiler into the cellar, particularly if there are landings or turns in the stairwell or other obstructions to negotiate. This is the reason why some contractors arrange for shipment of boilers and furnaces to coincide with the laying of the floor deck.

Since the connections and controls of each boiler will vary with the manufacturer's design and the actual layout of your system, a complete description of a hot-water installation isn't practical (see **16-36**).

Residential hydronic boilers are almost always plumbed with copper pipe. Nowadays, black iron pipe is used only with steam heat and commercial systems. Even though iron pipe costs less than copper, the labor involved in installing it is too expensive except where it can be offset by the even higher cost of the large-diameter copper piping that would be needed for steam or commercial installations. Because of the possibility of lead poisoning due to the formation of soluble lead salts in acidic water, codes now require *lead-free solder* for all sweated fittings.

The hot-water supply main begins with the *riser* that leaves a tap on the high side of the boiler and is sized to meet the flow requirements for the whole system (usually a 1¼-inch pipe). The riser turns 90 degrees at the ceiling into an *air scoop* fitting which purges potentially corrosive oxygen that dissolves in the boiler water through a float-type vent valve. On the bottom of the scoop is a tap for

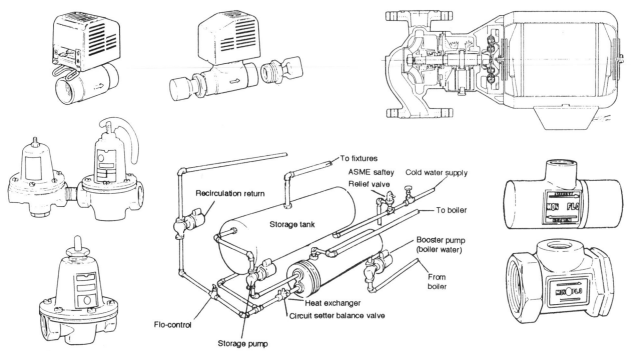

16-36 *Generic hydronic boiler connections. If complete installation instructions aren't included with your furnace, ask your supplier to draw a schematic for the system that labels each component and shows where and how it should be connected.*

a nipple to connect to the expansion tank. Since hot water is less dense than cold water, it expands. In a closed system it needs somewhere to go, which is the reason for the expansion tank. On some boilers, built-in or external *air separators* (or *air eliminators*) divert dissolved air into the expansion tank and vent assembly via a tap separate from the riser. Several different kinds of purge vents are used to expel air that becomes trapped in high points of the system as well.

Assuming a zoned series loop arrangement, the riser feeds into a manifold comprised of a horizontal line of reducing tees, each of which feeds into the ¾-inch zone valve that controls the flow of hot water to each heating loop. Each zone valve has a built-in check valve that conserves heat by preventing gravity recirculation and backflow. It also has a *balance valve* which can be set to balance the heat output of the zones by regulating flow volumes and a purge valve (*boiler drain valve*) to remove air from the system when it's first filled prior to start-up. Boiler drain valves have a hose fitting (which also helps facilitate collecting antifreeze in buckets). Some systems use a combination purge-and-balance valve instead.

Each zone should also have a gate valve so that it can be isolated from the rest of the system for servicing.

A separate zone valve feeds water into the *tankless* or *indirect-water heater* that provides hot water for household use. Since the heat-exchanger coil of the tankless water

heater, characteristic of older or cut-rate installations, is immersed in the boiler water itself, it's more vulnerable to corrosion and mineral buildup problems than one installed in a tank outside the boiler. Actual contact between boiler water and potable water is never allowed.

Likewise, the boiler feed-water connection with the household plumbing system must also be similarly isolated. A ½-inch feed line is fitted with a gate valve. Most codes require a one-way check valve next, which allows fresh water to flow towards the boiler but specifically doesn't permit boiler water to flow back into the household system. Boiler water is, of course, not safe to drink, especially if it has been fortified with glycol antifreeze. Since the household water pressure is typically around 45 psi and the boiler operates at pressures of 12 to 15 psi, a *pressure-reducing valve* (also called a *boiler-feed valve*) is installed next. At this point, the feed line must run horizontally, and the feed valve must be higher than the water level in the boiler. Before connecting the valve, open the feed-line gate valve to flush out any debris in the system that might otherwise interfere with the operation of the float inside the boiler-feed valve. The valve also opens to automatically feed water into the boiler when the pressure drops below the setting. A pressure-relief valve is next in line or else combined with the feed valve. Install a second gate valve after the boiler-feed valve so that the system can be isolated for repairs, if that should be necessary.

413

If not included in the feed valve, the pressure-relief valve can also be installed in a tap on top of the boiler. In either case, the relief valve must be connected to a pipe to drain within eight inches of the floor (or as per local code). It cannot be restricted in diameter and cannot have more than two 90-degree elbows. Relief valves are also generally required at the domestic, hot-water storage tank.

The ¾-inch return loops from the radiators flow back to a 1¼-inch return manifold at the bottom of the boiler. The circulator pump that drives the system is usually located between the return manifold and the boiler. Purge valves are also installed on either side of the circulating pump and/or at the lowest point of the system to aid in drainage. Gate valves are generally installed in both the return and supply mains.

The equivalent of the high–low limit control switch for a hydronic boiler is the *aquastat*. Depending on the system configuration, it will be installed in the riser pipe, strapped against it, or inserted in its own tap in the top of the boiler. Like most furnace controls, the boiler controls are operated by relays since the room thermostats which initiate the boiler cycling typically operate on 24 volts while the circulator pump requires 120 volts. Wires from each zone thermostat run to terminals on the zone valves and from there they run to a relay that connects with the low-limit control that operates the circulator. The low limit is set at 190°F (88°C) and the high limit is set at about 200°F (93°C). The low limit for the tankless water heater is set at about 125°F (52°C) instead.

As an additional safety measure, a low-water, cut-off switch is installed level with the top of the boiler in a special loop. This shuts off the burner if the water level in the boiler should drop and the automatic feed valve is malfunctioning.

Other controls include a temperature–pressure gauge (an altitude gauge, which shows the level of water in the highest radiator, is used with gravity or "open" hot-water systems). Codes require that the line-voltage wiring for electrical controls be run (from a junction box on the ceiling) through thin-wall metal conduit or with armored metallic cable.

Many professional contractors test the system for leaks by pressurizing the system with an air compressor, and reading the pressure from a gauge inserted in the water temperature tap. The system is filled with pressurized air, the line from the compressor is shut off, and the gauge is monitored for the prescribed length of time during which no pressure drop is permitted. The nonprofessional—and many professionals—prefer to find their leaks the "easy way," by turning on the water and looking and listening.

One other consideration which applies to all types of combustion heating systems is the provision of an adequate air supply. Normally, in an unobstructed basement, outside air infiltration is considered adequate. When a boiler or furnace is placed in a closet or boiler room, the code requires high and low openings in the interior walls with a "free area" of one sq in per 1000 Btuh of boiler input, each (metal grills are considered as having a 60 percent free area). In a tight house, infiltration won't suffice, and outside combustion air should be supplied instead. In fact, it's always a good strategy to supply outside combustion air. Use a free area ratio of one sq in per 4000 Btuh in an unobstructed basement.

FUEL SUPPLY LINES

Installing piping for LPG or natural gas lines is not any more difficult than water piping, but the consequences of a gas leak are a lot more lethal than a water leak. Consequently, the installation is justifiably subject to careful regulation and inspection.

Black iron pipe is used for natural gas and (where code requires it) for LPG piping as well (see **16-37**). Generally, the main line is either one-inch or ¾-inch pipe, with ½-inch feeds to the appliances. All pipe joints must be sealed with pipe joint compound. A shutoff is always installed ahead of the flexible metal connector that connects all moveable appliances (everything but the furnace). For LPG gas installations, ⅜-inch O.D. flexible copper tubing with flared fittings (also aluminum tubing in some locations) is more common than iron pipe. In a typical natural gas installation, a ½-inch pipe runs across or along the floor joists until it drops downwards to the furnace or water heater. A shut-off valve is inserted five-feet above the floor (refer to **16-37**). The pipe drops to a tee, the bottom end of which ends in a condensation trap fitted with a screw cap and the middle of which runs into the furnace or water heater automatic gas control valve. Be especially careful when screwing the tee leg into the die-cast body of the automatic gas valve. It's very easy to cross-thread or crack the soft metal with the hard pipe. And remember that backing off a pipe to tighten a loose joint at one end will loosen it at the other.

The specifics of the installation and the sizes of the gas lines are determined by the Btuh inputs and types of appliances they serve, the length of their runs, as well as the local gas pressure, *which varies with each utility*. Natural gas is supplied at high pressure which is generally reduced to seven inches WC (Water Column, equivalent to ½ psi) by a pressure regulator on the meter. A further pressure reduction may be required at the furnace. LP gas pressures are different. Fortunately, your gas company will provide you with the requisite information. In any case, you can't go ahead and install any piping until after you've contacted your gas company and/or obtained a permit from the local inspector.

You also aren't allowed to connect your gas pipes to the meter until after the installation passes a pressure test. Leave the union joint between the meter and the gas main disconnected (refer to **16-37**). Notify the inspector that you need an inspection. Install a pressure meter, and pressurize the system with a hand pump to the required level,

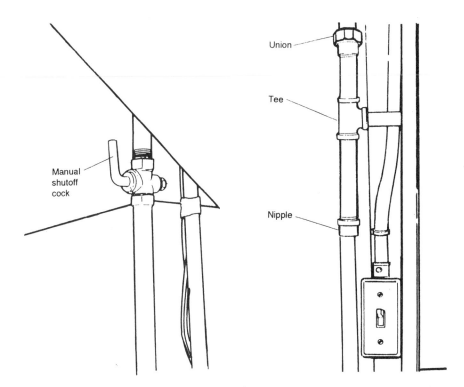

16-37 *Typical natural gas piping connections. Codes do not allow gas cocks to be installed anywhere in a line except at the end of a run ahead of the appliance. When the connection is between galvanized iron and copper use a dielectric coupler or union. These have steel bodies surrounding a threaded Bakelite plastic interior. A six-inch brass nipple can also be used for any such transition joints.*

and check it the required number of hours later. The pressure cannot drop at any time. Once you have the "green tag" that shows you've passed inspection, call the gas company to come and unlock the meter. Only then can you connect the union joint and turn the gas on.

If the gas is already hooked up (as, for example, it would be if you were extending a line to an addition), test the new connections for leaks by painting them with a soap-bubble solution (see **16-38**). *Never smoke* when working around live gas lines or have any other open flame. Use a flashlight to see the connections clearly. Even a tiny leak will make the solution bubble. Another way to test for leaks is to shut off the valves to all the appliances so that no gas is being drawn through the system, and watch the one-half to one cu ft dial on the meter. If it moves within two minutes, you've got a leak somewhere.

An LP gas leak is especially dangerous. Being heavier than air, the gas can flow downhill, collect in pools, and ignite explosively—even with nominally adequate ventilation that would dilute a lighter-than-air natural gas leak. Never take chances with gas lines or cut corners. Work carefully and meticulously observe all code requirements. If you aren't sure of your ability to do the job right, then it is always best to hire a professional.

Fuel oil isn't as explosively flammable as gas. A leak will create a smelly and obnoxious mess, but isn't life-threatening. The code requires that basement fuel oil tanks be located at least 10 feet from the oil burner. The soft, flexible copper lines themselves are buried in the concrete floor slab or are otherwise protected by plastic conduit in earth-floored crawl spaces. A filter is installed in the line after it emerges from the tank.

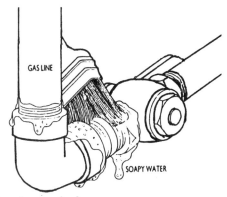

16-38 *Testing for gas leaks.*

415

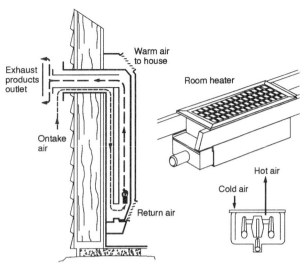

16-39　*Direct-vent room heater and a floor-mounted furnace.*

SPACE HEATERS AND OTHER COMPACT SYSTEMS

For very small houses or large room additions, or where the heating load is otherwise light, a space heater may be a cost-effective alternative to installing or extending a conventional heating system. Despite their erstwhile reputation for explosive unreliability, (modern) freestanding space heaters are safe, as long as they are installed to provide proper clearance to combustible surfaces (e.g., three feet minimum from walls on all sides). They are

16-40　*The refrigerant-filled, sealed tubing which connects the outdoor central air-conditioning condenser to the furnace-mounted indoor evaporator must be protected against kinking and any other injury that would make it useless. The rubber insulation conserves energy by keeping the refrigerant cold.*

fitted with safeguards that shut off the fire if the heater is overturned or overheats. But no fuel-burning heater should ever be used in an enclosed area unless properly vented to the outside. Electric resistance heaters or oil-filled electric radiators are the only kinds of heaters that don't emit poisonous carbon monoxide fumes.

Oil-fired space heaters which burn number one fuel oil, i.e., kerosene, have outputs of up to 50,000 Btuh. The large stationary models have an oil storage tank mounted at the rear of the unit fitted with a manually operated, constant-level control valve which governs the flame height (and heat output) by varying the level of the oil at the bottom of the firepot. Other heaters are portable kerosene burners.

Gas- or oil-fired wall and floor furnaces are designed to be concealed between wall studs. They function like a standard hot-air downflow or upflow warm-air furnace without the ducts. When mounted on interior walls, the flue gases are exhausted through a metal chimney pipe. Direct venting through an outside wall is more efficient since a single, short double-walled pipe both draws in combustion air and vents flue gases without using room air (see **16-39**). Since wall furnaces are controlled by a piezoelectric thermostat, they don't require any external electrical power source to operate unless they use fan-forced circulation. This makes them ideal for backup heat to keep a utility core from freezing during prolonged power failures.

Oil- or gas-fired floor furnaces that deliver heat through a register installed between the floor joists are another unobtrusive way to heat a small house or provide backup heat for a larger one (refer to **16-39**).

CENTRAL AIR-CONDITIONING

As mentioned earlier, one of the main advantages of forced warm-air heating is that the same ductwork can be used to provide cooled air without a great deal of extra cost or labor. Basically, the calculations for determining the hourly cooling load are the inverse of heat-load calculations. Instead of heating degree days, cooling degree days measure the average number of hours when the outside temperature is higher than the 65°F (18°C) indoor design temperature. Although intelligent siting and maximization of passive design strategies to encourage natural ventilation and high levels of insulation can significantly reduce summer heat gain, in large parts of the United States, at least, mechanical cooling is necessary to achieve the comfort levels considered acceptable today (see **16-40**).

Since ducts intended for cooling as well as heating are larger than ducts used only for heating, the system must be carefully planned ahead so that its heating and cooling components are compatible. Greater cooling capacity is needed in regions of endemic high humidity to remove the latent heat stored in moist air. For example, in the United States, a much smaller unit is needed in arid Arizona than humid North Carolina, although the average summer temperatures tend to be much higher in Arizona. As a rule, a 1600 sq ft house needs a 2½ ton or 30,000 Btuh (one ton = 12,000 Btuh) of refrigeration capacity. Even more so than with a furnace, short cycling an undersized air-conditioner will damage the compressor. And, as with heating systems, your dealer will determine the properly sized unit based on calculating the volume of the house, its window area, insulation R-values, appliance heat output, and solar orientation. You should also check the SEER (Seasonal Energy Efficiency Rating, which is the unit's cooling Btu's per watt of electricity). A SEER of 10 is good, 14 is best. Unlike heating systems that utilize a variety of fuels, modern air-conditioning runs on electricity. Although it may cost more initially, a unit with a high SEER rating will usually pay for itself in lower operating costs fairly quickly.

Because of the noise the condenser makes while operating, most residential central air-conditioners employ the *split system*, with a cooling coil (the evaporator) located in the furnace plenum, and the condenser outside on the north or east side of the house (see **16-41**). An ideal location would also be close to the furnace, where its noise wouldn't interfere with the use of the adjoining rooms, where it was shaded by tree plantings, yet where its hot-air discharge was unimpeded by any shrubs.

In the split system, the refrigerant flows between the evaporator and the condenser through measured lengths of precharged and factory-sealed tubing. In the "old" days, the entire system had to be purged and filled with refrigerant instead.

Refrigerant cooled by the condenser to about 45°F (7°C) flows to the evaporator cooling coil installed in the plenum of a forced, warm-air furnace, where air at about 80°F (27°C) is blown over it, dropping its temperature to about 55°F (13°C) as it's delivered to the supply ducts. To ensure efficient operation, the ceiling should be insulated with 12 inches of fibreglass, and any attic-installed ducts should also be covered with four inches of insulation and wrapped in a plastic vapor barrier to prevent condensation on the cold metal surfaces of the ducts.

Two lines run from the condenser to the evaporator. The smaller of the two (¼ inch to ⅜ inch O.D.) carries the refrigerant liquid. The larger (⅞ inch to 1⅛ inch O.D.) *suction line* returns the gaseous refrigerant. These lines are sold as a pair, in five-foot increments in lengths from 10 to 45 feet, prefilled with refrigerant and sealed by factory-installed, spring-loaded valves with special couplings at their ends. When mated with the equipment couplings, they fill the condenser and cooling coil with the proper amount of refrigerant. The liquid line is always insulated.

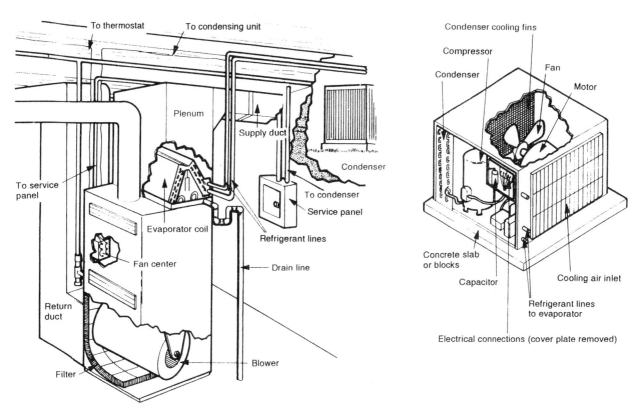

16-41 *Typical split, central air-conditioning system. Most central air conditioning systems are installed in tandem with a forced hot-air furnace.*

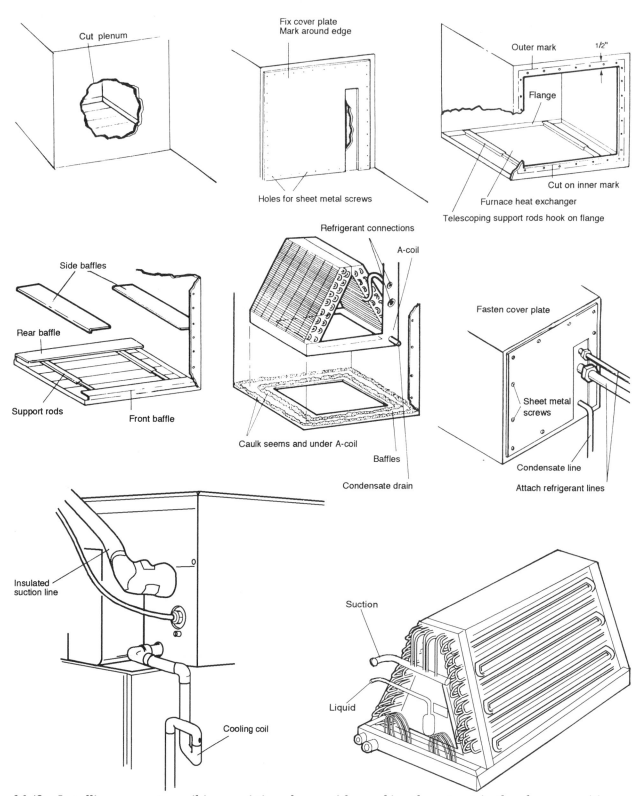

16-42 *Installing evaporator coil in an existing plenum. After making the cut out in the plenum, position the telescoping support rods. Cut the baffles to rest on the rods, caulk their joints and the area under the coil, and set the coil in place so that the condensate drain projects outward.*

418

You can find the length of the tubing to order by running a piece of clothesline along its exact route, stapling it to joists, and then bending it around corners as necessary. To avoid kinking (and ruining) the suction line, don't make any bends with less than a 12-inch radius (make sure you use a tubing bender on the real line). Lay the rope out straight, measure it, and round up to the nearest five-foot increment. It's better to have a little extra than to end up too short. The excess is coiled in a loop where it enters the evaporator.

The most common type of cooling coil (also called the evaporator) is shaped like an "A" and is designed to fit inside the warm-air plenum. The top of the A shouldn't stick up more than two inches into the hot-air duct, and its bottom must be at least three inches to four inches above the furnace heat exchanger. In most cases you can order a coil preinstalled in a modified plenum that is designed to fit your particular furnace plenum exactly. Otherwise, it's not too hard to adapt the plenum to fit the coil (see 16-42).

Unbend the corner tabs of the drive cleats that secure the plenum to the warm-air duct, and push the cleats off by hammering a heavy screwdriver or cold chisel against them. Then slide the S cleats off to free the plenum from the warm-air duct. Support the dangling warm-air duct from wires. Replace the plenum with the cooling section, and reattach it to the furnace and duct with new cleats. A short extension section may be needed to fill in between the cooling section and the duct. Use a fire-resistant cloth "flexible connection" between the cooling unit and the air duct to reduce the transmission of furnace noise and vibration into the ducts.

If the cooling coil doesn't fit your existing plenum, you can have a new one fabricated by a sheet metal shop. Sometimes, all you need to do is cut a hole in the existing plenum (refer to 16-42). Use the factory-supplied cover plate as a template for the cuts (which are 1/2 inch inside of the template outline). Lay a pair of telescoping support rods over the furnace heat exchanger, and then install side and rear baffles to make the opening the same size as the coil base (i.e., its intake). Caulk under the coil flange and set the coil into the plenum. Secure the cover plate with self-tapping screws.

Since warm air passing over the cold coils will shed its moisture, the bottom of the coil rests in a pan that catches the condensate. A fitting is provided for connecting the pan to a drain line that runs to a floor drain. Provide a trap in the drain line so that the plenum air pressure can't interfere with drainage. In a basement installation where the drain is higher than the pan outlet, a small electric condensate pump is installed in the drain line at the side of the furnace 12 inches below the catch pan or at floor level to automatically pump the water up to the drain. Provide a 120-volt outlet for the pump as well.

You can prepare the base for the outdoor condenser unit while you're waiting for the refrigerant tubing to arrive. Pour a four-inch-thick, reinforced level concrete slab over a four-inch gravel base or set four-inch solid concrete blocks in sand. The pad should be close to the house, but still leave access for servicing on all sides.

No matter what their size, condensers have a huge appetite for electricity. A 240-volt, 30-amp to 50-amp circuit is pretty much standard. If the electric meter is nearby, you can run a power tap from it through a waterproof, fused disconnect switch to the condenser. This saves the expense of otherwise running heavy cable from a distant service panel. However, *always* be sure to contact your power company before attempting to remove a sealed meter. If you're not comfortable with working in close proximity to live 240-volt lugs, farm this part of the installation out to a professional electrician.

The electrical code requires the use of time-delay cartridge fuses and an external disconnect switch even when the condenser circuit is protected by a breaker at the service panel. During start-up, the compressor motor draws three to five times as much current as it does once it's running. The time-delay fuse accommodates this initial surge without blowing.

Be sure when you order your heating system that the blower motor and fan volume are large enough for your cooling load as well. Blowers intended for heat-only systems need only a small, single-speed motor. Since more air must be moved across the cooling coil, combination systems require a three-speed motor and a larger fan. An air-conditioner will need less cooling capacity in a dry, hot climate like the Southwest of the United States than one for the humid South where a good deal of energy is expended in removing moisture as well.

Combination systems also use a different thermostat than heat-only systems. A heating/cooling thermostat has two levers: "HEAT–OFF–COOL" and "FAN–ON–AUTO." The first lever sets the system mode, and the second offers you a choice of either manual or thermostatic operation. More complex thermostats allow nighttime setbacks of heating and cooling levels and can be programmed for off-peak operation and other intervals.

Since the hook-ups for the furnace and the air-conditioning must be coordinated with each other, study the wiring diagrams carefully.

Always check the coupler connections for leaks as soon as they are installed. You can use a soap-bubble solution or a special leak-detection fluid supplied by the dealer. If the bubble test shows a leak, tightening the coupler an extra one-eighth turn usually takes care of it. Bubble tests aren't sensitive enough to detect a really slow leak. A professional halide flame detector or an electronic leak detector will detect refrigerant leaks as small as 1/2 ounce per year. If you buy your system from a supplier who actively deals with home-owner installations, you may be able to borrow these instruments. Otherwise, have the test done by a professional technician; you don't want Freon leaking into the atmosphere.

SEPARATE AIR-CONDITIONING SYSTEMS

When central air-conditioning is used in combination with hot-water heat, the evaporator coil is usually installed in the attic (see 16-43). Insulated ducts deliver cool air to each. A return plenum fitted with a removable grill for changing the air filter is placed in an easily accessible location. The condenser unit is still outside the house. In large houses, two outside condensers are often used in conjunction with an attic-mounted blower to cool air for the upstairs rooms with the second blower in the basement for cooling the downstairs rooms. Like heating ducts, air-conditioning ducts should be insulated from the summer heat, particularly when they run through an attic or any other space outside the building's thermal envelope. Flexible, insulated duct is expensive, not all that well-insulated, and its corrugations increase flow resistance. It is much better to use rigid metal with exterior insulation wrapped with an outside vapor barrier. Internally insulated ducts will deliver fibreglass particles along with cooled or warmed air.

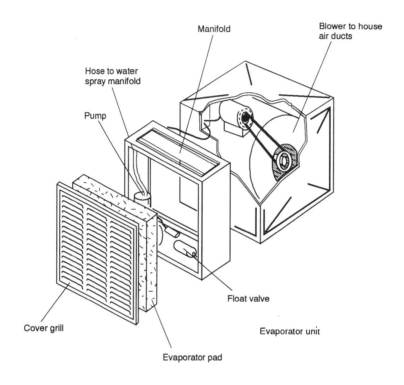

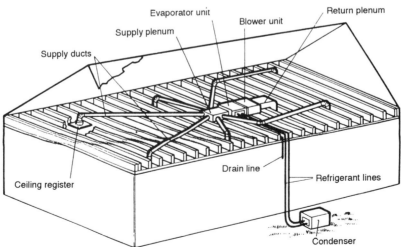

16-43 *Attic-installed central air-conditioning. Adequate insulation is critical for efficient performance of attic installations.*

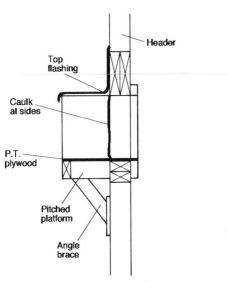

Header
Top flashing
Caulk at sides
P.T. plywood
Pitched platform
Angle brace

16-44   Window- and wall-mounted room air-conditioners. It's a better idea to install a room air-conditioner in a wall opening instead of a window. The operation of the window is not compromised, the installation can be more tightly sealed against both infiltration, and penetration by prowlers, and the unit can be placed in an optimal north wall which may not otherwise have a usable window opening.

ROOM AIR-CONDITIONERS

Another alternative to the combination heating/cooling system is to use individual window- or wall-mounted air-conditioners in bedrooms and other rooms frequently used during the summer months (see **16-44**). You can probably buy three or four window units for the cost of a do-it-yourself central-air installation. One fairly efficient option is to install an 18,000 Btuh window unit in the gable wall of the attic, and run a duct from the evaporator output to a grill mounted in the ceiling of the living room. Put the return-air grill in the ceiling of a back hallway, and run a return-air duct over or between the ceiling joists to the return-air opening of the evaporator blower. Downward cooling is very effective for the first floor areas. A ¾-ton unit mounted in a second floor window will cool upstairs bedrooms.

For best results, install window- or wall-mounted air-conditioners on the north and/or east sides of the house. The full sunlight of south and west walls robs the air-conditioner unit of its efficiency.

Follow the manufacturer's instructions for support and slant requirements; the unit must tilt slightly to the outside to drain the condensate from its cabinet. Window-mounted units are supplied with adjustable fillers that install between the cabinet and the jambs. These must be tightly caulked, both for waterproofing and to reduce out-side air infiltration. A special filler is supplied to stuff into the gap between the raised sashes of double-hung windows.

For a better-looking and much tighter job, set the air-conditioner in a hole framed in the walls instead. The unit can be left permanently in place and protected by an insulated plastic cover during the off-season. The bottom of the opening is tilted like a window sill. Caulk between the unit and the opening trim.

A small, ½-ton (6000 Btuh) "plug-in" window air-conditioner draws only 15 amps at 120 volts. A six-foot-long, grounded three-prong 14-2 extension cord is sufficient for powering it. Since there is a danger that the motor will burn out, and the house can burn down if you use under-sized extension cords, make sure that the cord matches the current draw of the unit and is specifically designed for air-conditioners. It's best to hard-wire permanent wall-mounted units into a junction box connected to a separate 20-amp, 240-volt circuit or provide a dedicated outlet for plug-in models.

EVAPORATIVE COOLERS

In hot and dry climates, evaporative coolers (also called *swamp coolers*) are efficient and much less expensive to operate than air-conditioners. When pulled through a water-soaked pad by a blower, hot, dry outside air gives up its heat to the water and emerges as humid and much cooler air, which is then forced through ducts to ceiling-mounted registers. Swamp coolers only work well where there is at least a 20°F (11°C) difference between the dry and wet air resulting in a cooled air temperature no higher than 79°F (26°C). This means that evaporative coolers won't provide enough cooling at outside temperatures of much more than 100°F (38°C) or where humidity levels are high. For example, in the United States, in Arizona, swamp coolers are efficient only at the beginning and the end of the heating system. The brunt of the cooling load must still be met by refrigerative air-conditioning. Even so, evaporative cooling can pay for itself very quickly.

A swamp cooler has its own separate thermostat. The cooling unit is normally mounted on the roof of the house. In addition to a 120-volt or 220-volt power line to the motor control relay, the unit is supplied with a water feed line. A float valve in the bottom of the cooler pan maintains a constant water level. An overflow drain is also provided.

When the thermostat calls for cooling, a pump sprays water from a manifold onto absorbent pads mounted against the louvered sides of the cooler. The blower draws air through the pads and pushes it down into a duct that connects to the heating/air-conditioning duct system. Since this increases the pressure of the inside air, barometric ceiling vents can be installed to relieve the pressure while the system is operating (some people just leave a window cracked open).

FAN-POWERED COOLING

Ceiling fans are a quiet, efficient way to move large volumes of air around the house (see **16-45**). Moving air makes you feel cooler by increasing the rate of evaporation from your skin. A ceiling fan can save money by allowing the air-conditioner to be set back five to ten degrees Fahrenheit (three to five and a half degrees Celsius).

For safety, allow at least seven feet of clearance under the paddles of a ceiling fan installation. Since their overall depth is about ten inches, you'll need to build eight-foot high ceilings if you plan on using ceiling fans. A 36-inch-diameter fan is large enough for a room with its largest dimension up to 12 feet. Use a 48-inch fan for rooms of 12 to 16 feet, a 52-inch fan for 16- to 18-foot rooms, and two fans for rooms whose longest dimension is over 18 feet. The fans are wired to ceiling junction boxes and can be combined with switch-controlled lights. Hard-wiring is neater and more convenient than pull-cord operation, but requires a special speed control/light switch combination.

ATTIC FANS

In summertime, the air temperature of an unvented attic can reach 150°F (66°C) or more. The attic becomes a radiator, supplying heat to the living area through the ceiling and greatly increasing the load on the air-conditioner. This is just one important reason for ventilating the attic. Roof, ridge, or gable-mounted ventilators exhaust the hot air and help reduce attic heat (see **16-46**).

With adequate levels of insulation and sufficient natural ventilation area, there is no need to use a powered fan to ventilate the attic. Indeed, research has shown that attic ventilating fans typically consume more energy than they save, except in the hottest areas of the country.

Powered attic ventilation isn't the same thing as powered *whole-house ventilation*, which can provide significant nighttime cooling in climates with hot days and cool nights (refer to **16-46**). A centrally located whole-house fan pulls air from open windows and exhausts it through the attic ventilation louvers. The total open window area

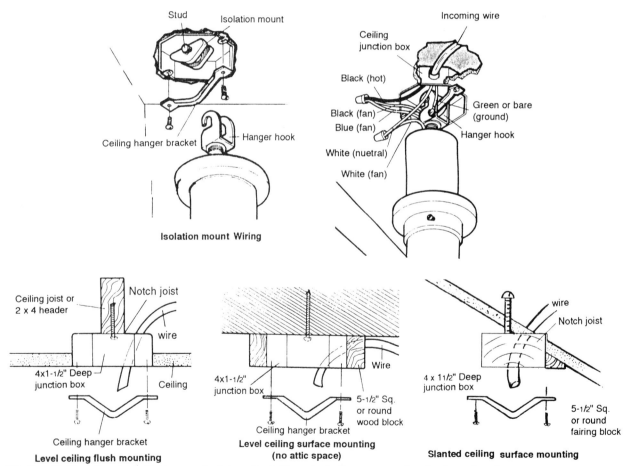

16-45 *Ceiling fan installation and wiring. Install an isolation mount in the junction box to absorb motor vibration and limit sound transmission into the framing. The optional blue wire feeds power to the fan light.*

422

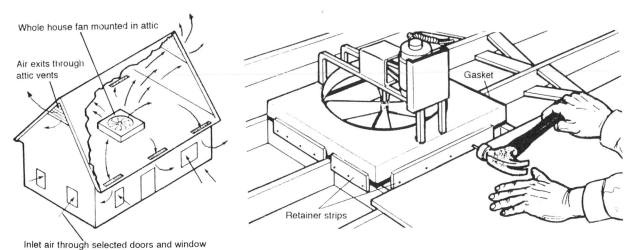

16-46 *A whole-house attic fan mounts on a header framed between the ceiling joists. Vibration-damping pads are inserted between the fan housing and the framework before nailing or screwing the fan to wood cleats.*

and the total attic vent area should be three times the total fan intake area, and the fan should be large enough to replace a third of the house air every minute. The fan will generally run at night, when it can draw cool air through the house as it pushes hot air out the attic ventilators.

There must be at least two to three feet of clearance between the fan and the underside of the roof to prevent back-pressure that will increase noise and lower efficiency. The net free area of the attic vents should be one sq ft for every 750 cu ft/min of fan capacity. The code also requires that an attic access door be provided whenever a fan is installed in the ceiling so that the fan can be quickly reached in case of an emergency. A high-limit, shutoff switch that will automatically turn the fan off in case of an attic fire is also a good safety precaution. Whole-house attic fans can be wired to operate manually and/or by a thermostat, or even a humidistat, in response to excessive humidity (see **16-47**).

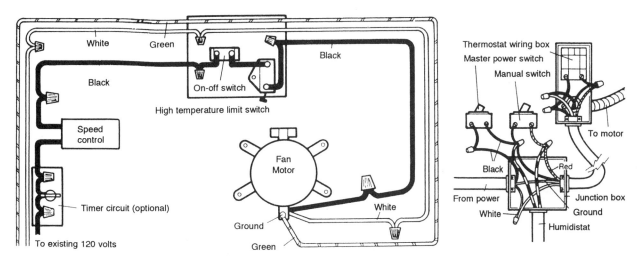

16-47 *Typical wiring for attic fan controls. In a standard installation, the fan is manually controlled by a switch or automatically by a manually set timer. The* ON-OFF *switch in the hi-temp limit box is left in the* ON *position. In the event of a fire, the limit switch automatically turns the fan off. The addition of a second switch and three-wire cable to the fan allows the thermostat to be bypassed and the fan to be operated manually by the master power switch when the manual switch is in the* ON *position. Adding a humidistat lets the fan respond to both high temperature and/or high humidity. Manual bypass operation is still possible as well.*

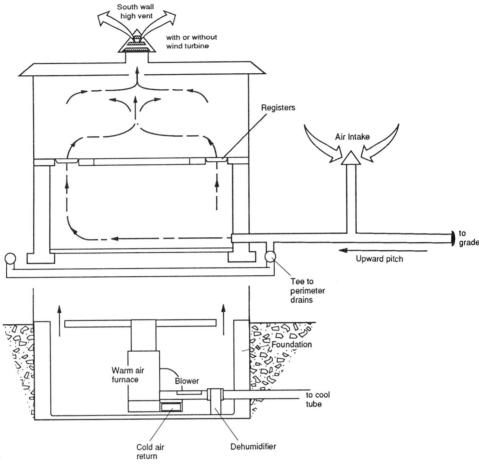

16-48 *Cool tubes.*

PASSIVE COOLING

During the late 1970s and early 1980s, considerable attention was focused on *cool tubes* or *earth tunnels* for passive cooling (see **16-48**). A cool tube basically consists of up to 300 feet of solid plastic pipe buried six to eight feet below the ground. The far end of the pipe extended to the surface, where it was open, but protected against weather and animals. The other end penetrated through the foundation wall into the cellar. In theory, air cooled by ground contact would flow into the cellar to replace hot air exhausted through high wall or ceiling vents. In reality, the air flow was negligible without the aid of a fan to pull the air through the pipes and into the warm-air furnace blower system.

Buried pipe is expensive; a low-cost alternative was to utilize the foundation-perimeter drain pipes as a cooler by teeing them into a cellar-mounted blower. Because of the complex dynamics involved, in virtually every case problems were encountered in calculating air flow and in sizing the pipes and fans in order to move the air slowly enough to allow appreciable cooling. Large-diameter steel culvert cooled faster than plastic pipe, but was more prone to condensation buildup. There was also a concern that the humid and cool interior of the buried pipes were an ideal environment for the bacteria that caused Legionnaires' Disease as well as other pathogens and molds. In any case, controlling infiltration of soil moisture was a significant concern. And, even worse, it would be hard to imagine a more obvious or more efficient pathway for radon infiltration than a cool tube.

Considerably more research is required before cool tubes can be considered a cost-effective and safe way to supplement household cooling loads.

17 Chimneys, Fireplaces, and Woodstoves

MASONRY OR PREFABRICATED CHIMNEYS—WHICH IS BEST FOR YOU?

Unless you plan to heat your home with a high-efficiency condensing gas furnace or with some form of electric heat, you'll need some sort of chimney to exhaust the high-temperature flue gases produced by burning oil, gas, coal or wood. You have a choice of building a masonry chimney (see 17-1) or installing a prefabricated, insulated metal chimney. There are good reasons for either choice.

Prefabricated metal chimneys typically consist of interlocking sections of asbestos-filled, double- or triple-walled stainless-steel pipe. This "insulated" chimney pipe shouldn't be confused with the galvanized, double-walled pipe used for direct venting of gas-burning wall furnaces, space heaters, and water heaters, which is not capable of withstanding prolonged high temperatures or corrosive fumes produced by other fuels.

Prefabricated metal chimneys are lightweight (compared to masonry), and easily and quickly installed, and less expensive than a masonry chimney. Even though materials for a concrete-block chimney cost about 25 percent less per lineal foot than a metal chimney, the block chimney will end up costing a lot more even if you build it yourself. Masonry chimneys require a foundation in the basement; a metal chimney only runs from the ceiling directly above the heating appliance through the roof. Its entire length can be supported on trimmers nailed between the ceiling joists or hung from the roof deck by a special section of pipe with factory-installed, adjustable mounting brackets. To run a chimney from the basement of a single-storey house to three feet above the ridge of a 4-in-12 pitch roof will require at least 24 feet of masonry. If the chimney is venting a wood stove in the living room, you'll need only about eight feet of insulated pipe to do the job. Since a metal chimney that vented a basement furnace would only be about six feet shorter than a masonry chimney, in this case you could save money by building your own block chimney.

Ultimately, like so many aspects of building, the real issue comes down to a question of up-front costs versus life-cycle costs. A top-of-the-line metal chimney has a 20-year warranty; a masonry chimney will outlast the house. But, if you only use a woodstove or fireplace for "ornamental" purposes rather than primary heating, both the life-expectancy and the cost-effectiveness of a metal chimney will be greatly increased.

17-1 *Temporary posts supported the cut ends of the girt beams as the massive fieldstone fireplace and chimney were built up under them. To prevent a fire hazard, it's critical that any wood framing be properly isolated from the chimney flue and its surrounding masonry by at least eight inches of solid masonry and/or firebrick between the flue and the wood. Check with your local fire inspector for the applicable clearances.*

425

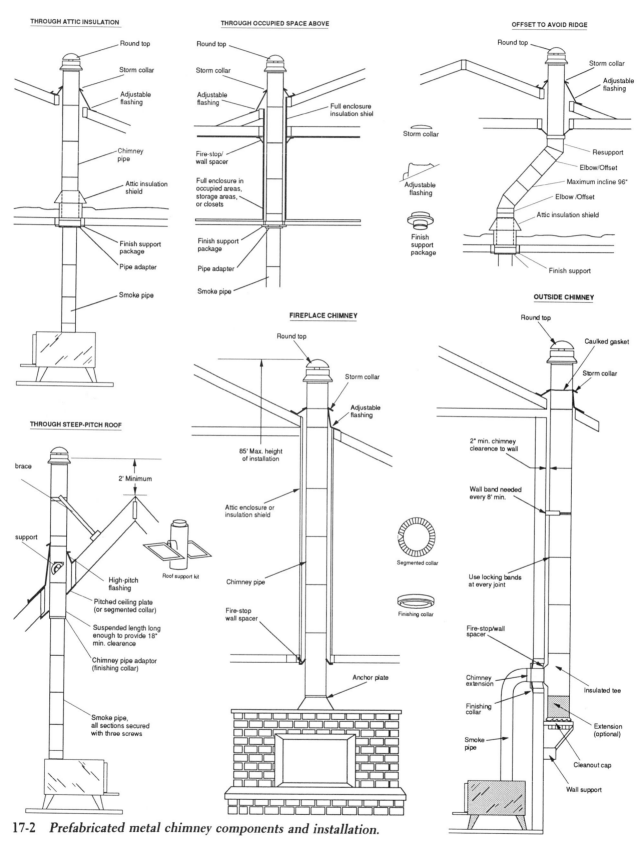

THROUGH ATTIC INSULATION

Round top
Storm collar
Adjustable flashing
Chimney pipe
Attic insulation shield
Finish support package
Pipe adapter
Smoke pipe

THROUGH OCCUPIED SPACE ABOVE

Round top
Storm collar
Adjustable flashing
Full enclosure insulation shiel
Fire-stop/ wall spacer
Full enclosure in occupied areas, storage areas, or closets
Finish support package
Pipe adapter
Smoke pipe

Storm collar
Adjustable flashing
Finish support package

OFFSET TO AVOID RIDGE

Round top
Storm collar
Adjustable flashing
Resupport
Elbow/Offset
Maximum incline 96"
Elbow /Offset
Attic insulation shield
Finish support

FIREPLACE CHIMNEY

Round top
Storm collar
Adjustable flashing
85' Max. height of installation
Attic enclosure or insulation shield
Chimney pipe
Fire-stop wall spacer
Anchor plate

Segmented collar

Finishing collar

OUTSIDE CHIMNEY

Round top
Caulked gasket
Storm collar
2" min. chimney clearence to wall
Wall band needed every 8' min.
Use locking bands at every joint
Fire-stop/wall spacer
Chimney extension
Finishing collar
Smoke pipe
Insulated tee
Extension (optional)
Cleanout cap
Wall support

THROUGH STEEP-PITCH ROOF

brace
2' Minimum
support
Roof support kit
High-pitch flashing
Pitched ceiling plate (or segmented collar)
Suspended length long enough to provide 18" min. clearence
Chimney pipe adaptor (finishing collar)
Smoke pipe, all sections secured with three screws

17-2 *Prefabricated metal chimney components and installation.*

A metal chimney warms up faster than a masonry one whose large mass must heat up before the chimney can draw efficiently. Since a cool chimney is one of the main causes of creosote buildup and downdraft problems, metal chimneys are ideal for intermittent use. But once a masonry chimney is warm, it radiates heat for a long time, even after the fire has died down. This ability to capture and release heat increases the net efficiency of the heating appliance by about 10 percent or more. A masonry chimney is particularly well suited to households where the fire, once kindled, isn't allowed to truly die out during the entire heating season.

Long-term safety and fire-resistance are probably the most important reasons to choose masonry over metal. The walls of a chimney rated for use with coal or wood-burning appliances must be able to withstand a continuous temperature of 1500°F (815°C) and a peak temperature of 2000°F (1093°C)—which can easily occur in a chimney fire—for at least an hour. Metal chimney pipe rated for temperatures below 1400°F (760°C) is acceptable only for gas- and oil-burning appliances. Check to make sure the metal chimney pipe you buy is rated for the type of fuel you're burning.

The code-mandated, fireclay flue liner of a masonry chimney will withstand temperatures continuously that metal chimneys can only handle intermittently. Although it can crack under the extreme heat stress which may occur in a chimney fire, a clay liner won't burn through, as metal can. Since a masonry chimney won't get as hot as a metal chimney, there's less chance of adjoining combustibles catching on fire during a chimney fire. It's also impervious to the corrosive fumes given off by coal-burning that will eventually rot out even the best metal chimney. But it's a potentially deadly mistake to assume that because masonry chimneys are more durable than metal, they are immune to the effects of chimney fires. Superheated gasses escaping through cracks in the tiles or their joints can heat up the outer masonry enough to ignite the surrounding walls. It's safer and smarter to adopt a program of regular chimney maintenance and good wood-burning habits than to wait for the chimney to cleanse itself by a spontaneous creosote fire.

PREFABRICATED CHIMNEY INSTALLATION

Some typical prefabricated chimney installations and their various components are shown in 17-2. Insulated chimney pipe is available in standard 18-, 24-, and 36-inch sections that typically twist-lock together. Always maintain a minimum two-inch clearance between the walls of the chimney and any wood structure (see 17-3). Don't fill the gap with insulation. Even though it won't burn, fibreglass can conduct enough heat to ignite surrounding combustibles. Metal framing shields and insulation shields are used to isolate penetrations. Various kinds of supporting packages provide structural anchorage and isolation. A *finishing collar* is used to make the transition from smoke pipe to chimney pipe. A round *trim collar* neatly covers the support collar and the hole in the wall or ceiling finish. A segmented trim collar which can be adjusted to the appropriate ellipse is used to trim an opening in a sloped ceiling. Depending on the slope of your roof, choose either a shallow or steep-pitched roof base flashing. To make a waterproof joint, seal the *storm collar* to the chimney pipe with flexible caulking or a compressible gasket.

17-3   One advantage of prefabricated, insulated metal chimneys is that unlike a heavy masonry chimney they can be enclosed in a wood or, as in this photo, stucco-finished surround above the roofline.

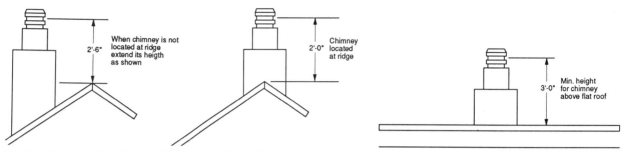

17-4 *Chimney heights and location. Check local code requirements for minimum heights in your area.*

Unless you have no other choice, avoid outside installations. Because of its exposure to the cold, the chimney will draw poorly and produce a rapid creosote buildup. (The same caveat applies even more to exterior masonry chimneys. Not only will they take forever to warm up, but the low R-value of brick guarantees a major heat loss if the chimney happens to be connected to a fireplace. The junction between brick and wall is also hard to waterproof.) To keep the creosote from blocking the bottom of the tee, add a short section of chimney pipe between the tee and the wall support. Close the end with a standard smokepipe cap that can be removed for frequent cleaning.

DESIGN CRITERIA FOR MASONRY CHIMNEYS

Several critical design criteria must be observed if a chimney is to draw well and be safe (see **17-4**).

The rule of thumb is that the chimney should be at least two feet higher than any ridge of the roof within 10

feet (measured horizontally). With a flat roof, the minimum height increases to three feet.

If your floor plan is such that the chimney is located closer to the eaves than the ridge, these height conditions will make for a tall (and potentially unstable) chimney. Because a greater surface area is exposed to chilling outdoor conditions, it could draw poorly and accumulate more creosote. If the chimney is more than six feet high, diagonal bracing is needed to keep it from blowing over (see **17-5**). The flat, steel band clamp and the two steel rod braces can be made to order by your local metal shop. The braces are a maintenance headache; unless they are kept well painted, they'll inevitably stain the roof with rust streaks.

If you can't avoid locating the chimney well below the ridge, you'll need to set up scaffolding on the roof to build it (see **17-6**). Blocking and adjustable extension legs make it possible to adapt standard pipe scaffolding to the roof slope.

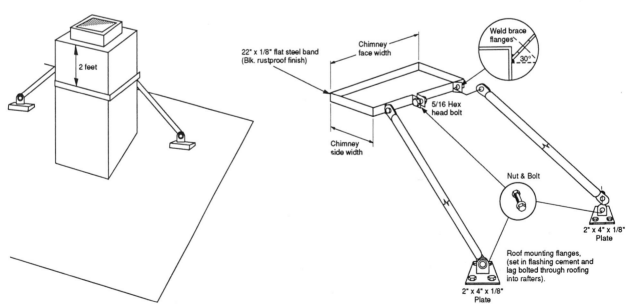

17-5 *Bracing for a tall chimney. Placing a chimney near the eaves should only be done if no other alternative is possible.*

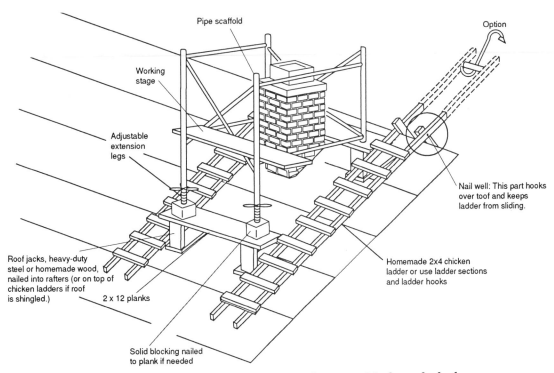

17-6 *Roof scaffold for chimney construction. At the very least, roof jacks and planks are needed to build a chimney on roof slopes greater than 3-in-12.*

Even if you've observed the height recommendations, nearby building surfaces and other obstacles such as trees can sometimes create turbulence that interferes with the air currents that promote a good chimney draft. A smokey fireplace or a furnace or stove plagued by frequent down drafting is probably the first evidence you'll have of such a problem. Often, adding extra height to the chimney will solve it.

The size of the chimney itself depends on the number of flues it contains and their cross-sectional areas, which, in turn, are determined by the output of the heating appliances* they serve and the overall length of the chimney itself, as measured from the *thimble* (smokepipe inlet) to the top of the chimney. A flue that is too narrow will restrict the draft. One that is too large will suck too much air out of the house and take too long to heat up. The ASHRAE guidelines for the chimney height and heating input (in Btuh) for the two most common standard size flues are listed in **17-7**. These are useful for matching flue size to fossil-fuel appliances and woodstoves. They can also be used to size round, prefabricated metal chimneys as well. Other rules govern the sizing of fireplace flues.

Although the calculations of heat input and flue size may seem to allow more than one heater to share a single flue, such a cost-saving shortcut is not only ill-advised, but generally not allowed by most codes. With the exception of a gas-fired water heater and clothes dryer, which may share the same smoke-pipe vent as the furnace, each heating appliance should vent into its own flue. Under some conditions, fumes from the lower heating unit could escape into living areas through the uppermost heater.

17-7 *Guidelines for chimney height and heating input for two common sizes of flues.*

8.5×8.5 flue = 52 in² net area/8.5×13 flue = 80 in² net area*		
Chimney height	Maximum input	Maximum input
10'	175,000 Btuh	300,000 Btuh
15'	210,000 Btuh	360,000 Btuh
20'	240,000 Btuh	415,000 Btuh
30'	275,000 Btuh	490,000 Btuh

*Actually, the flue areas are determined by the rated *input* of the heater which is measured in Btuh, since the actual output (the efficiency) of any heater is highly variable and can only be an estimate based on laboratory tests. The input, however, is a known quantity, that is, for a given number of Btu's contained in the fuel, only a certain percentage will go up the chimney in smoke. Woodstoves, on the other hand, are typically rated by their *output*. You'd have to work backward from the manufacturer's efficiency percent estimate to get the input Btuh (i.e., 100 percent).

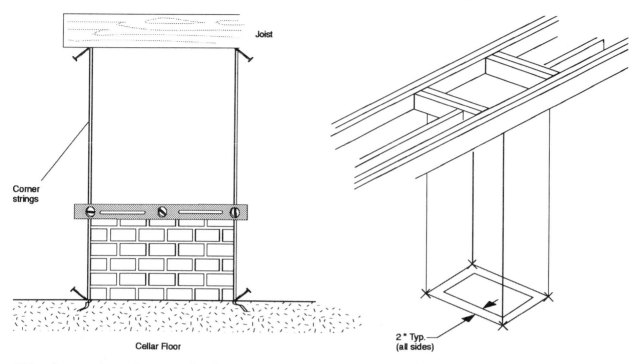

17-8 *Setting up guide strings for chimney construction. Vertical corner strings simplify laying up a plumb chimney.*

BUILDING A BRICK AND/OR PRECAST CONCRETE BLOCK CHIMNEY

Compared to concrete block or stone, bricks are probably the most comfortable masonry unit to work with. They're not too heavy, they're easy to lay, they look attractive, and you can leave off and resume working at any time. On the downside, bricklaying is slow, especially for beginners, and the bricks themselves are expensive. Two or three "common" bricks cost about as much as a single, concrete building block. This is one reason why the portion of the chimney that's in the cellar is usually laid up with inexpensive precast solid concrete chimney blocks instead, and the brickwork is reserved for the living areas where it can be shown to advantage. Likewise, fireplace foundations are built from standard $8 \times 16 \times 8$ concrete building block (and sometimes poured concrete, filled with rubble).

Precast concrete chimney blocks come in $16 \times 16 \times 8$ and $16 \times 20 \times 8$ to fit 8×8 and 8×13 flue liners, respectively. If two or more flues are needed, the blocks can be laid side-by-side and joined to each other with corrugated metal *masonry ties* embedded into the mortar joints of each course. Most codes require that each flue in a multiflue chimney be separated from the others by at least four inches of solid masonry or a course of brick. This divider (called a *wythe*) must be tied into the other masonry. Masonry ties are also used to anchor the chimney to the framing wherever possible and always where it passes through the roof to keep it from moving back and forth. Bend one end of the tie and drive a roofing nail through it and into the wood.

Precast chimney blocks are the fastest and cheapest way to lay up a masonry chimney, especially when it will be concealed behind a wall. You can also build a chimney from standard concrete building blocks as well, as long as their cores are filled with concrete to comply with the code. This sort of chimney is quite bulky. Space limitations may mandate brickwork instead.

Like a well-built house, a well-built chimney begins on a proper foundation. Because of the considerable weight of brick or block, (130 lbs/cu ft) the pad on which the chimney bears should be about one-foot thick and extend six inches beyond the outside dimensions of the chimney proper. Chimney and fireplace footings are normally poured and inspected at the same time as the house footings. Like the main foundation, they should always be poured on undisturbed soil, never on fill, and at the same level, or at least below frost. Foundations for exterior fireplaces and chimneys must also be likewise damp-proofed. When a chimney foundation is to be incorporated into a floor slab, excavate the area, and pour the chimney pad and floor slab at the same time.

Usually, the framing for the chimney opening is located on the floor deck from the plan dimensions, and the corners of the opening are "dropped" onto the floor slab or footing pad with a plumb bob or level and straightedge. Deduct the mandatory two-inch clearance between the masonry and the framing and connect the corner dots to outline the base of the chimney. Lay out the bricks on the lines, leaving gaps for the mortar beads. If you've framed the floor opening accurately, the trial layout will fit into the outlines. If you haven't, reframe the chimney opening to obtain the required clearance.

Drive hardened masonry nails into the concrete floor at each chimney corner and stretch guide strings up to cleats tacked across the floor opening (see **17-8**). With these strings to keep the outside corners plumb, all you have to worry about is holding the courses of bricks or blocks level.

A careful designer also coordinates the chimney location with the framing layout so that it fits between joists and (especially) truss rafters with the least possible accommodation (see **17-9**). For example, a 16-inch by 20-inch precast concrete chimney block suitable for a nominal 8×8 flue tile will require a 20-inch by 20-inch opening. The spacing between rafters at two inches o.c. is $21\frac{1}{2}$ inches. It's always a good idea to plumb up the chimney opening from one floor to the next and through the ceiling to the underside of the roof to keep it running straight and to head off any clearance problems in the framing before framing members are nailed off.

Usually the cast-iron cleanout door is installed in the first chimney block (assuming that you're starting with precast block in the cellar). To cut the opening, make repeated shallow scoring cuts with a circular saw equipped with a masonry blade (see **17-10**). If you try to saw through the block as if it were a piece of wood, you'll shatter the blade. As always, wear a dust mask and eye protection. Professional carpenters usually keep an old, half-worn-out saw around just for these types of jobs instead of clogging up their best, new framing saw with dust and grit. Using a power saw is also the easiest way to cut openings in the flue tiles. There's much less chance of breakage than with the traditional method, which is to pack the tile with shock-absorbing sand and then to punch a line of closely spaced holes through it with a nail set or to score it with a cold chisel.

Locate the cleanout door so that it will be easy to get to. If it's blocked by ducts or equipment, you won't use it. Set the first block in a bed of ordinary brick mortar (one part Portland cement, one part hydrated lime, and five to six parts sand, if you mix it yourself, or else add one part of brick mortar cement to five to six parts sand), and butter the door frame into its opening. Center and plumb the first flue tile in the mortar bed. Then lay more courses of block until you're ready for the next flue tile. According to the specifications in standard code, the flue tiles must be mortared together with a special heat-resistant *refractory cement* (you can pick up a pail of this premixed, putty-like compound at your local masonry supply dealer). Wipe the joint smooth on both the inside and outside so that it won't interfere with the draw or catch condensation which can cause ice damage.

17-9 *Framing for the chimney opening must be done carefully so that the chimney fits between the frame members with minimal trouble while maintaining the required two-inch clearance at all times. Note the tar paper flap that waterproofs the opening until the chimney goes through it.*

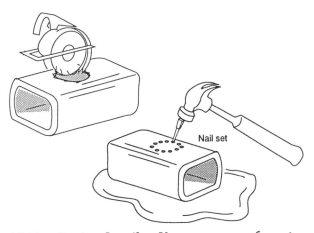

17-10 *Cutting flue tiles. Use a power saw for cut-offs. A nail set works well for making circular cutouts.*

431

Keep the tiles running square and plumb in the opening. Never fill the space between the flue and the inside of the chimney wall with mortar. Codes call for a minimum one-inch gap to provide a thermal break between the flue and the outer masonry as a safety measure against excessive heat buildup. The tiles themselves are held in place by the bits of mortar which inevitably drop from the trowel or ooze out the back of the mortar joints.

Special chimney blocks with a half-round cutout are used to accommodate the smokepipe *thimble*, a round clay tile which is cut to length to fit flush with the outside face of the chimney and the inside face of the flue (allowing the thimble to project into the flue will interfere with the draft). Seal the gaps between the thimble and the flue with *refractory cement*. If you're using brick instead of block, cut the arced filler pieces as carefully as possible, and fill in snug to the thimble with mortar. The thimble

should be placed so that the smokepipe from the heater will be at least 18 inches below the ceiling.

Even if you build the entire chimney from concrete block, it's recommended that you change over to brick at the point where it penetrates the roof. Brick weathers better than concrete block, the closer joint spacing requires less flashing metal, and the chimney simply looks better. (Refer to Chapter Nine for a description of proper flashing techniques.) Ideally, the roofing won't be installed yet, but if it is, be sure to cover it with a plastic sheet while you set the counterflashing pieces about 1½ inches into the mortar joints.

The last few courses of brick at the top of the chimney are generally *corbelled* (offset outward about an inch per course) both for an ornamental detail and to protect the sides of the chimney from weathering by making a drip edge for the chimney cap (see **17-11**).

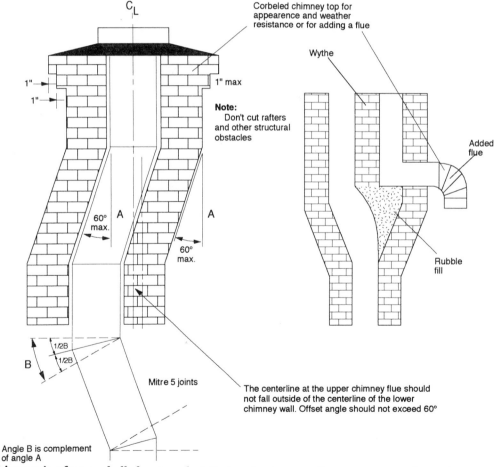

17-11 *A chimney is often corbelled outward at its top for improved appearance and weather resistance. Corbelling is also used to add a flue at an upper point or to make an offset when neither the rafters, beam, other structural framing members or the chimney location itself can be moved. The centerline of the offset chimney flue should not fall outside the centerline of the original chimney wall nor should the angle of the offset exceed 60 degrees.*

432

17-12 *Home-made staging for above-roof chimney work. A ladder laid across the roof deck is attached to the staging on the other side of the roof deck.*

Corbelling is also used to increase the size of the chimney when an extra flue must be added at some higher point or when the chimney must be offset to fit past an immovable obstruction. Offsets are safe as long as their angle doesn't exceed 60 degrees and the centerline of the offset flue doesn't fall outside of the centerline of the lower chimney wall. The flue tiles are cut on a mitre (bisecting the complementary angle of the offset, e.g., 15 degrees for a 60-degree offset) so that the cross-sectional area of the flue is not reduced.

When laying brick, take care to avoid spattering excess mortar on the bricks. Brush off any spills immediately. Once they've had a chance to set, removing mortar stains from the porous face of the brick will prove difficult, even with a wire brush and a muriatic-acid cleaning solution.

Strike the excess mortar from the joints with a brick-joint runner as soon as the mortar sets up enough to tool smoothly. Shape the joints to either a concave or a V-shaped profile to shed water and protect the mortar against premature failure. In the Southwest of the United States, where there isn't enough rain to matter, bricks are sometimes laid so that the excess mortar will leave a decorative, extruded bead, instead.

The fastest way to finish a chimney is to set a precast concrete cap on top of the last course of brick. To help promote a good draft, the lip of the last flue tile should project about two inches beyond the cap (see **17-12**). You can also cast the cap in place by bracing a simple board form to the roof.

A layer of ordinary brick mortar much more than an inch or two thick is brittle and unsuitable for casting. Use a mix of Portland cement and sand (basically concrete without the stones). Instead of a cast cap, some masons just trowel the mortar into a sloped finish (see **17-13**). When spread too thin, both brick mortar and concrete bond weakly and soon crack. Since the flue expands slightly as it warms up, it can crack the chimney cap.

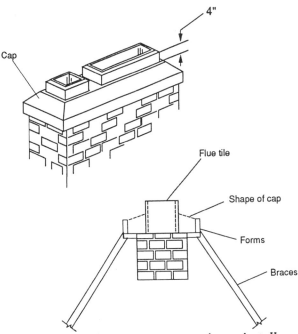

17-13 *Precast chimney caps are easier to install and longer-lasting than site-built caps made from mortar.*

433

Leave an ⅛- to ¼-inch expansion gap filled with flexible silicone or butyl rubber caulking. Other than the cap and a bit of corbelling, most chimney tops are otherwise unembellished. The normal updraft usually keeps most of the rain and snow out. But if there is a closed damper at the bottom of the chimney, the updraft will be reduced. Chimney caps of flat stone or traditional clay or metal can be both highly ornamental and functional. Since they can also complicate the chimney sweeps' routine servicing, they should also be removable, if possible.

An exposed block chimney is not very attractive. The usual cure—"disappearing" it behind a wall—blocks much of the heat that it would otherwise radiate into the living areas. However, installing a floor-level intake register and a ceiling-level outlet can actually improve the heat output by turning the chimney surround into a convective heater. Another solution is to parge the blocks with two coats of cement stucco. Unless tinted, ordinary stucco makes a dull grey finish. To brighten up the stucco, use a perlited gypsum plaster for a brilliant white finish or similar products for a softer, light-grey appearance.

HEATING WITH WOOD

The energy crises of the 1970s almost single-handedly brought about the renaissance of the wood stove. However, the modern, air-tight wood stove is anything but a low budget alternative heating system. Nevertheless, the pleasurable sensation of basking in the warmth of a wood stove on a cold night is a pleasure exceeded only by sitting in the rocker in front of a blazing fireplace. And, unlike a fireplace, a wood stove can be a very efficient source of heat for your whole house.

One reason the newer stoves have become even more expensive is that most of them are now equipped with costly catalytic combustors in order to achieve the EPA-mandated reduction of particulate emissions which were contributing to air pollution in valleys subject to wintertime temperature inversions. Woodstoves are now only 10 percent to 20 percent as dirty as the older models. Catalytic converters, when operating at the right temperature, also boost the efficiency of the stove to somewhere between 65 percent and 78 percent, which is close, if not better than, that of a standard oil burner.

There are so many different kinds of woodstoves and wood-burning furnaces widely available today that whole books have been written just to describe them and their applications.

While there are solid economic reasons for heating with wood where it's locally available, the decision whether to heat with wood (either for primary or backup heating) is ultimately a matter of personal preference. Until the fully automated wood-pellet-burning furnace becomes affordable for home use, heating with wood will continue to demand a high level of involvement, and the commitment which led people to embrace the convenience of fossil fuels in the first place.

SAFE WOOD STOVE AND SMOKE PIPE INSTALLATION

Adequate clearance between the stove and combustible surfaces is the most important element of a safe wood stove installation (see **17-14**). The NFPA (National Fire Prevention Association, which publishes standards on

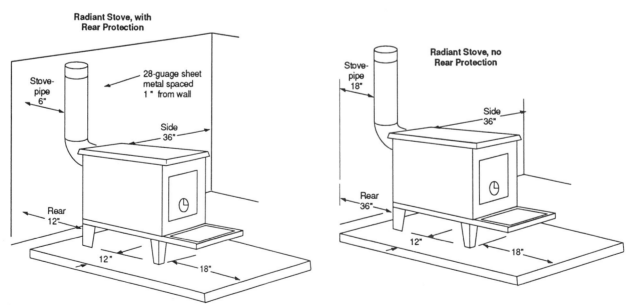

17-14 *NFPA-recommended clearances for wood stoves. Metal-jacketed, circulating-type heaters require the same clearances as radiant stoves with rear protection.*

which building codes are based) recommends a minimum clearance between the sides of a radiant-type stove and unprotected combustible surfaces of 36 inches and between the smoke pipe and all such surfaces of 18 inches. The required clearance between the bottom of the stove and the floor depends on the specific length of the stove legs and the type of protective covering used on the floor. Tall-legged stoves (more than 18 inches) are safe with only an apron of 24-gauge sheet metal. Mid-length stoves (six inches to 18 inches) require at least a sheet of ¼-inch asbestos millboard between the metal and the floor. Adding protection for stoves closer than six inches to the floor is achieved by replacing the millboard with a layer of four-inch hollow-core bricks (placed on edge to permit air circulation through them). A brick or slate hearth, bedded in an inch or so of mortar which is laid over an inch or more of sand will also provide good protection, as long as the overall thickness of the hearth is at least four inches. With circulating-type stoves (the ones jacketed with metal that heat primarily by convection), the side and rear clearances can be reduced to 12 inches. The recommended side and front clearances that these stove aprons should have to protect the floor from sparks and spilled hot coals is also shown in **17-14.**

It's easy to imagine a situation in which observing these recommendations can interfere with the use of the room. Fortunately, installing a protective fire-proof backing allows the required clearances to be safely reduced. A sheet of ¼-inch *asbestos millboard* or 16 gauge sheet metal mounted one inch off the wall shrinks the 36-inch clearance to 18 inches above, and 12 inches at the sides and rear. The 18-inch clearance for the stove pipe is reduced to nine inches above and six inches at the sides and rear.

With circulatory-type stoves, the 12-inch clearance becomes six inches and four inches, respectively.

If the side of the heat shield that faces the stove is painted with flat black, heat-resistant stove and grill paint, it will help heat the room by radiation. Unless kept highly polished, ordinary metal sheets aren't particularly effective reflectors or radiators.

Metal is probably a better choice for a heat shield than asbestos millboard, which can release asbestos fibres into the house air unless its cut edges are sealed with duct tape or paint. But whatever type of material you use for your heat shield, never, under any circumstances, allow it to make direct contact with a combustible surface. Use porcelain fence insulators or metal ferrules to maintain the minimum air space (see **17-15**).

Note that drywall and plaster, although themselves noncombustible, are considered combustible when attached to wood framing since they can conduct heat into it. Also, even though wood will not ordinarily ignite below 700°F (371°C), in close proximity to a source of high heat, it will, over time, undergo chemical changes that can cause it to smolder at temperatures as low as 200°F (93°C). This is a good reason for installing heat shields between the stove (and smoke pipe) and any nearby wood surfaces, even when they are technically within the domain of minimum clearance.

There's one other consideration which should not be overlooked. Besides cast-iron, some wood stoves contain "soapstone" (steatite or talc) panels which have excellent heat-retention capability and are, not surprisingly, quite heavy. Since the weight of your stove and its hearth can reach a half ton or more, be sure the floor framing that supports it is strong enough for the load.

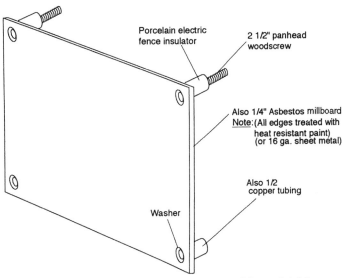

Porcelain electric fence insulator

2 1/2" panhead woodscrew

Also 1/4" Asbestos millboard
Note:(All edges treated with heat resistant paint) (or 16 ga. sheet metal)

Also 1/2 copper tubing

Washer

17-15 *Wood stove heat shields. To be safe and effective, any type of heat shield must always be isolated from direct contact with the walls by at least one inch.*

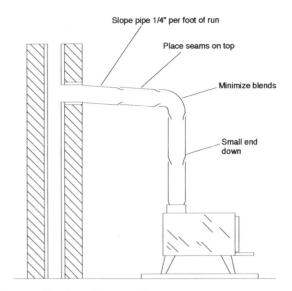

17-17　Smoke pipe installation safety. Smokepipes should enter the chimney thimble at least 18 inches below the ceiling.

17-16　The smoke pipe maintains a good, steep pitch upwards to join the chimney. The thermal mass of the chimney and the brick wall stores and releases heat after the fire dies down. The stove sits on a concrete slab so no additional hearth is needed. The fire inspector may require the brick wall to be separated from the wood framing by a ½-inch space, in which case, metal masonry ties inserted between the mortar joints and nailed to the studs will anchor the bricks to the wood.

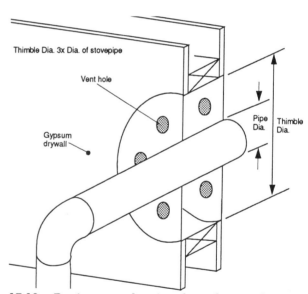

17-18　Passing a smoke pipe through a combustible wall. The vents in the thimble prevent dangerous heat buildup inside the wall cavity.

SMOKE PIPE INSTALLATION

A properly installed smoke pipe is another important part of safe wood heating (see 17-16). The operational principle is: *avoid the horizontal*. Horizontal pipes slow down the draft and collect creosote and ash deposits which will eventually corrode the pipe—if they don't burn your house down first. All horizontal runs should be kept as short as possible and pitch upwards towards the thimble at least ¼

inch per foot (see 17-17). Limit changes of direction to use as few elbows as possible. The ideal hookup would require just one 90-degree, adjustable elbow to connect the vertical riser from the stove top to the short horizontal that runs into the thimble. A second elbow is generally unavoidable with rear-mounted stoves. A good rule of thumb is to try to keep the overall length of the smoke pipe for a modern, air-tight woodstove under six feet. A

17-19 *This wood stove has been enclosed in a brick surround to capture heat and even out the wide room temperature swings typical of wood heat.*

longer pipe can be used to capture some of the excessive heat which old-fashioned, less-efficient wood burners let escape up the chimney.

To prevent creosote leaks when joining stovepipe sections, always insert the crimped end pointing downwards. It should overlap at least two inches. Some experts recommend sealing the joints with furnace cement. However, I've observed that, except at the collar of the stove outlet, the cement soon flakes off as the metal repeatedly expands and contracts. Use three self-tapping, sheet-metal screws to secure each pipe joint.

Unless it is properly protected, the smoke pipe should never pass directly through anything except a masonry wall. Support the pipe in a vented thimble inserted in a sheet metal flange three times larger than the diameter of the pipe (see **17-18**). Any wood framing within the area of the metal should be removed. If the code permits it, the metal can be covered with drywall, as long as no framing is within the underlying metal area. A vented thimble shouldn't be confused with the ornamental metal collar that's always used to cover the joint between the smoke pipe and the thimble. Although the same method has often been used to run smoke pipe through floors and ceilings, it's safer to use a section of insulated, prefabricated chimney for this purpose, instead.

FIREPLACES

It's been at least 150 years since fireplaces were the primary heaters in most homes. It's a commonplace that fireplaces are, from the standpoint of heat loss, almost an open window. In a traditional fireplace, the general outlines of which date back to the massive central hearths of colonial New England, not much more than 10 percent of the fire's heat is radiated out into the room. The rest goes up the chimney along with 10 to 100 times more air than is needed to support combustion. On really cold nights, a fireplace can actually achieve negative efficiency, losing more heat up the chimney than it gives off to the rooms while the furnace labors to replace the warm air sucked from the rest of the house.

Yet, for most people, the hearth is still the heart of the home. If not an outright necessity, a fireplace is at least a desirable amenity. The ascetic moralism of energy efficiency cannot hold a candle to the warmth of a crackling grate. People want fireplaces, not to heat their houses, but to warm their hearts. People have even gone so far as to set wood stoves in fireplace-like surrounds (see **17-19**). In the past few decades, the building industry has proffered several improvements in traditional fireplace design that mitigate some of the more egregious inefficiencies of fireplaces.

17-20 *Conventional and Rumford-type fireplace designs compared and contrasted.*

Dimensions for Conventional Fireplace with Outside Air (inches)										
Finished fireplace opening							Rough Brickwork		Flue size	Lintel length
A	B	C	D	E	F	G	H	J	L × M	N
24	24	16	11	14	18	8¾	32	19	8 × 12	36
26	24	16	13	14	18	8¾	34	21	8 × 12	36
28	24	16	15	14	18	8¾	36	21	8 × 12	36
30	29	16	17	14	23	8¾	38	24	12 × 12	42
32	29	16	19	14	23	8¾	40	24	12 × 12	42
36	29	16	23	14	23	8¾	44	27	12 × 12	48
40	29	16	27	14	23	8¾	48	29	12 × 16	48
42	32	16	29	14	26	8¾	50	32	16 × 16	54
48	32	18	33	14	26	8¾	56	37	16 × 16	60
54	37	20	37	16	29	13	68	45	16 × 16	72
60	40	22	42	16	31	13	72	45	16 × 20	72
72	40	22	54	16	31	13	84	56	20 × 20	84

Key
A = Fireplace opening width
B = Fireplace opening height
C = Firebox depth
D = Firebox width
E = Vertical wall of firebox
F = Sloped wall of firebox
G = Throat depth
H = Smoke chamber width
I = Depth to back wall
J = Smoke chamber height
K = Smoke chamber side slope
L = Flue liner inside depth
M = Flue liner inside width
N = Lintel width
O = Vertical distance from lintel to throat
P = Smoke shelf width

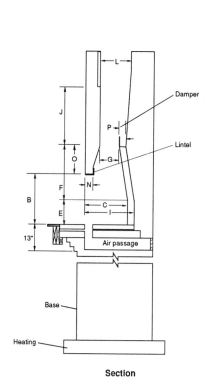

Section

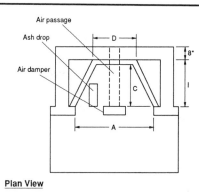

Plan View

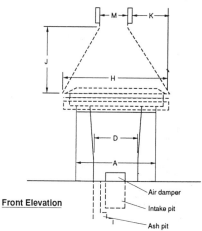

Front Elevation

Design Criteria for Rumford Fireplace with Outside Air	
1. D = C	7. G ≤ 3 inches or ≥ 4 inches
2. E = D	8. Centerlines of G and C are equal
3. I − C = 2¼ inches minimum	9. P = 4 inches
4. A × B ≥ 10 × (L × M)	10. N ≤ 4 inches or ≥ 5 inches
5. A approx = 2 or 3 × C, and B approx = 2 or 3 × C	11. O = or > 12 inches
6. B ≥ A	12. Damper is flat, opens towards P

The relationship between the dimensions of the various parts of the fireplace and the cross-sectional area of its flue are critical. Too small a flue will cause poor draw and downdrafting, while too large a flue will waste too much air. An awkwardly proportioned smoke chamber or firebox will make for a smoky fireplace, plagued by frequent downdrafts. The recommendations given in **17-20** are the result of a process of empirical and experimental refinement that has been more or less continuous since the 17th century. Yet, more than 200 years ago, Count von Rumford (Benjamin Thompson), an American expatriate and amateur engineer, realized that the design of the fireplaces of his time, upon which present-day fireplaces are still based, was inherently flawed. The low lintel and deep firebox and wide throat of the traditional fireplace are the cause of its low heat output. The characteristic narrow throat and shallow firebox with obliquely angled sides and back of a Rumford fireplace resulted in greater heat radiation to the room while drawing less air without down-drafting. The reason that Rumford fireplaces are not in wider use today probably has a lot to do with the fact that they take more skill to build than the conventional fireplace.

BUILDING A MASONRY FIREPLACE

As with a chimney, proper fireplace construction begins with a solid foundation (see **17-21**). If the fireplace is located against an outside wall, its foundation is usually poured as a closed box at the same time as the foundation wall, and filled with rubble stone. The foundation for a freestanding fireplace is generally built from ordinary concrete block.

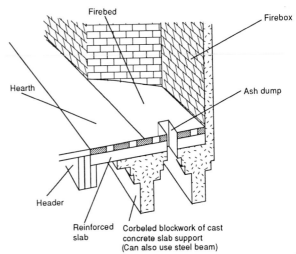

17-22   The subhearth slab. For both structural and fire safety reasons, the hearth should never rest directly on top of wood flooring or framing members.

To prevent cracking, and, even more important, to keep your house from burning down, no part of the hearth and its extension should contact the floor framing or be laid over a wood floor (see **17-22**). Shore up the form work for the cantilevered, reinforced concrete subhearth slab with temporary posts, and leave them in place until it is anchored by the weight of the rear chimney wall that is built over its back edge. If headroom permits, permanent support for the slab cantilever can be provided by corbelling out the block work or brickwork instead.

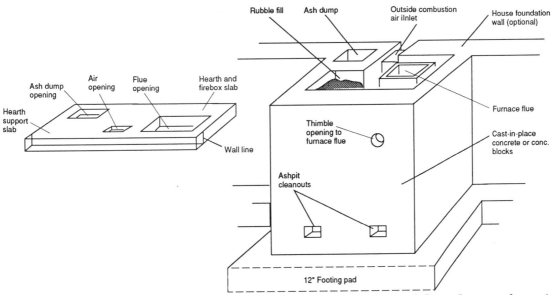

17-21   Fireplace foundations. Because it can contain numerous internal flues, ducts, and openings for cleanouts, a chimney foundation must be carefully planned before it is poured or laid up.

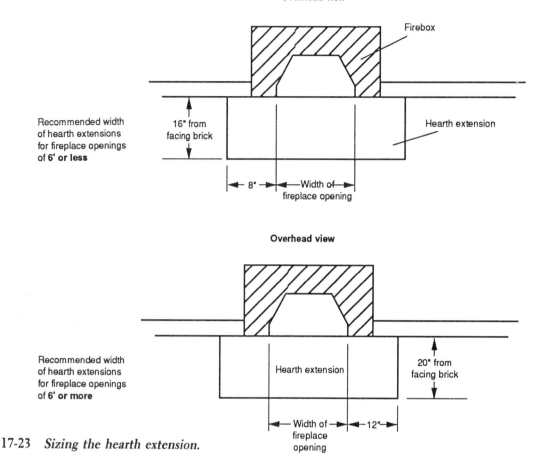

Overhead view

Firebox

Hearth extension

Recommended width
of hearth extensions
for fireplace openings
of **6' or less**

16" from
facing brick

8"

Width of
fireplace opening

Overhead view

Recommended width
of hearth extensions
for fireplace openings
of **6' or more**

Hearth extension

20" from
facing brick

Width of
fireplace
opening

12"

17-23 *Sizing the hearth extension.*

The NFPA recommendations for fireplace safety have been incorporated into building codes in the United States. If you are building in an area where no code holds sway, ask your fire insurance agent for a copy of NFPA standards for fireplace and woodstove installation. Usually, you'll need to have your work inspected after the firebox is complete up through the smoke shelf, but before the face bricks or the first flue tile are laid. The inspector's primary concern is to see that the proper clearances have been maintained. Measures designed to insure fire safety (such as the proper width of the hearth extension) are also another thing an inspector will look for (see **17-23**).

According to the code, the firebox must be lined with special high-temperature firebrick, cemented with refractory cement. Regular mortar is not permitted. The firebox must be surrounded by at least eight inches of solid masonry (this includes a minimum of two inches of firebrick). The smoke chamber walls should be solid corbelled brick, parged with refractory cement to make a smooth, finished surface. The angle of its sides should not be less than 45 degrees from vertical, and its height can't exceed the height of the fireplace room opening. If the smoke cham-

ber is lined with firebrick, its walls can be six inches thick, overall. Otherwise, eight inches of masonry is required.

The steel lintel that supports the top of the fireplace opening arch should be strong enough for the weight. Leave a gap between its ends and the masonry to prevent cracking when the metal expands. The ready-made damper should be in place so that it can be inspected for proper operation. In addition to a standard tight-fitting damper, you may wish to consider adding an external damper at the top of the chimney. Connected to a control rod by a stainless steel cable, this damper helps keep the chimney warm by blocking out the cold air that would otherwise flow down it when not in use. The chimney will draw better and stay cleaner, and infiltration-driven heat loss will be reduced.

The walls of the chimney must be of solid block or brick at least four inches thick. Rubble stone walls must be at least 12 inches thick. Maintain a two-inch minimum clearance between the chimney and fireplace walls, and all combustible framing and trim. Many builders have been unpleasantly surprised during an inspection to learn that the code also requires a four-inch clearance behind firebox

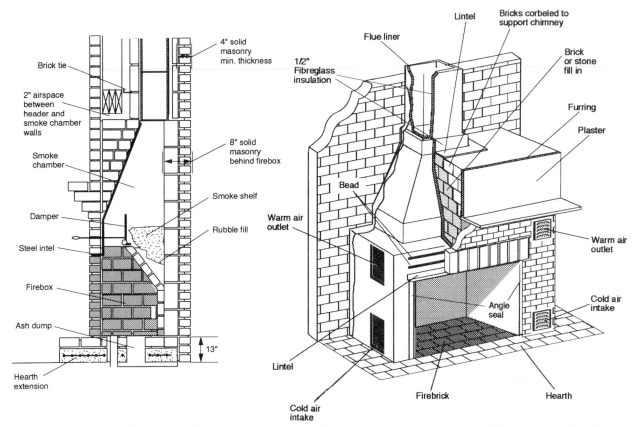

17-24 *Conventional masonry fireplace versus a prefabricated circulating fireplace. Since the steel shell of a prefabricated circulating fireplace makes a form for the brickwork, the problem of figuring the correct fireplace dimensions for a good draw is already solved.*

and smoke chamber. Install 26-gauge galvanized metal firestops at all floor and ceiling penetrations. There can be no wood trim within six inches of the fireplace room opening. Wood mantels or trim that project more than 1½ inches beyond the face of the opening must be at least 12 inches above it. A final inspection may be required before capping the chimney.

Even though not all codes require it (yet), it's a good idea to provide the fireplace with an external source of combustion air. This can be provided through a passageway (with a minimum cross-sectional area of 55 sq in) cast into the concrete foundation 13 inches below the surface of the hearth that opens into a closeable 4½-inch by 13-inch diffuser. If you use a metal duct instead (which would be the case with a central fireplace) it should be kept clear of the framing in case live coals happen to fall into it. Secure the joints with three screws as with stovepipe. The duct should have a conveniently accessible damper of some sort so that it can be closed off when not in use.

A Rumford fireplace, with outside combustion air, a tight-fitting damper, and a glass-doors closure will have the highest efficiency of any ordinary radiant fireplace.

Prefabricated steel, circulating fireplaces are widely promoted as an alternative to building your own fireplace (see **17-24**). In addition to the radiant heat emitted by an ordinary fireplace, circulating fireplaces supply extra heat to the room by warm-air convection currents. The units typically have a double steel wall with internal baffles designed to direct air over the hottest parts of the firebox. The intake vents are installed close to the floor. The outlets are placed higher up on the wall of the fireplace and can direct air out the front or sides or into another room. Some units use optional blowers to drive the circulation. Fitted with a closure and outside air supply, a circulating fireplace can raise heating efficiency up to 35 percent.

There's no reason why you couldn't build a circulating fireplace from masonry. But, by providing a template for the brickwork and eliminating the tricky work involved in building the sloped firebox and smoke shelf, the typical circulator makes it much easier to build your own fireplace. A masonry outer liner and hearth are still required for a safe installation. The masonry is separated from the steel frame by a ½-inch expansion gap filled with fibreglass insulation.

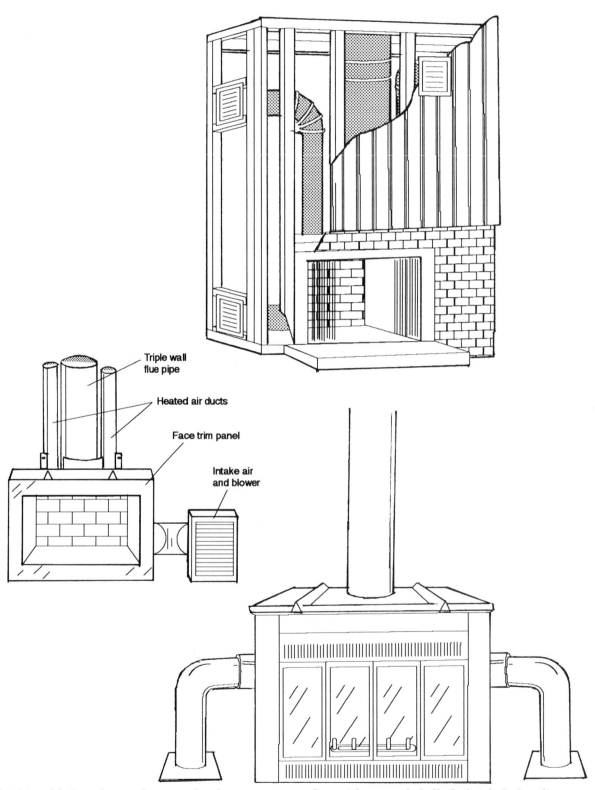

Triple wall flue pipe

Heated air ducts

Face trim panel

Intake air and blower

17-25 *A prefabricated zero-clearance fireplace comes complete with a metal shell, firebrick firebox liner, ductwork, and finished face panel. The entire unit can be installed in a wall opening in as little as a half hour. An optional blower and ducts can be used to blow heated air into one or more rooms.*

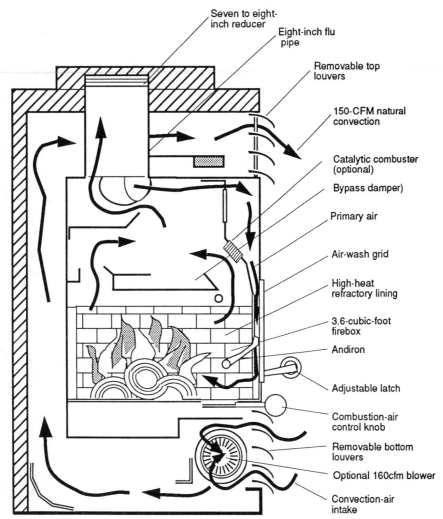

Seven to eight-inch reducer

Eight-inch flu pipe

Removable top louvers

150-CFM natural convection

Catalytic combuster (optional)

Bypass damper)

Primary air

Air-wash grid

High-heat refractory lining

3.6-cubic-foot firebox

Andiron

Adjustable latch

Combustion-air control knob

Removable bottom louvers

Optional 160cfm blower

Convection-air intake

17-26 *High-tech circulating fireplace/wood stove hybrid. Many municipalities, particularly where winter thermal inversions are common, have outlawed conventional fireplaces and wood stoves because of their contribution to particulate pollution. High tech alternatives that combine the functions of wood stove, fireplace, and furnace may be a reasonable alternative.*

Although they are an undeniable labor saver, the same objections lodged against prefabricated metal chimneys hold true for circulating fireplaces. A masonry fireplace basically lasts forever. In exchange for the equivalent of a mason's wage, the very best steel prefabs will provide you with a usable fireplace for about 30 years. Replacing a burned out liner surrounded by solid masonry is a major operation.

A prefabricated circulator isn't the same thing as an all-steel *zero-clearance* (so-called because they require no hearth) circulating unit intended for direct installation into the wall framing (see **17-25**). These units are typically vented by prefabricated chimneys. Other than the firebrick backing (which is supplied with the kit), any masonry is purely decorative. In fact, some of these units can be installed directly over a properly prepared, wood subfloor. Freestanding, all-metal fireplaces are really more a "species" of wood stove than a true fireplace.

The distinction between fireplace and wood stove or furnace is even more blurred with the latest generation of high-tech, zero-clearance fireplaces (see **17-26**). These appliances use sophisticated blowers, internal ducting and baffles, airtight glass and metal doors, secondary combustion chambers, and catalytic combustors to achieve heat output efficiencies that rival standard oil burners (up to 80 percent). They can even be integrated with warm-air ducts to provide central heating for an entire house. Beware that such high levels of performance are certainly not inexpensive, and with installation and ducting the costs can double.

17-27 *A Russian (or Finnish or Scandinavian, depending on the ethnic heritage of the apprentice stovemason's mentor) masonry heater employs an extensive system of flues and internal baffles and utilizes its tremendous thermal mass to capture most of the heat given off by a short intense morning and evening fueling so that it can be released slowly for even and comfortable heating throughout the rest of the day. The ornamental plates visible are actually control valves for the dampers that determine the various flue settings.*

ALL-MASONRY HEATERS

For about 500 years or so, people as diverse as the Finns, Russians, Koreans, and various northern Europeans have heated their homes quite adequately with huge central masonry heaters (see 17-27). The operative principle behind these remarkably efficient heaters is an immense amount of thermal mass to store heat in between firings, and a greatly-elongated smoke path to extract as much heat as possible from a short, hot-burning fire (see **17-28** and **17-29**). Since the 1970s, the construction of "Russian fireplaces," *Kachelofen*, and other variations on traditional masonry, whole-house radiant heaters has become something of a cottage industry. Skilled craftspersons, do-it-yourself workshops, and detailed published plans are all available. Albie Barden of Norridgewock, Maine, in particular, has designed and built extremely sophisticated heaters that combine the functions of a fireplace, wood stove, and cookstove into a single unit, complete with a family-sized warming bench.

17-28 *A side view of the masonry heater showing air ports. This owner-built heater contains over 5000 bricks and took several weeks to complete.*

17-29 *The rear of the same heater is the bathroom/laundry room wall. A small wood stove tucked into a nook makes for a cozy bath on cold winter nights. Note the cleanout doors for the heater flues.*

18 Electrical Rough-In

If you happen to make a mistake plumbing your house, the worst that can happen is that you'll get wet or you'll have to replace some drywall. If you do the wrong thing with your wiring, you can burn your house down or kill yourself or someone else. Safety is the main reason why electrical codes are so very fussy. Although they may vary in minor details, local codes generally conform to the NEC (National Electrical Code, which is published by the NFPA). The actual NEC book is so dense and impenetrable that almost no one (except maybe the electrical inspector) actually reads it. Instead, most electricians rely on any of several guidebooks to interpret the NEC. Since codes are constantly being revised and updated to reflect new materials and new ways of thinking about old methods, make sure that whatever guide book you use is based on the current code. Don't forget that local codes always take precedence over national ones. Check with your local electrical inspector to find out if there are any differences which will affect your house wiring (see 18-1).

Although they may seem like the consummate bureaucratic obstacle course, electrical codes are truly a repository of time-tested and proven wisdom. Bear in mind, the purpose of an electrical inspection is to guarantee the safety of your wiring. Even if you are building in a rural area beyond the boundaries of code jurisdiction, it would be utterly foolhardy to ignore or circumvent code recommendations.

Many do-it-yourselfers draw the line at electrical wiring because they're afraid of electricity. This isn't necessarily an irrational fear. Without an understanding of how it works, anyone whose ever been on the receiving end of a shock or seen the explosive flash of a short circuit can't help but regard invisible electricity as a menacing and capricious force.

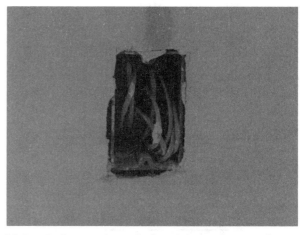

18-1 *Only experienced electricians who use the same system for each house will rough their wires into boxes without labeling them. Although it's a lot easier to do before the finish walls are installed, most building inspectors won't allow you to wire outlets and switches until after the drywall is up.*

Although it's a shopworn analogy, thinking about electricity as a kind of plumbing really does help demystify it (see 18-2). Water is pumped from a reservoir through a pipe under pressure, which is measured in pounds-per-square-inch (psi). A generator creates an electrical pressure, called *voltage*, forcing it to flow through a *conductor* (the wire). Just as the rate of flow as measured in gallons-per-minute depends on the diameter of the pipe, the *amperage* of an electrical flow depends on the size of the conductor (its *ampacity*).

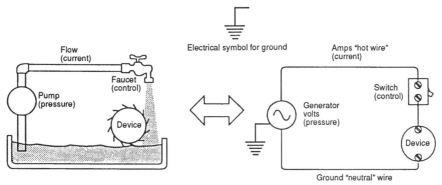

18-2 *The flow of electricity and the way it does work is similar to water power.*

18-3 *Electrical load calculation and typical appliance loads.*

	Item	Actual Rating	Result
Heating and Air-Conditioning Load	65% of central electric heat 100% of air conditioning	65% × 14,000 100% of 9,700	7,800 watts 9,700 watts
Required Other Loads	General lighting-3 watts per square foot Small appliance circuits-1,500 watts each Laundry circuit-1,500 watts or name plate	3,000 sq. ft. × 3 watts 3 circuits × 1,500 1,200-watts	9,000 watts 4,500 watts 1,500 watts
Other (Major Appliance) Loads	Clothes drier-5,000 watts or name plate Dishwasher Water heater Range Oven	5,500-watt 1,200-watt 4,500-watts 7,400-watt 9,500 watt	5,500 watts 1,200 watts 4,500 watts 7,400 watts 9,500 watts
	Total of other loads		**43,600 watts**
Derating the Total Load	First 10 kW of other load at 100% Remainder of other load at 40% Heating or air conditioning load, whichever is larger	100% of 10,000 40% × 33,600	10,000 watts 13,440 watts 9,700 watts
	Total derated load in watts		**33,140 watts**
Load in amperes (watts ÷ volts)		33,140 ÷ 240	**138 amperes**

Typical Appliance Loads

Appliance		Watts	Appliance		Watts
Air conditioner	Room, 7,000 Btu/hr	800	Humidifier	Portable	80
	Central, 35,000 Btu/hr	5,000	Iron		1,100
Blanket		200	Light bulb		rated
Blender		375	Microwave	Small	1,200
Clothes dryer	Electric	5,800		Large	1,800
	Gas	500	Mixer		200
Clothes washer		600	Motor, running	¼ hp	600
Coffee maker		1,000		⅓ hp	660
Computer	Personal	60		½ hp	840
Copy machine		1,500		¾ hp	1,140
Dehumidifier	25 pints/day	575		1 hp	1,320
Dishwasher		1,000		1-½ hp	1,820
Disposal		400		2 hp	2,400
Electric heat	Baseboard/foot	250		3 hp	3,360
Fan	Attic	500	Projector		360
	Bath	100	Range		12,000
	Kitchen	250	Refrigerator	Frost-free	350
	Ceiling	50		Regular	300
	Window, 20-inch	275	Sewing machine		90
Freezer		500	Stereo	40 watts/channel	225
Fryer, deep fat		1,500	Sunlamp		275
Frying pan		1,200	TV, color	9-inch	30
Furnace	Blower	1,000		21-inch	120
	Oil burner	300	Toaster/oven		1,200
Hair curler		1,200	Vacuum cleaner		650
Hair dryer		1,200	Waffle iron	Single	600
Heat lamp		250		Double	1,200
Heater	Portable radiant	1,500	Water heater	(per element)	4,500
Heating pad		75	Water pump	Shallow	660
Hot plate	Per burner	800		Deep	1,320

The friction that arises between flowing water and the walls of a pipe is measured in *poises*. The electrical equivalent to friction is *resistance*, which is measured in *ohms*. In plumbing systems, friction causes a pressure drop which is proportional to the length and size of the pipe. In electrical systems, resistance converts voltage into heat. The resultant *voltage drop* is also proportionate to the diameter of the conductor and its length. To keep the heat buildup within safe limits, electrical cables must be correctly sized for the loads they carry. Resistance heating elements exploit this property of electrical flow.

Together, the pressure and flow rate of a stream of water exerts a force (*horsepower*) that will do useful work when it encounters a device such as a turbine that converts it into kinetic energy. The measure of this force, electrically speaking, is *wattage*. Electrical energy does work when it is converted into other forms of energy such as heat, light, sound, and motion by devices such as heating coils, light bulbs, stereos, and motors. A *kilowatt-hour* (*kwh*, or 1000 watts used for one hour) is a measure of how much work is being done.

Other devices such as switches and circuit breakers act as control valves for the electrical flow just as a faucet or pressure-relief valve controls a plumbing circuit.

Although it stretches the plumbing analogy a bit, just as spent water ultimately returns to the reservoir or the pump through the ground water cycle, an electrical circuit isn't complete unless it returns to the generator, or, more accurately, to *ground*. While it's not quite that simple, you can think of an electrical circuit as a continuous loop between a distant source and your house, with a "hot" wire that carries the current to you and a "neutral" wire that returns it back to its source (i.e., the ground). Conceptually, a ground is the base state. It's where the difference in potential that gives rise to an electric current returns to zero. In practical terms, it's the actual connection of all parts of an electrical system to a conductor in direct contact with the earth, which is the ultimate ground. Because electricity, like water, seeks the path of least resistance to ground, a solid ground connection protects you against lethal shock since, under most circumstances, your body offers more resistance to an electrical current than a copper conductor.

The practice of wiring also has its plumbing analogs: to avoid leaks, use the right-size pipes, and the right kind of fittings, and orient them in the proper direction, install safety relief vents and traps in the right places, separate drainage from supply, and—most important—don't leave the water on while you work on the pipes.

The relationship between these various aspects of an electrical current are expressed mathematically in *Ohm's law* which states that $Amps = Volts/Ohms$ or, to put it in another more immediately useful way, $Watts = Volts \times Amps$ (also, $Amps = Watts/Volts$). As will be made clear elsewhere in this chapter, this equation is basically all you need to design your electrical system.

CIRCUIT DESIGN AND LOAD CALCULATIONS

Before you can bring power into your house, you'll have to estimate the overall system demand so that you can size the service entrance cable and other components accordingly. Today, a 100-amp *service* is the bare minimum for an average house without any electrical resistance heaters (this category includes an electric range or oven). A 150-amp or even a 200-amp service would be more sensible for a larger house or an ordinary house with a workshop. The extra capacity is a lot less expensive to install up-front than to retrofit in the future. A 200-amp service is always needed for any electrically heated house.

According to the NEC, all household wiring systems must have a base capacity of three watts per square foot of living area for lighting. For the purpose of calculation, "living area" includes the attic (if it's used for storage) and the basement. Crawl spaces, open porches, and garages are not included. In this case, "lighting" is assumed to provide receptacles for such appliances as the radio, TV, stereo, computer, vacuum cleaner, and so on.

The code requires at least two *small-appliance circuits* rated for 1500 watts each. These circuits serve such high-wattage small kitchen appliances as toaster ovens, blenders, and coffee makers and are included as fixed loads in the calculation.

The code specifically requires a *special purpose circuit* for the washing machine. This circuit is considered a fixed 1500-watt (or the name-plate rating of the machine, whichever is higher) load which must be included in the load base calculation, whether you have a washing machine or not. If you have an electric clothes dryer, it's entered at the higher of 5000 watts or 125 percent of the name-plate rating.

All other major appliances, such as the refrigerator, range, oven, freezer, dishwasher, air-conditioner, water pump, furnace blower, portable radiant heaters, fixed baseboard heaters, and stationary power tools or any other motor-driven device are entered into the calculation at their rated name-plate wattages.

Since some kinds of appliances will never be used at the same time (e.g., an air-conditioner and a central furnace), the code allows you to include the larger and ignore the smaller of these *noncoincident* loads in your calculations. But don't include either central air-conditioning or central electric heat in your load calculation just yet.

Begin by adding up the wattages of the general lighting load, the total for any fixed electric baseboard heaters, the small appliance circuits, the laundry circuit, the clothes dryer circuit, and all of the loads of the major appliances (see 18-3).

Since it's highly unlikely that all the appliances and all the lights will be on at the same time, the code *derates* part of the load. Use 100 percent of the first 10,000 watts and 40 percent of the remainder. Then add the greater of 65 percent of the heating load for central electric heat (i.e., an electric boiler, *not* baseboard heaters) or 100 percent of the central air-conditioning load to get the total derated load in watts. Multiply the total wattage by 240 (which is the household voltage at the service panel) to find the total load in amps.

After determining the capacity of the service entrance panel and its main breaker, you'll know what size cable to use for delivering power to it from the utility power drop. In the United States, most service cable is aluminum, since copper is just too expensive, even though smaller conductors can be used for the same amount of power (see **18-4**).

18-4 *Service cable selection.*

Service panel amperage	Aluminum cable	Copper cable
100	No. 2	No. 4
125	No. 1/0	No. 2
150	No. 2/0	No. 1/0
200	No. 4/0	No. 2/0

At the service entrance panel, the power feeds through a main breaker into individual branch circuits, each controlled by its own breaker. The capacity of your service isn't the same thing as the total amperage of your branch circuits. The demand calculation is for sizing service entrance capacity only and doesn't have anything to do with determining the actual number of individual branch circuits or their amperage rating. If all the breakers you could fit into a 100-amp panel drew a full load at the same time, you'd exceed the capacity of the main breaker by a factor of at least three.

Although the code doesn't tell you exactly how many circuits you need, it does tell you which ones are absolutely required and what their minimum amperage ratings should be (see **18-5**).

18-5 *Branch circuit amperages.*

Circuit purpose	Breaker Amperage
General lighting	15 or 20
Small appliance	20
Clothes washer	20
Non-motor appliance	Name plate rating (rounded up)
Motorized appliance	125 percent of name-plate rating*

*Motors initially draw more amps when they start than they do when running. If the motor drawing three amps or more is on the same circuit with other devices, the 125 percent rule is applied only to the largest motor and the name-plate rating is used for all the others.

The three watt-per-square-foot rule works out to one 15-amp circuit for every 600 sq ft, or one 20-amp circuit for 800 sq ft. The code doesn't specifically limit the number of fixtures and receptacles served by each general lighting circuit. But, as a rule of thumb, a 15-amp circuit shouldn't supply more than 12 outlets or a 20-amp circuit more than 16. Try to arrange it so that each general circuit carries, more or less, the same number of fixtures. When determining how many fixtures to run on a circuit, bear in mind that circuit design assumes a safe working load, not the maximum rating. Thus, although 15 amps times 220 volts equals 1800 watts, you shouldn't put more than 1650 watts worth of demand on that circuit. Likewise, for a 20-amp circuit (2400 watts maximum) limit the working load to 2200 watts.

What the code does require is a light controlled by a switch in each habitable room, hallway, stairwell, and attached garage. Except for the particular cases of the kitchen, bath, and entrance door, these lights don't necessarily have to be permanent fixtures; you can plug a lamp into a switch-controlled outlet.

Electric baseboard heaters require a 20-amp, 240-volt circuit for each individually controlled unit. However, units can be ganged in series as long as their total wattage doesn't exceed 2200 watts at 240 volts.

One duplex outlet should be provided for every six feet of uninterrupted wall space. The sum of all the appliance ratings served by a lighting circuit shouldn't be more than half the circuit rating, and no single appliance should exceed 80 percent of the rating.

The 20-amp small appliance circuits can't be used to serve receptacles in rooms other than the kitchen, dining, family room or pantry, or light fixtures in any room. But they can serve the refrigerator or freezer. The kitchen must have at least two circuits, each serving no more than six duplex outlets spaced four feet along the countertops. One or more of these circuits has to supply the dining room, family room, or pantry as well.

In addition to the laundry circuit, separate circuits are required for each fixed appliance that draws 1000 watts or more and for any motor larger than one-half horsepower. Special-purpose appliance circuits can be either 120 volt or 240 volt. The appliances can be wired directly to a circuit or else plugged into a receptacle located within six feet.

As a general principle, route the most circuits and put the most outlets where there is the greatest demand. Locate appliances so that those that draw the most power are closest to the service entrance. Shortening the cable run saves on expensive, large cables and also minimizes voltage drop.

Finally, the code also requires swimming pool, outdoor, bathroom, and other outlets in wet locations to be protected by a special *ground-fault interrupter (GFI)*. A "fault" is a technical term for a short-circuit. This is what happens when something crosses the hot wire and provides the current with a low-resistance path to ground. So much current flows through a short circuit that it blows the fuse or trips the circuit breaker almost instantly. However, there's another more insidious kind of short-circuit. In a *high-resistance fault*, minute leaks of current to a ground can occur without tripping the breaker. When a better path to ground is inadvertently provided, (for example, when you contact the hot wire of a frayed extension cord while standing barefoot on concrete), the current surge can be lethal. The GFI senses these microscopic current leaks and turns off the circuit.

GFI protection can be provided in two ways: either by special GFI outlets at the point of use or by installing a GFI breaker in the service panel to protect an entire circuit (see **18-6**).

As is the case for service entrance cable, there's an appropriate size wire for the amperage of each branch circuit (see **18-7**).

18-7 *Cable size for circuit load.*

Ampacity	Wire size (AWG)*	Use category
7	No. 18	Flexible cords, low voltage systems
10	No. 16	Extension cords, doorbells
15	No. 14	Lighting circuits (code permitting)
20	No. 12	Small appliance, lighting, general-purpose circuits
30	No. 10	Appliances 120v–240 volts
40	No. 8	Appliances 120v–240 volts
55	No. 6	Appliances, 240 volts, service ground wires
70	No. 4	Appliances, 240 volts, service ground wires
95	No. 2	Service entrance, service ground wire
110	No. 1	Service entrance, service ground wire
125	No. 1/0	Service entrance wires
145	No. 2/0	Service entrance wires
165	No. 3/0	Service entrance wires
195	No. 4/0	Service entrance wires

*AWG = American Wire Gauge, i.e., standard sizes.
NOTE: Ampacities listed are for *copper* wire, except SE cables, which are listed for aluminum. If you use copper, use the next lowest size.

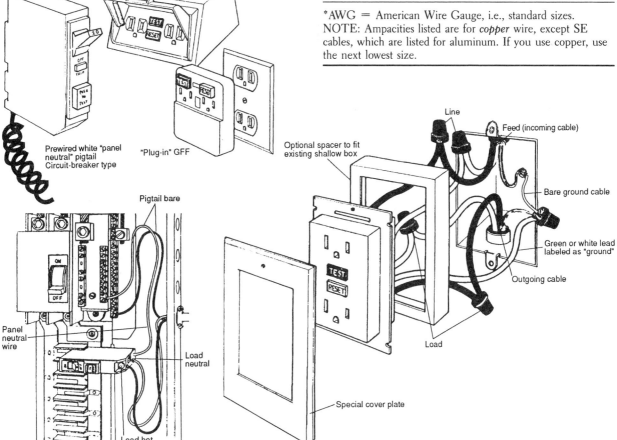

18-6 *Installing GFI protection. When more than one outlet on the same circuit requires protection it's more economical to wire them to a GFI circuit breaker installed in the service entrance panel.*

Amps	Watts	No. 14	No. 12	No. 10	No. 8	No. 6	No. 4	No. 2	No. 1/0	No. 2/0
1	120	450	700	1100	2800	4500	7000			
2	240	225	350	550	900	1400	2200	3500		
3	360	150	240	350	600	900	1500	2300	3750	
4	480	110	175	275	450	700	1100	1750	2750	3500
5	600	90	140	220	360	560	880	1400	2250	2800
7.5	900	60	95	150	240	375	600	950	1500	1900
10	1.2 kw	45	70	110	180	280	450	700	1100	1400
15	1.8 kw	30	45	70	120	180	300	475	750	950
20	2.4 kw	22	35	55	90	140	225	350	550	700
25	3 kw	18	28	45	70	110	180	280	450	560
30	3.6 kw	15	25	35	60	90	150	235	340	470
35	4.2 kw		20	30	50	80	125	200	320	400
40	4.8 kw		17	27	45	70	110	175	280	350
45	5.4 kw			25	40	60	100	155	250	310
50	6 kw			22	35	55	90	140	225	280
60	7.2 kw				30	45	75	120	185	240
70	8.4 kw				25	40	65	100	160	200
80	9.6 kw					35	55	85	140	180
90	10.8 kw					30	50	75	125	160
100	12 kw					28	45	70	115	140

**In the United States, the standard residential voltages are nominally 120 and 240 volts. At one time they were 110 and 120 volts. Until it was revised in 1987, the NEC used voltage values of 115 and 230 as a basis for calculations. This explains the confusion when an electrician or builder mentions "one-ten," "two-twenty," or "one-twenty two-forty" indiscriminately or you read 115 or 230 in older wiring manuals and find 110v or 220v ratings stamped on old wiring devices.

However, increasing the length of the wire increases its resistance which in turn lowers the voltage (see **18-8**). Excessive voltage drop not only burns out motors, but it creates heat which could melt the insulation, cause sparking, and a hazardous short-circuit. This is why it's always a good idea to keep all circuits as short as possible. The table below gives the maximum length for a circuit that will limit voltage drop to an acceptable maximum of two percent using type "T" or "TW" wires.*

To double the length of the run or the ampacity of the circuit without changing the wire size or rate of voltage drop, wire the circuit for 240 volts (e.g., a ⅖ service cable at 240 volts can be 280 feet long). The circuit length table in **18-7** is quite useful for figuring cable runs for heavy-appliance circuits.

*Cable type designations indicate the type of insulation and its properties: "T" denotes "Thermoplastic," "W" is "Water-resistant," "H" is "Heat-resistant" and "R" is Rubber. Type is printed on the cable jacket. Type T and TW are standard for residential wiring. Type RH, RHW, THW, are rated for higher ampacities. SE (Service Entrance), USE (Underground Service Entrance), and UF (Underground Feeder) cable are often marked with a temperature rating instead of type marker. 60°C is equivalent to type TW or T; 75°C is the same as types RH, RHW, and THW. Circuit lengths listed in italics cannot use Type T or TW cable. Use type THW, RH, or RHW, as local codes allow.

TYPES OF CABLE

Each kind of cable has special properties suited to its particular function. Service entrance (SE) cable has large-diameter, stranded conductors that can carry a heavy current. The thick, tough neoprene-rubber insulation resists moisture and heat. In the United States, since 1941, power has been delivered from the transformer at the utility pole to the house by a three-wire circuit. Two of these wires are hot, the third is neutral (see **18-9**). If you measure the voltage across both hot "legs," it will be 240 volts. If you measure it between either leg and ground, it will be 120 volts. This particular system makes it possible to deliver two different voltages to the house; 240 volts for power-hungry appliances and relatively safe 120 volts for general purposes.

Power from the pole can be carried either by three separate, insulated conductors, or by *triplex* cable which consists of two insulated conductors braided around a bare aluminum neutral conductor (see **18-10**). The conductors of *USE* (Underground Service Entrance) cable suitable for direct burial must be larger than above-ground cable since they won't be able to dissipate excess heat into the surrounding air. USE cable consists of three insulated conductors; two black live wires and one yellow neutral. Whether the cable is run through conduit or directly buried, all its conductors must be insulated.

If an overhead power connection is not run through conduit, type *SEC* (Service Entrance Concentric) cable

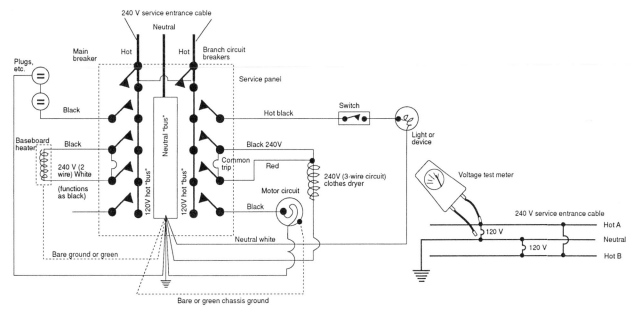

18-9 *Schematic of typical residential service circuit. The standard 240-volt service drop makes twice as much power (total wattage) available with minimal voltage drop. The schematic shows how the power is "split" into two legs for standard service circuits or combined for heavy-duty circuits.*

(refer to **18-10**) is used to bring it from the wall or roof anchor down into the meter box and from the meter box to the service entrance panel. This cable contains two insulated hot conductors completely wrapped in a braided aluminum neutral and covered with a sunlight- and water-resistant, grey plastic jacket.

In *SER* (Service Entrance Round) cable, the neutral is an insulated white or grey wire (refer to **18-10**). The plastic jacket also contains a separate, bare ground wire. SER is generally used only between an outside disconnect switch and the service panel.

Today, most residential wiring is done with inexpensive, lightweight plastic-jacketed *NM* (nonmetallic) cable, commonly known as *Romex*—the name of the most well-known brand (see **18-11**). Romex's flexibility makes it easy to connect to devices and snake through walls. It's available in No. 14, No. 12, and No. 10 gauges, with two or three, color-coded conductors and a bare ground wire, wrapped with paper. Since the paper coating can absorb water, Romex is suitable only for indoor use, in dry locations.

In *UF* cable, the insulated wires are embedded in a solid jacket of fungus-, sunlight-, and corrosion-resistant cable which allows it to be directly buried in the ground. UF cable is ideal for running branch circuits to outbuildings, under decks, or wherever the wiring will be exposed to the rigors of outdoor conditions.

NMC is another type of embedded, water-resistant cable (refer to **18-11**) suitable for both dry and damp locations such as cellars. But the plastic isn't quite as durable as UF cable; NMC can't be used underground.

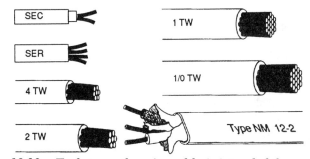

18-10 *Each type of service cable is intended for a specific, recommended use only. Always check your local code for permitted usages.*

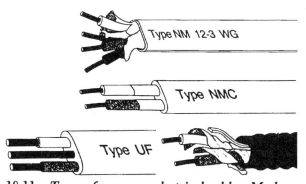

18-11 *Types of common electrical cables. Modern house wiring is done almost exclusively with easy-to-use, plastic-jacketed (Romex) cable.*

451

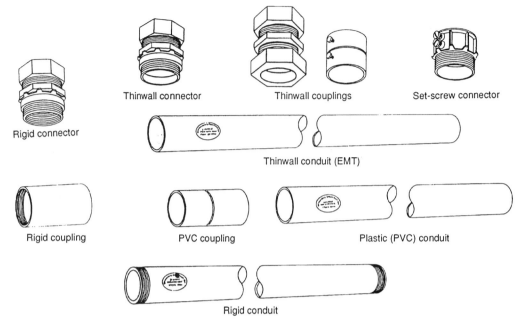

18-12 *Common types of conduit. Thinwall and PVC plastic conduit are easy to work with.*

Armored cable (AC), popularly known as "BX," is wrapped with a coiled steel jacket that protects the wires against physical damage. Because it will rust, BX cable is never permitted in damp locations, such as barns, outdoor structures, or basements. A special lead-clad, steel-jacketed cable (ACL) is used for damp locations instead. Local codes in some municipalities won't allow BX cable anywhere in the home; in other communities, the code won't permit anything else; and in still others, it's required only for certain special applications, such as furnace and motor control wiring or where a wire must be embedded in masonry or plaster.

There is also a great deal of local variation between codes on the need to run wires in conduit and on the type of conduit required (see **18-12**). The term *conduit* refers to any tubing through which individual wires are run. Conduit differs from pipe in that it is thinner and has a very smooth interior so that wires will not snag on it. Each

of the several different kinds of conduit is available in 10-foot lengths, in standard sizes ranging from ½ inch to 2½ inches (even larger-diameter, rigid conduit is used for commercial applications). A full range of fittings is offered for both wet (outdoor) and dry (indoor) locations.

As might be expected, the code is quite explicit about the number and type of wires that can be run in a conduit of a given diameter (see **18-13**). Most circuit installations use type THHN wire because its thinner size and high ampacity permit more wires or more amperage to run through the conduit than other types.

Basically, the NEC requires outdoor service wires to be protected by *rigid* (also called, *heavy-wall*) galvanized steel conduit wherever there's a risk of damage. Typical locations are where underground cable emerges from the ground and runs to a meter, or where the cable passes through a building wall or roof, or is laid beneath a concrete slab, sidewalk, or driveway.

18-13 *Conduit wire capacity.**

Conduit size, inches	No. 14		No. 12		Wire No. 10		Size No. 8		No. 6		No. 4		No. 2	
½	6	6	6	4	5	4	2							
¾			6	6	6	6	4	3	2	2				
1					6	6	5	5	4	4	3	3	2	2
1 + ¼							6	6	6	6	5	5	4	4
1 + ½									6	6	6	6	5	5
2											6	6	6	6

*The first entry in each column is for Type THW, the second italicized entry is for Type TW wire.

EMT (Electrical Mechanical Tubing) or *thin-wall* aluminum or steel conduit is used for many different applications. Almost all commercial or industrial wiring must be installed in conduit. The code often requires EMT conduit where wiring is run inside concrete blocks or over any masonry surface. It may be required for a wiring run over exposed ceiling joists or for furnace or other control wiring or for exposed outdoor wiring. EMT is soft enough to be bent with a special tool.

There are also two types of plastic conduit. Since it has fairly good UV-resistance, the familiar grey, PVC conduit is better for above-ground use than HDPE (high-density polyethylene) conduit which is primarily used underground. Where codes permit it, and there is no danger of mechanical damage, plastic conduit is an easy-to-use, low-cost alternative to EMT. Although it's completely waterproof and impervious to corrosion, it does have a tendency to sag when laid horizontally, especially outdoors, even with proper support. With inadequate support the sections can sag enough to pull wire connections apart.

Some applications may call for *Greenfield* conduit, which is basically identical to BX armored cable without the wires.

Whatever type of cable you use, the color code for the wires it contains is universal and must *always* be followed. A fundamental rule upon which the safety of the entire installation depends is: *the black wire is always hot.* In three and four wire circuits, *red and blue wires are also hot. White is always neutral.* There are only two exceptions to this rule. The first is where the white wire is used as an extension of the black wire in a *switch* leg circuit (refer to **18-44** below). The other is where the white wire is used as a hot lead for the other side of a 240-volt circuit where no neutral is required (the bare ground conductor does the job), such as a baseboard heater circuit. In both cases, the white conductor must be *painted black* (use a felt-tip marker) at the fixture connection.

The second fundamental wiring safety rule is: *never switch or fuse the white wire.* Circuit breakers, switches, or any other circuit control devices are always installed in the hot wire. The neutral wire must never be interrupted (when you connect the white wires to both terminals of a plug in the middle of a run they are joined by an internal jumper).

A bare copper conductor is the continuous, system *ground wire*, which must be mechanically bonded to every steel box, circuit device, and other ground wire. A green wire, or a green-and-yellow-striped wire, is a chassis ground. This is required for protection against a short circuit between a motor and its metal case. In an extension cord, it also functions as a continuous ground.

The color code also applies to the wiring devices themselves. The *black wire* is always connected to the *brass-colored terminals.* The *white wire* goes on the *silver-colored terminals.* Since switches are only installed across a hot wire, both terminals are bronze. With a three-way or four-way switch, two or three hot wires are required. To prevent mix ups, the terminal for the feed wire (the *common*) is black.

The bare *ground conductor* is always connected to the *green terminal.*

"Crossing" a wire by attaching a white wire to a bronze terminal or a black to silver will normally trip the circuit breaker. Installing a switch across the white wire will turn a light off or on, but it will also leave dangerous current flowing through the wires and could leave the rest of the circuit without a good ground.

WIRING THE SERVICE ENTRANCE

If you're going to install your own service entrance, you'll probably need to have your plans reviewed by the electric power company first. They may send a representative to show you where to put the meter and weather head or where the trenches for underground power will run. You'll need to prepare a drawing that shows the location of the service entrance and labels its components and the ratings of the cables and breakers in any case to get your electrical permit.

The choice of a wall-mount or a roof-mast weatherhead is decided by the code clearance requirements for overhead service drops (see **18-14**). Any overhead wires must be at

18-14 *A wedge clamp connects self-supporting "triplex" overhead service drop cable to a strain relief insulator on a crossbar clamped to the rigid conduit service mast above the roof. Note the service wires looped from the weatherhead to the overhead cables and the taped, split-bolt connectors ("bugs") that join them together.*

least 10 feet above lawns and patios, 12 feet above driveways, and 18 feet over streets and alleyways (see **18-15**). Furthermore, the weatherhead and the insulator rack must be at least three feet away from windows, porches, and fire escapes. If you can't gain the necessary height by running the service wire up along the rake, you'll have to use a roof mast instead. Any such mast must be at least 18 inches above the surface of the roof and no more than four feet in from its edge.

One advantage of triplex cable over the old-fashioned, three-wire service drop is that the bare stranded neutral conductor is also a guy wire that carries the weight of the other wires when it's attached to an insulated anchor screwed into the building wall or a bracket clamp on a roof mast, with a special wedge clamp.

In three-wire drops, each individual wire is anchored to a porcelain *insulator rack* lag-screwed through the wall into a stud (refer to **18-15**). Since your electric power company is usually responsible for running the cable from the pole to the weatherhead or mast, call them to find out which type of cable they use.

To install a wall-mounted service, plumb a line up from the meter box and screw the weatherhead mounting bracket into the wall at the appropriate height (see **18-16**). The center of the insulator rack or the screw-in triplex anchor must be 12 inches below the weatherhead and lagged into the closest stud. If there is no nearby stud,

nail horizontal blocking behind the wall, and bolt the insulator through it. Plywood sheathing alone won't hold an anchor against the weight of fifty or more feet of ice-coated triplex cable.

Center the SEC cable clamps over the plumb line, and screw them in loosely. The code requires a clamp every 4½ feet, starting above the top of the meter box. Measure the distance between the weatherhead and the meter box, and add five feet to get the length of the service cable. Electricians use a special, oversized nipping plier to cut service cable; you'll probably have to settle for a hacksaw. Strip three feet off the weatherhead end of the cable sheathing (make a cut along its length and a second cut around the base of the first, pull the jacket back and cut it off). Twist the neutral strands together at one side of the cable and trim the ragged ends even with a pair of diagonal cutting pliers.

Remove the weatherhead cap and slip the body down over the insulated wires, and bend them over the cut-out gaskets. Bend the bare neutral wire back so that it presses against the base of the weatherhead, and tighten the clamp screws. Snap the weatherhead cap back in place. Slip the weatherhead into its mounting bracket on the wall, and then feed the other end of the cable through a watertight hex-nut connector and into the meter box. Pull the cable tight, and then tighten down the cable clamps and the hex-nut fitting.

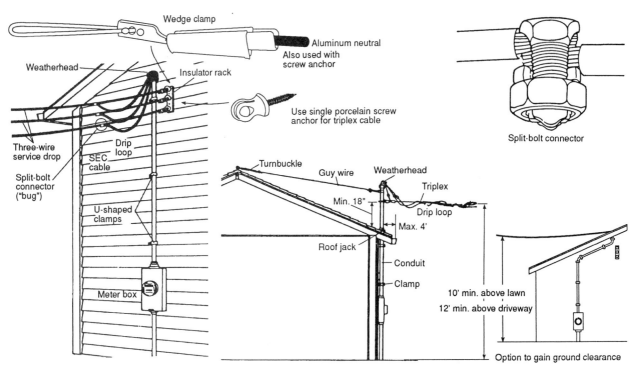

18-15 Triplex service drop cable has pretty much replaced the three wire service drop in modern installations. The electric power company normally runs this part of the service installation and "bugs" the cable (clamps with split-bolt connectors) to the service wire.

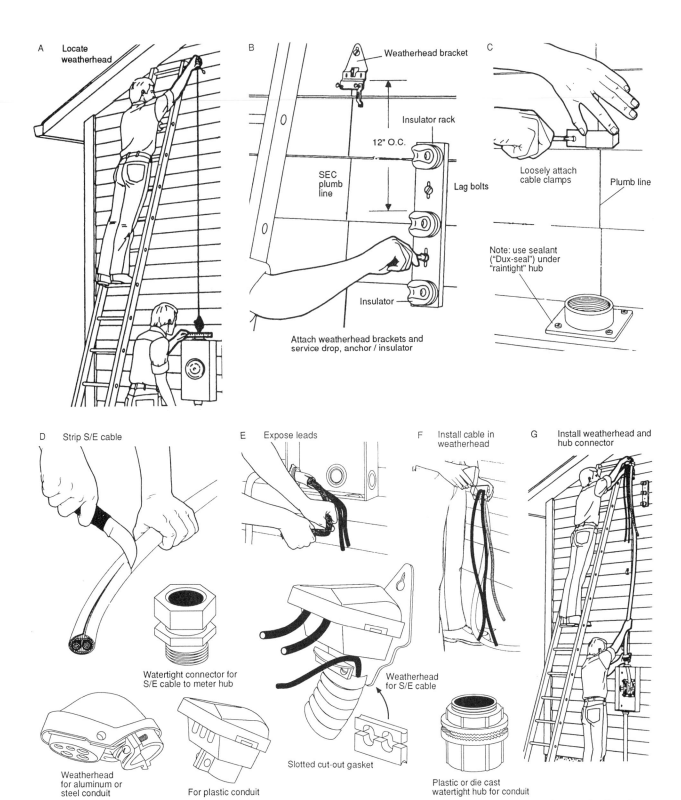

A Locate weatherhead

B Weatherhead bracket

Insulator rack

12" O.C.

SEC plumb line

Lag bolts

Insulator

Attach weatherhead brackets and service drop, anchor / insulator

C Loosely attach cable clamps

Plumb line

Note: use sealant ("Dux-seal") under "raintight" hub

D Strip S/E cable

Watertight connector for S/E cable to meter hub

Weatherhead for aluminum or steel conduit

For plastic conduit

E Expose leads

Weatherhead for S/E cable

Slotted cut-out gasket

F Install cable in weatherhead

Plastic or die cast watertight hub for conduit

G Install weatherhead and hub connector

18-16 *Installing a wall-mounted service drop. (A) Locate weatherhead on wall. (B) Attach weatherhead brackets and service drop anchor/insulator rack. (C) Loosely attach cable clamps. (D) Strip S/E cable. (E) Expose leads and twist strands together. (F) Install cable in weatherhead. (G) Hang weatherhead from bracket and run cable through raintight hub connector and attach to meter terminals.*

The electric power company usually connects the SEC wires when they run the service drop cable, after your installation passes inspection. If you ever have to work on this part of the power drop yourself or any part of the system ahead of the meter, have the power company shut off the service at the switch on the pole. To splice the weatherhead leads to the service drop cable, strip the insulation off the wires at a point about 18 inches back from the insulator (check local code). Coat the wires with *"No-Al-Ox"* (a special antioxidant compound which should always be used when joining aluminum wire to any terminal). The compound prevents oxidation which causes resistance and overheating and the eventual arcing that leads to short circuits and fires. (Since oxidation is also more rapid on roughened surfaces, take care to cut the ends of cables cleanly.) Clamp the wires together with *split-bolt connectors* (electricians call them *"bugs"*). Wrap each bugged splice completely with weather-resistant, *rubber* electrical tape. Ordinary vinyl tape breaks down when exposed to sunlight.

INSTALLING A ROOF-MOUNTED SERVICE MAST

Plumb a line up from the center of the meter hub to the eaves or rake soffit (see **18-17**). If the soffit board has already been installed, use a *bellhanger's bit* (a ¼-inch twist drill anywhere from one to three feet long, which is indispensable for running telephone wiring) to transfer the center mark to the top of the roof deck. Otherwise, drive a nail through the deck. Cut a hole through the roof (a reciprocating saw is handy for this job since it will cut shingles and wood with equal aplomb). Slide the rigid conduit mast up through it from below, and screw it into the hub. Slip a *roof jack* (which is what electricians call the preformed flashing boot that plumbers use to seal 1½-inch vent pipes) over the mast, and cut the shingles to fit around it as you would for any roof penetration. Slide the ends of the SEC cable (or individual conductors as code requires) through the weatherhead (leave three feet for the drip loop and drop splice), and pull the cable down into the conduit until you can slip the weatherhead over the end of the mast. Tighten the weatherhead set screws.

Attach a clamp to the mast just below the weatherhead and run a No. 6 steel guywire from the clamp to a turnbuckle hooked over a screw eye at the ridge of the roof (some codes may require solid bracing instead), and take up the slack.

Attach a clamp-on insulator to the mast 12 inches beneath the weatherhead for triplex service drop cable. Clamp-on racks are also available for three-wire drops. Secure the mast to the wall with circular conduit clamps spaced 4½ feet apart.

INSTALLING THE METER SOCKET

Although the electric power company owns the meter, it's your job to install the box that holds it (see **18-18**).

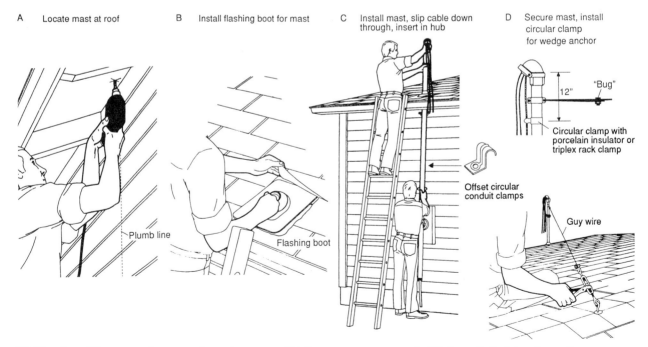

A   Locate mast at roof   B   Install flashing boot for mast   C   Install mast, slip cable down through, insert in hub   D   Secure mast, install circular clamp for wedge anchor

Plumb line

Flashing boot

Offset circular conduit clamps

"Bug"   12"

Circular clamp with porcelain insulator or triplex rack clamp

Guy wire

18-17   *Installing a roof-mounted service mast. (A) Locate mast at roof. (B) Install flashing boot for mast. (C) Install mast, slip cable down through, insert in hub. (D) Secure mast, install circular clamp for wedge anchor.*

Strip the appropriate amount of sheathing from the SEC and twist the ground conductors into a wire. The two hot leads from the weatherhead connect to the upper screw clamp terminals (see 18-19). The neutral wire slips into the center screw clamp. (If the meter is serving an underground conduit, the incoming wires must run up inside the box and bend so that they still enter the top side of the meter socket. Otherwise, someone could mistakenly assume that the power was off on the lower side when the meter was pulled.) The two hot wires that run to the service entrance panel are connected to the lower pair of side terminals. The neutral shares the same center terminal with the incoming neutral. As mentioned above, always coat the wires with No-Al-Ox before inserting them in the screw terminals. Make sure that the terminals are marked *Cu-Al*, which indicates that they're safe for use with either copper or aluminum. Never attach aluminum wire to a terminal marked *Cu*.

The body of the meter has four prongs that plug into the socket. "Pulling the meter" has exactly the same effect on the household electrical system as pulling the plug does on an appliance. Removing the meter is the easiest way to guarantee that all the power will be shut off when you need to work on the entrance panel or any point of the service run up to the meter input.

Unless you're experienced in working with electricity, it's a lot safer to hire an electrician when you need a meter pulled. Since there's no circuit breaker on the incoming line, *accidental contact with the live side of a meter is likely to be fatal.*

Before you can touch the meter, you'll need a *permit from the electric power company* to cut the sealed wire tag that locks the retaining collar clamp around the meter. Depending on the policy of your local utility, you may or may not be allowed to do this yourself. They might send someone out to do it for you, or tell you to hire an electrician. You'll also need to notify them when you reinstall the meter so that a new seal can be put on it.

18-18 *This meter socket has been wired by the owner with type SER cable. The primary side of the meter will be connected to the incoming service drop. Note the lugs in the bottom of the meter panel and the ground wire that connects to the buried ground rod. Also note the incoming telephone wires that will connect to the system interface visible in the lower right hand corner.*

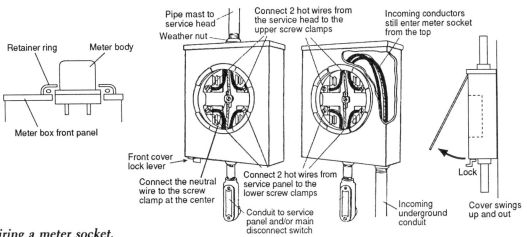

18-19 *Wiring a meter socket.*

Retainer ring   Meter body

Meter box front panel

Pipe mast to service head
Weather nut

Connect 2 hot wires from the service head to the upper screw clamps

Incoming conductors still enter meter socket from the top

Front cover lock lever

Connect the neutral wire to the screw clamp at the center

Connect 2 hot wires from service panel to the lower screw clamps

Conduit to service panel and/or main disconnect switch

Incoming underground conduit

Lock

Cover swings up and out

There are several safety precautions that will protect you from serious harm in case you accidentally contact the hot side of the socket while removing the meter. Wear rubber-soled shoes, and stand on a rubber door mat laid over a ¾-inch thick square of plywood to isolate you from direct contact with earth or concrete. After cutting and removing the seal, remove the retaining collar which is usually held in place by a tension tab (see **18-20**). If your meter has a screw-type clamp instead, loosen it with an insulated electrician's screwdriver (only the tip is exposed metal). Slide the locking lever of the meter box front plate out of its slot and lift the plate off the meter. If you didn't

wear them when cutting the seal, slip on a pair of heavy rubber gloves, and, grasping the meter with both hands, pull it downwards and outwards at the same time so that the live-side prongs slip out first.

Depending on your electric power company's requirements, you may have to insert a glass safety cover plate into the meter retaining collar and reinstall it, or slip plastic insulators over the live-side meter prongs and reinstall the meter.

With the exception of the heavy rubber gloves, which are too clumsy for delicate work, all of these safeguards should be observed whenever you work around a live ser-

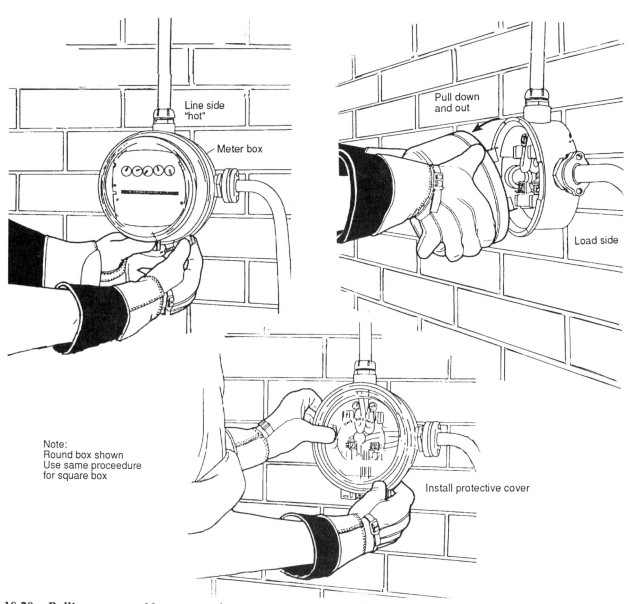

18-20 *Pulling a meter. Note: a round meter socket is shown. The procedure is the same with a standard rectangular meter box.*

458

vice panel or circuit. As a general rule, you should always shut off the power whenever you do any electrical work. But sometimes, there's no way to avoid working around a partially live panel unless you pull the meter. To reduce the chances of accidentally short-circuiting a live wire or getting a nasty shock, work with insulated screw drivers, pliers, and wire strippers. Always keep one hand in your hip pocket or behind your back; putting both hands into a live circuit lets current flow directly through your heart. Never assume a circuit is turned off just because the circuit breaker is switched off. Make sure there is no power in the location that you're about to work on by testing all the power leads and terminals with a meter (see 18-21).

INSTALLING A SEPARATE DISCONNECT SWITCH

One way to avoid the inconvenience of having to pull a meter when you want to shut off all the power to the panel is to add a separate main disconnect switch on the outside of the house between the meter and the panel (see 18-22). Locating a power shutoff outside the house is also a good safeguard for basements subjected to seasonal flooding.

A disconnect switch is simply a main circuit breaker mounted in its own weatherproof enclosure. In some installations (mobile home power drops, for example) the disconnect switch is combined with the meter enclosure.

The code requires the disconnect switch to be installed close to the meter. Connect the meter box to the disconnect box with a *nipple* (any short length of threaded conduit or pipe up to 12 inches long). Thread a lock-nut washer and plastic bushing over the ends of the nipple, and run SEC conductors from the meter output terminals to the hot side of the disconnect switch.

18-21 *Safety test for service panel. Touch one lead of the tester to the neutral bus (or box frame) and the other to the individual circuit breaker or power bus (when the main breaker has been shut off) to make sure there is no current in the circuit you intend to work on.*

18-22 *This outdoor service entrance contains a disconnect switch (under the cover immediately below the meter socket) a meter panel and a service panel all in one weatherproof unit. Note the telephone interface next to the conduit and the electrical inspector's approval ticket on the panel body.*

To remove a multiring *knockout*, drive the center knockout ring inwards with a nailset or screwdriver (see **18-23**). The tip should be placed halfway between the knockout ties. Work the knockout free from the inside of the box by twisting it back and forth with pliers.

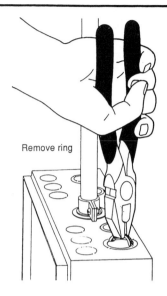

Remove ring

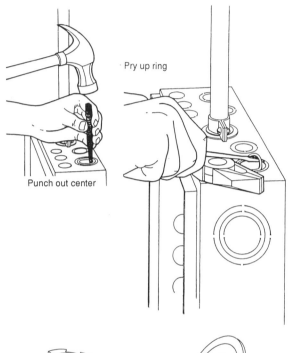

Pry up ring

Punch out center

Remove the next concentric ring by prying it upwards on both sides with the tip of a screwdriver until you can grip it with the pliers and twist it free. If you mistakenly remove a knockout or make it too large, the unneeded hole must be filled in with a snap-in filler blank or a *knockout reducing* washer. These fillers are a lifesaver for recycling second-hand panel boxes.

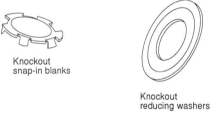

Knockout
snap-in blanks

Knockout
reducing washers

Fill-in unused knockout holes

Knockout
filler plate

18-23   *Removing and filling panel knockouts. (1) Punch out center. (2) Pry up ring. (3) Remove ring by twisting. The code requires any unused knockouts to be filled in.*

The code also requires the disconnect switch to be connected to the service panel by SER cable, which contains an insulated neutral as well as a bare stranded ground wire (see **18-24**). The neutral runs to the neutral lug on the service panel. The bare, SER ground wire runs to a separate grounding bar added to the panel. A heavy (No. 4 or No. 6) bare stranded copper ground wire runs from the input neutral lug of the disconnect to the system ground electrode. Depending on the type of cable used,

the location of the various components, and local code requirements, the connections between the meter box and/or disconnect switch and the service panel will most likely run through some form of conduit (see **18-25**).

With an overhead SEC drop, no conduit may be required. Instead, the cable bends to make a drip loop under the meter before running directly through a wood wall. It's protected at the point of entrance by a special *sill plate* and waterproofed with electrical sealing compound.

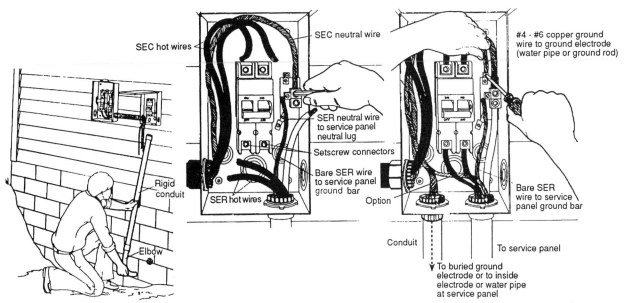

18-24 *Wiring for disconnect switch. Push SEC leads through a nipple from the meter box to the disconnect switch. A No. 4 or No. 6 bare copper ground wire is run from the disconnect ground lug to an outside buried grounding electrode, or else run in the same conduit as the SER cable and connected to an electrode inside the cellar or on a water pipe.*

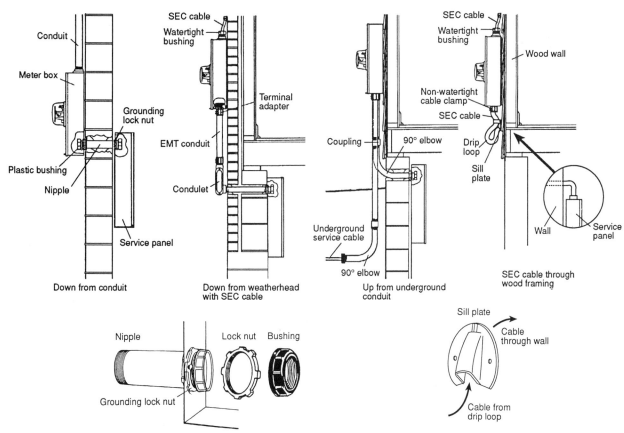

18-25 *Typical entrance configurations and hardware.*

Weatherproof pressure connector

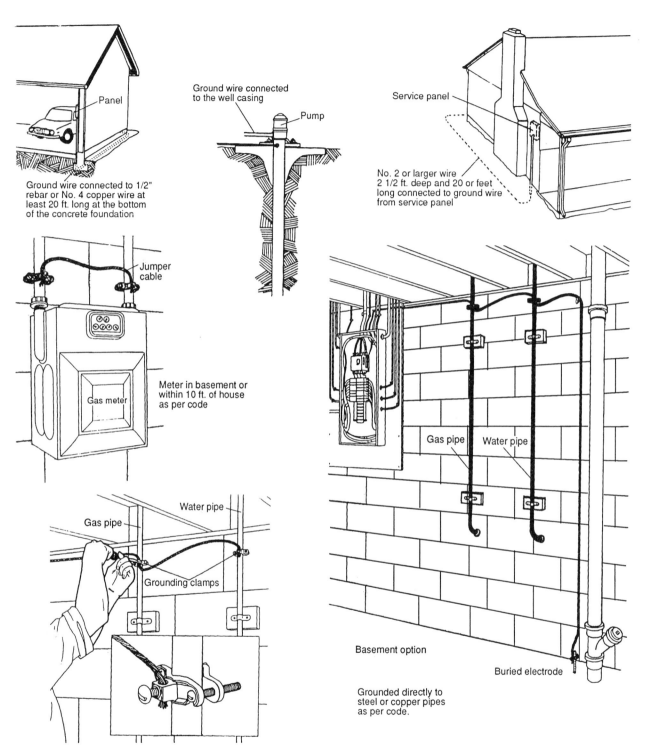

Panel

Ground wire connected to 1/2" rebar or No. 4 copper wire at least 20 ft. long at the bottom of the concrete foundation

Ground wire connected to the well casing

Pump

Service panel

No. 2 or larger wire 2 1/2 ft. deep and 20 or feet long connected to ground wire from service panel

Jumper cable

Gas meter

Meter in basement or within 10 ft. of house as per code

Water pipe

Gas pipe

Grounding clamps

Gas pipe   Water pipe

Basement option

Buried electrode

Grounded directly to steel or copper pipes as per code.

18-26 *Buried grounding electrodes are typically used in rural locations where the water pipe to the house is likely to be plastic. Some codes or local conditions may require grounding with a buried 20-foot-long copper cable. Where the municipal water service runs through steel pipes, the system is grounded to it inside the cellar. Since there may be no direct internal bond between the incoming and outgoing sides of a water or gas meter, a jumper cable is clamped to the pipes on each side of the meter to insure a continuous ground.*

462

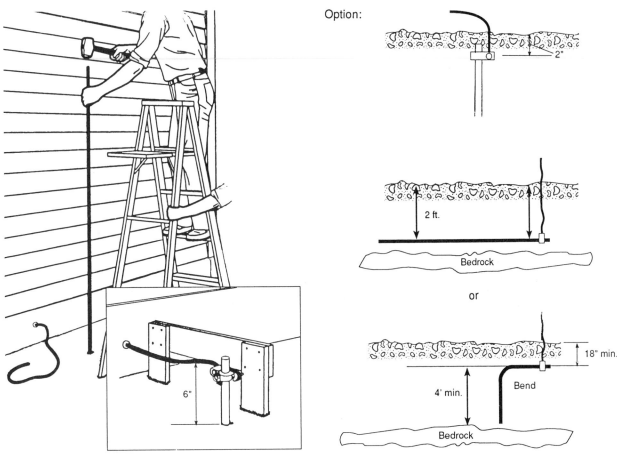

Option:

2"

2 ft.

Bedrock

or

18" min.

4' min.

Bend

Bedrock

6"

18-26 *(Continued)*.

GROUNDING THE WIRING

Until recently, most electrical systems were grounded by running a wire from the neutral bus to a clamp on the iron water pipe where it entered the cellar. Since water companies are increasingly using plastic pipe in place of steel, the old grounding method is no longer good enough. And, if your house has its own well, its water supply pipe is probably polyethylene in any case. The code now requires a separate grounding electrode, which is an eight-foot long, copper-clad ½-inch steel rod driven into the ground about 18 inches away from the foundation wall (see **18-26**). Some codes require the head of the rod to be driven below the surface; others want six inches left protruding. The ground wire is connected to the rod with a brass clamp, and the cable is protected against damage by either a conduit or barrier.

It takes a sledgehammer to drive a ground rod in anything but stone-free light soil. You'll need a brave helper to hold the rod as you hammer on it. Standing on a stepladder is unsteady; use a plank laid across a pair of sawhorses. If the rod hits solid rock within a few feet, the rod can be buried horizontally in a two-foot deep trench. The

electrode can also be buried beneath the cellar floor. Some codes require the electrode to be a 20 foot length of No. 2 copper wire buried 30 inches deep alongside the house or a ½-inch steel rebar buried in its concrete footings. A steel well casing can also be used for a ground electrode. Codes also vary as to whether the meter box, the service mast conduit, and both the service panel and disconnect switch have to be connected to the ground. When the meter box for underground power is located at a roadside utility pole, two electrodes are generally used; one at the meter/disconnect and another at the service panel. Always check with your inspector for local requirements.

In any case, metal water and gas pipes (if the gas company allows it) must always be *bonded* (the code term for a mechanical ground connection) to the ground wire. Grounding the internal piping carries any current leaks that could otherwise energize the pipes directly to the ground and is a safeguard against a shock if you wash the dishes in bare feet. A good ground is especially critical if your house is built on a concrete slab. In dry, sandy soils, this can be difficult to achieve with a single, short electrode.

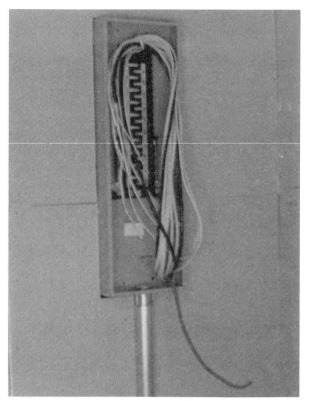

18-27 *This service panel has been installed in a garage. The cables for the individual circuits have been roughed in, but the circuit breakers and the underground service cable have yet to be installed.*

INSTALLING THE ENTRANCE PANEL

The wiring of the service entrance panel depends on whether the cables enter it from above or below (ends or sides) and on the type of cable used (see **18-27**). If you installed a separate disconnect switch outside the house, use the method shown on the upper left in **18-28** for SER cable. Note that an extra grounding bus is added to the panel box. Otherwise, the panel ground/neutral bar is bonded to the panel box by threading the special bonding screw or sheet-metal bonding clip supplied with the box into a pre-drilled hole (see lower left, **18-28**), and the leads from the SEC cable or the underground conduit are connected as shown in the top middle and upper right of **18-28**, respectively. Note that the hot leads are run to the left side of the panel and that the bare neutral is bent well away from the hot lugs to prevent possible arcing.

Entrance panels should not be mounted directly against a concrete or masonry wall (see **18-29**). Instead, attach a 2×2 frame to the masonry with powder-actuated fasteners or masonry screw anchors and construction adhesive, and cover it with ½-inch plywood. To allow room for attaching wires and future subfeed panels or other controls and outlets, cut the plywood larger than the panel. Service panels can also be installed between wall studs. To minimize heat loss, mount the panel in an interior, rather than exterior wall, and bring the cable in through the sill. Level the panel on the plywood backing and secure it with ¾-inch No. 10 or No. 12 pan-head wood screws.

If you live in an area where lightning storms are frequent, it's a good idea to install a lightning surge arrestor across the incoming service leads ahead of the panel main

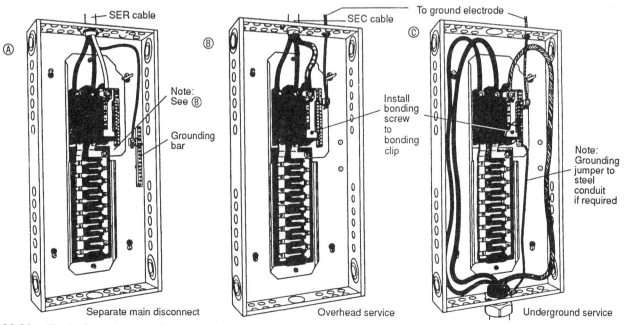

18-28 *Typical service panel wiring. Check your local code for neutral bus bonding requirements.*

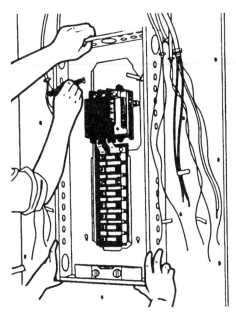

18-29 *Mounting the service panel. The moisture absorbed by masonry walls will cause a steel entrance panel mounted directly on it to rust.*

breaker to protect your electrical system from the powerful voltage surges which can occur when lightning strikes nearby (see **18-30**). While a lightning arrestor won't protect your system against a direct strike (only a properly installed lightning rod system can do that), it will keep the surge from a strike from travelling into your electrical system where it can explode your TV set or arc out of wall outlets. Since 75 percent of lightning damage can be traced to surges rather than direct strikes, a surge arrestor is good insurance. The arrestor will block spikes in excess of 2000 volts. You'll still need to protect delicate electronic equipment against lower voltage spikes with individual surge protectors.

Insert the arrestor into a knockout at the top of the panel, and fasten it with a locknut (refer to **18-30**). Run the white lead to the ground bar. Tap the hot leads just above the main breaker terminals by stripping ¾ inches of insulation from them. Clamp a plastic T connector on each lead, and run one of the hot wires from the arrestor to each tap. You can use a special main lug with an attached take-off tap.

INSTALLING BREAKERS AND WIRING THE BRANCH CIRCUITS

Even though the layout of all service panels is pretty much the same, the style of the circuit-breaker mounting lugs vary with the manufacturer. An attached label lists compatible brands or types of circuit breakers. The hot leads feed power to bus bars, which are mounted on insulated bushings that isolate them from the rest of the box. One

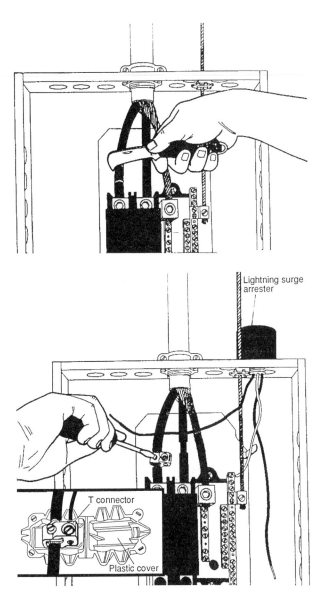

18-30 *Wiring a lightning surge protector across the main. Use special insulated T connectors to attach a lightning surge arrester to the hot service legs ahead of the main breaker.*

end of the circuit breaker fits onto a mounting flange or clip. Terminals on the other side of the breaker lock onto the hot bus. Depending on its service capacity, anywhere from a dozen up to 40 individual circuit breakers can fit into an entrance panel. Tapping 240 volts takes up two slots and requires a tandem breaker. If not quite enough slots are available for all your circuits, you can use a limited number of *split-breakers* to tap power for two 120-volt circuits from a single slot. Position the branch circuits on the power bus so that the load on each leg is more-or-less balanced.

465

Staple the cables from the branch circuits flat against the plywood (see **18-31**). Arrange the runs so that the overall appearance is neat and organized. Secure the cables to the knockouts with a Romex connector clamp, and strip the jacket off the wires inside the box. Leave enough slack so that you can route the cable from one side of the box to the other as necessary.

Begin by connecting the bare ground wires to the ground bus (refer to **18-31**). Route them across the bottom or top of the panel, taking care not to run them too close to the hot lugs. For a neater job, tape them together in bundles of three or four. Do the same with each white neutral lead. Leave slack for future wiring changes, and bend each lead into a long loop. Strip ½ inch of insulation off the wire, and slip it into the neutral bus terminal. The hot black and red leads slip into the power tap terminals on the circuit breakers. Label the leads for each circuit to keep them organized until they're all connected to their breakers and you can write the function of each circuit on the panel door label.

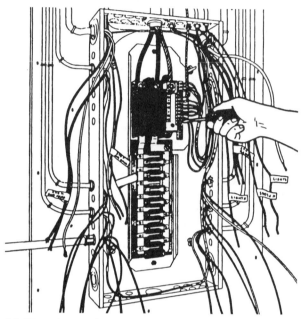

18-31 *Wiring branch circuits into the panel. The bare ground conductors are run in groups of two or three into the lugs on the bottom of the neutral bus. The white neutrals are run individually into separate lugs in the upper section of the neutral bus. Strive for a neat and orderly layout.*

RUNNING CABLE AND WIRING BOXES

When professional electricians wire a new house, they first "map" the plan onto the house by marking the location of the "boxes" on the studs with a felt marker, indicating various switches and receptacles with different symbols. Then they fasten the boxes to the framing and run the cable from box to box and, finally, to the service panel. This is a lot faster than puzzling things out step by step.

By convention, wall outlets are installed between 12 inches and 18 inches (note that the Americans with Disabilities Act specifies at least 18 inches) off the floor, which is high enough to reach without uncomfortable bending and low enough to use for powering appliances and floor lamps. Special floor-mounted outlets are equipped with protective brass cover plates. These are especially useful for powering floor lamps and convenience outlets in open-

18-32 *Next to mastering wiring hookups and circuit design, half the challenge of electrical work is becoming conversant with the many different kinds of wiring devices and their applications.*

space designs. Countertop and workbench outlets, especially those in the kitchen, are set above the backsplash to keep them from getting wet.

Backsplash height should be considered when you calculate kitchen window sill heights. A standard countertop is 36 inches high. Allowing for a four-inch backsplash, the outlet boxes should be between 42 inches and 46 inches from the floor. Light switches are set between 44 inches to 48 inches, which is a convenient height for most people. The switch is located inside the room opposite the hinge side of the door. Overhead fixtures are generally centered in a room.

There are many different types of electrical boxes, each of which is used for a specific purpose (see **18-32** and **18-33**). Because they are designed to mount in existing finish walls, "old work" boxes are primarily used for remodelling. The angled back of the sloped shoulder box (for example) leaves room enough to feed the wires into the box and to push it back into the wall without making an oversized hole or bending the cables too sharply. The reversible tabs on standard gangable boxes are designed so that they can be screwed into plaster lath or solid wood paneling with ¾-inch, No. 4 screws. When its tabs are folded into a box, the projecting "ears" of a *Madison clip* (sometimes called a *plaster ear*) hold the box tight against the back of drywall as tightening the cover plate draws the box forward. It's handy to keep these kinds of boxes in mind in case you need to retrofit a forgotten outlet.

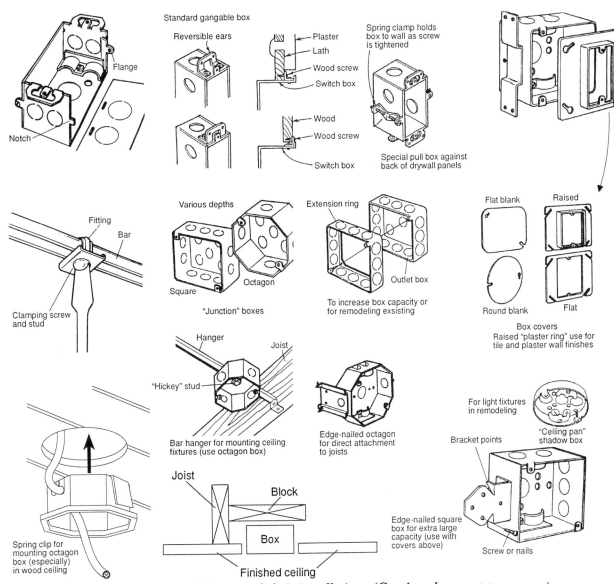

18-33 *Various types of electrical boxes and their installation. (Continued on next two pages.)*

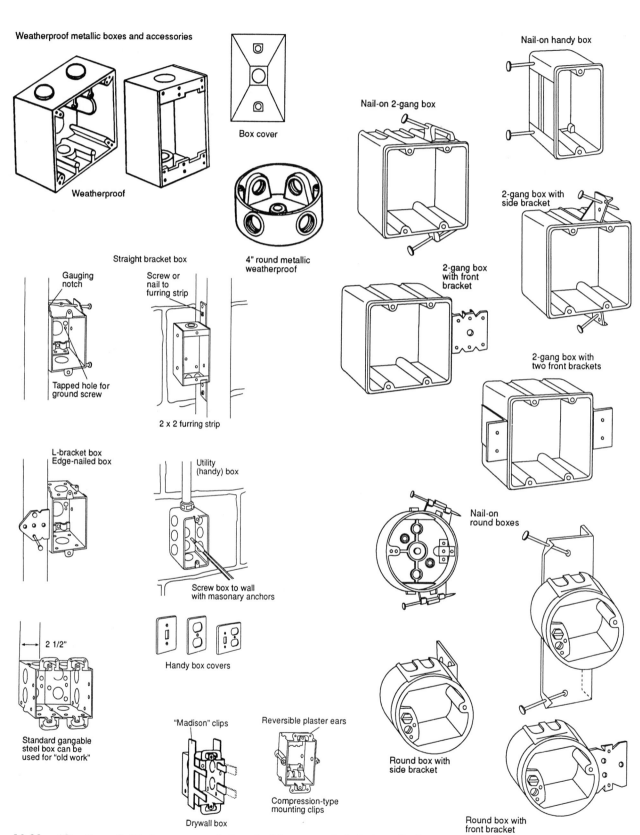

Weatherproof metallic boxes and accessories

Weatherproof

Box cover

Straight bracket box

4" round metallic weatherproof

Gauging notch

Tapped hole for ground screw

Screw or nail to furring strip

2 x 2 furring strip

L-bracket box
Edge-nailed box

Utility (handy) box

Screw box to wall with masonary anchors

Handy box covers

2 1/2"

Standard gangable steel box can be used for "old work"

"Madison" clips

Drywall box

Reversible plaster ears

Compression-type mounting clips

Nail-on handy box

Nail-on 2-gang box

2-gang box with side bracket

2-gang box with front bracket

2-gang box with two front brackets

Nail-on round boxes

Round box with side bracket

Round box with front bracket

18-33 *(Continued) Various types of electrical boxes and their installation.*

468

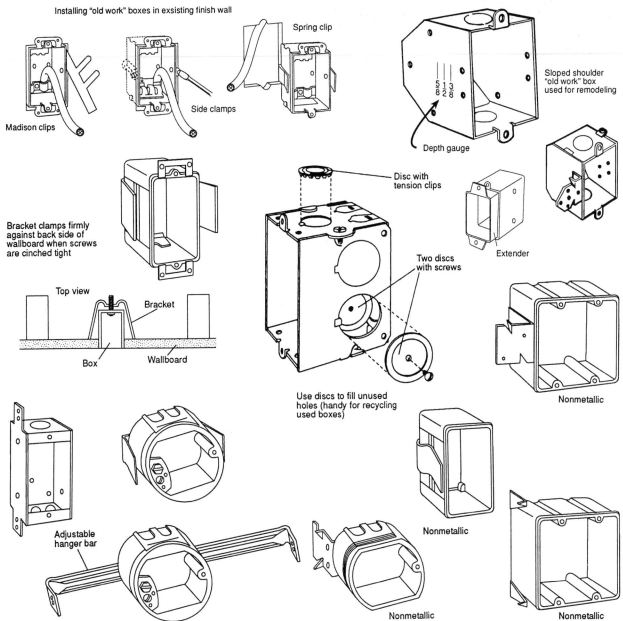

Installing "old work" boxes in exsisting finish wall

Madison clips

Side clamps

Spring clip

Sloped shoulder "old work" box used for remodeling

Depth gauge

Bracket clamps firmly against back side of wallboard when screws are cinched tight

Top view

Bracket

Box

Wallboard

Disc with tension clips

Two discs with screws

Use discs to fill unused holes (handy for recycling used boxes)

Extender

Nonmetallic

Adjustable hanger bar

Nonmetallic

Nonmetallic

Nonmetallic

18-33 *(Continued) Various types of electrical boxes and their installation. Boxes to right of center are nonmetallic (i.e., plastic) for use in "new" work.*

"New work" boxes attach directly to the framing studs, either with factory-equipped nails or else by side- or face-mounting brackets. Gauge notches or special markings on the side of the box guide you in placing the box on the edge of the stud so that it will be flush with the face of the finish wall. One or both side panels of a standard gangable box can be removed, and sections can be joined together to make multi-device boxes by loosening a screw. Gangable boxes can be screwed to strips of one-by blocking running behind their mounting tabs or else through their backs into a furring strip. "Handy" boxes (also called utility boxes) are used with conduit and other surface-mounted applications, such as barn and workshop wiring. Square boxes and octagonal junction boxes are used both with and without fixtures wherever extra capacity is needed. Bar hangers and a special clamping stud (a *hickey*) allow octagonal boxes to be conveniently mounted between ceiling joists to hold light fixtures.

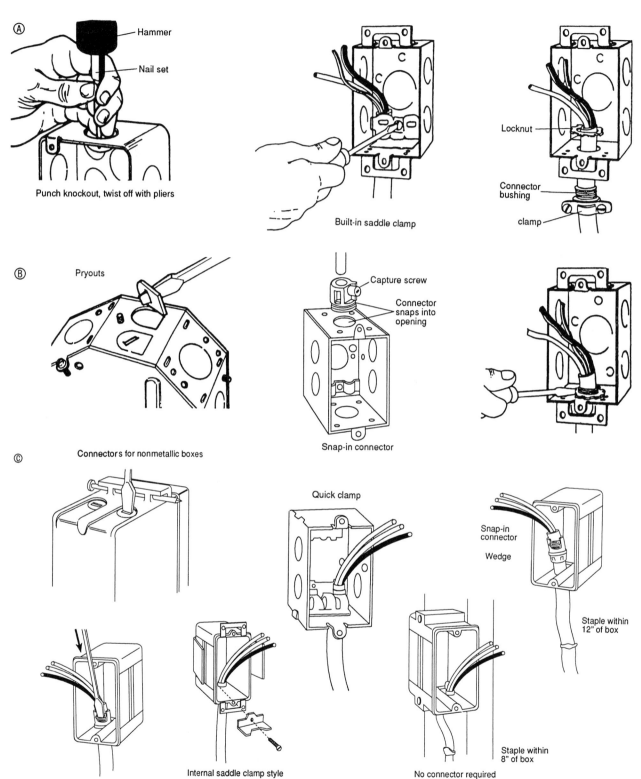

Ⓐ Hammer

Nail set

Punch knockout, twist off with pliers

Built-in saddle clamp

Locknut

Connector bushing

clamp

Ⓑ Pryouts

Capture screw

Connector snaps into opening

Snap-in connector

© Connectors for nonmetallic boxes

Quick clamp

Snap-in connector

Wedge

Staple within 12" of box

Internal saddle clamp style

No connector required

Staple within 8" of box

18-34 *Securing cables to a box. Connector clamps are generally only used for armored cable or with a metallic box that lacks internal saddle clamps or that must be side- or back-wired. Although not strictly required by code, its still a good idea to use snap in connectors with non-metallic boxes that otherwise have no internal clamps.*

470

Heavy cast aluminum boxes fitted with waterproof gaskets and covers are used for outdoor wiring with conduit or waterproof cable connectors. Unused holes are stopped with threaded plugs supplied with each fixture.

Inexpensive all-plastic, *nonmetallic* boxes have become quite popular with do-it-yourself electricians. Because the box is nonconductive, it does not need to be connected to the continuous bare ground wire.

The final phase of electrical rough-in is running the cables between the boxes. Most boxes use internal saddle clamps to hold the wires tight (see **18-34**). These are more convenient than punching the knockout and inserting a locknut and Romex cable connector. Slip a screwdriver

into the slot of the pryout, lift it up and twist it out. Internal clamps are optional when nonmetallic cable is run into single, plastic boxes but they must be used with multiple boxes. The code also requires cables to be stapled within eight inches of a plastic box and 12 inches of a metal box. Leave a loop of slack between the staple and the box for any future wiring changes.

Except for the definition of "conductor," the code is very precise about the number of wires permitted in boxes (see **18-35**).

The purpose of all these regulations is to prevent the box from being overcrowded, which could bend or break wires and cause short circuits.

18-35 *Number of conductors allowed in a box.**

Box size and type	Maximum number of conductors		
L × (W) × D	No. 14	No. 12	No. 10
Round & Octagonal Junction or ceiling			
4 × 1¼	6	5	5
4 × 1½	7	6	6
4 × 2⅛	10	9	8
Square ("major") boxes			
4 × 4 × 1¼	9	8	7
4 × 4 × 1½	10	9	8
4 × 4 × 2⅛	15	13	12
Switch or receptacle boxes			
3 × 2 × 1½	3	3	3
3 × 2 × 2	5	4	4
3 × 2 × 2¼	5	4	4
3 × 2 × 2½	6	5	5
3 × 2 × 2¾	7	6	5
3 × 2 × 3½	9	8	7
Weatherproof boxes, junction boxes			
4 × 2⅛ × 1½	5	4	4
4 × 2⅛ × 1⅞	6	5	5
4 × 2⅛ × 2⅛	7	6	6

*For the purposes of calculation, a wire that originates and ends in the box such as a jumper is not counted as a conductor. Nor are any wires from a fixture to the wires in the box. But both internal cable clamps count together as one conductor. So is the bare grounding wire that enters and leaves the box regardless of how many other wires are spliced to it. Any mounting studs, hickeys, or other attachments inside the box other than a switch or receptacle also count as one wire.

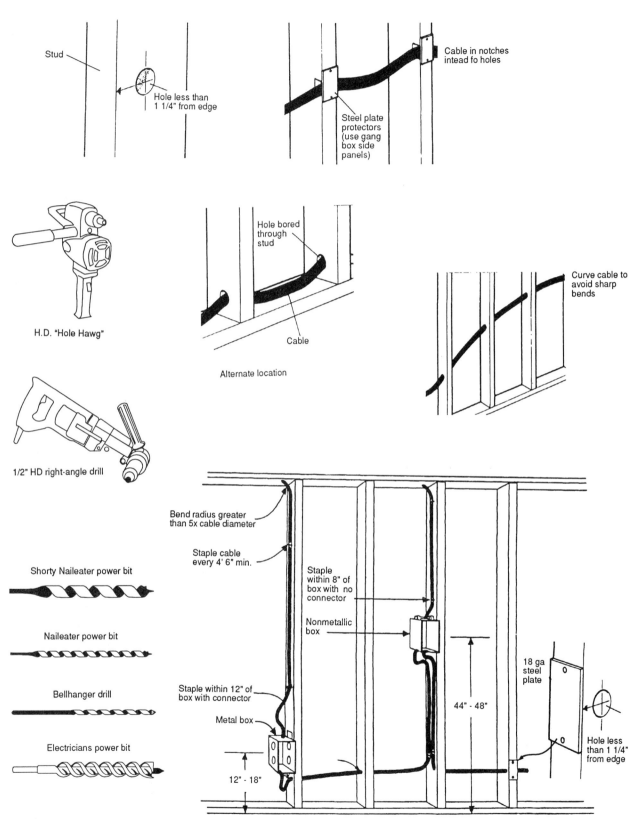

Stud

Hole less than 1 1/4" from edge

Cable in notches intead fo holes

Steel plate protectors (use gang box side panels)

H.D. "Hole Hawg"

Hole bored through stud

Cable

Alternate location

Curve cable to avoid sharp bends

1/2" HD right-angle drill

Shorty Naileater power bit

Naileater power bit

Bellhanger drill

Electricians power bit

Bend radius greater than 5x cable diameter

Staple cable every 4' 6" min.

Staple within 8" of box with no connector

Nonmetallic box

Staple within 12" of box with connector

Metal box

12" - 18"

44" - 48"

18 ga steel plate

Hole less than 1 1/4" from edge

18-36   *Running cable in walls. Leave slack in cable at boxes to facilitate any future wiring changes.*

472

Some of the code stipulations that govern the running of nonmetallic cable through the framing are shown in **18-36**. Here, the intent of the code is to protect the cable from being punctured by nails in the wall covering.

An ordinary ⅜-inch VSR (variable-speed, reversible) hand drill will get pretty tired drilling holes through studs for cables and, except for full-width bays, there isn't enough room between the studs to fit both the drill and the bit. Rent a right-angle drive, heavy-duty ½-inch drill (or a *Hole Hawg*, which is an extremely compact, heavy-duty drill for work in tight quarters). You'll also need a ¾-inch "shorty" naileater bit. Bore the holes as close as you can to the center of the studs. Any holes that are less than 1½ inches in from the stud face must be protected against nails by an 18-gauge steel plate. You can also notch the face of the studs with a saw and chisel where boring is impractical (a built-up corner, for example). All such notches should also be covered with steel plates. Avoid sharp bends in cable runs, which could kink the insulation. Raise or lower the cable gradually in a curve rather than in right-angle steps. The code calls for staples at least every 4½ feet.

Cables running at right angles to ceiling joists that will be finished are run through holes bored at least 1¼ inches up from the bottom edges (see **18-37**). Cables running lengthwise are centered on the sides of the joists. In an unfinished attic, you're allowed to staple the cable to the tops of the joists so long as it's protected by guard strips of 1×4 furring nailed alongside to form a channel. Lengthwise runs must be stapled to the sides of the joist. However, if the attic has stairs or a permanent ladder access, the cables must run through holes bored in the joists instead.

In unfinished basements, only No. 8 or larger cable can be strapped or stapled directly to the undersides of the joists. Smaller cable must run through holes or else be stapled to a 1×4. Some codes may require any exposed runs (e.g., in an unfinished garage or basement) to be protected by conduit.

WORKING WITH CONDUIT

Conduit runs must be planned carefully. Bends and offsets have to be precisely located. It takes a bit of practice to get the hang of making gentle bends in EMT thin-wall conduit without kinking the tubing. Although you can rent a conduit bender, it's probably cheaper to buy one if you have more than a little conduit to run. The handle is just a length of iron pipe.

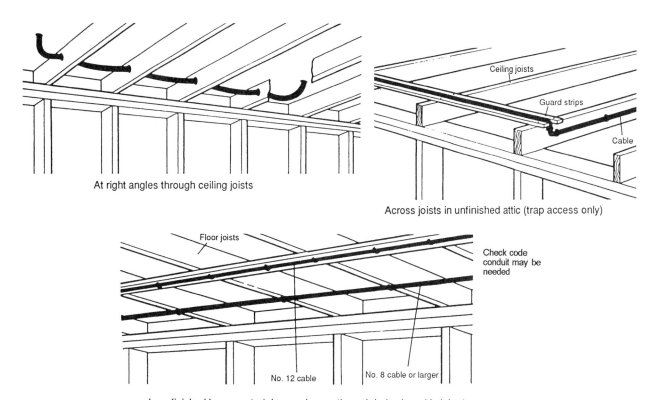

At right angles through ceiling joists

Across joists in unfinished attic (trap access only)

Ceiling joists

Guard strips

Cable

Floor joists

Check code conduit may be needed

No. 12 cable

No. 8 cable or larger

In unfinished basements (also can be run through holes bored in joists)

18-37 *Running cable in ceilings and attics. Where the attic area is accessed by permanent stairs or ladder, the code does not allow cables to run across the tops of the joists. They must be run through as in a finished ceiling.*

To make a bend, insert the tubing in the bender so that its hook is at the starting point of the bend (see 18-38). Put one foot on the foot piece of the bender and the other on the conduit to hold it, and pull the handle of the bender back slowly and steadily towards you until the conduit is bent to the desired angle as indicated by the level vials or the arrows on the body. When the handle is at 45 degrees to the floor, you've completed a 90-degree bend. Don't tug too sharply. A kinked conduit will have to be discarded. Don't be discouraged if it takes a few tries before you get it right.

When cutting conduit to length, don't forget to account for the *take-up* of the bend. Allow five inches for 1/2-inch, six inches for 3/4-inch, and eight inches for one-inch sizes. For example, if a box is located 15 inches from the corner of the bend, you'd set the arrow on the conduit bender at 10 inches from the end of a 1/2-inch conduit.

If the conduit is mounted against a flat surface, you'll need to bend 15-degree offsets—called a *kickbend*—so that it can be connected to a box (see 18-39). Lay the conduit flat on the floor, and pull the bender back to make the first 15-degree bend. Then, resting the tubing on a plank,

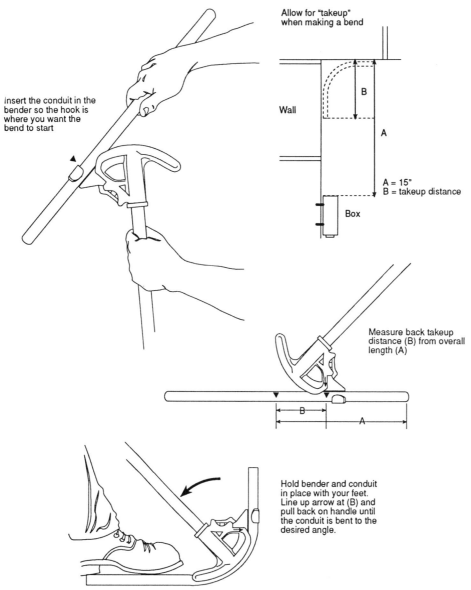

18-38 *Using a conduit bender. Slide the conduit into the bender so that the hook lines up with the start of the bend. Step on the conduit to hold it in place, and pull back evenly on the bender handle until the conduit is bent to the desired angle.*

slide the hook back to the beginning of the bend, and push the bender forward 15 degrees to complete the bend. You can also use offset connectors rather than having to make kickbends.

Rather than trying to figure the exact takeup of the bends in each section of conduit, you can add six to eight inches to the lineal length of the run, and cut off the extra later at the box. Conduit is easily cut with either a hacksaw or tubing cutter. Always file or ream the burr off the inside of the cut. Otherwise, it could snag and cut the insulation of the wires as they are drawn through the pipe.

The code doesn't allow more than 360-degree (a total of four 90-degree or one-quarter) bends in each conduit run between boxes. Each offset bend counts as a 45-degree (one-eighth) bend. If more bends are required, you can use a pulling elbow instead of a bend (see **18-40**). The removable cover facilitates pulling the wires through the conduit. You cannot splice wires in a pulling elbow, but you can splice them in conduit elbows or junction boxes, which are also considered as the start of another run. The more boxes, the fewer bends in each run, the easier the wire pull will be.

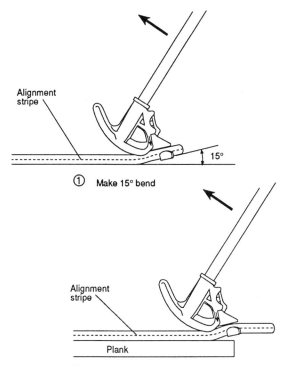

① Make 15° bend

② Flip tubing over, move bender further down, pull until tubing is parallel with floor

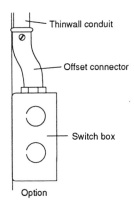

Option

18-39 *Making a kickbend. (1) Make 15-degree bend. (2) Raise tubing off floor on plank, turn over, set bender farther down and bend until tubing is parallel with floor—or use offset connectors instead.*

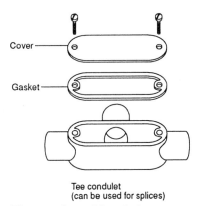

Pulling elbow (no splices allowed)

Standard octagon box with EMT connectors

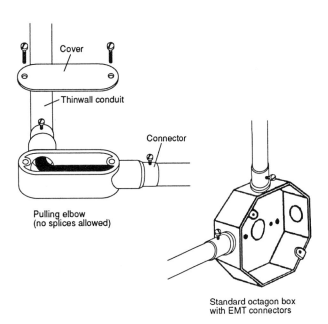

Tee condulet (can be used for splices)

18-40 *The number of bends in a run are limited by code. Pulling elbows, standard junction boxes, and condulet elbows are considered to start another run but no splices are allowed within a pulling elbow.*

475

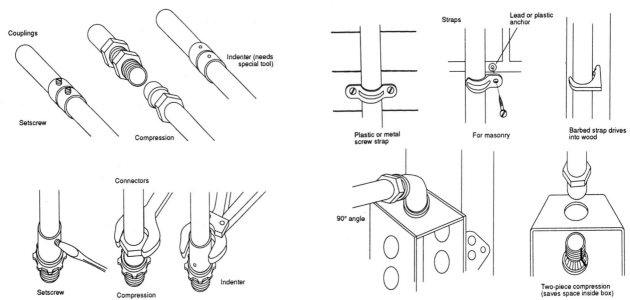

18-41 *The type of coupler, connector or anchor used depends on whether or not the connection must be watertight or mechanically strong.*

Straight sections of conduit are joined together with couplers (see **18-41**). Waterproof compression couplers and connectors are used for outdoor and damp locations. Setscrew fittings are the easiest and cheapest to use for runs in dry locations. A special indenting tool is needed to make crimped couplings which are mechanically strong. The fittings that join the conduit to boxes are threaded for locknuts. If space in the box is tight, you can use a special, slotted compression fitting instead of the regular standard locknut.

The conduit must be anchored at least every 10 feet and within 3 feet of each side of a box with a conduit strap (refer to **18-41**). Barbed straps drive into wood framing. Other types screw into wood or into plastic or lead masonry anchors. If concealed behind a wall or let in notches of studs, EMT must be protected by steel plates, since its walls are thin enough to be punctured by a nail or hardened drywall screw.

The wires are pulled through the conduit once it's been run between all the boxes (see **18-42**). Use type TW or THHN, solid conductors of the proper color code for each circuit. To make it easier to trace wiring, you can use red, blue, brown, or variously striped conductors (except for *green or yellow–green*) for the hot legs of additional circuits. Each circuit is required to have its own white neutral wire. With plastic conduit you'll also need to run a separate green wire for the continuous ground conductor.

For a relatively short and straight run, you can probably push a single pair or triplet of wires through the conduit. With longer runs, numerous bends, and more pairs of wires, you'll need to pull the wires through the conduit with a *fish tape* and a helper.

Starting at the far end of the run, feed the fish tape into the conduit until it comes out the other end. Strip an inch of insulation off the ends of the wires, and bend them around the hook of the fish tape. Wrap the con-

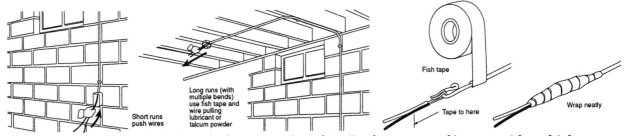

18-42 *Wires can be pushed through short runs of conduit. For long runs and/or runs with multiple bends, the wires are lubricated with talcum powder or pulling compound and pulled through with a fish tape.*

nection neatly with electrical tape so that it won't get hung up. Then, as your helper feeds the wires into the box to prevent snarling, pull the tape back towards you. Dusting the wires with talcum powder or special wire-pulling lubricant makes long pulls with lots of wires go easier. Leave at least six inches of wire sticking out of each box. It's always a lot easier to cut it off later than to end up too short. The code limitations on the number of wires permitted in conduit of a given diameter depends on the type of wire used as well as its size. In general, it's a lot more than you'd think could comfortably fit (e.g., up to seven No. 12 type TW conductors in a ½-inch or up to 19 in a one-inch conduit).

WORKING WITH FLEXIBLE METALLIC CONDUIT AND BX CABLE

Flexible metallic conduit, or *Greenfield* as it is known to the trade, is simply BX armored cable without wires. It's often used to wire devices such as motors, where vibration could loosen a rigid connection. The cable and the conduit can be concealed in walls and are often required for work within the cavities of block construction or when wiring must be buried under plaster. Because of its flexibility, bends, offsets, and couplers aren't needed.

To cut armored cable or conduit, saw through one of the jacket spirals at right angles with a hacksaw (see **18-43**). Take care not to cut past the metal into the wires. Twisting the armor snaps it free. Clip off any stubborn remnant with diagonal cutting pliers. To expose the conductors, make a second cut about a foot back of the end. Peel back the paper wrappers to expose the wires and the aluminum bonding strip (if there is one).

The key to a safe installation of cable or conduit is to protect the conductors from laceration on the sharp edges of the armor. Slip a nylon *anti-short bushing* into the cut end of the cable. In order for the inspector to verify the presence of the bushing, special *peep-hole connectors* are used to attach it to boxes. You can also use *insulated-throat connectors* that come with an integral bushing instead. Bend the bonding strip back before inserting the bushing. Wrap it around the head of the clamping screw when you install the connector.

Special 90-degree and 45-degree connectors are used to bring the cable into or out of a box with a sharp bend. Otherwise, any bends must be gentle enough not to snap the armor. Support the cable or conduit with straps or special BX staples placed at the same intervals as nonmetallic cable.

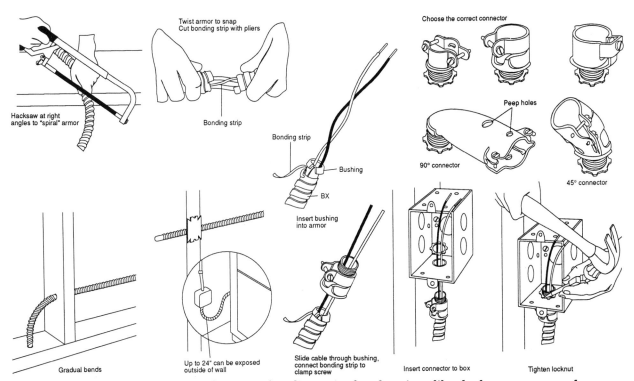

18-43 *BX cable often has a thin aluminum bonding strip that functions like the bare copper conductor in nonmetallic cable. When it's secured to the clamp screw of the cable connector, the box is electrically bonded to the cable. The wiring devices are grounded to the box by a grounding pigtail and a green grounding screw. A green-jacketed wire is run through Greenfield conduit when a separate continuous ground conductor is required.*

SURFACE RACEWAY WIRING

Surface-mounted raceways are a convenient way to run power to light fixtures mounted on exposed timber ceilings or to devices in other situations where it's difficult or impossible to conceal the wiring (see **18-44**). They are also widely used in remodelling to add receptacles, switches, and fixtures to existing wiring without fishing wires through walls.

The code permits surface raceways in dry locations protected from mechanical damage. The system consists of plastic or steel, hollow channel sections similar to flat conduit, joined by various slide-on or snap-in connectors. Once the conductors are fished through the raceways, cover plates are snapped over the connectors. Special adaptors allow power to be taken from a standard recessed outlet or junction box.

INSTALLING OUTDOOR POWER

In general, the easiest way to run power from the house out to the yard, garden, driveway, pool, or outbuildings is to lay UF cable in a two-foot deep trench (see **18-45**). Codes require that the cable be run through conduit at the point of entrance and exit into the ground. Install a waterproof connector at the end of the conduit. Leave a loop of slack for expansion and contraction at each conduit. An LB condulet connected to a short nipple is typically used to take power from a junction box inside the house.

In most cases, this circuit will be protected by a GFI breaker.

If your code permits it, you can also run TW wiring through conduit. Use either galvanized intermediate metallic conduit (between rigid and thinwall in stiffness) buried within six inches of the surface, or noncorroding, waterproof plastic conduit, buried at least 18 inches. Most codes require conduit for above-ground wiring.

Outdoor receptacle boxes and round fixture boxes are made from heavy cast aluminum and fitted with gasketed waterproof covers. Receptacles have spring-loaded covers. Switches are integral with the surface plate. Refer to **18-33** for common types of outdoor fittings.

If you need to do extensive trenching, you should probably rent a gas-powered trenching machine (see **18-46**). If your trench must cross an obstruction such as a sidewalk or driveway, drive a length of threaded, galvanized rigid conduit under it with a sledgehammer. Make a drive point by hammering the end of a nipple to a point, and thread it onto the head of the conduit. Screw a coupling onto the drive end of the conduit to protect its threads. Once the conduit has penetrated to the other side of the obstruction, remove the couplings, and install waterproof connectors for UF cable, adapters for plastic conduit or standard couplers for IMC.

Bury the cable or conduit in three inches of stone-free sand before backfilling the trench.

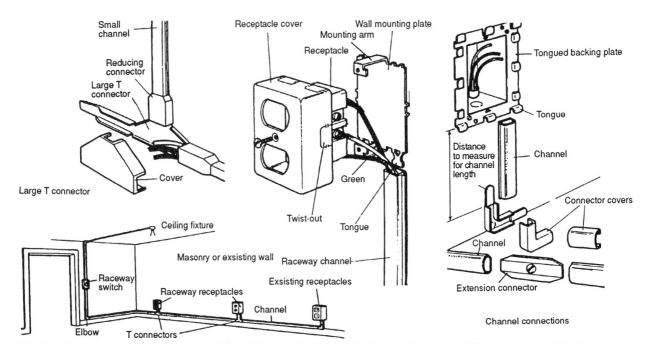

18-44 *Surface-mounted raceway wiring. Various fittings join channel sections. The wires are fished through the channels before the connector covers are snapped in place. A T connector is large enough so that it can be used as a junction box, allowing wires to turn or be spliced together. Fixtures are screwed to mounting plates that screw onto the wall. Extension covers add depth as needed for wire connections. Otherwise, the wiring devices screw to mounting arms on wall mounting plates.*

478

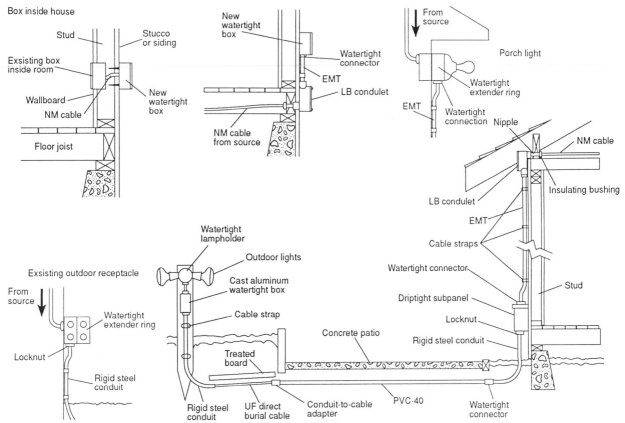

18-45 *Running underground wire. The closer to the surface, the greater the risk of damage, and, therefore, the more protected the cable must be. Check with local codes. Conduit should always be used to run wire under a patio, sidewalk, or driveway. Outdoor receptacles are typically added directly across from an indoor box using either a nipple or a short length of NM cable. Power for outdoor lights can be taken off an existing porch light as well or an existing outdoor receptacle can be used as a junction box for a new underground line. Where more than one outdoor circuit is required, use an outdoor subfeed panel.*

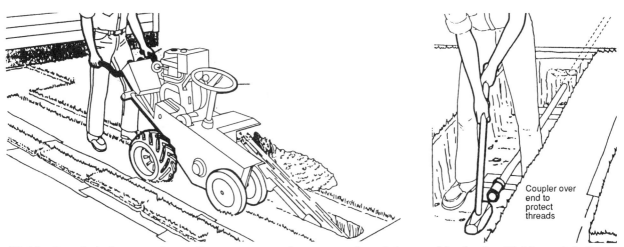

18-46 *In relatively stone-free soil, a power trencher saves a lot of time and backache. Rigid conduit fitted with a home-made drive point can be hammered under a walkway.*

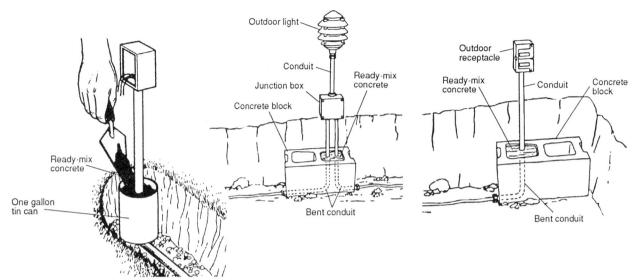

18-47 *Anchoring outdoor fixtures. Slip the concrete block over the conduit before attaching the receptacle or fixture and running the wires.*

The conduit must be firmly anchored where it emerges from the ground and terminates in an otherwise unsupported outdoor receptacle or lighting fixture (see **18-47**). The easiest way to do this is to route it through a concrete block, and fill the core with bag-mix concrete. A large coffee can also makes a good anchor.

SWITCHES AND RECEPTACLES

Various types of switches and receptacles are used in residential wiring in the United States. Since 1971, the terminals of wiring devices for 15- or 20-amp circuits have been either unmarked, signifying that they can only be used with copper (or copper-clad aluminum), or marked "CO-ALR" (Copper-aluminum revised) indicating that they can also be used with all-aluminum wiring. In light of the earlier problems with galvanic corrosion and loosening of terminals that were the direct cause of many aluminum-wired house fires, the chemical composition of both the aluminum wire and device terminals was altered to make them safe. However, except for service wiring, the bad reputation of aluminum has kept it from being more widely used in residential wiring today.

Some common kinds of toggle switches used in residential wiring are shown in **18-48**. The standard single-pole switch is used to control a device from one point. Three-way switches control devices from two points, and four-way switches are used for three or more points. A double-pole switch is used to shut off both hot lines in a 220-volt circuit (such as a heavy-duty saw motor).

The terminals can be located at the side, the ends, or the front of the switch body. The wire is always looped around the terminal in the direction that the screw tightens. Otherwise, turning the screw in tends to loosen the wire. Back-wired switches use spring-clip, push-in terminals into which the wires are inserted instead of screw terminals. Inserting a tiny, flat-bladed screw driver into the release slot undoes the grip. Back-wiring saves space in crowded boxes. As a safety measure to prevent accidental shorts between the terminals and the sides of a metal box, wrap the terminals with electrical tape after the wires are connected.

Although you can strip the jacket of NM cable by cutting carefully along its midline with a knife, a cable stripper does a better job without danger of nicking either the conductors or your hand (see 18-49). Squeeze the stripper around the cable so that its tooth pierces the insulation, and then pull it downwards to rip it. Pull the jacket back, and cut it off. Since UF cable is embedded in solid plastic, cut about an inch deep alongside the bare ground conductor with diagonal pliers, and then, gripping the ground wire with pliers, pull it upward to rip the jacket. Do the same with each insulated conductor.

When wires are spliced together inside a box, the connections must be both mechanically and electrically solid. Besides lights and plugs that don't work, a loose connection has high resistance which causes it to heat up. Arcing and corrosion are also side effects of poor connections. The threaded, tapered metal core of plastic-insulated wire nuts make a quick and solid connection on both accounts. As with pretty much all things electric, most wire nuts are color-coded to indicate the number and sizes of wires that they can accept. The standard "red cap" will splice two No. 10 or three No. 12 solid conductors. You can fit two No. 12 or three No. 14 wires into a yellow nut. Orange connectors are for No. 16 and smaller wires. Grey nuts

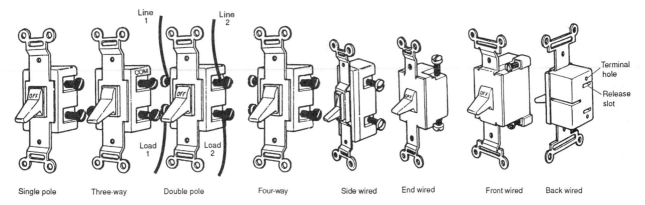

18-48 *Standard switches are rated for 15-amp service. Motors and some special circuits may require a 20-amp switch. Most side-wired switches are also back-wired.*

are good for four or five No. 12 wires, and the large blue caps handle up to No. 4 wires. Green nuts are reserved exclusively for bare and green ground wires.

Since the code won't allow more than one wire to be hooked to a terminal, multiple wires are spliced to a pigtail lead (refer to **18-49**), which counts as one additional conductor in the box (except for ground wires). The code also allows multiple wires to be twisted together with a projecting lead that attaches to the terminal. Since this particular splice must be soldered and taped, it's hardly used any more. Combination screw-terminal and push-in terminal receptacles are especially handy in crowded boxes or where three or four wires must connect to each side of the receptacle.

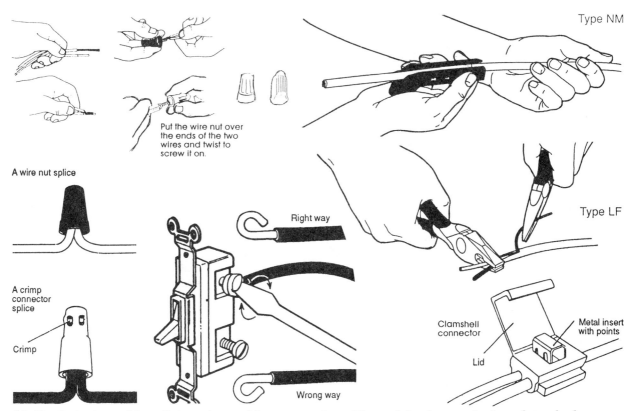

18-49 *Stripping cable, splicing wire, making connections. Upper right shows stripping of standard nonmetallic cable. Middle right shows stripping method for underground feeder cable.*

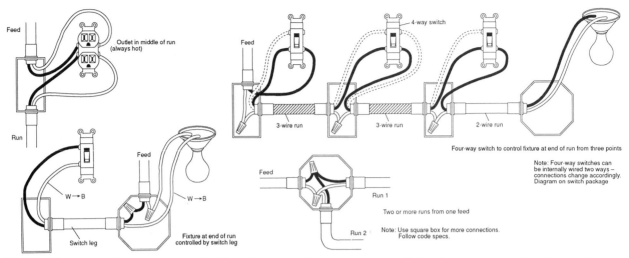

Feed

Outlet in middle of run (always hot)

Run

Feed

4-way switch

Feed

3-wire run   3-wire run   2-wire run

Four-way switch to control fixture at end of run from three points

Note: Four-way switches can be internally wired two ways – connections change accordingly. Diagram on switch package

Feed

W → B

W → B

Feed

Run 1

Switch leg

Fixture at end of run controlled by switch leg

Two or more runs from one feed

Run 2

Note: Use square box for more connections. Follow code specs.

18-50 *Representative examples of wiring diagrams. Your best approach is always to consult a licensed electrician.*

In most cases, the bare ground wires are spliced together with a green wire nut and connected by a pigtail to a green grounding screw or a snap-on grounding clip on the body of the box. One of the grounding wires also runs to the green terminal on the receptacle. Since plastic boxes are nonconductive, no ground wires are jumpered to it. In light of this, switches intended for use in plastic boxes are now available with a grounding screw terminal. At this writing, a revision of the code to require all switches to have a ground terminal is under consideration; so always check for current standards.

WIRING DIAGRAMS

As used in diagrams (see 18-50), a *feed* is the cable that delivers power from the source to the device. Think of it as incoming power. A *run* is the cable that carries the power from the device to the next device in the circuit. Think of it as outgoing power. A *leg*—or, generally, a *switch leg*—connects a control device (i.e., a switch) to another device (such as a light). It's basically an extended loop of the hot wire. Three-way switches control a single light from two locations with a three-wire cable that splits a single feed into two hot lines and a common neutral. The "common" terminal is always black (or copper-colored) and is usually by itself at one side of the switch body. Either or neither "traveller" leg of the circuit will be hot, depending on which switch is open or closed. If the red and black wires get mixed up, change them around until the circuit works. So long as you don't mix in white wires, there's no danger of a short.

Three-way switches are so called because they have three terminals, not because they work from three locations. A four-way switch does that. Since a four-way switch

can have one of two different kinds of internal wiring connections, getting the circuit to work right can be confusing if you don't know which way the switch is wired. Usually, a wiring diagram is printed on the switch packaging. By adding additional four-ways to the middle of a circuit, it's possible to control a fixture from as many locations as you desire.

When roughing in wires, don't trust your circuits to memory; you won't be able to remember which wires are connected to what and where (see **18-51**). Once the walls are up, it's a tedious job to trace circuits with a continuity tester. Label all the runs, switch legs, and feeds in each box.

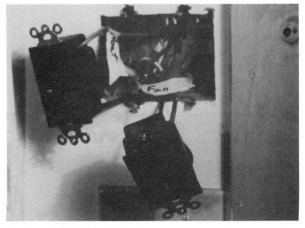

18-51 *Labelling the wires in boxes helps prevent confusion and short circuits when they're hooked up to their devices.*

19 Insulation

The popular notion that "heat rises" encompasses only a very small part of the phenomenon of heat transfer. Heat, the warmth we feel as we draw near to a fireplace, is the brain's interpretation of an increase in the kinetic energy of the molecules of the skin surface. All molecules at a temperature above Absolute Zero are in motion, i.e., they have kinetic energy. Heat is an increase in that energy— a speed-up of the random jiggling of molecules occasioned by the addition of some other form of energy, most often thermal or *radiant* energy. Temperature is a qualitative measurement of this energy change. It indicates the relative "hotness" or "coldness" compared to a standard. The Btu (British thermal unit) is a quantitative measure of heat. Think of it as a count of the number of molecules vibrating, kind of like a reading on a thermal odometer.

UNDERSTANDING HEAT FLOW

Heat transfer (or flow) takes place wherever there is a *difference* in temperature between any two bodies. Heat flow is always one-way—from the warmer body to the colder. The irreversibility of this flow is enshrined as the *Second Law of Thermodynamics*. Heat transfer is thus either a *heat gain* or a *heat loss*, depending upon your point of view. A cold window gains heat from a warm room which is losing heat to a cold window which is losing heat to even colder outside air.

Heat flow occurs through three basic processes: *conduction*, *convection*, and *radiation*. Conduction is heat transfer by the direct contact of heated molecules with unheated ones, by which a portion of their kinetic energy is exchanged. It's what happens when you grab the hot handle of a cast-iron frying pan.

Convection is heat transfer between solids by a fluid medium such as air or water. "Heat" itself doesn't rise, but rather the fluid that carries it does, since the increased energy of its molecules makes them move about more rapidly and spread farther apart. The measurable effect of this increased motion is a decrease in density; warmed air is lighter than cold air, so it rises. The warmed air transfers its heat to whatever cold surfaces it contacts and then, becoming heavier, it falls. The pressure of falling cool air helps push more warm air up. This cycle (that deposits dust particles on the ceiling cobwebs) is termed a *convective loop*.

Radiation is the most subtle and most direct form of heat transfer. All bodies above Absolute Zero emit radiation of various wavelengths—most commonly in that portion of the electromagnetic spectrum just below the threshold of visible light, called the infrared. As the temperature of a body increases, the frequency of its output of radiant energy rises at an exponentially proportionate rate to the input of energy until, at about 575°F (or 302°C), it enters into the visible spectrum (and your woodstove begins to glow dull red). Radiant energy travels outwards from a source in all directions at near light speed until it is absorbed by a body in its path, whereupon it is transformed into kinetic energy—or heat—and the intervening body grows warmer.

Since maintaining a comfortable difference between indoor and outdoor temperature and humidity is a major function of shelter, the Second Law of Thermodynamics has important consequences for house design, not only in heat loss calculations, but also in understanding how insulation works.

All matter, including building materials, has specific properties with regard to heat. Substances that transfer heat rapidly are called *conductors*. Those that impede heat flow are *insulators*. The *coefficient of thermal conduction*, or *k-factor* (*k*), is a measure of the rate of conductive heat flow through a unit area (one square foot) of a unit thickness (one inch) of a given material in Btu's per hour (Btuh) per degree Fahrenheit of temperature difference between its interior and exterior surfaces. The higher the k, the faster the heat flow through the material. What's important about the k factor is that it shows that overall heat flow is related to surface area, thickness, thermal conductivity, and temperature difference of the material. Engineers use the additive k-values of various materials to calculate the overall conductive heat transfer through composites of various materials, such as the components of a building wall.

Convective heat flows occur whenever warm air (or water) contacts a cooler surface. Such flows are either free or forced (that is, occur in either still air, fan- or wind-driven air, thermosiphoning, or pumped water). Thus the overall rate of convective heat flow is proportional to the velocity of the fluid movement across a surface as well as its temperature difference. (The faster the wind is blowing, the quicker your house will lose heat to the outdoors.) Another aspect of convective heat flow is that the thin films of air (or the viscosity of all fluids) which coat each side of a surface (its *boundary layer*) have a measurable thermal resistance which can be expressed as a mathematical entity (the *coefficient of fluid velocity*, or *f*) that plays a role in heat loss calculations.

Radiant heat transfer is extremely difficult to quantify. A radiant body is also losing or gaining heat by convection and conduction at the same time (to prove this, touch a hot stove). Only part of the energy a body (or material) absorbs is emitted as infrared energy. A very definite portion of its energy is *reflected* back as visible light, which gives the material its color. Materials which have a low emissivity often have high reflectivity—the net effect of which explains why shiny aluminum foil acts as a barrier to radiant heat transfer. This is also why, to be an effective insulator, aluminum foil must be separated from the heat-emitting surface by a dead air space (which doesn't transfer heat convectively). Aluminum is an excellent conductor and would otherwise rapidly transfer heat through both convection and conduction if it contacted the warmer surface.

The relative proportions of heat lost to conduction, convection, and radiation will change with the direction of the heat flow (see **19-1**). This has important consequences for the optimal placement and thickness of insulation. Convective transfer is always upwards. Convective and conductive heat losses are therefore the largest component of winter heat loss through a ceiling. In summer, heat absorbed by conduction from the hot roof deck radiates into the house from the ceilings while convective losses are to the floors. Thus, adequate attic insulation is important for reducing both summer heat gain and winter heat loss. Since the ground water temperature of the earth is always lower than a heated house, radiant heat loss is greatest through an uninsulated floor in winter.

The thermal resistance of both dead air spaces and the boundary films on their surfaces varies seasonally with their orientation and direction of heat flow (refer to **19-1**). The seasonal variations are understandable because the temperature difference between inside and outside surfaces generally reverses between winter and summer. These variations are one reason why *R-value labels* on insulation packages are often accompanied with an arrow that indicates the R-values (see below) in relation to the direction of heat flow.

The real significance of the k-factor for the home-builder is that it is used to determine the *R-value* which by definition is established as the reciprocal of k. The R-value furnishes a practical means of comparing the thermal resistance of various insulators and construction methods to heat flow. R-values are always additive. Since heat flow through a building occurs by all three methods simultaneously, the calculation of the total R-value of a given cross-sectional building construction adjusts for both (k) and (f) factors. Unless otherwise specified, listed R-values for insulation usually measure thermal performance at a temperature difference of 70°F (39°C). Should you ever need to do your own thermal calculations for heat loss or solar design, the *ASHRAE Handbook of Fundamentals* has many tables that list the various thermal coefficients of building materials.

The concept of *U-value*, or *overall coefficient of transmission*, which is defined as the reciprocal of the total R-value of a given composite construction (including constants for surface air films and outside air velocity) may

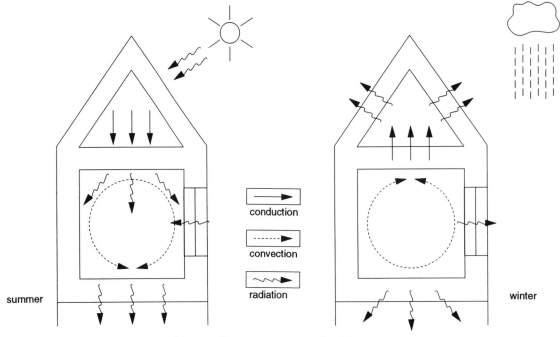

19-1 *Seasonal comparison of heat flow modes across various building surfaces.*

seem confusing at first. All you need to know about U-values is that heating engineers use them to make their heat loss calculations when designing heating systems. The difference between U-value and k factor is that while the k factor measures conductive heat flow in terms of Btuh per hour per square foot per inch of a given material per degree of temperature difference, the U-value does the same thing for the combined heat flows through all the components of a given building section, including dead air spaces, surface films, and its various construction materials and insulation. Since it's a number that expresses the thermal profile of a building cross section, it is obviously useful in figuring heat loss in Btuh, which is the main determinant for sizing heating and cooling equipment. Through algebraic manipulations, all these constants and coefficients can be boiled down to the basic heat loss equation:

$$Q = UA (\Delta T)$$

which basically states that the overall heat loss (Q) in Btu's per hour (Btuh) is the sum of the U-value of a particular building section, such as a wall, ceiling, floor, or window, multiplied times the area (A) of that section again multiplied times the difference between indoor and outdoor design temperatures (Delta T).

So, if you ever want to do your own heat loss calculations, you'll need to figure out the R- and U-values either step-by-step or from assumed typical cross-section values, and plug them into the actual room measurements. Your Delta T assumes an indoor design temperature of 70°F (21°C) and an outdoor design temperature that is an average of published winter lows or summer highs for your region.

Heat losses across building surfaces by conduction, convection, and radiation, are *transmission heat losses*. The heat loss which results from the exchange of air between the inside and outside of a building through the process of *infiltration* can comprise a large part of the overall building heat loss, especially once the building has been well insulated.

As mentioned earlier in Chapter Seventeen, the chimney effect (which is created by internal thermal pressures) and the external pressure difference between the windward and leeward sides of the house created by air velocity combine to force heated air to flow out of the house. Infiltration heat loss can be reduced by proper siting that shelters the house from winter winds or summer glare, by a house profile that presents a low windward surface area, and by rigorously caulking and weatherstripping all openings and penetrations to reduce the opportunity for heat "leaks." Adequate insulation also reduces infiltration by lowering the Delta T of the inside and outside walls, which is one of the main drives behind infiltration air flow.

In earlier times, before R-30 ceilings, R-19 walls, and insulated windows, it was assumed that most of the heat loss from the building envelope was through the ceiling

and windows. With the widespread adoption of more energy-efficient construction standards, the new heating short circuit looks something like this—

> Ceiling: 15 percent,
> Walls: 15 percent,
> Doors and windows: 15 percent,
> Basement: 25 percent,
> Infiltration: 30 percent.

Since the addition of nighttime insulation to windows, foam-core doors, and foundation perimeter and under-slab insulation reduce those structural components of heat loss even more, it becomes increasingly important to concentrate on blocking more subtle sources of infiltration heat loss (see **19-2**).

Although it is possible to pinpoint the sources of infiltration heat loss, it's just about impossible to quantify it. Arbitrarily assigning a rate for the number of whole-house air changes based on how "tight" the house is and multiplying that number by a coefficient (0.018) for the heat capacity of dry air (which is much lower than one might think) times the volume of heated air (cubic feet) in the house is one method that is supposed to give a reasonable estimate for the overall infiltration heat loss in Btuh. The so-called crack estimation method plugs the same coefficient into an equation that uses the lineal footage of window and door perimeters along with several other factors to arrive at the same estimate. Both of these methods are examples of what engineers call a SWAG (colloquially, a Scientific Wild-Assed Guess). As the *ASHRAE Handbook of Fundamentals* somewhat archly puts it: "It is necessary, therefore, to evaluate the conditions and select an appropriate (value) by judgement . . ."—which you would then plug into your heat loss calculations.

The significant point to take away from this extended discussion of heating physics and heat-loss theory is that proper insulation and control of infiltration is a critical component of maintaining a comfortable internal environment at an affordable cost.

19-2 *Components of infiltration heat loss in percent.*

Exterior walls, sills, holes in vapor barrier	25
Electrical outlets	20
Window frames and sashes	14
Heating ducts in cold spaces or untaped joints	12
Bathroom and kitchen ventilators	10
Doors	6
Fireplace (with damper, but no closure doors)	6
Recessed ceiling fixtures in attic	6
Miscellaneous penetrations (cable, wires, pipes, etc.)	2
	100 percent

(Source: Robert Argue, *The Well-Tempered House*)

Controlled air infiltration is *ventilation*. Fresh outdoor air must be exchanged for stale inside air at a rate sufficient for maintaining health and comfort and for reducing the buildup of indoor pollutants. The trick is to accomplish this exchange with a minimal loss of heat or "coolth" (this term was coined specifically to focus attention on the energy content of conditioned air). Present-day experts generally agree that 25 cubic feet per minute per person is the minimum amount of fresh air exchange needed for a healthy interior environment. A rule of thumb used by heating engineers is to provide one cubic foot per hour of outside air for every 100 Btuh of heat supplied by a combustion heating appliance. Under "normal" circumstances, one complete air change per hour will meet, if not exceed, these requirements. It's more than likely, after a conscientious effort to reduce heat leaks, that outside infiltration will supply just about the minimum amount of fresh air (as long as combustion appliances are supplied with sealed outside air sources). A tightly built house will always benefit from a daily airing out. This is one reason (besides fire egress) why building codes require an operable window in each room.

If the actual air exchange falls below the minimum one full change per hour, an air-to-air heat exchanger will be needed. Although technicians and energy-audit consultants specialize in measuring infiltration rates with special test equipment, if you need an air-to-air heat exchanger, it will be obvious; windows will fog up, walls will sweat even in mild weather, and cooking and other household odors will linger for days.

THE RELATIONSHIP BETWEEN RELATIVE HUMIDITY, INDOOR COMFORT, AND CONDENSATION

Comfort engineers generally agree that, depending on the activity level and season of the year, humans seem most comfortable when the *relative humidity (RH)* is between 30 to 70 percent. The idea of relative humidity can be a bit "slippery." The term refers to the ratio between the water vapor *actually held* by air at a given temperature to the total amount it *could hold* at that same temperature. Although the terms are often used interchangeably, strictly speaking, "moisture" isn't the same thing as water vapor. Moisture properly only refers to liquid water. Vapor is gaseous water. Preventing or controlling the change from one state to the other (i.e., condensation), especially within the cavities and on the surfaces of the building envelope, is an increasingly important consideration for today's homebuilders.

When the relative humidity is 100 percent, the air is said to be *saturated*, or at *dewpoint*. It simply can't hold any more water. As this vapor-filled air (for whatever reason) is cooled, its superfluous moisture condenses from a gas to a liquid, or, if the temperature is cold enough, a solid. The magnitude, as well as the rate of chilling, determines whether the moisture will be deposited as fog (tiny airborne droplets), dew (large droplets), or frost (ice crystals). To sum up: water vapor in still air will condense whenever it comes into contact with a surface that is cold enough. As the air loses heat by conduction, its dew point drops and its RH increases until it reaches saturation, at which point the excess moisture is shed.

The amount of water vapor in the air is always relative to temperature. The warmer the air, the more moisture it can hold. Air can't hold anywhere near as much water at 75 percent RH and 68°F (20°C) as it can at 75 percent RH and 90°F (32°C). In fact, at 100°F (38°C) and 100 percent RH, it will hold fifty times more water vapor than it will at 0°F (−18°C).

In the days before insulation and "tight" construction, keeping indoor air moist during winter was an uphill struggle. The RH of cold outside air would drop as it infiltrated into the house and was warmed to room temperature. For example, the RH of outside air at 10°F (−12°C) and 100 percent RH when heated to 70°F (21°C) indoors, drops to 8 percent. Traditionally, the problem was how to keep enough moisture in the house to make it comfortable. Although people commonly speak of "dry" or "moist" heat, the type of heating plant has only a marginal effect upon the moisture content of inside air. Except for an unvented, gas-fired appliance that would give off water vapor (and several other much more noxious pollutants) as a combustion by-product, all heat is "dry" heat, regardless of the fuel burned and the method of heat distribution. Convective heating by means of a forced, hot-air system is perceived as dry because it circulates large volumes of drying air over the skin. Since radiant heat (like that given off from hot-water baseboards and (to some extent) old-fashioned, cast-iron steam or hot-water radiators) doesn't cause as much convective air flow, the felt effect of this heat is less dry. Heat from a wood stove is not in itself more dry or moist than oil heat. But the large hot metal surfaces of the stove generate very strong convection currents. Winter air is simply dry air. The more of it brought into the house, the drier the indoor air becomes. This is the raison d'être for the original humidifier, the kettle kept boiling on top of the stove. Its modern successor is an electrically controlled device mounted on the furnace warm-air duct.

Contemporary air-tight construction has pretty much reversed the condensation problem. In a modern house, it's quite difficult to get the RH down to levels that would be considered too low for comfort and health. The superinsulated home, and even an ordinary "tight" house, is much more likely to suffer from the equally unhealthy and undesirable condition of excess humidity rather than that of dryness.

Condensation is usually the telltale sign of a moisture problem (it can also indicate ventilation problems and improper insulation, as is discussed later in this chapter).

The most obvious and most common site of condensation is a cold window pane. Not only will moisture col-

19-3 *Head casing attachment for owner-made thermal curtains sewn with special quilted fabric that contains an internal vapor barrier. The rings are linked by a chain sewn into the hem of the curtains so that pulling on the attached cords will open or shut the curtains.*

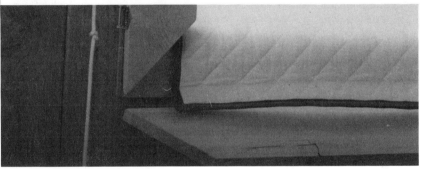

19-4 *The drawn curtain is held tight against the window side casings by spring-hinged wood clamps. Heavy chain sewn into the bottom hem pulls the curtain fairly tight to the spring-hinged sill.*

lecting on the lower sash stain and eventually rot the wood, but condensation of this kind further increases heat loss and chills the room. Heat loss is increased because when water vapor changes phase from a gas to a liquid, it gives off the "latent" heat it contains. Since this heat is immediately conducted to the cold window surface, it isn't available to warm the room.

The relationship between double-glazing and maintaining interior comfort without excessive condensation problems should be obvious; as vapor turns to water on the cold glass, the loss of that moisture from the interior air lowers the relative humidity. With added glazing, that moisture will remain in vapor form, and you'll be able to keep the humidity at a comfortable and healthy level.

As a rule of thumb, you can be fairly confident that as long as the drop in relative humidity doesn't exceed five percent for every 10°F (5½°C) drop in outside air temperature (calculated from a base of 30°F (1°C) and a RH of 50 percent), condensation won't occur on the panes of a double-glazed window.

Since the surface temperature of the glass is affected by solar radiation, windows, except for those on the north side, won't fog up as readily during daylight hours as they do at night.

Because of the potential for nighttime heat loss, it's recommended that the relatively large glazing areas of passive solar homes be fitted with some form of window insulation (see **19-3**). These can be either home-built or else purchased off the shelf (see **19-4**). Unless proper precautions are observed, thermal shutters can actually exacerbate an existing condensation problem (see **19-5**). Because an insulating shutter will prevent warm air from circulating over it, the temperature of the inside glass surface can approach that of the outside surface.

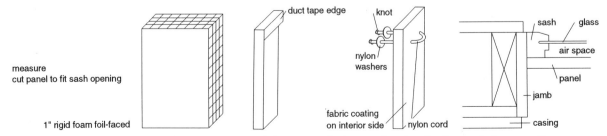

19-5 *Panels cut from inch-thick, foil-faced rigid foam insulation make simple thermal shutters. Protect the exposed edges of the insulation with duct tape. A loop of nylon cord makes a convenient handle for easy removal of the panel which fits snugly against the sash between the window jambs.*

The likelihood of frost accumulation increases the longer the shutter is left in place. If condensation problems are to be avoided, the shutter must seal tightly to the sides and bottom of the window casing. And it must be faced with a vapor-retardant material. Loose-fitting curtains or shades and quilts that lack an internal vapor-retarder will only make things worse. The energy savings gained by the shutters will be offset by an increased latent heat loss, first as the condensed moisture freezes during the night, and second, as it melts during the day. Sitting water will stain and eventually rot the window sashes and sills.

Excess humidity can be reduced by ventilation (which is not so desirable in the winter) and by source reduction, which involves changes in lifestyle as well as attention to building details. The amount of moisture produced by typical household activities is shown in **19-6**.

19-6 *Water vapor production in the household.*

Activity/Source	Vapor produced (lbs/day)
Unvented gas range (cooking for four persons)	4.7
Cooking, no lids on pots	2.0
Hand-washing dishes	1.1
Floor mopping	0.75
Clothes-washing (per load)	4.4
Clothes-drying (per load) unvented	26.0
Shower (per person)	0.5
Bath (per person)	0.1
Breathing (per person)	2.4
Houseplants (per plant)	0.15
Drying firewood (per cord)	30.0
Attached greenhouse	50.0
Humidifier (large)	40.0
Damp basement or crawlspace	50.0
Standing water in basement	60.0
Building materials during first year	80.0

Since a damp basement is one of the heaviest producers of moisture, good perimeter drainage and foundation waterproofing as well as a vapor barrier under concrete floor slabs and over earth-floored crawl spaces are integral structural components of interior moisture control. If the area of an earth-floored crawl space covered by the vapor barrier is gradually increased from an initial 50 percent to full coverage over a period of several months, trapped moisture in the cellar will have a chance to evaporate. In any case, all cellars and crawl spaces should be provided with operable windows or louvers for cross-ventilation. A minimum ratio of free vent area to floor area of 1:500 with two openings is recommended for spaces protected with a vapor barrier. If no vapor barrier is used, provide four openings and a vent ratio of 1:150.

Whatever its benefits, an attached greenhouse full of thriving plants is also a major contributor to household humidity. This is one reason why greenhouses should be isolated from the main living areas and fitted with a hygroscopically controlled ventilator or hand-operable vents.

A family of four going about their daily business, without doing any laundry, will add about 25 pounds of water vapor per day into the household air. The chart in **19-6** makes it clear that, at the very least, the clothes dryer should be vented to the outside. With the exception of the kitchen range and oven, gas appliances are already vented to the outside for health reasons. A range hood or kitchen exhaust fan will remove both water vapor and unhealthy combustion by-products. Never store green firewood in the basement. Up to 50 percent of its total weight is water.

In tight houses, cooking pots should be kept covered and the heat turned down once the water begins to boil. In summer, windows can be opened (except in humid climates) and laundry dried outdoors. Low-flow shower heads and faucet aerators together with a routine of wiping the bathroom glazing and sash dry after showering will also lower vapor production.

Condensation within the wall cavities was a rare occurrence in old uninsulated houses. Because of Dalton's Law (which states that the pressure exerted by water vapor is constant, regardless of its temperature), warm inside air will have a higher vapor pressure than outside air. It will actually force itself through the microscopic interstices of a wall. Although they might be impervious to moisture (liquid water), most building materials are permeable to water vapor (gaseous water). The water vapor will diffuse through an uninsulated wall cavity to the outside. Any condensation that does occur on the inside of the cavity will be as frost, which usually sublimates (changes directly from solid to gas) and doesn't cause any harm.

19-7 *Increase of weight of water by grains per pound of dry air as temperature increased at 20 percent, 40 percent, and 60 percent relative humidity. (7000 grains = one pound)*

20 percent relative humidity					
8°F	20°F	40°F	60°F	80°F	100°F
0	4 grains	7	16	30	59
40 percent relative humidity					
8°F	20°F	40°F	60°F	80°F	100°F
0	6 grains	15	31	62	118
60 percent relative humidity					
−20°F	+20°F	40°F	60°F	80°F	100°F
0	9 grains	21	46	90	169

(All figures for sea level)

19-8 *Due point for given temperatures and relative humidity.*

room temp. (degrees F)	Dew point at relative humidity percentage (degrees Fahrenheit)									
	(10%)	(20%)	(30%)	(40%)	(50%)	(60%)	(70%)	(80%)	(90%)	(100%)
50	−1	13	21	27	32	37	41	44	47	50
55	3	17	25	31	37	41	45	49	52	55
60	6	20	29	36	41	46	50	54	57	60
65	10	24	33	40	46	51	55	58	62	65
70	13	28	37	45	51	56	60	63	67	70
75	17	31	42	49	55	60	65	68	72	75
80	20	36	46	54	60	65	69	73	77	80
85	23	40	50	58	65	70	74	78	82	85
90	37	44	55	62	69	74	79	82	86	90

(Note: Convert Fahrenheit to Celsius by subtracting 32 and multiplying by 5/9.)

Introducing insulation into a wall cavity affects both heat transfer and vapor migration. Instead of the sharp temperature gradient between the inner and outer walls of the cavity, a more gradual gradient arises. As infiltration heat loss is also controlled, the relative humidity of the indoor air increases (see **19-7**). This moist air will reach its dewpoint at some point along the temperature curve within the insulation—or the exterior sheathing and siding (see **19-8**). Because there is little or no convective air flow within the insulation-filled cavity, condensed moisture cannot sublimate. It will become trapped in the insulation blanket or be absorbed into the sheathing and siding, eventually causing dry rot and peeling paint. Also, the lower R-value of wet insulation exacerbates the condensation problem. Inserting a vapor-impermeable membrane (the vapor barrier) between the insulation and the warm side of the wall keeps the water vapor in the heated rooms (see **19-9**). If no vapor can diffuse into the wall cavities, no condensation can occur.

The permeability of a vapor barrier is measured in *perms* (see **19-10**). Any material that has a permeability of less than one perm can technically be considered a vapor barrier. But an *effective vapor barrier* should have

19-10 *Vapor permeability of common building materials.*

Aluminum foil	0.00 (perms)
Polyethylene (4- and 6-mil)	0.05
Kraft paper, foil-faced	0.50
Kraft paper, asphalt-impregnated	1.00
CDX plywood, 1/2-inch	0.50
Vinyl wallpaper	1.00
Exterior oil paint	1.00
Urethane varnish	0.40 to 1.60
Styrofoam	1.20 to 3.00
"Beadboard"	2.00 to 5.80
15-lb asphalt felt (tar paper)	4.00
3/8-inch drywall	5.00

a perm of less than 0.10. The rule of thumb is that the permeability of the outside cold surface should be at least five times greater than the barrier on the inside warm surface. Thus covering the walls with vinyl wallpaper (perm = 1.00) will not stop vapor from migrating through a wall sheathed with plywood (perm = 0.50).

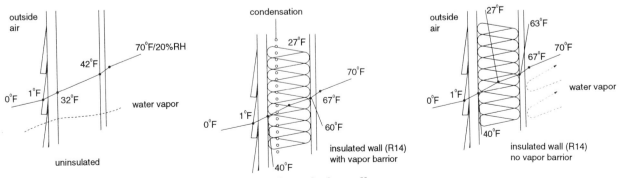

19-9 *A vapor barrier reduces vapor migration through the walls.*

Although both four-mil and six-mil polyethylene film have the same perm, the added toughness of the extra thickness makes the six-mil sheet a better choice. Puncturing a polyethylene film increases its net permeability by about a factor of three. The integrity of the vapor barrier is seriously compromised by electrical boxes, plumbing lines, and other penetrations. This can be remedied to some extent by sealing the edges of the film to the offending penetration with polyethylene tape. Any inadvertent cuts, rips, or tears should be repaired with tape as well. Codes now call for overlapping seams the width of a stud cavity. Research has shown, however, that this is incapable of resisting the force of vapor pressure. Acoustical sealant (a nonadhesive flexible type of caulking) will make a vapor-tight seam once the poly is stapled over it. Think of the house as a warm air balloon. The vapor barrier is the skin of that balloon. A leaky barrier is not much better than no barrier.

Ending the vapor barrier at the floor or a ceiling partition has the same effect as a large hole. Conscientious builders now lay a three-foot-wide strip of poly over the mudsill before setting the header and stringer joists, and then fold it up onto the subfloor before nailing down the sole plates (see **19-11**). The bottom flange of the strip is sealed to the foundation wall. Its upper edge is sealed to the wall vapor barrier which overlaps it. (Note: For this method to be effective, the header and stringer joists must be inset two inches so that a strip of rigid foam insulation can be laid over their faces. Otherwise, wrap the barrier

over the inside face of the joists and caulk the ends of each floor joist to the poly.)

Likewise, instead of cutting the vapor barrier at the ceiling where it's interrupted by an interior partition, tack a strip of poly to the top plate of the partition before you tilt it up (refer to **19-11**). The flanges on both sides can then be sealed to the cut ends of the main barrier.

Some builders prefer to solve the problem of maintaining vapor barrier integrity by nailing 2×3 horizontal furring to the studs after the barrier is in place. The furring makes a channel for wiring (you may need to use square boxes with plaster rings to gain enough room for all the wiring connections since deep boxes won't fit) and drain lines while leaving the underlying barrier intact. Rigid foam or more fibreglass can be added between the furring strips.

Actually, the term "vapor barrier" may be a misnomer. A more accurate term would be a "vapor retarder," in recognition of the practical impossibility of constructing a perfect vapor barrier in real-world houses.

There are still a few builders who will swear that "a house has to breathe." They maintain that wrapping the walls in plastic actually causes condensation. But in every case, the problems of structural rot, stud-cavity condensation, and mildewed or sweating walls or ceilings can be traced to improper or sloppy installation of the vapor barrier or to excessive levels of indoor humidity and poor ventilation, and not the presence of a vapor barrier *per se*. If, as sometimes happens, the barrier is mistakenly installed on the unheated side of the wall, condensation will occur within the wall since vapor cannot diffuse to the outside.

To be fair, the "breathing house" fallacy is only half wrong. The outside walls must indeed breathe. The insulated stud cavities and joist bays must be able to vent to the outside any vapor which does find its way through the membrane. Fortunately, wood and most other building materials are sufficiently permeable to water vapor that this process occurs unassisted. However, problems can arise when the outside walls are painted (especially with oil-based paints) and the vapor barrier is either absent or inadequate or interior humidity is excessive. As vapor diffuses through the wood, the pressure it exerts against the underside of the paint film is strong enough to blister the paint. This is a strong argument not only for careful barrier installation, but for the use of permeable penetrating stains instead of paint.

There is still some question among builders and technical experts as to whether a vapor barrier is needed in all cases and all climates (see **19-12**). In the Southeast of the United States, where cooling and high humidity are more of a concern than heating, any vapor movement would tend to be from the outside to the inside. This is one case where the film-forming effect of paint would be helpful. Some Southeastern building codes now require the vapor barrier to be installed on the outside of the house, under the finish siding and on the ground of a crawl space

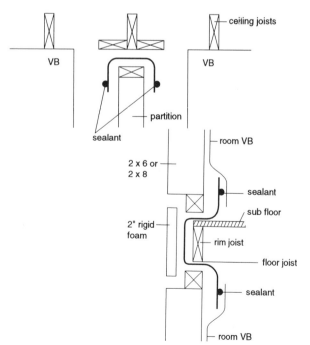

19-11 *Continuity of vapor barrier at interior partitions and at floor deck.*

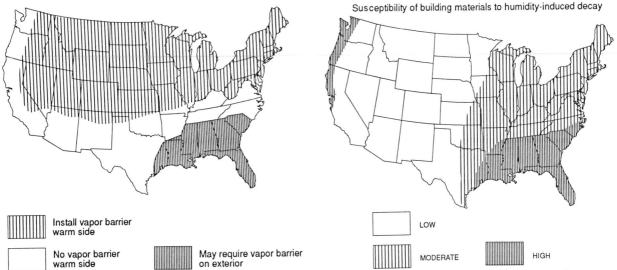

Susceptibility of building materials to humidity-induced decay

| Install vapor barrier warm side |
| No vapor barrier warm side |
| May require vapor barrier on exterior |

| LOW |
| MODERATE |
| HIGH |

19-12 *Where vapor barriers are needed. In regions where vapor barriers aren't used or are reversed, ventilation is extremely critical in preventing structural decay.*

or under a foundation slab. Engineers feel that this prevents condensation from occurring within the walls of an air-conditioned house. Other experts feel that installing any kind of vapor barrier in such climates causes more problems than it prevents, and they feel that it's more important to provide good ventilation for the walls and ceilings instead.

In climates that are hot and dry, like Arizona or the southern California deserts, there's not enough moisture in the hot outside summer air to condense when it infiltrates into cooled wall cavities. And, since there's little temperature difference between the inside and outside in winter, condensation isn't likely to occur then either.

The consensus among experts now seems to be that a vapor barrier should be used on the inside wherever the average January temperature is less than 35°F (2°C) and heating degree-days greatly outnumber cooling degree-days. Where this isn't the case, no vapor barrier is needed.

Some experts feel that in regions where inside temperatures normally exceed outside temperatures but the winters are mild, a vapor barrier should be installed on all the walls and only on the ceilings of humidity-generating rooms such as the kitchen, bathroom, or laundry room. It's thought that the absence of a barrier on the other ceilings allow excess vapor to vent into the attic where it can escape to the outside.*

***

*Water vapor held in rapidly moving air won't condense. For condensation to take place, the contact between the air and the cold surface must be maintained for some time. This explains why warm-air registers can be placed under windows without making them fog up.

The wisdom of depending upon ventilation to remove household water vapor through an attic ceiling is questionable. Granted, an attic can be very well-ventilated. But it also tends to be well-insulated, especially now that values of R-30 or more have become standard. The rate of diffusion through 12 inches or more of cellulose fill or fibreglass blankets may well be too slow to prevent condensation, especially if internal humidity is higher than optimum, which it would tend to be if the house were both well-insulated and tightly sealed against outside air infiltration (the higher the RH, the less the Delta T needed to reach dewpoint). In my opinion, if you use a vapor barrier on the walls, use it on *all the ceilings*. It can't do any harm, it may prevent some problems, and the added cost is insignificant.

The first map in **19-12** shows the approximate 35°F (2°C) January temperature line. Vapor barriers aren't needed below this line. The second map in **19-12** reflects the ambient humidity levels and thus, the vulnerability of the building walls to decay caused by moisture. In the Southeast, where buildings are very prone to decay, maximum ventilation is critical especially when no outside vapor barrier is used.

Vapor barriers should not be confused with *moisture barriers* (also called *house-wrap*). As mentioned in Chapter Eleven, this polyolefin sheet is installed on the outside of the house beneath the siding to block outside air from infiltrating through the walls. It allows one-way vapor diffusion from the inside to the outside. If it's put on inside-out, it will let vapor move into the walls from outside but block it from escaping from the inside. Rosin-coated building paper and tar paper allow vapor migration from both directions.

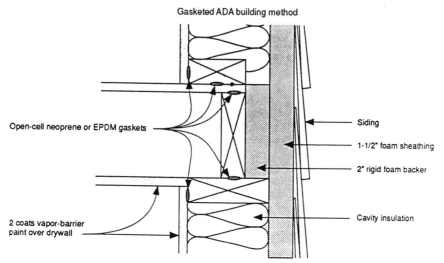

Gasketed ADA building method

Open-cell neoprene or EPDM gaskets

Siding

1-1/2" foam sheathing

2" rigid foam backer

Cavity insulation

2 coats vapor-barrier
paint over drywall

19-13 *The gasketed ADA building method essentially consists of completely isolating the interior building surfaces from the exterior so that infiltration pathways are effectively blocked and moisture-laden outside air cannot move into the house to replace the warm air leaving. Because the air in such a tightly sealed house would become rapidly unhealthy, mechanical ventilation and filtration is needed.*

19-14 *Properties of common residential insulations. Recommended R-values for insulation. R-values for electric resistance heat are generally higher. (Continued on next two pages.)*

Type	Average R/in	Cost	Application
Loose-fill			Blown into wall cavities and attics, can be spread by hand. Difficult to get exact density
Fibreglass (long fibre) (short fibre)	2.2–3.3 4.0	low medium	
pros & cons: short fibre more hazardous to health high densities can be achieved in attics good for filling irregular spaces			
Rock wool	2.9–3.3	medium	
pros & cons: more prone to settling than fibreglass			
Cellulose	3.3–3.7	low	
pros & cons: made from recycled newsprint nonirritating to skin (avoid breathing dust) cannot get wet, may not last in humid climates, combustible— will smolder			
Perlite (expanded glass beads)	2.5–3.8	high	
pros & cons: very heat resistant nonirritating can be added to concrete to decrease density, increases R-value Can compact and absorb water			
Vermiculite (expanded mica)	2.3–3.0	high	
pros & cons: can be poured into block cores noncombustible nonirritating, but may contain **asbestos**, avoid dust			

Now that more and more local building codes are requiring vapor barriers, we are faced with the situation in which new research claims are being made that moisture problems actually aren't caused by vapor diffusion at all. Instead, the thermally induced stack-effect of warm winter air is thought to be the culprit responsible for condensation. According to this theory, as warm air continuously pushes out the upper walls and the ceiling, the outside air that is drawn in through the basement and lower walls to replace it carries anywhere from 10 to 100 times the amount of water vapor that would otherwise enter the wall cavities by diffusion from indoor air alone.

The "air-barrier" or *Air-tight Drywall Approach* (ADA) uses continuous neoprene-foam or EPDM gaskets behind the top and bottom of drywall panels and between the plates, soles, band joists, and subfloor, to stop the air flow into and out of the building at the warm surfaces (see **19-13**). Some ADA advocates also install a polyethylene vapor barrier. Others recommend that a latex vapor-barrier paint be used over the drywall to retard diffusion instead.

Because of the extra labor and the somewhat tricky techniques involved, the ADA has been slow to win converts. As regional seminars intended to explain the system to professional builders and architects proliferate and enough ADA houses are built to evaluate their performance in the field, ADA methods may become the prevailing energy-efficiency standard.

Most of the materials commonly used as building insulators owe their thermal resistance (R-value) not to any intrinsic property of the substance from which they are made, but rather, the way in which they are put together. For example, glass has a k-factor of 5, which gives it an R-value of only 0.20 per inch. However, when spun into a blanket of fine fibres that trap air in their interstices, glass has an R-value of 3.5 per inch. Most insulators work because they contain dead-air pockets or a cellular structure filled with inert gasses (see **19-14**).

19-14 *(Continued) Properties of common residential insulations. Recommended R-values for insulation. R-values for electric resistance heat are generally higher.*

Type	Average R/in	Cost	Application
Rolls, Batts, Blankets			friction-fit or staple in stud/joist bays, stuff in cracks
Fibreglass	3.2–3.8	low	
pros & cons:	Nonflammable (except for facings) Moisture-resistant, won't rot, Doesn't degrade in sunlight Resilient, won't settle Easy for owner-builder to install Convenient sizes, easily cut to fit irregular spaces		
	Unpleasant to work with Skin irritant, avoid breathing fibres, wear mask, protective clothing		
High-density fibreglass batts	3.7–4.3	medium	
pros & cons:	up to 25% more R-value per inch but 50–100% more cost		
Mineral wool	3.2–3.8	low	
pros & cons:	same as fibreglass withstands high temperatures		
	same as fibreglass sharp glassy slivers, more irritating than fibreglass heavier than fibreglass, thick batts will settle		
Woven cotton	3.5	low to medium	
pros & cons:	same sizes and R-values as fibreglass batts and blankets up to 65% lighter no itching or irritation, no protective clothing needed		
	new product, not widely available, or proven in field		

19-14 *(Continued) Properties of common residential insulations. Recommended R-values for insulation. R-values for electric resistance heat are generally higher.*

Type	Average R/in	Cost	Application
Rigid foam boards			exposed crawl spaces, cathedral ceilings, under roofing, between studs, glued to interior masonry
Expanded polystyrene ("Beadboard")	4.0	medium	

    pros & cons: relatively inexpensive,
                    very light, 4×8 sheets up to six inches thick
                    nonirritating

                    interior use only
                    fragile, easily broken
                    compressible, moisture permeable, degrades in sunlight
                    attracts mice, flammable, toxic fumes, cover with drywall
                    some types made with ozone-depleting CFCs

Type	Average R/in	Cost	Application
Extruded polystyrene ("Styrofoam")	5.0	high	

    pros & cons: impermeable, relatively noncompressible, used for foundation and under-slab insulation, excellent for
                    filler between blocking, partition backer spaces component of many structural panels and insulated-core
                    foundation blocks and concrete forms.

                    combustible, toxic gasses, must be covered with drywall when used inside
                    must be protected from direct sunlight outside
                    some brands still made with CFCs

Type	Average R/in	Cost	Application
Polyurethane and polyisocyanurate	6.2–7.8	high	

    pros & cons: used for exterior wall sheathing, also excellent under roofing (with intervening plywood skin, used in
                    coolers, nighttime window shutters, pipe insulation

                    Brittle, irritating dust (with fibreglass reinforced types), degrades when exposed to sunlight
                    outgassing with some types lowers R-values. Toxic gasses if ignited, isocyanurates less combustible than
                      other plastic foams, cover with drywall on interiors.

Type	Average R/in	Cost	Application
Foamed in place			
Urea-formaldehyde foam **presently outlawed**	5.0–6.8	medium	

    pros & cons: combustible, outgasses formaldehyde and shrinks if improperly installed, requires skilled professional
                    application, still many problems.

Type	Average R/in	Cost	Application
Sprayed in place			
Cellulose	3.0–4.0	high	

    pros & cons: sprayed directly over wallboard, concrete, wood, no cracks or gaps—ideal for irregular surfaces
                    can be pigmented—makes a finish wall where abrasion is not likely
                    absorbs less moisture than loose-fill cellulose, won't settle
                    combustible
                    requires professional application

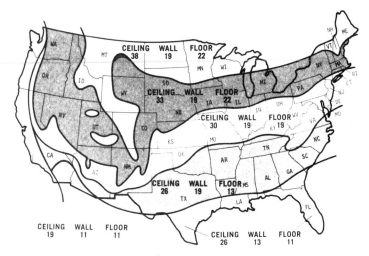

19-15 *Minimum recommended R-values for insulation.*

Each type of insulation has characteristics that make it uniquely suited to various applications. With insulation, "more is better" is true only up to a certain point. The optimal amount of insulation is a factor of initial material cost, present heating and cooling costs, projected increases in fuel costs, and climate conditions. It boils down to getting the maximum return on your investment in incremental R-value. The map in **19-15** gives minimum R-values that are presently considered to be the most cost-effective. Note that these recommendations are about half of superinsulated standards. I suspect that the current values will be revised upwards before long.

PUTTING IT ALL TOGETHER: INSULATING, WEATHERSTRIPPING, CAULKING, AND VENTILATION

The thermal envelope—which is the boundary between the heated and unheated zones of the house—is shown in **19-16,** as defined by the insulation.

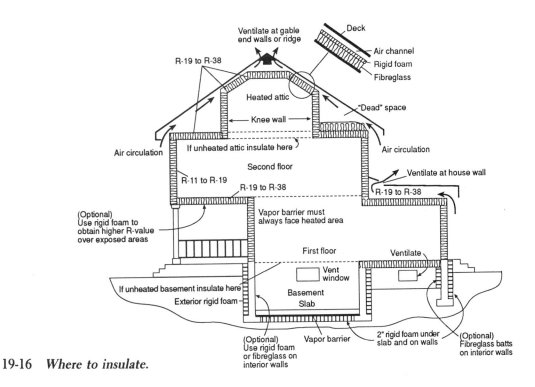

19-16 *Where to insulate.*

19-17 *One of the advantages of using rigid-foam exterior siding is that the house will stay fairly warm even before the ceiling insulation is installed, which makes it possible to heat it during rough-in.*

19-18 *No matter how or when you do it, installing fibreglass insulation is no fun at all. These batts will be friction-fitted into the stud bays. Note the flange of the poly vapor barrier in place over the ceiling insulation.*

There should not be any gaps in the continuity of the envelope or the vapor barrier which must always be installed on the heated side of the insulation (see **19-17**). The unheated side must always be vented to remove any vapor which has infiltrated past the barrier. The ventilation channels must run continuously between the back of the insulation and the underside of the roof decking, from the soffit inlet to the gable or ridge outlet.

I have a hunch that one of the reasons carpenters become contractors is so they can hire someone else to do the insulation (see **19-18**). No matter how you dress for it, installing fibreglass insulation is a pretty miserable job. The irritating fibres sift between loose-fitting garments or become trapped under the edges of tight sleeves. If it weren't for its low cost, there would be no reason to subject yourself to such misery. Fortunately, the ordeal is short-lived. Fibreglass insulation installs very quickly.

The kraft-paper and aluminum-foil facings on fibreglass insulation aren't very effective vapor barriers. Even if it

were possible to staple the pieces tightly to the studs without leaving any gaps or *puckers* (also called *fish mouths*), vapor can still move easily under their edges. The facing must be cut to fit around obstructions and gaps are left where it butts against the top and bottom wall plates.

Use unfaced blankets or batts instead. They cost less and are easier to install (see **19-19**). Ceiling insulation is the only exception. Friction won't hold unfaced batts over-

19-19 *Installing unfaced insulation. One way to increase the effectiveness of attic insulation is to lay a second layer of batts at right angles over the first.*

head. The paper facing keeps some of the dust from falling in your face and the stapling flange holds the insulation securely between the joists.

The batts should be carefully cut to butt snugly against the framing on all sides and at the top and bottom. Cut edges of adjoining pieces should also abut each other solidly. If a batt is too wide, don't compress it into the bay. Trim off the extra instead, leaving about one inch extra for a snug fit. Mark the length of the stud bays on the floor so that you can cut pieces all at once.

By compressing the insulation, you can cut it with a utility knife. But a 12-inch, serrated bread knife is a much handier cutting tool, especially for thick batts. If you're using faced insulation, cut through the paper side first. You'll know the knife is dull when it begins to tear the paper instead of cutting it cleanly. Resharpen the edge as needed with a mill file.

Install all the full-width pieces first. Use the trimmings from cut pieces for filling narrow bays and cracks around windows. Long vertical strips can be cut into short sections and installed horizontally to fill cripple bays under and over window openings. A little forethought keeps waste to a minimum.

Cut the insulation to fit around and behind electrical boxes (see 19-20). Don't leave any gaps. Slice the batt so that it will fold around cables and pipes. Slip high-R rigid foam behind warm-air ducts instead of stuffing the space with fibreglass.

When installing ceiling insulation, slit the insulation to fit snugly around any bridging. Always fill the spaces between the joists at the header joist with short pieces of batts or rigid foam. In a cold climate, forgetting to insulate against the rim of the floor deck can cause frost buildup that ruins the interior wall finish.

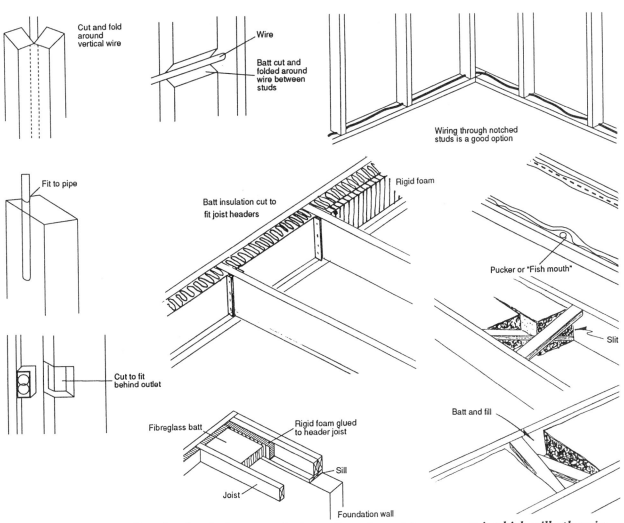

19-20 *When fitting fibreglass insulation around obstructions, try not to compress it which will otherwise reduce its R-value.*

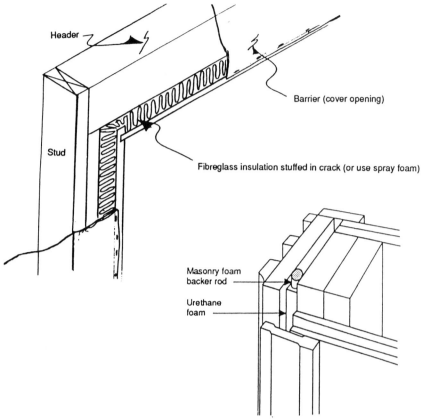

Header

Barrier (cover opening)

Stud

Fibreglass insulation stuffed in crack (or use spray foam)

Masonry foam
backer rod

Urethane
foam

19-21 *Filling cracks around windows and doors. Before installing the casing boards, cut the poly barrier back so that it overlaps the jambs but does not stick past the casing reveal.*

Don't neglect the gaps between window and door jambs and the studs (see **19-21**). An unfilled crack is a major route for outside air infiltration. Since the main idea is to block infiltration, it's better, in this case, to stuff the fibreglass into the crack than to worry about the loss of R-value that results from compressing fibreglass. Make a "stuffing stick," from a two- to three-inch-wide cedar shingle with its thin edge cut back to where it's about an eighth-inch thick.

For both high-R value and a tight seal, fill the gaps with urethane spray foam instead of fibreglass. Since the foam more than doubles in volume as it cures, avoid over-filling the cracks. The pressure exerted by excessive beads of cured foam can bow window and door jambs enough to interfere with their operation. Don't try to wipe excess foam off. Wait until it has hardened and trim it with a knife or plane.

Staple guns are inexpensive, but they are slow and awkward to use, particularly if you're stapling insulation to the ceiling. Although the best professional-grade staple hammer is fairly expensive, it will pay for itself in convenience and faster production many times over. It's indispensable for installing vapor barriers and house-wrap,

roofing tar paper, and almost any other stapling task. There's no general agreement on the best way to staple paper-faced insulation to the framing. Some recommend stapling the flanges over the face of the studs to make a tighter barrier. Others staple the flange to the inside edges of the studs (or joists), folding one or both flanges over on itself to stretch the facing tight (see **19-22**). Since the vapor barrier effect of paper facing is minimal at best, any advantage gained by overlapping the edges is offset by the difficulties it creates in locating studs for finish wall nailing. Unless very carefully stapled, lumps in the paper can make it impossible to pull the drywall tight against the framing.

To staple a less than full-width piece, cut the facing about 1½ inches beyond the edge of the batt, so that you can fold it into a flange (refer to **19-22**).

INSULATING THE ATTIC AND PROVIDING PROPER VENTILATION

Back when R-19 was the standard for ceiling insulation, the ends of the 5½-inch-thick fibreglass batts were laid directly over the top wall plate. There was usually enough space between the back of the insulation and the underside of the roof deck so that the path between the soffit air

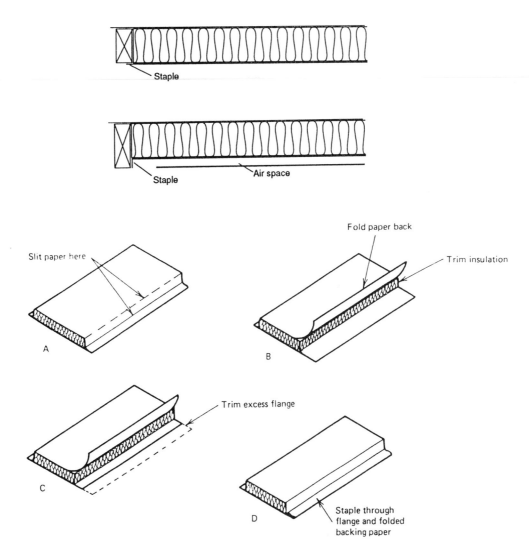

19-22 *Stapling flanges of paper-faced insulation. Stapling the insulation flange to the side of the stud instead of the face keeps the paper from bunching up under the wall finish.*

intake and the attic proper was unobstructed. Increasing the thickness of the batts to a 12-inch, R-38 created a problem: if the batts were laid across the top of the wall, they'd block off the air path. If they were cut back on an angle, they'd lose R-value. Stapling cardboard or corrugated plastic "chutes" between the rafters to keep the air channel open addressed the ventilation problem, but didn't do anything for the R-value problem since the ends of the batts still had to be cut or compressed to fit against the chutes. Since, as has been discussed earlier, an adequate air flow from soffit inlets to ridge or gable outlets is critical for controlling condensation and attic-heat buildup and preventing ice dams, it made sense to sacrifice R-values to ensure ventilation.

The problem is even worse with sloping ceilings between a knee-wall and the collar ties. Here, even 2×12

rafters don't have enough depth to accommodate both an air channel (minimum depth equal to 1½ inches) and 12 inches of fibreglass insulation.

One solution is to nail 1×2 cleats to the inside top edges of the rafters and push rigid foam insulation tightly up to them. Depending on the depth of the rafters and the desired R-value, either several thicknesses of extruded polystyrene or more expensive but higher-R polyisocyanurate boards or a combination of the two can be used. In the constricted area over the plates, substituting rigid foam panels for cardboard chutes compensates for the lower R-values of the fibreglass trimmed to fit against it. Depending on the relative cost of rafter stock versus rigid foam, it may be more cost effective to increase the rafters to a 2×12 and to use rigid foam in combination with fibreglass, especially if a cathedral ceiling is involved.

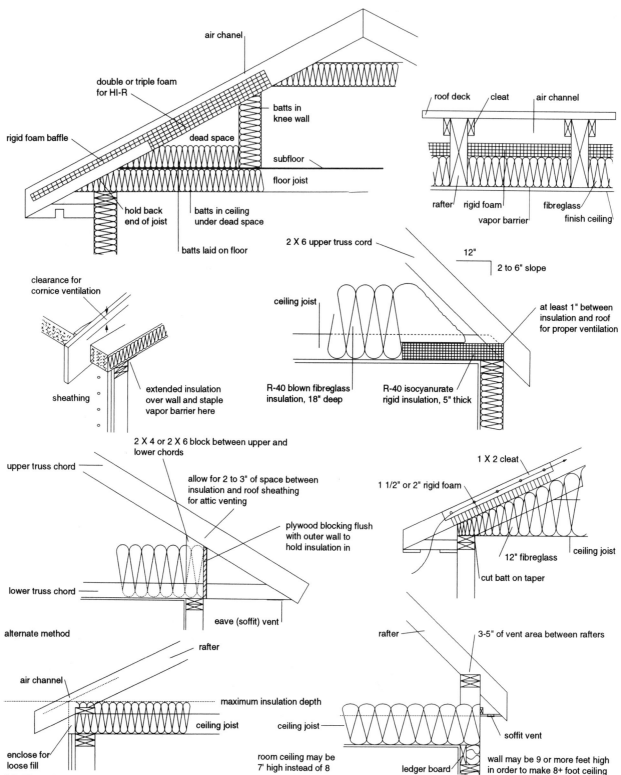

19-23 *Gaining extra depth for ceiling insulation. Adding an extra foot to the wall height and hanging the ceiling joists from ledgers below the plates is one possible way to gain extra space for attic insulation. Ordering wider trusses also has the same effect.*

500

Another solution, originally developed for the 12- to 16-inch depths of loose-fill insulation used with superinsulated construction, is to use raised roof trusses or special modified scissor trusses for cathedral ceilings. Nailing ordinary rafters to a plate placed on top of the ceiling joists instead of to the standard wall plate is another way to gain increased depth for accommodating insulation without the use of trusses (see **19-23**). If not otherwise enclosed by the soffit lookout, or if using loose-fill insulation, enclose the joist bays by extending the wall sheathing up between the rafters to the ventilation channel.

Using loose-fill insulation in the ceiling is also a good way to sidestep the unpleasantness of stapling fibreglass overhead. There's a difference between pouring and blowing type loose-fill insulations. There's also a difference between the blowing machines for mineral wool/fibreglass and cellulose. You can rent a cellulose blower, but, in most cases, only professional insulators have mineral and fibreglass machines. Blown-in insulation is mostly used for retrofitting old houses and other existing structures too awkward to reach by other means. It's seldom used in new construction.

Poured loose-fill attic insulation is easy to do yourself and considerably less expensive (see **19-24**). If you use cellulose or vermiculite, there's no irritation to contend with either (a respirator should be worn, however, to protect against the harmful effects of inhaling the dust). It's the most practical way to achieve the high R-values (R-40+) typical of super-energy-efficient construction. A nominal 12 inches is the upper limit of fibreglass-batt insulation. Even if the paper flanges could support the extra weight, it would tend to compress a super-thick standard batt (a higher-density fibre would be too expensive). Loose-fill vermiculite and fibreglass (and to a lesser extent, mineral wool) can be poured up to two feet thick with no significant settlement. (One possible option would be to fill the joist bays with loose-fill vermiculite, and then lay 12-inch fibreglass batts on top of them.)

Poured loose-fill is also ideal for fitting around obstructions (e.g., as in a truss roof). Nothing has to be cut or notched to fit. There are no gaps over the tops of joists or between joints.

To obtain the desired R-value, loose-fill insulation must be poured to the depth specified on the product label. Nail one-by "strike-off" boards across the tops of the joists as shown in **19-24** to make screeds for levelling off the insulation to the desired depth. Leave the strike-off boards in place. They can be used to support a plank walkway over the top of the insulation. An ordinary garden rake or a rake fashioned from 1×3 strapping and a scrap of plywood will let you push the insulation against the baffles and into other areas too low to crawl into. Install the ventilation baffles and any closures at the rafter plates before putting up the ceiling (likewise, staple the vapor barrier to the undersides of the joists, too). Extend the headers at the attic access opening to the level of the finished

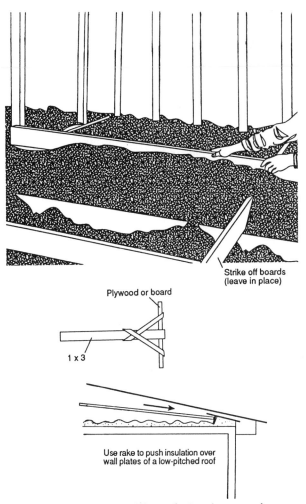

Strike off boards (leave in place)

Plywood or board

1 x 3

Use rake to push insulation over wall plates of a low-pitched roof

19-24 *Pouring loose-fill insulation in an attic. Failure to leave standard ceiling light fixtures uncovered by insulation creates a dangerous fire hazard.*

insulation. Always wear a dust mask or respirator when working with poured insulation.

Check with your local electrical inspector about running wires through loose-fill insulation. You may be required to use conduit or BX cable. The NEC requires a three-inch gap between any recessed light fixture or bathroom fan and the insulation. Build a metal box to keep loose insulation away. Or you can use special, recessed lighting fixtures designed to be covered by insulation.

If the pitch of the roof is sufficiently high to permit access near the eaves, you could opt to lay unfaced fibreglass batts between the ceiling joists after the ceiling is installed. Use 12-inch batts for truss roofs. For a tighter job with standard rafters, lay six- or eight-inch insulation between the floor joists, and lay a second layer over the joists perpendicular to the first.

When tongue-and-groove decking is laid out across exposed timber rafters in a cathedral ceiling, the insulation has to be put on the exterior side of the roof deck. Generally, rigid foam boards are laid over the decking (see **19-25**). Unless you use factory-made foam panels (urethane or Styrofoam with a waferboard nail-base skin which can be up to 12 inches thick), you'll have to overlap two or three layers of two-inch, polyisocyanurate panels to get enough R-value. Stagger and caulk the joints between the layers to reduce infiltration and to repel water. Two-by stock, ripped to the correct thickness, and nailed to the edges of the decking and a backer piece provide both a stop for the insulation and a subfascia for the finish trim boards. The decking should be covered with a poly vapor barrier before laying down the insulation panels. Nail the edges of the waferboard (or ⅜-inch plywood) to the backers. The rest of the sheets are glued to the top layer of insulation and anchored to the deck with six- or eight-inch (for four- and six-inches of insulation, respectively) ring-shank "pole-barn" nails driven through roofing tins to increase their holding power. Space the nails out at one-foot intervals along the edges and down the middle of each sheet.

As mentioned in Chapter Five, one problem with nailing the roofing over foam panels is that it may void the shingle manufacturer's warranty. There's a chance that, lacking the buffer of an attic or ventilated deck between them and the underlying insulation, the shingles will over-

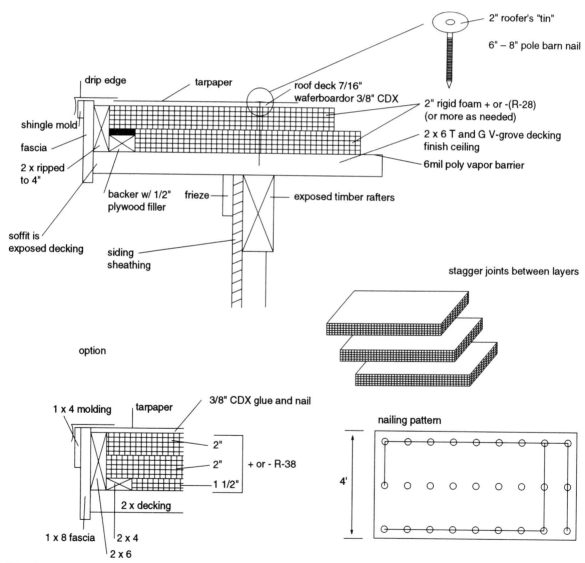

19-25 Rigid insulation laid directly on top of a roof deck does not require a ventilating air channel. Insulation panels with a factory-laminated nail base are an alternative to individual layers.

heat and break down. Structural stress skin panels designed for roofing have built-in ventilation channels, but they're very expensive. One option is to run vertical strapping at 24-inch centers over the insulation (drill pilot holes through the strapping so that the pole-barn nails won't split it), and lay plywood over it to form a ventilated deck—use H-clips to keep the edges from sagging (see **19-26**).

Extend the strapping over the eaves fascia board to make a screened inlet.

Laying rigid foam on top of a V-groove ceiling is the best way to achieve high R-values with the lowest profile at the rake and eaves. And, as long as it has a chance to dry out before laying down the waferboard, it will withstand an occasional shower with no ill effects.

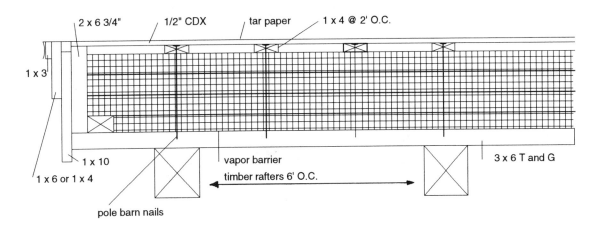

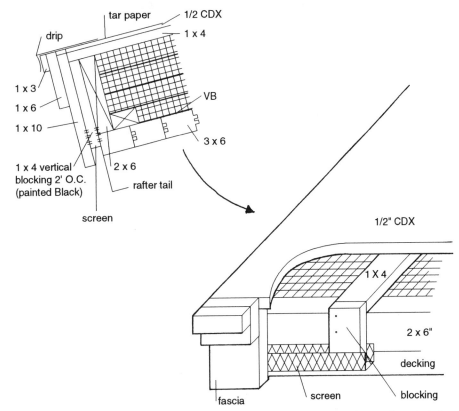

19-26 *Ventilation for rigid foam over decking. Because the soffit is solid decking, the air inlet for the roof deck is built behind the fascia board.*

19-27 *Two-by-sixes have been nailed to the roofside of exposed-beam ceiling boards for installing fibreglass insulation on top of the roof deck. Unfortunately, this inexperienced owner-builder neglected to drill air holes through the solid blocking (or use a 2×4) to make a continuous ventilation channel in each bay. Nor did he lay a poly vapor barrier over the boards before attaching the 2×6s. Since a 2×6 only allows enough room for R-19 fibreglass, the depth of the insulation cavity could be increased by using lightweight plywood and 2×4 I-beams in place of wider and heavier dimension lumber.*

Unfortunately, any roofing system that involves rigid foam insulation will be quite costly. A low-cost alternative is to run rafters on 24-inch centers over the decking and to fill the bays between them with ordinary fibreglass batts (see **19-27**). Because of the air channel requirement, you can't fit more than 9½-inch R-33 batts between 2×12 rafters. Since the exposed timber rafters and the decking are carrying the structural load, these secondary rafters need only to transfer the snow load to the decking. Simple site-built plywood and two-by box beams will provide enough depth for R-38 insulation and adequate stiffness to carry the roof load (see **19-28**).

Whether you decide to use structural foam panels, site-built layered foam roofing, or a fibreglass and secondary rafter system, careful attention should be given to the rake and eaves treatment to keep the bulk of the profile to a minimum.

The insulation panels can overhang the building line to form a full-depth, square-cut "railroad jet." But the insulation can also end at the walls and the cornices can be hung from the extended roof plywood. The extensions can terminate in lookouts for traditional cornices as well. Or, with unvented foam panels, the overhang can be clipped tight to the rake and terminate in a built-in wood gutter at the eaves. Another problem area, which was touched upon in Chapter Three, is insulating the floor above an exposed crawl space or unheated basement (see **19-29**). Since the vapor barrier must be installed between the floor and the insulation, the batts cannot be stapled between the floor joists. At one time, a special "reverse-flange" batt was widely used for this purpose. This batt was faced on both sides. An asphalt-coated paper faced towards the floor, and a plain paper flanged side faced the cellar. Unfortunately, for one reason or another this sensible product is no longer available. Nowadays, builders resort to stretching 16-gauge wire between roofing nails driven into the undersides of the joists to support the batts of unfaced insulation that are slipped between the bays. Special bowed-wire insulation supports are also available for this same purpose. Another option is to staple faced insulation to the joists, install wire supports, and then slice open the paper facing to short-circuit the vapor barrier.

I'd recommend using rigid foam or laying the insulation from above as described in Chapter Three. At the very least, staple it to the tops of the joists, lay down the vapor barrier and then lay down the floor deck, and, at a convenient time, cover the exposed face of the insulation with IB board or *Homosote* (a compressed paper panel often used for underlayments, roof decking, and, sometimes, finished walls and ceilings) to keep the fibres out of any area used for storage and to prevent vermin from nesting in the batts.

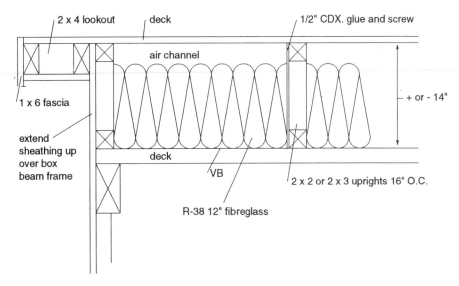

19-28 *Installing fibreglass batts over roof decking. The top chords of the box beams are extended to make a rafter tail that carries the eaves soffit, and a false rafter is attached to the sheathing at the rake end where it extends up over the box beam so that the profile of the fascia is of normal width.*

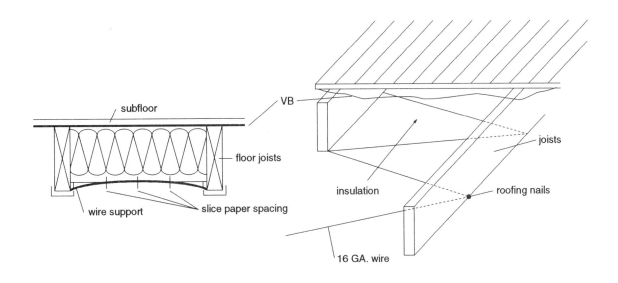

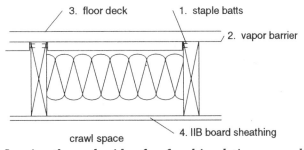

19-29 *Insulation of crawl spaces. Leaving the underside of unfaced insulation exposed to a crawl space makes it vulnerable to infiltration by pests as well as released glass fibres.*

INSTALLING VAPOR BARRIERS

The first step in installing a vapor barrier is to clean the floors. Pick up any stray nails or other debris that might puncture the film as you roll it out. The joint between the sole plate and the subfloor should be free of any dirt that could get trapped beneath the barrier.

Roll the poly out across the floor, allowing at least an extra foot for the lap onto the walls at its ends. Whenever possible, use sheets wide enough to cover the room with a single piece. Lift one edge of the sheet up and staple its edge to the wall studs about a foot below the plate. Then, unfolding the sheet and stretching it into the corner between the plate and ceiling joists, staple it to the joists. It's easier to run the sheet straight when you can eyeball the distance between the edge and the top plate instead of beginning at the ceiling. Work across the room, stretching the sheet evenly. Slice the corner folds so they lay flat against the walls. Cover over any electrical boxes or other obstructions (fold any projecting wires back into the boxes before putting up the barrier).

Staple the barrier to the walls next. Staple across the length of the top, and then work down the middle stud and downwards and outwards along the other studs towards the corners. Leave enough extra material to overlap the next stud bay at the corners, and let the barrier run out about six inches onto the floor. Cut the corners for a neat fold. If you used the technique described earlier in this chapter, lift up the flange of the vapor barrier strip that runs under the sole plate, and staple it to the studs. Then run a bead of acrylic copolymer caulk or staple polyethylene acoustical sealant along it before stapling the wall sheet over it.

Lay the film over windows and doors. Except for the doors, *don't cut out any openings* until after the wall finish is applied. Seal the barrier to the header and jack studs. Likewise, caulk the overlapping seams between sheets. Leaving the barrier in place until after the walls are painted saves a lot of cleanup work or protective masking. If you need ventilation, make a single slice in the sheet and reach behind it to open the windows.

Electrical boxes are a major source of vapor leaks and outside air infiltration (see **19-30**). If the boxes cannot be placed inside the vapor barrier, caulk the wires where they enter the boxes (use a highly flexible caulk). Any holes where the cable or pipes penetrate the top or sole plates or run to the outside should have been caulked before installing the insulation. Cut the barrier *inside* the boxes, leaving a ½ inch rim that can be stretched to fit tightly against the outside of the box—where it is then sealed to it with clear polyethylene tape. Insert a neoprene foam-rubber gasket under the cover plate.

Run a strip of tape down each stud to seal the staple punctures, and take care to patch any tears or punctures in the sheet with tape. Glue any poly film patches over large holes with sealant before taping. Some builders also run a bead of flexible sealant over all the studs and joists before putting up the finish walls to seal the punctures made by screws and nails.

CAULKING AND WEATHERSTRIPPING

The shelves of your local building materials dealer are stocked with what may seem to be a bewildering variety of caulks and sealants. In most cases, the best caulks are apt to be the most expensive ones. The table given in **19-31** compares the characteristics and performance of various readily available caulking compounds. A close reading of the product label will usually indicate the chemical family the caulk belongs to.

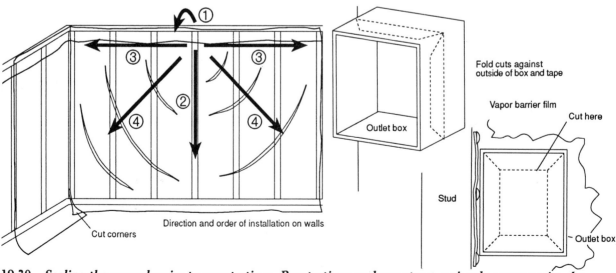

19-30 *Sealing the vapor barrier to penetrations. Penetrations and punctures seriously compromise the effectiveness of a vapor barrier.*

19-31 *Characteristics of common caulking materials.*

Type	Relative Cost	Durability	Flexibility (comments)
Oil-based	cheap	1–3 years	poor—dries out
(Don't use for permanent sealing, OK for window glazing)			
Vinyl latex	low	3–5	poor—shrinks
(Available in many colors; interior use only, degrades in sunlight, useful as a crack filler for painting)			
Acrylic latex	low	5–10	poor
(Same as vinyl latex, doesn't adhere well to metal)			
Silicon acrylic latex	low-medium	10–20	fair
(Best bet for low-cost caulking, adheres well to all materials except plastics, wide color range, fairly flexible, can be used outdoors, paintable)			
Polyvinyl acetate	low-med	10–20	fair
(Advantages similar to siliconized acrylic latex, also available in translucent color, adhesive, can be used as glue, will bond well on moist surfaces, useful in marine applications, wood-to-wood and wood-to-masonry joints.)			
Note: All vinyl-based caulks are noted for their easy application. Uncured caulk can be cleaned up with water. All acrylic caulks are excellent for wood-to-wood joints.			
Butyl rubber	medium	5–10	poor
(Sticky, hard to use, excellent water-resistance for roofing, degrades in direct sunlight, good for wood-to masonry and wood-to-metal joints.)			
Neoprene rubber rubber-asphalt	medium-high	10–15	good
(Patching foundations, concrete, sealing flashings, roofing, glazing)			
Polysulfide	medium	20+	good
(Difficult to apply, temperature must be over 60°F [15.5°C], requires special priming on many surfaces, will adhere to many problem surfaces [plastics, glass, wood-to-masonry, damp conditions], degrades in sunlight).			
Elastomeric acrylic copolymer	medium	25+	excellent
(Excellent adhesion to virtually any substrate, especially metal-to-metal joints with large range of motion, transparent or paintable and colored types, sticky and messy, difficult to apply upside-down, resealable, brushable grade for sealing large areas, won't degrade in sunlight.)			
Solvent-based acrylic	medium	20	very good
(UV-stable, excellent adhesion to glass, self-sealing, used for all glazing except polycarbonate or acrylic plastics)			
Silicone	high	25+	very good
(Cannot be painted, transparent and colored types, doesn't adhere well to plastics, pressure-treated wood, porous surfaces, very flexible, durable, can be applied over a very wide temperature range on dry surfaces, specialized RTV (room-temperature-vulcanized) type for high-temperature applications. Withstands high humidity situations and mildew better than other caulks, good for wood to metal, wood-to-wood.)			
Modified silicone			
(Same as other silicones, but paintable, doesn't hold paint as well as latex caulks.)			
Polyurethane (acoustical sealant)	high	20+	very good
(Excellent for filling large gaps up to ¾ inch, difficult to apply, requires staples or other support, remains flexible.)			
Urethane foams	high	10–20	poor
(Expandable foam sealants for filling cracks around windows, framing, plugging holes and penetrations, degrades in sunlight, messy to apply and cleanup.)			
Construction adhesives	low-high	varies	poor to fair
(For sealing vapor barriers, panel adhesives, bonding foam insulation, structural and non-structural uses, pressure-treated wood, wide variety of specialized applications, check for compatibility of solvents with substrate.)			

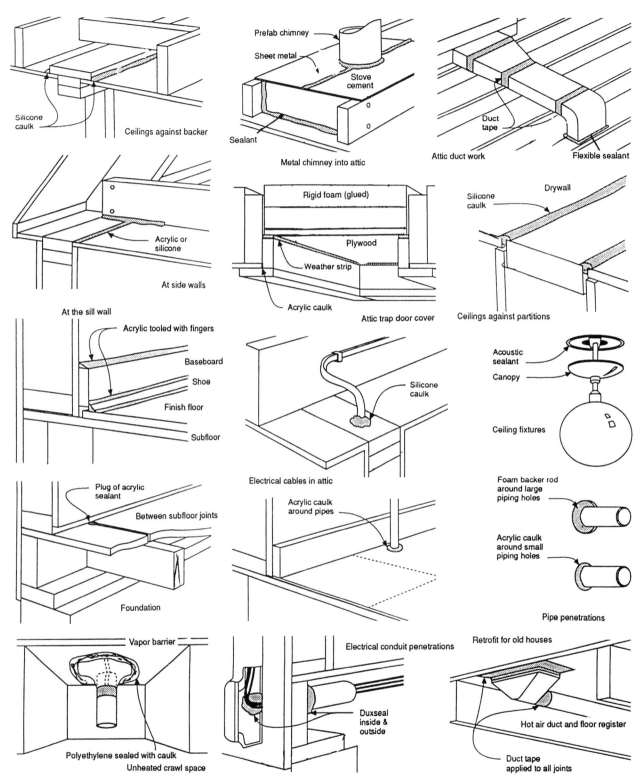

Silicone caulk

Ceilings against backer

Prefab chimney

Sheet metal

Stove cement

Sealant

Metal chimney into attic

Duct tape

Attic duct work

Flexible sealant

Acrylic or silicone

At side walls

Rigid foam (glued)

Plywood

Weather strip

Acrylic caulk

Attic trap door cover

Silicone caulk

Drywall

Ceilings against partitions

At the sill wall

Acrylic tooled with fingers

Baseboard

Shoe

Finish floor

Subfloor

Silicone caulk

Electrical cables in attic

Acoustic sealant

Canopy

Ceiling fixtures

Plug of acrylic sealant

Between subfloor joints

Foundation

Acrylic caulk around pipes

Foam backer rod around large piping holes

Acrylic caulk around small piping holes

Pipe penetrations

Vapor barrier

Polyethylene sealed with caulk
Unheated crawl space

Electrical conduit penetrations

Duxseal inside & outside

Retrofit for old houses

Hot air duct and floor register

Duct tape applied to all joints

19-32 *Caulking against infiltration within the thermal envelope. Only builders trained in the techniques of ADA and superinsulation will attempt to seal all the myriad sources of infiltration. If all these gaps are sealed, costly supplemental mechanical ventilation will be needed to keep the house air fresh and healthy.*

508

Caulking should be applied during construction between window and door casings and the exterior sheathing. Any penetrations through an exterior wall for wires, outdoor plumbing, antenna lead-ins, vents, and fans should also be caulked. Besides blocking infiltration, caulking must also keep water out of the building envelope. The tops and bottoms of all doors, the tops of window drip caps, and the joints between siding and trim should all be sealed with a high-grade, flexible and paintable siliconized acrylic latex, polyvinyl, or silicone caulk. Less-flexible caulks should be reserved for masonry joints where there is little movement. Large gaps should be packed with flexible polyurethane *backer rod* before caulking. Although even most professionals think otherwise, I am convinced that the proper application technique for caulking is actually *to push the tip* of the caulking cartridge *forward rather than pulling it back* as the bead is applied. To seal the edges of the bead to the substrate, "tool" them with a moistened fingertip.

In addition to the obvious sources of infiltration in the exterior walls, some typical *internal* heat leaks and the methods for plugging them are shown in **19-32**.

Caulks seal joints. Weatherstripping is used to seal the gaps between moving surfaces. There are almost as many types of weatherstripping materials as there are caulking compounds (see **19-33**). Unlike caulks, the quality and performance of weatherstripping tends to be less proportional to price.

19-33 *Comparison of common weatherstripping materials.*

Type	Cost	Durability	Installation (comments)
Wool felt	cheap	poor	staple or glue
(Easy to use, compacts and rots, mostly as backing for wood storm panels where there is no frequent movement.)			
Vinyl or aluminum-backed felt	low	poor	nail against side jambs
(Backing provides stiffness so that weatherstripping can be used on edge against door or window closure.)			
Vinyl self-adhesive foam strips	low	poor	self-sticking glue
(The glue dries out and the vinyl degrades and crumbles after exposure to weather, but it won't rot and so lasts longer than felt.)			
Closed-cell rubber strips (self-adhesive)	low	fair	self-sticking
(Neoprene rubber is more durable than vinyl foam. Works well as a compression-type seal for doors, hinged windows, and attic hatches.)			
Plastic V-spring	low to medium	good	self-sticking, staple, nail, slip into groove
(Versatile, works well with windows and doors, good for sliding joints.)			
Spring-and-cushion metal interlock	medium to high	excellent	surface nail or install in groove
(Gives years of service and tight seal under severe conditions, used for doors, windows, can require considerable skill and power tools to install.)			
Hollow and foam-filled vinyl or rubber bulb	Low to medium	good	Nail or slip into groove
(Requires little pressure for good seal, useful for doors and casement windows, heavy-duty type used for garage door seals, longer lasting than other types of vinyl, easy to install.)			
Wood-backed foam strips	Medium	good	nail to jambs or stops
(Two sizes, for light-duty doors and windows, large size for heavy doors, best installed over integral door stop, otherwise tends to move, not for sliding doors and windows, foam will eventually degrade, don't paint it. Easy to install/replace.)			
Vinyl-edge aluminum door sweeps	low	fair	screw to bottom edge of door
(Easy to install, adjust for seal, but vinyl edge becomes brittle and breaks off, cheap appearance.)			
Vinyl bulb gasket aluminum threshold	medium to high	good	screw to bottom of door or to sill
(Various configurations, create tight seal by compression of door- or sill-mounted heavy duty vinyl gasket set in aluminum stock, vinyl eventually wears out. Improper application interferes with operation of door.)			

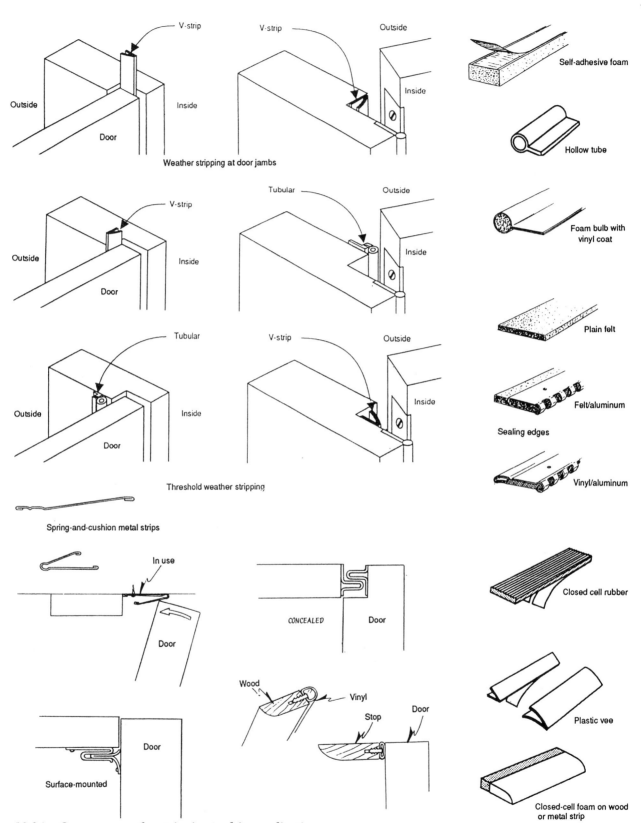

Weather stripping at door jambs

Threshold weather stripping

Spring-and-cushion metal strips

19-34 *Common weatherstripping and its application.*

Self-adhesive foam

Hollow tube

Foam bulb with vinyl coat

Plain felt

Felt/aluminum

Sealing edges

Vinyl/aluminum

Closed cell rubber

Plastic vee

Closed-cell foam on wood or metal strip

If not factory-installed, apply weatherstripping to all doors and operable windows, trapdoors, hatches, or any kind of closure or access panel between heated and unheated spaces (see 19-34). In addition to caulking and weatherstripping, seal the vapor barrier to any penetrations such as plumbing drain and vent pipes with duct tape. Tape all joints in air ducts and seal registers to the floor with tape or caulk.

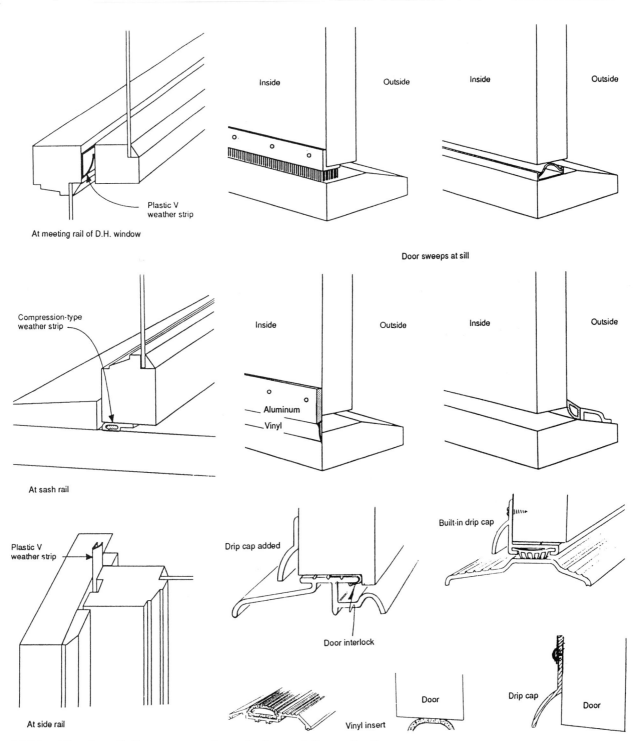

19-34 (Continued) Common weatherstripping and its application.

19-35 *Aluminum gable wall ventilators that can be adjusted to fit the roof pitch are quite commonly used in low-cost construction. A wood ventilator is much more handsome, but considerably more expensive. Angled wood ventilators are manufactured to fit a variety of typical roof pitches. Less expensive square and rectangular wood vents are also available.*

VENTILATION

As was discussed earlier, ventilating the attic is an important part of controlling interior moisture and heat build-up problems (see **19-35**). The effect of an unvented and a properly vented attic on internal comfort and structural integrity is shown in **19-36**.

Attic ventilation is usually achieved by the installation of a ready-made gable wall louver (see **19-37**). These can be either adjustable aluminum units in plain or white or brown enamel finish, wood units built to a predetermined pitch or rectangular wood or aluminum louvers. Continuous ridge ventilators are even more effective. Ready-made, perforated or louvered two-inch-wide aluminum strips are used for soffit inlets.

The code prescribes net free areas of the ventilation opening (see **19-38**). These will vary according to the presence or lack of a ceiling vapor barrier and the type of roof construction. Assuming that half the total area of the ventilation openings is distributed equally between a soffit inlet and a higher outlet, you can figure a ratio of free area to attic area of 1:150 for ceilings without vapor bar-

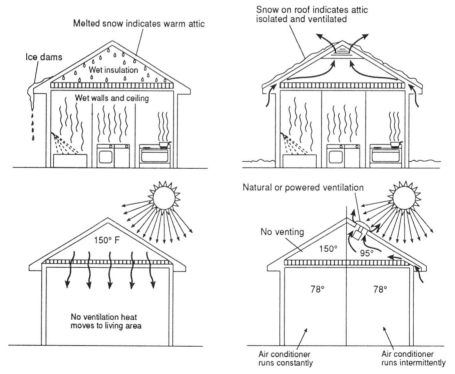

19-36 *Relationship between attic ventilation and indoor comfort. In winter, moisture that moves through the ceiling collects in an unvented attic where it condenses and saturates the insulation and leaks into the walls and ceilings; in a vented attic, the minimal amount of moisture that works into the attic past the vapor barrier escapes into the outside air without harm; in summer, the insulation absorbs heat which is radiated back into the living spaces through the ceiling. With an unvented attic, the air-conditioning must run constantly to maintain a comfortable temperature. With ventilation, the attic temperature can be almost 40 percent lower. The air-conditioner only needs to work intermittently.*

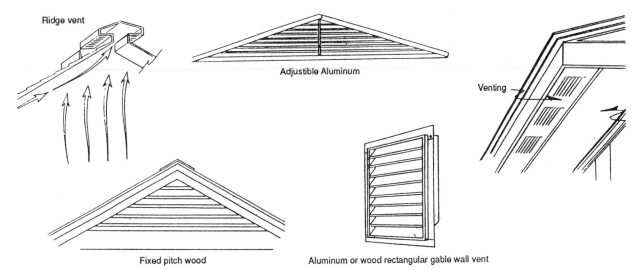

Ridge vent

Adjustable Aluminum

Venting

Fixed pitch wood

Aluminum or wood rectangular gable wall vent

19-37 *Types of attic vents. When an exterior chimney occupies the area that would normally be given over to a gable vent, the vent is sometimes built into the chimney itself.*

riers and a low-pitched roof with an outlet less than three feet above the inlet. Adding a vapor barrier or increasing the height of the inlets and outlet above the attic floor drops the ratio to 1:300. The same ratio is also required for cathedral ceilings (use a ridge vent). Where summer temperatures are high, a 1:150 ratio and/or a continuous ridge vent is recommended no matter what type of construction has been utilized.

A useful rule of thumb for figuring the ratio between the gross area of the ventilator and its free area is to use 1:3 for $\frac{1}{16}$ inch insect screen and 1:2 for $\frac{1}{8}$-inch screen or slit soffit louvers.

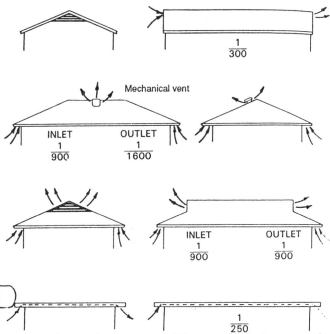

19-38 *Relationship between attic ventilator area and floor area. Codes prescribe the minimum ratio between ventilator area and attic floor area depending on the location and type of ventilation outlet and inlets used.*

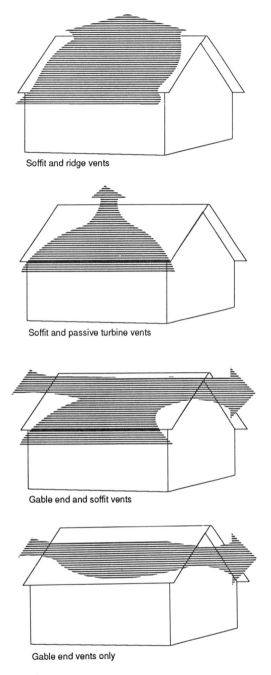

Soffit and ridge vents

Soffit and passive turbine vents

Gable end and soffit vents

Gable end vents only

19-39 *Providing continuous air flow above insulation.*

One condition which is often overlooked is that the ventilation channel above the insulation must be continuous (see **19-39**). If a skylight header or some other obstruction blocks off the air channel, notch or bore holes in the tops of the adjoining rafters to divert the airflow into an unobstructed bay.

While it may not make much difference if only one or two bays are blocked off, failing to provide an outlet for the channels beneath the roof of a heated attached porch or bump-out could cause serious condensation problems, particularly if the structure is an attached greenhouse. Ready-made, continuous side-wall ventilators similar to ridge ventilators have recently been introduced (see **19-40**). Prior to this, the only solution was to build your own outlet against the sidewall or to add strapping beneath the wall siding so that the roof could vent into it and up into the rake or eaves soffit.

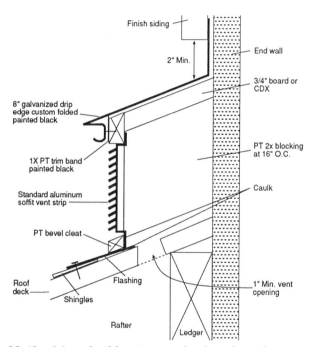

19-40 *Many builders ignore the fact that when the roof of any insulated structure such as an enclosed heated porch, shed, greenhouse, or lower storey "bump-out" ends against a building wall, an outlet for the ventilating channel between the insulation and roof deck must be provided.*

20 Stair-Building

Unless you're building a single-storey house on a slab foundation, your plans will include at least one set of stairs (see 20-1). Some builders like to build "rough" stairs immediately after nailing down the floor deck. Others (myself included) prefer to hold off until the roof deck is tarpapered. Whereas clambering up and down a ladder in the stairwell is inconvenient, leaving the stairs for "rainy day work" makes the best use of time in climates where closing in the house is a race against the weather. Another reason to hold off on stair construction is that there might not otherwise be enough clearance between the stair carriage and the floor header to slide the furnace or boiler down into the cellar (but, you can also avoid this problem by coordinating the delivery of these components with the floor framing).

Even more than rafter layout, building a set of stairs is one of those watershed skills that distinguishes an accomplished carpenter from a novice. While even utility stairs must be properly laid out for ease and safety of use, an exposed main stair is typically a prominent architectural feature of the house and thus requires the same careful attention, high-level skills, and quality materials to build as a fine piece of cabinetry or furniture. This is one reason that professional builders will often subcontract their stair work out to custom cabinet shops (or a stair-building specialist) or have their carpenters install factory-made prefabricated stairs instead of building them from scratch. So long as the stairwell opening is carefully constructed according to plan and the dimensions furnished to the mill are accurate, installing a factory-made set of stairs can be somewhat easier. It's certainly an option that a relatively unskilled owner-builder should consider.

As with roof framing and cabinetry, entire books as well as entire lifetimes can be devoted to the mastery of the stair-building art. But, as long as you understand the basic principles that underlie stair design, building a set of simple stairs should not be any harder than framing a simple gable roof.

20-1 *Even some professional carpenters find building a relatively simple set of straight-run stairs to be a formidable undertaking. Fitting the balustrade to the newel post calls for skillful and precise cutting.*

Stairs are best "built" on paper before they're framed with wood (see **20-2**). The actual stairs are an "in-the-field" adjustment of the virtual stairs as worked out in your scale drawings. The first consideration is finding the type of stair layout (or *run*) that makes the best use of the available space in your floor plan.

A "closed" straight-run stairway is the easiest to build. The stair carriage can be attached solidly to the enclosing walls. Only a simple, wall-mounted handrail is needed for safety. A stairway with one or both sides unwalled is called an "open" run. The unenclosed side must be protected by a railing (also called a *balustrade*) that is typically assembled with decorative, factory-milled components. The half-wall barrier is a much simpler alternative to the balustrade that's well suited to contemporary designs and the skills of a novice builder. The top edge of the barrier is usually trimmed with a flat wood cap that serves as a decorative handrail. Even though straight-run stairs are

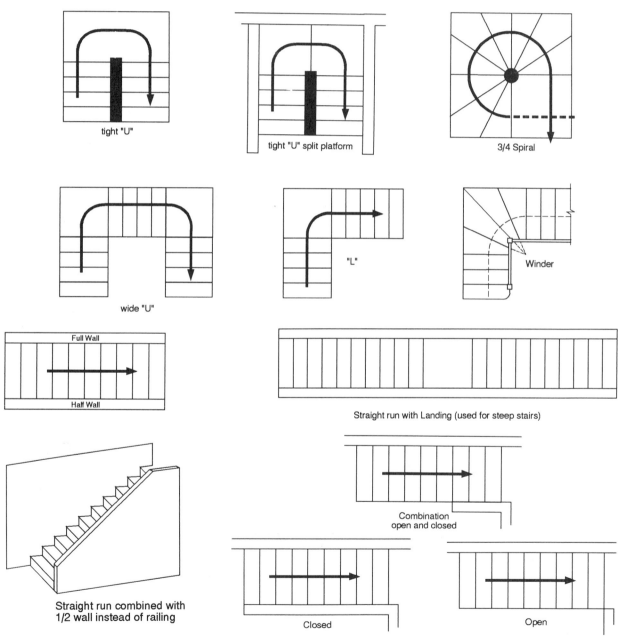

20-2   *The configuration of a stair run is mainly dictated by the volume of space available for the stairwell that is decided in the initial design phase of the project.*

the easiest to build, the run is often broken up by a landing platform for practical or aesthetic reasons. One or more landings permit changes of direction so that the stairwell opening can make the best use of the available space and headroom. Since a landing is also a safety feature that breaks up a potentially life-threatening fall into less hazardous lengths, U- and L-runs are a good choice for households that contain very young or very old inhabitants. The location and number of landings and the width of the stairwell for both L- and U-type stairways can vary in combination with open, closed, railing, or barrier treatments for aesthetic effect and space limitations.

When space is too tight to permit standard treads, *winder* stairs will subdivide a landing into triangular treads (refer to **20-20**). This gain in rise compromises safety. Even when properly laid out so that the point of convergence of the winder treads lies far enough outside of the corner so that a uniform 10-inch minimum tread width is maintained at the path of travel (about 16 inches in from the narrow end of the treads, which should be at least 4 inches wide at this point), a misstep can result in a nasty fall. Check to see if your building code even allows winders to be used on a main stair run in the first place.

A spiral stair run is another solution for extremely tight stairwell areas. Factory-made steel spiral staircases are most often used in such cases. Custom-built wood spiral stair runs are considerably more difficult to build but can be very dramatic and quite comfortable to travel if the stairwell area is large enough. Spiral runs can make a complete circle or a fractional portion or addition of one.

A set of stairs, as can be seen in **20-3,** is made up of two or three heavy *stringers*, which together comprise the *carriage* or *rough horse* that carries the *treads* and *riser* boards (risers are sometimes left out in modern designs).

The rules that govern staircase design, particularly the relationship between riser height and tread width, have been distilled from centuries of empirical experience. It's been established that stairs with a pitch of 30 degrees to 36 degrees instinctively feel the most comfortable and safe to climb. This pitch works out to a *unit rise* of 6½ to eight inches per step. Main stairs typically have a rise of around 7½ inches, while cellar and attic stairs tend to be steeper (up to nine inches) and outdoor public stairs shallower (four to seven inches). Any stair steeper than 50 degrees is just a ladder.

For the same reasons, the width of the tread is inversely related to the height of the riser: that is, as the rise increases, the tread width should decrease, and vice versa. Increasing the height of the risers also decreases the number of treads (and their width), which in turn shortens the overall length of the stairwell opening. This is why cellar, attic, and other "utility" stairs are so often built steep. However, it's a foolish economy to sacrifice safety to save space—even where codes permit nine-inch-high risers.

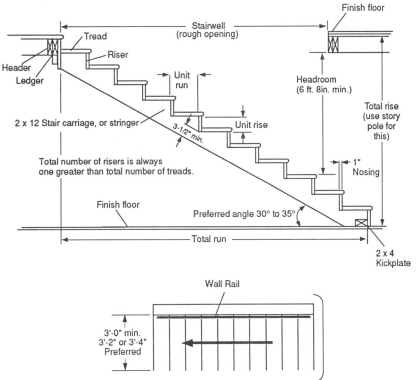

20-3 *Basic components of stair layout.*

Stair-building wisdom can be summed up in three rules of thumb, all of which must apply—although, in practice, only the first (which was promulgated by French architect François Blondel in 1672) is generally necessary, so long as you keep your stair rise within the 6½ to eight-inch range:

1. *The sum of two risers and one tread should equal 25.*

2. *The sum of one riser and one tread should be 17 to 18.*

3. *The riser times the tread width should be about 75.*

For the purposes of these calculations, tread width does not include the width of the tread *nosing*, which is the rounded leading edge of the tread that overhangs the face of the riser (see **20-4**). Although the resulting "toe space" is a necessary component of a safe stair, an excessively wide nosing has the opposite effect and can cause the stair climber to trip. For closed stairs, the ideal nosing is between ¾ inch to 1¼ inches wide and, in any case, not more than 1½ inches. If your stair design doesn't include riser boards, the overhang of the nosing should be increased to two inches. Some builders feel that since the riser-tread rules aren't perfect, they should not be relied on. Instead, they use the "7–11 Rule," which basically says that the stair run should always be designed so that its riser height and tread width end up as close as possible to 7 and 11 inches, respectively. In my experience, an (approximately) 7½-inch riser and 2×12 plank tread (actual width 11¼ inches, inclusive of nosing overhang) are an ideal combination.

Finally, there must be enough *headroom* between the treads and the stairwell ceiling and/or floor header so you won't smack your forehead into the stairwell header as you walk down the steps. Building codes require a minimum headroom of 6'-8". If space permits, 7'-4" is much better. Where stairwell space is tight, you can maintain the minimum headroom at the bottom of the stairs without sacrificing upstairs floor area by framing the upper level with 2×4 auxiliary headers as shown in **20-4**. Although not strictly necessary, tapered blocking will ease the transition between the two ceiling levels (see **20-5**).

Staircase width is also an important consideration. At the very minimum, a main stair should have a clearance of 32 inches between the handrail(s). Seldom-used utility stairs can be somewhat narrower; 30 inches is acceptable.

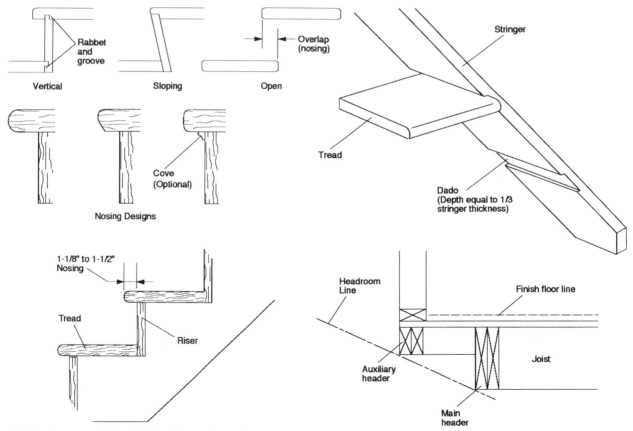

20-4 *Nosing widths and styles and auxiliary headers for conserving space.*

However, a 36-inch clearance will make it a lot easier to move furniture and people between floors. Where space permits, a 42-inch- or 48-inch-wide stair adds a touch of visual grandeur. Remember to allow for the thickness of the finish walls as well as the width of the handrail (or handrails) when rough-framing your stairwell opening.

Stair design requires the calculation of five variables from one given, the *total rise* of the stair. This is the distance (height) between finish floors, which is automatically established by the ceiling height, the depth of the floor joists, the thickness of the subfloors, and the finish flooring materials. (In actual practice, since the finish floors aren't normally installed until after the staircase, the total rise is measured from subfloor to subfloor and an adjustment is made for the thickness of the finish flooring.) Knowing the total rise allows you to find:

1. *the number of risers;*

2. *the number of treads;*

3. *the true riser height;*

4. *the tread width;*

5. *the total run or overall stairwell length.*

Begin by dividing the total rise by seven, which is the whole number closest to the optimum rise for a comfortable set of stairs. (Starting with this step usually eliminates the need to apply stair-building rules No. 2 and No. 3.) Since there can only be a whole number of risers, the result is rounded off to the nearest whole number. For example, assuming a total rise of 8'-5" (101 inches), then $101/7 = 14.42$, rounded off to 14, which is the number of risers. In standard stair construction, the stair carriage is normally set one step below the finish floor rather than flush to it. Since the face of the header is then the last riser, the number of treads will always be one less than the number of risers. Therefore, the number of treads in our example is 13. (If the stair carriage had been set flush with the finish floor, the number of treads and risers would be the same.)

Next, to find the true riser height, divide the total rise by the number of risers. Continuing with our example, $101/14 = 7.214$, i.e., approximately $7\frac{3}{16}$ inches. Applying stair-building rule number one ($7\frac{3}{16} + 7\frac{3}{16} + x = 25$), we find that the tread width (nosing not included) works out to $10\frac{5}{8}$ inches. The total run of the stairs is simply the product of the number of treads multiplied by the tread width. So 13 times 10.625 equals 138.125, i.e., 11'-6$\frac{1}{8}$". If your floor plan is too tight to permit an eleven-and-a-half-foot-long stair run, you could increase the rise to shorten the overall run. Eliminating one tread ($101/13$) gives a unit rise of just about $7\frac{3}{4}$ inches, which still meets the requirements of all three stair-building rules and results in a $9\frac{1}{2}$-inch tread width while shrinking the stair run down to 9'-6". (In practice, if the floor plan allowed

20-5 *This stairwell opening was deliberately rough-framed to a longer length than necessary. A secondary header was added later when there was more time to determine the exact layout dimensions in the field. Note the sloped ceiling frame that increases the storage space available behind the stairwell while maintaining adequate headroom.*

a 10-foot run, I'd probably increase the tread width to 10 inches for the extra comfort.)

The foregoing examples show that you have quite a range of flexibility in matching your stair rise to floor space and ceiling heights. They also show that it's a lot easier to make adjustments during the planning stages than it is to change a framed-in stairwell opening or floor level.

Before you can actually begin laying out and cutting the stair stringers, you must test your calculated riser heights against the actual overall rise. Multiplied 13 or 14 times, all those odd hundredths of an inch that were absorbed in your decimal-to-fractional transformations will add up to a significant discrepancy (in the case of our example, the difference between 0.214 and $\frac{3}{16} \times 13$ amounts to almost $\frac{3}{8}$ inch). Although you might not consciously notice that the last riser was a little shorter than the others, the human brain seems to assume that all steps are equal to the first and calibrates your stride accordingly. A difference between risers of no more than $\frac{1}{8}$ inch is enough to cause a misstep.

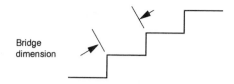

20-6 *Finding rough stringer length from the bridge dimension; multiply by the number of risers.*

Hold a storey pole against the stairwell header, and mark the total rise from floor to floor. If you're working off subfloors instead of finish floors, compensate for the difference by setting a scrap of finish flooring (or a block of equivalent thickness) against both ends of the storey pole and by scribing a line to show the finish floor levels. Set a pair of *wing dividers* (a compass-like tool that should be part of every basic tool kit) to the calculated unit riser height and, beginning at the scribe mark for the finish floor at the bottom, *carefully* "step off" the risers along the edge of the pole (if you don't make the marks all in the same line, they won't be accurate). The mark for the last riser should coincide exactly with the scribe line for the upper-level finish floor surface. If it doesn't, adjust the dividers slightly and step off the marks again. Keep repeating this calibration until the last riser is no more than 1/8 inch off the mark. This setting for the divider will correspond to your true riser height.

Since the edge of a stringer is the hypotenuse of the right triangle described by the total rise and run of a straight-run stair, like a rafter, the layout is done with a framing square. You can approximate the overall length of the stringer stock by scaling it off from the drawings, or you can stretch a string or tape measure diagonally across the stairwell opening from top to bottom. Another method is to draw the full-scale rise and run on a sheet of paper (or the subfloor) for a single step and measure the length of the *bridge dimension* (the hypotenuse of the triangle); then multiply it by the number of risers (see **20-6**). Whichever method you use, add a foot or two to give yourself a little margin for error.

Although, in some designs, the stringers are visible and become part of the overall decorative effect, with most stairs the edges of the stringers are concealed beneath the treads and riser boards and their face sides are covered by a piece of trim board called the *skirtboard*. While it doesn't have to be beautiful, stringer stock must be strong. Select kiln-dried, warp-free 2×12 spruce or Douglas fir planks, and avoid any pieces with large knots and/or splits that would weaken the stringer.

Crown your stringer stock (ideally, it should be dead-on straight), and set it across a pair of sawhorses. Hold your framing square so that its short blade is on your left as you look at it (see **20-7**). Position it on the stock so that the outside edge of the short blade marks the unit rise (as determined by your wing dividers) and the outside edge of the long blade marks the unit run (i.e., the tread

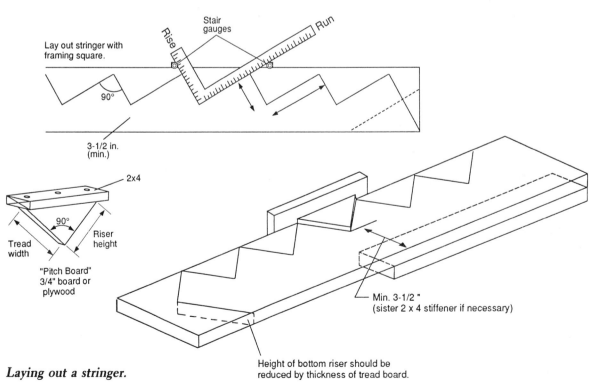

20-7 *Laying out a stringer.*

width) on the edge of the stringer. Clamp the square to the stringer and attach a pair of brass *stair gauges* to its edges to hold the square in correct alignment and keep the subsequent layout lines running true as you step the square up along the length of the stringer. You can also make a template called a *pitch block* from a scrap of plywood or board (refer to **20-7**). The layout lines should be set so that at least four inches of solid knot-free stock is left between the apex of the cutouts and the bottom edge of the stringer (bear this is in mind when selecting stringer stock). Use a freshly sharpened pencil or a knife to scribe the layout lines and check that all corners are at right angles to each other.

Draw a line parallel to the bottom of the stringer equal to the thickness of the tread. If the stringers are being set on the subfloor instead of the finish floors, add the thickness of the finish floor to the tread thickness cut mark before making the cut. For example, assuming a ¾-inch wood finish floor and 1½-inch-thick treads, you'd trim only ¾ inch off the stringers. Compensating for tread depth makes the first riser the same height as all the others (refer to **20-7**).

One more adjustment needs to be made before you cut the stringers. Check the stair landing for level (see **20-8**). It's possible, especially if you're installing stairs in an old house, for the floor to be off level across the width or length (or both) of the stairwell. If this is the case, use the lowest point as the control measurement when establishing your total rise. The bottoms of the other stringers can then be shortened as necessary to ensure that the treads themselves will be level. This is a more elegant and structurally sound approach than relying on shims to raise

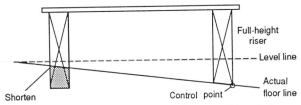

20-8 *Adjustment of stringers for out-of-level floor. It's better to shorten than to shim a stringer.*

up a short stringer. And, even though one side of the first riser may be higher than the other, relative to the floor, the results are less disastrous than a tilted staircase.

As when cutting a pattern rafter, make the cuts on the stringer as accurately as you can. Use a handsaw to finish the cuts at the back of the notches, and remove the kerf marks with a sharp chisel. Draw a level line across the stairwell header where the last riser of the stringer will fall (see **20-9**). Remember to account for the thickness of the finish floor and the last tread when making the calculation. For example, assuming a 7½-inch riser, a ¾-inch finish floor as yet uninstalled, and 1½-inch treads, you'd mark a line at 8¼ inches down from the top of the subfloor. If you've done your stringer layout correctly, this is exactly where the top of the stringer will line up when you set it in the stairwell for a test fit. The bottom cut will rest flush against the subfloor, and the cuts at the top will butt evenly to the header as well. A short level held against the face of the riser cuts and rested on the tread cuts will read both plumb and level. If it doesn't, something is off or you've made a mistake in either your layout or your cutting.

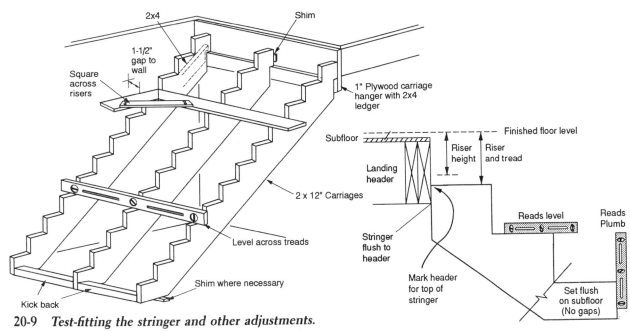

20-9 *Test-fitting the stringer and other adjustments.*

The number of stringers in a stair carriage depends on both the width of the staircase and the thickness of the tread material. Factory-milled, 1 1/16- or 1 1/8-inch-thick, clear vertical-grain Douglas fir or southern yellow pine stair tread stock needs three stringers for solid support on stairs up to three feet wide. If you fashion your treads from 1 1/2-inch-thick 2×12 plank, you could get away with only two risers, although I'd still recommend three on stairs up to four feet wide (for factory tread, I'd use four stringers for stairs over three feet wide). Plank stock makes a decidedly less traditional-looking tread, but it's also about six times less expensive than milled stock. You'll probably have to sort through quite a few 2×12s before you'll find enough straight pieces free of waney edges, objectionable knots, and milling blemishes and scratches to use for tread stock. Sand the face side before installation, and always lay the treads *heart-side up*.

If your test stringer fits, use it as a pattern to lay out the remaining stringers. Clamp or nail the pattern to the stock. If there's any difference in width between the two pieces, line up their bottom edges flush so that the finished stringers will be the same thickness.

There are several ways to attach the stringer to the header (see **20-10**). Since, with a closed stair, the outside stringers are solidly nailed to the stairwell framing, the tops of the stringers don't require much additional support other than toenails. However, with open stringers or wide stairs with one or more intermediate stringers, it's a good idea to notch the back faces of the stringers to accept a two-by ledger that can be spiked into the header. This can be strengthened by adding a cleat to the underside of the landing framing as well. An alternative is to cut a bird's-mouth-like notch in the stringer so that it fits up against the underside of the header. For a stronger connection, some builders use steel straps. Where space permits an extra tread, ending the stringer flush with the upper landing also makes a strong connection. Notch the stringers to fit over a ledger nailed across the bottom of the header. Depending on the thickness of the treads relative to the finish floor and/or subfloor, you also may have to rabbet out the top edge of the header or shim under the tread so that the last tread and the finish floor end up flush. For best results, ship-lap the joint between the tread and the flooring as shown in **20-10**.

Usually, the bottoms of the stringers are simply toe-nailed to the subfloor and then secured with 2×4 blocks nailed between them and into the subfloor and joists.

As with the rest of housebuilding, stair construction also has a rough-in and finish phase. In the rough-in phase, which is really part of the framing, the stringers are cut and nailed temporarily to the stairwell wall framing. Treads cut from scrap two-by stock are tacked to the stringers so

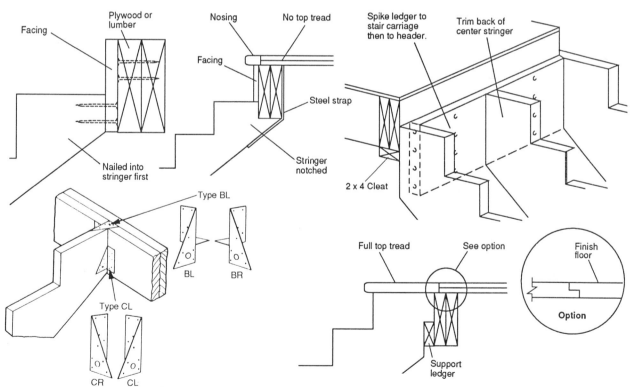

20-10 *Attachment of stringer to stair header and subfloor. A strong structural attachment is especially important when the stringers cannot be nailed to a supporting stairwell wall.*

that builders and subcontractors can use the stairs (see **20-11**). Later, the rough treads are removed, the stair stringers are remounted over the wall finish, and the finish treads and stair trim are installed as part of the interior trimwork (usually after the finish floors are laid).

You can avoid taking down the stringer by nailing a spacer to the stairwell wall framing before you install the stringer the first time (refer to **20-11**). Set the stringer in place against the studs, and snap two lines across them, one that marks the bottom edge of the stringer and a second with a ½-inch clearance below where the cutouts meet—the bottom corner of the triangles formed by the intersection of the treads and risers (see **20-12**). Screw or nail strips of plywood and board equal to the total thickness of the wall finish and the skirtboard to the studs parallel to, but about a half-inch above, the bottom line. The strips should be wide enough so that they don't extend past the second line. Then set the stringer in place even with the bottom line, and nail it permanently to the wall studs. Since you'll need 20d spikes to get a good purchase, predrill the stringer to prevent splitting. When it's time to install the wall finish, cut the panels and slide them into the channel behind the stringer, butting them against the spacer strip. Then slide the skirtboard down against the top of the spacer. The small gap between the underside of the stringer and the wall finish can be ignored. In any case, it will disappear if the underside of the stair carriage is covered with a wall finish.

20-11 *These stair stringers are permanently attached to the stairwell framing by nailing them through spacer shims that will allow the wall board and skirt board trim to slip behind them later. Professional carpenters often save their temporary treads for reuse with their next set of rough stairs.*

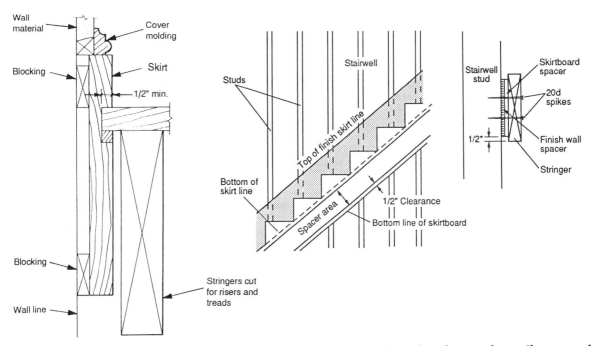

20-12 *Some builders prefer to tack the stringers to the stairwell studs so that they can be easily removed for wall finish installation; others prefer using spacers so that the stringer does not need to be taken down.*

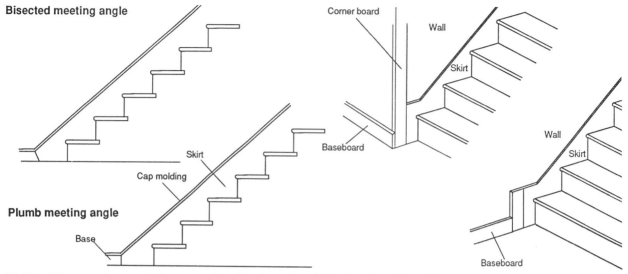

Bisected meeting angle

Skirt

Cap molding

Plumb meeting angle

Base

Corner board

Wall

Skirt

Baseboard

Wall

Skirt

Baseboard

20-13 *The meeting angle between the skirt board and the baseboard can be bisected or plumb.*

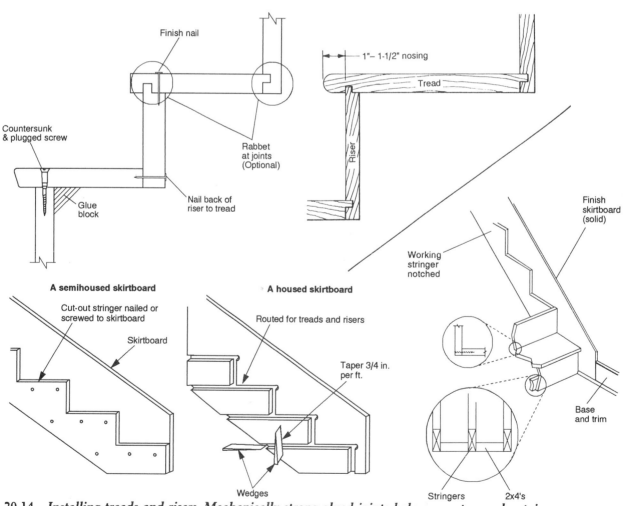

Finish nail

Countersunk & plugged screw

Rabbet at joints (Optional)

Nail back of riser to tread

Glue block

1"– 1-1/2" nosing

Tread

Riser

Finish skirtboard (solid)

Working stringer notched

Base and trim

A semihoused skirtboard

Cut-out stringer nailed or screwed to skirtboard

Skirtboard

A housed skirtboard

Routed for treads and risers

Taper 3/4 in. per ft.

Wedges

Stringers

2x4's

20-14 *Installing treads and risers. Mechanically strong glued joints help prevent squeaky stairs.*

When laying out the skirtboard, consider how you want it to terminate. It can either butt against a vertical corner trim board at the end of the stairwell or run into the baseboard moulding (see **20-13**). Allow enough extra length when cutting the stock so that you can scribe the actual location of the end cut.

Butting the risers and treads against the skirtboard of a closed stair is a lot easier than trying to cut trim boards or wall finishes to fit around tread nosings. The skirtboard also protects the wall finishes against any damage by traffic and appliances.

Attach the first riser to the face of the stringer with finish nails or countersink drywall screws, and plug the holes with dowels (see **20-14**). Install the second riser, and butt the first tread against it. For maximum strength, glue and screw or nail the bottom edge of each riser into the back of its tread. Although it's a lot more work, if you rabbet the top of each riser to fit into a dado cut into the front of each tread and rabbet the back of the treads to fit into a dado cut into the bottom of each riser as shown in **20-14,** the joint will be stronger and won't open up when the wood shrinks.

When butting risers and treads against the skirtboard, you shouldn't assume that the joints are square. In real life, each piece is likely to vary slightly. If you make square cuts, you'll end up with noticeable gaps between the ends of the risers and treads and the skirtboard. Even though any such gaps can be filled with putty if the stair trim will be painted, it's a much better idea not to have any in the first place. Cut the riser and tread stock just long enough so that you have to hold it at an angle to fit it between the skirtboards (see **20-15**). You can then scribe the actual cut line onto its end. Do the same with the opposite end as well. If you're using softwood, make the piece about $\frac{1}{16}$ inch longer than necessary, and give the cut a five-degree bevel. This backcut makes a snug joint against the skirtboards. Since hardwood fibres don't have any give, the cut and fit must be *exact*.

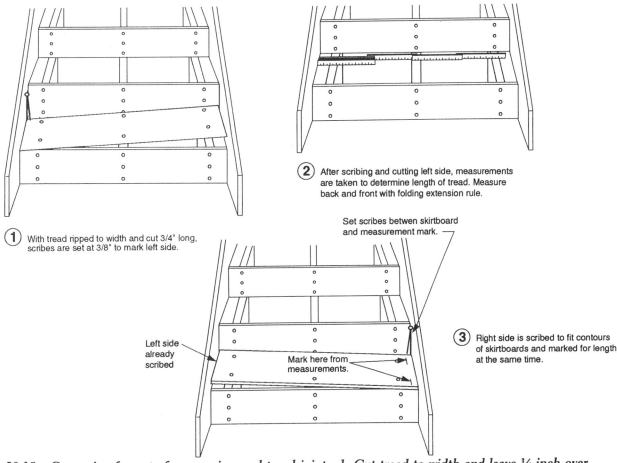

① With tread ripped to width and cut 3/4" long, scribes are set at 3/8" to mark left side.

② After scribing and cutting left side, measurements are taken to determine length of tread. Measure back and front with folding extension rule.

Set scribes betwen skirtboard and measurement mark.

Left side already scribed

Mark here from measurements.

③ Right side is scribed to fit contours of skirtboards and marked for length at the same time.

20-15   *Correcting for out-of-square riser and tread joints: 1. Cut tread to width and leave ¼ inch over-long. Set scribing tool at ⅛ inch and mark one side. 2. Cut tread on scribe mark. Measure front and back tread width with folding extension rule (more accurate than tape measure). 3. Mark tread for length and scribe opposite end.*

Most prefabricated and some high-quality, site-built stairs use *housed* stringer construction instead of the butt-joint and skirtboard method described above (see **20-16**). In this method, the treads and risers slide *from behind* into tapered grooves that have been cut into finish-quality stringer stock. Wedges and glue make this kind of stair extremely strong and squeak-proof. Another advantage is that they can be fitted to the skirtboards without any gaps and without fussy scribing. You'll need a router and a special template—as well as a very accurate layout—to make your own housed stringers.

Another option is to attach blocks to a finish backing stringer or to slide open treads into dado cuts or attach them to hardwood cleats screwed to the stringer.

Most amateurs should probably stick with closed or barrier-wall stair construction or else build open stairs that utilize treads set on simple cleats. A traditional open stair requires a skirtboard that is carefully mitred to form a tight joint with the riser boards (see **20-17**). These cuts must be made with a handsaw. The tread nosing must also be mitred so that it turns the corner where it overhangs the skirt. Thus, even without the complications attendant with the installation of a balustrade, a traditional open stair requires a great deal of skill and patience to build.

From the point of view of stair layout, a landing is only an oversize tread (see **20-18**). Use your storey pole to mark the height of the landing on the stairwell wall, and then draw a level line to indicate the top edge of the

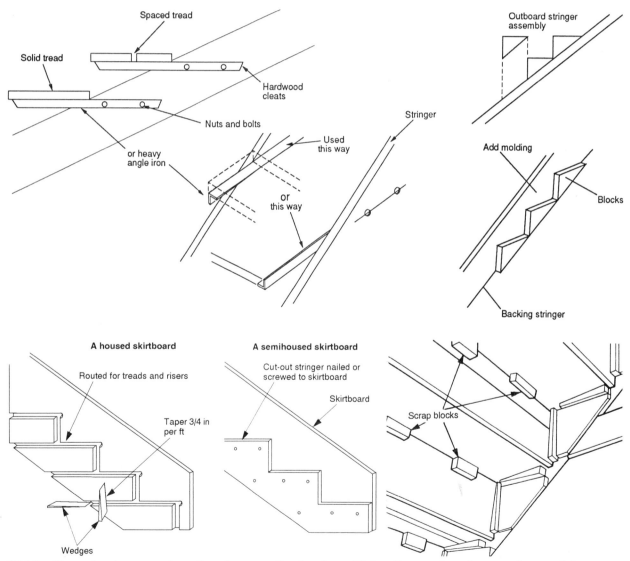

20-16 *Housed stringers make a first-class set of stairs that will last forever, but they require special equipment or a great deal of patience and skill to make.*

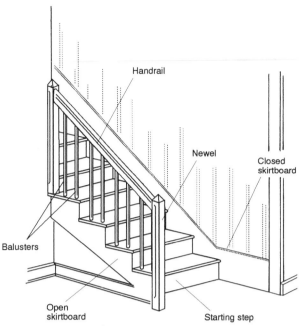

20-17 *Traditional open stair finish details. Even without the balusters, finishing a set of open stairs neatly is demanding and laborious work.*

framing. Remember to drop the mark a distance equal to the tread thickness. When establishing landing height, any subfloor decking is likewise considered as part of the framing dimension. Some builders just lay plank or milled stair tread directly over the framing, without any intervening subfloor. In this case, the edges of the planks or treads should be rabbeted to form a tight, strong shiplap joint. Otherwise, if you lay hardwood strip or standard, ¾-inch tongue-and-groove floorboards over a subfloor, rip a 3½-inch-wide strip off the nosing edge of milled stair tread stock, and cut a rabbet into its underside so that the piece will lie flush with the top of the finish floor.

The frame of the landing platform acts as a header for setting the lower set of stair stringers. If you lay out the landing joists to coincide with the upper-stair stringers you won't need to provide any extra blocking to support them. Since, in a closed stair, the outboard stringers are firmly attached to the wall anyway, only the intermediate stringer requires any blocking between joists under the subfloor. If you're setting the upper stringers on top of a finished floor instead, their bottom edges must also be trimmed to account for tread thickness. Since the finish wall and trim can be run directly down to the landing, the platform can be nailed directly to the stairwell wall framing without any need for the spacer shims required to set the stringers.

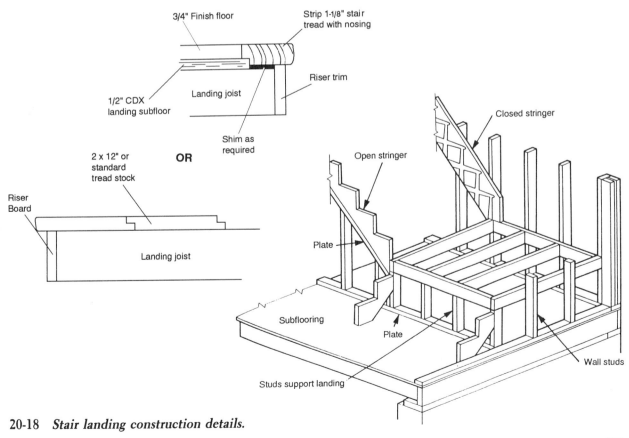

20-18 *Stair landing construction details.*

20-19 *Note how the skirt board of this riser stair drops vertically down the wall corner to merge neatly into the baseboard. Note the simple cleated bookshelves built into what would otherwise be dead space at the back of a closet.*

You can also utilize a landing to simplify the construction of a set of winder stairs. Winders can be thought of as two sets of ordinary stairs connected by one or more intermediate stairs that change direction. The difficulty with winders is that as the treads change direction, the angle of the stringer (and skirtboard) changes as well. The situation is analogous to the intersection of the fascia boards of two different-pitched roofs: the angle of intersection must be bisected. The difficulty of doing this neatly and accurately is one good reason why a novice stairbuilder shouldn't attempt to build an open-stringer winder stair. With a closed winder stair, you can frame a landing and use it as a platform for building the rest of the winder treads. Transfer the winder tread riser heights directly onto the stairwell wall from your storey pole. You can wait until after the finish wall surfaces are installed before beginning your winder layout, but I prefer to nail flatwise blocking between the studs to provide both solid attachment for the stairs and something to draw the layout lines on (see **20-19**).

Draw the layout for the riser tread directly onto the landing platform itself—or even better, onto a full-sized cardboard template (see **20-20**). As was mentioned earlier, the most important rule for safe winder layout is that the winder tread width at the line of travel (the average path

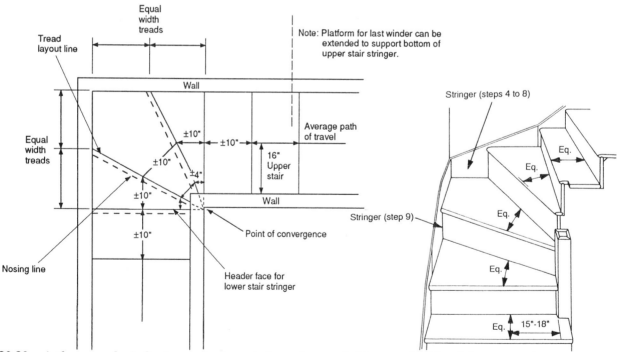

20-20 *A three-tread winder is easy to lay out since the treads bisect each side of the square described by the landing. With a closed winder, the stringer and/or skirt board layout or support cleat layout can be marked onto sheets of cardboard tacked to the wall studs or directly onto the installed finish wall. Only the upper and lower straight-run stairs will have stringers that end on the landing platform that supports the winder.*

taken up and down the stairs) should be the same width as the standard treads and that the narrow end of the winder treads should be about four inches wide. Since this means that the point of convergence for the angles that define the winder treads lies outside of the square formed by the intersection of the upper and lower staircases, the landing must be extended into the upper and lower stairwell areas the same distance that the point of convergence lies outside the stairwell. For example, assuming that the finished stairwell is three feet wide, and the point of convergence is four inches outside of this, the actual winder landing dimension (nosing excluded) will be three feet plus four inches square. These are the dimensions that your template will utilize when you trisect the square landing platform into three treads (typically all the winders that comfortably fit into a normal landing) by finding the halfway point along each wall and then connecting a line to the point of convergence.

After building the landing according to the dimensions determined by the template, notch the corner of the template, and lay it on the landing so that you can transfer the tread lines onto the stairwell wall. Plumb lines up from these marks to the horizontal lines marking riser heights. These lines indicate the position of the support cleats for each riser and tread. Use a sliding T-bevel and your tem-

plate to find the angles at which the supports must be cut. For maximum strength, rip two-by stock to the width of the riser height, and then cut the pieces long enough so that the tread-bearing portion of each successive riser rests on the one beneath it. Extend the back end of the topmost winder tread supports so that they make a base for attaching the upper stair stringers.

Installing the skirtboard trim is the tricky part. Just as the stringer does, the skirtboard angle also changes as it follows the turn of the winder treads (see **20-21**). This is one case where it's easier to notch the skirting to fit against the stringers (i.e., riser and tread cleats) rather than behind them and to draw the layout lines on the finish wall surface rather than over the framing. Snap chalk lines that connect the top points of all the riser/tread intersections. Then, using a spacer block or a square, mark a second line parallel to the first line to mark the top of the skirtboard. Bisect the angles by connecting the intersection of the top lines with the corresponding point of the bottom line. If you hold off on attaching the riser/tread cleats, you can use their layout lines together with the skirtboard top line and the bisecting angle lines as templates for cutting the skirtboard stock. Or, as an alternative to notching the skirtboards, plywood spacers can be installed beneath them and the cleats attached over them.

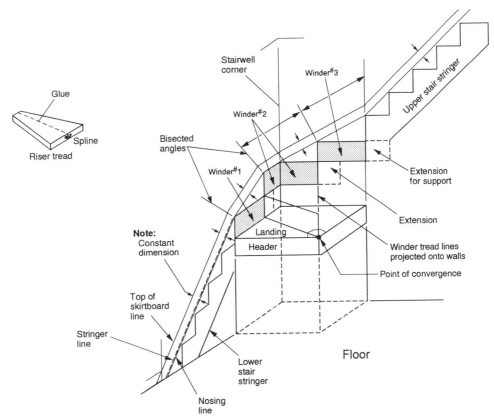

20-21 *Skirt boards for winders will consist of several short sections, each with a different slope angle.*

529

Returning to your landing template, draw a line for the nosing parallel to the front of each tread line and then use the pattern to mark and to cut each winder tread. Since the treads will be wider than a single piece of stock, try to lay out the pieces to reduce the chances of leaving weak grain exposed in the path of travel. For strength and stability, join the pie-shaped pieces of tread stock together with a glued spline joint rather than a shiplap.

Spiral stair layout uses the same basic principles as winder stairs. The major difference is that the point of convergence is at the center of the circle described by the stair-tread run (see **20-22**). The stairwell must be large enough to allow adequate tread width, and the center pole should be of sufficient diameter to support treads at least four inches wide at their narrow end. As with a winder stair, draw a full-sized layout onto a convenient subfloor area or a cardboard sheet. Use the storey pole to locate the treads on the finished stairwell wall and center pole. If the cleats are attractively finished, there is no need to close in the stairs with risers. Use metal angle braces or dadoed notches to join the narrow end of the treads to the pole. Since a skirtboard would require many angle cuts, the treads are normally butted directly against the finish wall (this is one case where a wood wall is definitely preferred over drywall).

One major advantage of closed stairs is that handrail installation is simple. The most basic balustrade for an open or partially open stair requires a great deal more labor to install. And, if the design calls for traditional turned balusters, newel posts, and gooseneck rail fittings, the installation is usually both costly and beyond the skills of more than a few professional carpenters, never mind the average do-it-yourselfer.

Since stairs are a common site of household accidents, building codes quite understandably prescribe such things as railing heights and spacings. In general, for residential applications, a railing height of 36 inches is common, although you should always check with your local code for specific requirements (see **20-23**). If balusters are used, their spacing should be close enough so that a four-inch sphere cannot fit between them. Previously, codes required only six-inch spacing, but studies have proved 95 percent of children under 10 years old are capable of slipping between the railings at that spacing. Although it's not uncommon for the first and second tread to extend past the handrail, it's much safer if the handrail termination coincides with that of the stairs (and code may require the handrail to extend well beyond the stairs). Handrails must be securely anchored to solid framing. Toggle bolts or other hollow-wall fasteners aren't strong enough to withstand a sudden impact.

Although 2×4 and other flat, banded profiles are used for railings in contemporary stair designs, the traditional 1½- to two-inch-diameter round or oval profile makes a much safer handrail. Unlike flat rails, a round rail can be gripped firmly and encircled by thumb and fingers. If you prefer a flat-style handrail, a narrow T-shaped profile furnishes a better grip.

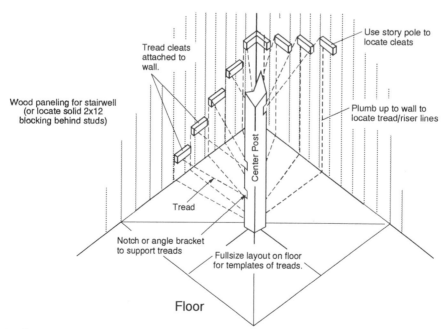

20-22 *Finishing the stairwell with board panelling simplifies spiral stair construction by allowing the tread support cleats to be attached directly to the boarding. Otherwise, solid 2×12 blocking must be nailed between the wall studs at the appropriate tread locations.*

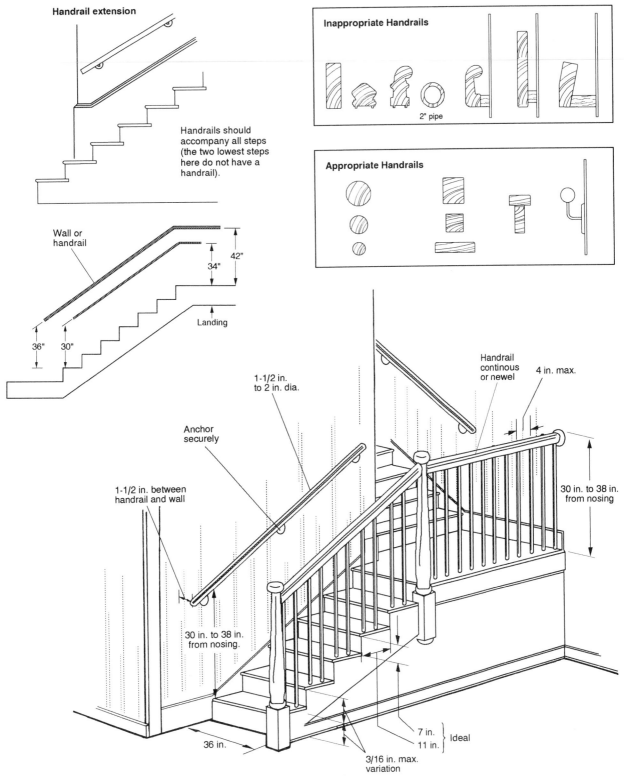

Handrail extension

Handrails should accompany all steps (the two lowest steps here do not have a handrail).

Inappropriate Handrails

2" pipe

Appropriate Handrails

Wall or handrail

42"

34"

Landing

36" 30"

1-1/2 in. to 2 in. dia.

Anchor securely

Handrail continous or newel

4 in. max.

30 in. to 38 in. from nosing

1-1/2 in. between handrail and wall

30 in. to 38 in. from nosing.

7 in.
11 in. } Ideal

36 in.

3/16 in. max. variation

20-23 *While codes do prescribe safe rail heights and baluster spacings, many of the handrail designs favored by contemporary designers are actually problematic from a safety standpoint. Always check your local code—especially for how far the handrail must extend beyond the final step.*

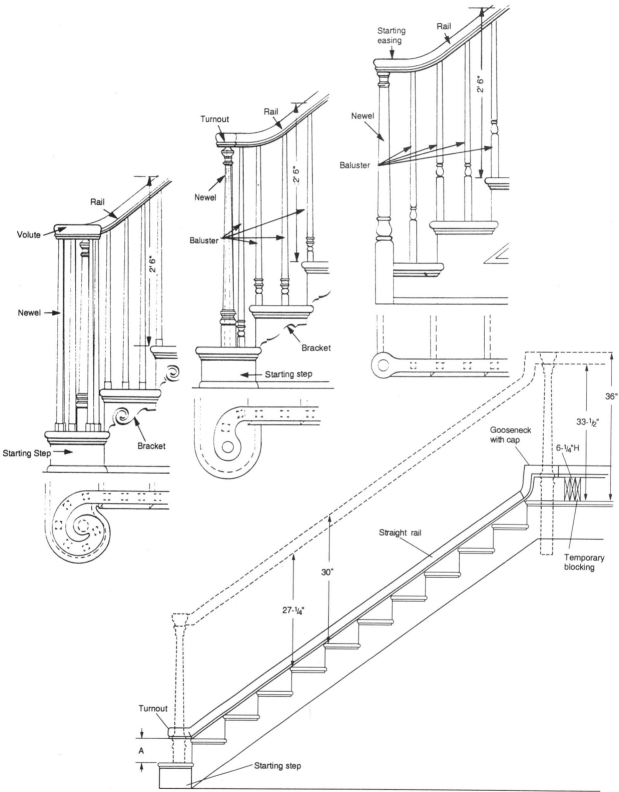

Rail

Volute

Newel

Starting Step

Bracket

Turnout

Newel

Baluster

Rail

2' 6"

Bracket

Starting step

Starting
easing

Rail

Newel

Baluster

2' 6"

36"

33-1/2"

6-1/4"H

Gooseneck
with cap

Temporary
blocking

Straight rail

30"

27-1/4"

Turnout

A

Starting step

20-24 *Handrail layout using factory-milled components is done by setting the rail on top of the finished stair treads.*

Two-by-two stock can be used for balusters in combination with one-by or two-by horizontal boards to make a simple contemporary balustrade for open stair runs and balconies. The balustrade support posts must be firmly bolted to the framing. These types of balustrade are simply more finished versions of outdoor deck railings.

When a railing is set at 36 inches off the floor of the upper landing, as shown in **20-23**, its height as measured at the *back* of the stair tread (i.e., at the face of the riser board) will be 36 inches, but, depending on the pitch of the stairs, will be less when measured from the *front* of the tread (i.e., where it would intersect the nosing). The simplest solution to this conundrum is to backset the upper support post so that it is centered under the intersection of the stair railing with the landing railing or else to run the stair railing into the side of a flat-faced newel post (which violates the safety rule about running railings continuously over newel posts). Still, running the baluster handrail between newel posts is a lot easier than installing an over-the-post railing.

Neither shortcut is possible, however, if you use a traditional turned newel post. Here a *gooseneck* fitting with a curved *easing* must be used to make the transition between the two railing levels. As shown in **20-24,** the best way to find the length of the handrail is to set the rail right on top of the finished stair treads and lay it out before the newel posts are attached. To find the distance to block up the upper-level railing so that you can find the length of the gooseneck, subtract the distance between the underside of the stair rail (at the nosing) from the distance between the underside of the level railing and the landing floor. (Given the tread width of the stairs shown in **20-24** and a 36-inch rail height, the top of the stair rail will be 30 inches from the nosing. Using a standard 2½-inch-thick railing, a plumb line drawn through the stair railing will be about 2¾ inches long at the pitch of the stairs used in our example. This explains where the numbers came from that were used to derive the amount to block up the gooseneck at the upper landing.) At the starting step, the turnout (or *volute*) is attached to the straight rail with its base centered over the starting newel location. The distance (A) between the turnout and the tread is added to the (30-inch) measurement of the distance between the nosing and the top of the stair rail to find the length of the starting newel post.

Using a *pitch block* takes some of the anxiety and difficulty out of determining the location and angle of cut for an easing or gooseneck fitting (see **20-25**). Set the pitch block run-side down under the easing piece, and mark where the curve of the fitting is tangent to the block. Then turn the pitch block over (rise-side down), and scribe the angle at which to cut the piece through the tangent mark. Since curved pieces will be difficult to hold against a chop saw or radial-arm saw table, screw a piece of plywood to its bottom to make a jig. As shown in **20-25**, the easiest way to locate the cuts on the straight rail sections that fit between the easings is to clamp the fittings to the stairs and then to hold the sections of straight rail against them. The straight rails require only a simple square cut to mate with the easings.

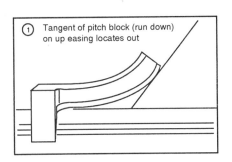

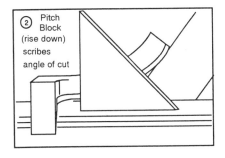

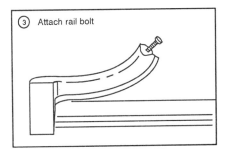

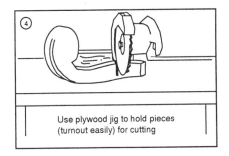

20-25 *Laying out and cutting handrail easings.*

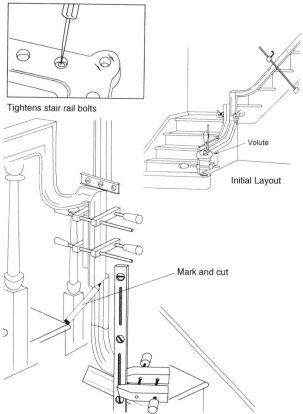

Tightens stair rail bolts

Volute

Initial Layout

Mark and cut

20-26 *Clamping the easings into position allows the 90-degree cuts for the straight rail sections that join them together to be precisely located.*

The sections are joined together with glue and a special double-ended 3½-inch by ⁵⁄₁₆-inch *rail bolt* that has a machine-screw thread on one end and a lag-screw thread on the other. Bore a center hole through a ³⁄₁₆-inch-thick section of handrail to use as a template for marking the rail bolt centers on the easing and the straight rails. Then drill a ¼-inch pilot hole into the fitting, and thread the lag screw end of the bolt into it by locking a pair of hex nuts against each other on the machine-thread end and turning them with a wrench. Next, drill a ³⁄₈-inch hole at least one inch into the end of the straight rail section. Then drill another one-inch-wide hole 1½ inches deep into the centerline of the underside of the straight rail 1³⁄₈ inches in from the end. Slip the machine-thread end of the rail bolt into the ³⁄₈-inch hole (remove the nuts first) and then, using the cavity in the underside of the rail, thread a nut onto the machine bolt, and tighten it down with a 12-point, box-end wrench. At this point, the installation is only temporary. Don't glue the sections together until after all the railing pieces have been cut and fitted and any imperfections in their mating edges smoothed out. Mark the alignment of each section with a pencil line so that you can reassemble them in the correct position when they're ready for final assembly and gluing (see **20-26**). The rail bolt access holes are filled with a dowel plug and sanded smooth.

To mark the location for the balusters, you can either set the fully assembled handrail temporarily in place on top of its supporting newel posts or else clamp it to the stair treads before the newels are installed (see **20-26** and **20-27**). With the former method, mark the treads for the

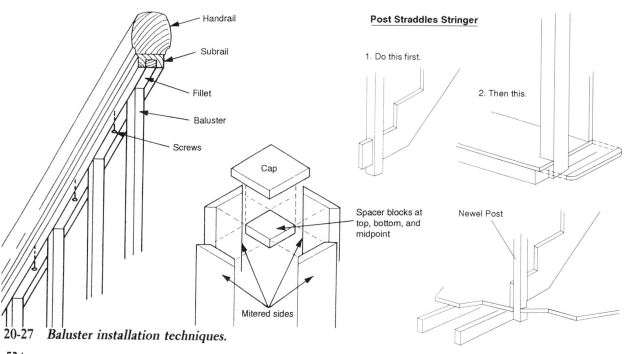

Handrail

Subrail

Fillet

Baluster

Screws

Cap

Spacer blocks at top, bottom, and midpoint

Mitered sides

Post Straddles Stringer

1. Do this first.

2. Then this.

Newel Post

20-27 *Baluster installation techniques.*

baluster centers, and then plumb up to the rail and mark its underside. With the latter method, simply transfer the baluster centerlines from the treads to the railing with a combination square. The face of the downstair baluster should line up with the face of the riser (not the nosing). Presuming that the balusters meet code spacing require-

ments, the center of the upstair baluster is set in the middle of the tread. Bore one-inch-deep holes in the underside of the railing and in the face of the treads for the balusters. If you use a pitch block as a guide for the drill bit, you can drill the railing without needing to place it on top of the newel posts first.

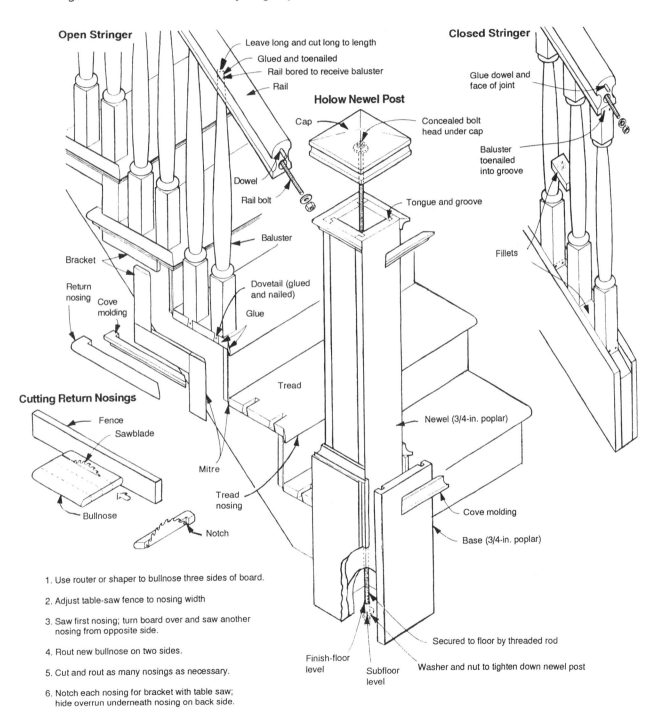

Open Stringer

Leave long and cut long to length
Glued and toenailed
Rail bored to receive baluster
Rail

Holow Newel Post

Cap
Concealed bolt head under cap

Dowel
Rail bolt
Tongue and groove

Baluster

Bracket

Return nosing
Cove molding

Dovetail (glued and nailed)

Glue

Closed Stringer

Glue dowel and face of joint

Baluster toenailed into groove

Fillets

Tread

Cutting Return Nosings

Fence
Sawblade

Mitre

Newel (3/4-in. poplar)

Tread nosing

Bullnose

Notch

Cove molding

Base (3/4-in. poplar)

1. Use router or shaper to bullnose three sides of board.

2. Adjust table-saw fence to nosing width

3. Saw first nosing; turn board over and saw another nosing from opposite side.

4. Rout new bullnose on two sides.

5. Cut and rout as many nosings as necessary.

6. Notch each nosing for bracket with table saw; hide overrun underneath nosing on back side.

Secured to floor by threaded rod

Finish-floor level

Subfloor level

Washer and nut to tighten down newel post

20-27 *(Continued) Baluster installation techniques.*

Cut the balusters just long enough to fit inside their rail holes. Smear construction adhesive on their ends, and insert them in the tread holes. And then, with a helper or two or three, begin setting the handrail in place on top of the balusters, starting at the bottom of the stairs. Construction adhesive has a fairly long "open" time during which you'll be able to twist the balusters as needed to line them up properly. Tap the handrail firmly into place on top of the balusters and newel posts with a rubber mallet, and check that there are no dips or crowns in it. Then finish the installation by toenailing the balusters into the treads and the underside of the rails.

Some balusters feature a dovetailed tenon at their base instead of a round peg. Each tenon slides into a dovetail slot cut into the ends of the treads (refer to **20-27**). The dovetail is glued and nailed to secure the baluster.

21 Interior Finish

Walls and Ceilings

GYPSUM WALLBOARD PANELS (Drywall)

There are many good reasons why drywall (or Sheetrock, one of its well-known trade names) as distinguished from traditional plaster, which I suppose could be called "wet-wall," is the most ubiquitous interior finish in use today (see 21-1). It's inexpensive, fire-resistant, relatively easy and quick to install, provides good thermal mass, and is versatile, being amenable to a variety of finish treatments including paint, texturing, plaster, and wallpaper, on both walls and ceilings.

Drywall panels are available in standard thicknesses of ¼ inch, ⅜ inch, ½ inch, and ⅝ inch. Because they will bend along a gentle radius without cracking, ¼-inch-thick panels, applied in two overlapping layers, are used for covering curved ceilings and walls. Three-eighths panels aren't rigid enough to span ordinary framing and are normally applied over solid substrates such as when renovating an existing wall or ceiling. Half-inch drywall is the standard thickness used for most applications. Codes normally require ⅝-inch "fire-code" panels for commercial construction and certain special conditions, such as fireproofing the walls of a boiler room or a garage under living areas. The extra thickness of the panels increases the amount of time it takes for the flames to ignite the wood framing beneath them.

Drywall panels are manufactured in a wide range of surface finishes, core materials, and edge treatments, most of which are intended for commercial and other specialized applications beyond the concern of the average residential builder. One special-purpose panel which you'll have occasion to use is "Type MR" (*moisture-resistant*). These light-green sheets are recommended either as a wall finish or base for ceramic tile in bathrooms and other rooms where high moisture levels would foster the disintegration of general-application drywall.

Although ½-inch and ⅝-inch, four-foot-wide drywall panels are available in two-foot increments in lengths from eight to 16 feet, the 4×8 size is the one most often used by nonprofessionals. Longer sheets cover more area with fewer joints, but their extra weight and size make them hard to handle, even with a helper. However, if you've got 9'-10" or 11'-2" ceilings or walls to cover, you should run 10-foot or 12-foot sheets instead of taping extra joints, even if the initial application is more physically demanding.

No matter what their size, the long edges of all standard drywall panels are tapered and the short ends aren't. When butted against another sheet, the tapered edges form a shallow trough that makes it easier to tape the joint. Since end (butt) joints or cut edges don't have a taper, it's much harder to do a satisfactory taping job. Hence, when deciding whether to run sheets horizontally or vertically and how long they should be, keep in mind that the goal is to eliminate as many joints as possible, especially butt joints. Drywall is relatively cheap. You won't save enough money by piecing together scraps to cover a wall to offset the time and effort it will take to finish the needless extra joints. As with plywood sheathing, drywall panels should be notched to run past the edges of window jambs rather than ending on them. Joints at the corners of window and door headers tend to crack.

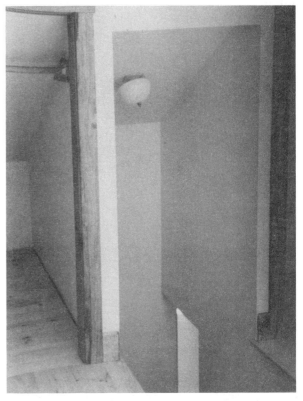

21-1 *The flat white surface of drywall finish sets off the rounded edges of the simple wood trim. If allowed to define space rather than just cover walls, drywall panelling can be a very effective design element.*

537

Some might object to the waste, but the supply of gypsum used to manufacture drywall is virtually inexhaustible, and the process is less disruptive than clear-cutting forests. Although drywall scraps do comprise a large part of all construction debris that accounts for 12 percent (as of this writing) of the total bulk in landfills, in many urban areas of the United States a market for recycled drywall has opened up.

INSTALLING DRYWALL

Drywall installation is a three-step process. "Hanging rock" (as tradespeople call fastening the sheets to the framing) is the first and easiest part (see **21-2**).

Unless you're planning on using some other ceiling finish such as boards, hang the ceiling first. Even with a helper, lifting and holding the awkward and heavy sheets in position long enough to attach them to the joists isn't easy. Working by yourself, it's not only potentially back-breaking, but damn near impossible. As you might expect, there are some aids and techniques that make the job easier (see **21-3**). You can tack a 2×4 across the wall studs about an inch beneath the ceiling and slip the end of the panel into the gap, and then, as you lift the other end upwards, have your helper wedge it tight against the joists with a *deadman* (also called a T-stick). You can make your own by nailing a three-foot-long 2×4 flatwise to the end of another 2×4, and bracing the connection with a plywood triangle. The overall length of the deadman should be about a half-inch more than the height between the floor and ceiling joists so that it can be wedged tight up against the sheet, clamping it to the ceiling. You could also use a second deadman in lieu of nailing the cleat to the wall—

21-2 *Drywall panels should be hung to minimize the number of seams to be taped. Although this complex surface has many edges, it has only a few long seams to tape. Inside and outside corner joints are much easier to finish than flat wall seams. Because the taping compound does not require a perfect fit between sheets, drywall is well suited for finishing complicated surfaces.*

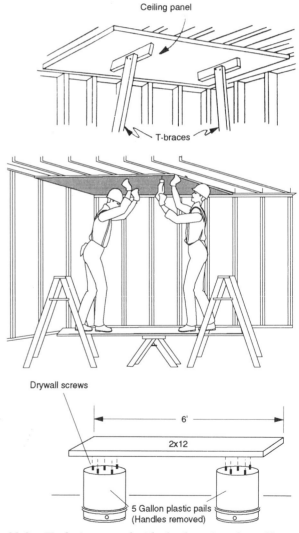

21-3 *Techniques and aids for hanging drywall on the ceiling.*

or else literally use your head to push the sheet up against the ceiling while standing on a stepladder or staging plank. Two empty five-gallon joint compound plastic pails screwed through their bottoms into a six-foot 2×12 make a stable staging that you can slide around the floor, which is exactly the right height for hanging and taping drywall ceilings (refer to **21-3**).

If you have a lot of ceiling to cover, or are using longer-length or heavy ⅝-inch sheets, you might want to rent a professional drywall lift. This device is equipped with rollers so that once the sheet is centered on the support, you can move it into position and, by turning the wheel crank, raise it up snug against the joists. You'll still need a helper to lift the sheets onto the jack without breaking them.

When hanging drywall or installing any kind of ceiling or wall finish, don't assume that the walls run straight or that the room corners are square—or that the ceiling joists are all in the same plane. If possible, measure the ceiling diagonals to check the room for square. If you can't do this, measure the ceiling at both ends, parallel to and at right angles to the run of the joists, and note any significant differences between the measurements that would show that the room is out of square (e.g., one end of the ceiling is an inch wider than the other). Try to find out which way the ceiling is running out of square so that you can trim the long edge of the starting sheets on a taper to correct for the error. It may help to hold a sheet in place against the ceiling, and, as you line up its butt end with the center of a joist, note the width of the gap that develops between one corner of the sheet and the wall. For example, if the gap tapers from zero to a half-inch, and the

ceiling is 24 feet long, you'll know it's 1½ inches out of square.

As when laying a floor deck, the first course of ceiling drywall is laid to a chalk line—and not necessarily against the edge of the ceiling framing (see **21-4**). Snap the line two feet out from the edge of the wall, and measure between it and the wall at several points along its length. Your tape should read two feet or slightly over, but not any less, if you don't want to have to trim off the edges of the drywall sheets. If you must move the line out much more than a half-inch to fit all the sheets without trimming, the gap won't be covered by the wall sheets, in which case you'll have to cut the edges on a taper or else cover them with moulding—or fill them in with joint compound. On ceilings, drywall panels are always installed with their long lengths perpendicular to the run of the joists.

As floor joists respond to live loads on the floor above a drywall ceiling, the drywall fasteners have a tendency to pull through the surface of the sheets. This kind of nail "popping" is much more likely with joists spaced on 24-inch centers than it is with 16-inch spacing (nail popping also results from the shrinkage of green or otherwise excessively moist framing lumber). Thus, even though 24-inch spacing may meet code requirements for deflection, it's still a good idea to frame your floors on 16-inch centers if you intend to use drywall ceilings. Another way to solve the problem is to screw the drywall to 1×3 strapping (called furring strips) nailed across the joists on 16-inch, or even 12-inch, centers. Some especially conscientious builders use strapping for drywall ceilings even with 16-inch joist spacing.

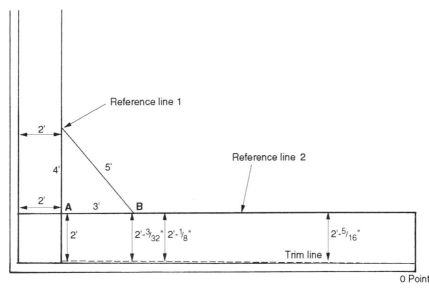

21-4 *One way to find if a ceiling or wall is square is to construct a 3–4–5 triangle on a reference line parallel to a wall and extend the adjacent triangle leg out into a second reference line. Measure to the wall from each end of this second reference line and note the difference between the two measurements. A wall ¼ inch out in four feet will be ¾ inch off in 12 feet.*

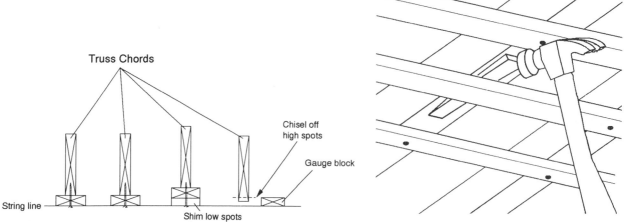

21-5 *Levelling a truss rafter ceiling for drywall. Strongbacks tend to even out many of the bows in the bottom chords of truss rafters.*

Although nail-popping is far less likely when the drywall is attached to truss rafters or ceiling, as opposed to floor joists on two-foot spacings, unlike deeper-dimension joists, the bottom chords of 2×4 truss rafters will seldom lie in more or less a flat plane. Any irregularities in the plane of the ceiling will be highlighted by the reflective drywall finish, especially where your sight lines are uninterrupted by partitions. Thus truss ceilings should be levelled before installing the drywall.

Snap chalk lines across the bottoms of the trusses (or ceiling joists) for the strapping layout (the first line is offset so that the lines mark the edges, not the centers, of the strapping). Nail strapping across the truss bottoms at each side of the building (or room) and stretch strings between them, running perpendicularly across the trusses. With a scrap of furring as a spacer, check the distance between the strings and the chalk lines on the bottoms of the trusses. Chisel out any high spots (i.e., where the distance is less than the thickness of the spacer). Then, as you begin nailing the strapping to the trusses with 8d box nails, use opposing cedar shingle wedges to shim any low spots (distance more than the thickness of the spacer) to the string (see **21-5**). You can also notch the strapping instead of the trusses, if you prefer. Although it's slow and tedious work, levelling the ceiling is a necessary step for installing a top-quality finish ceiling.

Stagger the panels so that there won't be any continuous butt joints. A "crossroad" is the hardest kind of joint to tape. The joint compound forms a hump that is virtually impossible to hide. Also, unless it's unavoidable, no piece should span less than three joists.

Hang the wall panels horizontally, working downwards from the ceiling (see **21-6**). That way, the cut edges of the panels will be at floor level, where they'll be covered by the baseboard moulding. Cut the bottom-most panel about ½ inch to one inch short so that it can slide easily

into place. If you try to force a tight panel to fit, you're likely to break its edge. There's no reason to worry about small gaps between panels anyway, since they will be filled with joint finishing compound. If, as sometimes happens, you must "persuade" a panel to fit, hammer on a length of 2×4 to distribute the force along the joint and to reduce the risk of cracking the sheet. Professionals use a *drywall jack* to lift the bottom edge of a wall panel and snug it up tight to the upper panels. A flatbar and a block of wood work almost as well.

Although drywall can be fastened to wall studs either horizontally or vertically, in most cases running the panels horizontally results in fewer joints to finish. Unlike several vertical joints, taping a single, long horizontal joint can be done without stagings or stooping that disrupt the control of your taping paddle.

Drywall is easily cut with a sharp utility knife and a metal straightedge, such as a drywall T-square (see **21-7**). Make a scoring cut on the finish face and, standing the sheet on edge, break it along the cut line. Finish by cutting through the paper on the backing side. Besides the convenience of its four-foot length, you can use your drywall T-square to make cuts along the length of the panels as well as across their width without having to snap or pencil guide lines first. Holding the blade of your knife at an angle against the square at the desired measurement, push its tip through the surface of the paper and continue holding the knife against the square as you pull it along the edge of the panel.

Cut edges are usually anything but smooth. Bumps and ridges not only interfere with a good fit, but can hang up the sheet and cause an edge to break. A Surform block plane is an ideal tool for trimming and smoothing rough edges, especially when the piece is too small to cut and snap. In a pinch, the flat edge of a steel hammer shaft is also a handy drywall edge trimmer.

Vertical corner

Nail this side only!

Drywall panel jack

Stud

Flat bar

Stud

Stud mark

Stud mark

Ceiling joist

First nail 7" from interior ceiling angles

Temporary support nail

2x4 Long Block

Tight butt edges

21-6 *Hanging drywall panels on walls. Use a lever the lift the lower wall panel snug up against the previously installed upper panel.*

When cutting holes for electrical boxes or other obstructions, take time to make careful measurements, and doublecheck the orientation of the sheets relative to the cuts. Even professionals occasionally mix up right and left when transposing cuts from front to back. A T-square is very helpful for laying out the cuts.

Holes for pipes and other small circular cuts can be neatly cut with an inexpensive hole saw that fits into your electric drill. Make yourself a template from a scrap of ⅛-inch hardboard to mark the cuts for electrical outlet boxes. You can buy a metal template for marking octagonal junction boxes or else you can make your own. You can also use a spare electrical box for a pattern as well.

Small openings, such as electrical boxes, can be cut with your knife. Make deep scoring cuts on the outline, and then score across the corners to make an X. Strike the center of the X with the butt of your hammer to snap the cuts inward, and then you can cut away the scraps with your knife.

You can also cut openings with special drywall saws. The handiest kind has a rough-toothed stiff blade about six to eight inches long that ends in an awl-like point that can be worked through the sheet to start the cut—saving the step of having to bore a starting hole first. A larger saw that resembles a pruning saw is used for cutting out windows or other large openings. Although you'll need to trim off the rough edges they leave with a Surform plane, a jig saw or a Sawzall make fast cuts without using any elbow grease.

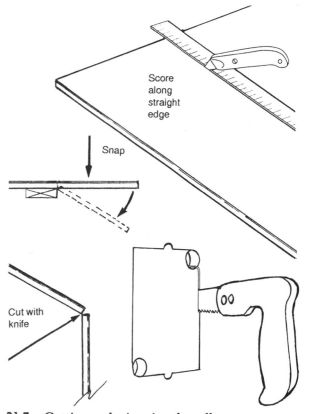

Score along straight edge

Snap

Cut with knife

21-7 *Cutting and trimming drywall.*

21-8 *The long horizontal joints on this wall have been feathered out to a perfectly smooth surface. This job was done by a professional crew using power equipment. If done with hand tools, the nail heads would be "spotted" rather than taped in a continuous line and the walls would lack the splotchy appearance.*

When making notch cuts, use a saw to cut the shorter sides, and snap-cut the longest side with your knife. Some installers prefer to cut window and door openings after they fasten the sheets to the wall. You can feel along the edge of the framing with the blade of your saw as you cut down through the drywall—or you can use a level to guide scoring cuts on the face side.

Sometimes, you'll find that the full-size piece you need to cover the inside of a closet wall won't fit through the door opening. Instead of cutting two smaller pieces and making yourself an extra joint to tape, "fold" the full-size sheet by making a scoring cut on its back side. As long as you handle the sheet carefully so as not to tear it, no crease will show on the face side after the piece is unfolded and fastened to the studs.

Among professionals, hardened Phillips-head drywall screws have largely replaced the blued-steel, barbed-shank nails that were formerly used to fasten drywall panels. If you use nails, drive them hard enough so that their heads are set in the slight depression (or "dimple") made by the crowned face of the hammer. Driving the nail too deep, or hitting it sideways, will cause the nailhead to break through the paper face and loose its holding power. If it's driven too shallow, it will stick up above the joint compound. Drywall screws hold better than nails, especially

if they are driven into strapping, which has enough "bounce" to make it hard to nail down tight. The screws are driven with a screw gun that has a slip clutch and a special dimple-forming nose piece that can be adjusted to set the screw at the proper depth. Screw guns are generally such a useful tool that you might consider buying one rather than renting it.

Whether you use nails or screws, the fasteners should be set in pairs spaced two inches apart on 12-inch centers. This double-nailing pattern has greater holding power than the formerly recommended eight-inch o.c., single-nail spacing. Use 1¼-inch nails or screws for ⅜-inch sheets, 1⅜-inch for ½-inch, and 1½-inch for ⅝-inch sheets.

Because it allows the sheet to move slightly—thereby preventing corner joints from cracking in response to normal structural stresses—some manufacturers recommend leaving the edge of the innermost corner sheet unfastened, and setting the fasteners seven inches back from the edges on the adjacent sheet. Nevertheless, most installers still fasten all the edges of all the sheets under the mistaken assumption that this is what keeps the corner joints from cracking.

TAPING AND FINISHING

Compared to taping, hanging rock is pretty much mindless "grunt work." Taping is definitely an art (see **21-8**). Don't believe anyone who tells you it's easy and fast. Professionals make it look that way because they've spent years acquiring and perfecting their skills. The novice taper will find it slow and frustrating going. Although, with patience and diligence, and some practice, almost anyone can do an adequate, if not quite perfect taping job, drywall taping (and painting) is one part of do-it-yourself homebuilding that you might be better off subcontracting out—particularly when time is in short supply. Even professional builders who can do their own taping will do almost anything they can not to—except when the job is too small or the notice too short to attract a specialist.

Unless you're a pro, there are only a few simple tools that you'll need for taping. An aluminum *hawk* (palette) holds the putty-like joint compound and provides a sharp edge to wipe your trowels clean against. A six-inch taping knife (which resembles a large putty knife but is more flexible) is used for spreading the first coat of compound. A 10-inch and a 14-inch knife (paddle) are used for the second and third coats. You can also use 10-inch and longer drywall trowels instead of paddles, which are similar in appearance to concrete finishing trowels except that they have a curved bottom (concrete trowels are flat) which flattens out as you push down on it, leaving a smooth finish. You might also want to have a smaller pointed taping knife for getting into tight spots.

You may find that your building materials supplier stocks more than one kind of joint-finishing compound. Commercial tapers often use a special "taping mixture" formulated to bond tightly to the drywall for first-coat work. They use an easier-to-spread-and-sand "topping mix" that also shrinks less for the second and third coats. Both kinds are available premixed or in dry powder form.

The residential drywall taper is more likely to be concerned with the difference between "all-purpose" and "setting" type joint compounds. All-purpose compound, or "mud," as it's called in the trade, is a vinyl-based mixture that hardens by evaporation. You can buy it either in premixed one- and five-gallon pails, or else in powder form (other than protection against freezing during storage, I can't think of any reason why a nonprofessional would want to mix his or her own). The main disadvantage of all-purpose compound is its slow drying time. It usually takes at least a day before you can safely recoat it. Under cold (below 60°F, 15°C) or damp conditions, it can take up to two or three days to dry. The bond between the paper facing and the underlying gypsum can loosen when the paper is soaked by excessively long contact with the moisture in the compound. If you try to rush the second coat, there's a good chance of ripping the soft joint tape with the edge of your taping knife or of ruining the finish as your knife plows up chunks of semi-hardened mud. To reduce waiting time and improve drying conditions, warm the rooms with a portable kerosene salamander or LP-gas heater (if there is no operating heating system yet installed).

Also, if all-purpose compound is spread too thickly, it shrinks and cracks, which makes it poorly suited for filling deep holes and gaps.

Like concrete or plaster, setting-type joint compound hardens by a chemical reaction—it must be mixed to the consistency of peanut butter in small batches on the job. Since it can't be retempered after it hardens, mix only enough to use right away. Pros use a mixing paddle (that looks something like a dough hook) powered by a ½-inch electric drill. The big advantage of setting-type compounds is speed. Compounds are available with setting times from 20 to 90 minutes. You can better than halve the drying time by mixing up the batches with warm water or with water in which you've just rinsed your tools. Each coat can be recoated as soon as it has set and the drying time is not seriously slowed by humidity. Since setting compound dries rock-hard and won't shrink, even when paddled on thickly, it's ideal for filling gaps and patching damaged areas and holes.

But setting-type compound dries too hard to sand easily, so inexperienced tapers should probably not attempt to use it except for preliminary patchwork. Even most professionals only use it as a first coat so that they can recoat with all-purpose compound on the same day.

When ready-mixed, all-purpose joint compound freezes, it becomes filled with soft lumps that leave frustrating gouges in your taping job. Allowing the mud to dry in the bucket is even worse. The hard, brittle flakes that form will not only ruin your taping job, but, if they get mixed in with the rest of the mud, will make it useless.

Keep the lid on the pail while using it, and scrape the inside of the bucket clean with a small taping knife. At the end of the day, smooth the surface of the remaining mud, and cover it with a piece of plastic wrap. If you're going to store it for any length of time, pour a cup of water over the plastic. Before reusing, stir the mud thoroughly after decanting the water to mix in any liquid vehicle that may have separated out. If you notice lumps in the compound, discard it or only use it for bedding coats. On the job, keep the pails in a warm place, and always let the mud warm up to about 70°F (21°C) before using it. Likewise, heat the rooms for at least a day before starting to tape and keep them heated until all coats are completely dry.

Formerly, you'd begin joint taping by spreading a coat of mud along a seam, into which you'd embed a two-inch-wide strip of paper joint reinforcing tape (see **12-9**). Nowadays, most professionals use self-adhering fibreglass mesh tape instead of paper tape to eliminate the bed-coat step. The tape is easy to apply, and, because of its open weave, it is less likely to trap bubbles or wrinkle than paper. But, because it's also only about half as strong as paper, it's a good idea to make up the difference by using high-strength setting type compound for the first coat.

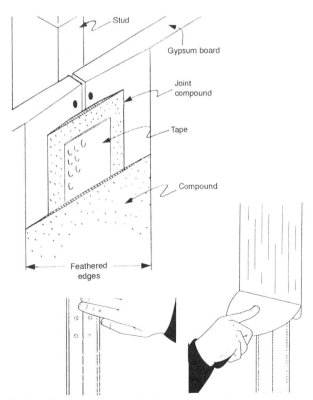

21-9   Two-coat embedded technique for tapered seams shown above in contrast to the first-coat technique that uses self-adhering fibreglass mesh tape.

543

Run the self-sticking tape over the butt joint seams first, beginning and ending on the centerlines of the tapered-edge or corner joints. Then run the tape along the tapered joints, covering the ends of any butt-joint tapes. Using a six-inch taping knife, spread the mud along the taper joints first. If you start with the bulk of the mud mounded up in the center of your knife, most of it will be deposited along the center of the seam and automatically feathered outward at the edges. Otherwise, spread the mud with your knife, and smooth it over and feather out the edges immediately afterwards with an eight-inch or 10-inch-wide paddle. Whatever you do, don't bury the tape under a thick layer of mud. Apply firm and steady pressure to the taping knife or paddle to squeeze most of the excess out of the joint. The mud should just barely cover the mesh of the tape, leaving the ghost of an occasional high spot barely visible. If you pay attention to smoothly feathering (blending) the edges of the compound into the paper, you'll save a lot of tedious sanding work later on. You may find that you get better results by making one pass down the center of the seam to squeeze out the excess mud and level the joint, and a second and third pass on each side of center to feather out the edges.

Wait until after the tapered seams are dry before mudding the butt seams (see **21-10**). In the meantime, you can fill in (or "spot") the nail holes. It takes at least three, and sometimes four, coats of mud to fill in the dimples. You can use a hammer to set a nail that's been left too high, but if you try the same technique with a screw you'll only succeed in breaking off the head. Use a hand-powered screwdriver to turn it deeper (the power driver will usually just strip the screw head). Don't use setting compound on nail holes. It's so dense that air can become easily trapped between it and the fastener and cause a lump in the finish surface. Most dimples usually dry so fast (even with all-purpose mud) that they can be recoated at least once during the same day.

The problem with butt seams is that their lack of a taper means you've got to feather the mud out over a much wider area if the joint is to be inconspicuous. "Double" the joint by running a full-width band of first-coat mud down each side of center, and feather it out with a 12- or 14-inch paddle.

After the butt joints have dried, you can tape the inside and outside corners (see **21-11**). Don't use mesh tape for corners. It won't fold into a neat crease and it's almost impossible to avoid cutting through it with the edge of the taping knife. Instead, fold a strip of paper tape along its precreased centerline and press the tape into a three-inch-wide band of mud applied to each side of the corner. Working from the middle outward, set and smooth out the tape one side at a time, and then go over it again to feather out the mud. Since there isn't any taper to set the mud in, the trick to mudding inside corners is to use as little as possible. The final coat should feather out only about six inches.

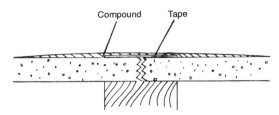

21-10 *First-coat taping technique for butt joints. If you don't let the tapered seams dry before you attempt to tape the butt seams, you'll find it difficult to do a good job where the two seams run into each other.*

Some experts recommend using a special right-angle-faced corner trowel for taping inside corners, but I've found them to be more hindrance than help. Most of the professionals I've known feel the same way. Usually, if one side turns out all right, the other won't. If you keep a steady hand so as not to dig the point of the knife into the side you've already feathered off, it's not too hard to get the hang of smoothing off the other side while it's still wet without leaving ridges and gouges.

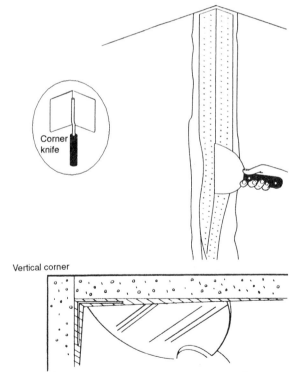

21-11 *First-coat taping technique for inside corners. Taping both sides of an inside corner while wet leaves a slight ridge of mud along one side of the centerline that can be struck off with the knife after it dries.*

21-12 *Taping ceiling and wall corner joint.*

In contemporary construction, the corner joint between the walls and ceilings is usually taped (see **21-12**). Where walls and ceilings will be covered with different finish materials, taping isn't necessary. Often elaborate plaster mouldings were traditionally used to ease the transition between walls and ceilings in the days before drywall. But the modern practice of using wood mouldings to avoid taping corner joints is, perhaps, just a hallmark of impatience, slovenliness, or both.

Metal corner beads are used to protect outside corners from damage (see **21-13**). The beads should be nailed, not screwed, to the drywall, since screw heads are tapered and will either not seat flat or else buckle the metal. Press the bead so that its edges spring flat against the drywall without leaving any gaps or buckles. Use only just enough nails to hold the bead in place. Too many can cause it to buckle. For extra impact resistance, even if you don't use it anywhere else, use setting-type compound for at least the first coat on all outside corners. Apply a thick layer and then, using the edge of the metal as a screed, feather off the compound with your taping knife in a continuous, even motion from top to bottom of the joint (see **21-14**). When taping fin walls, fill the space between the two corner beads level, running your paddle like a screed over their edges.

21-13 *Metal corner beads are used to protect the outside corners from damage. Some builders prefer to use rounded corner bead instead of square-edged corners.*

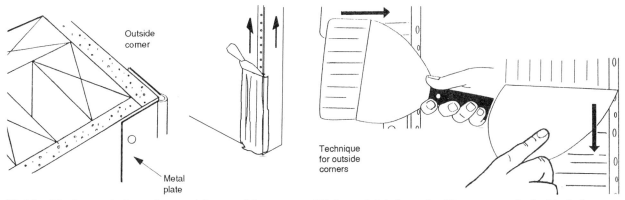

21-14 *Taping technique for straight outside corners. Flakes of dried mud will gouge tracks behind the knife. Flick them out of the joint with the corner of the knife and smooth over the compound once again. If the knife leaves behind depressions, spot-apply more compound and go over the joint again until the surface is level.*

545

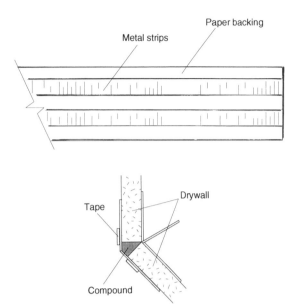

Metal strips

Paper backing

Tape

Drywall

Compound

21-15 *Metal tape for oblique outside corners.*

You can use paper tape on any inside corner but you can't use it or metal corner bead on outside corners that meet at oblique angles (see **21-15**). Instead, use a special paper tape reinforced with two parallel strips of thin galvanized steel that can be creased to form a crisp edge at whatever corner angle is called for. Metal tape is bedded in setting-type compound, and finished the same way as standard paper corner tape.

Not all suppliers stock the segmented metal corner beads that it takes to finish a curved outside corner. One way to solve the problem is to stick a strip of fibreglass mesh along the flat side of the curved corner, and to cut the other side in segments so that it can fold flat (see **21-16**). Then slice a length of reinforced metal tape in half, and bed the strip in setting compound so that its bottom edge extends about 1/16 inch beyond the corner to act as a screed for mudding in the opposite side.

An "L" bead is used to make a crisp joint where the edge of a sheet butts against a dissimilar material such as wood. L beads are applied over the face of the drywall, like corner beads (see **21-17** and **21-18**). When a cut edge

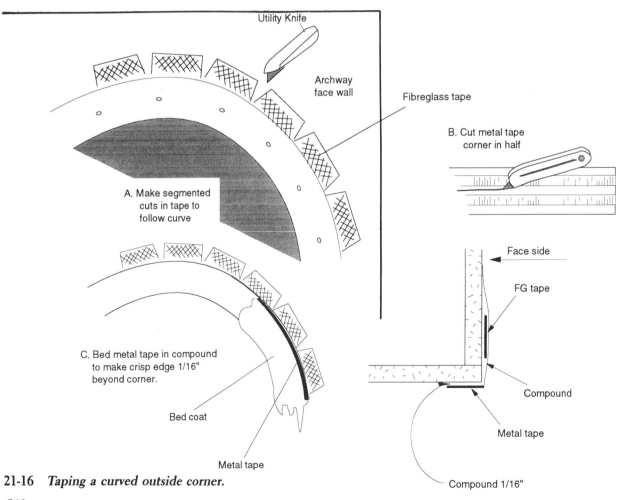

Utility Knife

Archway face wall

Fibreglass tape

A. Make segmented cuts in tape to follow curve

B. Cut metal tape corner in half

C. Bed metal tape in compound to make crisp edge 1/16" beyond corner.

Bed coat

Metal tape

Face side

FG tape

Compound

Metal tape

Compound 1/16"

21-16 *Taping a curved outside corner.*

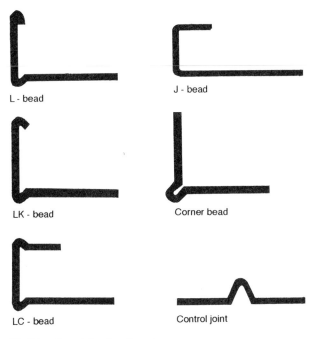

L - bead   J - bead

LK - bead   Corner bead

LC - bead   Control joint

21-17 *Special edge beads.*

of the panel overlaps a different material, a "J" bead is used both for protection and neat appearance. You can either nail the J bead in place first and slip the edge of the sheet into it or else slide it up under the un-nailed edge of the drywall and drive fasteners into it from the face side. L beads are filled with joint compound. The thicker J bead is usually simply painted. Both kinds of beading are available in several sizes to match the thickness of the drywall panels.

Don't start applying the finish (topping) coats of compound until after the first coat is completely dry. If you've done your taping coat carefully, you won't have too much sanding to do before you can apply the second coat. Professionals usually don't need to do *any* sanding until after the third coat. But as a beginner, it's likely you'll find yourself having to sand between each coat.

Go over the seam with your knife first to knock down any ridges or bumps. Then sand out any obvious high spots or ripples and poorly feathered edges with 150-grit sandpaper wrapped around a softwood block or else a fine-grit abrasive sponge sanding block. You might also consider buying a special sanding tool that comes fitted with a swivel extension pole so that you can reach ceilings and wall areas without having to stand on a ladder or staging (see **21-19**). The head of the sander is designed to use open-mesh abrasive screen that won't clog up like ordinary sandpaper. But, since it's harder to control, you may want to stick with ordinary sandpaper in critical areas. In any case, check the surface for smoothness by feeling it with your fingertips.

21-18 *The same rounded corner beads can be used to trim out a window in lieu of a wood casing.*

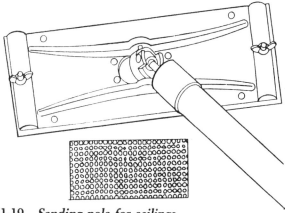

21-19 *Sanding pole for ceilings.*

547

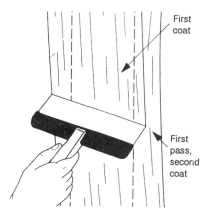
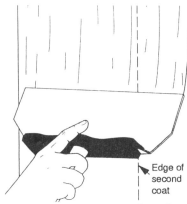

21-20 *It takes some time to get the feel of final coat taping. Control the pressure and angle of the blade so that it enters and leaves the joint gradually, like an airplane landing or taking off to leave only slight ripples in its wake.*

If you have a lot of sanding to do, you could use a palm-grip finishing sander to speed things up. Power sanders will do smoother work with coarser grits than hand sanding, but they can scuff the paper face much more easily. Since any such scuffs will show through the paint and their repair also needlessly complicates your taping job, be careful not too sand too hard or too much.

Although joint compound no longer contains asbestos fibres, you should still avoid breathing the sanding dust. Wear a particle mask or a respirator and eye protection when sanding ceilings.

The second coat should extend about two inches beyond the edges of the first, which is why you need to use ever-increasing widths of paddles to feather out the mud (see **21-20**). Double the mud on each side of the centerline with your taping knife, and then use a 10-inch paddle to smooth it off. You'll be tempted to make repeated passes to fill in small craters and feather out ripples and ridges, but too many passes can make more problems than they fix. If the surface is otherwise perfect, it's better to leave one or two imperfections for later sanding or filling with the third coat than to risk ruining it.

Because they usually aren't very conspicuous, inside corner joints usually only need two coats to finish. Straight joints, particularly on ceilings, are the most highly noticeable and call for three coats. It might even take four coats to hide an especially bad butt joint. Use a 14-inch paddle to feather out the third coat, which should ideally be only a light skim coat. Smooth the mud by making long runs over it while applying heavy pressure on the paddle.

Ideally, you should apply the tape and the first coats and the finish coats in a specific order and wait for each part to dry before starting the next. In reality, you'll find yourself crossing wet butt joints as you're doing the tapers. If you're careful, you can ease up on the knife as you cross a wet seam so that you don't leave ridges or tear up a partially dry surface.

Because a rough, reflective surface diffuses light and eliminates glare, drywall ceilings are most often given a *textured* finish. The textured effect is created by stippling a heavy, paste-like sanded paint with a large, coarse bristled brush or a special texturing roller. Drywall contractors usually achieve their distinctive fuzzy texture finish by applying any of several commercially available texturing compounds such as Imperial QT (a powder containing highly reflective brilliant white flakes of perlite and binders for combination with heavy ceiling paint) with a power spray gun similar to the kind used by modern plasterers. One advantage of using a textured ceiling finish is that the heavy paint coating hides a multitude of taping sins, so much so that the joints usually need only two coats of mud to finish.

In many parts of the United States, notably the Southwest, textured effects such as the "Mediterranean knock-down" are popular wall finishes. Here, the walls, which have been given a two-coat tape job, are coated with a texture-grade joint compound (which won't crack or shrink like all-purpose compound) applied with a coarse roller. Then the stippled surface is "knocked down" with random strokes of a drywall trowel.

A number of other texture effects can be achieved by applying techniques that make use of one or a combination of flat or notched trowelling, brushing, sponging, or brooming the compound while it is still wet.

ALTERNATIVES TO DRYWALL
Recently, fibre-reinforced gypsum plaster wallboard, which has been widely used in Europe for more than 10 years, has begun to be manufactured in North America by Louisiana Pacific Co. under the name of FiberBond. Unlike conventional drywall, FiberBond panels are non-laminated and lack paper facings, which gives a wall finished with them more of the look and feel of traditional plaster. The product is claimed by the manufacturer to be

stronger and more fire- and moisture-resistant than conventional drywall. Because of its greater density, which causes a ½-inch 4×8 sheet to weigh about 25 percent more than drywall, FiberBond also is more sound-deadening. The panels, which are also available in ⅜ inch and ⅝ inch thicknesses, come in 4×8, 4×10, and 4×12 lengths that are bevelled on all four edges.

In general, except for a few adaptations in response to its unique characteristics, FiberBond panels are basically installed the same way as conventional drywall.

Although its density makes it much harder to cut, scoring the face with a utility knife and a straightedge and snapping the opposite face still gets the job done. A drywall saw or jig saw is still the tool to use for cutting outlet holes and notching. But you'll need to drill a starting hole for the blade when you make cut-outs. You'll also need a Surform plane or a wood rasp file to trim away any tight fits. Your utility knife just won't cut it. You'll also need to use your Surform plane to chamfer a ½-inch-wide 45-degree bevel on the edges of any cut sheets that would otherwise end up with a butt joint.

You can use either nails or drywall screws to fasten the panels to the walls. Nails are actually easier to drive than screws, and there's no worry about over-driving them through the paper or crushing the core with an overzealous hammer blow. You can also drive the nails close to the edge without breaking it. On the other hand, drywall screws are a little harder to start, and it takes more pressure to keep the screwdriver bit seated in the screw head.

One big difference between FiberBond and ordinary drywall is that the fastest way to install the panels is to use an air-powered stapler (the same kind pros use to staple plywood and other solid sheathings). The staples won't pull through the material. Finally, when fastening the sheets, leave a ⅛-inch gap between them the same as for plywood.

But the real difference between fibre-reinforced panels and drywall is when it comes to taping and finishing; no tape is required at all for flat joints. Instead, the trough formed by the tapered edges is filled with a basecoat of specially formulated FiberBond Dri Mix joint compound. Unlike ordinary taping, only the trough itself is filled with the compound and the excess is screeded off with the taping knife rather than feathered out. After the base compound has dried (it shrinks slightly as it does so), the joint is topcoated with ordinary all-purpose mud, feathered out as usual a couple of inches beyond the basecoat. Sand the topcoat when it's dry.

Inside corners are taped first with creased paper tape bedded in a Dri Mix basecoat and then topcoated with all-purpose compound as above. Outside corners use standard metal corner beads and can be given two coats of ordinary mud without any need of a Dri Mix basecoat. Nails or other fasteners are spotted first with Dri Mix and finished with mud. Because there's no paper face to scuff, finish sanding is very easy.

TRADITIONAL PLASTERING

Like slate roofing, traditional plastering is one of those almost extinct crafts which has of late enjoyed something of a renaissance in high-end, custom-home building. There are at least three good reasons why plaster was superseded by drywall. First, even more than drywall taping, plastering is an art; it takes skill and experience to mix the plaster to the proper consistency and achieve a smooth and even surface when it's applied. Second, it's time-consuming work; two coats are the bare minimum, with three-coat work being the sign of a quality job. Even though spray machines allow modern plasterers to apply the material fairly quickly compared to hand-trowelling, each coat must damp cure for two to three days before it can be recoated. Finally, as the plaster cures, it releases huge quantities of water vapor into the house, much of which is absorbed into the wall cavities and framework. Applying plaster under humid conditions increases its drying time and can cause structural problems because of condensation and swelling and subsequent shrinkage of finish and structural materials. Even under normal conditions, plaster finishes would often crack as the framing beneath them settled or changed dimension with seasonal moisture variations. Balloon framing (which is more dimensionally stable than platform framing) became extinct about the same time that drywall was invented.

In addition, plaster can't be allowed to freeze while it's curing, which means that the house has to be kept heated in cold weather. Despite these drawbacks, some home owners feel that the look and feel of traditional plaster is worth the trouble and expense. Three-quarters of an inch of plaster makes a strong and solid wall with excellent sound-deadening and fire-resisting characteristics. Plaster can also be applied to curved and irregular surfaces much more readily than drywall or other panel-type finishes.

From the Middle Ages until the 1950s, plaster was applied over a base of thin wood strips called laths. Since then, specially treated gypsum panels and sheets of expanded metal have replaced wood lath as a plaster base.

Expanded metal lath, which is made from copper-alloy sheet steel, split and expanded into a diamond mesh or flat rib pattern and coated with rust-resistant black asphalt or galvanized zinc, in 27-inch-wide by eight-foot-long sheets, is mainly used as a base for commercial interior plastering and exterior stucco work. In residential work, metal lath is used in place of gypsum lath in high-moisture areas such as bathtub enclosures and shower stalls where it is less susceptible to moisture damage. The metal sheets are applied over 15-pound tar-paper underlayment stapled to the studs. They should overlap each other at their sides and ends. On inside corners, the sheets are "returned," i.e., bent and overlapped onto the next stud. Expanded metal lath, cut into eight-inch-wide strips, is also used to reinforce stress points over gypsum lath or other types of plaster bases. The pieces are stapled or tacked diagonally to the plaster base only (i.e., not to the underlying framing, which would otherwise transmit warping and shrinking stresses in the frame to the plaster finish and crack it), above the corners of doors and windows. Metal lath is also applied over the plaster base where it covers wood beams and other large structural timbers that are likely to change dimensions.

Gypsum plaster lath (or Rocklath), which comes in 16-inch by 48-inch by ⅜-inch panels that are nailed (or screwed) horizontally to the framing, is the standard plaster base for residential construction. It's also available with an aluminum foil vapor barrier backing or a perforated face designed for improved plaster bonding. A fibreboard lath product which has considerable R-value is also available.

Gypsum lath should be fastened to studs spaced 16 inches o.c. with galvanized roofing nails, offsetting the joints between courses. Leave a ⅛- to 3/16-inch gap between the edges of all sheets to help "key" the plaster to the base. Since, unlike drywall, you can use any piece of lath that will span a stud bay, there's very little waste. This makes up for the slightly higher cost of gypsum lath. *Cornerite*, a special five-inch-wide wire fabric bent to form a right angle, is stapled over the base to reinforce inside corners. Outside corners are reinforced with a metal bead similar to the kind used for drywall corners except that its outside edge is usually rounded over and raised above the base to make a screed for levelling the plaster to the correct thickness (see **21-21**).

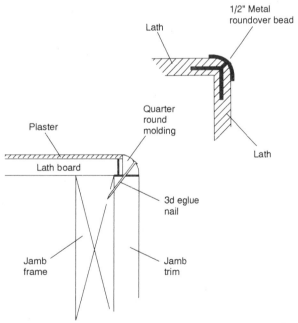

Plaster grounds are wood strips equal to the thickness of the plaster and the base (typically ⅞ inch, i.e., ⅜ plus ½) that are nailed around door and window openings and sometimes along the bottom of the walls or at the ceiling line (if a cove moulding will be used). The grounds not only serve as a gauge for maintaining plaster thickness and as a screed board for keeping the surface level and even, but also can be used as a nail base for attaching wood trim if left permanently in place. Extension jambs added to windows can be cut to act as plaster grounds as well.

Plaster grounds around door openings are usually removed after plastering. Using a spacing block, tack two strips of wood to the jamb sides of the door framing so that their edges line up with the desired thickness of the plaster coats. You can also use a single strip of plywood ripped to the correct thickness of the finished wall.

Although interior plaster can be applied directly over unpainted concrete, block, and brick surfaces, doing so would cause excessive heat loss. Instead, wood strapping is attached to the walls with special fasteners or adhesives. Hardened masonry nails can be driven into mortar joints with a hammer or a gunpowder-actuated tool. Special patented fasteners that screw directly into masonry are relatively costly, but take a lot less time and provide a more reliable grip than expansion fasteners or nails. To provide more resistance to heat loss, you can also glue rigid plastic foam directly to the walls and install strapping and plaster base over it. The reflective foil face of the insulation acts as a barrier to radiant heat loss, and the space between the strapping is handy for running wires. Otherwise, you can use the plastic foam itself as a plaster base, so long as you follow the manufacturer's recommendations for surface preparation and add the appropriate latex bonding agents to the plaster mix.

In three-coat plaster work, the first, or *scratch*, coat, is applied to the base and cross raked (scratched) after it has "taken up" (stiffened). It is then left to set and dry out for at least 48 hours. The second coat (the *brown* coat) is then trowelled on and levelled off by running a long, flat two-handed trowel called a *darby* across the surface, using a straightedge (a *rod*) and the plaster grounds to guide the screeding. In two-coat work, the scratch and brown coats are applied almost simultaneously. Since the brown coat is *doubled-back* over the scratch coat within a few minutes, there's no need to rake the scratch coat. With this method, small areas can be brought up to full thickness and used as a screed guide for the remaining surfaces. This is especially useful for maintaining an even finish on ceilings and other large areas.

Whichever method you use, the basecoats should end up even with the grounds and the final thickness of all the coats together should not be less than ½ inch. A ½-inch-thick coat of plaster is almost twice as rigid as a ⅜-inch one. At least ⅝ inch is required over masonry and, with metal lath, the overall thickness (as measured from the backside of the lath) should be ¾ inch.

21-21 *With a round-over corner treatment, wood casings and extension jambs can be replaced with a plaster finish. Order narrow jambs for the windows and run an L-bead where the plaster base butts against them.*

The scratch and brown coats are mixed (either on the job or at the factory) with aggregates that add strength, such as wood fibre or sand, and lightness, such as perlite or vermiculite. They also may leave a roughly textured surface. Although textured finishes of various kinds can be achieved by adding special sand to the final mix, and "floating" the surface with a wood trowel, the traditional hard smooth (or *putty*) finish is achieved by adding lime and cement to the mix and polishing it with a steel trowel, almost like finishing a concrete slab. Needless to say, this is demanding work. When mixing and using plaster, always follow the manufacturer's recommendations as printed on the bag, and use clean water of the correct temperature. Wash out the mixer, and rinse off your tools after each batch is mixed with clean water as well. Throw out any plaster that has begun to set, and rinse out the plaster tub.

A DO-IT-YOURSELF ALTERNATIVE TO TRADITIONAL PLASTERING

As is obvious from the preceding discussion, it takes more skill and patience to plaster a house than most do-it-yourselfers are apt to have. However, there's one kind of plastering technique which gives a rough and rustic but quite pleasing finish that has a more genuine feel to it than the textured-finishes that can be achieved with joint compound or textured paint mixtures. *Perlited gypsum plaster*

is normally used for basecoat work. However, it can also be trowelled directly onto gypsum lath boards with a steel trowel (the same kind that you'd use for drywall work) in one or two 1/8-inch-thick coats (see **22-22**). Since making a flat finish is not the objective, there's no need to set grounds or screeds. You can use ordinary drywall corner bead for outside corners. Although not strictly necessary, for best results reinforce inside corners and the corners of openings with metal mesh. To make a rounded-over corner, butt the lath against strips of half-inch wood quarter-round moulding tacked to the corners (refer to **21-21**). Or use 1/2-inch round-over profile metal corner bead instead of wood. The plaster will fill the gap between the lath and the edge of the bead.

Unlike conventional plastering, you should install the window and door casings, baseboards, and any ceiling moulding before applying the plaster. Otherwise, it won't be possible to get them to lie flat over the rough plaster surface (see **21-23**). If you're using two coats, you may want to apply 1/4-inch grounds for levelling the plaster adjacent to the trim if a reduced reveal is objectionable. If you stain, paint, and/or varnish the wood trim first (either before nailing it up or *in situ* before trowelling on the plaster) cleanup will be much easier. Screed the excess plaster off the edge of the wood with a taping knife, and rinse off the remaining film with a towel dampened with vinegar solution.

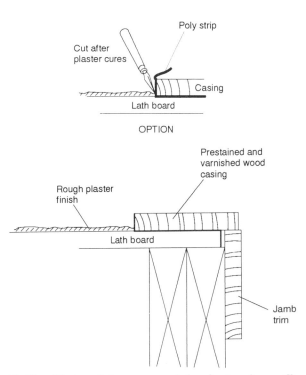

21-22 *Two coats of perlited gypsum plaster has been trowelled over gypsum lath to create this pleasing rough-textured wall finish which can be left natural or painted for washability.*

21-23 *Plaster stains are much harder to clean off bare wood. If used, the plaster grounds must be set carefully to the edge of the casing boards.*

Mix the plaster with a garden hoe in a shallow plastic mixing tub, and trowel it onto dampened gypsum lath with broad semi-circular strokes that leave their signature intact. Moistening the base helps prevent the shrinkage cracks that tend to develop as the paper wicks moisture out of the plaster. Work from top to bottom, and keep advancing the leading edge of the fresh material until you reach a corner or other natural stopping place. If you're using two coats, scratch the first coat with a notched trowel, and let it harden. Doubling back on semi-hardened plaster will just make a mess. You can experiment with trowelling techniques for different effects. The more you go over an area, the smoother it becomes. When dry, the plaster should have a pleasing light-grey appearance. But impurities in the water and other uncontrollable aspects of drying often cause mottled white patches and some surface crumbling. Prime the surface with heavy latex paint (primers especially formulated for drywall are ideal and inexpensive), and apply a finish coat of flat or semi-gloss latex to provide washability and prevent surface spalling.

I've heard of some do-it-yourselfers who have used ordinary drywall as a base for this kind of plastering. They claim that installing the sheets back-face outward and indenting them with a hammer claw provides a good bonding surface. In my experience, perlited plaster will bond well to just about anything, although shrinkage cracks often develop when the material is trowelled onto unsuitable bases, spread too thin, or dries out too quickly. Keeping the windows and doors shut will maintain high humidity and retard curing time, which prevents surface cracking.

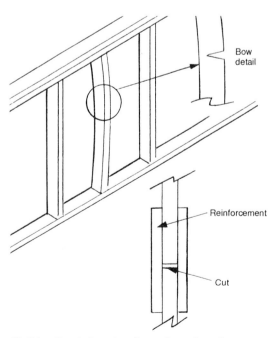

21-24 *Straightening bowed studs prior to panelling.*

A poor bond can also result from using stale plaster; plaster has a limited shelf life. It gradually absorbs moisture from the air and degrades, particularly if it's been allowed to freeze in a humid environment. Since there isn't ordinarily much demand for this type of product at your local building supply dealer's, whatever is in stock is likely to be old. If your plaster starts to set up almost as soon as it's been mixed, it's too old to use. If you buy your plaster from a masonry supplier, it's much more likely to be fresh. Don't store the bag in a cold place, and use it up quickly after the bag has been opened. Don't save partially used bags for later use.

PREFINISHED WOOD PANELLING

In my opinion, if there's a single product that epitomizes what's wrong with the modern building industry, it's probably prefinished wood "panelling" (plastic imitation ceiling beams are a close second). Plywood and hardboard panels are ubiquitous because they're light, easy to handle, simple to install, cover a lot of area quickly, and, once they are put up, basically maintenance-free. They're also just about the cheapest way to finish a wall.

There are literally hundreds of designs and patterns to choose from, running the gamut from real and/or simulated hardwood, softwood, and exotic wood veneers, to imitation barn board, marble, stucco, brick, stone, and linoleum, to textures and finishes unknown in the natural universe, such as the plastic-coated hardboard that is the finish of choice for mobile home bathroom and kitchen walls. My gripe with them is that, with the possible exception of a few top-of-the-line panels that look almost real, these products are the antithesis of a home improvement; they only cheapen and diminish the spirit of the home.

They are however, an economical wall covering for cheap commercial office space and for a basement workshop or other utilitarian space. Since anything under ¼ inch thickness is too flimsy to attach directly to the framing, ⅛-inch hardboard panels are normally glued over existing wall finishes or to an underlayment such as ⅜-inch drywall or rigid foam sheathing. Even the thicker plywood panels are likely to buckle if nailed to studs on 24-inch centers. To prevent this, nail horizontal strapping across the studs at 16-inch or even 12-inch centers.

Sight down the walls to check for bowed studs that will telegraph a bump through the panelling. This is more likely to be a problem with interior partitions that haven't had the bracing effect of plywood sheathing to keep their studs from warping as they dried out. Either replace the offending stud with a straight one, or saw through it and "scab" it back together (see **21-24**). This procedure should also be done before installing drywall.

Deliver the panelling to the job site about a week ahead of time, and store the sheets with stickers between. Allowing the panels to adjust to the moisture level of the rooms helps to keep them from buckling.

For best appearances, plan the layout of the panels so that the width of the starting and ending sheets are about the same on each wall and not less than three stud bays wide. If necessary, distribute the panels along the wall so that you can match their color and grain patterns.

Installation usually begins at a corner. If the corner is off, scribe and cut the first sheet so that its leading edge will fall plumb on the stud centerline.

The best way to cut panelling is on a table saw equipped with a fine-toothed carbide blade or a plywood blade. You'll need a helper or an adjustable roller stand to support the end of the sheet. Remember, the teeth of a handsaw or a tablesaw cut downward; so the sheet should be face-side up to prevent tearing the finish veneer. The rotation of a circular power saw or the stroke of a jig saw is upwards, hence the sheets are cut with the face (the "good" side) down. Splintering is much worse when sawing across the grain (*crosscutting*) than along it (*rip cutting*).

Hardened ring-shank, color-matched nails are normally used to secure the panels. General methods for nailing or gluing panels directly to studs or to underlayment are shown in **21-25**. Procedures for nailing differ only in nail penetration. For specifics, follow the panel manufacturer's recommended schedule. Panel adhesives (or general-purpose construction adhesives) are best applied with a caulking gun. The large one-quart cartridges are more economical than the standard 11½-ounce size.

Depending on their design, the edges of prefinished panels can butt together in a matched groove or a square joint. Various plain or profiled battens, mouldings, or inserts can also be used to dress up vertical joints and horizontal seams and trim out window and door casings. Standard wood cove and base moulding is used for ceiling and baseboard trim. In addition to wooden inside and outside corner and cap mouldings, manufactured metal or plastic trim and joiner strips are also available.

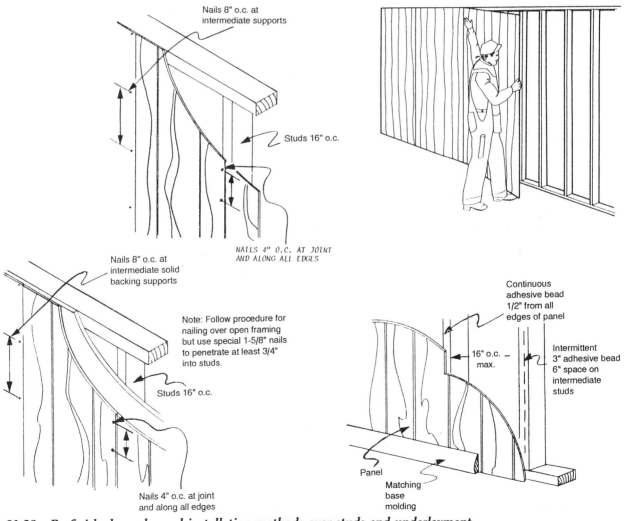

21-25 *Prefinished wood panel installation methods over studs and underlayment.*

553

21-26 *Vertical, 10-inch ship-lapped No. 3 pine boards combined with a V-groove spruce ceiling and 1×6 spruce floorboards and infused with light from tall windows create a warm and cozy living room.*

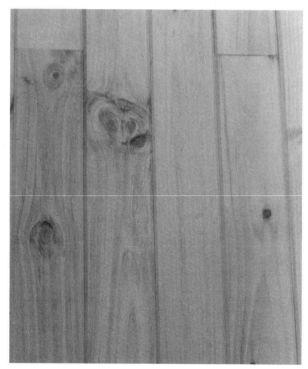

21-27 *Like a reveal against a window casing, by accentuating the line of the panelling, the bevelled profile of V-groove panelling makes the joints appear less conspicuous than they would if they were square-edged. The butt joints at the ends of boards are cut on matching 10-degree bevels for a tight fit.*

REAL WOOD PANELLING

In one form or another, solid boards have been used as a wall covering for centuries (see **21-26**). In late 17th-century America, what we think of as wood "panelling" today, that is, vertical boards (often with a decorative shiplap or tongue-and-groove bead along their edges) nailed to the walls, was called "ceiling." The term panelling referred to the early 18th-century practice of covering the walls with wide, thin-edged "panels" set in grooved horizontal rails and vertical stiles that looked almost as if a line of doors had been set on their sides and nailed to the studs. The term "wainscot" was originally also used for this floor-to-ceiling panelling, but by the 19th century it had come to mean the vertical narrow beaded "matchboard" that was run halfway up the wall and capped with a "chair rail" moulding or shelf. Today, the term panelling is generally applied to any matched (i.e., tongue-and-grooved), shiplapped, or square-edged boards that are nailed directly to the walls, regardless of their direction or coverage.

Just about any species of wood can be used for panelling. White and southern yellow pine, western red and eastern white cedar, redwood, and spruce/hemlock are some of the more common. When locally available, otherwise exotic species such as butternut, walnut, arbor vitae, or cypress can be quite affordable. Hardwood species such as maple, oak, and cherry tend to be considerably more expensive and are much more difficult to work with. Hardwood boards suitable for use as panelling should be dry and straight. Since hardwood has no appreciable "give" to it, you can't easily flatten out twisted boards or force

21-28 *In this room, weathered boards salvaged from the walls of an old shed are run both vertically and horizontally over tar paper to highlight the joints between them. The spruce floor resists wear better than pine.*

bowed pieces together as you can with softwoods. Cuts and joints must be precise since you can't force slightly oversized pieces together to make a tight fit. Holes for nails or screws must be predrilled to avoid splitting ends and/or bending the fastener.

Since weathertightness of the joint isn't a consideration, boards with any of the three basic milling patterns for exterior siding described in Chapter Eleven can be used for interior panelling. The desired appearance is the only criteria (see **21-27**).

Shiplap is the easiest of the sidings to install, but the nails are exposed. Depending on the type of nail head and the neatness of your nailing patterns, face-nailing can either add or detract to the overall appearance. Many builders prefer the look of tongue-and-groove boarding since it can be "blind" nailed. V-groove tongue-and-groove patterns accentuate the edges of the boards and also give a more finished appearance than straight-milled joints. Bear in mind that boards over six inches wide will need a face nail to hold them securely no matter what type of joint they have. Square-edged boards are considerably more rustic in appearance, but give quick coverage. For a crisp joint line—and so that the insulation won't be visible through the gaps between the boards—staple tar paper upside down (so the factory-applied chalk lines don't show) to the studs first. Some builders choose to emphasize this background joint line by using spacers to hold the boards ⅛ inch or ¼ inch apart (see **21-28**).

The easiest way to apply board panelling is to nail it horizontally across the studs. Horizontal application has the effect of lengthening a room. Some people find this appealing; others find it anything but (see **21-29**).

21-29 *Because it can be nailed directly to the wall studs, horizontal board panelling is easy to apply. However, because it tends to lower the apparent height of a room, it's not the best choice for a small room with low ceilings. Note how the V-grooves match up at the corner.*

555

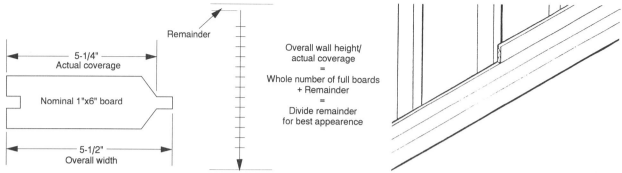

21-30 *Starting and ending horizontal panelling. For a balanced appearance, plan the installation before you begin nailing.*

You can start at either the floor or ceiling (see **21-30**). Divide the wall height by the actual coverage of each board to find out how many boards you'll need to cover it and how wide the last piece will be. Then you can decide whether or not to trim the starting board so that you don't end up with a narrow fillet, or whether to start with a full-width piece at the floor or ceiling and let the ending piece be covered by a baseboard and/or ceiling moulding. Where the ending piece works out to an inch or less, you can trim the edge of the next-widest board instead (e.g., trim an eight-inch board down to fit a 6½-inch width).

Many people feel that panelling with horizontal boarding to chair-rail height (32 to 36 inches off the floor) is better-looking than full-height panelling (see **21-31**). The last board can be full-width without any adjustments. A variety of cap treatments ranging from a simple overlapping flat band or outside corner moulding to a bracketed shelf with ornamental cove or crown mouldings are possible (see **21-32**).

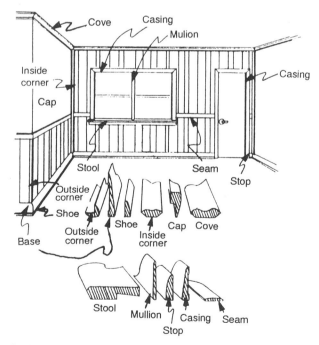

21-31 *Vertical or horizontal board wainscot capped with a simple, narrow, rounded-over band moulding goes well with drywall walls and ceilings, particularly in stairwells where the wood protects the drywall from impact and scuffing.*

21-32 *Cap details for horizontal half-wall panelling. Vertical half-wall panelling (wainscotting) requires horizontal strapping for a nailing base.*

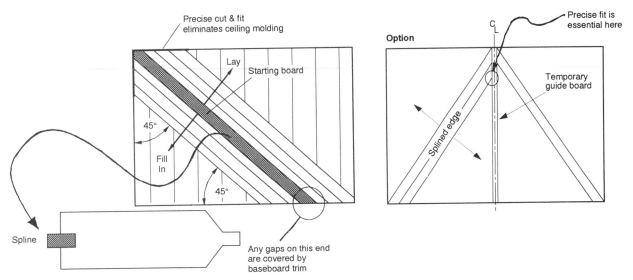

21-33 *Starting and ending diagonal panelling. When not covered by moulding, the ends of panelling boards may have to be scribed to the ceiling for a precise fit. If a textured ceiling finish will be applied, tack a temporary ground strip over the drywall so that the panelling will have a smooth surface to butt against.*

Boards can also be nailed directly to the studs on a diagonal (see **21-33**). The easiest way to install them is to make the cuts on a 45-degree angle. Other angles, such as 30–60 degrees, require resetting the sawblade with the concomitant increased chance of errors or else require two saws that can be set for one of each complementary angle pair.

When the boards all run in the same direction (as opposed to meeting at a centerline), it's a good idea to start the layout from the first full-length board at a corner. It's hard to check the angles for accuracy if you start with a short piece at the corner, and a slight error can add up to noticeable gaps as the boards increase in length.

Tongue-and-groove boards are always nailed tongue-out, with finish nails driven at about a 45-degree angle through the base of the tongue. Shiplapped boards are likewise nailed with the lap flat against the base so that, if needed, their joints can be driven tight together by a concealed toenail. When working with diagonal boarding, you'll have to change direction to fill in the short boards behind the starting board. Cut a *spline* (a thin, flat piece of wood used to join two pieces together), and glue it into the groove of the starting board. Tilt the closing boards upwards so they don't bind against the corners of the walls as you mate the joints—and then ease them down flat.

Most people prefer the look of vertical panelling. Nailing two-by-four blocking flatwise between the studs on alternating sides of two-foot centerlines is one way to provide a nailbase for the boarding (see **21-34**). But installing the blocking before the insulation makes it hard to fit the batts into the bays, and adding the blocks after the fi-breglass—and slicing the insulation to fit snug—is tedious and itchy. (Nailing the blocking sideways makes a thermal bridge between the wall surfaces and also increases air infiltration.) The most energy-efficient, quickest, easiest, and least costly method is to nail horizontal strapping across the studs.

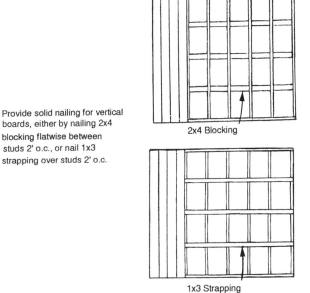

Provide solid nailing for vertical boards, either by nailing 2x4 blocking flatwise between studs 2' o.c., or nail 1x3 strapping over studs 2' o.c.

2x4 Blocking

1x3 Strapping

21-34 *Vertical boards need solid nailing. Where space allows, strapping is preferable to blocking.*

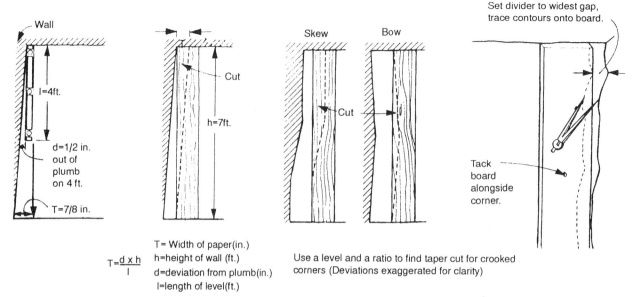

Wall

I=4ft.

d=1/2 in. out of plumb on 4 ft.

T=7/8 in.

Cut

h=7ft.

Skew   Bow

Cut

Set divider to widest gap, trace contours onto board.

Tack board alongside corner.

$$T = \frac{d \times h}{l}$$

T= Width of paper(in.)
h=height of wall (ft.)
d=deviation from plumb(in.)
l=length of level(ft.)

Use a level and a ratio to find taper cut for crooked corners (Deviations exaggerated for clarity)

21-35 *Scribing the starting edge of a board along an irregular wall using a compass or dividers. A formula can be used for a simple taper cut.*

As with prefinished panelling, begin installing vertical panelling by checking the starting corner for plumb. If it's off, the inside edge of the first board will have to be tapered so that its outboard edge is plumb. The easiest way to mark the cut is by setting a four-foot level plumb against the corner, and measuring the width of the gap between the level and the wall. Use this as a ratio to calculate the overall taper. For example, if there's a ½-inch gap between the bottom edge of your level and an eight-foot-high wall (assuming that the zero point is at the top of the wall), then you'll mark a point an inch in from the top edge of the board and snap a cut line that tapers to zero at the bottom edge of the board.

If the problem is not so much a taper as a bowed or otherwise irregular wall, the starting board should be scribed to fit (see **21-35**). Plumb and tack the board to the wall with its inside edge tangent to the outermost part of the wall bow. Set a compass or a pair of dividers—the kind that lets you interchange a pencil for the steel point on one leg—to the widest gap, and then scribe the edge of the wall onto the board. Be sure to hold the compass so that both legs stay in the same plane relative to the wall; tilting one leg throws off the scribe line.

Accuracy is especially hard to maintain when the compass must follow a very irregular surface such as brick or stonework. (You might consider notching the bricks to fit over the board instead. Soft brick is easily cut with a masonry blade.) A homemade pantograph is more accurate; drill a hole for a pencil socket through the centerline about a board's width in from the end of a piece of one-inch stock (see **21-36**). Cut the head of an 8d nail and stick its shaft into a second hole bored into the edge of the end of the block to make a point. Plumb and position the starting board so that its edge and the pencil point fall just inside the deepest reach of the pantograph, and then tack a small block to the other end of the stock at right angles to it and beneath it so that it lines up with the other side of the board, just like a T-square. This guide keeps the point and the pencil in the same line as you move it along the edge of the board.

Width of board (use wider board if needed to avoid small gaps)

Last board

Homemade pantograph

Offet board by width of distance from pencil to point of pantograph.

21-36 *Unlike a pair of dividers, a pantograph always stays in the same plane relative to the edge it's following, thereby guaranteeing the accuracy of the scribe line.*

The same scribing techniques are used for the ending (or *closing*) board, with one extra twist; since the width of the closing board is determined by the space between the preceding board and the end of the wall, the position of the scribe line must be adjusted accordingly. When tacked in place, the closing board should overlay the last full board by the width of a full board less an amount equal to the distance between the pencil and the point of the pantograph. If this is greater than a full-board width, either use a wider board or scribe a small filler piece to make up the difference.

Cut the scribe line with a jigsaw or on a band saw, try it for fit, "fair" off any places that don't fit right with a half-round wood rasp, and fill small gaps with translucent Phenoseal caulk (which dries to a clear amber color that blends in better with natural wood than most other caulks).

The same scribing technique can be used to match horizontal starting and/or closing boards to floors and ceilings or ceiling boards against walls. Some carpenters find it easier to use a *spiling batten*—a boat-builder's term for a ¼-inch-thick strip of softwood that's used as a scribing template in lieu of the closing board—especially if the ends of the board must also be scribed along with its edge (see **21-37**). The batten is cut about an inch shorter than the length of the boards and about ½ inch narrower than the gap that must be closed. It's tacked in place butted against the next-to-last board, and then scribed to the width of the maximum gap between the batten and the wall plus ¼ inch (just in case it should run off the edge). The scribed batten is then clamped to the closing board stock with inboard (bottom) edges lined up flush. The board is then scribed following the line drawn on the spiling batten. To make sure the compass setting hasn't been accidentally changed, draw a "reference" circle on the batten, and check it between the first and second scribing.

When cutting the inboard edge of a starting board or the leading edge of a closing board, a tighter fit will result if the cut is made on a slight bevel (about 5 to 10 degrees). This back-cut edge is easy to fine-tune for fit using a small block plane or wood rasp.

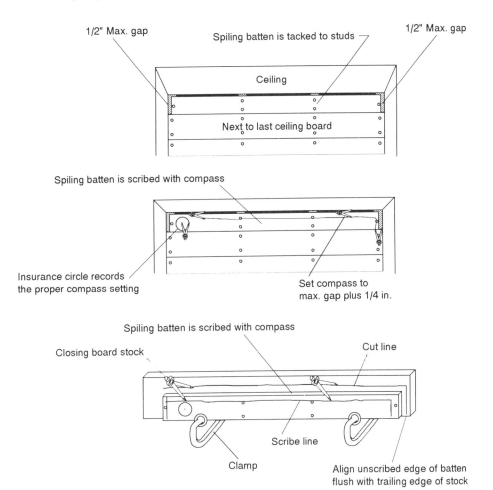

21-37 *Using a spiling batten to scribe the closing board. This technique works equally well for fitting closing boards on a panelled ceiling.*

559

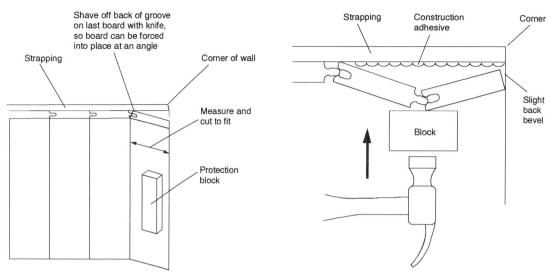

21-38 *Fitting tongue-and-groove closing boards. Face-nail the closing board with 6d finish nails, sunk and filled with wood dough.*

Unlike shiplap, which is always face-nailed, you won't have enough room to swing your hammer as you try to toenail the last few tongue-and-groove boards into a corner. Also, the bottom groove of the closing board won't fit under the tongue of the next-to-last board unless it's held at a steep angle (see **21-38**). Cutting a sharper angle on the backcut of the closing board usually let's you ease the board into place. Since the last two boards will be face-nailed anyway, you can also cut off the backside groove of the closing board. Another method, which results in a very tight fit, without any face nails, is to run a bead of adhesive across the strapping, and then tilt the leading edges of the next-to-last board upwards and the closing board downwards. Then, using a protective block and hammer, if necessary, force the two boards downwards.

The tongue will slip into its groove and the closing board will be jammed tightly against the corner. Wedge a 2×4 between the boards and a cleat to keep them flat until the glue sets.

Check every few courses to see that the boards are still running plumb or level as you continue running them out. Small differences in the tongue-and-groove or in the widths of the boards or the joint can cause them to run off. If you notice that this has happened, use the slack in the joint to make marginal corrections that will bring the boards back into true over several courses.

Even with the best-grade lumber, some of the boards won't mate perfectly without some persuasion. With *native lumber* (which is what the stuff you buy from your local sawmill is called) bowed boards can be fairly common.

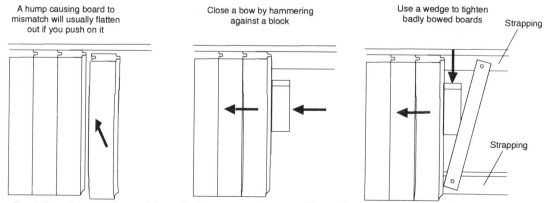

21-39 *Straightening out bowed boards. Even a wedge usually can't straighten out a bowed hardwood board—which is why only select boards kept properly stacked and stickered and stored in a dry place with an even temperature should be used for panelling.*

Sometimes the problem is caused by a warp in the face of the boards that prevents the joints from aligning. Simply pushing down on the problem area with the palm of your hand is usually enough to flatten the bow so that the edges mate (see **21-39**).

With shiplap boards, a box nail toenailed into the leading edge of the shiplap and driven home with a nail set will generally provide enough force to straighten out a bow in the edge of a board. If extra holding power is needed, drive two nails, side-by-side, at the same time. With tongue-and-groove boards, even if the head of a box nail weren't visible, it would tend to split the tongue before it moved it very far. Finish nails don't have enough holding power to straighten out anything more than a minor bow.

Often, the problem isn't a bow per se so much as it is a tight tongue-and-groove. Driving a scrap of matching board against the tongue with your hammer will usually suffice to coax the joint together, especially if you work along the length of the joint, nailing it as you go.

To straighten an especially stubborn bow (refer to **21-39**) tack a board (or 2×4 scrap) in line with the leading edge but at an angle across a pair of nailers or studs. Slide a tapered piece of matched board against the tongue and cleat. As you drive it downwards with your hammer, it will close up the bow. Any board that doesn't respond should be tossed into the scrap pile.

Finish nails (8d) are generally used for blind-nailing one-inch tongue-and-groove boards. Even though they have smaller heads than common nails, box nails are still too big for interior face-nailing. Although some builders use them anyway, the tiny heads of finish nails similarly don't have enough withdrawal resistance to hold a wide board flat against the wall. If you can find them, casing nails, with their slightly flared head, or 7d cement-coated crating nails with a small, checkered head, are ideal for face-nailing. Failing this, hardened spiral-thread flooring nails are another good choice, although they have an oily finish that tends to build up on your hammer head and leave telltale stains on the wood. Antique hand-forged nails or rectangular-cut flooring nails are another possibility, especially with rough-sawn square-edged boards.

Some builders try to hide face nails by setting the heads below the surface and filling the holes with colored wood putty. I favor using the nails as a design element. If you don't want to see nails, use blind-nailing or drywall. So long as the nail heads aren't too big and you maintain a consistent and even nailing pattern, the presence of nails will add to and not detract from the overall appearance. A jig drilled for the nail spacing that can ride along the leading edge of the board and is long enough to line up square with the last nail of the previous board ensures a neat nailing pattern (see **21-40**).

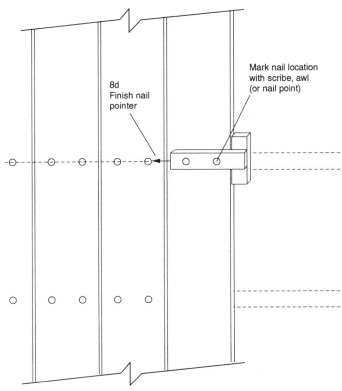

21-40 *This nailing pattern jig helps assure even and level spacing for face-nailed panelling.*

One of the advantages of vertical (and to some extent diagonal) panelling over horizontal is that it's unlikely that both ends of a board will have to butt perfectly against the floor or ceiling. Usually, it's one or the other end. If the boards are cut about ¼-inch shorter than the height of the wall, you can test the exposed end for fit, scribe and cut it, and recut it if you need to. The gap at the opposite end will be covered by an overlying moulding, typically the baseboard (see **21-41**).

An alternative is to run extra strapping or a backing course at the bottom of the wall, and attach the baseboards in the same plane as the panelling. The bottom ends of the boards will then butt onto the baseboard while the top ends are hidden beneath a ceiling cove or crown moulding or flat band.

A strip of shiplap set on shims so that its rabbet overlays the ends of the boards also makes a neat moulding with a slim profile. If you support the bottom ends of the boards on a temporary batten, you can use the shiplap at both the floor and ceiling (refer to **21-41**).

You shouldn't have to resort to inside corner moulding to hide a sloppy fit between vertical boards. With horizontal boarding, a tight-fitting inside-corner joint calls for more effort than most people are willing to give, especially if the corner is not quite square. As with fitting stair tread and risers to the skirtboard, cut the boards slightly longer, scribe each end for fit, and back-cut them. With softwood, you can make the final cut a smidgeon (a "hair") longer than dead-on, so that the boards have to be sprung into place.

One problem with horizontal boarding is that, even with careful attention, the joint lines can refuse to line up with each other on adjacent sides of a corner. It's just about impossible to prevent some joint "creep," even when you try to make up for it by playing with the joint width. Even worse, unless you pay careful attention to establishing and maintaining a level line, the joint lines won't end up at the same place as they started out when the panelling returns from its journey around the room. A square inside corner moulding will mask slight differences between the

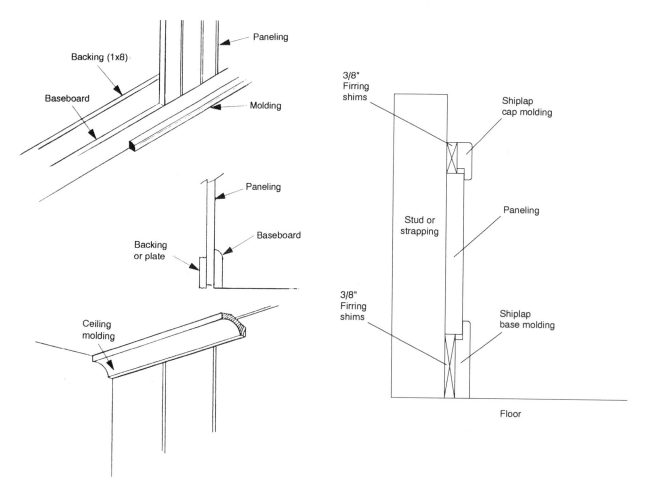

21-41 *Floor and ceiling moulding for vertical boards. Setting the baseboard in the same plane as the wall panelling gives the room an uncluttered, contemporary look.*

lines at adjacent corners while at the same time suggesting the visual continuity that it breaks. If you apply the corner moulding over the boards, they don't need to have a perfect fit as they would if they butted to it (see **21-42**).

As you might expect, outside corners can also be finished in several different ways. For vertical boards, the

edges of the last boards can be cut square so that they form an overlapping butt joint. The outside edge can be rounded over and sanded smooth, and/or one side of the joint can be held back to leave a ¼-inch reveal. The edges of vertical boards and the ends of horizontal boards can both be butted against a ¾-inch half-round moulding. Some builders prefer the tight fit of a 45-degree mitre joint. (If your saw can make oblique cuts, a 47-degree backcut makes a truly tight fit. You can also back-cut the edge with a hand or power plane.) Although it's considerably harder to make a good mitre with horizontal boards, it can be done. It's easier to butt them against a flat stop moulding. Finally, the simplest, but not necessarily most elegant, solution is to hide the joint beneath a milled outside corner moulding or a pair of corner boards.

Although wood panelling doesn't absolutely require any finish treatment (see **21-43**), one or two coats of linseed oil or Watco oil rubbed into the boards will protect it from dirt, bring out the grain, and give it a warm glow that darkens into a genuine patina with age. Where the wood will be subjected to more than occasional contact or moisture, it should be protected with a hard, urethane-type finish instead, particularly around food preparation areas.

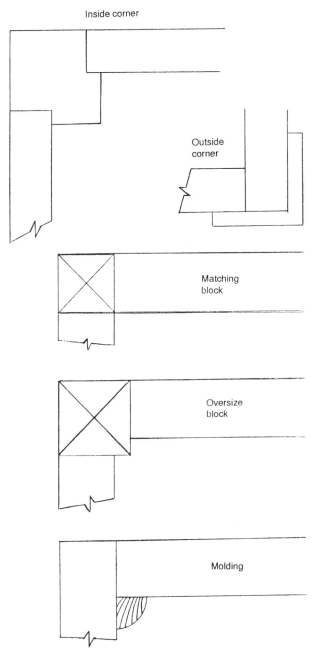

21-42 *The choice of treatment depends, to some extent, on whether the panelling is horizontal or vertical. The idea is to conceal exposed end grain whenever possible.*

21-43 *The line between wall finish and furniture becomes blurred in this panelled room. Note how the lines of the tongue-and-groove closet doors extend up into the wall above to the high storage cabinet to blend with the 1×10 shiplapped boards that cover the walls and ceilings. Unfinished bandsawn hemlock was used for all the interior woodwork.*

21-44 *Western red cedar boards run parallel with the rafters (across strapping) increase the apparent height of the ceiling. The boards are bevel-jointed at the peak for a clean line.*

CEILINGS

Wood panelling (i.e., real boards) can make a handsome ceiling, especially when combined with drywall or plaster wall finishes. There are even some structural advantages to attaching a board ceiling to truss rafters or floor trusses. Because you won't have to measure and cut pieces to fit the rooms, boarding a ceiling before the interior partitions are built is quick and easy. Since inch boards provide adequate top plate attachment for nonbearing walls, no nail backer blocking or partition ladders are needed for the partitions. This saves considerable time and materials. Unlike drywall, boarding is rigid enough to nail to joists on two-foot centers. Firring and shimming isn't generally needed, since the joint lines tend to obscure any dips in the plane of the ceiling. Finally, space permitting, you can lay fibreglass batt insulation between the trusses from above, sparing yourself the discomfort of stapling overhead.

Installing a board ceiling is the same as applying horizontal panelling to the walls (see **21-44**). With vaulted or cathedral ceilings, you might wish to run the boards parallel with the rafters instead of perpendicular to them, in which case you'd nail strapping across the bottoms of the rafters. Instead of mitring the ends of the boards to fit against each other at the inside corner formed by the peak of the ceiling, if you cut the boards on one side of the ceiling square and butt the boards on the other side against them with a bevel cut, the joint will be tighter.

With boards that run perpendicular to the rafters, either a mitre or a bevel joint will give good results at the peak so long as the boards meet evenly (see **21-45**). If the meeting at the peak is off, a strip of board with both edges bevelled is the easiest way to cover any gaps.

One difference between walls and ceilings is that, for some reason, narrow boarding (1×3 or 1×4) looks better on ceilings than it does on walls. An interesting treatment that takes advantage of this phenomenon is to ease the transition between the wall and ceiling by curving it (see **21-46**). Nail ¾-inch curved plywood brackets between the studs and rafters to make nailers for the boards. If you relieve the edge of their face joint slightly, narrow boards can follow a fairly tight arc.

As was discussed in Chapter Five, exposed ceiling beams present special problems for the finish carpenter, the chief of which is the concealment of wires and plumbing. "Dropping" the ceiling between the joists is the usual solution (see **21-47**). The depth of the beam reveal depends on how much space is needed for the wiring or plumbing.

A one-by or two-by cleat is nailed to each side of the beam at the desired depth. Either boards or drywall can be nailed to the cleats. Rather than scribe each board for a tight fit, cut them about a ¼ inch short and cover the

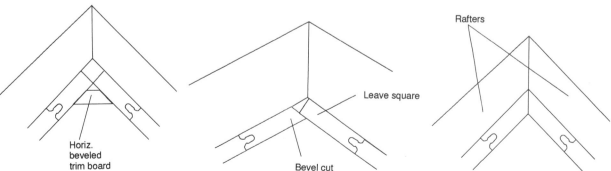

For vertical ceiling boards   For horizontal ceiling boards

Horiz. beveled trim board

Leave square

Bevel cut

Rafters

21-45 *It's very difficult to make a good butt joint between opposing vertical ceiling boards at the peak, which is why a cover moulding is the preferred treatment.*

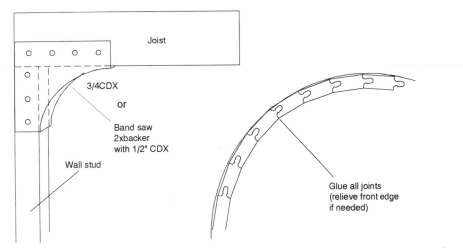

21-46 *Curved ceiling transition. This method only works when the joists line up directly over the studs. But you can add blocking to one or the other if they don't.*

gap with a quarter-round or a ½-inch by one-inch stop moulding.

Since the beams in an exposed timber ceiling are on 32-inch or 48-inch centers, a third cleat should be screwed and glued to the underside of the subfloor at the midspan of each joist bay to keep the drywall from sagging. If the depth of the ceiling is more than two inches or so, attach the center cleat to a one-by screwed flat to the subfloor.

If you wish to plaster the ceilings instead of paint them, nail Rocklath or expanded metal lath to the cleats.

If you staple strips of plastic film to the sides of the ceiling beams before installing the cleats, you won't have to worry about how to clean the joint compound, plaster, or paint off the faces of the beams. Force the point of a utility knife into the joint at a slight angle to cut the poly out after the job is done.

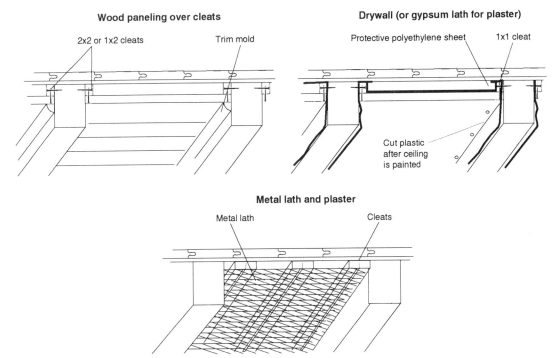

21-47 *Dropped ceiling finishes for exposed beams.*

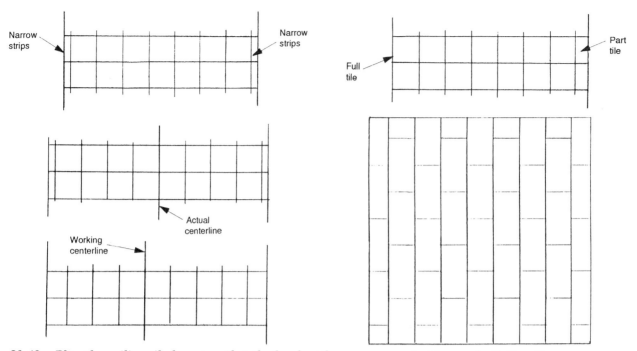

21-48 *Plan the ceiling tile layout so that the border tiles are even and at least a half-tile wide.*

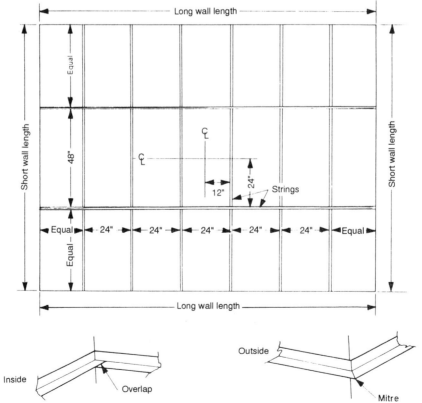

21-49 *Installing strapping for ceiling tiles. If the ceiling is out of square, splitting the difference between both walls is usually less noticeable than confining the taper to one side.*

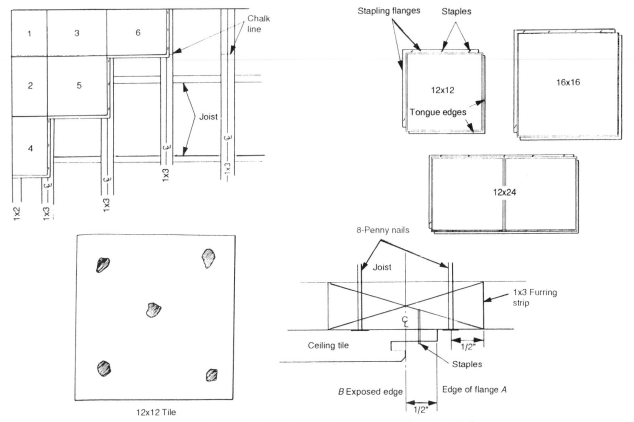

21-50 *Stapling or gluing ceiling tiles. Ceiling tile staples are generally ⁹⁄₁₆ inch long.*

CEILING TILE

Ceiling tiles are glued or stapled to 1×3 or 1×4 strapping set on appropriate centers. Plan the layout to avoid unsightly narrow strips or different-width tiles at the perimeter (see **21-48**). Mark the centerlines for each axis of the rooms on the floor (since most tiles are one-foot square or some other rectangular one- or two-foot module, you can also use graph paper, or tape off the spacing intervals on the ceiling itself) and lay out a course of tiles along both centerlines to see how the last tiles end up. Shift the actual centerline sideways so that the starting and ending tiles are at least six inches wide and of equal width.

Snap a chalk line for the working centerline across the run of the ceiling joists (see **21-49**)—since the first piece of strapping will fall over the middle of this line, the chalk line should actually be offset half the width of the strapping. Once the center strapping is nailed to the joists, you can use pieces of strapping cut to the correct length as gauges to space the rest of the strapping courses on the appropriate centers (typically 12 inches o.c.). Use 8d box nails to fasten the strapping. If necessary, string and shim the strapping as you nail it. Cut short pieces to fit between the strapping courses at the perimeter of the room, and nail them to the ceiling blocking. Locate and snap the

second working centerline at right angles to the run of the strapping (refer to **21-49**)—check the layout for square and then mark off and snap lines for the centers of the other tile courses. Rather than trust that the wall is perfectly straight or that all your starting tiles are exactly even, snap a line down the center of the first course of strapping so that you can line up the edges of the starting tiles. If the first course is laid out accurately, the rest of the tiles will automatically fall in line (see **21-50**).

Check the manufacturer's specifications for fastener spacing and length, and staple the tiles through their flanges to the strapping with a heavy-duty staple gun (this is one place where a staple hammer won't do a better job). Tiles can be cut by scoring with a sharp utility knife and snapping, but a cleaner cut results if you keep scoring the tile until you cut all the way through it. For fast and accurate cutting, use a table saw equipped with a fine-toothed blade.

Ceiling tiles intended for gluing usually have square instead of flanged edges. The adhesive is dabbed onto the back of the tile following the manufacturer's recommendations and the tile is pressed against the strapping, slightly out of position and slid into place (refer to **21-50**).

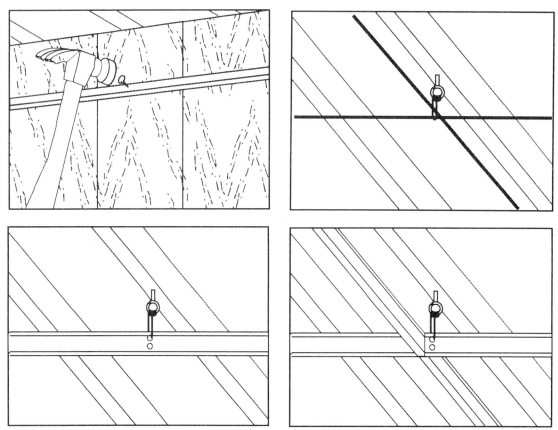

21-51 *Locate and mark off stud centers on the wall above the line of the perimeter moulding so you'll know where to drive the screws or nails. Main grid runners must hang in the same plane. The cut end of a short cross runner simply bears on the main runner and is held in place by the tiles.*

SUSPENDED CEILINGS

Suspended ceiling systems are popular because they are inexpensive and even easier to install than conventional ceiling tiles.

Once you've established a working centerline as outlined above, snap a level ceiling line on all the walls of the room. Attach the factory-supplied, metal perimeter moulding to the ceiling lines with drywall nails or panhead wood screws (see **21-51**). For concrete or masonry walls, use plastic anchors and sheet-metal screws. If you use a washer beneath the screw head, you can drill through the moulding and set the anchor without having to take down the moulding first.

Cut the bottom flange to make an overlapping fold for inside corners. For outside corners, the top flanges or each adjacent piece are cut on mitres and folded like the corner of a chimney base flashing. Joints between sections are overlapped about an inch.

Stretch strings across the run of the joists between the perimeter mouldings at the appropriate centerlines. These mark the level of the hangers that support the main grid runners. Nail the hangers to the sides of the joists. If your ceiling system uses wire instead of hangers, hold the top edge of the grid runners in line with the string as you bend the wire and slip it through the slots.

As you place each tile, insert the clips of a short interlocking crossrunner into the slots in the main grid runners to support the end of the tiles (refer to **21-51**).

Grid runners and crossrunners are easily cut with a hacksaw or a chop saw equipped with a metal-cutting blade. Fluorescent light pans, plastic light-diffuser grids and HVAC registers designed to fit into the grid of a standard tile module make it easy to install lighting and air outlets in the ceiling. Since any tile can be removed for access, changing or installing wiring or other mechanical systems can be done at any time.

22 Flooring

For most contractors and developers, speed equals profit. An entire house can be carpeted in a single day. The carpet can be glued to a concrete slab or laid on top of a tongue-and-groove underlayment-grade plywood subfloor. Resilient sheet vinyl usually requires an extra layer of underlayment and some surface preparation, but laying the vinyl itself doesn't take any longer than carpeting. Wood flooring, on the other hand, is labor-intensive *and* expensive. Once the boards are laid, they must be carefully sanded and finished with multiple coats of slow-drying varnish. Even with a small house, this can take a week or more. This probably is one reason why, despite the time-honored practicality, beauty, and durability of real wood flooring—except in high-end custom homebuilding—wall-to-wall carpet and sheet vinyl are the most common floor coverings.

Fortunately, one of the benefits of owner-building is that you can operate outside the strictures of the profit-or-perish syndrome. The time and effort that you put into laying a wood floor is insignificant compared to the years of service and enjoyment that it will give you. And, unlike vinyl or carpeting, which must be torn up and replaced when they wear out, a well-maintained wood floor is virtually immortal. It can be sanded and refinished again and again (see **22-1**).

TYPES OF WOOD FLOORING

Although there are many kinds of wood flooring available, all of them fall into one of the three general categories of strip, plank, or block.

Hardwood strip flooring is the most well known. Red and white oak, beech, birch, and maple are some of the more common hardwoods used for flooring. The boards are milled with a tongue-and-groove pattern on both their edges and ends (or "side- and end-matched," as lumbermen say) and planed to a thickness of slightly more than ¾ inch (²⁵/₃₂, to be exact). Standard widths are 1½, 2¼, and 3¼ inches. Troughs milled into the undersides of the boards increase their stability and stress resistance so that they tend to stay flat despite seasonal changes in moisture levels. End-matched strip flooring is sold in bundles of random length. The discount grades often have a higher proportion of "shorts" than the better grades. As might be expected, the quality of the milling, and the number and nature of visible defects, also vary with grade. Random variations in width and the fit of the tongue and groove are common in the lower grades. Since these kinds of defects make it almost impossible to lay a good-looking

22-1 *When given three or four coats of varnish, 1×6 tongue-and-groove spruce or pine boards blind-nailed through the subfloor and into the floor joists make a remarkably good-looking finish floor. Softwood boards are much less expensive and much faster and easier to lay and finish-sand than hardwood strip or plank flooring. Although they're not as impact-resistant as hardwood, there's no difference in the service life of the varnish between refinishings.*

floor, cheap wood-strip flooring can be a poor bargain. Oak, the most common hardwood used for flooring, comes in four grades: clear, select, No. 1 common, and No. 2 common. The other common hardwoods are graded as firsts, seconds, and thirds.

Clear-heart, vertical grain Douglas fir was widely used for porch flooring before the advent of pressure-treated boards. During the late Victorian era, and especially during the Craftsman-style architectural period of the first quarter of the 20th century, it was also popular for strip flooring and interior trim and case work. Douglas fir is harder and more resistant to impact than most softwood species. Today, fir suitable for flooring might be more expensive than most hardwoods.

569

As the name suggests, plank flooring is wider than strip flooring. Widths commonly vary from three to seven inches in two-inch increments and thickness runs from ⁵⁄₁₆ inch to ²⁵⁄₃₂ inch. In addition to solid boards, a laminated composite plank product is also available. The laminations add strength while the use of less-expensive plies beneath the face veneer lower cost. Some kinds of plank flooring are edge- and end-milled like strip flooring and are likewise installed by blind-nailing through the tongue. These typically are prefinished products with simulated pegs already in place. Other types of plank flooring come with counterbored holes through which nails or screws are driven into the floor joists. The holes are then filled with real wood plugs. These can be either edge-jointed or square-edged. Most plank flooring is sold in random-width bundles. There's no reason for varying the width of the boards between courses other than to follow the current fashion.

Block, or parquet, flooring, is also available in a variety of types and styles (see 22-2). These can be made from laminated plies, short blocks of solid wood, or short edge-joined pieces of strip flooring. Essentially, block flooring is a wood tile and is thus generally glued to the subfloor like standard vinyl tiles.

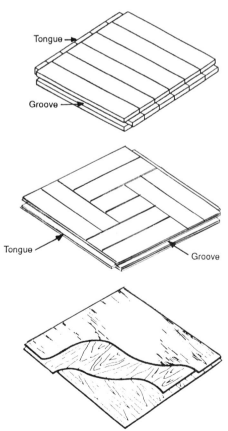

22-2 *Types of block, or parquet, wood flooring.*

Hardwood flooring, especially plank flooring, isn't cheap. When it has a factory-applied finish, it's downright expensive. Sometimes you can buy secondhand hardwood strip flooring or salvage your own. When refinished, recycled flooring has a handsome patina that's otherwise impossible to duplicate. It may even be that there's a flooring mill somewhere close by, in which case you can often pick up factory seconds at a heavily discounted rate. Although you may end up cutting defects out of a lot of boards and even throwing some into the kindling pile, the savings may be worth the wasted wood. Often, you can buy native hardwood boards from your local sawmill at a very reasonable price and have them edge-milled. Regional woods such as black cherry, hickory, ash, and walnut, which have rich color and grain patterns, make distinctive and uniquely beautiful flooring.

The use of softwood boards for flooring has a long history. One of the most desirable features of antique New England houses is their extravagantly wide, pine floorboards. Because those boards were cut from old-growth trees of gigantic girth and great age, their cells were densely packed and saturated with resins, giving them character, longevity, and much greater hardness than modern boards cut from the soft sapwood of fast-growing trees. As the ads in trade journals such as *Fine Homebuilding* and *Old House Journal* show, there's a thriving trade in recycled old-growth lumber. You can buy floorboards salvaged from architectural antiques or sawn from ancient semi-mineralized logs fished up from lake bottoms and swamps for about the same cost as premium hardwood strip flooring.

Softwood plank floors are inexpensive and easy to lay. But they *are* soft. Eastern white pine, one of the most common and sought-after species—and one from which it's still possible to get relatively wide boards (i.e., 16 to 20 inches)—scratches and dents quite easily in normal use. Spruce and hemlock boards are considerably harder, but more prone to shrinkage and warping. Douglas fir has comparable density and better stability, but the face grain of flat-sawn boards is too splintery for flooring and edge-grain quarter-sawn lumber is very expensive. Southern yellow pine ("hard" pine) is perhaps the best softwood species for flooring. The wood is dense, impact-resistant, and has a prominent grain pattern that is quite attractive and relatively inexpensive. Although yellow pine can shrink and warp considerably as it dries, once it reaches equilibrium, it's stable. To minimize waste, buy only a premium grade. Softwood boards used for flooring are typically milled with a tongue-and-groove pattern (but not a V-groove) and are blind-nailed. Widths vary from 1×4 to 1×8, with 1×6 being the most commonly used. Wide pine boards (eight inches plus) are usually square-edged, sometimes shiplapped, and always face-nailed. A tongue-and-groove joint would shrink too much to be effective.

Ideally, all flooring boards in general, and hardwoods in particular, should be carefully stored, stacked, and stickered in a heated room for at least six months prior to use, to let them reach equilibrium with their environment. Traditionally, floors were laid during the winter months when humidity levels tend to be low (except in the Pacific Northwest). Even when tightly laid, gaps will appear between the joints of summer-laid flooring during the heating season. Some seasonal dimensional change is inevitable, but the boards should never shrink so much that their tongues slip out of the grooves. If you buy your flooring from a reputable supplier, the boards should have a certified moisture content of nine to eleven percent, which is probably lower than summertime ambient moisture levels in most homes. This eliminates the need for long storage time and reduces the chances of winter shrinkage. For best results, don't store or install dry flooring during very humid weather. Because it was sealed when fully dry, prefinished flooring is less likely to be affected by fluctuations in humidity levels.

UNDERLAYMENT

The need for underlayment depends on the type of flooring material. As was mentioned above, $3/4$-inch underlayment-grade, tongue-and-groove plywood, when glued and nailed to the joists, is a suitable subfloor for wood and carpet—*as is* (see **22-3**).

Codes typically allow full-thickness ($3/4$-inch softwood or $25/32$-inch hardwood) flooring boards to be installed directly over a $1/2$-inch CDX subfloor without any intervening underlayment (so long as the seams between the sheets of plywood are supported by flatwise 2×4 blocking). However, $3/4$-inch tongue-and-groove plywood makes a much more solid and squeak-free floor. An underlayment, such as $1/2$-inch *PTS* plywood—which has a smooth "touch-sanded" (hence, the TS) surface and an impact-resistant core—should be used over $1/2$-inch CDX for thin, plank-type flooring and resilient sheet vinyl or carpeting. Depending on the thickness of the subfloor material and the type of flooring material and the desired degree of rigidity, various types and thicknesses of dense, smooth, *particleboard* are also used as an underlayment for carpeting and resilient sheet vinyl or vinyl tiles. Always check the flooring manufacturer's specifications and local codes for underlayment requirements. Finally, *hardboard* underlayment, a dense, grainless, and durable 4×4 sheet manufactured from hardwood sawdust bonded under heat and pressure, is the preferred choice when laying resilient flooring and carpeting over a firm but uneven subfloor such as $3/4$-inch CDX or tongue-and-groove planks. If the flooring material will be glued to the underlayment, the rough side should be laid face-up to provide a good bonding surface. Quarter-inch-thick *luan* (a plantation-grown species of Philippine mahogany) plywood also makes a comfortable, more-resilient underlayment.

Underlayment sheets are run across the joists, with their end joints staggered in relation to each other and falling over a floor joist. Their edge joints should also be staggered

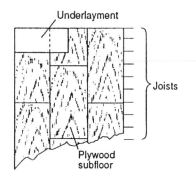

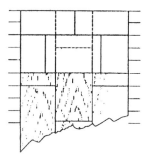

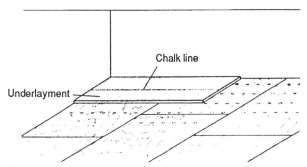

22-3 *Unlike vinyl or tile floors, wood floors don't usually require any underlayment. Using construction adhesive and a power nailer speeds up underlayment installation.*

in relation to the joints in the subfloor. Follow the manufacturer's recommendations for spacing between the edges of the sheets and against the wall. In general, with hardboard underlayment, which is more stable than particleboard or plywood, leave a $1/8$-inch gap between the underlayment and the walls and a $1/32$-inch between the sheets. The spacing should be increased to $3/8$ inch and $1/8$ inch, respectively, for particleboard and plywood. To reduce the chances of moisture absorption, especially with particleboard, which tends to swell up along its edges, install the underlayment just ahead of the flooring. As further protection, some experts recommend laying a vapor barrier between particleboard underlayment and the subfloor.

571

22-4 *Fastener schedule for flooring underlayment.*

Type	Nail size	Staple Size*	Edge Spacing**	Field Spacing
Plywood (½")	3d ring-shank/ CC-sinkers	16 ga. (⅝")	6" (⅜")	8" 6"
Particleboard	4d–6d RS CC box nails	16 ga. (1–1½")	6"/3" (½–¾")	10" 6"
Hardboard	4d annular or RS CC sinkers	18 ga. (⅝")	3"/4–6" (⅜")	6" 4–6"

* The second number, in ( ), in this column gives the minimum depth that the fastener should penetrate into the subfloor.
**The second number, in ( ), in this column gives the distance from the edge of the panels that the fasteners can be driven. The number in the first row in front of the / is the edge spacing for nails, the number following the / is the edge spacing for staples. The upper number in the "field" column is for nails, the lower is for staples. "Field" is the rest of the board.

Underlayment must be well fastened. The recommended nailing and stapling schedules for various types of underlayment are given in **22-4**.

Underlayment can also be used to make up for the difference in the thickness between different kinds of flooring materials so that all the floors of the house lie in the same plane. Slight changes can cause people to trip over thresholds. The alternative, varying the heights of the floor joists and/or the thickness of the subfloor is a lot more difficult, since it needlessly complicates wall and partition framing.

LAYING WOOD STRIP AND BOARD FLOORING

When wood strip (or board) flooring is used in more than one room of the house, the strips should all run parallel to each other, no matter what room they're in. Since it's also desirable that the flooring runs at right angles to the joists (you get a stiffer floor when the flooring nails penetrate through the subfloor into the joists), this generally results in the boards following the long dimension of the house.

If the house consisted of a single open room or there were no interior partitions perpendicular to the run of the flooring, you'd simply begin laying floorboards parallel to the longest sidewall and proceed across to the other side. But, because, in most houses, there are partitions that do run at right (and sometimes, stranger) angles to flooring, keeping the boards running parallel from room to room can be a problem. At some point, the direction in which the tongue-and-groove joint faces will have to be reversed if the direction in which the boards are running is to remain the same (see **22-5**). As was mentioned in Chapter 21, the switch is accomplished by gluing a spline ripped from the edge of a scrap piece of flooring into the groove joint of the transition piece. Before you begin actually nailing down the floor, it's a good idea to study the floor plan and determine the best layout for the least number of reversals and the lowest chance of running off parallel. For example, where the floor plan features a long central hallway, it makes more sense and means less work to start the flooring from the center of the hall and run it outward in both directions into the adjoining rooms, rather than to start at the long wall of the largest room.

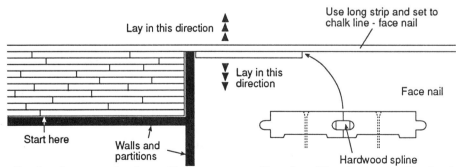

22-5 *Planning flooring layout and using splines to reverse direction. Flooring generally should run parallel with the long dimension of the house. Strip flooring can be laid independent of the run of the floor joists.*

Now that plywood has replaced matched or square-edged boards for subflooring, it's no longer necessary to lay down building paper (a stiff rosin-coated orange or pink paper that comes in three-foot-wide, 100-yard-long rolls) before installing the finish flooring. Besides keeping cold air from an unheated cellar from sneaking through cracks in the flooring, the main purpose of this underlayment was to keep coal dust from the cellar bin out of the living areas. Some writers on the subject—and some building codes—have yet to reflect this change.

Sweep and vacuum the subfloor and start the first strip of flooring. Leave a ½-inch expansion gap between the flooring and all walls. If the flooring were butted tightly to the wall, it would buckle as it expanded in response to normal moisture and temperature changes. The gap will be hidden beneath the baseboard moulding. As with wall panelling, the starting board must be face-nailed. Drill a pilot hole for a finish nail, set the head beneath the surface of the wood, and fill the hole with colored wood dough.

It's a good idea to lay out floorboards for each room loosely ahead of you so that you can show the natural variations in color and grain pattern off to their best advantage. This also helps you utilize the different lengths most efficiently. Use the longer pieces and save the shorts and cut-offs for filling in closets and end runs. End joints between successive courses should be staggered and offset at least eight inches. With end-matched strips, the joints don't have to fall over a joist. The butt joints of square-edge and softwood board flooring must *always* do so.

Fasteners for hardwood flooring are made from hardened steel that can penetrate the dense grain without bending. There are two types for hand-nailing, both of which can also be used with softwood (see **22-6**). The square-edged cut flooring nail has a blunt tip that reduces splitting of the tongue. When used for face-nailing, line up the long side of its rectangular head with the grain of the board. The screw-thread, round-head type has a much greater withdrawal resistance, although it does tend to split the boards at their end joints. As a safety precaution, drill a pilot hole for any type of nail that's driven close to the end grain. To avoid mashing the tongue, leave the nail head sticking out about ⅛ inch, and seat it with a nail set.

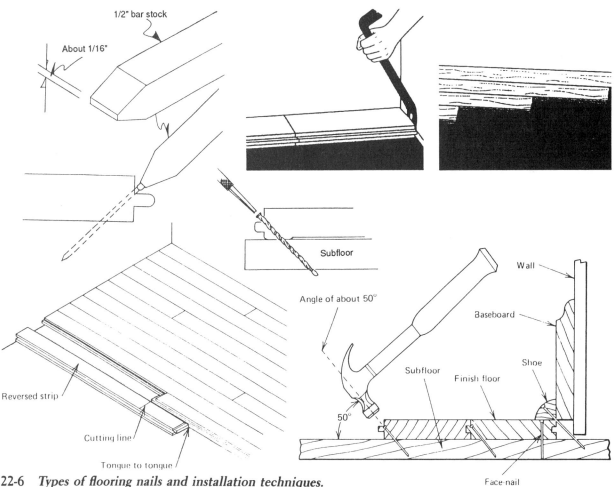

22-6 *Types of flooring nails and installation techniques.*

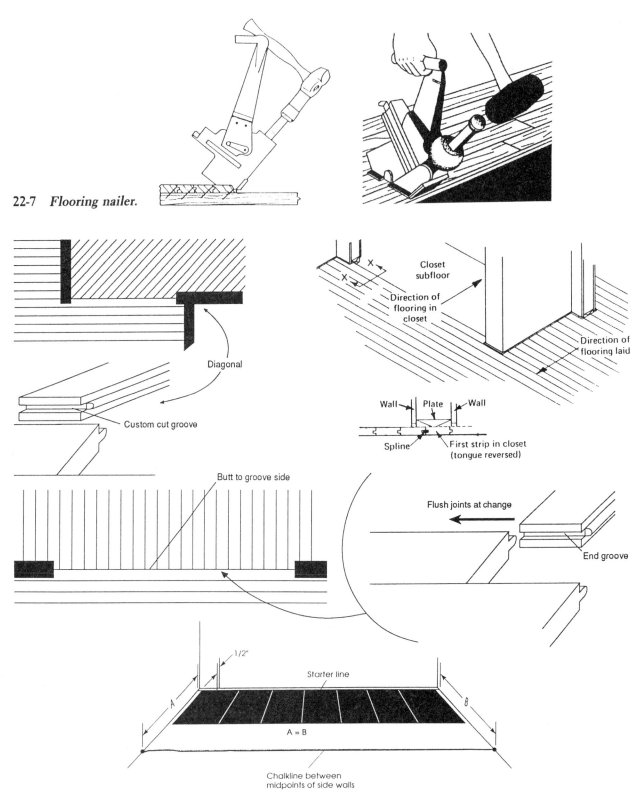

22-7 *Flooring nailer.*

Diagonal

Custom cut groove

Butt to groove side

Closet subfloor

Direction of flooring in closet

Direction of flooring laid

Wall Plate Wall

Spline

First strip in closet (tongue reversed)

Flush joints at change

End groove

1/2"

Starter line

A

B

A = B

Chalkline between midpoints of side walls

22-8 *Changes in direction of run. The starting line is established parallel to the room centerline. Check that the distance between the starter line and the walls is the same at both ends and that the opposite wall of the room is also parallel to the centerline. Split the difference for any tapers to both sides of the*

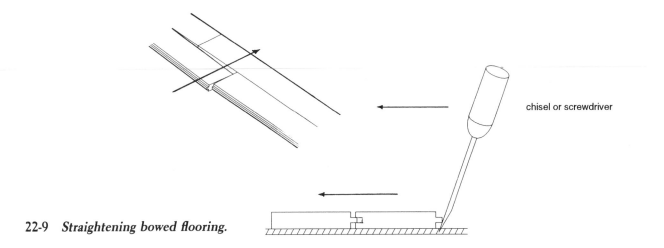

22-9 *Straightening bowed flooring.*

chisel or screwdriver

Actually, most hardwood floors are laid with a rented floor nailer, which is kind of an oversize, spring-loaded staple gun that drives a barbed fastener at the correct angle through the tongue of the board when its plunger is struck with a heavy mallet (see **22-7**). The shoe of the nailer is designed so that it pushes the board tightly into the preceding joint as the nail is driven home. Air-powered nailers are also available. Using a flooring nailer greatly speeds up the installation of flooring. The tool can also be used with softwood tongue-and-groove boards.

Although manufacturers recommend nailing strip flooring on 10-inch to 12-inch centers, if you drive a nail every eight inches, every second (or third) nail will penetrate into a floor joist. Snap chalk lines to mark the joist centers. For softwood, an intermediate nail is used only when the joists are spaced on 24-inch centers.

Check the run of the flooring from time to time to make sure that it isn't creeping off parallel. Measure the distance between the last board and the opposite wall. If there is a significant difference, the ending board will have to be cut on a taper. Since the fault may not be in the flooring but in the squareness of the room, you should always measure the rooms before you begin laying down the flooring. It may be possible to "split the difference" between both sides of the room or to make very slight adjustments in the joints between boards. If the length of the room can be spanned by a single, long board, you can also recut its tongue joint on a slight taper. If you spread the correction out over a few courses, it will be less noticeable than a sharply tapered ending piece. Of course, the best solution to the problem is to build partitions square with the walls in the first place.

If the run of the floorboards must change direction, the change should be made where it won't be obvious (see **22-8**). This is most often at the center of a doorway. The joint can be hidden under a bevelled piece of hardwood moulding similar to a threshold, called a *saddle*. If you prefer a flush junction instead, slide the end grooves of one side over the tongue of the last board that falls somewhere near the middle of the door opening. If the change of direction is at an angle other than 90 degrees, cut the ends to the correct angle, and then readjust your table saw so that you can cut a new end tongue or groove. A better-looking job is likely if you butt the boards for the new layout against the ending board rather than run them into it from the opposite direction.

Normally, a scrap piece of flooring and a hammer supply enough leverage to fit balky floorboards together. When this doesn't work, hammer a one-inch rough framing chisel or a stout flat-tipped screwdriver into the subfloor (over a joist if possible) at a slight angle next to the bowed tongue and use it like a lever to pry the offending board into place (see **22-9**). If this doesn't work, used the wedge technique described in Chapter 21 for stubborn panelling.

When an especially recalcitrant bow is at the end of a board, the board is likely to spring back and split apart on the nail as soon as the wedge pressure is released. Drill a pilot hole so that you can drive a nail sideways into the end of the abutting board and drive a second nail at the normal angle into the subfloor further up the tongue.

WOOD FLOORING OVER A CONCRETE SLAB

A concrete slab floor that is not in direct sunlight will still make a significant contribution to the overall thermal mass of a passive solar (or superinsulated) home, even if it is covered over with some other type of flooring material. Despite its benefits as a source of radiant heat, most people feel that concrete is a hard, unyielding, and often uncomfortable flooring material for living areas. Although certain types of wood, most types of vinyl and carpet, and all tiles can be laid directly over concrete, this approach won't "soften" the floor. The best way to do this is to lay the flooring over wood *sleepers* that rest on the concrete.

575

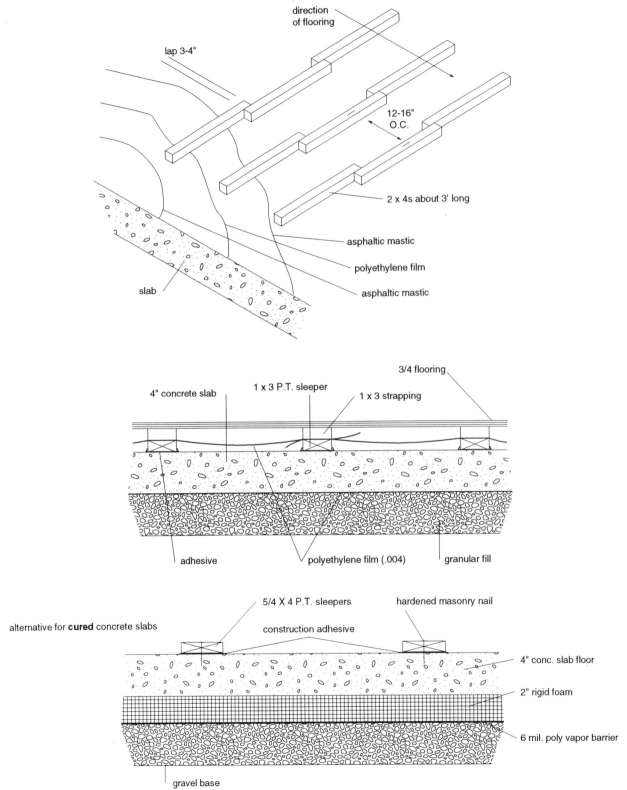

direction
of flooring

lap 3-4"

12-16"
O.C.

2 x 4s about 3' long

asphaltic mastic

polyethylene film

asphaltic mastic

slab

3/4 flooring

4" concrete slab

1 x 3 P.T. sleeper

1 x 3 strapping

adhesive

polyethylene film (.004)

granular fill

alternative for **cured** concrete slabs

5/4 X 4 P.T. sleepers

hardened masonry nail

construction adhesive

4" conc. slab floor

2" rigid foam

6 mil. poly vapor barrier

gravel base

22-10 *Laying sleepers over concrete. Coating the slab with mastic protects the flooring against moisture released from an uncured floor slab. Allowing the slab to cure for at least a month before laying the flooring will minimize this problem.*

The usual recommendation calls for the slab to be covered with an asphalt-based mastic (basically old-fashioned rubber floor tile cement) and a polyethylene vapor barrier before the sleepers are nailed to it (see **22-10**). This messy operation makes sense only if the slab has been poured directly over grade without the standard vapor barrier and rigid foam insulation that keeps it from absorbing ground moisture and that slows heat loss and helps retard condensation.

However, even when insulated, a concrete slab will be significantly cooler than the room. Under the right conditions some condensation is possible, given the dead air between the underside of the floorboards and the slab. But this condensation will occur just as readily on a film of vaporproof mastic painted over a slab as on bare concrete. The barrier film should be isolated from the slab by sandwiching it between two layers of 1×3 or 1×4 sleepers. I'd recommend this approach for any slab that has no underlying vapor barrier, particularly in humid regions where condensation is much more likely to occur. Having seen untreated sleepers that rested directly on a slab (albeit one that had a grade-level vapor barrier) in a cold climate for more than a decade without showing any signs of moisture damage or incipient rot, I can't find any compelling reason to bother with mastic and plastic.

But, whether or not you do add the vapor barrier, use pressure-treated wood for the bottom sleepers. Otherwise, any condensation or moisture absorption which does occur will rot the wood where it rests on concrete.

Although 1×3 or 2×3 stock is adequate for sleepers, the narrow width of the material makes it much more likely to split when you try to nail it to the concrete. It's better to use 1×4 or 2×4 instead. For blind-nailing, the sleepers should have a nominal thickness of two inches. Otherwise, the flooring nails will strike the concrete and bend. If you face-nail with countersunk screws instead of nails, the sleepers could be either a nominal or a full inch thick (a single layer of 1×4, or ⁵⁄₄×4, respectively).

Whatever its thickness, the sleeper course is fastened to the concrete with hardened nails. You can drive fluted masonry nails home with a two-lb hammer, but you'll have a better chance of the nails holding if you use a powder-actuated fastening tool and the nails that go with it (see **22-11**). Match the power range of the cartridges to the hardness of the material according to the color-coded chart on the cartridge packaging. "Yellow" loads are the most powerful and are used for cured concrete. "Green" loads work best for fresh concrete. Select nails long enough to penetrate ¾ inch into the concrete. Shorter nails won't have any holding power and longer ones will glance off sideways or stick out above the sleeper. When using a powder-actuated fastening tool for any purpose, always wear proper ear and eye protection.

Depending on the type of flooring, space the sleepers 10, 12, or 16 inches on center. The pieces should lay flat against the concrete. Cut any bowed pieces into shorter lengths. Otherwise, the nails won't have enough drawing power to flatten out the bow.

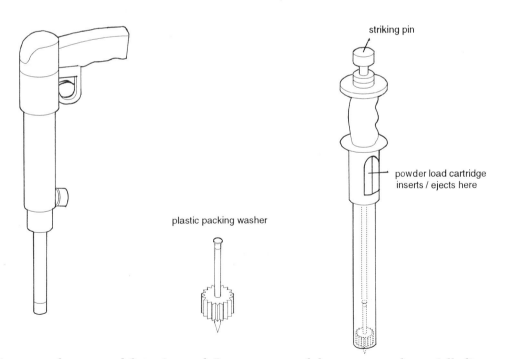

striking pin

powder load cartridge inserts / ejects here

plastic packing washer

22-11 *Using a powder-actuated fastening tool. In some parts of the country, only specially licensed operators are allowed to rent Ramset tools.*

Although concrete slabs under any living area should always be poured over rigid foam insulation, if you're converting former unheated space into living areas, the slab isn't likely to be insulated and will thus be a heat sink. You can slow the heat loss by installing rigid-foam insulation between the sleepers. So long as the top of the foam is flush with the top of the sleepers, their spacing can be increased to 12 or 16 inches. Rip equal-width strips of insulation on your table saw, and use them to space the sleepers as you install them. If a higher R-value is desired than can be provided by 1½ inches of rigid foam (± R-10 maximum), increase the depth of the sleepers to allow thicker insulation. Two-by-fours or even 2×6s set on edge and toenailed to 1×4 pressure-treated sleepers can be filled with economical fibreglass batts. Finally, if you intend to run or retrofit heating ducts between the sleepers, add insulation between the ducts and the underside of the

flooring (see **22-12**). Otherwise, the resulting "hot spot" will shrink or warp the boards.

The same sleeper system can be used to support a standard plywood subfloor for use with thinner wood flooring materials or provide a softer, more comfortable base than concrete for vinyl sheet and tile or carpeting.

A COMBINATION FLOOR AND CEILING SYSTEM

Back in Chapter Five, in the discussion of post-and-beam framing systems, I briefly touched upon some of the pros and cons of using solid decking over exposed timber joists (see **22-13**). In this system, 2×6 spruce/fir (pine and cedar are also used) V-groove, tongue-and-groove decking is blind-nailed to heavy timber joists set on 32-inch or 48-inch centers with 16d galvanized box nails. The heads of the nails are set with a ¼-inch pin punch (see **22-14**).

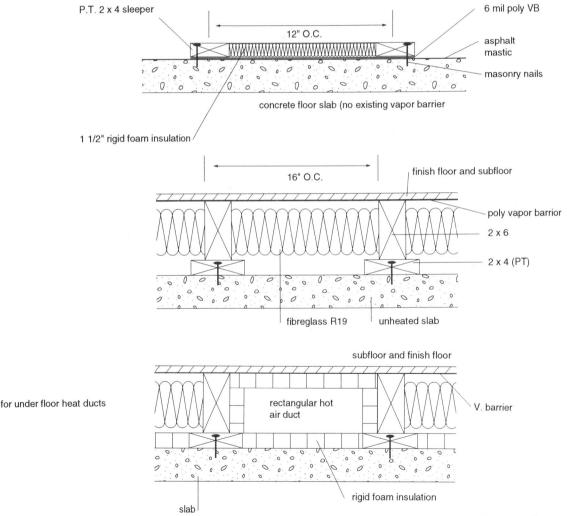

22-12 *Adding insulation between sleepers. Laying a wood floor over sleeper joists allows mechanicals and heating ducts to lie on top of the slab instead of being buried under it.*

Since the boards aren't end-matched, they are trimmed to break over the ceiling beams. For a tight butt joint, the end cuts are made on a five-degree bevel.

The thickness of the planking and the rigidity of the tongue-and-groove joint make a solid, strong floor deck. The V-groove side faces down, making a handsome finished ceiling that requires no further treatment other than a coat of oil or varnish.

Low cost is the biggest advantage of this system. Its most obvious disadvantage is the concomitant complications in routing wiring and plumbing. Typical solutions, for wiring, at least, include routing channels across the tops of beams for rigid-wall conduit that protects the wires against nails, (relatively) unobtrusive wire mould raceways along the upper edges of beams and across joist bays, and trying as much as possible to confine the mechanicals to partitions and perimeter walls. In small, two-storey houses, ceiling-mounted floor registers take the place of warm-air delivery ducts, and stairwells provide the cold-air return. Plumbing is usually concealed in dropped ceiling bays or in the soffits above kitchen cabinets or run through and above partitions.

There are three other less obvious drawbacks to this system. First, since the side of the decking that faces up is ostensibly its underside, the planing is often of poorer quality than the V-groove side. Not only will it be marred by almost indelible lumber grade stamps, but this is the face where the waney edges, planer gouges, and loose edge knots all show. The quality of the lumber varies considerably between different mills, even when it's ostensibly the same grade. Your local building materials supplier may not be particularly interested in special-ordering a better-quality product from a distributor with whom they don't normally deal. The search for a premium-grade product can be frustrating. Ask timber framers and other builders who use 2×6 decking which brands they use and where they got it from.

22-13 *V-groove, 2×6 decking makes a handsome ceiling/floor over exposed beams, particularly when combined with wood floors and drywall. However, the floor transmits sound readily, which makes it ill-suited to a house full of upstairs activity. It also complicates mechanical installation.*

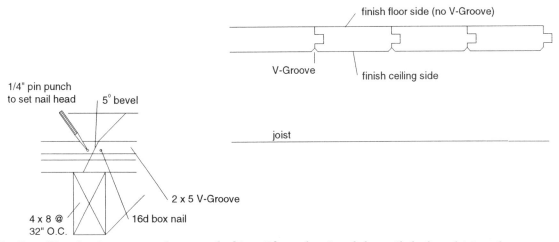

finish floor side (no V-Groove)

V-Groove

finish ceiling side

joist

1/4" pin punch to set nail head

5° bevel

2 x 5 V-Groove

4 x 8 @ 32" O.C.

16d box nail

22-14 *Installing 2×6 tongue-and-groove decking. Blunt the tip of the nails before driving them.*

The second problem is that the material must be protected against water damage until the roof is on. Water stains on the ceiling side and down the beams are very difficult and time-consuming to sand out. Waterproofing the deck with plastic sheeting as soon as it's installed offers only limited protection since the plastic is quickly torn or punctured as construction continues. (Water stains aren't a problem on a subfloor.) A related problem is the likelihood of damage to the decking itself. Boards and tools get dropped, the guards on circular saws sometimes stick open, nails, grit, and dirt are ground into the surface. You can protect the deck somewhat by spreading sheets of roof decking over it, or at least under your major work and traffic areas. Insult is added to injury when the interior drywall is hung or the walls are plastered and painted. Drop cloths or building paper are a necessity. One beneficial side effect of all this wear and tear is that when the decking is sanded prior to finishing (which would be needed in any case) the wood will have acquired a premature patina of age. Rather than spend time and money protecting the floor side of the decking, some builders simply use it as a subfloor and lay a finish floor over it. Quarter-inch hardboard or luan underlayment is required to keep the floor joints from telegraphing though resilient flooring or carpeting.

The final problem with this system is that the pitter-patter of little feet from above sounds more like the tap dance of pneumatic riveters from below. Dust and detritus also have a way of sifting down through the joints in the boards.

Carpeting alone will not deaden sound. Effective sound deadening depends on mechanical isolation (see **22-15**). Nailing sound-deadening underlayment to the deck gives only a slight reduction in noise level since the nails transmit the sound waves through the wood to the other side of the floor. The solution is to glue the 4×8, ½-inch sheets of sound-deadening board to the deck with an appropriate adhesive spread with a notched trowel, and then glue 1×3 strapping to the soundboard on 16-inch centers. Distribute weights such as concrete blocks over the strapping until the glue has set. Then blind-nail or face-screw 1×6 finish floorboards to the strapping, taking care that the nails don't penetrate into the sound board.

FINISHING WOOD FLOORS

Laying a wood floor is only one-third of the job. Unless you install a factory-finished product, you've got to sand and seal the floors.

For most people, the old saw "riding the tail of the tiger" is a reasonably accurate description of what it's like to operate a drum sander. To the uninitiated, it's a powerful, noisy, rebellious, dust-spewing "monster" that, in the hands of a careless or unskilled operator, can ruin a lot of expensive flooring in a very short time. Yet despite the intimidating aspect of the machinery, any reasonably conscientious and patient amateur can expect to do an entirely satisfactory job of floor finishing.

Although some professionals use even heavier and more powerful machines than the ones normally available for rent, the main difference is that rented machines aren't always in top condition, and the rental sales clerk might not have the slightest idea of how to run the machine anyway. Try to rent the newest machine you can find. Since there's a good chance you'll destroy one or more sanding belts before you get the feel of operating the machine, always take home more belts than you think you'll need. Any unused belts can be returned for credit.

In preparation for sanding, sweep and vacuum the floor thoroughly, and, if face-nailed, check to make sure that all the nail heads have been set about ⅛-inch below the surface of the boards. The edge of an exposed nailhead can shred a sheet of sandpaper in an instant.

When the sandpaper is clamped down tight, it should lay flat against the drum, without any slack, and the arrow printed on its backing should point in the same direction as the rotation of the drum. For new, unpainted wood, it will take at least three passes with progressively finer grades of sandpaper to give good results. Start with 36-grit paper for hardwood and 40-grit for softwood.

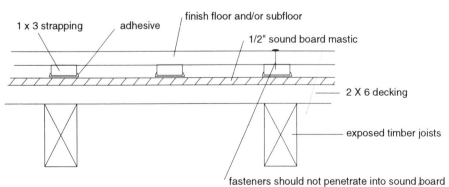

22-15 *Reducing sound transmission through decking. Mechanical isolation between the two surfaces is the key to sound reduction.*

Begin sanding on the right side of the room and leave yourself enough maneuvering room between your back and the wall. Push down on the handle, tilting the base of the sander back on its wheels, to lift the drum off the floor before starting the machine. The drum must *always* be turning at full speed when it contacts the floor. Lower the drum slowly, easing it onto the floor, and let the machine pull you along. The depth of the cut is controlled by the speed at which you allow the sander to pull itself across the floor. You can hold back on the handle to resist the pull and slow the machine, or just guide it with a light hand to speed it up. (If you've ever operated a rear-tine rototiller, you'll know the feeling.) Always let the sander pull *you*, never *push* the sander yourself. Pushing can cause the drum to bounce, rippling the floor and tearing the sandpaper. As you near the far side of the floor, ease the drum off the floor by pushing down on the handles. When you start or end a pass, imagine that the sander drum is an airplane and the floor is the runway and that the goal is smooth landings and takeoffs.

Always sand with the grain, never across it. Not only will cross-sanding leave deep scratches that will be hard to sand out, but the drum will follow the small humps and dips of the floor joints instead of levelling them out, leaving a rippled finish.

At the end of the pass, lower the drum back down onto the floor, and pull the sander backwards over the same path to smooth it out and pick up sawdust, being careful to end at the same place as you began. Then, with the drum raised, move the sander about four inches to the left, and start the second pass. Drum sanders are designed to cut a little deeper on the left side; thus the right side of the overlap is automatically feathered out (which is why you must always work from right to left).

When you've reached the left side of the room, turn the sander around and start sanding the part of the floor that was behind your back. Start the cut about a yard or so back on the floor you've already sanded so that you don't leave a ridge between the two areas.

Next, with a rented, circular edging sander fitted with the same grade grit as the drum sander, go around the perimeter of the floor, cutting in as close as you can get to the walls and any obstacles. Since the edger makes a circular cut, it can't reach all the way into a corner (see **22-16**). Use a palm-grip block sander or a hand scraper (a sharp paring chisel and/or a bullnose finger plane are also handy for levelling tight spots). The edger is also used to sand closets and other areas that are too small to maneuver the drum sander in or where it would have to be run across the grain rather than with it. Pay particular attention to the transition zone between the edger and the drum sander cuts. You might consider using an orbital-action finishing sander to blend them smoothly together.

After a few hours of "stoop labor" with an edge sander, running the drum sander will almost feel relaxing. Floor finishing is not a job for anyone with a weak back.

The entire operation is repeated a second and third time, using 50- or 60-grit and 100- or 120-grit sandpaper, respectively. If the finer paper clogs too fast, switch to the next-coarsest grit. Look at the surface of the floor obliquely under a strong light. Any dished-out areas, ripples, and scratches left by the sander will be visible. Since even tiny scratches will show up much more readily in hardwood than softwood, you may need to make a fourth pass, using 150-grit. For a truly perfect finish, some experts go over the entire floor with a six-inch belt sander, once with 150-grit and a final pass with superfine 220-grit. You'll know you're done when the floor feels satiny smooth to your touch and you can't see any scratches on the faces of the pin knots.

An inexpensive disposable dust mask like the kind used for insulation offers more than adequate protection for floor sanding (unless you're refinishing old, painted floors which are likely to be coated with lead-bearing paint). But you may want use a good-quality organic vapor respirator equipped with a toxic-dust filter anyway because you don't want to inhale any of the fumes given off by the floor finish. You should also wear hearing protectors while operating any sander.

If you empty the dust-collection bag at frequent intervals before it fills up, less dust will be released into the air. The accumulation of noticeable windrows of dust and grit on the floor are usually a symptom of a full bag or a clogged dust-collection system.

Finally, to protect the raw wood from scratches and scuffs, wear smooth, clean soft-soled shoes or work in your stocking feet during the final sanding and throughout the rest of the finishing process.

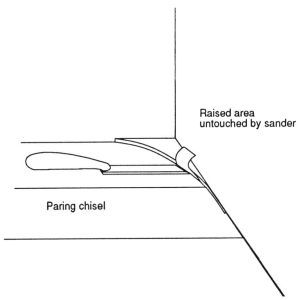

Raised area untouched by sander

Paring chisel

22-16 *A sharp, inch-wide hand scraper is a useful tool for smoothing off tight corners.*

APPLYING THE FINISH

Depending on the type of final finish you use and its manufacturer's recommendations, open-grained woods such as oak and mahogany may require a *filler* coat for a perfect finish. These are paste or liquid products that are applied to the wood after sanding and before finishing to fill in the tiny pores that are characteristic of such species. The floor must be sanded once more after the filler dries. No fillers are needed if you use a penetrating sealer or a polyurethane finish.

Vacuum the ceilings, walls, windowsills, the edges of trim boards, mouldings, warm-air grills, and any other surfaces where dust can collect, and then vacuum the floor. If you don't own an industrial-strength shop vac, rent one; most household vacuum cleaners aren't strong enough to suck the dust and grit out of the floor joints. Then wipe the entire floor with a *tack cloth* (a sticky open-weave cloth sold at paint stores) to pick up the dust that the vacuum cleaner missed.

Floorboards can be stained to change their color and highlight the grain. Although I think it makes more sense to pick a wood that naturally has the type of grain and color you like rather than try to mimic it with a stain, if you still want to stain your floors, there are some precautions that will ensure a good job. Since they apply to any wood that you might want to stain, such as casings, trim, and cabinetry, they're useful in any case.

Stains are either water-based or oil-based. Water-based stains *raise* the grain of the wood and so therefore require yet another light sanding after the stain dries. Oil stains don't raise the grain. But not all stains are compatible with the finish that may be applied over them or vice versa. Prepare a test sample by coating a scrap of flooring material with the stain and then applying the finish. When the finish is dry, lay a piece of duct tape on the sample, and see if the tape takes some of the finish with it when you pull it off. If it does, try a different combination of stain and/or finish. You'll want to make a test sample in any case just to see if the combination looks like what you want when it's dry.

As with paints and stains, choosing the right floor finish for your needs from the bewildering selection of products, which each claim superlative properties, is a mixture of blind luck and informed guesswork. All floor finishes fall into one of two basic categories: penetrating oils and surface resins. To put it another way, you have a choice between wrapping your floor in plastic or steeping it in oil. Penetrating finishes are absorbed into the cells of the wood and wear away with the floor. Surface finishes form a hard film on top of the wood. The two different types can be used in combination with each other, and sometimes the same material can be used for both, as for example, when a thinned-down varnish is applied as a base coat.

Penetrating finishes, such as linseed or tung oil or "Danish" oils such as Watco oil, are easy to apply and generally easy to renew without having to sand off the old finish first. They give the wood a warm patina but they offer little resistance to abrasion, unless given a protective wax coating (beeswax-, petroleum-, or tung-oil-based products) that must be frequently renewed or covered with a compatible harder surface finish. If you do mix different types of finishes, check the manufacturer's label for compatibility.

Penetrating sealers are usually thinned-down varnishes or lacquers that are absorbed into the wood to provide a base coat for the full-strength coats that follow. The slow-drying type is easy to use, while the much-harder-to-use, fast-drying type is favored by professionals since it allows them to recoat a floor in the same day.

Shellac is the traditional penetrating sealer. Multiple coats build to a strong and very glossy finish that can be spot-repaired as needed. Shellac is only compatible with other alcohol-based finishes and will spot easily if alcohol is spilled on it. It also tends to crack with age.

Lacquer is an alcohol-based sealing-type finish that dries very fast and fairly hard. Like shellac, it can be spot-repaired and recoated without sanding.

Modern synthetic varnishes form a durable, tough, glossy, and fairly elastic film. Alkyd resin varnishes are easily applied, while phenolic resin varnishes (spar varnish) tend to darken unacceptably with time and aren't often used for floors. What most people call "varnish" nowadays is actually oil-modified polyurethane, a plastic resin that dries very hard and has good resistance to abrasion, and, so long as you *carefully* follow the application directions, is fairly easy to use. Polyurethane floor finishes are noted for their somewhat unpredictable response to moisture and temperature conditions during curing, which can cause them to cloud. Their biggest drawback is that once they become scratched and worn, they can't be recoated without sanding off *all* the old finish.

Recently, water-based acrylic resins have become available that are fast-drying and that give off much lower levels of toxic fumes. But water-based acrylics are more easily scratched and less durable than urethane and other varnishes and also lack the wetting effect that gives the wood its pleasing hue. They also tend to be expensive.

All things considered, most home-owners will find that three or four coats of the best-quality gloss polyurethane varnish is the most practical, economical, and wear-resistant finish for their hardwood floors. Unless you are in the habit of walking around in your stocking feet and/or requiring your guests to leave their shoes at the door, you can expect to refinish high traffic floor areas like the kitchen every four or five years. Never wax polyurethane as it makes it almost impossible to sand.

Polyurethane varnish is best applied with a high-quality, extra-wide flooring brush or a lambs-wool applicator. Rollers should not be used since they create air bubbles that can become trapped in the film as it dries. The solvents in some kinds of urethane can also cause foam brushes and rollers to decompose, inoculating the finish with greyish crumbs of sponge.

Start at the wall opposite the door and paint in the perimeter first with a smaller brush. Then, following the grain, work a strip several brush-widths wide from one side of the floor to the other. Go back to your starting point and start the second strip, overlapping the previous section by about four inches. Overworking the varnish while you brush it or stirring it in the can creates bubbles and streaks. Pour the varnish into a paint roller tray in small batches, and don't try to save the leftovers, which will have picked up dust and dirt despite your cleaning.

The first coat should be thoroughly dry within 24 hours or less. If it feels at all tacky to the touch it isn't dry. Most urethanes must be second-coated within a specific time period to ensure proper adhesion between the coats. Follow the directions on the label.

After the first coat has dried, any nail holes or defects in the floor can be filled with wood putty. Filling the holes before the wood is sealed could cause solvents in the putty to stain the wood. Unless the directions indicate that it's unnecessary, sand lightly between coats with extra-fine (220-grit) paper to remove any dust marks and small imperfections and to increase adhesion. Vacuum and wipe the floor with a tack cloth between each coat, whether or not it's been sanded. As you continue applying the varnish, set up spotlights and make a point of getting down close to the surface to look for the inevitable specks of dust, grit, and animal and vegetable hairs that will "spontaneously" appear in the wet finish. Pick them up with your fingertip and wipe them off on the scrap of old bedsheet that you've kept hanging from your belt for the purpose.

The directions on the can typically state that you should provide "adequate ventilation" during and after application. As was mentioned in Chapter Fourteen, this can mean windows left wide open in the dead of winter. The problem with urethane is that it takes at least eight hours and as much as 24 hours to dry between each coat. Leaving the windows wide open isn't a problem in the warmer months. But, in cold weather, the air rushing in from open windows can chill the floors and retard the drying time

of the floor finish, even though the furnace is cranking out heat at full blast. Yet closing the windows also retards curing and increases your chances of a nasty headache by slowing down the dispersal of the volatiles. The best compromise is to open windows on an upper floor or in a different room than the one you're working in, and close them when you go home at night. (You'll have to do this from *outside* if the windows are in a room that's been freshly varnished.) If possible, it's better to do floor finishing at times when no supplemental heat is needed, since the convection currents set up by warm air (and to a lesser extent, hot-water baseboard heat) will stir up dust that becomes trapped in the drying varnish. This is one strong argument in favor of a radiant ceiling or floor.

RESILIENT SHEET-VINYL FLOORING

Resilient sheet-vinyl floor coverings (which aren't the same thing as the linoleum they've replaced) are often used in rooms subjected to high traffic and/or frequent wetting, where other types of flooring would be less than practical or too expensive. These typically include bathrooms, kitchens, laundry and utility rooms, breezeways, and entries ("mudrooms").

The reluctance that most do-it-yourselfers feel about installing sheet-vinyl themselves is understandable, particularly when the dealer usually includes installation at a nominal extra charge over the cost of the material itself—and one or two mistakes can ruin the entire sheet. If you have large areas to cover, especially where long seams will be unavoidable, sheet-vinyl installation is probably a job best left to professionals. But just about anyone can do a foolproof installation in a small room so long as you know some of the same tricks that professionals use to avoid costly mistakes.

The key is to make a *paper template* of the room and transfer the pattern onto the vinyl (see **22-17**). Then, every obstruction, skewed line, curve, and corner can be accurately cut without confusion or even a measuring tape. In fact, the Armstrong Co., a premier manufacturer of resilient flooring, offers a pattern kit that contains everything you need to install up to 600 square feet of flooring.

Lay paper sheets around perimeter. Fill in the middle and tape all sheets together

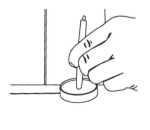
Scribe the exact perimeter of the floor with roller disc onto template.

Transfer template to vinyl

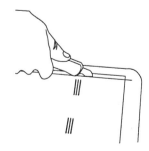
Cut with hooked blade

22-17 *Using a template to cut vinyl sheet flooring.*

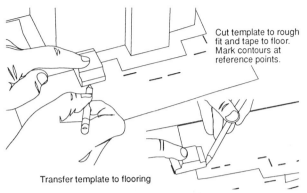

Cut template to rough fit and tape to floor. Mark contours at reference points.

Transfer template to flooring

22-18 *"Joe Frogger" method of fitting board or tile flooring around obstructions; the method is applicable to any type of flooring, including tile or sheet vinyl.*

Whether sheet or tile, a quality resilient flooring installation begins with proper preparation of the underlayment. For new floors, any depressions formed by the nail heads, scratches, and seams should be filled and brought flush to the surface with *embossing leveller* compound. The leveller is mixed with enough compatible latex bonding agent to give it the consistency of toothpaste. Use a flat steel trowel to spread it over the floor, and then scrape away the excess with the edge of the trowel, leaving the low spots filled. Check with your flooring dealer for the appropriate products and their proper usage.

The Armstrong layout kit includes 3×6 paper sheets. You could also use rolls of newsprint, food wrapping paper, examining bed paper, kraft packaging paper, or any other paper that comes in wide rolls. Lay the perimeter sheets first, holding their edges about a half-inch back from the walls or any other margins, and then fill in the midsections to cover the entire floor. Overlap the edges between sheets and tape them together with masking tape. To keep the paper from moving about and throwing off your measurements cut out one-inch triangles every few feet, and lay strips of tape across the slots.

The template kit contains a roller-disc scribing tool that has a hole in its center for holding a pen. As the tool follows the wall, it transfers the contours to the paper. A pointed transfer tool is provided to follow the contours of corners and other complicated and irregular edges. When scribing the cuts for pipes and other immovable obstructions, make a straight slice from the hole directly to the closest wall.

Leave the tape in place over the triangles as you take up the completed template and lay it out over the vinyl sheet which has been previously unrolled flat in another room. If the vinyl has a linear direction, line it up with the pattern. Then, following the scribe line on the paper with the inside edge of the transfer tool and holding the pen against the outside edge of the tool, transfer the pattern onto the vinyl. Carefully cut along these lines with a hook-bladed, vinyl knife and a straightedge.

The roller disc and the transfer tools described above are a slightly more sophisticated version of the *"Joe Frogger"* method known to any professional flooring installer and more than a few carpenters who have had to deal with cutting boards to fit complex profiles perfectly the first time (see **22-18**). Here, a small block of wood (the "frog") is held against the wall (or a doorframe with multiple corners, for example) and marks are made on a sheet of cardboard that's been rough-cut to fit and taped to the floor against the last floorboard, floor tile, or some other fixed reference point. The marks on the pattern are connected with a straightedge. The cardboard is then placed onto the workpiece, and the marks are transferred onto it from one side of the frog to the other. The result should be a perfect fit. For extra insurance, transfer the cut lines onto another piece of cardboard and make a trial fit with that before you cut the workpiece.

After the sheet has been cut and tested by dry-fitting, half the sheet is carefully rolled back, and mastic (adhesive) is spread on the exposed underlayment with a notched trowel (see **22-19**). Be sure that the trowel has the correct-size notches for the type of adhesive and the kind of flooring you are using. Spread the mastic evenly, but not too thick, leaving an arced pattern of distinct ridges without

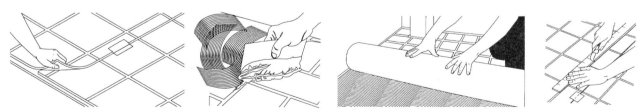

22-19 *Laying sheet vinyl flooring. Before positioning the template, unroll the two pieces of vinyl and overlap them two to three inches, face-up. Unroll the template, trace the outline on the vinyl, and cut the perimeters of the sheets to the scribe lines. Apply adhesive to the substrate, holding it back six to eight inches from the seam area. Unroll the vinyl in place from opposite walls. Line up the overlapping seams and cut through both sheets at the same time with a knife and straightedge. Remove the scrap, spread adhesive on the floor, press and roll the seam.*

any blobs. Roll the sheet back onto the mastic, and then repeat the process with its other half. Be careful not to fold or bend the sheet sharply or inadvertently step or lean on it while rolling or unrolling it. Vinyl is fairly brittle and will crack or tear easily when mishandled.

Professionals go over the newly laid sheet with a 100-pound rubber roller to seat it in the mastic. You can rent one of these from your flooring dealer or else you can use a wooden rolling pin borrowed from the kitchen. Bear down as hard as you can while rolling to exert maximum pressure.

Any seams that won't be covered by a moulding (usually where the flooring butts against the base of a bathtub or shower enclosure) should be filled with silicone tub-and-tile caulk and tooled smooth with your fingertip. Use latex caulk to seal the seam at the cut for a pipe. Spread a bead over the seam and then wipe it clean with a damp cloth.

Any of several different metal tack strips can be used to trim the joint where vinyl abuts carpet (see **22-20**). The strip is nailed over the vinyl, the edge of the carpet is locked onto the spikes, and the flange bent back down over the carpet with a rubber mallet. Various metal and wood strips also are used to join vinyl to wood. Adhesive and/or plastic expansion-type screw fasteners are used over concrete subfloors.

RESILIENT VINYL FLOOR TILE
Vinyl floor tiles are a lot easier to install than sheet vinyl. The tiles are also available in a much greater range of colors and styles than sheet flooring. Because different colors can be intermixed to create complex and interesting patterns, much more creative designs are possible than with almost any other kind of flooring except ceramics or stone.

The same basic principle of establishing a working centerline and two right-angle axes that has already been described for laying out ceiling tiles is used to set up the layout for floor tiles (see **22-21**).

To establish the diagonal lines needed to lay out a diamond pattern, measure off equal distances on two previously established intersecting right-angle lines, and connect the end points. Lay out the tiles to see how they end against the walls, and construct parallel lines to shift the base line, as necessary, for the best layout.

Once the lines have been set up, go over them with a red or black pencil to make them heavy enough to show between the ridges of the mastic. Spread the mastic as before with a notched trowel, over a comfortable work area that you can easily cover within the "open" time of the mastic. Some kinds of adhesive require time to get tacky before you can set the tiles, while with others, the tiles must be set immediately; follow the directions on the label. Mastic that sets too long will dry out and loose its adhesive qualities. Any such areas must be cleaned and recoated.

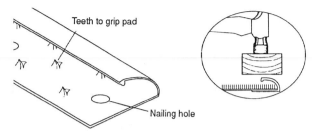

22-20 The change between vinyl and other types of flooring should always be protected by a metal transition strip even when both floors are at the same level.

New water-soluble mastics are available that give off a markedly lower level of toxic volatiles as they set. Cleanup of fresh spills, tools, and excess mastic that oozes out between the tiles is done with a moistened towel; mineral spirits must be used once the mastic has dried. "Organic," i.e., petrochemical-solvent-based, mastics do tend to bond better than the water-soluble products, but they are much more hazardous to your health and highly flammable. Cleanup requires mineral spirits or paint thinner. Take care not to soak the cleanup cloth with so much solvent that it runs down into the tile joints.

Mastics have a limited shelf life. Once the can has been opened, any leftovers will begin to harden fairly quickly. Pouring a cup of water over the surface of a solvent-type

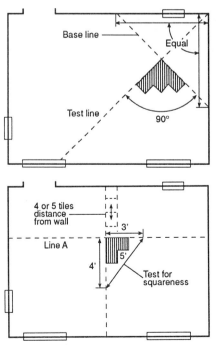

22-21 Laying out floor tiles is exactly the same as laying out ceiling tiles.

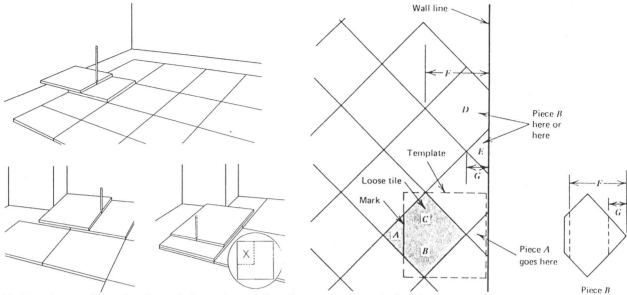

22-22 *Quite often, the discarded portion of the tile can be reused elsewhere.*

mastic will extend storage life by blocking air. Keeping the can in a cool place out of sunlight also helps. But adding water to a latex mastic will only dilute it. If, when you open a used (sometimes a new) can, the mastic has begun to harden, don't be tempted to add thinner. Hardened mastic is useless and should be discarded.

Place the tile exactly in position on the layout line. Don't try to twist or slide it into place, which flattens the ridges in the mastic and weakens the bond. The edges should butt firmly, but not so tight that they are forced together—which can cause the tiles to buckle and crack in the future.

Before spreading the mastic, sweep and vacuum the subfloor thoroughly. When laying tile, make sure that chips and shavings from cut edges don't fall onto the floor, where they will eventually work through the surface of the tile like a pimple.

Vinyl tile is easily cut by scoring with a sharp utility knife and a straightedge, such as a framing square, and snapping the tile along the score line. Complex cuts should be scored all the way through the tile to keep delicate pieces from breaking off. Special shears are also used to cut tile.

Many tile patterns have a subtle but distinct directional face grain. They should be placed and cut so that the grain lines up with that of the adjoining tiles. Cut edges should never butt against factory edges. The edge of a scored and snapped tile is usually a little uneven. If it won't be covered by a baseboard moulding, smooth it off with a Surform block plane. This tool is also handy for fine-tuning cuts to fit.

Lay as many full-sized tiles as you can and then begin cutting and filling in the border pieces. To find the cutline for straight, uncomplicated cuts, lay the border piece over the last full tile and then butt a full-size "gauge" piece against the wall and mark where its back edge falls on the face of the border piece. You can also use the technique for cutting end-wall shingles; lay the border tile upside down over the last full tile, and mark the point of overlap. For complex cuts, use the Joe Frogger method described above.

If the walls run square and parallel and your layout is accurate, all the border pieces will be (more or less) the same size. Check to see if the first border piece you cut will fit into the last space also. If it does, use it as a pattern for cutting the others (see **22-22**).

Avoid walking or kneeling on freshly laid tiles, at least until after you've laid enough of them to lock them between two opposing walls. Since the mastic remains quite flexible for a long time, it's very easy to inadvertently push the tiles out of alignment as you kneel and move about on them.

23 Tile Work

Like plastering or cabinetry, mastering the art of tile-setting can take a lifetime. Fortunately, you don't have to be a master craftsperson to tile your bathroom or foyer (see 23-1). The principles that govern the layout and installation of ceramic wall and floor tiles have much in common with those used for vinyl and wood flooring and ceiling tiles.

TYPES OF CERAMIC TILE

Modern ceramic tiles are produced in an amazing cornucopia of colors, sizes, and shapes. Yet all of them can be classified according to their permeability—that is, how much water they'll absorb. The ANSI (American National Standards Institute, which establishes specifications for just about every manufactured material in existence) has established four categories. In order of decreasing porosity (and increasing density), these are: nonvitreous, semi-vitreous, vitreous, and impervious. Since the density of a tile is primarily controlled by the temperature and the length of time at which it's fired, the hardest-fired tiles tend to be the most expensive (higher fuel costs).

The permeability of a tile is a consideration in deciding which kind of tile is best suited to a particular installation. For example, nonvitreous tiles shouldn't be used in cold outdoor locations since the water they absorb will freeze and crack the tiles. Nonvitreous tiles installed in wet indoor areas such as shower and tub enclosures are apt to fail sooner than a more costly semi-vitreous installation, even when extra waterproofing measures have been taken. And, since the pores of nonvitreous tiles can harbor pathogens and mildew, they can also cause health problems. But such considerations have not prevented their wide use in cut-rate installations.

With proper waterproofing, semi-vitreous tiles are suitable for wet indoor locations, but they shouldn't be used outdoors in cold climates. Vitreous tile is the best choice for general-purpose tiling in any type of location. Its high compressive strength enables it to bear heavy loads without breaking, making it ideal for flooring. Impervious tiles are, for all practical purposes, waterproof. Because of their cost, they're generally used only in hospitals, pharmaceutical plants, and other industrial and commercial installations where extreme sanitation is required.

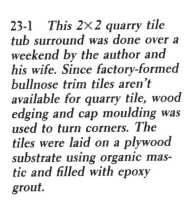

23-1 *This 2×2 quarry tile tub surround was done over a weekend by the author and his wife. Since factory-formed bullnose trim tiles aren't available for quarry tile, wood edging and cap moulding was used to turn corners. The tiles were laid on a plywood substrate using organic mastic and filled with epoxy grout.*

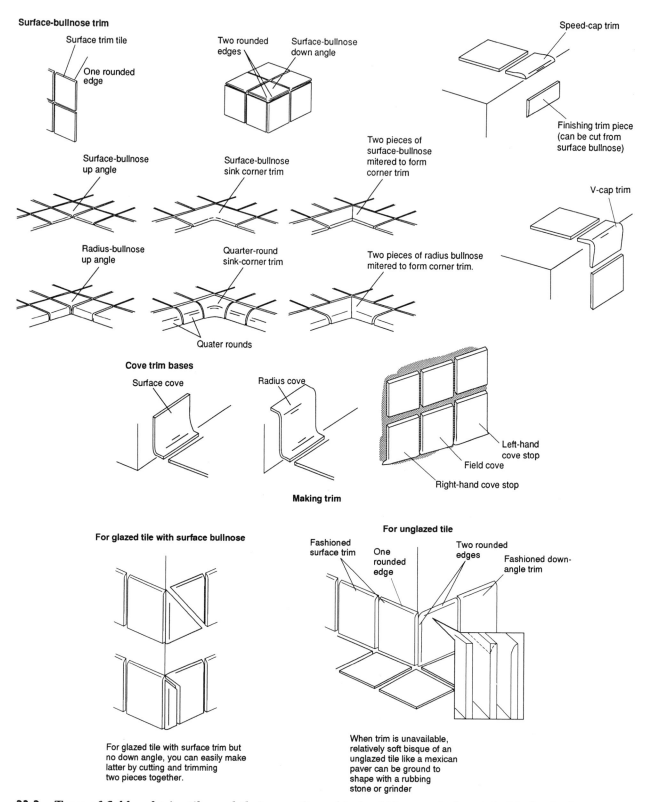

Surface-bullnose trim

Surface trim tile

One rounded edge

Two rounded edges

Surface-bullnose down angle

Speed-cap trim

Finishing trim piece (can be cut from surface bullnose)

Surface-bullnose up angle

Surface-bullnose sink corner trim

Two pieces of surface-bullnose mitered to form corner trim

Radius-bullnose up angle

Quarter-round sink-corner trim

Two pieces of radius bullnose mitered to form corner trim.

Quater rounds

V-cap trim

Cove trim bases

Surface cove

Radius cove

Left-hand cove stop

Field cove

Right-hand cove stop

Making trim

For glazed tile with surface bullnose

For glazed tile with surface trim but no down angle, you can easily make latter by cutting and trimming two pieces together.

For unglazed tile

Fashioned surface trim

One rounded edge

Two rounded edges

Fashioned down-angle trim

When trim is unavailable, relatively soft bisque of an unglazed tile like a mexican paver can be ground to shape with a rubbing stone or grinder

23-2 *Types of field and trim tiles and their uses. Some kinds of tile may lack certain kinds of trim. Others, such as unglazed Saltillo tiles, may lack trim altogether. These can often be custom-made.*

There's a big difference between the types of tiles used for walls and floors. Most wall tile is glazed and non-vitreous. But, even if the tile were vitreous, its glaze would be too soft and easily scratched to hold up on floors or countertops. Floor tile, which can fall into any of the four categories of porosity and can be either glazed or unglazed, is simply sturdier than wall tile.

Pavers, hand- or machine-made tiles at least ½ inch thick (and usually unglazed), are one of the more common flooring tiles. Most machine-made pavers are vitreous and, because they are freeze–thaw stable, they can be used in cold and wet outdoor locations. Nonvitreous handmade Mexican (*Saltillo*) and Mediterranean pavers from France, Portugal, and Italy, with their often quite crude and ir-regular appearance and rich unglazed earth colors, are quite popular for indoor floors throughout the United States and outdoor patios in warm climates. Because their porous surface is easily stained, they should be sealed (sometimes this is done by the retailer prior to sale) before grouting with at least two coats of tile sealer or a pene-trating oil finish. Sealers have to be reapplied annually.

Because of its density, vitreous or semi-vitreous un-glazed quarry tile (which is now made from fired clay and not, as was once done, from cut and polished stone) is especially well suited to floor and countertop service and for cold outdoor and wet locations. The tiles are sold unsealed. If you wish to seal them, you must apply a top-coat sealer made especially for use with quarry tile. The tiles won't absorb a penetrating sealer. As with urethane varnish on wood floors, any such sealer will have to be stripped prior to resealing.

Any tile two inches or less square is called a *mosaic* tile. Mosaic tiles are sometimes made of glass as well as ceramic, but in any case, they're almost always vitreous, and very tough, which makes them ideal for flooring and wet or freezing locations. To facilitate their handling and installation, mosaic tiles are almost always mounted on sheets of factory-applied backing. Careful application of the correct adhesive is required to prevent the backing from interfering with the bond between the tiles and the adhesive.

In application, tiles are either *field tiles* or *trim tiles* (see **23-2**). Those set in the main "field" are glazed only on their top face. Trim tiles, which define the margin of an installation and make the transition to other materials outside of it, are often glazed on one or more specially contoured edges to form inside and outside corners, mitres, and round-over edges at floors and the tops of walls. Despite the wide variety of trim tiles, you may still need to custom-cut your own for certain conditions.

TILE-SETTING ADHESIVES

Even more than tile composition, the type and proper application of a suitable adhesive is one of the most critical factors that affect the performance and durability of a tile installation (see **23-3**).

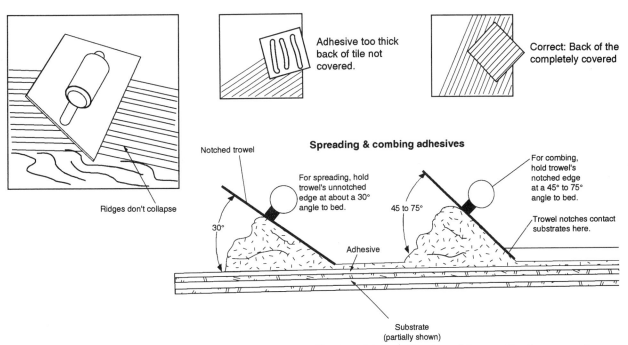

23-3 *Testing consistency, trowelling, and combing adhesives. To be effective, thinset adhesives must be mixed to the proper consistency. The angle of the trowel and the size and depth of its notches are important considerations for all types of adhesives.*

Ready-to-use petroleum or latex (water)-based "organic" (for their hydrocarbon content, not their freedom from chemical fertilizers) *mastics* are the most familiar to do-it-yourselfers. They're inexpensive, convenient, and easier and less time-consuming to apply than other forms of adhesives, particularly when setting wall tiles. Because their grip is immediate, there's far less problems with tile slippage.

Despite their widespread use, especially for setting wall tiles over drywall and plywood, organic mastics generally don't have as good a bond or compressive strength and as much flexibility as the cement-based *thinset mortars*. The organic mastics, in addition, aren't recommended for setting floor or countertop tiles, unless the area is subject only to very light traffic. They should never be used for wet floor installations of any sort nor where the tiles will be exposed to heat, such as part of a fireplace or woodstove hearth. Although, with proper waterproofing, they can be used for noncommercial wet-wall installations, they aren't the best choice for a top-quality trouble-free job.

Like the mastics used for setting vinyl floor tiles, solvent-based ceramic tile mastics also give off toxic—and potentially explosive—fumes as they cure. Wear a charcoal-filter organic vapor respirator, ventilate the work area, and extinguish all open flames, particularly gas pilot lights. While the fumes given off by latex-based organic mastics aren't flammable or as hazardous, it's still a good idea to wear a respirator while working with them. These precautions should be observed whenever you use any solvent-based product, whether it be for acoustical, vinyl, or ceramic tiles, contact adhesives for plastic laminates, or varnishes and sealers for floors and woodwork.

As used by tilesetters, the term "mortar" specifically refers to the cement mixture used to make the "floated" bed used as a substrate for tile installation, and not the cement-based thinset mortar adhesives that glue the tiles to it. To further confuse the issue, a floated mortar setting bed is sometimes called a "thick-bed" while any other type of setting bed is called a "thin-bed" or "thinset," regardless of the type of adhesive used.

As already mentioned, thinset tile adhesives are cementitious dry powders that are mixed with water, liquid latex, acrylic, or epoxy bonding agents to make an adhesive of superior qualities, well suited for setting tiles on floors, countertops, and other heavy-duty service areas and wet locations where strength and flexibility are potentially called for.

Water-mixed thinsets are used to set tile on concrete slabs or mortar beds for both wet and dry locations. With proper substrate preparation, some water-mixed thinsets can also be used for setting tile on plywood. Check the product specifications.

When combined with the dry ingredients, liquid latex and acrylic additives increase the bond and compressive strength of water-mixed thinset. Since the cement particles are essentially bound in a matrix of plastic or rubber, the cured adhesive is also much more flexible, which makes it suitable for use over plywood substrates as well as concrete or mortar. In fact, there are so many varieties of additives, each designed to enhance a specific quality, such as bond strength, tackiness, open time, faster or slower set, that experienced tiles setters constantly experiment with different recipes for different conditions. This improved and fine-tuned performance costs only a few cents more per square foot than organic mastics and straight water-mixed thinsets.

Epoxy thinsets are about four times more expensive than other thinsets, but they'll bond to problem substrates such as metal that are incompatible with other types of adhesives. Because of their high bond strength and unequaled flexibility, they're also ideally suited for tiling over plywood countertops and subfloors where movement is a concern.

Like other epoxy adhesives, epoxy thinsets consist of a resin and a hardener which must be mixed in very careful proportions before it can be blended with the sand-and-cement filler powder. The fumes are hazardous and the material is irritating to and difficult to remove from skin. Wear a respirator and rubber gloves.

Since thinset adhesives tend to set fairly quickly they're usually combined with a liquid additive that retards setting time. Pour clean room-temperature (65°F to 75°F, 18°C to 24°C) water and any liquid additives into the mixing pail first; gradually add the cement powder while stirring with a stick or trowel to remove the lumps. The powder is caustic; so wear a dust mask while mixing and rubber gloves while working with the wet adhesive. The mixture is allowed to *slake* (set) for 10 minutes and then stirred again to blend in any remaining lumps.

To check thinset for proper consistency, spread some on a small area of the setting bed and comb it with a notched trowel. If the mix is too thin, the ridges formed by the trowel won't hold their peaks. Press a tile into the adhesive, then remove it. If the mix is correct, the back of the tile will be completely covered with adhesive. If it's too thick, very little will adhere to the tile. Gradually add small amounts of liquid or dry ingredients to the mix and test each adjustment until you get the consistency right. The mix should be a little wetter for setting nonvitreous tiles than for vitreous tiles since they'll absorb water from it. Likewise, in hot and/or dry air, add more water than in cool or humid conditions.

Since organic mastics are ready-mixed, consistency is not a problem. However, both types of mastics require proper trowelling techniques to ensure a good bond. Dump a puddle of thinset or mastic onto your working area and spread it with the unnotched edge of a notched adhesive trowel. Hold the blade at about a 30-degree angle to the bed to work the adhesive into the pores of the setting bed. The thickness of the adhesive layer should be about the same as the depth of the trowel's notches, and, in any case, at least 3/32 inch thick. Then, using the notched

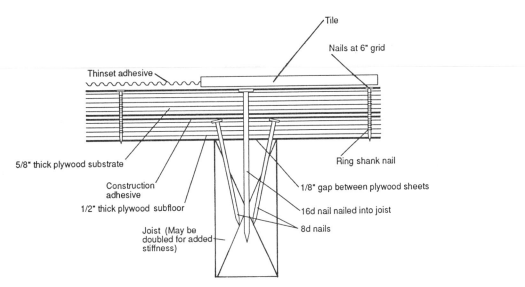

23-4 *Recommended substrate construction for plywood floor tile setting bed. Proper preparation of the substrate is critical to keep the grout joints from cracking when tile is laid over wood framing.*

side of the trowel, "comb" the material to form parallel ridges of uniform height. Hold the trowel at a 45-degree angle to the bed. If higher ridges are required, increase the angle of the trowel. Keeping the ridges at a uniform height is critical to obtaining a flat tile surface. Don't let the angle of the trowel change as you comb the adhesive and don't leave behind any globs (refer to **23-3**).

Since they make lower and narrower ridges, V-notched trowels are used to prepare the bed for mosaic tile and spreading organic mastics for standard 4×4 wall tiles. Square-notched trowels leave higher, wider ridges suitable for setting quarry, paver, and other large tiles.

When the adhesive is spread to the correct depth, half will adhere to the back of a test tile and half will remain in the bed. If only parallel lines of adhesive are stuck to the back of the tile, the bed is too thin. If adhesive oozes up along the edges of the test tile, the bed is too thick; it should be recombed with the trowel held at a lower angle. In most cases, a notch that's about two-thirds as deep as the tile is thick will leave ridges of just about the right height.

TILE SETTING BEDS

Plywood makes a good-quality substrate for wall and floor tiles in dry locations. With additional waterproofing measures, it can even be used for wet floors.

As was mentioned in Chapter Six, the floor joists under a tile floor should be beefed up to add stiffness and carry the extra weight of the tile. Doubled or deeper joists or 12-inch centers are some approaches. But even when so supported, a single-layer ¾-inch plywood subfloor may still be too flexible to make a crack-proof tile-setting base.

ANSI recommendations call for a 1⅛-inch minimum thickness. Instead of a single layer of (expensive) special-order 1⅛-inch plywood, which would still be subject to the seasonal changes that cause grout joints to crack, laminate two layers of ordinary CDX together (see **23-4**). Secure the subfloor layer solidly to the joists as shown with 8d nails and construction adhesive. Make sure the heads are sunk below the surface so that no bumps telegraph into the next layer. Then, glue a second layer of ⅝-inch CDX plywood to the subfloor with brushable construction adhesive. Stagger the sheets so that their joints don't fall over any subfloor joints, and nail them to the joists with 16d nails spaced about six inches apart as shown in **23-4**. For field nailing, use drywall screws (or ring-shank nails) six inches apart, just long enough to penetrate through the bottom of the subfloor layer. Leave ⅛-inch to ¼-inch gaps between the edges of the substrate sheets which will later be filled in with tile adhesive to allow room for the plywood to contract and expand without cracking the tile joints.

Use only a good-grade CDX that has no voids and splits or tears. But, unlike vinyl floor tiles, the underlayment for ceramic tiles doesn't have to be perfectly smooth. In fact, the rough finish of CDX ensures a better bond between the adhesive and the wood.

Unless taken into account during the design stage, the extra thickness of the tile substrate and the thickness of the tile itself will result in two different finish floor levels if, as is most often the case, more than one type of flooring material is laid over the same subfloor. While a bevelled wood or metal saddle can ease a slight transition (¼ inch or less), differences in level of an inch or more can cause people to stumble.

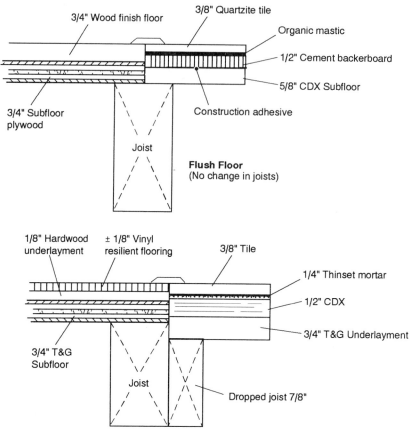

3/4" Wood finish floor
3/8" Quartzite tile
Organic mastic
1/2" Cement backerboard
5/8" CDX Subfloor
3/4" Subfloor plywood
Construction adhesive
Joist
Flush Floor
(No change in joists)

1/8" Hardwood underlayment
± 1/8" Vinyl resilient flooring
3/8" Tile
1/4" Thinset mortar
1/2" CDX
3/4" T&G Underlayment
3/4" T&G Subfloor
Joist
Dropped joist 7/8"

23-5 *Adjusting floor framing for tile base. The thickness of the tile, substrate, mortar bed, and the subfloor and finish flooring materials must be carefully coordinated during the initial design phase and checked in the field if a tile and other type of floor are to meet at the same level.*

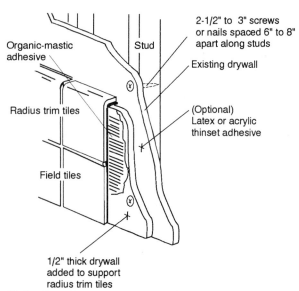

Organic-mastic adhesive
Stud
2-1/2" to 3" screws or nails spaced 6" to 8" apart along studs
Existing drywall
Radius trim tiles
(Optional) Latex or acrylic thinset adhesive
Field tiles
1/2" thick drywall added to support radius trim tiles

23-6 *Installation of radius trim tile over drywall applied over existing wall in a dry location.*

The floor joists can be dropped under the tile areas or the subfloor can be cut into strips that rest on ledgers nailed to the sides of the joists (see **23-5**). If necessary, the top edges of the joists can be notched so that the finished substrate and tile ends up flush with the other floors. So long as no layer is less than ½ inch thick and the overall thickness of the substrate and subfloor is at least 1⅛ inch, you can vary the thickness of its layers to match different flooring conditions. For example, you can use ½-inch CDX for the subfloor, or lay ½-inch cement tile backer board over a ⅝-inch subfloor. Tile should not be laid over 2×6 decking or 1×6 board subfloors without an intervening underlayment to isolate the joints so that they don't become stress points in the tile bed.

Ordinary unpainted drywall makes a good setting base for wall tiles in wet (and with proper waterproofing) dry areas (see **23-6**). Some tilesetters prefer to double up the drywall for extra strength, especially when remodelling over old, painted drywall.

Space the sheets about ⅛ inch apart, and cover the gaps with self-sticking fibreglass mesh tape. Fill the joints

Fill small dips with thinset adhesive

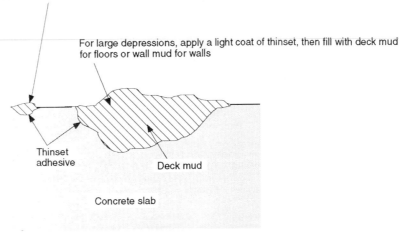

For large depressions, apply a light coat of thinset, then fill with deck mud for floors or wall mud for walls

Thinset adhesive

Deck mud

Concrete slab

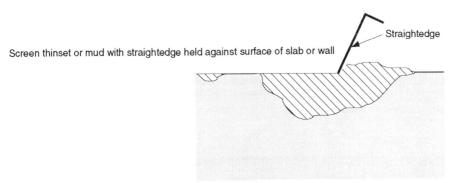

Straightedge

Screen thinset or mud with straightedge held against surface of slab or wall

23-7   Levelling a concrete slab for tile setting. Because of its greater thickness, a thinset mortar bed is considerably more forgiving of slight dips and bumps in the floor slab than organic mastics, which require a dead flat surface.

with thinset tile adhesive, and feather them out to a smooth flat surface. There's no need to fill and sand the nail holes. Some building codes require moisture-resistant drywall to be used on bathroom walls, in any case, and permit it for use as a tile-setting bed in wet areas. Since the material must still be properly waterproofed anyway, some tilesetters don't feel that it's worth the extra cost; others use nothing else.

Unpainted masonry (concrete block, smooth brick, and stucco) and concrete all make an excellent base for tiles so long as they are flat and have no major active cracks (see **23-7**). Block and brick walls with surface irregularities of more than an inch must be levelled first. Brush a coat of water-mix or latex thinset adhesive thinned to the consistency of heavy paint onto the walls. While it's still wet, float a layer of "fat mud" (also called "wall mud"—a sticky mortar especially mixed for coating walls) to even out the surface. As with plaster work, gauge strips should be temporarily tacked or bedded in thinset mortar to guide the screeding.

A concrete slab intended as a tile-setting base should be given a wood float finish—instead of the customary steel-trowel finish that is fine for organic mastics, but too slick to make a good bond with thinset mortar. If need be, rent a gas-powered abrasive wheel grinder to rough up the surface a little. Make sure the slab is not treated with curing compounds either, as these will also prevent a good adhesive bond. A slab that won't absorb water that's been sprinkled on it has probably been chemically treated.

Move a straightedge (a length of angle iron works well) over the slab to check for depressions and bumps. Any depressions deeper than ¼ inch should be given a light coat of latex thinset to strengthen the bond between the slab and the "deck mud" (thickset bed mortar) that's used to fill the hole. Back-butter the tiles with extra thinset to fill in any shallower depressions. Occasional bumps can be ground down with a carbide rubbing stone or with a hand-held electric grinder. But where the bumps are numerous and higher than ¼ inch, it's easier to float the floor level with a thin layer of deck mud.

Backer board (also available as Wonderboard) is a cement-cored ½-inch (or 7/16-inch) thick panel covered on both faces with a reinforcing mesh of fibreglass that makes a strong and rigid substrate for tiles. Since the backer boards themselves are waterproof, once the installation is properly protected so that water can't work into joints and seams, it's ideal for wet locations (see **23-8**). The sheets range in size from 3×4 to 4×8 with densities of 2.6 to 3.8 pounds per square foot. On walls, backer board can be nailed or screwed directly to the studs just like drywall. Leave ⅛-inch gaps between the sheets and a ¼-inch gap between the backer board and the sides of the wall framing to allow for seasonal movement of the wood. Tape the joints with fibreglass mesh tape, and fill them with thinset adhesive as for drywall. On floors, glue the backer board to a plywood or board subfloor of suitable thickness with thinset adhesive compatible for wood spread with a ¼-inch notched trowel before screwing it every six inches in the field.

The sheets can be cut by scoring and snapping—similar to working with drywall—using a special carbide-tipped scoring tool and a straightedge. After snapping the face side, score the folded fibreglass mesh on the back side to finish the cut.

Although they give superior results, particularly in wet areas and with floors and countertops laid over plywood that are subjected to heavy traffic, making a floated mortar tile bed is such a hard and lengthy process that only skilled tilesetters attempt it. For most home installations, any of the substrates mentioned above are more than adequate. But, if you're faced with turning an uneven concrete slab or masonry wall and/or an old, off-level wood floor into a level tile substrate, floating a mortar bed is the most practical way to do it (see **23-9**).

Like plastering, in theory the process is simple, but it takes skill and experience to do well. You basically position two parallel strips of wood several feet apart. These screeds (also called float strips or grounds) are anchored in windrows of mud with their top faces level with the desired thickness of the bed. The mortar is dumped between the strips and packed with a large wood float. A wood or aluminum screed bar is then drawn along the screeds while at the same time it is moved back and forth across the surface, similar to finishing a concrete slab. Any voids left in the surface are filled in with more mud and levelled with the wood float before the screeds are pulled up and set in the next area to be floated. The ruts left behind by the screeds are filled in, compacted, and smoothed with the wood float.

When mortar is floated over a plywood substrate rather than concrete, a layer of tar paper is glued to the floor with asphalt cold cement first. This *curing membrane* keeps the wood from sucking water out of the mortar as it dries. It can also serve to waterproof the substrate as is explained below. A layer of wire reinforcing mesh (which looks like chicken-wire fencing) is also bedded more or less in the middle of the mortar. It should be laid under the float strip when setting up the screed columns.

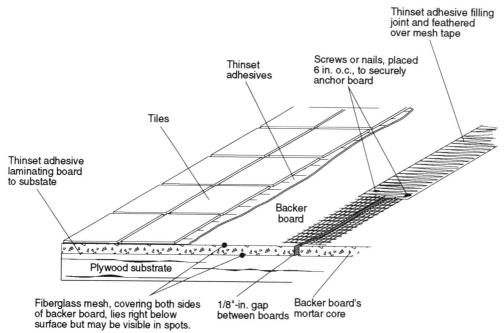

Thinset adhesive filling joint and feathered over mesh tape

Thinset adhesives

Screws or nails, placed 6 in. o.c., to securely anchor board

Tiles

Thinset adhesive laminating board to substate

Backer board

Plywood substrate

Fiberglass mesh, covering both sides of backer board, lies right below surface but may be visible in spots.

1/8"-in. gap between boards

Backer board's mortar core

23-8   Backer board should always be used for a substrate in a tiled shower or tub enclosure, particularly under benches or shelves subjected to standing water.

594

The "deck mud" used for floating a floor is similar to high-strength brick mortar. The approximate recipe calls for mixing one part Portland cement with six parts sand and one part water. The proportions are adjusted to accommodate any additives. A good deck mortar will be fairly dry and crumbly and will not puddle or slump readily.

To make "fat mud," add a half part lime to about five parts sand, one part Portland cement—and just enough water to produce a spreadable plaster-like mix. This gives the mortar the stickiness that it needs to grip both the substrate and the reinforcing mesh that keeps it from sagging off the wall.

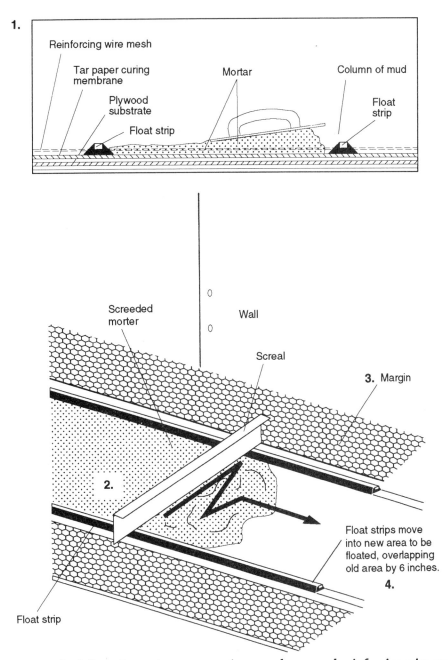

23-9 *Floating a mortar bed floor. Lay a tar-paper curing membrane and reinforcing wire mesh over the substrate, and set the float strips level in beds of mud. Dump mortar between the strips, and float it even. Screed off the mortar level with the float strips. Pull float strips forward into the next section and back-fill the ruts. Let dry overnight before laying tile.*

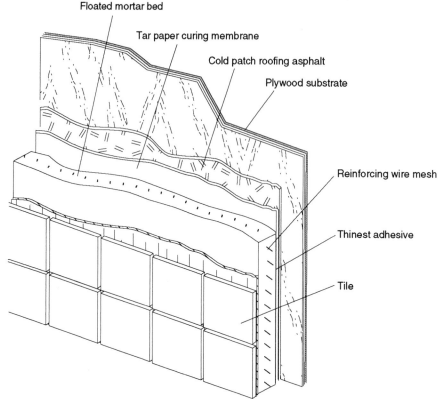

Floated mortar bed
Tar paper curing membrane
Cold patch roofing asphalt
Plywood substrate
Reinforcing wire mesh
Thinest adhesive
Tile

23-10 *Tar-paper waterproofing and/or curing membrane for mortar and backer-board setting beds.*

MEMBRANES

Membranes serve three purposes in tile installation. They're used to waterproof the substrate and prevent structural damage, to prevent premature curing of mortar beds, and to prevent movement between dissimilar materials from disturbing the tiles (*isolation membranes*). Often, the same materials or the same membrane may fulfill one or more of these functions simultaneously.

Although the tiles themselves may not be affected by water, the underlying substrate certainly is unless measures are taken to prevent water from seeping into it. Contrary to what many believe, the primary function of grout is to anchor the tiles. Grout alone offers little resistance to water movement.

The materials and method of installation used for a waterproofing membrane depend mostly on whether the membrane will be above or below the water line. On shower walls, for example, tar paper applied under the setting bed is the standard approach. A waterproofing membrane applied below the waterline, as, for example, with a shower base or sunken tub, is called a *pan* and must be made to much more exacting specifications.

For best results, a standard all-purpose tar-paper waterproofing membrane should be embedded in trowel-grade asphalt flashing cement (called *cold patch cement*) that has been brushed onto the plywood substrate beneath a floated mortar thickset or backer-board thinset tile bed. Overlap any joints two inches, and seal them with more cement. Although some builders just staple the tar paper to the substrate, the moisture in a freshly floated mortar bed can cause the paper to wrinkle and create voids in the mortar. The staples are also potential leaks.

As was mentioned earlier, tar paper applied over a plywood substrate also serves as a curing membrane to prevent excessively fast drying of a floated mortar bed, which will reduce the mortar to powder. Curing membranes in the form of four-mil poly film are also laid over fresh mortar beds and grout to prevent rapid curing in hot, dry weather (see **23-10**).

Since the manufacturer's specifications require backer board for floor tiles to be laminated to the substrate with thinset latex, any waterproofing membrane for a wet floor must be applied on top of the backer board instead. This is one reason why mortar beds are used for wet floors over wood.

Until very recently, there were no satisfactory products that could be applied over backer board, drywall, or plywood tile setting bases instead of beneath them. Fabrics made of 30-mil CPE (chlorinated polyethylene) sheets

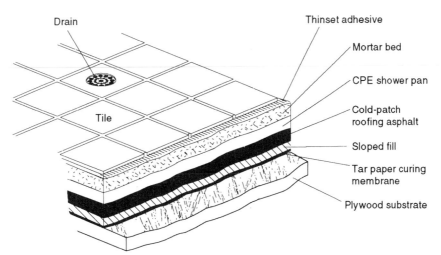

Drain
Thinset adhesive
Mortar bed
CPE shower pan
Cold-patch roofing asphalt
Sloped fill
Tar paper curing membrane
Plywood substrate
Tile

23-11 *Although costly, CPE membranes can achieve even better waterproofing than traditional soldered lead or copper pans with a lot less labor.*

laminated to polyester fibres have changed all that (see **23-11**). The material makes up for its cost by its versatility. It can be used with any substrate, including metal, backer board, drywall, concrete, and plywood, wherever the very thorough waterproofing is required.

The five-foot-wide sheets (sold in 100-foot rolls) are laminated by combing a $1/8$-inch to $3/16$-inch layer of thinset adhesive onto a clean, flat setting bed, placing the membrane over it, and smoothing it with a rolling pin to eliminate air bubbles and foster complete contact. If necessary, the edges of the sheets can be cemented together using xylene or Nobleweld 100 cement. After letting the thinset harden for 24 hours, a second layer of thinset or an organic

mastic can be spread over the membrane to set the tiles firmly.

Trowel-applied membranes, which are combinations of fabric and liquid latex, applied in alternating layers, can also be used to waterproof most substrates except wood (see **23-12**).

Traditionally, shower and tub pans were made from lead, copper, or galvanized steel flashing metal, with seams that were folded and soldered. Galvanic action would eventually corrode the joint where the pan connects to the drain flange. A hot-mopped pan, similar in construction to built-up roofing, prevented the corrosion problem but was a real challenge to build.

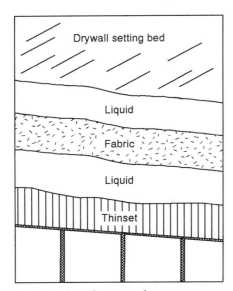

Drywall setting bed

Liquid

Fabric

Liquid

Thinset

1. Apply a thick coat of liquid part of membrane system to setting bed, using a roller, brush or trowel.

2. Cover liquid with fabric, allowing liquid to bleed through.

3. Apply thick top coat of liquid over fabric and let dry 24 hrs. before tiling.

23-12 *Trowel-applied waterproofing membrane.*

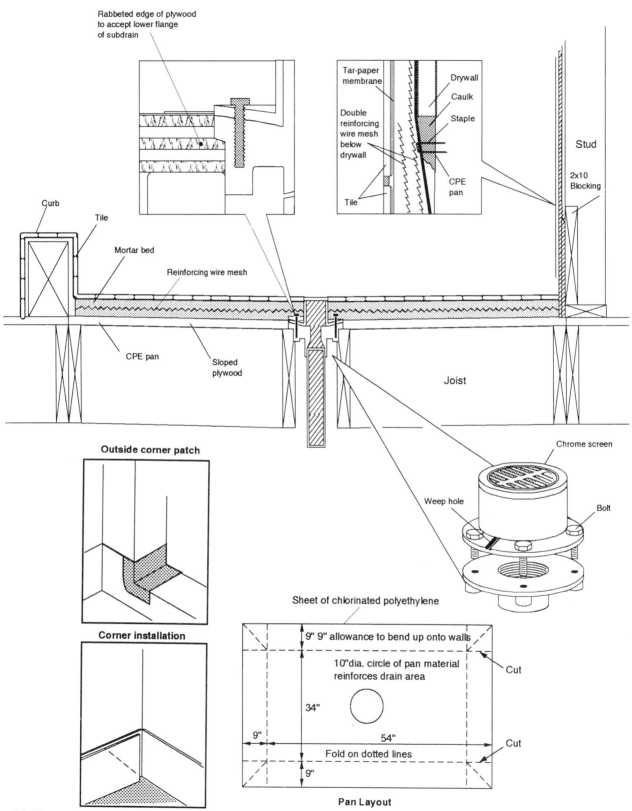

23-13 *Construction of a shower pan using CPE membrane.*

598

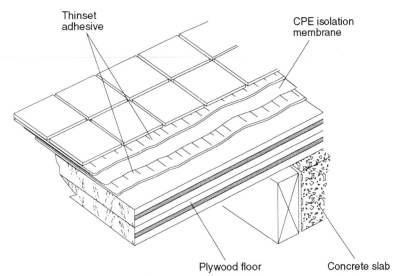

Thinset adhesive

CPE isolation membrane

Plywood floor

Concrete slab

23-14 *Isolation membranes absorb the stresses caused by differential movement in the substrate that would otherwise crack the tile bonds.*

Fortunately, there's a thicker, heavy-duty (40-mil) CPE-based membrane (Choloraloy 240) that can be easily formed into a waterproof pan in a single layer (see **23-13**). The corner folds are upturned to make a waterproof pan that covers the base of the shower or tub.

Another option is to construct the pan out of soldered copper and leave it untiled. Heavy flashing-grade copper can be purchased in 3×8 sheets and three-foot-wide rolls. The top edge of the copper forms a self-flashing lip against the substrate. The slanted plywood base should be coated with asphalt and tar paper for added protection. Isolate the drain flange from the copper with silicone caulk. The same approach can be adapted to make custom-built copper bathtubs.

Isolation membranes are used wherever there is a possibility of normal seasonal movement cracking a tile setting bed (see **23-14**). Although there are cases where isolation membranes are needed in new work, the majority of such conditions occur in remodelling work, when tiles are set over structurally weak areas or where different substrates abut each other. Because they consist of three separate layers, a bottom of a CPE membrane can stretch with the motion of the substrate without affecting the bond of the tile glued to the top layer.

TILE LAYOUT AND CUTTING

Because the pronounced regularity of a tile pattern is accentuated by its grout lines, for the best appearance the substrate of a tile installation must be as close to perfectly square, plumb, and level as is possible.

In practical terms, this means meeting or exceeding TCA (Tile Council of America) recommendations. These prescribe a tolerance of ⅛ inch in 10 feet for squareness, and ⅛ inch in eight feet for plumb on walls. Walls that meet at an inside corner can be up to ½ inch in 10 feet out of plumb without untoward problems. But at an outside corner they must be as close to dead-on accurate as possible. Likewise, the margin of error for floors and countertops shouldn't be more than ⅛ inch off level over 10 feet.

Tiles are laid out in the same manner as any regular modular wall- or floor-covering material. Plumb and level or right-angle baselines or centerlines are established and adjusted to yield the most even starting and ending filler pieces. If possible, narrow strips should be avoided. When figuring the number of tiles it will take to cover a given area, the width of the grout is included in the calculations. For example, the actual dimensions of a nominal 4×4 tile are 3⅞ inches by 3⅞ inches, which allows for a standard ⅛-inch grout joint.

With floors, it's especially important to establish accurate right-angle baselines, since any out-of-square tiles will show up unmercifully against a baseboard. When it's the walls rather than the tile layout that are out of square, you'll have to use your judgment as to the least obvious way to split the difference or the best place to hide the problem. Install any baseboard after tiling.

In small rooms, a framing square can be used to establish right angles. But in large rooms with several intersecting partitions, extending a 3-4-5 triangle from a baseline parallel to the longest (and hopefully straightest) wall is more accurate. If the distance between the wall and a right-angle baseline becomes skewed, you can determine how much to adjust the baselines to minimize the visual disruption caused by the out-of-square wall.

Before checking the walls and floors for level, plumb, and square, check your measuring tools for accuracy (see **23-15**). To check a straightedge, lay it on a flat surface and scribe a line along its length. Flip the straightedge over onto the other side of the line, and scribe a second line over the first. If the two lines follow each other exactly, the straightedge is, in fact, straight. If the lines are tangent, the edge has a convex bow. If the lines converge in a lens-shaped arc, the bow is concave.

To check a level, place it on a flat surface, and shim it as needed until the bubble reads in the center of the vial (refer to **23-15**). Scribe the outline of the level onto the surface and then rotate the level end-for-end and place it over the outline, making sure the shims haven't moved. It the bubble returns to dead center, the level is reading correctly. To check a level for plumb, rest the edge against a straight (plumb) wall stud. Note where the plumb vials read and then flip the level over. If it's accurate, the vials will still read the same.

Repeated shock and careless handling can bend a framing square out of true. A tiny crack can open up at the inside corner of the tongue and blade. To check a square, lay it on a straightedge with the tongue to one side, and scribe a line down the blade (refer to **23-15**). Flip the square over so the tongue points in the opposite direction, and rescribe the line. If the two lines coincide, the square is accurate. If the tongue was facing left when you started and the first line falls to the left of the second line, the square angle is acute (less than 90 degrees). If the first line falls to the right of the second line, the square is making an obtuse angle.

Usually, a square can be fixed rather than having to be replaced. Scribe a diagonal line from the inside to outside corners of the square. To increase an acute angle, use a hardened center punch and a hammer to make a few dimples on the upper half of the line. To decrease an obtuse angle, make the dimples on the lower half of the line. Try the square again and make a few more dimples if needed. These small deformations warp the square in the desired direction.

1. Lay-square with tongue to left, butting if firmly against straightedge, and scribe second line as before

2. Flip square over, as though it were hinged, align it with straightedge and scribe second line as before

3. Compare lines

Scribe second line here

Line 2   Line 1

Square is accurate (90°)

If first line falls to right of **V**, square is greater than 90°

1. Place level on flat surface, shimming level if needed to bring bubble to center of vial. Trace outline of level on surface

2. Rotate level 180° and place it on outline, keeping shims in place if used

3. If bubble returns to dead center, level is accurate

Line 1   Line 2

If first line falls to left of **V**, square is less than 90°

Adjusting a carpenters square for accuracy

1. To adjust square, first scribe line connecting inside and outside corners

2. To increase square's angle, use center punch to make dimples on center punch line

3. To decrease angle, make dimples on lower half of line

1. Lay straightedge on flat surface and scribe along its length

2. Flip straightedge, as though it were hinged, to opposite side of line and scribe another line over first

3. Compare lines

– A single line means straightedge is accurate

– A pair of diverging lines means straightedge is convex

– A pair of converging lines means straightedge is concave

23-15 *Since the tolerances in tile work are quite small, your straightedges, levels, and square must all be dead-on accurate. You should never assume they are.*

Since accuracy is important, construct a *trammel stick* by carefully driving 8d nails through the edge of a six-foot length of straight 1×2 stock (see **23-16**). The nail points should accurately mark three-, four-, and five-foot centerpoints. Use the trammel stick for laying out and checking your reference triangles.

A storey pole (also called a *jury stick*) marked with the average tile plus grout joint intervals is used to mark off the tile layout lines from the reference lines. Since tiles will vary slightly in width, the best way to mark off the storey pole is to lay ten actual tiles in a line. Butt self-spacing tiles (which have little lugs cast into their sides that are each half the width of a grout joint) tightly together. If you use plastic tile spacers instead, insert them between the tiles. Otherwise, space the tiles carefully with a wood spacer. Measure the overall length of the 10 tiles and divide by 10 to get the average tile and grout width. Set your dividers to this unit and step it off on the storey pole. A straight piece of 1½-inch by ⅜-inch lattice moulding makes a good storey pole. Cut a seven-foot length for walls and a shorter length for tighter areas.

Layout lines not only keep the tiles running straight and square, but they make it possible to cut tiles ahead of time. This keeps the adhesive from skinning over or setting up while you run back and forth to the tile cutter to trim each closing piece one at a time. The "boxes" of the layout lines also outline where to spread the adhesive without overspreading or leaving uncovered patches.

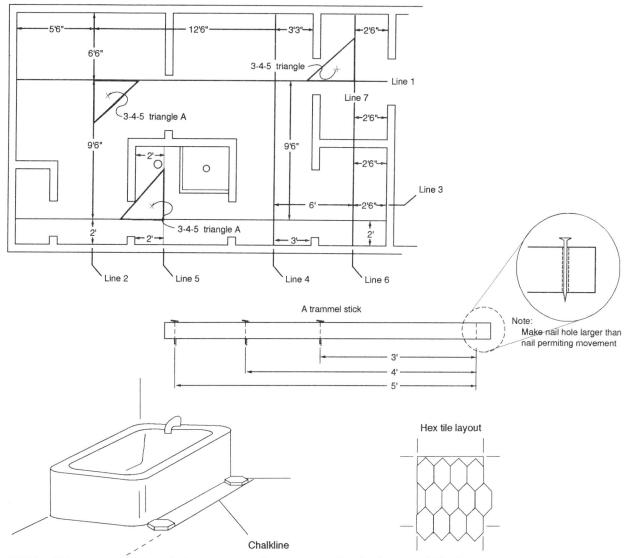

23-16 *Using a trammel stick for making reference triangles for layout of tile floor.*

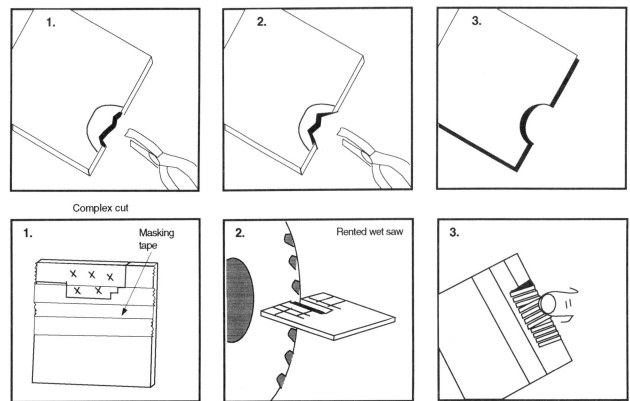

23-17 *Cutting tiles with a snap cutter and making complex cuts using a wet saw.*

TILE INSTALLATION AND GROUTING

Except for soft, nonvitreous tiles like Mexican pavers, most tiles are cut with a *snap cutter* (see **23-17**). Although a fairly decent-quality snap cutter isn't expensive, there's no reason to buy one since you can usually borrow or rent it from the tile dealer.

Mark the cutting line on the face of the tile with a fine-point felt-tip marker. Position it against the tool's bottom fence, aligning the cut mark with the cutting wheel. Hold the tile in place with one hand while you lift the handle to set the wheel on the upper edge of the cut mark, and draw the cutter steadily across the face of the tile. Don't exert too much pressure or you'll snap the tile. Then clamp the tile in place with the "wings" at the base of the handle and strike the heel of the handle lightly with your palm. The tile should snap cleanly along the cut line. If it doesn't, try hitting it a little harder. If it breaks unevenly or doesn't break at all, you didn't make a continuous or deep-enough score line. Don't be discouraged if you break a few tiles when you first start using the tool. It takes a while to get a feel for the right amount of force.

The snap cutter also has an adjustable fence that can be set for repetitive straight cuts.

Tile biters (or "nippers") are used to cut irregular shapes like fixture cutouts. After marking the cut, begin nibbling in from the edge, keeping the jaws of the tool more or less parallel to the cut line. It's better to take a lot of small bites than to risk ruining the tile with an uncontrollable big bite.

The snap cutter and nippers can't make complex notched cuts. You can use a rented diamond-blade wet saw to do the job quickly and accurately or you can do it with a hacksaw fitted with a tungsten-carbide rod blade. If you use the wet saw, make repetitive parallel cuts to the depth of the cut line, and then break out the pieces and trim the back of the cut with nippers (refer to **23-17**).

A wet saw must be used for cutting hand-fired pavers and other tiles too soft for the snap cutter. Unlike other kinds of cutters, the edge left by a diamond wet saw is perfectly smooth and slightly rounded-over, which makes it ideal for cuts that will be left exposed.

You can also use a Surform block plane equipped with a flat tungsten-carbide cutter to smooth the jagged edges of cuts and trim or enlarge them.

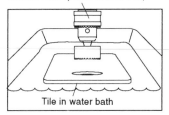

Cordless drill (Carbide hole saw)

Tile in water bath

23-18 *Cutting circular holes in tile. A single carbide-tipped hole saw costs more than an entire set of cheap ones; but, the bit stays sharp a long time and can cut through almost anything.*

A carbide-grit masonry blade set in a chop saw or radial arm saw can also be used to cut quarry tiles and standard wall tiles. But dry-sawing produces a great deal of dust, which, besides being a general nuisance, can clog the motor's bearings. Although it has no teeth, the high-speed blade can also shatter, throw off chips, or jam in the cut and twist the tile out of your hands, possibly causing serious injury. The blades don't last very long, either.

A diamond-blade wet saw runs cooler and more slowly, produces much less dust, makes thousands of cuts, and is considerably safer to handle. With a wet saw, there's very little danger of cutting yourself badly, even if you accidentally contact the blade. Its only disadvantage, other than its sheer bulk, is that the water bath makes a muddy mess and so the tool must be used outdoors. The biggest expense involved in renting these tools is the charge assessed for the blade.

A small diamond-tipped dry-cutting blade set in an electric hand-held grinder can also be a handy tool for cutting rough openings. Since the tool turns at high speeds, it throws off chips and will cut through skin and bone as easily as it cuts through hard tile.

A carbide-tipped hole saw and an electric drill are also indispensable for cutting circular openings in the center of tiles (see **23-18**). Since a tile that becomes overheated during a cutting operation can shatter, it's a good idea to immerse it in a water bath while drilling. But sticking a 120-volt power tool in water *isn't a great idea*, even if it's double-insulated and the circuit is protected with a GFCI. Use a fully charged heavy-duty cordless drill instead.

Tiles set in thinset adhesives should be firmly seated and levelled in their bed by striking a *beating block* (you can cut one from a six-inch by 10-inch scrap of plywood) with a rubber mallet. It's especially important to set sheet-mounted mosaic tiles with the block. Because of their uneven surface, you can't use a beating block to set Mexican pavers. Instead, tap them with the mallet itself.

Clean any adhesive that is left on the tiles or that has been squeezed up between the grout joints as soon as the tiles have been set in position. If you wait until the adhesive has hardened, the job will be a lot harder. Use a utility knife or a *grout saw* to clean out any adhesive that has worked into the grout joints. Vacuum the joints to pick up loose debris.

The tile should be allowed to set for at least 24 hours before grouting the joints. If the adhesive is not completely dry, it can discolor the grout.

Both kinds of tile grouts, plain or sanded, are basically mortar and additives mixed with water. Plain grout is used for joints $1/16$ inch or less in width. The stronger sanded grout is used for wider joints. Special latex and acrylic additives can be mixed with or used in lieu of water. Products are available which will enhance flexibility, increase water resistance or bond strength, eliminate efflorescence (whitish deposits on the surface of the grout), improve freeze–thaw stability, color retention, and stain resistance, or permit harder, denser joints.

Although the width and color of grout joints is ultimately a matter of personal taste, in general, narrower joints seem to go best with all but the largest tiles. A grout that contrasts strongly with the color of the tiles emphasizes the regularity of their geometric grid. Grout with a color that is closer in tone to the tiles tends to deemphasize the pattern. Cement-colored grout is a good choice for most applications. Wider joints (up to $1/2$ inch) will make the irregularities in the sizes of handmade paver tiles less obvious.

The key to mixing a strong grout is cleanliness and using only enough liquid to make the grout spreadable. Pour about three-quarters of the liquid you think you'll need into a clean bucket, and gradually add the powder. After all the dry ingredients have been mixed in, add the rest of the liquid little-by-little, checking the consistency as you go. The initial mix should be wet enough to spread with a trowel but stiff enough not to run. Let it slake for ten minutes, and then stir it to loosen it up. If it's so stiff that it won't stick to the sides of the tiles, add a little more liquid, let it slake again, and remix. Grout that's ready to use will have the consistency of creamy peanut butter: given a slight shove, it will slide rather than pour from the bucket, and it will hold peaks when spread.

The quantity of grout it takes to cover a given area depends on the width and depth of the grout joint as well as the size of the tile. But for an estimation, allow 15 pounds per $1/8$-inch joint width for standard $4 \times 4 \times 1/4$-inch tiles, 25 pounds per $1/8$ inch for $6 \times 6 \times 1/2$-inch quarry tiles, and about 13 pounds per $1/8$ inch for $8 \times 8 \times 3/8$-inch floor tiles for every 100 square feet of area. Allow 30 pounds per 100 square feet for 1×1-inch mosaic tiles with a $1/8$-inch joint. For example, increasing the joint width from $1/8$ inch to $1/4$ inch for a 6×6-inch tile doubles the grout amount from 25 to 50 pounds.

To ensure uniform coloration and drying characteristics, take care to use identical proportions and observe the same order of mixing with each additional batch. If you need more than one bag of grout, make sure that the batch numbers are identical.

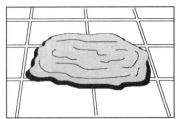
Dump grout on tiles

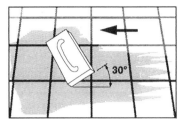
Spread with grout trowel

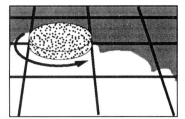
Repeatd circular passes with grout sponge

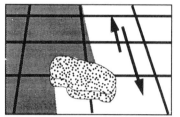
Parrellel long pulling passes

23-19 *Grouting tiles.*

Cheesecloth rub to remove haze.

Dump enough grout onto the tile to cover about 10 to 20 square feet—for walls scoop the grout from the bucket with a steel trowel, and deposit it onto the grout trowel (see **23-19**). Spread it over the tiles with a rubber-faced grout trowel held at about a 30-degree angle to the surface. Push and pack the grout into the joints by going over the surface at least two or three times. Then, holding the trowel at almost a right angle, strike the excess grout off the tiles by running the trowel diagonally across them (running the trowel square with the tiles tends to rake the grout out of the joints). Stir the grout remaining in the bucket before grouting a new area.

Start cleaning the grout residue off the face of the tiles as soon as the grout has started to set up (anywhere from five to 20 minutes). Grout joints that are ready for finishing should be resilient and firm, but not hard. If you wait too long to begin cleanup, the hardened grout can be removed with hard scrubbing by a plastic scouring pad.

As an inexperienced tilesetter, rather than trust the efficacy of your trowelling technique, it's good idea to compact the grout joints with a striking tool (a short piece of metal tubing or a teaspoon also works well) and fill in any voids or resulting low spots before proceeding to cleanup.

Every tilesetter has his or her own method for grout cleanup. Since the grout is quickly absorbed into the porous surface of unglazed and nonvitreous tiles, timely and thorough cleaning is critical if you wish to avoid staining the tiles or the tedious scrubbing and hazardous acid-washing it takes to remove the stains. One way to make grout cleanup easier is to seal the face of unglazed tiles before you install them so that both the grout and excess adhesive won't stick to them. A second coat of sealer is applied after the grout has fully cured. If you do seal the tiles, don't let any sealer run over onto their edges, where it will prevent a good grout bond.

Begin the cleanup by moistening a grout sponge (a $5 \times 7 \times 2$-inch high-quality sponge with rounded corners that won't rake out the joints) in a bucket of clean water. Wring the sponge out as dry as you can, and run it gently over the surface of the tiles in a circular pattern to loosen and pick up the grout particles, being careful not to gouge the joints. Turn the sponge over as soon as it fills with grout. The key to grout cleanup is to rinse out the sponge frequently and to wring it out well. As long as you keep the sponge rinsed and wrung, you won't need to change the water in the bucket very often.

The first pass of the sponge should pick up most of the surface grout. A second pass neatens and shapes the grout joints themselves. If the tiles have sharp, square edges, the grout is finished flush with the surface. If the tiles have a slightly rounded edge, the grout joints will be lower, and slightly concave. The important thing is that, whatever contour you give them, it should be consistent.

The third pass removes the residue from the surface of the tiles. Rinse and wring out the sponge. Then make a short straight pass (about three feet long), pulling the sponge *slowly* towards you without stopping (this prevents the sponge from leaving streaks). Turn the sponge over, and make a second parallel pass; then rinse and wring out the sponge. Continue making parallel passes across the entire area. Let the tiles sit for about 15 minutes so that the surface moisture left by the cleaning can evaporate. Then, rub the tiles with a cheesecloth or old diaper cloth to remove the grout haze.

If you didn't clean the tiles well enough during the initial sponging, or let the grout soak into a porous tile, the haze may resist your cleanup attempt. Sometimes additives in the grout cause cleanup problems too. If scrubbing with a damp plastic scouring pad followed by the cheesecloth doesn't do the trick, use a special nonacidic, nontoxic grout-haze cleaner that you can purchase from your tile dealer. If the haze still remains, let the grout dry for at least four days, and then try cleaning it off with a wet steel-wool pad or a stiff brush and a mild scouring cleanser.

Acid cleaners should be used only as a last resort when all other methods fail. Wait a month for the grout to cure completely. Try scrubbing the tiles with full-strength vinegar and a plastic scouring pad. Failing this, use a muriatic acid cleaner. Wear rubber gloves, goggles, and a toxic vapor mask for protection from fumes and splatters, and keep a bucket of clean water nearby in case of accidental skin contact. When diluting the acid, always mix the solution outdoors and pour the acid into the water to reduce the amount of heat and fumes given off.

Wet the area with water first, and then scrub the surface with a stiff brush dipped into the solution. After cleaning, rinse the area with water at least three times to remove all traces of acid residue.

LAYING A NATURAL STONE FLOOR

Natural stone floors are attractive and virtually indestructible. The key to a successful installation is to choose a stone that has a reliably flat surface and a fairly uniform thickness—and, most important, one that tends to break at a 90-degree angle to the face. It should also have a pleasing color and be porous enough to permit the application of a protective sealer. *Gauged stone* is any quarried stone that has been cut (and sometimes polished) to consistent dimensions. The gauged slate tiles popular for floors and hearths are installed in the same way as standard ceramic tiles. They're soft enough to rough-cut by breaking over an edge. For less waste and better cuts, use an ordinary masonry blade in a power saw. Since the blade can be lowered with each successive pass, a radial-arm saw is more accurate and safer than a hand-held circular saw for this purpose. With a chop saw, it's all too easy to jam the blade as it turns into the cut.

Cleft stone, such as flagstone, is split along natural cleavage planes and can vary considerably in thickness. The stones can be left natural on both faces or one face can be polished smooth.

Quarry stone typically sells by the *ungraded ton* or by *select*. The tonnage is cheaper, but much of it will end up as waste. Select stone costs at least twice as much as tonnage, but there will be very little waste. The most economical strategy is to buy a mix of about one-third select and two-thirds tonnage.

Like tile, a stone floor can be laid over either a wood or concrete substrate (see **23-20**). Over wood, the best and most durable job results if you lay a floated mortar bed as a base for setting the stone. Some stonemasons prefer to lay the mortar and bed the stone in a single

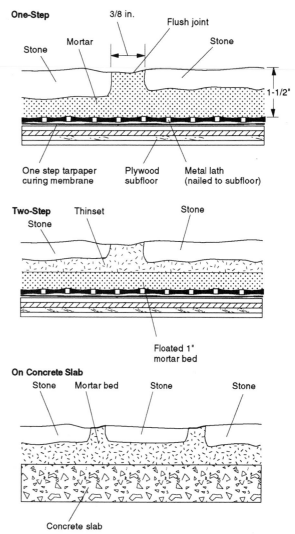

23-20 *Stones can either be set directly in fresh mortar, glued to a floated mortar bed with thinset, or mortared to a concrete slab.*

operation instead. In either case, mix a latex additive into the deck mud to prevent efflorescence between the joints. If a concrete slab is used for the setting bed, letting it cure for a full month should prevent this problem. A tar-paper curing membrane should be glued to a plywood subfloor. Nail galvanized metal diamond reinforcement lath to the floor with galvanized 8d nails as well.

Some masons prefer to dry-lay the stones in convenient sections first. They set the dominant stones, and then select others to fill in between them. The object is to strive for a balanced pattern, with a pleasing variety of stone sizes with few or no tiny filler pieces and a fairly consistent joint width. The process is akin to putting together a giant jigsaw puzzle. To save time and labor, try to use as many "naturals" (uncut stones) as possible.

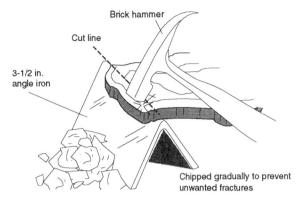

23-21 *Cutting natural stone. Chip gradually to prevent unwanted fractures.*

As you select the stones, check for internal fractures that would cause the stone to fall apart with use. Strike the stone with a hammer. A dull thud instead of a ringing sound indicates a reject.

To cut a stone, set it in place and lay the previously laid stones over it so you can scribe a line with a felt-tipped marker to guide the cut (this is one big advantage to dry-laying the stone). Then set the edge of the stone over an inverted length of 3½-inch angle iron, and chip away at it with a brick hammer (see **23-21**). To increase the odds that the stone will break where you want it to, don't try to make the cut all at once. Slide the stone forward over the cutting edge as you gradually break it off with the hammer. The process is similar to using nibblers to cut an irregular opening in a tile.

Some masons use a diamond wet saw to speed up the cutting process. But the cut edges made by a wet saw will have an unnaturally rectilinear appearance that is at odds with the reason for laying a stone floor in the first place.

Whether you opt for the one-step approach (see **23-22**) or lay the stones in a floated mortar bed, each stone is set one at a time.

With the one-step method, a dollop of mortar is thrown onto the floor and worked into the lath (assuming a plywood subfloor since no lath is needed with concrete). As with tile adhesives, the consistency of the mortar is very important. A good recipe for a strong mortar suited to high-traffic areas consists of 2¼ parts sand, one part masonry cement, and ¼ part lime with enough water to make it stiff enough to support the stone, but not so stiff that it won't ooze up between the stones. As masons say, it should have good "squeeze."

The stone is dropped onto the mortar bed and leaned or stepped on to set it approximately at its finish height. Level lines snapped on the walls or screeds set at the edges of the installation mark the desired level of the finish surface. The stones are checked for correspondence with the lines and for level across their surface with a four-foot level. Tap the stone with the butt of the trowel or a rubber mallet to bring it into final level and also to set it firmly. There shouldn't be any voids between the stone and the mortar bed. Tap the freshly bedded stone with a hammer. A hollow sound indicates a void. Lift the stone, add more mortar to the bed, and reset it. Starting off with enough mortar in the first place saves a lot of trouble. Set about 40 or 50 square feet of stone, and then start the finishing process.

If your mortar had the right squeeze, the joints between the stones will be fairly well packed with mortar. Fill in the rest of the gap with a tuck-pointing trowel (a skinny-bladed trowel used for packing mortar into joints). Then remove the excess mortar and float a thin layer of mortar over the entire floor with a damp sponge. After letting the mortar harden for a couple of hours, wipe off the stones with a wet sponge, being careful not to gouge the joints.

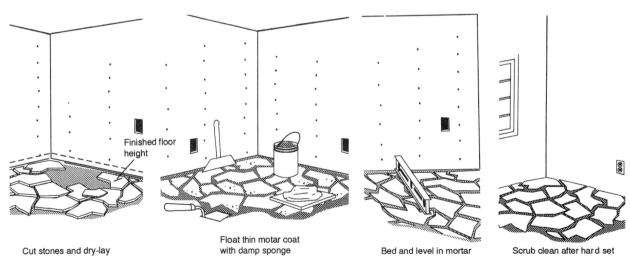

Cut stones and dry-lay   Float thin mortar coat with damp sponge   Bed and level in mortar   Scrub clean after hard set

Finished floor height

23-22 *One-step method for setting stones in mortar.*

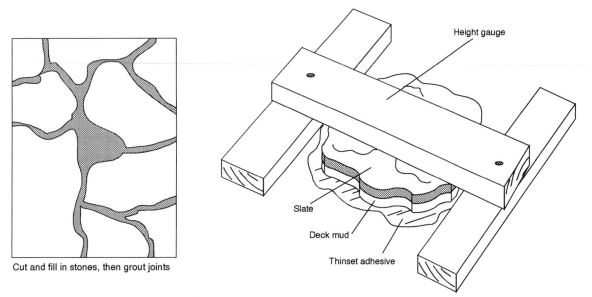

Cut and fill in stones, then grout joints

Height gauge

Slate

Deck mud

Thinset adhesive

23-23 *Setting the stones on a level bed allows you to use a height gauge instead of screeds or strings.*

Then let the floor set until the next day. Wet the floor with water, and then scrub it with a solution of one part muriatic acid to eight-to-ten parts water, using a stainless steel or green plastic scouring cloth. The floor must be kept wet throughout the acid wash to prevent the acid from burning the mortar and staining the stone. Mop up the acid solution with sponges, and scrub the floor with water until all traces of the acid are rinsed off.

If the floor begins to effloresce, scrub it with vinegar after the mortar has completely dried (it will turn light grey). Then apply a sealer to waterproof the stone. As with any tile or masonry sealer, the floor will have to be recoated annually to keep it looking like new.

The main difference between the above method and the two-step method is that the joints between the stones are filled with grout rather than mortar, which, if properly done, avoids the need for the acid-wash cleanup. Since the mortar should have very little squeeze, use a deck mud mix.

Instead of setting the stones a section at a time, you can also distribute the main stones across the entire floor and fill in between them. Apply a thin layer of thinset adhesive to the prepared concrete slab or the cured mortar setting bed. Then trowel deck mud over the thinset, butter the back of the stone with additional thinset, and lay it in the deck mortar. If the setting bed or concrete slab is perfectly level, you can use a height gauge instead of a four-foot level to set the stones to the correct height (see **23-23**). This is simply a length of 2×4 nailed to two pieces of blocking whose thickness equals the distance between the setting bed and the finish face of the floor. Straddle the stone with the gauge, and tap it with a hammer until its legs contact the setting bed. Remove the gauge and cut away the squeeze.

The principal stones are set like islands across the field of the bed. Then as the stones are filled in between them, they can be levelled with a straightedge resting on two previously set stones. Rake the excess mud from between the stone joints with a pointing trowel leaving about a ½-inch-deep joint to be filled with grout. Then clean off the surface of each stone with a damp sponge. Let the stones set until the mortar is fully dried, and then fill in the gap as you would for ceramic paver tiles. Since it's much easier for the grout to become trapped on the uneven surface of a cleft stone, it's critical to initiate cleanup quickly and do it very thoroughly. Since wide grout joints crack more easily than narrow ones, use an additive to increase grout flexibility and strength.

24 Interior Trim

24-1 *Finish work is ordered according to a slower, more carefully measured rhythm than frame carpentry; the mindset is different. The tools are kept sharp, the hands are kept clean.*

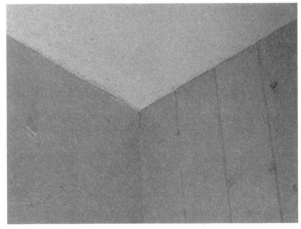

24-2 *Three textures meet in one corner: rough finished plaster and V-groove pine panelling meet a textured ceiling in a clean line. No mouldings are needed to cover up quick and dirty workmanship.*

There is a natural logic to finish work (see **24-1**). It begins at the ceilings and follows the curve of gravity down the walls to the floor. Paint splatters, dust rises, going against the grain makes extra work.

Interior trim proceeds at a different pace and with a different mindset than framing or rough finish. The wood tends to be expensive and easily damaged. Cleanliness is critical. The work area should be cleaned at the end of every day and kept as clean as possible throughout the day. Stray nails and grit seem to be attracted to finish lumber like iron filings to a magnet. Trim stock should be stored indoors, in a convenient place that's out of harm's way. Always wash your hands before handling or working with finish lumber. Be careful not to step on it or drop it. Sharpen your tools, and, if you've been using a general-purpose 20-ounce hammer, switch to a 16-ounce hammer. Some finish carpenters even use a 12-ounce hammer. These simple steps can save a lot of tedious sanding and wasted lumber.

MOULDINGS

Elaborate interior woodwork is one of the hallmarks of old-fashioned houses. Baroque layered and richly patterned crown mouldings ease the transition between walls and ceilings, wainscotted walls terminate in chair rails dressed out with cove and cap mouldings, window and door trim has beaded or raised profiles and ornamental stop blocks, the oversize baseboard where the walls meet the floors is capped and footed with profiled or rounded mouldings (as are the walls). The reductionist trend of twentieth-century construction has tended towards a simplification of the decorative exuberance (some might say excess) of the Victorian style. In contemporary homes, mouldings, when they're used at all, are decidedly less elaborate in profile. This is true even of the full-blown neo-Colonial houses of suburbia, where the trim evokes, but does not reproduce, the line of an earlier, more florid style. Part of the reason is fashion—but much of it is economics. Fancy mouldings are expensive and require skilled labor to install. At the same time, simple flat casings and band baseboards seem to suit modern tastes. They're also inexpensive and easier to install.

Builders in a hurry tend to use moulding as a substitute for careful work. Rather than make a neat joint between wall boards and ceiling (see **24-2**), they hide a gap with crown moulding. Mouldings are also part and parcel of a prefinished panelling installation. Moulding, from such a perspective, is dishonest and looks cheap. I'm thinking, in particular, of the imitation wood-grain "Colonial" or

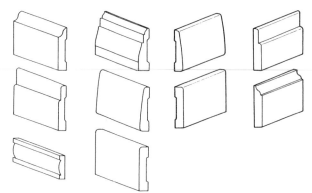

24-3 *Common casing and baseboard moulding patterns.*

Shingle

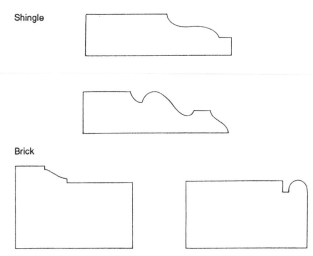

Brick

24-4 *Shingle and brick moulding. Shingle moulding is also used as a decorative band at the top edge of the fascia board, particularly with traditional wood shingle roofs which don't have a metal drip edge.*

"clamshell" window and door casings and baseboards that are the hallmark of prefabricated housing.

If you think of moulding as an "accessory" (in the haute couture sense of the word) to the rest of the house, then it makes sense to choose a pattern that is compatible with or complements the architectural style and line of the house. If your house is a reproduction of an earlier style, pick mouldings that are copies of or suggestive of the woodwork of that period. If your house is more contemporary, simple flat mouldings or none at all may be more appropriate.

That said, what follows is an outline of some of the most common types of standard factory-milled mouldings in use today. You'll notice that several different kinds of moulding can be combined for custom decoration. You can also make your own using any of a wide variety of profiled-cutting bits and a router or wood shaper.

Casing is used to trim around doors and windows and *baseboard* is used at the bottom of walls (see **24-3**). In general, baseboard mouldings are heavier or wider than casing mouldings, but many of the styles are, for all practical purposes, interchangeable, since each profile often is available in several different widths. Patterns that have a rounded-over edge that leads into a simple flattened arc are called "clamshell" casing. The patterns which feature compound curves and various reveals are classed as "Colonial" casing. Nowadays, most baseboard and a good deal of casing is cut on the job from square-edged 1×4 or 1×6 board stock. Depending on the style and the budget, these can be either hardwood or softwood, common (i.e., knotty), or clear/select grade. Number 2 pine is one of the most widely used woods for this purpose. Western red cedar and white oak are other popular choices.

Shingle moulding is ostensibly used instead of square-edged board to make a decorative joint where clapboards or wood shingles butt against the underside of a windowsill or against the soffit (see **24-4**). On the interior, it's sometimes used for shelf cleats and decorative banding at the top of wainscotting, wall and ceiling transitions, and as a

base for other more elaborate mouldings. Although *brick* moulding (also called *brickmould*) was originally used to trim joints between exterior brickwork and wood, today it's the standard exterior casing that comes with factory-built windows and prehung exterior doors. The thickened edge makes a good stop for bevel and shingle siding. Unlike other mouldings, brickmould is almost always factory-primed with wood preservatives and white, water-repellent paint and has no normal interior uses.

Drip caps are installed on the top edges of exterior window and door head casings to keep water from getting into the walls (see **24-5**). They are also used to waterproof the horizontal joints between sheets of panelling and courses of siding and any decorative horizontal trim. The joint between the drip cap and the wall sheathing is normally waterproofed with metal or vinyl flashing and caulking. Many builders find that it's less expensive to mill their own drip caps out of pressure-treated or rot-resistant cedar or redwood stock rather than buying factory stock.

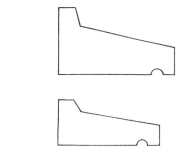

24-5 *Drip cap moulding.*

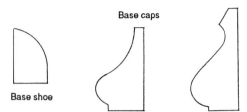

24-6 *Base shoe and cap mouldings.*

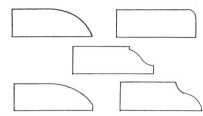

24-8 *Stop mouldings.*

Base shoe and *base cap* mouldings are installed over the floor against the bottom of the baseboard and against the wall on top of it, respectively (see **24-6**). The shoe moulding is useful for hiding expansion gaps, tapered floorboard joints, and gaps between the bottom of the baseboard and an uneven floor. Base cap mouldings add a decorative touch to the top of the baseboard. They can also be used as part of a more elaborate moulding on mantels and for trimming the open stringers of traditional stairs. Neither of these mouldings is widely used with baseboards today.

Crown-and-bed (also called *crown*) mouldings are used at the corners where ceilings and walls meet (see **24-7**). The present-day patterns are only a vestige of the elaborate plaster-of-paris cast crown mouldings of 17th- and 18th-century architecture. Crown moulding was also a prominent part of 18th- and early 19th-century cornice trim, formal porticos, fireplace mantels, and window header casings. The crown mouldings in use today are generally narrower than their Colonial prototypes, but they still use

various traditional combinations of convex and concave curves such as the S-shaped *ogee*, the *cove* radius, and the *round-over*. Simple ogee, round-over, and cove mouldings are also used for base caps and for decorative edge and corner treatment where the greater bulk of a crown moulding would be too overwhelming. Cove moulding is also used to trim inside corners, especially in combination with prefinished panelling. Round-over moulding is often applied to cabinets and doors to create a raised-panel effect. A round-over router bit is also used to make a decorative edge on square posts and exposed timbers.

Chair rail moulding is basically a flat crown moulding which is sometimes used in reproductions and renovations of traditional houses (refer to **24-7**). In lieu of wainscotting, it's applied horizontally to protect the walls from the backs of chairs.

Stop mouldings have many uses besides providing an edge for doors to close against (see **24-8**). These include guides for sliding and stops for hinged window sashes and edge trim for countertops.

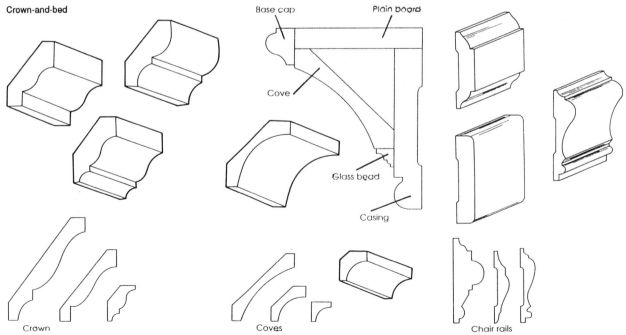

24-7 *Crown-and-bed, cove, and chair rail mouldings.*

24-9 *Screen and lattice moulding.*

24-11 *Round mouldings.*

As the name suggests, *screen* moulding is used to hide the raw edges and help hold screen in its sash (see **24-9**). The thin flat or fluted pieces are nailed into the sash rabbet over the tightly stretched and stapled screen. Screen moulding can also be used to hide the edges of plywood shelving.

Although it's unlikely that you'd build your own lattices since factory-made 4×8 panels are widely available, the thin flat bands of *lattice* moulding can be used for other purposes besides repairing damaged porch lattices. For example, they're often used in place of taping, to finish drywall joints. They also dress up the joints between Homosote (a 4×8×½-inch rigid panel made from compressed paper) porch ceiling panels.

Corner mouldings (also called *corner guards*) are used to trim outside corners, especially with horizontal boarding where a neat appearance is otherwise hard to achieve (see **24-10**). Various sorts of *ply cap* and *back band* mouldings can also be used for corner trim, especially where only one edge is showing. Ply caps and back bands can also be used to make a clean decorative edge on any kind of panel material and for adding a built-up profile to the edges of casings, baseboards, and wainscotting.

Quarter-, *half-*, and *full-round* mouldings have many decorative and practical uses (see **24-11**). Quarter-rounds are mainly used to trim inside and outside corners and as cleats for light shelving. Half-rounds are used for edge-banding shelving, covering joints, and as decorative surface trim. Full-rounds (also simply called "closet pole") are used for curtain rods, bannisters, and closet poles.

There are also numerous types of special-purpose mouldings available for such things as custom window sash construction (see **24-12**). Two of the most common are *astragals*, which make the closing edge of French doors, and *muntins*, which hold the glazing of divided light sashes and screens.

CUTTING AND INSTALLING CROWN MOULDING

Cutting and installing crown moulding well has always been one of those skills that separates the carpenters from the apprentices. It's also one of those things that are easy to forget unless you do it all the time.

Back when crown mouldings were milled by hand, they usually had a triangular cross section, which made the stock somewhat easier to position for cutting. But, since only the profiled face of the moulding is visible, all but the two narrow edges that bear on the wall and ceiling surfaces are now cut away to save material. While the relieved profile of modern crown moulding does make it easier to bend and twist the pieces to follow crooked walls and untrue corner angles, it also makes it very confusing to find the right orientation of saw blade to moulding angle. Eventually, I stopped trying to remember how I'd done it the last time and made the correct cuts for an inside and an outside corner on each end of a short piece of crown stock to make a pattern that I could keep in my toolbox.

The problem with crown moulding (and any other profiled moulding such as clamshell baseboard that meets in an inside corner) is that a mitred joint will almost always open up when you nail the pieces together. Also, a mitred joint can only fit perfectly into a perfect 90-degree corner. Since these are rare in real carpentry, most mitre joints fit poorly.

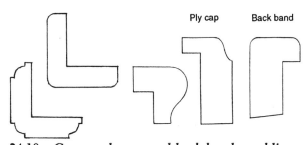

24-10 *Corner, ply cap, and back band moulding.*

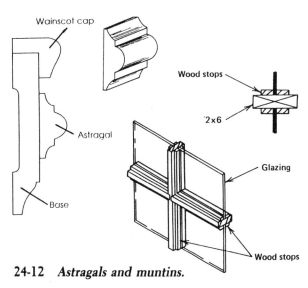

24-12 *Astragals and muntins.*

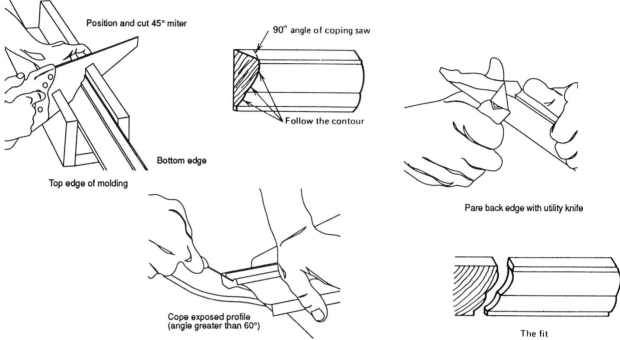

24-13 *"Upside down and backwards" method for cutting crown moulding.*

The solution is to *cope* the inside corners. A coped joint is a butt joint where one piece is cut to match the profile of the other. The first piece is cut square and butted into the corner. The opposing piece is cut on a compound mitre—at an angle to the face (the bevel) and at a 45-degree angle across the face (mitre)—which exposes the profile of the moulding. The back part of the stock is then sawn away with a fine-bladed coping saw, leaving only a thin edge showing that butts neatly and tightly against the first piece.

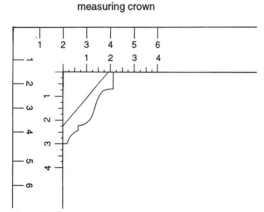

24-14 *Installed versus nominal width of crown mouldings.*

The tricky part is getting the compound mitre cut right the first time. Any old-time carpenter will tell you that the right way to cut crown moulding is "upside down and backwards" (see **24-13**). Because the profiled edge of a crown moulding is similar to a hip or valley rafter in that it's the hypotenuse of a triangle formed by the intersection of two sloping planes, it can't be cut by laying it flat on the saw table or mitre-box base and making a 45-degree bevel cut. Instead, it's cut on a 45-degree mitre (assuming a 90-degree corner, otherwise, the mitre is always half the corner angle) while being held in the same position it will occupy when installed against the wall and ceiling, only upside down and backwards—that is, the edge that will go against the ceiling is placed on the bottom of the mitre box (hence, "upside down"), which reverses the direction of the end that will be coped to the direction in which it will be installed (hence, "backwards").

When properly positioned in the mitre box or against the saw fence, the narrow flat sections at the back of the moulding which will bear against the wall and ceiling will rest square against the bottom and sides of the mitre box. The outside bottom edge of the crown moulding should be the same distance away from the fence as it will be from the corner of the wall. Although crown moulding is sold (and described) according to its overall horizontal width (3⅝ inches is standard), this measurement isn't the same as its installed "width"—i.e., the distance between the wall/ceiling corner and its leading edge (see **24-14**). Since this width will vary with the profile and angle of the moulding face relative to the wall, it's found by aligning a piece of moulding against the blade and tongue of a framing square.

If you're using a wooden mitre box to cut the moulding, you can tack a jig block to its base at the appropriate width to help hold the moulding in proper alignment (some power chop or mitre saws have adjustable clamps for the same purpose). Marking the installed width on the ceiling at the start and end of a moulding run also helps keep it running accurately when walls are less than perfectly straight.

While many professional finish carpenters still find that a simple hardwood mitre box and a 10 or 11 "point" (teeth-per-inch) handsaw are the only tools they need for all their moulding and trim cuts, most prefer the speed and convenience of a chop saw or a power compound-mitre saw over hand tools. If you already have a radial-arm saw on the job, you've got a power mitre box, too. Some trim carpenters use a *Lion trimmer* tool instead. This consists of a heavy, cast-iron fence in which a razor-sharp hand-lever-operated blade moves like a horizontal guillotine to shear off wood with a mirror-smooth cut. But with patience and a sharp, stiff high-quality saw, you can turn out perfectly adequate work with a wood mitre box—which is really nothing more than a jig for holding the saw at the right angle to the workpiece.

Once the crown moulding is cut in the mitre box, the back part of the exposed end grain of the profile must be cut away with a coping saw to leave only the profile. Rest the stock flat on a workbench, and begin cutting at the (true) top of the moulding. Hold the saw at a strong angle to remove as much back stock as you can while following the edge of the profile. End the cut carefully to leave the little triangular piece at the bottom of the moulding intact. This will later make a neat and very tight fit against the other half of the corner joint. Even when cutting at a severe angle, it's usually not possible to remove enough stock at the S-curved portion of the cove to allow a tight fit. Pare the excess away with a sharp utility knife. Try the coped cut against a scrap of moulding before trying it in place.

For the best appearance, give some consideration to the order in which you place the pieces of moulding around the room and where the butt and coped joints will go (see **24-15**). As a general rule, it's best to start by butting the first piece full length on the wall opposite the door. (Coped joints tend to look better when you look at the piece that was butted than they do looking at the pieces that were coped.) Before installing the moulding, locate and mark the studs on the wall with a pencil. Drive probe nails through the drywall where the holes will be covered by the moulding. Cut the starting piece snug enough so that you'll have to "spring" it into place. Drive 6d or 8d finish nails into the wall studs through the flat section at the top of the bottom cove and into the ceiling joists (or ceiling nailers) through the top of the S-curve just below the top of the moulding. If there's no ceiling blocking, drive longer nails directly into the top wall plate instead.

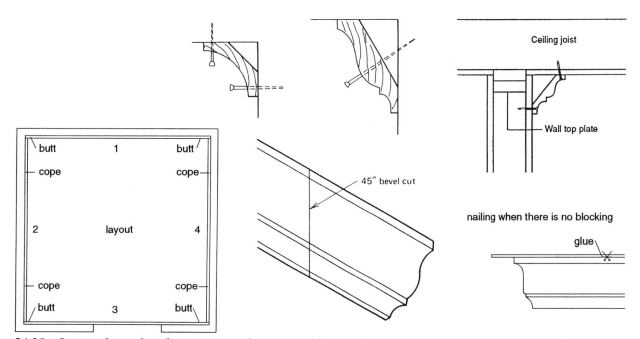

24-15 *Layout for and nailing crown and cove mouldings. When there's no backing behind the mould-ing, run a bead of glue and drive two finish nails at opposing angles to clamp the moulding against the wall until the glue sets.*

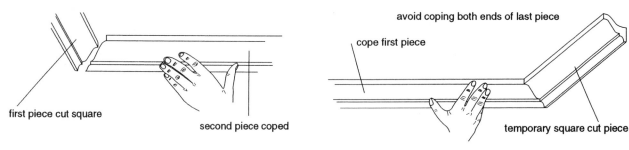

first piece cut square

second piece coped

avoid coping both ends of last piece

cope first piece

temporary square cut piece

24-16 *Avoiding having to cope both ends of the last piece to run cove moulding efficiently.*

To find the length of the coped piece of moulding that will fit against the first butted piece, measure from either of the flat surfaces of the installed piece to the opposite wall. Nail the moulding in place, working from the coped end back. Repeat the process for the third piece. The only drawback with this method is that the fourth (closing) piece will have to be coped on both ends. Since this is a little tricky, many carpenters prefer to cope the starting end of the first piece too, fitting it against a square-cut scrap tacked temporarily in place (see **24-16**).

Of course, not all rooms have just four simple walls. Where partitions form outside corners, the order of moulding layout should be determined with an eye to generating as little scrap as possible.

Outside corners are cut with the stock also held upside down and backwards. The only difference is that the angle of the saw is in the opposite direction. (Here's where that template I mentioned earlier comes in handy.) Since the exposed end-grain for an outside corner will be behind the edge, both sides of the joint must be mitred. Back-cutting the angles of the cuts slightly (about 47 degrees) helps ensure a tighter fit. If the corner isn't perfectly square, one side of the joint will overhang the other slightly. Trim the overhang off flush with a utility knife or a sharp chisel, and sand it smooth. The tiny bit of end-grain won't show up when its stained or painted.

For a variety of reasons, it's not uncommon for the profile to vary slightly between different pieces of moulding. The best way to avoid the frustrations that these variations can otherwise cause is to cut opposing corners or spliced pieces out of the same length of stock.

Finally, there are situations where a run of crown moulding must end on an open wall. Here, the end of the moulding should be mitred as for any normal outside corner so that it can be "returned" against the wall. The return piece is mitre-cut off a short scrap and then laid flat and square-cut to finish the return. Since such a delicate piece will crack if nailed, it's glued into place instead. If you need to hold it until the glue sets, drill a pilot hole and drive a 4d nail through the corner joint.

Because the wider the piece, the higher up it lies against the saw fence, crown moulding that's much wider than the standard 3⅝ inches can't be cut easily in the average

mitre box or a 10-inch chop saw using the upside-down-and-backwards method. Theoretically, if you knew the angle described by the face of the crown moulding relative to the wall (standard crown mould is supposed to be 38 degrees) it would be possible to determine the angle of the compound mitre cut that would allow the corner stock to be cut when laid flat on the base of a compound mitre saw or radial-arm saw table. Inside corner joints would require no coping and pieces of crown moulding too wide for the upside-down-and-backwards method could be cut to order. All it takes is a calculator that can do trigonometric functions and a few equations worked out by Stephen Nuding, a mathematically inclined New Jersey carpenter, in conjunction with a friendly neighborhood mathematics professor.

To figure the angles, measure the crown with a framing square to the nearest $1/16$th inch and convert the fractions to three- or four-place decimals to get the required measurements. The mitre angle (M) for a 90-degree inside or outside corner is the inverse tangent (arc tangent) of A (inside ceiling width) divided by C (crown hypotenuse length). Perform the division and then hit the inverse tangent key on the calculator to get the angle of the mitre cut in degrees.

To find the required bevel angle (B) for the same cut, multiply C by the square root of 2 and divide the answer into D (the inside wall width) and hit the inverse sine button.

For corners that meet at angles other than 90 degrees, first measure the corner angle (F) accurately and then apply the following formulas: $M = \tan{-1} \{A / C \times \tan (F/2)\}$; and $B = \sin{-1} \{D \times \cos (F/2) / C\}$. All the trig functions are standard calculator keys.

Coped joints can be used with any sort of profiled moulding so long as its curves don't approach horizontal. If they do, more stock than is practical or possible will have to be removed from the back cut to make a tight joint. Mitring is the only other alternative.

The difficulty in making tight corner joints is one reason why crown (and other types of moulding) are so often painted, instead of being varnished or stained. You can hide a lot of gaps beneath wood dough, sandpaper, and paint. Coped joints will make the tightest corners when working with hardwood. Softwoods can be forced together enough to make disappear small imperfections in a mitre cut. Otherwise, inside corners for mouldings with simple profiles like clamshell baseboard can be satisfactorily cut with a mitre saw. Even here, you'll still need to do a bit of backcutting and fudging with your utility knife. Freedom-form coping and tight, easily made mitre joints are one powerful argument for using square-edged board or simple, flat band-style mouldings in place of the more elaborate profiled traditional types.

INTERIOR WINDOW TRIM

Back when carpenters built their own windows and hung the doors in jambs they'd built from scratch, "casework" was an important part of the finish carpenter's repertoire of skills. The almost universal adoption of factory-built windows and prehung doors has greatly reduced the complexity of trimwork in modern construction (see **24-17**).

Unless they've been custom-built to your specifications (which cost more money and time) the jambs (side frames) of a factory-made window or door will be milled to one of two standard widths; the 4⁹⁄₁₆-inch jamb is intended to match a standard 2×4 wall section which assumes ½-inch exterior sheathing and ½-inch interior drywall; the 6⁹⁄₁₆-inch jambs are matched to the same wall finishes and 2×6 framing. In both cases, the extra 1⁄16 inch gives a bit of leeway in dealing with the usual slight variations in the width of the rough openings.

Since your particular wall may include some combination of rigid foam, strapping, and/or solid lumber panelling, exterior boarding, or thicker-than-normal sheathing, the factory-built jambs must be "extended" to bring them flush with the face of the interior finish wall. Adding the *extension jambs* is thus the first step in trimming out a window or door (see **24-18**).

24-17 *This double-hung window is classically trimmed in red oak. Note the reveal between the edges of the casing boards and the window jambs and how the horns of the stool overhang the apron and project past the face of the casings. The head casing is mitred to the side casings for a tight fit.*

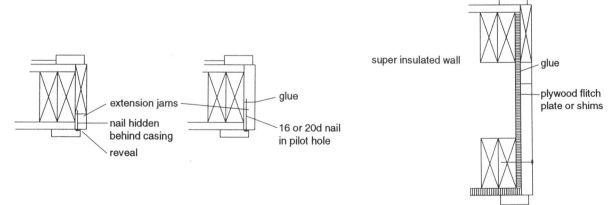

24-18 *Sometimes dealers will "throw in" the extension jambs with a complete window "package." Since most manufactured wood windows are made from pine or red cedar, it's not difficult to make your own jambs from matching wood.*

24-19 *Deep jambs are typical of superinsulated construction. Here the extension jambs frame the window and also serve as narrow casing boards. L-bead butted tight to the casings finishes the edges of the adjacent drywall.*

24-20 *With this window, the casing has been eliminated except for a narrow strip of ½-inch quarter-round moulding nailed and glued to the edge of the jambs and sanded smooth to fit the rough perlited plaster finish.*

Most window manufacturers offer extension jambs as an option with your window order. Although these wood strips are precut for length and rabbeted to mate with the rabbet cut into the standard jambs, they must still be ripped to width. They cost enough that a cost-conscious carpenter will usually find it not too much more trouble and considerably less expense to make their own from clear pine stock.

If the extension jamb is 1½ inches or less deep, it's simply glued and nailed to the existing jambs with finish nails. (Drive the nails slightly to the wall side of center so that they'll be covered by the casing boards.) If the extensions are deeper, predrill pilot holes through the jambs for long finish nails. With superinsulated construction and for extensions otherwise too deep to nail into the jambs, add shims and blocks to the frame as needed and nail through the sides of the extensions instead (see **24-19**).

Wipe off any glue that squeezes out of the joints. Sand the jambs smooth before applying the final finish (see **24-20**).

When the distance between the window jamb and the surface of the wall varies, cut the extension jamb pieces to the widest measurement on each side. Use a block plane or a finger plane to dress the jambs flush with the wall. Carefully level any areas beyond the reach of the plane with a sharp paring chisel.

Extension jambs are installed at the head and side jambs of the unit, before the window *stool*, the two side casings, and the head casing, and the apron are applied.

Unlike extension jambs, which are set flush with the face of the factory jambs, casing boards are always set back (typically about ³/₁₆ inch) from the edges of their jambs (see **24-21**). This detail (the same *reveal* first mentioned in conjunction with soffit work in Chapter Nine) is used

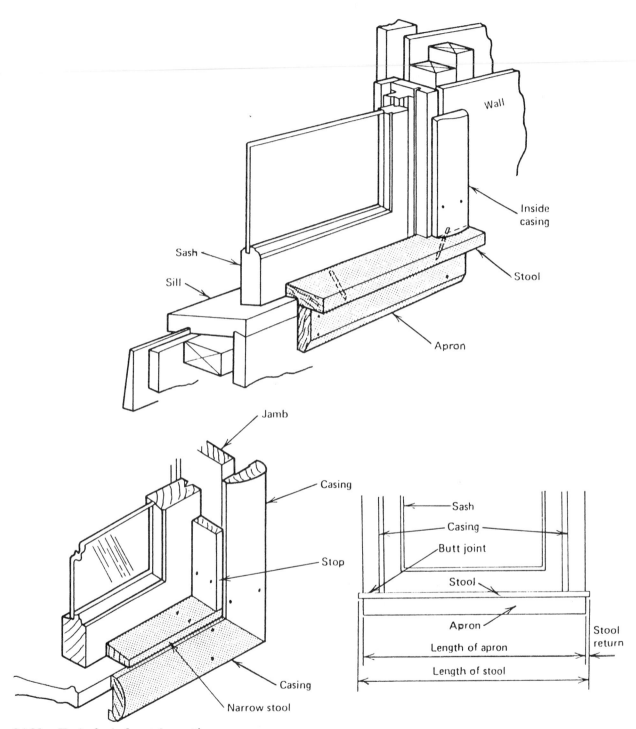

24-21 *Typical window trim options.*

almost anywhere two trim boards butt each other at right angles. Unless the pieces are glued tight together and sanded smooth, the joint between them will always be obvious. By breaking the visual continuity, a reveal trans-

forms what would otherwise be a clumsy butt joint into a deliberate design detail. Small discrepancies in the plumb and level of the jambs can be made to disappear by ever-so-slightly varying the width of the reveal.

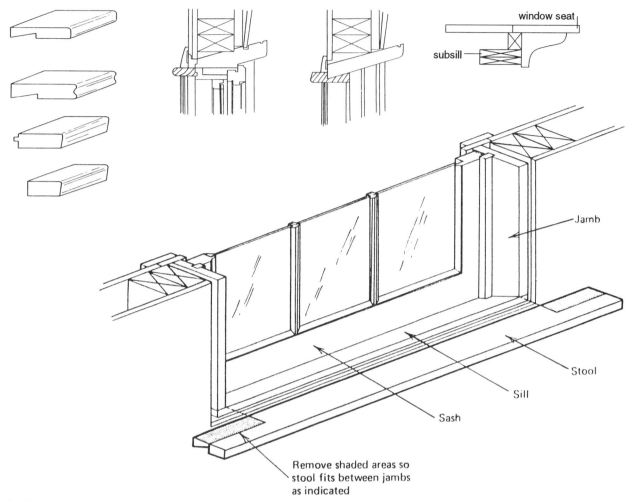

24-22 *Since modern windows mate easily with ordinary one-by stock, there's little need to buy expensive milled window stool moulding, which is typically bevelled to fit the sills of old-fashioned double-hung windows.*

Standard window stools are notched to fit in between the side jambs of the window and have "horns" at both ends on which the window side casings terminate (see **24-22**). At a minimum, a stool has to be deep enough and long enough to extend from the bottom jamb to just beyond the front face and the side edges of the window casings. Usually, the stool is cut slightly wider and longer to leave a half-inch reveal between the face of the casings and the front edge of the stool and between the side edges of the casings and the ends of the stool horns. The width of the stool can be increased even more to form a window shelf (see **24-23**) or even a window seat, in which case support brackets or trim of some kind are added beneath the stool.

Nail shims and blocking to the subsill framing to help support the stool at the correct height. To provide solid nailing for the apron trim board, run the blocking along the entire length of the subsill, and bring it flush with the wall finish (you can also set the blocking flush with the framing and fill in the gap with finish wall material).

It sometimes happens that the angle of the side jambs to the stool is something other than 90 degrees. To scribe the skewed cuts for a tight fit, first mark the room-side corner of the jambs onto the stool with a combination square. Next, use a sliding bevel square to find the actual angle between the jamb and the front edge of the tool and scribe it on the stool through the corner point. Then set a pair of dividers to the width of the jamb and scribe the stool horn from the wall. Check the jamb widths at each side of the window opening. If they aren't the same, one side of the stool will be wider than the other. In this case, you'll have to cut the butt edge (against the window bottom jamb) on a taper before laying out the horn notches. Cut the horn notches long enough to account for the

618

24-23 *This window stool has been extended to form a continuous countertop for the built-in cabinets below.*

width of the casings (on both sides) and their reveals, plus an optional reveal at the ends of the horns. Sand the exposed end-grain of the horns smooth before installing them (see **24-24**).

The side jamb casings are installed next. Mark a point on the edge of the head jamb to indicate the desired reveal and cut each jamb to that length. Before cutting, check across the marks to see if they're level. If not, you'll have to fudge the length of one of the casings and split the difference between the two sides. A taper in the width of

the head casing reveal is usually more obvious than a slightly off-level head casing.

Be sure to fill the gap between the jambs and the framing with fibreglass or expandable polyurethane foam insulation. Drive nails in pairs—one into the jamb, the other into the framing, working along the length of the casing so that you can pull or push a bowed jamb into line as needed. Cut the head casing to fit the outside measurement of the two side casings, sand the end grain, and nail the casing in place.

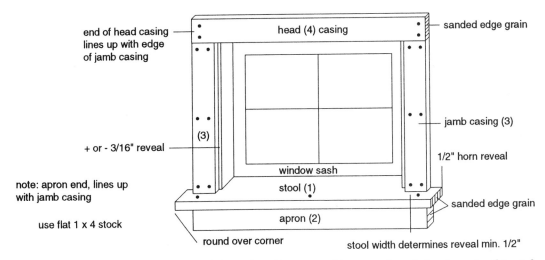

24-24 *Simple square-butted window casing. Because of its reveal and simple cuts, this style of casing is very forgiving of less-than-perfectly-square jamb construction.*

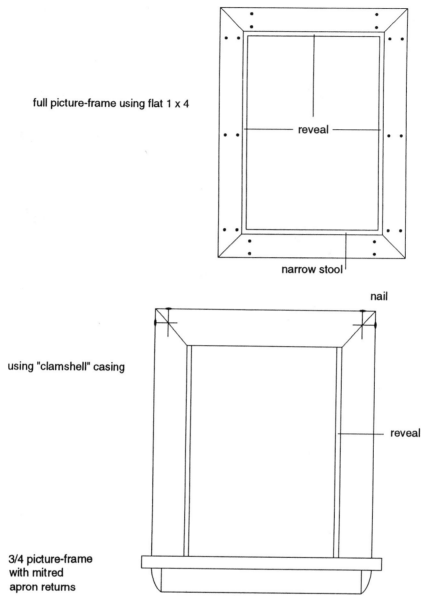

full picture-frame using flat 1 x 4

reveal

narrow stool

nail

using "clamshell" casing

reveal

3/4 picture-frame
with mitred
apron returns

24-25 *Picture-framed casing. Use returns to close off the ends if you use clamshell stock for the apron casing board.*

Finally, cut the apron piece that will be nailed below the stool. Aprons are usually cut to end flush with the ends of the stool horns, with no reveal.

The basic square-butted window casing described above is easy to install and looks good with almost any style of house from classic farmhouse to sharp-edged modern. Because boards shrink across the grain, butt-jointed casings do have a tendency to open up where the side casings meet the head casing. Because the shrinkage pulls the adjacent boards towards each other, the 45-degree mitre joints of a "picture-frame" casing are less likely to open

up (see **24-25**). But it's much harder to make a tight-fitting mitre joint in the first place. If the corners where the casing boards meet are less than perfectly square, the opposing faces of an accurately mitred joint won't line up or else the casings won't follow the edge of the jambs. If you can't make up the difference in the slack of the reveals, you'll have to fudge the mitre angle instead, which is hard to do in a way that isn't obvious. Face-nailing at the very tips of the mitre cuts can split the end grain. Drive a clapboard nail (finish nails don't have enough pulling power) down through the "point" of the head casing mitre into the point of the side casing mitre to close the corner tight. (You can also toenail through the end grain of a square-butted head casing board to pull it down tight against the side casing.)

The choice between mitred and square-butted corner joints is a matter of taste with flat boards (see **24-26**). With clamshell or Colonial casing, mitre joints are the only option. When ordering moulding stock, don't forget to allow extra length for the length of the mitres. Remember also that the header for a three-foot-wide window must be at least three feet and eight inches in length to cover the casings and their associated reveals. It's better to round off to the next-nearest foot than to try to piece in a short, spliced casing board. In general, avoid splicing by using full-length pieces wherever possible. If splices can't be avoided, cut them with a 22½-degree scarf joint (stain the end grain, if necessary) so that the joints will appear tight even if they shrink a bit.

If you use thicker stock for the head casing (e.g., 5/4 inch with one-inch side casings), the side jamb casings can slide up into a rabbet cut into the bottom edge of the head casing and no shrinkage will be visible. In Victorian houses, both the head and side casings were often butted into thicker decorative corner blocks (see **24-27**).

24-26 *The top edge of this red cedar square-butted window casing has been extended over the side jambs to match the apron. Note that the stool has been replaced by an extension jamb for a simple, sleek look. If mitred joints had been used at all four corners instead, the casing would be a true picture-frame type.*

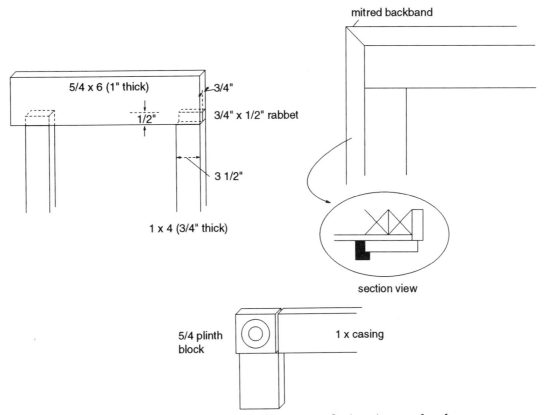

24-27 *More elaborate casing techniques can add elegance to the interior woodwork.*

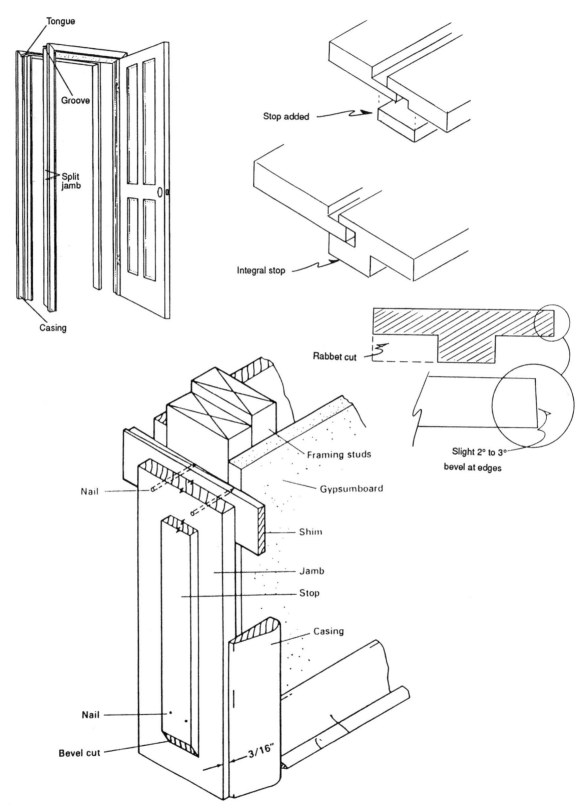

24-28 *Split jambs are also helpful when the walls vary in thickness from one side to the other or from top to bottom, as is sometimes the case in remodelling work.*

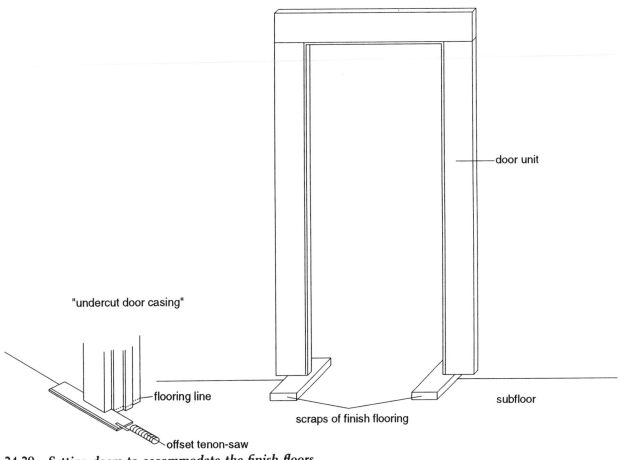

24-29 *Setting doors to accommodate the finish floors.*

Labels on figure: "undercut door casing", door unit, flooring line, subfloor, scraps of finish flooring, offset tenon-saw

TRIMMING INTERIOR DOORS

Much of the material on exterior door hanging that I already covered in Chapter Twelve also applies to interior doors. From the standpoint of installation, the major difference between exterior and interior doors is that because interior doors are lighter, their jamb stock can be thinner, and nailed rather than rabbeted stops are adequate. Interior doors also lack a sill. Their side jambs rest directly on the finish floor. A hardwood saddle is sometimes used to cover the transition when flooring material or its level changes in a doorway between rooms.

Unlike most exterior doors, prehung interior doors are more likely to be installed with ''split'' jambs, which consist of two interlocking sections that allow the jamb to be widened or narrowed to suit the wall thickness (see **24-28**). The stops can be either integral or added. Stops can also be eliminated if a home-built board door is hung flush with the casings, using H- or T-strap hinges. Here the reveal between the casing and the jamb functions as a stop. (This same method is used to hang storm doors.) Another advantage of split jambs is that the door can be ordered with its casings factory-installed on both sides to speed up installation. Despite their obvious convenience, some carpenters avoid split jamb doors because they feel that they (the cheaper brands, in particular) are flimsy and don't hold up well to years of hard service.

In the normal sequence of finish carpentry, the baseboard mouldings always butt against the side casings of the doors. Since the baseboards themselves normally are applied on top of the finish floors, it would seem logical to wait until after the finish floors have been laid to install the interior door units. At the same time, traffic over finish floors should be kept to a minimum to prevent damage to the finish. So most builders install their door units before the finish floors (see **24-29**). As was discussed in Chapter Twenty-two, scribing floors to fit complex profiles is tricky work, particularly when installing hardwood flooring as opposed to vinyl sheet or tile. It's a lot easier to avoid the need for a ''Joe Frogger'' in the first place. One method is to set the door jambs and side casings to height on top of a scrap of finish flooring. Otherwise, scribe the thickness of the finish flooring on the installed jambs, and cut out the bottom of the jambs and casings with an offset-handle, fine-toothed tenon saw.

The hollow-core interior door is the hallmark of low-cost construction. These doors consist of a honeycomb of corrugated cardboard sandwiched between two thin layers of luan mahogany or birch plywood with a band of solid wood around the edges to which the hinges and lockset can be attached. The face veneers are sanded and stained and/or varnished or painted. Use a fine-toothed plywood blade to trim the bottom of a hollow-core door (or any veneer-faced door). Score the cross-cut line with a utility knife first to reduce splintering of the face veneer by the saw blade.

The solid-wood blocking is seldom more than 1½ inches wide. If you ever need to cut a hollow-core door in half or otherwise need to trim it beyond its edge blocking, rip new blocking from a clear, straight 2×4, push the honeycomb material back, and glue the blocking between the veneer layers.

Hollow-core doors are inexpensive; unfortunately, they look it. New traditional raised-panel doors cost more than a budget-conscious builder can usually afford. Luckily, secondhand raised panel doors are a staple item of architectural salvage warehouses, and often they can be pur-

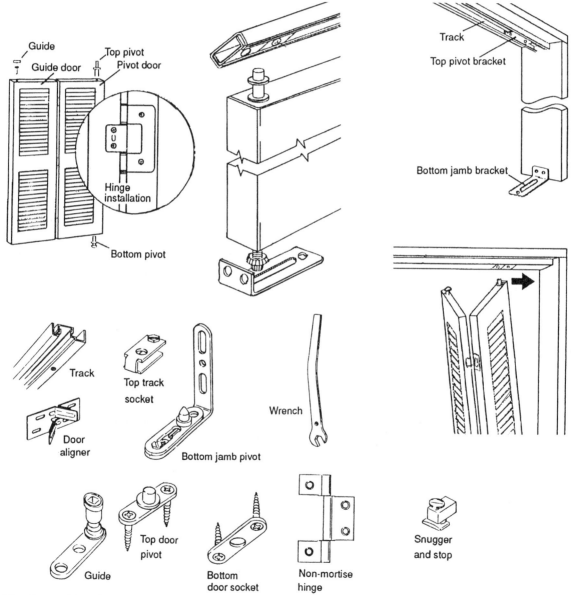

24-30 *Typical bifold door applications and hardware. Calculate rough opening dimensions from the finished opening requirements listed on the door package or dealer's spec sheets before you begin framing.*

chased for a cost comparable to or less than that of hollow-core doors. Since these doors are buried under thick layers of dense and possibly lead-bearing paint, they're best rejuvenated by a commercial strip shop rather than by the do-it-yourselfer. Hot-dip stripping is surprisingly affordable, and, so long as the doors themselves aren't oak (which turns black when exposed to hot-dip chemicals), it doesn't harm the wood. The doors will still require some hand scraping to remove paint residue from the mouldings and sanding to smooth off any "hairy" grain. But, after all costs are accounted for, the finished door will still cost far less than a new panel door, and, when oiled or varnished, it will have a matchless rich, dark patina.

BIFOLD, BYPASS, AND POCKET DOORS

Bifold doors are used for closets and other locations where swing room is limited. The doors are sold in kit form complete with all the necessary hardware and installation instructions. Styles include solid or louvred panel or half-solid-half-louvre and mirrored doors. The louvre doors are typically used for bathroom linen closets or furnace/utility rooms and laundry rooms where good ventilation is desirable. Bifold doors are sized to fit a finished opening. Obtain the correct dimensions from your building supplier. The rough opening should be large enough to accommodate ¾-inch finish jambs at the top and sides.

In a typical installation, a metal track is screwed to the head jamb along the centerline of the doors (see **24-30**). A metal pivot bracket is screwed to the finish floor at the bottom corner of the jamb. A nylon pivot bushing and a nylon guide bushing fit into predrilled holes in the top of the door and a single, adjustable metal pivot bushing fits into a hole in the bottom of the door. To mount the door, lift the top pivot bushing into its socket in the guide track while inserting the slide bushing into the track at the same time. Drop the bottom pivot bushing into the floor bracket, and adjust it for height by pushing on its cogs with a screwdriver. When correctly hung, the gaps between the door and its jambs should be even.

With *double bifold* doors a metal or plastic aligner is screwed to the bottom inside edge of one pair of doors to catch the back of the second pair of doors and push it forward so that they both close evenly. An adjustable spring-loaded "snugger" can also be installed in the top track to hold the doors tight against each other when they're closed.

A strip of trim is usually nailed to the head jamb to hide the edge of the metal track (see **24-31**). The strip can be offset in from the door casing or else the doors (and/or trim strip) can be set forward in the opening so that the strip is cased with a standard reveal. The side jambs can be treated in the same manner. In this case, the edge of the doors will close behind the side strip.

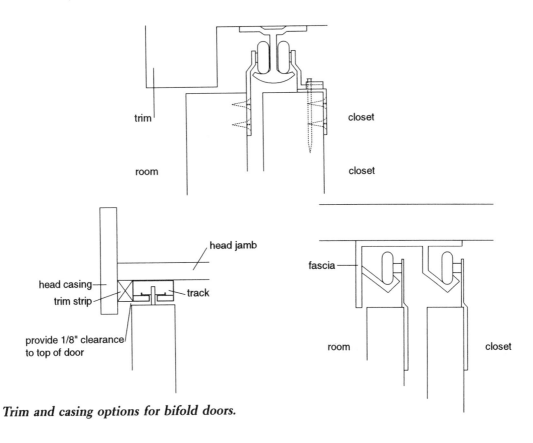

24-31 *Trim and casing options for bifold doors.*

625

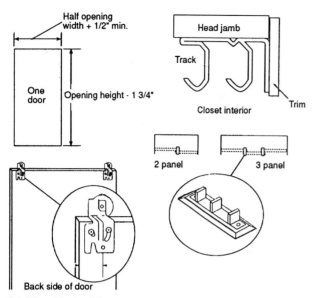

24-32 *Typical bypass door installation. When sizing the opening for bypass doors, allow an inch for the door overlap.*

Bypass (also called *"sliding" doors*) are also widely used for closets (see **24-32**). These units hang from double metal tracks screwed to the head jamb. Depending on the design of the track, it may feature an integral metal trim fascia or else require a wood trim strip which is installed after the doors are hung. As with bifold doors, bypass doors are sold in kit form with all the necessary hardware and mounting instructions included. Once the doors are hung and adjusted for height and plumb, a guide is screwed to the finish floor at the door overlap to keep the doors perpendicular as they move past each other.

A *pocket door* is a sliding door that disappears into the wall (see **24-33**). Pocket doors are installed as a unit in a rough opening large enough to include both the door and the factory-built pocket frame, which usually consists of horizontal 1×4 boards on 16-inch centers that furnish a nailing base for the wall finish, attached to metal verticals. The fasteners used to attach the finish wall to the frame shouldn't be so long that they penetrate through the frame and scratch or otherwise interfere with the operation of the sliding door. The better units have rubber bumpers so the door slides silently into its pocket.

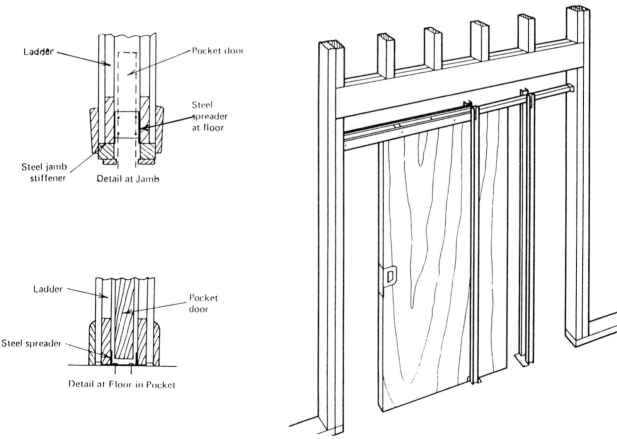

24-33 *Pocket door installation. Some of the less expensive units provide little support for attaching the finish wall.*

BASEBOARDS

Since (except for carpeting) baseboards are applied on top of the finish flooring, they're normally the last item to be installed (see **24-34**). But, as with door units, to limit traffic on the finish floors it's a good idea to precut the baseboards before laying the floors (see **24-35**).

Although compared to the current practice of a strip of clamshell or simple band of 1×4 board, a 1×6 topped with an ogeed cap might seem fancy, it's a pale vestige of the eight-or-more-inches-wide baseboard fitted with a cap and shoe mouldings that was de rigueur in the houses of yesteryear.

24-34 *This baseboard has a rounded-over edge that matches the profile of the door jamb casing and goes well with the rough plaster wall finish. Small gaps between the plaster and the baseboard were filled with paintable latex caulk.*

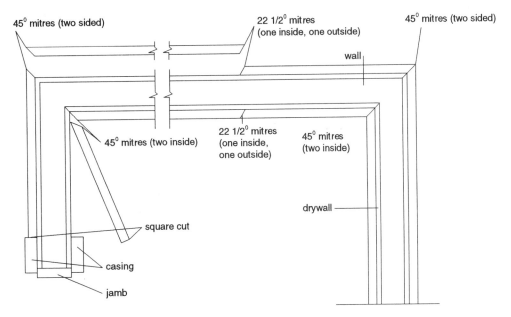

45° mitres (two sided)

22 1/2° mitres (one inside, one outside)

45° mitres (two sided)

wall

45° mitres (two inside)

22 1/2° mitres (one inside, one outside)

45° mitres (two inside)

drywall

square cut

casing

jamb

base board cuts

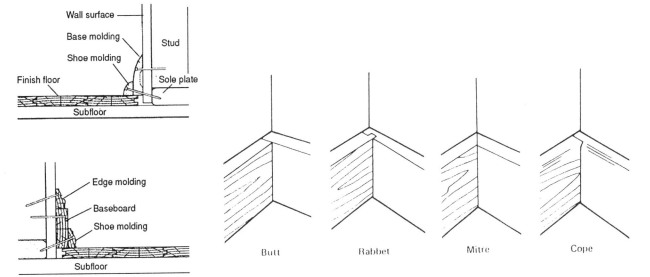

Wall surface

Base molding

Shoe molding

Stud

Finish floor

Sole plate

Subfloor

Edge molding

Baseboard

Shoe molding

Subfloor

Butt   Rabbet   Mitre   Cope

24-35 *Baseboard installation.*

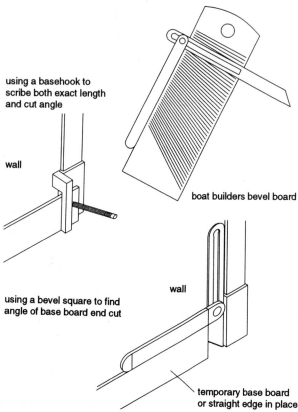

using a basehook to scribe both exact length and cut angle

boat builders bevel board

wall

using a bevel square to find angle of base board end cut

wall

temporary base board or straight edge in place

24-36 *Using a base hook and bevel board to scribe baseboard to door casings. A base hook scribes the exact length and intersecting angle.*

As has already been mentioned, baseboards are butted against door casings. Sometimes the floor or the casing won't run perfectly true and the baseboard will have to be scribed for a tight fit. Since there's no guarantee that the floor itself is perfectly level, laying a bevel square on top of the baseboard and butting it to the casing doesn't necessarily ensure a perfect fit. A U-shaped *base hook* is a homemade tool that slips behind the baseboard and is held tight against the casing so that its front leg transfers the cut line to the baseboard as shown in **24-36.** Another time-saving homemade tool that will prove handy whenever an angle from the bevel square must be translated into degrees of mitre or bevel cut for the saw is a *boat builder's bevel board.* This is simply a length of mahogany board or birch plywood that has been marked with angles from zero degrees to 45 degrees. Scribe the angle marks carefully with a sharp awl and fill them in with indelible ink. The bevel board makes it easy to read an angle from the square and adjust the saw to it.

Baseboard and all other interior trim should be stained (if desired), primed and painted, or varnished before installation to avoid tedious cutting in with the paintbrush against edges. This way, only a quick touch-up coat is needed on the face of the trim to cover any nail spots or other blemishes and to even out the finish. It's also a lot easier to clean water-based wall paint off a varnished edge than off raw wood. If you do stain your trim stock, be sure to tint any wood dough that you'll use to hide the nailheads. To prevent the dough stain from bleeding into the surrounding wood, wait until the trim has been given its first coat of varnish before filling the nail holes.

25 Kitchen Cabinets and Other Built-Ins

As it's generally understood in the building trades, cabinetry includes the construction of kitchen cabinets and countertops, the bathroom sink cabinet, medicine chest, and other "built-ins," such as bookshelves, custom bathtub surrounds, beds, window seats, planters, wardrobes and storage units, and workbenches.

Even though most experienced finish carpenters can build a pretty decent set of kitchen cabinets if they have to, most cabinets today are installed—rather than built on the job. Top-of-the-line manufactured cabinets are every bit as good as, if not better than, a custom-built installation, and comparably priced. The only difference is the added value of uniqueness. Whether the signature of a craftsperson is worth more than the anonymous perfection of the production line is a matter of personal taste. At the other end of the spectrum, cheap manufactured cabinets are markedly inferior to anything a reasonably skilled amateur cabinetmaker could turn out on his own—and they usually look it. Unlike prehung doors and factory-built windows, there isn't any inherent practicality and increased performance in buying rather than building your own cabinets. In fact, many do-it-yourselfers find cabinetry to be one of the most satisfying parts of the homebuilding experience. Just because you have neither the skills nor the tools to duplicate the look of a factory-made cabinet or the refined style of a master craftsperson doesn't mean that your cabinets will lack grace, or be poorly built. Owner-built cabinets may be simple and basic, even a little "funky," but that very lack of a professional appearance can give them a pleasing and unique quality that makes up for any failures in technique or design (see 25-1). Furthermore, since the installation of factory-built cabinets is complicated by walls and floors that are out of square or off level and plumb, building cabinets from scratch to fit the idiosyncrasies of your particular situation can sometimes be a lot less trouble than fudging and shimming store-bought units to fit.

Besides the lifestyle and aesthetic dimensions, one of the reasons so much attention and print is lavished on kitchen design and layout is that the concentration of appliances, specialized work and storage facilities, and the mechanical support systems that supply them with fuel, power, water, and ventilation, make even a small kitchen the most complicated and expensive room to build.

A pleasing and practical kitchen layout begins with the application of good kitchen design principles to the particular habits and living arrangements of the home-owners. Since everyone has a particular vision of his or her own "perfect" kitchen arrangement, what follows is only a general outline of some of the basic arrangements.

25-1 *Even though they may lack the polish and sophistication of a professional site-built or factory-made kitchen, owner-built kitchens typically exude a certain lively charm that more than makes up for flaws in design and technical execution.*

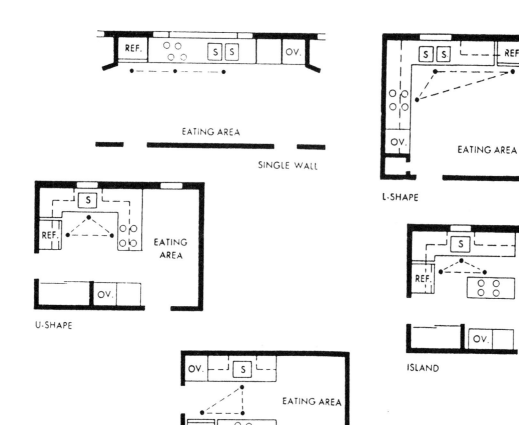

25-2 Most kitchens are some variation of these five basic plans.

25-3 This peninsula U-type kitchen is a classic example of the work-triangle principle. The stove, sink, and refrigerator form the apexes of the triangle and, as expected, the refrigerator is at the end of the longest leg.

25-4 *In this variation of the peninsula kitchen, the backsplash wall of the long, angled countertop which contains the sink and dishwasher separates the kitchen from the dining room and encloses it in a private space without isolating it. The stove is on the wall to the left of the picture. The refrigerator visible in the upper right-hand corner proved to be too far from the other work areas and was moved to the opposite corner, separated from the stove by a small countertop. The space occupied by the refrigerator was turned into a food-storage pantry.*

Kitchens are classified according to the circulation patterns between the various work and storage areas as single wall, corridor (or galley), corner, U, and island (see 25-2). The relationships between the different "work centers" of a kitchen are governed by the kitchen triangle principle (see 25-3). This principle states that the most efficient kitchen is one where the sum of the legs of the triangle formed by the paths between the sink, stove, and refrigerator doesn't exceed 25 feet (see 25-4) and where no leg is longer than 12 feet (25-5).

25-5 *The bulk of food preparation in this bachelor household centers on this compact island, while the rest of the kitchen provides auxiliary work space during social gatherings.*

Standards for the heights of kitchen work surfaces and cabinets embody what is felt to be most comfortable for the average person (see **25-6**). Although someone over six feet tall might find that a countertop set at 39 inches is less tiring to work at than the recommended 36-inch standard height, while a person who stands five foot tall might prefer a 30-inch countertop, bear in mind that nonstandard height counters can have an adverse effect on resale value.

Eat-at counters should be located outside the main work triangle or at least as far away from a cooktop or sink as possible. Stools or chairs shouldn't interfere with doors and kitchen traffic paths. Stools are used for standard 36-inch-high countertops with a 15-inch overhang. An alternative, which effectively separates the eating area of the countertop from the work area, is to build a ledge at 30 inches for use with normal chairs.

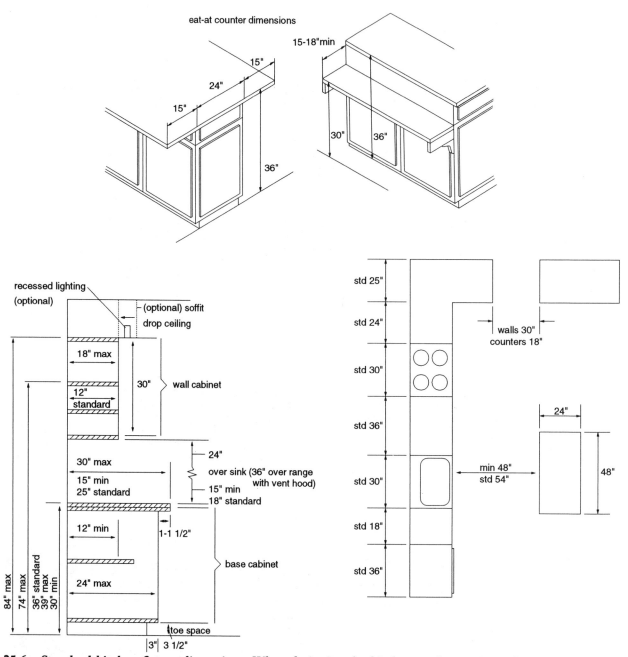

25-6 *Standard kitchen fixture dimensions. When designing the kitchen, make provision for concealing the range hood exhaust.*

The 24-inch minimum clearance of cabinets over a sink is increased to 30 inches over a range to accommodate the range hood. The ductwork for the hood will function more efficiently if it can be run straight up through the roof rather than horizontally through the ceiling and out the walls. Ductless range hoods, which theoretically filter the kitchen air instead of exhausting it to the outside, eliminate the need for a duct chase. Unfortunately, they don't work very well. Obtain the required clearances for your range hood from the dealer before designing the cabinets to which it will attach.

BASE CABINET BASICS

In principle, the simplest cabinets are all variants of the panel and face-frame system. Begin building the base cabinet (i.e., one that rests on the floor, as opposed to a wall cabinet) by framing a square and level base on the floor with 2×4s set on edge. Mark the layout full size on the floor, and check its front corners for square. Locate the

front of the base frame 3¾ inches back from the finished face of the cabinet to allow for the "toe space" that lets you stand close to the countertop when working (this assumes a three-inch-deep toe space and allows ¾ inch for the base trim board). Cover the base frame with ¾-inch AC plywood (the back side of the sheet will be hidden and does not have to be of paintable quality). This piece should overhang the toe-space frame by three inches to allow for the thickness of the cabinet face frame. The base panel ends flush with the frame at the sides.

Make any adjustment for an out-of-square wall by tapering the back edge of the base cover piece (see **25-7**). Likewise, when laying out the base frame, check the floor for level first, and use either the highest or lowest point, whichever will affect the toe-space height the least, as a benchmark for levelling the top of the base frame. Usually, it's better to shim the front frame up a bit rather than cut the back frame down. Nail a flatwise backer to the floor to provide extra support for nailing any shimmed front frame piece.

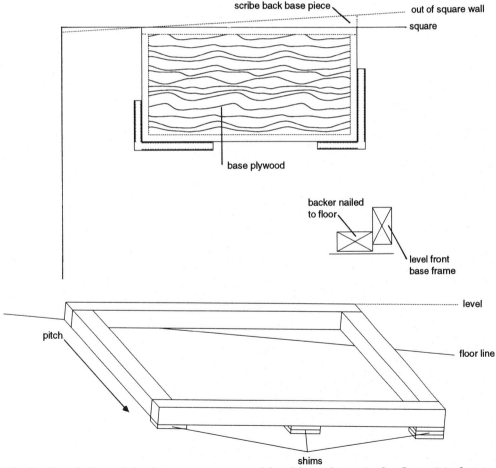

25-7 *As with the foundation of the house, a square and level base frame is the first critical step towards ensuring a good cabinet installation.*

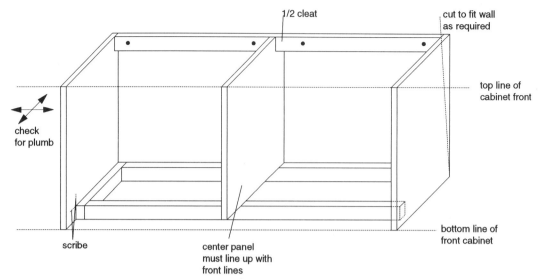

25-8 *Cutting and installing end panels. Check the wall for plumb. You may have to increase the panel width to keep the depth of the cabinet (and countertop) from shrinking too much.*

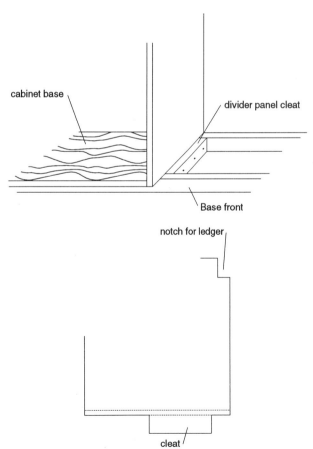

25-9 *Installing divider panels. Glue and finish nails are used when the divider panel is cut to fit on top of a continuous base.*

The side panels for the base cabinet are installed next (see **25-8**). The choice of plywood depends on whether or not the cabinets will be painted or varnished. AB fir plywood or birch plywood are good substrates for paint. MDO plywood is even better. You can also choose a decorative face-veneer plywood such as pine, cherry, oak, or mahogany for a clear varnish finish that highlights the grain pattern of the wood. While not cheap, veneer face plywood is stable, good-looking, and easy to work with. These plywoods are also available with a solid *lumber core* that finishes neatly along the edge, leaving no voids and fewer splinters than *ply-core* plywoods, which makes it ideal for doors with exposed lipped edges.

Check the wall and floor for plumb before cutting the cabinet end panels. Draw a level line on the back of the wall to mark the top of the 1×2 cleat that will support the countertop. Install the cleat, gluing it to the wall and screwing it into the studs. Cut the panel blanks slightly oversize in case you need to scribe their back and/or bottom edges to fit. The front and top edges should be perfectly plumb and level and line up with the other end panel and any intermediate panels the cabinet may contain. Once you're satisfied of the correct fit, notch the bottom of the panel to fit the toe space. Unless the baseboard will wrap around the corner, it generally runs into the end panel rather than over it.

Internal dividers are often installed in base cabinet units, particularly on either side of the under-sink area (see **25-9**). Although they can be cut to fit on top of the base piece, a stronger cabinet results if supports are built into the frame and the divider panels are notched to fit over and attach to them. Instead of a single base piece, separate pieces are cut to fit between each divider. The

634

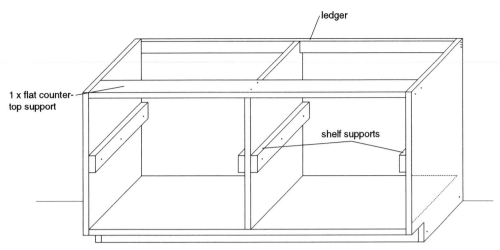

ledger

1 x flat counter-
top support

shelf supports

25-10 *Base cabinet ready for face rails.*

panels can either be notched to fit against the wall cleat
or else the cleats can be cut and butted against the panel
for added strength.

The end panels are glued and finish-nailed or (if a
baseboard will be used) screwed to the base frame and
nailed into the end grain of the wall cleats. Any divider
panels are notched along their top front edges so that the
front countertop support-frame rail can be run in one piece
(usually flatwise) between the two end panels. Before securing this piece and the divider panels, check them all
for plumb once more and tack temporary diagonal braces
across their top edges, if needed, to hold them in position
(see **25-10**).

The joinery involved in trimming out the cabinet face
frame can get quite complicated. Less experienced wood-

workers will do best to use the simple butt joints described
below (see **25-11**).

The end stiles (vertical pieces) are installed first by
gluing and finish-nailing them to the raw front edge of
the end panels. The width of the stiles is basically arbitrary,
depending on the desired width of the doors. One-by-
three (2½-inch) boards are one of the most common
widths. The stile should extend slightly past the bottom
edge of the plywood base panel (about ⅛ inch). Next,
glue and nail or screw the top horizontal to the countertop
front frame piece. Rails are normally narrower than stiles
(1¼ to 1¾ inches is typical). They should be wide enough
so that the overhang of the countertop lip (½ inch to ¾
inch) and the overlap of any drawer or cabinet door front
still reveals a satisfying amount of rail.

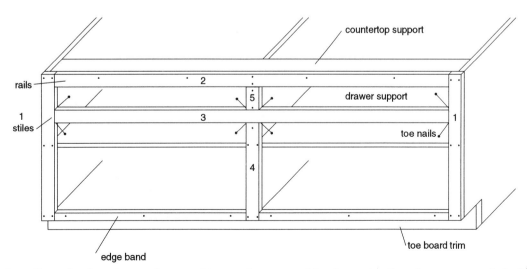

countertop support

rails

2

5   drawer support

1
stiles

3   1

toe nails

4

edge band

toe board trim

25-11 *Installing the face frame. Some cabinetmakers assemble the entire face frame as a unit before
attaching it to the front of the cabinet.*

The face stiles are nailed over the front edges of any divider panels. Some cabinetmakers prefer to fasten a second, continuous horizontal rail to the flatwise support for the drawer bottoms and fill in short vertical pieces between the two horizontal rails—rather than run the stiles full length—and fit the drawer bottom rails in between them. The rails and stiles can be joined with a simple, glued butt joint reinforced with toenailed 4d nails until the glue sets up. For decorative effect and added strength, you can also notch the rails and stiles into each other with a simple dado or a fancy dovetail joint.

Next, install any intermediate stiles, running them down from the drawer rail to the base. These provide supports for pairs of cabinet doors to hinge from or close against. Add additional drawer rails, as needed. These should be at least wide enough so that some reveal remains between closed drawer fronts. (For example, with a standard ⅜-inch drawer front lip, the drawer rails should be at least one inch wide to leave a ¼-inch reveal between the closed drawers. A 1½-inch-wide rail will leave a more robust ¾-inch reveal.)

Finally, cover the exposed front edge of the base plywood with a strip of trim wide enough to overhang the bottom by ⅛ inch to match up with the bottoms of the stile pieces.

WALL CABINETS

Wall-hung cabinets can be built in the shop and fitted with a back of ¼-inch luan plywood or MDO-type plywood or else built in place, utilizing the wall itself as the backing material. Although 1×12 or ⁵⁄₄×12 pine boards are often used to build wall cabinet carcasses and shelving, they limit the overall depth of the cabinet to 11¼ inches. Plywood or laminated shelving board are used if deeper cabinets are desired.

As with base-cabinet construction, check the walls for plumb before starting to build the cabinet frame (see **25-12**). The back edges of the side and shelving boards may have to be cut on a taper so that the cabinet fronts are plumb. For a backed cabinet, insert tapered shim pieces as needed between the cabinet back and the wall, and cover the gap at the wall with a flat band or a suitably profiled corner moulding.

Unless you don't mind using a stepstool to reach items stored on it, the top shelf of a wall cabinet unit shouldn't be any higher than 74 inches. Although some homeowners might wish to utilize the space above the standard cabinet top shelf for storing seldom-used items, the standard approach is to drop the ceiling height to about 7'-6" and hang the top of the wall cabinets from this soffit (see **25-13**). Since a seldom used area is a seldom cleaned one, for all practical purposes the storage space in extra-tall wall cabinets or between the top of a standard cabinet and the ceiling is more or less useless.

The cabinet soffit is usually framed directly below the finish ceiling using 2×2 lumber. It can also be built as part of the interior framing instead. This is often done when the soffit will also be used to conceal plumbing drains, water lines, and HVAC ducts—which are best installed prior to the wall finishes. If the soffit projects out beyond the face of the cabinets, it can contain recessed lighting fixtures which are ideal for supplemental task lighting. Otherwise, it can be treated as an extension of the finish wall or the cabinet top rail.

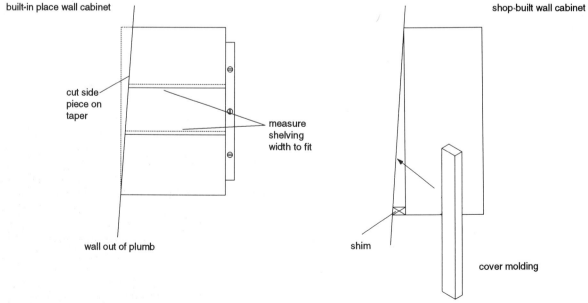

25-12 *When the wall is out of plumb, each individual shelf will have to be scribed for a good fit.*

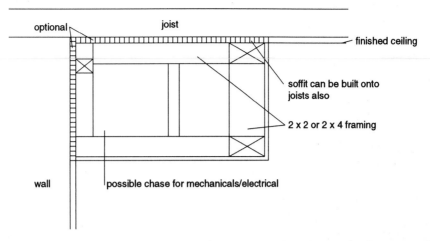

25-13 *Wall cabinet soffit. If recessed lights are to be installed in the soffits, locate the fixtures so that they do not interfere with the swing of the wall cabinet doors.*

As with every aspect of cabinetwork, there are any number of equally acceptable ways to support the shelving in wall cabinets (see **25-14**). The simplest is to use one of the prefabricated steel track and shelf support clip systems that let you change shelf heights as needed. The tracks can be screwed to the face of the cabinet side panels or semi-concealed in dadoes cut down their lengths. Some systems dispense with the tracks and use round pegs inserted into equally spaced, drilled holes to support the shelves.

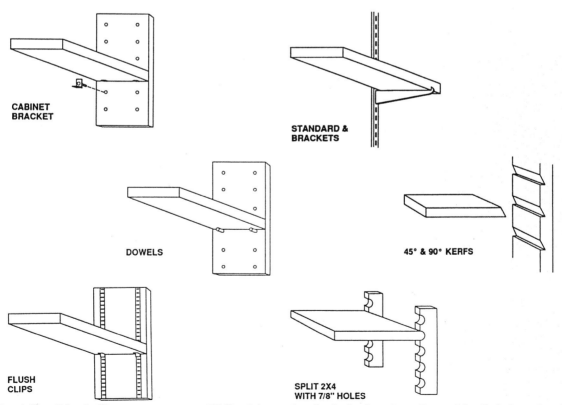

25-14 *Adjustable shelf-support systems. Wall cabinets that lack the bracing effect of fixed shelves should be stiffened with a ¼-inch plywood back.*

25-15 *This countertop ends in a storage shelf with a built-in copper-lined planter for kitchen herbs or house plants. Note the simple dadoed shelf supports cut in pine.*

25-16 *In this kitchen, dead space was turned into a useful storage unit by shrinking the back of the utility closet partition slightly inward and filling in the spaces with narrow shelving for hanging frequently used skillets. The family's wineglasses are stored behind the sliding door panels, which are made from ¼-inch hardboard covered with plastic laminate.*

If you have a radial-arm or table saw and the requisite carbide-tipped dado cutter head, quarter-inch-deep dadoes cut across the inside faces of the end panels make the strongest and least cluttered support for fixed shelving (see **25-15** and **25-16**). The shelves are slid into the glue-coated slots and screwed (or nailed) from the outside face (see **25-17**). If the cabinet frame is not already wall-mounted or is not held square by an attached back piece, check the carcass for square and tack a diagonal brace across its back to hold it until the glue sets.

When laying out the dado cuts, line both end pieces up side by side and draw the dado cut lines across both at the same time with your framing square. Use only flat boards for the end panels. Any bows will make the depth of the dado uneven and will affect the fit of the shelf boards, bowing out the end panels or leaving gaps in the dado joints. In most cases, a slight gap isn't a problem since the edges of the panels will be hidden beneath the face stiles that carry the cabinet doors.

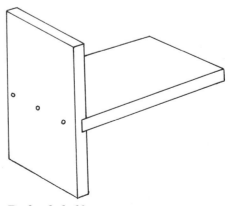

25-17 *Dadoed shelf support.*

Even when the shelving is left open and no doors are used, it's still a good idea to nail stiles at regular intervals across the front edges of the shelving to prevent the boards from twisting and to add stiffness to keep them from sagging. Brass or black iron pipe can also be used as an exposed shelf support (see **25-18**). The shelves are hung on metal pins driven into holes drilled through the edge of the shelf and the pipe itself. These are less cumbersome than the traditional means of supporting open shelving, which relies on triangular wrought-iron or wood brackets. If the shelving has a top as well as end panel, the resulting box-like unit can be screwed into the ceiling (or soffit) and given extra support by a cleat attached to the underside or top edge of the bottom shelf.

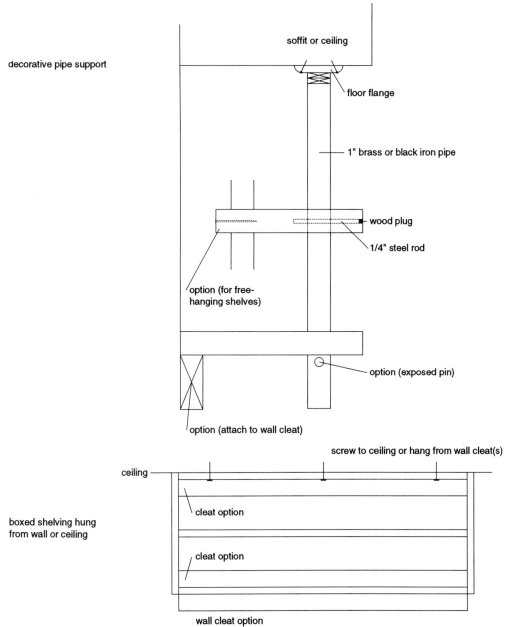

decorative pipe support

soffit or ceiling

floor flange

1" brass or black iron pipe

wood plug

1/4" steel rod

option (for free-hanging shelves)

option (exposed pin)

option (attach to wall cleat)

screw to ceiling or hang from wall cleat(s)

ceiling

cleat option

boxed shelving hung from wall or ceiling

cleat option

wall cleat option

25-18   *Pipe can be used to make an interesting shelf support that hangs from the ceiling. In light of the considerable weight kitchen shelves will often carry, the flanges that attach to the pipe should be lag-screwed into or through-bolted to solid backing.*

639

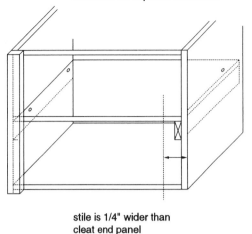

treatment for exposed cleat ends

stile is 1/4" wider than
cleat end panel

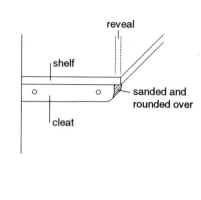

reveal

shelf

cleat

sanded and
rounded over

25-19 *Cleated shelving is simple and utilitarian, but not unhandsome.*

Shelf cleats are less elegant than dadoes, but they're a lot easier to make and much more forgiving of inexperience (see **25-19**). Cleats can be fastened to the end panels either before or after they're mounted on the wall. Unless the width of the cabinet unit varies from top to bottom or side to side, the shelf cleats can be cut all at once with a stop jig tacked to your saw table. If the ends are to be left exposed, cut the cleats a little short of full length to leave a reveal and sand the end-grain mirror smooth and round over the corners. Otherwise, cut the cleats flush with the front edges of the shelving, and nail a stile trim piece over the edge of the side panel to hide the end grain of the cleats and any gaps between the ends of the shelf boards and the side panels. Fasten the cleats to the side panels with three drywall screws and glue. Use two screws, driven at a slight angle to fasten the shelving to the cleats.

DRAWERS AND DOORS

Even more than with the construction of face frames, the level of skill and the complexity of joinery involved in building drawers can run the gamut from rudimentary to sheer artistry. Large sections of cabinetmaking and woodworking texts are devoted entirely to the many different types of intricate joints that can be used to secure the corners of cabinet drawers together. Nevertheless, it's possible to build a perfectly adequate and strong drawer using simple, glued butt joints and ordinary plywood or board stock. Easy-to-install drawer-slide hardware has taken much of the difficulty out of constructing integral wood slides and drawer tracks that don't eventually stick and interfere with the smooth operation of the drawer.

Drawer sides can be built from plywood or boards. Plywood is more stable, but its rough, exposed end grain along the edges of the drawer sides is hard to keep clean and doesn't sand well unless you use expensive lumber-core plywood. You could also glue a strip of shelf moulding or other wood to the cut edges. Half-inch AB or any veneer-faced plywood is suitable, although 3/4-inch panels are less likely to split when fastened together. Cheap factory-made drawers are made from particleboard, which is easily broken, doesn't hold fasteners well, and swells and disintegrates when wet. Half-inch-thick boards milled from stable, smooth-grained softwoods like basswood or tulip wood are also widely used for drawer sides in manufactured cabinets. But, for the typical do-it-yourselfer, a good grade of ordinary one-by No. 2 pine or cedar will be the most practical choice for building drawers.

The easiest kind of drawer to build that still is reasonably strong uses a four-piece side frame and a separate drawer front (see **25-20**). The side pieces are rabbeted along their bottom edge to accept a 1/4-inch-thick hardboard drawer bottom panel. The glossy, tempered side should face up. Glue the bottom to the frame rabbet, and secure it with small-headed brads or ringed panelling nails set just beneath the surface of the hardboard. Another method, which is a little more trouble, but a lot stronger since it does away with nailing, is to cut dadoes into the drawer sides about 3/8 inch up from their bottom edges. When the drawer sides are fastened together, the bottom panel is locked in the glued dadoes.

Drawer sides that meet at the corners in a butt joint, glued and screwed (or nailed), are perfectly adequate for years of trouble-free service and are easy to make. Because it's fastened from opposing directions, a rabbeted half-lap corner joint is stronger. But there's no need other than personal pride to use it or any of the even more elaborate corner joints such as the half-lap dovetail, now that modern wood glues that don't dry out are readily available.

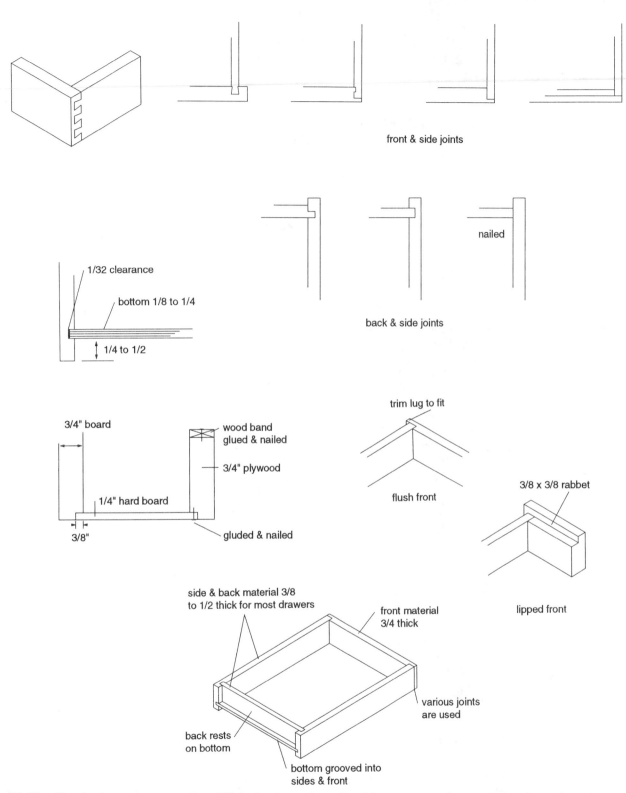

front & side joints

nailed

back & side joints

1/32 clearance

bottom 1/8 to 1/4

1/4 to 1/2

3/4" board

wood band
glued & nailed

3/4" plywood

1/4" hard board

3/8"

gluded & nailed

trim lug to fit

flush front

3/8 x 3/8 rabbet

lipped front

side & back material 3/8
to 1/2 thick for most drawers

front material
3/4 thick

various joints
are used

back rests
on bottom

bottom grooved into
sides & front

25-20 *Simple drawer construction. With the invention of stable, strong, and permanent glues, there is no longer any need for the intricate dovetailed corner joints that were once the hallmark of a well-built drawer.*

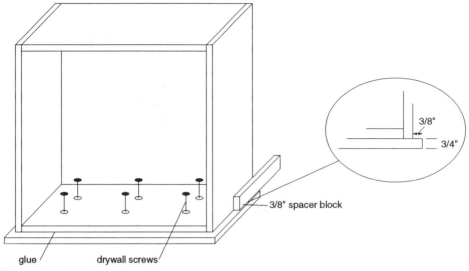

25-21 *Attaching the drawer front.*

If you try to draw two pieces of wood together with a screw-type fastener, the rotation of the screw as it enters the lower piece will tend to push the upper piece away, making it likely that the lower screw hole will strip before it grips. Drill a pilot hole through the upper piece that's slightly larger than the diameter of the fastener. This way, all the drawing power of the screw thread will be applied to the lower piece, pulling the two surfaces tightly together. This technique becomes increasingly necessary as the diameter of the fasteners increases (as with lag screws, for example).

The drawer fronts are cut from finish-grade veneer or board and attached to the front frame piece. The front piece should overhang the edges of the drawer frame about ³⁄₈ inch on all sides. This lip hides the necessary clearance gap between the sides of the drawer and the cabinet frame, and it also acts as a stop to prevent the drawer from sliding past the face of the cabinet. The edges of the drawer face can be left square and sanded or else rounded over or profiled with a decorative beading.

To fasten the drawer frame to its front piece, drill six slightly oversized pilot holes through the front of the drawer frame (see **25-21**). Lay the front piece facedown,

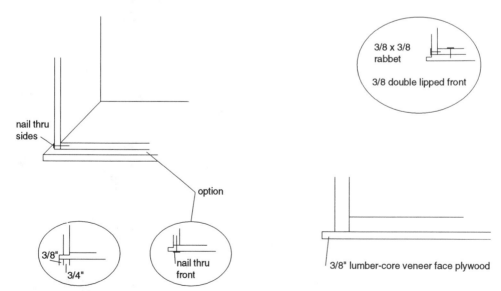

25-22 *The choice of drawer front construction is basically a matter of personal taste and a question of how much time you're willing to put into it.*

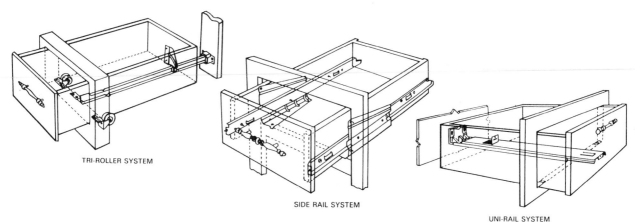

TRI-ROLLER SYSTEM

SIDE RAIL SYSTEM

UNI-RAIL SYSTEM

25-23 *Compared to center- or side-mounted built-in drawer slides, factory-made drawer slide hardware is much more likely to gives years of trouble-free operation.*

give it a coat of glue, and set the drawer front on top of it. Use a spacer block to line up the edge of the front lip with the sides of the drawer. Drive drywall screws into the back of the front piece. Use extra-long threaded screws for attaching the drawer handles or else bore a wider hole through the back of the drawer front frame to use a standard-length screw (designed for ¾-inch-thick stock).

The advantages offered by the double-front method described above are no fasteners visible in the drawer face and a very strong joint. The disadvantage is extra weight, bulk, and stock.

As you might expect, there are many other ways to build a drawer front (see **25-22**). For example, if you prefer to use a ⅜-inch-thick lip instead of a full-thickness front, the back of the drawer can be cut out on a table saw to form the lip and the front in just a single piece. When making the rabbet cuts, remove additional stock at the sides to accommodate the thickness of the drawer side pieces (e.g., ⅜ inch for the overlap width plus ¾ inch for the drawer side on each side of the front piece). If you prefer, you can still use the double-front method instead.

Various types of drawer slide hardware are available (see **25-23**). One of the best and easiest (the K-D drawer slide) consists of a two pairs of interlocking tracks, half of which are installed on the drawer sides and the other half of which are attached to the cabinet itself. The drawer thus slides back and forth in its cabinet-mounted track on nylon roller bearings. In order for the slides to function properly, the drawer must be 1¹⁄₁₆ inches narrower than the opening on which the slides are mounted (slightly more than ½-inch clearance for each set of tracks). This means that the drawer sides will be set in from the edge of the drawer front by the width of any lip plus ½ inch for the track. The distance between the cabinet frame members which support the tracks shouldn't vary more than ¹⁄₁₆ inch from front to back.

Another option is to install a flat piece of wood between the drawer front bottom rail and the cabinet back along the centerline of the drawer cabinet (see **25-24**). A second vertical center strip is attached to the underside of the countertop so that it projects down about ½ inch below the bottom edge of the top rail. A notch cut in the top edge of the drawer back piece guides the drawer along the upper track while rubber rollers mounted on the inside top edge of the drawer bottom front rail and the bottom back edge of the drawer itself let the drawer glide over the lower center strip. Leave about ¹⁄₁₆-inch clearance on each side of the drawer to keep it from jamming against the frame and wax the top guide strip.

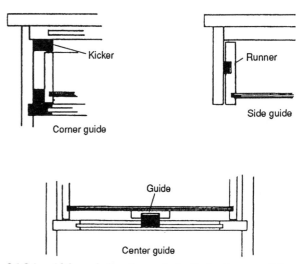

Kicker

Runner

Corner guide

Side guide

Guide

Center guide

25-24 *Although low in cost, built-in drawer slides take a lot longer to install than factory-made units. For smooth operation, use hardwood for the slides and give them a coat of wax.*

25-25 *Although the owner of this kitchen eventually built his own base cabinets, he found it easier to install factory-made cabinets with solid-oak framed glass doors than to build them himself.*

MAKING CABINET DOORS

Traditional raised-panel cabinet doors are smaller versions of the rail-and-stile wood doors used for exterior entries and interior rooms. As such, they require a good deal of skill and sophisticated machine tools to make. This is one case where factory-made doors may be a sensible option (see **25-25**). Plywood doors, on the other hand, are very easy to make with a table saw and a power sander.

Three-quarter-inch standard-thickness doors can be either flush-mounted or offset (see **25-26**).

Flush-mounted doors are hung so that they fit inside their openings when closed. Obviously, the margin for error required to ensure both a square opening and an even gap between the door and the cabinet rails and stiles is minute. But flush doors can look elegant, especially when installed with high-quality European-style concealed hinges.

Offset doors are much more tolerant of mistakes. With the most basic type of offset door, the entire door is set in front of the cabinet face frame so that it overlaps it on all sides by at least ⅜ inch. Special ¾-inch offset hinges are fastened to the back of the door and to the frame stiles.

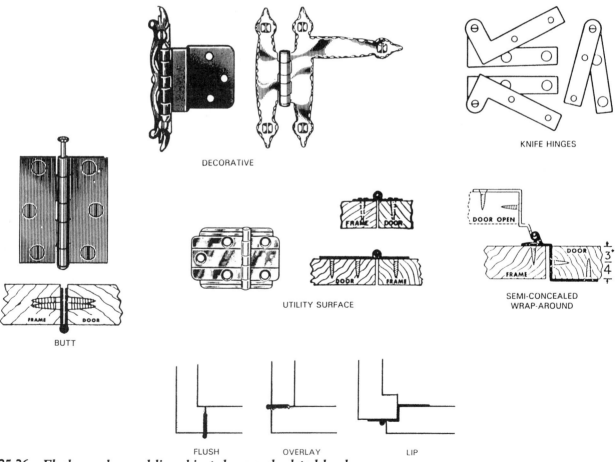

DECORATIVE

KNIFE HINGES

BUTT

UTILITY SURFACE

SEMI-CONCEALED WRAP-AROUND

FLUSH OVERLAY LIP

25-26 *Flush, overlay, and lip cabinet doors and related hardware.*

If the hinges are spring-loaded, no additional magnetic or mechanical cabinet catches are needed to keep the door shut tight. The only tricky part of installing full offset doors is making sure that their tops line up with each other and "read" level (that is, *look level* as opposed to actually being level) against the cabinet rails at the same time that their sides read plumb against the stiles and that all the frame reveals appear to be of even width (see **25-27**).

Although you can shape the edges with a router bit to soften their square profile, some people find the thickness of a full-offset door unattractive and prefer to use a ³⁄₈-inch lipped door instead. To make a lipped door, first measure the door frame opening (see **25-28**). Check its corners for square. Cut the door blank ¼ inch wider and longer than the widest and tallest measurements (if the door opening is out of square, one or more measurements will vary). Set the table saw blade to make a cut ³⁄₈ inch deep and ³⁄₈ inch wide (measured from the fence to the outside of the blade) and run the door blanks through the blade while holding them on edge against the saw fence. Check the rabbeted door blank for fit in its opening. There should be about ⅛ inch of play both vertically and horizontally. If the door pinches against the frame, cut the lip a little wider to increase its clearance.

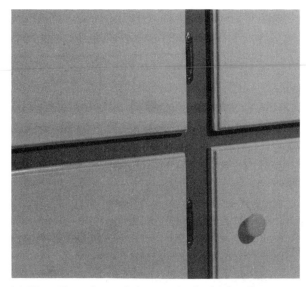

25-27   The edges of these ¼-inch-thick offset doors have been profiled with a router bit to soften them. The self-closing, surface-mount spring-loaded hinges hold the doors shut without any cabinet catches.

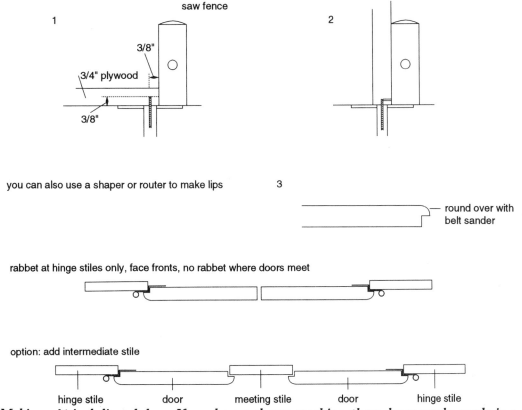

25-28   Making a ³⁄₈-inch lipped door. If you have a shaper machine, these doors can be made in a single pass. A table-mounted router will also do the job.

Mount ⅜-inch offset hinges on the doors and then screw the hinges to the stiles. Use only one screw in each hinge until you're satisfied with the fit. If you're not, remove the door, cut the lip on the pinched edge wider, and then trim it off so that it won't overhang the stile more than roughly ⅜ inch.

When testing doors (of any sort) for fit, avoid screwing and unscrewing the hinges repeatedly, which will enlarge the screw holes, causing loose hinges and sagging doors. If a hole becomes too loose, plug it by hammering splits of softwood dipped in glue into it before redriving the screw.

Finally, after all adjustments have been made, round over and/or smooth off the edge of the door lip with a power sander. A belt sander is also useful for smoothing out the rough bottom of the rabbet cuts.

When using lip doors, it's important to remember that half the thickness of the door will be inside the cabinet frame (see **25-29**). This means that the trim strips nailed to the edges of any plywood shelving inside the cabinets must not be more than ⅜ inch wide if the doors are to close. Use ¼-inch- or ⁵⁄₁₆-inch-thick edging to allow a little extra clearance.

A NOTE ON FASTENERS

Over the past decade or so, bugle-headed "drywall" screws have pretty much taken the place of ordinary wood screws and nails for most fastening purposes. Because of their narrow profile and coarse, sharp thread, they drive easily and hold well. But their tapered head requires them to be *countersunk* in hardwood and tends to split boards when they are driven too close to the end. Special pilots bits are used to cut a countersunk hole for seating the screw head

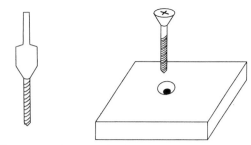

25-30 *Countersinking and plugging a screw.*

while boring a pilot hole (see **25-30**). Where visible screw heads are objectionable, the hole is bored deep enough so that it can be plugged with a scrap of dowel. Or you can use a plug cutter to make plugs out of matching or contrasting wood instead. Using a drill press, the plug cutter bit consistently turns out perfect plugs. The quality of the plugs turned out by a hand-held drill is not as good.

Despite their many advantages over conventional wood screws, drywall screws should *never* be used to hang regular doors. Their heads have too steep a taper to seat tightly against the hinges, and their narrow shanks let the hinges shift as the door swings until they eventually loosen and pull out.

A VERSATILE, EVEN SIMPLER CABINET- AND FURNITURE-BUILDING SYSTEM

Ted Zilius, a builder and designer in northern Vermont, has developed an extremely versatile low-cost method of building cabinets that can be used to build furniture, storage units, and closet shelving as well (see **25-31**).

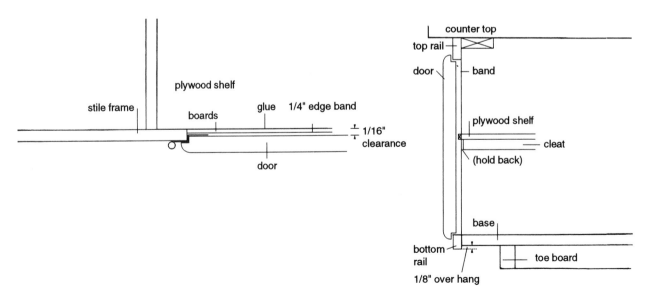

25-29 *Clearance between lipped door and shelf edges.*

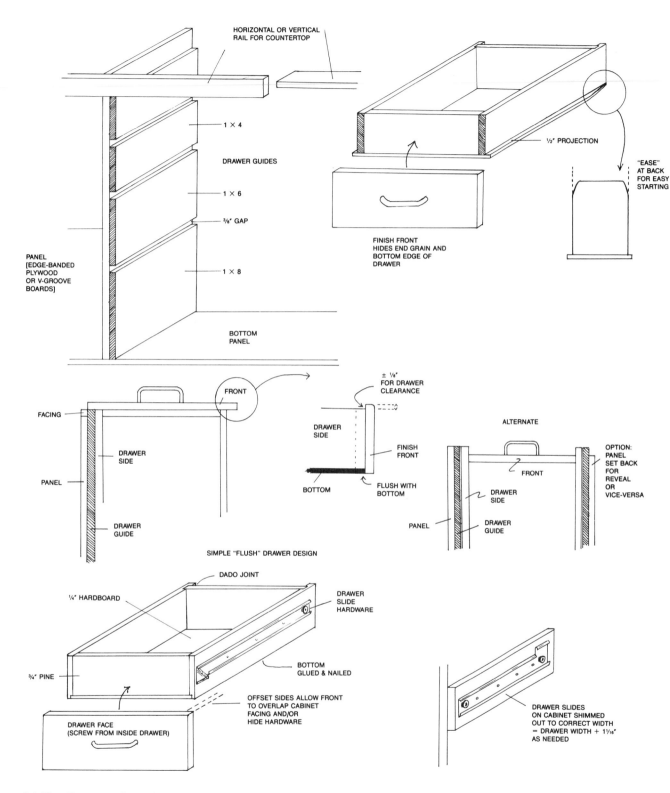

HORIZONTAL OR VERTICAL RAIL FOR COUNTERTOP

1 × 4

DRAWER GUIDES

1 × 6

³⁄₈" GAP

PANEL [EDGE-BANDED PLYWOOD OR V-GROOVE BOARDS]

1 × 8

BOTTOM PANEL

½" PROJECTION

"EASE" AT BACK FOR EASY STARTING

FINISH FRONT HIDES END GRAIN AND BOTTOM EDGE OF DRAWER

FACING

DRAWER SIDE

PANEL

DRAWER GUIDE

FRONT

SIMPLE "FLUSH" DRAWER DESIGN

± ⅛" FOR DRAWER CLEARANCE

DRAWER SIDE

FINISH FRONT

BOTTOM

FLUSH WITH BOTTOM

ALTERNATE

FRONT

DRAWER SIDE

PANEL

DRAWER GUIDE

OPTION: PANEL SET BACK FOR REVEAL OR VICE-VERSA

DADO JOINT

¼" HARDBOARD

DRAWER SLIDE HARDWARE

¾" PINE

BOTTOM GLUED & NAILED

OFFSET SIDES ALLOW FRONT TO OVERLAP CABINET FACING AND/OR HIDE HARDWARE

DRAWER FACE (SCREW FROM INSIDE DRAWER)

DRAWER SLIDES ON CABINET SHIMMED OUT TO CORRECT WIDTH = DRAWER WIDTH + 1¹⁄₁₆" AS NEEDED

25-31   *Because the Zilius system dispenses with the rail-and-stile facings of conventional cabinet construction, vertical stacking of drawers is much simpler. The drawers are also easier and cheaper to build and install than even the simple standard drawer with "K-D" slides shown here.*

647

25-32 *The cabinets in this kitchen were built using the simple "Zilius" system based on cleated V-groove pine panels and drawers that utilize a module based on the widths of standard boards.*

The end panels of the cabinets are built from 1×6 vertical V-groove pine (or other softwood) boards, secured by horizontal cleats glued and fastened with drywall screws that carry the base, countertop, and interior shelves (see 25-32, 25-33, and 25-34). The top front edge of the panels are held in place by a 1×4 laid flatwise into a notch that will later support the countertop and that functions as a stop/reveal against which the cabinet doors can close.

25-33 *Here, the base cabinet doors are sliding hardboard panels rather than cleated boards. Note how the end panel becomes the side wall of the refrigerator cabinet and how the open shelf unit is attached to the wall by a cleat under the second shelf.*

25-34 *These cabinet doors were cut from lumber-core knotty pine-veneer plywood, which is less likely to warp than cleated doors and which also gives the cabinets a less rustic, more contemporary appearance.*

Otherwise the panels can be fastened directly to the underside of the countertop, so long as you provide a minimum of ⅛-inch clearance between the top edge of any drawer and door and the lip of the countertop.

The big difference between the Zilius system and the conventional panel-and-frame system described above is in how the drawers are built and installed (see **25-35** and **25-36**). Depending on the desired depth of the drawers, lengths of 1×4, 1×6, 1×8, or 1×10 square-edged pine board are glued and screwed to the side panels, spaced ⅜ inch apart. The drawers are a simple frame of boards that correspond in width to the pieces glued to the side panels to which a ¼-inch hardboard bottom piece has been glued and nailed. The sides of the drawer bottom project outward about ½ inch beyond the drawer sides. This permits the drawer to slide in the track formed by the space between the side panel boards. The drawer bottom extensions are tapered slightly at their back ends to prevent them from binding as the drawer is closed. The end grain of the drawer sides can be sanded smooth and left exposed as a decorative touch that matches the end grain of the side panel cleats, or else covered by an overlapping drawer front that hides the ends of the cleats as well.

Where doors, instead of drawers, are installed, vertical cleats set back from the outside edge of the side panels provide a stop for mounting flush doors. The doors (and the side panels, too) can be made from either cleated boards or plywood. Cleated boards are less stable and will tend to warp slightly, even if you use dry lumber, but the imperfection could be considered as a positive feature of a rustic design.

25-35 *In this version of the Zilius drawer, the drawer sides extend beyond the drawer front to make a decorative edge that matches the end grain of the cleats which are screwed to the side panels. Note how the extended drawer bottom slides in the tracks formed by the cleats.*

25-36 *Here, in this somewhat more elegant version, the solid-core mahogany double drawer front hides the working mechanism of the drawer from view, giving the cabinets a more conventional Eurostyle appearance.*

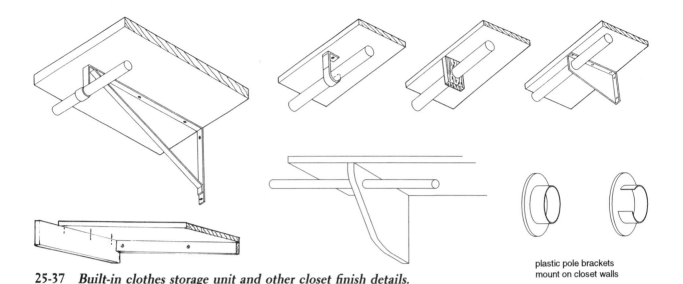

25-37 *Built-in clothes storage unit and other closet finish details.*

plastic pole brackets
mount on closet walls

25-38 *The lower part of this moveable bunk bed is a snug self-contained child's bedroom. Note how the same basic cleated board panel box is also used to make the armoire visible to the right of the bunk bed.*

25-39 *The upper part is a fun loft bed for a sleep-over friend or a change of view.*

Another option is to use sliding rather than swinging doors. These are cut from the same ¼-inch hardboard panels as the drawer bottoms. The hardboards can be left natural, painted, or faced with plastic laminate. The panels are installed in a metal sliding-door track (plastic is too flimsy for long service) fastened to the base and to a ledger on the underside of the countertop support rail. Sand the edges of the sliding panels and wax them for smooth operation.

CLOTHES STORAGE UNITS

The beauty of this system is that it can be used to build almost any kind of furniture. I've found it particularly valuable in building clothes storage closets that function like a built-in chest of drawers (see **25-37**). The units consist of at least three 1×12 to 1×16 panels, spaced 12 to 16 inches apart to which 1×6 drawer cleats are screwed. Squares of ¼-inch hardboard can be slipped into or out of the spaces between the drawer cleats as desired to create clothes shelving based on any desired combination of six-inch modules. Drawers for socks and underwear can also fit into the slots. If the edges of the panels are extended out beyond the cleats, bifold doors can be hung from them. Drill a finger hole through the fronts of any drawers since a knob would prevent the bifold door from closing.

The same principles can be applied to create custom units such as freestanding armoires or a moveable bunk bed (see **25-38** and **25-39**).

Bookshelves are basically floor-to-ceiling wall cabinets without a toe space (see **25-40**). In fact, it's not unusual for the lower section of a bookshelf to be a base cabinet which contains the home entertainment system. The cabinets can be deeper than the upper shelving. Alternatively, doors can be hung over the lower portion of a single, floor-to-ceiling shelf unit.

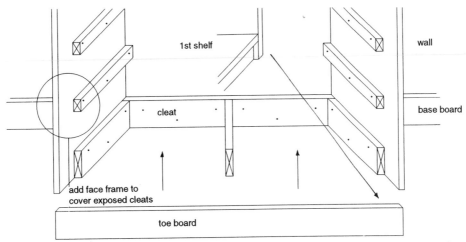

25-40 *Bookshelves are basically floor-to-ceiling wall cabinets. Construct the base frame so that the first shelf will overhang the toe board by about ¼ inch.*

The point is that almost the same methods can be used to build either wall cabinets, bookshelves, or open storage shelving in any room and for any purpose.

Even though a bookshelf ordinarily lacks a toe space, it shouldn't begin directly at floor level. Instead, use the 2×4-on-edge technique for making a base cabinet frame to make a flush base for the first shelf. If you use 1×12 boards for your shelving, screw a short 1×4 cleat to the bottom inside edges of the shelf side boards. These should be set back from the edges so that a 1×4 face board can be installed between them leaving a slight reveal under the lip of the first shelf board which will rest on top of these base pieces.

While 1×12 boards can make perfectly adequate bookshelves, shelves much more than three feet long will tend to sag when loaded with heavy books. For added strength and a more pleasing profile, you might consider using ⁵⁄₄ or even ⁶⁄₄ stock instead.

COUNTERTOPS

Plastic laminate is to kitchen countertops what plywood is to wall sheathing. No other countertop material—even wood—can match it for durability, economy, and versatility (see **25-41** and **25-42**). And, although you can order factory-built a custom-laminated countertop to fit your specifications, it's often easier and considerably less expensive to build your own from scratch, particularly when the kitchen walls or corners are slightly out of square.

A proper substrate is critical to the success of any laminate installation. Always use *high-density* (HD) particleboard (also called *core board*, which should not be confused with standard medium-density particleboard used for floor underlayment and cheap cabinet bases). The uniformly flat dense surface of HD particleboard bonds to the laminate much better than the uneven grain of ply-

25-41 *Despite its undeniable beauty, wood is actually a poor choice for a kitchen countertop that will be subjected to heavy-duty use. Varnishes and most other protective finishes are unsuitable for food-preparation surfaces and nontoxic salad-oil type finishes must be renewed regularly.*

25-42 *The only evidence that a properly glued-up wood countertop isn't a single slab should be the change in color and grain where the boards butt each other.*

651

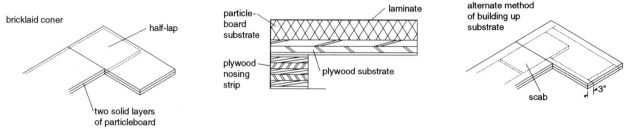

25-43 *A reinforced substrate keeps the laminate surface from pulling apart at the seams.*

wood. The material is available in ½-inch and ¾-inch thicknesses, in 25-inch and 30-inch widths sized especially for laminate work (a standard countertop is 25 inches wide), and in eight-, 10-, and 12-foot lengths as well as 4×8 sheets. If you buy 30-inch-wide underlayment you can rip a four-inch strip off the edge to use for the backsplash and have almost an inch of play left in the rough countertop for making any needed adjustments.

Glue three-inch- or four-inch-wide strips of ¾-inch underlayment-grade plywood to the underside of the particleboard along its perimeter, and secure them with 1¼-inch drywall screws, making sure to keep the screws clear of any proposed sink or other cut-out lines (see **25-43**). You can also use strips of particleboard to reinforce the countertop lip and base cabinet attachment zones, but plywood is stronger and holds fasteners better than particleboard. Add extra support around the edges of a cast-iron sink (stainless steel sinks are light enough that additional stiffening isn't called for). If two pieces of particleboard must be spliced together, span the seam with plywood at least 12 inches on each side. If the lip of the countertop will be cantilevered outward to form an eating area, run the underlying plywood at least a foot back beneath the main countertop area. Plywood strips should also be added to any part of the countertop that will bear on cross braces or top edges of divider panels in the base cabinet frame.

Set the rough countertop in place on top of the base cabinets, and check it for fit against the back wall (see **25-44**). If the front edge has been carefully aligned with the plywood strips, the final trim cut can be made along the back edge of the countertop where any wiggles in the cut line will be hidden beneath the backsplash. Some professionals prefer not to worry about a precise alignment of the underlayment edges. They set the countertop temporarily in place, mark the correct cut lines along the front, and with a wood or metal straightedge clamped along the length of the cut, saw through both pieces at the same time with a circular saw.

Although most carpenters make sink or cooktop cutouts after the laminate is glued to the underlayment, making the cutout first gives you a margin of safety in case you inadvertently overcut the opening (see **25-45**). Try the sink for fit in the rough opening. Then, if you have to, you can glue in filler strips of underlayment to the sides of the cut to fix the mistake.

To cut the opening, use a router equipped with a roller-bearing pilot bit. Drill a hole in the laminate, insert the bit, and follow the edge of the cutout in the underlying substrate. With this method, there's also less chance of cracking the laminate when the last bit of underlayment is cut through and the scrap piece drops downwards.

To fasten the countertop to the base cabinet, spread a bead of construction adhesive along all the bearing surfaces

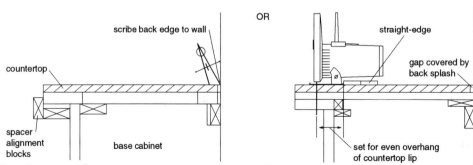

25-44 *Trimming a rough countertop to size. It's generally easier to scribe the back of a countertop to the wall than trim off the face edge.*

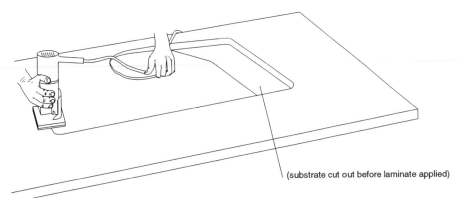

(substrate cut out before laminate applied)

25-45 *Foolproof method for cutting openings. Sometimes, if you wait to cut out a sink opening until after the countertop is installed, there may not be enough room between the backsplash and the cut line to maneuver a saw.*

of the cabinet frame, and then drive screws up through the frame members (drill a clearance hole first) and into the underlayment.

The sheets of plastic laminate come in nominal widths of 30, 36, 40, and 60 inches and lengths of 6, 8, 10, and 12 feet. The actual measurements of the sheets are one inch larger to allow for trimming waste and edging. Although you could conceivably cut a 25-inch countertop and a 4-inch backsplash out of a 30-inch-wide sheet and still have a 1¾-inch-wide strip left over for facing the front edge, it's a better idea to add at least ½ inch extra to all dimensions for finish trimming, particularly if you have limited experience working with laminates. If you buy the 36-inch-wide piece instead, you'll not only have plenty of allowance for trimming a crooked edge, but you'll also have enough stock to cut the edging pieces for the ends of the countertop and for the top edge of the backsplash.

Ordering laminate for a straight-run countertop is easy. But, since surface seams are both difficult to make and usually unsightly, sizing laminate sheets for a U- or L-shaped countertop that will require one or more seams can be problematic. As with drywall, it's better to end up with waste than it is to economize by joining smaller pieces. Whenever possible, try to locate otherwise unavoidable seams so that they run through a sink or cooktop cutout where only a few inches will show. If you do need to make a surface seam, position it as far as possible from any splices in the underlayment to prevent stress cracks.

Should you have to, the best way to make a tight seam that won't be too noticeable is to "mirror-cut" the two adjoining pieces (**25-46**). Butt the two pieces together in position on top of the underlayment after first sliding a scrap of laminate under the length of the joint. Clamp the pieces to the countertop so they won't shift while you cut them. Then clamp a straightedge to one side of the joint. Set a router equipped with a ⅛-inch straight-cutting bit so that it will cut through the top layer of laminate

and barely into the protective lower scrap strip and then feed the router evenly and smoothly along the straightedge to make the cut. Set a square against the straightedge, and draw an index mark across the seam so that you'll be able to realign each half of the joint precisely after you unclamp the sheets. If the fit isn't quite perfect, you can reset the straightedge and recut the seam, so long as there's still enough length on the sheets to overhang the ends of the countertop.

Before assembling the countertop, it's important to let both the substrate and the laminate acclimate to the ambient moisture and temperature levels of the environment in which they'll be installed for about 48 hours. Otherwise, there's a good chance that the two materials will contract and expand at different rates, causing the laminate to pull away from the underlayment after it's glued down. Store the materials so air can circulate freely around them.

Although laminates can be cut with a carbide-tipped scoring tool, the best tool for the job, particularly when long, narrow edging strips must be ripped, is a table saw equipped with a 60-tooth carbide-tipped blade. Hand-operated or motorized laminate slitters also do a nice job, but there's no reason for the nonprofessional to invest in such specialized tools.

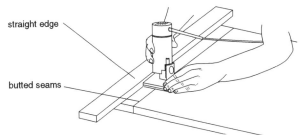

straight edge

butted seams

25-46 *Mirror-cutting a seam. The technique is similar to cutting a seam in resilient flooring.*

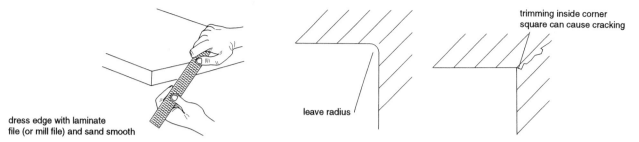

dress edge with laminate
file (or mill file) and sand smooth

leave radius

trimming inside corner
square can cause cracking

25-47 *It's a good idea to enlist at least one helper when setting the top sheet. To prevent cracks, pay particular attention to supporting the area around cutouts and ells or any other stress points.*

Use a small, lightweight easily maneuvered router that can be held in one hand (which is basically what a professional laminate trimmer is) for trimming the laminate after it's glued in place. Two kinds of bits are used to trim laminate. A straight cutter trims the excess off flush and square to the edge it overhangs. A bevel cutter trims it flush with a 22½-degree bevel along the top edge. For occasional work, a ball-bearing pilot bit equipped with carbide-cutting edges is more than adequate. Professionals use more expensive self-pilot bits that don't tend to seize up and burn the surface of the laminate.

Laminate is glued to the substrate with contact cement, which is one of the most obnoxious substances a builder will ever have to contend with. The fumes are not only toxic and intoxicating, but explosively flammable. As when applying organic tile and floor mastics, extinguish all open flames *including pilot lights*, open the windows, run a fan for good ventilation and wear an appropriate respirator.

Until very recently, contact cement was applied by brushing from a can. Aerosol spray cans are now available from professional suppliers that speed up application and drying time, produce fewer fumes and less mess, and cost only a little bit more than canned cement.

Both surfaces are coated with contact cement and allowed to dry. When the pieces come into contact with each other, they stick. They do so instantly and firmly, with no chance for adjustment in case of misalignment. This is the part of working with laminates that makes amateurs and even a few professional carpenters nervous. It's also why sheets of laminate are cut oversized and trimmed to size only after they're glued down.

Begin by gluing the countertop edge strips first. Since the edge-grain of both the underlayment and its plywood stiffener is more porous than the face, give it a double coat of contact cement. When the cement is dry (it will be dull and you'll be able to run your fingers across it without feeling any tackiness), bring the edge strip into contact against the edge of the countertop. Start at one end, and press the strip firmly into place. Have a helper hold the end of a long strip to keep it from snapping. The strip itself should be wide enough so that it sticks both up above

the surface of the countertop and down below the bottom of the edge. Then apply pressure to set the bond by moving a one-by block of softwood along the strip as you strike it with your hammer. After the edge strips are set, trim them off flush to the substrate with your router or laminate trimmer. Carefully remove any rough edges with a laminate file (similar to a fine mill file, but made especially for fine-tuning laminates, these files can be purchased from any supplier), filing towards the substrate to prevent chipping, gouging, or separating the edge (see **25-47**).

Next, coat the surface of the substrate and the top sheet with contact cement. With the exception of a short straight-run countertop, it's almost impossible to hold and maneuver a flimsy and brittle sheet of laminate into place while avoiding accidental contact. Fortunately, contact cement only sticks to itself. Pros use wax paper "slip sheets," flat wood stickers, or even slats of old venetian blinds to prevent the two surfaces from touching each other while the laminate is positioned.

Begin removing the slats or slip papers at the center of the sheet. Press it down and continue working outwards towards the edges. Otherwise, if you stick down the edges first, you could end up with a bubble in the middle of the sheet. Use a rubber hand roller and heavy pressure or else the hammer-and-cushion-block technique to bond the surfaces.

If, despite your best efforts, the top sheet fails to line up where it ought to, all is not lost. The glue bond can be dissolved with acetone or lacquer thinner. Carefully slip a drywall taping knife under the leading edge of the top sheet and pour solvent onto the blade, letting it seep into the crack. As the glue begins to loosen, continue working the knife and adding more solvent. With patience, you'll eventually be able to remove the entire piece, clean off the excess cement, recoat, and reset the top.

Trim the top flush with the edges, and then dress the slight ridge left by the router bit with a laminate file. Hold the file almost vertical and stroke downwards. When the edge is finished, the excess glue will peel off, leaving a thin, crisp edge. A bevel-cutter trim bit leaves a wider edge that takes less filing, but is more noticeable. The finished edge can be razor sharp; soften it with a few passes of a

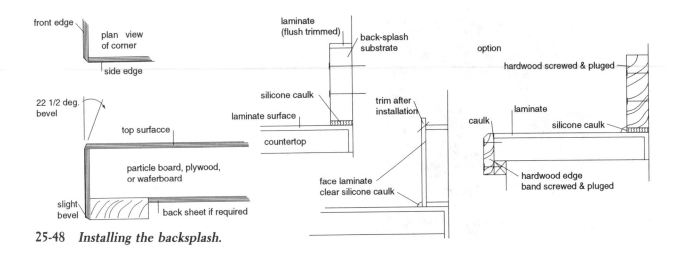

25-48 *Installing the backsplash.*

sanding block. To reduce the chances of a stress crack developing at the inside corners, leave the radius formed by the router-cutter bit instead of filing it square.

Some professionals use special clips to fasten the backsplashes, which have been previously laminated, to the countertop. Others glue them to the wall with silicone caulk (see **25-48**). The first method is quick and effective, but expensive, and requires specialized tools. The second method is easy but of questionable durability. I prefer to glue and trim only the edge strips onto the backsplash substrate before bedding it in a bead of clear silicone caulk and screwing it to the wall. Then I glue and trim the backsplash face piece and dress the edges as with the countertop.

Some installers prefer not to deal with edge and backsplash lamination at all. They glue down the countertop laminate first, trim it flush with the front edge of the countertop lip, and then glue and screw hardwood edge trim to the edges of the countertop. The backsplash is also a hardwood board, set in silicone caulk. The screws should be spaced evenly, countersunk, and plugged with wood dowels.

25-49 *This lavatory countertop was owner-built by diagonally gluing together thin strips of hardwood boards set on edge. Because a bathroom countertop receives far less abuse than a kitchen counter and can be sealed with epoxy varnish, wood is a quite suitable material.*

BATHROOM CABINETRY

Just as factory-built units have replaced site-built cabinets in the kitchen, the prefabricated lavatory base cabinet and moulded one-piece faux marble sink and countertop have become a standard part of the average bathroom, but many owner-builders still prefer expressing their individuality—especially in the bathroom (see **25-49** and **25-50**).

As far as construction details are concerned, there's no difference between a lavatory cabinet and a kitchen sink cabinet.

25-50 *The adaptability of the cleated-panel system to kitchen and bath cabinets is apparent in this partially completed lavatory countertop installation. Note how the top edges of the drawer cabinet panel provide the support for the countertop.*

655

25-51 *The walls of this bathtub enclosure were diagonally panelled with tongue-and-groove Western red cedar 1×6 boards. The underlying framing was waterproofed with tar paper and the joint between the tub and the boards sealed with clear caulk, as were all corner joints in the panelling.*

25-52 *The tub enclosure was made about 12 inches longer than the tub itself to leave room for a bench. The seat is tilted slightly to shed water and caulked to the walls. The woodwork of the tub surround flows into the wall panelling and lavatory bench. Note the custom towel rack and the ornamental cutouts in the enclosure wall.*

One type of cabinet work which is unique to bathrooms is a custom tub enclosure. These can range from setting an old-fashioned claw-foot bathtub into a tiled top to panelling the bath–shower stall walls with cedar or redwood boards or bevelled siding to building the bathtub itself from scratch.

Enclosing a standard bathtub with wood panelling or horizontal bevel siding is no more difficult than enclosing it with drywall or cement backer board (see 25-51 and 25-52). Waterproof the walls with tar-paper underlayment as described in Chapter Twenty-three. Pay particular attention to sealing the joint between the flange of the tub and the wall finish with silicone caulk.

Although no different in principle than setting an oversized, self-rimming sink in a countertop, setting an old-fashioned claw-foot tub in a tiled or wood enclosure poses special problems. Because the raised lip of the tub rests on top of the enclosure surface, a flat area is created between the tub and the enclosure walls. If the tub is fitted with a shower head, water falling on the countertop-like surface will run onto the bathroom floor. The simplest solution is to use the same old-fashioned circular shower curtain support that was used back when these old tubs were first retrofitted with overhead showers. Another approach is to have a separate shower stall and use the tub only for bathing. This is the same approach used with luxury bathrooms equipped with spa tubs (see 25-53). Because it can be supported by its lip alone, an old-fashioned tub makes a fine "poor man's" spa when set on a low pedestal or a low-cost sunken tub when dropped into the floor (see 25-54). If you insist on combining tub and shower functions in the same enclosure without the traditional shower curtain loop, use a modern square-cornered and flat-topped tub instead. Or build a raised lip across the front of the tub enclosure, and install an auxiliary drain in the surface of the tub base that empties into the regular tub drain. Standard V-cap trim tiles have an angled profile that also create a low lip that would divert water back towards the surface drain. To protect the substrate and underlying framing from water damage, run sheets of CPVC membrane-type waterproofing up under the lip of the tub and onto the enclosure walls before laying the finish surface.

To mark the cutout for a claw-foot tub enclosure, lay the tub upside down on the enclosure base underlayment (or else a cardboard template) and scribe its outline. Set a pair of compass dividers to half the distance between the outline and the inner edge of the tub lip, and transfer the line. Plywood underlayment, properly waterproofed, will make a solid substrate for a blind-nailed board finish. Seal the joints between boards with silicone caulk, and let it cure completely before coating the surface with a thick, waterproof epoxy finish. For ceramic or quarry tiles, laminate cement backer board to the plywood first. Tiles can be rough-trimmed to follow the edge of the cutout with a diamond-blade grinding wheel, a masonry blade in a skill saw, or a tungsten-carbide rod saw.

When wood is used for a tub surround or shower stall, a cloudy film of soap residue and mineral deposits tends to discolor the finish unless the walls are constantly scrubbed down. It takes about six or more coats of penetrating oil finish or warm linseed oil rubbed deep into the wood to retard this buildup.

HOMEMADE LIGHTING FIXTURES

Unless you buy the cheapest kinds, the cost of lighting fixtures can amount to a significant fraction of the construction budget. High-quality and good-looking, unpre-

25-53   Antique windows literally highlight this spa tub enclosure. The walls are 1×8 shiplapped clear redwood. A separate conventional shower was installed in a different part of the bathroom.

tentious lighting fixtures are both so expensive and so uncommon that cost-conscious owner-builders should consider building their own fixtures.

Reduced to its most basic elements, a light fixture, termed the *luminaire* by the trade, is a wall- or ceiling-mounted device that diffuses light over a wide area or focuses it onto a small one while safely dissipating the heat produced by the bulb, properly called the *lamp* (the "bulb" is only the glass surround). Everything else is decoration.

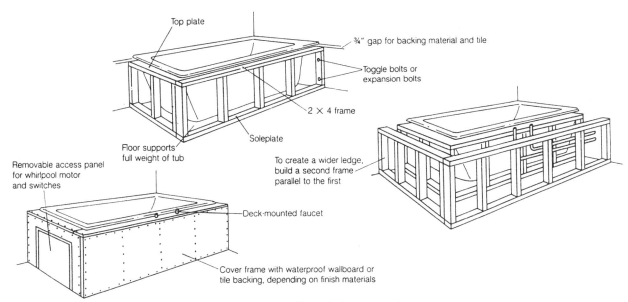

25-54   Construction details for various custom tub and shower enclosures.

25-55 *This simple yet elegant homemade light fixture is assembled from 1×8 boards with mitred corners and a bevelled edge using a G-40 globe lamp ("bulb") mounted in a standard porcelain socket.*

25-56 *Rice paper can be used to provide under-shelf countertop lights.*

25-57 *Wood slats can add a dramatic and aesthetically pleasing effect.*

25-58 *Overhead cathedral ceiling lights made with wood add to the ambience.*

A porcelain "bulb" holder is a lighting fixture reduced to its most elemental form. When surrounded by a wood frame, and fitted with a clear or frosted G-40 type globe bulb, you've got a simple, yet elegant, ceiling light fixture (see **25-55**). A reflector made from a square sheet of aluminum flashing metal will increase the effective light output and also help to dissipate heat buildup. The reflector also blocks light from escaping between the fixture and the ceiling to which it's mounted. Ordinary incandescent bulbs can also be used instead of globe bulbs if the room side of the fixture is fitted with a translucent plastic diffuser. This can slide into a saw-kerf groove in the lower inside edges of the fixture.

Various combinations of wood frames and rice paper or frosted glass and translucent plastics can be used to make fixtures as well (see **25-56, 25-57,** and **25-58**).

Simple board valances can also be used to direct light from wall-mounted fixtures downwards (e.g., over a bathroom sink) or upwards onto a reflective ceiling. Fluorescent tube lighting is especially well suited for this purpose.

You should always check local codes to see if home-built lighting fixtures are permitted. To prevent excessive heat buildup and a possible fire, the wattage of the bulb in any such fixture should not exceed 60 watts.

26 Finish Details

For professional and amateur homebuilders alike, getting the plumber and electrician to come back and set fixtures and install wiring devices and their cover plates and fix cross-wired circuits or the painters to return for the final coat can be a frustrating experience. In the meantime, there are nail heads to be sunk, filled, and finish-coated, dents and "dings" in the drywall and trim to be patched and refinished, walls and edges to touch up, appliances to connect, and seemingly spontaneously generated splatters, spills, and dust to clean. And there may be custom items begun that now need to be finished (see **26-1**). I'll consider one thing at a time with the hope that the whole of the finish details won't overwhelm you.

MECHANICAL FINISH

Except for the bathtub and shower stall, which is set before the walls and finish floors, plumbing fixtures are one of the last items to be installed. The toilet stool must wait until the finish floors are laid. Sinks and faucet fixtures can't be set until the countertops are built. The woodstove must wait until the hearth is complete, and hot-air registers and baseboard radiation all require the finish floors and walls to be in place, if not actually sanded, sealed, and/or painted. Likewise, kitchen appliance hookups should wait until the cabinets are built and the floors laid.

Obtain your appliance dimensions and recommended clearances and hookup requirements from the dealer before designing and building your kitchen cabinets. This is especially important for under-counter dishwashers, which typically have very tight clearances to the cabinet.

SETTING A TOILET

Before you begin to set the toilet, make sure the baseboard is installed on the wall behind it. Otherwise it may get hung up between the base of the toilet, the toilet tank, and the surrounding walls. And more than one freshly set toilet has been shattered by a slip of the hammer as a contorted carpenter tried to nail the baseboard to the wall behind it.

The top of the toilet closet flange is set flush to—or no more than ¼ inch higher than—the finish floor. Cut the flooring to fit within ⅛ to ¼ inch of the flange (which must be positioned so that the slots for the stool anchor bolts line up with the stool). Set a wax-ring gasket on the flange (use the type that has a tapered plastic collar which fits into the drain opening). With a helper, lift the toilet, center its drain flange over the gasket, and line up the toilet anchor bolts with the holes in the stool base. This must be done carefully since a misaligned stool will dent the soft gasket and cause a leak. Rather than try to hold

26-1 Handmade magazine and towel racks and toilet paper holders are just some of the many truly "custom" finishing touches that distinguish an owner-built home from the so-called custom homes of tract builders.

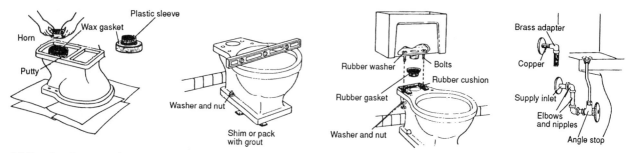

26-2 *Setting a toilet. Run a bead of tub and toilet caulk or plumber's putty around the bottom edge of the toilet bowl to seal it to the floor.*

a heavy porcelain stool while trying to center it over a hole you can't see, balance it on doubled-up 2×4 blocking. When properly positioned, pull the blocking to set the stool on the gasket, and gently and gradually rock the stool downwards until its base settles on the floor. Then tighten down the anchor bolt nuts and install the trim caps. The stool should rest firmly on the floor, and not rock from side to side or front to back when you sit on it. Connect the shutoff valve compression fitting to the coupling at the bottom of the tank with a flexible toilet riser tube, and your installation is complete (see **26-2**).

SETTING SINKS

Most of the sinks used today are *self-rimming*—that is, they have a lip which is set in caulk or putty on top of the finished countertop (see **26-3**). With stainless-steel kitchen sinks, screw or spring-type clamps attach to the underside of the sink lip and tighten against the bottom of the countertop substrate to anchor the sink in place. Cast-iron sinks have a rolled edge or flange that simply rests on top of the countertop. Self-rimming sinks are quick and easy to set. But, when a kitchen sink is set on top of a slightly irregular countertop (such as ceramic tile

or wood) the constant wetting and the differential in the movement of dissimilar materials eventually loosens the caulk bond so that water and food particles work their way under the rim. This not only makes a self-rimming sink hard to keep clean, but can cause the substrate to rot. Since bathroom sinks aren't subjected to the same sort of heavy use, caulk separation is seldom a problem.

Ring-mounted cast-iron sinks are attached to a stainless steel trim flange set in the sink opening on top of the finished countertop and the sink is lifted up to it from below. A bead of caulking applied to the sink flange seals it to the trim, and clamps pull it up tight against the underside of the countertop. Rimless sinks are flush with the countertop surface, which makes them somewhat easier to clean. The major advantage they offer over the self-rimming style is that it's possible to set tiles over their edge, reducing the chance of water seeping between the rim and countertop (see **26-4**). Bullnose-edge trim tiles make a neat finish.

Although it's a bit more trouble, you can set tiles over a self-rimming sink as well, especially if it's a low-profile stainless steel or pressed steel type rather than thicker cast iron or porcelain. The cement backer board that should

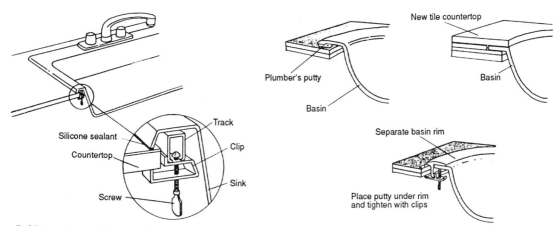

26-3 *Self-rimming sinks work best with smooth countertops such as plastic laminate or synthetic marble.*

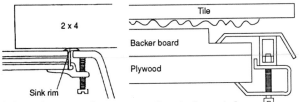

26-4 *Setting tile on top of a rimless sink.*

26-5 *Enclosing the toilet not only creates a novel effect, but eliminates the dirt-collecting area behind the bowl.*

always be used for a proper countertop tile substrate can be notched with a diamond cutting wheel so that the sink rim sets almost flush with its surface. The thin-set mortar bed also adds a little extra height to the tiles.

Incidentally, the same overlapping technique can be used to enclose a conventional toilet stool for an interesting "indoor outhouse" effect that does away with cleaning around and behind the base of the bowl (see **26-5**).

Although they've fallen out of fashion, there are still situations where a wall-mounted sink might still be used, such as in a small utilitarian half-bath. These sinks have cast-in mounting tabs that fit into slots in a wall-mounted steel bracket. (Solid blocking for the sink bracket should have been nailed between the wall studs.) Depending on their size and weight, wall-mounted sinks can either hang from the brackets with no additional support, or be braced by a pair of screw-on legs. The plumbing hookup is fairly standard (see **26-6**).

Pedestal sinks are an old-fashioned style that has been given a contemporary reinterpretation (see **26-7**). The pedestal base bolts to the floor, and the sink bowl bolts to the pedestal.

The shower-head gooseneck fitting isn't installed during the rough-in phase. Instead, a six-inch nipple fitted with a threaded can is turned into the shower pipe fitting while the wall finish and/or the shower/tub surround is installed. The nipple serves as a template for the gooseneck

hole and for trimming a tiled wall finish. Tub spouts are normally attached to a threaded fitting which must project the correct distance beyond the face of the finish wall. Protect the fitting with a threaded cap until you're ready to install the spout. When threading the spout or the shower gooseneck, wrap a rag or duct tape around it to protect the chrome finish while turning it with a pipe wrench or Vise-grip pliers.

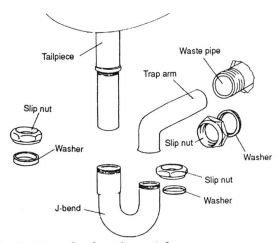

26-6 *Drainage hookup for a sink.*

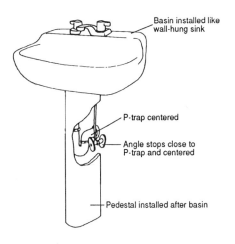

26-7 *Pedestal sink.*

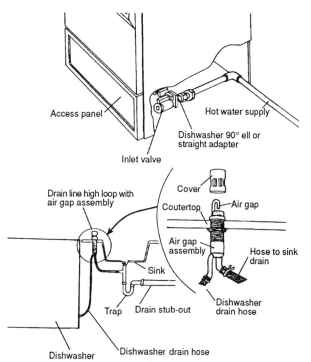

26-8 *Most codes require a one-way air gap installed in the countertop to prevent overflow from a clogged sink siphoning back into the dishwasher. If not required, then loop the drain hose up against the underside of the countertop and secure it with a clamp. Then drop the line down and tee it into the sink drain or garbage disposer drain.*

Shower faucets attach to internal threads in the valve body or external nipple-like extensions. The holes in the finished walls are covered by an escutcheon plate that often threads onto the faucet shaft to tighten the faucet against the wall. Always seal the gap between the finish wall and the pipe with silicone caulk. Oversize or ragged holes make it difficult to waterproof the wall around the fitting.

The hookup of appliances usually involves both electrical and plumbing connections (see **26-8**). Depending on local codes, the stub end of an LP or natural gas fuel line will come out of the floor as black iron pipe and terminate with an approved (for gas only) shutoff valve or stop cock. The actual connection to any movable appliance (such as a gas stove range or dryer) is normally made with coiled flexible metal tubing (which looks similar to Greenfield conduit) factory fitted with flare-type connectors. For LP gas installations, flexible copper tubing is usually used in place of black iron pipe. However, even if the code allows otherwise, it's always a good idea to use rigid pipe where the gas line exits from the floor and a flexible connector to the appliance to protect the line from accidental rupture if the appliance is moved for cleaning or repair.

If you plan to install a refrigerator equipped with an automatic ice maker, provide a ¼-inch ID flexible copper tubing water line. The tubing can tap off a nearby cold-water line with a reducing tee and compression fitting or else with a special saddle tap.

Finally, consider the quality of the plumbing fixtures you plan to buy. A little comparison shopping will reveal a wide range in prices of seemingly identical fixtures. With the possible exceptions of gold-plated faucets, cultured marble basins, and other high-end extravagances, the performance and durability of plumbing fixtures pretty well correlates with price and brand name. It won't be long before a cheap plastic or die-cast faucet begins to leak, low-quality fibreglass fixtures warp and crack, cheap enamelled sinks scratch and rust, and "economy" toilets break down. Instead of a possibly fruitless quest to find replacement parts for an off-brand fixture, it makes better sense to spend more money for a reputable fixture that will give years of trouble-free service. You don't have to spend a fortune on top-of-the-line fixtures that are basically intended for commercial applications or embody the latest fashionable status statement. Any mid-level fixture from a major manufacturer should be more than adequate.

Another caveat: Architects and interior designers have become enamored of high-style fixtures imported from Europe. Although they are usually manufactured to very high quality standards, finding spare parts for any fixture that does fail is apt to be a lengthy and difficult process. Furthermore, many of these fixtures don't fit standard North American mounting systems and have to be adapted at great expense and increased risk of future trouble to make them work, much less meet code.

TELEPHONE WIRING

Much to their chagrin, it's not unusual for a harried owner-builder (and even a few professionals), caught up in the press of larger considerations, to overlook small "details" like telephone jacks and wiring until after the drywall is up. To help ensure that this (and other low-voltage wiring such as thermostat control, door-chime, irrigation valves, security alarm, stereo speaker and TV-FM antenna cables) are included in the electrical rough-in, the location of the various jacks and outlets should always be shown on the electrical/mechanical drawings regardless of whether the actual installation is done by the owner or by a subcontractor.

Unless other arrangements are made for a complete installation (or "prewire"), the wiring provided by the telephone company normally ends at the interface jack. From there on, it's up to you.

A standard residential phone line provides enough power to ring five phones. The label on the underside of the phone will show its *ringer equivalence number* (REN—proportional to the amount of power it takes to ring the phone, usually 1.0 or 0.5). Add up the REN for all the phones you plan to use to see if there's enough power to make them all ring. (Instead of adding an extra line, you could disconnect the ringers of the least-used sets.) Of course, there's no reason that you couldn't provide more outlets ("stations") than phones so long as you place phone jacks close enough together and follow standard interfaces and connections (see **26-9**). A portable phone, particularly one with a satellite cradle that maintains battery charge, allows more flexibility with fewer jacks. Remember, however, that each portable base unit and satellite cradle also requires a 120-volt power outlet.

In houses with one or two phone lines, a special modular junction box that plugs into the company interface is the simplest way to wire in present and future capacity. Each of the (up to) four station wires from this junction

box can run to (as many as) three standard modular station jacks, wired either in series (from jack to jack) or parallel (branching off a single outlying jack) for 12 possible jack locations per line.

Station wire itself is not intended for outdoor use where it will be directly exposed to the weather. Nevertheless, particularly when retrofitting a jack, running the wire along the exterior of the building is often the only practical way to route it from one room to another. In such cases, any wire that can't be protected by the shelter of a soffit or moulding should be painted to protect it from UV degradation. An 18-inch- or 24-inch-long, $3/16$-inch- or $1/4$-inch-diameter *bellhanger's bit* is an indispensable tool for running station wire through walls and multiple layers of plates, flooring and sills.

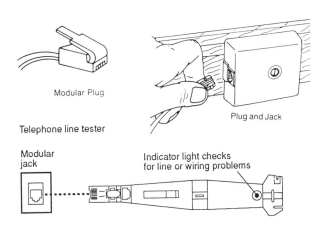

Telephone line tester

Telephone wire stripper

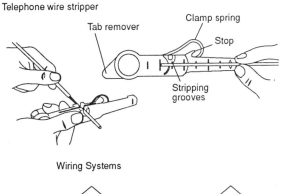

Wiring Systems

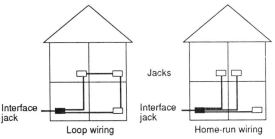

Loop wiring   Home-run wiring

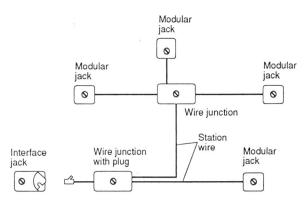

Installing a common connecting point

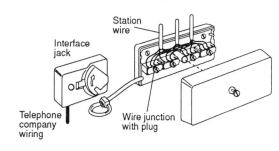

Extending new wire from a junction

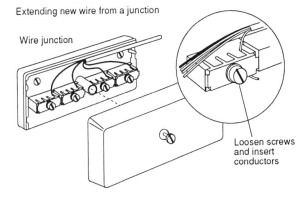

26-9   Telephone interfaces, connections, and jacks.

Although the plastic jacket of the round station wire which is always used between jacks can be cut with a utility knife (with great care), using a special cable slitter avoids the chance of cutting through the insulation of the underlying individual conductors. In lieu of a wire stripper, the conductors themselves can be easily pinched off between your fingernails. (To avoid possible damage to system components, always unplug the system at the interface connection while doing any work on it.) In any case, the terminals of most modular junction boxes actually require no stripping.

Although not strictly necessary, a crimping tool for attaching modular plugs to the base cord (the flat cord that plugs the phone into the jack and the handset into the receiver) is useful. If more than a few custom-length base cords are involved, it costs a lot less to make your own than to buy prepackaged ones.

THE PUNCH LIST

Professional contractors dread *punch lists* (see **26-10**). Architects seem to conspire with owners to search out every minute flaw in the finish, every overlooked detail, and anything the owners changed their mind about or decided to add at the last moment and neglected to inform the builder about. Together they draw up a check list of everything that must be done before the final payment, which represents the actual profit on the job, will be released. For some home-owners, it's a last chance to get something "for nothing" out of the builder or to redress slights, real or perceived. Yet the punch list is a vital and necessary part of the building process. Even in a small project, there are so much going on and so many details

to coordinate that it's inevitable that even the most conscientious and competent builder will miss a few things. The standard procedure is for the builder and the client and/or the architect (if there is one) to do a "walk-through" (and a "walk-around" the outside) together. Items remaining to be completed or mistakes that need to be fixed, and debris to be cleaned up and materials to be removed from the site are noted on a document and countersigned by all parties. Ideally, the builder then checks off each item as it's taken care of, a final walk-through is performed to confirm "satisfactory completion" (in practice a rather ambiguous phrase), and everyone signs off, the builder gets paid, the architect leaves, and the owner is given the keys to the house. Final inspections may also be performed by the local inspector before a certificate of occupancy is issued as well as by bank officers prior to the release of funds and the mortgage conversion, and, in the case of government-subsidized housing loans, by a HUD or FHA inspector. The owner-builder and family should go through the house room by room with the same eye for detail as a professional. Ticking completed items off a finite list can be a psychologically rewarding way to bring the project to a close.

The problem with many owner-built houses is that their builders often run out of steam once the work reaches a point of nominal finish and functional completion (see **26-11** and **26-12**). I can testify from personal experience about baseboards that were still waiting to be installed in closets that still needed the drywall taped and "temporary" 2×4 railings that took a dozen years to be replaced by a formal balustrade. As the frantic pace of construction winds down, the punch list of the minor "details" that stand between you and "final" finish seems to grow like

26-10 *The "punch list" includes such details as filling and sealing nail holes in the finish trim. To prevent stains from bleeding into the surrounding wood, don't apply the filler until after the first coat of varnish. Fillers should be colored to blend in with the wood.*

26-11 *Unless goaded to completion by a mortgage deadline, all too many owner-builders run out of energy once their project reaches "minimal habitability." The definition of this highly elastic term tends to vary according to personal tolerance for disorder and stress as well as financial liquidity.*

26-12 *For one owner-builder, "liveability" may be a place to put the stereo and tapes or a warm and dry roof over a mattress on the floor; for another it may not be reached until even the most minute details have been finished.*

26-13 *Site cleanup shouldn't be left until last. Dumpsters can be rented economically for the duration of a construction project.*

a malignant tumor. Unless you're under duress of a bank-imposed completion deadline (at which time the construction loan converts to a conventional mortgage) it's all too easy to let these seemingly unimportant and usually tedious tasks wait "until later." And, as every resourceful owner-builder knows, what the bank means by completion isn't quite the same thing as a house that's finished down to the last detail. My advice to you as you approach this final phase of building is: *don't surrender to the spirit of procrastination*. If you're like most owner-builders, it's almost a given that those unfinished little details will still need finishing when you put the house on the market ten years later.

Most of the final punch list consists of repairing the inevitable dents, bruises, and scrapes inflicted upon the finish surfaces during the last stages of construction and a marathon cleaning session with spills, spatters, and smudges. When I was in the building business, I found it very cost-efficient to hire a professional house-cleaner just before final inspection. Even though most contracts specify "broom clean," handing over the keys to a sparkling clean house goes a long way towards reinforcing goodwill between the builder and client (see **26-13**). The operative principle is that when everything is 99 percent perfect, your work will be judged by the one percent that "ain't." So, when you, the builder, have to repaint an entire wall surface because the paint dried to a different hue over the patch you put in the hole left by the electrician's mistaken outlet, that's what you'll do because that's what it takes to do the job right.

27 Landscape Construction

Oddly enough, except for high-end projects that involve landscape architects or designers from the very start, few homebuilders give as much consideration to the finish around the outside of their house as they do to its interior and exterior. Yet, attractive landscaping can add many thousands of dollars to the resale value of the house at a relatively small cost (see **27-1**). In a way this is quite understandable, since, other than initial siting considerations involving excavation and drainage, roadways, and perhaps the retention of certain vegetative features, the entire focus of housebuilding is on getting it up and getting in. In northern (colder) climates in particular, by the time the house is closed in, the outdoors is snowed under. Recognizing that further work is impossible until the following spring (which is also the height of the building season), most builders deliberately exclude all landscaping except for "finish grading" from their contracts and leave it entirely up to the discretion of the client to subcontract and deal with a landscaper for plantings, lawns, and other site improvements. As an owner-builder, you have the option of also being your own landscaping subcontractor.

A standard contract usually specifies that the site be graded for "positive drainage" around the perimeter of the house for a distance of at least 20 feet. Some FHA contracts also require the builder to finish-grade, rake, seed, and mulch the lawn areas to a certain specified distance on all sides of the house.

A conscientious excavator will wait until all the exterior work is finished and the stagings are taken down and debris removed before finish-grading. This not only prevents damage to the new lawn, but gives the excavation backfill a chance to settle over a few months and a few soaking rains. Additional fill can then be brought in with the backhoe bucket and distributed over any low areas around the foundation walls. If only a few wheelbarrow loads are needed, it can be spread by hand. The finished subgrade should pitch away from the foundation walls at least four inches over 10 feet before levelling out.

The topsoil which has been saved on site is then spread by machine to a depth of about four inches over the subsoil by machine. In the hands of a good operator, a backhoe, bucket loader, or even a back-dragged bulldozer blade can accomplish this with felicitous grace. In most parts of the country, topsoil will contain numerous small rocks and clods that must be hand-raked into windrows and wheelbarrowed to the margins of the property. This provides an excellent short-term employment opportunity for local youth. After seeding down the grass, protect it with a mulch of straw or old hay. Otherwise, between wind, rain, and birds, very few seeds will be left to sprout into lawn.

27-1 *Landscaping can be thought of as outdoor finish work. This owner-built fence, made from sawmill slabs, is anything but fancy, yet it definitely belongs to its landscape.*

Excavate outside of drip line   Backfill with compost or top soil not subsoil   Retaining wall

27-2 *Most excavators won't take any special steps to save or protect trees on site unless you specify this in the contract. Make sure that regrading does not alter the soil contour within the drip line of any tree you wish to leave.*

Many homebuilders go through trouble to save trees on the site only to have them die off a few years later. In most cases this is because their site modifications inadvertently or carelessly disturbed the tree roots or changed the oxygen content of the soil and/or its groundwater level.

Unless the original grade around the tree is maintained within the circumference of the *drip line* (the outermost perimeter of the tree's crown) the tree will die (see **27-2**). When excavating, stop the cut at the drip line, and protect the bank with a retaining wall. If the resulting hummock is too large for your site, consult a tree expert for advice on root pruning. By a combination of careful branch and root pruning, it's possible to tighten the perimeter of the drip line by as much as one-third.

It's also possible to raise the grade around a tree without harming it if air and drainage are provided for the roots (see **27-3**). The best way to do this is to strip the sod from around the tree to an area several feet beyond the circumference of the drip line and spread a few inches of compost

or peat/topsoil mix over it. Then lay short lengths of perforated plastic drainpipe (holes down) or clay drain tiles (even better) in a circle. Extend four to six pipes in a radial (spoke-like) pattern out to the circle from about six to twelve inches away from the tree trunk (the older the tree, the closer the ends of the spokes can be). Lay the pipes on the original grade, but make sure they slope away from the trunk at least $1/8$ inch per foot of run. Add vertical risers to the new grade line at the intersection of each spoke and rim pipe, and extend a drain line out to daylight or a dry well. Spread eight to 12 inches of crushed stone over the pipes (whose joints are protected with a loose wrap of tar paper) and then begin tamping down the backfill. Build a circular retaining wall from dry-laid stone or brick around the base of the trunk, leaving the ends of the drainpipes exposed.

If grade is being raised or lowered around only part of the tree, the retaining wall or spoke system need simply be installed in the disturbed area.

Install air and drainage

Build a retaining wall around trunk

Finish grade

27-3 *Raising the grade around a tree. Never push dirt against the trunk of a tree.*

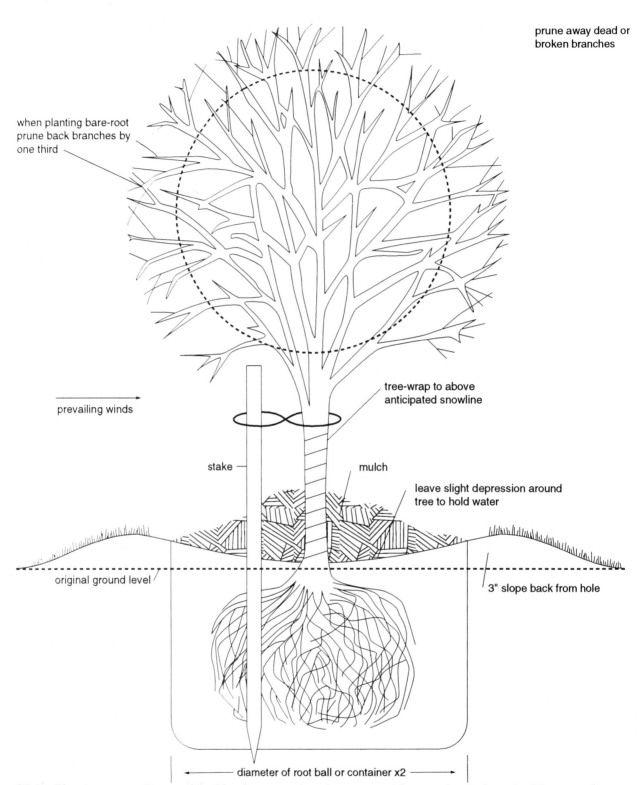

prune away dead or
broken branches

when planting bare-root
prune back branches by
one third

prevailing winds

tree-wrap to above
anticipated snowline

stake

mulch

leave slight depression around
tree to hold water

original ground level

3" slope back from hole

diameter of root ball or container x2

27-4 *Planting a tree. Be careful of landscapers who plant trees with a mechanical spade. They may be more interested in a quick job than in the careful steps it takes to ensure that the transplant will live and prosper. An experienced nurseryman can hand-dig and hand-plant trees of surprisingly large caliper (diameter at chest height).*

Instead of saving trees, you may wish to plant new ones or move and replant existing trees (see **27-4**). Digging up and replanting even a fairly small tree is a lot of work and requires expertise to keep from harming it. The key is to disturb as little of the root ball as possible, which requires knowledge of the different growth habits of each tree species. Unless you've had some prior experience digging tress, hire a professional or else buy a "B&B" (balled-and-burlaped) or container-grown tree ready for planting from a reputable nursery. You can also hire a truck-mounted tree spade to come on site to dig and replant trees up to any size whose root ball can fit into the jaws of the spade.

To plant a B&B or container tree, dig a planting hole about twice as wide as the diameter of the root ball or container, deep enough so that the tree will be at the same level as it was before planting. Remove the container carefully so as not to loosen the soil around the root ball or cut away as much burlap as you can after the tree is lowered into its planting hole. Bare-root trees should be placed in a hole wide enough and deep enough so that the roots can spread out naturally and so that the graft line remains above the soil and the tree is at its original depth.

Loosen the soil at the bottom of the planting hole so that it will be easier for the roots to expand and feed. Although many nurserymen will disagree, the latest research suggests that the best planting medium is the native soil removed from the hole, rather than planting soil or added organic matter. However, truly poor soil will benefit from the addition of about an equal part of quality topsoil, and sandy soils will increase their water retention with the addition of up to 50 percent peat moss.

Moisten the hole thoroughly before planting the tree. Have a helper hold the tree straight up while you fill in the soil around the roots. Tamp it gently but firmly to remove air spaces and continue adding soil and tamping until the new soil level forms a slight depression. Water the tree thoroughly and frequently after tamping.

The branches of a newly planted bare-root tree should be pruned back about one-third so that the tree doesn't lose more water through its leaves than it can take up with its roots. Trees planted in windy spaces should be braced by three staked guy wires spaced equally around the tree. Slip the wires through short lengths of hose to protect the bark.

When deciding where to plant trees, avoid close proximity to wells, sewers, septic tanks, and foundation walls. As the roots mature, they can crack concrete and lift sidewalks and footings in their relentless quest for nutrients and moisture.

Of course, landscaping is much more than planting lawns and trees. In fact, in some communities in the arid Southwest of the United States it may actually be against the local ordinance to surround your house with a water-guzzling lawn. *Xeriscaping* is the practice of landscaping with native plants—or, in other words, for the Southwest it means putting back the desert that you had to move in order to build your house. The concept is applicable to other climates and plant communities. Today, although many communities still enforce "weed control" ordinances, there is some acceptance of natural landscaping and "wildflower meadows" in place of manicured lawns. Consult your local library for guidance on plant species suited to local conditions.

There's also a thriving trade in "O.R.'s" (as professional landscapers call "ornamental rocks"). These can range in size from manually movable stones to gigantic boulders hoisted into place by a log-truck boom or small crane. Depending on the site contours, these rocks can be placed singly or in groups or even assembled on top of each other like giant building blocks to form retaining walls that double as rock gardens and steps.

Dry-laid stone walls have been a feature of the landscape for millennia (see **27-5**). Thus the art of stone masonry is literally as old as civilization. A beautiful stone wall is both artful and artless; the pattern of the stones is random, yet deliberate. A skilled stonemason lays stones with regard to their face color and grain as well as how they interlock with their neighbors. A big part of the battle is selecting good stones with regular faces in the first place.

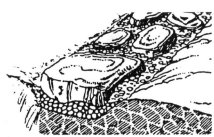

Irregular foundation stones in grade trench

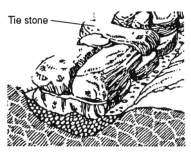

Tie stone

Start with largest stones at bottom course

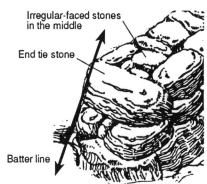

Irregular-faced stones in the middle

End tie stone

Batter line

Alternate courses, 2 over 1 and 1 over 2

27-5 *Building a dry-laid stone wall. No footings are needed.*

Unlike mortared stone walls, which must be laid on a foundation that is below frost line, dry-laid stone walls three feet or less high can be built directly on the ground with no digging required—other than removing the topsoil and levelling a strip equal in width to the base course of the wall, which should be about two feet. As the height of the wall increases, its base should be widened. Add four inches to the width at the bottom for every six inches of increase in height over three feet. Some stonemasons figure that the wall should have a enough *batter* (taper) so that its top will end up about 20 percent narrower than its base. Walls over three feet high will be stronger if their first course is set in a flat-bottomed trench that is about a foot deep. It doesn't hurt to dig a little deeper and add a layer of crushed stone or gravel either, particularly in wet, heavy soils.

To conserve good flat stones, lay the biggest and most irregular boulders in the first course at the bottom of the trench. If you've laid a gravel cushion, it will be easy to dig holes to fit stones that have only a single flat face. Stones below ground level should be spaced a few inches apart and the gaps filled with gravel and small rocks for good drainage. Lay the stones so that they tilt slightly inward towards the center of the wall from each side.

The guiding principle for laying dry stone is "One over two, two over one." One stone should always cover the space between at least two stones beneath it—exactly like the courses of brick or concrete block. Furthermore, try to set *tie stones* (a stone big enough to span the width of the wall) every six to eight feet apart. Tie stones should also be laid in alternating courses at the ends of the wall. As much as possible, save irregularly shaped stones for filling in the center portions of the wall.

Check the stones for level as you continue building the wall upwards. Obviously, individual stones won't be perfectly level, but their general axis and the run of each course should be so. If a stone rocks when set in place, try to knock off the offending high spot with a stone hammer or brick chisel. Failing this, shim it solid with wedge-shaped stones. Always face wedge stones towards the center of the wall, point end facing outward to keep them from eventually working out.

Not everyone will have a source of nice flat stones. If you find yourself working with a lot of rounded stones, place them in the middle of the wall and shim them so that they don't move. Then set stones that have at least one flat face against them on both sides. Each stone should touch at least five others: one at each end, two beneath,

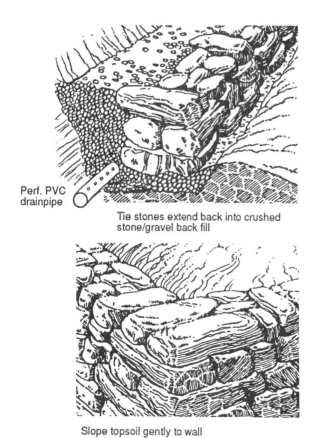

Perf. PVC drainpipe

Tie stones extend back into crushed stone/gravel back fill

Slope topsoil gently to wall

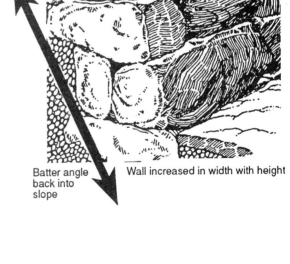

Batter angle back into slope

Wall increased in width with height

27-6 A dry-laid stone retaining wall. The stones "step" back into the bank to anchor the wall.

and at least one core stone. Save the very best long, flat large stones for tying the ends of the walls back into the wall.

When building a stone retaining wall, the wall should increase in width as it gains in height. It should also batter back slightly towards the bank (see **27-6**). Lay a perforated drain tile in a bed of crushed stone along the length of the back of the first course and continue backfilling with crushed stone and gravel as the wall rises. Try to find large heavy tie stones that are long enough to reach back into the gravel as you continue leaning the wall back.

Once a stone wall rises much above knee or waste level, getting the heavy tie stones up onto it becomes a problem. Sometimes the best stones will be heavier than even two people can safely lift. The rule for preventing injury is not to lift any more than you absolutely must. Using an inclined ramp (a stout plank resting on the top of the wall) to lift heavy stone is a technology at least as old as the pyramids (see **27-7**). And stones that you can't comfortably roll or push up a pair of planks can be coaxed into place with levers or rollers. If the stone itself is too irregular to sit on a roller, put the rollers under a short plank on which the stone can sit.

A well-built stone wall is beautiful and will last for centuries. But stone is expensive to transport, difficult to handle, and fairly limited in the ways in which it can be used. Treated-wood timbers, whether recycled railroad ties or new pressure-treated wood, are much easier to handle and work with than stone.

Salvaged railroad ties vary considerably in both dimension and condition. They're also very heavy as well as saturated with creosote and tar, which makes them hard to cut. It doesn't take too many crosscuts through railroad ties to gum up and dull a chainsaw. Creosote is not only a lot more toxic than CCA-treated wood, but more noxious. Gloves are a necessity as creosote is caustic and readily absorbed through the skin. Nevertheless, because used railroad ties are inexpensive and have a pleasing natural appearance compared to the sickly greenish hue of CCA-treated wood, many home-owners prefer to use them for landscaping projects. Having worked with both, I heartily recommend CCA pressure-treated 6×6 yellow pine timbers over railroad ties. For one thing, the preservative is nowhere near as hazardous to your health or to the immediate environment. The timbers themselves are milled to fairly consistent dimensions, which makes them a lot easier to build with. And the green color will weather to a natural-looking light grey in a couple of years or so. Treated timbers shouldn't be confused with the less expensive so-called "landscape timbers" that have only two flat sides and aren't usually treated all the way through the wood.

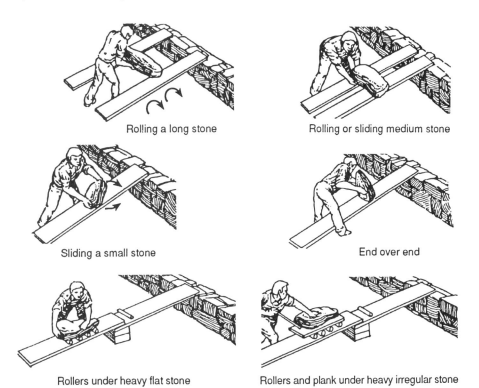

Rolling a long stone

Rolling or sliding medium stone

Sliding a small stone

End over end

Rollers under heavy flat stone

Rollers and plank under heavy irregular stone

27-7 *Lifting heavy stones to the top of a wall. As the incline of the plank increases, the stones become more difficult to move. You can increase the length of the ramp or rent a small tractor with a bucket loader.*

Because any retaining wall must resist a great deal of lateral pressure and accommodate drainage (and sometimes, frost heave) from the slope, careful design is important (see **27-8**). You may discover that retaining walls fall under the jurisdiction of your local building code and that a permit and even an engineered design may be required. Although walls four feet or less in height can be readily built by a beginner, you may want to consult an engineer for more complex projects.

The first step in building a timber retaining wall is to excavate the bank to make room for the "deadmen" that will anchor the wall to the bank. Set a grade string, and dig a foot-wide level trench at least 10 inches deep at its most shallow point along the entire length of the wall. Fill the trench with about four inches of crushed stone, and then set the first timber in it, lining it up to the string. Level the timber from end to end with a transit level or a four-foot level and a straightedge. But, instead of levelling the timber from front to back, give it a ¼-inch pitch so that the wall will lean towards the bank. Butt the timbers end to end.

While many professionals use a chainsaw to cut timbers, I prefer to use a circular saw. An eight-inch saw will cut through a milled 6×6 with a pass on either side. With a standard 7¼-inch saw, you'll need to saw through a one-inch-square section with a handsaw. Compared to a chainsaw, the tight joints made by a circular saw are well worth the extra effort, particularly if you need to make mitre cuts for angled walls.

Rest the timbers for the first course on blocks to hold them above ground to keep the drill bit from getting dulled while you bore pilot holes through them with an electrician's auger and a ½-inch heavy-duty drill on four-foot centers. Set and level the timbers, and drive 24-inch-long, No. 4 (½-inch-diameter) rebar pins through the pilot holes with a sledgehammer to anchor the timbers to the ground.

Set an eight-foot-long timber at right angles to the end of the first course and rest its other end across a three-foot-long cross block Pin the two timbers together with 12-inch-long rebars. Do the same at the far end of the wall and at six- to eight-foot intervals in between. When backfilled, the weight of the earth on these "deadmen" will resist the lateral force exerted by the fill on the wall and keep it from being pushed over. Lay perforated drainpipe along the backside of the wall pitched to daylight or a drywell, and cover it with crushed stone. Fill in the sections between the deadmen with timbers and pin them in place with rebar as well. Continue adding staggered courses of timbers pinning each to the one below, and, depending on the height of the wall, more deadmen (a course for every four vertical feet, except for the top). Backfill the area immediately next to the wall with crushed stone, and fill in the rest of the excavation with native soil or gravel. Maintain the ¼-inch pitch of the timbers so

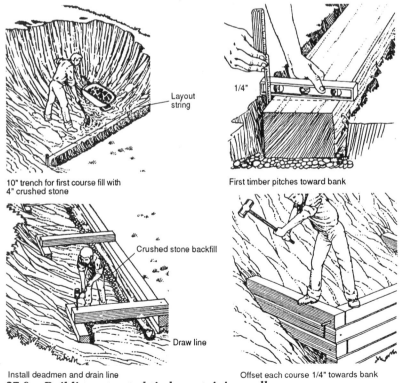

10" trench for first course fill with 4" crushed stone

First timber pitches toward bank

Install deadmen and drain line

Offset each course 1/4" towards bank

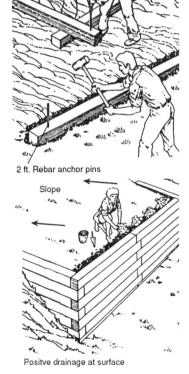

2 ft. Rebar anchor pins

Positve drainage at surface

27-8 *Building a treated-timber retaining wall.*

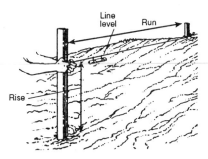

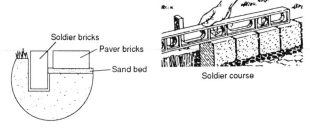

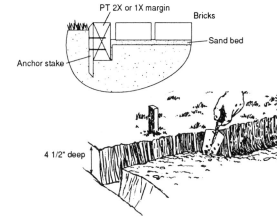

27-9 *Layout of outdoor timber stairs. Just like interior stairs, the risers of outdoor stairs must be equal. Since the riser height is the same as the timber depth, the grade will most likely have to be adjusted for the first or last step.*

27-10 *Margins for brick pathways. Setting soldier bricks level and plumb is tedious work.*

that the wall leans inward as it rises. Grade the backfill to slope away from the top of the wall for positive surface drainage.

Treated timbers can also be used to enclose planting beds, make terraced gardens, and for steps in walkways. Since the ideal rise-to-run ratio for comfortable outdoor steps is 6:15, a 5⅝-inch timber makes an almost perfect step (see **27-9**).

To calculate the number of steps you'll need for your timber stairway (or any other outdoor stair) drive a short stake into the ground at the high point of the stairway-to-be. Set a taller stake at the low point and stretch a line level between them—or shoot the elevation with a transit level or level between the stakes with a straight 2×4 and a four-foot level. The distance between the elevations is the stair rise, and the distance between the stakes is its run. Try to set the stakes at a distance that represents a convenient whole number to "cipher" with. Divide the rise by the thickness of the timbers and the run into evenly spaced tread intervals (they can be almost any length or combination of lengths so long as none are shorter than 15 inches). Unlike an interior set of stairs where the landing heights are fixed and the riser tread ratio varies, with timber stairs the riser height is fixed and the relative heights of the landings aren't. Fortunately, it's a lot easier to change the grade to suit the timbers than it is to raise or lower a floor deck.

Pin the stair riser timbers into the ground and to the header timbers that border the walkway (if any). Filling the walkway between the timbers with crushed white dolomite limestone improves nighttime visibility. Other types of stone or even bark mulch can be used for color and texture.

Dry-laying brick in a sand bed is another popular way to pave pathways and patios (see **27-10**). Although some landscapers prefer to set a *soldier course* (bricks set vertically on end in a margin trench) for the headers that form the margins of the pathway, it's a lot easier to use

treated wood for headers instead. Set level guide strings for the header layout, and stake the header boards in place as you would when building a footing form. Trim the header stakes off at a steep angle so that they can be buried in the backfill.

When laying a walkway in wet soil, excavate a foot-deep trench that slopes towards the center of the walkway (see **27-11**). Spread enough sand in the bottom of the trench to level it off and then run a perforated drainpipe down the center. Cover it with crushed stone, and then spread more sand on top of the gravel to form the bed for the bricks.

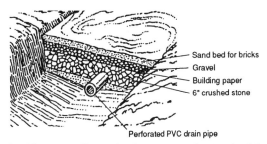

27-11 *A walkway bed in wet soil. Dry-laid brick will shift and settle in wet soil unless subsurface drainage is added.*

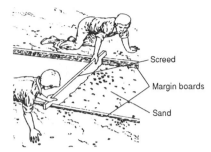

27-12 *A level tamped bed is a prerequisite for a quality brick walkway.*

The headers will make an excellent guide for screeding off the sand bed to make a level base for the bricks (see **27-12**). Settle the sand bed by watering it down and tamping it with an earth roller or mechanical tamper. Wait until the sand has dried before screeding it level. Cut the notches in the ends of the screed board about ¼ inch shallower than the thickness of a brick to allow for settlement of the bed. Otherwise, the bricks will end up below the headers.

Begin laying the bricks on the sand bed at a corner against the header board and check them for level with a straightedge resting across the headers (see **27-13**). Any bricks that are too high can be set deeper by pounding them with a rubber mallet or by removing a little bit of sand. Add sand to raise up bricks that are too low. Use spacers if you want to have a wide joint between the bricks; otherwise, butt them tightly against each other.

After all the bricks are laid, sweep dry sand back and forth over the surface, adding more until all the cracks between the bricks are filled. Water down the surface to settle the sand. After it dries add more sand and continue sweeping and hosing until the bricks won't accept any more.

Where heavy rains are the norm, it's a good idea to crown the brickwork rather than lay it dead level so that water will drain off to both sides. For patios and walkways that abut the house, the bed should slope away at about ⅛ inch per foot. A special curved screed is used to crown a sand bed (see **27-14**). Assuming a slope of ¼ inch per foot from centerline, screw spacer blocks to each end of a flat 2×4 screed (e.g., ½ inch for a four-foot-wide walk) and fasten a strip of ¼-inch plywood to the blocks and the center point of the screed board. Rest the ears of the screed on the header boards, and press the curved face down into the sand. Draw the board down the length of the compacted sand to form the crown. Remove the ears, and use the screed as a template for checking the set of the bricks.

Fencing is another important part of landscape construction (see **27-15**). Fences may make good neighbors but they can also lead to legal battles and bad feelings if you aren't careful about which side of the property line they're on. Issues of boundary lines, setbacks, fence height, and general appearance aren't as likely to become a source of contention in rural areas as in an urban or suburban setting, where fence building may be regulated by local zoning ordinances. For example, in some communities, boundary-line fences can't be more than six feet high. In any case, your neighbors have legal control over any part of a fence that you build on their side of the boundary line. Sometimes, neighbors will agree to split the cost or share in the labor of building a mutually desirable fence. In such cases, it's wise to add a clause to both property deeds that describes any agreements concerning repairs and maintenance should the property change hands.

The height of a fence depends on its purpose (see **27-16**). A privacy fence, for example, must be tall enough to screen neighboring houses and prevent passersby from seeing over it. This means that the height of the fence depends not only on your point of view looking out but

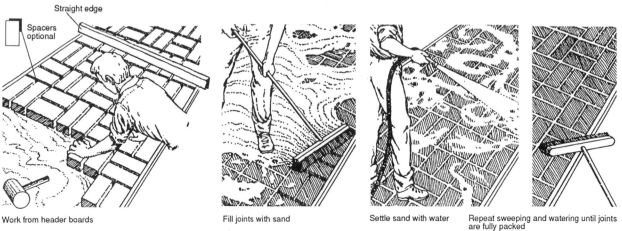

Work from header boards   Fill joints with sand   Settle sand with water   Repeat sweeping and watering until joints are fully packed

27-13 *Setting dry-laid bricks on a sand bed.*

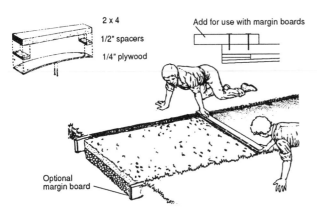

2 x 4
1/2" spacers
1/4" plywood

Add for use with margin boards

Optional margin board

27-14 *Crowning the surface of a walkway helps reduce the likelihood of settlement as the underlying bed becomes saturated.*

27-15 *In frost-free climates, concrete block fences and garden walls can be built upon a 12-inch-deep trench footing. This ornamental arch is supported by a simple plywood form until the mortar sets up.*

on the point of view of someone looking in. Distance and elevation of the object or view to be screened relative to the observer all affect the line of sight.

A fence that's intended to block movement but not the view (the traditional white picket fence, for example) doesn't have to be more than four feet high. An even lower fence or wall can act as a nominal barrier that defines an area without actually enclosing it.

A wood fence that is built to last must resist the forces of wind and frost heave and be rot-resistant. Achieving this requires some degree of what a more casual fence builder may regard as engineering overkill. Although you

can use untreated wood for the fence boards themselves, all the fence posts and any horizontal rails between them to which the fence boards are fastened should be pressure-treated lumber.

As a rule of thumb, post holes should be one third as deep as the post is long, typically, 24 to 30 inches deep (see **27-17**). In wet soils subject to deep frost penetration, extending the holes below the frost line will keep the fence posts from heaving. Pack a few inches of crushed stone into the bottom of the post hole to help promote drainage, and plumb the post with temporary braces as you backfill the hole with alternating layers of stone and soil. Tamp

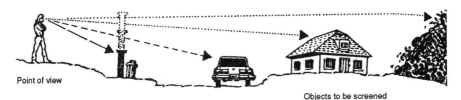

Point of view

Objects to be screened

27-16 *Privacy fences and lines of sight. When planning a privacy fence, try to check the line of sight from the outside looking in as well from the more obvious vantage point of inside looking out.*

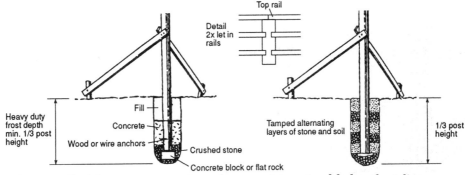

Top rail

Detail 2x let in rails

Heavy duty frost depth min. 1/3 post height

Fill

Concrete

Wood or wire anchors

Crushed stone

Concrete block or flat rock

Tamped alternating layers of stone and soil

1/3 post height

27-17 *Except in wet soils, it's not necessary for a fence post to extend below frost line.*

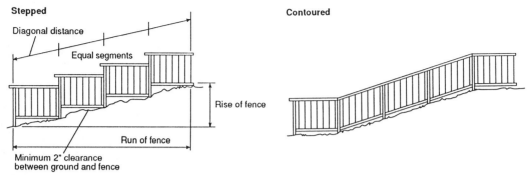

27-18 *Stepping a fence up a slope in equal segments looks more "architectural" than letting the fence follow the contour, which some feel looks more "natural." In any case, a stepped fence is easier to build. Another option, particularly on steep sites, is to slope the bottom rail and step the top rail.*

the fill with the flat face of a sledgehammer or a length of two-inch steel pipe with a cap on the end. You can spike short lengths of 1×2 across the post to help anchor it in the hole or else staple a tangled ball of chicken wire around the post and pour concrete halfway up the post hole. The bottom of the post itself should stick past the concrete into the crushed-stone base. After the concrete sets, backfill to grade and shoot level lines across the posts for setting the fence rails and cutting the posts to finished height.

For maximum strength, dado the bottom and any intermediate fence rails into the posts instead of toenailing them. The top rail can be nailed over the top of the posts or else dadoed in six inches or so below the top.

Although it's often done that way, fencing that runs along a slope usually looks better if it doesn't follow the contour of the ground. Instead, the sections of fencing between each post should climb the grade in a series of regular steps, just like outdoor stairs (see **27-18**). Stepping the fence up the slope maintains a constant height so that the security and privacy functions of the fence aren't compromised. Since the clearance between the bottom of the fence and the ground should be at least two inches at the uphill end, as the steepness of the slope increases the fence

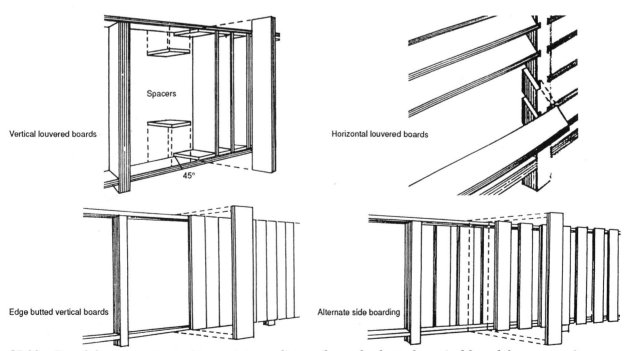

27-19 *Board fencing patterns. Use an intermediate rail on edge-butted, vertical board fences over four feet high to keep the boards from twisting.*

sections must become shorter to avoid excessive terracing of the grade on the uphill end and too much clearance at the downhill end of each fence section.

Vertical one-inch boards butted tightly together or overlapped board-on-board style and nailed to the fence rails make the most private and easiest-to-build fence (see **27-19**). However, since the boarding acts like a sail in the wind, the fence posts must be set deep and solid. Spacing the fence boards like pickets reduces wind resistance but surrenders privacy. Alternating the boards and spaces on both sides of the rail, so that a space on one side faces a board on the other, lowers wind resistance while still maintaining a fair degree of privacy. Boarding both sides also eliminates the definite front-and-back look of a single-side boarded fence, which is especially noticeable when intermediate rails are used to stiffen the fence boards. Depending on which side of the fence you have to look at, this could have an important effect both on the appearance of your property or a neighbor's feelings.

Vertical boards can also be nailed on a 45-degree angle in between the fence rails like vertical blinds. The fence rails can be dadoed for the boards or else angled spacers can be nailed to them between the boards. The fence boards can also be set in diagonal dadoes horizontally between the posts like an ordinary louvre. Although louvred fence boards provide both excellent privacy and wind protection, because they overlap each other more boards are needed to cover the same area as regular fence boards. Also, because they don't touch each other, louvred (and spaced) fence boards are more likely to twist (and sag if horizontal). Using kiln-dried, straight-grained boards will help minimize this tendency.

Special support is required at a gate hinge post to make the gate secure and to keep its weight from pulling the post sideways (see **27-20**). Gate posts can be strengthened by setting them deeper than the standard fence posts and/or casting them in a concrete threshold or pouring a concrete *strain plug* that resists sideways forces.

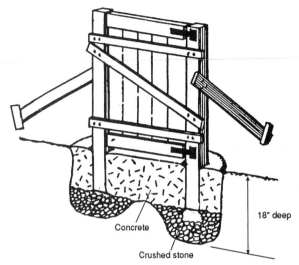

27-20 *This type of threshold can also be used to anchor a set of porch or deck steps.*

Dig a foot-wide trench at least 18 inches deep along the length of the gate and its posts (the trench need only be about a foot deep under the center of the gate itself). Shovel crushed stone into the trench under the gate posts. Nail the gate in position between its posts with temporary cleats and lower the assembly into the trench. Plumb, level, and brace it, and then fill the trench to grade with concrete.

To make a strain plug, dig a wider-than-normal post hole and nail a pair of 2×4 treated crossbars to the bottom of the hinge post (see **27-21**). Plumb the post on a base of crushed stone and then backfill the hole with alternating layers of crushed stone and earth to about 16 inches below finish grade. Tack a pair of 1×8s to the sides of the post parallel with the run of the gate and fill this form with concrete. After the concrete has set, remove the form boards and backfill to grade.

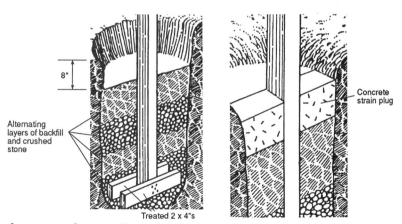

27-21 *A strain plug uses only a small amount of concrete yet imparts a great deal of stability.*

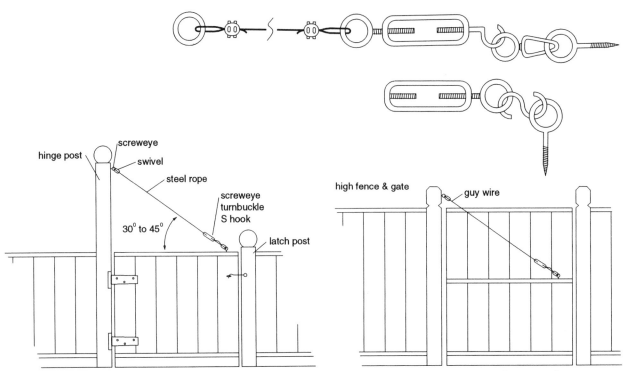

27-22   *Guy wires for heavy gates. Since steel contracts and expands with temperature changes, the turn-buckles will have to be adjusted seasonally.*

Depending on the length and weight of the gate, you may wish to use a bigger and heavier post (a 6×6 or even an 8×8, for example, with 4×4 fence posts). Any gate much over four feet wide should have a guy wire to relieve the strain on the hinges and prevent the gate from sagging (see **27-22**). Thus gate hinge posts are usually taller than fence posts (an exception would be a tall fence, where the guy wire can be run from the top of the hinge post to the middle of the far end of the gate itself). The post should be tall enough so that the angle of the guy wire to the top of the gate is between 30 degrees and 45 degrees.

To connect the guy wire, turn a ³⁄₈-inch zinc-plated screw eye into the side of the post a few inches below its top (screw eyes tend to pull out if screwed into the end grain on top of the post). Turn another eye into the top edge of the gate rail at its latch end. You can also use screw hooks with light gates. They usually bend under the load of a long (nine to 20 foot) heavy gate. Join ¹⁄₈-inch or ³⁄₁₆-inch galvanized steel cable to the latch-side eyebolt with an S-hook or self-closing connecting loop and a turnbuckle and cable clamps. Use a swivel connector at the hinge post end of the cable so that the gate will open and shut smoothly and so that the connecting loop won't pinch or wear against the eye hook. Install a turnbuckle at this end as well to make it easier to take the initial slack out of the cable and tighten it up as it stretches over time.

The gate itself can be hung with heavy-duty plated tee-strap hinges lag-screwed into the hinge post. Use a pair of two-part, lag-bolt hinges to hang a heavy gate (see **27-23**). The male parts, which end in a vertical pin, are screwed into the hinge post. The ringed female parts screw into the ends of the top and bottom gate rails or the sides of the gate stile and the gate is lifted up and set down onto the pins.

Depending on the level of security required and the type of gate, there are many different kinds of gate latches to choose from, including sliding bolts, hook-and-eye, drop latches, and various kinds of dead-bolts.

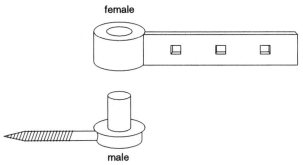

27-23   *Hinges should attach to a horizontal rail or an otherwise reinforced area of the gate.*

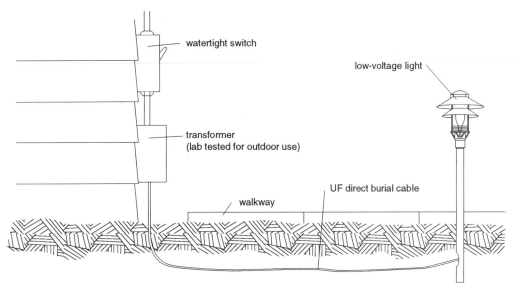

27-24 *Components of a low-voltage outdoor lighting system. The system must connect to a GFI-protected circuit. Leave some slack in cable to permit soil movement.*

LOW-VOLTAGE OUTDOOR LIGHTING

Line-voltage outdoor and underground wiring has been discussed in Chapter Eighteen. Low-voltage (12-volt) systems are widely used for lighting walkways, garden paths, patios, and other outdoor lighting needs. Special self-anchoring waterproof light fixtures with attached ground posts make it easy to set lights without any extensive digging or supplemental post anchors (see **27-24**). The power-supply wire can be buried directly in a shallow (six-inch-deep) hand-dug trench without need of conduit. The system is powered by a transformer that plugs into an outdoor receptacle. The transformer can also be set indoors in a garage, shed, cellar, or other convenient location.

AUTOMATIC WATERING SYSTEMS

Programmable digital electronic timers and PVC piping have made multizoned automatic watering systems affordable and easy to install. Because they deliver water according to a predetermined schedule precisely when and where it's needed, whether you're home or not, automatic systems conserve water, save time, and improve your home's value.

The number of sprinklers your system can run at the same time depends on the capacity of your domestic water supply, which is a function of the water meter, service line size, and water pressure. The size of the water meter is usually stamped on its body. If it isn't, your water company can tell you what size it is. Usually, this will be ⅝, ¾, or one inch. If you can't tell the size of your service line (the pipe that runs from the street or your well into the basement), wrap a string around the pipe and measure how long a piece it takes to encircle it (see **27-25**).

To ensure the maximum water pressure to your irrigation system, all the pipes from the supply line to the control valves and the sprinkler risers as well as the valves themselves should be at least the same size as the service line.

If you have a well with a pressure tank, all it takes is a glance at the attached pressure gauge while the pump is running to tell what your water system's pressure is. For municipal systems without pressure regulation, screw a water pressure gauge to an outside faucet—near to where you plan to locate your control valves, if possible—making sure all the water fixtures in the rest of the house are off, and turn the faucet wide open. Do this three times a day

27-25 *Finding the size of your service line.*

Length of string	2¾″	3⅜″	3½″	4⅛″	5³⁄₁₆″
Size of copper line	¾″		1″		
Size of PVC/poly line		¾″		1″	1¾″
Size of galvanized steel line	¾″			1″	1¾″

to get the average water pressure of your system. If you can't get a gauge or your water supply is pressure-regulated, call the water company and ask them what the average pressure is at the meter.

Use that figure and the chart in **27-26** to find the water capacity of your system in gallons per minute (gpm).

Make a drawing of your property on graph paper to determine the areas that need watering (see **27-27**). These will be your zones. Then, consulting a chart provided by your system manufacturer, determine which types of sprinkler heads and how many of them you'll need to water each zone. For example, there are pop-up sprinklers for lawns, "shrub heads" for shrubs and ground covers, "bubblers" for flower beds, planters, trees, and shrubs, and misters and drip irrigation lines for vegetable gardens, greenhouses, and container plants. All of these sprinklers have different "throw" patterns and delivery rates. Also, bubbler-type sprinklers can't be used in the same zone as pop-ups and shrub heads. It sounds a lot more complicated than it is. The manufacturer's brochures supply complete descriptions of their various sprinkler patterns and their coverage area and listings of their gpm output at given system pressures. Add up the gpm ratings for all the sprinklers in each zone. The total for any zone must be less than the calculated capacity of your water system in order for the sprinklers to work right.

The basic system consists of a controller/timer that is located somewhere convenient to a power source and protected from the weather, such as a garage or patio or basement. The 24-volt controller is powered by a transformer that plugs into a nearby outlet (see **27-28**). Color-coded wires from each controller zone terminal run to automatic valves that are grouped together in manifolds. Water is supplied to the manifold by a line taped in the water service line as close to the meter as possible. Distribution lines run from each valve to the sprinklers located in the zones.

From the tap in the service line, the pipe runs to a master gate valve that can shut the entire system down when necessary. From the shutoff, the pipe tees into an upward sloping supply line to the control valves and down into a boiler drain cock so that the system can be drained during freezing weather or for repairs.

Where freezing weather is normal, install *automatic drain valves* in reducer tees at the low points in the pipe run between each control valve and its sprinklers (preferably closer to the sprinkler than the manifold). Install an additional drain valve in the supply line between the control valve manifold and the point of entry into the house ahead of the system gate valve. The reducer tees should be angled 45 degrees downwards so that the water will drain into the bed of gravel that surrounds it. These valves open automatically whenever your system shuts off to drain the water left standing in the pipes.

Obviously, if freeze protection is a concern, you must pay careful attention to pitching the distribution pipes so that they'll drain back to the drain valves and the supply line so that it runs back from the manifold to the basement drain. Use strings and a level to lay out the pipe runs and to establish the depth of the trenches.

If your soil is hard to dig, soften it by watering the ground a day or two ahead of time. Use a mattock or a straight trenching spade to dig a six-inch-deep trench. Remove the sod first and place it on one side of the excavation. Put the soil on the other so that it's easier to put everything back after the pipe is laid. For more extensive installations, rent a gas-powered trencher.

If you need to tunnel under a sidewalk, thread a pipe-thread-to-hose-thread adapter onto the end of a male IP-to-PVC slip adapter and glue the adapter to the end of a length of PVC pipe. Connect your garden hose and turn on the water. At the pressure tunnels under the sidewalk, push the pipe forward until it clears the other end. Cut off the adapter (leaving enough length so that you can

27-26 *Finding the system's water capacity.*

Size of meter	Service Line	Water pressure (psi)							
		30	35	40	45	50	55	60	65
5/8″	1/2″	2.0	3.5	5.0	6.0	6.5	7.0	7.5	8.0
5/8″	5/8″	3.5	5.0	7.0	8.5	9.5	10.0	11.0	11.5
3/4″	3/4″	5.0	7.0	8.0	9.0	11.0	12.0	14.0	15.0
3/4″	1″	7.5	10.0	11.5	13.5	15.0	16.0	17.5	18.5
1″	3/4″	6.0	7.5	9.0	10.0	12.0	13.0	15.0	16.0
1″	1″	9.0	12.0	13.5	17.0	19.0	20.0	21.0	21.0

Note: For galvanized steel lines, use 65 percent of the gpm shown (there's more internal friction in steel pipe).
Irrigation systems can't operate with water pressures in excess of 80 psi. Install a pressure regulator in the supply line if this is the case.
Use 65 psi figures for determining capacity at pressures of 70–80 psi.
For pumped systems without a meter, use figures for the same size meter and service line.

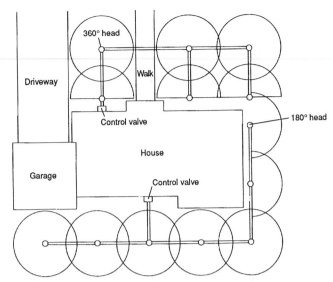

27-27 *Planning an automatic watering system. Ideally, the watering system is installed after the site is finish-graded and before the lawns are seeded.*

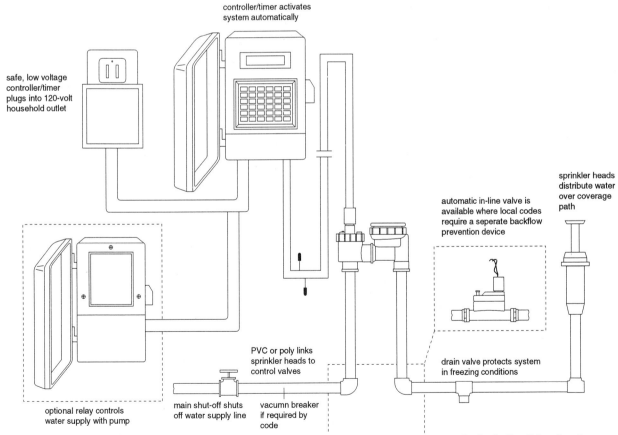

27-28 *Schematic of an automatic irrigation system. Drip irrigation systems use ¼-inch flexible plastic tubing and micro-sprinklers to distribute water from main lines. Unlike conventional irrigation systems, most drip systems require a pressure-reducing valve.*

use it again) and, after the water has drained off, clean the pipe and join it to the supply line with a coupler fitting.

When assembling the control valve manifold, the anti-siphon valves must be at least six inches higher than the highest sprinkler head on the system (local codes may require more separation) to prevent backflow from the sprinklers through the valves and into the household water system. Some local codes require the use of in-line valves and a separate *constant pressure backflow preventer* or *vacuum breaker* (basically a check valve) between the manifold and the supply line to prevent contamination of the household water system. Because water can flow through in-line valves and flush out dirt particles, they're recommended for use with irrigation systems that use unfiltered

water supplies, such as water pumped from a pond or well. In-line manifolds are set below ground in a wood-framed or plastic valve box. No matter which type of valve you use, it should be the same size as your service line (either ¾ or one inch).

From the manifold, the lines tee off into threaded risers for the sprinkler heads. All the distribution pipes and fittings should be the same size as the control valves also. Using smaller pipes does not increase the pressure, it only increases friction and actually reduces the output of the sprinklers and the number that can be installed on a single line. For runs over 100 feet, use pipe that's one size bigger than your control valves. Using as few turns as possible also helps to minimize pressure loss. As with zoned hot-

18-ga. color-coded multi-conductor wire

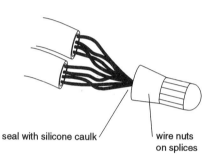

seal with silicone caulk

wire nuts on splices

schematic of connections to controller

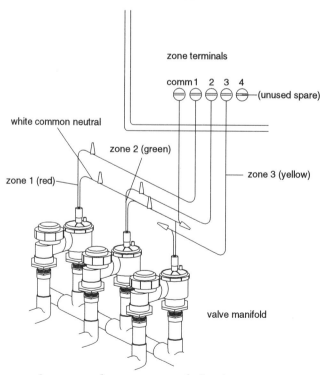

zone terminals

comm 1 2 3 4 (unused spare)

white common neutral

zone 2 (green)

zone 1 (red)

zone 3 (yellow)

valve manifold

27-29 *Use wire with as many conductors as there are control circuits on your master controller.*

water heat, it's better to tee branch lines off of the control valve output than to connect the sprinklers in series on a single line that makes multiple turns.

Once all the pipes have been assembled, seal all but the last risers on each circuit with threaded caps, and turn on the water at the main shutoff. Since the valves won't be connected to the controller at this point, turn the manual bleed screw on top of the valve body to open the valve and allow the water to flush the dirt from the lines. Check the system for any leaky fittings. Once the water runs clear and the leaks are fixed, close the bleeder screws, shut off the water supply, remove the riser caps, wrap Teflon tape around the riser threads, and install the sprinkler heads. Run the system again, adjusting the throw control screws on top of each sprinkler head for the most efficient pattern.

The manifold control valves are wired to the control panel with multi-conductor, 18-gauge plastic-jacketed thermostat control wire (see **27-29**). The number of conductors depends on the number of valves at each manifold. For example, if no more than three valves are on any manifold, use four conductor wires. Connect one of each pair of valve leads to a common neutral wire that runs to the controller common terminal. Each of the other valve wires connects to its own colored wire that connects to a zone terminal at the controller. It's not a bad idea to use wire with a spare conductor in case you want to add another zone at some future time (see **27-30**).

27-30 *A control valve manifold for an automatic sprinkler system. Each of the 24-volt solenoid-operated anti-siphoning valves supplies water to a separate zone according to a schedule programmed into the operating control. The white wire in the photo is the common neutral for the valves. Each of the hot wires is connected to one of three color-coded leads. The shut-off valve in the center line adjusts flow to mister sprinklers that water the vegetable garden beds.*

Common Woods and Their Uses

Dry Weight (lbs) represents pounds per cubic foot

DOMESTIC HARDWOODS Hardwoods are primarily used for furniture and cabinetry. Most are heavy and expensive. Use of tropical hardwoods should be avoided except where grown from sustained-yield plantations, as the production of hardwoods involves large-scale despoliation of ecosystems and aboriginal cultures.

Ash (white)
Fraxinus americana
41 lbs

Strong, pliant, hard, distinct grain, easily split. Works well with hand tools. Used for cabinet and trim work, tool handles.

Aspen (poplar)
Populus tremuloides
Populus gradidentata
25 lbs

Not very strong or suitable for structural work. Warps easily. Used for crating, cheap furniture, plywood cores.

Basswood
Tilea americana
26 lbs

Very soft, light wood. Weak, brittle, fine-textured and straight-grained. Very easy to hand-work, stable, resists warping. Used for drawer sides, casing, trimwork, and cheap furniture. Takes paint well.

Beech
Fagus grandifolia
44 lbs

Hard and strong, close, difficult grain, hard to work and finish smoothly, splits and checks during seasoning. Excellent for tool handles, used for flooring and furniture.

Birch (yellow)
Betula lutea
43 lbs

Prominent and beautiful grain. Hard, must be machine-worked. Finishes well. Used for flooring, woodenware, dowels, interior panelling.

Cedar (Eastern red)
Juniperus virginiana
30 lbs

Durable, close-grained, pungent, brittle. Used for closet and chest linings. Expensive. Cedar chipboard inexpensive replacement.

Cedar
(Northern white)
Thuja occidentalis
19 lbs

Rot-resistant, stable, soft and light-colored, splits easily, works well, finishes nicely. Used for shingles, fenceposts, boatbuilding, interior panelling, exterior siding, and trim. Log homes.

Cedar (Western red)
Thuja plicata
23 lbs

More durable than white cedar. Reddish to brown colored, pronounced grain. Soft, easily split, takes paint and stain well. Used for shingles, shakes, bevel siding. Lob and timber frames. Also boatmaking, interior panelling, exterior siding and trim. Increasingly scarce and expensive.

Fir (balsam)
Abies balsamea
26 lbs

Light, weak wood, rots easily. Used primarily for papermaking pulpwood, light framing where native species.

Fir (Douglas)
Pseudotsuga menziesii
34 lbs

Straight-grained, very strong, splintery. Used for structural timbers and common framing lumber, clear grades used for porch flooring, stair tread stock. Also widely used for structural and finish plywoods.

Fir (white)
Abies concolor
23 lbs

Common lumber tree throughout the lower elevations of the Southwest. Used for boards and light framing, similar to balsam.

Hemlock (Eastern)
Tsuga canadensis
Hemlock (Western)
Tsuga heterophylla
26 lbs

Comparatively weak for its weight, pinkish, brittle grain, more durable than balsam. Very heavy when green. Warps. Western hemlock much stronger than Eastern type. Both sold interchangeably with spruce lumber. Used for timbers, boards, and all general framing.

Pine (Eastern white)
Pinus strobus
25 lbs

Soft, light, very stable but weak wood. Works very easily. Widely used for millwork, casings, interior and exterior trim, siding, panelling, clapboards, cabinetry, and light-duty flooring.

Pine (ponderosa)
Pinus ponderosa
28 lbs

Light and soft, straight-grained, works easily, stable. Used for millwork. Stronger than white pine. Also used for cabin logs.

Birch (white)
Betula papyrifera
39 lbs

Tough, strong, fine-grained and smooth-grained. Used for dowels, plywood cores, veneer for doors and cabinetwork.

Butternut
Juglans cinera
25 lbs

Very light, soft-grained, weak, creamy brown, resembles walnut. Open-pored, easily worked. Takes finish well. Used for decorative trim, panelling, and cabinetry.

Cherry (black)
Prunus serotina
35 lbs

Medium hard, medium strong, beautiful grain and pinkish color. Machines and finishes extremely well. Used for fine cabinetry, panelling, furniture, trimwork, and plank flooring. Very stable when seasoned.

Elm
Ulmus americana
35 lbs

Very strong and tough, coarse-grained, difficult to work. Machines well. Used for handles, pallets, commercial flooring.

Maple (sugar)
Acer saccharum
44 lbs

Hard, very strong, fine texture and grain. Machines well. Used for flooring, furniture, cabinetry.

Oak (Eastern white)
Quercus alba
48 lbs

Very strong, durable, heavy, hard wood with blond color, visible grain. Machine workable. Used for furniture, flooring, millwork, cabinets, and heavy timber frames.

Oak (Northern red)
Quercus rubra
41.5 lbs

Medium strong, open-grained wood, pinkish color. Difficult to hand-work. Finishes well. Same uses as white oak.

Tulipwood
Liriodendron tulipifera
33 lbs

Weak, fine-grained greenish to brownish, easily worked. Very stable when seasoned, holds paint well. Used for food-packing crates, interior and exterior trim.

Walnut (black)
Juglans nigra
39 lbs

Very strong and durable, prized for fine and beautiful dark grain. Excellent finishing and machining qualities. Furniture and fine cabinetry. Scarce, very expensive.

DOMESTIC SOFTWOODS Used for structural carpentry and interior and exterior trimwork and cabinetry. Widely available, inexpensive, light, and strong. Some species are scarce and should be used sparingly.

Pine (sugar)
Pinus lambertiana
26 lbs

Very light and soft, extremely fine-grained. Weak, used for high-quality millwork, doors, window sash.

Pine (Southern yellow longleaf, loblolly)
Pinus balustrus,
Pinus taeda
38 lbs

Hard, dense, strong-grained yellowish wood. Very durable and strong. Used for pressure-treated lumber, structural timber and framing lumber, truss lumber, and flooring. Old-growth "hard" pine boards salvaged and recycled into new lumber.

Redwood
Sequoia sempervivens
28 lbs

Straight-grained, aromatic, reddish, easily worked, very rot-resistant wood. Widely used for bevel and board siding, exterior trim, outdoor decking, and structural lumber. Expensive. Wood harvested from vanishing old-growth forests poses ethical problems for many users.

Spruce (white) (black)
Picea glauca
Picea mariana
25 & 33 lbs

Eastern variety, more often used for pulp wood than lumber except locally. Also used for clapboards. Wood is relatively weak, similar to balsam. Western white spruce is stronger, widely used for framing lumber.

Spruce (red) (Sitka) (Engelmann)
Picea rubens,
Picea sitchensis
Picea engelmannii
24–28 lbs

Red spruce is an eastern lumber tree. Sitka and Engelmann are western varieties. All are strong, fairly dense, easily worked wood. Highest grades also used for instrument manufacture. Most common framing lumber, usually less expensive than Douglas fir. Also used for tongue-and-groove siding, sheathing boards, and structural decking. Pale white wood, tight hard knots.

Tamarck (larch)
Larix laricina
36 lbs

Very dense, hard, and strong wood. Difficult to season. Durable. Used for framing, flooring. Often mixed with spruce. Pale brownish color.

Western Dimension Lumber Base Values

For Sizes 2″ to 4″ Thick by 2″ and Wider
Courtesy Western Wood Products Association

USE WITH ADJUSTMENT FACTORS FOR BASE VALUES*
(Tables A through G follow)

Species or Group	Grade	Extreme Fibre Stress in Bending "F_b" Single	Tension Parallel to Grain "F_t"	Horizontal Shear "F_v"	Compression Perpendicular "$F_{c\perp}$"	Compression Parallel to Grain "$F_{c//}$"	Modulus of Elasticity "E"
Douglas Fir-Larch	Select Structural	1450	1000	95	625	1700	1,900,000
	No. 1 & Btr.	1150	775	95	625	1500	1,800,000
Douglas Fir	No. 1	1000	675	95	625	1450	1,700,000
Western Larch	No. 2	875	575	95	625	1300	1,600,000
	No. 3	500	325	95	625	750	1,400,000
	Construction	1000	650	95	625	1600	1,500,000
	Standard	550	375	95	625	1350	1,400,000
	Utility	275	175	95	625	875	1,300,000
	Stud	675	450	95	625	825	1,400,000
Douglas Fir-South	Select Structural	1300	875	90	520	1550	1,400,000
	No. 1	900	600	90	520	1400	1,300,000
Douglas Fir	No. 2	825	525	90	520	1300	1,200,000
South	No. 3	475	300	90	520	750	1,100,000
	Construction	925	600	90	520	1550	1,200,000
	Standard	525	350	90	520	1300	1,100,000
	Utility	250	150	90	520	875	1,000,000
	Stud	650	425	90	520	825	1,100,000
Hem-Fir	Select Structural	1400	900	75	405	1500	1,600,000
	No. 1 & Btr.	1050	700	75	405	1350	1,500,000
Western Hemlock	No. 1	950	600	75	405	1300	1,500,000
Noble Fir	No. 2	850	500	75	405	1250	1,300,000
California Red Fir	No. 3	500	300	75	405	725	1,200,000
Grand Fir							
Pacific Silver Fir	Construction	975	575	75	405	1500	1,300,000
White Fir	Standard	550	325	75	405	1300	1,200,000
	Utility	250	150	75	405	850	1,100,000
	Stud	675	400	75	405	800	1,200,000

*Design values in pounds per square inch. See Sections 100.00 through 170.00 in the *Western Lumber Grading Rules '91* for additional information on these values.

For complete information contact Western Wood Products Association, Yeon Building, 522 SW Fifth Avenue, Portland, OR 97204-2122 or other relevant regional association involved in the grading, manufacturing, and promotion of wood and related products.

Adjustment Factors for Base Values

SIZE FACTORS (C_F)
Apply to Dimension Lumber Base Values **A**

Grades	Nominal Width (depth)	F_b 2" & 3" thick nominal	F_b 4" thick nominal	F_t	$F_{c\parallel}$	Other Properties
Select Structural, No. 1 & Btr., No. 1, No. 2 & No. 3	2", 3" & 4"	1.5	1.5	1.5	1.15	1.0
	5"	1.4	1.4	1.4	1.1	1.0
	6"	1.3	1.3	1.3	1.1	1.0
	8"	1.2	1.3	1.2	1.05	1.0
	10"	1.1	1.2	1.1	1.0	1.0
	12"	1.0	1.1	1.0	1.0	1.0
	14" & wider	0.9	1.0	0.9	0.9	1.0
Construction & Standard	2", 3" & 4"	1.0	1.0	1.0	1.0	1.0
Utility	2" & 3"	0.4	—	0.4	0.6	1.0
	4"	1.0	1.0	1.0	1.0	1.0
Stud	2", 3" & 4"	1.1	1.1	1.1	1.05	1.0
	5" & 6"	1.0	1.0	1.0	1.0	1.0

REPETITIVE MEMBER FACTOR (C_r)
Apply to Size-adjusted F_b **B**

	Repetitive Member Use
Where 2" to 4" thick lumber is used repetitively, such as for joists, studs, rafters, and decking, the pieces side by side share the load and the strength of the entire assembly is enhanced. Therefore, where three or more members are adjacent or are not more than 24" on center and are joined by floor, roof, or other load-distributing elements, the F_b value can be increased 1.15 for repetitive member use.	$F_b \times 1.15$

DURATION OF LOAD ADJUSTMENT (C_D)
Apply to Size-adjusted Valves **C**

Wood has the property of carrying substantially greater maximum loads for short durations than for long durations of loading. Tabulated design values apply to normal load duration. (Factors do not apply to MOE or $F_{c\perp}$.)

Load Duration	Factor
Permanent	0.9
Ten Years (Normal Load)	1.0
Two Months (Snow Load)	1.15
Seven Day	1.25
One Day	1.33
Ten Minutes (Wind and Earthquake Loads)	1.6
Impact	2.0

Confirm load requirements with local codes. Refer to Model Building Codes or the National Design Specification for high-temperature or fire-retardant treated adjustment factors.

HORIZONTAL SHEAR ADJUSTMENT (C_H)
Apply to F_V Values   **D**

Horizontal shear values published by the Western Wood Products Association in Framing Lumber Tables are based upon the maximum degree of shake, check, or split that might develop in a piece. When the actual size of these characteristics is known, the following adjustments may be taken.

2″ Thick Lumber	3″ and Thicker Lumber
For convenience, the table below may be used to determine horizontal shear values for any grade of 2″ thick lumber in any species when the length of split or check is known and any increase in them is not anticipated:	Horizontal shear values for 3″ and thicker lumber also are established as if a piece were split full length. When specific lengths of splits are known and any increase in them is not anticipated, the following adjustments may be applied.

When length of split on wide face is:	Multiply tabulated F_v value by:	When length of split on wide face is:	Multiply tabulated F_v value by:
No split	2.00	No split	2.00
½ of wide face	1.67	½ of narrow face	1.67
¾ of wide face	1.50	1 of narrow face	1.33
1 of wide face	1.33	1½ of narrow face	1.00
1½ of wide face or more	1.00	or more	

FLAT USE FACTORS (C_fu)
Apply to Size-adjusted F_b **E**

Nominal Width	Nominal Thickness	
	2″ & 3″	4″
2″ & 3″	1.00	—
4″	1.10	1.00
5″	1.10	1.05
6″	1.15	1.05
8″	1.15	1.05
10″ & wider	1.20	1.10

ADJUSTMENTS FOR COMPRESSION PERPENDICULAR-TO-GRAIN (C_{C⊥})
For Deformation Basis of 0.02″
Apply to $F_{C⊥}$ Values   **F**

Design values for compression perpendicular-to-grain ($F_{C⊥}$) are established in accordance with the procedures set forth in ASTM Standards D 2555 and D 245. ASTM procedures consider deformation under bearing loads as a serviceability limit state comparable to bending deflection because bearing loads rarely cause structural failures. Therefore, ASTM procedures for determining compression perpendicular-to-grain values are based on a deformation of 0.04″ and are considered adequate for most classes of structures. Where more stringent measures need to be taken in design, the following formula permits the designer to adjust design values to a more conservative deformation basis of 0.02″:

$$Y_{02} = 0.73\ Y_{04} + 5.60$$

Example:	Douglas Fir-Larch: $Y_{04} = 625$ psi $Y_{02} = 0.73\ (625) + 5.60 = 462$ psi

WET USE FACTORS (C_M)
Apply to Size-adjusted Values   **G**

The design values shown in the accompanying tables are for routine construction applications where the moisture content of the wood does not exceed 19%. When use conditions are such that the moisture content of dimension lumber will exceed 19%, the Wet Use Adjustment Factors below are recommended:

	Property	Adjustment Factor
F_b	Extreme Fibre Stress in Bending	0.85*
F_t	Tension Parallel-to-Grain	1.0
F_c	Compression Parallel-to-Grain	0.8**
F_v	Horizontal Shear	0.97
$F_{C⊥}$	Compression Perpendicular-to-Grain	0.67
E	Modulus of Elasticity	0.9

*Wet Use Factor 1.0 for size-adjusted F_b not exceeding 1150 psi.
**Wet Use Factor 1.0 for size-adjusted F_c not exceeding 750 psi.

Conversion Diagram for Rafters

Courtesy of the National Forest Products Association

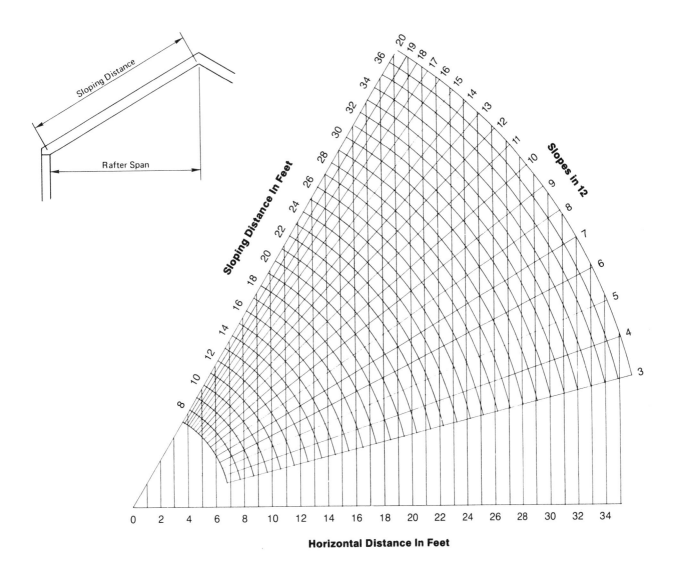

To use the diagram, select the known horizontal distance and follow the vertical line to its intersection with the radial line of the specified slope, then proceed along the arc to read the sloping distance. In some cases it may be desirable to interpolate between the one-foot separations. The diagram also may be used to find the horizontal distance corresponding to a given sloping distance or to find the slope when the horizontal and sloping distances are known.

Example: With a roof slope of 8 in 12 and a horizontal distance of 20 feet, the sloping distance may be read as 24 feet.

Western Lumber Span Tables

Representative Examples Courtesy Western Wood Products Association
(Empirical Design Values)

FLOOR JOISTS

Residential occupancies include private dwelling, private apartment, and hotel guest rooms. Deck under CABO and Standard Codes.*

40 psf Live Load, 10 psf Dead Load, ℓ/360

		2 x 6			2 x 8			2 x 10			2 x 12		
Species or Group	Grade	12" oc	16" oc	24" oc	12" oc	16" oc	24" oc	12" oc	16" oc	24" oc	12" oc	16" oc	24" oc
Douglas Fir-Larch	Sel. Struc.	11-4	10-4	9-0	15-0	13-7	11-11	19-1	17-4	15-2	23-3	21-1	18-5
	No. 1 & Btr.	11-2	10-2	8-10	14-8	13-4	11-8	18-9	17-0	14-5	22-10	20-5	16-8
	No. 1	10-11	9-11	8-8	14-5	13-1	11-0	18-5	16-5	13-5	22-0	19-1	15-7
	No. 2	10-9	9-9	8-1	14-2	12-7	10-3	17-9	15-5	12-7	20-7	17-10	14-7
	No. 3	8-8	7-6	6-2	11-0	9-6	7-9	13-5	11-8	9-6	15-7	13-6	11-0
Douglas Fir-South	Sel. Struc.	10-3	9-4	8-2	13-6	12-3	10-9	17-3	15-8	13-8	21-0	19-1	16-8
	No. 1	10-0	9-1	7-11	13-2	12-0	10-5	16-10	15-3	12-9	20-6	18-1	14-9
	No. 2	9-9	8-10	7-9	12-10	11-8	10-0	16-5	14-11	12-2	19-11	17-4	14-2
	No. 3	8-6	7-4	6-0	10-9	9-3	7-7	13-1	11-4	9-3	15-2	13-2	10-9
Hem-Fir	Sel. Struc.	10-9	9-9	8-6	14-2	12-10	11-3	18-0	16-5	14-4	21-11	19-11	17-5
	No. 1 & Btr.	10-6	9-6	8-4	13-10	12-7	11-0	17-8	16-0	13-9	21-6	19-6	16-0
	No. 1	10-6	9-6	8-4	13-10	12-7	10-9	17-8	16-0	13-1	21-6	18-7	15-2
	No. 2	10-0	9-1	7-11	13-2	12-0	10-2	16-10	15-2	12-5	20-4	17-7	14-4
	No. 3	8-8	7-6	6-2	11-0	9-6	7-9	13-5	11-8	9-6	15-7	13-6	11-0

*Deck spans are based on normal conditions of use and assume the moisture content of lumber used in decks will not be maintained at a moisture content in excess of 19% for an extended period of time.

FLOOR JOISTS

Residential occupancy sleeping rooms (BOCA only). Attics with storage under the Standard Code. Does not apply in UBC areas.

30 psf Live Load, 10 psf Dead Load, ℓ/360

		2 x 6			2 x 8			2 x 10			2 x 12		
Species or Group	Grade	12" oc	16" oc	24" oc	12" oc	16" oc	24" oc	12" oc	16" oc	24" oc	12" oc	16" oc	24" oc
Douglas Fir-Larch	Sel. Struc.	12-6	11-4	9-11	16-6	15-0	13-1	21-0	19-1	16-8	25-7	23-3	20-3
	No. 1 & Btr.	12-3	11-2	9-9	16-2	14-8	12-10	20-8	18-9	16-1	25-1	22-10	18-8
	No. 1	12-0	10-11	9-7	15-10	14-5	12-4	20-3	18-5	15-0	24-8	21-4	17-5
	No. 2	11-10	10-9	9-1	15-7	14-1	11-6	19-10	17-2	14-1	23-0	19-11	16-3
	No. 3	9-8	8-5	6-10	12-4	10-8	8-8	15-0	13-0	10-7	17-5	15-1	12-4
Douglas Fir-South	Sel. Struc.	11-3	10-3	8-11	14-11	13-6	11-10	19-0	17-3	15-1	23-1	21-0	18-4
	No. 1	11-0	10-0	8-9	14-6	13-2	11-6	18-6	16-10	14-3	22-6	20-3	16-6
	No. 2	10-9	9-9	8-6	14-2	12-10	11-2	18-0	16-5	13-8	21-11	19-4	15-10
	No. 3	9-6	8-2	6-8	12-0	10-5	8-6	14-8	12-8	10-4	17-0	14-8	12-0
Hem-Fir	Sel. Struc.	11-10	10-9	9-4	15-7	14-2	12-4	19-10	18-0	15-9	24-2	21-11	19-2
	No. 1 & Btr.	11-7	10-6	9-2	15-3	13-10	12-1	19-5	17-8	15-5	23-7	21-6	17-10
	No. 1	11-7	10-6	9-2	15-3	13-10	12-0	19-5	17-8	14-8	23-7	20-9	17-0
	No. 2	11-0	10-0	8-9	14-6	13-2	11-4	18-6	16-10	13-10	22-6	19-8	16-1
	No. 3	9-8	8-5	6-10	12-4	10-8	8-8	15-0	13-0	10-7	17-5	15-1	12-4

CEILING JOISTS

Use these loading conditions for the following: Limited attic storage where development of future rooms is not possible. Ceilings where the roof pitch is steeper than 3 in 12. Where the clear height in the attic is greater than 30 inches. Drywall ceilings.

20 psf Live Load, 10 psf Dead Load, $\ell/240$

Species or Group	Grade	2 x 4			2 x 6			2 x 8			2 x 10		
		12" oc	16" oc	24" oc	12" oc	16" oc	24" oc	12" oc	16" oc	24" oc	12" oc	16" oc	24" oc
Douglas Fir-Larch	Sel. Struc.	10-5	9-6	8-3	16-4	14-11	13-0	21-7	19-7	17-1	27-6	25-0	20-11
	No. 1 & Btr.	10-3	9-4	8-1	16-1	14-7	12-0	21-2	18-8	15-3	26-4	22-9	18-7
	No. 1	10-0	9-1	7-8	15-9	13-9	11-2	20-1	17-5	14-2	24-6	21-3	17-4
	No. 2	9-10	8-9	7-2	14-10	12-10	10-6	18-9	16-3	13-3	22-11	19-10	16-3
	No. 3	7-8	6-8	5-5	11-2	9-8	7-11	14-2	12-4	10-0	17-4	15-0	12-3
Douglas Fir-South	Sel. Struc.	9-5	8-7	7-6	14-9	13-5	11-9	19-6	17-9	15-6	24-10	22-7	19-9
	No. 1	9-2	8-4	7-3	14-5	13-0	10-8	19-0	16-6	13-6	23-3	20-2	16-5
	No. 2	8-11	8-1	7-0	14-1	12-6	10-2	18-3	15-9	12-11	22-3	19-3	15-9
	No. 3	7-6	6-6	5-3	10-11	9-6	7-9	13-10	12-0	9-9	16-11	14-8	11-11
Hem-Fir	Sel. Struc.	9-10	8-11	7-10	15-6	14-1	12-3	20-5	18-6	16-2	26-0	23-8	20-6
	No. 1 & Btr.	9-8	8-9	7-8	15-2	13-9	11-6	19-11	17-10	14-7	25-2	21-9	17-9
	No. 1	9-8	8-9	7-6	15-2	13-5	10-11	19-7	16-11	13-10	23-11	20-8	16-11
	No. 2	9-2	8-4	7-1	14-5	12-8	10-4	18-6	16-0	13-1	22-7	19-7	16-0
	No. 3	7-8	6-8	5-5	11-2	9-8	7-11	14-2	12-4	10-0	17-4	15-0	12-3

CEILING JOISTS

Use these loading conditions for the following: Ceilings where the roof pitch is not steeper than 3 in 12. Drywall ceilings.

10 psf Live Load, 5 psf Dead Load, $\ell/240$

Species or Group	Grade	2 x 4			2 x 6			2 x 8			2 x 10		
		12" oc	16" oc	24" oc	12" oc	16" oc	24" oc	12" oc	16" oc	24" oc	12" oc	16" oc	24" oc
Douglas Fir-Larch	Sel. Struc.	13-2	11-11	10-5	20-8	18-9	16-4	27-2	24-8	21-7	34-8	31-6	27-6
	No. 1 & Btr.	12-11	11-9	10-3	20-3	18-5	16-1	26-9	24-3	21-2	34-1	31-0	26-4
	No. 1	12-8	11-6	10-0	19-11	18-1	15-9	26-2	23-10	20-1	33-5	30-0	24-6
	No. 2	12-5	11-3	9-10	19-6	17-8	14-10	25-8	23-0	18-9	32-5	28-1	22-11
	No. 3	10-10	9-5	7-8	15-10	13-9	11-2	20-1	17-5	14-2	24-6	21-3	17-4
Douglas Fir-South	Sel. Struc.	11-10	10-9	9-5	18-8	16-11	14-9	24-7	22-4	19-6	31-4	28-6	24-10
	No. 1	11-7	10-6	9-2	18-2	16-6	14-5	24-0	21-9	19-0	30-7	27-9	23-3
	No. 2	11-3	10-3	8-11	17-8	16-1	14-1	23-4	21-2	18-3	29-9	27-1	22-3
	No. 3	10-7	9-2	7-6	15-5	13-5	10-11	19-7	16-11	13-10	23-11	20-8	16-11
Hem-Fir	Sel. Struc.	12-5	11-3	9-10	19-6	17-8	15-6	25-8	23-4	20-5	32-9	29-9	26-0
	No. 1 & Btr.	12-2	11-0	9-8	19-1	17-4	15-2	25-2	22-10	19-11	32-1	29-2	25-2
	No. 1	12-2	11-0	9-8	19-1	17-4	15-2	25-2	22-10	19-7	32-1	29-2	23-11
	No. 2	11-7	10-6	9-2	18-2	16-6	14-5	24-0	21-9	18-6	30-7	27-8	22-7
	No. 3	10-10	9-5	7-8	15-10	13-9	11-2	20-1	17-5	14-2	24-6	21-3	17-4

ROOF RAFTERS

No snow load.
Roof pitch greater than 3 in 12.
Heavy roof covering. No ceiling finish.

20 psf Live Load, 15 psf Dead Load, ℓ/180

Species or Group	Grade	2 x 6 12" oc	2 x 6 16" oc	2 x 6 24" oc	2 x 8 12" oc	2 x 8 16" oc	2 x 8 24" oc	2 x 10 12" oc	2 x 10 16" oc	2 x 10 24" oc	2 x 12 12" oc	2 x 12 16" oc	2 x 12 24" oc
Douglas Fir-Larch	Sel. Struc.	18-0	16-4	14-0	23-9	21-7	17-8	30-4	26-6	21-7	35-5	30-8	25-1
	No. 1 & Btr.	17-7	15-3	12-5	22-3	19-4	15-9	27-3	23-7	19-3	31-7	27-4	22-4
	No. 1	16-5	14-3	11-7	20-9	18-0	14-8	25-5	22-0	17-11	29-5	25-6	20-10
	No. 2	15-4	13-3	10-10	19-5	16-10	13-9	23-9	20-7	16-9	27-6	23-10	19-6
	No. 3	11-7	10-1	8-2	14-8	12-9	10-5	17-11	15-7	12-8	20-10	18-0	14-9
Douglas Fir-South	Sel. Struc.	16-3	14-9	12-11	21-5	19-6	16-9	27-5	24-10	20-6	33-4	29-1	23-9
	No. 1	15-7	13-6	11-0	19-9	17-1	13-11	24-1	20-10	17-0	27-11	24-2	19-9
	No. 2	14-11	12-11	10-6	18-10	16-4	13-4	23-1	20-0	16-4	26-9	23-2	18-11
	No. 3	11-4	9-10	8-0	14-4	12-5	10-2	17-6	15-2	12-4	20-3	17-7	14-4
Hem-Fir	Sel. Struc.	17-0	15-6	13-6	22-5	20-5	17-5	28-7	26-0	21-3	34-10	30-2	24-8
	No. 1 & Btr.	16-8	14-7	11-11	21-4	18-5	15-1	26-0	22-6	18-5	30-2	26-1	21-4
	No. 1	16-0	13-10	11-4	20-3	17-6	14-4	24-9	21-5	17-6	28-8	24-10	20-3
	No. 2	15-2	13-1	10-8	19-2	16-7	13-7	23-5	20-3	16-7	27-2	23-6	19-2
	No. 3	11-7	10-1	8-2	14-8	12-9	10-5	17-11	15-7	12-8	20-10	18-0	14-9

ROOF RAFTERS

Roof pitch 3 in 12 or less.
Light roof covering.
No ceiling finish.

30 psf Snow Load, 10 psf Dead Load, ℓ/240

Species or Group	Grade	2 x 6 12" oc	2 x 6 16" oc	2 x 6 24" oc	2 x 8 12" oc	2 x 8 16" oc	2 x 8 24" oc	2 x 10 12" oc	2 x 10 16" oc	2 x 10 24" oc	2 x 12 12" oc	2 x 12 16" oc	2 x 12 24" oc
Douglas Fir-Larch	Sel. Struc.	14-4	13-0	11-4	18-10	17-2	15-0	24-1	21-10	19-1	29-3	26-7	22-6
	No. 1 & Btr.	14-1	12-9	11-2	18-6	16-10	14-2	23-8	21-2	17-3	28-4	24-6	20-0
	No. 1	13-9	12-6	10-5	18-2	16-2	13-2	22-9	19-9	16-1	26-5	22-10	18-8
	No. 2	13-6	11-11	9-9	17-5	15-1	12-4	21-4	18-5	15-1	24-8	21-5	17-6
	No. 3	10-5	9-0	7-4	13-2	11-5	9-4	16-1	13-11	11-5	18-8	16-2	13-2
Douglas Fir-South	Sel. Struc.	12-11	11-9	10-3	17-0	15-6	13-6	21-9	19-9	17-3	26-5	24-0	21-0
	No. 1	12-7	11-5	9-10	16-7	15-1	12-6	21-2	18-9	15-3	25-1	21-8	17-9
	No. 2	12-3	11-2	9-5	16-2	14-8	12-0	20-8	17-11	14-8	24-0	20-9	17-0
	No. 3	10-2	8-9	7-2	12-10	11-2	9-1	15-8	13-7	11-1	18-2	15-9	12-10
Hem-Fir	Sel. Struc.	13-6	12-3	10-9	17-10	16-2	14-2	22-9	20-8	18-0	27-8	25-1	21-11
	No. 1 & Btr.	13-3	12-0	10-6	17-5	15-10	13-6	22-3	20-2	16-6	27-1	23-5	19-2
	No. 1	13-3	12-0	10-2	17-5	15-9	12-10	22-2	19-3	15-8	25-9	22-3	18-2
	No. 2	12-7	11-5	9-7	16-7	14-11	12-2	21-0	18-2	14-10	24-4	21-1	17-3
	No. 3	10-5	9-0	7-4	13-2	11-5	9-4	16-1	13-11	11-5	18-8	16-2	13-2

Bibliography

There's no shortage of books about every aspect of the building trade. Usually, almost every one of them contains at least one useful nugget of knowledge. A few are true treasures, bursting with real hands-on hints and well-organized and easily understood instructions. But unless you've spent a dozen or so years doing real-life building, it's not likely that you'll be able to separate the gold from the dross. The list that follows isn't intended to be comprehensive, much less listing all the sources that aided me in writing this book. What I've included instead, are those few titles that I think are most useful as either a more complete and detailed presentation of the subject than I had the space to cover, or else as a supplement to that information. Other titles are included simply because they are generally stimulating and thought-provoking and worth reading by anyone interested in design, architecture, and the less than strictly technical aspects of the building process. Books are listed in the order of the chapters to which they're relevant.

PREFACE: WHY DO PEOPLE BUILD THEIR OWN HOUSES?

Clark, Clifford Edward, Jr. *The American Family Home 1800–1960*; Chapel Hill, NC: University of North Carolina Press, 1986.

Leger, Eugene. *Audel Complete Building Construction*, 4th ed.; New York: Macmillan Publishing Co., 1993.

McLaughlin, Jack. *The Housebuilding Experience*; New York: Van Nostrand Reinhold Co., 1981.

Rybczynski, Witold. *Home: A Short History of an Idea*; New York: Viking Penguin, 1986.

————. *The Most Beautiful House in the World*; New York: Viking Penguin, 1989.

Watkins, A. M. *How to Avoid the 10 Biggest Home Buying Traps*; Naperville, IL: Caroline House, 1984.

1 GETTING ORGANIZED

Alexander, Christopher, et al. *Pattern Languages: Towns, Buildings, Construction*; London: Oxford University Press, 1977.

Cliffe, Roger W. *Portable Circular Sawing Machine Techniques*; New York: Sterling Publishing Co., 1988.

————. *Radial-Arm Saw Basics*; New York: Sterling Publishing Co., 1991.

————. *Table Saw Basics*; New York: Sterling Publishing Co., 1991.

De Christoforo, R. J. *The Complete Book of Stationary Power Tool Techniques*; New York: Sterling Publishing Co., 1985.

————. *The Complete Book of Portable Power Tool Techniques*; New York: Sterling Publishing Co., 1986.

Ferguson, Myron E. *Build It Right!*; Salem, OR: Dimi Press, 1994.

Kemp, Jim. *American Vernacular: Regional Influences in Architecture and Interior Design*; New York: Viking, 1987.

Kern, Ken, Ted Kogan, and Rob Thallon. *The Owner-Builder and the Code*; North Fork, CA: Owner-Builder Publications, 1976.

Langdon, Phillip. *American Houses*; New York: Stuart, Tabori & Chang, Inc., 1987.

McAlester, Virginia and Lee. *A Field Guide to American Homes*; New York: Knopf, 1984.

Prowler, Donald. *Modest Mansions: Design Ideas for Luxurious Living in Less Space*; Emmaus, PA: Rodale Press, 1985.

Spielman, Patrick. *Sharpening Basics*; New York: Sterling Publishing Co., 1991.

Stageberg, James, and Susan Allen Toth. *A Home of One's Own: An Architect's Guide to Designing the House of Your Dreams*; New York: Clarkson Potter Publishers, 1991.

Taylor, John S. *Commonsense Architecture: A Cross-Cultural Survey of Practical Design Principles*; New York: W. W. Norton, 1983.

Wolverton, Mike and Ruth. *Draw Your Own House Plans*; Blue Ridge Summit, PA: TAB Books, Inc., 1983.

2 GETTING STARTED

Hall, Walter, ed. *Barnacle Parp's New Chain Saw Guide*; New York: The Mother Earth News, 1985.

Jackson, W. P. *Building Layout*; Carlsbad, CA: Craftsman Book Co., 1979.

Scher, Les and Carol. *Finding and Buying Your Place in the Country*, 3d ed.; Chicago: Dearborn Financial Publishing, Inc., 1992.

Watson, Donald, and Kenneth Labs. *Climactic Design*; New York: McGraw-Hill Book Co., 1983.

3 FOUNDATIONS

Love, T. W. *Concrete and Formwork: Construction Manual*; Carlsbad, CA: Craftsman Book Co., 1973.

NAHB Research Foundation. *Residential Concrete*; Washington, DC: National Association of Homebuilders, 1983.

Pandrese, W. C., et al. *Concrete Masonry Handbook for Architects, Engineers, and Builders*, 5th ed., rev.; Chicago: Portland Cement Association, 1991.

4 PHYSICAL MATTERS

Allen, Edward. *How Buildings Work*; New York: Oxford University Press, 1980.

Hunter, Linda Mason. *The Healthy House*; Emmaus, PA: Rodale Press, 1989.

Parker, Harry. *Simplified Design of Structural Timber*; New York: John Wiley & Sons, 1979.

Philbin, Tom, and Steve Ettlinger. *The Complete Illustrated Guide to Everything Sold in Hardware Stores*; New York: Macmillan Publishing Co., 1988.

Salvadori, Mario. *Why Buildings Stand Up: The Strength of Architecture*; New York: W. W. Norton, 1990.

5 AN OVERVIEW OF FRAMING SYSTEMS

Benson, Tedd. *The Timber-Frame Home: Design, Construction, Finishing*; Newtown, CT: Taunton Press, 1988.

McClintock, Mike. *Alternative Housebuilding*; New York: Sterling Publishing Co., 1989.

Seddon, Leigh. *Practical Pole Building Construction*; Charlotte, VT: Williamson Publishing Co., 1983.

Spence, William P. *Residential Framing: A Homebuilder's Construction Guide*; New York: Sterling Publishing Co., 1993.

Sterling, R., et al. *Earth-Sheltered Residential Design Manual*; New York: Van Nostrand Reinhold Co., 1982.

Thallon, Rob. *Graphic Guide to Frame Construction*; Newtown, CT: Taunton Press, 1992.

US Dept. HUD with NAHB Research Foundation. *Reducing Home Building Costs with OVE Design and Construction*; Washington, DC: US Government Printing Office, 1979.

Williams, Benjamin, ed. *Reducing Home Building Costs*; Solana, CA: Craftsman Book Co., 1978.

6 FRAMING THE FLOOR

Todd, Ken. *Carpentry Layout*; Solana, CA: Craftsman Book Co., 1988.

7 WALL AND CEILING FRAMING

Sherwood, Gerald E., and Robert C. Stroh, eds. *Wood Frame House Construction: A Do-It-Yourself Guide*; New York: Sterling Publishing Co., 1992.

Syvanen, Bob. *Carpentry: Some Tricks of the Trade from an Old-Style Carpenter*; Chester, CT: The Globe Pequot Press, 1982.

8 ROOF FRAMING

Gross, Marshall. *Roof Framing*; Carlsbad, CA: Craftsman Book Co., 1984.

Siegele, H. H. *The Steel Square*; New York: Sterling Publishing Co., 1991.

9 ROOFING

Bolt, Steven. *Roofing the Right Way*; Blue Ridge Summit, PA: TAB Books, Inc., 1990.

Brunbaugh, James E. *Audel's Complete Roofing Handbook*; New York: Theodore Audel & Co., 1986.

10 ACCESS

Williamson, Dereck. *The Complete Book of Pitfalls: A Victim's Guide to Repairs, Maintenance, and Repairing the Maintenance*; New York: McCall Publishing Co., 1971.

11 EXTERIOR TRIM AND SIDING

Boericke, Art, and Barry Shapiro. *Handmade Houses: A Guide to the Woodbutcher's Art*; San Francisco: Scrimshaw Press, 1973.

12 WINDOWS AND EXTERIOR DOORS

Birchard, John. *Make Your Own Handcrafted Doors and Windows*; New York: Sterling Publishing Co., 1988.

Hiro, John E. *The Millwork Handbook*; New York: Sterling Publishing Co., 1993.

13 DECKS, GARAGES, AND OTHER ATTACHMENTS

Lees, Alfred, and Ernst V. Heyn. *Popular Science Decks and Sun Spaces*; New York: Sterling Publishing Co., 1991.

Yanda, Bill, and Rick Fisher. *The Food and Heat Producing Solar Greenhouse*; Santa Fe, NM: John Muir Publications, 1980.

14 PAINTING AND STAINING

Baer, M., E. Pomada, and M. Larsen. *Painted Ladies: San Francisco's Resplendent Victorians*; New York: Dutton, 1978.

Miller, Rex, and Glenn E. Baker. *Painting and Decorating*; New York: Bobbs-Merrill Co., 1984.

Swift, Penny, and Janek Szymanowski. *The Complete Book of Paint Techniques*; London: New Holland Ltd. (New York: Sterling Publishing Co.), 1994.

Wiles, Richard. *Decorative Papering*; New York: Sterling Publishing Co., 1993.

15 PLUMBING ROUGH-IN

AAVIM. *Planning for an Individual Water System*; Athens, GA: American Assoc. for Vocational Instructional Materials, n.d.

Alth, Max. *Do-It-Yourself Plumbing*; New York: Sterling Publishing Co., 1987.

Ingram, Colin. *The Drinking Water Book*; Berkeley, CA: Ten Speed Press, 1991.

Warshall, Peter. *Septic Tank Practices*; Bolinas, CA: Whole Earth Access, 1979.

16 HVAC SYSTEMS

Anderson, Bruce, with Michael Riordan. *The New Solar Home Book*; Andover, MA: Brick House Publishing Co., 1987.

ASHRAE. *ASHRAE Handbook of Fundamentals*; New York: American Soc. of Heating, Refrigeration, and Air-Conditioning Engineers, n.d.

Booth, Don, with Johnathan Booth and Peg Boyles. *Sun/Earth Buffering and Superinsulation*; Canterbury, NH: Community Builders, 1983.

Brumbaugh, James E. *Heating, Ventilating and Air Conditioning Library*, 3 vols.; New York: Macmillan Publishing Co., 1986.

Fossel, Peter V. *The Art of Keeping Warm: A Sensible Guide to Heat Conservation*; New York: Putnam Publishing Group, 1983.

Mazria, Edward. *The Passive Solar Energy Book: Expanded Professional Edition*; Emmaus, PA: Rodale Press, 1979.

Nisson, J. D. Ned, and Gautam Dutt. *The Superinsulated Home Book*; New York: John Wiley & Sons, 1985.

Shurcliff, William. *Super-Insulated and Double Envelope Homes*; Andover, MA: Brick House Publishing Co., 1981.

17 CHIMNEYS, FIREPLACES, AND WOODSTOVES

Barden, Albert A., III. *Finnish Fireplace Construction*; Norridgewock, ME: Maine Wood Heat Co., 1984.

Gould, Zack. *The Owner-Built Fireplace*; New York: Van Nostrand Reinhold, 1978.

Orton, Vrest. *The Forgotten Art of Building a Good Fireplace*; Dublin, NH: Yankee Books, 1969.

Shelton, Jay W. *Solid Fuels Encyclopedia*; Pownal, VT: Garden Way Publishing, 1983.

18 ELECTRICAL ROUGH-IN

Armpriester, K. E. *Do Your Own Wiring*; New York: Sterling Publishing Co., 1991.

Burch, Monte. *Basic House Wiring*; New York: Sterling Publishing Co., 1987.

Richter, H. P., and Creighton Schwan. *Practical Electrical Wiring*, 14th ed.; New York: McGraw-Hill, 1987.

Ritter, Keith. *The Residential Hydro Power Book*; Bridgeville, CA: Homestead Engineering, 1986.

Smead, David, and Ruth Ishihara. *Living on 12 Volts with Ample Power*; Seattle: Ride Publishing Co., 1988.

Strong, Steven J., with William G. Scheller. *The Solar Electric Home*; Emmaus, PA: Rodale Press, 1987.

19 INSULATION

Langdon, William K. *Movable Insulation*; Emmaus, PA: Rodale Press, 1980.

Schurliffe, William. *Thermal Shutters and Shades*; Andover, MA: Brick House Publishers, 1980.

Yost, Harry. *Home Insulation*; Pownal, VT: Storey Communications, 1991.

20 STAIR-BUILDING

Mannes, Willibald. *Techniques of Staircase Construction*; New York: Van Nostrand Reinhold Co., 1986.

Mowat, William and Alexander. *A Treatise on Stairbuilding and Handrailing*; Fresno, CA: Linden Publishing Co., Inc., 1985.

Schuttner, Scott. *Basic Stairbuilding*; Newtown, CT: Taunton Press, 1990.

21 INTERIOR FINISH

Allen, Sam. *Wood Finisher's Handbook*; New York: Sterling Publishing Co., 1984.

Ching, Francis D. K. *Interior Design Illustrated*; New York: Van Nostrand Reinhold Co., 1987.

Goad, Karen. *Drywall: Installation and Finishing*; New York: Sterling Publishing Co., 1993.

Van Den Branden, F., and Thomas L. Hartsell. *Plastering Skills*; Homewood, IL: American Technical Publishers, 1984.

22 FLOORING

Bollinger, Don. *Hardwood Floors: Laying, Sanding, and Finishing*; Newtown, CT: Taunton Press, 1990.

Burch, Monte. *Tile, Indoors and Out*; Passaic, NJ: Creative Homeowner Press, 1981.

23 TILEWORK

Byrne, Michael. *Setting Ceramic Tile*; Newtown, CT: Taunton Press, 1987.

24 INTERIOR TRIM

Lewis, Gaspar J. *Carpentry*; New York: Sterling Publishing Co., 1984.

Syvanen, Bob. *Interior Finish: More Tricks of the Trade from an Old-Style Carpenter*; Charlotte, NC: East Woods Press, 1982.

25 KITCHEN CABINETS AND OTHER BUILT-INS

Allen, Sam. *Cabinetry Basics*; New York: Sterling Publishing Co., 1991.

Grey, Johnny. *The Art of Kitchen Designs: Planning for Comfort and Style*; New York: Sterling Publishing Co., 1994.

Jones, Peter. *Shelves, Closets, and Cabinets*; New York: Sterling Publishing Co., 1977.

Murrell, Robin. *Small Kitchens: Making Every Inch Count*; New York: Simon and Schuster, 1987.

26 FINISH DETAILS

Spence, William P. *Finish Carpentry: A Complete Interior & Exterior Guide*; New York: Sterling Publishing Co., 1995.

Time-Life Books, eds. *Home Security*; New York: Time-Life Books, 1979.

27 LANDSCAPE CONSTRUCTION

Brimer, John Burton. *Homeowner's Complete Outdoor Building Book*; New York: Sterling Publishing Co., 1989.

Jacobs, David H., Jr. *Concrete: A Home Owner's Illustrated Guide*; Blue Ridge Summit, PA: TAB Book Co., 1992.

Self, Charles R. *Wood Fences and Gates: Plans, Designs and Construction*; New York: Sterling Publishing Co., 1986.

Stevens, David, Lucy Hunnington, and Richard Key. *The Complete Book of Garden Design, Construction and Planting*; New York: Sterling Publishing Co., 1994.

Metric Conversion

Inches to Millimetres and Centimetres						
MM—millimetres			*CM—centimetres*			
Inches	**MM**	**CM**	**Inches**	**CM**	**Inches**	**CM**
⅛	3	0.3	9	22.9	30	76.2
¼	6	0.6	10	25.4	31	78.7
⅜	10	1.0	11	27.9	32	81.3
½	13	1.3	12	30.5	33	83.8
⅝	16	1.6	13	33.0	34	86.4
¾	19	1.9	14	35.6	35	88.9
⅞	22	2.2	15	38.1	36	91.4
1	25	2.5	16	40.6	37	94.0
1¼	32	3.2	17	43.2	38	96.5
1½	38	3.8	18	45.7	39	99.1
1¾	44	4.4	19	48.3	40	101.6
2	51	5.1	20	50.8	41	104.1
2½	64	6.4	21	53.3	42	106.7
3	76	7.6	22	55.9	43	109.2
3½	89	8.9	23	58.4	44	111.8
4	102	10.2	24	61.0	45	114.3
4½	114	11.4	25	63.5	46	116.8
5	127	12.7	26	66.0	47	119.4
6	152	15.2	27	68.6	48	121.9
7	178	17.8	28	71.1	49	124.5
8	203	20.3	29	73.7	50	127.0

Feet and Inch Conversions

1 inch	=	25.4 mm
1 foot	=	304.8 mm
1 psi	=	6.89 kPa
1 psf	=	0.048 kPa

Metric Conversions

1 mm	=	0.039 inches
1 m	=	3.28 feet
1 kPa	=	20.88 psf

mm	=	millimetre
m	=	metre
kPa	=	kilopascal
psi	=	pounds per square inch
psf	=	pounds per square foot

Index

A

Air-conditioning
  central, 416–420
    and warm-air heating, 398
    separate systems, 420
  room, 421
Air filters, electrostatic, 398
Air-tight Drywall Approach (ADA),
    493
Allowable stress, 89
All-weather wood foundations
    (AWWF), 84
Aluminum siding, 302
Amperage, 445
  branch circuit, 448
Annual fuel utilization efficiency
    (AFUE), 394–395
Appliances
  circuit design for, 447, 448
  couplers for, 359
  electrical loads for, 446
  energy efficient, 385
  hookups for, 659, 662
Aquifer, 38, 379
Architectural symbols, 21
Armored cable (AC), 452
Artist's renderings, 20
Asphalt roofing, 234–253
  built-up, 248–250
  cold roof system, 252–253
  flashing conditions, 243–246
  for low-pitched roofs, 246–248
  installation of, 235–240
  protection against ice dams, 250–252
  valley treatment, 240–243
Asphalt-impregnated sheathing (IB)
    board, 157
Astragals, 611
Attic
  fans, 422–423
  insulation of, 498–505
  ventilation of, 512–514
Awning windows, 309

B

Backer studs, 105
Backfilling, 61–62
Ballast trench foundations, 78–79
Balloon framing, 102
Band joists, 104
Barrel hinges, 321
Base cap moulding, 610
Base shoe moulding, 610

Base values, 91
Baseboard, 609, 627–628
Baseline, establishment of, 30
Basements
  damp, 488
  see also Foundations, full-basement
Bathrooms
  cabinets, 655–656
  ceramic tile in, *see* Ceramic tile
  framing for
    floors, 128–129
    walls, 160–162
  sinks, 660–661
  toilets, 659–660
  tub enclosures, 656–657
Batter boards, 30, 32
Bay windows, 309
Beams, 90-91
  box, 148
  carrying, 104
  in mortise-and-tenon framing, 109
  steel, 121–122
Bearing partition, 105
Benches, deck, 334–335
Benchmark, 16, 115
Bevel siding, 289–292
Bifold doors, 625
Bird's-mouth, 174
Black-iron pipe, 364, 365
Blind valley rafters, 209
Blocking, 104, 131–132, 162
Board foot, 99
Board-and-gap siding, 294
Boards, 98
Boilers, 396n, 398–401, 412–414
Bookshelves, 650–651
Bow windows, 309
Box beams, 148
Boxboard siding, 292–293
Boxed cornice, 281–286
Boxes, electrical, 466–471
  vapor barriers around, 506
Brackets, roof, 278–279
Branch circuits, 448
  wiring, 465–466
Breakers, 465–466
Brick
  chimneys, *see* Masonry chimneys
  moulding, 609
  pathways and patios, 673–674
Bridging, 104, 131–132
Bright nails, 125
Bucks, 48–50

Building elevation drawings, 17, 20
Building lines, layout of, 30–32
Building permits, 23
Building process
  outline of, 23–25
  overview of, 20, 22–23
Building sections, 18
Building site, what to look for in, 13–15
Bulkheads, 56
Bull-nose moulding, 337
BX cable, 452, 477
Bypass doors, 626

C

Cabinets
  bathroom, 655–657
  kitchen
    base, 633–636
    doors for, 644–646
    drawers in, 640–643
    fasteners for, 646–647
    simple system for building, 647–650
    wall, 636–640
Cables, electric, 448
  running, 466–473
  securing to boxes, 470
  size for circuit load, 449
  types of, 450–453
California roof, 220–224
Cant strip, 248
Cantilevered beams, 91
Cantilevered retaining walls, 44
Carrying beams, 104
Casement windows, 308–309
Casing, 609
Cast-iron pipe, 374–375
Cathedral ceilings, insulating, 502
Caulking, 506–509
Ceiling
  combination wood floor and, 578–580
  drywall, 537–545
    textured effects on, 548
  framing, 164–170
  heating ducts in, 406
  insulating, 497, 499–502
  suspended, 568
  tile, 566–567
  wood panelling, 564–565
Cellars, *see* Basements

Cement sidings, 302
   stucco, 302–306
Chamfering, 112
Ceramic tile, 587–605
   adhesives for, 589–591
   beds for, 591–595
   installation and grouting, 602–605
   layout and cutting of, 599–602
   membranes for, 596–599
   types of, 587–589
Chair rail moulding, 610
Channel rustic siding, 294
Cheek cuts, 173
Chicken ladders, 279
Chimneys
   flashing, 244–245
   framing for, 196
   masonry, 425, 427
      building, 430–434
      design criteria for, 428–429
   prefabricated metal, 425–427
      installation of, 427–428
Cisterns, 379, 380
Clapboards, 289–292
Clay tile roofing, 264–267
Clear boards, 98
Clipped rake construction, 285
Clothes storage units, 650
Cold roof, 252–253
Collar ties, 107, 173, 183–185
Common boards, 98
Common difference method, 210
Common nails, 125
Common rafters, 172
   laying out, 174–179
Composting toilets, 384–385
Compound mitre, 173
Compression fittings, 369, 373
Compressive stress, 89, 90
Concrete, estimating, ordering, and
   placing, 50–52
Concrete block
   chimneys, see Masonry chimneys
   foundations, 79–83
      surface-bonded, 83–84
Concrete pier foundations, 70–72
   problems with, 74–78
Concrete tile roofing, 264–267
Condensation, 486–495
Conditions, 18
Conduction, 483–484
Conduit, 452–453, 473–477
   flexible metallic, 477
Construction-grade lumber, 99
Control point, 16
Convection, 483–484
Cooling systems
   energy conservation considerations
      for, 385–387
   evaporative, 421
   fan-powered, 422–423

passive, 424
   see also Air-conditioning
Copper tubing, 366–369
Corbelling, 432–433
Core boxes, 48–50
Corner posts, 144
Cornices, 280–287
Cottage-grade clapboards, 289
Countertops, 651–655
Cove moulding, 610
Crawl-space foundation, 64, 65
   insulation of, 505
Cripple jack, 173
Cripple rafters, 213
Cripple studs, 105, 140
Crown moulding, 610
   cutting and installing, 611–615
Curtains, thermal, 487

D

Deadbolts, 322
Dead-flat asphalt, 249
Dead load, 85–86
Decks, 327–335
   pressure-treated lumber for, 328
   rooftop, 340–343
Dehumidifiers, 398
Design
   foundation, 37–38
   overview of process, 11–23
Dimension lumber, 98
Disconnect switch, 459–461
Doors
   cellar, 56
   exterior
      building, 323–324
      drip caps for, 292
      hanging, 318–322
      insulation around jambs, 498
      locksets for, 322–323
      prehung, 314–318
      weatherstripping at jambs, 510,
         511
   garage, 345–346
   interior
      painting, 353
      trim for, 622–626
   kitchen cabinet, 644–646
Dormers, 191–195
   flashing, 245
Double-coverage roll roofing, 247
Double-envelope "geothermal" house,
   391–392
Double-hung windows, 308
   interior trim for, 615, 618
Double-pole site-built staging, 274,
   275
Double roof, 252–253
Dowels, 16

Drainage, 38
Drains
   foundation, 56–57
   plumbing, 360–363
Drawers, building, 644–646
Dressed sizes of boards, 100
Drilled wells, 376, 378
   pumps for, 380–381
Drip caps, 292, 609
Driveway, layout of, 28–29
Drywall, 537–538
   alternatives to, 548–549
   installing, 538–542
   taping and finishing, 542–548
Ducts, 406–412, 417
Dumpy levels, 30
DWV (drain/waste/and vent) system,
   356, 363
   cast-iron, 374–375
   plastic pipe for, 374

E

Earth-bermed foundation, 63–64
Earth tunnels, 424
Economy-grade lumber, 99
Edge-grained lumber, 97
Electric power lines, 33–35
Electrical symbols, 21
Electricity, 445–482
   heating with, 394
      compact systems, 416
      radiant, 402–403
      resistant, 401
   load calculation, 446
      circuit design and, 447–450
   types of cable, 450–453
   see also Wiring
Electrostatic air filters, 398
Elevations, 20
EMT (Electrical Mechanical Tubing),
   453
Energy conservation, 385–387
Envelope houses, 391–392
Evaporative coolers, 421
Excavation, 32–36
Expansion control joints, 48
Extended reducing plenum duct sys-
   tem, 408, 409
Extension ladders, 277
Extra clear clapboards, 289
Extreme fibre strength (Fb), 90

F

Factory and shop lumber (F&S), 98
False rafters, 173, 188
   hanging, 190–191
Fan-powered cooling, 422–423
Fencing, 674–678

Fibreglass insulation, 496–498
  for foundation, 55
Fibre-reinforced gypsum plaster wall-
    board, 548–549
Fin walls, 162
Fireplaces, 437–443
Firestops, 102
Fixed windows, 309
  building, 312–314
Flashing, 240–246
  in protection against ice dams, 251–
    252
  roll roofing, 248
  steel roofing, 258–259
  valley treatments, 240–243
Flat roofs, 171
  framing, 200
Flat-grained lumber, 97
Flood coat, 249
Floor, 569–586
  ceramic tile, 587–605
    adhesives for, 589–591
    beds for, 591–595
    installation and grouting of, 602–
      605
    layout and cutting, 599–602
    membranes, 596–599
    types of, 587–589
  framing, 115–138
    bridging and blocking, 131–133
    girder selection and construction,
      119–121
    job-site logistics, 138
    layout and installation of joists,
      122–125
    openings, 126–127
    porch, 336–337
    setting rim and stringer joists, 118
    setting sills, 116–118
    special conditions, 128–130
    steel beams, 121–122
    subframing, 134–137
    trusses, 133–134
  stone, 605–607
  vinyl, 583–585
  tile, 585–586
  wood, 469–583
    applying finish to, 582–583
    combination floor and ceiling sys-
      tem, 578–580
    laying, 572–575
    over concrete slab, 575–578
    sanding, 580–581
    types of, 569–571
    underlayment, 571–572
Floor plans, 15, 17–18
Floor slab
  controlling cracks in, 60
  draining water under, 59
  finishing, 60–61
  preparing for, 57

wood flooring over, 575–578
Fluid velocity, coefficient of (f), 483
Fly rafters, see False rafters
Footings
  layout, form work, and pouring, 40
  for special conditions, 43–46
Forced warm-air heating, 397
Foundations, 37–84
  all-weather wood, 84
  ballast trench, 78–79
  checking, 115–116
  concrete block, 79–84
  crawl-space, 64
  deck support post, 327
  drainage and, 38–39
  earth-bermed, 63–64
  estimating, ordering, and placing
    concrete for, 50–52
  frost-wall slab, 68
  full-basement
    backfilling, 61–62
    drains in, 56–57
    entrance to, 56
    finishing, 52
    floor slabs, 57, 59–61
    footing layout, form work, and
      pouring, 40–43
    forms for wall openings, 48
    pros and cons of, 39
    radon protection built-in, 58–59
    termite protection in, 62–63
    wall forms for, 46–48
  insulation of, 54–55
  partially enclosed, 63–64
  perimeter, 64
  pier and post, 70–78
  plans, 16–17
  slab-on-grade, 64–70
  soil mechanics and, 37–38
  waterproofing, 488
Fracture point, 89
Framing, 101–114
  ceiling, 164–170
  floor, 115–138
    bridging and blocking, 131–133
    girder selection and construction,
      119–121
    job-site logistics, 138
    layout and installation of joists,
      122–125
    openings, 126–127
    setting rim and stringer joists, 118
    setting sills, 116–118
    special conditions, 128–130
    steel beams, 121–122
    subfloor, 134–137
    trusses, 133–134
  lumber for, 99–100
  mortise-and-tenon, 107–112
  plans, 18
  roof, 171–231

alternate rafter layout method,
    181–182
  blind valley rafters, 209
  closing in, 228–230
  collar ties, 183–185
  cripple rafters, 213
  dormers and other openings, 191–
    196
  flat, 200
  gable wall framing, 231–233
  gambrel, 200–201
  hanging false rafters, 190–191
  jack rafters, 210–212
  laying out common rafters, 174–
    179
  mansard, 202
  no-valley technique, 220–224
  rafter installation, 182
  setting ridge, 179–180
  sheathing, 188–190
  shed, 197–199
  subfascias and lookouts, 185–188
  trusses, 224–228
  uncommon rafters, 202–209
  unequal pitch, 215–219
stick, 102–107, 110
structural engineering for, 90–98
wall, 139–164
  assembling, 148–152
  corner posts and partition backers,
    144–146
  double-sole-plate system, 141–142
  headers, 146–148
  interior partitions, 159
  layout, 142–143
  lining, 153–157
  nonstructural sheathing, 157–159
  special conditions, 160–164
Frieze board, 283
Frost heave, 38
Frost-wall slab foundations, 68
Fuel, heating
  cost comparisons for, 393–395
  supply lines for, 414–415
Fuel oil storage tanks, underground, 36
Furnaces, 396–398, 411–412
  floor, 416

G
Gables
  aluminum ventilators for, 512
  framing in walls, 230–234
  porches and, 336
  rafters, 173
  roofs, 171
  trusses, 225
Galvanized box nails, 125
Galvanized pipe, 364, 365
Galvanized steel-sheet roofing, 253–
    257

flashing, 258–259
Gambrel roofs, 171
  framing, 200–201
Garages, 345–346
Gates, 677–678
"Geothermal" house, 391–392
Girders, 104
  for decks, 330
  selection and construction of, 119–121
Girts, 107–109
Glazing, 310–311
  for greenhouses and sunspaces, 345
  heat loss and, 487
Grade-beam footings, 44
Grading, 666–667
Gravel stop, 249
Gravity-feed water supply, 379
Gravity-flow heating systems, 398–399
Greenhouses, attached, 343–345, 390, 391
  humidity from, 488
Ground-fault interrupter (GFI), 448–449
Grounding, 447, 453, 462, 463
Gutters, 266–269
Gypsum wallboard panels, *see* Drywall

H

Half-lap roll roofing, 247
Hardboard siding, 302
Header joists, 104
Headers, 105, 146–148
Health regulations, 13
Heat flow, 483–486
Heat pumps, 401–402
Heating, 387–416
  compact systems, 416
  electric resistance, 401
  energy conservation considerations for, 385–387
  fuel cost comparisons for, 393–395
  fuel supply lines for, 414–415
  heat pumps, 401–402
  hot water, 398–401
    installing, 412–414
  radiant, 402–404
    hot-water, 404
  solar, 387–393
  warm-air, 396–398
    installing, 406–412
  with wood, 434
High-resistance fault, 449
Hinges
  for cabinet doors, 646
  for exterior doors, 320, 321
  for gates, 678
Hip jack, 173
Hip rafters, 172
Hip roofs, 171, 202–208

Hip shingles, 240, 241
Honeycombing, 51
Hopper windows, 309
Horizontal sections, 16
Horsepower, 447
Hot water
  heating, 398–401
    installing, 412–414
    radiant, 404
  solar systems for, 392
House-wrap, 491
Howe trusses, 225
Hub-and-spigot pipe system, 375
Humidifiers, automatic, in forced warm-air heating systems, 398
HVAC systems, 385–424
  energy conservation considerations for, 385–387
Hydraulic head, 379
Hydronic heating system, 398–401
  installing, 412–414

I

Ice dams, protection against, 250–252
Infiltration gallery, 378
Infiltration heat loss, 485–486
  caulking against, 508
Insects, wood-destroying, 62–63
Insulation, 483–511
  of attic, 498–505
  foundation, 54–55
  heat flow and, 483–486
  installing, 495–498
  relative humidity and condensation and, 486–495
  R-values for, 492–495
  ventilation and, 512–514
Insulator racks, 454
Interior partitions, framing, 159
Isometric projections, 20

J

Jack rafters, 210–211
Jack studs, 105
Jacks
  ladder, 273
  roof, 279
Jamb studs, 139
Jet shingles, 235
Job-site logistics, 138
Joists, 99
  deck, 330–332
  floor, layout and installation of, 122–125

K

K factor, 483, 485
Kachelofen, 444

Keyways, 45
Kilowatt-hour (kwh), 447
King studs, 105
Kitchens, 629–655
  appliances
    circuit design for, 447, 448
    couplers for, 359
    electrical loads for, 446
    energy efficient, 385
    hookups, 659, 662
  basic plans for, 630
  cabinets
    base, 633–636
    drawers and doors, 640–646
    fasteners, 646–647
    simple system for building, 647–650
    wall, 636–640
  countertops, 651–655
  sinks, 660–661
  standard fixture dimensions, 632
Knee walls, 165
  framing, 185

L

Ladder jacks, 273
Ladders, 169, 277–278
  chicken, 279
Lally columns, 104
Landscaping, 666–683
Lattice moulding, 611
Lead paint, removing, 354
Leaders, 266–269
Ledgers, 102
Level, importance of, 92–94
Lifelines, 279
Light framing, 99
Lighting
  energy-efficient, 385, 387
  homemade fixtures, 657–658
  outdoor, 679
Line length, 174
Lineal foot, 99
Liquid propane gas
  heating with, 393, 395
  supply lines for, 414
  underground tank for, 36
Live load, 85, 86
Load, 85–87
Locksets, 322–323
Logistics, job-site, 138
Lookouts, 187–188
Lumber
  nomenclature for, 97–100
  pressure-treated, 328

M

Madison clips, 467
Mansard roofs, 171

framing, 202

Masonry
  chimneys, 425, 427
    building, 430–434
    design criteria for, 428–429
  fireplaces, 439–443
  heaters, 444

Mass-wall solar heating systems, 387–389

Master stud, 140

Measuring line, 173

Mechanical plans, 18, 19
  for slab foundations, 66

Mechanical symbols, 21, 22

Mechanics-grade clapboards, 289

Medium-density overlay (MDO), 300, 302

Metal chimneys, prefabricated, 425–427
  installation of, 427–428

Meter socket, 456–459

Mitre joint, backcutting, 286

Modulus of elasticity (E), 90

Moisture barriers, 491

Monolithic slab-on-grade foundations, 68–70

Mouldings, 608–615
  cutting and installing, 611–615
  for ends of porch floorboards, 337
  painting, 353

Mound system, 384

Mudsills, 104

Muntins, 611

N

Nails, 125
  roofing, 236

Natural gas
  for heating, 393–395, 412
  supply lines, 414–415

NMC cable, 451

Nominal sizes of boards, 100

Noncoincident loads, 447

No-valley roof framing technique, 220–224

O

Oakum, 375

Ogee moulding, 610

Ohms, 447

Oil heating, 393–395, 412
  supply lines for, 414–415

Outlets, 466–467, 480–482

Outrigger staging, 276

Overhanging beams, 91

Overhangs, cantilevered joists for, 130

Overturning, 88

P

Painting, 347–354
  exterior
    guidelines for, 347–348
    staining versus, 349–351
  interior, 351–354
    application tips and techniques, 352–353
    safety and, 354

Partially enclosed foundation, 63–64

Partition backers, 144

Partitions, framing, 159

Passive cooling, 424

Passive solar heating, 387–392
  insulation and, 487

Pathways, 673–674

Patios, 673–674

Perlited gypsum plaster, 551

Perforated plastic pipe, 56

Perimeter foundation, 64

Pier foundations, 70–72
  problems with, 74–78

Pilasters, 44

Pipes
  copper, 366–369
  for hydronic heating system, 399–400
  plastic, 370–375
  steel, 364, 365

Plain-sawn lumber, 97

Plancher board, 283

Planks, 99

Planned-and-matched siding, 293

Plans
  for kitchens, 630
  understanding, 15–20

Plastering
  do-it-yourself alternative to, 551–552
  traditional, 549–551

Plastic pipe
  DWV, 374–375
  supply, 370–373

Platform framing, 102–107

Plot plans, 15–16

Plumb, importance of, 92–94

Plumb cut, 174

Plumbing, 355–384
  developing on-site water supply, 376–381
  drainage, 360–363
  fixtures, installing, 659–662
  materials, 364–375
    copper tubing, 366–369
    plastic DWV pipe, 374–375
    plastic supply pipe, 370–373
    steel pipe, 364, 365
  outline of domestic system, 356–360
  sewage disposal, 382–384

Plywood siding, 300–302

Pocket doors, 626

Poises, 447

Polystyrene insulation, 54

Porches, 327, 336–340
  types of, 337

Positive drainage, 38

Post-and-beam framing, 107–112
  alternatives to, 111–112
  for ceiling, with stick-framed walls, 112–114
  closing in, 110–111
  difference between stick framing and, 110

Post foundations, 72–74
  problems with, 74–78

Prefabricated metal chimneys, 425–427
  installation of, 427–428

Prehung doors, 314–318

Pressure blocks, 168

Pressure-treated lumber, 328

Pump-jack scaffolding, 272–273

Pumps
  heat, 401–402
  water, 380–381

Punch list, 664–665

Purlin beams, 109

Purlin braces, 184

Q

Quarter-sawed lumber, 97

R

Rabbeted siding, 293–297

Racking, 94–96

Radial perimeter duct system, 406

Radiant heating, 402–404
  hot-water, 404
  masonry, 444

Radiation, 483–484

Radon, 13–14
  built-in protection from, 58–59

Rafter plate, 105

Rafter plate beam, 109

Rafter tails, 173

Rafters, 106, 172
  blind valley, 209
  cripple, 213
  installation of, 182
  jack, 210–211
  laying out, 174–179
    alternative method, 181–182
  setting, 179–180
  uncommon, 202–209

Railings, deck, 333–334

Railroad jet, 287

Rebar, 16, 46, 48

Receptacles, electric, 480–482

Register boots, 401

Registers, 406

Relative humidity (RH), 486–495

Retaining walls, 671–673
  cantilevered, 44
Reverse-osmosis water filtration system, 379
Ridge board, 106
Ridge caps, 240, 241
Rim joists, 104
  setting, 118
Risers, 412
Rocks, ornamental, 669
Roll roofing, 234, 235, 246–248
Romex cable, 451
Roofs
  asphalt, 234–253
    built-up, 248–250
    cold roof system, 252–253
    flashing conditions, 243–246
    installation of, 235–240
    for low-pitched roofs, 246–248
    protection against ice dams, 250–252
    valley treatment, 240–243
  closing in, 228–229
  concrete and clay tile, 264–267
  decks on, 340–343
  flashing steel, 258–259
  framing, 171–231
    alternate rafter layout method, 181–182
    blind valley rafters, 209
    collar ties, 183–185
    cripple rafters, 213
    dormers and other openings, 191–196
    flat, 200
    gable wall, 230–233
    gambrel, 200–201
    hanging false rafters, 190–191
    jack rafters, 210–212
    laying out common rafters, 174–179
    mansard, 202
    no-valley technique, 220–224
    rafter installation, 182
    setting ridge, 179–180
    sheathing, 188–190
    shed, 197–199
    subfascias and lookouts, 185–188
    trusses, 224–228
    uncommon rafters, 202–209
    unequal pitch, 215–219
  galvanized steel-sheet, 253–257
  gutters and leaders, 266–269
  insulation of, 502–505
  service mast mounted on, 456
  staging for, 278–279
  trusses, 107
  windows, 309
  wood shakes, 262–263
  wood shingles, 259–262
Room air-conditioners, 421

Rotation, 85
Round mouldings, 611
Round-over moulding, 610
Rumford-type fireplaces, 438, 441
Running foot, 99
R-values, 484, 492–495

S
Safety margin, 89
Salt-box-style roofs, 171
Sandwich door, 324
Scaffolding, rented, 271–273
School systems, 13
Screen moulding, 611
SEC (Service Entrance Concentric) cable, 450
Second clear clapboards, 289
Section modulus, 90
Select boards, 98
Select structural lumber, 99
Selvage roll roofing, 247
Septic system, 382–384
  building site and, 13
  installation of, 36
SER (Service Entrance Round) cable, 451
Service entrance (SE)
  cable, 450
  wiring of, 453–456
Service panel, 464–465
Sewage disposal, on-site, 382–384
Shakes, wood, 262–263
Shear, 89, 90
Sheathing, 153–157
  nonstructural, 157–159
  roof, 188–190, 228–230
Shed roofs, 171
  rafter layout for, 197–199
Shingles
  asphalt, 234–246
    installation of, 235–240
    valley treatments, 240–243
  wood
    roofing, 259–262
    siding, 298–299
Shiplap siding, 293, 294
Shoe, 104
Shutoff valves, 359
Shutters, thermal, 487–488
Siding, 288–306
  aluminum, 302
  board, 289–297
    bevel, 289–292
    boxboard, 292–293
    clapboards, 289–292
    rabbeted, 293–297
    tongue-and-grove, 293–297
  cement, 302
  hardboard, 302
  plywood, 300–302

  stucco, 302–306
  vinyl, 302
  wood shingles, 298–299
Sill sealer, 117
Sills, 104
  setting, 116–118
Simple beams, 91
Single-pole site-built staging, 274
Sinkers, 125
Sinks
  drain lines for, 360
  setting, 660–662
Site, 13–15
  cleanup of, 665
Site-built staging, 274–277
Site plans, 15–16
Site work, 27–36
Skylights, 309
  framing for, 196
Slab-on-grade foundations, 64–70
  frost-wall, 68
  monolithic, 68–70
Sleepers for rooftop decks, 341
Sliding doors, 626
Sliding windows, 308
Slope of roof, 173
Small-appliance circuits, 447
Smoke pipes, 434–437
Snow load, 86–87
Soffit, 285
  railroad jet, 287
  vents in, 283, 284
Softened water, 378–379
Soil mechanics, 37–38
Solar heating, 387–393
  insulation and, 487
Solar orientation, 14–15, 385, 386
Soldering, 368–369
Sole plate, 104
Solvent-welding, 372, 373
Space heaters, 416
Special purpose circuits, 447
Splash rib, 243
Split-breakers, 465
Springs, 376–378
Sprinkler systems, automatic, 679–683
Square, importance of, 92–94
Stack boots, 410
Staging, site-built, 274–277
  for above-roof chimney work, 433
Staining, 349–351
Stairs, 515–536
  outdoor, 673
Stairwells
  finishing, 530
  framing openings for, 126–127
Standard-grade lumber, 99
Steel beams, 121
Steel pipe, 364, 365
  cutting and threading, 365
Steel roofing, 253–257

flashing, 258–259
Steep asphalt, 249
Stepladders, 278
Stick framing, 102–107
  difference between timber framing
    and, 110
  for walls, with timbered ceiling,
    112–114
Stone
  floors, 605–607
  walls, 669–671
Stop mouldings, 610
Stoves, wood, 434–437
Strain, 89
Stress, 89–90
Stringer joists
  insulating, 132–133
  setting, 118
Strongbacks, 168
Structural engineering, 85–100
Structural light framing, 99
Structural lumber, 98
Stucco, 302–306
  foundation insulation, 55
Stud cavities, 102
Stud-grade lumber, 99
Studs, 105, 139–140
Subfascia, 173, 185–188
Subfloor, 104
  installing, 134–135
  protecting against weather, 137
Summer beam, 109
Sunspaces, 343–345, 390, 391
Super-insulated houses, 392–393
  window trim in, 116
Surface-bonded concrete block founda-
    tions, 83–84
Surface raceway wiring, 478
Surface runoff, 38
Suspended ceilings, 568
Swales, 39
Swamp coolers, 421
Sweat fittings, 366–368
Switches, electric, 480–482

T
Tail joists, 105
Tar paper, 228–229
Telephone
  lines, 33, 35–36
  wiring, 662–664
Tensile stress, 89
Termite protection, 62–63, 117
Thermal envelope, 495
Thermal mass, 387
Thermal performance, 310–311
Thermodynamics, Second Law of, 483
Thermosiphon system, 389
Tile

ceiling, 566–567
ceramic, 587–605
  adhesives for, 589–591
  beds for, 591–595
  installation and grouting, 602–605
  layout and cutting of, 599–602
  membranes, 596–599
  types of, 587–589
floors
  vinyl, 585–586
  substrate for, 129
roofing, 264–267
Timbers, 98
Toilet
  drain and vent lines for, 360, 362
  enclosing, 661
  setting, 659–660
  waterless, 383–384
Tongue-and-grove siding, 293–297
Tools, 25
  for do-it-yourself subcontractors, 25–
    26
Top plate, 105
Transit levels, 30–31
Translation, 85
Transmission, overall coefficient of, 484
Treated-wood post foundations, 70–72
  problems with, 74–78
Trees
  felling, 27–28
  grading around, 667
  planting, 668, 669
Trim
  exterior, 288–306
  interior, 608–628
    baseboards, 627–628
    doors, 622–626
    mouldings, 608–615
    windows, 615–621
Trimmer joists, 105
Trimmer studs, 105
Trombe wall, 388
Trusses
  floor, 133–135
  roof, 224–228
    erecting, 226–228
    site-built, 226
Tub enclosures, 656–657
Typical section view, 16

U
UF cable, 451
Unit strain, 89
USE (Underground Service Entrance)
    cable, 450
Utilities, installation of, 33–36
Utility-grade lumber, 99
U-value, 484–485

V
Valley jack, 173
Valley rafters, 172
Valley treatments, 240–243
Vapor barriers, 489–493
  installing, 506
Vent lines, 360–362
Vent stacks, flashing at, 243–244
Ventilation, 486, 512–514
  of attic, 498–505
  reduction of humidity by, 488, 491
  whole-house, 422–423
Vertical sections, 16
Vinyl flooring, 583–585
  tile, 585–586
Vinyl siding, 302
Voltage, 445

W
Wall forms, 40
  for full-basement foundation, 46
Wall sections, 18
Walls
  ceramic tile, 587–605
    adhesives for, 589–591
    beds for, 591–595
    installation and grouting, 602–605
    layout and cutting, 599–602
    membranes, 596–599
    types of, 587–589
  drywall, 537–545
  fibre-reinforced panels, 548–549
  framing, 139–164
    assembling, 148–152
    corner posts and partition backers,
      144–146
    double-sole-plate system, 141–142
    headers, 146–148
    interior partitions, 159
    layout, 142–143
    lining, 153–157
    nonstructural sheathing, 157–159
    special conditions, 160–164
  plastering, 549–552
  wood panelling, 552–563
Wallboard, *see* Drywall
Warm-air heating system, 396–398
  installing, 406–412
Washing machines, circuit design for,
    447
Water and sewer line connections, 36
Water softeners, 378–379
Water supply, on-site, 376–381
Water table, 38, 376
Watering systems, automatic, 679–683
Wattage, 447
Weatherstripping, 323, 509–511
Wells, 376
  drilling, 36
  pumps for, 380–381

Wet vents, 360
Wet walls, 160
Whole-house ventilation, 422–423
Wind pressure, 87–88
Windows, 307–314
    factory-built, installing, 312
    fixed, building, 312–314
    glazing characteristics and thermal
        performance, 310–311
    insulating around, 498
    interior trim for, 615–621
    manufacturers' specifications, 310,
        311
    openings, drip caps for, 292
    painting, 353
    types of, 307–310
    weatherstripping around, 511
Window wells, 62
Wiring
    boxes, 466–471
    for branch circuits, 465–466
    circuit design and load calculations,
        447–450

color code for, 453
conduits for, 452, 473–477
diagrams, 482
for disconnect switch, 459–461
grounding, 462, 463
for meter socket, 456–459
outdoor, 478–480
roof-mounted service mast, 456
of service entrance, 453–456
for service panel, 464–465
surface raceway, 478
switches and receptacles, 480–482
telephone, 662–664
Wood
    flooring, 469–583
        applying finish to, 582–583
        combination floor and ceiling sys-
            tem, 578–580
        over concrete slab, 575–578
        laying, 572–575
        sanding, 580–581
        types of, 569–571
        underlayment, 571–572

gutters, 267
lumber nomenclature, 97–100
nature of, 96–97
panelling, 554–563
    on ceilings, 564–565
    prefinished, 552–553
shakes, 262–263
shingles
    roofing, 259–262
    siding, 298–299
strength measurement for, 90–92
Wood-post foundations, 70–72
    problems with, 74–76
Wood stoves, 434–437

Y
Yarning iron, 375
Yield strength, 89

Z
Z-brace board-and-frame door, 323
Zoned heating systems, 400–401
Zoning, 13